The

ENCYCLOPEDIA

of

HIGHER EDUCATION

The

ENCYCLOPEDIA

of

HIGHER EDUCATION

VOLUME 1

*National Systems
of Higher Education*

Editors-in-Chief

BURTON R. CLARK
*University of California,
Los Angeles, California, USA*

and

GUY R. NEAVE
*International Association
of Universities,
Paris, France*

PERGAMON PRESS

OXFORD · NEW YORK · SEOUL · TOKYO

UK	Pergamon Press Ltd., Headington Hill Hall, Oxford OX3 0BW, England
USA	Pergamon Press Inc., 660 White Plains Road, Tarrytown, New York, 10591–5153, USA
KOREA	Pergamon Press Korea, KPO Box 315, Seoul 110–603, Korea
JAPAN	Pergamon Press Japan, Tsunashima Building Annex, 3–20–12 Yushima, Bunkyo-ku, Tokyo 113, Japan

First edition 1992

British Library Cataloguing in Publication Data
A catalogue record for this book is available from the British Library

Library of Congress Cataloging-in-Publication Data
The Encyclopedia of higher education/Burton R. Clark, Guy R. Neave, editors—1st edn.
 p. cm.
Includes index.
1. Education, Higher Encyclopedias. I. Clark, Burton R.
II. Neave, Guy R.
LB15.E49 1992
378′.003—dc20

ISBN 0-08-037251-1 (set)

∞ ™ The paper used in this publication meets the minimum requirements of the American National Standard for Information Sciences—Permanence of Paper for Printed Library Materials, ANSI Z39.48-1984.

Printed in Great Britain by B.P.C.C. Wheatons Ltd., Exeter

Contents

Volume 1   NATIONAL SYSTEMS OF HIGHER EDUCATION

Contents

Contents

Contents

Volume 2 ANALYTICAL PERSPECTIVES
Section I Higher Education and Society

Section II   The Institutional Fabric of the Higher Education System

Contents

Section III   Governance, Administration, and Finance

Contents

Volume 3 ANALYTICAL PERSPECTIVES

Section IV Faculty and Students: Teaching, Learning, and Research

Section V   Disciplinary Perspectives on Higher Education

Volume 4   ACADEMIC DISCIPLINES AND INDEXES
Part 1   Humanities

Contents

Part 2   Social Sciences

Part 3   Biological Sciences

Honorary Editorial
Advisory Board

Editorial Board

Preface

During the last half of the twentieth century, higher education has become a key institution in societies around the world. Nearly everywhere national systems of higher education have grown tremendously in size and scope in response to increased demand for access and the growing need to train experts for an expanding array of advanced occupations. Investing in research, these systems experience enormous growth in knowledge in numerous disciplines, specialties, and professional fields of study. They become elaborately involved with government and increasingly connected with industry. Nations seek to invigorate their higher education institutions in order to promote economic strength and enhance national standing in the world order. With each passing decade this central sector of society also becomes more international; advanced knowledge, its basic substance, flows readily across the borders of nations and regions. The idea of higher education has come into a new age.

The history of higher education shows that the traditional university is a uniquely durable institution. Despite war, pestilence, and the passing of all manner of political regimes, it has survived over some 800 years. It is one of a few societal institutions which serve as a repository of a nation's historic memory and identity. In newer nations and notably those which have achieved independence in the years since the Second World War, governmental officials and academic leaders, conscious of this particular role, have sought by various means to foster it as a foundation for nation-building and national unity. Other countries, and, at the time of writing, most particularly those in Central and Eastern Europe, look to the university to reassert a historic memory as a means of reviving earlier intellectual, political, and social values that are the necessary bedrock for reconstructing those societies. The citizens of a country may cast out a political regime and throw the statues of the Fathers of an earlier state onto the scrap heap of history. But instead of scrapping the university, they seek to strengthen it in the contexts of the new age.

There is little doubt that the monumental changes of the last half century have made higher education problematic. As demands mount and tasks proliferate, institutions, programs, and degrees increase in number and type. As systems struggle to combine elite operations and mass functions, overall purpose becomes ambiguous and confused. As the budgets of higher education rise dramatically, politicians, planners, and tax-paying publics seek accountability and cost containment. The fate of higher education becomes more intertwined with the development of science and technology, establishing imperatives that often contradict the demands of widened access and mass education. Set in motion in the twentieth century and destined to carry well into the twenty-first, such primary trends insure that faculty, students, officials, and the public will find this diverse institution an ever more complicated and perplexing realm. Seen as a tree of knowledge, higher education has become a veritable forest, exuberant in growth but tangled in character.

1. The Growth of Research and a Field of Study

When a sector of society becomes more important in the general scheme of things it elicits more scholarly attention. When costs increase, calls for expert analysis and advice are heard. When growing complexity confuses everyone, better understanding and problem-solving require systematic inquiry. Accordingly, higher education has developed in the 1960s, 1970s, and 1980s as an object of research and scholarship and as a field of knowledge. Research centers and policy institutes established in many countries now track and forecast the development of their higher education systems. "Institutional research" has become a subfield composed of many practitioners organized in national and international associations. International agencies, for example, the Organisation for Economic Co-operation and Development (OECD), the World Bank, and UNESCO, have systematized comparative and historical data. Private foundations have contributed substantially to the development of higher education as a field of self-standing study. Professorships have been created to integrate the growing body of theoretical and empirical materials and train new generations of analysts for basic and applied research. Sociologists, economists, historians, political scientists, educators, policy analysts, and others have developed research interests in this area and have brought new perspectives to bear. As an object of study, higher education now has a scholarly literature, significant in its breadth and depth, that offers a plethora of perspectives and a wide range of internationally derived descriptions and analyses.

On both practical and scholarly grounds, this current international knowledge about higher education warrants a far-reaching, extensive integration. We seek to provide that integration in the *Encyclopedia of Higher Education*. As an effort devoted to higher education alone, rather than to all of education, the *Encyclopedia* extends and deepens the encompassing work provided in 1985 in the Pergamon *International Encyclopedia of Education*, edited by Torsten Husén and T. Neville Postlethwaite. That valuable and highly successful encyclopedia provided only brief treatment of the development of research and scholarship in the study of higher education. When that work was planned in the early 1980s, there existed an earlier encyclopedia devoted to higher education, edited by Asa Knowles and published by Jossey-Bass in 1977. That encyclopedia has long been out of print; events of the last 15 years have also rendered it out of date. Much more theoretical analysis has become available, offering the opportunity not only to assemble materials but to synthesize them in useful frameworks.

2. Plan of the Encyclopedia

A distinctive feature of the *Encyclopedia* is exceptionally strong thematic organization. The articles and essays amounting to over 300 and contained within the following four volumes are not presented alphabetically. Instead, they are grouped under major topics and within particular themes or categories. Volume 1 is given over entirely to country reports: it includes more than 135 analyses of national systems of higher education. Volumes 2 and 3 present analytical papers, over 120 in number, organized within five themes. Volume 4 is an innovative effort to bring to a general international audience analytical accounts of the changing nature of the basic disciplines that form the knowledge core of higher education. Comprehensive subject and author indexes are found in the latter part of this concluding volume.

The principle point of integration in the *Encyclopedia* lies in the sequential organization of thematic sections in Volumes 2 and 3 and the use of four themes as parallel categories in a linked sequence in each country report in Volume 1. Much thought was given to the most salient, orderly, and useful set of major categories that would define and embrace the research and scholarly literature on higher education. We defined four themes that could be arranged in descending macro-to-micro order. The first is "Higher Education and Society." Here, 21 articles explore the many relations of higher education to other sectors of society. Edited and introduced by Gareth Williams, this section presents insightful and comprehensive statements on the connections between higher education and such other major institutions as the economic system, the political order, the structure of social stratification, and elementary and secondary schooling. The second theme is "The Institutional Fabric of the Higher Education System." Organized by Roger Geiger, this set of 30 articles analyzes the increasingly differentiated structure of higher education systems as they develop such types of institutions as research universities, polytechnics, liberal arts colleges, teachers' colleges, short-cycle colleges, and research academies; such different degree levels as short-cycle diplomas, bachelors' degrees, and doctoral degrees; and such detached or semi-autonomous "professional" or applied schools as medicine, law, engineering, and business.

Under the third theme of "Governance, Administration, and Finance," a section edited by Grant Harman, 27 related articles analyze the increasingly complicated webs of relationship involved in the governance and administration of higher education and the provision of finance at both governmental and institutional levels. Searching within the institutional fabric of the national system for additional conditions that determine academic behavior, this section moves the reader closer to the operational units of academic systems. In the overall descending order of the themes, we reach those units in the fourth theme, "Faculty and Students: Teaching, Learning, and Research." Edited by Ann Morey, this set of 24 articles concentrates on the micro settings in which professors teach and do research and in which students are engaged in learning. It examines such topics as faculty recruitment, faculty–student interaction, student learning and development, and undergraduate and graduate curricula.

The fifth theme, "Disciplinary Perspectives on Higher Education," completes the analytical reach of Volumes 2 and 3. Developed by Tony Becher, this section departs from the substantive sequence of the first four themes. Its purpose is to examine higher education through the eyes of different disciplines and academic specialties in which a significant amount of research and scholarship is now available. In 20 articles the reader may readily compare the perspective of history with that of sociology, economics with women's studies, law with literature, and organizational theory with philosophy. Concentrated on the study of higher education, this section also serves as a bridge to the disciplinary focuses of Volume 4.

We believe these five sections, organized by analytical category rather than by country or region, provide state-of-the-art coverage of what is currently known in the research literature on higher education.

In Volume 1, where extant knowledge is organized by country, the *Encyclopedia* deploys a common structure that links the country materials to the general analytical scheme. Each country article is structured sequentially by the first four categories of Volumes 2 and 3: namely, Higher Education and Society; The Institutional Fabric of the Higher Education System; Governance, Administration, and Finance; and Faculty and Students: Teaching, Learning, and Research. Edited by José Joaquin Brunner and José-Luis Garcia-Garrido, these 138 country analyses were prepared to the fullest possible extent by home-country experts. Authorship is as international as could be achieved in a protracted effort of commissioning, editing, and review that stretched over $2\frac{1}{2}$ years

(1989–91). Preparing country essays within a declared common structure proved a difficult task for authors and editors alike.

Volume 4 offers a unique comprehensive review of the core disciplinary composition of modern systems of higher education. Its substantial place in this *Encyclopedia* stems from a belief of the senior editors that the mainstream literature in research on higher education, concentrated on institutions and students, vastly understates the role and centrality of the disciplines. All too often the disciplines slip from view, contributing to a weak public understanding of their nature and importance. In all their modern specialized intensity, the basic disciplines are indeed hard to grasp. New disciplines and major specialties within them develop at a rate that defies exhaustive classification and coverage. Disciplinary alignments also vary among countries, and experts qualified to write a general essay on the entirety of a major discipline, for example, physics, economics, history, in their own country generally are not informed on a worldwide basis. But it is essential to the understanding of higher education that researchers and the general public attend to the development and structure, orientation and thought, of the disciplines. Toward this end, Volume 4 presents forty articles, including section editor overviews, grouped in five major subject areas: ten essays in the humanities, edited by Jan Sperna Weiland; eight in the social sciences, edited by Robert Scott; nine in the biological sciences, edited by Herbert Macgregor; six in the medical sciences, edited by William Rothstein; and seven in the physical sciences, edited by Carlos Kruytbosch.

As a result of its general structure, the *Encyclopedia* stresses a contextual approach in the first three volumes in which the conditions of teaching and learning in higher education are portrayed in a sequence that extends from the broadest level of societal determination to the immediate constraints and facilitations of faculty life, faculty–student interaction, and student learning. Volume 4 in turn is also heavily contextual in its portrayal of disciplines as ongoing concerns that stretch across institutions and nations, operating with patterns of thought, traditional symbols and identities, and distinctive practices that condition heavily the academic lives of professors and students.

In brief, the *Encyclopedia of Higher Education* is thematic, internationally comparative, logically integrated, and contextually explanatory. We have sought to provide a systematic organization of otherwise disparate materials that will help readers to move effectively from the specific to the general, and vice versa. Readers can turn to higher education in any particular country, aided in their understanding by the best analytical thought on various features. They can fashion their own comparisons of two or more countries on topics that vary from governmental control to student learning.

Two large topics that could have been included in the *Encyclopedia* were deliberately left out: a review of international and national organizations that are involved in the development of higher education, such as UNESCO and the Department of Education and Science (DES) in the United Kingdom; and a set of articles on important persons in the history of higher education, such as Cardinal Newman and Robert Hutchins. Either effort would have taken the size of the *Encyclopedia* beyond reasonable limits. Additionally, it would have been unnecessarily invidious to include the better known organizations and individuals and pass over in silence those which even if less well-known had nevertheless advanced the field substantially. We also took the view that the substantial nature of the work of various organizations and the influence of certain educational leaders would emerge in the references and materials used by contributors, thereby presented in context and in keeping with the judgment of those who wrote the articles.

In this extended effort, we have sought to balance scholarly expertise and international representation. The best thought on any particular research topic or theme may be largely located in one country or at best found in the scholarly communities of a handful of nations. If quality and insight are to be well-served, sheer expertise must necessarily come first. Yet an international or comparatively oriented *Encyclopedia* ought also to reach out to the widest possible base of scholarly participation, thereby enriching its contribution by perspectives born of a wide range of national cultures and regional settings. Our search for an international base began with the two Editors-in-Chief: one (Clark) from the United States, the other (Neave) from Europe. The Honorary Editorial Advisory Board consists of sixteen members drawn from all parts of the world: for example, Brazil (Goldenberg), India (Reddy), People's Republic of China (Wang Yongquan), Sweden (Husén), and Japan (Amagi). The twelve subject editors—two for Volume 1, five for Volumes 2 and 3, five for Volume 4—selected primarily for their expertise, were also widely distributed: one each from Australia, Chile, Spain, and the Netherlands; three from the United Kingdom; and five dispersed from San Diego to Washington in the United States. As previously noted, the Volume 1 authors are nearly all located in, or come from, the country on which they wrote. Volume 4 authors were drawn from Continental European countries, the United Kingdom, and the United States. The *Encyclopedia* as a whole represents an extended quest to mix the best possible expertise with the best possible international representation.

The most serious obstacle to true comparative coverage is not geographic representation but the difficulty of finding authors in any country who possess extended expertise on their topics beyond their own national boundaries and especially outside their own region of the world. Such expertise will be increasingly compelling, for if there is one facet of higher education which at the present time sets it off from its previous condition it is the intensification of international linkages. These linkages take many forms: students taking a year to study abroad; others going overseas to take a first degree; graduates enrolling at the world's major establishments to develop expertise not available at home; and the normal dialogue among professors and researchers engaged in knowledge exchange and collaborative research. What starts out with enterprising individuals seeking to broaden knowledge, contacts, and experience moves swiftly onward, bringing together institutions and eventually systems. Student mobility is one of the major and less recognized contributions that the developing world has made to the interdependence and internationalization of higher education. Additionally, governments are now turning their minds to mass student mobility, whether, for example, in the Commission of the European Community with its ERASMUS and TEMPUS schemes, or in the Japanese government's plans to attract in the 1990s some 100,000 foreign students to Japanese universities. The exchange of ideas is not far behind. The mass university is today an international phenomenon.

In the latter part of the 1980s, some examination of the plans and experiences of other countries has become a major input to national policy-making for systems of higher education. The pace of cross-national policy outlook has quickened, spurred by international economic competition and the fear that if one does not go down the road the winners have taken, one risks being among the losers. Regardless of motive, systems are now clearly interacting. What is perceived as the success of one quickly becomes the model for others to emulate. Whether the graft will take root in foreign soil is a matter of faith, hope, and money. As an example of this process, found in Western Europe at the beginning of the 1990s, the American "graduate school" is now actively studied and used as a point of reference by policymakers in the Federal Republic of Germany in the form of the *Graduierten Kolleg*, in France with the proposal by the Ministry of Education for the establishment of so-called *Ecoles Doctorales*, and in the Netherlands as a major idea for the reform of Dutch higher education. Such international borrowing illustrates the broader process of internationalization of knowledge that is fraught with challenge for faculty, students, administrators, and the system planner.

The widening search for answers drawn from the experiences of foreign countries places a particular burden on those whose knowledge of higher education goes beyond their own systems, if only to see whole features that are often taken out of context. Much remains to be done. In preparing the *Encyclopedia* we asked authors to be as international as they could be, but many essays reflect primarily the point of view and research base of a particular country and national system of higher education. Toward improvement in this state of affairs, in a relatively new field of study, we view the *Encyclopedia* as a research enterprise in itself, one that helps provide categories of thought and empirical foundations that will lead toward fuller comparative analysis. The *Encyclopedia of Higher Education* should serve as a footing in the 1990s and beyond for a growing international understanding of modern systems of higher education on the part of teachers, researchers, students, trustees, and lay members of governing bodies, local administrators, governmental officials, and the general public alike.

BURTON R. CLARK and GUY R. NEAVE

Acknowledgments

The authors and publisher would like to thank the following sources for permission to use their material:

Agathon Press for a revised and condensed version of Clark S M, Lewis D R "Faculty vitality". In: Smart J C (ed.) 1988 *Higher Education: Handbook of Theory and Research*, Vol. 4.

Agathon Press Inc. for Fig. 1 in Watkins D "Faculty and Student Interaction," from Pascarella E T 1985 Model of cognitive development. In: *Higher Education: Handbook of Theory and Research*, Vol. 1.

Association of Universities and Colleges of Canada for Fig. 3 in Watson C "Canada," from *Compendium of University Statistics*, 1987.

Beguin A for Table 8 in Woitrin M "Belgium," from *Une Face Cachée de l'Enseignement*, UCL, 1976, 1989.

College Entrance Examination Board, New York for Figs. 1–4 in Woodhall M "Financial Aid: Student," reprinted from Johnstone D B 1986 *Sharing the Costs of Higher Education*. Copyright 1986 by College Entrance Examination Board.

Conseil Central de l'Economie for information in Woitrin M "Belgium," from *Rapports et Avis Relatifs à la Position Compétitive de la Belgique*, 1989.

Conseil Interuniversitaire de la Communauté Française for citations in Woitrin M "Belgium," from *Le Financement de l'Enseignement Universitaire Francophone. Evolution Récente de Comparaison avec Quatre Pays Europeéns*, 1989.

Conseil National de la Politique Scientifique for Table 6 in Woitrin M "Belgium," from *Principaux Indicateurs de la Science et de la Technologie (1977–1988). Données de l'OCDE*, 1989.

Fondation Universitaire Brussels for Table 5 in Woitrin M "Belgium," from *Enseignement et Recherche Scientifique*, 1987.

HMSO for Figs. 5 and 6 in Woodhall M "Financial Aid: Student," from *Cmd 520: Top-up Loans for Students*, DES, 1988.

Institut de Recherches Economiques et Sociales for economic information in Woitrin M "Belgium."

Institute of Education, University of London/Kogan Page for Table 1 in Woodhall M "Financial Aid: Student," derived from Hansen J Cost-sharing in higher education: The United States experience. In: Woodhall M (ed.) 1989 *Financial Support for Students: Grants, Loans or Graduate Tax?*

Jossey-Bass for extracts in Nazombe A "Malawi," from Hunnings G 1977 University Education in Malawi. In: *The International Encyclopedia of Higher Education*, Vol. 6.

Malawi Department of Economic Planning and Development for extracts in Nazombe A "Malawi," from *Statement of Development Policies 1987–1996*.

Malawi Ministry of Education and Culture for information in Nazombe A "Malawi," from *Education Statistics of 1989*.

Malawi National Statistical Office for statistical information in Nazombe A "Malawi," from *Malawi Population and Housing Census 1987: Preliminary Report 1987*.

Ministry of Finance, Government of Pakistan for Tables 1–3 in Saqeb G N "Pakistan," from *Pakistan Economic Survey*, 1988–89.

Ministry of National Education, Brussels for extracts in Woitrin M "Belgium," from *Evolution des Effectifs des Enseignements de Plein Exercice*, 1988.

Netherlands Ministry of Education and Sciences for information in Tables 5–8 of Frijhoff W "The Netherlands," from *Dutch Higher Education and Research. Major Issues. Facts and Figures*, 1988.

Organisation for Economic Co-operation and Development for extracts in Woitrin M "Belgium," from *L'Enseignement dans les Pays de l'OCDE*, 1988.

Statistics Canada for Fig. 2 in Watson C "Canada," from *From the Sixties to the Eighties: A Statistical Portrait of Canadian Higher Education*, 1979.

The University of the South Pacific for an abridged version of Caston G "Academic Freedom," which also appeared in *The Contemporary Pacific*.

UNESCO for Table 4 in Saqeb G N "Pakistan," from *UNESCO Statistical Yearbooks 1971, 1975, 1980, 1985, 1987*. © UNESCO 1971/1975/1980/1985 and 1987 respectively.

Unwin Hyman Ltd for Fig. 1 in Little A "Diploma Disease," from Oxenham J (ed.) 1984 *Education Versus Qualifications*.

W. B. Saunders Company for extracts in Zimmerman M R "Pathology," from Zimmerman M R 1980 *Foundations of Medical Anthropology*.

The Western Australian Labour Market Research Centre for extracts in Hansen W L "Salaries and Salary Determination," from Hansen W L Salary flexibility and merit pay in higher education. *Labour Economics and Productivity* 2: 73–90, 1989.

VOLUME 1

National Systems of Higher Education

VOLUME 1

National Systems of Higher Education

INTRODUCTION

The purpose of this first volume is to provide sensitive, accurate, and up-to-date information on the state of higher education in most countries of the world. Many readers will turn to the *Encyclopedia* to learn more about a particular country or group of countries. We have taken this into account when planning the contents of the articles.

Yet clearly our aims are more ambitious. This *Encyclopedia* could, like many others in the area of comparative and international studies, have limited itself to providing information on the world's higher education systems. However, this we eschewed for reasons which have already been made plain by the Editors-in-Chief. Our editorial strategy sets major importance on in-depth examinations of such cross-national issues as institutional governance, diversity of institutional types, and the situation of teaching staff. Obviously, the overall structure of the undertaking must necessarily permeate each part and, in particular, the first. We set particular importance on ensuring a close and natural linkage between this first part and the remaining sections of the *Encyclopedia*.

When the *Encyclopedia* was planned in October 1988, it was decided to include only those systems of higher education with 3,000 or more students enrolled at institutions inside the country. In addition, the Editors decided that this cut-off point would take no account of those nationals studying overseas, whether for a first degree or for a graduate award. As a final condition, higher education systems were to be territorially defined, that is, higher education as it figures within a given nation-state and not, for example, "outreach campusses" set up abroad by institutions of higher education based in a third-party country. To achieve close coordination demanded that extremely clear criteria be employed in designing each case study. Given the diversity of institutional approaches and the specific development of the higher educational sector, we ran the risk that such diversity might lead either to an overly mechanical or an ill-structured report on each country. Either outcome would, in musical terms, have led to an excessively repetitive refrain or, on the contrary, to a symphony excessively complex in its themes and variations. We therefore opted for a simple chord of four notes, which we considered irreplaceable, as the basic line of argument.

The first of these, which provides the background, is the context of each particular system. One cannot grasp the nature of a system without referring to the setting within which it lies. Indeed, any system of human action or institutions is usually a subsystem of other, larger systems. The higher education system is set, first of all, within the larger system of education. At the same time it is also part of the political, or economic, or social subsystem of the nation. There are, of course, other systems which might apply in particular instances. To understand the often specific nature of a higher education system without considering aspects of the host country such as its geographical location, its frontiers and degree of isolation, the uniformity or diversity of the population, the broad outlines of its social, occupational, and economic structure, the political regime, and the population's system of beliefs that are present, would be exceedingly difficult—if not a sterile exercise. Nor should one forget that the university is an historical institution where present and future are always inexorably marked, explained, and often as not, influenced by past efforts. However appealing these factors normally are, we persisted in recommending to authors that they summarize this first block of information, which we have called "Higher Education and Society."

The notes which sound across the central body of our chord mark the two great structural elements in the higher education system: its institutional and administrative structures. This section carries the title "The Institutional Fabric of the Higher Education System" and deals with the first element. Here, the various sectors—the institutional building blocks—which make up the higher education system are analyzed. Whether university or nonuniversity sectors as well as other variations are set forth depends on the traditions of each country and, within these sectors, the typology of those institutions embedded in them. Other structural aspects are equally important—for instance the various routes which lead the student from secondary school to graduation and on towards graduate study programs. Furthermore this section also contains extensive information on the quantitative dimension and on the development of higher education in each country, as it has evolved over the last few decades.

Administrative structures are analyzed in the third section: "Governance, Administration, and Finance." There are two levels involved here: higher education systems at macro level and the institutional level—the latter is no less important since in many countries individual establishments often enjoy great autonomy.

Although crucial, structural data alone provide an overall vision rather more restricted than we would wish. There are other elements, especially of a functional nature, which impart both life and substance to structures. Of these elements none is more pertinent than those two lead actors of university life, the teacher and the student. The analysis focuses on three functional and basic activities of higher education: teaching, learning, and research. The various points brought into this view (e.g., the career paths of the teaching body, the social class composition of the student body, types of academic work, etc.), may serve as a dynamic tableau of higher education. It strikes the sharpest note in our chord, and is entitled "Faculty and Students: Teaching, Learning, and Research."

If these four sections stand as the core of each study case, authors were also asked to provide an assessment, critical and forward looking on the situation of higher education in their country, as a brief final conclusion. Authors were not obliged to concentrate their evaluation only in the latter section. Indeed, not a few decided to introduce a critical—sometimes deeply critical—note into other sections.

That each author had considerable latitude to interpret the topics in each of the four main sections as he or she judged appropriate, of course, implies a significant diversity in approaches. Formally speaking, such latitude might cause some problems in drawing exact comparative parallels between the various systems. We are convinced, however, that such problems are far outweighed by the advantages of not being limited by excessively rigid rules, which, almost always, are based on existing models in the wealthy and industrialized nations.

This *Encyclopedia* is the end product of a major exercise in international collaboration. Most authors invited to contribute to this first volume are both specialists and natives of the countries upon which they write. From the outset these criteria have guided us in our search for scholars whose knowledge of the subject was matched by their sensitivity to a broad international perspective. But inflexibility is not always a good thing. In some instances we have turned to scholars who, although not natives, nevertheless have a solid acquaintance with the country in question, on which they have published previously.

There remains one last point. Nowadays it is almost trite to invoke the acceleration of history which certain periods display. Yet the last three to four years have been one of those periods. If time and tide wait for no man then neither does history wait on the completion of encyclopedias. Our venture has been subject to two types of acceleration: the first is the intellectual evolution of those disciplines which contribute to the study of higher education itself. Of this we have been aware and have sought to take full account of it. The second are those events that can be foreseen neither by princes, nor by politicians, and certainly not by the planners and editors of encyclopedias. The planning and commissioning of articles for this section began well before the bicentenary of the French Revolution of 1789 and before those events which two hundred years later, profoundly altered the map, geographically, politically, and ideologically, of Central and Eastern Europe. The consequences of these events are still working their way through the life of the countries concerned and not least in the sphere of higher education. What their outcome will be, one may hope. But hope does not lend itself to precision and so certain of our entries must remain more than usually provisional, though one could also make the remark that by its very nature and its adaptability, the institution of higher education itself has, over the past three decades, been in a state of continual provisionality.

Faced with the unforeseen and certainly with the unforeseeable, some of our colleagues have, rightly, exercised caution and concentrated on the situation as it was at the time of their writing. And so, it may well be that entries which deal with countries whose history is accelerating, will appear less current than those where the pace of change is less frenetic.

Finally, we would wish to pay tribute to all those who contributed to this volume and to their willingness to accept the editorial Iron Law of length and datelines. If ours was the delicate task of imposing them, so theirs was the professionalism and dedication with which both were met.

José Joaquin Brunner
José-Luis Garcia Garrido

A

Afghanistan

Enrollment figures for higher education in Afghanistan are proportionally some of the lowest in the world which reflects the poverty and under-development of the country. The geographical and economic barriers to higher education expansion were exacerbated by war and severe political disruption in the late 1970s and 1980s, and participation rates declined in the 1980s. Dislocation has also been a constraint on the collection of systematic information.

1. Higher Education and Society

Geographical obstacles have included the isolation of a landlocked mountainous country with a sparsely distributed population (22.2 people per sq. km in 1987), and poor communications, with no railways. Dry conditions in much of the country encourage a nomadic pastoral economy while severe winters in other areas impede the operation of a settled and coherent society in which education can flourish.

The population of 14.8 million in 1989 is augmented by 5.6 million refugees in neighboring countries. The population is predominantly rural. Only 17 percent of the population lived in urban areas in 1983 compared to 10 percent in 1965. The capital Kabul (population 1.3 million in 1987) is the only city to have more than quarter of a million residents. Over two million people are nomads.

A Gross National Product (GNP) of US$230 per capita in 1985 places Afghanistan among the poorest countries in the world. Nomadic and pastoral ways of life contribute to very low levels of development in some respects. Natives of Afghanistan had the lowest life expectancy at birth (36) of all countries in the mid-1980s. The adult literacy rate is low (20%) as were the age participation rates in primary (22%) and secondary (7%) education in 1979. The involvement of women and girls in public life is limited, with educational age participation rates of seven percent at primary and two percent at secondary level in 1979.

Afghan society is divided into language and ethnic groups. Eighty percent of the population speaks one or other of the two official languages, Pashto Iranian or Dari (Farsi). These are the two languages of education, both employing Arabic script. The remaining 20 percent of the population speaks one or more of some thirty different languages. There are three major ethnic groups—Pushtuns (60% of the total population), Tajiks (30%), and Uzbeks (5%). The country is largely united in religion (99% Muslim of which 75% are Sunni) yet religious–secular tensions were an element in political conflict in the 1980s, seen, for instance, in reactions to literacy campaigns for women. Religious education at every level is conducted largely in Arabic.

The social structure has been little affected by political changes. Rural society is organized on tribal rather than conventional social class lines. The urban middle class has gained its position largely through education. Higher education was a locus of political activism in the 1970s and students played some part in the political changes of that decade.

The economy is predominantly agricultural. About 65 percent of the labor force are engaged in pastoral and arable farming. External trade is limited and exports consist mainly of agricultural products such as fruit, nuts, and cotton as well as traditional rural artifacts such as carpets, rugs, and hides. The limited industrial sector has developed through government agencies. Prospects of future development are restricted by a weak communications infrastructure and the effects of a long war.

Political instability has been acute since 1978. Afghanistan was founded as a state in 1747 and retained its independence in the nineteenth century despite pressures from both the British and Russian Empires. The monarchy developed parliamentary and constitutional forms after 1932. Modernization in social and economic spheres occurred in the period after 1930 and, from 1945 onward, was associated with external influences, including the United States, and international agencies, such as UNESCO. A republic was established in 1973 and emphasis was placed on central planning.

The accession of a radical socialist government and one-party state in 1978, allied to the Soviet Union, led to a civil war, primarily against Muslim traditionalists and nationalists, in which Soviet troops were heavily involved. The withdrawal of the Soviet army in 1989 has still not resolved the secular religious political conflict. The damage inflicted on Afghan society through civil war included an estimated one million casualties and the flight of over a quarter of the population as refugees to neighboring Pakistan and Iran. The war badly affected agriculture, industry, and communications.

The origins of higher education lie in Islamic centers—mosques with mullahs as teachers—which taught not only religion but also history, literature, philosophy, and, later, mathematics and geography. These institutions began with the Arab conquest in the seventh century and flourished in the seventeenth century.

2. The Institutional Fabric of the Higher Education System

Higher education is provided by the universities of Kabul, (*Pohantoon-e-Kabul*) and Nengarhar in Jalalabad. The Kabul Polytechnic, which is regarded as being on the same level as universities, provides courses in engineering and geology. There are also training institutes providing courses in agriculture, communications, finance and management, physical education and sport, and lower-level medical education. Higher teacher-training colleges provide two-year courses (one year of academic and one year of professional studies). Also at postsecondary level are higher technical schools, one-year primary school teacher-training institutes (often integrated with higher teacher colleges), and institutes of religious studies.

Kabul University was founded by decree in 1945, though its first faculty dates from 1932. Before 1960, the only other higher education institutions were seven *madrasahs* which were founded between 1919 and 1939. In the 1960s, the University of Nengarhar (1963), Kabul Polytechnic (1967), one training institute, two higher teacher-training institutes, and a second *madrasah* in Kabul were established. The remaining four training institutes, the two higher technical schools, four higher teacher-training colleges, and two schools of Islamic Education (*madrasahs*) were set up from 1970 onward.

3. Governance, Administration, and Finance

All higher education institutions are controlled and financed by the Ministry of Higher and Vocational Education. The universities enjoy a degree of autonomy in that they are answerable to the minister rather than to any department of the ministry. The universities and polytechnic are divided into faculties which are headed by deans. The historical associations of each faculty with external agencies in various countries has led to different foreign languages being used as media of instruction and to patterns of course organization and student assessment which vary between faculties. These associations have been between the faculties of engineering and agriculture and agencies and staff in the United States; the faculties of economics and science and (West) Germany; the faculties of law and medicine and France; the faculty of theology and Egypt; and Kabul Polytechnic and the Soviet Union.

Government expenditure on education as a percentage of GNP and of total government expenditure is low though the proportions spent on higher education are comparable with similar countries.

4. Faculty and Students: Teaching, Learning, and Research

University staff are ranked at five levels, from full professor to tutorial assistant. The majority of staff are full-time but the largest number (over 40%) are concentrated in the tutorial assistant grade. There were 1,418 staff in 1987, which differed little from 1979 (1,448).

Students are admitted to higher education on completion of the certificate of secondary education (*baccaluria*) and, for the universities, after success in an entrance examination. Traditionally, those passing this examination could enter the faculty of their choice. Since the 1970s, this right has been restricted as reference is made to government labor force plans in allocating students to areas of study.

Enrollments in higher education are distributed in a ratio of 2:1 in favor of universities. The main expansion was in the 1970s, progressing from a very modest provision in the mid-1950s when the total number of students was little more than a thousand. There were fluctuations in the number of students in the 1980s with an overall decline between 1979 and 1987, concentrated particularly in the nonuniversity sector. Despite the growth in student numbers in the 1970s, the age participation rates in higher education are very low by international standards.

First degrees lead to the title of bachelor or license in arts, science, law, engineering, or medicine. The normal length of bachelor degree courses is four years though courses last five to seven years in engineering, and veterinary and medical training. Graduate studies are available only to master's degree level.

Table 1
Numbers of students, and percentage of the 20–24 age group, in higher education 1965–88

	1965	1970	1975	1979	1987	1988
Numbers	3,451	7,723	—	22,944	17,509	—
Percentage	0.26	0.7	1.0	—	—	1.3

Table 2
Government expenditure on education

	1974	1980	1982	1987
Percentage of GNP	1.2	1.8	1.6[a]	—
Percentage of total government expenditure	15.3	14.4	6.9	3.7
Percentage on higher education	17.7	18.4	19.3	—

a Figure is for 1981

Table 3
Distribution of students by field of study

	1965	1970	1980	1987
Education	451	1,466	4,637	2,456
Humanities and Arts	555	1,239	1,595	2,257
Law	509	498	624	806
Social science	460	546	1,427	1,515
Business studies	—	—	420	1,307
Natural sciences	417	723	1,218	2,160
Medicine and health	615	1,184	3,279	2,653
Engineering	293	915	3,462	512
Agriculture	140	731	1,546	1,310
Other	—	—	1,444	2,533

Numbers of students in the different fields of study have changed quite dramatically over the years and particularly in the 1980s as facilities were affected by war. There has been a steep decline in engineering students, for instance. There has always been a concentration on humanities, medicine, education, natural science, social science, and agriculture.

Access to higher education is inevitably limited by the social origins of students. Those from regions and social groups with restricted opportunities for primary and secondary schooling have difficulty in competing for entry to higher education. There are no mechanisms such as private higher education or private schooling which restrict students from more disadvantaged groups, however. Female participation has been very limited in higher as in other forms of education. The first women were admitted as university students in the 1960s. The proportion of women in the 20–24 age group in higher education is minuscule but has been rising (0.3% in 1975, 0.5% in 1986). The overall proportion of female students has changed little—it was 14 percent in 1975 and this proportion remained the same in 1986.

5. Conclusion

Higher education in Afghanistan is precarious. It is based on an infrastructure of a poor and undeveloped country, and it developed in the 1970s from a very limited provision. The war and political instability of the 1980s damaged higher education and also the social economic base on which it was built.

Bibliography

Sen Gupta B 1986 *Afghanistan: Politics, Economics and Society.* Frances Pinter, London
Dupree L, Albert L (eds.) 1974 *Afghanistan in the 1970s.* Praeger, New York

M. McLean

Albania

1. Higher Education and Society

Higher education was established in Albania after the Second World War. The first teacher training institution was founded in Tirana in 1946 and from that time on higher education has been growing in scope and strength. National, democratic, and public in character, it is free for all citizens. Present and future needs and the conditions necessary for the socioeconomic progress of the country have defined the tasks of higher education and the dynamics of its development.

In territorial terms Albania has not changed since the Second World War. While the national frontiers have remained the same, however, the population has grown from 1,120,000 in 1945 to 3,183,400 in 1989, of whom 64.6 percent live in rural areas.

The government of Albania comprises the Council of Ministers, the State Planning Commission, the leading members of other central institutions of state administration and local administrative organs (executive committees of the district people's councils, etc.). The government is entitled to speak on all branches and fields of state administration, to run and coordinate all the questions of economy, politics, and defense throughout Albania.

The mission laid upon higher education by the government is the training of specialists in various broad aspects of economy and culture.

2. The Institutional Fabric of the Higher Education System

The higher education system of Albania comprises eight establishments, one university, and seven higher institutes, all of which are public. They specialize in various fields, acting independently of one another, but each directly dependent on the Ministry of Education. The establishments are as follows: Tirana University, founded in 1957, with its eight faculties (History and Philology, Medicine, Natural Sciences, Building Engineering, Mechanical and Electric Engineering, Geology and Mining, Economics, Political and Juridical Sciences); the Higher Agricultural Institute in Tirana (1959) and the Higher Agricultural Institute in Korça (1971); the Higher Institute of Fine Arts in Tirana (1966); the Vojo Kushi Higher Institute of Physical Training (1960); the Higher Pedagogical Institute in Shkodra (1957); the Aleksander Xhuvani Higher Institute in Elbasan (1971); the Eqerem Çabej Higher Pedagogical Institute in Gjirokastra (1971).

All higher education establishments were founded after the Second World War, in the period from 1946 to 1971. From its initiation in 1980 postuniversity training has been part of the higher education system.

Table 1
Students in higher education

	1960	1965	1970	1975	1980	1985	1989	1990
Admissions	1,818	3,492	6,120	2,623	3,790	4,907	4,881	—
Entire student population	6,703	13,700	25,469	21,606	14,568	21,195	—	27,000

Its goal is to train specialists in more specific areas and in greater depth than at the university level.

All citizens have the right to enter higher education. Admission policies are governed and planned by national legislation, and are based on high results in the four years of the secondary school. The area of study is mainly the choice of the students themselves, according to their qualifications and talents. Admissions to some disciplines are contest based. No tuition fee is paid, and students of limited economic resources receive state scholarships. Other students who are not granted scholarships also receive economic help because the state provides for student boarding, libraries, and so forth.

The number of admissions in five-yearly intervals as well as the total number of students are shown in Table 1.

Over 95 percent of full-time students are below the age of 25. The period spent in higher education ranges from three to five years. For all institutions the duration of study is defined by decree of the Council of Ministers. At the end of their studies, after a state examination or a thesis defense, the students obtain a diploma in accordance with their branch of study, for example "building engineer," "forestry engineer," "teacher of linguistics and literature," "teacher of mathematics and physics," and so forth. The diploma is awarded by the respective state institution and is signed by the rector, the chair of the commission, and the faculty dean.

State examination programs are worked out by the chairs of the respective institutions and are endorsed by the dean (director). For the higher schools, the state examination programs are unified and endorsed by the Ministry of Education. The diploma theses are given to the students before the beginning of the last year.

3. Governance, Administration, and Finance

3.1 National, Provincial, and Regional Administration

Higher education in Albania is organized, financed, run, and controlled by the Ministry of Education, which at the proposal of the higher schools is responsible for opening and closing departments and scientific sectors. Institutions of higher education (full- and part-time higher schools, their subsidiaries, new branches and disciplines, and the long-term post-university courses) are opened and closed by decree of the Council of Ministers.

Higher education develops in a structured way within the framework of national official plans. The defining of enrollments according to branches of study, new admissions, and the distribution into the workforce of diploma recipients is carried out under the Council of Ministers by the State Planning Commission which then informs the higher education authorities of plans through the Ministry of Education. The assignment of graduates to planned work places is made by respective ministries.

3.2 Institutional Administration

The higher school comprises faculties, specialist branches, subsidiaries and scientific sectors and, occasionally, laboratories, libraries, museums, campuses, and other experimental and aiding bodies. It is run by the rector, who together with assistants responsible for research and academic issues, make up the rector's office. The faculty is run by the dean's office, comprising the dean and his assistants. The basic unit of educational–scientific work, the department, is run by the head of department. All these bodies cooperate with other elements of the leading administrative structures of the higher school, to

Table 2
Teaching staff

	1960	1965	1970	1975	1980	1985	1990
Tirana University	317	436	584	679	621	861	1,051
Other institutions	78	190	232	417	482	607	715
Total	395	626	816	1,096	1,103	1,468	1,766

organize, run, and control the entire educational work, the postuniversity qualifications, and the research and scientific activity. Together they implement teaching plans, programs, and so forth.

Scientific councils headed by the rector, or on a faculty level by the dean, analyze the main problems in the teaching and scientific activities of every higher school or faculty. The scientific council is a collegial body responsible for advising on all educational problems and for awarding scientific degrees and titles.

In all institutions of higher education, authority is exerted through the coordination of individual management within a broad democracy. It is on this basis that regulations and statutes of the higher school, scientific councils, departments, and so forth, are compiled. Student representatives hold equal membership of all these bodies. Their number constitutes one-third of the total number of the departments and scientific councils.

4. Faculty and Students: Teaching, Learning, and Research

4.1 Faculty

The teaching body of higher education in Albania comprises professors, doctors of sciences, university readers, candidates of sciences, teachers, and assistants in the form of laboratory workers, for instance. The number of academic teaching staff has been growing rapidly. The dynamics of its development in five-yearly intervals is shown in Table 2.

One of the fundamental tasks of higher education is the appropriate qualification of the teaching body. It is compulsory for all the teaching staff to be suitably qualified. The indices of qualification are (a) scientific degrees: candidate of sciences and doctor of sciences; and (b) scientific titles: university reader or senior scientific associate.

The degrees of candidate and doctor are granted through the system of scientific qualifications being first and second degrees respectively. The degree candidate of sciences is defended through a system of postuniversity examinations and a dissertation that aims to solve a vital problem within a specialist field. The dissertation is defended before special commissions. Successful candidates of sciences then have the right to present a further dissertation and apply for the degree of doctor of sciences.

The scientific title university reader or senior scientific associate is granted to candidates of sciences or doctors of sciences, following a period of at least four years since they received their degrees. Candidates for these advanced titles should have achieved results in the solution of important scientific problems of economy and culture, and should have published monographs, articles, reports, or other scientific materials.

The title of professor is granted to faculty in teaching or scientific institutions who have the title university reader or senior scientific associate, and the scientific degree doctor of sciences. They must have extensive pedagogical and scientific experience, have reached a high level in their teaching and scientific work, supervising the qualification of young specialists, and publishing works of a high scientific level.

The scientific degrees and titles are granted by the Higher Commission of Attestation under the Council of Ministers and its sections. The interests of the teaching staff are represented through the trade union organization at the university and the other higher institute. The number of hours to be taught and the balance between teaching, research, and administration are defined by the Council of Ministers on a national scale.

4.2 Students

The distribution of graduate students across the main higher education institutions between 1960 and 1989 is shown in five-yearly intervals in Table 3.

The interests of the students are expressed through the Youth Organization. This organization operates in every faculty or branch of studies. It is concerned with advances in level of studies, out of class activities, and student participation in scientific associations. The scientific associations provide the means for students to expand their cultural and professional knowledge. The network of the scientific associations is tripartite, comprising: (a) the scientific society on a departmental basis (several societies can be set up depending on the disciplines the departments cover); (b) the scientific society of the faculty or the discipline; (c) the scientific association of the higher establishment on the university or institute basis.

Table 3
Graduate students

	1960	1965	1970	1975	1980	1985	1989
Tirana							
University	410	858	1,290	1,675	1,640	1,737	2,110
Other institutions	320	723	753	1,125	1,182	1,588	2,208
Total	730	1,581	2,043	2,800	2,822	3,325	4,318

Teaching programs are defined by the Ministry of Education and every change or amendment is made with the approval of the ministry. Subject programs, along with programs for productive labor and professional practice are worked out by the departments and endorsed by the dean's office.

Students are assessed by various means such as seminars, drills, laboratory work, oral and written tests, annual tasks, examinations, diplomas, final examinations, and so forth. Work is graded on a scale of one to ten and marks from five to ten are passes. Assessors give high value to the creative elements in a student's answer.

Bibliography

Ballanca Z 1987 *Administrative Law of* PSRA. Tirana University Publishing House, Tirana

Collection of Legislation in Force in PSRA *(1945–1985)*. 8 Nentori Publishing House, Tirana

Golemi B, Misja V 1972 *Development of Higher Education in Albania*. Tirana University Publishing House, Tirana

Regulations of the Higher Commission of Attestation 1988 Tirana University Publishing House, Tirana

Regulations of Higher Education 1983 Tirana University Publishing House, Tirana

Statistical Book of the Ministry of Education 1989 Tirana University Publishing House, Tirana

N. Konomi

Algeria

1. Higher Education and Society

Algeria is acknowledged throughout the world for the massive effort it has made since the mid-1960s in the development of its education sector. This effort reached 25 percent of its total budget in 1978 and nearly 11 percent of the investment budget of the 1980–84 plan.

Higher education existed in Algeria before independence in 1962; however under colonial occupation it was highly selective and catered mostly to the needs of the colonizers.

Algeria's frontiers have not changed since the French colonial occupation in the nineteenth century. It is bordered on the west by Morocco and Mauritania, on the east by Tunisia and Libya, on the south by Niger and Mali, and faces Europe with a Mediterranean coastline of 1200 km. With its huge size (it is the second largest state in Africa), it is in a strategic geographical position at the crossroads of Europe, Africa, and the Arab world.

The population has grown at a steady rate since the Second World War and at a more rapid pace since 1962. Estimated at 10.24 million inhabitants in 1962, the population grew at an average rate of 3.20 percent to reach 23.038 million in the last census of 1987 (Office National des Statistiques 1988a). At the beginning of the 1990s the estimate stood at around 24.5 million. The high rate of growth is attributable to cultural, religious, and economic factors.

From a regional point of view, 21.04 million inhabitants (91.3%) live in the narrow coastal band north of the Atlas Saharien (12% of the territory), while only 2 million live in the Sahara (88% of the territory). Starting essentially as a rural population at the beginning of the century, Algeria has become progressively urbanized and now the urban population represents 49.6 percent of the total (Office National des Statistiques 1988a).

The last published figures regarding the occupational structure of Algeria (1985) show a relatively important category of permanent wage-earners (66.6% of the total working population) which includes several income groups. Independent and self-employed workers comprise 20.12 percent while the number of employers is only 1.3 percent. Low wage categories are represented by seasonal workers (5.32%), apprentices (0.5%), and home helpers (6%), with a further unspecified 0.06 percent.

1.1 Structure of the Economy

The structure of the economy has been greatly influenced by the massive oil surpluses following the rise of oil prices at the beginning of the 1970s. During the first three development plans (1967–69, 1970–73, 1974–77) a major emphasis was put on the development of heavy industry and hydrocarbons. The last two five-year development plans (1980–84 and 1985–89) emphasized agriculture, infrastructures, housing, and services. In 1984, 30.5 percent of gross value-added came from the hydrocarbon sector (which contributes more than 80 percent to the balance of payments), 15.9 percent from industry, 8.8 percent from agriculture, 16.2 percent from building and civil works, and the rest mostly from transport and communications, trading, and other services (Office National des Statistiques 1988b).

1.2 Structure of Government and Main Political Goals

French colonial occupation was resisted since its inception in 1830. After independence the FLN (Front de Libération Nationale), which conducted the armed struggle, became the ruling party. Its political goals were to promote the masses, to establish a nonaligned socialist state, and to set the foundations for a strong industrial nation which would stand against any form of domination or exploitation. In 1989, a new constitution was approved which paved the way for democracy and pluralism.

Since the major reform of the higher education system (1971), its main goal has been to train the labor force for the urgent needs of the economy. Other objectives include strengthening the link between training and employment, improving the quality and performance of the higher education system, expanding the use of the national language (Arabic) in higher education institutions, promoting research, and finally opening up the university to external society (Ministère de l'Enseignement Supérieur 1987).

Islam is the state religion of Algeria; however, no particular religious body plays a direct or significant role in higher education.

As learning and science are fundamental to the Islamic religion and Koranic teachings, both have proved important in strengthening the population's will to pursue knowledge.

2. The Institutional Fabric of the Higher Education System

As is the case with many other strategic sectors of the economy, higher education has been under public ownership and state control since independence in 1962. Privately owned establishments for higher education have never existed, in part because of the limited role given to private capital in the economy and the socialist nature of the regime.

The higher education system started in 1962 with one university that was inherited from the French colonial period and was located in Algiers. The growth of university institutions was both vertical (through the absorption of existing establishments) and horizontal (through the creation of new establishments of higher education).

The system in the early 1990s extends to 92 very heterogeneous higher education institutions (50 uni-

versity and 42 nonuniversity). The university sector incorporates more than one hundred areas of study and extends over 28 cities. The nonuniversity sector (which had 40,198 students in 1989 and 5,030 teaching staff) covers several areas of professional training, such as forestry, fishing, building, agriculture, etc. (Ministère de l'Enseignement Supérieur 1989).

The creation of the Ministry of Higher Education and Research (1970) and the National Scientific Research Council, ONRS, (July 1973) illustrated the government's desire to integrate higher education and research. Research is conducted in two Research Centers (e.g., the Research Center for Astronomy and Geography) (CNAAG) and within universities, mostly in research units, which have an important role in postgraduate study. There are currently about 63 research units in all major disciplines distributed throughout 19 institutions and nearly 600 research projects in progress. Research benefits from a reasonable level of support from the government. The amount received has risen from US$4.2 million in the 1974–77 development plan to US$118 million in the 1980–84 plan and to an estimated US$450 million in the 1985–89 plan. The new philosophy that has been adopted extends research activities to other economic institutions (e.g., enterprise) and involves experienced practitioners.

In general the main qualification required to enter the higher education system is the baccalaureat, which was inherited from the French system. It contains four options: mathematics, philosophy and literature, science, and the technical option (the latter has assumed a new relative importance with the recent emphasis on technology). As a result of the

Table 1
Numbers of institutions by level of institution in the higher education system in Algeria (university sector only)

	1962–63	1967–68	1972–73	1977–78	1982–83	1988–89
Universities[a]	3	3	3	6	6	11
Polytechnics	1	1	1	1	1	2
Medical schools[b]	—	—	—	—	1	4
Teachers training school	—	1	1	1	1	6
Technical colleges	—	—	1	1	1	3
Agronomic institutes	—	1	1	1	1	1
Veterinary school	—	—	—	1	1	1
Higher education institutes[c]	—	—	—	—	7	13
Islamic institutes	—	—	—	—	—	3
Other specialized institutes[d]	—	—	—	—	1	4
Other specialized schools[e]	—	—	—	—	—	2
Total	4	6	7	11	20	50

Source: Ministère de l'Enseignement Supérieur
a These include the two new types of university of technology as well as the four old type universities   b Medical schools used to be part of the university until 1986 then became separate schools   c Higher education institute is the preliminary stage for an institution before becoming a university   d Town planning & urban studies, for telecommunications and for computer science   e These include the National School for Administration and the High School of Commerce

problems created by the previous admission system (overcrowding of certain disciplines and neglect of others) new admission conditions were set after 1983 which applied restrictions on access to certain subjects.

For the 1989–90 academic year, limitations (which can change from one year to the other) were placed on access to the medical schools, architecture, and computer science. All three require candidates to pass a competitive exam in addition to the appropriate type of baccalaureat. Though they are less stringent, conditions are also set for admission to other disciplines (e.g., exact sciences leading to engineering). Admissions rules and restrictions, in spite of their flexibility, are of a national character and follow state legislation.

There have been important increases in the total number of students enrolled between 1962–63 and 1988–89 (an increase of 6,000 students on average each year) with major increases in 1970–71, 1974–75 and 1982–83 corresponding either to new measures taken, like the reform (1971), or the opening of new universities (Berkane 1985).

The majority of the enrolled students are in the age group 20–24 years for undergraduate studies, as secondary schooling is generally completed at the age of 18 or 19. A recent study conducted on economics students, however, found that their average age in their last year of study was 26.06, which indicates that there are delays in completing degree courses (Ait Ahmed et al. 1987).

The first degree, generally called the *Licence* usually takes four years to complete. It is awarded by the Ministry of Higher Education and has both national, vocational, and international recognition.

Admission to graduate programs is by no means automatic. A select number of recent graduates have the alternative of studying locally or taking a government grant for study abroad.

Locally, admission to graduate studies, namely the Magister, created in 1976, is highly selective and restricted to only a few candidates each year. This is reflected in the figures for graduate study which, in spite of the three-fold increase from 3,965 in 1979–80 to 12,288 in 1987–88, still has a low rate of growth. Graduate students can benefit from a government grant (offered without restriction until 1985 and thereafter on a selective basis following the economic crisis and falling oil prices). The total number of students abroad fell from 5,737 in 1985–86 to 3,964 in 1987–88 (Ministère de l'Enseignement Supérieur 1988).

3. Governance, Administration, and Finance

3.1 National Administration

The government has prime responsibility for higher education since it is essentially part of the public sector. Major decisions concerning higher education are thus made by the government council (until the recent political changes the council of ministers). The Ministry of Higher Education implements major government programs and policies, but can also make independent decisions.

The budget is an important instrument for governmental direction and control of the higher education sector, while it is effectively shaped by decrees and ministerial decisions.

It was only at the beginning of the 1980s that a real planning policy for higher education started. This led to the introduction of the first "university map" (*carte universitaire*) in 1982. This drew the major lines of development of the university up to the year 2000 in

Table 2
Total enrollment by level of institution

	1962–63	1967–68	1972–73	1977–78	1981–82[a]	1988–89
Universities	2,696	8,096	25,114	48,718	62,163	109,260
Polytechnics	29	242	284	540	789	2,376
Medical schools	—	—	—	—	—	20,704
Teachers training schools	—	320	676	1,031	1,569	6,117
Technical colleges	—	—	219	362	217	2,570
Agronomic institute	—	77	457	565	536	1,424
Veterinary school	—	—	—	143	149	996
Higher education institutes	—	—	—	—	6,603	16,175
Islamic institutes	—	—	—	—	—	3,182
Other specialized institutes	—	—	—	564	572	2,035
Other specialized schools	—	—	—	—	—	2,549
Total	2,725	8,735	26,074	51,923	72,598	167,388

Source: MESRS 1982 *L'université en chiffres* pp. 5–13; MES 1989 *La formation supérieure en chiffres: année 1988–89*, pp. 8–11
a Exceptionally, figures for 1981–82 are used instead of 1982–83

Table 3
Evolvement of the local and foreign teaching staff in higher education

	1962–63		1967–68		1972–73		1977–78		1982–83		1988–89	
	L	F	L	F	L	F[a]	L	F	L[b]	F	L	F
Professors	9	57	10	44	46	132	120	92	260	168	362	128
Assistant professors	1	12	61	52	49	102	121	295	150	577	330	533
Lecturers	17	57	46	52	268	142	709	1,130	2.863	1,248	7,336	630
Assistants	54	84	214	197	402	420	1,868	1,147	5,625	767	4,719	49
Total	81	210	331	345	765	796	2,818	2,664	8,898	2,760	12,747	1,340

Source: MESRS, 1982 pp. 9, 20; MES 1985 p. 32; MES 1989 L'université en chiffres, p. 26
a The figures for foreign personnel used for 1972–73 are those of 1971–72 because figures for 1972–73 were not available
b The figures for assistants include technical collaborators

relation to the long-term development strategy of the country.

The prime source of finance for higher education remains the state budget. In theory, budgets are allocated by the Ministry of Higher Education on the basis of budget proposals, forecast by the various establishments of higher education according to their needs. The budget allocated to higher education has increased tenfold between 1962–63 and 1988–89. In terms of proportion, it rose from 2.2 percent of the total annual budget of the country in 1972, to 5.5 percent in 1989. The increase in the budget is due not only to the importance given by government to higher education, but also to the sheer increase in the number of students.

3.2 Institutional Administration

The organization, structure, and administering bodies of institutes of higher education are regulated by two main decrees dating from September 1983. Universities are headed by rectors (directors in the case of high institutes and specialized schools) appointed by the minister of higher education through a presidential decree as the post is also of a political nature. The rector of the university is assisted by two councils, the University Scientific Council, and the Orientation Council, whose members come from various external institutions.

The university is composed of various institutes (formerly called faculties) organized by single disciplines or groups of related disciplines (e.g., the institute of exact sciences) and run by a director designated by the rector and approved by the minister of higher education.

4. Faculty and Students: Teaching, Learning, and Research

4.1 Faculty

Initially the Algerian higher education system was dependent to a large degree on foreign teaching personnel. It has since managed to introduce a great number of Algerians to its academic staff, mainly through an adequate training policy for graduates (see Table 3).

The procedure of appointments follows several conditions which have been established by decree since 1968 and which were altered only marginally by a decree of 1977. The 1968 and the 1977 decrees relate to all four ranks in the academic profession. Full professors (who represent only 2.8 percent of the whole body of local teaching staff) are generally recruited from the body of assistant professors (*maitre de conférence*) who have completed two to three years experience in their tenure with the approval of the faculty and the university councils. Full professors represent only 2.8 percent of the whole body of local teaching staff.

The academic profession represents its corporate interests through a national union: the SNESUP (*Syndicat National de l'Enseignement Supérieur*), affiliated with the National Union of Algerian Workers (UGTA). The latter comes under the auspices of the ruling FLN party. Recent political changes are driving towards an independent union without affiliation to any political party.

4.2 Students

The student body has undergone a very rapid growth since 1962 and particularly since the reform in 1971 known as the democratization of higher education (see Table 4).

The rapid growth of the student body is followed by a similar growth rate in the numbers graduating from initial courses which indicate that the system did not improve its efficiency since the beginning of the 1970s (see Table 5).

Although scarce, some interesting studies have made a breakdown of the student body by social class (Kennouche et al. 1982, Glasman and Kremer 1978). Policy statements and programs to provide low income sectors of the population with access to higher

Table 4
Evolvement of the student body in higher education by major area of discipline (undergraduates only)

	1962–63	1967–68	1972–73	1977–78	1982–83	1988–89
Exact science[a]	1,530	4,807	12,423	29,494	64,467	117,498
Social sciences[b]	616	2,099	8,629	14,036	15,705	28,522
Humanities[c]	735	1,892	6,070	11,250	15,695	21,539
Total	2,881	8,798	27,122	54,780	95,867	167,559

Source: MESRS 1982: L'université en chiffres, pp. 6–14; MES 1989: L'université en chiffres, p. 12
a These figures include medicine, technology, exact sciences, veterinary and earth sciences (geology and geography)
b Social sciences include economics, law, and political science.
c Humanities includes sociology, psychology, French and Arabic literature from 1972–73 onwards, and languages.

education have not always been effective. Thus students with modest home finances are much less represented in higher education than students of higher income. Nevertheless in comparative terms, many social sectors that are denied access to higher education in other countries (e.g., the rural poor and the unemployed) are represented in Algeria.

The student union has evolved through three major stages. Shortly after independence it was formalized as the National Union of Algerian Students (UNEA). It lasted in this form until 1971, when for political reasons it was dissolved and replaced by another union, which was more law-abiding and had close connections with the ruling party, the FLN. It became part of the National Union of Algerian Youth (UNJA), which incorporates other segments of the young population. In the wake of recent political changes, there are indications that it might become independent again with no loyalty to any political party.

5. Conclusion

The Algerian higher education system has witnessed some remarkable achievements in its relatively short life, including 220,000 students (1% of the population) and more than 13,000 academic staff employed on a full-time basis. This has occurred in spite of the attractions of various other highly

Table 5
Numbers graduating from initial courses at university sectors

1962–63	1967–68	1972–73	1977–78	1982–83	1987–88[a]
93	654	2,355	5,928	9,584	15,323

Source: MESRS 1982: L'université en chiffres, pp. 10, 21; MES 1985: Annuaire Statistique Vol. 1 No. 13, p. 27; MES 1989: Annuaire Statistique No. 17, p. 9
a The figures for 1987–88 do not include the high technicians category which has recently been introduced into the higher education system: 959 in Technology, 190 in biology, veterinary and earth sciences and 173 in social sciences graduated in 1987–88

competitive sectors and the substantial brain drain, which has affected Algeria along with many other developing countries.

Despite its undeniable achievements, the higher education system still suffers from several weaknesses, such as the decreasing quality of graduates (particularly in social sciences), the problem of graduate unemployment and the relatively limited involvement of the university in social and economic development. Excessive centralization of decision making has contributed to part of the problem although there have been efforts to decentralize.

Initiatives have been taken recently with the intention of alleviating the problems presented by the exceptionally high number of students. Solutions include the acquisition of new buildings and infrastructures from other national institutions, and the establishment of the university map. Whenever possible the semester system is being replaced by the annual system, which should be much more time effective. In addition to these initiatives an intersectorial coordinating committee has been created to serve as a permanent link between employment requirements and the higher education system and a mixed commission has been established from the secondary and the higher education system to strengthen the coordination between the two sectors.

At the outset of the 1990s, the higher education system faces several issues likely to affect it until the year 2000 and even beyond. Among these is the need to create a correspondence between the output of the higher education system and employment requirements. There is also the question of the "Arabization" of the higher education system which is torn between its legitimate desire to contribute to the strengthening of cultural identity, and the scientific and technological progress in the world. Yet another problem occurs for the academics with rising expectations who suffer from low social status and a low standard of living. Finally there is a need for respect and cooperation from politicians who should not see the university merely as a source of criticisms, inefficiency, and opposition, but rather as a wonderful tool for training the elite of the country and for fulfilling the dreams of society for a prosperous and peaceful future.

Bibliography

Ait Ahmed B, Ferroukhi D J, Rabah A 1987 Le rendement du système d'enseignement supérieur, Research report 1, CREAD/MES, Algiers
Barkat M 1980 L'orientation, l'échec et la réussite des étudiants de 1ère année dans l'enseignement supérieur à l'Université de Constantine. Magister thesis, University of Constantine
Belgacem T 1989 Dynamique de la formation à l'étranger: Aspects économiques et impact budgétaire. Magister thesis, University of Algiers
Benachenhou A 1982 *Planification et développement en Algérie: 1962–1980*. Office des Publications Universitaires (OPU), Algiers
Benachenhou M 1980 Vers l'université Algérienne: Réflexions sur une stratégie universitaire. OPU, Algiers
Bencheikh-Lefgoun M S 1980 Développement universitaire et développement économique et social. *Les Cahiers de la Recherche* 8–9, 15 (59/60): 511–48 CURER-ONRS
Berkane Y 1985 Enseignement supérieur en Algérie et besoins de l'économie en cadres. Magister thesis, Constantine
Bertrand O, Kouacs J, Reves Z, Timar J 1974 Prévisions de main d'oeuvre et planification de l'éducation: Cas de l'Algérie. *Rev. Tiers-Monde*, 15: (59–60): 153–63
Bourdieu P 1984 *Homo Academicus*. Les Editions de Minuit, Paris
Cheriet A 1983 *Opinion sur la politique de l'enseignement et de l'arabisation*. SNED, Algiers
Djeflat A 1989 Développement économique et développement universitaire: Complémentarités et enjeux à la lumière de l'expérience algérienne, *Rev. CERES* 100: 26–33
Farhi M 1982 L'enseignement supérieur en Algérie et le recours à la formation à l'étranger. *Rapport de recherche*
Glasman D, Kremer J 1978 *Essai sur l'université et les cadres en Algérie*. Editions du CNRS, Centre Régional de Publications de Marseille
Haddad M 1986 Quelques problèmes de l'analyse des changements dans l'enseignement supérieur. *Rev. Algérienne Psychol. Sci. Educ.* 2: (59–67)
Kennouche B, Haddad M, Khenniche L 1982 *Les jeunes ruraux et l'école: Mythes et réalités*. Centre de Recherche en Economie Appliquée, Presses UAFA, Algiers
Ministère de l'Enseignement Supérieur 1985 *Annuaire statistique: Année Universitaire 1983–1984*, 1 (13). Algiers
Ministère de l'Enseignement Supérieur 1987 *Quelques données sur l'Enseignement Supérieur 1979/1986*. Second National Conference on Higher Education, Algiers
Ministère de l'Enseignement Supérieur 1989a *Annuaire Statistique: 1987–1988*, 17. Algiers
Ministère de l'Enseignement Supérieur 1989b *La formation supérieure en chiffres: Année 1988/89*. Algiers
Ministère de l'Enseignement Supérieur et de la Recherche Scientifique 1971 *Stratégies pour le développement du système de l'éducation post-secondaire*. Consultancy report. Artur D. Little, Algiers
Ministère de l'Enseignement Supérieur et de la Recherche Scientifique 1982 *L'université en chiffres*, Algiers
Ministère de l'Enseignement Supérieur et de la Recherche Scientifique 1983 Recherche Scientifique: l'essor et les moyens. *Rev. Univ.*, special edition Oct./Nov: 38–44. Algiers
Office National des Statistiques 1988a *Caractéristiques socio-économiques des pays du Grand Maghreb. Collections Statistiques, 10*
Office National des Statistiques 1988b *Les Comptes Economiques de l'exercise 1984. Revue Statistiques, 18*
Touati S 1981 *La formation des cadres pour le développement*. OPU, Algiers

A. Djeflat

Angola

1. Higher Education And Society

Angola, a former Portuguese colony, became independent in 1975. It lies on the southwest coast of Africa and is bounded by the Atlantic Ocean on the west, Zaire on the north and northeast, Zambia on the east, and Namibia on the south. It is roughly square, with a coastline of 1,000 kilometers, and occupies an area of approximately 1,200,000 square kilometers.

The main topographical feature of Angola is the high plateau, rising to an average altitude of 1,400 meters.

Climatic conditions vary according to altitude. On the plateau, they are generally refreshing and healthy. The cool Benguela Atlantic current means that it becomes warmer from the north to the south. Topography and climate create different natural regions. There are a variety of zones, including tropical forest, savanna, and even a desert on the south coast, which give rise to different possibilities in areas such as agriculture and settlement.

Angolan ethnic groups are closely related, having a common origin before the Portuguese arrival at the mouth of Zaire river in 1482. The colonial government was set up in Luanda in 1592 and the present boundaries were established by (1815), according to the Treaty of Vienna.

In 1961, uprisings against the Portuguese dominance began, leading to a colonial war which ended in 1974. Following negotiations, Independence was achieved on November 11 1975.

Independence was not peaceful and orderly. Civil war broke out, and is still going on. This has led to heavy economic disruption and instability in social organization and population distribution. An exodus has taken place from the countryside to the cities, mainly to Luanda, the state capital. It is estimated that of a total population of between six and eight million people, approximately one-third live here.

At the time of writing, in 1991, negotiations between the government and the guerillas are taking place, supported by the Portuguese government and the governments of the United States and the Soviet Union.

By 1974 the Angolan population was about five million people, of whom four and a half million were Africans and half a million were Portuguese Europeans. The events leading to Independence caused a massive exodus of the white population. In 1991 apart from a few thousand foreigners, the population was African. The African population consists of the Bantu ethnic group which is divided, in turn, into six main ethnic groups: the Ovibundu (the largest group), who live in central Angola; the Mbundu (the second largest group), who live in an area extended eastward from Luanda and to Bakongo in the north, and are related to the Zaire population in this area; the Lunda-Chokwe, who live in northeastern Angola; and the Nganguela and the Kuanyana-Humbi-Vanheca, both of which live in the south.

With the exception of a few small ethnic groups in the south, the population belongs to the same linguistic group, the Bantu. However, the different ethnic groups have their own languages and, in several cases, dialects still exist. Portuguese, the former colonial language, has been adopted as the official and common spoken language, because of this.

The Angolan population is very young. There are no official figures but it is estimated that half the population is under fifteen years old. This factor creates several difficult problems. Among these is the fact that the need for education has overwhelmed the nation's resources.

Angola has a rich agricultural, fishing, and mining potential. The climatic and topographical variety provide conditions for diverse crop and fruit cultivation, both tropical and temperate, and cattle raising. The long coastline and the calm seas also provide good conditions for fishing. Mineral deposits, namely diamonds, several ferrous and non-ferrous metals, and oil, are important. Unfortunately, all this potential has been jeopardized as a result of the civil war and its effects. Consequently, the occupational distribution of the active population does not follow the pattern that could be expected for such a country. Roughly 20 percent work in the primary sector, 20 percent in the secondary sector, and 60 percent in the tertiary sector. The exodus to the cities and the high percentage of the adult population enlisted in the army could explain this situation.

Since Independence, Angola has been ruled according to the Marxist–Leninist model of a one-party communist regime. All social organization is governed by central decisions of the political party. Policies of government and administration are subordinated to the party's political system, supported by the army's policy. The economy, social services, and domestic administration are controlled by the state, and the state is the Party. Ideas have been proposed to set up a pluralist regime, following the political events in Eastern Europe, but it is impossible to forecast the outcome of this.

2. The Institutional Fabric of the Higher Education System

Angola has one higher education institution, the university, with its headquarters and most of its schools in Luanda. It is a state university, embodied in the government framework.

The university has its origins in the former University of Luanda, set up in 1962 by the Portuguese administration. The university used to be attended mainly by white Portuguese students, the Africans representing less than 10 percent of the total enrollment. They reached about three thousand in 1974, the highest figure before Independence. Teaching was given in Portuguese, teachers were Portuguese, too, and it was also strongly supported by the local research institutes that were reasonably developed and staffed. The exodus of Portuguese settlers in 1974 and 1975 emptied the university of most of its teaching body and students, causing widespread disruption. With Independence, the university was renamed as University Agostinho Neto, after the nation's leader during the struggle for Independence. Efforts were made to rebuild the institution in line with the new political situation.

Admissions are open to those who have completed vocational studies at upper secondary level, lasting four years, or eight years of compulsory schooling. The latter policy, which does not seem to be developing very well, sought to accelerate expertise demanded for development needs. The former, based on vocational education, has also revealed some weaknesses. For these and other reasons, the entire educational system is under revision in the early 1990s.

Although statistics have not been provided, it is known that the humanities and social studies are more popular than science and technology. The scarcity of cadres and the youth of the active population mean that a significant number of students are engaged in occupational activities. This causes a lack of effectiveness in schooling standards, with some wastage of graduating students, which represents a serious problem.

The faculty and course structure is basically the same as that of the former colonial university. Nevertheless, a course in law, needed to frame the regime and the public administration, and another in architecture, were added. There are faculties or schools of law, economics, teacher training, sciences, engineering, medicine, agriculture, and veterinary sciences. Law, economics, and medicine are one-course faculties.

Courses in law, economics, engineering, medicine, agriculture, and veterinary sciences consist of a single cycle of study, and a single degree is awarded at the end, called the *licenciado*. Other courses were intended to follow a two-cycle pattern, the first three-year cycle leading to the *bacharelato*, followed by a two-year cycle leading to the *licenciado* degree. In practice, only the first cycle is in operation for sciences, which include mathematics, physics, chemistry, geology, and geophysics. The same is true of teacher training, where several courses are offered in line with the needs of the school system. Graduate studies are not yet organized.

3. Governance, Administration, and Finance

It is rather difficult to analyze systems of university governance in a context such as that found in Angola. Considering the nature of the regime, the war, and the scarcity of human academic resources, the peculiar system of governance is molded thereby.

The university is taken as an essential goal of nation building, and therefore is closely ruled by the government. The rector, the university head, is appointed by the President of the Republic. Directors of faculties and schools are appointed by the Minister of Education on the rector's recommendation. Although the system is clearly hierarchical, some academic participation is available through groups which include teacher and student representatives.

The university is financially supported by public funds and its management follows the public administration pattern. Students do not pay fees; their attendance is a matter of national interest.

4. Faculty and Students: Teaching, Learning, and Research

One of the most serious problems of the university limiting its development, is the composition and academic qualifications of the teaching body. This is especially relevant as regards recruitment. Angola has none of its own teachers, and conditions have not provided autonomy in this particular field, as well as in many others. Therefore, most of the teaching body is recruited from other countries on a cooperative basis. This scheme presents different problems: the academic quality is, in general, not up to the academic standards of some universities; there is no continuity in the academic staff, because of the temporary nature of their posts; the variety of the academic staff's origins (with differences in academic patterns and languages) results in serious communication problems.

Among the Angolans, the scarcity of an intellectual and professional elite, the Youth of the State Administrative Officers (part of them are university students, and even teachers at the same time), gives some indication of the parlousness of the situation.

5. Conclusion

The above description reveals a large number of problems. However, the fundamental problem is the instability of the country which is in turn reflected in Angolan university life.

Angola is a young country in two senses of the word: Its population is young, and it is itself a state recently born. Problems arising from this situation are common throughout Africa. The colonial inheritance, the administrative pattern, the need for change according to the new situation of independence, the shortage of qualified human resources, all represent an enormous challenge which is compounded by the war.

There are, however, hopes that the war will end and a democratic regime can be instated. The Portuguese-speaking world has shown great interest in aiding and participating in the rebuilding of the Angolan nation. One may hope for better days.

E. L. Pires

Argentina

1. Higher Education and Society

The development of a system of higher education in Argentina was a consequence of the strengthening of the national state in the 1880s. Although it was built upon institutions founded by the Church in the colonial days, or by provincial governments after Independence (1810), the system emerged as a small number of national universities located in the major cities. By far the largest and most important to this day is the University of Buenos Aires. By the late 1950s only seven national universities were in operation. Since then 22 others have been founded, many originally as provincial institutions and later absorbed by the national state; only one university remains within a provincial administration. Formally autonomous in government, they are financially dependent on the federal budget and have been subject to federal intervention frequently and for long periods. Private universities have been authorized to function only since 1958. There are 27 of them today, on average much smaller than national institutions. Prominent in number and size are those founded by the Catholic Church. The nonuniversity sector is made up primarily of teachers' colleges and technical schools. Enrollment in higher education is relatively high for world standards. It is largely concentrated in universities, and within them in national institutions.

Argentina is a large country with a relatively small population. Current population is estimated at 33 million, highly concentrated in the fertile Pampean region, whose natural, economic, and political capital coincides with the national capital city, Buenos Aires. This region includes about one-third of the country's territory and two-thirds of its population, one-half of which is in the Metropolitan Area of Buenos Aires. Total growth rates have been moderate to low since 1930, when mass immigration ended rapidly and natural growth rates were already showing clear signs of a decline, reaching a low plateau of between 1.3 and 1.5 percent per year (Recchini de Lattes and Lattes 1975). Already a highly urbanized country by 1930, internal migration has pushed urbanization even further, until to date, only a mere 15 percent of the population is rural. Urban population has been highly concentrated. The metropolitan area of Buenos Aires represents about one-third of the country's population. In recent years, however, it has grown considerably less than the rest of the urban system, which includes 18 other cities or metropolitan areas with over 100,000 population each, 13 of which are provincial capitals (Wilkie 1984).

Argentina is a culturally homogeneous country. Immigration played a very important role, but mass immigration was concentrated within a few decades two or more generations ago (1880–1930), 80 percent of which originated in Spain or Italy. Traces of the aboriginal population can be found easily in the interior provinces and among the lower urban strata, but they do not form the basis for cultural identity or political organization. Also, the African slave population was important during the late colonial days, but it left few demographic and cultural traces in the current Argentine population. Recent immigrants arriving from neighboring countries do not differ much from the population of the regions where they tend to live. Thus, most cultural indicators show considerable homogeneity, with only one major national language (Spanish) and religious affiliation (Catholic), while other languages and religions are visible and highly tolerated. Literacy is very high (93%), as is exposure to mass media. Regional differences in demographic, social and economic indicators are large, but there is no major area concentrating a large segment of the population in poverty.

Urbanization preceded and progressed faster than industrialization, reflecting initially the growth of a rich, export oriented, agricultural economy. The early development of manufacturing and a modern service sector in the cities was linked to the processing and administration of the export sector, to the growth of the state apparatus, and to the concentration in cities of high-income groups. Since the 1930s import substitution industrialization increased much faster than the primary sector, but so also did the public sector, including both administration, production of goods and services, and a spreading welfare system. These trends were linked to early massive growth of enrollment in higher education institutions, mainly but not only in professional schools (i.e., medicine, law, public accounting, engineering).

The agricultural sector in Argentina is largely modern, that is, it is wholly commercialized, highly mechanized, and in recent years has achieved levels of productivity similar to those found elsewhere in the developed world. Rural poverty and very small landholdings are limited to some backward areas. Thus, rural-urban differences in income and welfare are considerably smaller than in other Latin American countries. The urban economy includes an important but troubled manufacturing sector, which failed to modernize and become competitive in world markets, its post-1930 growth largely favored by protective policies. By the late 1950s it was evident that import substitution industrialization led to cyclical crises originating in the balance of trade. Although reforms lead to significant changes and growth during the 1960s and early 1970s, the economy has lost momentum since then. Furthermore, inflation which was already chronic, has become much higher since 1975 and has been steadily increasing to the present day. The rapid growth of the foreign debt, in spite of a much better performance in the agricultural sector, has generated a serious, long-term crisis since 1982, including recession, high inflation, and accumulated fiscal deficits.

The federal, republican political regime established with the 1853 Constitution, provided for the separation of the executive, legislative, and judicial powers. Argentina's democracy, however, has been subject to considerable instability since 1930, the date of the first successful military coup in this century. Elected, constitutional governments, have alternated with provisional, unconstitutional ones, which have often suspended civil and human rights of citizens. Major regime changes took place in 1955, 1958, 1962, 1966, 1973, 1976, and 1983, either through military coups or through a return to an elected, constitutional government. The executive branch has often encroached upon legislative and judicial powers even within democratically elected regimes, and the federal government has restricted the financial and political autonomy of provincial governments. Against this background, however, Argentina established a truly democratic, constitutional regime in 1983 which has survived the political and economic crises of recent years, without relying upon federal interventions or limitations of the legislative and judicial powers. In 1989 presidential elections were held, and the new executive, as well as a renewed parliament, came to power, showing signs of regime continuity.

The 1853 Constitution, combined with major laws enacted in the 1880s, gave priority to free and lay public education. Since then, universal, public primary school has been guaranteed to all children up to the age of 14. Literacy has become widespread as a consequence of the development of a system of federal and provincial public schools throughout the country. The private sector in primary and secondary education has also grown in cycles, competing with the federal and provincial educational systems. The federal government pays subsidies to many private schools at both levels. Currently, the public system at the primary level has been decentralized and it depends entirely upon the provincial governments. At the secondary level decentralization is more limited, but private schools play a major role. In higher education, the federal state plays the major role, but it does not subsidize private institutions at this level.

The Catholic Church is the main religious institution in the country, with some 95 percent of the population being nominally Catholic. Church and state are not entirely separate, since the 1853 Constitution established religious freedom and equality but the state sustains the Catholic Church. The peculiar arrangements established then have very often led to conflict. On the one hand, the Church is not entirely autonomous to choose its authorities in Argentina, and sometimes does not agree with the state on these matters. On the other hand, state support and supervision of educational institutions administered by the Church, as well as Church influence within the system of public education, have been chronic arenas for political conflict.

In fact, the Catholic Church and lay Catholic leaders have always aspired for a more active role in education, including higher education, both through the activities of its own institutions and within the public school system. This aspiration has conflicted with the views of other political sectors. Concerning higher education, the monopoly over professional diplomas granted until 1958 to national universities had been contested by the Church, which gained a major victory with the new legal framework allowing private institutions to enter into this market. The first few private universities, and the strongest, established since then have been linked to the Catholic Church. Competition with tuition free public institutions, and the lack of state subsidies at this level, have limited their ability to grow in quantity and quality.

2. The Institutional Fabric of the Higher Education System

The higher education system in Argentina is highly differentiated in finance and governance, but not in function, between the public and private sectors. All public sector institutions are state supported, while the private sector institutions receive very limited public support, depending almost entirely on private (including Church) funding and student fees. Institutions are also highly differentiated in two broad categories—universities and other. The former compose a rather homogeneous group, while the latter

Table 1

Argentina: Enrollment in higher education by sector and type as percentages 1987

Type Sector	University	Other
State: national	89.9	32.9
State: provincial	0.3	37.3
Private	9.8	29.8
Total	100.0%	100.0%
	(755.000)	(203.000)

Source: Secretaría de Educación, Estadísticas de la Educación

are more heterogeneous. Universities are considerably more important in terms of enrollment, expenditure, political visibility, and functions. Since they differ in many ways from nonuniversity institutions, we will now discuss the two categories separately. In both cases we find differentiated public and private sectors. A summary view of the proportion of total enrollment in each category is found in Table 1.

There are currently 29 national (i.e., federal) universities in Argentina, plus three provincial institutions, among which only one is comparable to the national ones. (The other two are a police academy and a school of aeronautical engineering.) One of the national universities is in fact a large technical school, with many regional branches throughout the country. In sum, there are 26 public universities *strictu sensu*, 25 of which are federally supported. All of them are constituted by a small number of schools, or *facultades*. Exceptionally, the latter have been replaced by departments in some small universities. Schools, between six and fourteen, are quite autonomous bodies, mainly in the older and more traditional universities. Most of them have a professional orientation, that is, they are organized around teaching for the professions which require diplomas in order to practice legally, and subsequently, schools have been authorized by the federal government to award such diplomas to practice medicine, law, engineering of various kinds, architecture, pharmacy, psychology, and the like. Also, there are schools awarding degrees in disciplines with no clear professional boundaries, except in the teaching of such disciplines. The most prominent examples are schools or *facultades* of philosophy and letters, sometimes called humanities, and of exact and natural sciences.

Public universities may be grouped in two major categories. On the one hand, the older and larger universities, which include one giant (Buenos Aires, with over 200,000 registered students), and the universities of Córdoba, La Plata, Litoral (now divided in two—Litoral proper and Rosario), Tucumán, and

Cuyo (also divided in two—Mendoza and San Juan). All of them were founded before the 1950s, and have between 10,000 and 75,000 students. They are all located in major cities. On the other hand, the new universities are usually much smaller, normally around 5,000 to 10,000 students, with one exception (Nordeste, with 37,000 students), and include schools in various cities within a certain area or region. A number of them were founded as provincial institutions in the early 1970s in a larger attempt to decentralize and deconcentrate the older university system, but soon afterwards were absorbed by the federal government.

There are 27 legally authorized private universities. Among them, however, there are a number of small, specialized schools, very different in structure and function from the public universities (i.e., technical or business schools). The larger institutions include the two older Catholic universities (*Universidad Católica Argentina* and *Universidad del Salvador*), authorized to function in the late 1950s, and some private non-Catholic ones which grew mainly in the late 1970s (i.e., *Universidad de Belgrano* and *J F Kennedy*). They range in enrollment between 4,000 and 10,000 students, and are located in the Buenos Aires Metropolitan Area. Smaller universities, which tend to be located in provincial cities, are predominantly recent Catholic institutions. Private universities are also organized in schools or *facultades*, and do not differ in function and organization from public universities.

There are no research universities *strictu sensu* in Argentina. However, all public universities claim to include research within the normal activities of its faculties, and major universities in fact do have important research components. In private universities, and in smaller institutions in both sectors, research is conducted only in exceptional cases. Although most schools within large public universities have research centers or institutes, research is largely concentrated within a few of them. At the University of Buenos Aires, for instance, bio-medical research is quantitatively the most important, and it takes place within institutes located at the schools of medicine, biochemistry, and veterinary science. The school of exact and natural sciences' institutes are also very important, and this school is, comparatively speaking, much more research oriented than the rest of the university. A university-wide division of science and technology grants fellowships and subsidies to faculty and student applicants in Buenos Aires.

Research is coordinated, promoted, and to a large extent financed, through a specialized body, the National Council for Scientific and Technological Research, or CONICET, administratively independent from the university system. The council supports research through several mechanisms, including subsidies, fellowships, and incorporation into the so-

called research career. From its inception in 1958, the council developed special relationships with national universities, but these have fluctuated over time. During the 1970s and early 1980s the council's policy was to create autonomous research institutions, while in recent years it moved back to its older policy of supporting university research, although not with the exclusion of other nonuniversity, public and private organizations. Currently, over 2,000 researchers hold positions within the research career, and a majority of them are affiliated to national universities.

The university system also includes two large institutions highly specialized in the training of professionals for private industry which do not fit easily within the description of universities offered above. The *Universidad Tecnológica Nacional*, within the public system, is a large technical school with branches throughout the country. It trains engineers in various specialities with a practical orientation, as contrasted to the relatively more academic orientation of other schools of engineering in public universities. The *Universidad Argentina de la Empresa* is a business supported, private school, oriented towards the training of executives for private industry, both at the undergraduate and graduate levels.

Outside the university system, higher education in Argentina includes mainly two types of institutions. The first category, the larger one includes teacher-training colleges, which carry out programs to train pre-primary, primary, secondary, and specialized school teachers. The bulk of students are enrolled in institutions training pre-primary and primary teachers. Diplomas for secondary education are granted both by university and nonuniversity institutions. Programs in teacher colleges are shorter than university programs, lasting from two to four years. The second category is that of technical and semi-professional schools, including those training para-medical personnel, social workers, artists, and technicians. They are also short-cycle institutions.

While the university system is largely dominated by national institutions, this is not the case with the nonuniversity sector. Provincial institutions, as well as the private sector, are as important as national institutions in terms of total enrollment (see Table 1). Their weight is also shown in the relative importance of the Metropolitan Area of Buenos Aires as compared to the rest of the country: while nonuniversity institutions are distributed following closely the total population distribution, this is not the case with universities, which are more heavily concentrated in the metropolitan area and in other large cities. In other words, nonuniversity institutions are placed closer to where the demand is, while universities have found it more beneficial to locate themselves where power and resources are based.

The nonuniversity sector serves largely as the training ground for the rest of the educational system. However, this is not its only and exclusive field of operation. Universities also train teachers, and nonuniversity institutions train specialists who engage in other activities. Such is the case, for instance, of schools training artists and performers. Also within this sector one should include non-training institutions, such as the official academies. While these are often honorific societies supported by the national state, with limited academic or professional functions, there are exceptional cases with important research components, such as the National Academy of Medicine.

National universities have currently an open admission policy. Entrance examinations, which were previously administered autonomously by each school, have been eliminated. All students with a high school diploma are eligible to register in the university, and school, of their choice. Furthermore, public universities have free tuition. This has resulted in a dramatic increase in university enrollment since 1984 from the already high levels achieved before. Private universities have their own admission policy, but have also refrained from establishing entrance examinations. Although the tuition fees they charge vary considerably, it is always significant as compared to free public institutions. Thus, even with an open admission policy, and given the relative lack of differentiation in terms of programs and quality with the public sector institutions, private universities have not grown as rapidly as public ones in recent years.

By Latin American standards, enrollment in higher education was already unusually high in Argentina during the first half of this century, due to the growing demand for education arising from rapid urbanization and industrialization, and also due to public policies favoring expansion of the national universities (Levy 1986). From the 1960s, when private universities were authorized to function and award diplomas, growth has continued, although unevenly. Figures shown in Table 2 indicate that enrollment has tended to double each ten years, but growth has been highest in the early 1970s and during the recent few years, from 1984. They happened to be periods when democratically elected regimes favored an open-policy admission. This policy resulted in a more dramatic growth when it followed, as it did in recent years, a period of restrictive policies which even led to a decline in absolute numbers. Restrictions, in other words, created an unsatisfied demand which was channeled soon afterwards.

Growth rates of the nonuniversity sector have tended to be much higher than those in the university sector. The former made up only 11 percent of total enrollment in the early 1960s, while it now makes over 20 percent. The big change, however, took place mainly during the late 1970s and early 1980s, when public sector restrictions were applied to the university public sector, channeling unmet demand to the nonuniversity institutions and the private sector

in general. The private sector ceased to grow in the most recent period of open admissions. A comparison of nonuniversity institutions between 1983 and 1987 is illustrative: while private sector enrollment has stabilized, public sector enrollment has increased to 34 percent at the national level and 41 percent at the provincial one.

Growth of enrollment in higher education has far surpassed population growth in Argentina. While students enrolled made up 11.3 percent of the population aged 20–24 in 1960, they increased to 15.1 percent in 1970 and 22 percent in 1980. The rate was around 37 percent in 1990. Of course, students in Argentina are spread over a wider age range, but as an approximation those figures are indicative of the tendency.

Official statistics systematically over-estimate university enrollment, since inactive students are seldom excluded from registers. A recent census carried out at the University of Buenos Aires counted approximately 50,000 students less than the official enrollment figure, for a loss of over 20 percent. The same source indicates that a very large proportion of the total student body is enrolled in the first year or university-wide cycle instituted several years ago, where drop-out rates are known to be very high. To summarize, a more restrictive definition of university enrollment would bring down the figures presented in Table 2 to perhaps one-half, and also would seriously reduce yearly variations.

University first degrees are usually professional diplomas (i.e., for lawyers, physicians, engineers, architects, or public accountants) or so-called *licenciaturas* (licences) in a given discipline. The former usually require six, and the latter five, years of study. They are both called "basic careers" offering terminal degrees. In a few cases students may choose an intermediary degree when they have completed some requirements of a basic career. There are also "technical careers" or short-cycle ones, offering terminal degrees geared toward semiprofessional activities. They are granted by the technical universities, and last normally four years. A few university schools also offer short-cycle degrees (e.g., for laboratory technicians) lasting two to three years. In all cases, degrees are awarded by schools within each institution, but have to be authorized by the national Ministry of Education. Professional diplomas have to be registered by the appropriate governmental office, but there is no system of state examinations to practice the professions. The market demand for nationally valid diplomas has placed a premium on national authorization of public and private schools, and thus has limited the operation of provincial universities within the public sector.

Graduate training programs admit only candidates with a first degree, that is, a *licenciatura* or professional degree. University doctorates are not professional diplomas, neither are they normally

Table 2
Enrollment in higher education and annual percentage growth[a] 1960–87

	1960–64	1965–69	1970–74	1975–79	1980	1981	1982	1983	1984	1985	1986	1987
University												
Number	175.208	230.937	347.853	458.546	393.828	402.070	411.113	416.571	507.994	664.200	707.016	755.206
% Annual growth	—	6.4	10.1	6.4	-4.1	2.1	2.2	1.3	22.0	30.7	6.4	6.8
Other												
Number	21.904	28.082	52.407	73.476	93.645	123.618	130.443	164.055	169.541	181.945	195.866	203.336
% Annual growth	—	5.6	17.3	8.0	8.2	32.0	5.5	25.8	3.3	7.3	7.7	3.8
Total												
Number	197.113	259.019	396.532	532.622	487.473	525.688	550.556	580.626	677.535	846.145	902.882	958.542
% Annual growth	—	6.3	10.6	6.8	-2.0	7.8	4.7	5.5	16.7	24.9	6.7	6.1

Sources: Cano 1984 (1960–82), Estadísticas de la Educación 1983–87
a Annual growth rates calculated using five-year average enrollment 1960–79

required for university teaching or research appointments. Recently the National Research Council (CONICET) has established a system of fellowships addressed to candidates in graduate training programs. Graduate training is a relatively neglected area in all universities, including the major ones, as is also research. Requirements vary regarding the number and type of courses to be taken, but the major one is always a doctoral thesis. In recent years MA programs, as well as a number of short-term graduate courses leading to graduate certificates, have grown in both private and public universities. However, they have little formal recognition in the market.

3. Governance, Administration, and Finance

3.1 National Administration

The legislation regulating the higher educational system has changed frequently in Argentina since 1955. The legal framework was altered with regime transitions in 1955, 1958, 1966, 1973, 1976 and 1984. Throughout this period, however, the national government has regulated, controlled, and financed the public higher educational system. Although autonomy of academic institutions has been established as a goal, it has only exceptionally been granted to them. In fact, only between 1958 and 1966, and since 1984 to the present, have institutions been academically and administratively autonomous, even if financially dependent from the federal government. The following discussion centers upon the current, that is, post-1984, situation.

The constitutional government elected in 1983 decreed a federal intervention in all 26 national universities. In 1984 new legislation was approved by congress which determined the "normalization" of university institutions, that is, established procedures for faculty appointments by open competition and for free elections to be held among the three university bodies which were to choose representatives to university councils: faculty, graduates, and students. In each university the highest academic authority is exercised by a university council composed of those representatives. After normalization was achieved and councils were constituted, each council elected the president or rector, the highest administrative officer, replacing the one previously appointed by the central government. A parallel system of representation was established within each school or *facultad*, which after normalization elected a dean from among its faculty. All deans are ex officio members of the corresponding university council, together with elected faculty, graduates, and students.

The national Ministry of Education, through a special department of university affairs, regulates the relationship between the national government and each autonomous national university. The major role of this department is to supervise the implementation of the current legislation at each institution, and to negotiate the yearly budget. Central planning and evaluation is very weak. The law established the National Interuniversity Council as the main body coordinating university policy in the public sector. It is made up of all university presidents and a representative from the national ministry. Although this Council has a very broad mandate, including coordination of programs and degrees awarded, as well as of relations with other public and private institutions, it has no authority over the autonomous institutions represented there.

The nonuniversity sector within the public higher education system is a residual, highly heterogeneous category, which includes a variety of institutions not included within the rule of the university law. Most of them are teacher-training institutions, and administratively they depend upon the area into which that particular teaching takes place. Thus, the national Ministry of Education has specialized divisions in charge of secondary schools, technical schools, adult education, art education, physical education, and so on. Institutions training teachers for each of these areas are included administratively within the corresponding division. Not all of them, however, depend on that Ministry. Many are dependencies of provincial governments. Also, police academies, schools for librarians, aeronautical engineering, and many other specialized, tertiary level institutions, belong administratively to other national ministries. Nonuniversity institutions are not autonomous: their authorities, programs, and budgets, are dictated by the division and ministry within which they are located. A few older and more prestigious institutions do have some academic autonomy.

Private universities are not included within the same legislation as public universities. In this case the legal framework has been more stable: since originally authorized to function in 1958, it was only partially modified in 1967 and has not changed substantially since. Private universities are nonprofit organizations with full academic, administrative, and technical autonomy. They choose their own officers, with no provision for student or faculty representation. They also determine their own curricula, which must be approved by the Ministry of Education. Professional degrees are granted under a system of supervised examinations. The government also reserves the right to inspect administrative and financial procedures, and may intervene in institutions which fail to follow regulations.

The federal government is the major, and almost only, source of finance for national universities. This is, also, the main expenditure for higher education in the national budget, since there are no subsidies to private universities (unlike primary and secondary private schools) and the cost of nonuniversity higher education, which is much smaller, is shared partially

Table 3
Federal budget spent in education and percentage spent in higher education 1961–87

	1961–65	1966–70	1971–75	1976–80	1981–85	1986–87
Federal education budget (in million australes of 1987)	1.698	2.643	3.332	2.652	2.530	2.557
Percentage in higher education	25.7	26.3	24.2	29.2	34.4	45.3

Source: Petrei and Montero 1989 pp. 79 and 81 (in Petrei (ed.) 1989)

with provincial governments. In theory, each university elaborates its own budget, which is included by the Ministry of Education in the educational budget, and submitted by the Finance Ministry to congress for approval. In practice, the process tends to work the other way around: the central government, through its Finance Ministry, does the budgeting exercise, negotiating with the Ministry of Education, and universities have little to say about how much they receive from the latter, although some negotiating takes place between the university presidents and the department of university affairs within the ministry.

As can be seen in Table 3, the higher education budget has tended to include a growing percentage of the total federal expenditure in education. During the 1960s and 1970s higher education was about 25 percent of the total, but it started to increase as a consequence of the transfer of much of the primary and secondary educational budget to the provinces, resulting in the decline in the total federal expenditure in education. In recent years 45 percent of the latter was spent in higher education, over 90 percent of which is spent in the public universities. Federal spending in higher education has fluctuated for the last three decades. Increase in the recent two years reflects an expansion in spending associated with higher enrollment under conditions of a sluggish economy.

3.2 Institutional Administration

As indicated above, there are marked differences in models of governance between the public and private sectors, and among the former, between universities and other institutions. University councils, formed by elected representatives, rule over national universities. Their power is quite limited, however. On the one hand, they appoint an executive with considerable authority; as legislative bodies they can hardly supervise day-to-day operations of large scale, complex institutions. On the other hand, *facultades* or schools, mainly the traditional professional ones, maintain a strong identity and autonomy. In fact,

many observers see the Argentine public universities as loose confederations of professional schools. The attempt in recent years to centralize the first, or basic cycle, through which all incoming students have to go, was geared to increase overall university power in the teaching process. The relative failure of this reform can be blamed on the opposition of those schools, which did not want to lose control over admissions, appointments, and a portion of their budget. The third, or graduate, cycle, is also supposed to become centralized, with university doctorates coordinated by graduate schools. However, no university has taken steps towards this kind of centralization and coordination of graduate training.

Schools or *facultades* are the main units into which university life is organized, both in public and private institutions. Elected councils at the school level are today the seats of power, appointing and supervising the deans. The tradition of federal interventions and the large size of most schools, however, have resulted in considerable administrative autonomy on the part of the latter, who until 1984 were normally appointed from above. Councils also appoint a number of committees, normally including faculty and students, to oversee particular areas, that is, graduate programs, curriculum, budget, and the like. Within each school, departments and chairs are the main teaching units. In some of them, chair holders still enjoy considerable teaching and administrative autonomy, but the trend has been towards greater departmental coordination.

Nonuniversity institutions, as well as all private sector institutions, are considerably more vertical in organization, with less participation in collegial bodies. Private university presidents are chosen by university boards, whose composition reflects the orientation of the founding organization (i.e., the Church, a religious order, or business interests). Faculty representation is very limited, and university presidents appoint deans and departmental chairs. There is no formal mechanism for student representation in most private universities. Nonuniversity institutions in the public sector are administered by authorities appointed by the corresponding area of government, and seldom are open to faculty or student participation in the decision-making process.

4. Faculty and Students: Teaching, Learning, and Research

Teaching in Argentine universities is largely carried out by part-time teaching staff, including the highest and most prestigious appointees. The full-time system in public universities was only introduced in the 1950s, but in spite of a rapid growth in the initial years, the number of full-time faculty has not increased proportionally since then. Full-time faculty has fluctuated around 10 percent with higher figures among the professorial ranks (10% of assistant professors, 20% of associate and full professors), as compared to teaching assistants (5%). This proportion is slightly higher in the smaller, provincial universities, as compared to the larger ones. In the last ten years, the proportion declined, since part-time faculty more than doubled, while full-time faculty increased only 70 percent (see Table 4). Private universities have an even smaller proportion of full-time faculty.

Normalization of public universities in 1984 led to the appointment of faculty in all ranks through open competition. Juries were chosen to make the appropriate recommendations to school councils, based upon degrees, teaching experience, publications, and teaching performance. Appointees enjoy a limited tenure status. A large proportion of all faculty members are still under yearly contracts, since expansion of enrollment led to a growing demand for teaching staff.

First-cycle university degrees are normally required for all faculty ranks. Graduate degrees are not mandatory. Professorial ranks (i.e., assistant, associate, and full professors) are established on the basis of teaching experience and, to a lesser degree, professional experience and publications. Career paths are not clearly institutionalized, with the partial exception of the more traditional professional schools, since for a long time most appointments were made under contract by university authorities, with no academic review system. Advancement has been largely a function of seniority, and instability often resulted in career breakdowns. Also, the predominance of part-time teaching has worked against such institutionalization. The normalization process described above has resulted in a limited trend towards more universalistic, academic criteria for career paths in the public universities. Private universities, as a general rule, do not formalize those criteria, although they do use similar ranks. The non-university institutions place almost exclusive attention to seniority, while ranks are not clearly defined.

Part-time faculty is appointed to teach a specified number of classes, and may accumulate hours of teaching in different units or different institutions. Only full-time appointments assume some time for research. Each school determines the teaching load associated to each rank and status. There are no overall, university rules in this respect. Faculty unionization has grown in recent years, linked to teachers' unions, but there is no all-university representation of faculty interests.

The distribution of university students across subject areas has changed substantially in the last two or three decades. By the early 1960s, students in the medical areas (including medicine and dentistry), made up around 30 percent of the total, while they declined to less than 15 percent in the 1980s. Science

Table 4
University faculty, by status, Buenos Aires and all other national universities 1977–87

	1977	1978	1979	1980	1981	1982	1983	1984	1985	1986	1987	Total 1987
University of Buenos Aires												
Professors												
Full-time	100	102	108	111	—	121	119	180	188	166	170	(757)
Part-time	100	116	119	121	—	126	136	162	175	215	237	(6,362)
Assistants												
Full-time	100	98	94	96	—	100	101	135	140	123	127	(852)
Part-time	100	101	102	103	—	104	111	126	154	194	206	(14,595)
All other national universities												
Professors												
Full-time	100	110	111	115	—	115	119	134	144	151	176	(4,192)
Part-time	100	108	110	113	—	112	117	143	156	176	194	(27,076)
Assistants												
Full-time	100	97	96	99	—	104	107	121	133	141	167	(2,242)
Part-time	100	103	104	106	—	107	111	134	144	152	167	(34,494)

Source: Estadísticas de la Educación 1977–87

and technology, within which engineering is the major career, has taken up that difference and now includes around 40 percent of the total university enrollment. The third major category includes the social sciences, which has maintained its share from around 36–38 percent, but has changed greatly in composition: law students used to be the major component here, but it has now been replaced by economics (which largely means public accounting as a career) and administration. Finally, the humanities have increased their share from around 7–10 percent of the total. This distribution is quite different when comparing public and private universities, although the former weigh much more in the total: the medical professions and science are overrepresented in the public institutions (58% as against 26% in private institutions); social sciences and humanities are underrepresented (34% vs. 57% in the former, 8% vs. 17% in the latter) (Cano 1985 p. 68).

Students also tend to be part-time. Surveys indicate that between 40 and 70 percent of students also work (Pérez Lindo 1985 p. 233). They normally take two or three years longer to graduate than what is expected in the formal program. Also, the age range is wide, since many are enrolled for long periods, or actually enroll at later ages than normal.

The proportion of females among students has grown constantly during the last three decades throughout the higher education system. On average they represented an important minority in the early 1960s (around 35%) while they are a majority today (53% in 1986). Their percentage declines, however, if we only consider universities (47%) as compared to nonuniversity institutions (78%), reflecting their relative weight in the teaching professions. Within the universities, females are overrepresented today in the medical careers and the humanities, while the reverse is true for science, engineering, and the social sciences.

Surveys conducted in various national universities throughout the 1970s, and more recently in Buenos Aires, indicate relative stability of social origins, as indicated by father's occupation. Between 15 and 30 percent of students, depending on which university, are of working-class background (including blue-collar as well as low white-collar occupations); around 10 percent come from upper-class origins, and the rest is middle class (including professionals) (Pérez Lindo 1985 p. 209). There is no comparable data for the private universities, nor for nonuniversity institutions.

Student unions have been legalized since 1984 in all public universities. Elections have been held periodically since then in all universities and schools for student representatives in councils, as well as for union authorities. All students are formally members of student unions, and participation (as indicated by voting patterns) is quite high. Unions have a strong political life, and in recent years the various student factions have been related to major national political parties, and student vote has reflected to a large extent the vote for those parties. This is a major change from the past, when student party preference was out of tune with national public opinion.

First degree programs are now initiated by a one-year cycle for all students in Buenos Aires, an attempt to reform higher education by including some "liberal arts" components. However, even such limited attempts has met with considerable opposition, largely re-directing it to a more specialized training. By and large, most programs include only specialized courses, organized within a rather strict curriculum allowing few choices to be made by students. Programs are decided by each school council, and change frequently in their details but seldom in general orientation. Degrees are supervised by each school, and there is normally neither a final examination, nor periodic assessments of student performance: students are examined, or otherwise evaluated, in each of the courses taken, and there is seldom an overall evaluation of their work.

5. Conclusion

The last attempt to reform higher education in Argentina dates from the mid-1950s, and many of the goals were never achieved. Since then, enrollment has grown dramatically, and the system has diversified to include a much larger number of institutions, both private and public. Old problems have not been solved, and new ones have emerged. The capacity to cope with them has also declined, to the extent that the Argentine economy has done quite poorly in the last two decades. The prospects for a prompt recovery are dim, and the Argentine state, the main source of financing for the system, is facing a deep fiscal crisis.

The old problems had to do with an outmoded system of professional schools, the low professionalization of teaching and research careers, the weakness of graduate programs, and the marginal role of scientific research within the university. It was deeply felt by reformers that the university had grown out of tune from society demands for human resources and knowledge. There was also a growing concern with the large size of university institutions and the effects of dispersion within large cities. In spite of some progress during the late 1950s and the 1960s, none of these problems were actually solved. Since then, higher education became more massive, and quality deteriorated, partially as a consequence of a less selective process in recruiting both students and teachers, and partially due to increased pressure upon resources. The emergence of a private system of higher education served only marginally to alleviate this pressure, and the duplication of functions without an improvement in overall quality did little to change the picture.

The system and its many components have not been evaluated properly. This is, in fact, one of the many symptoms of trouble, which does not allow us to know where we stand regarding quality of higher education in Argentina. Although most observers agree that it has deteriorated in the long run, many feel some components (i.e., particular medical or engineering schools) still train their graduates reasonably well. The main qualitative problems, however, seem to lie in the global picture. First, the system generates too much waste in the form of drop-out students and those who remain very long within the system without graduating. Second, even if the average training of graduates is acceptable, there is little differentiation: academic excellence is to be found almost nowhere. As a consequence, there are few chances of training very high-level students and of keeping first-rate scientists and scholars as teachers. This, of course, reinforces low quality throughout. Finally, the system works against innovation of all sorts, since there is no premium posed on change within it. Thus, the visible lack of coordination between the higher education system and society demands will tend to increase.

There is currently no overall plan to reform higher education in Argentina. In fact, in spite of its many obvious problems, university reform is not high in the priorities set up by the political agenda, given the current economic crisis. It seems that the major difficulty, however, is to be found inside the system, where corporate interests seldom favor innovation and change. Most probably the better chance for renewal would come from establishing high quality, even if small, programs, protected from institutional rules prevalent in the rest of the system. Other urgent transformations could be introduced gradually in some institutions: higher selectivity in admission, increase in full-time faculty, fellowship systems and selective fees, further formalization of graduate programs, expansion of middle-level diplomas, and so on. Larger institutions would have to stop growing first, and then study carefully programs for reorganization.

Bibliography

Cano D 1985 *La educación superior en la Argentina*. FLACSO-CRESALC/UNESCO, Buenos Aires
CONICET 1985–88 *Boletin Informativo*. CONICET Buenos Aires
Levy D 1986 *Higher Education and the State in Latin America: Private Challenges to Public Dominance*. University of Chicago Press, Chicago, Illinois
Pérez Lindo A 1985 *Universidad, política y sociedad*. EUDEBA, Buenos Aires
Petrei A, Montero H, Montero M 1989 El gasto público en educación en la Argentina. In: Petrei A (ed.) 1989 *Ensayos en economia de la educación*. Fundación Mediterránea, Buenos Aires
Recchini de Lattes Z, Lattes A E (eds.) 1975 *La población de Argentina*. CICRED, Buenos Aires
Secretaria de Ciencia y Técnica 1989 *Relevamiento de recursos y actividades en ciencia y tecnologia, 1988: Resultados preliminares*. Buenos Aires
Secretaria de Educación 1982–86 *Estadisticas de la educación: Educación superior, cifras provisionales*. Departamento de Estadistica, Buenos Aires
Secretaria de Educación 1988 *Universidades argentinas: Guia de carreras, 1988–1989*. División Nacional de Asuntos Universitarios, Buenos Aires
Tedesco J C, Braslavsky C, Carciofi R 1984. *El proyecto educativo autoritario: Argentina, 1976–1982*. FLACSO-Grupo Editor Latinoamericano, Buenos Aires
Universidad de Buenos Aires 1988 *Programación cientifica 1987* UBACYT. EUDEBA, Buenos Aires
Wilkie R W 1984 *Latin American Population and Urbanization Analysis: Maps and Statistics 1950–1982*. UCLA Latin American Center Publications, Los Angeles, p. 99

J. Balan

Australia

1. Higher Education and Society

Like other national education systems, higher education in Australia is a product of Australia's unique history, geography, and demography. It has a number of major characteristics, not least its strong urban concentration in the state and regional capital cities which cling to Australia's coastline. It has a predominantly public character and substantially expanded and diversified from an elite system prior to the Second World War towards a mass system in the early 1990s. It has been almost totally dependent on federal government funding since 1974 and experimented with free tuition from 1974 to 1988. There is remarkable uniformity in its institutional quality with nothing faintly resembling "Oxbridge" in the United Kingdom or the United States "Ivy League." A so-called "binary division" of higher education (comprising universities with research as well as teaching responsibilities and colleges of advanced education (CAEs) with a mainly undergraduate teaching mission) lasted from 1965 until the 1988 adoption of a sweeping federal government plan to restructure and reform higher education dramatically by both abolishing the "binary system" and more closely harnessing higher education to the needs of the economy. The increasing trend towards privatization of higher education in the second half of the 1980s, culminated in full cost-fees for overseas students, the reintroduction of modest tuition fees for Australian students, and the establishment of Australia's first private universities and colleges.

Australia is an island continent of 3.2 million square miles, which is approximately the same size as the United States. However, unlike the United States much of its interior is largely uninhabited desert. Its European settlement commenced as a series of six separate British colonies during the late eighteenth and early nineteenth centuries. These independent colonies (and two territories) united to form the federated nation of Australia in 1901 and the state boundaries have remained unchanged since that time. The national or federal government is also commonly referred to as the Commonwealth (Government).

Prior to the outbreak of the Second World War, the sparsely settled continent of Australia had a predominantly Anglo–Celtic population of just 6.6 million. Then, as now, the majority of that population was located in the handful of large urban state capital cities, most of which are clustered on the southern and eastern seaboard. The two capital cities of Sydney in the state of New South Wales and Melbourne in the state of Victoria alone accounted for almost half the nation's population. In 1939 there were just six universities, one in each state capital, and they were all small, narrow, parochial institutions whose *raison d'être* was undergraduate teaching.

However, in the five decades following the Second World War, the size and makeup of Australia's population has changed dramatically, as has the provision for higher education. In particular, Australia's expansive postwar refugee and immigration policies have resulted in substantial inroads into Anglo–Celtic predominance and the achievement, by 1989, of a diverse multiracial society in which one person in every four was born beyond Australia. Australia's population crept from 9 million in 1954 to 11.5 million in 1966, to 14 million in 1976, and to 16 million in 1986. The major successive waves of postwar migrants have included eastern and southern European refugees immediately postwar; British, Italians, and Greeks in the 1950s and 1960s; and increasingly, Middle Eastern and South East Asian groups (including Vietnamese refugees) in the 1970s and 1980s, as British migration has slowed to a trickle.

The phenomenon of the concentration of Australia's population in its major capital cities has continued apace since the Second World War. Thus in 1988, the cities of Sydney and Melbourne alone accounted for almost 8 million of Australia's 16 million inhabitants and fully two-thirds of Australia's people lived in urban locations. English remains the sole official language, though, in the last several decades, teaching and learning of English as a second language has become a significant element in the education system. In addition, the emergence in the late 1980s of a major new category of full-fee-paying overseas students (38,000 in 1988)—primarily from non-English-speaking countries in South East Asia— has contributed greatly to a thriving private education sector in ESL.

Approximately 60 percent of Australia's wealth is owned by only 10 percent of the population and there is a very strong correlation between socioeconomic status and wealth, together with membership of the prestigious professions such as medicine and law. Although there is no hereditary aristocracy, numbers of "old" families— very often descendants of the owners of large nineteenth-century rural properties—are prominent in the upper echelons of the socioeconomic hierarchy (Higley et al. 1979, Connell and Irving 1980, Connell 1983). While most members of Australia's elites are of Anglo–Australian background, numerous influential business leaders come from Eastern European backgrounds, having migrated to Australia in the immediate post-Second World War period.

There are strong links between social class and schools attended. Those of higher socioeconomic status—Australia's elite—have predominantly been educated at non-Catholic private ("independent") schools and send their children to such schools. By contrast, those at the lower end of the same spectrum go to government or Roman Catholic schools (Higley et al. 1979, Connell et al. 1982).

1.1 Structure of the Economy

Australia's mixed economy is a legacy of the country's large size and its relatively small population, and of the differing orientations of its national governments since Federation. These have been coalitions of the conservative and business-oriented parties of both city and country (at the beginning of the 1990s the representatives of these interests were the Liberal Party and the National Party—previously the Country Party—respectively), and alternatively the Australian Labor Party which has been concerned with social welfare, the interests of working people, and the creation of state-owned enterprises—including railways, airlines, banks, water and energy bodies, and telecommunications— free of overseas control.

Despite extensive state ownership, the private sector remains dominant, employing 75 percent of the civilian workforce. Moreover, public expenditure is a relatively small proportion (36%) of gross domestic product (GDP). In spite of this, graduate employment is concentrated in the public sector, which includes community services (such as teaching, health services, etc.) and public administration. Manufacturing industry, which employs 17 percent of the workforce, recruits barely 9.4 percent of graduates (Australian Bureau of Statistics 1987a).

The structural imbalances of the Australian economy—the dominance of primary production, a relatively small secondary manufacturing sector oriented almost solely to the domestic market, and a substantial tertiary sector—ensure that Australia is particularly vulnerable to the vicissitudes of international trade. Export income is almost exclusively reliant upon primary products including coal, wool, wheat, iron ore, alumina, beef, and gold. Whilst there is some value-added processing, such as steel making and refining, the bulk of Australia's commodities are exported in unprocessed form. The manufacturing sector has been in decline since at least the 1960s, and while in 1990 the Hawke government is attempting to restructure the economy towards value-added industries and particularly the export of high-quality manufactured goods, Australia continues to import substantial quantities of manufactured goods. A rapidly growing trade deficit, together with substantial international borrowing, contributes to a disturbing overseas debt approaching 40 percent of GDP.

The dramatic Commonwealth-initiated reforms in higher education of the late 1980s constitute a major part of the government's microeconomic reforms for greater international competitiveness.

1.2 Structure of Government and Main Political Goals

Australia has a federal system of government comprising a national government in Canberra, six state, and two territorial governments. Although education is constitutionally a state responsibility, since the Second World War the federal government has become increasingly involved in financing and making policy for both schools and higher education (Smart 1990). In fact, in 1973 the Whitlam socialist Labor government took over from the states the total financial responsibility for higher education (universities and colleges of advanced education [CAEs]) —which had previously been shared—and simultaneously abolished tuition fees, with the explicit goal of increasing the proportion of working-class students undertaking tertiary study. As a consequence, since 1973 Australia has had the somewhat anomalous situation of divided financial and administrative responsibility for its universities and CAEs. While the tertiary institutions are established by state Acts of Parliament and the state minister is technically responsible for their welfare and administration, the federal government now provides virtually all of their capital and recurrent funding (Beswick 1987). This situation can and does produce conflict and confusion in higher education policy when, as they often do, the two levels of government disagree. In 1988–89 the federal government's endeavor to force many supposedly autonomous state institutions of higher education to amalgamate produced some classic illustrations of this federal-state conflict.

Since the Second World War, the goals and structure of higher education have been systematically reviewed at intervals by a succession of national committees of inquiry (Murray 1957, Martin 1964, Williams 1979, Dawkins 1987). All of these committees, with the exception of Williams, justified expansion of higher education based essentially on human capital arguments about the benefits to the individuals, the society, and especially to the national economy. The Martin Report in 1964 recommended

an important diversification of the higher education system into a binary system through the creation of new CAEs—that is, colleges with a strong orientation towards business and industry— and the associated expansion of Australia's technological labor force (Harman and Smart 1982). In the 1980s the economic goals of higher education has become even more dominant in federal government policy. Thus in 1987–88 the main thrust of the ministerial Green and White Papers on higher education was the urgent necessity to harness higher education more directly to the needs of the national economy (Dawkins 1987).

Apart from provision of some university residential colleges and several small Roman Catholic teachers colleges, the churches have been conspicuously absent from Australian higher education. However, in July 1989 the Roman Catholic Church announced its intention to open in 1992, Australia's first Catholic university, the University of Notre Dame Australia, in Western Australia.

2. The Institutional Fabric of the Higher Education System

Until 1986, Australia's higher education system was composed exclusively of public sector institutions. Since then, the private Bond University was established in Queensland, several small business-program oriented universities with United States connections have been mooted for Sydney and Melbourne, and the Roman Catholic university mentioned above is to be established in Western Australia. In addition, there are a small number of profit-oriented, narrowly focused, small private colleges which have sprung up in recent years, largely to cater for the growing full-fee paying overseas student market and often affiliated with public universities and colleges. In the public sector, in the late 1980s there were: 24 universities which enrolled approximately 200,000 students; 47 CAEs which enrolled upwards of 200,000 students; and 220 Technical and Further Education (TAFE) colleges which enrol over one million students in a vast variety of vocational and leisure courses.

In Australia, the term "higher education" is commonly used to refer only to universities and CAEs. This is a more restrictive use than in some other countries where the term often means all postschool or at least all postsecondary education. Australians now use the term "tertiary education" to refer to all-embracing postsecondary education (Harman 1989).

Prior to 1989 there were three clearly defined and hierarchically differentiated levels of tertiary education: universities; colleges of advanced education (CAEs); and TAFE colleges. These were funded and administered differently by the federal government's Commonwealth Tertiary Education Commission. Since 1 January 1989, however, following the ministerial White Paper on Higher Education

Table 1
Number of higher education institutions 1987

Type of institution	No. of institutions	No. of students enrolled (in thousands)
Universities	19	183.1
Colleges of advanced education	46	201.3
Commonwealth institutions	1	0.2
Non-government–teachers colleges	3	1.7
Institutes of tertiary education	1	0.3
TAFE institutions providing advanced education courses	16	5.9
Other institutions providing higher education	3	1.2
Total	89	393.7

Source: Dawkins 1987 p. 94

(Dawkins 1988), the "binary division" between universities and CAEs has been officially abolished and replaced by a single "unified national system" (UNS). The practical implications of this new policy are still being worked through. One major outcome has been the encouragement of smaller CAEs to merge with universities to form larger institutions.

The distinguishing feature of the universities has been their responsibility for undertaking research and postgraduate training in addition to the teaching of undergraduates. The 24 universities fall into three categories: the older (usually larger) and more traditional original capital city institutions which tend to have highest status; the newer second (and sometimes third) established capital city and regional universities, mostly built during the rapid expansion phase of the 1960s and 1970s; and the most recent group of universities (4 in 1990, but there will shortly be others), which have achieved university status since 1986 by "upgrading" from institute of technology (CAE) status and which currently bear the title of University of Technology.

The CAEs were established as a separate sector following the Martin Report in 1964 and were intended to fill the gap between universities and technical colleges (Wark 1977). They were meant to prepare middle-level personnel for industry and government and were to concentrate on subdegree (mainly diploma) courses. However, as a result of "academic drift," by the late 1970s many of the larger CAEs were emulating universities and nationally almost 70 percent of CAE students were enrolled in bachelor level or graduate courses. There was substantially greater diversity in the CAE sector, ranging from the large multischool central institutes of technology (which concentrated on applied science, technology, engineering, and business) to the large multicampus former teachers colleges which expanded into business and other nonscience areas, and a multiplicity of small specialist CAEs for such vocations as pharmacy, agriculture, physiotherapy, music, and the like.

There were almost 90 CAEs in the early 1970s and many were small and regarded by the federal authorities as educationally and economically unviable. Consequently, mergers were encouraged and by 1988 the number of CAEs had been reduced to 47. Even so, in 1986 the average CAE enrollment was only a little over 3,000 compared with over 7,000 in universities (Harman 1989). When the round of mergers precipitated by the 1989 White Paper has been finalized, it is likely that the approximately 65 universities and CAEs which existed in 1988 will be reduced to a UNS in 1990 of no more than 40 institutions.

Unlike the universities, the CAEs have not traditionally been funded for research in their general operating grant by the federal government, and so, to the extent that they have pursued research, they have been obliged to look to industry and commerce for support. Nor have they been permitted to award doctoral degrees. However, under the new UNS, from 1989 onwards, most CAEs will be permitted to offer doctoral degrees and encouraged to compete with universities for federal research funds.

The Technical and Further Education (TAFE) area finally received recognition as a separate sector of tertiary education in 1974 following the Kangan Report which reviewed the role, function and funding of TAFE in Australia. It is perhaps the most versatile and adaptable of the sectors. In 1986, some 886,679 students took vocational and preparatory courses while another half million were enrolled in adult education, recreation, and leisure courses. In recent years some TAFE colleges have begun teaching certain undergraduate courses for universities and

CAEs by contract. Under the UNS, there is strong pressure on universities and CAEs to give better credit transfer to students completing TAFE qualifications. There are likely to be increasing links between TAFE and traditional higher education in the future.

Governments, primarily the Commonwealth, fund the great bulk (90%) of all research undertaken in Australia. The two main vehicles for research have been the federal government's vast public corporation—the Commonwealth Scientific and Industrial Research Organisation (CSIRO), founded in 1926—and the universities.

The total research effort is relatively small. Thus Australia spends approximately one percent of GDP on research and development as compared to the United States (2.5%), United Kingdom (2.2%), Japan (2.3%), Sweden (2.3%) (OECD 1987). Over 90 percent of this funding is provided by government. Moreover, the investment of Australian business and industry in research and development is extremely low when contrasted with that in comparable Organisation for Economic Co-operation and Development (OECD) countries, which is 0.39 percent of GDP (OECD 1987). Barely 0.19 percent of graduates are employed in business-funded research and development (Australian Bureau of Statistics 1987b).

The universities have traditionally been funded for research in two ways. The first is directly through various federal research grant bodies such as the Australian Research Council (ARC) and the National Health and Medical Research Council (NHMRC) which allocate grants on the basis of competitive review of research proposals. The second way of funding research is indirectly through the federal government's general recurrent operating budgets for the universities which contain an unspecified notional allocation for research purposes.

Traditionally, the bulk of the research funds have been notionally allocated to the universities in this general recurrent operating budget and it has been left very much up to the academic decision-making bodies of the individual universities to decide how much of their operating grant to spend on teaching and how much on research. The research moneys have so far tended to be spread broadly, and fairly thinly, across the university faculty. Under the Dawkins (1988) White Paper reforms of higher education which are being implemented in the early 1990s, the federal government has opted for a much more selective, centralized, and concentrated approach to research and research funding, though. Over the three years 1989–91 the federal government is "clawing back" from the universities' general operating grants over A$125m (US$100m) which is to be used to build up the ARC central pool of funds. These central funds are available for competitive allocation to university (and now also CAE) faculty, based partly on national research priorities and partly on the pure merit of research proposals. It is anticipated that this new procedure will lead for the first time to significant numbers of university academics being denied any research funds and thus being reduced to a *de facto* teaching only role. (Smith Report 1989, Dawkins 1988).

Two observations can be made about graduate training in Australia. First, it is a relatively new field (for example, the first Australian university doctorates were not awarded until the 1950s); and second, the British pattern has been predominant until fairly recently, so that the doctorate by research thesis (without coursework) has been the traditional model. Another feature derived from the British influence has been the fairly elitist, selective, and restrictive approach to admission to graduate study, and hence the quite small proportion of the population with a graduate qualification. The traditional view was that graduate study was primarily for research training purposes and the usual route was either selection on merit to undertake an honors bachelor's degree (usually taken as an extra year of study after the pass degree and combining both coursework and a research thesis) or a master's degree by research thesis only, perhaps followed by a doctorate by research thesis only. It is only since the mid-1970s that the United States pattern of coursework master's degrees as a terminating vocation or professional upgrading qualification has become common as a form of graduate training. Even so, as a legacy of the research model, most Australian coursework master's degrees still insist on a substantial research thesis as part of the program requirement.

3. Governance, Administration, and Finance

3.1 National Administration

Despite the fact that education is constitutionally a state responsibility, the federal government has gradually come to dominate the macro policy and planning of higher education through its acquisition of total responsibility for its funding. Each state minister of education has an advisory planning and coordinating body for higher education. These bodies are in some cases statutory authorities but in most cases not. In recent years, such bodies have become, like their state ministers, relatively powerless and passive onlookers as the federal minister and the federal higher education body has assumed more and more control.

Historically, federal ministers have relied not on their Department of Education but rather on specialist federal higher education agencies for policy advice and for administration of higher education. From 1959 to 1977 the statutory Federal Australian Universities Commission (modelled somewhat on the British Universities Grants Commission) effectively ran the national planning and financial administration of the Australian universities with relatively little input or interference from the federal minister. Similarly, from 1971 to 1977 the Federal Commission on Advanced Education did the same for the colleges sector. Sensing the need for better budgetary and sectoral coordination of higher education, the Federal Government merged these two commissions and the parallel TAFE Commission into a single Commonwealth Tertiary Education Commission (CTEC) in 1977. The CTEC retained within its structure separate advisory councils for each of these three sectors. It proved to be an effective agency which, despite increasingly rigid financial guidelines from the federal treasury and cabinet, managed fairly successfully for over a decade to act in some measure as a buffer between the politicians and the higher education institutions. In this way it protected their autonomy in the determination of their academic and research agendas despite seriously dwindling real resource levels (Marshall 1988).

However, the CTEC did not survive the dramatic restructuring of the whole education portfolio which occurred in 1987–88 under the new reformist Minister of Education, John Dawkins. In 1987, the Hawke socialist Labor government, on being re-elected for its third consecutive term, undertook simultaneously a major restructuring of the public service and of ministerial portfolios. In an effort to improve national economic policy coordination a series of so-called "mega-ministries" was created. As part of this process, Dawkins was appointed in July 1987 to head the newly merged departments of employment, education, and training (DEET). As part of his efforts to improve ministerial control over the hitherto relatively autonomous education bureaucracy, Dawkins abolished both the statutory Schools Commission and CTEC and absorbed most of their staff into his "mega-department." In place of CTEC and the Schools Commission, Dawkins created a relatively small advisory body, the National Board of Employment, Education, and Training (NBEET). Within NBEET there is a small Higher Education Council to advise the minister on higher education policy (Marshall 1988, Harman 1989, Smart 1989a).

The net effect of these ministerial reforms has been to shift higher education policy control from CTEC to the minister. This is a dramatic move, for it has removed the CTEC buffer and made the hitherto autonomous higher education institutions much more vulnerable to direct ministerial and bureaucratic intervention in their affairs. Furthermore, the Commonwealth has changed the focus of its intervention from "macro" financial concerns to the "micro" level of internal institutional decision making concerning teaching and research (Marginson 1989).

In the CTEC era (1977–88) each tertiary institution had the certainty of clear and relatively stable budgetary guidelines and unambiguous national policies publicly reported by CTEC. Each institution was able to negotiate its overall financial allocation either directly with the large professional staff at CTEC or indirectly through its state coordinating body with CTEC. From 1989, however, under the new federal ministerial White Paper policies, each institution must negotiate its internal "institutional profile" with DEET officers and will have its financial allocation determined accordingly. The negotiated profile will comprise "mission statements" concerning specific permissible areas of teaching and research. Never before has the federal bureaucracy or the minister sought to intervene in this way so as to dictate the content of the academic and research programs of the institutions (Smart 1989a).

The relatively clear and stable processes of central coordination and planning which operated up until 1988 under the extensive expertise within CTEC, have now been replaced by procedures the details of which are still in many cases unclear. Consequently, the pre-1989 processes will be described below, along with any known changes to operate from 1989.

Prior to 1989, a national triennial planning and funding cycle was the basic model for higher education, though it had suffered occasional interruptions due to federal budgetary problems in the late 1970s and early 1980s. The procedure would commence with federal treasury-approved financial and enrollment guidelines being publicly announced and presented to the CTEC. These broad national guidelines signalled to CTEC the overall financial budget and enrollment targets for the higher education system for the triennium. The CTEC would then call for triennial submissions from all institutions.

Triennial planning was an interactive two-stage process involving the individual institutions, their state coordinating authorities and CTEC. Each institution would prepare a triennial submission which provided a broad overview of its existing programs, additional student places sought, and fields of study for expansion and new initiatives. The emphasis was on consultation. Members of the state coordinating bodies would consult with business and industry representatives as well as institutional representatives including chief executive officers, academics, planners, student and staff representatives, and members of the academic board and governing bodies.

Each state coordinating body would then prepare a comprehensive state triennial submission which set out broad state views on issues and on priorities for recurrent and capital expenditure, before providing detailed recommendations on each institution's budget and enrollment targets.

Following analysis of the state triennial submissions, CTEC would publish a national report listing the capital works allocation program it proposed for each institution, the total recurrent budget for each institution, and the upper and lower range of student enrollments which each institution must seek to achieve.

Under CTEC, higher education was informally linked to a "national plan" by virtue of the financial and student growth guidelines laid down by federal cabinet. It is clear that under the Dawkins reforms, higher education will be much more closely linked to national economic planning. What is not yet clear, however, is how, in the absence of CTEC, this national plan will be transmitted to the higher education system in a public fashion that permits informed debate and consequent alteration.

In the past, the formal mechanisms for quickly assessing and evaluating higher education's broad response to national goals have been the annual reports of CTEC. In future, the annual profile negotiation process between each institution and DEET will no doubt provide a much more precise micro process for assessing the institution's contribution over the previous 12 months and reassessing its mission for the period ahead. Whether NBEET will have the staffing and resources to provide the macro-evaluation of higher education formerly provided by CTEC remains to be seen.

The federal government provides almost all of the (A$4b, US$3b) annual operating and capital budget of the public higher education institutions. However, as a result of federal budgetary cost-cutting the proportion of GDP being spent on higher education has decreased from 1.36 percent in 1975 to 0.99 percent in 1988 (Hilmer 1988). Some of the older universities have modest endowment and bequest income and, in addition, alumni associations are a very new but promising fund-raising phenomenon. Joint venture research partnerships with business and consultancy income are, again, relatively new but growing sources of institutional revenue.

As from 1989, uniform tuition fees of A$1,800 (US$1,300) per annum for all Australian students will have been reintroduced, but it is expected that most students choose to defer payment and pay later through an income tax surcharge once they have graduated and are employed. All tuition collections will go, however, direct to the federal government for redistribution. Since 1985, all those overseas students who are not either wholly or partly subsidized as part of Australia's foreign aid program, have paid a full cost-fee direct to the institution and this is becoming a modest source of growth income for some institutions. Since opting out of shared funding with the Commonwealth in 1973, the state governments have made little financial contribution to higher education. There have been some occasional isolated instances of states providing special capital or recurrent funds, but these have been the exception rather than the rule.

3.2 Institutional Administration

Higher education institutions in Australia are governed by senates or councils comprised of members of the external community as well as representatives of each institution's students, academic and general staff, and graduate body. Each higher education institution is established by a separate state Act of Parliament which sets out the powers, duties, and membership of its senate or council. According to a Western Australian government review of such bodies, "... in broad terms Senates and Councils are responsible for ensuring that the institution provides an intellectual and physical environment conducive to the attainment of excellence in learning, teaching and research" (Hetherington Report 1985).

While the membership of senates and councils shows considerable variation, it is generally structured to ensure representation through appointment and election of various categories of people and interests in order to achieve a balance of perspectives and skills. The size of governing bodies varies from 10 members to over 50, with most having 15 or more. The issue of the size and functioning of senates and councils has been hotly debated since the release of the White Paper in 1988. In that document (Dawkins 1988) the federal minister for education urged institutions to streamline their governing bodies more along the lines of business company boards and has offered institutions financial assistance to encourage reviews of these bodies. In general, the institutions have rejected the minister's proposed 10–15 person membership as too small to provide adequate representation and balance, though most appear to accept that in excess of 30 is too large.

The pivotal internal committee within each institution is that dealing with academic matters, usually called the academic board or council. Traditionally it was chaired by the vice-chancellor or director, though less universally so in more recent times, with the role often being filled by one of their deputies. The size and membership of this academic committee varies considerably: because of its collegial style it is usually large. Historically it was largely—or in some cases totally—composed of full professors, and was sometimes known as the professorial board. In more recent times, this committee, while still weighted towards senior academics, will typically have some representation of all levels of the academic staff and sometimes of students. This is usually achieved by making ex officio membership inherent to certain senior academic positions while other committee members are elected from different promotional levels of academic staff and the student body.

Governing bodies' relationships with their academic boards/councils always need sensitive handling. On the one hand they need to uphold academic freedom and on the other they have an obligation to ensure the most effective disposition of resources. Traditionally, senates and councils have placed great reliance on the initiation and direction of education policy from their senior academic body.

In recent years, senates and councils have become more interested in long-term educational planning and development. They have begun to take the initiative more frequently in suggesting to academic committees the possibility of new courses, new teaching approaches, and worthy projects for research. It remains to be seen whether the more corporate and managerial role envisaged for governing bodies in the 1988 White Paper will enhance or retard such initiatives.

Academic boards and committees have also suffered increasing criticisms similar to those levelled at governing bodies. It is frequently argued that these large, collegial bodies are too slow and cumbersome in their decision-making processes to cope with the pace of change and the demand for more rapid determination of academic issues. The result has been a tendency for academic boards and councils to make greater use both of their standing committees (e.g., education, planning, finance, admissions, postgraduate, and research) and of ad hoc committees appointed to deal with specific issues or problems as they arise. In addition, of course, a good deal of power and responsibility for decision making and resource allocation has increasingly been delegated to the faculty and department level where the power of professors is now relatively weak, as authority is often broadly shared and leadership may be rotated.

The roles of nonacademic staff and students in the authority structure vary. The nonacademic staff have usually had at least one elected representative on governing bodies, though they may be one of the groups disenfranchised in the general streamlining process of the early 1990s. Apart from possible representation on the governing body, nonacademic staff tend to be relatively unrepresented and invisible in the decision-making processes on most campuses.

Academic work has traditionally been organized in "base units" called departments and/or schools and faculties controlled by an appointed or elected head or dean. In the CAEs, heads tend to be permanent appointments, whereas in universities they have increasingly been elected for a three-year term and often incumbents are of nonprofessorial rank.

The White Paper (Dawkins 1988) advocates a more managerial, less collegial approach with heads being appointed by the institution's chief executive rather than being elected by colleagues.

Simultaneously, in the larger institutions, there has been a trend towards grouping faculties/departments together into "divisions," primarily because larger units will enable more efficient resource management. The base units, however, remain responsible for the teaching and examining/assessing of students and for the allocation of resources for these functions. They usually also have some responsibility for allocating both research funds and administrative tasks between academic staff.

4. Faculty and Students: Teaching, Learning, and Research

4.1 Faculty

Australian academics are appointed directly by autonomous or quasi-autonomous institutions. They are not public servants as are public school teachers. Positions are advertized both internationally and within Australia, and applicants are selected on the basis of such criteria as research performance, experience, academic record, references, and personal qualities. Selection committees—reflecting the collegial mode of governance—determine appointments. Increasingly, reflecting equal opportunity policies, these committees are becoming more broadly based. It is usual for them to include, for example, a proportion of women and the institution's equal opportunity officer.

In universities, research performance has remained of higher priority for appointment than teaching competence, and increasingly, a doctorate is becoming a necessity for appointment to the rank of lecturer or above. While the CAEs were originally established and envisaged as teaching only institutions less attractive to academically qualified staff, since the late 1980s their research aspirations have led

Table 2
Full-time and fractional full-time[a] academic staff in higher education—Australia 1987

	Tenured	Untenured	Total	Untenured percentage
Above senior lecturer	3,560	84	3,644	2
Senior lecturer	5,971	239	6,210	4
Subtotal: senior lecturer and above	9,531	323	9,854	3
Lecturer	6,142	2,676	8,818	30
Tutors and others	279	2,441	2,720	90
Total	15,952	5,440	21,392	25

Source: Dawkins 1988 p. 109
a Fractional full-time for universities only.

to appointment criteria similar to those in universities and hence to enhanced status.

The career ladder in both universities and CAEs is roughly similar and the salary scales are now uniform, though the White Paper has suggested institutions might look to introducing salary "loadings" based on meritorious performance and market demand. The career ladder ascends from tutor, to lecturer, to senior lecturer, to reader/associate professor (principal lecturer in CAEs) to professor (dean, head of department in CAE).

Each of the levels below associate professor has an incremental salary scale with a number of annual steps. For each of associate professor and professor there is a single uniform fixed salary. Thus with a few minor exceptions such as "clinical salary loadings" for medicine, all professors in Australia, whatever their discipline, received a salary of A\$63,919 (US\$47,939) in 1989.

To be promoted from one classification to the next in the career ladder requires application for promotion and rigorous assessment by an institutional committee of peers, based on institution-wide criteria primarily related to teaching, administration, and research. In universities, the greatest weight has traditionally been given to research performance. A senior lectureship has traditionally been regarded as the "career grade" (comprising 29% of all academics in 1987), and only a small proportion of staff (17% in 1987) ever attain promotion to associate professor/principal lecturer, or appointment to a chair (see Table 2). Appointment to a chair (full professorship) cannot be achieved by promotion but only by application for a vacant chair (which is advertised internationally). In very rare cases, universities may create "personal chairs" for outstanding scholars whom they wish to retain or reward.

Traditionally, in Australia, tenure has been granted more liberally—following the British rather than United States model—and so up until the financial crisis of the 1980s, perhaps 90 percent of full-time academic staff in universities and colleges had tenure. Until this crisis, virtually all positions were advertized as tenured track and it was almost routine for staff to be granted tenure following a probationary review in their third year of appointment. Senior academics recruited from one institution to another were normally granted immediate tenure. Since the crisis there has been a decline in tenured positions (75%), particularly at junior levels, and an increase in contract or limited-term appointments (which are not promotional positions). At senior levels tenure is almost universal. In 1987, barely 2.5 percent of university staff at the rank of senior lecturer or above (reader/associate professor, professor) were untenured, though 31 percent of all academic staff were untenured. By contrast, 99 percent of tutors were untenured. The situation in CAEs is very similar. Other trends which have become

evident in recent years include greater numbers of fractional appointments, and the introduction of casual staff for junior teaching. The number of full-time equivalent teaching and research staff at the tutorship level has declined markedly in the 1980s. A significant proportion of support teaching at the undergraduate level is being carried out by casual tutors—often women—who have no promotional prospects, very heavy teaching loads, and seemingly no academic future.

Further outcomes of the "decade of neglect" are deteriorating staff to student ratios (from 11:1 in 1975 to around 13:1 in 1988) and the steady aging of Australian academic ranks (the 40–50 age group is now dominant) (CTEC 1986).

While the autonomy of institutions and academics in determining their teaching and research priorities has gradually been eroded by the establishment of state and federal coordinating bodies, the current White Paper reforms (Dawkins 1988) pose even greater threats. Academics fear that such long-standing principles as tenure, uniform salaries, the collegial governance of institutions, and, particularly, the right of university academics to undertake research, are now at risk. Indeed the whole culture and traditional solidarity of academia may be under challenge (Marginson 1989).

Australia's tertiary education institutions (particularly the universities) were modelled largely upon their nineteenth-century British counterparts. While United States practices have become increasingly influential, the character and academic values of the British model have remained embedded in Australian academic culture. Scott (1984) argues that the solidarity of British academics is characterized by, and can be explained by the comparative equality of status and privilege between junior and senior staff, the lack of any research/teaching distinction, the lack of any formal distinction between institutions and the worth of their awards, and finally, a degree of homogeneity of academic and cultural values within academic ranks. This generalization has been equally applicable to Australia, but seems likely to be less so after the White Paper proposals (Dawkins 1988) are implemented.

Under the White Paper reforms, the traditional (binary) "teaching and research"/"teaching only" dichotomy between university and college academics is being recast according to merit, institutional size, and whether the researcher's field accords with the national economic priorities specified by DEET and the ARC. Thus the traditional pattern of all university academics having a somewhat higher status than CAE academics is likely to be fractured by a new pattern in which funded researchers—wherever they are located—will have higher status than "teaching only" staff. Further fracturing is likely following the proposals for the implementation of "market differentiation" of salaries.

Another major source of potential disunity comes from the White Paper's proposals for administrative reform. The active participation of academics in the administration and policy determining processes of institutions is discouraged by the White Paper. In the interests of efficiency and effectiveness, it is proposed that the teaching and research roles of academics be separated from the task of administration. Administration will be the domain of a new stream of academic managers, who will not necessarily have any substantive academic expertise. While some academics maintain that professional autonomy and academic freedom would be fatally compromised, other academics feel more sanguine about probable outcomes.

The traditional solidarity of Australian academia can be explained—at least in part—by the similar backgrounds of Australian academics in terms of social class, gender, and ethnicity. The historical elitism of Australia's higher education system, in which access has been "restricted" to Anglo–Celtic Australians of higher social class, particularly to the products of private education, has resulted, not surprisingly, in the socioeconomic characteristics of the teaching body paralleling those of the student body from which it has been largely drawn. Moreover, the predominance of British academics recruited from similarly elitist universities in the growth phase (1950–75) of Australian higher education, reinforced this trend.

In 1987, women constituted barely 26 percent of academics and tended to be concentrated in the CAEs and the lower ranks of the universities. Only two of 24 vice chancellors are female. Most importantly, only 6.7 percent of academics are tenured females while tenured males make up over 50 percent of the academic ranks. The majority of women still tend to be found in such traditionally female areas as the social sciences and the "helping professions" (teaching, nursing, etc.), whilst science, mathematics, economics, and commerce are dominated by males. However, as a result of equal opportunity policies and an expanding range of academic disciplines, women and academics of non-English speaking background are beginning to dent this homogeneity, while indigenous Australians (Aboriginals and Torres Strait Islanders) remain an almost insignificant proportion of academic staff.

Historically, the autonomous universities and colleges have individually determined their own work patterns and allocations of duties. In both the universities and colleges, for example, senior academic committees determine the allocation of teaching resources for each faculty or department and then the faculty—either collegially, or through its head—determines the allocation of teaching loads, committee membership, and other administrative duties. In the universities, some research funds are allocated to faculties for their own determination, while others are allocated from a central university research committee by competitive bidding and peer review. The individual operating grants of institutions and their modes of organization and teaching effectively determine the number of staff contact hours of teaching in each institution. Their higher levels of per capita funding and research obligations, mean that the university staff have had generally lower teaching loads than the colleges. This difference, however, is destined to cease as the White Paper reforms equalize per capita funding across the UNS. In addition, state and federal arbitration process in higher education, which is developing rapidly in the early 1990s seems likely to lead within a few years to the external determination and uniform codification of academics' rights and obligations in such areas as sabbatical leave, long service leave, superannuation, hours of work, consultancy rights, tenure, patents, publishing rights, royalties, and so on.

4.2 Students

As in most OECD countries, growth in student numbers has been dramatic in Australia: from less than 30,000 in 1946 to over 400,000 in 1989. Table 3 shows the growth in student numbers during the halcyon era of the 1960s and early 1970s, followed by much more modest growth in the 1980s as demography and financial stringency made their impact on expansion.

Demographic projections predict a decline in the absolute numbers of 16 to 18 year-olds in the Australian population between 1989 and 1996, with numbers increasing to 1987 levels by 2003. Despite this demographic decline, government policy, driven by

Table 3
Higher education enrollment 1960–87

	1960	1965	1970	1975	1980	1985	1987
Universities	53,391	83,349	115,630	147,754	162,484	174,817	180,803
CAEs	—	24,330	37,625	125,383[a]	165,070	195,231	212,931
Total	53,391	107,679	153,255	273,137	327,554	370,048	393,734

Source: Adapted from Anderson and Vervoorn 1983; CTEC 1986, 1987
a The federal government's decision to incorporate state teachers colleges into the CAE sector is responsible for the dramatic increase in CAE enrollments between 1970 and 1975

economic competition, is to increase higher education enrollments from 400,000 to around 675,000 by the year 2001 in order to compete with comparable OECD countries (Dawkins 1987). Although such policies are primarily oriented towards increasing participation by school leavers, there is also a strong emphasis on equity policies oriented towards increasing participation by mature age and other disadvantaged and nontraditional higher education students.

For young people, admission to higher education is effectively determined by competitive examination after 12 years of schooling (including 2 years of postcompulsory schooling). Aspirants to mature aged student admission status (those over 25 years) must also sit an entrance exam, or provide proof of previous comparable educational qualifications. At present, while there is no active discrimination against any student on the basis of race, gender, religious, or political affiliation, there is little provision for the special entry of those disadvantaged social groups presently underrepresented in higher education, particularly indigenous (Aboriginal) Australians.

In the late 1980s a relatively stable 41 percent of Year 12 students transferred to higher education immediately after completing schooling (Dawkins 1987 p. 14). Thus a primary focus of policies to extend access and increase participation is increasingly being directed towards improving upper-secondary retention rates, particularly of the socially disadvantaged. In 1982 Year 12 retention rates were 36 percent, in 1986, 48.7 percent, and in 1987, 53 percent. The Commonwealth's goal for the 1990s is 65 percent.

A majority of students (55 percent) study full-time on campus, though a substantial 32 percent study part-time and over 12 percent study externally (at a distance, by correspondence, etc.). Full-time enrollments dropped substantially from 63.6 percent in 1975 to 55.2 percent in 1985 as more students opted for the part-time and external modes. The White Paper reforms seem likely to lead to a trend back towards full-time enrollments, though external study may also expand substantially.

As Table 4 indicates, approximately one quarter of students are engaged in the study of the exact sciences (which include medicine and the health sciences), one-quarter in the humanities, and a half in the social sciences (which include education, economics, law).

However, the impression given by Table 4 that there has been a strong drift to the exact sciences since 1979 is somewhat misleading, as the "drift" is almost totally accounted for by the transfer of nursing education from hospital-based training to higher education in 1984. In fact, the numbers of students in the traditional exact sciences have continued to decline as they have in education, while the dramatic growth areas have been law, business studies, computing, and economics and commerce.

Historically, Australian higher education has been an elite system. At present, with barely 20 percent of young people continuing to higher education, it narrowly fulfills Trow's primary criterion for "mass" higher education (Neave 1985). However, in spite of the abolition of tuition fees, and the provision of student allowances, many of the characteristic features of an elite higher education system remain. Tertiary students are predominantly from higher socioeconomic groups while, within higher education itself, the more prestigious faculties and the older institutions attract greater numbers of students from privileged backgrounds and the academically more "able" (Williams 1987). Anderson and Vervoorn assert that ". . . higher education in general and universities in particular remain socially elite institutions. The over-representation of students from high socio-economic backgrounds has remained constant, at least since 1950, as has the under-representation of those from lower socio-economic backgrounds . . ." (Anderson and Vervoorn 1983 p. 120).

This lingering elitism is supported by the strong link between access to higher education and private education.

> . . . compared with public school students those who attend private schools are much more likely to complete secondary school and, of all who do complete, private students are more likely to transfer to higher education. Within higher education their choice is for university (and the prestigious faculties) rather than CAE. (Anderson and Vervoorn 1983 p. 77)

This link is both cultural and economic, and is effected through both the academic orientation and the higher upper-secondary retention rates of most private schools (Smart and Dudley 1989).

Women constitute 51 percent of enrollments at undergraduate level, a proportion which has been increasing steadily since the mid-1950s, and particularly the 1970s. However, they are under-represented in those undertaking higher degrees particularly at PhD level (Anderson and Vervoorn 1983 pp. 44–63). Moreover, women tend to be concentrated in nursing and teaching, and in the arts,

Table 4
Higher education students by field of study 1979 and 1985 (percentage)

	1979	1985
Exact sciences[a]	27	31
Social sciences[b]	46	42
Humanities	26	26

Source: Adapted from CTEC 1986 p. 81.
a Includes medicine, nursing, and dentistry b Includes education, law, and business studies

humanities, and social sciences, also in the visual and performing arts.

Increasing female participation rates reflect the greater tendency for girls to complete secondary schooling. In 1977, female Year 12 retention rates overtook male Year 12 retention rates for the first time. However, the incorporation of teacher education into CAEs in the 1970s and of nursing education in the 1980s have boosted the statistics for female participation in higher education while masking the relatively small real gains in areas of traditional male study.

There is growing evidence that a non-Anglo–Celtic ethnic background (apart from Aboriginality) is no longer a barrier to access to higher education and the professions. Anderson and Vervoorn (1983 p. 98) report a Victorian study from the early 1970s which concluded that "those of non-English background were at least as likely to continue to higher education as those of English speaking background . . . whilst "Other" students [mainly Asian] achieved an even higher continuation rate."

Beswick (1987c) reports that "immigrants from non-English speaking backgrounds are now graduating at significantly higher rates than the old Anglo–Australian population." In particular he notes that for second generation immigrants (those born in Australia of immigrant parents):

> Entry to the professions has clearly been identified as a means of social mobility. . . . In the most recent cohorts admitted to the course in medicine at the University of Melbourne, in one of the most competitive entry processes in Australia, less than half of the students have Australian born parents. (Beswick 1987c p. 8)

Universities have traditionally insisted on their right to control their own course offerings and content. However, when the CAEs were being established after the mid-1960s, state coordinating bodies were created to regulate, rationalize, and approve their course offerings and development. Increasingly, the universities too, have found themselves subject to some degree of scrutiny and *de facto* control by these state bodies. In addition, the colleges (but not the universities) were obliged to have their awards accredited by the Australian Council for Awards in Advanced Education. Following the changes at the end of the 1980s it is unclear whether a new national accrediting body will be appointed to interact with the UNS.

Most higher education in Australia is effectively vocational/professional in character. Training in medicine, law, and latterly education, engineering, and technology, together with nursing, the health sciences, and a range of more recent specializations, has always been the primary focus of Australia's universities and colleges. The concept of a broad liberal education has been strongest in the humanities. Although some institutions have attempted to incorporate a wide general education into professional/vocational degrees, they have been relatively unsuccessful in changing the instrumentally oriented culture of Australian higher education.

Apart from the longer professional courses such as medicine, dentistry, veterinary science, teaching, and so on, three years is the most usual length of an undergraduate degree, with an additional year of study to complete an honors degree. The traditional British model of honors degrees and pass degrees having different curricula is no longer the norm, though most honors degrees still have a research thesis requirement.

Graduate degrees include coursework degrees (which usually include a minor dissertation) such as MSc, MEd, MBA, and research degrees—MPhil and PhD. Most institutions also provide a range of graduate diplomas, the most common being the diploma of education (the qualifications required for teaching in the state education systems). However, an increasingly wide range of specialist diplomas are offered in fields such as computer studies, environmental science, management, library studies, and health sciences.

The traditional pattern of assessment of elite higher education systems—end of course exam—is no longer the norm in Australian institutions. There is growing emphasis on continuous and multiple mode assessment (e.g., essays/assignments, plus exam) rather than the once traditional single assessment by final examination. Increasingly, too, the trend is towards greater flexibility and choice within courses, while three terms have given way to two semesters, and year-long courses have been replaced by shorter semester-long courses. Greater provision for credit transfers—not only between comparable institutions, but also from TAFE to higher education— is a feature of the Dawkins (1988) reform proposals. There is a strong push towards breaking down the fairly rigid access barriers between university, college, and TAFE. The present tensions between maintaining standards and traditional institutional autonomy while widening access and increasing the participation of nontraditional higher education students through more flexible entry provisions and credit transfers nicely illustrate the strains Australian higher education is experiencing as it moves from an elite to a mass higher education system.

5. Conclusion

Like many of its counterparts throughout the Western world, Australian higher education since 1975 has experienced a period of stability if not decline, following the period of rapid growth and development during the 1960s and early 1970s. Since the mid-1970s, Australian higher education's woes have been exacerbated by total reliance on federal finance, at a time when the national government has been essaying severe restraints in public sector expenditure. Higher education's share of the total federal budget declined from 4.5 percent in 1976 to 3.0 percent in 1986.

As a result of higher education's quite severe and prolonged financial neglect, recent years have witnessed a serious deterioration in provision and maintenance of capital buildings and research equipment; in staff–student ratios; provision of student places; and academic salaries, conditions, and morale.

Not until 1987 did the Hawke Labor government, under its new Minister for Education, John Dawkins, begin seriously to address the parlous state of the higher education sector. The ministerial Green and White Papers (Dawkins 1987, 1988) have mapped a radical reform agenda which promises dramatic reshaping of the face of Australian higher education. The ambitious targets set for student growth (from 400,000 in 1988 to 625,000 in 2001) and the limited finances available to achieve them have made radical change and restructuring inevitable.

Clearly, the significant changes initiated by the federal government mean that higher education in Australia faces historically unprecedented turbulence and ferment over the next few years. While the possibilities for progress are great, there are also many potential pitfalls. It will be particularly important that educational quality is carefully monitored and protected against the potential dangers of an excessive reliance on the White Paper's as yet untested assumption that "bigger is better." Equally important will be careful monitoring, and if necessary correction, to ensure that research output and efficiency is not damaged by excessive research concentration and dictation of funding priorities from the central government.

Perhaps the biggest gamble of all is that the federal government, while preaching the rhetoric of deregulation and autonomy, appears to have imposed much more central control on, and regulation of, the tertiary institutions. Whether this will produce a better higher education system for Australia is an open question which history will now put to the empirical test.

Bibliography

Anderson D S, Vervoorn A E 1983 *Access to Privilege: Patterns of Participation in Australian Post-Secondary Education*. Australian National University Press, Canberra

Australian Bureau of Statistics 1987a *Labour Force Status and Educational Attainment: Australia*. ABS Cat No 6235.0. Australian Government Publishing Service, Canberra

Australian Bureau of Statistics 1987b *Research and Experimental Development: All Sector Summary 1985–86*. ABS Cat No 8122.0. Australian Government Publishing Service, Canberra

Australian Science and Technology Council 1987 *Improving the Research Performance of Australia's Universities and Other Higher Education Institutions* (The ASTEC Report). Australian Government Publishing Service, Canberra

Beswick D G 1987a *Prospects for the 1990s: A New Phase of Development in Australian Higher Education*. Centre for the Study of Higher Education, University of Melbourne, Research Working Paper 87.17

Beswick D G 1987b *The Role of Government in Higher Education in Australia*. Centre for the Study of Higher Education, University of Melbourne, Research Working Paper 87.16

Beswick D G 1987c Trends in higher education. In: Keeves J (ed.) 1987 *Australian Education: Review of Recent Research*. George Allen and Unwin, Sydney

Commonwealth Tertiary Education Commission 1986 *Review of Efficiency and Effectiveness in Higher Education*. Australian Government Publishing Service, Canberra

Commonwealth Tertiary Education Commission 1987 *Selected Higher Education Statistics*. Australian Government Publishing Service, Canberra

Connell R W 1983 *Which Way is Up? Essays on Sex, Class and Culture*. George Allen and Unwin, Sydney

Connell R W, Ashenden D J, Kessler S, Dawsett G W 1982 *Making the Difference: Schools, Families and Social Division*. George Allen and Unwin, Sydney

Connell R W, Irving T H 1980 *Class Structure in Australian History*. Cheshire, Melbourne

Dawkins J 1987 *Higher Education: A Policy Discussion Paper* (Ministerial Statement—The Green Paper). Australian Government Publishing Service, Canberra

Dawkins J 1988 *Higher Education: A Policy Statement* (Ministerial Statement—The White Paper). Australian Government Publishing Service, Canberra

Harman G 1989 The Dawkins reconstruction of Australian higher education. Paper delivered to Annual Meeting of American Education Research Association, San Francisco

Harman G, Smart D (eds.) 1982 *Federal Intervention in Australian Education*. Georgian House, Melbourne

Hetherington R et al. 1985 *Senates and Councils of Tertiary Institutions in Western Australia: Review of Structures and Functions* (The Hetherington Report). Tertiary Institutions Governance Committee, Perth, Western Australia

Higley D, Deacon D, Smart D 1979 *Elites in Australia*. Routledge and Kegan Paul, London

Hilmer F G 1988 Higher education under scrutiny—Another view. *Aust. Q.* 60(1): 27–39

Marginson S 1989 Is there life after Dawkins? *Soc. Alternatives* 7(4): 30–36

Marshall N 1988 The failure of the academic lobby: From policy community to bureaucratic management. *Politics* 23(2): 67–79

Martin L 1964 *Tertiary Education in Australia: Report of the Committee on the Future of Tertiary Education in Australia* (The Martin Report). Government Printer, Canberra

Murray K et al. 1957 *Report of the Committee on Australian Universities* (The Murray Report). Government Printer, Canberra

Neave G R 1985 Elite and mass higher education in Britain: A regressive model? *Comp. Educ. Rev.* 29(3): 347–61

Organisation for Economic Co-operation and Development 1987a *Post Graduate Education in the 1980s*. OECD, Paris

Organisation for Economic Co-operation and Development 1987b *Structural Adjustment and Economic Performance*. OECD, Paris

Organisation for Economic Co-operation and Development 1987c *Universities Under Scrutiny*. OECD, Paris

Partridge P H 1973 *Society Schools and Progress in Australia*. Pergamon, Sydney

Scott P 1984 *The Crisis of the University*. Croom Helm, London

Smart D 1989a The Dawkins 'reconstruction' of higher education in Australia. Paper delivered to Annual Meeting of American Education Research Association, San Francisco

Smart D 1990 The Dawkins Reconstruction of Higher Education in Australia. *Educational Research and Perspectives* 17(2): 11–22

Smart D, Dudley J 1989 Private schools and public policy in Australia. In: Walford G (ed.) 1989 *Private Schools in Ten Countries: Policy and Practice*. Routledge and Kegan Paul, London, pp. 105–32

Smith R et al. 1989 *Report of the Committee to Review Higher Education Research Policy* (The Smith Report). Australian Research Council, Canberra

Wark I 1977 Colleges of advanced education and the commission on advanced education. In: Birch I K F, Smart D (eds.) 1977 *The Commonwealth Government and Education 1964–1976*. Drummond, Melbourne, pp. 153–76

Williams B R et al. 1979 *Education, Training and Employment: Report of the Committee of Inquiry into Education and Training* (The Williams Report). Australian Government Publishing Service, Canberra

Williams T 1987 *Participation in Education*. ACER Research Monograph 30. Australian Council for Educational Research, Hawthorn, Victoria

Wilson G 1989 *Review of the Commonwealth Postgraduate Awards Scheme* (The Wilson Report). Australian Research Council, Canberra

D. Smart

Austria

1. Higher Education and Society

Austria is a democratic republic in the center of Europe which in 1955 regained national independence after seven years of annexation by Nazi Germany and 10 years of Allied occupation. Most of the 7.6 million Austrians speak German, although small minorities speak Slavonic languages. Vienna, the capital, which until 1918 was the administrative and intellectual center of the multinational Hapsburg empire, has retained its academic predominance: it is the seat of several universities and other institutions of higher education. The University of Vienna, founded in 1365, is the oldest in the German-speaking countries.

For centuries the Roman Catholic Church, especially the Jesuit and Benedictine orders, played an important role in Austrian higher education. The establishment of the universities of Graz (1585), Salzburg (1622), and Innsbruck (1669) was a joint effort of the House of Hapsburg and the Catholic Church to stem the tide of Protestant Reformation. Only the rise of liberalism during the second half of the nineteenth century brought the tight control of state and church over the universities to an end. The Constitution of 1867 secularized the whole education system and proclaimed the "freedom of science and teaching."

The saddest chapter in the long history of Austrian higher education was undoubtedly the 1930s. Austria's universities, which during the decades before the First World War had become centers of excellence in areas such as medicine, physics, engineering, economics, and philosophy, recruiting brilliant scholars and scientists from all over the Hapsburg empire, suffered two terrible blows which cost them many fine teachers and destroyed unique schools of thought. A first purge by the Austro-fascist government of the early 1930s removed all socialist and Marxist professors and lecturers. The second and certainly most severe loss was the emigration and expulsion of a large number of Jewish professors and lecturers in the wake of rising antisemitism and Nazism. (The philosophy faculty of the University of Vienna lost more than one-third, the medical faculty more than half of their professors and senior lecturers.)

Since the Second World War a succession of single party and coalition governments have been following policies which had three basic aims: to bring Austrian higher education back into line with the scientific developments of the Western industrialized world; to keep it open to all those qualified to study; and to make it responsive to the needs of Austria's rapidly changing economy. There was, however, never a "national plan" for higher education with explicit enrollment target figures: the extraordinary growth of university studies since the mid-1960s was the product of an unrestricted social demand. The rise of the overall number of students in higher education by more than 500 percent from 1961 to 1988 (see Table 1) was partly caused by population growth between 1950 and 1965 (the birthrate rose by nearly one-third) but much more by the massive trend towards continued higher and postsecondary education.

There are two major reasons why the decline in the birthrate which started in the mid-1960s is not expected to have a reducing effect on student numbers before the early 1990s. Austrian expansion of higher education started from a lower level than in most other European countries; Austria is still catching up.

Secondly, the level of qualifications required by the labor market is rising. The Austrian economy is sharing the Europe-wide shift from the primary sector to the secondary, and increasingly to the tertiary,

Table 1
Demographic data from Austrian population and educational statistics (index 1961=100)

Absolute figures	1961	1971	1981	1988	Index
Population	7,073,808	7,491,526	7,555,338	7,596,081	107
People in employment	3,369,815	3,097,987	3,411,521	3,430,000	102
Birth rate	131,563	108,510	93,942	88,052	67
Maturanten[a]	12,223	16,755	27,517	31,684	259
First year students[b]	7,480	8,998	17,314	20,194	270
Overall number of students[b]	31,858	49,063	112,930	164,937	518
Graduates[c]	2,170	4,483	6,606	8,877	409

a Annual output of secondary school leavers entitled to study   b Universities and Colleges of Art and Music (Austrians only)   c First degrees (Austrians only)

service sector. Employment in agriculture has dropped from 23 percent in 1961 to 8 percent in 1990 and industry and manufacturing are gradually shrinking below the 40 percent mark while the service sector (e.g., commerce and personal services, the social services, and public/civic service) now employs more than half of the Austrian labor force. Finally, there remains the motive of gaining higher education qualifications in order to have an academic title. To be a graduate (*Akademiker*) in the still rather hierarchical and formal Austrian society entails elevated social status and respect, even in everyday social interaction.

2. The Institutional Fabric of the Higher Education System

Austrian postsecondary education comprises three types of institutions: universities, colleges of art and music, and a group of so-called "academies." While access to all of them normally requires university entrance qualifications, that is, the upper-secondary school leaving certificate *Matura*, only the universities and colleges of art and music are perceived as institutions of higher education. The academies are predominantly teacher-training institutions and despite their name they have nonacademic status and should be regarded as the "nonuniversity sector."

2.1 The Sectoral Organization of Higher Education
The University Organization Act of 1975 designated 12 institutions as universities, all of them public. They vary enormously as to their age, size, and the range of studies they offer. While the three old universities of Vienna, Graz, and Innsbruck have retained and expanded the traditional European faculty structure, a number of universities have grown from nineteenth-century foundations originally specializing in fields such as engineering, mining, economics, or agriculture and forestry. The University of Vienna is Austria's largest higher edu-

cation institution with more than 61,000 students in 1989. The two other original universities are also large: Graz has 23,000 students and Innsbruck 19,000, while the University of Mining in Leoben and the new University of Educational Sciences in Klagenfurt cater for 2,000 and 4,000 students respectively.

The post-Second World War foundations—Salzburg (where a university already existed from 1622 to 1810), Linz, and Klagenfurt—do not have the traditional range of faculties: Linz does not have a humanities faculty, Klagenfurt does not have a law faculty, and none of them has a medical faculty. Klagenfurt has recently begun to offer economics and business studies to take some of the pressure off the Vienna University of Economics whose enrollment exceeds 20,000. All universities offer undergraduate and graduate studies and have the right to award academic degrees and honors.

The principle of "unity of research and teaching" entitles and obliges all units and members of the Austrian higher education system to participate both in teaching and research. Consequently there are no research professorships, but in order to strengthen the research capacity of certain disciplines, 21 university research institutes have been established since 1975, some of them in cooperation between the federal government and private bodies and enterprises, some for specific research projects.

The link between research and teaching should guarantee that teaching takes account of state-of-the-art science. Involving students in the research process is seen as part of their academic education and also as an opportunity to identify and select able young scientists. On average 40 percent of the working hours of university personnel are devoted to research. In recruiting and advancing professors and junior staff members their achievements in science and research are fundamental criteria.

All six colleges of art and music are public, financed and controlled in the same way as universities. Their artistic and teaching freedom is guaranteed by constitutional law. There are three colleges located in Vienna: the College of Fine Arts, the College of Applied Arts, and the Vienna College of Music and Drama. Probably the best known of the three colleges of music is the *Mozarteum* in Salzburg. The unique feature of the colleges is the artistic "master schools" and "master classes" operating alongside chairs for academic subjects. While graduates of degree courses are awarded master's degrees and—to a limited extent—doctorates, graduates of artistic or vocational courses finish their studies with nonacademic titles.

Some colleges have extraordinarily high proportions of foreign students: at the Vienna College of Music and Drama about 40 percent of the student body are of foreign nationality; at the Salzburg *Mozarteum* almost half.

The nonuniversity sector of postsecondary education consists of a heterogeneous group of academies and other institutions which predominantly train teachers for primary and lower secondary schools, religious education, and vocational instruction, but also train social workers and medical-technical assistants. Unlike the all-public higher education system, some of these—usually fairly small—institutions are owned and run by regional bodies or private organizations. Eight of the fourteen teacher-training colleges are public ("federal"), while the others are totally or partly owned by the Roman Catholic Church. They were established in 1962 when teacher training was reformed, extended, and upgraded from the upper-secondary to the postsecondary level. In the late 1980s, fewer than 10 percent of Austria's students took part in this type of education. As a university alternative their significance has been decreasing since the 1960s in spite of the massive expansion of postsecondary education.

2.2 Admission Policies

One of the most marked features of Austrian higher education is its open, nonselective admission policy. All Austrian holders of the upper-secondary school leaving certificate (*Matura*) are legally entitled to study free of fees any subject at the university of their personal choice. (Only certain courses at the colleges of art and music or those for physical education teacher training require entrance examinations to be passed which test artistic talent or physical fitness.) There is no competitive selection or meritocratic limitation, not even in such highly attractive fields as medicine, business administration, or journalism, nor is there a national student placement agency. The unavoidable consequences of this liberal, if not *laissez faire*, approach are overcrowded institutes, gross imbalances between universities, and startlingly high drop-out rates.

That Austria should nonetheless have comparatively low university enrollment rates—in 1988 16.5 percent of the relevant age group were students—must be seen in the light of the secondary school system through which students must first pass. Austria has retained the traditional European bipartite system of secondary education with selection for the eight-year general education secondary school at the age of 10. Although in 1962 a short-cycle upper-secondary school for the 14 to 18 age group was established which also awards the *Matura*, early selection has proved to be socially biased and far from efficient in mobilizing (working-class) talent. Other significant factors are the marginal status of the nonuniversity sector and the popularity of the vocational upper-secondary schools. While graduates from the general education secondary schools have few career options but to move on to higher education, the alumni of these technical or commercial schools gain both the *Matura* and vocational qualifications which give them excellent employment prospects on the labor market. At present only 38 percent of the graduates of vocational education move on to a university.

2.3 Quantitative Developments

Between 1970 and 1985 both the universities and the colleges of art and music underwent an explosive growth, even though at very different levels of scale. Within that period, university enrollment increased by approximately 100,000 students from 43,122 in 1970 to 141,144 in 1985. The "master class" principle

Table 2
Enrollment in higher education (regular Austrian students only)

	1960	1965	1970	1974/75	1980	1985	1988
Universities	27,237	38,057	43,122	62,481	100,114	141,144	158,396
Colleges of Art and Music[a]	—	—	1,457	2,928	3,744	4,372	4,508
"Academies" (Nonuniversity sector)[a]							
Teacher training academies	—	—	5,997	8,111	7,431	5,576	5,294
Other academies	—	—	305	703	1,665	2,217	1,935

a Incompatible data before 1970

and the artistic entrance examinations prevented the colleges of art and music from turning into mass institutions, but their student population exactly tripled between 1970 and 1985, growing from 1,457 to 4,372.

The proportion of students between the ages of 18 and 26 years rose from 3.9 percent in 1961 to 11.7 percent in 1981 and to 16.5 percent in 1988, which is still on the lower end of the European spectrum. The number of graduates in the adult working population increased from 2.6 percent in 1961 to a relatively low 4.4 percent in 1988.

While the universities and colleges continue to grow at a reduced rate, the teacher-training academies of the nonuniversity sector have begun to feel the impact of the worsening employment prospects for primary and lower-secondary school teachers in the wake of the declining birthrate: since the all-time high in the mid-1970s the number of teacher trainees has been falling from 8,111 to 5,294 in 1988.

2.4 Structure of Qualifications

The General Act on University Studies of 1966 and subsequent legislation systematized and homogenized all university studies, degrees, and graduation requirements and introduced a two-tier structure for all courses except medicine. Traditionally, university studies in Austria led to a doctor's degree or a state examination. Nowadays only medicine, whose minimum length of study is 12 semesters (six years), can be studied as an all-through doctoral course. All other first-degree studies end with a master's degree. They are divided into two stages, each of which has to be completed with a diploma examination. Before being admitted to the second diploma examination, students have to submit a thesis.

The minimum length of each course of study is laid down by law. Most master's courses require at least eight semesters (four years), although some are longer (e.g., agriculture and engineering nine semesters, chemistry and psychology ten semesters). The three-year courses at teacher-training academies terminate with teaching certificates, which do not carry credit at universities.

At the graduate level, doctoral studies have to be based on a master's degree in the same or a closely related subject. The minimum duration of a doctoral program is two years, but completion usually takes considerably longer. There is no formal admission or selection procedure, but candidates have to find a supervisor for their dissertation who accepts them on the merits of their previous studies. Doctorates are awarded after the submission of a dissertation based on independent research and a viva voce examination (*Rigorosum*).

While the courses and curricula of university studies are closely controlled by the Ministry of Science and Research, the decision to award master's degrees and doctorates is an autonomous function of the universities and colleges of arts and music.

3. Governance, Administration, and Finance

3.1 National Administration

All Austrian universities and colleges are institutions of the state, centrally governed and administered by the Ministry of Science and Research on the basis of a comprehensive corpus of higher education legislation. Some provincial authorities have encouraged the establishment of higher education institutions in provincial capitals (e.g., Klagenfurt and Linz) and they support "their" universities and colleges with extraordinary donations; they have, however, no say in the process of higher education decision making where a legally defined balance of power between ministerial administration and institutional autonomy prevails.

Ministerial competence includes decisions on university organization and the establishment of new institutes; the allocation of funds and the creation of new posts; the construction and management of university buildings; the structure and organization of study courses and examinations; the range of courses offered at individual institutions; and the appointment of university staff, including professors.

In some of these decisions (e.g., the appointment of professors) the universities and colleges have the right to recommend or nominate.

University autonomy is clearly circumscribed, safeguarding against ministerial interference in matters of teaching and research, including the selection and recruitment of staff and the granting of teaching authorization. College legislation is very similar but the teacher training academies of the nonuniversity sector do not have an autonomous sphere; they are controlled and administered by the Ministry of Education, Arts, and Sports, as are secondary schools.

The legal framework of study courses has reached a degree of complexity which is increasingly criticized as being bureaucratic and too rigid. It consists of a four-tiered system of regulations, of which two have the rank of laws to be passed (and amended) by parliament while two have the nature of decrees issued by the ministry. The most general regulations concerning organizational principles, enrollment procedures, the structure of studies, examinations, and degrees, etc. are laid down in the General Act on University Studies. On the next level, a series of analogous laws provide the common features of certain large fields of studies such as medicine, law, or the social sciences. Ministerial decrees then prescribe in general terms for each single subject the curriculum to be followed at all universities offering courses. Finally, "study orders" formally establish the preceding hierarchy of regulations as the actual curriculum of a given university department or institute.

The planning role of the Ministry of Science and Research is not strong. Given the fact that Austrian students are not selected, but free to choose any university and any subject, the minister can regulate the flow of students only indirectly: by information campaigns or by failing to increase the capacity of overcrowded courses which are ascribed low national priority. One important means of influencing public opinion and setting priorities is the "Higher Education Reports to Parliament" which the minister has to publish at least every third year. These reports provide a kind of continuous assessment and evaluation of the achievements and needs of universities and colleges.

3.2 Finance

Universities and colleges are financed almost completely (96%) by central government. Only about 4 percent of the higher education funds come from other sources such as foreign students' fees, donations, contracted research, and consultancies. In 1972 study fees for Austrian students were abolished. Fees had been very low while the costs of collecting them had become untenably high.

The higher education part of the annual national budget is drawn up by the science and research and finance ministries, which in turn base their estimates on the financial and personal resource requirements that universities have to submit annually with a three years projection.

Most decisions on higher education expenditure are either taken by or have to be approved by the Ministry of Science and Research. Universities have at their disposal only modest lump sum allocations for administrative and operating expenditure. All larger payments, such as for the purchase of scientific and technical equipment and furniture, are made by the ministry. The construction and maintenance of university and college buildings are the responsibility of the Ministry of Construction and Technology.

Since the beginning of the rapid expansion in the 1960s, public spending on higher education has increased fivefold, peaking between 1970 and 1980 and levelling off towards the end of the 1980s. This increase did not just offset the general rise of costs during this period, but allowed the modernization of old facilities and new building as well as the widening of teaching and research capacities. The higher education allocation in the national budget shows a stable, continuous rise from 2.3 percent in 1970 to 2.9 percent in 1989. In 1987 the share of the gross national product devoted to higher education approached 1 percent.

3.3 Institutional Administration

The university reform of 1975 abolished the traditional pattern of governance that divided decision making between all-professorial faculty boards and individual chairs held by full professors. In the post-1968 drive for more democracy and accountability, power-sharing ("codetermination") between professors, assistants, and students was introduced in several newly created university and college bodies.

The rector, a full professor, is elected by a university assembly comprising representatives from all university staff groups for a two-year term of office during which he or she acts as the highest official of the university or college. In the old universities which all have retained the faculty structure, the rector is responsible for the internal regulation of university life and executes the decisions of the academic senate, a body composed of delegates from all faculties; in the new generation of universities the rector cooperates with university committees. The general management of universities is in the hands of university directors appointed by the Minister of Science and Research. In matters of public administration these managers are subordinate to the minister; in autonomous academic matters to the rector.

The deans who head faculties also have to be full professors elected for periods of two years by faculty committees comprising all the faculty professors but also representatives of assistants, students, and other staff. They are responsible for routine administration, the execution of faculty committee decisions, and the coordination of teaching and research. (Colleges of art and music do not have faculties but departments, otherwise their governance is similar to the university pattern. Teacher-training academies are headed by directors appointed by the Minister of Education, Arts, and Sports.)

Since the abolition of chairs, the base units for research, teaching, and administration are the institutes. The heads of institutes are elected by their respective institute assembly in which professors, assistants, and students have proportional representation. Associate professors are eligible as well. Although they are mainly advisory bodies with the right to be informed and to make suggestions, institute assemblies have made decisions on teaching, staff appointments (except for professorships, which are the responsibility of faculty commissions), and the use of resources much more transparent and accountable than before.

Normally institutes are established for whole disciplines, but subdivisions for specialization in large fields such as history or physics do exist. Although it

Table 3
Higher education expenditure

Higher education budget	1970	1975	1980	1985	1987
As percentage of the national budget	2.28	2.60	2.79	2.82	2.86
As percentage of the gross national product	0.62	0.78	0.86	0.96	0.97

was the aim of the university reorganization of 1975 to create larger, more efficient, and cooperative units most institutes are still small: in 1987 out of a total of 814 university institutes 510 had only one full professor, 235 institutes comprised two or four full professors, and only 17 institutes had from five to nine full professors. A number of institutes were headed by associate professors. From 1975 to 1987 the proportion of "one-professor institutes" sank from 75 to 63 percent.

The adequacy of teaching and of the curricula of all courses of study is monitored, and decided on, by study commissions with proportional representation of professors, assistants, and students. In most cases they are organized within single subject institutes, in studies like law or medicine however, they are organized on faculty level.

4. Faculty and Students: Teaching, Learning, and Research

4.1 Faculty

The rapid growth of the student population and the differentiation of modern science and scholarship have drastically changed the size and career patterns of university teaching staff. In addition to the fully employed university personnel shown in Table 4, a large number of university assistants and external experts were given limited contracts as part-time lecturers. They widened the range of specialist classes offered and took over a substantial part of the continually growing teaching load.

At the top of the academic hierarchy are full professors with tenured civil servant status until they retire at the age of 68. Many professors begin their careers as assistants, acquire the status of reader through the postdoctoral *Habilitation* process and are eventually called to a professorship. When a vacancy arises for a full professor, a faculty appointment committee advertises the post both nationally and in relevant professional journals abroad. The committee assesses the candidates and proposes three of them to the minister of science and research who makes the final selection. Like all high-ranking civil servants, full professors are appointed by the Austrian president. Full professors do not have a fixed teaching load; the scope of their duties is laid down in rather free terms in individual contracts. Associate professors are usually recruited from the group of readers of a given university at the proposal of faculty committees. They have more or less the same duties as full professors but they are subject to clearly defined civil service work regulations, have a minimum teaching load of 6 to 8 hours per week, are on a lower pay scale, and are not eligible for certain higher university offices such as dean or rector.

Readers are either senior assistants or scientists working outside the university system who have obtained a teaching authorization (*venia docendi*) through a *Habilitation*. This postdoctoral qualification is normally gained after 10 to 14 years of research. It involves the submission of a thesis (*Habilitationsschrift*) to an autonomous faculty committee, a viva voce examination, and the proof of teaching competence. The awarding of reader status by the university has to be formally endorsed by the ministry.

By far the largest group of university staff are

Table 4
Higher education academic staff

	1970	1975	1980	1985	1989
Universities					
Full professors	806	1,093	1,119	1,134	1,152
Associate professors	100	300	470	560	580
Assistants	3,653	4,697	4,882	5,178	5,294
Other teaching and scientific staff	317	667	690	864	806
Universities total	4,876	6,757	7,161	7,736	7,832
Colleges of Art and Music					
Full professors	57	152	253	312	393
Associate professors[a]	84	136	107	64	—
Assistants	13	48	66	104	132
Other teaching and scientific staff	121	135	134	153	196
Colleges total	275	471	560	633	721
Higher education total	5,151	7,228	7,721	8,369	8,553

a During the 1980s associate professorships at colleges were turned into full professorships and phased out assistants, who enter the academic profession after their master's degree or their doctorate. *De jure* they have a supportive function in the teaching, research, and administration of a given institute, *de facto* they tend to have a strong attachment to one professor in whose field they do research and who supervises the progress of their thesis. Assistants are temporary civil servants with renewable contracts of initially two and then four years. Until 1988 assistants were granted tenure only after having passed the *Habilitation*. Now they can apply earlier. In each individual case a faculty committee has to make a recommendation to the ministry on the basis of two independent references and an overall assessment of the applicant's research and teaching record. Although the work of assistants is regulated nationally by general public employment legislation, there exists considerable variance at institute level. It is a widely observed informal convention that assistants spend half their working time supporting professorial teaching and research and departmental administration and the other half doing their own research.

The corporate interests of the various subgroups of the academic profession are represented by national associations: the Austrian Rectors' Conference, the Federal Conference of Academic Staff and—from 1990—the Federal Conference of University and College Professors. In the process of higher education policy making these bodies have to be consulted and the ministry is obliged to submit to them for comment the drafts of all higher education legislation.

4.2 Students

During the 1980s, new students increasingly based their choice of subject on career prospects and employment chances, which explains both the growth of fields like technology and economics and the marked decline of medicine and teacher training. Since the middle of the 1970s, the latter two have

Table 5
Distribution of students across the main subject areas (percentage)

	1980/81	1983/84	1988/89ᵃ
Theology	2.3	2.3	1.9 (1.4)
Law, social sciences, and economics	27.0	28.5	32.3 (34.4)
Medicine	14.5	12.8	8.3 (4.7)
Humanities and natural sciences	38.2	37.6	36.5 (35.2)
Technology	14.0	14.5	16.3 (20.0)
Agriculture and veterinary medicine	3.3	3.8	4.0 (4.3)
Others	0.7	0.5	0.7 (—)

a The figures in brackets show the distribution of 1988 first year enrollments

Table 6
Female participation in higher education

Percentage of females	1961	1971	1981	1988
Population	53.4	52.8	52.7	52.4
*Maturanten*ᵃ	38.5	44.7	48.5	51.3
First year students	29.2	34.8	47.2	46.6
Overall number of students	26.2	27.7	41.2	44.8
Graduates	27.4	26.1	35.5	43.3

a Secondary school leavers entitled to study

been suffering from substantial graduate unemployment.

While the overall participation of women in higher education has been rising steadily since the early 1960s, their distribution across the main subject areas varies considerably, ranging from 68 percent in the humanities, 56 percent in medicine, 46 percent in law, and 37 percent in theology to 19 percent in technology/engineering in the academic year 1987–88.

The reduction of gender inequality in higher education was not accompanied by a comparable shift in the social composition of the student body. It was the daughters of the "new middle class" who profited most from the widening opportunities. Since the mid-1970s the proportion of students with a working-class background has remained low and stable at around 13 to 14 percent.

The introduction of so-called "codetermination" in 1975 gave students a certain amount of academic power at national, university, faculty, and institute level. Like other academic interest groups, the Austrian Students' Union has to be consulted in matters of university legislation. The major students' factions are affiliated with national political parties. Although union membership is compulsory, only about one-third of the students have bothered to vote in the biannual elections recently. At institute/study course level individual candidates are elected who represent students' interests in curricular matters. Study course commissions monitor the study programs at university level and nationally. They can propose changes and new study programs, but ultimately the decisive authority over the structure and curricula of all undergraduate courses is the Ministry of Research and Science.

Austrian pupils have to follow a broad 12–14 subject general education curriculum throughout their upper-secondary education. Consequently undergraduate programs are either specialist single-subject courses or combination courses with a major and minor subject. The standardization of all undergraduate courses has led to an abolition of the traditional study freedom and an increase in examinations which is widely criticized as counterproductive. Students are normally assessed in each class at the end of the semester.

Two problems give cause for serious concern: the high dropout rate and the fact that most students need much longer to complete their studies than the regulations stipulate. The long-term average success (i.e., graduation) rate is only 51 percent. Twelve percent of the male and 17 percent of the female students drop out after their first year; and those who graduate exceed the minimum length of undergraduate studies on average by five semesters. Unsurprisingly "quality" and "efficiency" have become leitmotivs in the ongoing Austrian higher education debate.

5. Conclusion

At the beginning of the 1990s, Austrian higher education is faced with three strong challenges: (a) the reform of the existing legal framework; (b) the strengthening of short-cycle nonuniversity study alternatives; and (c) the initiative of the Austrian government to join the European Community (EC).

Draft amendments to the University Organization Act and the General Act on University Studies circulated for comment in early 1990 signal the intention of the ministry of research and science to strengthen institutional autonomy and to introduce notions of "market," "accountability," and "quality control" into the Austrian reform debate. The two proposals which received most public attention were the introduction of professorships without tenure and the recognition of private higher education by the ministry. However, the opposition to "private universities" among all academic interest groups and the Socialist Party was so fierce that the (Conservative) minister withdrew the proposal before the end of the consultation period.

The high dropout rates in research-oriented undergraduate courses raised the question of whether a substantial part of the student population would not be better served by shorter, practice-oriented, non-degree alternatives. Various models of an expanded nonuniversity sector are under consideration.

Austria is eager to join the emerging multinational network of European scientific cooperation. In the establishment of new study programs, in the fight against insufficient resources and obsolete equipment, and in the ministerial drive for efficiency and quality in teaching and research, *Europareife*, that is, being up to an (imaginary) all-European standard of science and scholarship, has become a powerful argument for innovation.

Bibliography

Bundesministerium für Wissenschaft und Forschung (ed.) 1985 *Berufliche Situation und soziale Stellung von Akademikern.* Bundesministerium für Wissenschaft und Forschung, Vienna

Bundesministerium für Wissenschaft und Forschung 1987 *Higher Education in Austria.* Bundesministerium für Wissenschaft und Forschung, Vienna

Bundesministerium für Wissenschaft und Forschung 1987 *Hochschulbericht 1987.* Bundesministerium für Wissenschaft und Forschung, Vienna

Bundesministerium für Wissenschaft und Forschung 1989 *Studieren in Österreich.* Bundesministerium für Wissenschaft und Forschung, Vienna

Burkart G (ed.) 1985 *Maturanten, Studenten, Akademiker.* Kärntner Druck- und Verlagsgesellschaft, Klagenfurt

Dell'Mour R, Landler F, Rabitsch W 1985 *Bildungswesen und Qualifikationsstruktur.* Bundesministerium für Wissenschaft und Forschung, Vienna

Findl P, Holzmann R, Münz R 1987 *Bevölkerung und Sozialstaat.* Manz, Vienna

Gruber K H 1982 Higher Education and the State in Austria. *Eur. J. Educ.* 17(3): 259–70

Kellermann P (ed.) 1988 *Universität und Hochschulpolitik.* Böhlau, Vienna

Lassnigg L 1989 *Ausbildungen und Berufe in Österreich.* Institute for Advanced Studies, Vienna

Lassnigg L, Pechar H 1988 *Alternatives to Universities in Higher Education. Country Study: Austria.* Organisation for Economic Co-operation and Development (OECD), Paris

K. H. Gruber

B

Bahrain

1. Higher Education and Society

Bahrain is a group of islands in the Arabian Gulf, long ruled by the Al-Khalifa family. It was a British protectorate from 1860 to 1971, when it regained its independence and joined the United Nations. Its frontiers remained unchanged throughout those years. It is an emirate with a cabinet appointed by H.H. the Amir Sheikh Issa Bin Salman Al-Khalifa.

The population in 1988 was estimated at 473,300 including 34 percent non-Bahrainis. The ethnic structure is mainly comprised of Bahrainis (68%), other Arabs (4.1%), and Asians (24.7%) with a variety of other nationalities making up the remaining 3.2 percent (1981 census). The age distribution in 1988 was 0–14: 34.6 percent; 15–64: 63.2 percent, 65+: 2.2 percent. Although 82 percent of the population is said to be urban, any rural/urban distinction is inapplicable because, with an approximate area of 692.5 square kilometers, the country is too small to be categorized in those terms.

Although in the 30 years from 1959 the indigenous Bahraini population has almost trebled, the non-Bahraini population has grown to nearly five times its previous size. The increase in the Bahraini population is attributed to the high birth rate, a higher life expectancy due to improved health care, the spread of education, and a better standard of living. The increase in the non-Bahraini population arose because of the country's need for a more skilled and qualified labor force as industry and commerce grew.

Bahrain's principal industries are oil products and aluminum smelting. Pearls, fish, fruit and vegetables were the economy's mainstays until oil was discovered in 1932. Oil reserves were depleted by the 1970s but international banking thrived.

Higher education has developed slowly but steadily with the main aim of training Bahrainis for the professional jobs currently held by foreigners. It is largely devoted to engineering, business, teaching, nursing, and medical studies. Religious organizations play no role in higher education.

2. The Institutional Fabric of the Higher Education System

There are three institutions of higher education and training: the national University of Bahrain (UB), established in 1987, which is funded but autonomous; a state-owned College of Health Science (CHS), established in 1976 and administered directly by the ministry of health; and a regional Arabian Gulf University, (AGU) established in 1982 and owned jointly by Bahrain, Iraq, Kuwait, Oman, Qatar, Saudi Arabia, and United Arab Emirates. Although all three institutions are primarily concerned with teaching and training, UB and AGU have developed research activities as an integral part of their system.

There is also a government organization, Bahrain Center for Studies and Research, which was established in 1981 and plays a dual role as it is both a funding agency for selected research, and also carries out its own research in socioeconomic fields.

All three institutions charge fees, operate on the credit hour and semester system, and have academic faculty members from throughout the world. In both UB and AGU, most faculty members hold research degrees.

Earlier institutions of higher education were reorganized in the 1980s. The Teacher's Training College for Men (TTCM) was established in 1966, and the Teacher's Training College for Women (TTCW) in 1967; both were phased out in 1980 with the establishment of Bahrain University College of Arts, Science and Education (UCB) in 1979. The Gulf Technical College (GTC) was established in 1967, converted to Gulf Polytechnic (GP) in 1983, and merged with UCB in 1987 to form the University of Bahrain.

Before 1966, no institution of postsecondary education existed. Bahrainis went abroad for higher education either on government scholarships or at their own expense. Even after the establishment of such institutions in their own country, several students continued their higher education abroad, because the programs offered locally were limited, geared only to the needs of Bahrain, and had a limited intake to ensure quality. In 1987–88, 1,612 Bahraini students were studying abroad. Thirty-nine percent of those students were women.

The admission qualification for all institutions in Bahrain is a certificate of secondary education equivalent to that issued by the Ministry of Education, with an achievement level above a specified minimum. These are determined by the government representatives who form the governing bodies. Admission qualifications reflect government policy. Quotas for various colleges are specified annually by the university council for UB and AGU, and by the Board of Education for CHS. Most students are at least 18 with the majority in the age group 20–24. Accurate data are not available for different years, however.

The programs offered at UB are:

(a) A two-year technician diploma in engineering followed by a three-year bachelor's degree.

(b) A two-year associate diploma in business or accounting, followed by a two-year bachelor's degree in the same field.

(c) A two-year diploma in commercial studies.

(d) A four-year bachelor's degree in science, arts, education, or physical education.

(e) A two-year associate diploma in office management, followed by a three-year bachelor's degree.

(f) A graduate diploma in education (PGDE) for teaching in secondary schools.

(g) A master of education degree (MEd) in curriculum development.

(h) A part-time studies diploma in business and a master's degree in business administration.

The programs offered at CHS are:

(a) Two two-and-a-half year programs for an associate degree in Health Sciences (ADHS) in general nursing, laboratory technology, pharmacy, radiography, public health, medical equipment, sports medicine, or dental hygiene.

(b) A one-year post-ADHS program in teacher training, psychiatric nursing, midwifery, or community nursing.

(c) A six-month maternal and child health program for trained practical nurses.

(d) A two–three year post-ADHS bachelor's degree in nursing.

(e) A two-year public health inspector program to train middle-level health personnel.

(f) A middle-level health management program leading to a Certificate in Health Care.

The programs offered at AGU are:

(a) A two-year premedical program, followed by a five-year bachelor's degree in Medicine and Medical Sciences.

(b) Graduate diplomas, and higher degrees in various specializations in desert sciences and arid lands, biotechnology, technology management, and energy.

(c) Programs for master's degrees in educational administration or special education.

3. Governance, Administration, and Finance

The governing body for higher education is (for UB) a board of trustees, chaired by the Minister of Education; a board of education chaired by the Undersecretary of the Ministry of Health, is responsible for CHS; and, for AGU, a board of trustees, chaired by an official representative of one of the participating states. The boards meet biannually.

Funds for both UB and CHS are allocated by the government, and for AGU by the participating states. Contributions from private individuals and industries have been rare.

Budgets have increased with the expansion of higher education. The annual operational budget for UB in 1990 was 11.7 million Bahraini dinar (BD) (US$31,350,000); for CHS it is around BD 1.5 million (US$3,980,000); the AGU operational budget is a biennial Saudi Riyals (SR) 120,500,000 (US$32,000,000).

Members of the board of trustees of UB are appointed by an Amiri decree and those of the board of education of CHS by an edict issued by the Minister of Health. The board of trustees of AGU consists of one official representative from each of the participating states, the chair of the Executive Council of the Arab Bureau of Education for the Gulf States (ABEGS), the director general of the Bureau, and the president of the university.

The respective boards oversee the administration. This includes setting up goals and general policies; approving academic programs and entry requirements, the size of student intake, and so forth; ensuring the implementation of the statutes; monitoring the progress of the institutions; and submitting and seeking budget approvals from respective authorities.

Academic authority at both UB and AGU rests mainly in the university council, consisting of the president, vice-presidents, and deans. At UB the council also includes between one and three outside members while AGU puts forward a representative from each college elected by its faculty. Each college has its own council, which is presided over by the dean and consists of department chairs, and at UB one other senior member from each department, and three external members nominated by the university council and appointed by the board of trustees. At AGU these additional council members are three of the faculty and one or more external members. For CHS, there is a faculty council and an academic committee, both chaired by the dean. The faculty council is a decision-making body within the college charged with establishing guidelines regarding rules, regulations, policies, and procedures, and serving as administrative and academic council to the dean. The academic committee supervises all educational activities—planning, implementing, coordinating and evaluating curricula—and initiates action on the development of new programs, curricula, and instructional materials.

In UB and AGU, appointments, renewals of contracts, and promotions are recommended by depart-

Table 1

Members of faculty in the University of Bahrain, the Arabian Gulf University, and the College of Health Sciences for the Year 1988–89

	UB	AGU	CHS
Professor	17	13	—
Associate professor	37	11	—
Assistant professor	114	62	—
Lecturer	44	3	50
Instructor	60	—	6
Researcher	—	8	—
Language instructor	26	—	—

Sources: University of Bahrain Directorate of Personnel
Arabian Gulf University Bulletins 1988–89
College of Health Sciences Dean's Office

mental committees and routed through the college council to the university council. Academic power is therefore collegial. In CHS, such tasks are the domain of faculty council and academic committee, routed through the dean to the college board.

The fundamental units in the organizational structure of both UB and AGU are academic departments.

4. Faculty and Students: Teaching, Learning, and Research

4.1 Faculty

Overall members of faculty in UB, CHS, and AGU are shown in Table 1 for the academic year 1988–89. Faculty ranks are professor, associate professor, assistant professor, and lecturer or instructor in UB; professor, associate professor, assistant professor and researcher in AGU. With the exception of lecturers, anyone filling one of these positions should hold a doctorate. At CHS, the majority of faculty are instructors and lecturers.

Promotion from assistant professor to associate professor and from associate professor to professor requires a minimum period of four to five years' relevant experience and published research work. Applications are screened by university committees, and confidential evaluation reports are sought from external referees.

Recruitment is the responsibility of the individual institution. The University of Bahrain and AGU advertize vacancies. Relevant departments evaluate and route their choices through the deans for approval at the university council. At UB, non-Bahraini staff are normally employed on a two-year contract. Bahrainis become permanent staff after a two-year probation period. At AGU, all staff are employed on a contract basis. At both UB and AGU, staff are considered to be employees of the establishment; at CHS they are civil servants.

The rights and responsibilities of faculty members are specified in contracts and statutes. The teaching load is defined in the contract and the balance between teaching, research, and administration is specified in the statutes of both UB and AGU.

4.2 Students

The distribution of students at UB, AGU, and CHS by level of study, is shown in Table 2. With the expansion of higher education, there has been an increase in the number of graduates in all major areas of specialization.

The majority of students are Bahrainis, except at AGU where they come from all participating states and from all social levels. Female students constitute over 50 percent of the student community at UB, over 67 percent at AGU, and over 80 percent at CHS. At UB, gifted but needy students are given financial aid and sometimes tuition fees are waived.

There are no student or staff unions or organizations. Students join specialized university societies and clubs which organize activities and have faculty members as advisors.

The ultimate approbation for academic programs rests with the establishment concerned. Thus at UB

Table 2

Student enrollment in the University of Bahrain, the Arabian Gulf University, and the College of Health Sciences by level of study for the years 1987–90

	Year	Undergraduate	Graduate
University of Bahrain	1987–88	4,109	133
	1988–89	4,623	174
	1989–90	4,655	176
Arabian Gulf University	1987–88	245	26
	1988–89	303	61
	1989–90	343	111
College Health Sciences	1987–88	800	—
	1988–89	716	—
	1989–90	750	—

Sources: University of Bahrain Directorate of Admissions and Registration; Arabian Gulf University Directorate of Student Affairs; College of Health Sciences Dean's Office

and AGU, the college concerned defines the structure of its course studies and turns for approval to the university council, whereas in CHS, it is the college board which grants final approval.

At UB, undergraduate studies in arts, science, and education are based on a "liberal arts" approach. Its engineering and business courses have structured programs, which concentrate on professional training as does CHS's bachelor's degree in nursing. At AGU too, the bachelor's degree in medicine is also structured, it uses the "innovative curriculum" approach and is "problem-based." Student assessment in each course is based on classroom participation, mid-semester and final examinations, report writing, and project work. Graduate studies at UB and AGU require the completion of a specified number of courses and writing a thesis based on research, and in some cases completing a project. In order to continue studies towards any degree or diploma, students must maintain semester and cumulative grade point averages above specified minimum levels.

5. Conclusion

The merger of GP and UCB which formed the University of Bahrain was the most significant recent development of higher education. Neither GP nor UCB could have developed alone into a fully-fledged university. However, as both GP and UCB were entirely different in their earlier developments, their original philosophy and mission, and their academic and administrative structure, the merger has been a difficult and complicated undertaking.

Higher education in Bahrain currently faces three problems:

(a) Maintaining the proper balance of autonomy and dependency in the relationship of the university to the state and society;

(b) Maintaining the university as a corporate entity "with a sufficient freedom of choice not to be mere administrative structure for the local implementation of national plans" (Lockwood and Davis 1985);

(c) Ensuring the quality of education in the face of external pressures for higher enrollment, limited resources, and increasing financial constraints.

These are likely to become major concerns unless proper measures are taken to deal with them.

Bibliography

Al-Shirawi M 1989 *Education in Bahrain: Problems and Progress.* Ithaca Press, Oxford
Daniels D, Issan S 1985 Bahrain: System of education. In: Husen T, Postlethwaite T N (eds.) 1985 *The International Encyclopedia of Education*, Vol. I. Pergamon, New York, pp. 399–402

Kurian G T 1982 *Encyclopedia of the Third World*, rev. edn. Vol. I. Mansell Publishing Limited, London, pp. 113–23
Sabie T 1988 Bahrain. In: Kurian G T (ed.) 1988 *World Education Encyclopedia*, Vol. III. Facts on File Publications, New York, pp. 1464–69
State of Bahrain Amiri Decree Number 12 for the year 1986 for the establishment and organization of the University of Bahrain. *State of Bahrain Official Gazette*, 1696: May 29, 1986.
State of Bahrain Ministry of Education, Directorate of Educational Statistics, *Annual Reports 1974–75 to 1986–87.* State of Bahrain Ministry of Education, Bahrain
University of Bahrain 1989 *Statistics 1988/89.* Directorate of Planning, Development and Public Relations, Bahrain
Lockwood G, Davies J 1985 *Universities: The Management Challenge.* The Society for Research into Higher Education and NFER-Nelson, Windsor, p. xii

J. E. Al-Arrayed

Bangladesh

1. Higher Education and Society

Education opportunities have always been meagre in Bangladesh. The British rule introduced modern secular education to meet the needs of colonial rule, yet the education system carries the stamp of diverse religious heritage, of which Islamic *madrasah* education is predominant.

The boundary of the land that now constitutes Bangladesh has changed with the change of rulers. In 1947, when Britain granted independence to British India, Bangladesh, being the eastern part of the contiguous Muslim majority area, formed part of the dominion of Pakistan. Political and economic differentiation by the dominant western wing forced an armed conflict on the eastern wing, and liberated Bangladesh emerged in December 1971.

Bangladesh has an area of 143,998 square kilometers with a population of 114 million in 1990. The intercensus growth rate of population for 1974–81 was 2.9 percent. The urban population is estimated at 5.6 percent. The annual growth rate of households is estimated at 8.9 percent in urban areas and 1.3 percent for rural areas. The male–female ratio is 1.05:1. The majority of the population (85%) is Muslim. The regional distribution of population, except for an urban pull, has remained reasonably stable.

The civilian labor force has been estimated at 35 million for 1989–90. The refined activity rate was variously estimated at 43.2 (urban), 40.2 (rural), 7.5 (female), and 69.1 (male) in the 1981 census. The rate is declining over time, and there are wide regional variations.

Agriculture is still the main source of employment. In 1985–88 about 57 percent of the labor force was employed in that sector. Employment in the industrial sector has remained generally static and a significant increase has occurred in service sector employment, including professional, technical, managerial, clerical, and sales areas.

Social class structure, defined by income distribution, indicates that 12.8 percent of households were in the high-income category, 31.7 percent in middle-income, and 55.5 percent in low-income categories. The gini coefficient indicates increasing inequality of income over time. The pressure of a rapidly increasing population on scarce resources has increased landlessness, unemployment, and poverty amongst the masses.

The economy of Bangladesh is predominantly agricultural, and this sector contributes about half of the gross domestic product. The manufacturing sector has grown slowly and productivity in this sector remains low. There has been rapid expansion in the construction and utilities sectors as well as in the service sector.

In 1972, after liberation, Bangladesh adopted a constitution in which democracy, socialism, secularism, and nationalism were guiding principles. The government was parliamentary and a multiple party system operated. However, in January 1974, the presidential form, along with a one-party system was proclaimed. In August 1975, a coup d'état took place and the new government reintroduced a multiparty system under a presidential government with an elected parliament. A second coup in 1983 displaced the elected president but preserved the structure of government with the addition of smaller administrative units (*upazila*) to undertake developmental work.

Various socioeconomic goals, as expressed in development plans, have evolved. The first five-year plan placed priority on meeting basic needs, including education and restructuring the economy to avoid a concentration of economic power. The subsequent plans have discounted equity, poverty alleviation, and meeting the basic needs of the toiling masses in favor of augmentation of output, and in recent years structural readjustment and liberalization of trade and investment have become important policy targets.

Bangladesh currently has three basic trends in education: (a) the expensive English-medium education, patronized by high-income groups with implicit linkage with educational systems in the United Kingdom and United States; (b) the less expensive Bengali-medium secular education, which greatly varies in quality and standards and is patronized by middle-class groups; (c) religious education, which as it is the least expensive, is the resort of the poor. This latter has recently gained political importance due to patronage from rich Muslim countries. A tendency to introduce Arabic as part of the curriculum in these schools has recently emerged with the expressed intent of forging links with educational systems in Middle Eastern countries.

2. *The Institutional Fabric of the Higher Education System*

The usual system of education in Bangladesh consists of five years of primary schooling followed by five years of secondary education. The next tier consists of two years of higher secondary education followed by an undergraduate education of between two and five years, depending on subject (medical, engineering, or general) and type (pass or honors level). Consequently, graduate level education could be of one or two years duration for a master's degree or a postgraduate diploma. A research degree (MPhil or PhD) requires two to five years study.

The higher education system comprises three general teaching and affiliatory universities, one residential teaching university, one university for engineering and technology, one university for agriculture, and one Islamic university. Another university of science and technology is likely to become functional and a general university is being planned for the south-west region, while an affiliatory and an open university are in the offing.

Dhaka University, established in 1921, has 10 faculties, 7 institutes, and 36 departments, 23 constituent colleges and 198 affiliated colleges. Rajshahi University, established in 1953, has 6 faculties, 1 institute, 26 departments, 7 constituent colleges, and 169 affiliated colleges. The University of Chittagong, established in 1965, has 4 faculties, 1 institute, 21 departments, 9 constituent colleges, and 88 affiliated colleges. Jahangirnagar University, established in 1970, has 3 faculties, 2 institutes, and 12 departments. The Islamic university, established in 1986, has 2 faculties and 8 departments. Bangladesh University of Engineering and Technology, established in 1960, has 4 faculties, 2 institutes, and 14 departments. Bangladesh Agriculture University, established in 1960, has 6 faculties, 1 institute, and 42 departments.

Admission policies are determined by each institution and so (except for military and medical colleges) is selection. Admission to professional, technical, and general universities is highly competitive. Good performance at the secondary and higher secondary level public examinations conducted by external boards set up by the Government Directorate of Secondary and Higher Secondary Education, is required as is a good performance in admission tests and interviews. Entrance to affiliated general colleges is less demanding and even less demanding in private colleges.

In the departments within the science faculties at the universities and the science (including medical) colleges, laboratory work is a requirement for a degree. In some departments in other faculties, research papers are required for graduate level courses. Some departments, particularly in science, allow completion of master's degree requirements partly or fully through laboratory/field research. The MPhil and PhD degrees require submission of a thesis based on research under a supervisor's guidance. Research degrees are becoming more popular. Dhaka university seems to be leading in this area. However, opportunities for interdisciplinary research and interdepartmental or interuniversity collaborative research are few. Dhaka university has set up research centers. However, the research institutes in social sciences or in physical and industrial sciences, funded by the government, have few links with the university. The relationship with the government is limited to commissioned research related to projects and development plans. Relationship with business and industry is largely absent and whatever exists is almost totally linked to the public sector. Relationship with nongovernmental organizations is strictly at a personal level. The donors have utilized university personnel for research consultancy on a fairly regular basis, as have the national consultancy organizations. In the university grants commission and similar agencies, funding for research has been very limited. Universities do not have any meaningful plans for organizing research.

Admission to general universities between 1960 and 1965 increased at an annual average rate of 4.8 percent, while in the next five-year period it increased at an average annual rate of 17.6 percent. The rate declined to 16 percent in the following five-year period, further decreased to 3.2 and 1.04 percent in the succeeding five-year periods. The decrease is largely due to the lack of further capacity in the existing universities, because of the restrictive policies dictated by the government through budgetary allocation. For the Engineering University, the annual average rates for corresponding five-year periods are 2.0, 3.8, 6.0, and 5.0 percent respectively. For the Agricultural University, similarly, the rates were 6.0, 6.4, 5.7, and 1.2 percent respectively. However in the college sector, the increase has been impressive. In the medical colleges, despite fallback in 1980–85, the annual average increase in the period of 1960–70 was 3.5 percent and in the following 10 years it was 5.1 percent; the rate for the next five-year period was 0.8 percent. The corresponding rates for agriculture were 6.3, 3.9, and 2.1 percent; for engineering (−4.0), 35.7, and 1.5 percent respectively. In law colleges over the 25 years, the average rate of annual expansion in enrollment has been 30.6 percent. In government colleges, owing to the takeover of nongovernmental colleges, the corresponding annual rate for 25 years was 25.3 percent, and for nongovernmental colleges it was 5.3 percent only. However, the participation rate, calculated on the basis of total enrollment in higher education over the estimated 20–24 age group, increased from 1.5 percent in 1960 to 2.5 percent in 1980 and has remained there.

Twelve years of preuniversity schooling is a pre-requisite for undergraduate level entry. Superior performance (i.e., being amongst the top 5% of students) at secondary and higher secondary level is required for medical and engineering education. University admission is also selective, being open only to the top 20 percent of students on the whole and in certain departments to students who were amongst the top 10 percent. College education is available to the rest but government colleges in urban areas are also restrictive in qualification for entry. Thus courses are structured and only limited flexibility exists. Changing courses, except for science students, is impossible. Master's level education is basically a continuation of undergraduate level entry except in business administration. At this level, rigidity with respect to institutional affiliation inhibits flexibility and mobility of students. Admission to research degrees, though selective, is less restrictive as the number of entrants is still limited.

3. Governance, Administration, and Finance

3.1 National Administration

Universities are established under an Act of Parliament or an ordinance of the government, while colleges are established under executive order or permission. There is no legal framework for educational institutions in general, except that some may have been registered under the Society Act and the government has passed certain orders with respect to governance, control, and fund management if they wish to be eligible for financial assistance and/or affiliation. Affiliatory universities provide for certain requirements as to governance and academic management for purposes of affiliation. The Ministry of Education controls the vast expanse of primary, mass, secondary, technical, teacher training, and some but not by any means all of the institutions of higher education.

The president of the state is the ex officio chancellor of the universities while the secretary of the Ministry of Education (MOE) functions as secretary to the chancellor. When this tradition began in the days of British rule it was designed to provide academic autonomy free of political intervention; this is no longer assured under changed circumstances.

The chancellor appoints the vice-chancellor, who is the executive and academic chief of the universities. In four general universities, appointment is made from a panel of three elected by senate, where government retains control through representatives of colleges, registered graduates, and ex officio members. The chancellor also appoints pro-vice-chancellors (where such provision exists) and treasurers of the university; the chancellor also nominates members to syndicate, senate, and selection committees for teachers.

The University Grants Commission (UGC), created to coordinate and advise, is technically responsible for allocation of budgetary funds provided by the government. The UGC consists of a chair, a full-time member, and some part-time members including some government officials. Increasingly, despite being an autonomous body, it seems to have become ineffective vis-à-vis the ministry.

In the government colleges, the control is direct, as the ministry and the director general exercise complete control over all matters except academic programs. Similar control is exercised in non-governmental colleges through the governing body and financial grant.

The primary goal of higher education, as reflected in reports of the Education Commission, is the development of a knowledgeable and socially committed labor force for development. The development plans place emphasis on qualitative improvement in higher education through development of teachers, libraries, and laboratories; expansion of science and technical education; and encouragement of female participation. The plans, prepared by respective institutions and coordinated by UGC and the Ministry of Education, have, however, failed to reach the said objectives because of a paucity of funds and inappropriate prioritization due to pressure for quick expansion.

The prime source of finance for the universities is the government, which provides more than 90 percent of the revenue and capital expenditure.

The proportion of the gross domestic product spent on the education sector as a whole is around 1.5 percent. The higher education share of GDP is estimated at 0.3 percent. As a proportion of the total government budget, the education sector's share came down from 15 percent in the 1960s to about 10 percent in the 1980s. Actual developmental outlay was reduced from 5.3 percent in the first development plan to around 3 percent in the third one.

3.2 Institutional Administration

Vice-chancellors administer the universities with the advice and consent of various statutory bodies. The senate, with representation of teachers, students, alumni, government, parliament, and colleges is required to sit at least once a year to consider the annual report and the budget along with any amendments to statutes. The academic council, with representation of professors, deans, chairs, directors of institutes, and representatives from colleges is responsible for admissions, examinations, curricula, academic standards, and affiliation of colleges. In matters of research degrees (MPhil, PhD) it acts on the recommendation of the board of advanced studies. In all administrative and policy matters, the vice-chancellor works in conjunction with the syndicate, which has representatives from among teachers, university administration (including deans and provosts), government, and senate. A finance committee and a planning and development committee (and/or tender committee) assist in the process.

The registrar is in charge of the registry and general administration. The controller of examinations acts on the decisions of the academic council in this regard, in conjunction with examination committees of the departments. The controller of accounts, acting under the advice of the treasurers, is responsible for keeping account books and audits. In the general universities the inspector of colleges is responsible for the supervision and inspection of affiliated colleges and works according to the decisions of the academic council. Development and maintenance work is supervised by the chief engineer.

The departments are the basic unit of academic administration. Coordination and development committees, consisting of senior teachers, and academic committees consisting of all teachers, play their respective roles. The leadership role of the chair has been diluted in recent years as the position is filled by all the senior members in rotation. The faculty under the chairmanship of an elected/nominated dean fulfills a screening function only.

Student administration is the function of the provosts who are in charge of the residential halls. The director of guidance and counselling (where one exists) still plays a minor role in this area too.

The vice-chancellor wields extensive authority, while the pro-vice-chancellor can only perform delegated functions. The treasurer is unable to exercise independent authority, since this position is treated to be a subsidiary appointed official. Teachers' participation is a basic part of decision making at all levels, but their position is weakened by unnecessary division among them. Participation by employees and students is marginal but that of the government is significant.

4. Faculty and Students: Teaching, Learning, and Research

4.1 Faculty

The number of teachers employed in universities and colleges increased from a total of 2,312 in 1960 to 12,088 in 1985. The teacher–student ratio has not suffered an overall decline in the universities, but in the general colleges the case is quite different. The number of teachers with high academic qualifications from study abroad increased from 17 percent in 1965 to 59 percent in 1985. This qualitative change has occurred largely in the universities, in the professional institutions, and partly in government colleges. The composition of faculty has also changed in favor of senior posts. In 1985, 31 percent of teachers were professors or associated professors, compared with only 16 percent in 1960. Within the university system, the proportion of teachers in sciences and technology has marginally increased, while that for humanities has declined.

In the universities, one must obtain at least a first class degree at the bachelor's and/or master's level to be eligible for appointment; a deficiency in this respect could be covered by a research degree. Similar academic qualifications are required along with an active teaching record of at least three years and publication in recognized journals for appointment to the post of assistant professor. In turn, five years service at that level and a required publication record are necessary for appointment as an associate professor. After seven years of service in that position and an acceptable record of publication, one becomes eligible for appointment to the post of professor. The limitation of the sanctioned post has recently been circumvented in general universities through a system of restructuring, which allows upgrading of posts. The technical universities have so far avoided such a procedure. Appointment to positions in government colleges is made by the Public Service Commission at entry level, while promotion to the next level is through administrative review. The nongovernment colleges, particularly in nonurban areas are very relaxed as to qualifications for appointment, because there are not enough qualified teachers.

Each university and college has a teachers' association, and these have increasingly assumed the role of trade unions. There exist national federations of university teachers, government college teachers, nongovernment college teachers, and university and college teachers. These associations have been vigilant in protecting their members' interests, at times at the expense of institutional interest. The government has patronized various sections within such bodies for divisive purposes.

In the universities, according to the decision of the syndicate, a lecturer is supposed to take 19 hours of classes, including tutorials, or laboratory work; an assistant professor 16 hours; an associate professor 12 hours; and a professor 9 hours. In the colleges the workload is higher because of vacant positions and adverse teacher–student ratios. Lecture hours may be reduced in order to handle administrative work, but no such provision has been made for supervision of research work, except in the Bangladesh University of Engineering and Technology.

4.2 Students

Between 1960 and 1985, the number of students taking degree courses in institutions of higher education increased from a total of 55,675 to 184,854 indicating an average annual rate of growth of 9.4 percent. The growth has been higher in the universities. In the nonuniversity sector, increases in social sciences and commerce far exceeded those in science and humanities.

All available surveys indicate that students from higher income and urban groups increasingly dominate the universities which is contrary to the situation in the 1950s and 1960s. This is more pronounced in science, technology, and professional subjects. On the basis of gender, the dominance of urban higher income groups among female students is quite perceptive.

In the universities, students are encouraged to form associations in the departments as well as in the residential halls to advance extramural activities. There is also a university-wide students' union. Close affiliation of student organizations with political parties has created problems of discipline and order. Institution-wide associations are prevalent in colleges. Students in general universities are represented in the senate.

The curricula for various degree programs are defined by the department concerned and/or the faculty, and submitted for approval to academic council. The system of examination, written, practical, and viva, is similarly devised.

Compartmentalized models according to areas, without optimal flexibility for broad undergraduate education is the norm.

Bibliography

Ahmad M 1981 *Progress of Science Education and Research: Papers on higher education in Bangladesh.* Dhaka University Alumin Association, Dhaka

Ahmad M 1988 *Efficiency and Accountability in Higher Education. Prospective in Social Science 1.* Dhaka University, Dhaka: 200–263

Ahmad M 1988 Equity, efficiency and excellence in higher education. *Bangladesh Journal of Political Economy* 8: 234–50

Ahmad M 1989 An overview of education sector in Bangladesh. *Bangladesh Journal of Political Economy* 9: 73–94

Ahmad M 1990 Higher education in Bangladesh. *Bangladesh Journal of Political Economy* 10: 1–26

Ahmad M 1991 An induced human resource development. *Bangladesh Journal of Political Economy* 11: 108–132

Ahmad M 1991 Empowering people through education. *Bangladesh Journal of Political Economy* 11: 281–93

Bureau of Statistics *Statistical Yearbook.* Annual Publication. Government of Bangladesh, Dhaka

Hug M S 1983 *Higher Education Development in Bangladesh.* University Press Ltd, Dhaka

Jahan R 1988 *Participation of Women in Higher Education.* Dhaka University Alumni Association/United Nations Association of Bangladesh, Dhaka

Sharafuddin A A M (ed.) 1987 *Cooperation in Education, Science and Culture in South East Asian Region.* United Nations Association of Bangladesh, Dhaka

UNESCO 1988 *Higher Education and National Development in Four Countries.* Principal Regional Office of Education for Asia and the Pacific, PROEAP—UNESCO, Bangkok

UNESCO 1990 *Mobilizing Additional Resources for Higher Education* PROEAP, Bangkok

University Grants Commission *Annual Reports*. University
  Grants Commission, Dhaka
World Bank 1989 *Bangladesh recent economic development
  and short-term prospects*. World Bank, Washington, DC

M. Ahmad

Barbados

1. Higher Education and Society

The term "higher education" is used by the educational authorities in Barbados to refer to a particular type of tertiary education, namely, the type
which universities and/or colleges offer in degree
programs, or in advanced diploma and certificate
programs, whether autonomously or in affiliation
with institutions which award degrees (see Government of Barbados 1988 pp. 67–69). Thus, while there
are four public sector educational institutions in Barbados which have officially been classified as tertiary
level, it is the University of the West Indies (UWI),
and specifically the Cave Hill Campus of the UWI,
which forms the main focus of this article. The UWI
is a regional institution which was opened in 1948
with a single campus at Mona in Jamaica. Today it
has three campuses since a second was opened at St.
Augustine in Trinidad during 1960–61, and a third
was officially opened at Cave Hill in Barbados in
1968. While considering the question of higher education in Barbados, it is necessary to begin by providing some information on the social context of
higher education there.

Barbados has a total population of about 254,000
(Inter-American Development Bank (IADB) 1989).
The population grew at average annual rates of 1.3
percent during 1946–60, 0.2 percent during 1960–70
and 0.4 percent during 1970–80, and, according to
the IADB, 0.3 percent during 1981–88. The very low
rate of population growth in Barbados since the
Second World War has been due to an energetic
Family Planning Program which got underway in
1955, and to the relatively high level of emigration
of persons of child-bearing age during the 1950s and
1960s. Almost 85 percent of the population lives in
urban areas. The latest available population census
data, which are for 1980–81, indicate that Blacks
account for 91.9 percent of the population, Whites
for 3.3 percent, racially-mixed persons for 2.6
percent, East Indians for 0.5 percent, and others for
1.7 percent. The official language is English.

In 1967, the year succeeding the one in which
Barbados gained its political independence, the occupational structure of the working population was as
follows: professional, technical, and related workers
8.0 percent; administrative, executive, and managerial 2.7 percent; clerical 10.4 percent; sales 9.2

percent; farmers and fishermen 21.3 percent; quarrying and transport and communication 8.2 percent;
skilled craftsmen and production process workers
22.3 percent; and textile workers 17.9 percent
(Government of Barbados 1973). With the intensification of the effort at development planning in
the postcolonial period, there has been a further
opening up of opportunities near the top of the
occupational structure, that is, at the level of professional, technical, and related occupations. However, only a very small proportion of the labor force
continues to be found in the administrative-execu-
tive-managerial category. In 1986, for instance, professional, technical, and related workers accounted for 11.1 percent of the employed labor force
but administrators, executives, and managers for
only 3.6 percent (Barbados Statistical Service
1988).

The Barbadian economy was dominated by the
sugar industry at the end of the Second World War,
but is heavily service-oriented today. In 1987, the
sugar industry accounted for less than 3 percent
of Gross Domestic Product (GDP) and the entire
agricultural sector for under 7 percent. On the other
hand, the major contributions to GDP were made by
the wholesale and retail trade (21%), government
services (17%), financial insurance and business services (13%), and tourism (11%) (Government of
Barbados 1988). When one examines the various
sectors in relation to their contributions to foreign
exchange and employment, the tourism and manufacturing sectors assume a role of critical importance.
Together these two sectors generate about 70 percent
of the foreign exchange and provide jobs for more
than one-third of the employed labor force.

2. The Institutional Fabric of the Higher Education System

In describing the sectoral organization of higher education in Barbados, attention will be focused on the
objectives and programs of the tertiary-level educational institutions. Within the public sector, there
are four tertiary-level educational institutions: the
Samuel Jackman Prescod Polytechnic (Polytechnic),
Erdiston Teachers' College (Erdiston), the Barbados
Community College (BCC), and the Cave Hill
Campus. Strictly speaking, the Polytechnic is not an
institution of higher learning. It is an institution
which was officially opened in January 1970, to develop trade skills and occupational competencies up
to the level of skilled craftsmen as well as to prepare
students for entry into the Division of Technology of
the BCC. However, the Polytechnic has not been
excluded completely from the discussion since (a) it
has links with the BCC and (b) the Government
has made it clear that during the current five-year
development plan period "Consideration will be

given to the award of special scholarships as a logical extension to the Associate Degree programmes being offered at the Barbados Community College" (Government of Barbados 1988 p. 69).

Erdiston, which was opened in 1948, is an institution which provides a basic two-year teacher education program for those teachers in primary and secondary schools who are not university graduates. This certificate program is endorsed by UWI. In addition, Erdiston cooperates with the Polytechnic and the BCC to provide certification in selected technical and vocational areas (business education, industrial arts, and home economics). These courses are mainly for secondary-school teachers. Erdiston offers a number of postbasic and continuing education courses designed to meet the special needs of teachers and the public. Among these are one-year, in-service, part-time courses in the teaching of reading and remedial education, along with one-year full-time courses in early childhood education and physical education.

The BCC was established in 1969 as an institution to improve the facilities available to the community for a wide range of skills at the technician, paraprofessional, middle-management and preuniversity levels. It offers courses in the Divisions of Liberal Arts, Fine Arts, Health Sciences, Sciences, Commerce, Hospitality Studies, Technology, General and Continuing Education, the Language Centre, and the Departments of Computer Studies and Physical Education. In addition, the BCC offers a wide range of evening and summer courses as part of its service to the community. The courses of study are of two years' duration, and lead to the "associate degree" in arts or applied arts and sciences or applied sciences. During 1988–93, the government plans not only to expand the system for the award of the associate degree for two-year programs of study, but also intends to have the BCC devote efforts in articulating its associate degree programs with the programs at UWI and other universities in order to facilitate transfers.

The Cave Hill Campus, which is at the apex of the system of tertiary education in Barbados, is, it must be stressed, still a regional institution. However, under the new funding arrangements which took effect from October, 1984, the Government of Barbados now has direct responsibility for the financing of the Cave Hill Campus, on the understanding that the regional governments would reimburse the Government of Barbados for any expenses incurred by that government on behalf of students from their countries who attend the Cave Hill Campus. As at the other two campuses of the UWI, the Cave Hill Campus offers courses leading to the bachelor's degree in arts and general studies, education, natural sciences, and social sciences. The University of the West Indies has a special arrangement where the first part of the law program is done only at Cave Hill,

the first part of the medical program only at the Mona Campus, and engineering and agriculture only at the St. Augustine Campus. At Cave Hill, courses leading to the licentiate in theology and the BA Degree in theology are offered in the Faculty of Arts and General Studies, and these courses have been offered in affiliation with Codrington College. In addition, a number of certificate, diploma, and graduate degree programs are offered.

Enrollment at the Cave Hill Campus stood at 2,264 persons in 1989–90, almost 20 times the number of registered students with which it opened its doors in 1963–64. Over the last decade, enrollment at the Cave Hill Campus has continued to grow, but at a slow rate, with the highest annual increase for the 1980s being in 1984–85 when there was an increase of 149 students (University of the West Indies 1991). Since 1984–85, the annual increase in student registration at the Cave Hill Campus has varied between 79 and 112 students. Attention should be drawn to the fact that there are Barbadians enrolled at the other two campuses of UWI, and that there are more than 200 Barbadian students studying at universities outside the region with the aid of government scholarships, exhibitions, bursaries, and loans. It may be interesting to note that altogether there were 6,147 students enrolled in tertiary educational institutions in Barbados in 1989–90: 1,621 at the Polytechnic, 122 at Erdiston, 2,140 at BCC, and the remaining 2,264 at Cave Hill.

3. Governance, Administration, and Finance

The body which has prime responsibility for higher education is the Ministry of Education. The government has made it unmistakably clear that now that it has the responsibility for the financing of the Cave Hill Campus, it will continue to support UWI as a regional institution of higher learning and research, but will "encourage" UWI to "continue to liaise more closely with other tertiary institutions and to continue to respond to national development needs" (Government of Barbados 1988, p. 69).

The affairs of Erdiston and the BCC are run by Boards of Management which are appointed by and answerable to the Minister of Education. These Boards are normally appointed for three years. The governing body at the Cave Hill Campus is the Campus Council. The Campus Council has very wide powers, including control of the finances of the Campus and the appointment and promotion of faculty employed at the Campus up to the level of senior lecturer. It is made up of: (a) senior members of the Cave Hill Campus and the University; (b) persons appointed by the governments of the Campus countries; (c) student representatives; and (d) the Campus Registrar as Secretary. It is chaired by an appointee of the governments of the Campus countries.

4. *Faculty and Students: Teaching, Learning, and Research*

Data on the overall size of the teaching staff at the Cave Hill Campus at five-year intervals since 1960 were not available at the time of writing. It should be noted, however, that while the Cave Hill Campus started out in the 1960s with a teaching staff of around 20 persons, it had a total of 124 full-time members of teaching staff at November 1, 1989 (University of the West Indies 1991).

The conditions for being granted tenured status at UWI have to do with the applicant's research, publications, ability as a teacher, contribution to university life, public service, and scholarly and professional activity. The body which is responsible for recommending the renewal of an appointment on indefinite tenure is the University Assessment and Promotions Committee (UAPC). As it goes about its work of making recommendations to the University Appointments Committee, the UAPC is also expected to take into account the expectation that there would be different standards of achievement at different stages of the career of a member of staff. A member of staff other than a professor is not normally considered for indefinite tenure before that member has accumulated a total of six years.

The Cave Hill Campus produced its first graduates in 1967. In that year, 35 persons graduated from there with first degrees: 30 in arts and general studies and five in natural sciences. Today, the number of persons graduating from the Cave Hill Campus with first degrees is around 10 times larger than it was in 1967, and it is the Faculty of Social Sciences which produces most of such graduates. Of the 393 persons who graduated from the Cave Hill Campus with first degrees in 1990, 30.8 percent were in social sciences, 27.7 percent in law, 23.7 percent in arts and general studies, 15.5 percent in natural sciences, and 2.3 percent in education (University of the West Indies 1991).

5. *Conclusion*

Space does not permit an identification of all the major difficulties currently facing higher education in Barbados or which are likely to affect higher education on the island over the coming decade. However, there are at least three such difficulties worth mentioning.

The first difficulty, and perhaps the greatest one, is financial. As in other Third World countries, the cost of higher education has been escalating in Barbados, and the government has been forced to find ways of restricting the rate of growth of its expenditure on education at this level. A vitally important mechanism in this respect has been the Student Revolving Loan Fund (SRLF), which has been ongoing since 1977 with assistance from the IADB, and which has provided Barbados with a mechanism of loan grants to reduce the financial burden of providing scholarships, grants, and awards for tertiary education in general and higher education in particular. Secondly, there is need for tighter articulation of the teacher-training program at Cave Hill with that at Erdiston, and to resolve the difficulties linked to demands by the BCC for more ready accreditation of its associate degree by UWI. Finally, there is the issue of whether the Cave Hill Campus can remain a regional institution, when, in the "restructuring" process which has taken place since October, 1984, the Cave Hill Campus has been brought increasingly under the financial control of the Campus Council and the Government of Barbados.

Bibliography

Barbados Statistical Service 1988 *Labour Force Report 1981–1986*. Barbados Statistical Service, Bridgetown
Drayton K B 1981 UWI at the Crossroads. *Caribbean Contact*
Goodridge R V, Layne A 1984 *A Digest of UNESCO Studies and Documents on the Democratization of Higher Education*. UNESCO, Paris
Gordon S 1963 *A Century of West Indian Education: A Source Book*. Longman, London
Government of Barbados 1973 *Barbados 1973–1977 Development Plan*. Ministry of Finance, Bridgetown
Government of Barbados 1988 *Development Plan 1988–1993: A Share for All*. Ministry of Finance and Economic Affairs, Bridgetown
Inter-American Development Bank 1989 *Economic and Social Progress Latin America: 1989 Report*. Inter-American Development Bank, Washington, DC
Layne A 1989 *Higher Education in Barbados*. CRESALC-UNESCO, Caracas
Marshall R et al. 1986 *Review Report on the Cave Hill Campus*. Ministry of Education, Bridgetown
Shorey L, Layne A 1986 Research and the university teacher: the Caribbean context. *Revista Interamericana de Desarrollo Educativo* 99: 68–78
University of the West Indies 1991 *Official Statistics 1989/90*. Office of Planning and Programming, University of the West Indies, Mona, Jamaica

A. Layne

Belgium

1. *Higher Education and Society*

The origins of the higher education system in Belgium can be traced to the foundation of the University of Louvain in 1425 and the establishment of the State Universities of Ghent (1816) and Liège (1817), and the Free University of Brussels (1834).

The universities have undergone a considerable development, both quantitatively and qualitatively, since 1960. The higher education system of Belgium is characterized by the dominance of private, but state-subsidized institutions (69 percent of the total enrollment) and by the fact that the main universities are very comprehensive (including engineering or polytechnics, agriculture, medicine, architecture, business schools, etc.) leaving almost no room for separate *grandes écoles*, at the university level; this favors great interdisciplinary opportunities for professional studies. The universities also enjoy something of a monopoly in basic research, since most of the public research funds are directly or indirectly, allocated to them instead of going to parallel bodies in other sectors.

The national boundaries of the country did not change after the Second World War but internally, the political geography of Belgium has been progressively reorganized since 1963 into three regions (Flanders, Wallonia, and Brussels) and two main languages communities (Flemish and French, with another small, German-speaking community). Since 1989, the education budgets for the various communities have been entirely distinct and are managed autonomously, except for the financing of foreign students which remains national. The national population is not increasing significantly but the Flemish community has been growing in proportion to the rest of the nation and has therefore assumed a greater relative importance. In 1950 it stood at 4,551 million and in 1987 it had reached 5,685 million and, moving from 53.5 percent of the total population to 57.6 percent.

The occupational and social class structure of Belgium has been changing since the early industrialization of the nineteenth century. Flanders, previously dependent on agriculture and textile industries has changed to a quickly developing and dense economy including automobile industry (52,000 workers), electrical goods, chemicals, steel, nonferrous metals, and telecommunications. The coal and steel industry of the south (Wallonia) has been replaced by a smaller more specialized steel industry, chemical industry, including pharmaceutical, glass, and cement industries, the cost of which has been highly reduced employment. The central region, Brussels, is more and more devoted to service industries which now comprise 84 percent of the employment in the area.

Nationwide, agriculture accounts for 2.5 percent of the total employment, the secondary sector declined from 47.5 percent in 1950 to about 28.5 percent in 1987, and the tertiary (services) grew from 40.0 percent in 1950 to 70 percent in 1987 (IRES 1989).

The structure of government and the distribution of power between the political parties did not undergo very fundamental changes after the Second World War. The Social Christian party (Christian Democrats) were almost always in power, usually within a coalition with the socialist parties or the liberal (free enterprise neo-conservative) parties. Even under a coalition with the socialists, no nationalization took place. The main political tendency is rather to trust to market forces, and to favor (or subsidize heavily) the private sector (including private education). Government, society, and industry expect that the education system and the universities will provide them with ready-made human resources, with little state interference.

Religion and the powerful Christian organizations (Church, Christian trade unions, Christian hospital networks, and the private religious school system) play a very important role in society and politics. The two largest and oldest universities (Leuven and Louvain) are part of the Roman Catholic education network. Any attempt in the past to reduce public aid to private schools led to a sort of school war and the final consolidation of the private system with religious groups. The period of university expansion (1960–75) favored the social image and the financing of universities, but with the problems of public budget deficits from the mid-1970s and the policy of austerity since 1982 both have deteriorated sharply.

2. The Institutional Fabric of the Higher Education System

Tables 1a and 1b summarize the present structure of higher education and its quantitative development since the Second World War, showing the distribution between languages, public or private status, and the rates of expansion.

If one considers the levels of institutions, research is largely located in the university system, except for applied research developed in industry. The complete universities and their graduate schools are normally the research universities, especially for basic research. However, all teaching institutions are developing some kind of research, especially in cooperation with regional authorities. University education is then closely linked to research. No Nobel Prize has been awarded outside the strict university structure.

Besides the university network, nonuniversity higher education attracts slightly larger numbers of students. It includes short course studies of two to three years (nurses, librarians, primary school teachers, etc.) and long courses of four years and more (architects, industrial engineers, business studies, etc.). Teachers for pupils in the final years of secondary education must, however, be university graduates. Nonuniversity higher education totalled 125,804 students in 1988 (Ministry of Education 1988). Their degrees are favored by industry, and bridges are provided to university curricula. Some institutions of the long course type have, in the past, been integrated within the universities.

The twofold increase in the number of university students has not entailed the creation of many new institutions (except where language differences made it the best option). Instead the existing network

Table 1a

The institutional framework of the Belgian university system 1959–60 to 1987–88[a]

		1959–60	1964–65	1969–70	1974–75	1979–80	1984–85	1987–88
Public								
Flemish		4,435	7,017	13,006	14,869	15,998	18,546	17,205
complete	Ghent	4,055	6,099	11,093	11,523	12,025	13,503	12,685
incomplete	UIA, Antwerp	—	—	—	1,090	1,403	1,755	1,795
	RUCA, Antwerp	380	918	1,913	1,686	1,724	2,349	1,965
	ULC, Limburg	—	—	—	570	846	939	760
French		5,022	6,568	9,996	11,209	12,346	13,035	13,469
complete	Liège	4,452	5,622	8,189	9,104	9,617	9,790	9,639
incomplete	UMS, Mons	162	338	892	1,098	1,433	1,814	2,003
	POLYTECHN, Mons	258	389	483	548	511	567	862
	AGRO, Gembloux	150	219	432	459	785	864	965
Total Public		9,457	13,585	23,002	26,078	28,344	31,581	30,674
Private								
Flemish		6,869	10,937	17,744	23,955	28,779	33,453	34,843
complete	Christian, KUL, Leuven	6,005	9,256	13,810	17,325	20,603	22,855	23,280
	Non-Christian, VUB, Brussels	218	870	1,936	3,782	5,103	6,370	7,094
incomplete	Christian, UFSIA, Antwerp	646	811	1,923	2,470	2,595	3,439	3,764
	UFSA, Brussels	—	—	75	378	478	789	705
French		11,565	16,187	24,262	30,426	34,493	36,474	37,020
complete	Christian, UCL	6,123	8,031	12,794	15,155	16,510	17,011	16,744
	Non-Christian, ULB, Bxl	4,420	6,472	8,652	11,603	13,743	13,835	14,047
incomplete	Christian, FNDP, Namur	421	838	1,746	2,523	2,898	3,691	3,947
	FUCAM, Mons	258	411	492	428	415	861	1,174
	FUSL, Brussels	343	435	578	717	927	1,076	1,108
Total Private		18,434	27,124	42,006	54,381	63,272	69,927	71,863
Bilingual								
UCL-KUL, ULB-VUB until 1970, with language sections								
Private	Protestant Theology Faculty	—	46	71	70	130	116	136
Public	Royal Military School	210	181	511	451	738	730	849
Total		28,101	40,936	65,590	80,980	92,484	102,354	103,522

a Figures at 1 February for each academic year

Table 1b

Analysis of total

	1959–60	1964–65	1969–70	1974–75	1979–80	1984–85	1987–88
French	16,957	23,182	34,607	41,893	47,202	49,818	50,934
Flemish	11,144	17,754	30,983	39,087	45,282	52,536	52,588
Male	22,658	31,833	47,605	54,576	59,290	61,123	59,523
Female	5,355	9,103	17,985	26,404	33,194	41,231	43,999
Belgian	26,253	37,310	58,731	71,611	79,795	89,706	91,224
Foreign	1,760	3,626	6,859	9,369	12,689	12,648	12,298
Six complete universities	25,273	36,350	56,474	68,492	77,601	83,364	83,489

Sources: Bureau de Statistiques Universitaires 1989
Service d'études-UCL 1989

Table 2
Number of institutions (not including Protestant Theology and Military School)

	1960	1970	1989
Public			
Flemish	2	4	4
French	4	4	4
Private			
Flemish	1	4	4
French	3	5	5
Bilingual	2	0	0
	12	17	17

was developed, for example Leuven expanded to Kortrijk.

The number of institutions (see Table 2) appeared to increase between 1960 and 1989. However, one should bear in mind that new names are the result of splitting previously bilingual universities or merging and upgrading preexisting smaller institutions.

Admission policies are defined by national law. Any citizen completing secondary education with the appropriate certificate of ability is entitled to enter university. Only at polytechnics (schools of engineering) is an admission examination required, focusing mainly on mathematics. There has been some discussion about introducing a *numerus clausus* for medicine, but a policy of information to prospective students proved sufficient: market forces played their role radically reducing the number of students in medicine and veterinary science.

The universities are, then, legally committed to admit any qualified candidate; financially they are also unrestricted inasmuch as the state pays the universities a subsidy for every accepted student. The tuition fee, paid by the student, is limited to about US$445 (for the Flemish-speaking community) and US$645 (for the French-speaking community). How-

ever, figures show that access is essentially reserved to higher or medium income families.

Liberal admission policies entail a very high rate of failure for first-year students (up to 60 or 70 percent), quickly corrected in the succeeding years (40 percent), or where there is an entrance examination (27 percent) (*Le Soir* 18 April 1989).

Foreign students are readily accepted and account in some cases for 20 or 30 percent of the enrollment of a university; 81 percent are in the French-speaking institutions. Belgian universities are also very willing to recruit teachers from abroad: international scientific cooperation is already very developed across the Atlantic, and is expanding within Europe.

Total enrollments in higher education since 1960 are shown in Table 3 in spite of unfavorable demographic trends within the 18–20 age group since 1980, and the severe drops in enrollment that are forecast, total numbers are rather stable, thanks to longer studies and an increased number of female students. The time of expansion has passed however.

Increasing numbers of young people are choosing the nonuniversity sector and opting for shorter studies and more practical and professional education (e.g., a 34 percent increase in economics in three years in Flanders): they are in competition with university graduates (Bonte 1987).

The percentage of the age group 20–24 years enrolled in higher education is comparatively good. Students of higher education entering into short courses accounted for 26.8 percent of the age group and students of long courses 19.1 percent (1985–86). Recent figures have shown a decreasing proportion of high school leavers entering university, from 52.4 percent in 1972–73 to 31.8 percent in 1979–80 (Ancion 1982).

The length of first and second degree courses is shown in Table 4. The name of the degree and the length of studies for what are called "legal" degrees is still organized nationally for private and public institutions in a rather rigid system. Other than following the list of courses imposed legally for medicine, engineering, and law, individual uni-

Table 3
Total enrollments in higher education

	1960	1965	1970	1975	1980	1985	1988
Universities	28,101	40,936	65,590	80,480	92,484	102,354	103,522
Non-university	20,839	34,532	53,694	72,259	96,845	116,738	125,804
University-level institutions (long course)	—	—	—	—	—	33,765	37,702
Higher technical education (short course)	—	—	—	—	—	82,973	88,102
Total	48,940	75,468	119,284	153,239	189,329	219,092	229,326

Table 4
Length of course and titles of degrees

	Social Science	Science/Engineering	Medicine
First degree studies (undergraduate)			
Candidat–Kandidaat	2 years	2 years	3 years
	(age 18–20)	(age 18–20)	(age 18–21)
Second degree studies (graduate)			
Licencié–Licenciaat	2–3 years	2–3 years	—
Maitre–doctorandus	one extra year		
(or Master of Arts)	after second degree		
Docteur–Doctoraat	3 years	3 years	4 years
(with thesis except			
for medicine)	and more		+specialization years

versities are largely responsible for the content and level of their teaching.

Graduate training starts after four or five years of candidature and licence, but only students gaining 70 percent of the marks at the *licencié* level are usually admitted to doctoral programs. This admission is really the introduction to university research programs, through the tutorship of the professors supervising the doctoral thesis.

Numerous courses of graduate study are rather freely organized by the universities.

3. Governance, Administration, and Finance

3.1 National Administration

From 1989 onwards, the role of national government has been changed: the Ministry of Education of each language community is responsible for the development of higher education (budgets for current expenses as well as for investment, budgetary control, appointments in public universities, etc.). The national or federal authorities retain responsibility, at present, though, for the minimal conditions of degrees, as well as rates of pay and pensions for the various types of personnel.

Since 1989 coordination has taken place at the community or regional level rather than at the national level. This is managed rather marginally through special research grants, on top of the budgets of the ministries of education, which are really the main method of public intervention.

As far as planning, implementation, or evaluation are concerned, there is no central allocation of student places or staff resources. Long political discussions about the expansion of education between 1960 and 1975 have established a system of public financing, peculiar to Belgium that leaves substantial autonomy to the institutions. The state pays the same amount of annual subsidy per student to the private as well as the public universities. This amount will be lowest for a student in the social sciences and

highest (four times as much) for a student of the final years of engineering or medicine (Ancion 1982).

The amount of the grant is supposed to ensure a different student–teacher ratio for the various disciplines. In fact, the financing system is mainly a way to compute the yearly budgets allowed to universities. These are allocated according to the number of students who meet the standard requirement for financing (i.e., those matriculating for a program of 300 hours/year of lectures recognized by the Ministry). The number of effective students not accounted for public financing can reach 10 percent or more.

The system of financing per head is degressive at a level over 9,500 students. In the past when a particular institution did not reach the minimum critical size, the state would still pay for a theoretical "floor number" of students. These artificial benefits are disappearing. The combination of economies of scale in large universities and hypothetical of "ghost" students in small institutions explains why the cost to the taxpayer of a particular student can vary greatly according to the type of institution concerned.

The investment budget of the private universities was also financed by loans from the communities (or by the state until 1989) at a very low rate of interest (1.25%). The state for its part directly finances the construction programs of the public universities.

Under this neo-conservative system of financing (current and investment), universities in Belgium are largely subsidized by the state but have responsibility for the allocation of their global resources, provided they do not run into deficit. The public universities themselves are gaining more autonomy and responsibilities, especially when the public budgets for universities have to be reduced. This financing system made it possible to double enrollment between 1960 and 1975, just by adapting the annual subsidy to the number of students matriculating, without defining precise goals or national plans.

The various universities traditionally attract their own "clientele" and obtain the means to accept all

65

students applying for matriculation without any intervention from a central allocation body. The system is probably responsible for the relatively lower enrollment figures in public universities (1960: 9,457, 1988: 28,879) and higher figures in private institutions (1960: 18,434 or 65%, 1988: 73,658 or 69%), which is economical if one recalls that the cost per head is lower in large scale (usually private) universities.

This rather noninterventionist system on behalf of the education ministry leaves responsibility for the future of education with the universities, depending on their sense of social responsibility and their capacity to self-evaluation. The future of each university depends largely on the dynamism of the team at the top.

Since 1977 each language community has had a council composed of representatives from the various universities (The Conseil Interuniversitaire de la Communauté Française or CIUF for the French includes administration, personnel, and students; Vlaams Interuniversitaire Raad or VLIR for the Flemish includes only the rectors and their deputies). The objective of the councils is to favor cooperative discussion between universities and consultation with the minister.

Faced with repetitive cuts in university financing from the state since 1974, universities are increasingly concerned with rationalization, evaluation, cooperation, and the search for extra resources, but these moves depend on their own initiative. The Ministry of Education can only require progressively balanced budgets and accounts, according to a seven-year plan (1982–89) launched after severe cuts in 1982.

This system which essentially finances the universities by individual head of the student population has been criticized as leading to a hunt for students, but so far no better system has been seriously proposed. There can be no doubt that it maintains a sense of competition between institutions as far as image, pedagogy, scientific level, social services, cost of living, lodging, and so forth, are concerned. Students pay the same very low tuition fee in all the institutions of the same community, however: about US$645 for the French Community and about US$445 for the Flemish in 1989 in any institution of the same region. The choice is, then, not directly financial.

The labor market seems to be the driving force in this system. In all universities the number of students and the curricula are being adapted to the expectations of society (both industry and the state). The problem will be to preserve, in spite of the pressures of utilitarianism and pragmatism, enough basic and independent science and humanities study in order to maintain the critical mission of the university (Wielemans 1988).

The main source of finance is still the state grant per head of students admitted, in keeping with the law of July 1971. The amount of public finance per head of university students, however, decreased by

Table 5
Evolution of current cost per head in education

	1960	1970	1975	1980	1984
As percentage of national income per capita					
Inc capita					
Primary	0.21	0.18	0.24	0.27	0.29
Secondary (and higher non univ. ed.)	0.44	0.44	0.49	0.56	0.50
University	1.03	0.98	1.02	0.84	0.68
Compared to the cost of a pupil in					
Primary ed.	100	100	100	100	100
Secondary (and higher non univ. ed.)	214	239	205	209	173
University	498	537	427	314	234

Source: Baeck (Fondation Universitaire) 1987

29 percent from 1960 to 1985, while public financing was increasing by 41 percent for a pupil in primary school, and by 14 percent for secondary education (Baeck 1987).

This general deterioration in the public financing of universities (as well as in their social image) took various forms after 1980: no indexation of subsidies, limitations on the admission of Belgian or foreign students, cuts in social allowances, and increased enrollment fees. This tendency, illustrated in Table 5, was influenced also by decreasing numbers in primary and secondary education.

The proportion of the Belgian gross national product (GNP) devoted to public financing of all levels of education is high in overall comparison with most other European countries. This is not the case for the public financing of higher education, though, where the contribution of GNP to university expenses is comparatively small.

This overall tendency is confirmed in the comparative figures of public expenditure in research and development as a percentage of GNP (CCE 1989). With 0.54 percent (1987) of GNP, Belgium is almost at the bottom of the list of OECD countries and is about half of the corresponding figure for the Netherlands (CCE 89).

For research and development confined to universities, Belgium ranks 13th at 0.25 percent (CIUF 89). If one includes the research and development financed by industry, which at present is at the average European level, Belgium's GNP would be low at 1.65 percent (1987). The official proposal is to reach 2 per cent (the European average being 2.33%) mainly through increased public contributions and fiscal measures promoting industrial research and development, development of science parks, and so forth (Wielemans 1988).

This past trend has forced universities to collect

extra resources (public and private) from scientific foundations in Belgium and abroad and from contract funded research with industry. These extra resources can reach 25 percent of the present budget of a university, and require for their collection the management of hundreds of agreements, depending on the foundations or industry resources. The contribution from private sources is reaching 25–30 percent and is still increasing.

3.2 Institutional Administration

On principle, the organizational structure of all institutions appears much the same. At the highest level there is a board, chaired by a president, which recruits its members not only among academics but also from economic, social, and political circles. A rector selected from the academic body is responsible for academic affairs for a period of about five years. A general administrator manager is, on the other hand, responsible for financial and investment problems. Rector and manager are in full-time charge of the daily life of the institution, provided there is no veto from the government commissioner (public universities) or the government representative (private universities).

An academic council represents the various bodies of the university, especially the faculty, through elected deans of the various schools. It has a largely consultative power and the right of recommendation of candidates for the highest positions. It is in the council that academics have the maximum power.

Although this structure seems very similar from one university to the other in fact the distribution of real power varies. In private institutions the power is largely concentrated with the board and the record for all kinds of appointments, programs, budgets, and so forth. In public institutions more power is left to the Ministry of Education for appointments of professors on recommendation by the university authorities.

Table 6
University personnel

	1980	1987
Teachers and scientific personnel	3,062	3,085
(with tenure)	4,784	4,409
(short-term contract)	1,614	1,943
Total	9,460	9,437
Administrative and technical personnel		
(with tenure)	9,086	8,391
(short-term contract)	2,375	2,230
Total	11,481	10,621

Source: CNPS 1989

At the two universities of Louvain a board of trustees, including the bishops of Belgium and laity from various sections of society, has the final say over top appointments and over strategic decisions.

The students and administrative personnel are represented at the level of the board or the academic council, according to the institution. It is clear that their real influence is limited even if their particular viewpoint is heard regularly.

Besides being headed by the board and the academic council, the university structure includes a great number of consultative councils, within the *faculté* (faculty or schools) and departments, in a very decentralized grouping. At this level, nonacademic staff and students are more effectively represented.

Power is collegial, shared by all members and not concentrated around the full professors. Various checks and the general atmosphere of collegial management limit the power of the chair, especially as far as replacement, programs, or new appointments are concerned.

In a typical, complete university of large size, one could number 10 *facultés* (or schools), 50 departments, and 250 academic units defined according to a scientific discipline. The disciplinary units are responsible for their own organization and scientific initiatives, but must have both been approved by the higher echelons.

4. Faculty and Students: Teaching, Learning, and Research

4.1 Faculty

The teaching body experienced what was possibly too rapid an increase from 1960 to 1980, subsequently numbers have fallen for mainly financial reasons (see Table 6). Restrictions have been more sensitive in the French-speaking universities, due to the more pressing rationalizations. To compensate for this, the proportion of short-term contract personnel has been increasing. To illustrate this tendency, in the French-speaking universities, from 1982/83 and 1987/88, academic staff has been reduced by 7.8 percent, the scientific staff 3.4 percent, and the administrative and technical staff by 9.9 percent, while the number of students increased by 9 percent (CIUF 1989). Under these conditions, the ratio of the number of students per head of academic and scientific staff is, at 14.2, that is, higher than the ratio contemplated in the 1971 law.

Academic staff are usually recruited from among the doctoral graduates of the same university (most often having a graduate degree from a foreign university). The selection is influenced by the present faculty, but the decisive power rests with rectors and their advisors in private universities, and with the Ministry of Education (until the early 1990s) for the public universities. As a matter of principle, there is no nationality requirement.

Table 7
Development of student numbers by field of study and percentage of total 1959–60 to 1987–88[a]

	1959–60	%	1964–65	%	1969–70	%	1974–75	%	1979–80	%	1984–1985	%	1987–88	%
Theology, Philosophy and Arts	4,051	14.42	6,126	14.96	8,125	12.39	11,182	13.81	14,560	15.74	15,035	14.69	12,364	11.94
Law	2,720	9.68	3,335	8.15	7,433	11.33	10,080	12.45	10,934	11.82	13,203	12.90	14,366	13.88
Sciences	3,495	12.44	5,556	13.57	7,179	10.95	8,496	10.49	9,477	10.25	10,639	10.39	9,748	9.42
Medical and veterinary sciences	7,952	28.30	10,067	24.59	18,665	28.46	25,742	31.79	28,579	30.90	25,419	24.83	22,780	22.00
Engineering	3,794	13.50	4,769	11.69	5,834	8.89	6,326	7.81	7,125	7.70	8,340	8.15	9,811	9.48
Agriculture	574	2.04	783	1.91	1,445	2.20	2,111	2.61	3,014	3.26	3,656	3.57	4,034	3.90
Social Sciences	4,541	16.16	7,955	19.43	13,077	19.94	12,571	15.52	12,802	13.84	19,093	18.65	23,895	23.08
Psychology	885	3.15	2,095	5.12	3,508	5.35	4,117	5.08	5,531	5.98	5,924	5.79	5,327	5.15
Interfaculty Sciences	89	0.32	250	0.61	324	0.49	355	0.44	462	0.50	1,045	1.02	1,197	1.16
Total	28,101		40,936		65,590		80,980		92,484		102,354		103,522	

a Figures at 1 February of each academic year.

The usual academic career starts at the level of *chargé de cours-docent* (assistant professor) with tenure after the doctorate between the ages of about 35 and 40. The level of associate professor should be reached after eight years; becoming a full professor is a matter of 10–15 years unless serious defects or a financial crisis intervene. These intervals were much shorter in the period of expansion.

The legal status of the tenure, in a private or public university, is comparable to the status of a civil servant. The rates of pay are at the level of the highest civil servants (*secrétaire général*) of a government ministry.

No central agency intervenes in recruitment, which is typically the responsibility of the various bodies of the university (and also of the Ministry of Education in the case of a public university).

By law, status, career, and rates of pay are identical in all the subsidized institutions and schools. This aspect is closely controlled by a representative of the Minister of Education whose presence on the board of the various universities is required by law. No competition between universities could be accepted at the level of pay or even career. Rates of pay are supposed to be the same for all the professors, any differentiation is legally and socially problematic in the early 1990s.

Faculty interests are represented at university level and also nationally by an association of academics. A trade union type of association is, on the whole, confined to the nonacademic or scientific staff.

As a guiding principle it is recommended to teachers of full-time courses that 5 hours a week should be spent in teaching. This is a minimum which is intended to allow time for research or administration loads; in fact, the average number of hours is higher and can reach 10 hours in the case of some teachers. The distribution of time between teaching, research, and administration is organized internally, by consensus between colleagues, everybody being supposed to share the burden of administration.

4.2 Students

Table 7 shows the distribution of students across the main subject areas from 1960 to 1988. All fields expanded in numbers but the relative share for sciences, including medical and veterinary sciences, decreased from 1970. Humanities have also declined in this period while social sciences, especially economics and business education, have increased their share considerably.

There is no nationally available breakdown of the social class of students' parents nor even something similar for every university, but studies for particular universities (see Table 8) show a rather constant pattern: the middle class is still the dominant group attending university. Lower income groups tend to favor nonuniversity higher education (Lammertijn 1987).

In spite of the numerous scholarships and loans to students (up to 20 percent of students benefit from social help in a particular university), little progress has been made towards the participation of less advantaged groups in university education. Students from working-class families (skilled and unskilled) account for only 13.6 percent in the universities, against 25.9 percent in the nonuniversity sectors (Wielemans 1988).

Limited openings are offered to students who do not have a secondary education degree, but show maturity and experience. For example, at Louvain, the "Open Faculty for Economic and Social Policy" offers a master's degree in three years of part-time study.

The university system could then be considered to be relatively elitist, but this is corrected by a large nonuniversity system of higher education.

The proportion of women students has grown steadily from 1960 to 1988, although they are still slightly outnumbered by men (see Table 1b).

Student interests are represented by unions at the university or schools levels. Representatives from these unions are members of the boards or of the academic councils and while the percentage of participation at elections is constantly limited (about 15%) the elected representatives are available for dialogue.

After 1968 student unions were largely politicized and leftist. In the 1980s, although still greatly concerned by the problems of the Third and Fourth

Table 8
Social origin of entrants to Louvain (French) University, percentage distribution

Social class of parents	1967–68	1971–72	1984–85	1987–88
Agriculture	6.8	6.2	3.9	3.4
Manual workers	4.5	7.6	8.9	8.9
Nonmanual, lower management	52.6	53.1	43.1	42.5
Graduate managers/professionals	31.7	33.1	40.9	39.4

Source: Beguin 1976, 1989

World, they were more interested in the defense of the interests of the student body (examinations, social budgets, sports, and cultural activities).

Student organizations comanage, with the academic authorities, very substantial social budgets which cover subsidies to restaurants, lodging, and social and cultural activities. These sums are a part of the general university budget rather than an independent budget derived from extra-university authorities.

Examinations and programs are typically organized by the various universities and their constituent bodies (i.e., faculties, and departments). New study programs are initiated by the universities without the intervention of accreditation bodies. For financial reasons, however, the ministries of education have refused since 1982 to finance new programs. This slows down substantial adaptations of existing programs.

The undergraduate courses generally offer a rather broad general content (e.g., mathematics, statistics, philosophy, history, sociology, law) in social sciences, which allows a progressive reorientation during the first two years. This general, liberal orientation (with common basic courses) tends to be jeopardized by the demand for more specialized professional courses from the first years.

A credit system is in place which favors limited but none the less effective bridges between the programs of various institutions, especially from undergraduate to graduate schools.

Students are assessed at term (semesters) and yearly examinations. Examinations are most frequently written but there are also oral examinations, especially at the graduate and final dissertation level.

5. Conclusion

The evidence is that Belgian universities, compared to others, are largely open, private although publicly financed, not costly, autonomous, monopolistic, and responsible for their own strategy and evaluation.

The quality of the education provided should be considered to be good, judging from the easy access of Belgian graduates to the best foreign universities with, as a result, a brain drain from Belgium. The quality of research is improving as is reflected in an honorable number of Nobel prizes and other international scientific prizes.

The difficulties present in higher education in Belgium at the beginning of the 1990s stem from the demographic stabilization of numbers, the continuing decline in public financing, and the ageing (owing to the lack of recruitment possibilities) of the academic and scientific staff. Possible remedies could be found in new sources of finance, more specialization and a greater degree of complementary work between institutions, and new programs (e.g., adult education, new technologies). The most obvious

solution in addition to the above would be to finance higher education and research to the level of the most developed European countries. For some time governments have promised to correct this Belgian weakness and to adapt the level of financing to average European standards.

With more finance and good strategic management (including creativity, flexibility, modernization, and opportunities for adult education), the geographical, scientific, and cultural assets of the Belgian system could lead to a bright future. Over the coming years, the main problem will be winning the competition for talented staff from the best brains of a prosperous Belgian economy and from other developed countries in Europe and from the United States.

Bibliography

Ancion W 1982 *Evaluation du système de financement et de contrôle de l'enseignement universitaire en Belgique de 1977 à 1981*. AUPELF-OECD/CERI-IMHE, Paris

Baeck L 1987 *Enseignement et Recherche Scientifique: les options prioritaires*. Fondation Universitaire, Brussels

Beguin A 1976 *Une face cachée de l'enseignement*. Doctorat, Institut des Sciences Politiques et Sociales. UCL, Louvain-la-Neuve (updated in 1989)

Bonte A 1987 Economisch Hoger Onderwijs in drie jaar met 34% gegroeid. In: *De Standaard* December 9th 1987

Bureau des Statistiques Universitaires 1989 *Rapport Annuel 1988*. Fondation universitaire, Brussels

"Comment diminuer les échecs en candidature?" in *Le Soir*, 18 April 1989

Conseil Central de l'Economie (CCE) 1989 *Rapports et avis relatifs à la position compétitive de la Belgique*. Conseil Central de l'Economie, Brussels

Conseil National de la Politique Scientifique (CNPS) 1989 *Principaux indicateurs de la science et de la technologie (1977–1988). Données de l'OCDE*. Conseil National de la Politique Scientifique, Brussels

Hecquet I 1984 Prospects for revitalizing the Belgian university system. *Eur. J. Educ.* 19 (2)

Institut de Recherches Economiques et Sociales (IRES) 1989. UCL, Louvain-la-Neuve

Lammertijn F 1987 Sociale ongelijkheid en universiteit. In *Onze Alma Mater* Leuven 3: 151–85

Ministry of Education 1988 *Evolution des effectifs des enseignements de plein exercice*. Etudes et documents de la Direction Générale de l'Organisation des Etudes. Service Statistiques et Programmation. Ministère de l'Education Nationale, Brussels

Organisation for Economic Co-operation and Development 1988a *L'enseignement dans les pays de l'OCDE (1985–86)*. OECD, Paris

Organisation for Economic Co-operation and Development 1988b *OECD Statistics*. OECD, Paris

Wielemans W 1988 The labour market as the driving force of Belgian higher education. *Eur. J. Educ.* 23(1/2)

Conseil Interuniversitaire de la Communauté Francaise (CIUF) 1989 *Le financement de l'enseignement universitaire francophone. Evolution récente et comparaison avec quatre pays européens*. Conseil Interuniversitaire de la Communauté Française, Brussels

M. Woitrin

Benin

1. Higher Education and Society

The political, economic, and educational systems in Benin are in transition from highly centralized systems to more flexible decentralized ones. Over-reliance on the state is gradually giving way to a tendency to make students and their parents bear some of the cost of their education. The state no longer guarantees employment in the public sector after the completion of higher education.

Still, due to the substantial rise in primary and secondary school enrollments in the 1970s and 1980s and the deep-rooted belief that education is the main channel for upward social mobility there is considerable demand for higher education and serious pressures on governments to provide it.

Despite the economic recession and the encouragement of private sector intervention higher education is high on the current government's agenda. Steps are being taken to reorganize and improve existing structures to ensure a high quality and better value for money.

2. The Institutional Fabric of the Higher Education System

Soon after Benin's independence from France in 1960 negotiations started between the two countries for the promotion of higher education. A series of agreements were signed between 1961 and 1970 when the University of Dahomey (UD), replaced the common higher education institution opened in 1965 for both Togo and Dahomey (now Benin) called the Benin Institute for Higher Education (IESB). Only three departments and an institute were opened at the foundation of the university: the Department of Medicine (DEMP), the Department of Letters and Humanities (DELL), the Department of Science and Technology (DEST), and the National Institute for the Training of Public and Private Administration Personnel (INFCAP).

Over the last 20 years the university has grown into a fully-fledged higher education institution with several faculties and institutes which replaced and developed the former departments. They can be grouped into three main categories: professionalized, nonprofessionalized, and para- and postuniversity establishments.

2.1 Levels of Institution

Professional establishments train qualified cadres and higher technicians in specific fields of development. Until the mid 1980s graduates were automatically employed in the public sector by the state. Candidates are selected from baccalaureate holders (secondary school-leaving diploma) after a com-petitive entrance examination. Promotion from one cycle to the other requires an average of 12 marks out of 20 over the two or three years of the first cycle. High demand for higher qualifications led to the opening of a second cycle or level two training in many establishments. The length of studies in the second cycle is also two or three years except in medicine where it is four years with an additional internship year.

Currently the Faculty of Medicine also offers a four-year specialization program for general practicians.

The full list of these establishments is as follows:

(a) the Faculty of Health Science (FSS) or National Institute of Health Science (INSS) which train general medical doctors and specialists;

(b) the Faculty of Agronomy or National Institute of Agronomy which prepares students for the general diploma of agronomy and the diploma of agricultural specialist;

(c) the Higher Polytechnic College (CPU) which prepares students for the diploma of higher technician (DTS) in a single cycle of three years;

(d) the National School of Administration (ENA) which prepares students for the diploma of junior inspector or higher technician in the first cycle and for the diploma of administrative officer;

(e) the National Institute of Economics (INE) which prepares students for the diploma of higher technician (DTS) in the first cycle and for the diploma of executive officer or economist–engineer in the second cycle;

(f) the National School of Social Workers which trains students for the diploma of social worker in a single cycle of three years;

(g) the Advanced Training College (ENS) which trains students for the teaching certificate for junior-secondary teaching in the first cycle and for the teaching certificate for senior-secondary teaching (CAPEM or CAPES) in the second cycle;

(h) the Integrated Normal School (ENI), of which there are three—the ENI Natitingou (north) which trains primary school teachers; the ENI Parakou (north) which trains junior secondary-school teachers in the exact and social sciences; and the ENI Lokossa (south) which trains junior secondary teachers in letters and humanities. The last two ENI replaced the first cycle of the Advanced Training College mentioned above;

(i) the National Institute of Physical Education and Sports teaching (INEEPS) which trains junior certified physical education teachers in the Level I courses open to selected holders of BEPC (end of junior secondary-school diploma). The Level II course open to selected holders of baccalaureate trains students for the certificate of aptitude for senior-secondary physical education and sports teaching.

Nonprofessional establishments are classic academic institutions which admit any baccalaureate holder or any one who has passed the special university entrance examination. Students may apply for scholarship only after the first year. There is no obligation on the state to employ them after graduation. Courses are divided in two cycles of two years each. The first cycle leads to the first degree of literary studies (DUEL), scientific studies (DUES), and law and economic studies (DUEG). The second cycle leads to the graduate diploma called *licence* after which students write a research report or a dissertation to obtain what is called *maitrise* in the same year.

Para- and postuniversity establishments aim to improve, complete, or help students acquire skills and knowledge needed for specific professions and to encourage further studies and research in specific fields of inquiry. Studies last between a few months and four years. The following are in this category:

(a) the Benin Center for Foreign Languages (CEB-ELAE), known mainly for the training of English speakers in French and for research and pedagogical activities in languages and social sciences;

(b) private language centers—the American Cultural Center offers advanced English courses to help students intending to go for university training abroad and professionals who need English for their jobs; the Soviet Union Cultural Center offers Russian courses to candidates for further studies in the Soviet Union; two other private institutes organize university-level courses in English, Spanish, and German as well as in translation, interpretation, and bilingual and trilingual secretaryship (the AudioVisual Center of Modern Languages (CAVILAV) and the International Communication Center (INTERCOM) which also runs courses in tourism and hotel sciences);

(c) the Regional Institute of Public Health (IRSP) which trains practising medical personnel and people from other sectors concerned with public health. Courses last nine months and lead to a public health diploma, a graduate degree in public health (MSP), and a doctorate in public health (DSP), according to entrance qualifications;

(d) the Institute of Mathematics and Physics (IMSP) which is an international third-cycle postuniversity institute founded in 1987. Courses last four years and lead to a doctorate degree;

(e) the Institute of Advanced Biomedical Sciences, which is a research institute which provides research facilities to research units inside and

outside the university as well as training facilities for research personnel.

2.2 Graduate Training Programs

Each higher education institution in Benin combines teaching and research. In their final year of training students from professionalized institutions and graduates in universities are required to investigate a topic of their choice and present a written report. But this work appears more as an initiation to research and a *rite de passage* than research proper.

Until recently there was no clearly defined research policy coordinating and integrating research activities in the university and in other sectors into a coherent endeavor to shed light on to development problems.

This policy is, however, necessary because research is carried out elsewhere than in university institutions, in autonomous research structures. These include: the Bureau of Agronomic Research (DRA); the National Institute for Training and Research (INFRE); the Bureau of Research in Traditional Medicine and Pharmacology (DRMPT); the Institute of Advanced Biomedical Sciences (ISBA); the Benin Office of Mining (OBEMINE); the National Center for Testing and Research in Public Works (CNERTP); the National Institute of Statistic and Economic Analysis (INSAE); and the National Center of Documentation and Computing (CENADI).

In 1986, two main research institutions were created under the Ministry of Education, the first of which is the National Council of Scientific and Technical Research (CNRST) responsible for developing national research policy and its execution. In 1989, it laid down a policy which stressed that all development projects should be research based and evaluated, and that a national research program should be rooted in the natural and traditional values and potentialities of the country, based on a multidisciplinary approach. The state was called upon to set aside a sizeable part of the higher education budget for research funding. The second institution is the Benin Center of Scientific and Technical Research (CBRST), an executive and coordinating body for the application of the research policy elaborated by the National Council.

These institutions will hopefully improve the quality of research and ensure a wider dissemination and use of its results. Care needs to be taken, however, to avoid stifling individual initiatives and intellectual creativity by overcentralization and narrow utilitarian views of state-regimented research.

3. Governance, Administration, and Finance

3.1 National Administration

Higher education in Benin is organized by the state and administered through the Ministry of Education. All professionalized and nonprofessionalized establishments as well as public para- and postuniversity establishments are under the responsibility of a central administration called the *Rectorat* (vice-chancellor's office) of the National University of Benin. The *Rectorat* is composed of the deputy vice-chancellor's office, a bureau of academic affairs and its units, and a bureau of administrative and financial affairs and its units.

This central administration works in collaboration with other central service institutions, that is, the National Center of Student Welfare (CENOU), the university library, and the National Center of University Publications (CNPU) and the University Scientific Council. The management of the university is administered by the Central Council of Administration (CCA) to which all the above-mentioned administrative structures and establishments as well as the students and the university teachers' unions send representatives. It meets twice a year and elects a governing committee (*Comité de Direction*) which is a democratic executive body running the university between the two meetings of the CCA.

3.2 Institutional Administration

Each institute or school is run by a director. Each faculty has a dean. Directors and deans are helped by a director of studies, a head of administrative and financial affairs, and a principal secretary (SP). Each institute or school is divided into sections according to the main subject areas of each. Directors are appointed by ministerial decree. Deans and heads of sections or departments are democratically elected among full-time professors and assistant professors.

4. Faculty and Students: Teaching, Learning, and Research

4.1 Faculty

The university teaching staff belong to the state civil service in category A according to the general statute of full-time state civil servants. There are two branches: the general higher education teaching staff, and the technical higher education teaching staff.

The former is composed of assistants and professors. Each category has two subcategories. Lecturers start from assistantship and progress to full professorship in four stages on the basis of qualification (doctorate degree), job experience, and scientific, technical, or literary publication. Teacher shortage has made it necessary to recruit nonstatutory staff consisting of qualified and experienced senior-secondary school teachers called *assistants stagiaires* (student lecturers). They work under the supervision of assistant professors or professors.

Technical higher education teaching staff is composed of three categories: higher technicians, assistants, and professors. Progress from one category to the other is dependent on the same criteria as for general higher education staff.

The university also employs part-time as well as expatriate lecturers. The teaching staff corporate interests are defended by the National University Teachers' Union (SNES).

In 1991 the university employs some 671 lecturers including about 10 percent expatriates, and excluding about 40 percent part-time lecturers. The university still relies heavily on part-time lecturers and also on expatriates. More full-time local teaching staff need to be trained so that the university can grow into a fully-functioning institution with its own contribution to the development of science, technology, and culture worldwide.

4.2 Students

From less than 2,000 students in 1975 the university student population grew to 3,390 in 1980, 7,305 in 1985, and 9,705 in 1990 (Hode 1987, personal communication for 1990 figures). There has been a rapid increase of the student population over the last 15 years.

The bulk of students enroll in general academic education mainly in humanities and social sciences. In addition the proportion of female students is weak and appears to be falling from 20 percent in 1982 to 14 percent in 1988. The number of students graduating from the university has rapidly increased in the last decade.

Table 1 suggests there are more highly qualified trained personnel than can be employed in the public sector since only 60 percent of the highly qualified cadres are needed. However, there seems to be a shortage of intermediary cadres and skilled workers

Table 1
Evolution of the student enrollments across the main subject areas and proportion of female students

Year		1979	1982	1985	1988
Exact sciences	Total	1,071	1,275	1,782	1,846
	Women	196	148	193	187
	Percentage of women	18	12	11	10
Humanities and social sciences	Total	1,942	3,912	5,541	7,024
	Women	336	915	1,115	1,074
	Percentage of women	18	23	20	15
Total	Total	3,013	5,187	7,323	8,870
	Women	532	1,063	1,308	1,261
	Percentage of women	18	20	16	14

Source: Ministry of Education Statistics yearbook in Ahouandjinou (1990)
(Exact sciences include medicine, exact and natural sciences, agronomy, biological and industrial techniques. Humanities and social sciences include law and economic planning statistics and management, physical education, teacher training, law and administration sciences techniques, social work and public health.)

Table 2
Comparative study of provision of labor needs and provision of graduates from the school system for the period 1989–90

Professional categories	Needs in labor	Graduates from the school system	Balance
A	3,105	5,914	+2,809
B	4,347	1,055	−3,292
C	9,936	4,258	−5,692
D	13,041	39,687	+26,646
Total	30,429	50,919	20,485

Source: Hode (1987 p. 32)

of categories B and C, of which only 24 percent and 43 percent respectively are provided by the school system (Hode 1987 p. 32) (see Table 2).

5. Conclusion

Higher education in Benin has come of age after twenty years of existence. However, it still suffers from two immature and developmental diseases: on the one hand a chauvinistic and narrow utilitarian view of culture, science, and development; on the other hand a lack of faith in national creative capacities leading to a tendency to copy models of curriculum, evaluation procedures, organizational structures, research, problems, and approaches from developed Western universities. Both may be manifestations of a complex dependency which should be left aside for a truly relevant higher education that solves individual as well as societal development needs while reducing intellectual dependence on the West but without avoiding world issues.

Growing unemployment in the public sector and increasingly crippling financial difficulties require a rethinking of curriculum planning, teaching, pedagogy, research programs, and funding strategies which closely associate economic operators to education and training of "usable," creative, and versatile cadres. It should dispel the myth that diplomas are the "open sesame" to the doors of the civil service, life-long careers, and higher social status.

Bibliography

Ahouandjinou G S 1990 Contribution à l'étude de l'évolution des effectifs. Etudiants de l'Université Nationale du Bénin de 1979 à 1989. Unpublished dissertation. Institut National d'Economie, Cotonou
CNRST (National Council of Scientific and Technical Research) 1989 *Politique nationale en matière de recherche scientifique et technique pour une recherche scientifique et technique dynamique et efficace au service développement de la République Populaire du Bénin.* CNRST, Cotonou
Hode M S N 1987 L'Ecole nouvelle et la problématique de l'emploi en Republique Populaire du Bénin. Unpublished dissertation. Ecole Nationale d'Administration, Cotonou
Presidence de la République 1986 Decret No. 86-23 du 29 Janvier 1986 *portant création, compositions et fonctionnement du conseil national de la recherche scientifique et technique.* Presidence de la République, Cotonou
Presidence de la République 1986 Decret No. 86-24 du 29 janvier 1986 *portant approbation des statuts du centre Béninois de la recherche scientifique et technique* (CBRST). Presidence de la République, Cotonou
UNESCO 1982 *World Guide to Higher Education: Comparative Survey of Systems, Degrees and Qualifications. Benin.* UNESCO, Paris, pp. 28–30
UNESCO 1986 *Bulletin of the* UNESCO *Regional Office for Education in Africa. Special Vol. 1 December 1986: L'Enseignement Supérieur en République Populaire Benin.* UNESCO, Dakar, pp. 9–19

J. Akoha

Bolivia

1. Higher Education and Society

Bolivia is situated in the heart of South America. It is bordered by Brazil to the north and east, Paraguay to the southeast, Argentina to the south, Chile to the southwest, and Peru to the west.

According to the last population census, in 1976, the Bolivian population was just over five million, and it is estimated to have reached six million by 1983. The population is heterogenous and the impact of traditional cultures is demonstrated by the persistence of native languages. According to the 1976 census 36 percent of the total population spoke only Spanish, 8 percent only Aymara, and 14 percent only Quechua. Sixteen percent of the total population spoke Spanish and Aymara, 21 percent spoke Spanish and Quechua, and 5 percent spoke other languages.

According to the National Institute of Statistics, the annual rate of population growth for the 1985–90 period was 2.8. In 1985 life expectancy was 50.7 years, and it is calculated that by that year, child mortality was 124.4 per thousand.

Primary sector activities are important in Bolivia, although the number of people employed in this sector has been decreasing. Secondary activities show almost no change in their capacity to absorb labor. The most important increases have occurred in the commerce and service sector.

The socioeconomic process of the last few decades had its origin in the 1952 Revolution which produced very important changes in the productive structure and in social and political relations. The most outstanding transformations were the emergence of state capitalism, agrarian reform, the nationalization of mines, the growth of state bureaucracy, and the emergence of medium-sized private mining enterprises and agro-industrial activities.

From 1981 to 1984 a severe socioeconomic and political crisis developed, giving way in 1985 to the implementation of a new model based on neoliberal stabilization policies and a structural adjustment of the Bolivian economy. These policies reduced public expenditure, especially in the social areas of education, health, and housing. Nonprofitable state-owned mines were closed, some public enterprises were privatized, and market relations were opened to offer and demand. Unemployment increased and the economy underwent a "tertiarization" and informalization process. The result was economic stabilization and the curtailment of inflation, but there are still serious problems that limit the possibility of a reactivation of the productive sector. Although there has been some economic growth from 1985 on (an average of 2 percent annually), the lowest sectors of the population have not benefited from this growth and there are indications of a polarization of income with no redistribution.

2. The Institutional Fabric of the Higher Education System

Higher education in Bolivia comprises universities, teacher-training institutions (which prepare teachers for primary and secondary schools, both urban and rural), and technical institutes. There is also a military school for engineering. Higher education is predominately public at the university and teacher-training levels. In the 1980s many private institutions were created, especially in fields related to computer science, accounting, and secretarial and managerial skills.

Table 1
Higher education student population 1988

	Population	Percentages[a]
Total population 5–19 years old	2,215,900	
Total of primary and secondary school students (public and private education)	1,394,089	62.9
Total population 20–24 years old	488,200	
Students in teacher-training institutions (urban and rural)	8,996	1.8
Students in the Bolivian University	51,000[b]	10.4

Sources: National Institute of Statistics (Instituto Nacional de Estadísticas, INE, Encuesta Nacional de Población y Vivienda). Ministry of Education. Executive Committee of the Bolivian University (Comité Ejecutivo de la Universidad Boliviana, CEUB).
a These percentages give only a rough approximation because the age of students does not correspond exactly with the age groups of the data obtainable from INE. In the case of the 5–19 year-old population, children begin primary school at seven. In the case of higher education, the age of students may go beyond 25. b Estimate

There are eight national universities, one in each capital department of the country, except for Pando. There is one private university with official recognition, the Bolivian Catholic University in La Paz. There are also four private universities, three in Santa Cruz and one in Cochabamba, which have been recently created, but have yet to obtain official recognition. These universities are raising an important issue in Bolivia, that is, the privatization of education, an issue previously raised regarding primary and secondary education. Over the last few years, because of the political crisis and weakening of the state, the private sector has emerged as a power willing to act, in some cases, through a sense of community service, and as a means to improve academic levels and to create employment possibilities for teachers.

Universities cover around 30 fields of study and grant the academic degree of *licenciado*. There is only one graduate course at the university in La Paz, which was created in the middle 1980s and offers a master's degree in socioeconomic development. There is no PhD program. The duration of university courses varies between five and seven years, though very few students finish their studies in the established period of time. After the thesis is completed and defended the degree of *licenciado* or engineer is awarded.

Teacher-training institutions have a lower academic level than universities, and they have no graduate studies. Courses are four years in duration. The teacher-training institutions are under the authority of the Ministry of Education and Culture. In 1984, there were 18,178 students studying in 27 institutions (10 urban and 17 rural). Between 1982 and 1985, around 500 more students graduated each year than was required by the public school system. Therefore, beginning in 1986 registration was closed to first year students (UNESCO 1986). Registrations reopened in 1989.

Technical education is affirmed in a great variety of institutions, and is heterogenous in the types of courses offered, their duration and academic level.

Scientific research is conducted in some university institutes, but in general these institutes have scarce human and material resources and almost no link with other academic and nonacademic (e.g., industrial) activities.

A high school diploma is generally the only requirement for entrance into higher education institutions. This has been true for universities since 1979, when admittance of all high school graduates became an important goal for low-income students who wanted universities to become "popular and democratic" academic centers. This decision gave rise to an accelerated growth of student population, with no parallel improvement of infrastructure or academic standards. As a result, an attempt has been made to reduce the number of new students and a preuniversity course of three to six months in length has been established, at the end of which an examination must be passed before the student may enter the university.

3. Governance, Administration, and Finance

3.1 National and Regional Administration

The eight Bolivian public universities all have an autonomous structure. This involves the free and independent management by each university of its resources, the election of rectors, teaching faculty, and administrative personnel, the development and approval of statutes, educational programs, budgets, and contracts, and the approval of new institutes and facilities. All universities have the same basic bureaucracies, and at the national level they are coordinated by the Executive Committee of the Bolivian University (CEUB) located in La Paz. This body executes resolutions issued by university congresses, and represents the university system both nationally and internationally. Even though the principle of autonomy means independence and freedom for the universities, the creation of the CEUB is an attempt at coordination among them.

The importance of CEUB as a coordinating organization has lessened. Relations among universities, through congresses, for example, are now characterized by dialogue and the expression of needs by the representatives of these universities, but institutional mechanisms for real decision and action are lacking.

The university reflects the crisis of Bolivian society as a whole, as well as the scarce resources of the country. These resources are not sufficient to meet the needs of university infrastructure, faculty salaries, and so on. Young people see the university as a means of upward mobility, and very few other alternatives are offered to them. If they graduate they find jobs scarce and very few ways to develop personally and professionally.

The problems of teacher-training institutions are very complex and reflect those of Bolivian education in general. Even though the schools are under the authority of the Ministry of Education and Culture, this alone does not assure an adequate orientation of their objectives to the fundamental needs of education in the country, nor the existence of institutional mechanisms for the formation, orientation, and placement of future teachers. Not much progress has been made beyond traditional educational methods, and there is, in general, a low level of academic achievement.

Additional problems include limited financial resources, poorly prepared teachers, and poorly paid teaching faculties. Furthermore, those students who graduate enter into the range of low-paid public servants. In spite of this, from 1982 to 1985 registration increased by 67 percent, mainly because of a lack of employment alternatives.

Very little information is available regarding higher education financing over the last few decades. When information exists it is not easily comparable, which is why Table 2 only refers to 1988.

The national budget of the public education sector accounts for 5.3 percent of the total national budget. The university budget comprised 1 percent of the total national budget for 1988, and 20.2 percent of the national education budget. Although this budget may seem large in relation to the rest of the sector, it remains insufficient. The percentage of the public education budget assigned to teacher education is only 2.3.

3.2 Institutional Administration

The autonomous public universities constitute a system called the Bolivian University, with a complex structure. At the national level, the National Congress of Universities is the highest policy and decision-making body. Congress meets every four years, gathering delegates from all the eight public universities.

The National General Conference of Universities is the main decision-making body between congresses. Conferences meet twice a year, with all eight universities represented. They also have other functions, such as the approval of the university budget, the modification of statutes, the approval of reports presented by CEUB, and so on. The Executive Committee of the Bolivian University (CEUB) is the national organism for planning, coordination, and execution of resolutions issued by National Congresses and Conferences.

At the local level the university congress is the highest decision-making organism, with attributes similar to those of the National Congress. The University General Assembly is the highest decision-making organism between congresses, at the local

Table 2
Higher education budget 1988

	US$
Gross national product	4,370,419[a]
Total national budget (approved)	2,418,080
National budget of the public education sector (approved)	128,841
National budget assigned to the Bolivian University (approved)	26,086
National budget assigned to public teacher education (approved)	2,923

Sources: Banco Central de Bolivia. Ministry of Finance
a Preliminary data

university level. It sets the general university policy, approves and modifies university statutes, determines the position of the university at the National Congress of Universities, and approves and promotes new faculties and areas of study. The membership of this university assembly includes the rector and vice-rector, the faculty deans and delegates from the various teaching faculties, and university students. The university general secretary and director of administration and finance are also members, but without a vote.

The rector and vice-rector are elected every three years by a universal vote of students and faculty. Deans of each faculty or areas of study are selected by students and teaching faculty every two years. These authorities plus the secretary-general, the director of administration and finance, and faculty and student delegates, form what is called the university council.

In the governing bodies of the Bolivian University mentioned above, the representation of university authorities and faculty is equal to that of students. This is known as cogovernment.

4. Faculty and Students: Teaching, Learning, and Research

The total number of teachers at the Bolivian University was 3,480 in 1983 (the last year for which official data is available at CEUB). The census carried out at the Universidad Mayor de San Andrés of La Paz shows that 40 percent of the total number of teachers worked full-time. The requirements to become a university teacher are: to have a university degree, to have working experience, and to have publications related to the speciality. The university selects the candidates through an examination and evaluation of previous work. The examining committee is formed by teachers and students. There exists a category of invited professors who do not go through this procedure. In La Paz, according to the data of the 1988 census, almost 9 percent of teachers fall in this category. The selection of teachers is the responsibility of each university.

Labor relations between the teacher and the university are set by special university rules. The teacher cannot be removed and has the right to retirement. The levels of salaries for full-time teachers are higher in average than those of civil servants. University professors' prestige is also high. There are university teachers' associations which are exclusive to the universities. The curricula of the courses are determined by the university council. The academic faculty council of each university determines the number of class hours for each subject. From the first year on courses are focused on a specialized field. The liberal arts system does not exist.

In 1986 the distribution of students at the Bolivian University in different fields of study was as follows: social sciences and humanities, 51 percent; health sciences, 20 percent; and pure, natural, and technological sciences, 29 percent.

According to official data provided by CEUB the number of students registered at the Bolivian University has increased from 21,001 in 1972 to 33,330 in 1976, 56,632 in 1982, and 93,387 in 1988. According to CEUB, in 1982 only 1,272 students finished their studies, which does not necessarily mean having obtained their degree.

Students pay virtually nothing for their education, and as a result there is a large number of middle- and lower middle-class students of urban origin. There are few students of peasant origin, and for some years there has been a demand for the establishment of peasants' universities in rural areas. Owing to the existing cogovernment system, students participate fully at all decision-making levels. There is also permanent participation of students in the formulation of university policies.

5. Conclusion

There is a lack of adequate and systematic information to allow the analysis and evaluation of higher education in Bolivia. For decision making, planning, and evaluation, accurate data is imperative. At various times, both in universities and in the Ministry of Education and Culture, attempts have been made to develop information systems, but they have not been followed through.

There is a lack of human resources in Bolivia, at all levels of education. There has not been a clear policy at the highest levels of government to improve the academic standard of education, partly because of the financial implications, and partly because the so-called "social aspects of development" (education, health, and housing) come well after economic priorities of growth.

As there is no clear policy regarding the importance of the role of education in the process of development, there are no coherent and effective relations between education and other sectors of society, nor among the various levels and fields within the educational system. There is no dialogue nor interchange among the different areas of higher education. The autonomy of the university means an atomization, where the only interaction is having the CEUB act as a channel through which the annual budget is approved.

There is no unifying principle regarding the function of higher education within a national context. There is also a lack of capacity to express and satisfy regional needs. However, democratic governments have decided that social issues should be addressed, after coping with the economic crisis. This could make education an important focus, as the source of the formation of human resources. It could also open new opportunities for the emergence of creative capacities and the affirmation of integration and growth.

Bibliography

Capra G G 1989a Problemática de la Universidad Boliviana, Primera parte-Diagnóstico. *Temas en Crisis* 11 (33): 48–51

Capra G G 1989b Problemática de la Universidad Boliviana, Segunda parte. *Temas en Crisis* 11 (34): 50–52

Comité Ejecutivo de la Universidad Boliviana 1985 *Estatuto Orgánico de la Universidad Boliviana.* CEUB, La Paz

Mankiewics V 1989 *Teoría y práctica de la crisis universitaria.* Imprenta Llajtamasi Producciones, La Paz

UNESCO 1986 *Bolivia, Opciones y Estrategias para el desarrollo de la educación regular.* UNESCO, Paris

UNICEF 1986 *Grupos Postergados de Bolivia.* UNICEF, La Paz

Universidad Mayor de San Andrés 1988 *I Congreso Interno. Censo Académico-social-docente, Tomo VII.* UMSA La Paz, 1988

Universidad Mayor de San Andrés 1989 *Propuesta de Reforma Institucional* UMSA, La Paz

M. I. Pérez de Castaños

Botswana

1. Higher Education and Society

The primary role of higher education is to develop the high-level labor force required to sustain Botswana's rapidly expanding economy. The university strives to meet this role by developing academic and research programs that are relevant to labor needs. Consequently, academic programs tend to emphasize courses that are utilitarian in nature. Courses with aesthetic and intrinsic appeal are offered only on a limited scale.

The university also has special programs that are intended to extend its resources and services to the society at large. The National Institute of Development Research and Documentation (NIDRD) research focuses on education and society, agriculture, trade and labor, the environment, and rural development, as part of the mechanism through which the university directly contributes to societal development.

The Institute of Adult Education (IAE) distance education program also extends the university's academic resources to the general public. The program offers short nonaward bearing and award bearing courses in different fields of study. University resources are also made available to different government ministries and to the private sector through individual and collaborative staff consultancies and voluntary services. These latter include inservice training as well as voluntary service on different professional committees of the government and the private sector.

In future, these services will be coordinated by the planned Center for Continuing Education. The center will strengthen the university's links with the outside community through public lectures, conferences, distance learning, and part-time courses (University of Botswana 1987).

2. The Institutional Fabric of the Higher Education System

In Botswana, higher education constitutes the third level of education following seven years of primary and five years of secondary schooling. Education at this level is provided locally by the University of Botswana (UB) and its affiliated institutions. These institutions include four primary teacher-training colleges, two secondary teacher-training colleges, Botswana Agricultural College, Botswana Polytechnic, and the National Health Institute. Affiliation allows the university to monitor academic standards and to award the University of Botswana qualifications in the institutions. However, the control and financing of affiliated institutions remains the responsibility of the relevant government ministries under which they fall. Botswana also enrolls an annual average of 200 students abroad in areas and or levels that are not locally available (Ministry of Finance and Development Planning 1984).

The University of Botswana (UB) is one of the two youngest higher education institutions in Africa, having acquired full university standing only in 1982. Its origin can be traced back to 1945, however, when the Pius XII Catholic University College (CUC) was established in Lesotho. This college was established in 1945 by the Oblates of Mary Immaculate to provide higher education for Roman Catholic African students. Though in Lesotho, CUC accepted Batswana students who were pursuing degree studies of the University of South Africa. "From 1952, the Nationalist government of the Republic of South Africa began imposing restrictions on the admission of foreign Black students to South African universities" (University of Botswana 1985). Neighboring sovereign African states had until then relied on South African universities but following the restrictions it was necessary for them to establish higher education institutions of their own. Owing to resource limitations, the three British colonies of Basotholand, Bechuanaland Protectorate, and Swaziland, (then known as the High Commission Territories), prepared to establish a joint university. In 1964, with the help of the British government and the United States Ford Foundation, CUC campuses were bought and incorporated into the University of Basotholand, Bechuanaland, and Swaziland (UBBS). Though still established in Lesotho, UBBS was governed by an autonomous council that included representatives from the member countries. As the three territories gained political independence in the late 1960s, UBBS became known as the University of Botswana, Lesotho, and Swaziland (UBLS) but remained in Roma, Lesotho (University of Botswana 1985).

The university became physically present in Botswana only in 1971 as a university campus of UBLS. The establishment of university campuses in Gaborone, Botswana, and Kwaluseni, Swaziland followed the recommendations of Sir Norman Grey's Academic Planning Mission to decentralize the control of UBLS. In October 1975, the government of Lesotho challenged the authority and autonomy of the university council, which led to Lesotho's withdrawal from the original confederation. The university campuses in Botswana and Swaziland were reconstituted as the University of Botswana and Swaziland (UBS), with the two campuses acquiring the status of University Colleges. The University College of Botswana (UCB) was established under an Act of Parliament of 1976.

In 1982, the two university colleges became independent universities. The University of Botswana (UB) was established in July 1982 by an Act of Parliament, and formally inaugurated in October 1982 by His Excellency Dr Q K J Masire, the President of Botswana, who is also the university chancellor. In 1990, UB is one of the fastest growing universities in Africa and is a member of the Association of Eastern and Southern African Universities, The International Association of Universities, The International African Institute, The Association of Commonwealth Universities, and the Association of African Universities. In addition, UB has cooperative links with The Free University of Amsterdam, The State University of New York, Ohio University, Manchester University, and The University of Edinburgh.

The university academic year has two semesters. The first semester runs from late August to early December and the second from late January to late May. Instructional sectors are organized into a combination of the course system and subject system with a move towards the subject system since 1983. A full course runs for nine hours per week (excluding laboratory sessions where applicable) for a 14-week semester while a subject runs for the same number of hours over the whole academic year (28 teaching weeks). A full-time student must attend a minimum of nine hours per week; or three courses per semester.

Departments within the different faculties are responsible for the design and development of academic programs. Programs are offered at the certificate, diploma, junior degree, graduate diploma, and master's degree levels. University departments offer four-year junior degree level programs. Master's and graduate level programs are only avai-

lable in the faculties of education and humanities. Three-year diploma programs are offered on a limited scale by the IAE and the faculties of education and the social sciences. Programs at this level are mainly offered by the university's affiliated institutions. The specific instructional and curricula materials are selected and developed by individual staff members under the auspices of their departments.

2.1 Admissions Policies

Although the specific admission criteria differ by department, a first class or good second class pass in the Cambridge Overseas School Certificate with a credit in English language admits a student into a four-year junior degree program. Achievement lower than a second class pass may gain a student admission either to the degree program through the mature entrance scheme or to diploma or certificate level program offered mainly by the affiliated institutions. The mature entrance scheme allows individuals 25 years or older with compensatory professional experiences, admission to the university. Mature applicants also have to pass a selection examination. Although there are no age limits for admission to the university, restrictions may apply to those students seeking government scholarships.

Eligibility for government scholarships is based solely on merit. Nearly 80 percent of Batswana university students receive government scholarships with the remaining 20 percent sponsored by foreign governments, especially in the case of foreign students, or privately by employers or families. Government bursaries cover room and board, food, books, supplies, and a subsistence allowance. In return for the bursaries, students are bonded to work for the government for a number of years equal to one more than the number they spent in school. In addition, they contribute 5 percent of their monthly salary to the bursary fund for the duration of the bond (Ministry of Finance and Development Planning 1984).

3. Governance, Administration, and Finance

3.1 Institutional Administration

The major governing bodies of the university are the council (which regulates the administration and policy-making processes) and the senate (which is the university's academic authority). Council membership includes the university principal officers, senior personnel, and prominent national figures. Also represented on the council are the university alumni, academic and senior administrative staff, and the student body.

In accordance with university statutes, council powers include: making university statutes, articulating university policy to establish procedures for the overall governance of university organizational life, and approving university programs and plans. The council is also responsible for the provision of funds for the smooth running of the university and for the resources required to support both the academic activities and the physical development and maintenance of the university.

While retaining overall control, the council delegates the daily running of the university to its committees and consults the senate on academic matters. The main standing committees of the council are the academic and senior administrative staff appointment and promotions committee, the non-academic staff appointment and promotions committee, the finance committee, and the development and estate maintenance advisory committee.

The senate is comprised of senior members of the academic staff and the students' representative. The senate is responsible to the council, and is accountable for the general control and direction of the teaching and research activities, for examinations and the conferment of degrees, and for awarding diplomas and certificates. The senate exercises its statutory powers mainly through its approval of academic regulations pertaining to admissions, examination procedures, degrees and programs of study, curricula and library regulations. Like the council, the senate delegates much of its detailed responsibilities to its committees such as the senate executive committee, the academic planning committee, the admissions committee, and the general maintenance committee.

In accordance with university statutes, the principal officers of the university are the chancellor, the chairman of council, who is appointed by the chancellor and acts in his absence, and the vice-chancellor. The president of the Republic of Botswana holds the office of chancellor, and is therefore the head of the university. The vice-chancellor is the chairman of senate as well as the chief administrative and academic officer for the university. He is assisted by the deputy vice-chancellor, the registrar, the bursar, and the librarian. Under their leadership, the university is organized into three divisions: administrative, academic, and nonacademic (University of Botswana 1985, 1987).

The academic division is organized into four faculties: education, humanities, science, and social sciences, all of which are headed by a dean, and all of which run their activities through the faculty boards. They are further organized into departments which are responsible for the development of programs of study offered by the universities. Each department has a head who may also be the senior department professor. The faculty is represented by the dean, either personally or through delegates, in all the university's decision-making bodies. The dean's office consults the faculty board on the coordination of all faculty activities.

The faculty of education is composed of the departments of educational foundations, languages and social sciences, nursing education, primary education, adult education, and science and mathematics education. The faculty of humanities includes the departments of African languages and literature, English language and literature, French, history, library studies, and theology and religious studies. The faculty of science has the following departments: biology, chemistry, geology, environmental science, mathematics, physics, and pre-entry science. The social science faculty consists of the school of accounting and management studies and the departments of: demography, law, political and administrative studies, social work, sociology, and statistics.

In addition to the four faculties, the university has two institutes. The Institute of Adult Education (IAE), and the National Institute of Development Research and Documentation (NIDRD), which coordinates and promotes university research activities. The institutes are headed by directors.

The nonacademic staff includes technicians, clerks, janitors, and other support staff who provide the essential facilitative services for the general running and maintenance of the university.

3.2 Finance

The government of Botswana provides up to 58 percent of the university's recurrent expenditure. The rest of the recurrent expenditure is derived from lump-sum government tuition transfers (10.5%), tuition and fees (4%), auxiliary enterprises (20%), external support (6.5%), and others (0.3%) (Ministry of Finance and Development Planning 1984).

The university receives external support from various donors from all over the world. The major donors include the government of the United Kingdom, the World Bank, the European Development Fund, UNICEF, and the Swedish International Development Cooperation. The university also receives gifts and grants from the international development agencies of Norway, The Netherlands, Canada, the United States of America, the United Kingdom, France, and Sweden. Assistance has also been received from the United Nations Development Program (UNDP) and the Fulbright program. Donor support has been directed mainly to capital costs as well as sponsored posts. Donor contributions to recurrent expenditure are mainly to support expatriate academic staff (Ministry of Finance and Development Planning 1984).

4. Faculty and Students: Teaching, Learning, and Research

4.1 Faculty

Acting on behalf of senate, the Academic Staff Appointment Committee has the authority to appoint the university teaching staff. The actual selection of applicants is done by members of the relevant department, however, with the faculty dean presiding as the chair of the selection meeting. The minimum qualification for full lectureship is a master's degree in the relevant area. Botswana nationals with outstanding academic performance may, however, join the teaching staff as staff development fellows. (Staff development fellows are members of the university academic staff who have not acquired the status of full lectureship. Such members would be equivalent to teaching assistants in United States universities. However, the term may also be used to refer to staff members who are still on training, even though they have acquired full lecturer status.) Foreign applicants (referred to as expatriates) are considered only in the event of there being no Batswana with the requisite qualifications for the advertised post. Expatriates are employed on a temporary two-year renewable contract. In addition to their salary, they receive a contract and inducement allowance in lieu of pension. Local staff are employed on a permanent and pensionable basis but have to serve a two-year probationary period before their appointment may be confirmed. Once appointed, staff members are annually reviewed for promotion within the ranks of lecturer, senior lecturer, assistant professor, reader, professor, and professor with personal chair. Promotions are based on excellence in teaching, professional and scholarly activities, and publications.

Since the establishment of UCB in 1976, the academic staff has increased by an average of 10 percent annually, with the overall figure reaching 242 by 1989. The highest increase (23%) occurred in 1981–82 as a result of the separation of UBS. The university academic staff are predominantly expatriates because of the shortage of adequately qualified Batswana. Until 1980–81, only 10 percent of the teaching staff were Batswana. Owing to an ongoing rigorous staff development program, the proportion of local staff increased to slightly below 50 percent by 1988–89. Despite this overall increase, the local staff remains grossly underrepresented in the law, chemistry, physics, statistics, mathematics, and science and mathematics education departments. Further, the university appoints staff to policy and decision-making committees on the basis of seniority; so by default, local staff members are at present underrepresented in the major policy-making bodies.

4.2 Students

Since the establishment of UCB in 1971, overall student enrollment has had an average annual growth rate of 16 percent. Between 1971 and 1980, enrollment increased by 625 percent (from 204 to 1,481) and is projected to increase between 1980 and 1990, by another 132 percent (from 1,481 to 3,440). Notwithstanding this expansion, labor forecasts sug-

gest the need for greater expansion in enrollment. It is projected that there will be a shortfall of about 1,599 graduates and diplomats in the market by 1995 (Ministry of Finance and Development Planning 1984).

Prior to the establishment of UB (1982), Batswana students constituted 80 percent of the university student body. The remaining 20 percent was composed of international students mainly from Swaziland, South Africa, and Zimbabwe (then Rhodesia). After 1982, the percentage of foreign students declined to about 10 percent due to Zimbabwean independence and to the withdrawal of Swati students as the two university colleges gained full university standing. The nursing education and the library studies programs remain the most popular among foreign students.

Within the Batswana student population (90%), about 10 percent are part-time, enrolled mainly in the certificate or diploma programs in accountancy, business studies, and theology extension studies. Though female students constitute 40 percent of the total enrollment, they are underrepresented in the natural sciences (21%) and overrepresented in education (48%). Except in the natural sciences, retention and progression rates average 75 percent. The retention and progression rate of the (1978–81) cohort in the science department was 15 percent and 9 percent for males and females respectively (Ministry of Finance and Development Planning 1984).

The student body is organized through the Student Representative Council (SRC) which works with the dean of students' affairs to promote the welfare of students. Students also have their elected representation on the residence committee, the faculty boards, the senate and council.

Because the university predominantly serves undergraduate level students, it accords comparable weight to excellence in teaching as to academic research. The regular full teaching load is nine hours per week but ordinarily extends above this level because of staff shortages.

In order to retain full-time student status as well as the government bursary, a student must maintain a satisfactory academic performance as well as attend a minimum of three out of four of the weekly lectures. Students' yearly progression is determined through a combination of continuous assessment and an "external" yearly comprehensive examination. Students who do not pass the examination on the first occasion may write a supplementary examination. If they fail this attempt, they may be allowed to repeat the subject or year, transfer to another program of lesser academic challenge, or discontinue their studies.

Over the years, maintenance of high academic standards has been impeded by the fact that most incoming students are not adequately prepared to undertake university studies. Consequently, the university plans to develop a university pre-entry program similar to the one already offered in the science department in order to bridge the gap between high school and the first year of the university.

Bibliography

Coulclough C, Cumming C, Sekgoma G 1988 *Investment Options in Post-Secondary Education*. University of Botswana, Gaborone

Council of the University of Botswana, Lesotho, and Swaziland 1974 *Further Devolution Report of the Devolution Team*

Ministry of Finance and Development Planning 1984 *Botswana Education and Human Resources Sector Assessment*. IEES, Florida

Ministry of Finance and Development Planning 1985 *National Development Plan 1985–1991*. The Government Printer, Gaborone

Rose B 1970 Education in the former high commission territories of Basotholand (Lesotho), Bechuanaland (Botswana), and Swaziland. In: Rose B (ed.) 1970 *Education in Southern Africa*. Macmillan, Johannesburg

Stevens R P 1967 *Lesotho, Botswana and Swaziland: The Former High Commission Territories in Southern Africa*. Praeger, New York

University of Botswana, Lesotho, and Swaziland Reports of the Vice-chancellor to Council for the years 1967 to 1972

University of Botswana, Lesotho, and Swaziland 1969 Report of the Academic Planner as submitted by Sir Norman Alexander to the Council of the University

University of Botswana, Lesotho, and Swaziland 1970 Report of the Academic Planning Mission as submitted by Sir Norman Grey

University of Botswana 1985 *Development Plan 1985/86–1990/91*. University of Botswana, Gaborone

University of Botswana 1987 *Calendar 1988–89*. University of Botswana, Printing and Publishing, Gaborone

University of Botswana and Swaziland 1976 *Development Plan 1976/77*. University Council, Gaborone

M. Marope

Brazil

1. Higher Education and Society

Brazilian institutions of higher education were, from the beginning, one part of a peculiar project of modernization from above. The project began in Portugal at the end of the eighteenth century, was transplanted to Brazil with the Portuguese court in 1808, and continued after political autonomy in 1822. It was led by Sebastião José de Carvalho Melo, the Marquis of Pombal, minister of King D. José I from 1750 to 1777, known for the expulsion of the Jesuits from the Portuguese empire and the renovation of the traditional *Universidade de Coimbra* in Lisbon.

Pombal hoped to free Portugal from the grips of Catholic restoration and conservatism, allowing it to share the benefits of the spreading scientific and industrial revolution without, however, incorporating new sectors in the ruling circles, or any major change in society or the economy. The Portuguese experience should be contrasted with that of other Western European countries, where evolution of higher education was part of a much broader process of social and political modernization, mediated by different sorts of new professional groups—lawyers, the military, engineers, university professors, scientists— responsible for the progressive rationalization and institutionalization of the new social order. Neither Portugal nor Spain participated in the great religious and cultural transformations marking the end of the European Middle Ages, and neither developed the strong professional, academic, or religious corporations and movements which were present in different degrees in societies like Britain, France, or the German states.

The enlightened elite of Brazil, like their counterparts elsewhere in Latin America, entered the independence years of the early nineteenth century admiring and copying the French opposition to all forms of corporatist arrangements and privileges, including those of the church and of the traditional universities. Once free from colonial rule Brazil created different versions of the Napoleonic system of higher education which took away from the church most of its role as an elitist educator. When the first professional schools were established in Brazil in 1808, they were meant to prepare cadres for public administration—in the military forces, the engineering corps, the hospitals, and in the handling of legal affairs—but they lacked the professional and scholarly traditions which were necessary for the modernization of Western university systems. They also lacked the pressures for performance and competence which would be required in conditions of intense competition for social mobility. Members of Latin America's enlightened elite were able to speak French, to travel to Europe, and to handle French concepts, including the democratic and rationalist ideals. Their societies, however, remained restricted to the limits of their economies with a few export products, large pockets of traditional or decadent settlements, one or two major administrative and export centers and, in the case of Brazil, a slave system lasting almost to the end of the nineteenth century. This additional disincentive led to the general lack of intellectual and institutional vigor typical of most of the scientific and higher education institutions in Latin America throughout the nineteenth century.

The first higher education institutions were established in Rio de Janeiro (military engineering, medicine), Salvador (medicine), Recife, and São Paulo (law). After 1850, under Emperor D. Pedro II, Brazil entered a long period of political stability and economic growth, which allowed for the gradual expansion of its educational institutions and the consolidation of a few scientific centers, like the National Observatory, the National Museum, and the Imperial Geological Commission. At the end of the nineteenth century, following the expansion of coffee plantations and the arrival of several million European immigrants to the Brazilian southern states, the old imperial regime was replaced by a federal republic, and dozens of "faculties," as well as a few new research institutions, were created in the State of São Paulo and in other regions. Brazil's first university, however, the *Universidade do Rio de Janeiro*, was inaugurated only in 1920 by the federal government, as a loose federation of previously existing professional schools.

The current institutional and intellectual framework of contemporary Brazilian educational institutions was established in the 1930s, with a major overhaul in 1968. The Getúlio Vargas period, from 1930 to 1945, was a time of growing political and administrative centralization, culminating in the fascist *putsch* of 1937. Italy, and the 1923 Giovanni Gentile education reforms, were permanent sources of inspiration, both for the reform of secondary education and the organization of universities, all under close ministerial supervision. In 1931 the new government established a Ministry of Education and Health, and legislation was introduced defining the framework for the country's university system, which was to combine a faculty of philosophy, sciences, and letters, in charge of basic research and teacher education, with independent professional schools in law, medicine, engineering, pharmacy, and others. The curricula for all careers were to be defined by law and to be mandatory for all; a national council of education was to supervise and give stability to educational policies. In 1934, the Vargas regime sealed a political pact with the conservative Roman Catholic church, granting it control of education policy and institutions. In 1939 the *Universidade do Rio de Janeiro* was reorganized along the lines of the 1931 legislation, with the creation of its *Faculdade de Filosofia*, to be led by Catholic intellectuals, and a new name, *Universidade do Brasil*. It was supposed to provide the model for all other higher education institutions in the country.

The politically and economically advantaged citizens of the state of São Paulo, already the country's economic hub, manœuvered to keep their autonomy from the center, and in 1934 created their own university, which was the first to follow the letter of the 1931 legislation, whilst remaining under local control. Its *Faculdade de Filosofia*, fully staffed with European academics, became Brazil's first university

institution to carry on research as a permanent and recognized activity and to grant advanced degrees.

Political centralization, authoritarianism, and enthusiasm for European fascism receded in the early 1940s, after Brazil joined the allies in the Second World War. However, the centralizing and bureaucratic tendencies of the 1930s remained through the years to follow, less from ideological choice than from institutional inertia. A network of federal universities developed after 1945. Initially this was mainly due to the federalization of several state universities created in the 1930s and 1940s and later its development was enhanced by the notion that each state in the federation was entitled to at least one federal university. The state of São Paulo kept its tradition of regional independence and self-sufficiency, and developed its own system of public higher education. The Church and state pact of 1934 left its imprint, but receded with political liberalization, and the early 1940s saw the establishment of the Pontifical Catholic University in Rio de Janeiro, the first of a series.

Isolated schools continued to be created both privately and by the federal, state, and local governments in the following years, leading to the current *de facto* diversification of Brazilian higher education: a network of federal universities, a large state system in São Paulo, and other smaller state and local institutions in other regions. Growing demands for higher education since the late 1960s met with limited growth in the public sector and a rapid and uncontrolled expansion of private institutions, which accounts, in the late 1980s, for more than 70 percent of a total enrollment of about 1.5 million students, as against 30 percent in a total of about 300,000 in the mid-1960s (see Table 1 and Fig. 1).

Higher education in Brazil was traditionally the channel by which a social elite educated and reproduced itself within a highly stratified, regionally unbalanced, and unequally developed society. As the educational institutions began to expand, access to culture and expert knowledge provided new grounds for claims to social and political leadership, which changed in character as the number and social origins of the student body also evolved. In Brazil, as elsewhere in Latin America, political activism has

Table 1

Brazilian higher education 1960–86: New students, total enrollment and graduating students

	1960	1970	1980	1986
New students	35.4	145.0	404.8	442.3
Total enrollment	93.2	425.5	1,377.3	1,418.2
Graduating students	16.9	64.0	222.9	234.2

Source: Gusso et al. Table V.1, p. 239

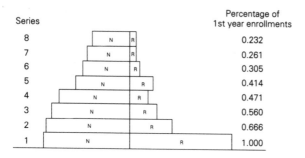

Series			Percentage of 1st year enrollments
8	N	R	0.232
7	N	R	0.261
6	N	R	0.305
5	N	R	0.414
4	N	R	0.471
3	N	R	0.560
2	N	R	0.666
1	N	R	1.000

Figure 1
Brazil, educational pyramid 1982
Source: Instituto Brasileiro de Geografia e Estatística, Pesquisa Nacional por Amostra Domiciliar (PNAD, 1982), as analyzed by Philip R. Fetcher and Sérgio Costa Ribeiro, *Profluxo: Uma Realidade Educacional do Brasil*

been a permanent feature of university life. Political leadership, social mobility, and, more recently, professional credentials and job security, have frequently overshadowed the acquisition of professional skills required by the job market as the main motivations for higher education.

Only about a third of the country's 150 million inhabitants can be said to participate to some degree in the organized and modern sector of society, in terms of consumption, employment, living conditions, and access to education. In the past, most people lived in the countryside; today, more than 70 percent are urban dwellers, which leads to serious problems of housing, transportation, overcrowding, violence, and other manifestations of social marginality in large urban centers. Modern industry is concentrated in São Paulo and other southern states; large, capital intensive rural enterprises dominate extensive parts of the land, including some of the largest frontier and demographically rarified states. The occupational structure shows a strong dominance (70%) of urban as against rural occupations. The densely populated northeastern states, dominated since the seventeenth century by sugar cane plantations and industry, have remained in a state of chronic misery for centuries, and are a source of steady population migration to the southern and urban regions.

Population growth was extremely high between 1940 and 1960, when it grew by 70 percent from 41.2 to 70.1 million; the 1980 census registered 119 million, indicating a similar increase rate. In the 1980s, however, birthrates have dropped dramatically while earlier increases in life expectation have leveled off, leading to downward estimations in population growth for the coming decades. The high rates of rural–urban migration in the last decades also seem to have passed their peak; in the early

1990s the fastest growing regions are the frontier areas and middle-range cities. There are already signs of migration from the largest metropolitan areas to smaller ones.

Ethnic differences are also apparent. Brazilian Blacks are at the bottom of the social pyramid in every respect, such as education, employment, and wealth. The Indian population that existed in the colonial period was either substantially reduced or fully assimilated, except for small pockets of a few hundred thousand who remain, in fact, outside society. There is only one spoken language, Portuguese, but socially unrecognized linguistic differences do exist, not only among regions, but mostly among social strata, a condition presumably accounting for the serious learning difficulties of lower-class students in public schools. Italian, German, and Japanese immigrants were forced to close their schools in the 1930s, and it is still forbidden in Brazil to provide basic education except in the Portuguese language. A few private foreign schools provide bilingual education in the main cities. There are no higher education institutions, however, organized along linguistic, ethnic, or cultural lines.

There are no major religious cleavages in Brazil. When asked, most Brazilians declare themselves Catholic. However, Roman Catholicism coexists with different forms of African and spiritualist cults, and some forms of Protestant fundamentalism have made substantial inroads among the poorer strata. The Roman Catholic Church has traditionally been very active in educational matters, and still runs about a dozen universities, as well as a large number of secondary and fundamental schools. There are also a few Protestant higher education institutions, but none related to the Afro-Brazilian religions.

Brazil was formally a federation of states, further divided into thousands of municipalities and local districts. Political and economic power has usually remained in the hands of the central government, a tradition of central dominance which has only been challenged in the São Paulo region and occasionally elsewhere. The 1988 Constitution leaned towards decentralization, a process which has still to take place. Public subsidies, public employment, and special access to privileged business opportunities are still the main source of income for the upper strata of the country's poorer or economically decadent regions, and not only there; economic transfers to the poorer sectors, however, have not been significant, through lack of motivation, administrative incompetence, or sheer lack of resources. The educational system closely reflects this picture. Although access to first year, public basic education is now generally available except in the poorest areas, the quality of educational services is very unequal. Repetition and dropout rates are extremely high, and correlate strongly with socioeconomic conditions. The average number of years of schooling in the whole of Brazil was as low as 5.12 years in 1982; in rural areas it was 3.17, and in the northeastern region, 3.8 years. Given the extreme variations in terms of quality, the number of functional illiterates in the country, although unknown, is probably very high. Instead of investing in the solution of this problem, Brazilian society has moved towards the expansion of higher educational levels, leading to an increasing gap in the country's educational inequalities. Secondary education today is mostly provided by private institutions, which are only accessible to children of middle- or higher-income families who can pay and remain in good schools until the age of 15. Attendance at a good private school is a necessary condition for passing the entrance examinations for access to the public universities, which are usually the best, and free of charge. The alternative, for those who are not admitted, are the private institutions, where one has to pay for a lower quality education.

2. The Institutional Fabric of the Higher Education System

Brazilian higher education was formally unified along two lines: one, more traditional, related to the public regulation of professions; and the other, more modern, oriented towards the organization of knowledge in academic disciplines. These two unifying principles are not recognized as different, and their uneasy coexistence helps to explain the deep contradictions, differentiation, and contrasts among Brazilian higher education institutions which occur in practice.

The 1931 university legislation reinforced the traditional Napoleonic notion that higher education institutions were schools licenced by the state to teach and certify for the established professions. Each teaching institution was a *faculdade*, in the sense that they were granted the faculty, or franchise, to act on the state's behalf in providing education and extending legally binding professional credentials. This franchising system worked both for public and private institutions, with several important consequences. Since all units had to provide the same education, there was little room for academic autonomy. Educational credentials acquired a value that was fairly independent from their knowledge content, so increasing the demand for formal education with an incentive to do it as easily and cheaply as possible. Holders of diplomas in new fields of knowledge and education, like economics, journalism, or administration, lobbied to create their own franchises, and therefore brought their courses under the same principle of national uniformity and federal regulation. There was neither place nor incentive for research or nonprofessional degrees, and no role, except a ceremonial or a purely bureaucratic one, for a unified university authority and administration.

An elaborate system was set in place to keep this system under control. Each profession was to be controlled by a professional council, whose members would be elected by their peers under ministerial supervision. They would be responsible for keeping the standards of the profession, protecting the market against uncertified persons, and helping to draft the mandatory basic curricula for the schools. All institutions were supposed to provide the same core curricula, with freedom to add options and special emphasis. In fact, given the link between courses taken and professional privileges, the mandatory curricula in most cases occupied the whole four or five years of study for each profession. This complex system was to be further controlled by a federal council of education and its state counterparts, which were supposed to authorize the establishment of new institutions and care for their quality and reliability.

Such a system generated a large bureaucratic paraphernalia of rules and regulations to be followed by the schools. This extended from elaborate degree registration procedures to admission procedures and faculty hiring and promotion practices, all inspected by the Ministry of Education and supervised by the education and professional councils. The public universities, as part of the civil service, were also subject to the administrative and financial regulations emanating from the central administration and the government's accounting offices. Most of this control, however, dealt with formalities. In practice, once an institution received authorization to teach, it would almost never have it revoked, and the basic equivalence of skills to be provided by the different schools throughout the country was never achieved. Moreover, as the higher education system expanded, differences in quality tended to increase, and to become publicly recognized.

A 1968 reform bill sought to reorganize the traditional Napoleonic system along the North American model, centered on academically defined departments geared towards research and graduate education. The traditional chair system, led by prestigious part-time lawyers, medical doctors, and engineers was to be replaced by full-time researchers organized in departments and research institutes. A two-year, college-like "basic cycle" was to precede professional education in all careers. The traditional course sequences were replaced by the credit system, for greater flexibility of course choices. The students were supposed to fulfill the educational requirements for their professional careers by picking their credits from among the different departments; the careers were supposed to be coordinated by interdepartmental committees, with the disappearance of the traditional *faculdades*. Isolated and independent professional schools were supposed to disappear or to combine into university structures of the new pattern. This whole conception was to be helped by the building of integrated campuses in the outskirts of Brazil's main cities, which were to replace the old faculty buildings which were scattered in downtown areas.

This reform faced from the beginning at least three serious obstacles: the overall political climate in which it was conducted, the explosion of demand for higher education, and the resistance of the traditional *faculdades*.

In the year 1968 political mobilization and youth protest was almost everywhere. In Brazil this took the shape of huge student demonstrations against the military government that had seized power in 1964. Repression followed, and between 1969 and the mid-1970s urban guerrillas clashed with the military in a climate of political repression and fear which was particularly hard on the academic institutions. The implementation of a university reform law in such a context could only be perceived as part of the government's repression of the students and the liberal academic community, and as such be viewed with suspicion. The fact that the innovations introduced by the reform had been taken from the North American system only contributed to this perception. This was regardless of the fact that placing research at the core of the universities, ending the chair system, and establishing graduate studies had been central to the aspirations of many who now confronted the military authorities.

More serious, in the long run, was that the 1968 reformers had failed to anticipate the huge increase in demand for higher education already taking place in Brazil as elsewhere in Latin America and the Western world. This expansion was, in part, a consequence of more students coming out of an increasing number of secondary schools. It was also caused, though, by whole new segments of the population suddenly aspiring to higher education: women, older people already employed, holders of secondary degrees in search of an upgrade in their academic credentials. Admittance to Brazilian universities has always been through entrance examinations, and in 1968 the large number of candidates left out of the system simply due to lack of places became a political embarrassment for the government. A decision was made not only to increase the number of openings in the universities, but also to allow for the creation of a large number of private and isolated *faculdades*. These new institutions were mostly low-cost teaching schools staffed with part-time and inadequately qualified professors, working mostly in the evenings, and catering to students unable to meet the university's entrance requirements, usually because of the low quality of their secondary education. Thus, while the reform postulated a gradual convergence of higher education towards a unified university model, it started at the same time to diverge into a strongly stratified system, with a free, more prestigious, and usually better public sector at the top

and an extended, low quality, and fee-paying private system at the bottom.

The traditional faculties of law, medicine, engineering, dentistry, and a few others were fairly successful in resisting the new legislation within the universities. They often kept their old buildings downtown, never moving to the new campuses. When they introduced the department structure and the credit system, they did it internally while resisting disciplinary unification with other career and discipline-based departments and institutes. The chair system disappeared, but was often replaced by oligarchies of full professors. They resisted the introduction of full-time employment, and were slow in establishing their graduate programs. In short, the faculties kept the dominance of professional over disciplinary identity almost everywhere. The traditional professions' ability to resist came partly from the fact that the new legislation did not change the rule, nor the general assumption, that each higher education career was supposed to lead to a nationally valid professional entitlement. As the system expanded, new professions were added to the old ones, each able to gain, in due time, its own legal status and protection: pharmacists, veterinarians, psychologists, librarians, nutritionists, educational supervisors, nurses, journalists, social workers, statisticians, geologists, economists, and so forth. They did not, however, attain the institutional and career organization that existed previous to the 1968 reform and which only survived in the more traditional professions.

In spite of these difficulties, the new legislation led to the creation of discipline-based departments and institutes from the old *Faculdades de Filosofia, Ciências e Letras*, which became responsible for teaching in the basic cycle, for education of secondary school

Table 2
Graduate student enrollments 1987

	Degree Level		
	Total	MA	PhD
Arts	373	309	64
Biological sciences	3,235	2,115	1,120
Health professions	5,367	4,173	1,194
Physical and earth sciences	4,882	3,479	1,403
Engineering	5,550	4,550	1,000
Social sciences and humanities	11,195	9,433	1,763
Social professions	5,581	4,959	622
Rural and industrial professions	3,294	2,701	570
Total	39,478	37,719	7,759

Source: Gusso et al. Table V. 13, p. 249

Table 3
University teachers with graduate degrees 1987

Region	Type of institution				
	Federal (44,179)[a]	State (20,330)	Municipal (4,847)	Private (51,872)	Total regional percentage
North (3,578)	31.2	14.0	—	11.9	27.0
Northeast (21,933)	40.3	14.0	0.5	13.4	30.1
Southeast (66,421)	52.8	67.4	14.2	22.6	37.9
South (22,678)	46.0	25.7	10.5	15.4	28.2
Center-west (6,618)	38.45	0.2	0.7	17.1	29.0
Total Institute Percentage	45.1	49.6	10.1	20.3	33.9

Source: Adapted from Gusso et al. Table V.21, p. 254
a Figures in brackets indicate actual numbers

teachers, and also for graduate education and research. They also took charge of professional education in the "new" or politically weaker professions, alone or in cooperation with other departments. As the teaching load increased, the departments expanded very quickly, often by hiring young teachers without graduate degrees for full-time teaching tasks.

Graduate education and research expanded dramatically after 1968, which was partly due to the new legislation, but also because of the presence of new governmental agencies working in the field of science and technology. The 1968 legislation required graduate degrees for career advancement in the universities, generating a strong and sudden demand for graduate studies. At the same time, the National Development Bank and other agencies related to the Ministry of Planning (the National Research Council and the *Financiadora de Estudos e Projetos*—FINEP) began to provide money for new graduate and research programs within and outside the universities. Fellowships were created for studies abroad and for sending university teachers to complete their degrees in other universities in the country, and a sophisticated peer review system for continuous evaluation of all graduate programs was created by the Ministry of Education. The number of graduate students rose rapidly from almost zero in the mid-1960s to nearly 40,000 in 1986 (see Table 2). The percentage of university teachers with doctoral degrees rose from 6.6 percent in 1974 to 12.7 percent in 1987, while those with master's degrees increased from 9.7 to 21.2 percent in the same period (see Table 3). The distribution of the better qualified teachers at the beginning of the 1990s is very uneven,

with a strong concentration in the public universities, on the one hand, and in the southeast of the country on the other.

The end result of these developments is an extremely differentiated system of higher education, which is made particularly difficult to understand because the differences are not formally acknowledged. From the legal point of view, there are only research universities, or institutions evolving towards this model. In practice, there are profound regional inequalities, traditional professional schools, graduate programs with strong research components, low-quality undergraduate courses in the "soft" disciplines, a large private sector with evening courses and lax admittance requirements, and a relatively small number of highly prestigious public institutions.

3. Governance, Administration, and Finance

In 1988 Brazil adopted a new constitution restating the unity of its higher education system around the research university model, and granting full academic, financial, and administrative autonomy to its universities. The constitution also guaranteed that public education should remain free of charge, and forbade any kind of public subsidy to the private sector, except for research projects or for "community" institutions (a concept applying to a few universities in the state of Santa Catarina and other southern regions). Many issues are left unresolved: the true extent of "autonomy," the regulation of nonuniversity institutions, the role of the federal and state councils of education, the legal status of universities and professors regarding the civil service, and so forth. The Brazilian congress was supposed to vote in 1991 for an education bill to complement the constitutional tenets. Whether legislation will be able to solve the problems of governance, administration, and finance which became particularly acute at the end of the 1980s, in a context of extremely high inflation, economic crisis, and political mobilization, that brought about the country's first presidential election in 25 years, is doubtful.

One of the most difficult issues to be handled involves governance of public universities. Brazilian *faculdades* have traditionally been ruled by their schools' "congregations," or academic senates made up of full professors with token representation from the students and lower rank faculty. Appointments for the main executive positions—rectors and the schools' directors—was usually made by the federal or state government from lists produced by the institutions.

The 1968 reform strengthened the powers of the rectors and the government's control upon them, by requiring a list of six names to be produced by the universities, instead of the traditional three. Political liberalization after 1985 opened the way to pressure from students, teachers, and employees' associations towards equal weight in one-person-one-vote elections for executive posts at all levels in the public universities, and equal representation in all deliberative bodies. After 1988 there was also pressure to accede to the notion that the universities were free to choose their authorities internally, without consulting any kind of external body or public authority. Most public universities adopted these procedures in one way or another, and the government usually appointed rectors from candidates who had received most votes in the lists supplied by the universities. In this way it kept the formalities of the law without entering into conflict with the universities. This practice, however, has generated tensions in some of the best public institutions, where the senior academic staff finds itself often overwhelmed by the mobilization of students, employees, and junior assistants. It is also already clear that university authorities need an external mandate, emanating from the government or from some kind of board of trustees, to enable them to handle their own institution's internal matters effectively. Brazilian public universities are likely to be governed through some combination of these practices at some time in the 1990s, neither returning to strong oligarchic or bureaucratic rule nor settling for an overwhelming prevalence of electoral and corporatist power. Private institutions, universities or not, have no tradition of administrative autonomy vis-à-vis their owners or the controlling institutions, and it is unlikely that this picture will be significantly changed.

Another problem is that of evaluation and quality control. The Federal Council of Education is legally responsible for the quality of higher education institutions, as well as for authorizing the establishment of new universities and isolated courses. In reality, appointments to the council have often been political in nature, and its work has been mostly formal and bureaucratic, with no established mechanism for the regular evaluation of the universities and schools under its jurisdiction. Evaluation of graduate education and research has, on the other hand, been carried out regularly by *Coordenação de Aperfeiçoamento de Pessoal de Nível Superior* (CAPES), an agency within the ministry of education concerned with graduate education, research, and the upgrading of university teachers. This agency has developed a fairly reliable data basis on the academic production of the country's graduate courses, and makes extensive use of peer review committees which rate each program from A to E every two or three years. Their ratings are used by CAPES to allocate fellowships to graduate students and to provide other kinds of support to the graduate programs. The reputation and reliability of CAPES's evaluations has led to their routine use by other government and nongovernment institutions in their dealings with the country's university research and graduate education programs. It would seem obvious that a similar evaluation mechanism should be extended to the undergraduate level of education as well, and the Ministry of Education has stimulated discussions and studies in this direction in the 1980s. There are, however, both technical and political difficulties in this extension. Undergraduate education is more multidimensional than graduate education, leading to serious problems of comparison among courses and institutions geared towards different sectors of the public and diverse educational goals, even in the same fields of knowledge. Since the quality of many undergraduate courses and institutions is obviously not good, they offer strong resistance to any attempts at external evaluation, very often presenting their case as a defense of academic and institutional autonomy.

In the absence of a nationwide evaluation system, several partial initiatives have emerged since the mid-1980s. Some universities have developed their own systems of internal evaluation, and these are starting to provide them with decision-making instruments they did not have a few years before. Some professional associations are starting to talk about the introduction of board examinations for diploma holders, as a condition for professional affiliation and peer recognition. At least one private publisher has started a yearly guide to the Brazilian universities; aimed at potential students and their families it includes a course-by-course rating of university education in all fields of knowledge.

It is clear that, regardless of the legislators' intentions, sectoral differentiation will continue and will increase in the near future. Besides the known differences between the public and the private sectors, regional initiatives are likely to grow and to find their own solutions to the problems of governance and financing. The São Paulo state system was formed by the *Universidade de São Paulo*, the *Universidade de Campinas*, and the *Universidade Estadual de São Paulo*. In 1988 it was granted full administrative and financial autonomy vis-à-vis the state government, and a fixed percentage of the state main excise tax for the university expenses. The state council of rectors was to take responsibility for the distribution of resources among the universities, and also for the definition of salary levels. This move freed the state government from the constant pressures for salary increases for teachers and administrative personnel, and placed the decision fully in the rectors' hands. A limit was also set on the percentage of the state's budget that could be allocated to higher education. The assumption seems to be that the university sector has grown as much as possible in consideration of the other educational levels. Further growth, according to this assumption, can only be obtained when the state economy grows, or through access to contract research and other forms of loans and donations, since tuition cannot be charged. As the state universities adjust to the new situation, they will be the first public universities in Brazil to face the possibilities and dilemmas of extended autonomy.

Another significant regional experience is that of the southern state of Santa Catarina, which developed a network of small community universities throughout the state's territory. This pattern is partly the result of Santa Catarina being a small state with multiple urban centers, modern agriculture and industries, and a fairly highly educated population that could not rely on either federal or state resources to meet their educational needs. The state's community universities and schools are run by a combination of local authorities, business groups, and the church. They are entitled to charge tuition, but in many cases such costs are covered by fellowships from local business firms; and they can also receive federal support, since they do not fit the definition of "private" in the country's Constitution.

3.1 Finance

Public resources for higher education in Brazil grew steadily until the early 1980s, and then stabilized, with abrupt variations from one year to another, due to high inflation rates and general economic depression. Brazilian public universities have traditionally been free of charge, and are fully maintained by the federal or state governments. Most of the money goes towards salaries, which accounts for 80 to 90 percent of all expenses in the early 1990s. Salary levels and privileges for professors and administrative employees in the public sector have been defined through bargaining between the government and the teachers' and employees' associations. This has left little latitude for the universities to make internal decisions on salary levels, promotion rules, and alternative allocations of salary money.

Resource allocations are supposed to be made once a year in the federal and state budgets. However, high inflation has required a large number of ad hoc decisions on budgetary supplements, leading to uncertainty about the future and deteriorating conditions. Money for research, student fellowships, and unusual projects has to be sought outside the regular budget. The National Research Council, the *Financiadora de Estudos e Projetos* and São Paulo's *Fundação de Amparo à Pesquisa* are the usual sources of support for university research, while student fellowships for graduate studies can also be obtained from CAPES, an agency within the Ministry of Education. Universities can also establish cooperative agreements with public corporations, some branches of the government, and the private sector. Foreign foundations and intergovernmental organizations also provide funding. Certain departments in some universities have become extremely skilful in tapping these external sources.

Tuition can be charged in the private sector, but, because of the usually lower socioeconomic origin of its students, there are inherent limits on fees, and they are often controlled by the government. The alternative is for the private sector to provide the cheapest possible type of education for the largest possible number of students. One strategy has been to concentrate in fields not requiring expensive equipment and teaching materials; another has been to hire only part-time teachers, who are sometimes full-time professors in a public institution nearby. A third strategy is to press for public subsidy, which was never very high, and has been practically forbidden by the 1988 Constitution. The only major kind of public support for the private sector has been a system of student loans, which in 1988 helped about 200,000 students, around one-fourth of the total in the private sector.

4. Faculty and Students: Teaching, Learning, and Research

Diversification in both the institutions and sectors of Brazilian higher education has led to profound differences in the nature and role of teaching and research staff, as well as in the quality of educational experiences the students receive.

At the top of the system there is a fairly small elite of about 14,000 faculty with doctoral degrees or equivalent titles and about 40,000 students in master's and doctoral programs in the best public universities, mostly in the southern part of the country. Professors are endowed with reasonable salaries and can complement them with fellowships, research money, and good working conditions (in spite of declining resources in the 1980s). Graduate students are selected from the best of those coming from public universities; they do not pay tuition, and receive a fellowship for two or more years.

The middle strata is composed of about 45,000 teachers in public universities attended by about 450,000 undergraduate students. Many teachers are active in professions outside the universities, and only teach on a part-time basis. A large proportion of them, however, are part of the new breed of full-time teachers hired after 1968, very often on a provisional basis, with the expectation that they would eventually obtain their academic degrees. They are mostly all tenured now, regardless of their academic achievements, and in most universities they can be promoted to the level of assistant professor by dint of seniority. Courses and facilities at this level are uneven, with the best in the center–south and in the traditional professions, and the worst in the public universities of the northeast. Students in public universities have almost free access to restaurants and a few other facilities, but university lodgings are very unusual, and physical installations, laboratories, research materials, and teaching aids are scarce. Students usually come from the best private secondary schools (and thus from middle- to high-class families) and often go through cramming courses to prepare for the university's entrance examinations (these are private, profit-oriented courses outside any kind of government supervision, which tend to be quite efficient in their purpose). As the educational system expands, these students are faced with increasingly serious problems of unemployment, in spite of the relative quality of their education.

Finally, at the bottom, there are around 60,000 teachers serving about 600,000 students in private institutions. Most of these teachers work part-time, are not well-qualified, and have to accumulate a large teaching load in several institutions—or a combination of jobs—in order to survive. Some have full-time appointments in public universities, and "moonlight" in private schools where courses are usually given in the evening. They are not organized, and do not have equivalents to the teachers' associations which prevail in the public sector. Tuition fees are low and government-controlled. However, the students can barely afford them. Facilities and teaching materials are minimal or nonexistent. Students tend to be poorer and older; courses are mostly in the "soft" fields. Most students are already employed in lower middle-class or white-collar jobs, and look to education as a means for job improvement or promotion; they are usually more interested in credentials than in knowledge or skills.

All these differences are combined with profound regional imbalances and contrasts between the southern states, more specifically the state of São Paulo, and the rest of the country. São Paulo is Brazil's biggest and most industrialized state, encompassing about one-fifth of the national population, and one-

third of its graduate enrollment. It is also the region in which the dual nature of the Brazilian higher education developed more fully. There is proportionally less enrollment in public universities than in other regions, but the universities are far better than in the rest of the country, while the private sector is much more complex and differentiated than elsewhere. There are few federal institutions in the state, in contrast to the country's poorest region, the northeast, where more than 70 percent of the students are enrolled in federal universities and have few alternatives in the private sector.

4.1 Career Paths

Career paths vary greatly throughout this diversified system. At the *Universidade de São Paulo* a doctoral degree recently became the minimum requisite for admittance to an academic career. In other public universities, a graduate degree is not an absolute requisite for first-level entrance. Regular academic appointments are made after elaborate and formalized procedures which include written examinations, a public lecture, and evaluation of the candidate's curriculum. Promotion to the higher ranks—associate and full professorship— requires similar procedures. Many Brazilian universities still accept the institution of *livre docencia*, an adaptation of the old German *Privatdozent*, which in practice is obtained through public examination and the presentation of an academic dissertation, and assures an academic status immediately below full professorship. In the past, *livre docência* was a mechanism to assure academic quality; today, it is most often a mechanism to circumvent the doctors' degree requirement for admission and promotion, except again at the Universidade de São Paulo, where the *livre docência* remains a required step in the path towards full professorship.

Once admitted at any level, tenure is assured in practice except for extreme cases of misbehavior. Brazilian public universities are part of the civil service and, in the past, professors were hired as civil servants, which meant, among other things, employment stability after a few years and retirement with full salary after 25 years (for women) and 30 years (for men). In the late 1980s the federal universities began to hire in accordance with the labor legislation for the private sector, where people can be dismissed at any time at one month's notice and retirement benefits are very limited. These differences, however, have been narrowed by pressure from the professors' unions. In the private sector, on the other hand, there is a general absence of career structures and tenure mechanisms. Professors are hired as teachers when needed, and usually dismissed at will.

The rigidity and formality of appointment and promotion procedures in the public sector have led to the introduction of alternative mechanisms. The University of São Paulo, for instance, can appoint professors by invitation for limited periods; to be admitted to the regular career they are required to pass a formal examination, however. In the past, and mostly in the federal universities, similar mechanisms have led to the admission of large numbers of people who were later granted the rights of stability and career promotion through ministerial decrees or judiciary decisions. One consequence has been the low academic level of many institutions; the other is their inability to hire new and supposedly more qualified personnel for lack of academic slots. Another characteristic of this arrangement is that mobility between universities is almost nonexistent, since jobs and ranks are not transferable between institutions, even within the same system.

Academic power within Brazilian universities usually rests in the hands of academic units (schools, faculties, institutes), within the limits set by the government, on the one hand, and the professors' and employees' associations and unions, on the other. Curricula for the legally recognized professions and careers are established by the Federal Council of Education, and can only be expanded or interpreted locally. Universities are free, however, to establish new courses and careers, and have no limitations regarding their graduate programs, except the periodical evaluation from CAPES. Nonuniversity institutions, even in the private sector, can only be created or offer new degrees with the formal authorization of the Federal Council of Education. The government has the power to establish salary levels and the availability of posts in the public sector, and also tuition prices and salary levels in the private institutions.

Academic power in the public sector is also exerted by the universities' teachers' associations, which are nationally organized as the *Associação Nacional de Docentes do Ensino Superior* (ANDES) and affiliated with the country's more militant central union, the *Central unica dos Trabalhadores* (CUT). The militancy of ANDES in the 1980s has been instrumental in assuring the salary levels and job stability of university professors, but has also paralyzed many of the government's initiatives in terms of university reform. It has also led to rigidity in the rules and procedures of the public universities over academic careers, placing, therefore, a clear limit to the universities' formal autonomy. The employees' associations are a relatively new phenomenon in Brazilian universities. They have followed the general pattern of political and union organization of Brazilian civil servants and have been active in several strikes at the federal and state levels, participating wherever direct elections for executive offices in public universities are held.

Political mobilization is a much less salient feature among Brazilian students in the late 1980s than it was in the 1960s and 1970s. The National Union of Students (UNE) was organized in the early 1940s, and

played an important role in the popular demonstrations that led to Brazil's entrance into the War against the Axis alliance. In the 1950s and 1960s UNE was at the forefront in all libertarian and nationalist campaigns that culminated in the large public demonstrations against the military regime in 1968. Many student leaders were killed by political repression, or went into exile in the early 1970s. Later, as the students' ranks swelled and lost the memory of the past, many of those active in the 1960s joined the teachers' association movement of the 1980s, while the new students entered a period of political indifference not dissimilar to that found in so many other Western societies.

5. Conclusion

The challenge to Brazilian higher education as it faces the turn of the millennium is whether universities will be able to accommodate the country's growing educational demands while at the same time fulfilling their role as centers for academic excellence and scientific research. The current situation, in which better quality education is provided free in the public sector, while low quality, mass schooling is only available privately, is not likely to last. In the next decades, the public sector is likely to come under increasing pressure to broaden its coverage, and while doing this it will either keep its remaining standards of quality, or leave that task to the private sector. The educational role to be fulfilled by Brazilian universities in the near future is not limited to their current or prospective students. As it enters the last decade of the twentieth century basic and secondary education in Brazil is plagued by an acute lack of qualified teachers, and it is not clear how the universities can recover their traditional role of teacher education, given the low prestige of the teaching profession and the poor educational background of those willing to join its ranks. The universities will also have to play a growing role in continuing education for all professions, and in providing nonconventional courses for those who want to learn more but are unable to attend the regular courses given along the traditional curricula.

All these challenges will have to be met in a context of economic constraints. The Brazilian state is not likely to increase the universities' share of the national budget in the near future, nor its share of educational expenses vis-à-vis other educational levels. Pressures for evaluation, administrative efficiency, and accountability are likely to increase alongside a growing movement towards new sources of income, including cost recovery from the better endowed students. The full administrative, patrimonial, and academic autonomy granted to the Brazilian universities by the 1988 Constitution could become a precious instrument in the search for a broader and more diversified role, and a larger and more equitable financial basis. On the other hand, autonomy can also provide more traditional and short-sighted sectors within the universities with a weapon for retrenchment, isolation, and resistance to the realities of the external world. This is the dilemma for the future.

Bibliography

Azevedo F de 1963 *A cultura brasileira*, 4th edn. University of Brazil, Rio de Janeiro

Barros R S de 1959 *A ilustração brasileira e a idéia de universidade*. University of São Paulo, São Paulo

Bethel L (ed.) 1986 *The Cambridge History of Latin America,* Vol. 5. Cambridge University Press, Cambridge

Carvalho J M 1978 *A Escola de Minas de Ouro Preto—o peso da glória*. Cia. Editora Nacional and FINEP, Rio de Janeiro and São Paulo

Cidade H 1969 A reforma pombalina da instrução. In: *Liçoes de cultura e literatura portuguesa*. Coimbra Editora, Coimbra, Portugal

Costa V 1986 Brazil: The Age of Reform, 1870–1889. In Bethel L (ed.) 1986, pp. 728–78

Cunha L A R da 1980 *A Universidade Temporã: o ensino superior da colônia à era de Vargas*. Civilização Brasileira, Rio de Janeiro

Cunha L A R da 1983 *A Universidade Crítica: O Ensino Superior na República Populista*. Francisco Alves, Rio de Janeiro

Dean W 1986 The Brazilian Economy, 1870–1930. In: Bethel L (ed.) 1986, pp. 685–724

Fausto B 1986 Brazil: The social and political structure of the First Republic, 1889–1930. In Bethel L (ed.) 1986, pp. 779–830

Furtado C 1968 *The Economic Growth of Brazil—A Survey from Colonial to Modern Times*. University of California Press, California

Gusso D A, Tramontin R, Braga R 1987 Ensino Superior. In: IPEA-IPLAN-SEC *Educação e Cultura 1987—Situação e Políticas Governamentais*. Secretaria de Planejamento, Instituto de Planificação Econômica e Social—IPEA, Brasilia

Levy D C 1986 *Higher Education and the State in Latin America—Private Challenges to Public Dominance*. University of Chicago Press, Chicago, Illinois

Oliveira B A 1973 *As Reformas Pombalinas e a educação no Brasil*. Universidade Federal de São Carlos, São Carlos

Paim A (ed.) 1982 *Pombal e a Cultura Brasileira*. Tempo Brasileiro, Rio de Janeiro

Prado C Jr. 1967 *The Colonial Background of Modern Brazil*. University of California Press, Berkeley, California

Schwartzman S 1978 Struggling to be born: The scientific community in Brazil. *Minerva* 16 (4): 545–80

Schwartzman S 1988 Brazil: Opportunity and crisis in higher education. *Higher Educ.* 17(1): 99–119

Schwartzman 1991 *A Space for Science: The Development of the Scientific Community in Brazil*. Pennsylvania State Press, University Park, Pennsylvania

Schwartzman S, Bomeny H M, Costa V M R 1984 *Tempos de Capanema*. Ed. Paz e Terra and Editora da Universidade de São Paulo, Rio de Janeiro and São Paulo

Stepan N 1976 *Beginnings of Brazilian Science—Oswaldo Cruz, Medical Research and Policy, 1890–1920*. Science History Publications, New York

Wirth J D 1970 *The Politics of Brazilian Development 1930/54*. Stanford University Press, Stanford, California

Withaker A (ed.) 1961 *Latin America and the Enlightenment*. Cornell University Press, New York

S. Schwartzman

Brunei

1. Higher Education and Society

The development of higher education in Brunei has been rapid, particularly since Independence was declared in 1984. The University of Brunei Darussalam was established in 1985, with the Brunei Institute of Technology and the PAP Rashidah Sa'adatul Bolkiah College of Nursing opening in the following year. Prior to 1985, the only higher education institutions were the Sultan Hassanal Bolkiah Teachers College which was upgraded to an Institute of Education in 1985 and integrated into the University in 1988, and the Seri Begawan Religious Teachers Training College. The limited higher education provision in Brunei meant that many students had to go abroad for their tertiary education prior to the mid 1980s. The government supported such overseas study through a scheme of scholarships, but policy from the mid-1980s has been to limit assistance to courses which are not presently available in Brunei such as degree courses in medicine, law, dentistry and engineering.

A number of economic, social, and cultural factors help to account for the growth of higher education. These include the need for a trained and experienced local workforce, and for a reduction in the dependence on expatriates who presently comprise almost one-third of the working population. A local skilled workforce is required in the oil and gas industry which produces three-quarters of the nation's Gross Domestic Product; for the rapidly expanding public sector; and for those industries which, under the Fifth National Development Plan, 1986–90, diversify the economy in preparation for a post-oil era.

The growth of higher education can also be seen as part of the expansion of the nation's education system in general. With half of the population of 241,000 under the age of 20 years (this figure is increasing annually at a rate of some 2.5 percent), the education system had to expand rapidly in the 1980s. This has also meant an increased emphasis on local teacher training in the new University.

Higher education has a central role in the implementation of national education objectives. These include the establishment of bilingualism where Bahasa Melayu is the official language and English the second language; and the promotion of Islam in the context of Malay culture and the monarchy. Programs are therefore offered in both Bahasa Melayu and English, and include compulsory courses on Malay culture. Higher education is central to nation building in an Islamic nation which resumed full independent sovereign status in 1984.

2. The Institutional Fabric of the Higher Education System

Higher education is entirely sponsored by the government and is mainly the responsibility of the Ministry of Education. The University and the Institute of Technology are the direct responsibility of the Minister of Education who is also the vice-chancellor of the University.

The Nursing College is presently under the director of schools—an administrative arrangement which is under review; and the Religious Teachers' Training College is under the Ministry of Religious Affairs.

The University's admission requirements for its degree programs include credit-level passes in four subjects at Ordinary level, including Bahasa Melayu; two passes at Advanced level; and, for English-medium programs, a pass in English at Ordinary level. The entry requirement for the University's three-year Certificate in Education program which was formerly offered by the Institute of Education is four credit-level passes at Ordinary level including Bahasa Melayu and English.

Applicants for entry to the Institute of Technology require a credit-level pass in Bahasa Melayu at Ordinary level or, in the case of applicants from technical schools, a credit in Bahasa Melayu at Brunei Junior Certificate in Education level. In addition, specific course requirements must be met in each of the three areas of Higher National Diploma studies offered by the Institute. These areas are computer studies, business and finance, and electrical and electronic engineering. For each the entry requirement is either four passes in appropriate subjects at Ordinary level and at least one pass at Advanced level, or a pass in BTEC National Certificate, or a diploma in the relevant field.

The College of Nursing and the Religious Teachers' Training College require credit passes in at least four subjects at Ordinary level, including Bahasa Melayu.

Applicants to the above institutions must be citizens of Brunei or, in the case of the College of Nursing, hold permanent resident status. However, a small number of overseas students are admitted to the University under the Brunei-ASEAN scholarship scheme. A policy relating to the numbers of foreign students attending the University under this scheme was being formulated in 1989.

Tables 1 and 2 show the enrollment patterns in each of the higher education institutions. In the case of the University, the Institute of Technology, and the College of Nursing the first intakes were in 1985 and 1986, with increased enrollment levels reflecting the development of the new programs in each institution. Enrollments in the former Institute of Education were transferred to the University as from the 1988–89 academic year.

Enrollments in the former Institute of Education declined from a peak of 572 in 1981. This was largely because the need for Malay-medium teachers was reduced after the introduction of a bilingual system of education in 1985. From 1985 onwards there has been a surplus of Malay-medium teachers, with the increased demand for bilingual teachers at primary and secondary level being met by degree programs and a three-year Certificate in Education program in the new University.

The University of Brunei Darussalam offers six honors degree programs, each spread over a minimum period of four years, and leading to the award of the following first degrees:

(a) Bachelor of Arts Education (Malay-medium): education with either Bahasa Melayu and Malay literature, or Islamic studies.

(b) Bachelor of Arts Education (English-medium): education with two subjects chosen from economics, geography, history, and English.

(c) Bachelor of Science Education (English-

Table 1
Enrollments in higher education in Brunei 1985–89

	1985–86	1986–87	1987–88	1988–89
University of Brunei Darussalam	164	338	510	899
Institute of Education	221	270	260	—[a]
Institute of Technology	55	65	85	92
Nursing College	—	24	12	22
Religious Teachers' Training College	344	249	248	211
Total	784	946	1,115	1,224

a 239 Certificate-level student enrollments transferred to University

Table 2
University of Brunei Darussalam: Total enrollments by field of study 1985–89

		1985–86	1986–87	1987–88	1988–89	1989–90[a]
Education	Degree	60	158	254	339	335
	Nondegree	—	—	—	239	233
Management and Administrative Studies		44	85	124	164	160
Arts and Social Sciences		51	95	132	157	131
Total		164	338	510	899	879

a Projected enrollments

medium): education with two subjects chosen from biology, chemistry, mathematics, and physics.

(d) Bachelor of Arts, Primary Education (English-medium).

(e) Bachelor of Arts (Malay-medium): two subjects chosen from economics, geography, history, Malay language and linguistics, and Malay literature.

(f) Bachelor of Arts (English-medium): management studies or social policy and public administration.

Provision also exists for experienced teachers to upgrade from certificate to degree level with up to one year's credit granted for previous studies. In addition, the University offers a one-year postgraduate certificate in education and a one-year postgraduate diploma in educational management.

The Institute of Technology offers Higher National Diploma programs in business and finance, computer studies, and electrical and electronic engineering. Each of these courses has a duration of two and a half years including a six-month period of industrial placement. The Nursing College offers a course lasting just over three years and leading to a diploma in general nursing. The Religious Teachers' Training College offers a three-year course leading to a certificate for teachers of religion.

3. Governance, Administration, and Finance

Higher education is centrally funded by the government through its Ministry of Finance. The Ministry of Education and the Ministry of Religious Affairs each submit an annual budget which is considered by the National Budget Committee. In addition to annual budgeting there has been a development budget for major capital works under each of the Five-Year National Development Plans. The Economic Planning Unit of the Ministry of Finance also acts as a secretariat for the Five-Year Development Plans. The secretariat assists in the coordination of budgeting and planning at the national level.

The overall control of the University is the responsibility of the University council which is presided over by an appointed chairperson. The policies of the council are implemented through the vice-chancellor as principal executive officer of the University. Membership of the council is determined in accordance with the policy of the government.

The senior academic body of the University is the senate. Members of the senate include the vice-chancellor as chairperson, deans, heads of departments, professors, the registrar, and such other members as the vice-chancellor may decide.

The University was established with two faculties which were expanded to four in 1987. These are the faculties of arts and social sciences; education; science; and management and administrative studies. It is also intended that the Brunei Institute of Technology be incorporated into the University to form a faculty of engineering. Each faculty is administered by a dean who is also chair of the faculty board which is directly responsible to the senate, which in turn is subject to the overall control of council.

The teaching and research programs of the four faculties are organized in departments as follows:

(a) Faculty of arts and social sciences: economics, geography, history, Islamic studies, Malay language and literature.

(b) Faculty of education: language education, educational psychology, science and mathematics education, arts and social sciences education, educational foundations, in-service education, and teaching practice.

(c) Faculty of science: mathematics, biology, chemistry, and physics.

(d) Faculty of management and administrative studies: management studies, social policy, and public administration.

The academic administration of the other institutions differs from that of the University. The Institute of Technology has three teaching departments responsible to an academic board chaired by the director. The size of the College of Nursing allows it to function as a single administrative unit without departments. Its principal is responsible to the director of schools within the Ministry of Education.

4. Faculty and Students: Teaching, Learning, and Research

In 1989 there were 164 academic staff in the University, 39 in the Institute of Technology, 32 in the Religious Teachers' Training College, and 12 in the College of Nursing. Because all of these institutions are relatively new, the only trend which can be noted is that the number of staff in the Religious Teachers' Training College has almost doubled since 1978. With the exception of the Religious Teachers' Training College, most staff are recruited on contract from overseas, although the policy is gradually to replace expatriates with local staff.

Within the University, levels of academic appointment follow a common pattern from tutor through assistant lecturer, lecturer, senior lecturer, associate professor, and professor. The rank of assistant lecturer was introduced to accommodate some staff from the former Institute of Education prior to the upgrading of their qualifications. The three levels of appointment within the Institute of Technology are lecturer, senior lecturer, and principal lecturer, which are equivalent to the salary levels of assistant lecturer, lecturer, and senior lecturer within the University. The Nursing College appoints staff at the levels of education officer and nursing officer (teaching), while the Religious Teachers' Training College appoints staff at the levels of religious education officer and religious teacher. For each institution recruitment is through the establishment department of the prime minister's office.

New programs within the University require the approval of senate. A system of external examination has been established to monitor the content, method, and standards of assessment in all courses. The University functions on a semester system. Depending on the degree program, students are required to accumulate between 120 and 128 units over their four years of study. Assessment is based on a combination of cumulative assessment and final examinations with the latter normally carrying a heavier weighting.

5. Conclusion

The rate of development of higher education in Brunei in the immediate future will be limited by the number of potential applicants. However, a predicted increase of 40 percent in the size of the 15–19 age group over the decade (1990–2000), together with school-level policies designed to increase pupil retention and pass rates at the senior secondary level, promise a larger pool of school leaver applicants by the mid-1990s. It is expected that the new University's target of the year 2000 will be met at that stage, by which time its new campus will have been completed.

The expansion and diversification of the Brunei economy assures a strong and continuing demand for graduates. Over the period 1986–91 the number of university graduates required in the total workforce is expected to double. This increasing demand for graduates will continue to be met in part by expatriate contract staff; partly by local staff trained in overseas institutions, especially in such fields as medicine, law, dentistry, and the paramedical professions; and increasingly by graduates from Brunei.

Bibliography

British Council 1977 *The Feasibility of a Centre of Higher Education in Brunei.* British Council, London
Economic Planning Unit, Brunei 1986 *Brunei Statistical Year Book.* Bandar Seri Begawan, Brunei
Education Council, Brunei 1976 *Scheme for the Implementation of the New Education Policy Report of the Education Commission of 1972.* Bandar Seri Begawan, Brunei
Ministry of Education, Brunei Department of Planning, Research and Development n.d. *Educational Statistics of Brunei Darussalam.* Bandar Seri Begawan, Brunei
Ministry of Finance, Brunei, Economic Planning Unit 1986 *Fifth National Development Plan 1986–1990.* Bandar Seri Begawan, Brunei
State Secretariat, Brunei 1972 *Report of the Education Commission Brunei.* Bandar Seri Begawan, Brunei
State Secretariat, Brunei, Economic Planning Unit 1980 *National Development Plan 1980–1984.* Bandar Seri Begawan, Brunei

F. Coulter

Bulgaria

1. Higher Education and Society

Bulgaria's national frontiers have not changed since 1940. The territory consists of 110,994 square kilometers, with a population in 1988 of nine million people.

Until November 10, 1989 Bulgaria was an exemplary totalitarian state under Soviet influence. The communist takeover started in September 1944, when the country was occupied by the Red Army, and was completed by the end of 1949. By 1950 there were no more political parties—the remaining Communist party and the Bulgarian Agrarian Union during the last almost half of a century having never acted as political parties in a parliamentary framework—no private agriculture, and no private business or industry. Most of the basic human rights were often violated or heavily restricted.

As in the other parts of Eastern Europe the situation has changed drastically in 1990. After the first

Table 1
Development of population growth since 1939

	1939	1960	1970	1980	1988
In millions	6.319	7.905	8.515	8.877	8.986
Density per square kilometer	61.3	71.3	76.8	80.0	81.0
Percentage of urban population	22.7	38.0	53.0	62.5	67.0

Source: Statistical Yearbook 1989

parliamentary elections for 40 years in June 1990, the communists, now calling themselves socialists, won a majority of 210 out of 400 seats in a new Grand Assembly. Until December 1990 the cabinet was a totally communist one. Since then a new cabinet with the participation of a newly emerging opposition has been designated. In this new government the Ministry of Science and Higher Education has instructed a new policy of "de-ideologization" in higher education. This occurs within the framework of an economic crisis of catastrophic dimensions, and a teaching staff which, in its majority, were members of the former communist party.

Higher education has always been secular in Bulgaria. Sofia University had a Department of Theology until 1946, which became a separate religious academy within the High Synod of the Bulgarian Orthodox Church, but its alumni were not granted the state diploma of higher education.

All institutions of higher education in Bulgaria are public and are subsidized by the state budget. By 1989 there were 30, among them three universities.

2. The Institutional Fabric of the Higher Education System

Until the 1940s there was one university—the Saint Clemens of Ochrida University of Sofia. Its history till 1938 is still the fullest and unique account of the first half century of higher education in Bulgaria (see Arnandov 1939). After the late 1940s several departments were detached from the university (e.g., medicine, agriculture, theology, forestry) and reorganized as independent higher education institutions, mostly called institutes.

The situation at the beginning of 1990 was as follows: three universities; three pedagogical institutes (teacher-training colleges); three business institutes; two agricultural institutes; ten technological institutes; five medical schools; three in art and music; and one in sports (see Table 2).

Nominally, there are no levels or hierarchy within the establishments in the Bulgarian higher education system. Study lasts at least four years and six years for medicine. There are no reliable statistical data of

the number of semesters an average student needs to complete his or her studies, but it is in practice higher than 10 semesters, that is, five years.

There are about 50 so called semi-higher institutes with six-semester courses. Ten of them are primary-teacher-training colleges and the remainder are vocational. Most of them are functionally integrated to higher institutions.

Research activities are presumed to exist in all higher education institutions, but the level and range differs considerably between the different faculties. With few exemptions faculty members are over-burdened with much formal teaching *ex cathedra*. The departments lack adequate equipment, laboratories, and libraries to do research that would reach international standards. One cause is the existence of a big parallel system of research institutes—the Bulgarian Academy of Sciences. Efforts in the early 1970s to integrate educational and pure research institutions of the academy for a common purpose failed because of the resistance of a *nomenclatura* on both sides.

Admission to higher education is centralized. There are uniform entrance examinations based on Bulgarian, mathematics and other disciplines. Usually, a candidate can apply for one and in exceptional cases two higher institution(s). A prerequisite is a diploma for the completion of secondary school. For all departments the number of enrollments are fixed by the government. This system has been in place since the 1950s.

The length of the first and unique degree is four-and-a-half to six years. The minimum applies for some economics institutions and high school teacher-training colleges, and the maximum for medicine. For the universities and the engineering institutes the course is ten semesters long. There is no division between bachelor's and master's degrees and there is a uniform diploma for higher degrees. For most of the courses longer than ten semesters, there is a final state examination, awarded by a committee of the individual establishments without special representations by the government.

With very few exemptions, the major subjects are chosen at the moment of enrollment, the curriculum is rigid and the students have almost no choice.

Table 2
Bulgarian higher education institutions with year of founding in brackets

Institution	Number of students	Number of foreign students	Technical staff	Full and associated professors
Universities				
Sofia (1888)	15,560	1,100	1,188	485
Plovdiv (1961)[b]	4,500	—	345	90
Veliko-Tirnovo (1963)[b]	4,500	—	380	70
Higher teacher training				
Shumen (1964)	3,700	—	265	71
Blagoevgrad (1975)	3,600	—	266	60
Plovdiv (1964)	650	7	92	18
Higher economic				
Sofia (1920)	7,500	700	513	194
Varna (1920)	4,700	250	223	68
Svishtov (1936)	4,000	—	179	59
Higher agricultural				
Plovdiv (1945)	3,000	348	252	119
Stara-Zagora (1921)[a]	200	132	265	121
Mechanical and electrical engineering				
Sofia (1945)	13,000	950	1,219	450
Varna (1963)	5,746	225	455	118
Gabrovo (1964)	3,000	—	194	57
Rousse (1954)	5,000	320	520	143
Chemical engineering				
Sofia (1945)	2,400	140	427	164
Civil engineering				
Burgas (1963)	1,200	250	205	59
Mining				
Sofia (1945)	2,000	100	247	128
Forestry				
Sofia (1925)[a]	1,500	70	130	62
Sports				
Sofia (1942)	4,700	620	437	217
Sofia (1942)	2,800	300	270	73

Source: Kunev 1989
a Until 1945 departments of Sofia University   b Teacher training institutes until 1972

even when options do exist, they are hampered by tunnelization."

Graduate studies are called "aspirantura" and the PhD students "aspirants." Nominally, the length of a graduate course is three years and leads to the degree of "candidate of sciences" where the specialization can be in mathematics, physics, economics, history, and so on. The number of "aspirants" is determined by the government every year. To enroll, it is necessary to have a diploma of higher education, and to compete in an entrance examination. A graduate course is also available at research institutes of the Academy of Sciences and other research organizations.

The candidate's thesis is defended at a public session of the respective scientific council, and needs the approval at two levels (area commission and presidium) of the Higher Attestation Commission—a governmental institution directly under the rule of the government. This commission is entitled to award all degrees: candidate (PhD), doctor of sciences, docent (associate professor) and professor. The research institutes have two grades: first-level senior research fellow, and second-level senior research fellow which correspond to professor and docent. The Higher Attestation Commission can confer a degree even if the candidate has been rejected at the lower level.

3. Governance, Administration, and Finance

The prime responsibility for the development and governance of higher education has a ministry called the Ministry of Science, Culture and Education (during the period 1986–89) and now the Ministry of Science and Higher Education.

Table 3
Enrollments during the last decade

Academic years	1980–81	1985–86	1987–88	1988–89
Universities and teacher-training colleges	21,051	27,155	33,442	34,895
Medicine	12,218	12,539	11,566	12,065
Economics	14,162	15,324	17,384	19,215
Agriculture and forestry	3,815	5,075	5,484	5,870
Engineering	29,960	36,463	42,761	49,688
Arts	2,056	2,418	2,824	2,026
Sports	2,068	2,533	2,946	3,205
Total	85,330	101,507	116,407	126,964

Source: Statistical Yearbook 1989

The system is centralized so there is no provincial or regional administration.

The top coordinating agency shaped the higher education through budgetary control, by decrees, by approving all curricula, personnel assignments and so on.

The goals set by the central coordination agency have been to ensure the role of the ruling political party. There were no formal mechanisms for assessing or evaluating higher education, but voluntarist decisions of the respective political bodies. National plans were formulated in a vague and unrealistic way, "creating higher specialized professional intellectual workers for a future communist society." It is only the intrinsic value of scientific knowledge, especially in the natural sciences, that has preserved and saved a low, but acceptable level of higher education, not as a result of the actions of central planning, but despite it.

The only resource for the financing of higher education is the state budget. There are no reliable data on the Gross National Product (GNP) and what proportion was devoted to higher education.

The typical scheme of governance is as follows: the institution is governed by the rector, two or three vice-rectors and an academic council. The academic council is elected by a general assembly, including both representatives of the academic staff and of the students and technical personnel. This council elects the rector. But all the elections have been ficticious and the real decisions were taken by the communist party. The same model then applies to the different departments. The mandate is always for four years but can be repeated. The secretaries of the party organizations at all levels were members with voting power in all ruling bodies.

The higher institutions are organized in departments, called faculties, which have chairs. The head of the chair is not elected but assigned by the depart-

mental council. Students and nonacademic staff are represented only in the general assembly. The formal responsibilities of the chairs are: the assignment of teaching hours among academic staff, discussion of research done by staff and all daily problems. A base unit exists which has no responsibility to assign personnel or to decide on curricula.

4. Faculty and Students: Teaching, Learning, and Research

The overall number of teaching staff in higher education was 13,200 in 1983/84 and 16,000 in 1987/88 (Kuner et al. 1989).

An academic career commences by becoming an assistant. A necessary qualification is only a diploma of higher education, but a "candidate" degree gives priority. The procedure of appointment consists of a competition with entrance exams and interviews. An assistant is then assessed every five years. The assistant position has three levels: assistant, senior assistant and head assistant. Every level has a mandate of three to five years. After each period the holder has to be reassessed.

The next stage in the academic career is the position of docent or assistant or associate professor (Prior to 1950 another rank existed, that of "extraordinary professor," before the full professorship. This is the first "habilitation" level. A prerequisite is a candidate degree. The criteria now required are research results in corresponding areas, but also teaching abilities. The same criteria also apply for the full professor with the prerequisite of a doctor of sciences.

Recruitment starts at the individual establishment and finishes in the High Attestation Commission.

Prior to 1990, virtually no organization represented the corporate interests of the academic staff. Academics were automatically members of one section of the trades unions, dominated by the ruling party. Since then a variety of newly created unions has emerged.

Norms are laid down for the teaching load. They are divided into two main groups: formal lecturing (*ex cathedra*) and exercises (problem solving, seminar discussions, laboratory and field work, etc.). The average teaching load for a lecturer is four to six hours per week, and in the case of tutorials 10–12 hours per week. The distribution between teaching, administration and research, though decided at the level of the chair, and formally subjected to nationally defined norms, were never enforced.

Data on the social class origin of students is unreliable, as is that on ethnic origin. Until 1989 and the early part of 1990, students' interests were represented via the Komsomol organizations, the youth branch of the Communist party, which also served as a channel of recruitment to the *nomenclatura* (party elite). With their diminishing, smaller organizations were set up and are currently growing. What their impact will be is too early to assess. In the summer of 1990, student strikes had a significant impact on the political life of the country. The erection of a "City of Truth"—a camping site in front of the Presidential office, which stayed in place for more than a month—forced the last communist head of state to step down. Nevertheless, at the time of writing, no clear characteristics of the student movement have crystallized.

5. Conclusion

This article was written at a very difficult time—in the Spring of 1991. After the crucial year of 1990, when most of the Eastern European political systems collapsed, much of what has been written is of historical interest. A number of new measures stand in the offing. By the end of 1991, a new bill on higher education—as too on education in general—will be drafted by the new parliament. And, at the time of writing, it is difficult to foresee what its provisions will be. One thing is clear, however: government interference will be diminished, the possibility of private and company based higher education, on lines comparable with practices found in Western Europe, will be developed in order to ease the integration of Bulgaria into the different settings—political and economic—of Europe.

Such reforms have wide support among today's students and some of the teaching staff, too. But a number of years will have to pass for it to become operational, and this will not make the burden of many members of teaching staff any easier. Yet, nobody doubts that a liberalized economy, and an openness to the outside world will have effects similar to those over a century ago, when the first Bulgarian university was established, and which after 50 years reached international standards.

Bibliography

Arnandov M 1939 *History of Sofia University*. University of Sofia Press, Sofia
Central Statistical Office 1989 *Statistical Yearbook*. Central Statistical Office, Sofia
Kunev S et al. 1989 *Establishments of Higher Learning in Bulgaria*. Sofia Press, Sofia

B. Penkov

Burkina Faso

1. Higher Education and Society

Burkina Faso, the former Upper Volta, is a land-locked country situated in the heart of West Africa and belongs to the group of Sahel nations. It has a surface area of about 274,000 square kilometers and—following the most recent census in 1985—a population of 8.7 million. The population is divided into several ethnic groups, but the Mossi account for half of the population. Population growth is rather high at 2.68 percent. Burkina Faso has a population density of 32 people per square kilometer, but a highly uneven geographical distribution. Migration movements, both intranational, towards the more fertile Volta Basin, and international, especially towards the Ivory Coast, are very important. Between 700,000 and one million Burkinabès are said to live and work abroad.

Burkina Faso is a former French colony which became independent in August 1960. The recent political history of the country has been characterized by a succession of different governments. In 1983 a radical regime came to power, proclaiming a democratic and popular revolution. Under the leadership of the charismatic Afro-Marxist Thomas Sankara and his successor, Blaise Campaoré, attempts were made to break with the past and with international imperialism and to promote rural development.

The majority of the population—about 95 percent—derive their livelihood from subsistence agriculture, especially millet and sorghum, and animal husbandry. Consequently agriculture is the most important source of revenue for Burkina Faso's economy. It is responsible for about 40 percent of the Gross National Product (GNP). Unfortunately, due to drought, desertification and obsolete agricultural techniques, productivity is low and is hardly sufficient to fulfill national food consumption needs. Since the Sahel crisis of the seventies, there have often been food shortages. Wage employment is insignificant at about 1 percent of the active population, and is mainly accounted for by the public and semipublic services sector. The general consequence of all this is that the mean income per capita barely reaches US\$160 per year. Thus Burkina Faso is among the poorest countries of the world.

The education system of Burkino Faso broadly follows the pattern of other French-speaking Sub-Saharan African countries. A six-year primary school, starting at seven and leading to the certificate of elementary education (*certificat d'études primaires*), is followed by four years of lower secondary and three years of higher secondary education, respectively leading to the certificate of lower secondary education (*brevet d'études du premier cycle*) and the *baccalauréat*. After taking the *baccalauréat*, one has the right to follow higher education abroad or at the University of Ouagadougou in the capital.

Burkina Faso's education enrollment (26.8 percent at the primary level, 4 percent at the secondary level and about 1 percent at the tertiary level) is among the lowest of the continent, while the illiteracy rate is 82.5 percent. Therefore, the expansion and improvement of educational services is an absolute priority of the government. Total educational expenditure amounts to almost 25 percent of total government expenditure. Since 1983 public educational expenditure has increased by 8 percent every year. Nowadays, mainly in cooperation with the World Bank, serious efforts are being made to expand the education system by means of a more efficient use and allocation of existing funds, and the allocation of extra money for education.

2. *The Institutional Fabric of Higher Education*

The University of Ouagadougou is the single most important establishment of higher education in Burkina Faso. Founded in 1965 as a rather modest institute of higher education, it obtained university status in 1974. Nowadays, the University of Ouagadougou contains the following faculties and schools: the Institute of Humanities and Social Sciences, the Institute of Language, Literature and Arts, the Law School, the College of Economics, the University Institute of Technology, the Institute of Mathematics and Physics, the Institute of Chemistry, the Institute of Natural Sciences, the Institute of Rural Development, the College of Medical Sciences, and the National Institute of Education.

The first stage of university education takes two years (three for medical studies) and leads to the graduate degree (*diplôme d'études universitaires générales*). For students attending the University Institute of Technology, which prepares them for the management and administration of public and private enterprises, this is at the same time their leaving certificate. A third year of university studies leads to the *licence* or degree; the *maîtrise* or master's is awarded after one or more extra years. The qualification for teaching at the higher secondary or higher education level can be obtained after one further year of pedagogical training at the National Institute of Education.

Other institutes of higher education include the National School of Administration and the Magistrature and the Inter-State School of Rural Engineering. Both are located in the capital. The National School of Administration and the Magistracy provides graduate courses in economics, development planning, administrative law, and so on for civil servants seeking jobs as senior executives in the public office. The Inter-State School for Rural Civil Engineering is a joint initiative of the governments of 13 francophone African states. It offers three-year graduate courses in hydraulics, civil and sanitary engineering, refrigeration technology, and hydrology.

Postsecondary training is provided for in the National School of Public Health (*Ecole Nationale de la Santé Publique*) (nursing), the National School of Sports (*Ecole Nationale des Sports*) (sports administrators), and the National School of Primary School Teachers (*Ecole Nationale des Enseignants du Primaire*) (teachers) but this should not be considered as higher education, because these types of further training can be started after taking the certificate of lower secondary education. One should also note that, in the eyes of the public, the course of training for army officers is considered to be a highly respectable form of higher education.

3. *Governance, Administration, and Finance*

The Higher education policy belongs within the competence of the Ministry of Secondary and Higher Education and Science. The University of Ouagadougou is a public institution, enjoying considerable academic and financial autonomy. The National Center of University Works, responsible for the provision of student services such as medical care, transportation, and food and lodging, has a comparable statute. Both institutions are subsidized by the government. The government also takes care of the salaries of teaching and nonteaching personnel.

In 1985–86 the government's support for the University of Ouagadougou amounted to 275 million francs CFA (US$1 million). About 75 percent of this sum was intended to pay for operational expenditures and the rest for salaries of supplementary administrative and technical personnel, employed by the university. In addition, one should add the salaries of the academic and nonacademic university staff and ad hoc donations in materials, amounting to 657 million francs CFA (US$2.387 million). In the same year, the National Center for University Works received a subvention of 320 million francs CFA (US$1.175 million) and student fellowships added up to 2,928 million francs CFA (US$10.755 million)—a 70 percent share of the total higher education budget. This means that public expenditure for higher education for 5,273 students totaled 4,184 million francs CFA (US$15.368 million) in 1985–86 (Mingat and Jarousse 1987). In contrast, it is worth noting that during the same year government spent 4,940 million francs CFA (US$18.145 million) on primary education which serves 350,000 children. Only 25 percent of the public higher education budget was spent on pedagogical expenditures such as salaries of staff and teaching materials, whereas 75 percent was spent on such items as student scholarships and welfare services. One third of the budget was used to finance studies abroad.

The unit cost of higher education in Burkina Faso amounts to 764,951 francs CFA (US$2,810) per student per year and is 46.3 percent higher than the unit cost of primary education (Ministère de l'Education de Base et de l'Alphabétisation de Masse 1990). In absolute as well as in relative terms, this unit cost is among the highest in the region. The extremely generous public policy over the award and the

Table 1
Evolution of total university enrollment in Burkina Faso

	1967–68	1970–71	1975–76	1981–82	1983–84	1985–86	1986–87	1987–88
University of Ouagadougou	51	193	677	2,568	3,406	4,100	4,405	4,656
Study abroad	348 (87%)	710 (79%)	—	1,399 (35%)	1,405 (29%)	1,173 (22%)	1,203 (21%)	—
Total enrollment	399	903	—	3,967	4,811	5,273	5,608	—

Source: Mingat and Jarousse (1987) and Jarousse and Rapiau (1988)

amount of student scholarships is to be held responsible for this phenomenon. Almost 90 percent of Burkinabè students receive an average scholarship of 478,000 francs CFA (US$1,755) per year (8.6 times the per capita GNP). Criteria for awarding studentships are almost nonexistent and contribute considerably to the mechanical growth of the student population. As the number of secondary school leavers grows (8 percent per year during the last decade) so does the volume of studentships. The award of studentships for higher education ignores criteria such as school performance, economic need, or labor market requirements. The only restrictive element is a rather generous age limit. For holders of the *baccalauréat* it is sufficient to be under 23 before matriculating at the University. Criteria for admission to certain high status faculties such as science, maths and physics and medicine, however, are very strict. Judging from their school career, the type of *baccalauréat*, and student preferences, the National University Scholarship Commission decides autonomously on the field of study of individual students. Only the most capable and best prepared are allowed into the Institute of Mathematics and Physics, the Institute of Chemistry, the Institute of Natural Sciences or the College of Medical Sciences.

4. *Faculty and Students: Teaching, Learning, and Research*

The number of academic staff has increased considerably since the University of Ouagadougou was founded. In 1975 the teaching staff hardly exceeded 50 persons. In 1980 the total teaching staff amounted to 143; by 1986 staff amounted to 256 persons. About one third of the actual academic staff is foreign.

Over the past two decades impressive gains have been achieved with regard to access to higher education in Burkina Faso (see Table 1).

Figures on higher education enrollment growth between 1970 and 1980 reveal an average growth rate of 23.1 percent (Salifou, 1983). Between 1980 and 1986 the annual enrollment growth at the University of Ouagadougou was 18 percent. Recently, enrollment growth rates have dropped to about 10 percent per year (Jarousse and Rapiau 1988). Over time, the proportion of students studying abroad has fallen from 79 percent in 1970 to 35 percent in 1981 and 21 percent in 1986. Nowadays scholarships for study abroad are only given for fields of study which are not available in Burkina Faso such as engineering, technology, and veterinary surgery.

As in most other francophone African countries, university enrollment in Burkina Faso is marked by a high concentration of students in the humanities and social sciences (66 percent in 1986–87). It is simplistic to attribute this literary bias exclusively to inappropriate student preferences. It is at least partly

a consequence of the rigid admission policies of the National University Scholarship Commission.

Wastage is considered another problem typical of francophone African universities. Overall promotion rates at the University of Ouagadougou are estimated at between 50 and 60 percent. This figure, however, conceals considerable differences between promotion rates in the humanities and social sciences (almost 80 percent), and maths and natural sciences (barely 20 percent) (Jarousse and Rapiau 1988).

Burkinabè authorities have stressed more than once the necessary development of a national scientific research capacity, especially in the fields of agriculture, linguistics, rural development, hydrology, modern technology, and education. At university level, interesting research activities, especially in the social sciences and the humanities, take place in research centers, attached to different schools and institutes. In addition, important research programs are developed at the National Center for Science and Technology in Ouagadougou and at the West African Center for Economic and Social Research in Bobo-Dioulasso.

5. *Conclusion*

Paradoxically, Burkina Faso's system of higher education is at once overdeveloped and underdeveloped. Actual problems facing the development of higher education in Burkina Faso include the high unit cost and the pressing need to adapt higher education to national realities. The higher education system of Burkina Faso seems to be oversized in relation to budgetary perspectives and the needs and the financial possibilities of the economy. Although the University of Ouagadougou produces only 700 or 800 graduates per year, the problem of unemployment of highly educated personnel has emerged. Following recent data of the National Employment Office, university graduates make up 11 percent of the unemployed under 30 years of age. As anticipated, the problem is most threatening in law, economics, and the humanities (Adams, Bah-Lalya and Mukweso 1991). This situation is the more precarious as the estimated growth in university output will substantially surpass the expected demand for personnel at graduate level.

The disproportionately high unit cost is another element in the overdevelopment of higher education in Burkina Faso. High unit costs can be explained by the particularly generous scholarship policy, manifesting itself at the same time in the relatively high number of beneficiaries and the considerable amount of money awarded to each scholarship-holder. Recent government measures limiting access to university education to a maximum of 1,000 students per year until 1992, and a maximum 750 after that, and proposing new criteria for student scholarship awards, are hardly surprising.

Without questioning the plausibility and the reasonableness of these policy measures, one should not forget that the higher education system of Burkina Faso, in another sense, is still clearly underdeveloped. The tertiary level enrollment rate of about 1 percent is among the lowest of the continent and one can reasonably ask if national development can be realized without a certain number of highly skilled university graduates (Adams, Bah-Lalya and Mukweso, 1991).

Bibliography

Adams M N, Bah-Lalya I, Mukweso M 1991 Francophone West Africa. In: Altbach P G (ed.) *International Higher Education.* Garland, New York, pp. 349–74
Jarousse J P, Rapiau M T 1988 *Coûts, production et difficultés de l'enseignement supérieur au Burkina Faso.* The World Bank, Washington, DC
Mingat A, Jarousse J P 1987 *Coûts, financement et politique de l'éducation au Burkina Faso.* The World Bank, Washington, DC
Ministère de l'Education de Base et de l'Alphabétisation de Masse. 1990 *Education de base pour tous au Burkina Faso (situation et perspectives).* Ministère de l'Education de Base et de l'Alphabétisation de Masse, Ouagadougou
Salifou A 1983 *Perspectives du développement de l'enseignement supérieur en Afrique dans les prochaines décennies.* UNESCO, Paris
Sanou F 1988 Politiques éducatives du Burkina Faso. *Annales Serie A: Sciences humaines et sociales* 1: 9–64
Wetta C 1989 Marché et mobilité de l'emploi au Burkina Faso. *CEDRES-études. Revue économique et social burkinabé* 27: 1–34

K. Potemans

Burundi

1. Higher Education and Society

Burundi is situated between Rwanda and Zaire in Central Africa. It has a surface area of 27,834 square kilometers and a population of some 5,000,000, divided into several ethnic groups, the principal ones being the Tutsis and the Hutus. After having been administered by Belgium since the First World War, it became a republic in 1966. A military régime was installed after a coup in 1976 by Colonel Bagaza, a Tutsi. He was overthrown by Major Buyoya, also a Tutsi. Struggles between the two major ethnic groups continue to cause tension in the country's affairs.

Essentially agricultural, Burundi's economy depends very much on food production. Estimates suggest that 50 percent of the population are illiterate (UNESCO 1990). This is why education is considered a major priority by the government. Economic fluctuations affect the development of higher education as well as other aspects of society. Institutions of higher education are being encouraged to take part in the country's economic development by laying emphasis on practically oriented training. Twenty-two percent of the educational budget is devoted to higher education, whose main purposes are to train national cadres in the university faculties and institutions of higher education and to promote research.

2. The Institutional Fabric of the Higher Education System

The main institution of higher education is the University of Burundi (*Université du Burundi*), founded in 1960. It incorporated the *Institut agronomique du Ruanda-Urundi*, previously the Faculty of Agriculture of the *Université officielle du Congo belge et du Ruanda-Urundi*, founded in 1958, and the *Centre universitaire Rumuri*, founded in 1960. The University comprises faculties of letters and human sciences, law, economics and administration, science, psychology and education, agriculture, and medicine, and institutes of education, physical education, and technology. An Institute of Applied Science was created in 1982. New courses have been introduced in rural economics, pharmacy, geology, and Kirundi (the national language). New facilities have been built at the Faculty of Agriculture. Moreover, the number of research centers to support teaching within the faculties is increasing.

Other institutions of higher education include the *Ecole supérieure de Commerce*, founded in 1981, the *Ecole de Journalisme*, founded in 1981, the *Institut supérieur d'Agriculture*, founded in 1983, the *Institut supérieur des Techniques de l'Aménagement et de l'Urbanisme*, founded in 1983, and the *Institut supérieur de Gestion des Entreprises*.

The *Ecole supérieure de Commerce* trains administrators and managers who will work in public and private administration. The *Institut supérieur d'Agriculture* trains specialized engineers in the zootechnology of tropical regions and in disciplines considered useful for the development of agriculture and animal husbandry.

The *Ecole de Journalisme* trains personnel for the various departments of the Ministry of Information and other services that require communications specialists, the *Institut supérieur des Techniques de l'Aménagement et de l'Urbanisme* trains town and regional planners, and the *Institut supérieur de Gestion des Entreprises* trains business managers for both the private and the public sectors.

Higher education is open to students who have passed the *certificat d'humanités complètes*, a school-leaving certificate awarded after six years of primary and seven years of secondary education. In some faculties, they must also sit a competitive entrance examination (e.g., engineering, medicine). Selection for entrance to the University is carried out by a commission that sits in July. It takes into account the places available and national requirements.

Qualifications awarded in higher education tend to follow the Belgian model. Studies at the University of Burundi lead to a *licence* in law, history, geography, African language and literature, French language and literature, English language and literature, administration and management, political economics, rural economics, educational sciences, or physical education after four years' study or to a diploma in engineering after five years. The Faculty of Science confers a *licence* in biology, chemistry, earth sciences, physics, or mathematics after four or five years' study. The Faculty of Medicine awards a *diplôme de docteur en médecine générale humaine* after six years. It is the only doctorate conferred in the country. All these courses include a first cycle of two years leading to the *candidature*, which parallels Belgian practice.

The Institute of Education delivers the *diplôme universitaire d'études pédagogiques* after two years and the Institute of Technology awards a *diplôme d'ingénieur technicien* after three years.

The *Ecole supérieure de Commerce* offers two-year courses in commerce, accountancy, customs, statistics, management of health institutions, secretarial studies, and library studies. The diploma it awards is academically equivalent to the *candidature* delivered by the University.

The *Institut supérieur d'Agriculture* offers four-year courses. The first year is common to all courses and the other three years are divided into four sections: agricultural zootechnology, rural engineering, forestry, and agricultural and nutrition technology. The *diplôme d'ingénieur technicien* it delivers is academically equivalent to the *licence*.

The *Institut supérieur des Techniques de l'Aménagement et de l'Urbanisme* provides four-year courses in urbanism and town planning, architecture and construction, and roads and communications, leading to a *diplôme d'ingénieur technicien* that is academically equivalent to the *licence*.

The *Ecole de Journalisme* offers two types of courses: the printed press and radio and television. They both last two years. The diploma awarded is academically equivalent to the *candidature* conferred by the University.

The *Institut supérieur de Gestion des Entreprises* offers long specialization courses for high-level personnel and short courses for middle-level personnel in the same fields. Candidates must have a higher education qualification in economics and one year's professional experience to enter the long course. They must be sponsored by their employer. Priority is given to national personnel. Studies lead to a *diplôme de spécialité* and a *certificat de réussite* respectively.

The number of students at the University of Burundi has increased considerably. In 1963, there were 104 students, in 1969–70 300, in 1975–76 648, in 1981–82 1,901, and in 1987–88 almost 3,000 students were enrolled. Some 500 students are enrolled in the other institutions of higher education.

3. Governance, Administration, and Finance

Most institutions of higher education fall under the jurisdiction of the Ministry of Higher Education and Research (*Ministère de l'Enseignement supérieur et de la Recherche*), although certain specialized institutes have been created by other ministries according to national needs, such as the *Ecole de Journalisme* and the *Institut supérieur d'Agriculture*.

The University of Burundi is an autonomous institution, under the jurisdiction of the Ministry of Higher Education and Research. It is directed by an administrative council, a rector and a vice-rector, all nominated by the president of the Republic. The administrative council is appointed for a renewable term of four years, the rector for four years and the vice-rector for three years. The University has a directorate of academic affairs and a directorate of research, as well as a unit for interuniversity cooperation. Academic and social services were separated in 1984 when the *Régie des Oeuvres Universitaires* was created to deal with the social and cultural problems of the students. The University receives an annual grant from the Ministry of Higher Education which is topped up by external funds from bilateral and international cooperation agreements and student fees.

The *Ecole supérieure de Commerce* is headed by a director and an assistant director who are both nominated by the president of the Republic on the recommendation of the Minister of Education. It is an autonomous institution responsible to the Ministry of Higher Education.

The *Ecole de Journalisme* is responsible to the Ministry of Information. It is headed by a director who is appointed by presidential decree, and is assisted by a council of professors.

The *Institut supérieur d'Agriculture* is responsible to the Ministry of Agriculture. It is headed by a director and two assistant directors, one for administrative affairs, the other for academic affairs. It receives an annual grant from the Ministry and financial contributions from cooperation agreements and student fees.

The *Institut supérieur des Techniques de l'Aménagement et de l'Urbanisme* is responsible to the Ministry of Public Works and Urban Development (*Ministère des Travaux Publics et du Développement urbain*). It is headed by an administrative council and a council of professors who assist the director. The institution receives an annual grant from the Ministry, which is topped up by financial contributions from other countries and student fees for traineeships.

4.1 Faculty and Students: Teaching, Learning, and Research

Academic staff is divided into *assistants, maîtres-assistants, chargés d'enseignement, chargés de cours, chefs de clinique, adjoints, professeurs associés, professeurs,* and *professeurs ordinaires.* In addition to their teaching duties, they also carry out research.

Higher education teachers are recruited from among holders of the *licence* and engineers who have distinguished themselves during their university studies. Since no doctorate level education is offered in Burundi, they are also recruited from among holders of doctorates and engineers who have been trained in universities abroad. The *assistants* are often sent abroad to complete their studies and receive grants for this purpose.

The academic staff at the University of Burundi has developed considerably. In 1963–64, there was a total academic staff of 28, in 1969–70 there were 60, in 1975–76 they numbered 133, and in 1981–82 there were 277. However, their number had dropped to 217 in 1986–87.

Students usually begin their higher education studies at the age of 20. They are awarded a monthly grant that enables them to pay the registration fees and covers their living costs. It must be remembered that more than 80 percent of school-age children remained outside the educational system in the 1980s.

5. Conclusion

The main problems facing higher education in Burundi are costs, the lack of properly trained teachers, and adapting academic programs to the needs of the country. These problems are heightened by the fact that all the institutions of higher education depend on public funds. Moves are being made by the government to get the support of the private sector, which at present is more active in the fields of nonformal education and literacy development at the secondary level.

International cooperation has played a major part in the development of higher education. Through Associations of Universities to which the University of Burundi belongs, academic staff have been sent for short periods to teach at the University. International organizations have provided grants for students to study abroad and have provided equipment for the institutions of higher education.

There are plans to reorganize the faculties and create new courses to meet national needs, to organize teacher training more efficiently to avoid having to send future teachers abroad to complete their training, to introduce graduate education, and to develop higher education in such a way as to obtain better academic results. The government is also planning to place all the institutions of higher education under the responsibility of a single ministry in an attempt to pool resources. A government study is being carried out to examine the feasibility of integrating the *Institut supérieur de Gestion des Entreprises* into the Faculty of Economics and Administration of the University.

Burundi is greatly concerned with improving the educational level of its citizens, as can be seen from recent developments and the aid it offers to its students. Great efforts have been made to increase secondary school leavers' chances of having access to higher education by multiplying the number of institutions over the 1980s. Training is very much centered on the economic needs of the country. Fields such as communications, town planning, and agriculture have been developed.

Although the total number of students and teachers in the institutions of higher education may appear relatively small in comparison to other countries, it must be remembered that Burundi is a small country with only one university. Its student numbers have increased considerably and every effort is being made to improve opportunities to study.

Bibliography

Burundi 1988a Ministère de l'Education nationale. *Développement de l'éducation, 1986–88: Rapport national du Burundi.* International Conference on Education, 41st session, Geneva, 1989. Ministère de l'Education nationale, Bujumbura

Burundi 1988b Ministère de l'Education nationale. *Questionnaire du Bureau International de l'Education sur l'éducation post-secondaire et sa diversification face à la situation de l'emploi.* International Conference on Education, 41st session, Geneva, 1989. Reply to questionnnaire ED/BIE/CONFINTED/41/Q/87. Ministère de l'Education nationale, Bujumbura

UNESCO 1990 *News Bulletin*, July 1990. UNESCO, Paris

Université du Burundi 1985 *Le Règlement général: Textes fondamentaux.* Université du Burundi, Service des Presses et Publications, Bujumbura

C. Keyes

C

Cameroon

1. Higher Education and Society

The structure of the education system of the Federal Republic of the Cameroon has certain unique features which arise from its occupation, prior to Independence and reunification in 1961, by two colonial powers, Britain and France. The western parts of the country display school structures and examination forms at secondary level which are based on English models. The other regions were heavily influenced by French practice. Cameroon is officially a bilingual state with both French and English as the official languages.

Cameroon has a surface area of some 183,567 square miles (475,000 square kilometers). It is bounded in the west by Nigeria and by the Gulf of Guinea, in the north by Chad, in the east by the Central African Republic, and with the Republics of the Congo and Gabon on its southern frontiers. With a population of approximately 10.8 million in 1989, Cameroon is climatically varied ranging from the Sahel semidesert region to the north through to the African rainforest in the south. The country is divided by a mountain range, some of whose peaks are still volcanic, which cuts off the northwest from the rest of the country. With a crude birthrate of 42.5 per thousand and a relatively low life expectancy of some 44 years, more than half the population (54.7%) is under the age of 19. Just over four out of ten live in urban areas (42.4%) and the Gross National Product (GNP) per capita is US$1,059.

There are five major ethnic groups, the largest of which is the Cameroon Montagnards which account for 31 percent of the population, the Equatorial Bantu (19%), the Kirdi (11%), the Fulani (10%), and the Northwest Bantu which, combined with other residual groups, represent some 29 percent of the population. The religious composition is rather more eclectic with Christians making up around one third; Moslems approximately one sixth. More than half the country subscribes to indigenous beliefs.

The economy of Cameroon is overwhelmingly agricultural, though there are significant natural resources such as bauxite, iron ore, and oil. However, only the first has given rise to a substantial industry. Yet, with GNP growing at an estimated 5.5 percent per annum, the development of a textile industry, a chemical industry, and the generation of hydroelectric power may form the base from which future expansion grows. The major exports are crude oil, cocoa, coffee, wood, and aluminum. The occupational structure comprises some 24 percent of the workforce in agriculture, 31 percent in industry, with approximately 45 percent employed in the services sector.

The Federal Republic came into being in 1961. Independence from France was achieved in 1960 and after a referendum held the following year in those regions which fell under British mandate, the southern portion of the ex-British Cameroons voted for unification. The northern parts opted to join with Nigeria. The political regime is that of a one-party republic, built around Cameroon People's Democratic movement. For the 22 years following Independence, the nation's president was Ahmadou Ahidjo. He was succeeded in 1982 by Paul Biya.

2. The Institutional Fabric of the Higher Education System

In purely nominal terms, "higher education" in the Cameroon first took shape in 1921 with the creation of the curiously named "higher" primary school at Yaoundé, subsequently extended to Douala, Dschang, and Ebolowa. Though clearly such establishments had little to do with higher education in the strict sense, such a situation nevertheless allowed the French authorities to argue before the League of Nations that the way for establishing a genuine higher education system was thereby opened in principle (*Rapports annuels* 1925 p. 3). The gradual development from bottom up of public *lycées* alongside missionary schools, both Protestant and Catholic on the one hand, and the policy of sending school graduates to study abroad in metropolitan France on the other, acted as a further stimulus to the demand among Camerounais for higher education to be provided. Such demands became particularly acute in the immediate postwar period and during the period leading up to Independence.

During the decade following Independence, the Cameroon higher education system grew to 11 establishments, a rate of growth driven forward by the need to meet the needs of the country's economic, political, and social development. (*Topic* 1987 p. 7). Two fundamental features characterized the higher education policy of Cameroon during this period: its accelerating rhythm and its emphasis on diversification. Higher education system developed in two phases.

The first phase which lasted from 1961–62, saw the

foundation of the Higher Teacher Training College (*Ecole Normale Supérieure*) and what was later to become the University of Yaoundé, then known as the *Fondation Française*. Three faculties were established in science, law and economics, and humanities. The policy of diversification was also pursued in parallel with the setting up of four university centers of Buéa (humanities), Douala (economics), Dshang (agronomy), and with sciences at the center in Ngaoundéré.

The second phase took place between 1969 and 1972 and involved the setting up of specialized establishments which are held by the authorities to be *grandes écoles*. *Grandes écoles*, a specifically French variant of higher education establishment, are not only selective in their admissions policy, they tend to be oriented toward the development of specific sectoral skills either in public administration or in the private sector of the economy. Thus, in 1969, the University Center for Health Sciences was founded and the following year, the Higher Institute for Information Sciences and Journalism, later known as the Higher Institute for Information Sciences and Technology (*Ecole Supérieure des Sciences et Techniques de l'Information*). The National Higher Technological Institute (*Ecole Nationale Supérieure de Technologie*) and the Institute for International Relations were founded in 1971, and a year later the Institute for Demographic Studies and Research.

In addition there is a diverse nonuniversity sector which includes among others, the Civil Service Staff College (*Ecole Nationale d'Administration et de la Magistrature*) which also trains legal administrators, and the National Institute of Youth and Sport.

Access to the university reflects the dual origin of Cameroon's education system. It is open to holders of the *Baccalauréat* which is sat after 13 years of primary and secondary education, or to holders of the General Certificate of Education Advanced level which is awarded after 14 years of primary and secondary schooling. The former qualification is French in origin and the latter its English counterpart, current in the northwestern parts of the country. Following the French model, access to the "higher schools"— *grandes écoles* or *écoles supérieures* — is competitive and is based on sitting a special entrance examination which is open to those who already hold one of the two school leaving certificates mentioned above. Special entry conditions attach to the Civil Service Staff College. An additional condition of eligibility to sit the competitive examination is extended to holders of the West African School Certificate, the *Brevet Elémentaire* or the *Brevet d'Etudes* who have four years seniority in the civil service.

The structure of university qualifications bears a certain similarity to the French model prior to 1968 and is divided into three distinct levels. The first cycle lasts three years and, in law and economics, the humanities and in the sciences, leads to the award of the *Licence*. Completion of second cycle studies lasts a further year and, after the submission of a dissertation, results in the award of the *Maîtrise*. Third cycle studies require a minimum of three further years before sitting for the "short cycle doctorate" (*Doctorat Troisième Cycle*) or a minimum of five years before submitting for the State Doctorate (*Doctorat d'Etat*).

Specialist qualifications are delivered by the corresponding specialist institutes. Thus, the International Relations Institute awards a *Maîtrise* two years after the *Licence* and the *Doctorat Troisième Cycle* after a further two years study beyond the *Maîtrise*. The University Center for Health Sciences offers training at three levels: first, for the diploma of medical doctor, which is a six-year course; second, a three-year course leading to the health technicians' diploma; and third, a two-year program leading to the higher diploma in nursing studies.

Teacher education, which takes place in teacher training colleges, organizationally separate from the university, also has its distinctive qualifications—the *Certificat d'Aptitude de Maître d'Enseignement* for primary school teachers and the various diplomas for teaching at the lower or upper secondary level, whether general academic education or for technical schools. Teachers for upper secondary schools take a five-year course in the Ecole Normale Supérieure which leads to the *Diplôme de Professeur des Lycées d'Enseignement Général*.

The diplomas awarded in higher education are state awards.

3. Governance, Administration, and Finance

The University of Yaoundé comes under the responsibility of the Ministry of Higher Education, Computer Sciences, and Scientific Research. As a highly centralized system based on one major university, and with the whole of the financing coming from public funds, control exercised by the Ministry follows the usual combination of financial oversight and the use of legal steering through decrees and ministerial circulars. Since, formally speaking, the degrees awarded by the university are state degrees, the state has formal responsibility for ensuring their quality and thus, at least formally, has the power to exercise an evaluatory function. The national goals attributed to higher education are the classic triptych of economic development through the supply of a qualified labor force, the reinforcement of national identity and the modernization of both social and administrative structures. Such objectives are set out nationally in successive five-year plans. Yet modernization does not demand the simple importing of legal frameworks, political institutions and economic patterns found in the major industrialized countries (Davidson 1979 p. 225). They require the appropriate adaptation to the society in which they are set.

The University is headed by a chancellor who is nominated by the government and who in turn is chair of the Administrative Council of the University. The academic organization of the University follows the usual departmental structure grouped by cognate areas in faculties. A slightly different pattern is to be found in the various nonuniversity establishments whose administrative structure is based on departments or sections.

4. Faculty and Students: Teaching, Learning, and Research

The need to develop a body of university teachers and researchers drawn from Cameroons itself was one of the major priorities following Independence, hence the emphasis placed from the first upon founding an advanced teacher training establishment (*Ecole Normale Supérieure*) at the same time as the University. If faculty were at first constituted by considerable numbers of non-Camerouni nationals, this situation has since been remedied. However, difficulties still remain in integrating the skills, techniques, and approaches often developed by study abroad, with the needs and materials that local conditions require. Teaching staff are civil servants and are paid directly by the Ministry of Higher Education and Research. Appointments, as well as promotions, are subject to oversight by central administration.

About half the students in the University receive scholarships. Yet the lack of appropriate financial support is one of the major reasons for students dropping out. In some of the nonuniversity establishments, particularly those associated with future government service, all students receive a stipend. This means, however, that the number of places available are tied to the number of bursaries.

Bibliography

Davidson B 1979 *L'Afrique au XXè siècle*. Jeune Afrique, Paris

Joseph R 1986 *Le Mouvement nationaliste au Cameroun*. Karthala, Paris

Kange E 1985 *Sémence et moisson coloniales*. Centre de Litterature Evangelique, Yaoundé

Kange E 1988 Etude critique des tendances observées dans les universités et instituts de recherche de l'Afrique centrale. *Actes du colloque de Dakar, mai 1987*. UNESCO, Paris

Rapports annuels a la Commission des Mandats de la SND. Commission des Mandats, Yaoundé

Sengat Kuo F 1950 A propos de l'éducation de base au Cameroun. *Présence Africaine* 7: 74–84

Topic 1987 164:7

E. Kange

Canada

1. Higher Education and Society

To understand higher education in Canada one must first understand the country itself, a strange hybrid nation, often baffling to foreigners. It is an affluent country, peaceful, democratic, conservative, fairly generous and caring. To foreigners it appears to be administratively untidy, unorganized, and unfocused, tolerating wasteful duplication of effort with overlapping jurisdictions and responsibilities, and having little unified sense of purpose or consciousness of national identity. Most Canadians see this decentralization and individualization as strength, not weakness. Without them, a country of such disparate parts and diverse origins would probably not have survived as a nation.

Canada is a federation of ten provinces and two territories. Like many later developments, the impetus to found the country was, in part, a reaction to external events. After the American Civil War, it was felt in 1867 that a confederation of the five small British colonies to the north would both strengthen them and provide for self-government, while heading off any move toward republicanism. As settlement moved westward, Canada expanded to its present size (Fig. 1).

The original colonies had been settled by France and Britain, so the new country had two founding cultures and legal and administrative traditions, two official languages, and representatives of many Christian faiths. Since its inception, Canada has grown due to immigration as well as to fertility; it is now a mosaic of most of the world's ethnic and social groupings.

Canada is an immense country, in geographic size comparable to the Soviet Union or China. Its population of about 26 million is unevenly distributed, being densest in the southern cities and towns within a hundred miles of the United States border. The physical geography and climate meant that there was evident from the outset, in all aspects of Canadian life, an intense and independent localism. In universities this takes the form of a determined defense of institutional autonomy. Only in a very loose sense can one speak of even provincial "systems" of higher education, let alone a national system. Canada has 10 such systems. Thus, although the terms "higher education system" and "university system" are commonly used in this article and are in current vogue, they are not to be taken as precise. Despite repeated calls for greater centralization since the mid-1960s (OECD 1976, Sheffield et al. 1982), this national nonsystem remains essentially unchanged.

In this article, the term "higher education" is used in the broad sense to cover all formal education beyond schooling, synonymous with the terms "tertiary level" and "postsecondary" education.

Figure 1
Administrative regions of Canada

1.1 Historical Background

The earliest institutions of higher education in Canada were denominational, founded exclusively by, and for, the adherents of particular religious sects, whether by papal charter or crown charter. At the time of confederation they were small, numerous, and widely dispersed (18 for 3.5 million people). All but three—Dalhousie in Halifax, McGill in Montreal, and the University of Toronto—had religious affiliations (Harris 1976). As the west was settled, each province created a university and, unlike eastern and central Canada, concentrated its resources in one nondenominational public institution after the manner of the land-grant universities of the American midwest. This policy continued until the great expansion following the Second World War.

The denominational character of the older universities changed in the 1950s and 1960s as the costs of higher education grew and the importance of provincial grants increased. Public funds were not available to religiously exclusive institutions. In response they either became wholly secular or separated from those parts of their organizations which were devoted to theology and the training of clergy, so that they would be eligible for public funding.

If there has been one constant policy preoccupation for Canadian higher education since the 1950s, it has been with "access". Facilitating access to institutions and programs has been the main means of improving equality of educational opportunity.

The number and capacity of universities, and then the number and capacity of nondegree-granting institutes and colleges were increased to ensure that "every qualified applicant who wished to attend could be admitted." In one form or another that phrase was used by the educational representatives of provincial governments and the federal government as, from the end of the 1950s to the mid-1970s, they provided funds for the expanding systems (Watson 1973).

It is not unrealistic to argue that the social policy goal of greater equity was one of the paramount motives for the expansion of higher education. Governments were experiencing an unusual set of circumstances. Canada, in common with other western nations, had experienced the postwar baby boom. By 1951 the first large cohorts from the boom were entering the school systems, and increases continued each year until 1971–2. In the 1950s and early 1960s the secondary schools had been transformed from academic to comprehensive institutions, and participation beyond the compulsory years of schooling (which ended when the child reached 16) had soared. Fortunately, apart from a short recession, these were decades of high economic growth. The economic boom brought about an immigration boom, which in the 1960s averaged 142,890 net per year. The migrants' children further swelled the school population.

By the mid-1960s the increased flow of pupils had reached the secondary education/higher education transfer point. It would have been unwise politically,

Table 1
Population in Canada by province (in thousands)

	1941	1946	1951	1956	1961	1966	1971	1976	1981	1986	1989
Newfoundland	0.0	0.0	361.4	415.1	457.9	493.4	522.1	557.7	567.7	568.3	569.2
Prince Edward Island	95.0	94.0	98.4	99.3	104.6	108.5	111.6	118.2	122.5	126.6	130.0
Nova Scotia	578.0	608.0	642.6	694.7	737.0	756.0	769.0	828.6	842.4	873.2	885.7
New Brunswick	457.4	478.0	515.7	554.6	597.9	616.8	634.8	677.3	696.4	708.4	717.6
Quebec	3,331.9	3,629.0	4,055.7	4,628.4	5,259.2	5,780.8	6,027.8	6,234.5	6,438.4	6,532.4	6,679.0
Ontario	3,787.7	4,093.0	4,597.6	5,405.9	6,236.1	6,960.9	7,703.1	8,264.5	8,625.1	9,101.7	9,546.2
Manitoba	729.7	726.9	776.5	850.0	921.7	963.1	988.2	1,021.5	1,026.2	1,063.0	1,083.3
Saskatchewan	896.0	832.7	831.7	880.7	925.2	955.4	926.2	921.3	968.3	1,009.6	1,007.1
Alberta	796.2	803.4	939.5	1,123.1	1,332.0	1,463.2	1,627.9	1,832.0	2,237.7	2,365.8	2,423.2
British Columbia	817.8	1,003.0	1,163.2	1,398.5	1,629.1	1,873.7	2,184.6	2,466.6	2,744.4	2,883.4	3,044.2
Yukon	5.0	8.0	9.1	12.2	14.6	14.4	18.4	21.8	21.8	23.5	25.7
Northwest Territories	12.0	16.0	16.0	19.3	23.0	28.7	38.8	42.6	42.6	52.2	53.1
Total	11,506.7	12,292.0	14,009.4	16,081.8	18,238.3	20,014.9	21,552.5	22,992.6	24,338.5	25,308.1	26,164.3

Source: Statistics Canada Catalogue No. 91–201 June 1982, 93–901 (Vol. 1) 1981, 92–101 1986

seeing the United States example of mass higher education, to try to dam the student flow.

1.2 Population and Demographic Factors

The population of Canada, which in 1941 had been 11,506,700, had grown to 16,080,000 by 1956; to 19,644,000 by 1965; to 22,696,000 by 1973; and to 25,309,331 by 1986 (Statistics Canada 1973, p. 93, 1986, p. 241).

The population of the provinces in 1986 varied from 126,646 (Prince Edward Island) to 9,101,694 (Ontario) (see Table 1). By 1986 the population of Ontario had grown to about two and a half times its 1941 size, while that of Prince Edward Island had increased by only about one third.

The demographic turning point occurred in the early 1970s. Fertility dropped sharply and the number of school entrants began to decrease. By the late 1970s enrollment was declining everywhere, immigration had dropped to an annual average of 108,800 (1977–79) and planners were advising governments and institutions of higher education to expect a continuing decline in enrollments throughout the 1980s.

As the value of the per capita grant began to falter in the late 1970s and the grant continued to be set below annual inflation rates throughout the 1980s, institutions used vigorous marketing tactics to increase the number of both full-time and part-time students.

1.3 Economic Factors

Canada is rich in primary resources, a great agricultural producer, and highly industrialized, with a considerable manufacturing sector and the transportation and communications infrastructure of a modern state. The most noticeable change since the Second World War has been to the labor force, with the growth of the service sector, partly due to the development of "big government" (i.e., government providing support programs in health, housing, welfare, and comparable social services). This is high-technology economy with a growing service sector requires a work force and managerial cadres which are highly educated technically and professionally, persons whose lifelong education and reeducation needs will be met, to a large extent, by recurring study in universities and colleges. In the 1970s and 1980s this led to a growth in part-time enrollment and a rise in student age.

A labor force with high levels of female participation, coupled with women's demand for gender equality of opportunity in the workplace, has created a demand for study to obtain qualifications. There has been considerable feminization of the student body. In 1945 20.8 percent of the full-time undergraduate university enrollment was female, in 1986 the figure was 48.9 percent (Statistics Canada 1978 p. 208, 1986 pp. 96–97).

2. The Institutional Fabric of the Higher Educational System

2.1 Sectoral Organization of Higher Education

Structurally, the 10 provincial higher education systems of Canada differ considerably from each other, but all are binary in character in that they have both a degree-granting sector and a nondegree-granting sector. In 1987–88 there were 67 universities in Canada and 199 nondegree-granting institutions.

The traditional terms "university," "college," and "institute" are misleading in that they cover considerable variation. A small university may offer only undergraduate programs in arts and sciences; a very large one provides a vast array of baccalaureate, master's, and doctoral programs, with faculties covering all the professional schools, specialized research institutes, centers for interdisciplinary studies, and federated colleges.

A "college" may refer to an undergraduate institution affiliated to a university, or a special-purpose institution like a teachers' college, college of art, or community college. Even the common use of the adjective "community" does not accurately reflect the nature of the latter institution. In the provinces of Alberta and British Columbia until about 1970, the community college was a junior college modeled on the United States pattern, providing vocational studies and transfer programs consisting of the first two years of certain four-year undergraduate programs. Although the purpose of these colleges has been broadened, the provision of the transfer opportunity remains their main mission. Community college programs in other anglophone provinces (i.e., all but Quebec) are not designed for transfer to universities. Quebec's *Collèges d'Enseignement Général et Professionnel* (CEGEPs) are different again. In Quebec the articulation between school, college, and university is close. This province has an 11-grade schooling system (compared with 12 or 13 in the anglophone provinces), after which the student who wishes to undertake any type of higher education enters the CEGEP. This institution offers two-year preuniversity programs in the humanities, social sciences, and physical sciences. It also provides three-year vocational programs leading to employment.

The general structure of education in Canada from nursery school to postdoctoral studies is shown in Fig. 2.

2.2 Levels of Institution and Structure of Qualifications

Since the Second World War, diploma level work below the baccalaureate has virtually disappeared from the anglophone universities, although they still confer some graduate professional diplomas. The universities award bachelor's, master's, and doctoral degrees. The colleges and institutes award diplomas and certificates, and for many of the graduates of

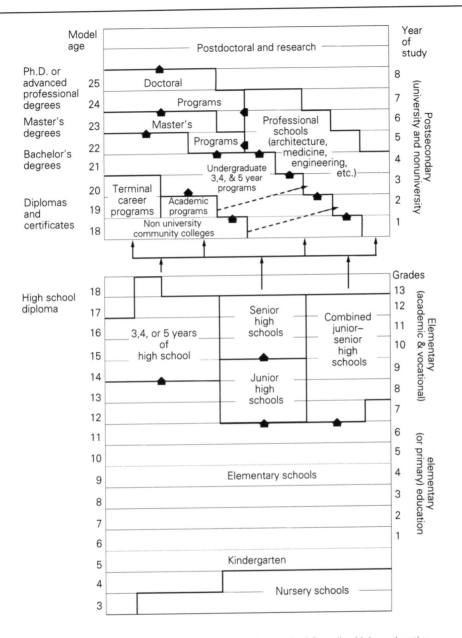

Source: *From the Sixties to the Eighties: A portrait of Canadian higher education*
Education, Science and Culture Division, Secretary of State, Feb. 1979, p.4

Figure 2
General structure of education in Canada

their vocational programs there are, in addition, provincial licensing or credentialing examinations.

The common duration of the undergraduate university program in Canada is four years; there are some five-year programs (e.g., architecture); and in Ontario, following on from the fact that students spend longer at the secondary school, there are three-year general and four-year specialized baccalaureate programs. Master's programs take one or two years to complete, and doctoral programs another four to five, at least two of which must be spent in full-time study on campus.

An academic year's full undergraduate load usually consists of five full courses (or equivalent) extending over two terms. The academic year in Canada is short, lasting from mid-September to mid-April with short breaks at Christmas and mid-winter. Most students work the four months of late spring and summer to earn part of their expenses for the following year.

Many professional faculties (e.g. medicine, library science, management studies) recruit only from applicants holding a first degree in prerequisite subjects. Students are admitted directly from secondary school graduation into bachelor of commerce, social work, forestry, engineering, agriculture, and veterinary science programs. After two years of undergraduate study students may be admitted into faculties of law and dentistry. Teacher education has gradually been transferred from colleges to faculties of education in universities. Both the concurrent and end-on (degree then professional) programs take some four to six years of full-time study.

The common community college program in Canada (excluding Quebec) is a two-year diploma course; however, some take three years. There are also one-year certificate courses.

Following the Second World War, several Canadian provinces created institutes of technology in the tradition of those seen in the United Kingdom. Subsequently there developed a few polytechnical institutes whose vocationally oriented programming spanned both diploma courses and first degree courses. The "poly" has been slow to develop in North America, however. As the college systems were set up in the mid-1960s to the mid-1970s, many technical institutions were absorbed into the new systems to complement programs in business, allied health, and applied arts. Outside the college systems, however, there still remain some notable technical institutions of high repute.

The most common nondegree-granting institution in Canada is the so-called community college, which is the most radical innovation in Canadian higher education since the Second World War. In almost all provinces there is now a network of provincially funded colleges, relatively unselective and open door as to admission, operating with many branch campuses, providing postsecondary programs by full- and part-time study, giving courses on contract for local employers and agencies, conducting labor force upgrading classes, and providing general interest courses. Their admission regulations for mature students ignore their secondary school achievement and completion record. Admission for young people entering directly from secondary school does not require graduation, and selection is at a lower academic achievement level than for the universities.

Colleges are scattered throughout a province, although there tends to be a concentration of large ones in the big cities. It is expected that most students will commute from home, so residential colleges are rare. The universities, on the other hand, provide subsidized student residences on their campuses.

2.3 Admissions Policies and Selection

Universities in Canada control their own admissions. The *de facto* choice is made at the level of the department or program, although the large universities have a separate admissions office and staff to review undergraduate applications.

Young people graduating from secondary school are judged by the average of their final year's marks, even though their nonstandardized nature is recognized. There are no longer public matriculation examinations. In the 1960s attempts were made to supplement marks with standardized tests of the United States variety, but Canadian educators have been mistrustful of their validity. However, some universities do require the Educational Testing Service's College Entrance Test for undergraduate applicants, and the Graduate Record Examination for applicants to master's and doctoral programs.

Although secondary school average marks are important, universities may use additional criteria according to the program's needs and capacity. Government's access policy does not necessarily commit the system to providing a place in a particular institution or the program of the student's choice.

The same admissions criteria apply whether entrants wish to study part-time or full-time, except where the applicant enters as a mature student (over age 21 and at least one year out of school) where selection depends on judgment of the individual's potential ability to do academic work. Generally the mature student is on probation until the equivalent of the first year's study has been successfully completed, after which the same rules apply for regular and mature students.

Community colleges also exercise autonomy in selecting students, but they are encouraged to follow an "open door" policy and admit on a "first come, first served" basis. In practice, however, they are more open-door as to the institution than to the program. Colleges have the difficult task of trying to reconcile conflicting demands; as community colleges they are expected to serve their own areas and be academically nonselective yet the students, many of whom are not well prepared, must complete rigorous study programs. The institutions are judged by the success of the employment placement of their graduates, the satisfaction of employers, and their graduates' pass rates in public and professional licensing examinations. They are criticized for having high failure and dropout rates early in their programs. In an effort to achieve a higher rate of successful completions, colleges have gone well beyond the universities in providing counseling, study skills coaching, and a preparatory year. Unfortunately, once students have taken a whole year's additional preparation in a college, there tends to be a high sense of obligation to admit them. However, the success rate of such students is not high.

2.4 Quantitative Developments in Higher Education

Both full-time and part-time enrollment in universities increased rapidly in the 1960s and 1970s (see Table 2), but it was expected that the 1980s would be a period of consolidation. There were indeed a few years in the late 1970s when this seemed likely. However, from the mid-1980s there has been an unexpected upsurge in applications, which has raised anew questions about the continuation of the provinces' policy of ensuring access to higher education.

Community college enrollments showed comparable rapid increases in the late 1960s and the 1970s when the new systems were being established and funds for vocational training were readily available from the federal government's policy of buying training places in provincial institutions' programs. However, the mid-1980s witnessed the beginning of a sharp decrease in college applications, and a federal policy change providing substantial public funding for skill training within industry has deflected considerable income elsewhere.

Canada prides itself on having a large number of higher education institutions and offering a wide range of programs to a large student body. While not yet a "mass" system (Trow 1973), its participation rates are second only to those of the United States. In 1961–62 the total full-time university participation rate was 7.5 percent of the 18 to 24 age group; in 1971–72 it had risen to 13.7 percent, and in 1987–88 to 16.5 percent. By 1987–88 the variance by province for total undergraduate study ranged from 23.4 percent to 38.4 percent of the 18 to 21 age group, and for graduate study from 2.3 percent to 5.0 percent of the age group 22 to 24.

Where community colleges are concerned the diversity in participation from province to province is considerable. In 1987–88 it varied from 4.2 percent to 16.8 percent of the 18 to 21 age group (excluding Quebec, whose CEGEP population includes students who would be in secondary school in the other provinces).

2.5 Graduate Training Programs

Universities normally exercise control over admissions to their graduate and professional programs, although in some areas the total number of places is decided only after consultation with government (e.g., in the number of admissions to teacher education, nursing training, and medical education). In anglophone universities, at the master's level a mid-B (good second class) first degree is desired and, if the applicant is "changing field," make-up work is required; thus whether a master's program will take one or two years to complete depends on the applicant's baccalaureate discipline. There are several professional master"s degrees (e.g., in education, the MEd) which can be obtained entirely by part-time study, but for the most part master's programs in the anglophone universities require a full-time residence period.

Admission to a doctoral program usually requires a B+ (upper second class) master's degree or equivalent, as well as written evidence of research ability. There may also be interviews, admission tests, and—for foreign students—a test of their command of the English (or for francophone universities the French) language.

There are professional doctorate degrees (e.g., Doctor of Social Work, Doctor of Education) but the trend has been to replace them with the PhD. Precise regulations governing PhD programs vary from university to university, but all share certain common features: at least two consecutive academic years of full-time advanced coursework on campus; a comprehensive examination (written or oral or both); and a written, orally defended dissertation describing a piece of original scholarly research. The anglophone universities of Canada do not follow the

Table 2
Full-time enrollment in higher education in Canada 1961–87

	1961–62	1971–72	1976–77	1981–82	1986–87	1987–88
Community colleges	53,400	173,800	226,161	273,398	321,483	319,115
Universities: Undergraduates	121,283	287,118	335,559	334,503	418,270	427,873
Graduates	7,347	35,908	40,947	47,159	57,147	58,189
Subtotal	128,630	323,026	376,506	401,662	475,417	486,062
Total	182,030	496,826	602,667	675,060	796,900	805,177

Sources: *Historical Compendium of Education Statistics*. Statistics Canada Catalogue 81–568, Ottawa 1978 *A Statistical Portrait of Canadian Higher Education*. Statistics Canada, Ottawa 1983. *Education Canada*. Statistics Canada Catalogue 81–229, Ottawa. *From the Sixties to the Eighties, A Statistical Portrait of Canadian Higher Education*. Statistics Canada: Education, Science, and Culture Division, Ottawa 1979

United Kingdom's model of doctorate by thesis only but, although their degrees are United States style, they lack the flexible arrangements of some United States institutions which avoid the necessity for several years of full-time study on campus. The francophone universities of Quebec permit more part-time study and have fewer full-time residence rules in their master's and doctoral processes.

The average time taken to complete a PhD in Canada is about five years, and there is a high non-completion rate (about 50 percent) with candidates ABT ("all but thesis") largely because they have left the university after the residence years and taken a demanding full-time job.

3. Governance, Administration and Finance

3.1 National and Provincial Administration

When Canada was created, it was not envisaged that higher education would become an enterprise of central importance to the nation. It was entirely a provincial responsibility. This situation prevailed until the Second World War; federal governments showed no tendency to interfere, although they supported research, particularly in agriculture. During the Second World War there arose the question of national military service and how the staff and students of universities were to be treated. To solve the matter the government of Canada took advice from the National Conference of Canadian Universities (NCCU). This is the first example of a Canadian government dealing directly with university representatives. When the Canadian constitution was patriated in 1982 the division of powers remained unchanged.

However, although Canada does not have a federal minister of education, or an office or department of education, federal governments do claim an interest in, and exercise an influence upon, higher education. This is accomplished largely through financial support provided under federal policies. The provinces are, however, assiduous in protecting their ultimate jurisdiction over education.

Following the Second World War, the federal government adopted a policy of sponsoring veterans' higher education. In order to avoid the appearance of direct intervention, these grants to the universities were justified as buying "training services," part of the veterans' settlement policy of the Department of National Defense.

The education of veterans was a one-off task. The universities' plea for continued federal financial support was presented to the Royal Commission on National Development in the Arts, Letters and Sciences (the Massey Commission), which had been set up in 1949 (Canada 1951). Two of its recommendations had lasting importance for higher education in Canada: that the federal government give universities direct nondesignated operating grants; and that it create a funding council to encourage research and scholarly work in the arts, humanities, and social sciences (the Canada Council, set up in 1957). The grants were provided for the 1951–52 academic year. Quebec objected to them as an infringement of its jurisdiction, and after the first year forbade its universities to accept them. To appease its sensibilities, the federal government has adopted a number of devices to allocate its grants.

Although Canadian governments have no general jurisdiction over higher education, they have jurisdiction over policy areas which impinge upon its activities (e.g., labor force training, and research funding). This was stressed by Prime Minister Lester Pearson at the 1966 federal–provincial conference on financing higher education (Pearson 1966). In addition, because of their general commitment to the welfare of Canadians, federal governments must serve the national interest by trying, through their financial power, to equalize conditions fairly throughout the country.

3.2 Finance

The higher education institutions of Canada receive their main operating funds in the form of an annual grant from the provincial government; even though a substantial portion is federal, its monies have become "invisible" given the current funding mechanism (see Table 3). It is not surprising, therefore, that the important political level for institutions of higher education is the province. Provincial civil servants, provincial intermediary agencies, and provincial representative associations are more important than national ones. National academic associations perform important coordinating, communicating, and lobbying functions, but their provincial counterparts deal with the agents of power. The complex framework of organizations is shown in Fig. 3.

Provincial governments long ago decided that dealing directly with universities' finances was a politically unrewarding activity. It was impossible to satisfy all institutions equally. Instead, a complex formula, related to enrollment and weighted as to program, decides institutions' block allocations. By a series of adjustments the formulae are made independent of year-by-year enrollment fluctuations. By a series of earmarked grants some of the funds can be separated from the basic grant and reserved for specific purposes.

The formula calculates the institution's total grant. There is no pressure to spend the operating grants according to the program enrollments by which they are calculated. Universities are free to decide how they spend their income. As autonomous institutions, they do their own institutional planning using the budget as the major allocative intervention tool to create change.

The relationship of community colleges to provincial governments is closer and more dependent. In some provinces they are managed directly. In others there is a council of lay persons appointed by the provincial government to supervise the system. College financing, however, has an important difference from that of the university: substantial ancillary income is derived from federal sources through the sale of program places for labor force and skills development, and also through contracts with local industrial, commercial, or professional organizations.

An important indirect source of public support for universities and colleges is the financial assistance to students. Traditional financial support, in the form of scholarships, bursaries, and fellowships, comes from both public and private sources. Much more important, however, is "student aid." Provincial student assistance plans vary, but all share certain features: they are a combination of loan and grant, are means tested, and assume that undergraduates' families will take major responsibility for their costs. The loan portion is interest-free until the student graduates and is employed; then it is repaid in installments with interest charged at the market rate on the outstanding balance.

Total assistance is expressed in terms of a maximum number of dollars and years of funding. The longer the program the more the student receives, so *de facto* university students receive more than college students. Individual grants and loans are calculated in terms of expected income (part-time or summer earnings, and parental contribution) and expenditure (tuition and other fees, living expenses, transportation, books, health care, and incidental costs).

Initially, part-time students were not eligible for financial assistance. Even under the most generous schemes they now receive only small grants to cover direct costs.

As well as provincial plans there is also a federal loan program. Students not eligible for provincial grants may be able to obtain a federal loan. In 1986–87 250,930 full-time students received CDN\$711.47 million (US\$630.51 million) under the Canada Student Loan Program; the total provincial assistance to full-time students was CDN\$660.32 million (US\$585.18 million). For part-time students the comparable federal figures that year were 1,080 students receiving CDN\$1.45 million (US\$1.28 million) (Government of Ontario 1987, pp. 38, 43).

Financial support for graduate students, particularly doctoral students, is generous. It includes a variety of publicly and privately funded scholarships, fellowships, and postdoctoral fellowships, many awarded by the research-supporting national councils. Each province also has an assistance scheme for graduate students, combining grants and loans to some permitted maximum dollar amount for a maximum number of years. No parental support is expected, and in the assistance scheme the students may obtain cost of living expenses for dependent spouses and children.

However, the most important financial support for doctoral students comes as payment for work as parttime teaching assistants under the supervision of the professors responsible for the undergraduate introductory courses.

3.3 Institutional Governance

The common organizational pattern found in Canadian universities is usually depicted by a line chart showing the president, vice-presidents, and assistant vice-presidents at the top. On the administration side below the vice-presidents are a plethora

Table 3
Canadian expenditure on higher education by source of funds (in millions of US\$)

	Universities				Colleges		
	1960–61	1970–71	1980–81	1985–86	1960–61	1970–71	1980–81
Federal government	47.2	185.9	434.8	515.9	12.1	44.6	51.7
%	19.5	11.7	11.1	9.1	23.6	11.7	3.2
Provincial government	105.3	1,055.9	2,756.2	3,522.0	36.7	266.4	1,364.5
%	43.5	66.5	70.1	61.8	71.9	69.9	84.5
Municipal government	0.6	0.9	0.6	1.5	0.0	3.0	0.0
%	0.3	0.1	0.0	0.0	0.0	0.8	0.0
Fees	40.7	168.8	354.5	638.0	2.2	26.0	111.3
%	16.9	10.6	9.0	11.2	4.3	6.8	6.9
Other sources	47.9	176.1	385.8	1,021.9	0.09	41.0	87.9
%	19.8	11.1	9.8	17.9	0.2	10.8	5.4
Total	241.7	1,587.6	3,931.9	5,699.3	51.1	381.0	1,615.4
%	100.0	100.0	100.0	100.0	100.0	100.0	100.0

Sources: Statistics Canada *A Statistical Portrait of Canadian Higher Education, from the 1960s to the 1980s.* Ottawa 1983, pp. 62, 63. Association of Universities and Colleges *Compendium of University Statistics.* Ottawa 1987, p. 28 *Education Canada: A statistical review for 1987–88* 81–229. Ottawa 1989, p. 218

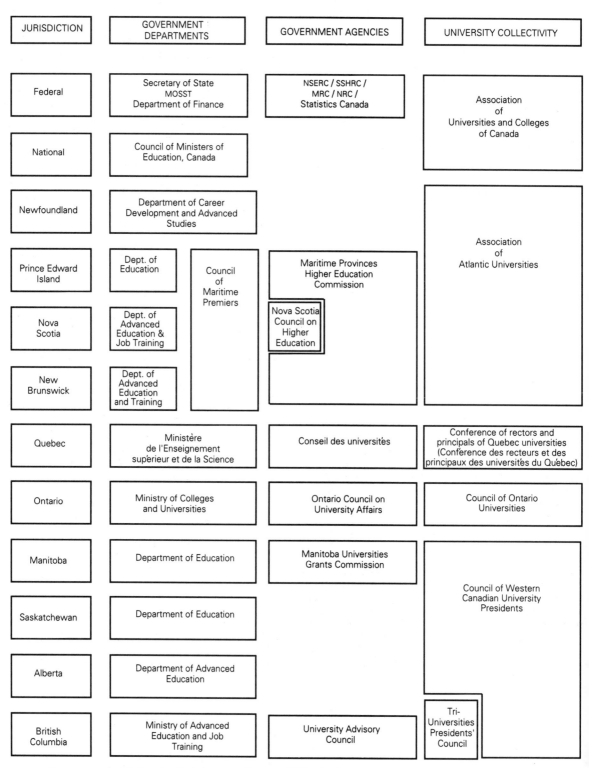

JURISDICTION	GOVERNMENT DEPARTMENTS	GOVERNMENT AGENCIES	UNIVERSITY COLLECTIVITY
Federal	Secretary of State MOSST Department of Finance	NSERC / SSHRC / MRC / NRC / Statistics Canada	Association of Universities and Colleges of Canada
National	Council of Ministers of Education, Canada		
Newfoundland	Department of Career Development and Advanced Studies		Association of Atlantic Universities
Prince Edward Island	Dept. of Education	Council of Maritime Premiers	Maritime Provinces Higher Education Commission
Nova Scotia	Dept. of Advanced Education & Job Training		Nova Scotia Council on Higher Education
New Brunswick	Dept. of Advanced Education and Training		
Quebec	Ministère de l'Enseignement supérieur et de la Science	Conseil des universités	Conference of rectors and principals of Quebec universities (Conférence des recteurs et des principaux des universités du Québec)
Ontario	Ministry of Colleges and Universities	Ontario Council on University Affairs	Council of Ontario Universities
Manitoba	Department of Education	Manitoba Universities Grants Commission	Council of Western Canadian University Presidents
Saskatchewan	Department of Education		
Alberta	Department of Advanced Education		
British Columbia	Ministry of Advanced Education and Job Training	University Advisory Council	Tri-Universities Presidents' Council

Source: *Compendium of University Statistics AUCC Ottawa, 1987 p.1*

Figure 3
The higher education framework of Canada

118

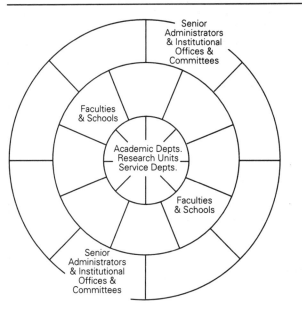

Figure 4
Organizational structure of Canadian universities

Departments are grouped into faculties, each headed by a dean. Like their colleagues, department chairs, nowadays deans are generally appointed from within the current teaching staff for a (renewable) short term of three or four years. There will be a faculty council as well as department councils, by which decisions are made collegially. Usually they have student and support staff representation, but the faculty always has the preponderant voice.

The third circle is occupied by the senior administration. Their power lies in the ability to respond, encourage, support, or veto; but it is constrained by committees and councils like the Academic Council.

Large universities are such complex organizations as almost to defy description, which is why the general support staff who work in the various offices and understand the procedures and regulations of the institution exercise considerable *de facto* authority.

For the most part, community colleges do not share the tradition of collegial decision making. Although this varies with the province, they tend to have a hierarchical, managerial style of operation. Their presidents, vice-presidents, and deans have authority to make independent decisions without consulting their teachers, students or staff. To some extent this power is exercised because their teachers do not expect, or even try, to control the academic enterprise, so administrative decisions are seldom challenged.

In some provinces, particularly the western ones, there is token representation of teachers and students on college councils. In others there is none. The large college system of Ontario (the Colleges of Applied Arts and Technology, or CAATs) until recently had no provision for college councils. Recently, by government decree, they have been instituted but it is not clear precisely how they will operate and what authority they will wield.

of service offices; and on the academic side are a series of faculties, and below them a number of departments. Another way of depicting universities would be as a series of concentric circles, with departments, research units, and service offices, which run the institution day by day, at the center (see Fig. 4).

The department is the main operating unit of a university. Its faculty controls the curriculum, which includes the content of the courses, the teaching process, the learning experiences the student is expected to encounter, student advising, and examining. It is the focus of the student's life in other important ways, as it organizes the enriching colloquia, conferences, and off-campus visits which supplement formal studies. The department is not only a teaching unit; it is a research-producing, disseminating, and evaluating unit, and the focus of the faculty's academic life no less than the student's.

4. Faculty, Students, and Learning

4.1 Faculty

The growth in the number of teachers employed in higher education is shown in Table 4, and their

Table 4
Full-time postsecondary teachers in Canada 1961–87

	1961–62	1971–72	1976–77	1981–82	1986–87	1987–88
Community college	4,400	14,100	18,775	20,535	23,550	23,780
University	8,755	27,600	31,648	33,244	35,570	35,844
Total	13,155	41,700	50,423	53,779	59,120	59,624

Sources: *Historical Compendium of Education Statistics*. Statistics Canada Catalogue 81–568, Ottawa 1978 *A Historical Portrait of Canadian Higher Education*. Statistics Canada, Ottawa 1983 Education Canada. Statistics Canada Catalogue 81–229, Ottawa *From the Sixties to the Eighties. A Statistical Portrait of Canadian Higher Education*. Statistics Canada: Education, Science, and Culture Division, Ottawa 1979

Table 5a
Full-time enrollment and educational attainment by province 1987–88

	Newfoundland	Prince Edward Island	Nova Scotia	New Brunswick	Quebec	Ontario	Manitoba	Saskatchewan	Alberta	British Columbia	Canada
Community college	3,016	907	2,438	2,367	159,940	95,029	3,839	2,916	23,865	24,547	319,115
University	10,872	2,030	24,317	15,200	116,627	192,717	19,606	20,729	46,614	37,350	486,062
Total	13,888	2,937	26,755	17,562	276,567	287,746	23,445	23,645	70,479	61,897	805,117
Educational attainment[a]	6.3	7.2	10.0	7.9	10.0	12.4	9.9	8.4	12.2	11.4	11.0

a Percentage of population of 15 years and over having university degrees (figures for 1986–86)

Table 5b
Full-time teachers by province 1987–88

	Newfoundland	Prince Edward Island	Nova Scotia	New Brunswick	Quebec	Ontario	Manitoba	Saskatchewan	Alberta	British Columbia	Canada
Postsecondary	293	32	62	202	—	2,172	383	218	767	983	5,143
Community college	215	65	300	250	11,350	6,750	380	380	2,130	1,920	23,780
Subtotal	508	97	363	452	11,350	8,922	763	598	2,897	2,903	28,923
University	971	136	2,031	1,190	8,050	13,809	1,732	1,580	3,280	3,065	35,844
Total	1,479	233	2,393	1,642	19,400	22,731	2,495	2,178	6,177	5,968	64,767

distribution by province in 1987–88 in Table 5b. In 1950 there were some 5,539 full-time teachers employed in Canadian universities. By 1976, when the rapid expansion of higher education was subsiding, the total was 31,648, an average annual increase of more than 1,000. It takes 22 or more years of full-time study to prepare an assistant professor, and prior to the 1960s Canada's capacity for doctoral studies was slight. It was not capable of supplying the required volume of highly qualified teachers rapidly. So, just as Canada imports a great many other commodities, it imported the additions to the professoriate.

However, by the second half of the 1970s, higher education had entered a period when Canada's economic growth was faltering; there was rapid inflation and rising unemployment. Public health costs were high, and in the competition for funds the health services won over education, which could be cut with fewer adverse results politically. Moreover, the decline in school enrollments made it reasonable to expect a reduction in higher education enrollment and costs. So, the university full-time teaching force and (slightly later) the community college teacher cadres were virtually frozen.

Although their real income was not growing, universities and colleges found that their enrollments continued to increase. They could seldom replace the full-time tenured teachers who moved or retired, let alone make new appointments; so they turned to the extensive use of part-time and short-contract staffing. One difficulty in demonstrating meticulously when and in what disciplines this change occurred, and where it had grown by the end of the 1980s to unacceptable proportions, is that Statistics Canada's file on part-time teachers is inadequate. What will probably prove to have been the most far-reaching and serious change in Canadian university life in this generation has been carried out almost unnoted.

The change has been achieved at the expense of a generation of young scholars, the first products of the postwar expansion of doctoral studies in Canada, who arrived on the academic market just too late to find employment in the institutions which had reached their full complement. As Rajagopal and Farr noted (1989 p. 267), "Even where part-timers are unionized, they remain outside the academic decision-making processes."

The Canadian professoriate is still a masculine enclave. In 1961, of the full-time teachers, women represented 11.4 percent, and in 1988 17.8 percent. They too came to the academic market too late. The gender revolution in undergraduate enrollment took place after the great expansion was complete, so only men were included. Even today, qualified female candidates in some fields are scarce. Although their numbers in doctoral studies are increasing, female students are still a minority. Women academics who do obtain employment are concentrated in the lower ranks at the lower end of the salary scales, and in the humanities, social sciences, and such fields as nursing and teaching.

In the mid-1980s gender inequities in employment became a major political issue. A series of bills at the federal and provincial levels set up machinery to review and adjust the salary scales of female-dominated jobs in relation to male-dominated jobs of "equal value." Provincial and federal faculty organizations set up status-of-women committees to monitor developments. Provincial governments urged that Faculty Renewal Funds be used to increase the number of women faculty.

4.2 Career Paths

Canadian faculty have the familiar United States rank structure: assistant, associate, and full professor. Prior to the Second World War there were a number of titles below assistant professor, but in the expansion period many titles disappeared. In recent years they have begun to reappear: new appointments are being made in such categories as "lecturer," "fellow," "laboratory assistant," and "teaching assistant." Those holding such appointments were traditionally not fully qualified, but now many hold the doctorate and have a considerable dossier of research publications.

In theory, progress through the university teaching ranks is based on a combination of teaching excellence and research excellence: the former attested by favorable ratings from students and peers, and the latter attested by the number of research grants from the national funding councils or international foundations, and by favorable assessments of the candidate's published research work, carried out by peers from other universities. In practice the evidence of research capability is crucial to obtaining tenure and promotion.

The composition of the community college teaching force is quite different, and career expectations vary accordingly. In provinces where these colleges have transfer programs, the universities which receive their graduates require the teachers to have at least master's level qualifications in appropriate disciplines. The vocational teachers have qualifications similar to those demanded of community college teachers in the provinces where there is no transfer function. They are chosen for their employment, craft, or professional practice experience. Their salary scales are based on seniority and do not greatly reward formal qualifications. Community college faculty are judged on their teaching alone. The conduct of research is neither expected nor encouraged.

4.3 Representation of Faculty Interests

In each university a faculty association negotiates teachers' salaries, benefits, and conditions of work

Table 6
Degrees awarded in Canada

	1960	1970	1987
Bachelor and first prof	19,797	67,100	103,070
Master's	2,227	9,638	15,978
Doctorate	306	1,625	2,384

with the representatives of the board of governors (usually senior administrators). Many faculty associations are "unionized," that is, they operate under the aegis of provincial legislation on collective bargaining. Most of the others have some "special plan," that is, are recognized as the sole bargaining agent for faculty, have formal contracts, and seem to have all the trappings of a union without actually being one. Collectively the universities' faculty associations support a provincial association.

The support staff of a university do not belong to the same association as the faculty. The precise arrangements vary: they may have an independent institutional association, or they may vote to join one of the large public service unions.

The most serious challenge to traditional university process was the rapid development of faculty unionism about 1975 to 1980, during the period when it became clear that financial constraints would be a continuing condition, not a short-lived aberration. In the 1990s it seems likely that the general support staff and the research and technical employees of universities will become more militant, demanding some of the work conditions and benefits (like sabbatical leave) enjoyed by the teaching staff.

In many provinces the community colleges do not share the traditions of the university and its faculty association. Their teaching staff tend to be more formally unionized.

4.4 Students

Growth in the total number of degrees awarded may be seen in Table 6.

The greatest increase in undergraduate degrees has been in the social sciences and in commerce (business studies). The number of degrees in education grew rapidly in the 1950s and 1960s but thereafter declined sharply as the number of teacher education places was reduced to reflect the surplus of teachers due to declining school enrollment.

Statistics on the number of certificates and diplomas awarded by nondegree institutions in the 1950s and early 1960s are fragmentary. In 1964–65 there were 3,493 diplomas of various sorts conferred. By 1970 most of the new provincial college systems had been established and the statistics had become more comprehensive. In 1970–71 43,633 diplomas were awarded. In 1975–76 the total had grown to 54,348; and by 1986–87 to 82,326.

4.5 Social Class Origins

Equality of access to tertiary studies has been endlessly researched in Canada since the mid-1960s, with the varying percentage representation of different subgroups in different types of institution and program providing the evidence of inequities (see Fortin 1987, Anisef et al. 1985, Pineo and Goyder 1988, Guppy 1987, Guppy 1988, Breslauer 1985, Hum and Strain 1988, Stager 1984). Public statistics have not been gathered according to ethnic, racial, or religious categories, so participation studies have been based on sample surveys. Their theoretical models, definitions, and criteria for judging the source, nature, and degree of inequalities have so differed that the studies cannot be compared.

The gender imbalance has been redressed in undergraduate studies and improved in many professional areas. In 1985–86 female students formed 45.7 percent of the enrollment in law, 43.8 percent in medicine, and 67.5 percent in pharmacy (Statistics Canada 1986 pp. 90, 92, 96), but female participation is still low in doctoral studies. Professions dominated by women persist (e.g., social work, nutritional science, nursing, and physiotherapy) and female students in engineering, technology, and physical sciences are still a small minority.

Several new access preoccupations have now emerged: geographical equity across the provinces; age equity of middle-aged and elderly versus young applicants; and status equity for part-time as opposed to full-time students. In Quebec there is concern that the francophone student is overrepresented in nondegree programs and part-time study; and underrepresented in doctoral level graduate study (ASOPE 1976, 1980, 1981, 1982).

All these issues are complicated by the institutions' claim that to redress such inequities they need more money, and governments' scepticism that better funding alone will achieve the goal of greater equity. There is now renewed questioning of the policy emphasis on access. There has always been a school of thought (see Bercuson et al. 1964) which alleges that standards and quality have been adversely affected by rapid expansion and the quest for social equity. Critics have also complained that preoccupation with access has led to neglect of the issue of survival: wastage rates are too high. The study of participation rates ought to be supplemented by analysis of graduations.

4.6 Learning and Examinations

First degree programs tend to be broad: even honors programs are much less specialized than would be common in the United Kingdom or Europe. By a series of prerequisite and corequisite courses, students are directed to take a substantial number of their courses in departments other than their own. Degree requirements are expressed in course credits at the first, second, third, and fourth year levels.

There are extensive offerings in intersession, summer session, and evening classes for part-time students and for full-time students who wish to speed up the program.

There is no central agency which regulates the course structure of undergraduate programs. Internal procedures approve new programs and program changes; these are initiated at the level of the department, receive academic scrutiny by faculty committees at faculty and senate; and are confirmed by the board of governors. Uniformity throughout a province of course content and program design is neither valued nor sought. Universities take pride in the uniqueness of their courses and programs.

Provincial governments have councils to advise on professional programs. Usually there is some stated required content and number of hours of practical work. Some professions are licensed by a provincial college or have a credentialing agency; these undertake site visits and approve the courses, physical facilities, and faculty qualifications. This ensures that a university keeps its investment in professional programs at a very high level. Quebec has an Office of Professions to supervise licensing and prepractice educational requirements.

For graduate programs some provinces have a council of university faculty which carries out periodic evaluation of programs to ensure that their academic standards remain high. These are peer reviews; assessments are made by eminent academics, invited from other countries (or other provinces) to make site visits.

In general, Canadian university curricula are less likely to be radically innovative than those of the United States, but are less conservative than those of Europe. There have been some notable program innovations, particularly in education and medicine.

Community college programs are more innovative and market oriented. They owe much to the ingenuity and initiative of their teachers and their advisory curriculum committee members, who are drawn from industry. However, the colleges enjoy less program autonomy than the universities. Program changes are not only subject to internal review, administrative approval, and acceptance by the board of governors, but they must then be submitted to a provincial level authority for approval (see Dennison and Gallagher 1986, Murphy 1983, Hart 1988).

Across anglophone provinces, college programs of ostensibly the same type will differ as much as university programs. They have superficial similarities in terms of the number of courses and the total number of student hours, but course sequences, the "core" and range of options, and balance of practical and academic work all differ from place to place. So, although in theory a student's credits are portable, in fact transferring from one community college to another, even within the same province, is not easy.

Quebec officials exercise much greater control over the CEGEP system's curricula. Programs are designed by groups of CEGEP teachers working under the direction of the Minister's College Council. Programs are uniform in outline, providing details of the required and optional courses, course units, hours of laboratory and practical work, and the facilities and amenities to be provided. Program implementation and standards are monitored by periodic reviews of samples of examinations, students' projects, and term papers.

5. Conclusion

Four aspects of the expansion of Canadian higher education in the postwar period have created the issues likely to dog higher education in the future. It is not the fact that development of the system occurred but how it occurred that still arouses controversy. The first aspect is the question of what "equality of opportunity" means; the second, the separation of the degree-granting and nondegree-granting institutions into isolated sectors; the third, how higher education is to be financed; and the fourth, how academic standards are to be set and monitored, and by whom.

Following the Second World War, the need to create new universities and expand the capacity of existing ones was argued primarily by the use of demographic data: the effects of the baby boom, rising secondary school completion rates, and annual increases in applications to universities. Governments were impressed with evidence of a strong social demand for access to higher education. And there was all-party agreement that greater access was desirable. However, there was no suggestion that universities should not continue to be the sole arbiters of what represents a "qualified" applicant.

Within the academic community, particularly among professors of education, sociologists, and feminists, dispute recurs periodically as to what constitutes equality of educational opportunity and how it might be achieved. There is no evidence that this is currently a serious issue outside academe, but the need for more money to serve atypical students whose preparation for university study has not been satisfactory is used to try to influence governments' fiscal policies. So it is quite likely that awareness in Canada of the lack of participation of certain subgroups of the population will grow and become a politically sensitive issue. If that occurs, it is possible that a degree of infringement of university autonomy will result.

When the community college system was initially set up, the question of providing an option for students to transfer from college to university was hotly debated. The transfer issue has not receded. In the 1990s it will likely take a new form. It will not be argued in terms of social and educational philosophy, but in terms of logistics, capacity, and costs.

Per capita college costs are lower than university costs. As student preferences shift back and forth between the two sectors and pressure on the capacity of one shifts to the other, it makes sense to consider the total number of student places available. The colleges are not degree-granting institutions, but there is no legal prohibition on their developing cooperative programs with the local university. There is no legal impediment to some of the large urban colleges offering programs which lead to a degree through some agency like the British Council for National Academic Awards.

Canadian universities and colleges draw their income primarily from government grants, supplemented by research and service funds, tuition fees, and gifts. Fees have been kept artificially low, pegged to the grant system, and their value has reduced steadily since the 1960s. There is little fee variation between programs and institutions. By linking tuition to grants, governments have ensured that raising fees is a zero-sum game. If institutions realize more by fees they thereby lower their grant income. Governments desire to substitute private for public funds, but this has not yet been realized to any great extent.

With enrollments continuing to grow, class sizes and student–faculty ratios have risen to an unacceptable level. As the 1989 brief of the Ontario Confederation of University Faculty Associations to the Ontario Council on University Affairs stressed, the "huge surge in enrollment is causing deterioration in the quality of education. What is clearly needed is a Faculty Growth Fund to increase the number of tenure-stream positions" (1989 p. 3).

Debate on how to address financial problems will likely bring together the issues of fees, privatization, and institutional differentiation. Some institutions might be freed of financial constraints by becoming private, foregoing grants but charging high fees and seeking large endowments. Less drastic than creating a private sector would be to allow tuition fees to float according to market demand.

"It takes an academic to judge another academic or academic enterprise, academically," seems to be the maxim which applies throughout the world. The matter of standards, however, is a public concern: there is not only the question of accountability to show that public money was spent honestly, but that it was spent well. Academics have a profound mistrust of lay ability to pronounce on the latter question. Until recently, Canadian governments have left judgments of quality entirely to academics. Questions are now being raised, though, as to whether the nation needs to have all these programs of a similar type, however academically acceptable, and some academics have asked whether the accepted standard is sufficiently high.

The postwar expansion of universities in all provinces was carried out by, and supervised within, the academic community with little regard for costs. Enrollment expansion caused by the transfer of teacher training into the universities was also accomplished without systematic periodic evaluation of the new programs and with little regard for costs.

Expansion of graduate studies followed, and here some provinces did institute a periodic review and approval system. The difficulties are that such systems are time-consuming, deflecting academic time from academic tasks; existing programs are at an advantage over all attempts to establish new ones of comparable nature; and while review may ensure high standards, it also ensures that small institutions cannot compete. There is the fiction that all universities achieve the same academic standard, when this is patently not the case.

With economic constraints emerging in the late 1970s, claims for accountability and questions about standards were raised. They have not become strident in Canada, but in the 1990s periodic evaluation of programs standards will likely be imposed more generally.

Canadian community colleges have a different problem. Even today they have variable academic standards, but consciously play the "second chance" role for much of their work, and this requires an "open door" policy. However, their craft, technical, and professional programs must face the scrutiny of employers and credentialing associations. So, to enable their graduates to have a high probability of success in the credentialing examinations, they will be forced to become academically more selective in the future.

Ironically, the factor which is likely to have a major impact on Canadian higher education in the 1990s is one which, at face value, has nothing to do with universities and colleges. In December 1988 a free trade agreement with the United States was ratified, North America's answer to Europe's agreement for 1992. One of the agreement clauses permits the professionals of one country to work in the other. How this will affect the free flow of professional and academic labor is not clear. What effect this will have on the institutions which educate this level of labor is even less clear. Professional and academic curricula vary greatly in both countries. However this problem is solved, the agreement will make it more difficult for Canadian institutions to create and maintain their unique quality.

Bibliography

Anisef P, Bertrand M A, Hartian U, James C E 1985 *Accessibility to Postsecondary Education in Canada, A Review of the Literature.* Department of the Secretary of State, Ottawa

Anisef P, Okihiro N R, James C E 1982 *Losers and*

Winners: The Pursuit of Equality and Social Justice in Higher Education. Butterworth, Toronto

ASOPE 1976, 1979, 1980, 1981, 1982 A series of publications of the research project "Aspirations scolaires et les orientations professionelles des étudiants québecois"

Bercuson D J, Bothwell R, Granatstein J L 1964 *The Great Brain Robbery: Canada's Universities on the Road to Ruin.* McClelland and Stewart, Toronto

Breslauer H 1985 Women in the professoriate—the case of multiple disadvantage. In: Watson C (ed.) 1985 *The Professoriate–Occupation in Crisis.* Higher Education Group, The Ontario Institute for Studies in Education, Toronto, pp. 82–104

Campbell G 1971 *Community Colleges in Canada.* Ryerson-McGraw-Hill, Toronto

Canada 1951 Report of the Royal Commission on National Development in the Arts, Letters and Sciences. King's Printer, Ottawa

Clark W, Laing M, Rechnitzer E 1986 *The Class of '82: Summary Report of the Findings of the 1984 National Survey of the Graduates of 1982.* Secretary of State and Statistics Canada, Ottawa

Dennison J 1987 Universities under financial crises. The case of British Columbia. *Higher Educ.* 16: 135–43

Dennison J, Gallagher P 1986 *Canada's Community Colleges: A Critical Analysis.* University of British Columbia Press, Vancouver

Fortin M 1987 Accessibility to and participation in the postsecondary education system of Canada. *Forum Papers,* National Forum on Postsecondary Education. Institute for Research on Public Policy, Halifax, Nova Scotia pp. 1–19

Government of Ontario 1987 *OSAP Report,* Toronto

Guppy N 1987 *Limiting Access: The Social Impact, B. C. Under Restraint.* Conference papers. University of British Columbia, Vancouver

Guppy N 1988 Accessibility to higher education—New trend data. *CAUT Bulletin* June, pp. 15–16

Harris R S 1976 *A History of Higher Education in Canada, 1663–1960,* University of Toronto Press, Toronto

Hart J D 1988 A history of the development of the curriculum guidelines for postsecondary programs of the Ontario Colleges of Applied Arts and Technology, 1972–1986. Unpublished EdD dissertation, University of Toronto, Toronto

Hum D, Strain F 1988 Fiscal transfers, horizontal equity and postsecondary education. *Can. J. H.E.* 18(2): 15–36

Leslie P 1980 *Canadian Universities 1980 and Beyond: Enrolment, Structural Change and Finance.* Association of Universities and Colleges of Canada (AUCC), Ottawa

Maritime Provinces Higher Education Commission (MPHEC) 1988 *Financial Plan 1989–90.* Fredericton, New Brunswick

Maritime Provinces Higher Education Commission (MPHEC) 1988 *Statistical Compendium, 1988.* Fredericton, New Brunswick

Maritime Provinces Higher Education Commission (MPHEC) 1988 *Annual Report, 1987–88.* Fredericton, New Brunswick

Murphy M N 1983 An analysis of the general education component in curricula of the Ontario Colleges of Applied Arts and Technology. Unpublished EdD dissertation, University of Toronto, Toronto

Ontario Confederation of University Faculty Associations (OCUFA) 1989 *Forum* 6(13): 3

Organisation for Economic Co-operation and Development 1966 Training and Demand for High Level Scientific and Technical Personnel in Canada, Review of National Policies for Education. OECD, Paris

Organisation for Economic Co-operation and Development 1976 *Review of National Policies for Education: Canada.* OECD, Paris

Pearson L B 1966 Opening Statement. *Report.* Conference on Financing Higher Education in Canada, Montreal

Pineo P C, Goyder J 1988 The growth of the Canadian education system: An analysis of transition probabilities. *Can. J. High Educ* 18(2): 37–54

Rajagopal I, Farr W D 1989 The political economy of part-time academic work in Canada. *High. Educ.* 18(3): 267–286

Roberge P 1982 *Les étudiants à temps partiel des universitaires québecois.* Conseil des Universités, Gouvernement de Québec

Sheffield E, Campbell D D, Holmes J, Kymlicka B B, Whitelaw J H 1982 *Systems of Higher Education: Canada,* 2nd edn. ICED, New York

Skolnik M L 1986 If the cut is so deep, where is the blood? Problems in research on the effects of financial restraint. *Rev. High. Ed.* 9(4): 435–55

Slaughter S, Skolnik M L 1987 Continued efforts to cope with declining resources: Selected postsecondary education systems in the United States and Canada. An introductory essay. *Higher Educ.* 16: 125–143

Stager D 1984 Accessibility and the demand for university education. In: *Report,* Commission on the Future Development of Ontario's Universities, Toronto

Statistics Canada 1973–1986 *Education Statistics.* Catalogue No. 81-229 1973; 1986: 90, 92, 96, 97; Catalogue No. 81-568, 1978 Ottawa

Trow M 1973 *Problems in Transition from Elite to Mass Higher Education.* Carnegie Commission on Higher Education, Berkeley, California

Warme B, Lundy K 1988 Erosion of an ideal: The "presence" of part-time faculty. *Stud. H. Ed.* 13(2): 201–13

Watson C 1973 *New College Systems in Canada.* OECD, Paris

C. Watson

Central African Republic

1. Higher Education and Society

The Central African Republic has been independent since 1960. Situated in the heart of Africa, it stretches over 623,000 square kilometers between Zaire and the Congo to the south, Chad to the north, the Sudan to the east, and Cameroon to the west. The population, an estimated 2,583,000 inhabitants in 1975, is increasing at the rate of 2.4 percent a year. It is basically rural. Seventy-four percent of people live in the countryside, and 26 percent in urban areas.

Numerous ethnic groups live in the Central African Republic. The Pygmies were the first inhabitants; tribal groups are the Gbaya, Banda, Yakoma, Sango, Banziri, Mandja, Nzakara, Zandé, Ngbaka, Gula, Kara, and the Mbororo, among others. Despite its ethnic diversity, the Central African Republic has a national language (Sango) and an official language (French).

The economy is based on agriculture (coffee, cotton, tobacco, etc.), wood, and mining (diamonds and gold). The Gross Domestic Product (GDP) was estimated to be US$318,677 in 1985. The active population represents 55 percent of the total population and is divided as follows: primary sector 88 percent, secondary sector 4 percent, and tertiary sector 8 percent.

From 1960 onwards, the Central African Republic has tried numerous forms of government. After being a republic from 1960 to 1965, the following forms of government were tried in succession: dictatorship (1965–76), empire (1976–79), a multiparty republican regime (1979–81), rule by the Military Committee for Rectification (1981–86), and the republican regime (from 1986), based on a constitution that provides for the division of power, the rule of law, and democratic freedom. It is a presidential regime, where the ministers who answer to the president are responsible for applying sectoral policies.

Political restructuring in 1987 placed higher education under the responsibility of the Ministry of National Education. The post of Secretary of State for Higher Education was established in 1989 within the Ministry of National Education and Higher Education. These agencies have a multifaceted mission: to conceive, elaborate, apply, and monitor the execution of the government's higher education policy.

Religious personnel were very active in primary education before Independence. This ended with the nationalization of religious schools in 1960. They have only recently become involved in higher education, and this is limited to religious training.

2. The Institutional Fabric of the Higher Education System

The basic goal of the colonial educational policy was to produce civil servants. That goal changed in 1958 with France's creation of a subregional institution in Brazzaville, in the Congo—the *Institut d'Etudes Supérieures* (IES), whose mission was to supply high-level personnel to the colonies of French Equatorial Africa.

After 1960, the former colonies of French Equatorial Africa (Congo, Gabon, Chad, Central African Republic, and Cameroon) created, with the help of France, the Foundation for Higher Education in the Central African Republic (FESAC), which was not destined to last long. Each country decided to have its own organization. Then, in 1969, the University of Bangui was created. Higher education is represented in the public sector by the University of Ban-

gui and in the private sector by the School of Theology and Biblical Studies, St Mark's Major Seminary and the International Preparatory College (a commercial institution).

The University of Bangui is comprised of four faculties—liberal arts and social sciences; law and economic sciences; health sciences; and science and technology—and two institutes—a management institute and an institute of rural development. The University is also the site of a teacher-training college, and research institutes of applied linguistics and mathematics.

The entrance requirements for higher education as set by the Ministry of Higher Education are a second-level baccalaureate or equivalent diploma, or the passing of a special test. Restrictions, often subject to change according to the specialization of each institution, take into account age (maximum 25 years old) and the number of places available. The number of students at the University of Bangui has increased from 1,808 in 1981–82 to 2,698 in 1987–88.

The student body at the University of Bangui is growing slowly. Three principal factors explain this slow growth: low percentages of students passing the baccalaureate examination; high dropout rates in the first few years; and study abroad of sciences and technology.

The study programs at the University of Bangui are mostly divided into two cycles. The first cycle imparts general education and lasts two years. The second cycle, also two years in length, gives a basic professional grounding. The faculty of health sciences is the only one to have a third cycle, dedicated to research. The other faculties send their students abroad for this level of studies. The private institutions have adopted this structure of studies in their system.

3. Governance, Administration, and Finance

The University is administratively and financially autonomous, but the Ministry of National Education and Higher Education directly intervenes in the appointment of officials and in the decisions on actions suggested by the university council. Following the States-General (1987), a program adopted by the government for the restructuring and operation of the University redefined the University's role and its goals for the next five years. These are: to adapt the program of studies in line with development; to intensify and adapt research in line with development; to participate actively in the task of promoting national culture and the national language (Sango); and to restructure in order to respond efficiently to these goals, despite the modest means available.

The public sector of higher education is financed by the budget allotted by the state to the Ministry of

National Education and Higher Education (8.561 billion Central African Francs); 23.5 percent of this goes to higher education. Expenditures basically cover students' scholarships, wages, and daily operation.

The Minister of Higher Education is the chancellor of the University and grants the degrees. The president is named by decree and has authority over the academics. He or she supervises the proper functioning of the institutions and oversees the university budget. The administrative council, presided over by the Minister and comprised of people nominated by the Minister of Finance, implements the University's development plan, set out by the government.

The university council, presided over by the president of the University, plans the budget, approves proposed official documents to be submitted to higher authorities, and suggests members for the teaching faculty. It is consulted about the regulations, organization, and program of studies.

The dean, named by decree, is in charge of the faculty. The faculty is divided into departments, created by the Ministry, and consisting of one or more specific disciplines, in which both teaching and research are carried out. The scientific commission of the department proposes the programs of studies, and gives its opinion about recruiting and promoting professors. The number of professors is small. Specialists are lacking in several fields.

4. Faculty and Students: Teaching, Learning, and Research

The permanent members of staff are divided into the following ranks: professors, lecturers, teaching assistants, and assistants. Each group chooses a representative by department and institution. The studies and research programs, schedules, and types of examinations established by the departmental councils are examined by the councils on the institution level and by the University council before being approved by the president of the University or the Minister.

Success rates are low among students at the University of Bangui and vary from one institution to another. The high failure rates reflect more the difficult study conditions at the University of Bangui (no policy regarding numbers, poor orientation, poor infrastructure, etc.) than the social situation of the students. It is also difficult to speak of a minority. The Pygmies do not participate in higher education because of their lack of integration into Central African society.

The students are organized in associations to represent their material and moral interests on the departmental, faculty, and university level. An arbitration council has been established to hear their complaints and demands.

5. Conclusion

Higher education is going through a difficult period because of the political and economic crisis affecting the country. Lack of financial resources for education and research has led to a brain drain. A government organized seminar in 1982 attempted to formulate new guidelines to integrate higher education and national development. No real improvement has happened, the university still being too powerless. Each year new graduates enter the job market with no hope of finding work. In spite of the critical analysis of the situation and the concrete proposals made by the States-General on Higher Education in May 1987 (especially that the University be effectively integrated into the development of the nation, by making education more professional and intensifying research), much remains to be done.

Bibliography

Jeune Afrique, University of Bangui, Ministry of National Education and Higher Education 1987 *Atlas of Higher Education in the States of the Central African Republic*, Bangui
Yearbook of Statistics 1987–88
World Bank 1985 *The Central African Republic. Report of the Mission of August 22, 1985.* World Bank
World Bank/IDA/RCA 1989 *Flow of Students and Internal Structure of the University of Bangui*, Bangui

M. F. Mbringa-Takama

Chad

1. Higher Education and Society

The Republic of Chad is located in north central Africa, bordered by Libya to the north, the Central African Republic to the south, Niger, Nigeria, and Cameroon to the west, and Sudan to the east. Colonized by the French within their zone of influence in French Equatorial Africa, Chad became an autonomous state within the French community in November 1958. Independence followed in 1960.

A population growth rate in the order of 2 percent meant that by 1985 the population of Chad was estimated at about five million inhabitants, within an area of 1,284,000 square kilometers, giving an average density of population of around 2.5 inhabitants per kilometer. This average figure, however, hides the geographical and economic configuration of Chad. The north is dominated by desert, the Sahel, in the center, is devoted to livestock production, and the greatest actual density of population is in the south, in the savannah area.

Within this regional pattern, agriculture is the main base of the economy. It created about half the Gross

Domestic Product (GDP) in 1988 and employed about three-fourths of the labor force. The principal cash crop is cotton from the south, and it is the major export commodity, accounting for 70 percent of export earnings in the late 1980s (*World of Learning* 1990). The difficulties in improving agricultural production have included a major five-year drought starting in the mid-1960s, a phenomenon which has since recurred, and the loss of livestock production amid the instabilities of war.

Industry (mining, manufacturing, construction, and the power industry) contributed 15 percent of GDP in 1987. The manufacturing sector is dominated by agroindustrial activities, such as brewing, and notably the processing of the cotton crop by the state-owned cotton monopoly. Sources of power are scarce, however, and Chad is heavily dependent on imports of mineral fuels for the generation of electricity (*World of Learning* 1990). Its own petroleum resources have not yet been fully developed.

As a consequence of the basic economic configuration and occupational structure, together with the terms of international trade and internal and external political difficulties, Chad in 1987 had a trade deficit of US$116.5m, and a total external debt of US$27m. The Gross National Product (GNP) was estimated by the World Bank in 1988 at about US$160 per head which is extremely low in comparative terms (*World of Learning* 1990). The implications of this economic situation for the provision of education are extremely serious, but they are made even worse by political instabilities. Some educational progress was made in a twenty-year period after Independence, but even in the 1960s there were civil disturbances and riots in the capital, N'Djamena. There was also a rebellion in the north in 1965 and a military coup in 1975, and a civil war began in 1979. The pattern of political conflicts, with army coups, assassinations, imprisonment of political and military leaders, guerilla warfare, and the Libyan occupation of the "Aozou strip" in the north and tensions with the Sudan, has resulted in the intervention of a variety of peace-keeping forces or assistance, from the Organization of African States, France, and the United States, and the involvement of a number of other states, notably Algeria, in a range of peace initiatives. A variety of domestic and international agreements have been made, aimed at stabilizing the area, though how long they will last is unclear, and a certain amount of pessimism is probably justified.

Renegotiation of formal political structures has been part of the search for stability. Under the Constitution of 1989, executive power is vested in the president, elected by direct universal suffrage for seven years. Legislative power is exercised by the Council of Ministers, which is appointed and led by the president. The Constitution envisaged the reestablishment of the National Assembly, to be elected for a five-year term, although only one political party was foreseen (*World of Learning* 1990). It is clear that the political fabric of the country is weak, and this is compounded by cultural and linguistic differences, notably between the north and the south, and ambiguities about the national language. Almost half of the population are Muslims (living mainly in the north); 6 percent are Christians; and most of the remainder of the population (mainly in the south) follow a variety of animist beliefs. The official languages are French and Arabic and various African languages are widely spoken; but the illiteracy rate is high. In this political context, educational resuscitation, which would be difficult anyway, is made more so because of the inheritance of an exceptionally weak educational base.

2. The Institutional Fabric of the Higher Education System

The development of publicly supported schooling was particularly slow in Chad, even within the context of African educational history. Secondary education, for example, had to be obtained outside Chad before the Second World War, and a government-sponsored secondary school system did not take shape until the 1980s (Kurian 1988). Remarkable progress was made in the 1960s and 1970s in primary education, when primary school enrollments grew from under 5 percent to over 40 percent (Miaro 1985). This progress was blocked by the impact of the civil war from 1979 onward, when many schools were closed; since then, educational reform has been given low priority on the political agenda.

The position of higher education and the university should be understood in the context of the education system which precedes it. One aspect of Chad's educational inheritance is the high average rate of adult illiteracy which, in 1985, according to UNESCO estimates, was 74.7 percent. Another important aspect of Chad's educational inheritance is that the school system follows a traditional French model, and is highly selective. It has been neither culturally indigenized nor significantly modernized to meet or anticipate demands for science, engineering, technology, and agriculture (Miaro 1985).

Secondary education officially starts at the age of 12, though entry can take place at 15 years of age. The official length of secondary-school studies is seven years. The enrollment ratio for secondary education in 1986 was 16 percent of boys in the relevant age group and 2 percent of girls (*World of Learning* 1990). Partly as a consequence of the low figures at this level, higher education contains something under 1 percent of the age cohort. Entry to higher education studies must be preceded by enrollment in secondary education at either the *lycée*, which offers both first and second cycles of secondary education, or a *collège d'enseignement générale* which concentrates on the first cycle. Entry to secondary education requires success in the *concours d'entrée en sixième* and this examination is in itself a highly selective process. Four years of study in the first cycle of secondary education leads to the *brevet d'études du premier cycle*. The second cycle is of three years, and leads into higher education via the *baccalauréat* and its four specialities (philosophy and literature, economics and the social sciences, mathematics, and the natural sciences) (Kurian 1988, Miaro 1985).

The main institution of higher education is the University of Chad, founded in 1971 in N'Djamena with French as the language of instruction. It is state controlled. It has four institutes: Law, Economics, and Management; of Letters, Modern Languages, and Human Sciences; the Institute of Sciences; and an Institute of Animal Husbandry and Veterinary Medicine for Tropical Nations. A faculty of medicine is to be inaugurated (*World of Learning* 1990). In addition there are a range of postsecondary professional training schools, including a National School of Administration, a National School of Telecommunications, a National School of Nurses, and a National School of Police. There is a tradition of training secondary-school teachers outside Chad at the *Ecole Normale Supérieure de Brazzaville*, although some groups of teachers in the social sciences and letters receive their academic training at Chad University (Miaro 1985).

The course of study in the University is divided into two levels: a two-year diploma course and a three-year course leading to the first degree (*licence*). One or two years more lead to a master's degree (*maitrise*). The doctorate of the third cycle (*doctorat du 3e. cycle*) is awarded to students who present a thesis corresponding to two or three years of research work after a master's degree. While a doctorate is available on the basis of further research, the normal pattern is for advanced qualifications to be sought overseas, although the precise numbers are not clear. Third-level education is free. There is no provision for halls of residence, cafeterias, and other services, however. All students are awarded scholarships, and higher education is free (Kurian 1988).

3. Governance, Administration, and Finance

The administration of public education, including higher education, is structured around the national Ministry of Education. With a minister of cabinet rank at its head, and assistance from a secretary of state, administration is through the National Directorate of Education. As well as directorates for primary and secondary education and so on, there is a section of the General Directorate which deals directly with the University. From 1974, the newly created National Institute of Education undertook a number of review and advisory planning functions. Within the University itself a university council, whose membership is broadly drawn from pro-

fessions outside the university, assists the rector who is appointed through presidential decree.

The general financial situation of education in Chad is poor. Only about 3 percent of national income and about 15 percent of public expenditure is devoted to education, and most of this money goes on teachers' salaries and school materials (Kurian 1988). Priorities for public expenditure up to 1985 have been the military and the police. Such extra money as there is comes from foreign loans or assistance. For example, in 1988 the International Development Association gave US$22m in support of a program to reconstruct schools in areas affected by the conflict with Libya, and to provide teacher-training facilities. In 1989 the African Development Bank approved a loan of more than 3,500 million francs through the scheme Financial Cooperation on Central Africa (c. US$11,000 at 1989 exchange rates). This loan was for the construction of 40 primary schools (*World of Learning* 1990), but the fact remains that there is extremely little public money available for research and development within the higher education sector.

4. Faculty and Students: Teaching, Learning, and Research

Academic staff in Chad are drawn from different nations, with 50 percent of the staff being French. The figures for the number of teachers in tertiary education vary, with estimates of between 85 and 141 teachers. There are three ranks of teaching staff: professor, assistant lecturer, and assistant. National academics hold their tenured position as civil servants, while foreign academics are hired for varying periods. Research is carried out mainly in research institutes, such as the National Institute of Human Sciences, the Institute of Husbandry and Veterinary Medicine for Tropical Nations, and the Research Institute of Cotton and Exotic Textiles.

In 1975, 1,435 students were enrolled in higher education institutions outside the country while the University of Chad had 388 students. About 90 percent of the overall student population was male. In 1985, 550 students were enrolled at the University of Chad itself with no significant change in the proportion of male and female students. That year, the teacher–student ratio was 1:6.

5. Conclusion

It is difficult to see the education, including higher education, system in Chad in a positive light. The ambitions of nineteenth-century educational reformers and governments in Europe to provide elementary education for all built upon a partial, existing base. Even the efforts of the newly developing nations in Africa in the 1960s were normally buttressed by the inheritance of a mixed pattern of traditional education, missionary schools, and some provision of schooling, including secondary schooling, by colonial powers. Chad's quantitative educational inheritance was notably poor, partly because of the difficulties of providing education to a scattered population and partly because of tensions over Western and Islamic models of education. Resources, which are in short supply anyway, have been needed for defence and efforts to create internal stability. Such educational improvement as is underway is heavily dependent upon foreign aid—which by and large is merely replacing some of the educational fabric which has been lost.

While statistics indicate that an educational system exists, therefore, (even though there is a very low secondary-school enrollment ratio and very low access to education for girls) and while an administrative structure for education is formally in place, it may be questioned whether an educational system, in the sense of the standardized, national distribution of education, has been made a reality in Chad. Against this background, and the manifest lack of political stability, it is doubtful whether the concept of a higher education system is appropriate to understand the realities of higher education and its social standing in Chad. The development of such a system within the reconstruction of the education system as a whole will probably require major international assistance, the development of a powerful political ideology centering around national mobilization, reconstruction, and new definitions of political responsibility and, at least during a transition period, some notion of regional cooperation in higher education.

Bibliography

Europa World Yearbook 1990. 31st edn. Europa Publications, London
Kurian G T 1988 Chad. In: Kurian G T (ed.) 1988 *World Education Encyclopedia*. Facts on File Publications, Oxford
Miaro-II B-R 1985 Chad. In: Husen T, Postlethwaite T N (eds.) 1985 *The International Encyclopedia of Education*. Pergamon, Oxford
World of Learning 1990. 40th edn. Europa Publications, London

R. Cowen

Chile

1. Higher Education and Society

Chilean higher education attempts to provide for all high school graduates by including in its system a vast array of private nonuniversity institutions, and of course, it also trains highly qualified professionals in the traditional universities. Despite its efforts there remain problems: there is little information for potential students to make rational decisions about their postsecondary education; there is a large internal brain drain as the good high-school graduates from low socioeconomic levels are financially unable to apply for university admission; there are poor incentives for attracting good candidates into academic courses; there is too much emphasis on "competitive" research; and the training of researchers is carried out in small isolated units.

The present-day Chilean higher education system has mainly been shaped by the evolution of the interest in it over the years, by the types of university institutions available, and by the changes in political ideas or groups in power. In 1713, 60 years after the foundation of the capital, Santiago, the city council asked the King of Spain to open a university to train students in law, mathematics, and medicine. The University of San Felipe was established by royal charter in 1738 and inaugurated six courses of study in 1747 using the available infrastructure from the earlier confessional universities. In 1842 the University of Chile was established by Andres Bello to give special attention to research. New concepts and courses of studies, largely shaped by parallel changes in Europe were gradually included in studies of medicine, engineering, and agriculture. In 1843 the first Primary Teachers' Training School (*Escuela Normal*) was created at the secondary level by Sarmiento. During the reform movement in Cordoba in 1918, students actively joined in the fight for control of the University of Chile.

In the early 1950s, research attained a higher profile in Chile, most especially in the University of Chile. By law 0.5 percent of all taxes were allocated to it. Promising scholars were trained in the United States and European universities of high standing and basic equipment was acquired. Eventually research quality improved in several areas including: physics, mathematics, electronics, geology, chemistry, astronomy, economics, anthropology, and agriculture (Saavedra 1986). An eighth university was created in 1956.

There were no further university foundations until 1981. In 1960 a two-year Community College system was launched. Traditional university schools failed to enroll graduates from the community colleges, however, and eventually the seven colleges had to be transformed into provincial university campuses offering traditional university careers. As a by-product of the otherwise failed experiment, well-trained scholars settled in parts of Chile removed from the capital and major cities and expanded the possibilities for further training.

The 1960s brought both a massive expansion and a change in university management. In the mid-1960s the collection, processing, and economic analysis of basic information helped to coordinate university investment. Expansion was negotiated with selective institutions operating with very low enrollments; overly small specialized courses were streamlined. In 1967 the worldwide revolution among university students hit Chile. Students and administrative staff obtained voting power and participation became an end in itself. Enrollment expanded and research centers focusing on social problems were created. However, despite the enthusiasm of the time not all aspirations were realized: while it was felt that university activities were crucial for future national development and deserved special funding, a proposal for a national doctoral program (to operate as a cooperative effort of all universities) did not succeed. Each university sought to develop its own research capacity. Optimistic expectations about future university funding may have been one of the reasons why a cost recovery proposal submitted to the congress during the Frei regime was rejected. A massive expansion of free tuition enrollments followed during the Allende regime (1970–73).

Until 1973 universities were governed by rectors and by councils made up of deans and, in the case of the public universities, some public officials. Student power in university government had increased since 1967. Although the official sources of power were internal there were also powerful external influences. By 1970 some 80 percent of the eight public and private universities were financed with public funds. However, dependence on government finance was not without difficulties such as a lack of long-term planning; high prices from suppliers who risked delays in payments; too much time spent by managers in lobbying government officials.

Through a mixture of vertical authority and market competition, the 1973 military coup shifted the emphasis in university education toward professional training and later on forced conditions on the autonomy of the universities by linking the use of funds to the market demand for new students. Members of the armed forces were appointed as university presidents (*rectores delegados*), some 2,000 liberal scholars and 20,000 students were summarily expelled, social studies courses were eliminated or restricted, and some 25 research centers in the social sciences were closed or limited (Brunner 1986). The school year was fully devoted to classes. The teaching load was increased and loyalty to deans and the government was made an important element in salary determination. Mastery of accepted knowledge and the ability to apply that knowledge in the solution of practical problems were the main criteria for reviewing curricula, selecting instructors, and testing students. In 1974 higher education received a larger share (41%) of a smaller pie, as the total education share of government spending declined to 14 percent from 20 percent in 1969.

As national frontiers have not changed this century and less than 5 percent of the population do not use Spanish as their first language, geographic, ethnic, and demographic factors have had little effect on higher education. Economic and social factors are important considerations in understanding the present situation in Chile, however. The growth rate of the population decreased from 2.6 percent in the 1950s to 1.2 percent in the early 1990s. Universal primary education was achieved in the late 1960s. There has been social pressure for further expansion of higher education opportunities. The percentage of the labor force involved in agriculture dropped from 31 percent in 1960 to 15 percent in 1985 as the workforce moved into the service industries increasing representation there from 44 to 60 percent. The productivity level in agriculture is still half the level of industry, however. The urban population, as a percentage of the total population, increased from 68 percent in 1960 to 83 percent in 1980. Although the gross national product (GNP) per capita was lower in 1986 (US$1,320) than in 1965, the economy was by then somewhat diversified and no longer depended only on copper, but also on the acceptance of its agricultural and other products in the markets of the developed world. The use of modern technology that has been forced on Chile by liberal trade policies may be related to the increment in the percentage of the labor force with a background in higher education (from 4% in the 1960s to 12% at the time of writing).

Religious organizations have played an important role in the development of higher education. Aristocratic and confessional colonial universities were established in Chile by the Dominican (1619) and Jesuit (1620) orders to teach theology and canon law, philosophy, and the arts. This model of higher education continued into the republican period when the Instituto Nacional was created in 1813. As the number of enrollments grew and the social base of the student body broadened, the university became a center for political debate, and in 1888 the first Catholic University was created by papal decree as an alternative to the secular influences in the University of Chile.

2. The Institutional Fabric of the Higher Education System

In January 1981 four major reforms were instituted in Chile's higher education system. From then on the traditional universities (those which had been operating in 1980) had to compete not only among themselves but also with a wide range of new private education institutions including the professional institutes (IP) and technical centers (CFI) which were established. Universities were forced to increase tuition fees as the only alternative means of finding additional financing. As a means of circumventing the poverty trap which prevented students from low-income homes entering higher education student loans were made available for all students. It was intended that quality should be raised by allocating half of the public funds devoted to universities to be apportioned between the new students with highest scores in the university entrance examination test (UEET) of each year (private IPs and CFTs could not benefit from this incentive). A four-year transition period allowed gradual implementation of the new norms (Castaneda 1986). Fourteen different campuses of the former two public universities were transformed into separate traditional universities. During the first five years potential new universities (institutions granting degrees in 14 professional subjects defined by law as a university level) were to seek approval from the Ministry of Internal Government. Only three universities were granted such approval in the 1983–87 period. Thus, a total of 23 universities operated in that period.

Although there was intense competition among traditional universities from the outset, it was based on the expansion of those courses chosen by students with high scores in the UEET (but there were few efforts to improve the quality of courses on offer), the hiring of marketing agencies, and the offers of scholarships and fringe benefits that were made to the best students. Within the first year the number of new places in medicine, engineering, and economics doubled. There was a consensus of opinion that the only result of the highly expensive university training would be underemployment for most of the future graduates. In November 1981 initial results forced a crucial change in the new system. It was decided that the mechanisms for improving quality would not be applied to new universities. Student loans were to be used only by students enrolled at the traditional universities. Students from new universities and IP would be approved by examiners from the traditional universities in order to enroll in upper courses. The creation of new courses and the number of places available on them was controlled by the government in 1982. In 1983 subsidies were reshaped on a five-level scale, linked to scores in the UEET. The amount was frozen in pesos in spite of inflation.

In 1987 there was a fresh purge of scholars, more emphasis was put on efficiency, and the political control on the opening of private universities was halted. Professors were fired, university funds further reduced (and transferred to research). In 1989, 14 new private universities started operations with some 3,000 new places for initial admission. New higher education institutions have concentrated their efforts on relatively low-cost fields. There are now seven research universities (two public and five private with public subsidies); 34 nonresearch universities (12 public); 56 IP (one-fourth of which are teacher training establishments); and some 150 short-cycle nonuniversity CFTs.

Research is undertaken not only by universities, but also by public and private research institutes and enterprises. Although research received high priority only after the mid-1950s, there is a strong empirical research tradition in a few faculties of seven universities and in half a dozen isolated technological centers (ACICH 1987). The support for research started in the mid-1950s in the Universidad de Chile and was quickly followed in other universities. In 1965 the University of Chile created a Faculty of Sciences to train students in research and the University of Concepcion created a group of science departments (biology, physics, mathematics, chemistry, sociology, and anthropology) that provided instruction to students in all vocational courses. In 1979 there were 74 graduate programs, and by 1984 there were 160 in 11 universities, including 23 doctoral programs (Brunner 1986). In spite of these efforts there is still no systematic support for developing doctoral training in Chile. This style of graduate study is tailored to a future academic career. It is not organized, either in purpose or design, to provide high level labor for a range of professional or occupational settings.

There were several nonuniversity research efforts. The National Development Corporation (CORFO) created technological centers in geology (1957), forestry (1961), natural resources (1964), fishing (1964), and technology-INTEC (1986). INTEC has been selling about US$1 million in annual services since the mid-1970s. Several public research and development centers were also created by other institutions in the last two decades, including agriculture-INIA (1964), nuclear energy (1964), mining and metallurgy-CIMM (1970), and Fundacion Chile (1975). Public and private enterprises producing copper, explosives, cement, or wood have also embarked on research programs.

Research productivity has gradually increased over time. In 1967, 123 publications in international scientific journals were produced by a total of 14 authors per million residents; in 1980 the number of publications had increased to 619 and the number of authors to 56 per million residents (ACICH 1987). The number of authors per resident is much higher than in other Latin American countries (Argentina has 37 and Venezuela 40). Competition for Fondecyt funds has stimulated externally-reviewed research projects.

While admission to traditional universities is quite selective few constraints limit admissions of students to the new private institutions. There is an efficient admissions system to publicly financed institutions based on the UEET. The UEET is jointly sponsored by all traditional universities. Students can apply for places on five alternative courses from the pool of options available in all universities. A computer assigns students according to their weighted averages of UEET scores, grades in secondary education, and special tests in certain areas. One in four applicants is finally admitted to the traditional universities. Additional specialized tests are applied at several institutions. In some institutions admission policies for new students include a psychological test about attitudes and values with respect to the armed forces and their political views (Ormeno 1988).

The pattern in enrollments in higher education reflect changes in structure described above. In 1940 there were five universities and 7,846 students (1,959 females); 14,917 students in 1950 (5,368 females); 24,703 in 1960; and 41,801 in 1965 (16,750 females). From 1970 when there were 76,795 university students (50% females) enrollment jumped to 146,451 in 1973. Over 10 percent of the 18–22 year-old age group was enrolled at the university in that year. Figures reached a peak in 1975 with 147,549 students, but dropped in 1980 to 118,978 students, a slow increment followed as figures rose to 127,496 in 1985 and 134,300 in 1989. Although many of the declared objectives of the 1981 reform became obsolete with the ensuing changes, the number of students in the new private higher education institutions increased dramatically, while traditional, publicly funded universities levelled off at some 127,000 students. From 12,000 students in nonsubsidized CFTs in 1981, private enrollments (including non-traditional private universities) increased to 106,000 in 1989 (8,000 in new universities, 24,000 in new IPs, and 74,000 in CFTs).

In 1989 some 100,000 students started postsecondary education (40 percent of the 18-year-old population). Some 30,000 enrolled in universities and the balance in IPs (10,000) and CFTs (60,000) offering short (two- or three-year) careers. There were at the time 233,000 students already in the postsecondary system (19 percent of the 18–22-year-old-population) including 126,300 in traditional universities. The preference for higher education can be explained to some extent by the positive rates of return, which will be examined below (representing some social value allocated to university careers), and the relatively low rates of graduate unemployment. It is true that there was a rise from the 5 percent unemployment rate for those with higher level education in 1980, to 6.6 percent in 1984, (IDB 1987), but the unemployment of people with no university education was more than double these levels.

The length of first-degree studies is usually five years (six years for engineers and seven for physicians), but four years for primary teachers and courses in IPs and two or three years for technical degrees in CFTs. Lawyers are accredited by the Supreme Court, but all other careers only require the higher education diploma. A diploma from a five-year (or longer) course is the usual requisite for admission to graduate studies. Graduate studies are now isolated efforts and each program defines its own special admission requirements.

3. Governance, Administration, and Finance

There are three management issues regarding policy implementation in Chilean universities (the rest of this article refers only to universities). They concern the lack of opportunities for potential students from low socioeconomic groups; redistribution of public resources allocated to public universities towards the wealthier groups of society; and the unequal gender, age, and geographic distribution of access to, and quality of, the higher education system.

3.1 National, Regional, and Provincial Administration

The military system of governance—the institutional framework for setting priorities, making policy decisions, and allocating resources—was a serious constraint on improvements to internal efficiency. By making the appointment of rectors a political decision, the allocation of funds a function of the Ministry of Finance, and supervision the responsibility of the Ministry of Education, the government implemented its higher education policies. Attention was paid to discipline, training of efficient professionals, and political control rather than to academic outcomes.

Measured by performance in the labor market and by some subjective evidence of academic performance in other countries, professional training in Chile is of high quality. The evidence also suggests that the social returns of investment in higher education have been substantial. The last available estimate, using data for 1982, is 6.8 percent rate of return (Riveros 1986), much lower than the 12.2 percent estimated for 1959. However, these are likely to be underestimates, because they do not reflect nonmarket effects, which are also expected to be substantial. In any case, rates of return measured by specific vocational courses would probably show much higher rates for graduates in medicine, engineering, or economics, with education yielding the lowest return. These differences are generated by entrance constraints on courses and by lack of relevant information to candidates.

The central agency created in the Ministry of Education to oversee the higher education system has not been able to prepare the basic information necessary to any discussion of the key questions about the present or future state of the higher education system. One such question would concern the provision of relevant and timely information about the labor market. There are no follow-up studies of graduates from the new institutions. Some graduates from CFTs may experience difficulty in finding a job. Low-income students and their families need information and assistance in making academic and career choices. The high-income students in new universities may find places in the labor market more easily given their family connections and support.

High education subsidies (about 40 percent of teaching unit costs) have stimulated high-income families to invest in quality fee-paid private high schools in order to gain access to good tuition-subsidized public universities. Students from high-income families who have done well tend to go on to careers with higher unit costs (medicine, odontology, or engineering). Scholarships for deprived students are scant (Arriagada 1989). Among students with low academic performances only high-income students can attend the new private universities, because public loans are not granted to deprived students willing to attend them.

Subsidized university education most benefits students whose families have been able to invest in their previous training by enrolling them in private schools; supplying all required textbooks and reference materials; providing them with special coaching when facing learning problems; preventing health problems in order to help them to attend on the maximum number of days in the school year, and providing them with opportunities to learn a foreign language. Over 70 percent of university students belong to families included in the high or medium groups of the socioeconomic distribution. These data, together with the fact that about 20 percent of the resources for education are apportioned to higher education, show that about one-tenth of total public resources allocated to education (about US$48 million) are transferred as subsidies to a select group of some 85,000 wealthy students.

Three areas of educational inequity should be highlighted. While overall female participation is approximately equal to male participation, significant differences persist across fields of specialization. There are relatively few female engineering students while they are overrepresented in education or nursing (Schiefelbein and Farrell 1980). There are no opportunities for workers to study in night shifts (even though the most cost-effective means of improving access to higher education is either to offer night and weekend classes or distance learning alternatives) or to certify for self-teaching by enrolling in (and passing) isolated courses. Finally, the smaller or poorer the location the worse the educational opportunities, it provides to its students. The subsidy per student received by regional institutions tends to be one-fourth of the average subsidy received by the eight universities operating in 1980 (Lavados et al. 1986).

3.2 Institutional Administration

The absolute power given to the *rectores delegados* has generated inefficiency in higher education as has the lack of incentives for management to improve quality in academic performance. There are neither external examiners for students presenting theses, no visiting committees to assess recruitment and remuneration of personnel, nor rewards for funds obtained from external sources. In 1988, in one Teaching College (*Universidad Metropolitana*), there were 458 academic staff (256 full-time) and 409 full-time administrative personnel including a huge and well-paid university police (Ormeno 1988). Administration costs accounted for 45 percent of the budget. This allocation of resources resulted in lower faculty salaries, smaller outlays on supplies and equipment, and losses in the quality of instruction. An instructor in Calculus II for engineers in the University of Chile (six sessions per week) earned the equivalent of 50 subway tickets per month.

Although new private institutions generate some of the same social benefits as public ones, they do not receive subsidies. The new universities created in the early 1980s are not highly efficient. In 1984 and 1985 about 20 to 30 percent of their students were dropping out each year. Among those that remained the promotion rate ranged between 65 and 90 percent (Sanfuentes 1988). Although there is a larger proportion of teaching staff with graduate training in the new universities than in the traditional universities (24 versus 20 percent), the new universities only have part-time staff drawn from among the full-time staff of traditional universities. The new universities only pay the bare minimum required to entice professors to moonlight in this way. No research is carried out by these new universities.

While new private resources finance a large part of the two or three-years degree courses, the real expenditure per student in traditional universities has declined in recent years and enrollment in them has levelled off. Average annual tuition fees are estimated at US$500 in CFTs, per student, US$800 in IPs, and US$1,200 in new universities. The financial contribution of the private sector increased from zero to about US$55 million per year in the period 1981–88. In the same period the public contribution was reduced by US$56 million, while traditional university enrollments increased from 99,428 to 126,300.

Public funds are allocated mainly as direct transfers. Public funding goes to either public or private universities (private institutions created after 1981 notwithstanding) in three forms; direct institutional support (65%), indirect support in the form of financial aid to students (24%), and support in the form of performance incentives (11%) to enroll greater proportions of the most highly qualified students (Arriagada 1989). These figures are far away from the 1981 targets.

Until 1973 the private sector had relied virtually as much as the public sector on government finance. Since the military coup in that year, this approach has been modified; all the universities operating in 1980 depended on a mixture of public and private financing. Universities now charge significant student fees, and cost recovery exceeds 25 percent of total income, in the region of 60 percent of the instructional unit cost, when expenses for research, services, and extension are deducted (Arriagada 1989). The government has not interfered in the tuition fees institutions can charge, thus, fees have been adjusted according to market trends, to some US$1,200 in the case of new private universities (Sanfuentes 1988). Unfortunately, along with the increment in tuition fees, access for students from low income backgrounds has not been protected. Over half of the income from tuition is obtained through student loans (*credito fiscal*), but provision of financial assistance to low income students is lacking.

Higher education charges for a number of services. Apart from instruction (tuition), there are products sold by auxiliary enterprises such as hospitals, laboratories, testing, bookstores, publishers, cafeterias, TV stations, cinemas, theaters, music, social or sports clubs, sports events, sports fields, and student housing. Most of these are usually subsidized. Although revenues from these products may be increased, there are great political disadvantages in advocating price increases. One factor further limiting the revenue-raising capacity of public institutions is the lack of incentives in terms of corporate taxes for charitable funding of education, but some incentives were included in a 1987 law.

Although specific funds for research and technology (FONDECYT) have been gradually channeled through the Research Council (CONICYT), they represent only some 10 percent of the total funds used in research activities. FONDECYT transfers some US$5 million each year in a competitive process. All institutions (including newly created universities) can apply for grants. International technical assistance worth about US$5 million per year (30%) is also channeled into research. Still these are small amounts and some equilibrium between targeted and competitive research must be eventually reached.

4. Faculty and Students: Teaching, Learning, and Research

4.1 Faculty

The massive growth in higher education, along with academic traditions and pressures for common salary and equipment levels makes it difficult to initiate the required conditions for research at the third level. With 126,300 university students and 12,000 professors, every change and proposed charge affects a large number of people who will react to those changes and transform proposals into political issues. Pressures for common salary levels mean that better salary conditions intended only for a select number of researchers will immediately be demanded by the whole teaching staff (which cannot be afforded). Until more resources become available access to data banks, equipment, reactives, and other elements cannot be provided to all higher education institutions.

The tradition of academic research is kept alive only by a select number (1,500 to 2,000) of university research scholars, while the remaining 10,000 university professors, though willing and able to transmit the core of accepted knowledge, are not really willing to further the frontiers of their disciplines. Additions to the body of highly qualified professors is rather slow. Only 220 scholars received grants to study abroad at the master or doctoral level in the 1977–85 period. This group represents an investment of some US$5 million (ACICH 1987).

Although the allocation of scholarships is centralized, recruitment of academic teaching staff is the responsibility of each individual establishment and significant differences exist between the career and status of faculty in different types of institutions. The reduction in financing forced the universities to provide differential salaries for full-time work according to academic training. Senior professors with the ability to carry out independent research are paid some US$15,000 per year, while associate professors get half that much, assistants one-third, and instructors only about US$3,000 per year.

In spite of this salary structure, academic power is concentrated in deans appointed by the rector. Deans are key elements because they decide the balance between teaching, research, and administration. Only recently has the academic staff been able to elect deans and thus gradually increase its collegial academic power in university affairs.

4.2 Students

The military intervention is also reflected in a greater access to engineering and technology. Enrollment in the exact sciences and technologies rose from 43.7 percent in 1970 to 53.4 percent in 1985, while social sciences figures reduced from 49.1 percent to 39.4 percent with the humanities accounting for the remaining 7.2 percent.

Half of the university students come from families in the highest quintile of the income distribution and 20 percent in the fourth quintile, while only 5 percent are in the first or lowest quintile (Petrei 1987). The probability of the children of agricultural workers reaching university is around 5 percent (Schiefelbein and Farrell 1982).

During the period 1973–84 student unions were controlled by the government which appointed the leaders. Later, students elected their leaders. Some 40 to 50 percent of the student body cast their votes. All enrolled students may vote; no special membership is required. University authorities seldom talk with elected student leaders.

Each faculty proposes the program or courses necessary for an area of study and the University Council or rector makes the final decision. Courses are usually specialist and single subject. There are a few universities operating with a limited (constrained) credit unit system.

Some indication of the quality of professional

training can be obtained from the performance of the best graduates who go on to further studies in developed countries. For example, there is a 30 percent approval rate for Chilean physicians taking the Foreign Medical Graduate Examination for the Medical Sciences (FMGEMS) even though it is in a foreign language. It is more difficult to know their professional level after graduation given the increasing isolation from a supervised medical practice. Chilean economists usually score in the upper quintile in the Graduate Entrance Examination Test required to enroll at graduate schools of economics in the United States. Chilean economists are regularly accepted on graduate courses in Chicago, Harvard, MIT, Berkeley, and other leading universities. Even though one-third of university graduates needs some further training related more directly to their jobs they do not have special problems in coping with professional challenges.

What is less clear is whether graduates will have those capacities beyond professional expertise that are now critical in Chile: the ability to be creative, the willingness to take risks, and the desire to participate constructively in the civic affairs of the country. In addition, privatization of the health sector will probably affect the graduate training of medical doctors and the quality of future health levels.

5. Conclusion

The difficulties facing unemployed or low-paid students who have to repay student loans and the means of support for research and graduate studies are two crucial problems that should be critically assessed.

The rapidly increasing dependence on loans as a means of financing students is alarming and must end, but some type of financing through work–study programs should be arranged. The 1981 reform established that all students able to prove that they or their family could not pay the tuition (some cases were checked by social workers) were allowed to receive a loan (the average loan was US$750 in 1984). Loans are supposed to be paid back in 10 to 15 years with a two-year period of grace after graduation, but those dropping out are required to start payments the following year. About one-third of the student body has received student loans. Repayment of loans started in 1989; the default rate is over 40 percent. There are 30,000 default cases in judicial collection. Many of these cases are students who dropped out early, have no jobs (the rate of unemployment for youngsters is over 20 percent) and have been unable to pay in spite of court orders obtained by the treasury.

An alternative to this system could be the introduction of income-contingent loans. Income-contingent loans would directly reduce the level of subsidies received by high-income groups and make loans more acceptable to low-income students as the

risks would be reduced. Moreover, Chile should help students to pay for their higher education. A work-study program encourages the development of values needed in our society, and it allows the opportunity to create public-service roles for students both on and off campus.

The amount of research and development expenditures is low and has levelled off in the 1970s with a decreasing share of universities. About 0.4 percent of the gross domestic product is allocated to research. This figure is lower than four other Latin American countries, and much lower than the 2.2 percent observed in developed countries. The total support for basic research should grow. At present some US$100 million are spent each year in research and two-thirds of that amount is used by universities. In 1965 the university sector was using 80 percent of the US$75 million then allocated to research. Chile is the only South American country allocating more than 50 percent of research resources to universities.

The reduction in the amount of research funds used by universities may be related to funding mechanisms that fail to separate research support from general funding. During periods of sharp resource constraints research activities are probably going to be reduced. This problem was partially addressed by the creation of the National Research Funding Agency (CONICYT) in 1967. Still, the massive development of higher education, academic traditions, and pressures for common salary and equipment levels makes it difficult to create the required conditions for research at the university level.

The principal problems of graduate education are the total amount of resources and the dispersal of funding across too many programs. Graduate enrollment is only 2 percent of the university total. However, growth in graduate education programs has to some extent resulted in too many programs relative to available funding. Class sizes are small, student–teacher ratios are low, and facilities are poor. In 1984 there were 2,371 graduate students in total in some 100 programs. The dispersal of programs makes it impossible to use funding mechanisms to provide performance incentives and prevents the development of the critical mass of both students and faculty needed to develop true centers of excellence.

There are several conditions necessary to the improvement of the country's ability to carry out the research demanded for social and economic development and to train graduate students at a doctoral level. The long-term development of research and doctoral training is conditioned by competitive salaries and job stability protection against political onslaughts; national research data banks and access to international data banks; computing facilities; libraries and documentation centers; travel and per diem expenses; and editing facilities. The number of institutions (41 universities) and the large size of the teaching staff do not allow comprehensive collaboration between the universities. A consortium of centers of excellence is necessary where selected scholars from all universities may cooperate in research, use all available facilities, and complement their salaries up to the nationally competitive required levels. The creation of a consortium or specialization of an academic institution in research and graduate education would result in an improved management of resources, but the basic diversity of research laboratories should be retained.

Economic and social development in Chile depend in the end on production systems that are more skill and knowledge intensive and employ more advanced technologies. This larger role for science and technology within the Chilean economy requires, in turn, major investments in the scientific and technological infrastructure and in high-level labor force development. These investments should take into account both public and private sectors. New institutions and new linkages among available institutions are required to implement the investment program and to cover a range of functions including development of the workforce, basic and applied research, technology and development, and application to production.

Bibliography

Academia de Ciencias del Instituto de Chile (ACICH) 1987 *El Desarrollo Cientifico y Tecnologico en Chile*. Corporacion de Promocion Universitaria, Santiago.

Academia de Medicina del Instituto de Chile 1985 *Educacion Medica en Chile*. Corporacion de Promocion Universitaria, Santiago

Arriagada P 1989 *El Financiamiento de la Educacion Superior en Chile 1960/1988*. FLACSO, Santiago

Bowman M J et al. 1986 Adult life cycle perspective on public subsidies to higher education in three countries. *Econ. Educ. Rev.* 2: 135–45

Briones G 1981 *Las universidades chilenas en el modelo de economia neo-liberal 1973–1981*. PIIE, Santiago

Brunner J J 1986 *Informe Sobre Educacion Superior en Chile*. FLACSO, Santiago

Brunner J J 1988 La reforma de las universidades Chilenas: implicaciones intelectuales. *Material de Discusion No 114*. FLACSO, Santiago

Bustos E 1989 Educacion superior crecio en 700% desde ano 1981. *El Mercurio*, 19 July p. C6. Santiago

Castaneda T 1986 *Innovations in the Financing of Education: the Case of Chile*. Discussion paper report EDT35, World Bank, Washington, DC

Centro de Estudios de la Realidad Contemporane. *Realidad Universitaria 1968–1988*. Santiago

Consejo de Rectores 1986 *Anuario Estadistico*. Santiago

Courard H 1989 Notas acerca del Plan Nacional de Desarrollo Cientifico y Tecnologico PLANDECYT–1988. Documento de Trabajo 397, FLACSO, Santiago

Cox C 1989 *Informe Sobre los Institutos Profesionales*. Documento de Trabajo 418, FLACSO, Santiago

El Mercurio 1989 Guia de ingreso a las instituciones de educacion superior privadas 1989. 1 March Supplement, Santiago

Inter-American Development Bank (IDB) 1987 Informe del progreso social. Washington, DC

Lavados H, Hill E, Apablaza V 1986 *El Sistema Educacional Chileno*. Corporacion de Promocion Universitaria, Santiago

Ministerio de Educacion Publica 1988 *Estadistica Educacionales 1987*. Santiago

Ormeno A 1988 *Educacion y Universidad*. Proyecto Universidad y Democracia, Centro de Estudios de la Realidad Contemporanea (CERC), Santiago

Petrei H 1987 *El Gasto Publico Social y sus Efectos Redistributivos*. Estudios Conjuntos de Integracion Economica de Latinoamerica (ECIEL), Rio de Janeiro

Riquelme S 1989 Las platas de la Educacion. *El Mercurio*, 23 April pp. B1–2, Santiago

Riveros L 1986 *The Rate of Return to Schooling in Chile: a Long-term Overview*. World Bank, Washington, DC

Saavedra I 1986 El desarrollo cientifico universitario. In CPU *Juan Gomez Millas (1900–1987) El Legado de un Humanista*, Corporacion de Promocion Universitaria, Santiago

Saavedra I, Lavados I 1982 Las activadades de Investigacion y Desarrollo en Chile. In CPU *Conocimiento, Educacion Superior y Desarrollo Nacional*, Santiago

Sagasti F, Cook C 1985 *Tiempos Dificiles: Ciencia y Tecnologia en America Latina Durante el Decenio de 1980*. Lima

Sanfuentes A 1988 *Desarrollo de la Universidades Privadas en Chile*. Ilades, Santiago

Schiefelbein E 1987 *Education Costs and Financing Policies in Latin America. A Review of Available Research*. World Bank, Washington, DC

Schiefelbein E, Farrell J P 1980 Women, schooling and work in Chile. *Comp. Educ. Rev.* 24(2):112

Schiefelbein E, Farrell J P 1982 *Eight Years of their Lives: Through Schooling to Labour Market in Chile*. International Development Research Center (IDRC), Ottawa

E. Schiefelbein

China, People's Republic of

1. Higher Education and Society

As an important component of China's brilliant classical civilization, Chinese higher education dates from the early Zhou Dynasty (eleventh–eighth century BC). The modern Chinese higher education system, however, started in the later Qing Dynasty, and was symbolized mainly by the establishment of the Metropolitan University (predecessor of Peking University) in 1898, the first comprehensive university of China. During one century of development, the system has undergone dramatic changes. The basic characteristic of current Chinese higher education is its socialist nature. It emphasizes the all-round development of the students—morally, intellectually, and physically—and the aim of serving the social and economic development needs of the country. It is mainly a centrally planned system based on its own cultural tradition but absorbing foreign experiences. Accompanying the newly adopted policies of reform, and open to the outside world, Chinese higher education is undergoing profound reform in almost every aspect of the system, readjusting its structure and function, in order better to serve the construction of a high level of socialist material and spiritual civilization.

The People's Republic of China (PRC) is situated in East Asia. It covers an area of about 9.60 million square kilometers, typically divided into three major topographical regions: the eastern, northwestern, and southwestern zones. The latter two regions cover more than 60 percent of the total area of the country, but, because of the poor natural conditions, their agricultural output value and industrial output value were only 10.3 percent and 5.8 percent of the corresponding national output values in 1987. Consequently, education, especially higher education, is underdeveloped in the northwest and southwest but more developed in the east. In 1987, more than 88.5 percent of higher education institutions were located in the east, enrolling more than 91.1 percent of students.

China has the largest population of any country in the world. In 1949, when New China was established, the population totalled 541.67 million, and it has continued to grow rapidly. The birthrate up to 1971 was always higher than 30 per 1,000, with exceptions only during 1958–61. Owing to the implementation of family planning policy, the birthrate has decreased since the 1970s. The 1987 registration reported that the total population numbered 1,080.73 million (Taiwanese and overseas Chinese are not included), and the birthrate was 21.04 per 1,000. The population of China is quite unevenly distributed. In 1987, the broad northwest and southwest region was inhabited by only 12.3 percent of the national total population. The rural–urban population ratio has decreased due to industrialization and intensive urban construction. In 1949, 89.4 percent of the national total population inhabited rural areas. This fell to 53.4 percent in 1987.

Besides the majority Han nationality group, China has 55 minority groups. According to the 1982 census, ethnic minority people numbered 67,233,254 or 6.7 percent of the country's total. Han Chinese is the most widely spoken language and the most important Chinese dialect is Mandarin. The government has paid great attention to helping minority groups promote their national languages and introduce written languages where none existed previously.

According to the 1 percent population sampling survey, in 1987 the occupational structure of the labor force was as follows: 70.9 percent work in farming, fishing, animal husbandry, and forestry; 16.4 percent work in industrial production and transportation; 4.5 percent are teachers and various other specialized personnel; 1.4 percent are office workers; 1.8 percent are officials of government and mass

organizations; 2.7 percent work in commerce; and 2.4 percent are in the service sector. According to the needs of state plans for socialist modernization, the percentage of farmers should be reduced, and that of teachers and specialized personnel increased.

The economic system of New China had been a state-planned system until the end of the 1970s. In order to overcome the shortcomings of this over-centralized system, a comprehensive restructuring of the economy has been carried out, and a new planned-commodity economy has been established. Collective-run and individual-run enterprises have developed. The value of industrial output produced by enterprises other than state-run ones accounted for 40.2 percent of the national total in 1987. Agriculture was the most important sector of the national economy in the early years of New China. At the same time, the government gave priority to the development of industry, especially heavy industry. The value of industrial output has thus increased rapidly, and surpassed the value of agricultural output from 1956 on. In 1987, the gross national product (GNP) stood at US$ 201 billion, of which the primary economic sector accounted for 28.8 percent, the secondary 45.7 percent, and the tertiary 25.5 percent.

The 1982 constitution defines the socialist system as the basic system of the state and forbids any organization or individual to disrupt the socialist system. The National People's Congress is the highest authority of state power. The standing committee of the National People's Congress exercises the functions of the Congress between its annual sessions. According to the decisions made by the National People's Congress and its standing committee, the chairman of the state promulgates laws, appoints and removes the premier and other senior officials, and represents the state in foreign countries.

The State Council is the highest administrative organ of the state. In 1988, the administration beneath it developed into 86 ministries, commissions, and other central organs. The State Education Commission (SEC, formerly the Ministry of Education or Ministry of Higher Education) is in charge of higher education affairs. For administrative purposes, China is divided into 22 provinces, 5 autonomous regions, and 3 municipalities directly under the central government, which, in turn, are divided into 326 prefectures and cities at the prefecture level, and 2,194 counties and cities at the county level.

Since 1978, the government's political goals have been to achieve the "four modernizations" (of agriculture, industry, defense, and science and technology), adhering to the "four basic principles" (socialism, dictatorship of the proletariat, leadership of the Communist Party, adherence to Marxist–Leninist and Maoist ideology) to build China into a powerful socialist country. The government set targets of quadrupling the GNP between 1980 and 2000, and has stressed that education must serve socialist construction, which in turn must rely on education, to achieve these goals.

The mission of higher education is to train tens of millions of advanced specialized personnel so they are equipped with up-to-date knowledge of science, technology, and management; imbued with a pioneering spirit; and can keep abreast with developments in science, culture, and the technological revolution. According to the Decision of the CPC Central Committee on Reform of China's Educational Structure in 1985:

> China's strategic goal in developing higher education is: By the end of the century, China will have built a well-proportioned, rationally tiered system embracing a complete range of disciplines and areas, on a comprehensive scale conforming to its economic strength; senior specialists will be trained basically at home and the institutions of higher education will contribute substantially to China's independent scientific and technological development and to solving major theoretical and practical problems that crop up in the course of socialist modernization.

China is a multireligious country but has no official religion. The major religions are: Buddhism, Taoism, Islam, and Roman Catholicism. These are adhered to by a small portion (about 8.4% in 1980) of the total population. The constitution of China stipulates that Chinese people possess religious freedom, but religious bodies are forbidden to intervene in education. Under these conditions, there is no direct relation between higher education and religious bodies.

2. The Institutional Fabric of the Higher Education System

In 1949, there were 205 institutions of higher learning in China, of which 86 were private. After the founding of PRC, all private institutions became public by the end of 1952. There has been no private sector in Chinese formal higher education system since then. However, in recent years, as a result of reforms, about 200 higher education establishments run by some social groups and individuals have been founded. Most of their programs are short-term vocational or supplementary and no valid certificate recognized by the state is awarded.

Chinese higher education institutions fall into two main categories: regular institutions and adult institutions. Regular higher education institutions enroll mainly high school graduates in full-time programs for a degree or a diploma. The largest group of regular institutions is the comprehensive universities and independent specialized colleges, including colleges of engineering, agriculture, forestry, medicine and pharmacy, teacher training, language and literature, finance and economics, political science and law, physical education, and art. Before the end of

the 1950s, comprehensive universities consisted of departments in the field of humanities, social sciences, and natural sciences only. However, since the 1960s, many comprehensive universities have also provided certain engineering or other professional programs. Since the early 1980s, a number of specialized colleges have established departments in natural sciences or social sciences and even humanities. All of the universities and colleges offer a full range of baccalaureate programs. In addition, some of them are committed to graduate education through the doctorate degree, and some through the masters degree only. The others do not offer graduate education. However, many universities and colleges also provide regular short-cycle programs and programs in adult higher education and continuing education.

Since 1954, the government has successively designated certain universities and colleges as national key higher education institutions. In general, these key institutions have better faculties, laboratories, libraries, and other facilities than other institutions of the same kind. They are required to concentrate their efforts on improving the quality of teaching, research, and institutional management, and providing expertise and assistance for other institutions. However, this policy has proved a controversial issue.

The second group of regular institutions is the short-cycle specialized institutions, which train mainly for practical work at junior college level by providing two to three year short-cycle courses. They are also engaged in adult and continuing education at the same level.

The smallest group is the short-term vocational universities. Such institutions were first established in the early 1980s. They offer vocational training at junior college level and set up programs mainly according to the needs of the local community.

Adult higher education institutions offer higher education to people with a high school education who are already holding a job. There are six main types of institution.

Broadcasting and televisual universities are open institutions which conduct teaching by means of radio, television, publications, and audiovisual teaching materials mainly at junior college level. The students can study full-time, part-time or in their spare time. The China TV Normal College is a program run by the State Education Commission. It conducts its courses via television satellite and aims at training primary and middle-school teachers in an effort to improve their educational level in special fields.

Universities for staff and workers form the largest category of adult institution. Some of these institutions, offering mainly junior college courses and a limited number of undergraduate courses, are established and administered by institutions and enterprises for their own employees. Others are organized and administered by local education authorities or a workers union, and students attend in their own time.

Management personnel colleges are administered by the central or local governments. This type of institution offers mainly a junior college level education. The objective is to train mainly personnel who have practical management experience.

Educational colleges are responsible for the in-service training of primary and secondary school teachers and educational administrators at junior college or undergraduate level. They are run by local governments and administered by the related education authorities.

Peasants' colleges are junior college level institutions run by local governments. They offer programs to adult technical personnel in farming, young farmers, and forestry workers who have finished senior secondary education.

Independent correspondence colleges are long-distance adult higher education institutions at junior college level, organized and administered by the ministries concerned and local education authorities.

In addition, since the early 1980s, a state higher education self-study examination system has been established. By passing the examinations, students can obtain a graduate diploma of regular college level, a certificate of short-cycle program level, or an individual course certificate.

Conducting scientific research, as well as teaching is an important function of Chinese higher education institutions. The scientific research system consists of four kinds of institution: higher education institutions; the Chinese Academy of Sciences and Chinese Academy of Social Sciences; research institutes under enterprises or related governmental departments; and local research institutes. In higher

education institutions, faculty members are expected to carry out research work. In a few key universities and colleges, certain National Key Laboratories of different disciplines sponsored by the state have been established. There are also research institutes in many universities and colleges. In those which do not have research institutes, the research work is done in the "teaching and research section," the grassroots unit of Chinese higher education institutions. Research projects are sponsored by the government, enterprises, other establishments, and universities and colleges themselves. Joint research with organizations outside the universities and colleges is encouraged.

Tables 1 and 2 give the numbers of institutions in both main categories. Since 1949, the number of regular higher education institutions and those for adults had increased from 205 and 1 respectively to 1,075 and 1,373 in 1988. However, dramatic fluctuations took place in the growth rate between 1958 and 1962 as well as in the Cultural Revolution (1966–76). From 1958 to 1960, the central government, local governments, and all enterprises stressed the need for massive increases in agricultural and industrial production, as well as growth in education and other spheres of society. The number of regular higher education institutions rose from 229 in 1957 to 1,289 in 1960, and institutions for adults spiralled from 92 in 1957 to 877 in 1962. Around 1961, the national economy went into recession. The number of higher education institutions sharply declined. During the Cultural Revolution, normal instruction and the admission of new students were suspended for four consecutive years from 1966, and many institutions were closed. At the same time, the so-called "July 21 University," developed. These were mainly run by enterprises, recruiting workers or pea-

Table 1

Numbers of regular higher education institutions 1965–88

	1965	1970	1975	1980	1985	1988
Short-cycle specialized institutions	52	—	—	171	325	345
Short-term vocational universities	—	—	—	—	118	119
Universities and colleges						
Bachelor and graduate diploma granting	248	—	—	188	265	215
Masters granting	—	—	—	—	148	207
	134[a]			316[a]		
Doctorate granting	—	—	—	—	160	189
Subtotal	382	—	—	—	573	611
Total	816	434	387	675	1,589	1,686

a Institutions offered graduate programs when there were no degree systems

Table 2
Number of higher education institutions for adults

	1958	1965	1975[a]	1980	1985	1988
Radio & TV universities	—	—	—	29	29	40
Universities for staff & workers	—	—	—	1,194	863	888
Agricultural universities	—	—	—	165	4	5
Educational colleges	—	—	—	1,290	216	265
Management personnel colleges	—	—	—	—	102	171
Independent correspondence colleges	—	—	—	4	2	4
Total	265	758	10,836	2,682	1,216	1,373

a Including evening universities and correspondence colleges run by regular higher education institutions

sants without entrance examinations, and with no guarantee of the educational quality of their courses. As many as 10,836 higher education institutions for adults had been set up by 1975. Since 1979, China's focus has shifted to economic development, and within nine years, the number of regular higher education institutions increased by 70 percent. The institutions for adults decreased in number after a series of readjustments until all conformed to a standard of educational quality.

The general admissions policy is intended to ensure that the students who are enrolled meet the country's needs both in quality and in quantity. From 1952 on, with the exception of the Cultural Revolution period, a national unified admissions system has been in practice. Every year, a uniform entrance examination is given simultaneously in all parts of China. The SEC organizes groups of experts to set the examination papers. In addition, applicants for programs in foreign languages take oral examinations and those in fine arts, applied arts, and sports take an additional examination corresponding to their options. People up to the age of 24 who graduate from the senior middle schools, and those with the same educational level, are eligible to take the examination. No restrictions on sex, nationality, birth place, or family background have been imposed. Certain physical criteria have to be met, however. The minimum entry marks for different levels of institutions are determined by the provincial admissions committee according to the overall performance of applicants and the number of students to be enrolled in the province, laid down by the annual state plan. This differs from province to province and year to year.

Higher education institutions themselves determine their minimum entry marks for different programs on condition that they enroll sufficient students according to the plan approved in advance by the SEC or local education authorities. Admissions policies favor applicants who are "students good in three areas" (good academic performance, good physical health, and good moral record), a few excellent graduates recommended by relevant high schools, ethnic minorities, overseas Chinese, and students with good athletic records. Somewhat lower entry marks can be set by the institutions subject to approval by the provincial admissions committee.

Total enrollment in higher education is shown in Table 3. Enrollment in regular higher education institutions changed dramatically during certain periods, in line with the changes in the numbers of institutions described above, and for the same reasons. Since 1980, enrollment has increased. Enrollment increase peaked around 1985, because the decision to award higher education prior to the year 2000 was made in 1983. That decision resulted in institutions immediately facing serious shortages of funds, workspace, and other conditions for a wide range of development. The quality of instruction was also affected. After 1985, a policy was introduced to slow down the development of higher education. Growth rate in enrollments decreased from 22.0 percent in 1985 to 4.9 percent in 1988. By 2000 the increase of total enrollment in regular institutions might well be small.

Due to the encouragement of government and the willingness of many staff and workers to become qualified, enrollment in higher education institutions for adults has continuously increased, especially since 1980. These enrollment figures may increase faster than those of the regular institutions.

The proportion of the 20–24 age group population enrolled in the whole higher education system is shown in Table 4. It is below the average of other developing countries. Owing to limited funds and limited vacancies of posts available to graduates, the Chinese higher education system is unlikely to expand rapidly.

141

Table 3
Total enrollment in higher education by type of institutions (in thousands)

	1960	1965	1970	1975	1980	1985	1988
Regular higher education							
Universities & colleges[a]	778	649	48	479[c]	884	1,210	1,448
Short-cycle specialized institutions[b]	187	30	—	22[d]	282	580	731
Subtotal	965	679	48	501	1,166	1,790	2,179
Adult higher education[e]							
Higher education institutions for adults	—	—	—	—	308	1,232	1,092
Adult education institutions run by regular higher education institutions	—	—	—	—	189	493	635
Subtotal	300[f]	413	—	729	497	1,725	1,727
Total	—	1,092	48	1,230	1,663	3,515	3,906

a Including both undergraduates and graduates   b Including enrollment in short-term vocational universities and that in the short-cycle programs offered by universities and colleges   c 2–3 year regular courses   d 1–2 year refresher courses mostly for employed staff and workers   e Data since 1980 not including enrollment registered in single courses   f Data refer to 1959

The Regulations Concerning Academic Degrees in PRC in 1981 established the degree system in New China. Previously, students graduated from higher education institutions at different levels obtaining the appropriate diploma. No degree was conferred. According to the "Regulations," there must be three grades of Chinese academic degrees: the bachelor's degree, the master's degree, and the doctor's degree. Students graduating from short-cycle specialized institutions do not receive a degree but a short-cycle courses diploma. Degrees are conferred by institutions authorized by the State Council accredited by the Committee of Academic Degrees under the aegis of the State Council.

Table 4
Numbers (in thousands) and percentage of 20–24 year olds enrolled in higher education

	1964	1982	1987
20–24 year olds	50,821	74,363	121,514[a]
Enrollment			
Short-cycle programs	23	225	681
Undergraduates	662	929	1,278
Graduates	5	26	120
Adult higher education	435	1,173	1,858
Total	1,125	2,353	3,937
Percentage	2.22	3.16	3.24

a Estimate based on one percent sampling survey

Bachelor's degree studies usually last for four years, with a few exceptions which last for five years. In institutions with a credit system, about 140 semester credits (or equivalent class hours in institutions without a credit system) are required to graduate. The bachelor's degree is conferred on graduates who attain the following: (a) a good command of basic theories, specialized knowledge, and basic skills in the branch of learning concerned; (b) some ability to undertake scientific research or engage in technical work. A few students who perform badly in their studies but pass all the courses required do not obtain the bachelor's degree but have instead a diploma of graduation from their university or college.

When the Regulations Concerning Academic Degrees came into force in 1981, China's graduate education divided into two consecutive stages. The first leads to the master's degree; the second to the doctorate.

Graduating students in universities and colleges, and those under 35 who have graduated from universities and colleges or hold an academic record of equivalent education level, are eligible to apply as a master's degree candidate. Applicants take the entrance examination which covers subjects including general and specialized courses assigned by SEC and the institutions involved. The minimum entry marks are set by the SEC. Besides taking the entrance examination, graduating students must submit their graduate thesis or graduate project in order for their research ability to be evaluated. There are also entrance examinations set by individual institutions for candidates for doctoral degrees to which those aged under 40 with a master's degree or equivalent may apply. In recent years, a small number of graduate students (less than 30 percent of the total) have been permitted to enter through recommendation alone, without taking the entrance examination. In general the master's degree program lasts three years including course work and more than one year of thesis work. The doctoral degree program also lasts three years with dissertation work thoughout the program and some course work in most cases.

3. Governance, Administration, and Finance

3.1 National and Regional Administration

Higher education institutions are either directly under the State Education Commission (SEC) (e.g., Peking University), or relevant departments under the State Council (e.g., Beijing Agricultural University under the Ministry of Agriculture), or the provincial governments. Higher education institutions for adults run by enterprises or other organizations are also supervised by the central or local authorities. The SEC shapes higher education mainly in the following ways: (a) implementing policies and decrees drawn up and enacted by central government as well as its own regulations; (b) working out the long-term and annual development programs for higher education in accordance with the strategies drawn up by central government; (c) funding higher education institutions under it with the government expenditure allocation for education; (d) administering personnel affairs, for example, appointing the presidents and drawing up regulations for the staff of the institutions; (e) supervising teaching and scientific research work in higher education institutions; and (f) internationalizing higher education. It must be pointed out that the administrative system of China's higher education was highly centralized prior to 1980. However, the situation was constantly changed throughout the 1980s and decentralization has become the main tendency.

The State Education Commission is in charge of national planning in higher education in keeping with the overall state plan for the social and economic development of the country. Formerly, strict implementation of the national plans was required.

Since 1980, a series of reforms have been carried out. Provided they implement national planning, regional governments and higher education institutions may develop higher education according to their specific conditions.

The main goals set by the top coordinating agency and how they are transmitted to higher education are described below.

(a) Standardizing the general training objectives and the specifications for different fields of study: the SEC stipulates the general requirements of morality, health, and academic performance for all students. It determines specialized fields of study and approves the establishment and closure of specialist departments in regular higher education institutions. Formerly teaching programs drafted by the SEC were mandatory, but now they may be drawn up by the individual institutions.

(b) Standardizing higher education institutions and controlling their number: the SEC is in charge of approving the establishment and closure of all institutions of higher education.

(c) Allocating student places: the SEC works out the annual plan of enrollment. In the past, this was an overall state plan which included the total number of students admitted and the numbers distributed to different levels, fields of study, provinces, and institutions. Now, higher education institutions not only enroll new students in accordance with a state plan, but also admit students on the basis of contracts with employers and those who are self-supported with the approval of the SEC.

(d) Allocating graduates to jobs: the SEC draws up the annual plan for job assignments for graduates. At present, self-supported students seek jobs independently; students enrolled by contract go to work in the contractor units; and the job assignments for graduating students enrolled according to the state plan follow a process which combines graduates' preferences, institutions' recommendation, and employers selection.

Table 5
Higher education expenditure as a percentage of GNP (in billions of RMB yuan)

	1960	1965	1975	1980	1985	1986
GNP	140[a]	160[a]	300[a]	433.6	833.0	945.7
Higher education expenditure	1.36	0.74	0.83	2.81	6.48	7.99
Percentage	0.97	0.46	0.28	0.65	0.78	0.84

a Estimated numbers

(e) Determining the authorized size of the higher education institutions: the SEC draws up regulations for staff. According to these regulations, the SEC, relevant departments under the state council, and provincial governments determine the number and structure of staff in different institutions under them.

(f) Internationalizing higher education including sending students to study abroad, admitting foreign students, exchanging visiting scholars with foreign countries and other academic activities. Before the late 1970s, all these activities were planned, organized, and funded by SEC. Now, in addition to the governmental plan, institutions may manage these activities on condition they use self-raised funds.

The evaluation of higher education's response to these goals is done mainly by the central government and by the SEC. Self-evaluation is also encouraged. The SEC assesses higher education at irregular intervals. The participation of leading officers of other departments (e.g., State Planning Commission, the Ministry of Labor and Personnel Affairs, and so on) in the SEC makes its assessment more objective. Beneath the SEC are different bureaus in charge of different types of higher education institutions. They evaluate institutional performance and the sector of higher education through surveying and investigating the responses from employers and society in general to the output of higher education. They report to the SEC. The establishment of a formal evaluation system has been discussed, but as yet nothing has been done.

3.2 Finance

Except for a very limited amount from the social sectors, funds for higher education in China are mainly allocated by government. The SEC and other relevant ministries as well as local governments allocate funds to the institutions directly under them according to the state budget. Allocation is formula-based in that the amount appropriated is determined by the number of students multiplied by a quota of expenses per student, derived by the SEC. The quota varies by levels and by field of study. The appropriation covers all expenses of the institutions. Certain items may receive special funds if approved by governmental agencies responsible for finance. State appropriations for higher education since 1960 are shown in Table 5.

The funding level of Chinese higher education institutions is low in comparison with that of most countries. Shortage of funds creates a series of problems at the institutional level: bad maintenance of buildings, equipment, and other facilities; lack of funding for instruction and administration; and low faculty salaries leading to an unstable teaching force. To solve these problems, the government has increased appropriations to education. In addition,

raising funds from other channels is not only permitted but encouraged. Institutions may obtain funds from different sources by training contract students for them; undertaking research and development projects sponsored by enterprises and governmental agencies; by transferring their scientific and technological knowledge into the technology market; by offering correspondence or short-term courses; by providing social, technical, and consulting services; and finally by raising donations.

3.3 Institutional Administration

In Chinese higher education institutions, the president is the highest executive authority. In the 1990s most institutions practice an administrative system termed "presidential responsibility under party committee guidance." This means that major decisions on governance of the institution are made by the party committee or by the president with the approval of the party committee. Beneath the president, several vice presidents are in charge of academic, student, personnel, business, and other affairs. Below the vice-president level, the administrative structures differ between various institutions. However, in large institutions the general model of governance can be described as follows.

The dean of studies or provost reports to the president and vice-president for academic affairs, and is in charge of teaching and research in the institution. The director of general affairs reports to the president and vice-president responsible for general affairs, and is in charge of the institution's business and support services. A vice-president responsible for academic affairs is concurrently dean of the graduate school. Under the deans and the director are divisions, with sections under them, responsible for related administrative affairs. In small institutions the head of the division of teaching and studies and head of the division of general affairs are responsible for administering the relevant areas.

Presidents of certain famous universities and colleges are appointed by the state council. All others are appointed by the SEC or other departments and provincial governments responsible for them. Vice-presidents may be nominated by the presidents and are then approved and appointed. Provosts, directors of general affairs, and heads of divisions and sections are all appointed by the president. Of course, especially for top posts, certain kinds of negotiation and soundings are always taken before the appointments. "Professional" administrators may be former members of teaching staff or graduates of higher education institutions, or those qualified in other spheres, such as accountancy.

According to regulations drawn up by government, a faculty post qualification committee should be set up in all institutions of higher learning. In institutions authorized to confer degrees, there should be, in addition, an academic degree evaluation committee.

In some institutions there are academic committees. In general, the three committees are all established at both institutional and departmental level. Within the academic committee, important academic affairs (such as improving and reforming teaching and research, assessing significant achievements in teaching and research, deciding on awards, and so forth) are discussed, and suggestions are put forward. The faculty post qualification committee is in charge of the promotion of faculty members. The academic degree evaluation committee is responsible for awarding degrees. The decisions on awards and promotion made by these committees are generally approved automatically by the president. However, in other academic affairs the ultimate decision rests with the president.

The academic committee generally numbers several dozen members and is determined by individual institution. It usually includes the president, vice-president, provost, heads of department, and leading professors and associate professors. The faculty post qualification committee consists of 15 to 25 members, of whom professors and associate professors form more than two-thirds of the total. Under this committee, the disciplinary level qualification body consists of five to nine professors and associate professors, of whom no fewer than half should be full professors. The academic degree evaluation committee is selected from those above the rank of lecturer and generally from those above the rank of associate professor. In a doctor's degree-conferring unit, more than half of the members are full professors. The subcommittees for different branches of learning consist of seven to fifteen members.

The congress of staff has been established in order to ensure participation of nonacademic staff and more democratic management and supervision. The delegates to the congress are elected directly by the staff in each electoral unit—department, division, or other basic unit of the institution—for a term of three years. About 40 percent of total delegates are nonacademic staff members. The congress meets once a year to hear the president's annual report, to discuss the institution's annual plan and other important issues, and to put forward suggestions. It also discusses regulations on the staff's work and welfare and makes relevant decisions which are put into practice if the president agrees. In addition, congress has the right to supervise the administrators of the institution, to comment on or criticize them, and to make recommendations for promotion or dismissal to the appropriate department of the institute. In some institutions, a university senate headed by the president and composed of a certain number of prestigious people exercises the power of review and supervision.

Students may have one or two seats on the senate of the institution. In addition, the student union and graduate union often transmit student's opinions and proposals on teaching and learning, and institutional life and administration to the administrators and faculty members.

The "base units" which organize the academic work are teaching and research sections under the departments in most cases, or the departments themselves where no such sections exist under them. Teaching and research sections are set up in accordance with the programs or courses offered. Their responsibilities are: (a) organizing teaching, including setting syllabi and offering courses, compiling teaching materials, improving the quality of teaching, and so forth; (b) organizing the scientific research of faculty members and organizing various academic activities; (c) administering and constructing laboratories and reference rooms; (d) organizing faculty development work. In many institutions, there are separate research institutes, which are "base units" of scientific research. However, assuming the work load of teaching, offering relevant courses, and advising on the thesis work of undergraduates or graduates, are also amongst their responsibilities.

4. Faculty and Students: Teaching, Learning, and Research

4.1 Faculty

The teaching body of China's higher education system has made great progress. In 1949 the overall teaching staff in regular higher education institutions numbers only 16,059. It had increased by a factor of 5.2 10 years later. The overall number of full-time faculty members since 1960 is shown in Table 6.

The trend of development of and fluctuations in the overall number of faculty members is similar to that of the total enrollment as shown in Table 3, and the explanation is the same. Since 1980 the rate of increase of faculty members has been lower than student enrollment, so the student–teacher ratio has increased.

Full-time faculty members in regular higher education are shown in Table 6. In adult higher education, full-time faculty members have increased rapidly, while the number of part-time teachers has fallen. Figures for part-time faculty members in regular higher education are unavailable and negligible in any case. Table 7 gives the number of part-time faculty members in adult higher education.

In China, employees of state-run enterprises and institutions are called "state staff and workers." Almost all faculty members in China are state staff members. They are on the government pay roll, enjoy public health services and certain labor protections as well as labor insurance, and retire with a pension. In principle there is no tenured status to faculty members. Individuals are obliged to transfer from one post to another as approved by the organ-

Table 6
Number of full-time teaching staff

	1959	1965	1972	1975	1980	1985	1987
Regular higher education	99,657	138,116	130,175	155,723	246,862	344,262	385,352
Adult higher education	2,119	8,493	1,422	18,312	34,903	69,261	84,282
Total	101,776	146,609	131,597	174,035	281,765	413,523[a]	469,634[a]

a Not including teaching staff in adult institutions run by higher education institutions

ization for which they work. However, the regulations on transferring posts are very complicated, and most faculty members hold their position until retirement. Similarly faculty members may be dismissed or resign from public employment though this is rare, unless they commit a crime, or in certain other exceptional cases. Tenure exists *de facto* in China though not *de jure*. Recruitment is the responsibility of individual institutions.

Reforms introduced a new "faculty posts appointment system" aimed at motivating academics' enthusiasm for their work. Under the new system, posts of faculty members are created according to each institution's actual needs in teaching and research. Each post has clearly defined responsibilities and workloads. There are four types of post or rank: assistant, lecturer, associate professor, and professor. One is appointed to hold a certain rank, once qualified by the faculty post qualification committee at departmental and institutional level, if there is a vacancy. Appointments usually last for two to four years, and can be renewed.

Qualifications for different posts and the criteria for promotion are as follows: a master, a double bachelor degree holder, or a bachelor having worked for one year on probation, are qualified for a post as assistant. A doctor is qualified for a post as lecturer. A master or a double bachelor degree holder who has worked as an assistant for two years or more, or a bachelor who has worked as an assistant for four years or more, can be promoted to a lectureship after review. Those who have been lecturers for five years or more or who hold a doctorate and have worked as a lecturer for two years or more are eligible for promotion to an associate professorship provided they have a strong theoretical base, deep specialist

experience, a good teaching and publishing record. Associate professors who have worked for five years or more at that level can be promoted to full professor on the condition that their teaching is excellent and they have published papers and books with important, original, and creative ideas. The ability to organize and administer teaching and research is also requisite in a professor. Not all higher education institutions in China may qualify professors and associated professors by themselves. Those which are not authorized to qualify faculty members for such high ranking posts make recommendations to the faculty posts qualification committee at provincial level.

Nongovernmental learned societies in China are the major organizations representing faculty interests. They are organized by disciplines, for example, the Chinese Physics Society, the Chinese Association of Historical Science, and so forth. Some make awards to distinguished scholars.

Another kind of organization representing faculty interests at different levels is the school staff's union, which covers staff from kindergarten to university. The National School Staff Union is a branch union of the Chinese National Labor Union. Beneath the provincial staff union are branch unions in every higher education institution. The staff union attends to the interests of its members in educational work, institutional management, and staff welfare.

The Ministry of Education attempted to define faculty workload and formulate "tentative regulations" in 1981. After experimenting in some institutions for four years, it was found to be difficult to implement uniform regulations and calculate methods on faculty workload in diversified institutions. Since 1985, higher education institutions have been authorized to define faculty workload according to their own regulations, taking the 1981 tentative regulations of the ministry as a reference.

In general, faculty workload varies between different ranks in that the higher the rank, the heavier the workload. Faculty workload consists of teaching, research, administration, laboratory construction, and other responsibilities. In institutions where

Table 7
Number of part-time teaching staff in adult institutions

	1959	1965	1972	1975	1980	1987
Total	4,045	5,096	618	74,740	34,894	28,845

Table 8
Percentage of students enrolled in regular higher education institutions by level (5, 6 and 7) and field of study

	1960	(%)	1965	(%)	1970	(%)	1975	(%)	1980	(%)	1985	(%)	1988	(%)
Exact sciences														
5	107,436	57.4	15,670	51.5	—	—	16,198[b]	75.3	85,148	30.2	189,107	32.6	262,564	35.9
6	577,107	74.5	487,936	75.8	30,635[a]	64.1	332,546[a]	69.4	603,767	70.0	752,190	67.0	878,907	65.8
7	1,594	43.9	4,191	92.2	—	—	—	—	16,286	75.4	67,528	77.3	96,511[c]	80.3
Social sciences														
5	2,120	1.1	1,157	3.8	—	—	328[b]	1.5	6,588	2.3	87,350	15.0	113,808	15.6
6	17,448	2.6	21,106	3.2	90[a]	0.2	7,033[a]	1.5	36,523	4.3	96,322	8.6	135,934	10.2
7	184	5.0	24	0.5	—	—	—	—	622	2.9	7,619	8.7	10,526[c]	8.8
Humanities[d]														
5	77,552	41.5	13,601	44.7	–	–	4,976[b]	23.1	190,050	67.4	304,015	52.4	354,331	48.5
6	179,960	23.2	134,966	21.0	17,090[a]	35.7	139,912[a]	29.2	221,636	25.7	274,131	24.4	320,379	24.0
7	1,857	51.1	331	7.3	—	—	—	—	4,696	21.7	12,184	14.0	13.154[c]	10.9

a Two–three year regular courses   b One–two year courses mostly for employed staff and workers   c Data refers to 1987   d Including students enrolled in teachers' colleges

faculty are required to do both teaching and research, teaching in general accounts for two-thirds of the total workload. For those with some administrative work and other duties, the teaching workload is reduced. The balance between teaching, research, and administration is determined by the head of the teaching–research section in general or sometimes by the department chairperson.

4.2 Students

The development of the student body is shown in Table 8. The fields of study and levels being grouped here are both according to UNESCO categories. Before the 1980s, the structure was lopsided with a very small proportion of enrollment in the social sciences and at the sixth and seventh level. Since the early 1980s, reforms to the higher education structure (the proportion of enrollment in different fields of study and different levels) have been pursued, thus making the structure more balanced both between the fields of study and levels.

The number of graduates is given in Table 9. The figures declined sharply in the early 1970s because of the abolition of higher education institutions and the suspension of admissions during the Cultural Revolution. It has increased tremendously in recent years, especially at short-cycle program level and in adult higher education because the government has given a favorable reaction to their development.

The breakdown of the student body by social class, gender, and ethnicity are shown in Table 10. Since the early 1960s, the government has consistently paid great attention to providing higher education for minority nationalities. In 1987, 17 institutions, including 10 institutions for specifically minority nationalities, enrolled mainly minority students. Autonomous regions and prefectures of minority nationalities established 79 higher education insti-

tutions of various types. More than 60 institutions of higher learning in the hinterland had set up classes catering to the needs of minority regions. Moreover, all higher education institutions are open to minorities. Preferential treatment for minorities in entrance examinations has been mentioned earlier.

To help qualified students receive higher education free from financial constraints, a grant system was established to provide financial aid to all students. Financially disadvantaged students could receive a higher stipend. In 1987, this system was replaced by a scholarship system and a student loan system. Students receive different types of financial aid according to certain regulations. About 15 percent of undergraduate students receive scholarships and 85 percent are given an educational loan from the state bank. Special grants exist for students doing certain subjects and for those willing to work in remote parts of China. These policies, in addition to free tuition and free accommodation, enable financially disadvantaged students to enter higher education.

Every higher education institution in China has its own student union, which represents students' interests and links students to the institutional leadership. In general, student unions aim to encourage institutions to improve instruction and administration. They organize various student activities; develop relationships with student organizations in other establishments; and aim to promote mutual understanding and friendship with students in foreign countries.

At institutional level the students' union is organized in three groupings: institution, department, and class. Every student is an ex officio member. Regional associations of student unions exist in each province and the National Student Association of China acts at national level. The student union of

Table 9
Number of graduates

	1960	1961	1962	1963	1964	1965	1966	1967	1968	1969	1970	1971	1981	1982	1983	1984	1985	1986	1987	1988
Regular higher education Universities and colleges[a]	89,758	100,450	123,010	162,766	187,351	178,001	134,647	113,694	136,931	150,119	102,672	5,945	112	368,217	252,571	204,248	201,885	227,764	252,973	279,791
Short-cycle specialized institutions and others	46,380	50,833	54,245	35,988	17,148	7,520	6,023	11,142	13,263	—	—	—	139,528	89,027	82,773	82,689	114,499	165,028	278,957	273,675
Subtotal	136,138	151,283	177,255	198,754	204,499	185,521	140,670	124,836	150,194	150,119	102,672	5,945	139,640	457,244	335,344	286,937	316,384	392,792	531,930	553,466
Higher education institutions for adults	—	—	—	—	—	—	—	—	—	—	—	—	94,224	226,969	136,245	163,936	347,031	450,054	481,311	753,844

a Not including graduate program diploma and degree holders

148

Table 10
Percentage of students by gender, social class, and ethnic minority[a]

	1958	1965	1970	1983	1988
Gender					
Male	76.7	73.1	75.9	73.1	66.6
Female	23.3	26.9	24.1	26.9	33.4
Social class[b]					
Workers	13.2	8.6	44.8	70.6	63.7
Peasants	44.6	60.5			
Staff and others	42.2	30.9	55.2	29.4	36.3
Ethnic minorities	3.4	3.2	4.2	4.9	6.1

a Not including graduate students and those in adult higher education institutions   b Data refers to first-year students only

each institution can apply for membership of those associations.

Students in Chinese higher education are trained according to "specialities" which break down disciplines into special fields of study. This breakdown may differ due to different circumstances; for example, historical science may be *a* speciality, but it can also be divided into two narrower specialities: Chinese history, and foreign history. Every first-degree speciality has its own teaching program, in which the training goals of the speciality, years of schooling, minimum total course hours (or credits) required for graduation, lectures, and laboratory work (prescribed, restricted elective, free elective), field work, thesis, and requirements regarding labor work and military training are stipulated.

The form of undergraduate courses has been in transition. At one time, socialist construction needed huge numbers of specialized personnel in various areas, of which most were new to China. The goal of training in general is to specialize in a certain field. Furthermore, there is no special training provided by the employer units for new employees. Employer units expect graduates from higher education to handle their work independently as soon as they are assigned to the posts. Graduates are required to master increasingly specialized knowledge and even specialized techniques and skills. Thus it was necessary to set up ever narrower specialities and this is being done. All courses required for graduation are prescribed by the teaching program. Specialized training occupies a large proportion (at least one-third) of undergraduate studies. In the remaining "basic studies," a number of courses, such as physics and mathematics for engineering specialities, are offered as preparatory courses for specialized training but are not based on a "liberal arts" model. This form of undergraduate studies trained students to meet the demands of the labor force in the early days of the New China. However, along with economic

and social development, shortcomings appeared and became increasingly serious.

The areas covered by different specialities have now been broadened. Of the 1,039 specialities set up in Chinese regular higher education in 1980 mergers and readjustment created 870 in 1988. Elective courses and the credit system have been set up in most institutions. Students are encouraged to broaden their basic training. For example, students of science and technology specialities are permitted, and even encouraged, to take courses in the fields of humanities and social sciences, and vice versa.

According to the regulations concerning undergraduate studies and the requirements for graduates drawn up by the SEC, students are assessed mainly on the following points: the command of basic theories; specialized knowledge and basic skills in the branch of learning concerned; and the ability to undertake scientific research, or to engage in technical work. Assessment of students' basic skills is through laboratory and field work. Finally, the graduation thesis (or project or other form of graduation practice) provides the basis for assessing the students' ability to do research and technical work.

5. Conclusion

Higher education in the New China has made great progress and accomplished remarkable achievements without parallel in Chinese history. Nevertheless, it cannot yet meet the needs of the economic and social development of the country. The major problems are discussed below.

Though reforms have been implemented in recent years, the earlier overcentralized model of higher education administration has not completely changed into a more rational one. Government departments in charge of higher education administration still, in many ways, exercise a rigid control over higher education and undertake a great many aspects of institutional administration. Yet they do not effectively manage many of the matters that are within their jurisdiction. The current administration makes many standardized requirements, criteria, and regulations which do not reflect the diverse needs of the country and sap both competition and vitality in the higher education system. It dampens the enthusiasm of individual institutions to promote teaching and research work in keeping with their own strong points. It lacks the self-adjustment and integration which could be used to fight off the unfavorable effects resulting from errors in planning or decision making.

To overcome this, the CPC Central Committee began a policy of transferring certain powers of decision making in regulating, planning, funding, personnel administration, and teaching and research to units at lower levels, thus extending institutional decision making to administration of its own affairs.

Higher education administration will be more decentralized and streamlined in the future. Institutional management will become more motivated and vital and will have a self-adjustment mechanism capable of ensuring higher education meets the country's needs in time.

The structure of higher education does not serve the needs of economic and social development satisfactorily. For example, the proportion of students enrolled in humanities and pure science is too large; the numbers involved in engineering, agriculture, medicine, and social sciences are not balanced; and graduate education is too broad in scale due to over expansion, and so on. To reform this irrational structure, the government has readjusted the annual admissions plans, and formulated new policies for student grants, graduate job assignment, and resource allocation to encourage more students to enrol in those departments to which priority is given.

The quality of higher education leaves room for improvement. First, ideological and moral education offered in higher education institutions is very weak. The outlook of some students on the world, life, and values is incorrect or confused. To change this situation, courses in these fields have been reformed. Teacher supervision of students has been strengthened. The campus environment for extracurricular activities has been improved.

Second, teaching needs further improvement. The areas covered by different specialities have been broadened, course content upgraded, practice sessions added, the number of required courses reduced and electives increased.

The efficiency of higher education is low. In 1987, 903 out of 1,063 regular higher education institutions enrolled fewer than 3,000 students. Most institutions are inefficient because they lack the economics of large-scale operations. The overall student–teacher ratio is 5:1, much lower than most other countries. The utilization of laboratories, equipment, and other facilities is also low. To raise internal efficiency, the government strictly limits the number of new institutions and the size of staff of each institution. It has carried out a contract appointment system for teaching staff and encouraged interinstitutional cooperation and exchanges.

In the last decade of the twentieth century China is at a critical moment of reform in its economic and political system. By the year 2000, the gross national product (GNP) will be doubled. A socialist planned commodity economic system will be established. The socialist democratic and legal system will be greatly strengthened and the scientific and technical gap between China and the developed countries will be narrowed. However, the population will exceed 1.2 billion which will be a heavy burden on the country. Against this background, Chinese higher education in the coming years will emphasize improving quality rather than broadening scope. The system will become more diversified to meet the various needs of economic and social developments, more socialized to enable greater social involvement, and internationalized. A socialist higher education system with China's own characteristics will be established by the end of the twentieth century.

Bibliography

CEYB Editorial Department 1984 *China Education Yearbook 1949–1981*. China Encyclopedia Press
CEYB Editorial Department 1986 *China Education Yearbook 1982–1984*. Hunan Education Press, Changsha
CEYB Editorial Department 1988 *China Education yearbook 1985–1986*. China Encyclopedia Press, Beijing
Chen Lie 1987 *An Introduction to Collegiate Teaching* Zhejiang University Press, Hangzhou
Chen Mokai (ed.) 1988 *An Introduction to Evaluation of Higher Education*. Jilin Education Press, Changchun
Chinese Encyclopedia Editorial Department 1985 *Chinese Encyclopedia: Education*. China Encyclopedia Press Beijing
Chinese Higher Education Society 1987 *On Chinese Higher Education*. Beijing Normal University Press, Beijing
Conference of Registrars and Secretaries and Conference of University Administrators 1983 *University Administration in China*. University of Reading, Reading
Department of Planning, Ministry of Education 198? *Achievement of Education in China, Statistics 1949–1983* People's Education Press, Beijing
Department of Planning, State Education Commission 1986 *Achievement of Education in China, Statistics 1980–1985*. People's Education Press, Beijing
Educational Fund and Teacher's Salaries Research Group of State Education Commission 1988 *Educational Fund and Teacher's Salaries*. Educational Science Press, Beijing
Fu Juanming (ed.) 1987 *Comparative Higher Education* Beijing Normal University Press, Beijing
Hao Keming, Wang Yongquan (eds.) 1987 *A Study of China's Higher Education Structure*. People's Education Press, Beijing
Hawkins J N 1974 *Mao Tse-Dong and Education: His Thoughts and Teachings*. Shoe String Press, Hamden Connecticut
Hawkins J N 1978 *China, People's Republic of*. In: Knowles A S (ed.) 1987 *The International Encyclopedia of Higher Education*. Jossey-Bass, San Francisco, California, pp 880–88
Huang Jinghan (ed.) 1988 *Ideological and Political Education of College Students in the New Period of China* Huazhong Normal University Press, Wuhan
Institute of Higher Education, Peking University 198? *Research in Higher Education*. Peking University Press Beijing
Li Hanyu (ed.) 1987 *Evaluation of Engineering Higher Education*. Zhejiang People's Press, Hangzhou
Li Yining (ed.) 1988 *A Study on Economics of Education. China's Education Fund*. Shanghai People's Press Shanghai
Lin Yuqi 1987 *On Learning in University and College*. Xian Jiaotong University Press, Xian
National Research Society of Faculty Administration in Higher Education Institutions 1986 *A Study on Faculty*

Administration in Higher Education Institutions. East China Normal University Press, Shanghai

Pan Maoyuan (ed.) 1985 *Foundations of Higher Education*. People's Education Press and Fujian Education Press, Beijing, Fuzhou

Reform of China's Educational Structure: Decision of the CPC Central Committee 1985. Foreign Language Press, Beijing

Shanghai Research Institute for Higher Education 1988 *A Study of Strategy of Higher Educational Development*. Shanghai Jiaotong University Press, Shanghai

State Education Commission 1986 *The Development of Education in China*. Paper presented at the 40th International Conference on Education, Geneva

State Education Commission 1989a *The Development of Education in China*. Paper presented at the 41st International Conference on Education, Geneva

State Education Commission 1989b *Post-Secondary Education in China: Present State and Trends*. Paper prepared for the 41st International conference on Education, Geneva

Student Administration Bureau, State Education Commission 1986 *A Prospect of the Reform of College Entrance Examination in China*. Higher Education Press, Beijing

Tao Zengpian (ed.) 1984 *Higher Education Administration*. Liaoning People's Press, Shenyang

Wang Shanmai (ed.) 1988 *Educational Investment and Reform of Finance in Higher Education Institutions*. Beijing Economy College Press, Beijing

Wang Yapu, Ying Jianzhi 1983 *Management of Higher Education*. East China Normal University Press, Shanghai

World Bank 1981 *China: University Development Project I*, Report No. 3366-CHA. World Bank, Washington, DC

World Bank 1983 *China: Polytechnic/Television University Project*, Report No. 4406-CHA. World Bank, Washington, DC

World Bank 1985 *China: Long-Term Issues and Options*, Report No. 5026-CHA. World Bank, Washington, DC

World Bank 1986 *China: Management and Finance of Higher Education*. A World Bank Country Study Report. World Bank, Washington, DC

Xiong Mingan 1983 *History of Chinese Higher Education*. Chongqing Press, Chongqing

Yu Li, Xue Tianxiang (eds.) 1988 *A System of Higher Education Management Science*. Education Science Press, Beijing

Zhang Guangdou (ed.) 1987 *Studies in Reforms of the Structure of Engineering Education*. Chongqing University Press, Chongqing

Zhang Guocai 1989 *Higher Education Research in China, an Annotated Bibliography*. Research Institute for Higher Education, Hiroshima University, Hiroshima

Zhang Jingying 1986 *University Psychology*. Qinghua University Press, Beijing

Zhang Zengjie 1986 *The Mentality of College Students*. Southwest Normal University Press, Chongqing

Zheng Qiming, Xue Tianxiang 1985 *Foundations of Higher Education*. East China Normal University Press, Shanghai

Zhu Jiusi, Cai Keyong, Yao Qihe (eds.) 1983 *Administration of Higher Education Institutions*. Huazhong Institute of Technology Press, Wuhan

Wang Yongquan

Colombia

1. Higher Education and Society

Higher education in Colombia has a long tradition, going back to the sixteenth and seventeenth centuries when its first universities, *Universidad de Santo Tomas de Aquino* (1580) and *Pontificia Universidad Javeriana* (1623), were founded. They, in turn, were modeled on the philosophies and teaching methods of the Spanish universities of Salamanca and Alcala.

This long tradition has been enriched by the efforts of private institutions, especially the Roman Catholic Church. Today the higher education system contains a number of national and regional public universities, religious and secular private universities, and public and private institutes of higher education, which are not universities in the formal sense.

Recent economic problems have had a negative effect on the availability of resources. At the same time the universities have had to face new demands on their social and scientific capabilities. All these pressures have to be met in conditions of severe restriction at home, and a changing world scene.

Located in the north-west corner of South America, Colombia is a gateway to the continent through which various cultural influences have passed, as can be seen from the changes which have taken place in its educational system over the years. Colombia is an Andean country, but is also Caribbean, closely related to Central America, and bordered by Brazil. Most of Colombia's frontiers with its neighbors have been defined, although some sea and undersea areas are still disputed, with Venezuela, for example.

Colombia's population is estimated at 30 million, the result of a high birth rate in the 1970s and a slow decline in infant mortality. The fertility rate has recently dropped, with substantial variations from region to region. Life expectancy at birth has risen, especially in the major cities, and today the average stands at 65 years overall.

The population of Colombia is an ethnic mosaic, with three main strains in its make-up: White, Black, and Amerindian. The different cultural traditions infused by these races have given rise to a variety of regional types of very distinct characteristics. Most of the population is of mixed descent—the mestizos—and only 2 percent of the total is of pure Amerindian blood.

1.1 Social Class and Occupational Structure

While institutions of higher education have proliferated, there is a sector of the population which is hardly represented in the educational system as a whole: children and adolescents from the poorest families. For them income, access to public services, and participation in society are all extremely limited. Some calculations suggest that 20 percent of the

151

Colombian population lives in conditions of critical poverty.

The fluctuations in the Colombian economy and the effects of the world recession of the late 1980s are reflected in changes to the structure of employment. Urban unemployment accounts for between 14 and 15 percent of the total workforce. However, since 1984, it has fallen considerably. The highest rate of unemployment exists among those who have some secondary instruction. During the 1970s people with no formal education showed the lowest unemployment rates; this trend began to change in the following decade. The unemployment rate among university graduates is lower than the overall average. The gross structural unemployment, however, is explained by the unemployment of women between the ages of 25 and 35 with incomplete secondary education.

A recent report on labor problems in Colombia (Chenery Mission 1986), concluded that a constructive response to the challenge of a more educated workforce is, in addition to the creation of more new jobs, the development of sectors which can use more educated labor more intensively, and can give support to science and technology.

1.2 Structure of the Economy

Agricultural production has declined as a percentage of Gross Domestic Product (GDP), from about 30 percent in 1960 to 20 percent in 1989. In the same period the manufacturing sector has grown rapidly during the 1950s and 1960s, to reach 21 percent of GDP.

The contribution of mining to the economy at the beginning of the 1980s was minimal; but the exploitation of discoveries has now made it one of the most dynamic sectors in the economy and it has now recovered the importance it had in the 1950s. Oil, finance, public services, and transport have also played a dynamic part in Colombia's economic development.

A number of studies have suggested that the economic structure of Colombia as it stands at the beginning of the 1990s contains a relatively small industrial sector in comparison to other similar countries.

1.3 The Structure of Government and Political Goals

Colombia has a presidential form of government, with direct elections. The state has three arms: executive, legislative, and judicial. The executive is made up of the president and the cabinet of ministers, the decentralized institutes (one of which is the Institute of Higher Education, ICFES) and the administrative departments.

In the political arena, the parties play a major role. The two large traditional parties are the Conservatives and the Liberals. Between them they hold most posts at the different levels of government,

although other minority parties are represented in the legislative bodies and in local government.

Colombia is a unitary republic, but it has introduced a novel element into its political organization with the direct election of mayors in the municipalities. The object of this innovation is to decentralize the administration and give more autonomy to the departments and municipalities and to strengthen their revenue base by allowing them to manage their own public services.

The constitution as it stands guarantees freedom of education, while the state has ultimate powers of inspection and control of public and private educational institutions. Each government has drawn up its plan for social and economic development. The current development plan for 1987–90 contains three programs to support higher education, which commits it (a) to consolidate a state university system, (b) to raise the quality of postsecondary education, and (c) to restore its financial base. Government priorities are concentrated, however, on three other main programs: (a) the plan to eradicate absolute poverty, (b) the national rehabilitation plan, and (c) the integrated rural development plan.

1.4 Relations with the Church

The first Colombian universities had a clearly ecclesiastical origin, guided by the spirit of the Counter Reformation. Moreover, the Dominicans, Jesuits and Franciscans brought with them the teaching methods of St Thomas Aquinas, Suarez, and Dun Scotus. The curriculum was directed towards speculation and deduction in the world of dogma, and away from any knowledge of the real world.

Paradoxically, it was the Catholic Church which itself supported a major ideological revolution in higher education in Colombia. In the eighteenth century it introduced inductive and positive reasoning in the Botanical Expedition, the most important scientific project of the colonial period, which continued through to the early days of independence.

The relations between church and state, particularly with regard to education, have been regulated since 1889 by diplomatic agreements or concordats. With some interruptions, the church has continued to administer its own universities, which remain among the most prestigious in the country and are a formal part of the higher education system.

2. The Institutional Fabric of the Higher Education System

2.1 Sectoral Organization

Colombian higher education is at present regulated by Decree 80 of 1980, complemented three years later by the establishment of open education and the correspondence system to coexist with the traditional system.

All these alternatives are offered by private and public institutions classified as nonprofit organizations. In 1986 there were 226 such institutions, 70 of which were state run and 156 private. The Constitution still confers on the state the power to supervise all higher education, which has the stated objects of:

(a) broadening the access to education for young people;

(b) conducting programs designed to make the inhabitants of rural areas, city fringes, and indigenous peoples a part of Colombian society;

(c) encouraging integration between research organizations and other sectors of Colombian society;

(d) training instructors as scientists and teachers; and

(e) promoting decentralization and contributing to the development of the regions in which the institutions are located.

2.2 Levels of Institutions

Institutions in higher (postsecondary) education are of four kinds, depending on the education they provide: (a) intermediate professional institutions, (b) institutes of technology, (c) universities, and (d) graduate institutions.

The intermediate professional institutions are designed to prepare students for practical activities in secondary tasks within the economy, as accounts clerks, sales assistants, operators of small agricultural businesses, and so forth. Research in this area is directed at a greater understanding of and efficiency in the specialist subjects taught. The successful student earns the title of Intermediate Technical Professional in the subject of study.

The institutes of technology prepare students for a technological activity, that is, the practical application of basic theories. The programs lead up to the title of Technologist or Specialist Technologist in the subject concerned. Research in these institutions has centered mainly on the creation or adaptation of technological innovations.

Undergraduate university courses consist of academic programs and formation in the liberal professions. They provide basic education in the humanities, research, and the professions. The graduate earns the title of doctor, biologist, lawyer, engineer, and so forth depending on the area studied.

Advanced or graduate studies are the highest level of education, preparing students for research, scientific activities, and specialization.

The universities offer at least three undergraduate programs, and many also have advanced graduate programs. The distribution of higher education institutions by academic type and origin (public or private) appears in Table 1, which also shows the growth of institutions between 1983 and 1986.

Table 1
Higher education institutions 1983–6

Academic type and Origin	1983 Number	%	1986 Number	%
Total general	217	—	226	—
Public	65	30	70	31
Private	152	70	156	69
Universities	67	—	71	—
Public	30	45	30	42
Private	37	55	41	58
Other university level institutions	54	—	60	—
Public	16	30	18	30
Private	38	70	42	70
Institutes of technology	29	—	35	—
Public	10	35	13	37
Private	19	65	22	63
Intermediate professional institutions	67	—	60	—
Public	9	13	9	15
Private	58	87	51	85

Table 2
Research and development projects by institutions 1982

Institutions	Number of projects
Central Government	38
Universities	1,140
Public	938
Private	202
R & D institutions	418
Public	221
Private	160
Mixed Ec.	29
Internal. public organisms	4
Internal. private organisms	4
Scientific & technological services	114
Public	94
Private	20
Industry (productive)	61
Public	20
Private	17
Mixed	24
Total	1,771

Scientific research in Colombia is mainly carried out at the universities, at private research centers, and in public institutions created for that purpose. There is no central organization to determine scientific policy for all institutions, although the Ministry of Education, through the research fund COLCIENCIAS, sponsors research in various areas of knowledge, and assigns priorities depending on the government policy.

The universities conduct most of the research and development projects, as can be seen in Table 2, which uses data from 1982 onwards. However, the universities do not have the resources to fully utilize their research capacity and to work with the production sector.

The institutions of higher education offer instruction in both day and night courses, and sometimes correspondence courses. Some of them, such as the universities, use all the media of higher education (see Table 3).

2.3 Admission and Selection Policy

Each of the universities has an admission department or registry to determine admissions policy, subject to the general requirements laid down in the law concerning higher education. These requirements include both the high school diploma and the state examinations, which are standardized tests designed to show knowledge and abilities. The universities decide on the score level required for each course of study. The National Testing Service, a department of ICFES, is responsible for preparation, applying, and processing the state examinations.

The universities also establish other requirements for admission, such as interviews, additional examinations, and high school grades. In general terms, admission is highly selective, especially where courses are much in demand, such as medicine. The institutes of technology, the intermediate professional institutions, and the National University for Correspondence Studies, are, on the whole, less demanding.

2.4 Quantitative Development of Higher Education

Higher education has been very much a service for the elite; the slow process of democratization began only in this century. Only since 1960 has there been any rapid increase in the number of students enrolled and in the number of institutions offering non-university higher education (see Table 4).

In 1960 only 2 percent of Colombians aged 20–24 had access to higher education; in the late 1980s, the figure was almost 15 percent (see Table 5). During the 1960s and 1970s there was a huge expansion in the number of university places available, and from 1983 correspondence courses began in both public and private universities.

2.5 Graduate Programs

As in the rest of the universities of Latin America, the increase in graduate studies in Colombia has been particularly marked since the 1950s. Before then, there were only two graduate programs available. In 1989 there were nearly 400 (see Table 6). There are now some 10,000 students taking graduate courses for master's degrees and specialist qualifications.

Table 3

Institutions and academic programs by levels and modalities 1986

Institutions (total numbers)	Number of institutions	Number of programs							
		Total	Modalities			Levels			
			Day	Night	Distance	Technical	Technology	Univ.	Graduate
National	226	2,069	1,380	590	99	303	270	1,079	417
Public	70	938	720	154	64	38	129	523	248
Private	156	1,131	660	436	35	265	141	556	169
Universities	71	1,323	1,001	263	59	1	70	859	393
Public universities	30	758	631	95	32	1	50	468	239
Private universities	41	565	370	168	27	—	20	391	154
University institutions	60	229	180	96	23	—	57	218	24
Public univ. inst.	18	92	46	28	18	—	28	55	9
Private univ. inst.	42	207	134	68	5	—	29	163	15
Technological institutions	35	162	76	71	15	17	143	2	—
Public techn. inst.	13	52	30	8	14	1	51	—	—
Private techn. inst.	22	110	46	63	1	16	92	2	—
Technical professional inst.	60	285	123	160	2	285	—	—	—
Public technical prof. inst.	9	36	13	23	—	36	—	—	—
Private technical prof. inst.	51	249	110	137	2	249	—	—	—

Table 4
Student enrollment

	1960	1965	1970	1975	1980	1985
University	23,013	44,403	85,560	178,576	234,705	319,532
Non university	—	—	—	8,106	36,925	71,958
Total	23,013	44,403	85,560	186,682	271,630	391,490

The development of the graduate system has not been the result of any government strategic planning nor of any specific policy. It has been more of a spontaneous event related to: (a) interaction of the Colombian education system with those of other countries through scholarships, visiting professors, and a closer relationship with international literature; (b) the expansion of schooling at all levels; and (c) the greater demand for educational qualification at higher levels.

The policy problem the education authorities now have to resolve is the reorientation of an unstructured mass of graduate programs into a coherent whole, particularly with reference to new graduate programs, that is, the doctorates and postdoctorates.

Graduate studies, however, face some limitations. One such is the universities' shortage of resources for scientific research in support of advanced studies and specializations; another is the lack of scientific information and connections with scientific institutions in other countries. The few international links of the graduate program have been made with the United States and Europe rather than the rest of Latin America or international or regional organizations. Despite these limitations, the potential of Colombian universities in many areas of higher research and instruction is outstanding, as can be seen from Table 7, which shows the areas in which research is being carried out.

3. Governance, Administration, and Finance

3.1 National Administration

Universities are classified as public—i.e., national, departmental, and municipal—and private. Although all higher education institutions are regulated by Decree 80 of 1980, the National University has a greater degree of independence. The president of Colombia appoints and removes the rectors of their various establishments. The departmental governors, as representatives of the president, appoint the rectors of departmental universities, and the mayors appoint the rectors of the municipal universities.

The government supervises the functioning and administration of the universities through the Ministry of Education with its dependent institution ICFES, created in 1968.

The function of ICFES is to regulate the physical structure, budget, costs, and academic activities of educational institutions. It approves the creation of new institutions of higher education and new academic programs.

In the private sector, higher education finances itself with matriculation fees and other fees paid by the students, and from other services provided to the community, such as studies, hospital services, consultancy, and so on. Since the institutions of higher education are nonprofit organizations, they are also in a position to receive donations from government and other Colombian and foreign organizations.

The public universities are financed out of state revenues, with small regional contributions. A structural analysis of their budgets, made in 1990, showed that 10.5 percent of their resources come from their own assets and matriculation fees, 4 percent from credit and unspent balance of previous fiscal years, and 85.5 percent from central government.

About one quarter of the country's education budget goes to higher education, although most of this is allocated to the maintenance of existing institutions rather than to expansion or the development of new programs.

The government institute for technical specialization abroad, ICETEX, has loan programs to allow young Colombians access to higher education.

3.2 Institutional Administration

Legislation decrees that the national, departmental, and municipal universities must have a higher council, an academic council, and a rector.

The private religious foundations follow the same structure, but in such a way as to work within the

Table 5
Number enrolled in higher education as percentage of population aged 20–24

	1960	1965	1970	1975	1980	1985
Percentage	2	3	5	7	11	13

Table 6
Graduate programs 1955–86

	1955	1960	1965	1971	1975	1979	1980	1983	1986
Total number of programs	16	32	45	129	124	254	278	262	417

rules of the orders which own them. The private secular foundations, as nonprofit organizations, have governing bodies made up of their founders, directors, benefactors, ex-alumni, and so forth, which determine the guidelines for the functioning of their institution. Their work is complemented by other bodies parallel to those in the public system.

The higher council is the senior administrative body in the state universities, and it defines and evaluates administrative and academic policy. It consists of the Minister of Education, the governor or mayor, a representative of the president, the rector of the university, a dean named by the academic council, a representative of the teaching staff and a representative of the student body; sometimes an alumnus is also included.

The academic council is the seat of academic authority. It is responsible for course programs, academic

Table 7
Graduate programs, areas of knowledge and levels 1985

Areas of knowledge	Number of programs	Levels		
		Specialty	Master	Doctorate
Natural sciences	31	3	27	1
Agriculture and veterinary	12	3	9	—
Health	212	187	25	—
Engineering, architecture, urbanism	50	16	34	—
Sub total	305	209	95	1
Social sciences and law	57	39	15	3
Economy, adminis., accounting	89	63	26	—
Humanities & religious science	16	—	13	3
Fine arts	1	1	—	—
Education	52	4	48	—
Sub total	215	107	102	6
Total	520	316	197	7

regulations, and research policy. Usually it is composed of the rector—to whom the rest of the body act as advisers—the academic vice-rector, the administration director, the various faculty deans, a representative of the teaching staff, and a representative of the student body.

Each faculty is administered by a dean, who is advised by a faculty council.

Although lines of authority are clearly defined, effective participation from each group concerned varies greatly from one university to another. The representatives of the teaching staff and of the student body are usually elected by popular vote, but the rectors are appointed by higher authority. Although all teaching staff may participate in the election of their representative, usually each university selects its staff; lays down the mechanism for promotion and development; and allocates scholarships, sabbatical leave, and other benefits. Private universities on the whole have smaller resources in this area.

4. Faculty and Students: Teaching, Learning, and Research

4.1 Faculty

In 1986 there were 43,469 teaching staff in higher education, of whom 17,653 were working in public institutions and 25,816 in private establishments.

The educational level of teaching staff is as follows: 28,479 have a professional title or *licenciatura*; 1,939 have a lesser qualification, as intermediate professional or technologist; 11,827 have some specialist or master's qualification; and only 1,224 have doctorates. The largest number of teaching staff with master's degrees or doctorate are to be found in the area of social sciences. The full-time teaching staff take the most active part in university administration.

In the public universities, a teaching career passes through four levels of qualification: instructor or auxiliary lecturer, assistant lecturer, associate lecturer, and professor. Each institution has its own requirements for moving up the scale, including publications and research, academic qualifications, training courses, teaching experience, and professional performance.

Although there is nothing corresponding to the tenure system, labor law provides relative stability

Table 8
Graduates from higher education 1970–84

Subject areas	1970 No.	1970 %	1975 No	1975 %	1980 No	1980 %	1984 No	1984 %
Science								
Natural sciences	191	2.3	306	2.1	600	2.4	346	1.2
Agriculture and veterinary	608	7.4	970	6.7	838	3.4	622	2.2
Health	975	11.9	1,276	8.7	2,583	10.4	3,993	13.7
Engineering	1,401	17.1	2,036	13.9	2,623	10.6	4,341	14.9
Sub total	3,175	38.7	4,588	31.4	6,644	26.8	9,302	32.0
Social sciences and humanities								
Social Sciences	579	7.1	820	5.6	1,447	5.9	1,765	6.1
Administration and economy	1,403	17.1	3,319	22.7	6,399	25.9	7,180	24.7
Law and humanities	1,303	15.9	2,395	16.4	3,491	14.1	3,856	13.3
Architecture and fine arts	440	5.3	526	3.6	1,017	4.1	1,119	3.8
Education sciences	1,309	15.9	2,970	20.3	5,747	23.2	5,840	20.1
Sub total	5,034	61.3	10,030	68.6	18,101	73.2	19,760	68.0
Total	8,209	100	14,618	100	24,745	100	29,062	100

Source: ICFES. *Estadisticas de la Educacion Superior*, corresponding years

for full-time teaching staff, especially at public universities.

There exist, particularly in the public sector, organizations representing the interests of the teaching staff, but there is no national organization to which most staff from both public and private sector become associated. The university teachers' association ASPU has only attracted some 5 percent of university teaching staff throughout the country. The influence of all of these bodies in decision making has varied widely over time and from one university to another.

4.2 Students

In general, graduates from higher education have been increasing in numbers in recent years: in 1970 there were 8,209 graduates and in 1984 there were 29,062. The increase of 254 percent is higher than the increase in university matriculations for the same period. Figures for the subject areas studied appear in Table 8.

The role of the student organizations has changed over the history of the universities and other institutions. Student concern is not confined to academic considerations, but has spread to more general policy matters. The student organizations have been unstable, fragmented, and influenced by political interests, and this has prevented the formation of representative organizations at a national level.

The widening of access to higher education is no automatic guarantee of the arrival of social equality, and recent experience in Colombia has proved this.

The late 1980s saw a proliferation of entities offering higher education, which immediately fitted into their place in the structure of society. The technological and intermediate programs have meant that education is reaching sectors of the population which previously had no access to universities; but their qualifications are looked down upon in the labor market. Most of their students belong to the lower-middle and lower classes.

Night studies have been introduced to allow lower-middle and lower-class employees to reenter universities and be able to work and study at the same time. The public universities are taking increasing numbers of students from these levels of society, but they still have serious underrepresentation of the lower classes, and overrepresentation of the upper and upper-middle classes. Aside from this, the quality of higher education has now become a matter of political importance.

5. Conclusion

The headlong rush of progress in Colombian higher education since the 1960s can provide some useful lessons for this country and Latin America as a whole as they face the challenges of a changing world.

Latin America must adopt new economic, political, scientific, and technological strategies, all more closely related than ever before, to become part of the modern world.

In the case of Colombia, coordinating the public and private sectors to make use of the scarce resources available for education has shown that there are great possibilities. The goals of equality in society or employment, which have motivated politicians to open up the higher education system, are not achieved simply by increasing the number of places available though. Equality has other demands, such as the provision of education of a similar quality for all, and the search for similar conditions and performance.

Also, any expansion of the number of places should entail a concomitant expansion of resources, but these are not necessarily available, and this can lead to a reduction in quality. Moreover, there is no direct relationship between training received at the university and a steady offer of employment, which is affected by many extraneous and constantly changing factors.

The function of graduate study in Colombian society requires careful analysis, especially in the context of the current vertical and horizontal explosion in programs. This fourth level of education must be differentiated from the other three, and the scientific work done at graduate level must be linked to the research centers of the countries at the forefront of technology. This does not stop graduate study from being a bridge to other social sectors such as politics, production, and academic duties. The twin openings to domestic and international integration can be complemented by a closer relationship between the universities of all Latin America.

Bibliography

Alvarez B, Ortiz A 1988 The University: An ambiguous symbol of social mobility. *J. Popular Culture* 22(1): 121–9

Amaya P, Mesa G, Velásquez A 1986 *Colombia: Política Científica, Formación de Recursos Humanos y Utilización en Investigación* (mimeo). Red de Recursos Humanos para la investigación en los paises de América Latina y del Caribe. CIID, Bogotá

Chenery Mission 1986 El Problema Laboral Colombiano: Diagnóstico, Perspectivas y Políticas. Informe Final de la Misión de Empleo. *Economía Colombiana*. Bogotá: Revista de la Contraloría General de la República, serie documentos, separata No. 10, Bogotá

Instituto Colombiano para El Formento de la Educacion Superior (ICFES) 1986 *Estatisticas de la Educacion Superior 1986* ICFES, Bogota

Jaramillo J 1982 El proceso de la Educación, del Virreinato a la época contemporánea. *Manual de Historia de Colombia* 3: 325–37

Parra Sandoval R, Jaramillo B 1985 *La Educación Superior en Colombia* (Monograph). CRESALC–UNESCO, Caracas

Vélez Bustillo E, Caro B L 1986 *Postgrado en América Latina: Investigación sobre el caso de Colombia.* CRESALC–UNESCO, Caracas

B. Alvarez; A. Alvarez

Congo

1. Higher Education and Society

The People's Republic of the Congo is situated in equatorial Africa, facing onto the Atlantic Ocean on its Western frontier, with the Gabon to the northwest, the Cameroon and the Central African Republic to the north, and Zaire to the east and south. With a total surface area of 342,000 square kilometers and a total population estimated at around 2.3 million in 1990, it has as its capital, Brazzaville with around 600,000 inhabitants. Just under four out of ten Congolese live in urban areas, and with a population growth rate held to be around 3.4 percent per year and a crude birthrate of 46 per thousand, the Congo is a country under considerable population pressure though the number of inhabitants per square kilometer is estimated around 17. Actual estimates in the early 1990s give an average life expectancy of 54 years for men and 58 for women.

Until 1958, the Congo was part of the French colonial dependencies and French remains the official language though there are in addition some six indigenous tongues—Kongo, Kago, Mbosi, Mbene, Teke, and Munukutuba. Just over half the population are Kongo speakers. Officially, more than half the population are Catholic, with approximately a quarter Protestant and 19 percent Animist. A small minority of some 3 percent holds to the Muslim faith.

The economic structure of the country owes much to its geographical position at the confluence of the Congo and Oubangui rivers and was, when under French occupation, a major point of outlet for raw materials coming from inland. It commands considerable natural resources, among which are petroleum, lumber, copper, uranium, and phosphates. Its petrol reserves were reckoned in the early 1980s to account for some 2 percent of Africa's total reserves (*New Encyclopedia Britannica* 1986 p. 533). Its principal exports are, in order of importance, petroleum products, lumber, diamonds, sugar, and tobacco. Though the agricultural sector employs some 60 percent of the labor force, it accounts for only 15 percent of Gross National Product (GNP)—the industrial sector generating some 33 percent and servicing a further 55 percent. Estimates as to GNP per capita vary from US$830 through to US$930, an estimate given by the World Bank at 1986–88 average prices.

Recent years have seen a dramatic fall in GNP which some sources reckon to have fallen by more than 4 percent since 1988. Much of this has been due to the condition of the extractive industries principle of which is the oil industry. With the fall in oil prices since 1985, the income generated by this sector has fallen by more than half. The policy of economic reconstruction has had wide-ranging consequences in all areas of national life. In 1990, negotiations with the World Bank placed a ceiling on the national budget of francs CFA 193,600 million (US$711 million). An additional part of the program of reconstruction was the elimination by 1992 of the public sector deficit. Foreign assistance programs above all from French sources have been restored and entered into operation in 1991.

In the early 1990s, the Congo is in the midst of major political reconstruction, a situation made no easier by its parlous economic condition. Following Independence in 1958 and the establishment of the Congo as a fully independent state in 1960, a series of coups in 1962 and again in 1968 made the Congo one of the first African states to opt for a Marxist–Leninist regime. The State was developed around the formula of a Peoples' Republic along socialist lines organized around the Congolese Peoples Party.

As is customary under such regimes, a high degree of state intervention accompanied by insensitive planning, based on the precepts of "scientific socialism," has been *de rigueur.* Changes in Eastern Europe and a deteriorating economy have put this into sharp reversal from the end of 1989. In that year a number of major reforms were announced including the introduction of a multiparty democracy and the shedding of Marxism–Leninism, though scientific socialism will apparently remain as the main national goal.

The upshot of these measures has been to put a brake on previous modes of development. In June 1991, a national congress elected a provisional government and assumed the role which hitherto fell to the Head of State. General elections are purportedly to be held in 1992.

It is against this background and in a country which UNESCO estimates reckon has a 37 percent illiteracy rate (one of the lowest in Africa and due in large part to the priority accorded to education under the earlier regime) that much remains in a state of flux.

2. The Institutional Fabric of the Higher Education System

At the time of Independence, the Congo was not well-provided with higher education establishments. What was later to become the country's only university—the Marien Ngouabi University—then formed part of the French Foundation for Higher Education in Central Africa and covered both the Gabon and what was later to become the Central African Republic. In 1959, shortly after Independence within the French Commonwealth, the Foundation was transformed into the Center for Higher Administrative and Technical Studies. It acquired full university status as the *Université de Brazzaville* in 1971. Its designation as the *Université Marien Ngouabi* dates from 1977.

Despite formal separation from France, the organizational model as well as the basic qualifications which result from attendance are firmly rooted in French practice. The language of instruction is French. The University is organized along faculty lines, there being four—law, sciences, economics, and letters and human sciences. There are, in addition, a number of specialized institutes located within the University dealing with such areas as management, rural development, education, and health sciences. The University also includes two higher institutes, one dealing with technical education and the other mainly training civil servants and future members of the magistrature. Over and above these responsibilities, the University also has formal responsibility for diffusing distance education throughout the country. This task is assumed by the Department of Distance Education.

As with many universities based on the French model of higher education, entry is open to all those holding the upper-secondary school-leaving certificate—the *baccalauréat* or its equivalent qualification. If this qualification provides general access to higher education, the facility nevertheless exists for individual institutions to operate their own specific conditions of entry. Competitive entry examinations do operate in the case of the Civil Service College and the school for the training of magistrates.

The structure of studies bears considerable similarity to the structures found in the French University prior to the reforms of 1968 and 1972. The first university degree in the *Université Marien Ngouabi* is the licence which, in contrast to the first French qualification (the DEUG, which lasts two years), is a three-year program. Formal provision is made for higher degrees in the shape of the *diplôme d'études supérieures* which requires a further two years' study. Time required for an engineering diploma varies from two to five years. Provision is made for doctoral level studies which require a further five years after the *diplôme d'études supérieures*, making a ten-year course from the start of undergraduate study. These degrees are national degrees, that is to say, they are awarded by the University on behalf of the State. The latter lays down the conditions of validation and formally underwrites their quality.

Though institutes exist within the *Université Marien Ngouabi* which are clearly not of full university status, it is probably not entirely correct to draw a hard-and-fast distinction between two formal sectors, university and nonuniversity higher education, along lines that are often classically associated with this type of demarcation in Western Europe. The training

159

of primary-school teachers takes place in normal schools (*écoles normales d'instituteurs*), which are generally equated with a level of upper-secondary schooling, a pattern which resembles one well-established in France 20 years ago. More close to the university/nonuniversity divide is the Paramedical School for nurse training and other medical technicians. Specialized institutes have played a key part in the country's development, and particularly the Institute for Rural Development which trains engineers and agronomists through a program lasting five years.

3. Governance, Administration, and Finance

As with many developing countries, the prime role of the university is to assist in the cultural, economic, and political progress of the nation. National planning objectives, as befitted a regime drawing its inspiration from Marxist–Leninist principles, were centrally determined and drawn up in the form of five-year plans. Education figured prominently in these and most particularly in the plan running from 1982–86. It placed particular emphasis upon developing primary schooling. Such plans were sectorally implemented through the appropriate ministries and transmitted from there to the University via a Directorial Committee (*Comité de Direction*).

As the country's single university and located in the capital, the *Université Marien Ngouabi* comes under the control of the Ministry of Education. It is headed by a rector, appointed by the government. Administration, again following the French lines, comes under the general oversight of a Secretary General, who reports both to the rector and to the Ministry of Education. It must, for the moment, remain a matter of conjecture how far these relationships will be revised. Whether a greater degree of institutional autonomy will develop and the degree of self-government that will emerge from political regime less wedded to central control are aspects which only the future can reveal.

4. Faculty and Students: Teaching, Learning, and Research

The latest figures available on both staffing and students are not the most up-to-date and relate to the year 1987. The total number of academic staff was then in the region of 783, though no breakdown between rank appears to be to hand. In that same year some 12,043 students were enrolled. Of these, women accounted for approximately 18 percent of all enrollments. In addition, 10 percent of enrollments are students from abroad, mainly from neighboring Francophone countries with which the

Table 1
Student enrollments 1975–87

Year	1975	1980	1984	1985	1986	1987
Total	3,249	7,255	10,444	10,684	11,008	12,043

Source: UNESCO 1990 Table 3.11 pp. 3–248

University has cooperation agreements. To offset this, UNESCO estimates reckon that in 1988 approximately 3,283 Congolese were studying abroad, more than eight out of ten in France (UNESCO 1990 pp. 3–382). Enrollment figures for the period 1975–87 for the whole of the Congolese higher education system are set out in Table 1.

Though doctoral programs do formally figure in the courses available for students, much of the training for the future cadres of higher education takes place abroad.

5. Conclusion

As with many African countries, the future pattern higher education will assume in the Congo is difficult to foresee. The vital importance of higher education for national development remains uncontested. Yet the country's difficult economic situation places it under severe stress. The use of foreign assistance in developing primary education has been marked and the signing of a cooperation agreement with the People's Republic of China in 1989 is an indicator of this. Clearly, the introduction of a multiparty regime on the one hand, and the strictures imposed by the International Monetary Fund to reduce the public sector deficit by 1992 on the other, will have considerable effects, if only indirect, on both higher education finance and upon the relationship between higher education and government. It remains to be seen whether the close political control exercised over the University will be replaced by more flexible arrangements. In itself, this issue is not unique to the Congo. However, both the shedding of the major part of the official ideological overlay and the move towards a certain measure of economic liberalism highlight the difficulties involved in this transition.

Bibliography

International Association of Universities 1990 *International Handbook of Universities*. Stockton Press, London
New Encyclopedia Britannica 1986 15th edn., Vol. 3
UNESCO 1990 *Statistical Yearbook 1990*. UNESCO, Paris

M. Vansteenkiste; G. Neave

Costa Rica

1. Higher Education and Society

The first institution of higher education in Costa Rica was the University of Saint Thomas, founded in 1843, which concentrated on legal studies. It was abolished in 1888, as part of a global educational reform. Higher education subsequently rested with various professional schools until the creation of the University of Costa Rica (UCR) in 1940. In the 1970s, public higher education expanded with the establishment of the National University (UNA), the Technological Institute (ITCR), the Open University (UNED), and several community colleges offering short technical courses. The 1980s saw the growth of private higher education with emphasis on commercial and business courses.

Costa Rica, embracing 51,100 square kilometers, is located in the Central American isthmus between Nicaragua to the north and Panama to the south. Border problems were resolved by the 1940s. The mortality rate decreased from the 1930s onwards with improved hygiene and health services. By the end of the 1950s, population growth, almost 4 percent yearly, was among the highest in the world. As prosperity subsequently increased and lifestyles changed, voluntary contraception became widespread. By the 1980s, the population growth rate had decreased to 2.9 percent.

With almost three million inhabitants, half of them living in urban areas. Costa Rica has an average of 350 persons per square kilometer. The central valley contains over 50 percent of the population, as well as the most modern infrastructure and services. Costa Ricans are predominantly Caucasian, with Mestizos in the Pacific northwest, Blacks in the Caribbean lowlands, and a few thousand scattered Indians. Spanish is the official language and Roman Catholicism the official religion, though Protestant evangelical activity has increased.

Urban growth has transformed the occupational structure of Costa Rica. Coffee production and other agricultural activities, formerly dominant, now occupy only a quarter of the labor force. Nevertheless, the economy still relies heavily on the export of coffee, bananas, sugar, and cattle. Manufacturing contributes nearly one-fifth of the national production and jobs. Industry is concentrated in the central valley. Beverages, food, textiles, furniture, and shoes are produced for domestic consumption, and medicines, electrical machinery, sheet metal, textiles, and paper products for export. The tertiary sector employs over half the labor force. The growth of the public sector has been particularly dynamic, with government employees, including teachers, constituting approximately one-third of the tertiary sector.

The 1949 Constitution defines Costa Rica as a sovereign, democratic republic. The government has three branches: legislative, executive, and judicial. A president, two vice-presidents and a unicameral assembly are elected every four years by universal suffrage. The Supreme Court of Justice has jurisdiction throughout the country. The autonomous Supreme Election Tribunal acts as a fourth power.

The Catholic Church has influenced primary and secondary education, but its role in higher education has been minimal. An Adventist University, created in 1986, is the only religious institution of higher education.

2. The Institutional Fabric of the Higher Education System

The higher education system contains parauniversity or community colleges and university studies (see Table 1). The parauniversity subsystem offers short, complete courses in public colleges specializing in technical and agricultural studies, and private schools offering commercial and business education. The state universities are the UCR with five campuses, the ITCR with three, the UNA with three, and the UNED with five. The four private universities are the Central American Autonomous University (UACA), the Central American Adventist University, the Latin American University of Science and Technology, and the International University of the Americas.

In addition, various programs at foreign universities have been established in recent years. The National University (Florida), the Central American Institute of Business Administration (INCAE), the Friends' World College, and the Interamerican University of Puerto Rico provide short courses,

Table 1
Number of institutions in each level 1960–85

	1960	1965	1970	1975	1980	1985
Research universities (UCR, UNA)	1	1	1	2	2	2
Technological institutes	0	0	0	1	1	1
Open University	0	0	0	0	1	1
Parauniversity state institutions	0	0	0	4	4	4
Specialized institutions[a] (Agriculture, business, teacher training, and nursing)	5	5	6	1	1	2

a The School of Nursing, three normal schools, and the Inter-American Institute for Agriculture Science (IICA) existed in 1960. The Higher Normal School for Secondary Teachers was created in 1968. In 1973 UNA incorporated the normal schools and in 1974 the UCR incorporated the School of Nursing. In 1984 the INCAE was created.
Source: Primary data supplied by each institution

seminars, and master's degrees in Business Administration. The Tropical Agronomical Center for Research and Teaching (CATIE), by agreement with the UCR, offers master's programs in agronomy, animal husbandry, and natural resources.

Most scientific research is carried out by the state universities, which concentrate human resources, technology, and the accumulated experience of more than five decades. Some governmental institutions also participate in research, particularly in agriculture, forestry, fishing, health, and natural resources. Private research centers are few.

The secondary school diploma is required to enter an institution of higher education. Each institution, being autonomous, also has separate admission requirements. The UCR, ITCR, and UNA require a minimum average grade from the last two years of secondary school, plus a minimum admission examination grade. Most courses in these universities also require specific minimum average grades. The UNED and the UACA have no special admission requirements.

The state universities offer short and long courses. The former lead to a diploma. Longer courses conclude with the bachelor's or *licenciatura* degree. Courses are taught in seven areas: arts and humanities, basic sciences, social sciences, education, agriculture, engineering, and health. Graduate studies begin after the conclusion of the bachelor's or *licenciatura* degree. Qualifications for admission vary according to the type of graduate training. For master's and doctor's degrees, centered on research, a high, minimum average grade and command of one or two foreign languages are common requisites.

3. Governance, Administration, and Finance

3.1 National Administration

Article 84 of the Constitution gives the state universities full autonomy in their functions, organization, and government. However, dependence on state financing greatly diminishes their real autonomy.

The state universities are coordinated by the National Council of Rectors (CONARE). A Coordinating Commission *(Comisión de Enlace)*, formed by the Ministers of Education, Treasury, Planning, Science and Technology, and the four university rectors, provides a liaison between CONARE and the government. The Planning Office for Higher Education, (OPES), headed by the executive secretary of CONARE, plays a technical and consultative role and draws up five-year plans. In addition, the education and human resources sector, which consists of the Ministries of Education, Planning, and Science and Technology, CONARE and OPES, the University Colleges, the Central American School of Agriculture, the National Council for Educational Loans, the National System of Cultural Radio and Television,

and the National Institute of Technical Training (INA), coordinates activities in the fields of finance, study programs, the quality of education, recognition of studies and degrees, and labor policies. One of the main achievements of the coordinating mechanisms—considered vital for the state universities—was the creation in 1976 of the Special Fund for Financing Higher Education.

Private universities are supervised by the National Council of Private Higher Education (CONESUP).

The main source of finance for higher education has been central government; additional income is generated by the universities themselves and foreign loans. Prior to 1972, the UCR received 10 percent of the Ministry of Education budget. The proliferation of other institutions meant that their funding required special allocations from central government, administered by the Special Fund for Higher Education. Since 1981, the state universities have negotiated jointly for central government funds, always receiving less than requested. State university education absorbs 7–8 percent of the national budget and more than 30 percent of the education budget. The national percentage has decreased slightly over a few years as a consequence of Costa Rica's severe economic crisis and the allocation of resources to other sectors such as housing and foreign debt service.

3.2 Institutional Administration

The universities all have a similar hierarchical structure. The highest ranking body, the university assembly, is made up of all tenured teachers plus student representatives. It defines general university policies, elects the rector and the university council, approves and modifies the organic statute, decides on the creation or suppression of centers, faculties, and regional sections, and resolves appeals from the university council.

The university council comprises representatives from each academic area, elected for two-year periods. It supervises university activities in accordance with the policies dictated by the university assembly, approves the annual budget, and draws up agreements with other institutions.

The rector, elected by the university assembly, heads the executive hierarchy. He or she is the legal representative of the university, implements university council resolutions, controls university activities, confers degrees and presents nominations for the vice-rectors to the university council. The vice-rectors are the rector's closest colleagues. Liaising among themselves, they supervise fulfillment of the rector's dispositions in their respective vice-rectories.

Public nonuniversity institutions are under the direct control of the Ministry of Education, which appoints the director and the teaching and administrative staff under the auspices of the civil service. Private nonuniversity institutions, though controlled

Table 2
Total enrollment in higher education 1960–85

	1960	1965	1970	1975	1980	1985
Research universities	3,828	5,824	12,913	32,515	42,523	47,338
Technological institutes	—	—	—	279	2,420	2,709
Open University	—	—	—	—	5,869	8,346
Parauniversity state institutions	—	—	—	—	10,178	5,378
Specialized institutions[a]	—	—	—	—	—	225

Source: CONARE and primary data supplied by each institution
a IICA does not have regular students

by the Ministry of Education, appoint their own directors and academic and administrative staff. In the universities, academic decision making is largely in the hands of individual professors, whereas in nonuniversity institutions, decision making is predominantly collegiate.

The universities are organized into area faculties, subdivided into schools and departments. These are headed by deans and directors and governed by area councils and faculty and school assemblies. Nonuniversity higher education is organized according to curricular options. In public institutions, academic work conforms to the parameters set by the Ministry of Education. Private institutions are organized around "career units."

4. Faculty and Students: Teaching, Learning, and Research

4.1 Faculty

In 1985, the total number of faculty staff in the state universities was 3,913, of which one-third were full-time. To obtain tenure, candidates with a *licenciatura* or higher degree participate in an open competition. All appointments must subsequently be ratified by the school assembly and the vice-rector of teaching.

Tenured staff progress through four ranks: instructor, adjunct professor, associate professor and full professor. Other categories of professors are: retired, emeritus, interim, ad-honorem, invited, and visiting. All professors are recruited and employed directly by an institute of higher education, except in public parauniversity institutions, where appointments are made by the Ministry of Education. The most highly qualified staff are predominantly in the UCR.

All professional staff must, by Costa Rican law, belong to their respective professional college. Each university also has one or more trade unions, voluntary membership of which is open to all employees. Academic activities and work loads are decided separately by the university assembly and university council of each institution. Within each school, the director assigns specific tasks to each professor.

4.2 Students

A generous scholarship system has opened higher education to a wide range of social groups, though the UCR in particular still draws most of its students from the middle classes. In higher education as a whole, there are slightly more men than women students. Costa Rican law prohibits discrimination by ethnic group. All the institutions of higher education have recently stimulated participation by handicapped students and senior citizens. Table 2 shows the total enrollment in higher education between 1960 and 1985.

Each institution of higher education has a student union; the universities also have student assemblies in each school. Participation is open to all students, but, in practice, less than one-third are involved. The structure of first degree programs is defined by the individual institutions. Their content is drawn up and modified by the respective school. In the universities, they must then be ratified first by the vice-rector of teaching and then by CONARE or CONESUP; in the para-universities, it must be ratified by the Minister of Education.

In the universities, the first courses of undergraduate studies follow the liberal arts model of

Table 3
Number of university graduates in university institutions by area of study 1960–85

	1960	1965	1970	1975	1980	1985
Arts and humanities	16	—	—	252	213	203
Basic sciences	4	—	—	121	135	172
Social sciences	52	—	—	435	947	1,368
Education	61	—	—	1,437	1,500	1,198
Agriculture	0	—	—	71	263	288
Engineering	32	—	—	229	328	480
Health	18	—	—	356	565	526
Others	0	—	—	1	26	3
Total	183	—	—	2,902	3,977	4,238

Source: CONARE and primary data supplied by each institution

broad, general content; the student subsequently takes specialized courses in a single subject. (Graduate figures are shown in Table 3.) In the para-university institutions, all undergraduate training is specialized. Students gain credits for each course approved. Evaluation takes place within each course. The grade is based on examinations and other forms of assessment.

5. Conclusion

Historically, education has been an important aspect of the democratically oriented nation state. The state commitment to the improvement of education in Costa Rica is visible in the overall achievements that the country can claim with respect to coverage and quality in the higher education field.

Bibliography

CONARES-OPES 1986 *Cifras Relevantes de las Instituciones de Educación Superior Universitaria.* CONARES-OPES, San José

CONARES-OPES 1987 *La Educación Superior en Costa Rica.* CONARES-OPES, San José

CONARES 1987 Posibilidades de Estudio en la Educacion Superior Universitaria Estatal de Costa Rica. CONARES-OPES, San José

Congreso Costa Rica 1960–86 *Memorias de Educación.* CONARES-OPES, San José

Fischel A 1987 *Consenso y Represión. Una Interpretación sociopolitica de la educación costarricense.* Editorial Costa Rica, San José

ITCR 1973–89 *Statistics.* Register's Office

Ministerio de Educacion 1988 *Plan Operativo Anual.* San José

UACA 1976–89 *Statistics.* Register's Office

UCR 1983 *Regimen Academico y Estudiantil.* UCR, San José

UCR *1960–89 Statistics.* Register's Office

UNA 1974–89 *Statistics.* Register's Office

UNED 1978–89 *Statistics.* Register's Office

A. Fischel

Cuba

1. Higher Education and Society

The Republic of Cuba is made up of the island of Cuba and a great number of small adjacent islands and cays, in the Caribbean subregion of Latin America. The Cuban archipelago comprises an overall land area of 110,860 square kilometers.

Cuba's total population is close to 10.5 million and the demographic density is 94 per square kilometer. Some 72 percent of the population live in urban areas and the remaining 28 percent in rural areas. The official language is Spanish.

The basic means of production in Cuba belong to the state, and the economy is essentially agro-industrial. The distribution of the labor force by occupational category is as follows: executive personnel, 7.2 percent; services workers, 13.4 percent; administrative personnel, 7.3 percent; technical personnel, 21.2 percent; and workers, 50.9 percent.

The levels of education reached by the labor force are as follows: elementary school, 23.5 percent; junior high school, 37.8 percent; high school, 11.5 percent; vocational training, 18.3 percent; and higher education, 8.9 percent.

Article 1 of the constitution proclaimed in 1976 states that "Cuba is a socialist state of workers and farmers and other manual and intellectual workers . . ." and Article 50 states that "Everyone has the right to an education." This right is ensured through a comprehensive and free system of schools, semi-boarding schools, full boarding schools, and scholarships for all academic and vocational levels. The fact that all the school materials and services are also free ensures that all young people, irrespective of their families' financial situation, have equal access to all the education that social requirements, economic and social development needs, and their own capabilities allow.

Before the revolution in 1959, higher education in Cuba was a facet of the underdeveloped neocolonial system prevailing in the country, and was a privilege of the upper classes. Until then the country's only three public universities provided training for traditional careers, essentially in the humanities, social sciences, and medicine, while ignoring to a large extent engineering, natural sciences, mathematics, and agricultural sciences, which are essential for economic and social development.

As a result of the deep economic, political, and social changes that began in 1959, it was possible to extend educational opportunities to the entire population, effectively and free of charge, at all academic levels. This provided the foundations for truly democratic higher education.

At present, higher education is a functional link in the national education system. Its objectives include the training of high-level professionals and specialists, and the conducting of research in priority areas of the national economy.

2. The Institutional Fabric of the Higher Education System

Higher education is a subsystem comprised exclusively of public institutions. The majority of these higher education institutions were founded after the higher education reform of 1976.

The 1970s were characterized by an important quantitative growth. This was a result of the need to provide higher education for a large number of students in many different fields, in order to meet the highly trained labor requirements of Cuba's new national development program.

Table 1
Evolution of the network of higher education institutions

	1959–60	1970–71	1976–77	1980–81	1988–89
Universities	3	4	4	4	4
Higher polytechnic institutes	—	—	1	1	2
Higher institutes	—	1	20	31	41
University centers	—	—	3	3	1
Total	3	5	28	39	48

By the end of the 1980s, higher education had 48 institutions classified as follows: universities, higher polytechnic institutes, higher institutes, and university centers.

The universities are in charge of training professionals in the following fields: natural sciences, mathematics, social sciences, humanities and economic sciences. Some also provide training in the fields of engineering and agricultural sciences.

The higher polytechnical institutes train students for the engineering and architecture professions. The higher institutes produce professionals in specific fields of science, such as pedagogy (teachers and professors), agricultural sciences, medical sciences, art, international affairs, and physical culture.

The university center will ultimately become one of the aforementioned institutions. It provides professional training in diverse fields.

There are two types of subordinate teaching units: the branch units that provide part-time training, and the comprehensive teaching–research–production units where part of the normal curriculum is offered.

In Cuba scientific research is an essential and integral part of higher education. In actual practice professors and students participate together in research projects, thus making education and research at the universities an important factor in the country's scientific development.

Fields of study are grouped in compliance with the country's main areas of development: geology, mining, and metallurgy; energy; machine industry; chemical and sugar industries; electronics, automation, and communications; transportation; the building industry; agricultural and animal production; economics; public health and physical culture; natural sciences and mathematics; humanities and social sciences; pedagogy; and the arts.

The structure of the different fields of study has gone through successive transformations in keeping with the national social and economic structure. From 28 fields that existed in 1959, the number increased to 115 by 1977 and is currently being revised.

Students are offered three different types of course: regular day courses, regular courses for workers, and "free" or "directed" courses. The regular day courses require full-time study. The regular courses for workers are based on part-time study and occur in the evening or on a "consultation" basis.

The free or directed courses have no attendance requirements. Students work with their texts and recorded lectures.

Selection for the regular day courses is based on a combination of the student's academic record in high school and the results of an entrance examination in three subjects: mathematics (common to all), and two others depending on the particular course of study chosen.

Acceptance to the regular course for workers is based on two requirements: affinity with the work the candidate is doing; and a two-subject entrance examination (Spanish and mathematics).

Access to the "directed" or "free" courses requires only the completion of high school. This option is ideally suited to satisfying personal interests while acquiring a college education.

In 1959 there were barely 16,000 students in higher education. During the 1960s enrollment increased at an average annual rate of 6.1 percent. From 1970 on, however, enrollment increased sharply, peaking at 15 percent. By 1980 total enrollment had gone from 35,000 in 1970 to 151,700. During the 1980s enrollment tended to stabilize and the figure for the 1988–89 academic year was 283,000 (43 percent of these students in regular day courses). This means that 2.7 percent of the Cuban population are enrolled in higher education.

Currently, 24 percent of the population between 20 and 24 years of age attend educational establishments. The distribution of students in higher education centers shows that 15 percent are at the universities and the remaining 85 percent are in the other types of higher education institutions.

All the degrees are equivalent, irrespective of the type of course or institution; all imply the same job opportunities and social recognition.

Graduate education includes a professional upgrading system which certifies the development of higher scientific and technical skills, although not in the form of a degree.

Table 2
Total enrollment in higher education (in thousands)

1960–61	1965–66	1970–71	1975–76	1980–81	1985–86	1988–89
19.5	26.2	35.1	84.0	178.4	269.5	283.6

The Cuban higher education system also grants the following two scientific degrees: doctoral candidate (roughly equivalent to a PhD) and doctor of sciences. Access to the scientific degree program is highly selective.

3. Governance, Administration, and Finance

3.1 National Administration

The Ministry of Higher Education is the governing body in higher education nationwide. It is in charge of implementing the educational policy at this level and of providing the methodological orientations for all institutions.

Planning for higher education is also a part of the country's overall planning effort. This task is in the hands of the Ministry of Higher Education and other relevant ministries and agencies with institutions for higher training, working jointly with the national global planning bodies, such as the Central Planning Board (JUCEPLAN), the State Committee for Finance, and the State Committee for Labor and Social Security. The country's main employers also participate actively in this process.

Certain relevant provisions defined after broad consultation with professors and students govern, among other matters, management, academic planning, and scientific development policies. In establishing these policies, institutions have the necessary autonomy and can, therefore, participate actively and creatively in the educational process.

Higher education is financed primarily by funds appropriated from the state budget. There are other sources of finance, particularly for research breakthroughs achieved in higher education institutions and other scientific research centers, but these funds are not significant.

3.2 Institutional Administration

Institutionally speaking, governance is effected through a blend of democracy and centralization. Institutions have a leading authority, the rector, invested with the power and responsibility to run the higher education center. There are other collegiate authorities which comprise heads of the various academic and administrative levels and representatives of students' and trade union organizations.

The academic departments are the basic element in the institutional structure, responsible for scientific research and professional upgrading.

The collegiate governance bodies in higher education centers are: the board, the central methodological committee, the scientific council, the faculty, and the workers' assembly.

4. Faculty and Students: Teaching, Learning, and Research

4.1 Faculty

During the 1988–89 academic year, Cuban higher education professors totaled 23,700, 20 times as many as in 1959. Of them, 20,800 worked full-time and 2,600 were mostly prestigious and experienced professionals from the various branches of production and services.

The overall student–faculty ratio in higher education is approximately 12:1, although this indicator may vary according to groups and courses.

Higher education workers are affiliated to a national organization, the National Trade Union of Education and Culture Workers. Professors and researchers can also be members of other scientific and technical associations in keeping with their professional interests.

4.2 Students

Professional training has embarked on a new trend aimed at a relative reduction of enrollment in traditional social sciences and economics courses and an increase in priority courses for the country's economic development, such as engineering and agriculture. There has also been a boost in the training of professionals in medical and pedagogical sciences, areas of vital importance for the social and cultural development of the country.

The main part of the student body of pedagogical sciences, designed to turn out elementary and secondary school teachers, is made up of people who are teaching at those levels and studying part-time to acquire their *licenciatura* degrees.

Since 1959, professionals who have graduated from higher education total 317,000. Graduation classes average some 30,000 a year. At the end of the 1980s, 3 percent of the population had completed higher education.

Dropouts have been reduced by half since 1970, although the rate is still high, particularly in the first two years of college life. Among the main causes for full-time student dropouts are high standards (students are only allowed to repeat a year in exceptional circumstances) and poor academic performance.

Higher education students in Cuba are part of the Federation of University Students. This organization plays a prominent academic role and looks after the students' interests and demands.

Women make up 57 percent of the student population, most of them in pedagogy, economics, social sciences, humanities, natural sciences, and mathematics. The Cuban higher education system also includes a large number of foreign students, mostly from underdeveloped countries. In the 1988–89 academic year there were 5,800 foreign students from 98 countries studying in Cuba, a great many of them from Latin America and the Caribbean.

The country's economic and social development plan has made it possible to ensure jobs for all graduates from full-time courses. This is the main way young professionals are introduced to an economically active life.

To diversify graduates' placement prospects and enhance their ability to adapt to the changing demands posed by scientific and technological progress, curricula are now being modified to broaden professional profiles. One variant is a two- to three-year hands-on training period under the direct supervision and control of the employing enterprise or agency, prior to enrollment in specialized graduate courses.

Other programs link student teaching units and production as a significant step toward integrating academic activities, research and production. One of them is the improvement of diploma dissertations and projects which require a technical study or scientific research on a specific production- or services-related problem and which may be tutored either by professionals or professors in higher education centers. Other experiments are under way to link students to their future work: for example, production practice at different stages during college training and, in the final stage, direct contact with the future workplace. Another project is the linkage of students to production in their teaching units as a significant step toward integrating academic activities, research, and production.

In general, undergraduate courses (*licenciatura*) last five years, and each term is divided into two semesters of 14 to 18 weeks in length with three weeks for examination; the only exception is medicine which lasts six years. Curricula generally contain some 50 subjects and a total of 4,000–4,500 hours, not including practices in production and services centers as part of the professional training or the time employed in preparation of the diploma dissertation.

5. Conclusion

Cuba is no longer affected by a shortage of professionals, so it is possible for higher education to concentrate on other objectives.

Future development strategy is geared to the training of broad profile graduates capable of adapting to the country's changing needs.

The higher education network needs to level out in quantitative terms and work at reducing its over-specialization problem. Course structures must reflect scientific and technological progress and also turn out the professionals needed in the provinces where the institutions are located. Interinstitutional relations and cooperation must be enhanced.

The access system is still undergoing constant review and improvement with the aim of arriving at the fairest possible selection of candidates on the basis of their academic achievement and social conduct.

Scientific research and the constant upgrading of the faculty will continue to have the undivided attention of the authorities, for they are the key elements in the drive for greater quality. Efforts will be focused on attracting the finest production and services specialists to higher education so that they may enrich the educational process with their expertise.

A high priority will be assigned to improving all levels of management in higher education, finding alternative sources of financing, and making the best possible use of human, material, and financial resources.

The new curricula must be such that they will develop the qualities of creativeness, independence, cooperation in the graduates, and the ability to work on interdisciplinary projects, to have self-discipline and dexterity in the use and manipulation of the instruments of their profession. They must learn to assimilate modern methods and high technology in their jobs, and have the ability to adapt. Efforts will also be made to make teaching forms and methods more flexible and effective.

Bibliography

Anuario Estadístico de Cuba 1987 Comité Estatal de Estadísticas, Havana

Consejo Superior de Universidades 1962 *La Reforma de la Enseñanza Superior en Cuba*. Consejo Superior de Universidades, Havana

Consejo Nacional de Universidades 1965 *Conclusiones del Primer Seminario de Evaluación de las Universidades Cubanas*. Consejo Nacional de Universidad, Havana

Comité Estatal de Estadísticas 1989 *Boletines de inicio y final del año escolar a partir de 1977–1978*. CEE, Havana

Ministerio de Educación 1972 *Estudio diagnóstico: Análisis cuantitativo y cualitativo, sistema universitario; período 1959–1971*. MINED, Havana

Ministerio de Educación 1976 *Poryecto para la Organización y Desarrollo de la Educación Superior*. MINED, Havana

Ministerio de Educación 1981 *Informe a la Asamblea Nacional del Poder Popular*. MINED, Havana

Ministerio de Educación 1986 *Pedagogía 86. Conferencia: Desarrollo de la Educación en Cuba*. Palacio de las Convenciones, Havana

Ministerio de Educación Superior 1982 *Dirección de Desarrollo, Estudio Diagnóstico del Desarrollo de la Educación Superior; período 1959–1980.* MES, Havana
Ministerio de Educación Superior 1984 *Informe a la Asamblea Nacional del Poder Popular.* MES, Havana
Ministerio de Educación Superior 1990 *Informes anuales; a partir del año académico 1976–77.* MES, Havana
Documentos del Primer Congreso del Partido Comunista de Cuba 1976 DOR, Havana
Documentos del Segundo Congreso del Partido Comunista de Cuba 1981 DOR, Havana
Documentos del Tercer Congreso del Partido Comunista de Cuba 1986 DOR, Havana
La Educación Superior en Cuba 1985 Monografía. CRES-ALC-UNESCO, Caracas
Martin E et al. 1986 *Aspectos socioeconómicos de la preparación de especialistas con educación superior en Cuba.* Ediciones ENPES, Havana
Vecino Alegret F 1983 *Tendencias en el desarrollo de la educación superior en Cuba; significado del trabajo didáctico. Tesis.* MES, Havana

E. Martin Sabina; Y. F. Fernández

Cyprus

1. Higher Education and Society

This article deals only with higher education in the southern two-thirds of Cyprus which is inhabited by 80 percent of the population. On account of the 1974 invasion by Turkish troops and the separation of Cyprus into two, between which there is no physical or other contact, there is no information available about higher education in that part occupied by Turkish troops and inhabited mainly by Turkish Cypriots.

There are several paradoxes surrounding higher education in Cyprus. The first is that in a population of 600,000 there are nearly 10,000 students studying at foreign universities all over the world but Cyprus has no public university. Secondly, at least four private institutions call themselves universities, polytechnics, or colleges but there is no public institution with this name, although there *are* public institutions of higher education. Although hundreds of Greek Cypriot professors, associate professors, and lecturers at foreign universities have expressed their wish to offer their academic services to Cyprus, there is no opportunity for them to do so. Finally, the number of students is increasing (48% of total secondary school leavers continue their studies), although there are at least 8,000 unemployed university graduates.

These paradoxes reflect social and political values, institutions, and circumstances, which explain on the one hand the strong tendency to enroll in higher education among Greek Cypriot youth, and on the other the failure of the Cyprus government to establish a university.

According to the Second Five-Year Development Plan (1967–71) issued by the Ministry of Finance in 1968, "the culture of Cyprus possesses ideologies and value systems which attach great importance to individual achievements and is very responsive to innovations, new ideas and new opportunities" (p. 273). This culture has strengthened enormously the social and economic significance of education in general and higher education in particular. Higher education has traditionally been very important to the realization of individual social and economic expectations. In a largely agricultural society with no deep social divisions, it has been the most effective promoter of social mobility and equity.

The traditional social and economic value of higher education was strengthened by the establishment of conditions of service in public employ which stipulated that only people with university degrees could be appointed to some posts and promoted to others. In addition the five following factors were important:

(a) the creation, after Independence in 1960, of many highly paid jobs—administrative, diplomatic, political, and specialist—reserved almost exclusively for university graduates;

(b) the destruction after the 1974 Turkish invasion resulting in the loss of immovable and movable property of great value but not the economic value of a university degree;

(c) the large number of scholarships offered by foreign governments through the Ministry of Foreign Affairs for the purpose of helping the development of Cyprus;

(d) the tendency of many Cypriots settled in the United Kingdom to invite young relatives from Cyprus to the United Kingdom and offer them hospitality and financial assistance for higher studies there;

(e) the long-term policy of Greece to attract Greek Cypriot students to Greek universities by waiving fees and offering scholarships and subsistence allowances to a great number of them.

Despite its failure to establish a university, the government of Cyprus has not been inactive in the field of higher education. It has established new schools, improved the quality of those existing, and at the same time prepared the ground for the establishment of a university. A decision in principle to establish a university was taken by the Council of Ministers as early as December 1978.

On 13 July 1989 the House of Representatives passed unanimously Law No. 144/1989 "for the establishment and operation of a public University," planned to start operating in September 1991. The provisions of the law were based on the proposals of a preparatory committee consisting of Cypriot academics working at foreign universities. Nearly all the members of the House described the law as a historic act that would enhance the emancipation of higher education in Cyprus.

2. *The Institutional Fabric of the Higher Education System*

During the academic year 1988–89 there were seven public and 18 private institutions providing higher education and awarding various diplomas, usually below first university degree level.

The public institutions of higher education are the following:

(a) The Pedagogical Academy, which offers three-year courses in primary school teaching and nursery school teaching.

(b) The Higher Technical Institute, which offers three-year courses in electrical, civil, mechanical, and marine engineering and computer studies.

(c) The School of Nursing which offers three-year courses in general nursing and psychiatric nursing (registered nurses) and 18-month courses in general nursing and psychiatric nursing (assistant nurses).

(d) The Hotel and Catering Institute which offers a two-year course in cookery and one-year courses in reception, waiting, and housekeeping.

(e) The Cyprus Forestry College which offers a two-year diploma course and a six-month post-diploma course in forestry.

(f) The Mediterranean Institute of Management which offers a one-year training program in management for university graduates.

(g) The Pedagogical Institute, which offers inservice training to primary and secondary school teachers.

The private institutions were mostly established during the 1980s and offer courses of one to four years' duration.

During the academic year 1988–89 there were 5,066 students enrolled in the higher institutions of Cyprus (35%), and 9,410 students enrolled in universities abroad (65%). This distribution is rapidly changing in favour of the Cypriot institutions. Since 1989 nearly half of the new students have registered in Cypriot institutions.

Of the students staying in Cyprus 33.3 percent attend public institutions while the rest attend private institutions. Of the students studying abroad 39.8 percent receive higher education in Greece, 21.9 percent in the United Kingdom, 20 percent in the United States, 6.6 percent in the Federal Republic of Germany, 3 percent in Italy, 1.9 percent in Austria, 1.8 percent in France, and the rest in nearly all the other European countries. The above distribution has varied over the years due to various factors, including the cost of living, tuition fees, admission restrictions, and future employment prospects.

Both public and private institutions of higher education in Cyprus are professionally oriented and try to meet the demands of the labor market. At the public institutions the number of students admitted to every program or field of study is in keeping with the estimated short- or long-term labor needs of the specific field in industry or profession. Students are usually employed immediately after graduation without having to take further professional examinations. Private institutions also cater for local labor needs in a more flexible way and in a broader field. They offer courses in such fields as secretarial studies; business administration; electrical, civil, and mechanical engineering; wireless communications; catering; banking; accountancy; and computer studies.

All public schools of higher education demand at least 12 years of schooling as a prerequisite. Candidates for admission need to be holders of a leaving certificate from a six-year secondary school. This will also be true of the University of Cyprus.

The Pedagogical Academy, the School of Nursing, and the Higher Technical Institute admit students mainly on the basis of the grades attained by the candidate in the entrance examinations. These are organized by the Examination Service of the Department of Higher and Tertiary Education of the Ministry of Education. The exams cover blocks of different subjects according to the field of intended study. Other schools set up their own exams which vary, again according to the type of institution. The university will also have its own entrance examinations.

Transfer from one institution to another in Cyprus is not usually possible at any stage of the study course, nor is it possible to transfer from one program to the other in the same institution.

3. *Governance, Administration, and Finance*

3.1 *The National Level*

The seven public institutions of higher education are run by various ministries, according to the content of their programs. The Pedagogical Academy and the Pedagogical Institute are under the Ministry of Education; the Higher Technical Institute, the Hotel and Catering Institute, and the Mediterranean Institute of Management are under the control of the Ministry of Labor; the School of Nursing is under the control of the Ministry of Health; and Cyprus Forestry College is under the control of the Ministry of Agriculture and Natural Resources. In each case the ministry responsible approves the regulations, type of programs, level of courses, admission standards, examination rules, evaluation and revision of curricula, grading system, and supervision and enrollment.

Private institutions are run by their Board of Governors according to the provisions of Law 1/1987, which regulates the establishment, control, and operation of institutions of higher education. This law has set procedures for the registration, supervision, and possible accreditation of private schools. The schools are subject to inspection by the Ministry of Education with regard to virtually all matters (staff qualifications and pay, school buildings, facilities and equipment, content of programs, and standards of performance). Indirect government control can be secured through the provision for accreditation of schools. In order to secure validation for their certificates and a kind of indirect accreditation of their courses, a number of private institutions of higher education have been affiliated with universities or polytechnics in the United Kingdom or the United States.

Public institutions are financed by public funds in various ways as they come under different ministries. Private institutions are owned and administered by private individuals or bodies and raise their funds primarily from tuition fees.

Local higher education absorbed 3.3 percent of the total expenditure on education and the unit cost per student in 1987–88, measured in terms of recurrent and capital expenditure, was US$4,173 for public education and US$1,771 for private education. The total expenditure on students abroad as derived from the Central Bank records in 1987 is estimated at US$53.3 million. This corresponds to about 1.3 percent of the Gross National Product.

With the establishment of the University of Cyprus the Government plans to increase public expenditure devoted to postsecondary education in terms of absolute expenditure and in relation to national income.

3.2 The Institutional Level

For each public and private school of higher education there is provision in its regulations for the establishment of academic, administrative, and disciplinary committees, in which both the faculty and the students are represented. The academic committee advises the board of management and the director of the institution.

The University will consist of schools, and each school will consist of departments. The department will constitute the basic unit of the university. There will be a chancellor in charge of the university, deans in charge of the schools, and presidents in charge of the departments.

The University will be governed, according to Law 144/1989, by the Council of the University and the Academic Senate. The council will be responsible for administrative and financial affairs and will consist of

the chancellor and the vice-chancellor, three members of faculty, four persons to be appointed by the Council of Ministers, three nonacademics who will be appointed by the senate, and one student representative. The senate will be in charge of the academic work of the university and will consist of the chancellor, the vice-chancellor, and the deans of the schools; three members of the academic staff of each school, and three student representatives. Its main tasks will be to approve the decisions of the chancellor, the academic programs, the entrance and year examination standards, the evaluation system, and the award of diplomas and degrees.

For the establishment of new schools and departments, and the abolition of existing ones, the senate will make suggestions to the council of the university and the council will issue relevant regulations on the approval of the Council of Ministers.

The individual schools of the university and the departments of each school are to be governed by their respective councils and thus the power will be shared among all teaching staff. The decisions of the council of each school will be under the approval of the Senate, and those of the council of each department under the approval of the council of the respective school. The council of each department will define the general academic policy of the department and will have the responsibility for the research and the teaching work.

4. Faculty and Students: Teaching, Learning, and Research

4.1 Faculty

The educational personnel of public and private institutions of higher education varies according to the different types of educational establishments and the specific educational and training activities. It usually consists of secondary school teachers who have received appropriate graduate (MA, PhD level) pedagogical as well as academic training in a specific field of study at a foreign university.

The staff of the university to be established will consist of lecturers, assistant professors, associate professors, and professors. Moreover, there will be visiting professors, special lecturers, and teaching assistants. The posts of professor and associate professor will be permanent while those of lecturer and assistant professor will be on renewable three-year contracts.

The first members of the faculty will be appointed by the selection bodies which will be appointed by the Temporary Directing Committee. The latter has already been appointed by the Council of Ministers and has been charged, according to the provisions of Law 144/1989, with taking all the initial steps for the establishment of the university. After the university begins to operate, the selection of the academic

Table 1
Distribution of students by field of study

	Students at foreign universities		Students in Cyprus	
Exact sciences/engineering/ medicine	4,544	49.4%	2,421	47.7%
Social sciences	3,135	33.3%	1,782	35.1%
Humanities	1,325	13.0%	863	17.2%
Preparatory studies	406	4.3%	—	—

staff will be the responsibility of the councils of the individual departments and schools.

4.2 Students

Almost half of Greek Cypriot students both abroad and in Cyprus study exact sciences and engineering. This is a reflection of the utilitarian and highly instrumental attitudes which prevailed in Cyprus immediately after Independence. The distribution of students with regard to the field of their study is shown in Table 1.

The new university will consist at the initial stage of the following three schools: (a) the School of Pure and Applied Sciences, (b) the School of Humanities and Social Sciences, and (c) the School of Economics and Administration.

Progress of study at public and private institutions of higher education is evaluated by continuous assessment and final written examinations. The latter are held for a number of courses, as a supplement to continuous assessment, at the end of each semester or at the end of the academic year. In some institutions final year assessment requires the preparation of a major project report.

The course of study in all institutions combines academic instruction and practical training, but the emphasis put on each aspect varies according to the aims of the institution.

The students of the public postsecondary institutions are organized in individual student unions which are usually very active. As mentioned above, the students will be represented at both the council and the senate of the new university.

5. Conclusion

Clearly, higher education has played a very important role in Cyprus's economic, social, and cultural development. It is hoped that the establishment of a university will greatly increase this development. The expectations of the university are also high in other fields, like the promotion of equality of opportunity and local research, which is almost negligible at the moment. However, unless the university gains high status from the very beginning the trend towards studying abroad will be difficult to weaken.

Bibliography

Ministry of Finance 1968 *Second Five-Year Development Plan (1967–71)* Planning Bureau of the Republic of Cyprus

Report of the Cyprus Government on Higher Education 1982. In: *World Guide to Higher Education*, UNESCO, Nicosia

P. Persianis

Czechoslovakia

1. Higher Education and Society

The Czech and Slovak Federal Republic is a federal state in Central Europe consisting of two equal republics, the Czech Republic (CR) and the Slovak Republic (SR). National frontiers have not changed since the Second World War.

In the period following the Second World War there has been a slight increase in the population size (see Table 1). The average annual rate of population growth between 1950 and 1988 was 0.6 percent. Government measures to control natality had a small effect for a short time only.

Czechoslovakia occupies an area of 127,900 square kilometers and has a population density of 122 per square kilometer. Regional distribution of population is relatively level.

The majority of the population is Czech (63.3 percent) and Slovak (31.3 percent). Minorities form a relatively small group—only 5.4 percent of which 3.8 percent are Hungarian, 0.5 percent Polish, 0.4 percent German and 0.3 percent Ukrainian.

Table 1
Population of the Czech and Slovak Federal Republics (in millions)

Year	1950	1960	1970	1980	1988
CR	8.92	9.66	9.80	10.32	10.36
SR	3.46	3.99	4.53	4.98	5.27
Total	12.38	13.65	14.33	15.30	15.63

Czechoslovakia is a developed industrial country. In 1988, 11 percent of the total workforce was employed in agriculture, 46 percent in industry, and 43 percent in the tertiary sector.

Since the Second World War society has made efforts to develop the national economy, improve living standards, and create favorable conditions for the cultural development of the population. Great attention is therefore paid to the development of higher education.

The social class structure of Czechoslovakia is very homogeneous. Marked differences in per capita income as well as in living standards have been eradicated.

Such development is centered around planning for student enrollments and resources for the maintenance and growth of higher education institutions.

1.1 The Development of Higher Education

Higher education within the territory of present-day Czechoslovakia has a long tradition. It can be traced back to 1348 when Charles University, the first Central European university, was founded in Prague by Charles IV King of Bohemia and Holy Roman Emperor. Even at that early date its international commitment was evident, illustrated by the participation of Czech, Saxon, Bavarian, and Polish students, representatives of the four "university nations." At the time of its foundation it consisted of four faculties: arts, law, medicine, and theology.

In Slovakia, the first higher education institution, called Academia Istropolitana, was founded in Bratislava in 1467 by Matthias Corvinus King of Hungaria.

A significant role in the development of technical higher education was played by the Engineering School of the Estates which was founded in Prague in 1707 and was reorganized as a high school in 1863. Since 1879 it has been called the Czech University of Technology.

From 1918, when the Czechoslovak Republic was promulgated as independent, up to 1937 another two universities, one polytechnic institute, and three higher education institutions were founded.

During the Second World War when a majority of the Czechoslovak territory was occupied by Fascist Germany, all the Czech higher education institutions were closed. The great majority of higher education students were imprisoned in concentration camps for protesting against the Fascist occupation. Some lecturers were also imprisoned and executed. In memory of the heroic demonstration by Czech students which was brutally oppressed by the Nazis, 17 November is annually celebrated as International Students' Day.

Another significant period in the development of higher education began after the liberation of Czechoslovakia in 1945. Between the years 1945 and 1948 two universities and nine higher education

institutions of different professional orientation were established.

2. The Institutional Fabric of the Higher Education System

In Czechoslovakia all higher education institutions are organized on a state basis. They can be established, amalgamated, divided, and abolished only by laws issued by the Federal Assembly.

In 1988 there were 29 institutions of higher education, and seven independent pedagogical faculties which have the status of higher education institutions. They are governed by the Ministry of Education, Youth, and Sport of their particular republic. In addition there are seven army institutions supervised by the Federal Ministry of National Defense, one institute subject to the Ministry of the Interior, and six faculties of theology of different churches which come under the Ministry of Culture. They are situated in 23 towns throughout Czechoslovakia, with the majority clustered in Prague, Bratislava, Brno, and Košice.

Out of the overall number of higher education institutions there were at the end of the 1980s five universities, two veterinary universities, two economic universities, ten technical institutes (of which four were polytechnic universities), four institutes of agriculture and forestry, and six academies of fine arts.

The universities follow a traditional pattern: they are made up of faculties of social sciences, natural sciences, and medicine. Polytechnic universities contain facilities of engineering, electrotechnics, civil engineering, and so forth. All higher education institutions have teaching and research responsibilities.

Equal legal status is enjoyed by all the teaching and research institutions and their graduates. Those differences that do exist between individual establishments are nonformal. They emerge from the tradition, the structure of qualifications of university teaching staff, the level and outcomes of research, and so on.

The structure of higher education has remained stable for more than twenty years. The number of faculties has only increased slightly, with the exception of a period of rapid growth in the first half of the 1950s.

2.1 Participation in Research

Higher education institutions contribute significantly to the research base of the country. Internally their research potential covers both basic research (about 65 percent) and applied research (about 27 percent). Of the total basic research of the country 31 percent or so is carried out by the institutes of higher education, in accordance with the state plan.

Major responsibility for basic research is ascribed to the Czechoslovak Academy of Sciences (ČSAV) and the Slovak Academy of Sciences (SAV) in the Slovak Republic, the latter institution being an integral part of the former. Their joint contribution accounts for about 48 percent of the overall basic research carried out by academic and non-academic institutions combined.

The academies are made up of 120 research institutes which maintain close cooperation with the higher education institutions. From the legal, organizational, and economic viewpoint, however, both systems are virtually self-sufficient.

Their cooperation is organized and ensured by collegial bodies consisting of representatives from the higher education institutions. The collegial bodies have responsibility for planning basic research at state level. Other important vehicles for cooperation are the agreements made between separate higher education institutions (or faculties) and the academies. In addition, ČSAV and SAV researchers have a responsibility to work part-time in higher education institutions, just as university teaching staff are obliged to become members of the academies, representatives in collegial bodies, academic research councils, and so forth.

Higher education institutions also participate in the applied research controlled by the State Planning Commission (established to oversee the role of applied research in the economy), by the State Commission for Scientific, Technological and Investment Development, and by the respective ministries. They also form contracts with enterprises involved in research to satisfy the needs of the production sector.

Participation in research is mandatory for all university teaching staff with the exception of lecturers. It is believed that research activity improves the quality of their teaching performance and benefits the content of the instruction they provide. From the teachers' point of view it is a criterion for promotion.

2.2 Admission to Higher Education Institutions

It is a basic requirement for admission to higher education that secondary education has been completed. Admission policies and selection are based on an overall assessment of an applicant. Under consideration are the candidate's achievements over the course of secondary education and entrance examination results. An evaluation is also made of individual dispositions for study in the chosen field.

Preliminary planning of student enrollments aims to secure the balance of university output and the needs of employers, and, consequently, to prevent unemployment.

In the 1980s the number of applicants to higher education was double the number it was possible to enroll. In some subject areas a balance is maintained between the number of applicants and the planned number of places (for example, in technical and teacher training institutes) in contrast with fine arts, humanities, psychology, philology, sociology, medi-

cine, and so forth. It is generally considered that rejection of young applicants may be less psychologically traumatic than is later unemployment for graduates.

The general policy on enrollments is worked out by the State Planning Commission. The number of places available in the individual institutions and subject areas is set by the Ministry of Education, Youth and Sport in the respective republic. In arriving at the final figure account is taken of the average dropout rate.

There are no special quotas for social classes or ethnic groups. Selection is organized on the principle of social, national, and territorial balance among the students and the overall population structure. Preference is shown on a regional basis in the fields of teacher education and medicine. Students from the remote regions are given preference over other candidates with the one stipulation that their study achievements are equal.

Since 1950 there have been periods of both development and decline in student enrollments. In the period 1950 to 1965 there was a rapid upturn in student enrollments, while between 1966 and 1972 falling numbers of part-time students caused an overall decline in the enrollment figures. From 1973 to 1981 another upturn took place and then in the years 1982 to 1985 there was a further decline caused this time both by a shortening of the duration of studies in some subject areas from five to four years, and by an economic stagnation during which highly educated graduates were less in demand. Since 1986 the trend has once again been towards a gradual increase of enrollments.

The enrollment pattern from 1960 onwards is illustrated in Table 2 which gives total enrollments of full- and part-time students and foreign students in absolute figures.

The proportion of full-time students of higher education in the age group 20–24 years is to be found in Table 3.

2.3 Structure of Qualifications

The system of higher education in Czechoslovakia is one-tier and nondifferentiated. The length of time taken to attain first degrees varies according to the fields of study. The majority of studies last for four or five years. Technology, chemistry, agriculture, and some social sciences are included in the 49 percent of first-degree courses that are studied for four years. Five-year courses include the natural sciences, more complex technical subject areas, pedagogy, and part of the social sciences. Only medicine and fine arts are studied for six years.

In medicine and veterinary medicine, first degrees are awarded after success in the state examination (*rigorosum*). Graduates receive the degrees MUDr (doctor of medicine) and MVDr (veterinary doctor). In all the other institutions of higher education

Table 2
Development of the student body (in thousands)

Year	1960	1965	1970	1975	1980	1985	1990
Total full-time students	65.5	91.7	103.0	119.0	147.8	136.9	149.0
Full-time foreign students	1.8	3.3	3.6	3.6	3.6	4.1	4.8
Part-time students	26.7	49.9	24.4	32.0	45.2	27.6	28.1
Total	94.0	144.9	131.0	154.6	196.6	168.6	181.9

studies, success in the state final examination, which testifies the student's knowledge and ability to apply the knowledge in practice, completes the course of study. The state final examination involves the defence of a diploma thesis prepared by final-year students under the supervision of an experienced teacher.

Graduates of technical institutes, institutes of agriculture, and economic universities are awarded the title "Ing" (engineer) immediately after successfully passing the state finals.

Graduates in other than the above mentioned institutes are not awarded any title, with the exception of the high achievers with excellent outcomes both in the course of first-degree studies and in the state final examination. In such cases the state final has the same status as the state *rigorosum*.

Those graduates of universities and of other institutions in the university sector who have completed their first-degree studies with the state finals are allowed to take the state *rigorosum*. The *rigorosum* is aimed at assessing graduates' expertise in their chosen specialization. On passing the *rigorosum*, a graduate is awarded a doctorate in law, philosophy, natural sciences, pedagogy, pharmacy or socio-political sciences, according to the field of study. These diplomas indicate that graduates have completed their first-degree studies and thus are highly skilled in a particular subject area.

Either on their own initiative or encouraged by their employers, graduates may progress to postgraduate courses. These courses are organized by higher education institutions and have a minimum

length of 200 teaching hours. The postgraduate courses fulfill the functions of innovation, specialization, and requalification. That is to say, they aim to improve and update the graduates' knowledge in accordance with scientific and technological advancements, to provide in-depth knowledge and expertise necessary for the performance of special professions and functions; and to enable them to change their profession or qualifications, or to apply their existing knowledge and skills in other domains and so forth.

Graduates may begin postgraduate courses immediately after finishing their first-degree studies. The overwhelming majority of graduates, however, enter the course after several years of practice.

One form of graduate training program is research training organized by higher education institutions and the research institutes of the Czechoslovak Academy of Sciences and the like. Applicants for research training are competitively screened and must also pass an entrance examination. The aim is to ascertain whether the applicants' knowledge exceeds the average knowledge of first-degree graduates, and to determine whether they are suitable for research work.

Research training, from the viewpoint of legislation does not equal first-degree studies carried out at a top level. It is a specific form of qualification improvement. Taken as a full-time course it lasts for three years; part-time it lasts for five years. At the end of this period examinations must be passed and the candidate must make a successful defence of a dissertation. (The dissertation is individual research work in which the applicants prove their expertise and ability to carry out research work.) If these two conditions are met the academic council or the presidium of the academies of science awards the degree CSc (candidate of science).

University teachers and researchers who have achieved excellent outcomes in their performance can submit their doctoral dissertations for defence. After a successful defence the academic council or the presidium of the academies of science awards the degree DrSc (doctor of science).

Table 3
Proportion of full-time students in the age group 20–24 (percentages)

Year	1960	1965	1970	1975	1980	1985
Rates	10.8	13.8	10.4	12.1	17.5	15.4

3. Governance, Administration, and Finance

3.1 State-based Governance of Higher Education

Higher education is governed by the Federal Assembly, the legislative bodies of both republics and by the government of both republics. There is one Ministry of Education, Youth, and Sport in each republic which exercises its responsibility in the domain of higher education.

The document that is fundamental to the shape of higher education is the Higher Education Act approved by the Federal Assembly (that is, at parliamentary level). It defines the status, organization, and operation of higher education.

In both republics the Ministry of Education, Youth and Sport issues mandatory general legislation concerning the course of higher education studies, their forms, curriculum development, interdisciplinary programs, and the organization of the academic year; admission procedures and the conditions for the exemption from entrance examinations; leaving requirements; postgraduate courses and the general professional inservice training; students' rights and duties, their participation in the research and artistic activities and in educational measures; and the procedures of admission of new teachers in the tenure track, the organization of faculty and other staff development.

The ministries are also responsible for the operative administration of higher education institutions. They submit suggestions for the appointment and removal of rectors to the government; appoint deputy vice-rectors and deans of faculties; and submit suggestions for the appointment of professors to the President of Czechoslovakia via the government.

Higher education was formally organized around the principle of state planning. This included the input and output of higher education institutions as well as allocating finance and overseeing staffing policy. The numbers of personnel were controlled indirectly by determining salary scales.

The financing of higher education is based on the state budget. The Ministry of Education, Youth and Sport submits a proposal for the allocation of finance to higher education to the Czech and Slovak National Councils. The overall amount of state budget as well as the amounts to be allocated to individual sectors of both republics are validated by the Czech and the Slovak National Councils. Earmarked financing of individual higher education establishments is carried out by the Ministry of Education, Youth, and Sport. Within this framework, specific allocations are made for investment resources, resources for teachers' salaries, for the operation of the institution, for the students' scholarships, and so on. These resources may not be utilized for other than the specified purpose.

In addition to the resources obtained from the state budget, higher education can obtain finance

Table 4
Expenditures on higher education (in millions of Czechoslovak crowns)

Year	1960	1965	1970	1975	1980	1985
Millions of Kčs	1.0	1.5	2.8	3.8	4.5	5.1
Percentage of the gross national product	0.43	0.71	0.65	0.77	0.65	0.62

from the sale of research results to firms, for professional services, graduate studies, and so forth. These financial resources have an additional function. It is likely that in the future their role will increase.

The overall amount of financial resources devoted to higher education in Czechoslovakia and their proportion in the gross national product are given in Table 4.

3.2 Institutional Organization and Administration

The principles of academic organization and administration are set down in the Higher Education Act. The internal structure of higher education institutions and their administrative bodies are established under a unified system. Most higher education institutions are divided into faculties which conduct teaching and research in one or several related subjects. Faculties are staffed by teachers and have various numbers of students, depending on the perceived national needs for output in the respective field. Some smaller ones (veterinary universities and academies of fine arts) are not divided in faculties at all. Those small institutions that are structured into faculties have their activities centralized to the detriment of individual faculties. On the other hand, large institutions tend to delegate part of the rector's responsibility to deans of faculties and thus to promote their independence.

Higher education institutions are headed by rectors who are appointed by the President of Czechoslovakia after being recruited from among the university teaching staff. As a rule rectors are distinguished specialists in the subject area of the institution to which they are nominated. Deputy vice-rectors are responsible for the administration of the institutions. Their duties lie in specific domains of academic life: in education, research, postgraduate courses, exchange programs, and international cooperation, the development and further expansion of higher education institutions, and other connected areas. Material and technical resources and the economic operation of the institution are controlled by a bursar.

The academic council is an advisory body to the rector, who acts as chair. The other members are the deputy vice-rectors, deans, bursar, and others nominated by rector from among faculty and staff of the institution as well as external experts. There are also members of the student body. Besides this social association, trade union representatives also sit on the council.

Faculties are headed by deans who are recruited from among the professors and associate professors. Faculty administration is the concern of the deputy vice-deans who are responsible for similar academic fields as deputy vice-rectors. The dean of faculty is also assisted by an advisory body known as the academic council which is established and organized around the same principle as the council of the higher education institution.

Faculties are subdivided into departments which are the basic units of the faculty. They conduct educational, research, and other professional work. They are staffed with teachers who work either in one or several related disciplines. The head of department is usually a professor or an associate professor.

Departments are responsible for the content and methodology of teaching, updating it according to the advances in science and technology. They are self-sufficient in the development of instructional materials for students, or at least share in the development. The head of department supervises teachers' class performance and encourages the staff to improve their qualifications. The departments that provide instruction in the main disciplines in the respective field of study exercise their responsibility for the particular field of study as well as for their students.

4. Faculty and Students: Teaching, Learning, and Research

4.1 Faculty

The university teaching staff are divided into several categories. Their proportion is as follows:

(a) professors   10.0%

(b) associate professors   22.0%

(c) senior lecturers   62.5%

(d) lecturers   0.2%

(e) *assistants*   5.3%

Professors are appointed by the president of the republic and are recruited from among associate professors, researchers, and acknowledged experts in their field of study. The academic condition for appointment is the DrSc degree (doctor of science) or at least a CSc (candidate of science); experience in educational practice is also mandatory. Suggestions for appointment are considered by the academic council of the faculty and the whole institution of higher education. The rector submits the result

of their deliberations to the Ministry of Education, Youth and Sport from where it is passed on to the president via the federal government. Among the professors' duties are reading lectures, presenting seminars, and supervising students' diploma theses. They also act as educators in graduate research training.

Associate professors are appointed by the Minister of Education. They are promoted from among senior lecturers, researchers, and outstanding experts in the field. It is necessary for them to have the CSc degree and be skilled and experienced in educational work. Associate professors are also responsible for giving lectures, leading seminars, instructing students on their diploma theses, and teaching postgraduate research trainees.

Senior lecturers are obliged to have a CSc degree, or to be working for it. They give seminars and perform other tutorial duties such as holding laboratory courses. Lecturers are neither obliged to have academic degrees nor to be working for one, or carrying out research work. Instead they have extended teaching duties in comparison with senior lecturers.

Assistants are on the lowest rung of the academic ladder. They are graduates who are studying to become university teachers. Their main duty lies in intensive professional and pedagogical training.

The proportions of university teaching staff and their structure are given in Table 5.

Recruitment of faculty is the responsibility of each individual establishment. As a rule, vacancies are filled through competitive election. The status of university teaching staff of equivalent rank is the same throughout the higher education system.

The interests of the academic profession are represented by the Trade Union of Educational and Scientific Personnel. The Union has membership of collegial advisory bodies attached to the Ministry of Education, Youth and Sport, and of academic councils, and collegia. It also forms part of the com-

Table 5
Development of the teaching body (in thousands)

Year	1960	1965	1970	1975	1980	1985	1988
Professors and associate professors	1.7	2.8	3.6	3.5	4.5	5.8	6.8
Senior lecturers, lecturers and assistants	8.8	12.5	12.8	13.5	13.8	13.3	13.5
Total	10.5	15.3	16.4	17.0	18.3	19.1	20.3

missions established in higher education institutions and their faculties.

Teachers are expected to maintain a high quality in their work, reflecting in how they teach recent outcomes of scientific and technological progress, and to carry out their own research for the benefit of themselves and their students. Overall proportions of teaching and research work are mandated by the Ministry of Education, Youth and Sport. Individual proportions are given by head of department.

4.2 Development of the Student Body

Higher education is conducted either as full- or part-time study. In the 1980s full-time students accounted for 80 percent of the student body. The distribution of students across the main subject areas is illustrated in Table 6.

The proportion of students across the different social classes is more or less proportionate to the overall social class structure of Czechoslovak society. Meanwhile there has been an increase in the number of female students entering full-time education; nearly doubling since 1950, to stand at 43.9% in 1985.

Studies in higher education are free of charge, operating costs are covered entirely by the state budget.

Every student has the right to a scholarship the amount of which will vary dependently on his achievements. Those students who are either orphans, or whose parents have too low an income for them to support a student's living costs are provided with welfare scholarships to help with accommodation, board, expenditures on clothing, books, and the like, as well as the expenses of the student's cultural and physical development.

The students who do not live in the town where the institute is situated, or nearby, can stay in student hostels. Accommodation and the cost of food are subsidized; students pay only a small amount, the rest is covered by the state.

4.3 The Organization and Supervision of Study

Tertiary level education is organized by the Ministry of Education, Youth, and Sport, by rectors, deans, and by heads of departments. The scope of their responsibilities is set by the Higher Education Act and its regulations.

Higher education studies are either ordinary, leading to first-degree diplomas, or extraordinary during which students acquire and extend their knowledge in some of the disciplines.

Ordinary studies are organized in two forms: full-time and part-time. The length of full-time courses varies from 4 to 6 years, of part-time from 4 to 7 years. Part-time studies also include evening courses.

Significant for the planning of student enrollments and for shaping the content of education is the structure of subject fields, which is defined by the Federal Government via the respective ordinances. The structure is updated every five years as a rule, in the light of advances in science and technology and in the whole national economy. For the period 1986–90 the structure comprised 184 subject fields.

The content of studies in individual fields is defined in the document called "A Graduate's Profile" which includes basic qualification parameters in the respective domain, and in the curriculum. The curriculum, or study program, encompasses the distribution of disciplines across semesters; the numbers of hours to be devoted to lectures, seminars, and other tutorial systems, examinations and credits; student practice, and the like.

The approved curriculum is mandatory for all students in their respective subject field. Student choice takes place only in case of nonobligatory and alternative seminars and lectures. Gifted students as well as sportsmen and students with children to take care of can study according to an individualized curriculum.

The content of particular disciplines is defined in the syllabus. It includes topics outlining certain problem areas of the respective field of science. The structure of subject fields, graduate profiles, curricula and syllabi of individual disciplines are developed by the Ministry of Education, Youth, and Sport on the recommendations of advisory bodies whose members are recruited from outstanding academic staff, scientific and research personnel, and other field experts.

The graduates' profiles, curricula, and syllabi of individual disciplines undergo recurrent innovations in accordance with scientific, technological, and overall economic progress. In the second half of the 1970s a reform of the content of higher education took place with the aim of cutting down the number of study fields, strengthening academic background, and enlarging the proportion of student practice, and so forth. As a result of the rationalization of curricula and the intensification of studies some subject fields have been shortened from five to four years.

In the Czech Republic the official teaching language is Czech, while in the Slovak Republic it is

Table 6
The distribution of students across the main subject areas (in thousands)

Subject areas	1960	1965	1970	1975	1980	1985
Technology	4.3	5.8	5.8	7.4	10.9	14.0
Agriculture	1.1	2.2	1.8	2.3	3.0	3.7
Natural sciences	0.2	0.5	0.8	0.6	0.9	1.1
Medicine	1.2	1.6	1.6	2.5	3.1	2.4
Social sciences[a]	5.4	6.9	8.1	8.7	12.3	13.5
Fine arts	0.1	0.2	0.2	0.4	0.5	0.5

a Social sciences includes teacher training

Slovak. Both teachers and students use their mother tongue in the teaching or learning process if they work or study in the other republic though; the languages are very similar to each other.

Students are assessed after each semester. Each semester has a defined number of credits for seminars, laboratory courses, and student practice, and a defined number of examinations (no more than five) to be passed.

5. Conclusion

Higher education in Czechoslovakia contributes positively to the overall progress of society. It has reached a relatively high standard, although problems still remain.

The proportion of university students in the respective age group is lower in comparison to other countries of the same level of economic advancement. It can be foreseen that within the 1990s, regardless of the planned upturn in overall student enrollments, the proportion will stagnate. The reason is a rapid growth of the respective age group expected to take place in the second third of the 1990s.

The increase in the proportion of higher education students in the 1960s and 1970s resulted in higher differentiation of students' abilities and their motivation for studies. Unfortunately this differentiation has not been countered with sufficient flexibility in the studies they pursue to achieve an optimum result. As a matter of fact, a tendency has emerged for students to be satisfied with only average achievement. Central agencies as well as higher education institutions devote considerable efforts to nurturing talented students. Among other options, the introduction of a two-tier system of studies including short cycles is subject to debate.

The distribution of students across subject fields has not responded to changes in the demands of employers. Moreover, innovation in the content and methods of instruction has not been carried out in a desirable way. It is generally considered that such insufficiencies derive from overcentralization in decision-making in education.

The range of graduate studies has so far been small. It is expected that in the 1990s the role of lifelong education will increase and, consequently, higher education institutions will devote more resources to graduate courses.

A decisive task of higher education institutions in the future will be to enhance the quality of graduates so that they are skilled and able to work under conditions of rapid scientific and technological advancement. Hence it is necessary to improve the effectiveness of the educational process, especially independent learning, and to extend the application of new communication technology, such as microcomputers and videotechnology.

It is expected that at the beginning of the 1990s the Higher Education Act will be updated. At the center of attention will be an enhanced decision-making role for individual higher education institutions and their democratization. Moreover, the role of the academic research councils of the institutions and their faculties will be strengthened. Rectors and deans will be elected by academic councils, as was the case in the past.

Several measures are to be taken in order to support economic self-sufficiency of the higher education institutions. To supplement the finances supplied by the state budget, higher education institutions will assume greater responsibility for obtaining resources by the sale of their research, especially in the domain of research and professional services. Graduate and extraordinary studies will be fee-paying while first-degree studies will remain free of charge both for students and their would-be employers.

The development of higher education will be ensured by setting aside further resources from the gross national product for the purpose both of investment and of operating higher education.

Bibliography

Hartman J 1981 *Vysoké školy, Seznam studijních oborů a jejich rozmístnění na vysokých školách. Profily absolventů.* Státní pedagogické nakladatelství, Prague

Jůva V 1981 *Vysoká škola a výchova.* Universita J E Purkyně, Brno

Kotásek J 1985 *Kapitoly o vysokoškolské výuce, sv. I, II, III.* Ústav rozvoje vysokých škol ČSR, Prague

Kotásek J, Koucký J 1988 *Možnost realizace vícestupňového studia na vysokých školách v ČSSR.* Ústav rozvoje vysokých škol ČSR, Prague

Mates P, Průcha P, Svatoň J 1984 *Vývoj organizace a řízení československých vysokých škol v letech 1918–1983.* Ústav školských informací MŠ ČSR, Prague

Ministry of Education 1976 *Další rozvoj československé výchovně vzdělávací soustavy. Dílčí projekt č.9 – Vysokéškoly.* Státní pedagogické nakladetelství, Prague

Ministry of Education 1984 *Soubor základních právních předpisů pro vysoké školy.* Státní pedagogické nakladatelství, Prague

Ministry of Education, Youth, and Sport 1988 *Analýza československé výchovně vzdělávací soustavy.* Státní pedagogické nakladatelství, Prague

Mokošín V 1988 *Koncepce rozvoje vysokého školství v ČSSR v devadesátých letech.* Ústav rozvoje vysokých škol ČSR, Prague

V. Mokošín

D

Denmark

1. Higher Education and Society

In 1980, the population of Denmark (a territory of approximately 43,000 square kilometers) rose to over five million persons. The Faroe Islands have been a self-governing society within the Kingdom of Denmark since 1948, and in 1979 Greenland achieved the same status.

Denmark is a constitutional monarchy. National affairs are governed by a parliament consisting of one chamber, while regional affairs are conducted by county and municipal councils.

Denmark's first university, the University of Copenhagen, was founded in 1479. For the next 300 years, this was the only institution of higher education in Denmark. The nation's second university, the University of Aarhus, was founded in 1929. While various specialized educational institutions appeared in the course of the eighteenth and nineteenth centuries, it was not until the beginning of the 1960s that a marked development of the entire higher educational system took place. During that period, educational policy encouraged enrollment in higher educational institutions by individuals from all social classes. The objective was to remove economic and geographical barriers to individual advancement. Educational planning was based on free admission to all forms of education and on developing possibilities to absorb the increasing numbers of students. However, during the 1970s it became necessary to check educational expansion because of a surplus of graduates and excessive expenditure of public funds. By the end of the 1980s, educational debate was characterized by pressure for significant cuts in the funding of higher education, more stringent entrance requirements for institutions of higher education, and by calls for increased control of the quality of education.

Universities and other institutions of higher education are all state-run and are administered by the Ministry of Education (with the exception of the Royal Academy of Music and the Royal Academy of Architecture and Fine Arts, both of which are administered by the Ministry for Cultural Affairs). Traditionally, institutions of higher education tend to enjoy a high degree of autonomy. The total amount of funding at the disposal of each institution is determined by provisions in the national budget. However, the allocation of funding within each institution is internally administered by its governing bodies.

1.1 The Economic Situation

In comparison with many other European nations, Denmark emerged from the Second World War in tolerable material condition. Nevertheless, the nation experienced marked economical difficulties, and reconstruction of the organization of production was essential. Despite this, by 1947, Denmark had achieved a level of production surpassing prewar levels. By the end of the 1940s, Danish agriculture and trade had eliminated most of the economic effects of occupation. These results were achieved partly by the help of trade agreements, the European Recovery Programme, the Marshall Plan, and low-cost loans. In 1950, however, the upswing in the economy was arrested when sterling was devalued, which caused a significant fluctuation in the balance of trade and an increase in the nation's foreign debt.

The end of the 1950s saw revitalization of economic development, occasioned in part by falling prices of raw materials abroad and by favorable conditions in the economies of Denmark's trading partners. The national debt was paid and the national budget yielded a modest profit. The economic stagnation of the 1950s was followed by a period of expansion resulting in a level of prosperity that had never been experienced previously. Private consumption increased. The amount of public expenditure rose from US$0.56 billion in 1953 to US$0.92 billion in 1965. In the same period, the population increased by only 0.4 million. An increased amount of goods and services, including educational services, were now available to the public at large.

During the 1960s, unemployment was exceptionally low at a level of 1 to 3 percent. Despite a gradual shortening of the working week, total production increased annually at an average of 4.4 percent until 1973. The total labor force rose slightly from 2 million in 1960 to 2.2 million in 1970. However, its structure altered markedly in this period.

No less than 170,000 individuals employed in agriculture changed sectors in the 1960s. The urban occupations witnessed an influx of some 270,000 individuals. While the percentage of young people in urban occupations decreased, the number of women entering the labor market offset this decline.

The 1960s were characterized by a substantial increase in the standard of living and in the provision of social security. However, these conditions altered drastically in 1973. The recession resulting from the oil crisis of 1973 and 1974 was the most dramatic check to economic development experienced by Denmark since the war.

From 1973 to 1982, economic growth was approximately 1.5 percent, or one-third of what it had been in the period 1960–73. The level of unemployment increased to almost 10 percent of the labor force. By 1986, employment figures were 21 percent higher than in 1960. At that time, the public sector employed 500,000 more individuals than in 1960. Agriculture lost 250,000 in the same period, while the service sector gained a corresponding number.

In 1986, the private service sector and the public sector accounted for two-thirds of the labor force as compared with two-fifths in 1960.

In macroeconomic terms, Denmark's economy has not been balanced since the end of the 1950s, despite the apparent prosperity of the following period and the liquidation of the foreign debt. Although the gross factor income has experienced considerable growth since then, the increasing deficit has meant that the foreign debt, measured as a part of the gross factor income, has been steadily increasing since 1960, reaching a level of 47 percent in 1986. The Danish national debt is one of the largest in the OECD countries, only exceeded by those of Iceland, Ireland, Portugal, Greece, and Turkey.

In the educational sector, these problems made themselves felt at the beginning of the 1980s

2. The Institutional Fabric of the Higher Education System

2.1 Categories of Educational Institutions

In Denmark, a distinction is drawn between institutions of higher education and institutions for further education. Institutions of higher education are also institutions for research, and teaching must relate to the research being conducted there. Teachers in these institutions are obliged to spend 40 percent of their working time on research activities. Teaching activities must account for approximately 50 percent of working time, with the remaining 10 percent or so to be used for various forms of administration. This division of working time applies in principle to all permanent members of the teaching staff of higher education institutions, regardless of grade, that is, for full professors as well as for associates and lecturers.

The University of Copenhagen is traditionally structured, with five faculties or departments, namely, theology, social science, medicine, the humanities, and the natural sciences, Aarhus University operates along the same lines.

A new concept in the area of education—the university center—was introduced for the first time in Odense in 1964. A university center provides both academic and nonacademic courses, whilst the content of such courses may transcend traditional divisions between disciplines. However, Odense

Table 1

Total number of students enrolled in institutions of higher education (1987)

University of Copenhagen (1479)	26,491
Aarhus University (1928)	13,336
Odense University and University Center (1964)	6,246
Roskilde University Center (1972)	2,994
Aalborg University Center (1974)	5,736
Specialized institutions	
Denmark's Technical University, Lyngby (1829)	5,312
The Dental College, Copenhagen (1888)	395
The Dental College, Aarhus (1958)	304
The Royal Veterinary and Agricultural University, Copenhagen (1856)	2,610
The Royal Danish School of Pharmacy, Copenhagen (1892)	868
The Copenhagen School of Economics, Business Administration, and Modern Language (1939)	14,030
The Aarhus School of Economics, Business Administration, and Modern Language (1939)	5,814
The Royal School of Educational Studies, Copenhagen (1956)	2,403
Total	86,577

maintained aspects of the traditional university structure. Education is offered there within three main areas: (a) the humanities, social science, business administration, economics, and modern languages; (b) the natural sciences; and (c) medicine and physical education.

The Roskilde University Center was established in 1972. The interdisciplinary content of the various courses of study is characteristic for this institution.

An overview of all institutions of higher education is given in Table 1, including their founding dates and the number of students enrolled as at 1987.

There are considerable numbers of institutions of further education, including, among others, 8 technical colleges; 60 training colleges for various kinds of teacher training and kindergarten teacher training; 11 state colleges for social educational training; and colleges for training nurses, midwives, dieticians, physiotherapists, occupational therapists, and other health personnel.

Entrance requirements for institutions of further and higher education are normally either (a) 12 years of education with a concluding examination, and the student examination (*Examen Artium*), or (b) the Higher Preparatory Examination (HF), or (c) the Higher Commercial Examination. Individuals possessing other qualifications are matriculated only by individual assessment and dispensation. Until 1976, anyone possessing the *Examen Artium* could be matriculated. However, the pressure upon facilities of the educational system in the 1960s and early 1970s forced the Ministry of Education to be more restrictive.

Virtually all courses of study lead to candidate degrees, abbreviated to such academic titles as cand.jur., cand.med., cand.mag., and so forth. The academic title for graduates from Denmark's Technical University is civil engineer.

The group of institutions of higher and further education which comes under the jurisdiction of the Ministry of Cultural Affairs is atypical in relation to other institutions of higher education and will not be dealt with here.

2.2 Development of Higher Education since 1960

Like many other countries in Europe, Denmark experienced general growth in the area of education during the 1960s. Approximately 18,000 students were enrolled in institutions of higher education in 1960. By 1970, the number of students enrolled had increased to approximately 53,000. At the largest single institution, the University of Copenhagen, the 1960 enrollment figure of 6,697 increased to 23,447 in 1970.

At Aarhus University, the only other university existing at that time, the increase in number of students enrolled was, relatively speaking, even more marked, with 2,000 students enrolled at the beginning of the 1960s and approximately 10,000 in 1970. The development in the numbers of matriculates to institutions of higher education up to 1987 is shown in Table 2.

Danish educational policy in the 1960s was based

Table 2
Admission to higher education

	1960	1965	1970	1975	1980
University studies					
Sciences	350	720	1,010	1,890	1,520
Social science and law	380	1,240	1,470	2,430	1,891
Arts and theology	570	1,930	3,020	4,070	2,001
Medicine	470	1,030	1,100	1,470	865
Specialized studies					
Technical university	560	800	1,080	1,070	1,250
Pharmacy, dental colleges, agriculture and forestry	600	710	610	750	818
Schools of economy, business administration, and modern languages	460	800	1,030	2,340	2,583
Total	3,390	7,230	9,320	14,020	10,928

Source: *Admission to Higher Education 1960–1980*. Ministry of Education. Economic–Statistics Division, Copenhagen 1984

on the objective of free admission to all forms of education. In addition, the OECD economic perspective, which at that time, related economic growth to investment in education, was also a part of Danish policy. This view was introduced in Denmark by the "Technician Commission," a government commission which was established in 1956 to ensure a more socially equitable policy of admissions to all forms of higher education. There was particular interest in ensuring equality in matriculation to technical studies and the natural sciences. The concept of equality in matriculation to all forms of higher education as a means to realize social equality was generally accepted throughout the 1960s, as was the belief that all graduates would be absorbed by the labor market. The government initiated a series of measures intended to attain the goal of social equality, and, in the late 1960s, the state opened admission to higher education. The Higher Preparatory Exam (HF) was introduced, to allow socially and culturally disadvantaged students to prepare for higher education.

One of the most important initiatives was the further development of financial support for students (*Ungdommens Uddannelsesfond*). Its objective was to provide financial support for students engaged in different forms of educational activity, but had particular regard for higher education. The guiding principle was the will to ensure that no one could be denied an education on economic grounds. It was thought that improved economic conditions during studies might not only bring more students into higher education but also reduce dropout frequency. Hence, social equality and the development of the national economy would be achieved.

The development of higher education in this period was based upon the "social-demand" principle. However, it proved difficult to anticipate the number of those matriculating. In the 1960s, the forecast called for an increase from approximately 9,000 in 1959/60 to 18–20,000 by 1970. However, by 1963 the number of enrolled students had already reached the level anticipated for the 1970s. The Ministry of Education set up a commission to assess the need for a new university.

As the outcome of their recommendations, Odense University was established and existing institutions were considerably expanded. The university centers at Roskilde and Aalborg were also planned. These centers were first opened to matriculation during the 1970s.

Throughout the 1960s, educational policy endeavored to extend the resources of buildings and staff to keep in step with the anticipated numbers of new admissions. The political objective was to prevent the introduction of restricted admissions or *numerus clausus*, particularly in relation to admissions policies for universities. Thus, the government sought to meet the avalanche of new students by founding new institutions for further and higher education both in Copenhagen and in the provinces.

From 1965 to 1969, construction costs amounted to US$194 million. Running expenses increased from approximately US$32 million in 1960 to approximately US$227 million at the end of the decade. The numbers of full-time teachers employed in the same period increased from approximately 1,050 to 3,500, while numbers of part-time teachers increased from 850 to 3,500. In 1970, the total government expenditure for higher education amounted to 1.4 percent of the Gross National Product.

By the middle of the 1960s, it became apparent that universities faced an administrative crisis that threatened their traditional autonomy. University professors were unable to cope with the rapid and sizeable increase in the numbers of teaching staff and students. The content of traditional disciplines was undergoing change, encouraged by the increase in numbers of new teachers. In addition, many of the new, younger university teachers were critical of the research, teaching, and administrative capabilities of the full professors. This, in turn, raised the issue of retaining special privileges for professors. The dissatisfaction with professorial autocracy was reinforced by student demands for participation in various administrative decisions regarding university management.

In the 1960s, the positive benefits of investment in education were unquestioned. By the 1970s this view changed. An increasing skepticism was accompanied by doubt as to whether there would be sufficient employment opportunities for future graduates. It became apparent that a reduction in the growing deficit in the balance of payments would demand a significant reduction of growth in the public sector.

Belief in social equality began to wane, partly because, despite considerable expansion of the educational system during the 1960s, there was no noticeable change in the social imbalance in recruitment to higher education. A committee appointed by the Ministry of Education was assigned the task of reviewing problems related to the overwhelming increase in numbers of admissions. In 1973, the committee reported that if graduate unemployment was to be averted in the 1980s, restrictions upon admissions must be imposed in the 1970s. A total plan for higher education was made for the period up to 1987. Presented in 1973, this plan recommended control of admission to studies in higher education and of funding, and changes in the structures of studies.

In 1973, the average prescribed length of study was about five years. However, certain courses of study, for example in humanities faculties, had an actual average of more than 9 years and medical studies around 8.6 years.

Following ministerial negotiations at the start of the 1970s, a quota for the number of collective admissions to institutions of higher education was established for the first time in 1975. The social demand approach had been replaced by a labor market approach. New criteria for admission were set down. Coordinated procedures for all institutions of further and higher education were established in order to control the number of students admitted. These also allowed potential students to apply for admission to more than one institution or study program, in order to increase their chances for admission.

In June 1976, the law restricting admission to tertiary education was passed. Table 3 shows the numbers of applicants in relation to admission limitations for respective institutions. While applicants could seek admission to more than one institution, their applications were made in order of priority. For example, 6,413 applicants in 1977–78 and 10,233 in 1987–88 cited admission to the University of Copenhagen as their first priority.

During the 1970s, the university centers at Roskilde and Aalborg introduced various innovations in the traditional university structure, including an interdisciplinary approach to study. A new basic education program was introduced. After two years of basic education, students could continue in a more specialized program for two to four years.

A general reform of studies in the humanities was introduced in 1985, and in the sciences in 1989. The Ministry of Education sought to coordinate Danish studies and academic degrees with those of other countries in the European Community by 1990. In

Table 3
Number of applicants and limitations upon admission to institutions of higher education

	Applicants/admission limitations			
	1977–78	1980–81	1984–85	1987–88
Universities in Copenhagen, Aarhus, and Odense	13,295/ 6,607	13,820/ 5,947	17,658/ 7,054	19,289/ 6,904
Technical university, veterinary and agriculture university and the university centers	5,360/ 2,330	6,056/ 2,799	8,717/ 3,884	9,198/ 4,101
Royal school of pharmacy and the dental colleges	999/ 372	1,192/ 385	1,044/ 326	914/ 317
Economy and business on academic level	319/ 309	362/ 359	800/ 587	1,166/ 1,166/

Table 4

Total research expenditure in Denmark in 1985 as distributed by sectors, in millions of Danish crowns and as percentage of total expenditures

Sector	Millions of Danish crowns	percentage
University sector	1,874	24.4
Remaining public sector	1,503	19.5
Private noncommercial sector	65	0.8
Business and trade sector	4,250	55.3
Total	7,692	100.0

Source: Forskningssekretariatet, Copenhagen 1987, p. 10

1990, the Bachelor of Arts (BA) and of Sciences (BS) was introduced in Danish universities and colleges for the first time. The prescribed length for bachelor studies is three years. These initiatives by the Ministry of Education were part of a general attempt to shorten previously lengthy university studies. After obtaining a BA or BS degree, a limited number of students may continue their studies towards candidate degrees.

In addition to candidate degrees, which are regarded as professional degrees, some institutions also prepare students for research degrees, that is, the magister and the licentiate degrees. The licentiate may be compared to the PhD. The universities also confer doctorates. The doctorate is conferred in recognition of an outstanding, original, and mature contribution to research. It is granted on the basis of a published thesis which must be defended in public.

2.3 Research

Research in Denmark is conducted within four sectors established by agreements with the OECD and drawn up to provide statistical information about research activities. The research sectors are (a) business and trade, (b) universities and other institutions of higher education, (c) all other areas of the public sector, and (d) private, noncommercial institutions.

Expenditure for research and development in Denmark amounted to approximately US$1.2 billion in 1985. The distribution of research funds throughout the sectors is shown in Table 4. Approximately 52 percent of total expenditure is taken by salaries, 27 percent by running costs and 15 percent by investments in buildings and equipment.

Despite a margin of uncertainty in the figures pertaining to research activities, it is apparent that real growth took place in the period 1976 to 1985, in expenditure, numbers of individuals involved, and of full-time annual works. This development is assessed in terms of key statistics in Table 5. The

Table 6

Research expenditures in millions of Danish crowns in actual costs

	1976	1979	1982	1985
University sector	761	881	1,352	1,874
Remaining public sector	577	732	1,154	1,503
Private noncommercial sector	27	33	43	65
Business and trade	1,125	1,672	2,744	4,250
Total	2,490	3,323	5,293	7,692
Index (1976=100)	100	133	213	309

Source: Forskningssekretariatet, Copenhagen 1987

Table 5

Danish research in the period 1976–1985

	1976	1979	1981	1985
Population (in millions)	5.1	5.1	5.1	5.1
Labor force (in millions)	2.4	2.5	2.4	2.6
Persons engaged in research (in thousands)	25.2	27.7	30.5	35.9
Manpower full-time equivalent (in thousand hours)	13.2	15.1	17.2	19.9
Full-time manpower (per thousand inhabitants)	2.6	3.0	3.4	3.9
Gross national product (in billions Danish Crowns)	251.0	347.0	464.0	615.0
Research expenditures (in billions Danish Crowns)	2.5	3.3	5.3	7.7
Research expenditure as percentage of GNP	0.99	0.96	1.14	1.25

Source: Forskningssekretariatet, Copenhagen 1987

share of total research expenditures for business and trade in the same period rose from 46 percent in 1976 to 55 percent in 1985 (see Table 6).

3. Governance, Administration, and Finance

3.1 National Administration

Responsibility for the educational sector rests with the Danish state, county authorities, municipalities, and private institutions and individuals.

Every significant field of education is regulated by legislation. Generally speaking, parliament is responsible for formulating educational goals. Under the Appropriation Act, parliament is responsible for determining the allocation of public funds to educational institutions.

In accordance with legislation, the chief responsibility for education in Denmark rests with the Minister of Education, who is the only elected official in the ministry. The ministry consists of one department containing three major sections and six directorates, each of them responsible for a specific area of education. The Directorate for Further and Higher Education (DVU) was established in 1974, partially reducing the traditional autonomy of individual institutions of higher education. Included in the restructuring of the administration of higher education which took place in the mid-1970s, six national planning committees were established, each of which represented a major area of research and study. Their function was to advise the ministry, and, more specifically, the Directorate for Further and Higher Education.

Since their establishment, there have been running discussions about the actual status of such committees, whether they are autonomous in policymaking or whether they only have an advisory function in relation to the directorates. The directorates themselves have gained increasing importance in planning, controlling and supervising the implementation of policies.

3.2 Institutional Administration

In 1970, a law on the administration of higher education was passed, since amended several times. In its original form it provided greater democracy in the administration of academic affairs by including collegiate governing bodies in administrative processes. It also introduced elected representation in such governing bodies for students and technical and administrative staff. In the 1980s, this law came under attack from the political Right for undermining the ability of institutions to provide education and conduct research of high standard. The ministry intends to amend the law in the early 1990s.

Under the Act of Administration of Higher Education, each institution is governed by a rector together with a number of collegiate governing bodies. The rector is elected from among the academic staff by the members of the governing bodies of the institution for a term of three years. The group of rectors for all institutions of higher education makes up the Danish Conference of Rectors (*Rektorkollegiet*). The Conference of Rectors promotes cooperation between universities and other institutions of higher education.

Several committees were established during the 1960s to deal with problems within the educational sector. In committee reports from 1964, the traditional autonomy of the universities was in debate as, too, the wish to adjust administrative structures and procedures to meet demands arising from the general development of all educational sectors.

Conflicts between teaching staff and between students, teachers, and administrators led to student strikes in 1968. The Rector of the University of Copenhagen responded to student demands by forwarding proposals for a new structure of university management, a proposal which was ratified in parliament in 1970. The new law abolished the autocracy of university professors virtually overnight. The universities were managed by democratically elected governing bodies consisting of teachers, students, and members of the technical and administrative staff.

In principle, the legislation of 1970 remains in force today, although considerable changes have been made in regard to proportional representation for the relevant groups which participate in the governing bodies.

The same legislation stipulates that the Ministry of Education has supreme authority over the institutions covered by the Act. The minister sets down regulations for the following areas: (a) admission to studies, (b) study programs, (c) the granting of licentiate degrees and doctorates, (d) the employment of teachers and researchers, and (e) the expulsion of students.

The management of each institution is conducted by the rector, together with a certain number of collegiate boards and committees. The constitution of the managements is fixed in statutes which must be authorized by the Ministry of Education.

The rector is the institution's public representative and is responsible for daily administration. The vice-rector, elected for a term of two years, assists the rector and may deputize at public functions. Members of all governing bodies are elected. Half of the members of The Academic Council of the university are teachers, one-fourth are student representatives, and one-fourth are representatives for the technical and administrative staff. The Academic Council deals with all matters concerning the institution as a whole.

Education and research is conducted within faculties or departments. Each faculty is administered by a faculty board and by the dean, elected by the same procedures which apply for the governing board. Research activities in each area of study are normally conducted in institutes governed by a director and an institute board. A study board is set up for areas of study or for individual courses of study. Each study board is made up of an equal number of teacher and student representatives. Members of the study board are elected from the teaching staff and the student body in the relevant institute or faculty. The study board has jurisdiction in all matters pertaining to the contents of courses, and the organization of instruction and examinations. The study board can recommend the establishment or abolition of teaching posts and reviews the qualifications of applicants for new posts.

3.3 Finance

In 1980, a new budgetary system was created. Whereas previously, the budget was annually adjusted, resources are now distributed in relation to the number of students graduating each year. The concept of the "effective student" was introduced in this context. Students who abandon their studies or who are not actively engaged in studies are not resource-productive. Similarly, considerable changes were effected with regard to the allocation of funds to research activities. It is now possible for the ministry to earmark funds for research in specific areas or disciplines, instead of merely allocating research funds in relation to the size of the institution in question, as had previously been the case. According to the Act of Administration of Higher Education, the ministry has no authority in the daily administration of institutions, as in matters pertaining to the curriculum, employment of staff and so on. However, changes in the practice of allocating funds to institutions of higher education has given the ministry and the directorate considerable influence in such matters. The university has traditionally received a considerable portion of the nation's total research funds. However, as the total demand for research gradually alters, this tendency, too, is likely to change, with an increasing share of the research budget being allocated to ministries other than the Ministry of Education.

As shown in Table 7, the 1980s witnessed significant "rationalization", if the so-called S/T ratio—the proportion of numbers of study level increases in relation to the numbers of full-time teachers—is an adequate measure for such rationalization. In the ministerial paper on higher education policy delivered in December 1988, a demand was made for even greater effectiveness in the coming years.

Cutbacks in appropriations to education are part of the government's efforts to reduce public spending. While it is not the government's policy to reduce the numbers of educational opportunities, as such, long-term studies within the higher educational system have been reduced in order to finance less costly, short-term, nonacademic training courses.

Table 7
S/T Ratios (target ratios) 1982–89

	1982	1985	1989
Humanities	13.0	13.5	14.0
Business languages	15.0	15.5	17.0
Social science and law	20.0	20.0	20.5
Business economics	17.0	20.0	20.5
Natural sciences	7.0	8.5	9.5
Technical sciences	7.5	9.0	10.0
Medicine	13.0	13.5	14.0

Source: Ministry of Education Economic–Statistical Department, Copenhagen, 1989

4. Faculty and Students: Teaching, Learning, and Research

4.1 Faculty

The number of permanent posts is determined by the annual allocations provided by financial legislation to research and instruction in respective institutions. In periods of cutbacks, teachers are dismissed. Only full professors have the status of public servants (which gives them tenure) and cannot be dismissed from their positions without difficulty. All members of the teaching staff are remunerated under the provisions of permanent agreements drawn up by the Central Association of Academics (AC) and the Ministry of Finance. Salaries are set in relation to seniority and grade, but do not otherwise vary in terms of area of specialization or by institution.

The cuts of recent years have meant stagnation in the employment of full-time teachers. The majority of teachers in employment in the early 1990s were taken on in the 1960s and 1970s. If budgetary policy permits, they can remain in their posts until retirement at age 70.

Recruitment problems raise further issues related to innovation in research. Although institutions continue to offer special fellowships with limited teaching obligations to younger scholars, these individuals tend to leave the university when their term of research expires. Until 1984, university teachers were usually promoted after a four-year trial period, if their research and teaching qualifications were accepted by a professionally qualified jury. Since 1984, such "junior" posts have served as temporary fellowships not necessarily leading to permanent employment at the institution in question.

In general, when a teaching post is to be filled, a professionally qualified, interinstitutional and/or international jury is convened to consider the qualifications of applicants. In principle, the final decision is made by the faculty and must be accepted by the rector or the ministry. Full professorships are made by royal appointment.

In order to stimulate the research environment, the ministry founded an interinstitutional academy,

The Danish Research Academy, in 1987. Its aim is to support and stimulate further studies for research scholars in cooperation with individual institutions of higher education. In addition, The Danish Research Academy offers scholars economical opportunities for travel and research abroad. However, despite these measures, research activities will continue to dwindle in the university sector.

4.2 Students

Higher education in Denmark is provided without fees of any kind. However, the cost of living for students is considerable, particularly because dormitories and halls of residence cannot meet the demand for student housing. In the 1980s, the State Educational Support scheme was extended in order to provide students over 18 years of age with grants, as well as with state-guaranteed bank loans. Grants are awarded in relation either to the financial circumstances of the applicant or, for those under 22 years of age, their parents. The revisions are subject to constant changes reflecting alterations in government policy on cuts in public spending.

Since the regulation of admissions policies in 1976, there have been considerable changes in matriculation patterns. The control of matriculation is manifested in the creation of more places for study courses that show reasonable graduate employment prospects and the corresponding cuts in admissions to courses which have fewer employment openings. There has been a considerable development of technical education as also studies in business administration. While previously furnishing graduates to the public sector, higher education is now directed towards the private domain. In 1976, a little less than half (47.6%) of students commencing long-term studies were directed towards employment in the public sector. In 1987, this was the case for only 22.3 percent of new students.

5. Conclusion

The present situation in higher education poses the question of whether there are any general guidelines for educational policies in the 1980s.

Policies of the 1960s were characterized by a desire for social equality, later replaced by a labor market orientation.

Increasing centralization has destroyed the traditional autonomy of the university sector, while political centralization, in itself, has created new problems. Despite continual regulations of educational supply in relation to market demand, the numbers of highly educated unemployed continue to be distressingly high.

At the end of the 1980s, development policies were characterized by greater market influence on curriculum content, over control of the budget, and demands for controls upon quality and effectiveness.

At the time of writing, however, no one has been able to agree upon the criteria for such controls.

In conclusion, it is interesting to note that, despite party-political disputes about the nation's educational policies, the tendencies and policy planning of the 1980s will undoubtedly be realized in the 1990s, no matter how governments are constituted politically or to which political party the Minister of Education may belong.

Bibliography

Brynskovudvalget 1975 *2. beretning om budgetterings-normen for videnskabelige ansatte ved de højere udd-annelses-institutioner.* Undervisningsministeriet, Copenhagen

Christensen J P 1981 *Den højere uddannelse som politisk problem.* Samfundsvidenskabeligt Forlag, Copenhagen

Danish Ministry of Education 1987 *Education in Denmark. The Education System.* Ministry of Education, Copenhagen.

Forskningssekretariatet 1987 *Forskningsstatistik 1985.* Forskningssekretariatet, Copenhagen

Minister of Education and Research 1988 *Report on the Danish Government's Policy in the field of Higher Educational.* Ministry of Education, Copenhagen

Pedersen M N 1977 *State and University in Denmark.* Odense University, Odense

Pedersen M N 1982 Denmark: state and university—from coexistence to collision. In: Daalder H, Shils E (eds.) 1982 *Universities, Politicians and Bureaucrats.* Cambridge University Press, Cambridge, pp. 233–75

Pedersen P J, Sørensen C, Vadstrup C 1987 Træk af udviklingen i Dansk Økonomi efter 1960 In: *Dansk Økonomi—Råd og realiteter 1962–1987.* Det økonomiske Råd, Copenhagen, pp. 7–35

Planlægningsrådet 1967 *Skitse for udbygningen af de højere uddannelser i tiden indtil 1980.* Planlægningsrådet, Copenhagen

Planlægningsrådet 1971 *De videregående uddannelsers udbygning 1971/72–1975/76.* Planlægningsrådet, Copenhagen

Von Eyben udvalget 1968 *Økonomisk støtte til unge under uddannelse.* Betænkning nr. 506, Undervisningsministeriet, Copenhagen

Whitehead J S 1981 Denmark's two university centers: The quest for stability, autonomy and distinctiveness. *Higher Educ.* 10: 89–101

J. Conrad

Dominican Republic

1. Higher Education and Society

The Dominican Republic has a total population of 6,803,000. Of that total, 3,990,000 are urban residents, while 2,815,000 are rural dwellers. Approximately one million Dominicans live as immigrants in the United States and Venezuela.

The most dynamic sectors of the national economy are tourism, agro-industry, foreign trade, and the financial sector. In recent years, the informal economic sector has grown rapidly, while the importance of agriculture and mining has diminished considerably. The majority of the economically active population work in the service sector, although the industrial sector has been favored by the tax-free zones.

After 31 years of the Trujillo dictatorship (1930–61), the nation finally has a constitutionally based, democratic political structure. Despite tendencies toward authoritarian and personalistic rule, the transition of power since 1966 has been determined by elections.

2. The Institutional Fabric of the Higher Education System

2.1 Organization of Higher Education

University education in the Dominican Republic dates back to the founding of the Dominican-run University of Saint Thomas Aquinas. The modern day University of Santo Domingo was formed by a 1938 statute which determined the curriculum. The university was entirely dependent on the state, which nominated all personnel.

The university reforms initiated in 1962 resulted in the institution's autonomy, turning over its direction to professors, students, and employees. That same year, the *Universidad Católica Madre y Maestra* (UCMM), created by the Catholic Church and important business sectors in the north, received accreditation. Neither the laws which establish the autonomy of the *Universidad Autónoma de Santo Domingo* (UASD) nor the creation of the UCMM established an overall university system. A 1970 decree permitted the creation of new universities. From that date until 1983, 23 such institutions were formed.

In 1983, the National Higher Education Council (CONES) was formed by representatives of the public and private sectors as a first effort towards creating a unified university system. However, its functions are limited to the approval of applications, fiscal management and accreditation of degrees, it does not have overall responsibility for higher education policies.

2.2 Enrollment Expansion

The university population has undergone sustained growth since 1960, when there were only 3,732 students, to reach a total of 128,748 students in 1985. This expansion has been largely conditioned by the democratic conquests of 1961, which have fostered the growth of the middle class as well as the broader inclusion of this class in the secondary and higher education systems. An additional factor without which this rapid growth would not have been possible, has been the growing number of women in the student and working population (Silié 1988). The expansion of the curricular programs offered has also contributed to the enrollment boom.

Table 1
Students enrolled in higher education, public and private sectors 1970–84

Year	Public sector	Percentage	Private sector	Percentage	Total
1970–71	17,854	83.0	3,646	17.0	21,500
1971–72	18,039	81.4	4,110	18.6	22,149
1972–73	23,028	79.9	5,792	20.1	28,820
1973–74	24,425	77.1	7,270	22.9	31,695
1974–75	23,248	63.2	13,557	36.8	36,805
1975–76	29,210	57.9	21,235	42.1	50,445
1976–77	32,228	57.3	24,023	42.7	56,251
1977–78	31,971	51.5	30,138	48.5	62,109
1978–79	38,359	50.9	36,974	49.1	75,333
1979–80	50,787	55.0	41,473	45.0	92,260
1980–81	60,039	55.5	48,098	44.5	108,137
1984–85	67,122	44.2	84,776	55.8	151,898

Source: Fundación de Crédito Educativo and Consejo Nacional de Educación Superior

The overall number of universities, as well as the regionalization of higher education, has facilitated university access for students from the provinces. At present, the Dominican Republic boasts 26 regional universities.

The student population, which in former years was almost entirely in the UASD, has gradually been concentrated in the private universities. At present, private institutions account for 60 percent of the student enrollment. The university population is composed of students from all social classes, although the upper middle class is most heavily represented.

2.3 Curricula Offered

Almost all the universities begin their study programs with a basic course, which, although structurally distinct all have the same formative objectives.

Three levels of study are offered: technical, undergraduate, and graduate. The technical study programs are generally considered intermediate. A total of 89 such courses are offered in the various faculties and their average length is two years. The majority of students are enrolled in undergraduate programs with an average length of four years. The nation's graduate programs are undergoing an expansion and the university system now offers a master's program. There are still no PhD programs available.

3. Governance, Administration, and Finance

3.1 University Governance and Planning

The UASD governing structure is democratic and includes participation by students, professors, and certain levels of the administration. The UASD does not receive fiscal aid from CONES. The university's highest governing body is the Council (*Claustro*) comprised of professors and students. The University Council, headed by the president, is responsible for the executive direction of both itself and the *Claustro*. Each faculty and department has a technical council, which is the body responsible for the direct administration of the fields of study and research activities. All directive positions are elective.

The private universities establish their philosophical orientation and administrative structures in accordance with their sponsoring bodies and without state interference. There is no student participation in the direction of these universities. The university's sponsoring body designates the president who in turn designates administrative officials.

Central university planning does not exist in the public or in the private sector. Attempts to organize programming do not go beyond certain market strategies or the formation of occasional new programs. Since the state also lacks a planning system, budgeting allotments are undertaken using political criteria.

3.2 Finance

The UASD is financed almost entirely by the state on an annual basis. Additional revenue sources are student fees and donations. Private universities are funded primarily through tuition, donations, loans, and investments. To date, only six private institutions receive state funding, which represents 45 percent of the state budget for higher education.

4. Faculty and Students: Teaching, Learning, and Research

4.1 Faculty

While UASD faculty are selected through open applications, their private counterparts are designated by the university president. There are 6,000 university professors in total. The majority of these began their faculty careers without special educational preparation, professional experience, or research backgrounds. Very few have completed graduate degrees (in the UASD, only 19 percent had master's or PhD degrees). Seventy percent of the faculty work on an hourly part-time basis. The majority of the remaining 30 percent either divide their time between teaching and administrative duties or devote a portion of their efforts to research. The average time commitment per professor is 15 hours per week. Employment contracts must be renegotiated every academic period. The sabbatical still does not exist in the Dominican Republic, although in 1989 the UASD began efforts for its implementation.

The professors' union at the UASD is the only organization of its type in the country. Although the union is active in making its demands known, it has not been able to extend itself beyond the public university.

4.2 Students

Since 1961, the student body has undergone changes in its social composition, largely due to the growth of the middle class on a national level. However, the majority of the student population comes from the upper-middle class (Menéndez 1987).

In order of preference, the most highly demanded subject areas are: social sciences, humanities, and natural sciences. The latter category is dominated by medicine and related fields (CONES 1986).

The union of students limits its activities to the state university. The private institutions permit representation only from those student organizations with scientific and cultural objectives. Although once quite active, the union of students now limits its endeavors, increasingly reduced in scope, to the university arena.

All students have access to university financial aid which is administered by a private, nonprofit organization. Scholarships, financed by the universities or cooperating entities are also available.

4.3 Research

Although the majority of the nation's universities recognize the importance of research, this activity has been reduced considerably in recent years. Just 181 professors, approximately 3 percent of the total, have some connection with research activities. Of this reduced percentage, only half are employed on a full-time basis (Castillo and German 1988).

5. Conclusion

Massive increases have occurred in student enrollment without the necessary planning to support them. Among the serious consequences this has provoked are overcrowded classrooms, inexperienced professors, lack of teaching equipment, inadequate facilities, and research difficulties. The net result has been a reduction in the quality of education.

Additionally, adverse economic factors limit students' dedication. Forced to seek paid employment, students increasingly devote less time to their studies. This tendency undermines attempts to maintain academic standards.

In light of these difficulties, demands are being formed for the creation of legislation which would take into account the entire university structure and give it greater coherence.

Bibliography

Castillo G, German A 1988 *La investigación en la Universidad Dominicana*. Editora UASD
Consejo Nacional de Educación Superior (CONES) 1986 *Diagnóstico de la Educación Superior Dominicana*. CONES
Menéndez A 1987 *El Universitario Dominicano*. Editora INTEC
Silié R 1988 *Educación Superior Dominicana: Situación y Perspectivas* (mimeo)

R. Silié

E

Ecuador

1. Higher Education and Society

Higher education in Ecuador is primarily the state's responsibility. The country's social polarization meant that higher education traditionally constituted a class privilege. In the second half of the twentieth century this situation has changed as the result of a series of socioeconomic transformations. Consequently, people from a greater range of social backgrounds have been able to seek higher education. The phenomenon of mass education and a decrease in the levels of academic excellence have accompanied these changes. The dynamic of these developments in society and higher education institutions has contributed to the fact that universities have experienced severe academic, financial, and administrative crises over the 1970s and 1980s.

Ecuador's national boundaries have not been altered since 1942 when the country signed the Rio de Janeiro Treaty with Peru, effectively reducing its surface area to 270,670 square kilometers. Ecuador disputes the legitimacy of this treaty.

In 1950 Ecuador's population was 3,310,080 and had risen to 10,823,000 by 1990. The population increases at a rate fluctuating between 2.8 and 3.1 percent annually. The majority of people are located in two of Ecuador's four regions: the Sierra and the coast contain 95 percent of the total population. The Amazonian jungle and the Galapagos account for the remaining 5 percent.

It is important to note two population distribution characteristics. First, the Sierra's population has been decreasing as a result of migration, whereas that of the coast has been increasing. Second, changes have occurred in the ratio of rural to urban population. In 1950 the urban population was 30 percent, whereas in 1990 it had reached 54 percent. These changes may be attributed primarily to changes registered in socioeconomic development.

The highest percentage of employed people are located in agriculture, which accounts for 35 percent of total employment. The service sector employs 26 percent, business 11 percent and manufacturing 10 percent. This structure is the result of changes which have occurred since the early 1960s, a period in which both services and business have grown in comparison to agriculture. For example, in 1960 agriculture employed 56 percent of the working population. These modifications are the result of the indus-trialization process and migration and urban movements. The economic changes have affected the social structure as well. A shift of economic development from agricultural to business, industrial, and financial sectors has also produced an increase in salaried sectors and a diminution of precarious semifeudal forms which prevailed among rural workers.

Similarly, the middle class and mestizo sectors have grown. It is estimated that the Ecuadorian population is presently distributed as follows: 10 percent Whites (pure Latin-Spanish), 60 percent Mestizos, and 30 percent Indians. This racial division corresponds to a social one; the upper and middle classes are primarily found within the White and Mestizo populations, whereas Indians are generally located in the lower social classes. Nearly 90 percent of the population speaks Spanish. Indians speak diverse languages according to their tribal affiliation, but Quechua is the most commonly spoken Indian language.

Three levels of government exist in Ecuador: the central government (Ecuador is a centralized, not federal, state); provincial councils; and municipal councils, which are the district governments. Higher education is primarily the responsibility of the central government. The universities and polytechnic schools are autonomous institutions and are associates of a collegiate body, the National Council of Universities and Polytechnic Schools (CONUEP) which serves mainly to coordinate administrative matters.

In addition to its traditional political functions (administrative, legislative, and judicial), the post-Second World War Ecuadorian state has come to assume an active socioeconomic role. The state intervenes in the economic and social spheres. This was especially so in the 1960s when oil revenues grew but intervention in the economic sphere decreased in the 1980s as a result of the economic crisis.

State financial assistance is evidence of its commitment to higher education. The government's education policy is oriented towards establishing greater cooperation between the Ministry of Education and CONUEP for the purpose of furthering pragmatic and methodological links, especially between secondary and higher education. It also seeks to improve levels of academic excellence as a means by which to curb unemployment among university graduates. This latter problem has been intensifying.

Higher Education is primarily controlled by the Ecuadorian state. Nevertheless, certain religious institutions of the Roman Catholic Church also participate in the higher education process, especially at the university level. A number of private associations have also been participating in the administration of some universities in recent years.

2. The Institutional Fabric of the Higher Education System

The higher education system is composed of five types of institution: (a) universities; (b) polytechnic schools; (c) military institutions of higher education; (d) international advanced degree institutions with offices in Ecuador, which include the *Facultad Latinoamericana de Ciencias Sociales* (FLACSO) and the *Centro Internacional de Estudios Superiores para América Latina* (CIESPAL); and (e) technical institutions, separated into those which develop human resources in technological fields through associate degree programs and those which train primary school teachers, providing two years of post-secondary school instruction as opposed to higher education as such. Only the first four types of institution form part of the higher education system.

The four classes of specifically higher education institutions include various establishments. First, 19 establishments exist as central universities and 34 as extension programs (types of branch institutes). A total of 53 universities were operating in 1990, therefore. The universities are of two basic types: the first is commonly referred to as "classical" and covers all kinds of knowledge fields, whereas the second is "technological" and primarily provides teaching in technical fields (although over time the technical schools have extended their programs to include humanities as well). Both types of institution offer full degree (bachelor, engineering, and doctorate) programs which last five, six, or seven years, as well as what are referred to as intermediate programs which generally last two or three years (for technological degrees). The state runs 34 of the 53 university institutions. The remaining 19 are run by religious communities and private associations.

Second, there exist three central polytechnic schools. Like the universities, they offer full and intermediate degrees.

Third, there are two military-run higher education institutions which provide professional training (not necessarily military): the *Escuela Superior Poli-*

técnica del Ejército (ESPE) and the Instituto de Alto Estudios Nacionales. These two institutions offer graduate programs in which both civilians and military personnel may participate.

Finally, the *Facultad Latinoamericana de Ciencias Sociales* (FLACSO), which is the Ecuadorian office of an international institution that covers all of Latin America, and the Centro Internacional de Estudios Superiores de Comunicación para América Latina (CIESPAL) offer special graduate courses at both doctorate and master's level, in addition to nondegree courses.

A certain amount of importance has been given to research since 1972, following the oil era. During an initial phase, research capacities have improved through methodological training; CONUEP has been vital to this process through its funding of research projects. Through institutions such as the National Council of Science and Technology (CONACYT) and the universities associated with CONUEP, the state has been the main impetus for research development.

Research develops primarily through four channels: university institutes; private academic institutions; state centers, organizations, and dependencies; and international graduate programs. Private enterprise also provides some research activity in technological applications, but this is of little significance.

Admission requirements differ according to the institution. Admission to the universities and polytechnic institutions generally requires a high school diploma in a given specialization as well as the payment of registration fees. These are the only requirements in state institutions. The private universities also require an entrance examination, to show students' aptitude and general knowledge. The fees are significantly higher than in state universities. The other higher education institutions establish their own requirements. The enrollment figures in Table 1 refer only to universities and polytechnic schools. It is estimated that 18 percent of the population in the age group 20 to 24 entered the university and polytechnic system between 1970 and 1990.

Degrees granted differ from institution to institution in the higher education system. Those obtained most often are: bachelor's (after four years of study); economist's, engineer's, and lawyer's (after five or six years of study). Occasionally lawyers, as well as all medical and odontological

Table 1
Higher education enrollment

	1970	1975	1980	1985	1990
Students registered	20,396	66,366	122,646	163,366	192,000[a]

a Approximate figure

raduates, are granted degrees with the title of Doctor." In order to graduate it is usually necessary o submit a thesis and defend it before a committee.

Some fields in certain universities, polytechnic chools, and other higher education institutions offer raduate studies. Most of these studies finish at the aster's level. However, several doctorate and pecial courses also exist. In both cases, it is the astitution which bestows the degrees. Where state astitutions are concerned (universities and poly-echnic schools), the degree is given in the name of he Republic and by legal authority.

Although graduate studies demand research skills, hese are usually limited in scope. This is due to the act that Ecuador's research infrastructure is mini-ally developed. Also, graduate work is generally atended for professional as opposed to academic urposes.

. Governance, Administration, and Finance

.1 National Administration

ligher education is the responsibility of each of the niversities, polytechnic schools, and special insti-utions, and of the Ministry of Education and Culture a the case of technical institutes.

Ecuador has a decentralized government for igher education, particularly in the university and olytechnic sectors. The government respects the adependent nature of these institutions. Never-heless, all higher education institutions receive econ-mic aid from the state and must submit to the state reasury for financial review.

Universities and polytechnic schools have planning epartments and state universities generally do not nforce limitations on admissions. Other higher edu-ation institutions establish their own planning, nplementation, and evaluation mechanisms in ccordance with the needs of the institution.

Links between higher education institutions' plans nd programs and those regarding national dev-lopment generally do not exist. However, the need or such coordination began to emerge in the 1980s.

The state is responsible for financing higher edu-ation. Percentages of the Gross National Product GNP) allocated to higher education are as shown in able 2.

The state allocates funds according to the number f students registered in each university and poly-echnic school.

In addition to obtaining state funds, the uni-versities and polytechnic schools charge student fees and specific research and consulting fees. Income from these sources covers about 10 percent of the total expenses of the state universities.

3.2 Institutional Administration

Universities and polytechnic schools are governed through collegiate bodies and elected authorities which are ordered as follows: (a) the assembly (com-posed of all full professors, student representatives, and administrative personnel); (b) the rector; (c) department (teaching) and institute (research) coun-cils; (d) department and institute directors. The members of the collegiate governing bodies are democratically elected.

Other higher education institutions have various systems of government, consisting of collegiate bodies responsible for decision making, and admin-istrative authorities that enact resolutions.

A system of cogovernment exists in all higher education institutions except for the technical insti-tutes, which are dependent upon the Ministry of Education. Academics and students, as well as administrative personnel, participate. In the uni-versities and polytechnic schools students account for 50 percent and administrative personnel 10 percent of the total number of academic respresentatives.

The higher education institution's academic work comprises both teaching and research. The uni-versities and polytechnic schools also sponsor exten-sion or "social service" activities. Teaching takes place in the departments and schools. The institutes are responsible for research.

4. Faculty and Students: Teaching, Learning and Research

4.1 Faculty

Table 3 shows the number of professors (academic) and researchers since 1980.

Table 4 illustrates the breakdown of academic positions in state universities and polytechnic schools.

According to both the University and Polytechnic School Law (LUEP) and past legislative decisions, it is necessary to hold a university degree in the respective

Table 2
ercentage of GNP allocated in higher education

	1970	1975	1980	1985	1990
ercentage	0.46	1.04	1.15	0.92	0.80

Table 3
Professors and researchers

	1980	1985	1990
Professors and researchers	6,884	9,992	11,200
Average student–staff ratio	18.1:1	17.0:1	17.0:1

191

Table 4
Breakdown of academic positions

	1980	1988
Principal	14.7	14.5
Full professor	53.8	55.5
Associate professor	12.0	9.8
Assistant professor	3.7	8.9
Student assistant	12.5	9.0
Other	3.3	2.3
Total	100.0	100.0

field, win a competition (based on a test of knowledge), and show merit (proof of past experience) in order to obtain a teaching or research position.

State university and polytechnic professors are regarded as special public employees since they are governed by the LUEP. This permits them to maintain two public sector jobs at the same time.

University and polytechnic school professors and researchers belong to the National Federation of Ecuadorian University and Polytechnic School Professors (FENAPUPE). Each university also has a teacher and researcher federation. Postsecondary school institutions' staff may form part of the National Educators Union (UNE) which represents primary and secondary school teachers.

Faculty and researchers fulfill their academic obligations according to annual work plans which are elaborated by the governing bodies of the individual institutions. Individual proposals are usually respected, especially if they apply to teaching and research matters. The greater amount of time is usually spent on teaching. Nevertheless, in some universities full-time professors can spend 30 of their 40 work hours on research.

2. Students

The higher education student body is composed of individuals from middle- and upper-class homes. Students from the middle class constitute the majority of the state university and polytechnic school populations. The economically privileged frequently pursue studies in private institutions.

The majority of higher education students are mestizo. There is a minority of Indians, blacks, and other races.

Liberal admissions and free education represent university policies which are based on the need to make higher education accessible to less privileged economic sectors. In practice however, these policies have not proven feasible.

The right to free association is established in the universities and polytechnic schools through two types of collegiate organization: Student federations encompass all of university or polytechnic school students, and school associations group together students in the same field. Together, various federations constitute the National Student Federation. This federation represents a vital political force in the country.

The structure of each of the university and polytechnic fields' study plans is defined by the faculty governing councils. These councils subsequently submit proposals. The university or polytechnic school council ultimately approves and authorizes the programs.

The governing councils review the organization and content of each program course submitted by professors and researchers who are grouped according to the fields.

The country's higher education system does not have a uniform student evaluation policy. Each institution formulates its own procedures. Nevertheless certain similarities do exist. The final grade reflects the sum or the average of three different grades classwork, research, and examinations (both tests and final exams). Professors usually submit grades each trimester. However, course duration may vary. Certain institutions follow a semester system, while others have year-long courses. Only a few institutions utilize the credit system (completion of individual subject matters).

5. Conclusion

Higher education in Ecuador is undergoing a severe crisis, which is most evident in the low levels of academic performance. This crisis may be attributed primarily to financial restrictions. The planning and policy separation which exists between the state and the universities and polytechnic schools has also intensified unemployment in professional fields.

Bibliography

Institute Latinoamericano de Investigaciones Sociale (ILDIS) 1985 *Guía del Estudiante Universitario del Ecuador.* Quito

Malo G H 1980 *Pensamiento Universitario Ecuatoriano estudio introductorio y selección.* Biblioteca Básica de Pensamiento Ecuatoriano XIV. Banco Central del Ecuador-Corporación Editora Nacional, Quito

Moreano A 1984 Universidad, crisis y reforma. In: Moreano A et al. (eds.) 1984 *Situación y Desarrollo de la Universidad.* Universidad Central del Ecuador, Quito

National Council of Universities and Polytechnic School (CONUEP) Problemas universitarios: Cuadernos de análisis. *Weekly Journal* (1–6). CONUEP, Quito

Pacheco Prado L 1990 Evaluación de la situación actual y perspectivas para el corto y mediano plazos de la Universidades y Escuelas Politécnicas. Internal document. CONUEP, Quito

Pacheco Prado L La Educación Superior no universitari en el Ecuador. Unpublished manuscript. Quito

Pareja F 1986 *La Educación Superior en el Ecuador*. Centro Regional para la Educación Superior en América Latina y el Caribe (CRESALC-UNESCO), Quito

L. Pacheco Prado

Egypt

1. Higher Education and Society

The Arab Republic of Egypt (ARE) is situated in the northeastern corner of Africa. It is bounded in the north by the Mediterranean Sea, in the east by the Red Sea, in the south by the Sudan, in the west by Libya and in the northeast by Israel.

The population of the ARE is 55 million (1989 census). Cairo, the capital, has a population of 12 million. The population increase in the ARE is 2.9 percent per annum (see Table 1). Since the beginning of the century there has been a great increase in the urban population due to the accelerated development in the industrial and services sectors. A study of the last seven censuses reveals that the urban population has risen to 40 percent of the total population.

After the Revolution of 1952, radical economic changes were put into practice to improve living standards. The dominantly free enterprise policy was replaced by a socialist one based on economic planning and state control. Article 23 of the 1971 Constitution stated: "The national economy shall be organized in accordance with a comprehensive development plan which ensures raising the national income".

Before the revolution there was an agrarian economy, where 66 percent of investments were in agriculture, with heavy stress on cotton plantation, and low-land productivity. This was replaced by an agro-industrial economy. Investments in agriculture from 1970–80 were estimated at 36 percent while in industry it was 49.5 percent.

Considerable attention was given to agricultural expansion through land reclamation. Almost 1.04 million acres were reclaimed: 16 percent of the whole cultivable area at midcentury. In industry, evident care has been given to the existing industries as well as to the newly established ones. Since 1952, 800 new industrial projects have been established, costing £E 1,000 million (US$299 million). Consequently, a clear change in the distribution of the labor force took place. Between 1960 and 1970 the number of agricultural workers declined from 58 percent to 51 percent of the labor force while in industry it rose from 12.6 percent to 18.5 percent.

Ownership, dominantly individual before the Revolution, has been changed through a series of nationalization schemes to three styles of ownership: public, cooperative, and private.

The structure of government and main political goals are set out in the permanent Constitution of the ARE of September 1971. This defines the form and essence of the State, its economic and social foundations, the political system, as well as the rights and duties of the citizens as follows:

(a) The ARE is a democratic and socialist state.

(b) Islam is the religion of the State and Arabic its official language. Islamic jurisprudence is the principal source of legislation. Freedom of religious practice is guaranteed.

(c) Sovereignty is of the people alone and they are the source of authority. Sovereignty is practiced and protected by the people, who undertake to safeguard national unity in the manner stipulated in the Constitution.

The economic foundation of the ARE is a socialist system based on sufficiency and justice to prevent exploitation and to remove class discrimination.

The Government is the supreme executive and administrative organ of the State. It is formed of the prime minister, the prime minister's deputies, the ministers, and their deputies. The prime minister supervises the work of the government; the government undertakes the execution of the general policy of the State in accordance with the laws and republican decrees.

The Cabinet exercises the following functions:

(a) laying down the general policy of the State, and controlling its implementation;

(b) controlling the implementation of laws, the upholding of state security, the protection of citizens' rights and the state's interests;

(c) preparing draft laws and decrees;

(d) directing, coordinating and following up the work of the ministries, and public organizations and institutions.

2. The Institutional Fabric of the Higher Education System

In 1906 a group of eminent Egyptians began to discuss the feasibility of founding a national university,

Table 1
Population in Egypt

	1947	1960	1971	1989
Population in thousands	19,0222	26,085	34,076	55,000
Average annual rate of growth as a percentage	1.78	2.36	2.62	2.90

193

and began to collect contributions for this purpose. The university was officially inaugurated in 1908.

The university sent several students abroad in order to create a staff of qualified lecturers. Meanwhile, distinguished scholars from European universities were invited to come to Cairo and, in collaboration with their Egyptian colleagues, set up courses in history, Arabic literature, philosophy, and economics. Together they created the concept of university education in the modern sense.

In 1917, government authorities considered the foundation of a state university, and a committee was constituted to study the question. But it was not until the year 1923 than an agreement was reached with the government, by which the existing National University became the nucleus of a Faculty of Arts in a new State University with an independent status in respect of both its administration and the organization of its faculties and departments.

In 1925 a decree founded the State University under the name of the Egyptian University, comprising the Faculty of Arts, the new Faculty of Science, and affiliating the higher schools of medicine and law with the status of university faculties. In 1935, the higher schools of engineering, agriculture, and commerce were also incorporated into the new university. In 1940 the university was named the Fouad 1st University, and in 1946 the school of Dar El-Oloum was also affiliated to the university. After the July Revolution of 1952, the university was renamed Cairo University.

Until 1938 higher education was concentrated in the city of Cairo. In that year two branches of the Faculties of Arts and Law were established at Alexandria. In 1941, a branch of the Faculty of Engineering was added and the three faculties became the nucleus of Farouk 1st University, which was founded in 1942. After the revolution it was renamed Alexandria University.

The need occasionally arose for the establishment of some institute or higher school to meet the requirements of the country in some areas. Examples of these were the Higher Training College for Secondary School teachers, the Commercial Institute, and the Agricultural Institute. But no sooner had these been established than they had become a nucleus for Ibrahim Pacha University, later known as Ain Shams University, founded in Cairo in 1950. There was also a movement towards the establishment of regional universities. All of these began as colleges affiliated to one of the existing universities, and the new universities when complete replicated the mother universities. In this way the following universities were established:

(a) the University of Assiut in 1957;

(b) the University of Tanta in 1972;

(c) the University of Mansûra in 1972;

(d) the University of Zagazig in 1974;

(e) the University of Menia in 1976;

(f) the University of Menofia in 1976;

(g) the University of Suez Canal in 1976.

The University of Helwan, established in 1975 comprised institutes of a type previously rejected by existing traditional universities. Examples of these are the Institutes of Tourism and Hotels, Physical Education, Social Services, Music, and Arts Education.

There is also a branch of Cairo University located in Khartoum and a branch of Alexandria University located in Beirut.

In addition, there is The American University in Cairo, a private institution, founded in 1919, and providing a liberal arts education for approximately 9,000 students. Courses are offered in several departments, including Arabic studies, economics and political science, materials engineering and physical sciences. The American University in Cairo is multinational in its origins and its outlook. Its cosmopolitan character is evident in both the faculty and student body. Teachers come from the Americas, the Middle East, Europe, and Asia. More than sixty nations are represented in the student body although the majority of the students are Egyptian. It offers limited enrollment and concentrated programs.

A variety of postsecondary institutions exist outside the university system. These institutions, commonly known as institutes, developed in the late 1950s in response to the enrollment pressure on the universities and the country's need for technically trained personnel.

Industrial and commercial technical institutes are considered as the basic model of higher education particularly after the transformation in 1975–76 of the majority of higher institutes, once attached to the Ministry of Higher Education, into university colleges which formed part of Helwan University. The technical institutes were first established in 1956 as vocational training centers, and were open to holders of the general Secondary Education Certificate. In 1966, the centers were upgraded as regards their training, duration of study, and curricula, and renamed technical institutes. Institutes provide training for specialized technicians in the various fields of economic, commercial, industrial, and scientific employment.

At the end of the 1980s, the number of technical institutes amounted to 35—16 commercial and 19 industrial. These institutes accept holders of the General and Technical Secondary Education Certificate. The period of study is two years, at the end of which a student is awarded a diploma in one of the specialist study branches. All technical institutes are governmental and are affiliated to the Ministry of Higher Education. Eight Health Technical Institutes offering two-year programs in related health fields are administered by the Ministry of Health. As of 1986–87, eight intermediate institutes under private auspices were in existence. They come under the general supervision of the Ministry of Higher Education but are relatively independent in determining the curriculum and course syllabus. The Ministry approves but does not define these areas. Programs are offered in the fields of management, secretarial skills, social service, and commercial studies.

Admission to private intermediate institutes is based on the General Secondary Education Certificate and is coordinated by the same office that administers admission to universities. Study in these institutes runs for two years, at the end of which a student is awarded a diploma in one of the specialized areas.

Higher institutes are either private institutes attached to nongovernment associations or governmental institutes attached to government bodies. There are nine private higher institutes: six for social service, two for agricultural cooperation, and one for administrative and cooperative studies. Study lasts for four years, at the end of which students are awarded the university first degree.

Other types of higher education attached to ministries apart from the Ministry of Higher Education also exist. Thus the Sadat Academy For Administrative Sciences is attached to the Cabinet Presidency. The Police Academy comes under the Ministry of the Interior, and military colleges under the Ministry of Defense. The Ministry of Culture is responsible for the Academy of Arts, which comprises art institutes for the theater, the cinema, Arabic music, the conservatoire, and the ballet. There are, in addition, two higher institutes awarding the master's degree. These are the Higher Institute for Literary Criticism and the Higher Institute for Popular Arts (folklore).

Research has assumed an important role in Egyptian universities. A presidential decree of 1972 established a separate budget for university research. Funds are also provided by business firms and individuals. Members of the university teaching staff are encouraged to undertake research, and original research is a prerequisite for academic promotion. Teaching staff are particularly encouraged to participate in applied research projects in cooperation with commercial or industrial institutions.

All research in the university is supervised and coordinated by the Academic Board for Postgraduate Studies and Research, which takes steps to prevent duplication and to foster interdisciplinary or interdepartmental cooperation.

Research is also carried out in various specialized institutes throughout the country. Some are affiliated with the universities, while others are attached to ministries.

Admission to the various faculties of universities has, since 1954, been based on the principle of equal opportunity among applicants. The only criterion for preference among applicants is their intellectual ability, which is assessed by examination. Hence, admission to a university is, for the most part, determined by the result of the national examination for the General Secondary Education Certificate.

Holders of the Secondary School of Commerce certificate are admitted to the Faculty of Commerce; holders of the Secondary School of Agriculture Certificate to the Faculty of Agriculture; and holders of the Technical Secondary School Certificate to the Faculty of Engineering. Holders of the General Certificate of Nursing are admitted to the Higher Institute of Nursing. In all cases, the candidate should have obtained at least 70 percent of the total marks, and pass a supplementary examination of the General Secondary School Certificate.

3. Governance, Administration, and Finance

3.1 National Administration

There had long been a Department of Higher Education within the Ministry of Education, but with the multiplication of universities and higher institutes, a Ministry of Higher Education was set up in 1961. It acts as a governing and coordinating body for planning, monitoring, and developing the system of higher education. Another trend connected with the multiplicity of universities was the establishment of the Supreme Council of Universities. It was established in 1950 as a central body for planning and coordination among the universities. These 11 member universities now comprise 175 faculties and institutes.

The universities carry the responsibility for training the labor needed for social and economic development; for conducting scientific research to deal with issues of concern to the nation; for preparing cadres of teaching staff; and giving expert advice in all that concerns society in view of their role as centers of ideological and cultural enlightenment. To allow for maximum drive and independence, the Supreme Council of Universities approved the following principles:

(a) University autonomy is a recognized principle stipulated in Egypt's Constitution. It is also provided for in the university rules and regulations and backed by the political leadership.

(b) University autonomy does not mean alienation from society. The universities are part and parcel of society, and they reciprocally affect each other.

(c) The universities enjoy academic freedom and autonomy. They exercise self-management within the framework of the regime and laws of the nation, with a view to enhancing academic freedom and freedom of thought in the university world.

(d) The universities are also autonomous in that they apply controls and determine criteria for the evaluation of standards of performance.

(e) The universities have the right to exercise their responsibilities concerning education and scientific research, which are their basic functions, in addition to their third function as ideological and cultural beacons in society. Thus they are responsible, through their leadership, their faculty, and departmental councils, for establishing courses and examinations and granting academic degrees.

(f) Although it is necessary that universities enjoy autonomy and self-management, university education should be planned on a nationwide base in the light of plans setting out targets for social and economic development, especially since there are now 12 universities (Al Azhar included). This task is undertaken by the Supreme Council of Universities, which carries out the planning of university education, the general supervision of university degrees and performance rates, and general follow-up of the results of such planning.

The major source of university finance is the national budget, supported by local funds in each region and by loans negotiated at the international level. However, universities receive around 20 percent of the national education budget.

3.2 Institutional Administration

The university is administered by a president as well as a university council. The president is the head of the university and presides over the university council meetings. University presidents are appointed by presidential decree following nomination by the minister of higher education, and should have occupied professorships for at least five years at any of the Egyptian universities. The term of office is four years, subject to renewal. The president administers the educational, administrative, and financial affairs of the university within the policy formulated by the Supreme Council of Universities. The university president exercises the powers of a minister.

The president is assisted by two deputy presidents. One of them is responsible for graduate studies, research, and cultural relations. The other deputy president is in charge of undergraduate studies and student activities in general. When a new branch of the university is established, a deputy president of the branch will be appointed. The deputy assists the president in managing the educational, administrative, and financial affairs of this branch. The senior deputy president would assume control in the president's absence. The deputy presidents are appointed by presidential decree on recommendation of the minister of higher education, in consultation with the president, and are expected to have held professorship for at least five years at one of the universities.

The university council is the governing body of the university and consists of the university president as chair, the deputy presidents, deans of faculties, secretary general of the university, and four members with experience in university education who are appointed for two years, subject to renewal.

The university is administered according to a system of decentralization. Each faculty is, to a great extent, a separate entity, managing its own academic and administrative affairs and regulating its finances according to the budget allocated to it. The faculty is administered by the dean and its council.

The faculty council comprises the dean, who acts as chair, the vice-deans, the heads of departments, a professor from each department, the senior assistant professor and lecturer in the faculty, in addition to three members experienced in the disciplines of faculty.

The faculty consists of a number of departments, each enjoying independent status in academic, administrative, and financial affairs. The department is headed by the most senior professor. The department council comprises professors, assistant professors, and five lecturers to be chosen every year, in order of seniority.

Each university has two main academic boards. One of them is the Academic Board of Education and Student Affairs, which is presided over by the deputy president for undergraduate studies and student affairs. This board is made up of the vice-deans of faculties and institutes for undergraduate studies; and three to five members experienced in academic education and public affairs, to be appointed for a renewable term of two years. The other academic board is for graduate studies and research, presided over by the deputy president for graduate studies and research. It consists of the vice-deans of faculties

Table 2
University faculty

	1965–66	1970–71	1974–75	1979–80	1988–89
Staff	2,497	2,969	5,219	8,924	15,828
Assistants	2.427	4,169	6,659	13,436	17,067
Total	4,924	7,138	11,878	12,360	32,895

and institutes for graduate studies and research; and three to five members experienced in production and public services, to be appointed for a renewable term of two years. This would be according to a resolution of the university president, in consultation with the board, following approval of the university council.

4. Faculty and Students: Teaching, Learning, and Research

The teaching staff comprises professors, assistant professors, and lecturers. Demonstrators and assistant lecturers are expected to continue their graduate education and obtain a doctoral degree, after which time they may be considered for appointment to the permanent staff of the university (for numbers of university teaching staff 1965–89, see Table 2).

To be appointed to any teaching staff post, the minimum requirement is a PhD (or an equivalent degree in the field of specialization), plus other conditions to be specified for each teaching post. A lecturer should have graduated at least six years before the appointment. Lecturers constitute the basis of the teaching staff. They may participate (as part-supervisors) in the supervision of research work leading to an MA, MSc, or a PhD degree, provided that a professor or an assistant professor is chief supervisor.

An assistant professor should have spent at least five years as a lecturer; whereas the professor should have spent at least five years as assistant professor. Professors and assistant professors, besides teaching, supervise research work done in the department, especially by demonstrators and assistant lecturers reading for their graduate degrees.

The work load of a professor is 8 hours per week; for an assistant professor, 10 hours per week; and for a lecturer, 12 hours per week. If the demonstrators and assistant lecturers are given a teaching task, their work load is usually 14 hours or less, according to circumstances. These rules apply for all faculties and all disciplines. Members of staff whose timetable hours exceed the prescribed workload are paid on an hourly basis for these extra hours.

The university avails itself of the services of its former professors on pension (from the age of 60), who are reappointed as part-time professors. Also scholars holding key positions in the government or in private bodies are eligible for the post of part-time professor. This system of employing part-time teachers helps to overcome the retirement age problem, which otherwise deprives the university of the services of academics aged over 60. Also professors given key positions in the government (as often happens) may thus continue to teach at the university.

Whenever there is a shortage of teachers in any department, nonpermanent teachers from other universities or from similar departments at the same university are employed and paid on an hourly basis.

Members of the teaching staff may be transferred from one department to another, to other faculties within the university, or to other universities with the approval of the appropriate university council. Teaching staff also may be assigned to other universities abroad for a period of up to four years, or may serve for the same period in positions outside the university, for example, in government departments, international agencies, and nongovernmental organizations. Some teaching staff, by special permission, hold part-time positions outside the university in addition to their work in the university.

The number of students to be admitted to each faculty is determined by the Supreme Council of Universities at the end of each academic year (for enrollment figures 1960–87, see Table 3). The Council also establishes the regulations for admission. Students are placed in a particular faculty through an Admission Coordination Office, affiliated to the Supreme Council of Universities. The students who succeed in the General Certificate of Education examination and seek admission to university apply to this office in Cairo or one of its branches in the provinces. Students list the faculties they wish to join in order of preference. Admission of students indicating the same preference depends on the examination result of each student.

Bibliography

This article is based mainly on: Supreme Council of Universities (SCU) 1989 *University Eduction in Egypt.* SCU Press, Cairo

Abu Ismail A I 1964 Some aspects of the industrial structure in Egypt. *Inst. Nat. Plann. Bull.* 432

Egypt, Central Agency for Public Mobilization and Statistics 1978 *Statistical Handbook.* Nahdet Misr, Cairo

Egypt, Ministry of Education 1988 *Annual Report on Education Development in Egypt.* Ministry of Education Press, Cairo

Egypt, Ministry of Information 1971 *The Constitution of the Arab Republic of Egypt.* Ministry of Information Press, Cairo

El Fiki H S 1974 *The Cultural History of Education in Egypt.* Dar El Maarif, Cairo

Harbi M K 1970 *The Development of Education.* Ministry of Education Press, Cairo

Helmi M K 1978 *Education in Egypt.* General Egyptian Book Organization, Cairo

Table 3
Student enrollment in universities

	1960–61	1965–66	1969–70	1981–82	1986–87
Students	84,704	123,732	122,049	504,368	506,232

Mabro R 1974 *The Egyptian Economy 1952–72.* Oxford University Press, Oxford

W. A. Boulos

El Salvador

1. Higher Education and Society

El Salvador is a small country with an area of 21,000 square kilometers. It borders Guatemala on the west, Honduras on the north and east, and the Pacific Ocean on the south. It won its independence from Spain in 1821 along with the other Central American countries.

The estimated population in 1990 was 6.4 million, with equal numbers of males and females. The population growth in this century has been substantial. It is estimated that between 1987 and 2000 the average population growth will be 2.1 percent annually. Life expectancy at birth is 62.

The urban population made up 44 percent of the total (1987); 55 percent of the population is less than 20 years old and 10 percent is 50 years old or older. The illiteracy rate is 57 percent.

According to the World Bank classification, El Salvador is a lower middle-income economy; its gross national product per capita in 1987 was US$860.

As a consequence of the internal armed conflict, which became acute in 1980, the economy has deteriorated; the average annual growth was 4.3 percent between 1965 and 1980, and it has been −0.4 percent between 1980 and 1987. The 1990s must be a time of recovery.

Government expenditure is 12.4 percent of the gross national product (1987). Between 1972 and 1987 certain percentages of government expenditures varied dramatically; for example defense allocations increased from 6.6 to 26.8 percent, while education fell from 21.4 to 17.1 percent and health expenditures declined from 10.9 to 7.4 percent.

There is no official religion in El Salvador, as state and Church have been separated since the 1860s; however, virtually all the population is Christian and the vast majority are Catholic.

The current political constitution specifies that higher education must be regulated by a special legislative act. The University of El Salvador and any other public universities that may be established will enjoy autonomy in academic, management, and financial matters. Moreover, the public universities must provide a social service and respect academic freedom. Private universities must be nonprofit, provide social service, and abide by the norms of academic freedom.

Finally, the political constitution stipulates that each year the government budget must include resources sufficient to support the public universities which will be subject to constitutional controls by the Court of Public Accounting.

2. The Institutional Fabric of the Higher Education System

Higher education in El Salvador dates from the birth of the state itself. Indeed, the legislative and constitutional body—the Constituent Assembly of the State of El Salvador—that created El Salvador as an independent nation in 1841, established in the same year the University of El Salvador, the cornerstone of higher education in the country. For more than a century—from 1841 to 1965—higher education was synonymous with the University of El Salvador.

In 1965 the government passed legislation that allowed the opening of private universities. This was an attempt to counterbalance the University of El Salvador, which strongly criticized the government and the conservative sectors of Salvadoran society. After 1965—and certainly since 1980—there has been an accelerated, although sometimes erratic development of higher education, mainly of universities.

Before 1965, the structure of the university was based on a set of seven classic schools (medicine, engineering, law, humanities, economics, dentistry, pharmacy). In the early 1960s, however, a reform movement improved and modernized the university.

Other smaller nonuniversity postsecondary public institutions were established in the 1950s: The School of Social Work and the Higher Normal School for teacher training for the secondary level.

Between 1965 and 1979 four private universities were established. In 1980 civil war started and the campuses of the University of El Salvador endured a four-year military occupation. Between then and the late 1980s, 27 private universities were established, some of them small and very specialized (there is, for example, one named "University of the Salesman").

In 1989 the basic organization of higher education was composed of 32 universities (31 of which were private) and 29 postsecondary nonuniversity institutions (16 of which were small private institutions offering two- and three-year programs).

Public nonuniversity higher education includes nine technological institutes (which provide training for technicians and teachers for primary and secondary education) and four specialized schools: the National Agriculture School, the Military School, the Higher School of Physical Education, and the Military School of Nursing.

Usually, the universities offer long-course programs which require more than four years of full-time studies to obtain a degree. A few of them house certain research activities and publish professional journals, mainly in the social sciences (e.g., the

Jesuit-run University José Simeón Cañas and the University of El Salvador).

Virtually all university degrees are linked to a first higher education degree, regardless of the period of time needed to fulfill them. Graduate studies are almost nonexistent. Salvadorans who want to pursue graduate studies go abroad, mainly to the United States or Europe. There are no precise figures on the consequent brain drain in El Salvador, but it appears to be relatively high.

There are minimal formal constraints on entering higher education: a high school diploma—granted officially by the Ministry of Education—is the single general requirement of all higher education institutions. In some instances admission tests are also required. The law stipulates that no higher education institution can deny admission to students because of race, creed, sex, or political affiliation.

In the late 1980s there was a total enrollment in higher education of 85,500 students, compared with 5,000 students in the early 1960s. Of that enrollment, 72 percent was in university institutions (engineering-related 18 percent, health professions 12 percent, economic/business 19 percent, humanities/teaching 23 percent); 28 percent was in postsecondary non-university institutions (engineering-related 2 percent, health professions 2 percent, economic/business 3 percent, humanities/teaching 21 percent).

In terms of enrollment the University of El Salvador is the foremost institution admitting 44 percent of the total while the University José Simeón Cañas accounts for 10 percent of the enrollment.

Sixty percent of nonuniversity, postsecondary enrollment is in private institutions. The latest figures indicate that 51 percent of the total enrollment in higher education is in public institutions.

In the late 1980s an average of 3,090 persons graduated annually from universities (most degrees are granted after a period of five years of full-time study). The University of El Salvador awarded 30 percent of degrees and 70 percent graduated from private universities. Nonuniversity higher education institutions graduated 2,600 persons in 1988.

3. Governance, Administration, and Finance

3.1 National Administration

In general, the Ministry of Education is responsible for the management of the educational system. However, for higher education there is a constitutional provision that grants autonomy to the University of El Salvador. For the other higher education institutions, especially those publicly funded, the Ministry of Education has a greater role in terms of coordinating activities and authorizing initiatives.

Since 1987, there has been a General Directorate of Higher Education within the Ministry of Education. This unit is responsible for overseeing the functioning of all higher education institutions, with the exception of the University of El Salvador, which has its own special bylaws. It is intended to be a major vehicle for liaison between the Ministry of Education and the private higher education institutions.

The establishment of private higher education institutions is authorized through a specific legal procedure. First, the candidate institution must obtain the approval of a set of bylaws from the Ministry of Education. Secondly, the Ministry of the Interior (*Ministerio del Interior*) grants the institution legal status as a nonprofit organization designated as a public service. Thirdly, an ad hoc committee, composed of representatives of the University of El Salvador, the Ministry of Education, and the candidate university, must approve the curricula. Finally, the Ministry of Education inspects the facilities to be sure that they meet the minimal requirements established for higher education. After these steps, the Ministry of Education decrees the full functioning of the new university.

The Ministry of Education, through its General Directorate of Higher Education, is responsible for monitoring the approval of curricula of public higher education institutions, such as the above-mentioned technological institutes. In this case a similar ad hoc committee serves to approve the curricula.

The main source of financing for public institutions is the central government budget; other sources are the tuition and fees paid by the students. The main source for the private institutions are tuition and fees paid by students and grants provided by supporting organizations. To give an example of the levels of financing: the annual budget for the University of El Salvador for 1989 was US$12.5 million.

3.2 Institutional Administration

The basic model of governance in the universities is (a) an electoral body in charge of electing the rector and deans, and composed of faculty, students, and alumni; (b) a Higher Council in charge of the policy-making process, usually composed of the president or rector, the deans of the schools, and senior students.

This structure has remained unchanged in the history of higher education in El Salvador. The University of El Salvador has always followed it or has struggled to retain it and all other higher learning institutions have attempted to emulate the pattern, although the emphasis on student representation can vary from one institution to another. The tradition of university students in El Salvador is to seek full participation in the decision-making bodies. The private universities encourage student participation in different proportions. The other public institutions of higher learning usually depend upon the Ministry of Education, and their students have relatively little participation in the decision-making process.

It is unusual for nonacademic staff to be present on the governing boards of the universities, although in some instances their representatives participate in meetings as observers.

In the most common academic organizational structure in Salvadoran universities work is carried out in schools (*facultades*) made up of departments. In some cases there are institutes within the universities, usually research-oriented, that are in charge of special programs or projects. The University of El Salvador has regional centers, or decentralized units which provide more opportunities to students who do not live in the capital city. Some private universities function exclusively in cities other than the capital city.

In the case of nonuniversity institutions, the model is more varied, although basic academic organization typically rests on departments or degree programs.

Regarding the learning process, the University of El Salvador has autonomy in the establishment of its curricula and testing, assessment, and graduation procedures. Other institutions have their own similar procedures, but, as explained above, they must submit these procedures for approval to the University of El Salvador and the Ministry of Education.

4. Faculty and Students: Teaching, Learning, and Research

4.1 Faculty

Before the 1960s, university professors were usually part-time employees. They were paid on an hourly basis for their teaching, and the lecturers were professionals were devoted a small part of their time to teaching. During the 1960s, full-time lecturers, professors, and high-level administrators were assigned to virtually all the schools of the University of El Salvador, and the first private universities started their operations with some full-time faculty and staff.

In 1989 there were more than 4,700 faculty members in the Salvadoran university education system, 78 percent of whom were male. As a whole, 8 percent of faculty are full-time; 11 percent are part-time; and 81 percent are so-called "hourly teachers." In the University of El Salvador 65 percent of faculty are full-time; 22 percent are part-time; and 13 percent are hourly teachers.

The percentage of university faculty at the University of El Salvador is 32, and 68 percent work in private universities. However, while all of the University of El Salvador's faculty hold university degrees, 20 percent of the faculty in private universities do not. Figures for the faculty of nonuniversity higher education institutions are not available.

During the 1960s, the faculty of the University of El Salvador started to organize itself in unions along with nonacademic staff; however, there are also other professional associations that have as their members only university teachers.

Faculty members in El Salvador are teaching-oriented; the amount of their time devoted to research is not significant. However, faculty members are sometimes involved in community development and forms of social action as part of their academic work. This, of course, varies from one university to another.

4.2 Students

In a developing society like El Salvador virtually all higher education students come from the upper strata of the socioeconomic structure of the country as defined by income. The percentage of the 19–24 year age group enrolled in higher education is 15.6, and 55 percent of university graduates are male.

In El Salvador students often form or join guilds and associations to defend their interests. Many also become involved in social issues, and participate in national politics. Historically the General Association of Salvadoran University Students (AGEUS) has represented university students. At the same time, each school has its own association.

In order to participate in internal university politics, students form groups that can represent a specific ideology. It is common to have Christian Democratic, Social Democratic, Revolutionary, and a wide range of Marxist-oriented groups competing through secret and direct elections for positions in the different governing bodies of the university and the students associations.

5. Conclusion

The roots of higher education in El Salvador reach back to the very birth of the country. To be understood it must be seen in the light of the overall conditions, the history, the environment, and the socioeconomic circumstances of the country. It should be pointed out that in some instances there have been points of academic excellence in Salvadoran university institutions.

It is a widely recognized fact that the University of El Salvador has clashed with the government and conservative sectors of society on issues such as human rights, budgetary matters, and academic freedom. Since the 1970s these confrontations have extended to other universities, mainly the University José Simeón Cañas.

For 124 years, university education was the responsibility of one autonomous institution, the University of El Salvador. After 1965, and particularly after 1980, small private universities have proliferated. The civil war, military intervention in the University of El Salvador (1980–84) on behalf of the government, and the growing expectations of emerging social sectors of the population have encouraged such proliferation. The risk of institutional weakness and academic mediocrity as a result of this proliferation is high.

The government has taken over certain functions of higher education in order to train teachers and technicians for short careers and to oversee private institutions.

Some major areas of the higher education institutions (graduate studies, research, basic science) need to be enhanced. Currently the emphasis of higher education institutions is on teaching and granting undergraduate degrees. Coordination, accreditation, financing, management information systems, and faculty career and development are areas that also have to be developed.

In the near future, the Salvadoran higher education system must meet the challenge to improve its processes and outcomes, to contribute to the national recovery, and to become a major and respected social institution in the country.

Bibliography

El Salvador, 1966 *Ley de Universidades Privadas,* Legislative Decrees 244 (1965) and 250 (1966)
El Salvador 1983 *Constitución Política.*
Inter-American Development Bank 1989 *Economic and Social Progress in Latin America. 1989 Report.* Inter-American Bank, Washington, DC
Merlos S R 1960 El Constitucionalismo Centroamericano en la Mitad del Siglo XIX *La Universidad* 3–4: 9–53
Ministerio de Educación 1989a *Diagnóstico de la Situación de la Educación Universitaria en El Salvador*
Ministerio de Educación 1989b *Educación Superior en Cifras 1987–1988.* Dirección General de Educación Superior
Ministerio de Educación 1989c *Memoria de Labores* [Annual Report] 1988–1989
Vu My T 1985 *World Population Projections 1985.* The World Bank/Johns Hopkins University Press, Baltimore, Maryland
World Bank 1979 *Demographic Issues and Prospects (A World Bank Country Study).* World Bank, Washington, DC
World Bank 1989 *World Development Report.* Oxford University Press/World Bank

V. M. Valle

Ethiopia

1. Higher Education and Society

Ethiopia, the seventh largest country in Africa, has a total land area of 1,251,282 square kilometers with a central highland mass surrounded by lowlands. The country is largely a high plateau with elevation ranging from 100m below sea level to 4,000m above sea level. Its frontiers have remained the same for quite a long time.

According to the census of the Ethiopian central statistics office (CSO 1987), its population is estimated to be 46 million, of which about 88 percent live in rural areas. Age distribution shows predominantly young people (i.e., below 30 years of age). The total population is estimated to grow at 2.9 percent per annum, while the urban population is growing at an average rate of 4 percent per annum.

Agriculture is the principal natural resource. Major cash crops are coffee, oil seeds, cotton, sisal, tobacco, fruit, pepper, and sugar cane (Pankhurst 1955, CSO 1987). Ethiopia is first in Africa and tenth in the world in livestock production. The manufacturing sector, which is largely state owned, plays an important role in the country's Gross Domestic Product (GDP). Handicrafts and the small-scale industries sector also contributed significantly to the GDP. Gold, platinum, salt, and industrial minerals are also important in the Ethiopian economy (CSO 1987).

Ethiopia has one of the longest histories of sovereign statehood in the world. The country had been ruled by various feudal kings until 1974, when a popular revolution brought the Provisional Military Administrative Council (PMAC) into power. This administration ruled the country until 1987 when the people's Democratic Republic of Ethiopia (PDRRE) was formed.

Religious schools of Christian and Muslim origins were the earliest Ethiopian schools. Apart from religious teaching, those schools also taught literature, reading, simple arithmetic, and so forth. The main purpose of the religious schools was further strengthened when a modern theological school was founded in 1944. The so-called Western-style modern education attained momentum between 1908 and 1935, when schools of this type were opened in different parts of the country. Teachers were mostly from Britain, France, Egypt, Syria, and Lebanon. French and English were the alternative mediums of instruction in the Ethiopian school system, but at present English is the language of instruction at the secondary and tertiary levels.

The schools that were suspended during the Italian occupation (1935–41) were reopened in 1942, when educational expansion started its evolutionary growth. The first higher education institution, University College of Addis Ababa, was established in 1951.

2. The Institutional Fabric of the Higher Education System

After the first higher education institution, the University College of Addis Ababa, was established in Ethiopia, the demand for such institutions began to grow rapidly. As a result of the demands and the needs of the country, various colleges were established in the 1950s, including the colleges of Engineering and Agriculture, the Public Health College, and the Building College. Later the Ambo Agricultural School was established and in 1974 a commercial school and a school of theology were upgraded to the level of higher education institutions. Thus, higher education was expanding horizontally at a very slow rate but it saw no vertical development until 1961 when the University College of Addis Ababa was upgraded to a university (Trudeau 1964). In the early 1990s there are three universities and several colleges and junior colleges.

Unlike the general education system, where there were public, private, and mission schools, higher education institutions were only government owned. It is true that missionaries, especially Canadians, played a very crucial role in designing, establishing, and administering higher education institutions, as well as advising Ethiopian authorities on the strengthening and expanding of these institutions. The sectorial organization of higher education varies from a situation of strong charter rights and autonomy to being accountable to the appropriate ministry. Thus the University College of Addis Ababa was the only autonomous higher education institution for a long time, while the Colleges of Engineering and Building were accountable to the Ministry of Education, the College of Agriculture came under the Ministry of Agriculture, the College of Public Health under the Ministry of Health, and so forth (Trudeau 1964).

In 1977, a separate governmental body, the Commission for Higher Education (CHE), was established to coordinate all the higher education institutions in Ethiopia. At present there are three universities and five colleges and institutes which operate under the Ministry of Education, and about four colleges which are not directly the responsibility of the higher education department of the ministry but are also governmental responsibilities. The ministry has a special department headed by a vice-minister charged with the responsibilites of overall coordination, determining policy, guidelines, selection, and certification of students; coordinating research and publications, and accrediting the programs and evaluation of higher education institutions. Most of these responsibilities also extend to those higher education institutions which do not fall directly under the Ministry of Education.

One category of higher education institutions in Ethiopia is the university. For a long time Addis Ababa University was the only one of its kind in Ethiopia, until Asmara and Alemaya Universities attained university status.

Research is an integral part of the three universities and even the other colleges where staff members are encouraged and expected to carry out some research while they are teaching.

Besides the three universities, there are five other institutions of higher studies directly subject to the Ministry of Education which can be categorized as agricultural, technical, teacher training, and business colleges (Ministry of Education 1988). There are two agricultural junior colleges (Ambo and Jimma), one institute of animal health assistants (Debre Zeit), one college of teacher education (Kotebe), one junior college of commerce (Addis Ababa) and one polytechnic institute (Baher Dar). Research is supposed to be an integral part of all of these institutions. In fact most of them have research and publication units of varying strengths and experiences. Higher education institutions in Ethiopia can be categorized under three major divisions. The first category consists of universities (those offering undergraduate and graduate degree programs); the second category consists of those colleges or institutes offering graduate degree programs; and the third group comprises junior colleges or institutes offering diploma or certificate courses. The number of institutions in the levels mentioned above is given in Table 1.

The Ethiopian school leaving certificate examination, which is awarded to those candidates who have successfully completed 12 years of education, is the criteria of selection for admission into higher education institutions. Probably any candidate obtaining a satisfactory overall grade point average in any five subjects, including mathematics and English, which are compulsory for all candidates, could enter the higher education institutions. The grade point average requirement is set up by the department of higher education in the Ministry of Education. The admission requirements change from year to year depending on the performances of the candidates and the available places in the institutions.

Table 1
Higher education institutions in Ethiopia

Institutions	1960	1965	1970	1975	1980	1985	1988
Universities (degrees)	—	1	2	2	2	3	3
Colleges/institutes (degrees)	5	—	—	—	—	—	3
Junior colleges (diplomas)	1	1	—	—	5	5	6
Total	6	2	2	2	7	8	12

Table 2
Enrollments in higher education (1960–88)

Institutions	1960	1965	1970	1975	1980	1985	1988
Universities (undergraduate degree)	—	—	—	6,127	—	11,780	10,935
University (graduate degree)	—	—	—	—	—	279	431
Colleges/institutes (degree)	—	—	—	—	—	—	—
Junior colleges (diploma)	—	—	—	918	—	5,866	5,654
Total	883[a]	—	—	7,045	—	17,925	17,020

The entrants to the higher education institutions in Ethiopia come from the following categories:

(a) Regular entrants who are regular and extension students completing high school and passing ESLCE in their first registration.

(b) Private entrants who once failed ESLCE but have improved their results in the successive years.

(c) Quota entrants selected on the basis of the low level of economic development of a particular region, and the background and standard of the high school in which they were trained.

(d) International or miscellaneous students from comparable standards other than ESLCE.

In Ethiopia, the requirement for degree and diploma offering higher education institutions is set centrally by the ministry, which controls institutional variation during selection. Thus there are no regional or institutional variations in selection for higher education, although there have been some incentives to encourage disadvantaged groups by using the quota system without violating the minimum grade point average requirement. The minimum grade point average, however, required for admission for the three categories of regular, private and quota entrants varies on a yearly basis, but the majority of entrants are regular students.

The University College of Addis Ababa started with the initial enrollment of only 72 students in 1951 and there has been only a very gradual quantitative increase. In fact, this was the trend for all higher education institutions until 1974, after which date enrollments in higher education changed drastically. Enrollment, which was only 7,045 in 1973–74 increased to 17,925 in 1985–86 (an increase of about 154 percent). This tremendous growth in a very short period, can only be truly appreciated when one considers the various calamities the country was facing at the same time. Table 2 illustrates the figures for total enrollment in higher education since 1960 at five-yearly intervals by level of institution as it was

categorized earlier (Trudeau 1964, MOE 1986, CHE 1989).

The government provides full scholarships to all students from outside Addis Ababa and tuition is free for every citizen of the country.

It is not easy to get a precise picture of the proportion of age group (20–24 years) enrolled in the whole higher education system from 1960 to the present, but CHE (1989) indicates that the participation rates were 0.54 percent (1984); 0.53 percent (1986); 0.51 percent (1987); and 0.45 percent (1988). These rates are quite low even by African standards.

The higher education institutions which are categorized as junior colleges and other similar colleges offer courses leading to a diploma. These programs take two to three years of full-time study, after which those who have outstanding results could be recommended for first degree programs. The colleges and universities offer courses leading to undergraduate degrees (BA or BSc) depending on the area of specialization. The length of study varies from department to department, but generally it takes four to five years for all faculties except medicine which takes seven years for the MD degree. Agriculture, arts, science, law, business, public health, and social work offer four-year courses leading to a bachelor's degree, while architecture and engineering offer five-year courses for the first degrees (Amare 1982). Similarly, the College of Town Planning, Institute of Water Technology and Health Science offer four years bachelor's degree programs (CHE 1989). All of the degree and diploma awarding higher education institutions are public and the institutions themselves award degrees or diplomas. The higher education department at the ministry is responsible for overall coordination and therefore controls academic accreditation in the country.

Graduate studies begin after the completion of undergraduate degrees. The major criteria for admission to graduate study is a good grade point average in undergraduate studies. At present there are a total of 28 areas or programs of graduate studies in Ethiopia (CHE 1989 p. 12).

3. Governance, Administration, and Finance

3.1 National Administration

Until 1977, Addis Ababa University was responsible for the control and accreditation of all higher education institutions. The Commission for Higher Education which was established in 1977 was charged with the following responsibilities:

(a) planning the expansion of higher education institutions in accordance with the national requirements of the country;

(b) approving short- and long-term budgets for higher education;

(c) evaluating higher education institutions;

(d) controlling the quality and quantity of labor development in higher education institutions.

After 1987 the Ministry of Education was invested with powers and duties concerning higher education. It is now the case that the Ministry of Education is the top coordinating agency, and shapes higher education in Ethiopia.

The goals that are set by the central agency are reflected in the duties and responsibilities of the Ministry of Education according to Proclamation No. 8/1987 of the National Shango (parliament). Planning for higher education institutions, actually starts at the institutions themselves. The respective department and unit initiates short- and long-term plans based on the responsibilities charged upon them. The lower units pass on their plans to the heads they are accountable to, who in turn pass them to their superiors until all converge at the Ministry of Education level. It is the department of higher education of the Ministry of Education which consolidates all plans of the institutions and presents them to the policy committee of the Ministry of Education or to the Board of Governors for higher education, where certain adjustments could be made on the basis of the directives given by the National Planning Office. Once they are approved by the Ministry of Education or the board, the short- or long-term plans are sent to the National Planning Office, which may, in turn, make certain adjustments and present them to the Council of Ministers where they get final approval.

The goals that are set up for higher education within the national plan (short- or long-term) are mostly quantitatively assessed at various levels. Each institution is responsible for quarterly reports on the implementation of the plan which finally has to be evaluated at ministry level and reported to the central planning. Thus the mechanism set up by the government allows each level of institution to evaluate the implementations of its plans.

Although it was intended to increase the student enrollment by an average rate of 5.4 percent in the 10-year plan, it was actually observed that at the end of the five-year period it had increased by an overall average rate of only 1.6 percent. Meanwhile the individual rates had increased by 2.5 percent in teacher training, 10.4 percent in health science, 4 percent in agriculture, 6.2 percent in technology, 3.2 percent in sociological science, and 5.2 percent in natural science. However, if one evaluates the overall quantitative achievements of 1985–89, the results were satisfactory, as was stated earlier (CHE 1989 p. 19).

The prime source of finance for higher education is the central government. No qualified Ethiopian candidates pay tuition fees; they receive scholarships which cover all living expenses.

Despite the serious problems facing the country, a substantial amount of the total requested budget for higher education was approved for the 1985–89 period, which was 88 percent, 86 percent, 85 percent, 77 percent and 64 percent respectively for each year.

Almost all of the higher education institutions offer evening extension courses leading to various qualifications, including undergraduate degrees. Most of the participants are office employees or members of business organizations. Unlike the regular program, which is financed by the government, the extension courses are run on a tuition basis.

Trudeau (1964) has indicated that the total budget of the University College of Addis Ababa for the years 1950–61 was about US$6,145,000, while a budget of about US$1,993,645 was approved for all the higher education institutions in 1962–63. The total recurrent budget for the years 1974, 1985, and 1988 was approximately US$8,345,000, $25,430,000, and $26,935,000 for each year respectively.

3.2. Institutional Administration

Until the formation of the Commission for Higher Education (CHE) in Ethiopia, Addis Ababa University was the only institution chartered in full control of all existing colleges and of all future developments of formal postsecondary institutions of learning in Ethiopia. The head of state, who was the chancellor, used to appoint the board of governors, the president, and the two vice-presidents. Before the revolution of 1974, the board of governors used to have nine members including the president and eight members nominated by the emperor himself, three of whom were representatives from the ministries of education, agriculture, and public health, respectively. According to Trudeau (1964), the Board of Governors was the principal policy-making corporate entity of the university. It had the power to establish and determine the general academic and administrative policies of the university. For many years the ministers of education, health, agriculture, foreign affairs and finance served as board members. This composition of board members gave the university great influence and was a distinct advantage to it.

The overall aim of CHE was to coordinate and administer all higher education institutions so as to avoid duplications and to create a shared information system. Thus, according to Proclamation 109/1977 of the Ethiopian government, a board of higher education has been established with the Minister of Education as chair, and the ministers of health, agriculture and resettlement, and industry; the commissioner for national planning, and the Ethiopian Science and Technology Commissioner as members. The Commission was the executive office of the Board of Higher Education, in charge of the following functions:

(a) planning and furnishing staff, material, and curriculum needs of the higher education institutions in the country;

(b) providing guidelines for the selection of students for all higher education institutions;

(c) approving certifications to be awarded to graduates of higher education institutions;

(d) giving directives for each institution about its internal organizational structures;

(e) guiding the research activities of each institution in accordance with the national plan;

(f) planning and coordinating foreign aid and ensuring its congruity with national needs;

(g) guiding the publication and dissemination of texts, journals, and research reports of higher education institutions;

(h) promoting research in higher education institutions and facilitating the generation of internal revenue;

(i) issuing or approving general guidelines for the coordination of higher education institutions;

(j) limiting the number of higher education institutions with the consultation of appropriate government bodies and ministries;

(k) giving general directives, guidelines, or policies for all higher education institutions;

(l) accrediting higher education institutions;

(m) expanding or integrating higher education institutions;

(n) approving plans and budgets of higher education institutions for both short and long terms;

(o) making and signing agreements with any other institutions about higher education;

(p) evaluating or giving directives for the evaluation of higher education institutions in Ethiopia;

(q) assessing the labor development progress of each institution within the national needs of the country.

The political system of Ethiopia as it stood in 1987 has been transformed. The newly emerged National Congress (Shengo) issued a proclamation coordinating all educational institutions in the country under one ministry. However, the Board of Education still maintains its position.

Each department of a higher education institution has a general staff meeting where the democratic exercise of power begins. These units are responsible for planning and preparing the budget of each department that is finally submitted to the academic commission. The formal committees through which academic power emerges include the departmental general staff meeting, the academic commission, the Faculty Council and Educational Advisory Committee of Higher Education, and finally, the Board of Higher Education.

The Faculty Council consists of all deans, academic staff representatives, and student delegates. The composition is the same for academic commissions at the university and junior colleges as well. Thus, department heads are nominated at staff meetings, elected by members, and approved by the appropriate dean. The deans of faculties are nominated by each faculty's academic commission, appointed by the president, and approved by the senate or faculty council. The president is nominated by the faculty council if it is a university and appointed by the government with the participation of the Higher Education Department and the Ministry of Education. The heads of nonuniversity institutions are nominated by the respective academic commissions and appointed by the Department of Higher Education.

Each department is responsible for initiating courses of study in the field and allocating credit hours. Admission policies are standardized by the Department of Higher Education in the Ministry of Education. Each institution has its registrar who deals with student registration and documentation when the applicants have been assigned by the department of the ministry. For universities the curriculum committee of the Faculty Council approves the curricula for the entire period of study and for junior colleges the academic commission fulfills the same function. The department also plays a crucial or active role in determining the length and content of the curriculum.

4. Faculty and Students: Teaching, Learning, and Research

4.1 Faculty Development

In the early years of higher education in Ethiopia the faculty was composed entirely of foreigners. Ethiopianization of the teaching staff has been gradual but at the beginning of the 1990s a great majority of the staff members are nationals. Full-time teaching staff has increased from 181 in 1960 to 1,682 in 1989. More than half of the total teaching staff have graduate degrees in the field in which they are teaching.

Employees of higher education institutions are civil servants. Any Ethiopian 18 years of age or older with the requisite qualifications, who has not been sentenced for an offence reflecting moral turpitude or an offence related to the post to which he or she is applying may compete. Ethiopian nationals are given priority. Procedures for recruitment, probation, appointment, promotion, training, working hours, and other relevant issues have been standardized for all higher education institutions through the service regulations issued by the Higher Education Commission.

Because of these standardized regulations, there are no significant differences between the career and status of faculty in different types of institutions. Recruitment is the responsibility of the institution and in some cases subject to approval by a higher body or the Department of Higher Education within the ministry. Any position which is to last longer than three months must be approved by the ministry.

The criteria for promotion consists of the total number of years of service, academic qualifications, publications and contributions to knowledge in the field, academic commitment, and the dedication of the applicant. Candidates are nominated by the head of the institution and approved by the staff promotion committee.

Faculty interests are represented at various levels of the institution. At the department level, the general staff meeting is the site of overall participation in planning academic programs, and nominating members to serve in higher bodies of the institution, like the academic commission of a faculty. The academic commission decides various academic and administrative issues, including curriculum, employment, and promotion. In the case of a university, the senate or faculty council is composed of deans, faculty members elected by the staff, teachers' union, and student unions. All the higher education institutions have student representatives who are members of the Ethiopian Youth Association. The campus teachers association is also a branch of the National Teachers' Association in Ethiopia.

4.2 Students

The total number of students enrolled in higher education grew at something of an evolutionary pace until 1974 after which a significant change of enrollment has been indicated by various sources. According to Trudeau (1964), there were about 883 students in six institutions of higher learning or colleges but according to CHE (1989), there were about 16,945 students in higher education institutions in Ethiopia, and MOE (1988), indicated that there were about 16,589 students enrolled. The data from these three sources have been combined and indicated in Table 3.

Table 3
Distribution of students in general areas of studies

Years	1960	1965	1970	1975	1980	1985	1989
Students	883[a]	—	—	7,045[b]	—	16,815[c]	16,945[c]

a Trudeau (1964) b MOE (1988) c CHE (1989)

The only type of social classification for which there exists reliable data for students is that of gender. Available data does not indicate any other social breakdown. Thus this section concentrates on gender issues as they are reflected in the available sources.

The Ministry of Education (1988) reported that for the years 1974–88 the percentage of female primary students was 32, 38, 39, 39 and 38 percent while for junior secondary it was 30, 36, 38, 39 and 39 percent and for senior secondary it was 24, 35, 38, 39 and 38 percent for the respective years. In literacy classes the picture reverses for women and men. There are more female literacy participants than males. In higher education, the percentage of females was 8 percent in 1973–74 and still only 10 percent in 1987–88.

Students in higher education institutions have their own unions which organize political, social, and economic as well as cultural activities for the whole student body. The University Students Union of Addis Ababa (USUAA) and the National Union of Ethiopian Students (NUES) effectively mobilized students against the feudal system in 1974. They even reached the peasants and workers through literacy campaigns and the Ethiopian University Service programs. Although these and other unions are not political organizations, they have served as such and have exerted tremendous pressure on the feudal system, demanding radical land reform, freedom of speech and justice. These student unions played a substantial role in the 1974 mass movement against the feudal system.

Today, students have unions that are in fact branches of the national youth association. The Ethiopian Youth Association is a strong union that has representation in many important forums, like the National Shengo and the Party Central Committee. The higher education institutions invite student associations or unions to participate in important meetings, like the senate or faculty council and also in academic commissions in all institutions. Thus, students are represented in various policy and decision-making bodies.

Conclusion

The Commission for Higher Education has made various recommendations with regard to the further development of higher education in Ethiopia. Concerning the curriculum it proposes:

(a) Establishing and strengthening curriculum development, and establishing a coordination and evaluation body within the Higher Education Department to avoid duplication, and waste.

(b) Conducting a tracer study in consultation with graduates and employers to get the necessary feedback for the training program.

With regard to teachers, it suggests:

(a) Mandating one of the institutions to carry out inservice training for beginning teachers of higher education institutions.

(b) Formulating a regulation that stipulates the balance between teaching, research, and preparation of teaching materials and standardizing it for all higher education institutions.

(c) Improving the service regulations for the retirement of experienced teachers, based on experiences of other countries and the Ethiopian situation.

(d) Intensifying training for teachers of higher education institutions by procuring more scholarships, awards from foreign donor agencies, and the government budget.

(e) Recruiting more graduate assistants for teaching posts.

As for students it recommends:

(a) Replacing the ESLCE qualifications for entry into higher education institutions (in which weaknesses have been perceived in many studies) with another system of evaluation in which academic achievement, aptitude, and continuous evaluation summaries for grades 9–12 are components of the selection process.

(b) Formulating clear and standardized guidelines and admission policies concerning socially disadvantaged groups, such as women, residents of remote and extreme rural areas, and so forth.

Bibliography

Aggarwal J C 1971 *UNESCO's Contribution Towards World Education*. Arya Book Depot, New Delhi
Alemayehu R 1984 *Literacy for Work: A Comparative Study of Literacy Campaigns in Tanzania and Ethiopia*. MA thesis, McGill University, Montreal
Amare G 1982 Education in Ethiopia. In: Fafunwa A B,
Aisiku J U *Education in Africa: A Comparative Survey*. George Allen and Unwin, London
American Association for Higher Education 1981–86 *Current Issues in Higher Education*. AAHE Press
Brubacher J S, Rudy W 1976 *Higher Education in Transition*. Harper and Row, New York
Central Statistics Office 1987 *Facts and Figures about People's Democratic Republic of Ethiopia*. Bole Printing Press, Addis Ababa
Commission for Higher Education (CHE) 1989 *Evaluation of Higher Education in Ethiopia and Recommendations for Future Actions*. CHE Press, Addis Ababa
Curriculum Evaluation and Educational Research Division (CEERD) 1986 *Evaluative Research of the General Education System in Ethiopia (ERGESE): A Quality Study*. EMPDA, Addis Ababa
Eurich N P 1981 *Systems for Higher Education in Twelve Countries: A Comparative View*. Praeger, New York
Fagerlind I, Saha L 1985 *Education and National Development: A Comparative Perspective*. Pergamon, Toronto
Gordon M S 1974 *Higher Education and the Labor Market*. McGraw-Hill, Toronto
Joint Committee on Standards for Educational Evaluation 1981 *Standards for Evaluations of Educational Programs, Projects, and Materials*. McGraw-Hill, Toronto
Ministry of Education (MOE) 1987 *Educational Activities and Developments in the Past 13 years*. EMPDA, Addis Ababa
Ministry of Education (MOE) 1988 *Basic Education Statistics*. EMPDA, Addis Ababa
Mitzel H E 1982 *Encyclopedia of Educational Research*, 5th edn. The Free Press, London
National Comission on Excellence in Education 1983 *A Nation at Risk: The Imperative for Educational Reform*. US Government Printing Office, Washington, DC
Nigussie B 1988 *Traditional Wisdom and Modern Development*. University of Stockholm, Stockholm
Pankhurst S 1955, *Ethiopia: A Cultural History*. Fletcher and Son, Norwich
Provisional Military Administrative Council (PMAC) 1977 *Proclamation No. 109/1977 for Administration of Higher Education Institutions in Ethiopia*. Duplicated copy of the proclamation from CHE. Addis Ababa
Schaeffer S, Nkinyangi J H 1983 *Educational Research Environments in the Developing World*. IDRC, Ottawa
Stewart I 1978 Problems of teacher education in developing countries with special reference to Papua New Guinea: Some current strategies. *Br. J. Teach. Educ.* (3)
Trudeau E 1964 Higher education in Ethiopia. Doctoral dissertation, McGill University, Montreal
WPE 1985 *The Ethiopian Economic and Social Development Ten Year Plan*. WPE Press, Addis Ababa
Ayano T 1981 Evaluative Study of the Ethiopian Literacy Campaign Program (1979–81). Master's thesis University of Ibadan, Ibadan
UNESCO 1988 *Ethiopia-Development of University Education*. UNESCO, Paris.

T. Ayano

F

Finland

1. Higher Education and Society

The first Finnish university was established in 1640 in Turku. The Academy of Turku had four faculties: philosophy, theology, law, and medicine. When Finland came under Russian domination in 1809, a new period began. Czar Alexander I endowed 20 new professorships at the Academy. When fire destroyed most of Turku in 1827, Czar Alexander moved the academy to Helsinki and called it the Imperial Alexander University. It remained as the only university until 1908 when the Polytechnic Institute became the University of Technology. Higher education for business studies began with the Swedish School of Economics and Business Administration (until 1928 the Swedish Institute of Economics) in 1909, and then the commercial institute of Helsinki became the Helsinki School of Economics and Business Administration in 1911.

In 1917, after Finland had declared her independence, the Alexander University was renamed the University of Helsinki. Higher education developed rapidly in the early part of this century. Institutions of higher education were set up in Turku by private initiative: Åbo Akademi, The Swedish-language University of Turku, in 1917, and the University of Turku in 1920. In 1927 Turku gained its third institution of higher education when the Swedish School of Economics and Business Administration was established with Åbo Akademi. In 1980 it merged with Åbo Akademi. At the same time small institutions of higher education were created.

Most notable in the development of Finnish higher education has been its regional expansion since the end of the 1950s. The University of Oulu was established in 1958 to increase educational opportunities in northern Finland. Tampere University of Technology was established in 1965, and the University of Vaasa (until 1980 the Vaasa School of Economics and Business Administration) was founded in 1968. Eastern Finland received three new institutions of higher education during the 1960s and early 1970s: The Lappeenranta University of Technology, the University of Joensuu and the University of Kuopio. The University of Lapland was established in Rovaniemi in 1979.

In the 1960s and 1970s the major Finnish institutes were granted the status of institutions of higher education. Thus the institute of music became the Sibelius Academy in 1966, the institute of industrial arts became the University of Industrial Arts in 1973, and the institute of theater became the Theatre Academy in 1979. All of them are situated in Helsinki.

In the early 1990s Finland has 20 university-level institutions of higher education, including the three arts institutions.

After the Second World War Finland ceded certain areas of eastern Finland to the Soviet Union. Some 400,000 Karelians moved to Finland. After the war indemnities were paid in 1952 the economic development of Finland took off. Today Finland ranks eighth in the world in terms of national income.

The Finnish population began to grow immediately after the war. From 3.8 million in 1945 it increased to 4.9 million by 1985. Change was most pronounced in the 1950s and 1960s. After the Second World War most people lived in rural areas (67.7%), but in the 1950s many moved to towns to work and study. At the same time agriculture became highly mechanized meaning that fewer workers were needed. Urbanization continued up to the 1990s. However, some townspeople now want to return to the countryside. For example, small rural factories are being established by young well-educated people who wish to work and educate their children in a peaceful environment.

The Finnish have two official languages: Finnish and Swedish. The majority are Finnish-speaking: 91 percent in 1950 and 94 percent in 1987. The ever increasing numbers have major consequences for education planning. Swedish speakers live on the south and west coasts of Finland. Otherwise there is a very small Russian-speaking population and two other minority ethnic groups, the Lapplanders (Samis) people and gypsies. The former now number 1,710.

Finland's occupational structure changed considerably after the Second World War. Agriculture was a major source of employment until the 1960s, but lost workers to manufacturing from the 1970s, and to services and commerce in the 1980s. Economic development was very positive in the 1980s and at the beginning of the 1990s unemployment remains at only five percent. The forestry industry has a good export record. There is an agriculture surplus in Finland and difficulties in export along with this.

The political development of the country has been very consistent since the Second World War. Finland has emphasized its independence and neutrality. The Finnish Parliament had a nonsocialist majority from 1948 except between 1972 and 1978. The Conservative President Paasikivi held office from 1946 to 1956 when President Kekkonen of the Agricultural party (1956–81) displaced him. Kekkonen aimed to attract members of the government both from right and left. He was followed in 1982 by President Koivisto who appointed a coalition government from the Social Democratic Party, the National Coalition Party, the Swedish People's Party of Finland, and the Finnish Rural Party.

With the upturn in the economy, Finnish governments paid closer attention to higher education. One starting point was the principle of equal education for all, which emerges clearly in the regional distribution of institutions of higher education from the 1960s. Nowadays, the generally accepted goal of education is to promote equality among the population and to provide all young people with appropriate knowledge and skills. In the final analysis, education also helps to raise the standard of living and improve the quality of life. Educational equality requires an even distribution of schools and other educational facilities throughout the country. Further development of the education system will be based on the principle of continuing, lifelong education.

The new Higher Education Development Act came into force at the beginning of 1987. The Act governs all 20 institutions of higher education. It lays down a planning system, sets certain objectives for higher education development, and guarantees increases in higher education resources up to 1996. The main duties imposed by the Act relate to performance evaluation and to the intensification of research and graduate training.

Finland is possibly the most Lutheran country in Europe. In 1987, 88 percent of the population were members of the Lutheran Church, while 1.1 percent (56,428) people adhered to the Greek Orthodox Church. The University of Helsinki faculty of theology awards master's degrees in theology. Most graduates, both women and men, become priests of the Lutheran Church. The faculty is, however, independent of the Church and gives an academic training in theology. Once the Greek Orthodox Church had its own seminary in Kuopio, but in 1989 a new degree program began in the University of Joensuu.

2. The Institutional Fabric of the Higher Education System

In Finland the main responsibility for higher education rests with the state. All institutions of higher education were taken over by the state in the 1970s and 1980s. Figure 1 shows the various fields of study in the 20 institutions of higher education. Ten have multiple faculties: the Universities of Helsinki, Turku, Jyväskylä, Tampere, Vaasa, Joensuu, Kuopio, Oulu, Lapland, and the Swedish language University of Åbo Akademi. Ten are specialist institutions: the three universities of technology in Espoo, Tampere, and Lappeenranta; the two Finnish

Schools of economics and business administration in Helsinki and Turku; the College of Veterinary Medicine in Helsinki; and the three universities of the arts. Several universities have institutes of translation studies and further education units which are situated in another town.

Finnish educational policy aims at securing further studies for all students graduating from the comprehensive and upper secondary schools. Approximately one-fifth of these openings are in institutions of higher education. The formal requirement for higher education studies is the matriculation examination, taken at the end of the upper secondary school. The number of matriculated school leavers per year is around 30,000, while intake to higher education is slightly over 13,000.

All fields of higher education have a *numerus clausus*. As a rule, students are selected on the basis of their matriculation and school-leaving certificates and the entrance examination (and in some fields, an aptitude test). Each institution determines its own selection criteria and methods. Faculties of a given field may cooperate in selection. Measures have been taken to secure admission to higher education for nonmatriculated students. At present they represent about 1.5 percent of the total enrollment.

The Ministry of Education decides on the annual intake on the basis of proposals made by the universities.

Between 1960 and 1987 the number of students increased from 22,981 to 99,246, a positive development in which the establishment of new universities has been an essential factor. University students represented six percent of the population of 20–29 year olds in the year 1967–68 and by 1979–80 the figure was eight percent; by 1987 the percentage of university students aged 20–24 years represented 11.6 per cent of their age cohort and the 25–29 year olds accounted for 7.7 percent of that age group.

The Finnish basic qualification is the candidate degree. The average time needed for a basic degree varies according to the field of study. Those taking the Master of Education in 1985–86 studied for 4.9 years on average (the shortest time needed), while it took up to 10 years to complete the Master of Science in Architecture. Overall, the average length of course was approximately 6.5 years. In medicine, dentistry, and veterinary medicine, however, the basic degree is the licentiate, which is the first graduate degree and requires seven or eight years of study.

Higher education in Finland is free of charge: there are no tuition fees to be paid to the institute of higher education. Eligible students studying for a basic degree may obtain government assistance in the form of a state study grant and/or a state guarantee and interest support on loans from private financial institutions.

Graduate studies are divided into licentiate and doctorate degrees. The licentiate degree is optional

Name of Institution	Theology	The Humanities	Law	Social Sciences	Economics and Business Administration	Psychology	Education	Natural Sciences	Agriculture and Forestry	Sport Sciences	Engineering and Architecture	Medicine	Dentistry	Health Care	Veterinary Medicine	Pharmacy	Music	Industrial Arts	Theatre and Drama
University of Helsinki	●	●	●	●		●	●	●	●			●	●	●		●			
University of Joensuu	●a	●		●		●	●	●	●										
University of Jyväskylä		●		●	●	●	●	●		●				●					
University of Kuopio				●				●				●	●	●		●			
University of Oulu		●		●			●	●			●	●	●	●					
University of Tampere		●		●	●	●	●	●				●		●					●
University of Turku		●	●	●		●	●	●				●	●	●					
Åbo Akademi	●	●		●	●	●	●	●			●b			●					
University of Lapland			●	●			●												
University of Vaasa		●		●	●														
Helsinki School of Economics and Business Administration					●														
Swedish School of Economics and Business Administration					●														
Turku School of Economics and Business Administration					●														
Helsinki University of Technology											●								
Lappeenranta University of Technology											●c								
Tampere University of Technology											●								
College of Veterinary Medicine															●				
Sibelius Academy																	●		
University of Industrial Arts																		●	
Theatre Academy																			●

a Orthodox theology b Only forestry c Only engineering

Figure 1
Fields of study in the institutions of higher education

211

in the new system and the doctorate can now be taken without it. Everyone with a basic degree has the right to pursue graduate study in either form.

The optimum study period for the licentiate is two and a half years and four years for the doctorate. In practice the length of studies is significantly longer. Both degrees are predominantly research based. In addition to a thesis, each includes a total of one year of studies. Graduate studies are pursued quite independently, but some disciplines have organized special doctorate programs.

In 1987, 9,920 first degrees were obtained and 780 graduates received a further degree. In 1985 the latter numbered 650 (28 percent women). The distribution of doctorates and licentiates was: medicine 107, mathematics and natural sciences 191, technology 136; all others 216.

More than one-third of those taking a graduate degree obtained university posts, about one-fourth other research posts, and over a third found other jobs. The number of those obtaining posts outside the universities is rising and the rate of increase will be accelerated by various measures taken by the authorities.

3. Governance, Administration, and Finance

3.1 National Administration

The central administration of higher education is described in Fig. 2. Institutions of higher education are directly subordinate to the Ministry of Education. Matters involving higher education and scientific research are dealt with by the Department for Higher Education and Research at the Ministry. Tertiary-level education in the arts is administered by the Arts

Department of the Ministry, although there are plans to transfer it to the Department for Higher Education and Research in 1990.

The functions of the Department for Higher Education and Research include general development and the planning of higher education. The most important tasks relating to education are activity and economic plans, planning the distribution of study places, general planning of degrees and teaching, and administrative planning. Other tasks of the Department include preparing the annual budget and legislation on higher education to be considered by the Council of State or parliament. Development work is done in cooperation with institutions of higher education. Similarly, preparation of the annual budget and regulations involving institutions of higher education are mainly done on the basis of proposals made by these institutions.

The expert body consulted by the Ministry of Education in these matters is the Council for Higher Education, appointed by the Council of State for three years. The council formulates policies connected with the development and planning of Finnish higher education. It has five sections for different scientific fields: medicine, education, psychology, and so on. Members of these sections are professors or associate professors of the universities.

Since the 1980s all institutions of higher education have been state run but they can receive further private financing for various purposes, to establish new professorships and research projects, for instance.

University funds are allocated through the state budget approved by parliament. The Ministry of Education supervises expenditure and drafts the

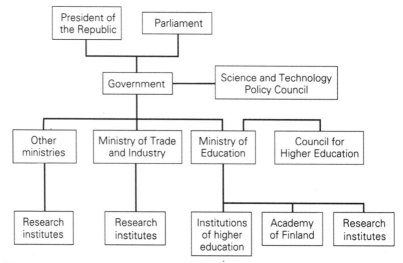

Figure 2
The administration of higher education and research in Finland

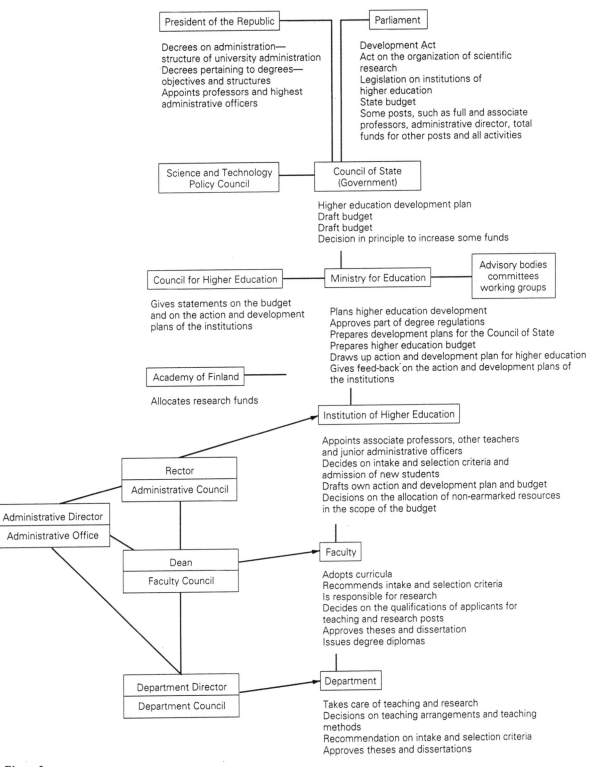

Figure 3
Levels of decision making for higher education

213

annual higher education budget on the basis of suggestions put forward by the institutions themselves and a statement on the matter made by the Council for Higher Education. The general framework for the proposal is grounded in the Higher Education Development Act. This contains minimum target numbers of study places in relation to facilities and teaching staff.

In higher education finance, a major step was taken when this Act came into force at the beginning of 1987. The government then took a decision which would in principle increase some important appropriations. This government decision guarantees an annual real increase of 15 percent in certain pivotal appropriations over the period 1988–91. The structure of the higher education budget has been gradually revised since 1987. Institutions have been granted considerably greater power to decide on the allocation of their resources. Now they can make the decisions on how to use their budget, for instance for establishing new professorships, or for purchasing new instruments.

Higher education expenditure, as a percentage of gross national product, was 0.61 percent in 1985, 0.66 percent in 1987, and 0.70 percent in 1988.

3.2 Institutional Administration

All institutions of higher education have their autonomy guaranteed by law for the administration of their internal affairs. A separate law has been passed for each institution, with a related statutory order stipulating in greater detail the limits of this self-regulation. The autonomy of the University of Helsinki is defined in the Constitution.

The traditional pattern of university administration has evolved toward a more democratic model. Thus, not only professors but also other teachers and staff, as well as students, are allowed to participate in the administration.

The reform introduced in the 1970s revised the administration of 11 institutions on a tripartite basis: one-third of the membership of administrative bodies to represent professors and associate professors, one-third other personnel, and one-third students. In the early 1980s these principles were again revised. In university administration, the trend (still current in the 1990s) is to simplify administrative procedures. New principles have also been adopted in the composition of the bodies. Figure 3 shows the main tasks in different levels of decision making for higher education, as well as the internal administration of some universities.

The administrative council is the supreme decision-making body of a university. It takes care of the overall administration and makes proposals for legislation and for the budget. The council approves the medium-term plan and other major plans and fills some posts. In certain regulations the administrative council is known as the government of the university.

A university is headed by a rector who is elected from among the professors to direct and supervise the activity of the university and to chair the administrative council. In the 1980s some universities have elected one rector and either one to two vice-rectors; the increased task load of the rectors was too much for one person to cope with. The administrative office prepares matters for different administrative bodies and implements decisions. It may also make decisions on minor issues. It is headed by an administrative director who is the rector's closest assistant and who supervises the work of the office.

Matters concerning teaching and studies are dealt with by faculty and department councils. The faculty councils develop instruction in the faculty, confirm curriculum proposals put forward by the department councils, supervise the administration of new students, and organize entrance examinations. The faculty councils also nominate candidates for vacancies at the professorial or associate professorial level. The department is the basic administrative unit for teaching and research in one or several subjects of study or fields of research. The department council is responsible for practical matters related to the organization of teaching. It also appoints professors to examine and approve graduate theses and equivalent levels of study.

4. Faculty and Students: Teaching, Learning, and Research

4.1 Faculty

Table 1 shows the development of academic teaching staff during 1960 to 1987, in which period their number increased from 2,496 to 7,538. Traditionally the main tasks of universities have been teaching and research. Full professors have the main obligation in this area. Associate professors, who often have similar qualifications in their specific field as professors, supervise the research of graduate students. Their number rose very quickly in the 1970s and 1980s.

The second teaching group comprises lecturers who have concentrated teaching tasks. Their teaching duty is 396–448 hours per academic year. The

Table 1

The number of teaching staff in the universities 1960–87

	1960–61	1970–71	1980	1987
Professors	477	648	829	980
Associate professors		364	628	753
Lecturers	156	451	1,470	1,681
Chief assistants				380
Assistants	1,863	1,595	1,893	1,803
Hourly, special, and docent	—	1,885	1,374	1,941
Total	2,496	4,943	6,194	7,538

third group is composed of assistants and chief assistants. Their main concern is research, and the writing of a thesis for which they have four years. According to regulations they can actually work in a department for ten years. Assistant positions are filled by graduate students. Beside their research, they have teaching duties on some courses. The fourth teaching group covers hourly, special, and docent teaching. The qualification for docent is a doctorate and wide research activity. Thus, a doctor must continue his or her research and publish several papers before applying for a docent post. Two experts within a faculty, usually professors or associate professors, will evaluate a scientific qualification. If their reports are positive, the faculty recommends to the chancellor or the administrative council of the university that the candidate be appointed as docent. Docents do not command good salaries; they are only paid for their teaching hours, which amount to 28–56 hours per academic year.

A major responsibility of each faculty and each department is the recruitment of new teaching staff. In Finland there is no central recruiting body. Information about new professorships or posts for lecturers or assistants is published in general and academic newspapers. The faculty directly elects new lecturers and assistants from among the applicants. For professorial positions they submit the three candidates they consider best for final selection by the chancellor or the administration council. The President of the Republic appoints professors to their posts.

Professors, lecturers, assistants, and docents have separate national staff associations which all belong to the central trade union (AKAVA). This body incorporates all academic professional associations. The union (AKAVA) organizes staff benefits and negotiates salaries and other matters with representatives of the state. There are also many scientific associations which have as their nucleus the delegation of the Finnish scientific associations. The association had 183 members in 1990.

Academic work in the universities is planned so that each member of teaching staff is subject to regulations influenced by legislation and by collective bargaining contracts. These regulations set down norms of teaching hours and other tasks. Standard teaching hours per academic year vary according to status. A professor's annual total is 144 hours, an associate professor's is 186 hours, while lecturers have a 396–448 hour teaching load and assistants between 60 and 120 hours.

4.2 Students

The number of students in the universities has increased greatly between 1960 and 1987, as is shown in Table 2. More detail of the situation in the late 1980s is given in Table 3.

The number of foreign students in Finnish universities has also increased, as Table 4 indicates.

Among student organizations are the national Union of Finnish Students, the student unions in all institutions of higher education, faculty and subject organizations, and various cultural and political organizations. These organizations are active in questions related to study, in student welfare, in international affairs, and, to an increasing degree in recent years, in cultural activities.

The most important student organization is the National Union of Finnish Students (SYL), established in 1921. It is an umbrella organization whose members are the student unions of institutions of higher education and a number of student organizations in other higher level educational institutions. Combined membership is approximately 86,500 students.

Legislation ensures that all undergraduate students enrolled in an institution of higher education are automatically members of a corresponding student union. The Ministry of Education approves the annual membership fee of the student unions. The administration of each student union is composed of an assembly, which is usually elected every two years and which in turn elects a cabinet and decides upon the need for hired staff. Candidates for student union elections often affiliate themselves with the Finnish political parties, but independent candidates have recently enjoyed a growth in popularity.

The student union plays an important role in the development and organization of housing, health care, and catering for students. Foreign students are usually admitted and have, with a few exceptions, the same rights and duties as Finnish members. There are, however, a few restrictions concerning the right of a foreigner to participate in the activities of a political party.

Before the 1970s the universities made independent decisions about their examinations. Their

Table 2

Number of students between 1960 and 1987

	1960	1965	1970	1975	1980	1987
All universities	22,981	38,337	58,751	71,011	82,996	99,246
Universities of science	22,261	37,416	57,476	69,607	81,379	97,454
Universities of arts	638	751	1,051	1,092	1,256	1,792

Table 3

Number of students in the 1987 autumn term and number of examinations passed in 1987 in universities and specialized institutions[a]

Field of study	Number of students in the autumn term				Examinations passed	
	total	of which female	new entrants	of which female	total	of which graduate
Teacher education	11,373	8,064	2,118	1,515	1,651	11
Fine and applied arts	1,792	967	282	154	208	—
Humanities	17,398	13,079	2,220	1,657	1,039	80
Religion and theology	1,721	798	183	98	116	17
Social and behavioral sciences	9,807	5,785	1,086	672	820	78
Commerce and business administration	12,101	5,607	1,712	863	1,355	31
Law and jurisprudence	4,022	1,753	503	234	551	15
Natural science	8,716	4,192	1,340	653	812	169
Mathematics and computer science	5,423	1,570	912	288	384	49
Medical science and health	6,672	4,455	964	699	997	161
Engineering	15,114	2,170	2,238	407	1,161	141
Architecture and town planning	1,457	605	113	53	91	4
Agriculture, forestry, and fishery	2,993	1,417	343	166	371	32
Home economics	178	168	18	17	24	1
Mass communication documentation	297	160	51	27	29	—
Others and unspecified	182	80	11	8	43	7
Total	99,246	50,870	14,094	7,511	9,652	796

a According to the UNESCO International Standard of Classification of Education

own basic regulations provided for undergraduate and graduate studies. In 1974 the government reformed basic degrees broadening their scope, to stress professional aspects in planning study courses, and to facilitate a more efficient integration of both professional and scientific elements. Each university department also reformed its own degree course according to the general framework outlined by the Ministry of Education. Within this framework the

Table 4

Foreign students in the Finnish universities

	1978	1984	1987
Nordic countries	94	148	177
Sweden	68	99	118
Norway	10	22	21
Denmark	10	12	22
Iceland	6	15	16
Other Europeans	211	291	375
Asia	91	168	211
Africa	86	170	218
North America	85	118	141
South America	34	24	21
Australasia	3	7	5
Unknown	1	3	20
Total	605	929	1,168

universities may determine curricula and degree courses themselves. Universities criticized the reform for laying too much stress on the professional dimension of higher education.

A degree course concentrates upon a specific, socially relevant field where scientific expertise is needed. As a multidisciplinary and objective-oriented whole, the degree course aims at the combination of scientific knowledge, theory, and practice. Students may concentrate on a main subject, studying this in depth, while also following studies in two to four subsidiary subjects. For example, a student might have education sciences as a main subject with further studies in perhaps history, psychology, archeology, and psychiatry.

Basic degrees are assessed in credit units. One credit unit refers to an input of approximately 40 hours of work. The usual minimum for a degree course is 160 credit units. To obtain a medical degree 240–250 credit units are required.

5. Conclusion

All 20 institutions of higher education in Finland stress their extensive autonomy in teaching and research and in other internal matters. Their tasks were defined in the 1986 Higher Education Development Act as being: "to promote and undertake free research, give tertiary-level academic and art instruction based on it, and otherwise promote culture and academic education." Autonomy means that universities wish to develop liberal education rather than to reinforce vocational aims. Universities are not business institutions and cannot follow their norms. The Academy of Finland has evaluated some fields of science since the early 1980s. This evaluation is valuable and will continue. Considerable criticism has been levelled at national resource allocation. The Ministry of Education has turned its attention to the length of study in basic degree and graduate courses. Basic degree studies take six or seven years on average, but there are fields in which they may even take 10 years. One purpose of higher education reform is to reduce the average to five or six years. The reason for delayed graduation is usually that students have part-time or full-time jobs or study a great number of secondary subjects. The students have stressed their desire for freedom in their studies and dislike exact time limits.

Bibliography

Martti K 1985 Degree reform of higher education in Finnish Universities in 1966–1974. In: *Seventh International Standing Conference for the History of Education*, Vol. 1. Salamanca, pp. 362–71

Ministry of Education 1984 *Educational Development in Finland 1981–1984*. Reference Publications 12. Ministry of Education, Helsinki

Ministry of Education 1987 *Higher Education Development Program for 1987–1992 Approved by the Government*. Ministry of Education, Department for Higher Education and Research, Helsinki

Ministry of Education 1988 *Development of Education 1986–1988*. Reference Publications 14. Ministry of Education, Helsinki

M. T. Kuikka

France

1. Higher Education and Society

The University of Paris, along with the University of Bologna, and Montpellier were the founding models of the European university. First recognized by the Papal Bulls issued in 1208–1210 by Innocent III, which conferred the rights of internal autonomy on those teaching in Paris, the University underwent various fortunes. The Sorbonne was founded in 1257 by Robert de Sorbon, confessor to St Louis, and in 1292 a further Papal Bull conferred the right to grant *licencia ubique docendi*. Prior to the Revolution of 1789, universities in France found themselves in frequent conflict with the authority of the Church Universal as well as that of the King. Though enjoying considerable status and esteem for some 300 years, they underwent a marked decline in the course of the eighteenth century.

The French Revolution of 1789 abolished the universities on the grounds that, as guilds and corporations, they constituted a privileged body. They were swept away under the Le Chapelier Law of 1791, though many historians argue that their intellectual death took place well before.

The creation of the Imperial University (*l'Université Imperiale*) by Napoleon I between 1806 and 1808 marks the establishment of the modern French higher education system. Strictly speaking, the Imperial University was not a university in the modern sense. It was, from a legal and organizational perspective, a public foundation in which was vested the responsibility for the whole of educational provision in France, enjoying monopoly powers *de facto* and *de jure* under the Catholic Church and under the state in law only.

The French Revolution and the First Empire also took the initiative of founding a number of *grandes écoles*, essentially specialized institutions, closely linked to the service of the state. Among them one may note the *Ecole Polytechnique*, first established in 1795 to provide artillery officers for the Army and the *Ecole Normale Supérieure* in 1808 to provide teachers for secondary and higher education.

After the reconstitution of the faculties and the establishment of universities in the latter part of the nineteenth century, French higher education assumed its most noteworthy feature: a structural segmentation between the universities on the one hand and the *grandes écoles* on the other. A further dichotomy resulted from the decision, taken by parliament in 1875 that higher education was to be free. The Law on the Freedom of Higher Education of that year, set down a second division between the private sector *grandes écoles* and private sector universities and the public sector—legally designated as the *service public de l'enseignement supérieur* that came under the state.

1.1 Relationship with Religious Bodies

With the promulgation of the Law on the Freedom of Higher Education, the Catholic Church expected a major expansion in Catholic higher education to take place. This did not happen. In fact, church universities existed in Paris, Lyon, Lille, Toulouse, and Angers, but they were—and today remain so still—the only religious institutions of higher education. The public sector retained its supremacy.

For reasons of history and its particular geographical location, the University of Strasbourg, which is a state university, includes faculties of both Protestant and Catholic theology. This springs from the fact that for some 47 years between 1871 and 1918, Alsace-Lorraine was part of the German Empire. With the return of the two provinces to France, French legal judgment took the view that the separation between Church and state which took place in the rest of France in 1905, did not apply to the newly recovered territories.

For the major part of the higher education system which in fact covers not only public institutions but also those in the private sector where members of the Church do not teach, the fundamental legal principle is that of secularism (*laïcité*).

1.2 Occupational and Social Class Structure

Throughout the nineteenth century and well on into the twentieth, France was predominantly a rural country. In 1911, for instance, some 17,444,948 people lived in towns with some 22,096,052 in communes of 2,000 inhabitants or less. The major period of urbanization took place in the 1950s and 1960s when a quite massive exodus from the countryside set in, thus shifting radically the balance between urban and country dwellers firmly in favor of the former.

Higher Education was within reach of only the offspring of the upper and middle classes. For the most part, higher education was organized around the major faculties of medicine, science, law, humanities and a few engineering schools, which were often organized separately from the university. The government faced considerable difficulties in developing such areas as technology.

The situation just described changed quickly. By 1980, some 33,633,168 people lived in urban areas and 17,207,309 in what was officially designed as rural areas. In the 1990s some 80 percent of the French population are urban dwellers.

In the postwar period and most particularly during the 1950s France, like many other European countries, saw a demographic upsurge. Often popularly known as the "school explosion" (*l'explosion scolaire*), it bore down particularly heavily upon the National Ministry of Education, and over the past 20 years has worked its way up to higher education. Student numbers in higher education rose massively from 265,000 in 1960–61 to 747,000 a decade later to reach 1,488,651 in the academic year 1988–89. For establishments coming under the administrative oversight of the Ministry of National Education the age participation rate in higher education for the university year 1988–89 was 31.2 percent of 20 year-olds, 20.4 percent of 21 year-olds, 13.7 percent of 22 year-olds, and 9.6 percent for those aged 23 years. This is certainly lower than the corresponding statistic for the United States, Japan, and West Germany. The participation rate for the age group 18–24 is lower than that found in the United States and Japan, but higher than Germany or the United Kingdom. Today (1991) around 30 percent of the age group 20–24 are studying. By the end of the century the French government aims at a total enrollment in higher education of 1,800,000 students in which case some 60 percent of the cohort aged 20–24 will be made up of students. Since 1984 successive governments, both right-wing coalition and socialist have set an extremely high target for the numbers of

school students reaching a level of academic attainment equivalent to the *baccalauréat*, that is, the school-leaving certificate normally sat by upper-secondary school students in their last year at around 18 years of age. To give some measure of the degree of expansion that has taken place over the past thirty years, one has only to remember that in 1960–61 those in higher education accounted for 2.7 percent of the whole population of pupils and students. Today, the similar statistic is 9.1 percent.

Government policy, the attitudes freely developed in the family, the condition of France in the world market, social demand for higher education, the successful increase in the numbers of students passing the *baccalauréat* and last, but not least, demography are all factors which contribute to the development of the role and the functions that higher education is called upon to assume.

In the earlier part of the 1980s, the enrollments in higher education increased on average by 2.3 percent per annum, and during the two years from 1988 to 1990, reached 4 percent. Thus, in the space of seven years, higher education has seen its numbers swell by 208,000. First-cycle studies which last two years after entry to higher education, face the prospect over the next ten years of an extra 300,000 students.

Of all those enrolled in higher education, 12.5 percent come from abroad and of these more than 40 percent are congregated in Paris. By far the larger part come from the North African Arabic-speaking states or from the former French-speaking colonies in West Africa.

1.3 Structure of the Economy

If the agricultural sector is important even today it is a fact that the number of those engaged in this occupation is falling. For this reason, the number of students admitted to higher education institutions that correspond to this area of activity are kept to a strict minimum. In the primary economic sector, control over higher education is exercised by the Ministry of Agriculture. Teaching is given in secondary schools of a technical nature and at post-secondary level and leads to a technical qualification called the *brévét de technicien supérieur* (BTS) which is usually sat two years after the *baccalauréat*. Such courses are also provided in technical engineering establishments, either public or private in nature, following on from two years of study in specialized classes in the top section of the academic upper-secondary school—the *lycée*—and termed classes in preparation for *grandes écoles*. These classes are highly selective. In the university year 1987–88, the number of students following courses in agricultural sciences was 8,060, of which 2,389 were in private establishments. Some 8,500 were in state sector secondary schools preparing a BTS with a further 3,619 studying for the same qualification in private schools. Most institutions teaching agronomic sciences and agricultural engineering are located in the Paris region, in the West of France (Rennes, Nantes, or Angers) or in the South at Montpellier and Toulouse.

The way higher education develops has implications for the secondary and the tertiary sectors of the national economy. Even so, the number of students following engineering courses, a key element in a modern day economy, has increased far less rapidly than the rest of the university population. An official enquiry, recently conducted in 1989 by the Commission of Enquiry into Higher education and the state of the economy (*Haut Comité Economie Education*) reckoned that the outflow of graduates from the engineering schools—approximately 14,000 per year—is only half of the country's needs. In addition, France faces a shortage in business studies graduates not to mention a shortfall of some 120,000 people, both men and women, needed for the sales force in the tertiary sector.

1.4 Structure of Government and Main Political Goals

The Fourth Republic (1946–58) was a regime not over-remarkable for the efforts it made in the area of higher education. With the advent of the Vth Republic in 1958 a more interesting period set in, highlighted with the Student Revolution of 1968. In the aftermath of those events, the Parliament voted a Bill in November 1968 which today bears the name of its instigator Edgar Fauré, then Minister of Education. This law served as the overall legal framework for university education in France until the return of the Left to power in 1981. The then Minister of Education, Alain Savary, drew up a new bill which, voted by parliament on January 24, 1984 stands as the basic law for that part of higher education which falls under the remit of the Ministry of Education, though by no means exclusively so.

The tasks and goals set down in the 1968 Higher Education Guideline Law were maintained and developed further by its successor of 1984, though the Savary Law, for political reasons, applies across the board irrespective of the particular ministry which exercises oversight—and this can extend to the Ministry of Defense and as we have seen earlier, the Ministry of Agriculture. There are, however, certain exceptions, principally the private sector higher education system existing in the sense that the tasks laid upon state sector higher education are not mandatory on the private sector. Organizationally, however, each sector often retains its own particular forms.

The tasks of higher education are set down as follows:

(a) to develop research and advance the level of science, culture, and vocational training for the nation as well as the individual citizen;

(b) to advance the development of the nation and its regions in the areas of the economy, politics, and employment;

(c) to take a positive stance against social and cultural inequality between the genders, and to provide as far as possible, access to culture, knowledge, and research.

The Guideline Law of July 10, 1989 gave further confirmation to these tasks. Much of the public discourse of successive governments have stressed the responsibility which higher education has in determining the place of the nation in an economically competitive world, both in the European Community and also worldwide.

2. The Institutional Fabric of the Higher Education System

In France, the legal tradition is one in which, except for private sector education, the state exercises control over the public sector institutions and universities in such domains as political decision making, as well as those decisions of a financial and administrative nature.

2.1 The Sectoral Organization of Higher Education and Levels of Institution

Private sector higher education in France accounts for a very small proportion in terms of both institution and enrollment. In the academic year 1988–89 for instance, there were some 13,050 engineering students in private sector establishments, compared with 10,224 in public sector higher education coming under the oversight of ministries other than education and a further 29,588 engineering students in state sector higher education. A not dissimilar situation is found with regard to student enrollments in business studies. Private sector business schools totaled 28,999 with a further 6,230 enrollments in the highly selective preparatory classes (*classes préparatoires aux grandes écoles*) located in certain *lycées* but 43,632 business studies students in the state sector. In the area of higher technicians' studies, students numbered 58,475 in the private and 75,056 in the public sectors respectively. Finally, enrollments in universities were 18,361 for the private sector and 1,036,628 in the public sector.

The degree of formal independence which the private sector enjoys vis à vis the overall decisions reached by the state is relatively restricted. Certain laws permit different ministries to grant financial assistance. Nevertheless, the state reserves the monopoly over validation and accreditation of degrees and diplomas. It may, if it is so disposed, grant recognition to a private establishment (*habilitation*) or it may also grant validation of its courses certifying that they are of a standard equivalent to that of the public sector (*homologation*). Both practices are not infrequent in the case of business schools. However, such validation or recognition is not general. Rather, it is the result of decisions reached at different times by different ministries. From a legal perspective, many private sector institutes of higher education are formed as associations, a device that is particularly useful for private sector institutions specialized in agriculture, business studies, nursing, and paramedical fields—with the exception of medical doctors and pharmacists—and private sector arts academies.

The private sector can be divided into three parts:

(a) The first is fully independent with control only exercised over the formal qualifications of those teaching. Such establishments may themselves determine student admission, select their own teachers, draw up their own courses, award their own diplomas, and manage their own affairs. There are both good and less good establishments in this category. Included are establishments teaching such fields as music, fine art, business, informatics, and foreign languages. A few even award first degrees from United States universities.

(b) The second deals with vocational training in the main. In this area the state gives its assent, financial support, and in those instances where students are not enrolled in officially recognized state diplomas, will grant some degree of validation. Schools in this sector tend to specialize in marketing, medical technology, and nurse training. Those business schools which are organized out of the Chambers of Commerce figure here.

(c) The third is composed of those universities or selective schools which operate within the framework of legislation governing state recognized courses and prepare their students for state degrees and diplomas. In law, such establishments have private status. In organizational matters they are free to set their own teaching methods, choose their own teachers, select their students, and also set the fee levels.

The state sector comes under the responsibility of the state. Here again, we may subdivide this sector into two parts. The first part, made up of the *grandes écoles*, comes under the responsibility of various different ministries. Among them are the various national agronomic institutes and schools of fine arts, music, dance, and theater, some of which come under the state, while others are the responsibility of local government. Also included under this head are the Civil Service Staff College (*Ecole Nationale d'Administration*), various military and engineering schools such as St. Cyr (army officer training), the *Ecole Polytechnique*, establishments training admin-

istrators for the Health Service, schools of architecture and town planning, and merchant marine and cadet naval officers' training establishments. Students are rigorously and highly selected by competitive entry examination which are becoming increasingly selective.

The second part is composed of engineering schools, the universities, and those *grandes écoles* which come under the direct responsibility of the Ministry of Education.

Research training begins with the so-called third cycle, that is, after a minimum of five years' study in higher education, and is marked by the *diplôme d'études approfondies*. Academic staff undertake research both individually and as members of a team in laboratories. University research is naturally significant but a large proportion is carried out under contract with the major research establishments that are organized in parallel to the university, examples of which are the *Institut National de la Recherche Agronomique*, the *Commissariat à la Recherche Atomique*, the *Centre National d'Etudes Spatiales*, the *Centre National de la Recherche Scientifique*, and the *Institut National de la Santé et de la Recherche Médicale*, and so on.

Students undergoing training to become primary-school teachers follow courses in normal schools (*écoles normales d'instituteurs et d'institutrices*). Secondary-school teachers are recruited by national competition and subsequently undergo a period of induction. If some among them are graduates from the *écoles normales supérieures*, others were until recently trained in *centers de formation pédagogique*—teacher-training centers. One of the most recent reforms introduced by the government in 1991 has been to revise the institutional base of teacher education and to bring it into the universities in the form of *instituts universitaires de formation*.

Higher education includes all programs after the *baccalauréat*. Universities also operate a special examination for entry for those young people who have not obtained the *baccalauréat*. Work experience can also be taken into consideration when applying through this route.

2.2 Admissions Policies and Selection

Selective entry to higher education including the *grandes écoles* has been dealt with above. Within the selective sector these establishments go under various different names—national school (*école nationale*), institute, and school. They recruit very well qualified students who are usually destined for high level specialized training of a professional nature. These schools—engineering schools, *écoles supérieures*, and *grandes écoles*—are part of a very tight hierarchy often commanding considerable prestige and repute. To graduate and be in the upper part of the rank order of graduation is often extremely important through an individual's later career.

Table 1
Enrollment trends within the selective sector 1960–88

Year	1960–61	1970–71	1980–81	1985–86	1987–88	1988–89
Engineering schools	20,770	30,512	36,952	45,095	49,287	52,782
Business schools	5,286	9,395	17,730	28,633	28,993	33,265
Preparatory programs for engineering and business schools	21,038	32,349	39,357	47,334	53,267	57,940

Though in the past, some students have gone forward to doctoral level study, this is not a usual pattern for this type of establishment. Table 1 sets out the enrollment trends for certain types of establishment in the selective sector.

There is no selection for entry to university for those entering on a first degree. However, some exceptions to this general rule exist in the form of the two-year University Institutes of Technology, founded in 1966 and now numbering some 56 across the country. Enrollment patterns for the University Institutes of Technology are set out in Table 2. Entry to medicine, dentistry, and pharmacy is also selective; enrollments are set out in Table 3.

If entry to first-cycle studies which last two years is open with the exceptions noted above, the second cycle—also of two years' duration, is open to all who have passed a first-cycle diploma. One ought to bear in mind that any subject area can, if it wishes, impose selection either via competitive examination or by an examination of the student's school record sheet.

The third cycle involves training for research and training by research with all students being selected after their *maîtrise* (master's examination).

Of those entering higher education in the early 1990s around two out of five are in the selective sector: 9.2 percent in health sciences; 9.8 percent in the preparatory classes, and 27.5 percent in technological education. In 1988, first-time entrants to higher education were 10.6 percent in preparatory classes, 10.5 percent in the University Institutes of Technology, and 24.2 percent in the higher technicians sections which are post-*baccalauréat* studies usually located atop certain specialized secondary schools. The nonselective tracks of universities accounted for 53.8 percent of enrollments in higher education. Whether to select or not is a highly charged issue. But the current trend among students

Table 2
Enrollment patterns for the University Institutes of Technology 1970–88

1970–71	1980–81	1985–86	1986–87	1987–88	1988–89
24,195	53,826	62,867	63,705	65,769	65,941

Table 3
Enrollments for medical sciences 1960–88

1960–61	1970–71	1980–81	1985–86	1987–88	1988–89
40,235	136,162	188,802	170,353	157,167	154,881

and also among their families has had the effect of extending the selective sector farther across the higher education system.

2.3 Structure of Qualifications

Whether in the public or the private sector, the duration of studies for engineering and business schools is between two to three years. In effect, if one counts the time elapsed since the individual passed the *baccalauréat* this is around four to five years once one takes account of the two years spent in a *classe préparatoire*. The diplomas awarded as well as the title, which in the case of engineers is state protected and the conditions of certification, all come under state control.

With the exception of the University Institutes of Technology which have already been described, the structure of studies in university is based on three cycles. The first, with the exceptions mentioned earlier, lasts two years. At the end of the first year, a selection is made for those who wish to proceed into the area of health sciences. At the end of the first cycle, students will obtain a *diplôme d'études universitaires générales* (DEUG). The time taken to complete the first cycle is, in point of fact, often nearer three years than two, though the latter is the normally expected time required. Pass rates vary: in law and economics 37 percent are awarded the DEUG after two to three years; 44 percent in sciences; and 50 percent in humanities and social sciences. Dropout rates after one year in humanities and social sciences are in the order of 85 percent—40 percent in sciences and 45 percent in law and economics.

Clearly, all is not well with the first cycle. Graduates holding the DEUG are approximately 25,000 in humanities and social sciences, 20,000 in law and economics, and 15,000 in science. In addition, some 22,000 students from the University Institutes of

Technology obtain a *diplôme universitaire de technologie*.

If the second cycle lasts two years, students are allowed to take only one year to complete their *licence*. In 1988, for instance, some 58,493 *licences* were awarded: 10,077 in law; 4,664 in economics; 25,514 in the humanities; and 12,943 in science. The following year moves on to the *maîtrise* of the master's degree in applied science (*maîtrise de sciences et techniques*). Some 42,983 masters' degrees were awarded in 1987: 8,818 in law; 5,891 in economics; 13,387 in humanities, and 12,275 in science.

Those wishing to study further may opt either for the *diplôme d'études supérieures spécialisées* (in 1988 some 10,502 did so), or they may choose the *diplôme d'études approfondies* (17,915 students elected this track). The doctorate lies at the end of this path. In 1988 doctors were capped in the following areas: 408 in law; 425 in economics; 1,871 in the humanities; and 4,070 in the sciences.

3. Governance, Administration, and Finance

Private sector higher education was discussed in Sect. 2. In the case of the public sector there are three aspects to be considered: (a) the power of the state; (b) the situation of local government; and (c) the civil service.

(a) Though Parliament votes on laws for higher education, the last two major bills have been drawn up by government. The latter has responsibility for drawing up the law. The exercise of formal responsibility in higher education falls to the government with certain minor exceptions which relate to teaching in the private sector. This responsibility extends to course outline approval, the quality and award of diplomas, and the financial domain in the public sector, and involves the organizational form and control over institutions, schools, and universities. The state opens establishments and determines the programs taught either by dint of formal regimentation or by the application of financial resources.

The proportion of Gross Domestic Product (GDP) spent on higher education was 0.41 percent in 1957, 0.39 percent in 1980, and 0.4 percent in 1988. In a few years one may anticipate an increased amount of public expenditure under this head and it is one of the more pressing issues in France. During the five years of the Ninth Plan, both central and local government set aside 750,000,000 Ffrs (US$126,063,130)—and this does not include the state budget—on higher education expenditure. The equivalent sum estimated for the Tenth Plan has been set at 2,085,000,000 Ffrs (US$350,455,500). The Financial Law of 1990 underwrote an increase of 54 percent in the public expenditure for building and other equipment compared to the figures of 1989. And in January 1990, the Minister of Education, Lionel Jospin, unveiled an emergency plan which set aside some 400,000,000 Ffrs (US$67,233,670) for the coming year.

(b) The effect of demography plus the demand for higher education, both of which have direct repercussions for the universities have obliged the state to seek the support of local government. Thus, the voluntary support the latter has given is on a level with the amount the state set aside for the building budget. Not surprisingly, local government is looking for a greater share in power to match the burden it has assumed.

(c) Outside the administration of the Ministry of Education, the *grandes écoles*, civil servant colleges, and engineering schools are often part of the service of the Ministry to which they are attached.

Those establishments coming under the ambit of the Ministry of Education, however, that is, institutes, higher teacher training colleges (*écoles normales supérieures*), and the *grandes écoles* are administered by a director and an advisory body. The director is usually a ministry appointment. The advisory board (*conseil*) is elected on the basis of electoral colleges with constituencies composed of teachers, students, and technical, administrative, and clerical personnel.

The 73 universities and the three National Polytechnic Institutes of Grenoble, Nancy, and Toulouse are officially *établissements publics* of a scientific, cultural, and vocational nature. They have a juridical personality and thus have financial and administrative autonomy. They are administered by an administrative council, a scientific council, and also a council for teaching and university affairs. All involve election including the university president. They exercise legal oversight and for this reason stand as an important element in the relationship between each university and school. The central ministry is the *recteur d'académie, chancellier de l'université*. He or she is appointed by government and represents the official power of the ministry in the appropriate educational region of which there are 27 in France.

Central administration determines the number of student places in those areas subject to a *numerus clausus* as is the case for medicine, dentistry, pharmacy, and engineering schools. It also allocates staff to posts. Under previous governments, the state made appointments in the case of teaching staff, administration, and technical services. It also assigns buildings and allocates money. In the interests of equity, formula financing was used and based on a complex equation which took account of student numbers, surface area equipment costs, and the type of teaching undertaken, for example, science, law, and humanities. These norms, having been introduced in 1977, are now surpassed and a new system is being introduced. Each university is called upon to draw up a forward plan encompassing teaching, research, international collaboration, and so on. After scrutiny by the Ministry, this plan is translated into a contract between the Ministry and the submitting party, be it university, *grande école*, and so on, which will last for a period of four years. As partner of the state, the establishment can be assured of receiving salaries for posts, expenditure, and for the upkeep of buildings. Evaluation will subsequently be made a posteriori by the National Evaluation Committee which, established in 1985, was given independent administrative authority in 1989.

4. Faculty and Students: Teaching, Learning, and Research

4.1 Faculty

Sixty percent of teaching staff are in the areas of science or medicine. Full professors account for some 25 percent of all academic staff, and *maîtres de conférences* (roughly equivalent to the American associate professor) constitute 40 percent of all academic staff in establishments coming under the ambit of the Ministry of Education. In 1988–89 the total academic strength of university teachers was 45,570. Of these 13,162 were full professors, 19,487 were *maîtres de conférences*, and 8,523 were *assistants*.

Appointment to professorial posts in the fields of law, economics, and management is subject to a nationwide competitive examination, centrally set. In other fields, selection is made by committee on the basis of the qualifications and publications of the individual applicant. All tenured academics are civil servants. If careers are primarily a matter for the state, it remains a fact that the individual university may choose its appointments, and furthermore, promotion to the grade of *maître de conférence* is determined by peer review. Each major academic discipline has a national disciplinary council which exercises oversight and upholds quality, so that even with the status of civil servant, the individual's status is dependent on a jurisdiction emanating from the discipline of which he or she is part.

In medicine, teachers have two institutional bases—the hospital and the university.

The exact balance between teaching and research is not laid down in formal statutes. Only in teaching are the number of hours laid down and this tends to apply more to the *maître de conférence* than for the full professor whose obligations though expressed in total hours per year are not fixed in terms of hours per week. Even so, these norms are determined nationally.

The use of part-time teaching staff is a feature among others of the University Institutes of Technology. The advantage of this is held to be that it gives opportunities for those who are practitioners in business or public service to be able to convey their expertise to students.

Apart from their formal representation on the three university councils, academic staff have their own representative structures in the form of a national consultative council and commissions that deal with promotion. There are three main trade unions. In addition, various associations often nationally organized are to be found among alumni, sometimes to represent the interests of their alma mater, sometimes as discussion and debating bodies. Among them are the Association of Engineering Schools, the Association of the Deans of Law Faculties, and so on.

Nonteaching technical and clerical personnel coming under the administrative ambit of the Ministry of Education number some 40,000.

4.2 Students

We have already attended to trends in overall student enrollment (see Table 1). Overall student numbers for the period 1960–61 to 1987–88 for all higher education minus private universities and inter- or multidisciplinary programs are set out in Table 4.

Student social class background on the basis of the social status of the head of the family as of 1987–88 is set out in Table 5, which is broken down according to the level of studies—first, second, and third cycles.

Though student unions exist, their membership accounts for only an extremely small percentage of all

Table 4
Enrollments in public sector universities in France 1960–88[a]

	1960–61	1970–71	1980–81	1985–86	1987–88
Exact sciences	132,107	294,413	397,842	423,273	418,491
Social sciences (law, economics, and business)	41,807	166,734	223,114	285,758	292,545
Humanities	66,814	233,605	262,665	309,959	322,644

a Private sector and interdisciplinary programs not included

Table 5
Student social class background according to level of studies 1987–88

Social status of head of family	First cycle	Second cycle	Third cycle
Farmers	3.7	3.6	3.2
Agricultural workers	0.6	0.5	0.5
Industry or business employers	8.2	7.9	7.5
Liberal and *cadres supérieurs*	25.6	32.5	35.7
Cadres moyens	19.6	17.6	13.9
Employees	9.3	7.5	5.2
Workers	15.4	10.8	6.7
Service personnel	1.6	1.3	1.2
Others	16.0	18.3	26.1
Total	100	100	100

in higher education. Student unions are considered primarily to be political affiliations as opposed to student welfare or sporting associations. Students have the right to be kept informed of developments in the university. They have formal rights of participation on the various university councils. Even so, student participation in the elections to student office is minimal.

5. Conclusion

French humor which is always critical and sometimes wry has a neat comment to make about the differences in the nation's higher education system. It is extremely difficult to get into the *grandes écoles*, but one can graduate having done little work. On the other hand, it is easy to get into university, but it is hard to graduate without working inordinately hard. That said, there are three major problems that face France. The first of these is the sharing of the rising burden of the cost of higher education between central and local government. This contains a potential for political conflict between the two parties. It also has a high potential for student unrest. The second is that the *grandes écoles* and other national schools maintain a Malthusian policy to preserve their reputation and the excellent job prospects their graduates enjoy on leaving which revolves around highly competitive and selective entry examinations. But this shortage of well-qualified people has its consequences for firms. Often they find the cost of employing such brilliant youth too high. And the needs of business are not always met in the training the young and talented receive. The third problem is that the universities take the remainder who have not been selected, and do so without sufficient teachers, without adequate equipment, and without suitable buildings. And then, the internal selection whether self-selection or not, nevertheless excludes large numbers of able students who find their needs unmet. In truth, the social and financial costs of the French higher education system are very high.

Bibliography

Bienaymé A 1986 *L'enseignement supérieur et l'idée d'université*. Economica, Paris

Boisanté J L, Jouve H 1989 *L'enseignement agricole à l'horizon 2000*. Rapport au ministre de l'agriculture et de la forêt collection des rapports officiels. La documentation française, Paris

Bonhotal J P 1989 L'autonomie financière des universités. *Revue du Trésor*

Bonhotal J P 1989 L'organisation budgétaire, financière et comptable dans l'enseignement supérieur. *Actualité juridique droit administratif*

Carpentier A 1988 *Le mal universitaire*. R. Laffont, Paris

Clerc D 1987 Enseignement supérieur: l'intendance ne suit pas. *Alternatives économiques*

Comité national d'évaluation 1989 *Priorités pour l'université*. Rapport au Président de la République (1985–1989). La documentation française, Paris

Devaquet A (ed.) 1988 *L'amibe de l'étudiant. Université et recherche: l'état d'urgence*. Odile Jacob, Paris

Durand-Prinborgne C 1988 Evolution et juridication de l'enseignement supérieur en France in Recent Trends in European Higher Education. *Eur. J. Educ.* 23(1/2)

Durand-Prinborgne C 1989 *Propos impertinents à une vieille dame: l'education nationale*. Retz, Paris

Durand-Prinborgne C 1990 Politique nationale? Politiques régionales? Les contrats de plan etat-régions. *Savoir Education Formation* 1

Eicher J C 1979 *Economie de l'éducation*. Economica, Paris

Eicher J C Pauvre université française. *Projet* 205

Friedberg E, Musselin C 1989 *En quête d'universités étude comparée des universités en France et en R.F.A.* Logiques sociales L'Harmattan, Paris

Le Bris R F 1985 *Les universités à la loupe*. Economica-Atlas, Paris

Miquel A 1989 *Les bibliothèques universitaires*. Rapport au ministre d'état chargé de l'education nationale de la jeunesse et des sports collection des rapports officiels. La documentation française, Paris

Paye-Jeanneney L, Payan J J 1988 *Le chantier universitaire: "Bâtir l'avenir"*. Beauchesme, Paris

Prelot P H 1989 *Les établissements privés d'enseignement supérieur*. Bibliothèque de droit public tome 154. Librairie Générale de Droit et de Jurisprudence, Paris

C. Durand-Prinborgne

G

Gabon

1. Higher Education and Society

The Republic of Gabon lies across the Equator. Its northern frontier is bounded by Cameroon, with its eastern and southern boundaries abutting onto the Congo. Its western coastline is bordered by the Atlantic Ocean. With a total surface area of 267,667 square kilometers and a population estimated in 1990 at 1,365,400, of whom 47.3 percent live in urban areas, Gabon achieved independence from France in 1960. The population increase is estimated at 2 percent per year and the Gross Domestic Product (GDP) per head in 1989 has been reckoned at around 881,000 francs CFA (US$3,236).

Estimates place the literacy rate at 65 percent. The number of students enrolled in secondary education represented some 26 percent of the age group 12–18 years in the school year 1989–90. The statistic for higher education enrollments expressed as a percentage of the age group 20–24 years was 3.46 percent in the same year. The national budget for 1990 was 400,000 million francs CFA (US$1,469 million) of which 12.94 percent was allocated to education, with higher education accounting for some 3.45 percent of the total.

Gabon's economy is dependent on government loans and the major part of its resources originate from its oil and mining deposits. Nevertheless, the primary sector contributes only 11 percent to the GDP although it employs nearly 50 percent of the population. The tertiary sector is also dependent to a very large degree on help from abroad and at the start of the 1990s has been facing a crisis for a few years.

It is difficult to evaluate with great accuracy the wage-earning population in Gabon. However, it is estimated at 33,000 persons in the public sector and 5,500 in the private and semipublic sectors. A link between the level of study and the level of employment can be established, as shown in Tables 1 and 2. The distinctions shown in Tables 1 and 2 are not clear-cut. There are people from the bottom level at the top of the hierarchy.

1.1 Political and Administrative Structures

Gabon has a semipresidential regime and is divided into nine provinces administered by governors. Despite this organizational structure, the Gabonese administration is highly centralized. At the political level, Gabon has known several regimes since 1960. From 1960–67 a system of multipartism existed. This was replaced by monopartism from 1968–90, when a return to multipartism occurred. Since the last elections, the former single party (PDG) has had a majority at the National Assembly. It is concerned with the question of continuity in higher education policy as well as in other fields.

Table 2
Relationship between level of employment and level of study in public service

Category	Level of study
A1	graduate studies
A2	undergraduate studies
B1	professional training after the baccalauréat
B2	baccalauréat
C	completion of the first cycle at secondary school

Table 1
Relationship between level of employment and level of study in the private sector

Level of employment	Level of study
Senior and middle executives	holders of the *baccalauréat* and higher diplomas
Technicians	upper and lower sixth forms
Apprentices	secondary school, fourth year
Highly specialized employees and workers	secondary school, third year
Specialized and labor force employees	on-the-job-training
General labor force	no particular level

1.2 Relationship with Religious Bodies

There are four official religions in Gabon: Catholic, Protestant, Muslim, and Animist. Christianity plays a role of paramount importance in primary and secondary education. This is not, however, the case in higher education, which is strictly publicly run.

2. The Institutional Fabric of the Higher Education System

Higher education "contributes to the intellectual and cultural promotion of the Gabonese society; in other words, it participates in its evolution toward a greater responsibility for each citizen." Among the main objectives assigned to higher education are: the elaboration and transmission of knowledge; research development; and training.

Higher education is provided by two universities— Omar Bongo University at Libreville and the University of Science and Technology of Masuku (USTM at Franceville)—and also by various independent institutions. These are all public and receive little or no subsidies from the private sector.

2.1 Organization of Studies at the University

The Omar Bongo University at Libreville is composed of seven establishments, comprising three faculties, three high schools, and one institute, as follows: the Faculty of Law and Economics (FDSE); the Faculty of Literature and Humanities (FLSH); the Faculty of Medicine and Health Sciences (FMSS); the Higher Normal School (ENS); the High School of Technical Education (ENSET); the Secretarial High School (ENSS); and the National Institute of Management Science (INSG). The institutions partially linked with the Omar Bongo University (UOB) are the National School of Magistrature (ENM) and the National School of Water and Forestry (ENEF).

The University of Science and Technology is composed of two establishments: the Faculty of Sciences, and Masuku Polytechnic (for engineers [PhD level] and skilled technicians).

2.2 Organization of Studies in the Nonuniversity Institutions

There are several autonomous institutions of higher education which are independent of the universities

Table 3
Total number of students by establishment, nationality, and sex 1989–90

	Gabonese			Foreigners			Total		
	Male	Female	Total	Male	Female	Total	Male	Female	Total
Omar Bongo University									
Faculty of Law and Economics[a]	453	206	659	38	15	53	491	221	712
Faculty of Literature and Humanities	465	199	664	22	22	44	487	221	708
Faculty of Medicine and Health Sciences	178	222	400	35	37	72	213	259	472
National Institute of Management Science	157	115	272	9	13	22	166	128	294
Secretarial High School	0	65	65	0	11	11	0	76	76
Higher Normal School[b]	157	56	213	1	0	1	158	56	214
High School of Technical Education	83	5	88	3	1	4	86	6	92
Subtotal	1,493	868	2,361	108	207	207	1,601	967	2,568
Masuku University of Science and Technology									
Faculty of Sciences	206	25	231	11	2	13	217	27	244
Other departments	225	14	239	14	2	16	239	16	255
Subtotal	431	39	470	25	4	29	456	43	499
Other establishments									
School of Teacher Education	283	130	413	9	2	11	292	132	424
National School of Administration	32	6	38	0	0	0	32	6	38
Preparatory School for Careers in Administration	21	10	31	0	0	0	21	10	31
National School of Magistrature[c]	31	17	48	0	0	0	31	17	48
National School of Forestry	23	6	29	10	0	10	33	6	39
Institute of Economics and Finance	20	6	26	0	0	0	20	6	26
National Institute of Management	178	22	200	2	1	3	180	23	203
Subtotal	588	197	785	21	3	24	609	200	809
Grand total	2,512	1,104	3,616	154	214	260	2,666	1,210	3,876

a not included   b Including 28 pupils who are educational advisers and 17 who are inspectors   c Not including 10 pupil-magistrates

and the Ministry of Higher Education. These are: the African Institute of Computer Science, founded in 1971 by the members of OCAM; the National School of Administration (ENA); the Preparatory School for Careers in Administration (EPCA); the Institute of Economics and Finance (IEF); and the National Institute of Management (INC).

2.3 Levels of Institution

The required starting level of studies in higher education is generally the *baccalauréat*, obtained after seven years of secondary studies and six years at primary school. For certain branches, there is a special entry examination at the university or a preparatory year. Working people or those who do not hold the *baccalauréat* are legally entitled to two years. The entry requirements for different higher education establishments, the length of studies, and the degrees offered vary from institution to institution. Most of the institutions including departments other than higher education are postuniversity, that is to say, they admit graduate students by entry examination. Moreover, while undergraduate studies are common to all colleges, graduate studies are not available in all education units or establishments. Hence the Faculty of Sciences offers only undergraduate studies, so students have to pursue their studies abroad, particularly in France.

2.4 Quantitative Developments in Higher Education

The development of the numbers enrolled in higher education since the foundation of the National

Table 4
Number of students by field of study, 1989–90

	Female	Total
Education sciences and teacher training	70	213
Letters, religion, and theology	110	329
Fine arts and applied arts	—	—
Law	164	431
Social sciences and behavioral sciences	221	756
Business and management training	251	566
Data processing and documentation	51	136
Home economics	—	—
Training for the service industries	—	—
Exact sciences and national sciences	24	186
Mathematics and computer science	8	84
Medical sciences of health and hygiene	222	400
Engineering sciences	14	239
Architecture and town planning	5	38
Industrial production professions	0	80
Transport and telecommunications	2	8
Agriculture, forestry, and fish-farming		
Grand total	1,158	3,530

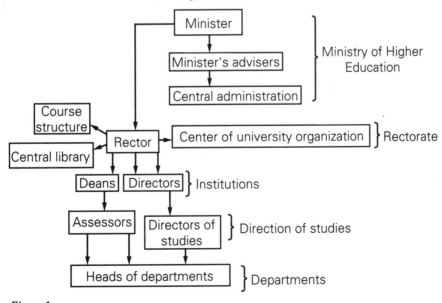

Figure 1
Organizational structure of the University

Table 5
Number of grant-holding or paid university students, 1989–90[a]

| | Grant-holding | | | | |
	Number	Percentage of total	Paid Number	Percentage of total	Total
Omar Bongo University					
Faculty of Law and Economics	229	32.2	30	4.2	712
Faculty of Literature and Humanities	280	39.5	26	3.7	708
Faculty of Medicine and Health Sciences	223	47.2	6	1.3	472
National Institute of Management Science	216	73.5	2	0.7	294
Secretarial High School	48	63.2	3	3.9	76
Higher Normal School	98	45.8	49	22.9	214
High School of Technical Education	87	94.6	—	—	92
Subtotal	1,181	46.0	116	4.5	2,568
Masuku University of Science and Technology					
Faculty of Sciences	160	65.6	—	—	244
	240	93.3	—	—	255
Subtotal	400	80.2	—	—	499
Grand total	1,581	51.5	116	3.8	3,067

a The Gabonese government also awards grants to national students for the following establishments: National School of Forestry—18 grants, National School of Magistrature—46 grants, National Institute of Management—106 grants

University (which became the UOB in 1977) in 1970 and also the amalgamation of the Faculty of Sciences and School of Engineers into the USTM, has been steady. Table 3 summarizes the total numbers enrolled in higher education in Gabon in 1989–90. The number of Gabonese students in higher education in 1990 can be estimated at approximately 5,000 (3,647 + 830 + students abroad without grants).

Table 6
Grant-holding students from outside Gabon, according to source of funding, 1989–90

Source of funding	Number of grant-holders
Gabonese government	665
French financial aid	74
United Nations National Development Program[a]	—
Canada	4
China[b]	32
Germany	1
Tunisia[b]	2
Soviet Union[b]	50
Yugoslavia[b]	2
Total	830

a Information not provided   b Grants subsidized by the Gabonese government

Table 4 shows Gabonese students by field of education in 1989–90, as per the UNESCO classification.

3. Governance, Administration, and Finance

The Ministry of Higher Education is organized as shown in Figure 1. The universities benefit from a certain degree of autonomy. They are headed by rectors who are solely responsible for the university. The establishments are controlled by deans or directors who are assisted by tutors or directors of studies and general secretaries. The establishments are divided into departments (education and research units).

Higher education is financed exclusively by public funds. The system of allocation of student grants is one of the largest sections of the budget (see Table 10). The funding can prove to be very expensive if internal resources are low. The number of grants awarded in the two universities in 1989 is set out in Table 5, and the sources of funding for non-Gabonese students in Table 6.

4. Faculty and Students: Teaching, Learning, and Research

4.1 Faculty

Table 7 shows the distribution of teachers by grade, nationality, and sex. Table 8 shows the growth in

Table 7
University teaching personnel according to status and sex, 1989–90

	State employees M	F	Total	Contracted employees M	F	Total	French aid workers M	F	Total	Others M	F	Total	Total M	F	Total	Teacher–student ratio
Omar Bongo University																
Faculty of Law and Economics	28	0	28	3	0	3	5	1	6	—	—	—	36	1	37	1:19
Faculty of Literature and Humanities	53	13	66	17	6	23	4	0	4	1	0	1	75	19	94	1:8
Faculty of Medicine and Health Sciences	36	7	43	2	0	2	5	0	5	1	0	1	44	7	51	1:9
National Institute of Management Science	6	2	8	—	—	—	3	2	5	—	—	—	9	4	13	1:23
Secretarial High School	0	2	2	—	—	—	—	—	—	—	—	—	0	2	2	1:38
Higher Normal School	11	4	15	8	1	9	8	2	10	7	2	9	34	9	43	1:5
High School of Technical Education	10	0	10	5	0	5	6	0	6	5	0	5	26	0	26	1:4
Subtotal	144	28	172	35	7	42	31	5	36	14	2	16	224	42	266	1:10
Masuku University of Science and Technology																
Faculty of Sciences	18	2	20	5	3	8	12	0	12	4	0	4	39	5	44	1:6
Other departments	8	1	9	1	0	1	27	1	28	8	0	8	44	2	46	1:6
Subtotal	26	3	29	6	3	9	29	1	40	12	0	12	83	7	90	1:6
Grand total	170	31	201	41	10	51	70	6	76	26	2	28	307	49	356	1:9

numbers of academics since 1970–71. The number of teaching hours per week for teachers varies with their grade: professors teach for three hours per week; senior lecturers for five; assistant lecturers for seven; and assistants for eight.

Scientific research and higher education, which were under the supervision of the same ministry for years, are now separate. This reveals the low opinion that the authorities have of research in Gabon. As it was impossible to pursue research (because of obsolete facilities and insufficient means), Gabonese teachers and researchers stopped working for a period of five months in 1991 to claim better working conditions, especially taking into account that they cannot fulfill their careers without carrying out research.

Table 8
Development of the numbers of academics in Gabon from 1970–71 to 1989–90 (Gabonese and foreigners)

	1970–71	1975–76	1980–81	1985–86	1989–90
Faculty of Law and Economics	80	279	511	767	712
Faculty of Literature and Humanities	29	237	475	582	708
Faculty of Sciences[a]	53	73	162	174	244
Faculty of Medicine and Health Sciences	—	60	209	345	472
National Institute of Management Science	—	46	159	187	294
Secretarial High School	—	—	—	77	76
Higher Normal School[b]	—	122	170	225	214
High School of Technical Education	—	8	53	95	92
Total	162	887	1,889	2,607	3,067

a Within the framework of the University of Omar Bongo from 1970–71 to 1985–86, and part of the University of Science and Technology of Masuku from 1986–87   b In 1971–72, the numbers of pupil–professors were combined with those of the Faculty of Law and Economics and the Faculty of Sciences

4.2 Students

Owing to a lack of information, it is not possible to examine distribution of students by social origin. The students' origins have been calculated according to a highly representative sample of establishments. It appears that the economics and law courses are well ahead of the others. The province of Woleu-Ntem provides the highest number of students, followed by the province of the estuary.

J. Obone

Gambia

1. Higher Education and Society

The Gambia, Africa's smallest mainland country with an area of 10,490 square kilometers and a population of approximately 750,000, offers few opportunities for postsecondary or tertiary education. The period 1976–86 witnessed an unprecedented expansion in education. Total school enrollment from 1982–83 to 1985–86 rose from 66,398 to 85,007. Structures and facilities for both formal and nonformal education were enhanced and the heavy enrollments referred to above surpassed planned targets, although universal primary education has yet to be achieved. Major problems exist throughout the system in terms of the supply of qualified teachers, classrooms, furniture, and instructional materials. Secondary school places are oversubscribed both at the secondary technical and high school levels. There is mounting pressure for increased access to tertiary education.

The quality of schooling leaves much to be desired at all levels. During the period 1982–83 to 1987–88 education's share of recurrent government expenditure fell from 20 percent to just over 12 percent. Despite these constraints, ambitious targets have been set for education for the period 1988–2003 (see *Education Policy 1988–2003* p. 8ff) and the demand for higher secondary and postsecondary education, including vocational education, is expected to rise rapidly.

The *Education Policy 1988–2003* document indicates (p. 41ff) that the government of The Gambia will "as a long-term objective in the latter stages of the policy period 1988–2003 and beyond, seriously examine and pursue the possibility of establishing the nucleus of a university at the Gambia College." If this policy is pursued, as seems likely, the government of The Gambia would do well to examine its options carefully. Other "small" African countries like Botswana, Lesotho, and Swaziland manage to sustain their own universities, but with high unit costs and many other problems. Wandira's (1977) classic analysis of the "one–country–one–university" syndrome points out many of the social, economic, and political problems surrounding this type of insti-

tution. The government of The Gambia would do well to weigh the pros and cons of establishing an institution which may prove to be more of a drain on the economy than an engine of development.

2. The Institutional Fabric of Higher Education

No tertiary or higher education is available as such in The Gambia in 1990. Successful students who have completed high school and who wish to take courses above this level proceed to foreign institutions. The last available figures indicate that some 163 Gambian students were enrolled in foreign universities or colleges of education, mainly in West Africa. A special arrangement with Sierra Leone's Milton Margai College allows for the admission of Gambian students to tertiary level courses at that institution. The Gambia relies on universities and colleges in the Commonwealth, the United States, Europe, the Arab world, the Soviet Union, and other Eastern Bloc countries for the education of its labor force to the graduate and postgraduate levels.

The obvious economic advantages of avoiding the high recurrent and capital costs of establishing a national university for limited numbers of students have to be set against the inherent disadvantages of a general rise in fees for foreign students, the increasing difficulty of admission to a foreign university in the face of rising local demand for places, and the problem of the functional relevance of overseas training. The Gambia's *Education Policy 1988–2003* document indicates the desire of the government to "define a clear policy on higher education in the country." Educational developments taking place in the rest of West Africa will undoubtedly have an influence on the establishment of any tertiary level institution in The Gambia. The policy document suggests that such an institution would focus on priority labor needs and would be set up in close collaboration with established overseas universities. Priority human resource development needs identified include teacher education and training of agricultural scientists and technicians, public health workers, and nurses. These fields already form the main activities of the major postsecondary institution in the country—The Gambia College—which itself forms the probable basis for eventual expansion and development into a university.

With its main campus situated at Brikama, some 35 kilometers from the capital Banjul, The Gambia College is made up of four constituent schools: Agriculture, Education, Nursing and Midwifery, and Public Health. The latter two schools are located in Banjul itself. Admission to The Gambia College is after four or five years of secondary education and the courses offered are of two or three years' duration. A recent innovation is the establishment of a Higher Teachers' Certificate (HTC) program, developed through a link with the University of Bristol School of Education in the United Kingdom. It is hoped that this innovation will provide a model for further developments in tertiary education in The Gambia.

Bibliography

Education Policy 1988–2003 1988 Ministry of Education, Youth, Sports, and Culture, Banjul
Education Requirements Study 1984 Cambridge Education Consultants, Cambridge
Gambian Education Sector Study 1981 Ministry of Education, Banjul
Lauglo J (ed.) 1980 *Universities, National Development and Education. A Report of a Workshop.* University of London Institute of Education, London
Wandira A 1977 *The African University in Development.* Ravan Press, Johannesburg

R. L. Smith

German Democratic Republic

1. Higher Education and Society

The social development of the German Democratic Republic (GDR) since its foundation in 1949, has had a clear influence on the organization of its entire system of education (Schulz 1983, GDR Today 1987). The political, economic, social, intellectual, and cultural renewal of society that began in late 1989 will also require the complete reorganization of science and education. This article predates any such changes and refers to the established higher education system in the eastern part of Germany prior to reunification in 1990.

Higher education in the GDR was closely interwoven into social development. This emerges in the growing part in society of science and higher academic education and the expansion of its humanistic, progressive nature. Yet, the influence of science has far-reaching effects on society, economy, the quality of life, and culture. Revolutionary restructuring society includes therefore the reform of research and teaching at university level.

The social controls in the higher education system are the result of centuries of historical development. Several universities have venerable histories. Karl Marx University in Leipzig (now University of Leipzig) had its origins in 1409; Wilhelm Pieck University in Rostock (now University of Rostock) dates from 1419; and Ernst Moritz Arndt University at Greifswald was founded in 1456. They were followed by Wittenberg (1502), which later merged with Halle University (1694), and Friedrich Schiller University in Jena founded in 1558. Humboldt University in Berlin (1810), of which Wilhelm von Humboldt was a founder, became a leading establishment during the nineteenth century.

Until the middle of the nineteenth century mining and technological disciplines developed in specialist nonuniversity institutions. The Mining Academy in Freiberg (founded 1765) is the oldest mining college in the world. The Technological University of Dresden, which was founded as a technical education institution in 1828, has achieved international significance. In addition to these many technical colleges were founded, especially at the end of the eighteenth, and in the first third of the nineteenth century.

The GDR is situated in the heart of Europe and borders on the Federal Republic of Germany, Czechoslovakia and Poland while the Baltic Sea is its natural frontier in the north. Covering an area of 108,333 square kilometers, the GDR is one of the world's smaller countries. The north is agricultural, while the largest industrial centers are in the south.

The GDR had a total population of 16,639,877 in 1986, of whom three quarters were city dwellers and one quarter lived in the countryside. The working population was 8,548,000 comprised of 7,555,000 workers and employees, and 815,000 members of production cooperatives. Ninety-one percent of all women of working age were either students or workers. In the process of the changes in society the population of the GDR was reduced.

One hundred thousand or so Sorbs form the only national minority. They enjoy full equality and freely cultivate their own traditions and customs.

The social agenda is planned and led by the People's Chamber (*Volkskammer*) as the Parliament of the GDR, the Council of State, and the Council of Ministers.

The GDR has been a member of the United Nations since 1973, and maintains diplomatic relations with 135 countries. Its policy towards states with different social systems is aimed at strengthening relations of peaceful coexistence. In accordance with social goals, science and education were oriented towards the progress of society, and were thus among the most important factors of growth in society.

Living and working conditions, all branches of the economy, science, education, and culture, were subject to central planning. Plans covered five-year periods that were then subdivided into annual plans. However, this did not entirely allow for the essential creative contribution of working people.

The constitution guaranteed division between church and state. There was, though, close cooperation in many issues of life in society between nonreligious people and people belonging to the church and religious groups.

It is a priority of society that science and education are used for the welfare of the people and of humankind in general. Progressive aspects of academic and cultural heritage must be preserved, while science and education must correspond to social requirements. The most important task of higher education is to prepare academically trained personnel for all fields and to ensure that their education is of the highest quality.

Graduates of higher and technical education must be further educated to higher levels so that they may use the latest research findings creatively.

Universities and university colleges should advocate and advance intellectual and cultural life, and thus respond to the political, academic, and cultural needs of the population. Also important is the development of international academic relations.

The GDR was, and hopefully remains, a developed industrialized country with an advanced agricultural sector.

The major industries are energy and fuel, chemistry, metallurgy, electrical engineering and electronics, and mechanical engineering. The only raw materials in the GDR are potash, rock salt, barite, lime chalk, gravel, and lignite. The most important of these is lignite. The GDR produces more than one third of world production; 83 percent of electricity is generated from lignite, causing great environmental pollution. In recent years, microelectronics has become a major industry.

Agriculture covers 6 million hectares with emphasis on grain (wheat, rye, barley, and oats), potatoes, sugar beet, animal fodder, fruit, and vegetables. More than 82 percent of the permanent agricultural workforce are members of the 4,211 cooperatives which cultivate 87.5 percent of the farmland and keep 89 percent of the livestock.

The GDR produced a national income of 252,210 million marks in 1986. Far-reaching reform to establish a socially and ecologically sensitive market economy is emerging.

2. The Institutional Fabric of the Higher Education System

Higher education has always been adaptive. It underwent three reforms after 1945.

After the liberation that followed the Second World War, a new system of higher education was started on the territory later to become the GDR. A further reform of higher education followed at the beginning of the 1950s. The establishment of a socialist higher education was accomplished in the 1965 law on the unified education system which, in turn led to the third higher education reform of 1968.

Higher education in the GDR traditionally consists of two levels, university education, and technical education. All educational institutions are run by the state; there are no private educational institutions.

Universities and university colleges are the highest institutions of education. Universities are distinguished by a wide academic profile. Some also offer technical sciences. In 1969 a new type of institution, the *Ingenieurhochschule*, was introduced. It concentrates on the transfer and use of technological

Table 1
Number of universities and university colleges

	1960	1970	1980
Universities	6	6	6
Technical universities and university colleges	10	19	18
Medical academies	3	3	3
Agricultural and forestry university colleges	2	2	2
Economics and law university colleges	3	3	3
University colleges of education and physical education	9	10	10
Art university colleges	11	11	11
	44	54	53

knowledge and economic knowledge. At university colleges of education, pedagogical and psychological subjects are, for example, combined with social sciences, mathematics, and science. In order to satisfy the accelerating demand for highly qualified specialists, the number of universities and university colleges grew significantly over three decades. The situation was also improved by the establishment of regional university colleges.

In the unified education system both engineering and technical colleges are deemed to be part of higher education. The country's economic requirements are met by 237 engineering and technical colleges. These include: 52 engineering colleges catering to industry, construction, engineering, transport, postal services, and telecommunications; 39 agricultural engineering colleges specializing in agriculture, forestry and the food industry; 9 colleges of economics and state administration; 62 medical colleges; 50 colleges of education; 12 colleges of art and culture; and 8 colleges of librarianship, archive science, and museum administration.

Social change is bringing about fundamental reappraisal of the skill characteristics and job profiles of engineers, economists, agricultural engineers. These workplace changes are reflected in changes in the aim, content, and methods employed in teaching and organizing initial and further education. The division of higher education into two profiles ensures that the demands of research and development as well as the leadership and organization of production will be safeguarded. Technicians and economists are being trained to new levels in technical colleges. The merging of technical colleges into universities is consistently linked with this; in other cases technical colleges will be reprofiled. The reformed initial and inservice higher education of engineers, economists, and agricultural engineers was critically assessed in the current discussion on the reform of higher education.

232

Universities and university colleges can only realize their aims in initial and further education if they also fill a research function. It is the role of the institutes of the Academy of Sciences of the GDR, however, to concentrate solely on research. They, along with universities and university colleges cooperate in the work of the research establishments of state industry. A similar process takes place in agriculture. These collaborative projects are the outcome of long-term national planning for research. Concentration on key areas and high technologies, peace research, and so forth, is essential given the limited research potential available. Fundamental research is primarily developed by universities and university colleges with the aim of combining with and complementing applied research. Interdisciplinary research, often specific to the universities, which brings together mathematics, the social and natural sciences, agriculture, and medicine, is also a feature of strength.

Thus the essential purpose of education is defined as continually supplying graduates well-prepared for professions and careers which will continuously evolve over the next three to four decades. Research depends on redefining the content of basic education, which will certainly need to expand. It also should promote independent academic work amongst undergraduates and participants in courses of further education while motivating them to further heights.

International collaborative research is a constituent part in the international relations of higher education, and supports national research, especially in universities and university colleges.

2.1 Admission Policies and Selection for Initial Higher Education

The university entrance certificate (*Hochschulreife*), usually acquired in the *Abitur* examination, is the basic requirement for admission to higher education. Education leading up to university entrance is provided in extended secondary schools, in the *Abitur* sections of vocational schools, adult education centers, those higher education institutions which offer preliminary or pre-academic courses, and the Workers' and Peasants' Faculty of the Mining Academy in Freiberg. These serve as extensions of the ten-year general secondary education which is received by about 95 percent of boys and girls in the GDR.

Young people applying for admission to university courses in technological or economic subjects or a university college of engineering must have completed vocational training in a relevant field in addition to meeting standard university entrance requirements. The three-year combined vocational and pre-academic program leading to the *Abitur* and the preliminary courses for young skilled workers provided at university colleges are the main routes for such qualifications.

Since the late 1970s practical experience and a pre-academic practical placement period (*Vorpraktikum*) lasting up to one year have gradually been established as compulsory entry conditions for students applying for matriculation in technical and economic sections of universities, university colleges of technology and of economics, and at institutions of agricultural and medical higher education. Work experience is designed to acquaint future students with the professional environment they hope eventually to enter.

In contrast, for technical education, the certificate of ten-year secondary education is normally sufficient. In addition, applicants for technological and economic courses must have completed vocational training and had at least one further year of work experience.

Course requirements are high for all applicants regardless of whether they apply for full-time or distance education, or for evening courses. Moreover, applicants to distance or evening courses are expected to have both substantial work experience and good results in their jobs.

There are no entrance examinations. In some subjects, however, for example, in the arts, in physical education and in interpreter's courses, applicants must pass an aptitude test.

Every citizen of the GDR fulfilling these requirements has the right to apply for a course at a university, university college, or technical college. Those who wish to apply must submit an application to the central office for admissions of their chosen institution. Selection is based on the number of applications, which go for assessment to the institution's admissions committees. The committees include experienced members of staff and student and trade union representatives. They recommend the admission of the ablest and most talented applicants, taking into account projected enrollment figures. The rectors of universities, the directors of engineering or technical colleges, or their deputies make the final decision.

Those rejected are invited for counseling at which they may be advised to apply elsewhere or in a different subject.

2.2 Quantitative developments

Investigations have shown that about 32 percent of those born each year pass through a course of higher education. This has remained constant for many years (Schulz 1983).

Preparation for entry to higher education took place mainly at extended secondary schools (*erweiterte Oberschulen*); vocational training, plus preparation for a course in higher education (*Berufsausbildung mit Abitur*) has also developed. For adults, the route to higher education lies via university extension institutions (*Volkshochschulen*) or via preparatory courses at university colleges.

Table 2
Admissions to universities and university colleges between 1960 and 1987

	1960	1965	1970	1975	1980	1985	1987
Full-time students	20,699	16,360	30,786	27,783	26,761	26,474	25,351
Distance/evening students	9,382	8,375	13,189	6,607	5,188	5,109	5,513
Total admissions	30,081	24,735	43,975	34,390	31,949	31,583	30,864
Percentage of female students	—	33.9	44.7	49.0	53.1	51.5	51.2

Table 3
Admissions to engineering and technical colleges between 1960 and 1987

	1960	1965	1970	1975	1980	1985	1987
Full-time students	19,477	21,509	22,991	34,484	35,547	32,999	31,605
Distance/evening students	38,356	21,748	33,538	17,779	16,582	16,700	16,781
Total admissions	57,833	43,257	56,529	52,263	52,129	49,699	48,386
Percentage of female students	—	46.4	62.9	80.3	83.6	80.3	78.9

Table 4
Graduates of universities/university colleges and technical colleges between 1960 and 1987

	1960	1965	1970	1975	1980	1985	1987
Graduates of universities/ university colleges	15,005	20,878	22,312	36,521	24,200	25,046	22,762
Graduates of technical colleges	24,544	33,633	36,265	43,030	42,038	43,201	42,118

Since 1952 one characteristic of tertiary education in the GDR is that traditional universities, university colleges, and technical colleges have, together with full-time courses, provided distance and evening courses specifically designed for working people (Möhle 1983). Distance and evening courses in about 130 subjects leading up to degree level exist at 20 universities and university colleges. These courses have the same aim and almost the same content as full-time degree courses, differing mainly in their teaching and organization, but not in the level of attainment. Preference has always been given to running both full-time and distance courses at traditional establishments of higher education rather than establishing a separate open university.

Admissions to university and technical education between 1960 and 1987 show there has always been a constant number of applications to higher education, in relation to demographic development. The proportion of female students has also risen considerably.

The graduate growth rate is considerable. Between 1960 and 1975 the number of graduates rose by a factor of almost 2.5, and since then numbers have

remained constant. This pattern differed slightly at technical college level. Between 1960 and 1975 the number of technical college graduates almost doubled; and has since not varied. One fifth of all graduates of tertiary education obtained their degree by distance study.

The graduate stock in the national economy has risen considerably. The percentage of higher education and technical college graduates in the national economy rose from 11.7 percent in 1971 to 21.6 percent in 1987. This trend continues.

2.3 Structure of Qualifications

Higher education normally takes five years full-time study ending with exams for the diploma degree. Medicine is the exception requiring six years full-time. The duration of degree courses by distance study is more protracted.

In courses for engineers, economists, and agricultural engineers, students take their final exams (*Hauptprüfung*) at the end of their fourth year. Thereafter there are two routes to obtaining their diploma degree: by a fifth year of full-time study, or by entering work and continuing as external students obtaining their degrees within one-and-a-half years. The degree dissertation forms part of the department's research and is defended before an expert committee. The first degree (*Diplom*) is the lowest academic grade to be awarded by an establishment of higher education in the GDR. This structure is set out in the 1968 Decree on Academic Qualifications.

A technical college course lasts three years, or correspondingly longer when taken as a distance course. The certificate is awarded after the successful completion of examinations and a final project. It is awarded by the relevant engineering or technical college.

2.4 Further Education of Graduates

In important social areas, and especially in the economy, as for instance the development and application of microelectronics, of robotics, the optimal use of raw materials, energy, and biological processes, which often involve computer technology, graduate inservice training has been updated to correspond with growing demands for such qualifications (Möhle 1988).

In the 1970s inservice education at universities and university colleges was a separate activity, but nowadays it enjoys equal status to teaching and research.

Such vocational inservice education combining social and discipline-based education, enhances further specialization, updates knowledge, skills and finally provides a second qualification or a retraining program. Further education (*Weiterbildung*) is becoming increasingly interdisciplinary and is always activity-oriented.

At graduate level further education is carried out under the distance education system. There are 160 graduate courses which last two to four terms. The law guarantees release from work for 36 working days per academic year for participants. In addition they are granted a month to complete their final thesis. Intensive short courses that last approximately 150 hours operate in strictly defined fields. More than 500 such courses are offered in each academic year.

Further education centers depend on coordinated cooperation between universities and technical colleges, in order to raise standards and efficiency. The microelectronics center brings together 13 universities and university colleges and two technical colleges.

Contractual agreements for further education between firms and universities are growing in number. Firms' educational requirements form the basis for planning in further education both in the universities and in cooperative efforts between the two. Further education attracted 118,500 university and college graduates at graduate level in the period 1976–80. Between 1981 and 1985 there was a 66 percent growth rate as the number of participants rose to 367,400.

3. Governance, Administration, and Finance

3.1 National Administration

As an organ of the Council of Ministers of the GDR, the Ministry of Higher and Technical Education is centrally responsible for all matters relating to higher and technical education. It therefore ensures that a common policy is implemented by all ministries with remits covering the development of higher and technical education (Schulz 1983). It formulates legal regulations and then verifies that these have been implemented.

Different advisory bodies existed inside the Ministry: the Council of Higher and Technical Education (*Hoch- und Fachschulrat*), Academic Advisory Bodies (*wissenschaftliche Beiräte*), representing different fields, and the Council for Academic Awards (*Rat für akademische Grade*).

The Ministry is also assisted by special institutions which research the development of higher education, among which are the Central Institute of Higher Education in Berlin and the Institute of Technical Education in Karl-Marx-Stadt (now called Chemnitz). All such bodies work in conjunction with research teams in universities and colleges.

The new-found autonomy of universities and colleges will limit ministerial responsibility for higher education to coordinating academic development. The Ministry will ratify the appointment of rectors and appointments to leading academic positions. It will have responsibility for the basic organization of education, the definition of academic degrees, and the annual budget. This will entail supporting important areas and projects. International scientific and higher educational contacts serve this intention. Governance and management are being progressively rationalized, reorganized, and computerized.

Almost all plans of higher and technical education are financed from the state budget, which constantly increases. Annual state expenditure on higher and technical education doubled between 1971 and 1987. It has provided for new university centers in Leipzig and Jena.

About 100 cooperation contracts (*Koordinierungsverträge*) and 1,500 research contracts (*Leistungsverträge*) have been entered into with industrial partners in which scientific and technical research was almost completely financed by client firms. Interdisciplinary and social science research was financed by the state.

3.2 Institutional Administration

The head of every university or university college is the rector (*Rektor*) who is elected from among the chairholding professors every three years by the scientific council. Rectors are confirmed in post by the Minister. The rector is required to have all-round competence, and is given executive decision-making powers.

Table 5
Money available from the state budget for education (in millions of marks)

	1971	1975	1980	1985	1987
Total for education	6.369	8.276	9.836	12.404	13.406
Higher and technical education	1.455	1.721	2.016	2.699	2.910

Central to university planning are the long-term plans for institutional research. Such strategic frameworks impose on the rector the duty of upholding and initiating high standards in research and in initial and further education. The teaching role of the university must be of particular importance as the means of ensuring noteworthy academic achievement in the future. Finally, the rector must ensure close cooperation and good relations with other academic institutions both nationally and internationally.

The rector has a formal obligation to guide and oversee sections, clinics, and separate institutes of the university, and is supported in this by prorectors and university directors. Among these are the first prorector, the permanent deputy of the rector, and prorectors of training, social, natural, and medical sciences.

The rector and the pro-rectors are supported by the directors of the university. The organizational model provides for directors of student affairs, further training, research, staff development and qualification, and international relations. The administrative director coordinates the administration and planning of financial matters, equipment and the provision of materials, as well as economic and social affairs.

In future the coordination of all matters pertaining to universities, university colleges, and their submission to government will be carried out in a Conference of Rectors of the GDR.

Engineering and technical colleges are administered along essentially the same lines as universities and university colleges. They are headed by a director. Depending on the size of the institution, the director is supported by either one or two deputy directors to whom is delegated certain administrative functions.

A system of individual leadership has thus developed. It is based upon creative consultation and cooperation. The rector has, in the scientific council, an important "academic parliament" whose rights of decision making must be extended. Rectors work with the senate, faculties, and in the plenum. The members are leading academics, newly recruited staff, and students all of whom are elected every three years. The scientific council of the university is concerned with the following areas:

(a) The development of academic disciplines and interdisciplinary work;

(b) evaluation of the quality of training;

(c) long-term research planning;

(d) the evaluation of scientific achivements;

(e) the development of the teaching body and of newly appointed academic staff;

(f) the business of promotion and *facultas docendi*;

(g) the preparation and implementation of investments, and the budget;

(h) the development of scientific–cultural life.

The recommendations and decisions of the scientific council are implemented by the rector and the prorectors in their leadership and planning capacity.

In technical colleges special advisory bodies exist as in universities; for example, the Council of the Technical College (*Rat der Fachschule*).

In 1968 the third higher education reform created sections (*Sektionen*) as the basic unit of academic work in universities and university colleges. The former faculties, to which a large number of different institutes belonged, were no longer liable. Each section is headed by a director, who is supported by a deputy director of initial and further training, and by a deputy director of research. The section director has responsibility for the following areas:

(a) developing scholarship, especially teaching areas, and establishing research priorities;

(b) maintaining quality in training and study, as well as in scientific output;

(c) implementing relevant research, and fostering scientific publication;

Table 6
Development of higher education personnel

	1951	1970	1975	1980	1985	1987
Total	—	80,068	89,941	96,661	102,541	104,269
Teaching staff	1,395	4,621	5,284	6,333	7,180	7,362
Junior academic staff	1,879	16,598	20,828	22,515	23,151	23,111
Doctors/dentists	—	4,050	4,303	5,088	5,385	5,589

(d) developing an efficient team of new academic recruits;

(e) ensuring close cooperation with partners in industrial programs.

The director is responsible for the section's work, appointing and leading the subdepartment (*Wissenschaftsbereich*) heads and reviewing their work. The subdepartments are the smallest academic units. Their heads provide leadership for the associated lecturers, academic personnel, and students, and endeavor to ensure high achievement in the main areas of activity.

The director is backed by the section council, comprising members of the section and representatives of the main industrial partners. In the end, crucial departmental problems are properly the concern of the entire department.

4. Faculty and Students: Teaching, Learning, and Research

4.1 Faculty

Following the Potsdam Agreement at the end of the Second World War, all fascist teachers were expelled from higher education. A new teaching body then had to be established to promulgate the reform of universities and university colleges which a new generation has since inherited.

Academic staff in higher education are grouped into two major categories: senior academic staff (*Hochschullehrer*) comprising professors (*Professoren*) and lecturers (*Dozenten*); and junior academic staff (*wissenschaftliche Mitarbeiter*), with lecturers (*Fachschullehrer*) at technical colleges a distinct group from both of these.

The number of personnel has steadily increased. At universities and university colleges the number of teaching staff grew by 60 percent in the period 1970–87. The number of junior staff (excluding medicine) rose by 40 percent in the same period while the number of teachers working in technical colleges doubled (the exact increase was 107.3%). This has greatly benefited the student–teacher ratio. In 1970 there were four full-time students to every teacher; in 1987 the ratio was 3.1:1. Over the same period in technical colleges the ratio has improved from 11.1:1 to 8.1:1.

Since the quality of research, and of initial and

further education, is determined by the qualifications of teaching staff and junior academic staff, their systematic training is of great importance to society (Schulz 1983).

The responsibilities, rights, and duties of senior academic staff were laid down in the "Decree on the Appointment and Positions of Senior Staff at Higher Education Institutions" (*Hochschullehrerberufungsverordnung*) of 1968. These include organizing teaching courses in initial and further education—lectures, seminars, and tutorials (*Konsultationen*). The senior academic staff's own research is an essential prerequisite for teaching. It is the duty of every senior staff member to contribute significantly to the development of his or her specialist field, and to organize students' participation in research. Further to this, it is their responsibility to cooperate with the appropriate firms and cultural institutions to ensure rapid dissemination of research results.

In view of the importance of these obligations the appointment of senior academic staff is undertaken with great care. Proposals for appointments are drawn up by the Section councils to which the successful candidate will be appointed. The council undertakes selection on the basis of proven academic ability.

As a prerequisite the candidates require a senior doctorate (*Promotion B*) and the *facultas docendi* (*Lehrbefähigung*). Finally, the respective trade union committees will also give their views. The rectors of the universities or university colleges submit proposals for appointments to the Minister. A list of three candidates is submitted to the Minister in the case of a full professorial appointment. Chairs and lectureships which fall vacant or are newly created are publicly advertised.

Experienced lecturers and other academic staff may be appointed associate professors (*außerordentliche Professoren*) and associate lecturers (*außerordentliche Dozenten*) in recognition of their achievements and merits. Academics employed outside the universities and university colleges but with qualifications suited to senior appointments are appointed to part-time professorships (*Honorarprofessuren*) or part-time lecturerships (*Honorardozenten*) to establish links between training, research, and the rest of society.

The high social esteem senior academic staff enjoy is reflected in the salaries they are paid.

Junior academic staff include assistant lecturers (*wissenschaftliche Assistenten*) and assistant physicians (*Assistenzärzte*); specialist lecturers (*Lehrer im Hochschuldienst*) and senior specialist lecturers (*Lektoren*); senior assistants (*wissenschaftliche Oberassistenten*) and senior physicians (*Oberärzte*); and academic secretaries (*wissenschaftliche Sekretäre*). In general, they are supervised by senior academics responsible for their special fields.

Specialist qualifications closely linked with

Table 7
Development of technical college personnel

	1970	1975	1980	1985	1987
Total	13,460	18,739	20,193	21,745	22,017
Teaching staff	5,683	8,451	9,851	12,254	11,781

research are expected of all junior staff. This is reflected in the increase in the numbers of first and second doctoral theses completed between 1971 and 1987, and particularly in the growing percentage of women completing a doctorate.

There are three different academic degrees in the GDR: the first—the diploma (*Diplom*)— is awarded in a particular discipline. This second is the first doctorate (*Promotion A: Doktor eines Wissenschaftszweiges*). The highest or senior doctorate (*Promotion B*) gives the title of *Doktor der Wissenschaften*. All theses are publicly defended, and evaluated by three assessors. Academic degrees are awarded by the universities or university colleges.

The training of researchers is clearly a major concern throughout higher education. Training programs leading to higher academic degrees include research studies (*Forschungsstudium*) and supervised advanced research for doctorates (*Aspiranturen*). Research study courses have been developed to enable highly able students to receive rapid training as research workers. In general, students take three years to complete their research studies. They work towards the first doctorate.

Aspirantur research courses involve graduates who obtained particularly good results over several years of practical research experience, taking into account their involvement in working for society. Two types of such advanced research courses result in these doctorates: first, a three-year full-time research course (*planmäßige Aspirantur*). Candidates hold scholarships usually amounting to 80 percent of their previous salary. Candidates also take part in part-time advanced research courses (*außerplanmäßige Aspirantur*) over four years. Such students are entitled to one day paid study leave per week plus four weeks per year. *Aspirantur* research courses may be taken for either a first or a second doctorate.

The new generation of academics receive an introductory course into teaching methods in higher education at the beginning of their working life, plus a one-year graduate course which includes an introduction into teaching methods for a special subject. Though the *facultas docendi* are issued on an optional basis, their possession is obligatory for later appointments.

College lecturers (*Fachschullehrer*) must fulfil basic qualifications. They should have first degrees in fields corresponding to the area in which they work and specific qualifications acquired within the framework of further education; and evidence of teaching knowledge and skills acquired through graduate courses in technical college teaching methods. They undertake research and contribute to development activities both at universities and colleges or in industry. Specialists with professional experience outside the academic world who meet these specific requirements may be employed as part-time college lecturers.

The social and professional interests of all teachers in higher education are represented by the trade union at both a national and a local level, as well as at their work place. Competition between establishments of higher education, mainly led by the trade union, compares performance of institutions. Those with the best results pass their experience on.

Academics who distinguish themselves through their outstanding commitment to academic and social progress command great authority. Academics are delegated by their sections to work in all the major academic aspects of higher and technical education, in staff development, initial and further education, as well as in research, management, and planning. Setting a minimum number of teaching hours for professors and senior lecturers was not constructive and was therefore abolished. Teaching staff may be temporarily relieved of teaching to concentrate on research or writing books.

4.2 Students

Tables 2 and 3 (Sect. 1) showed the rising number of female students in higher education. Clearly this illustrates the equal rights women enjoy in the GDR.

The proportions of women admitted to full-time and to distance and evening courses, do, however, show changes. Prior to 1970 a high proportion of female admissions was to distance and evening courses. After 1975 this fell considerably, and the figure as a proportion of all admissions was hence also reduced.

Classification according to study choice is of interest. In 1987, the main emphasis was on the technical sciences and economics; teacher training was equally important. The training of mid-level medical personnel is assigned to technical colleges. It is still true that too few women study technical sciences. The situation is reversed in other fields; the proportion of women in teacher training, medicine, and health-related subjects is above average. The health service, together with trade and the service industry, are traditionally female-dominated professions. The social and cultural sciences, together with languages and linguistics, are present in relation to their importance to society.

Since 1981 all full-time students in the GDR have been entitled to a grant freeing them from social pressure and allowing them to concentrate fully on study. Additional awards are made to those with good or outstanding marks. The grant is not to be paid back by the student later nor do GDR students pay fees. Moreover, in 1987, 72.9 percent of university and university college students and 64.4 percent of technical college students were lodged in subsidized halls of residence.

Legislation guarantees working people in higher education either in distance or in evening study to have up to 48 days per year paid educational leave.

They are also given three months off work to finish their final theses.

The higher education system of the GDR fulfills its international commitment by qualifying foreign citizens at its universities, university colleges, and technical colleges. Between 1975 and 1987, the number of foreign undergraduate and graduate students rose from 4,747 to 12,745.

The body representing the interests of students in higher education is the elected Students' Council, both universities and technical colleges.

The content of teaching and studying at universities and university colleges is characterized by three main elements: general basic education, subject-related education, and specialist education.

General basic education provides a thorough grounding in social problems and in the subject field. The study of two elective foreign languages, as well as physical education on a voluntary basis, is continued.

In the first stage all students receive a computer-based foundation course in information science. For some 15 percent a more in-depth training in information science is provided as a second stage (Möhle 1989b).

Subject-related education develops theoretical knowledge in academic disciplines relevant to the students' later careers. This provides a broad foundation for the further assimilation of new academic knowledge. Specialist courses equip students with particular knowledge and skills necessary for their professional work.

University teaching methods give particular emphasis to every student's ability, through independent study to become acquainted with research, and develop the capacity to recognize and solve academic problems and questions.

An academic session (*Studienjahr*) extends over 10 months covering academic training, periods of practical work (one lasting one semester), and examinations. It is subdivided into two semesters of equal duration.

As the aims in initial education both full-time and distance education are the same, study areas are fixed in the one curriculum. In the light of the different backgrounds and circumstances of students the choice of content is differentiated. Individual study of special printed materials (*Lehrbriefe*) is an important part of distance studies for initial education. Individual study is supplemented by seminar courses (seven a year) with student groups. The second part of initial distance studies accentuates long periods of individual study and independent work. In the preparation of the final thesis, research is carried out (Möhle 1988c).

In the past, centrally validated curricula and teaching programs formed the basic elements and the foundation for teaching and studying. In future graduate profiles (*Absolventenbilder*) of each individual discipline will be developed. Teachers and students will be responsible for their implementation as well as for content and teaching methods. The students, for example, will construct their own curriculum from a number of subjects and classes suggested for their field of study.

Technical education offered by colleges of tertiary education includes:

(a) social sciences, courses in German, foreign languages, and physical education;

(b) professional basic education, that is mathematics, natural sciences, technical sciences and economics, educational sciences and psychology, and culture and art;

(c) subject areas specific to particular economic sectors and related practical courses and work placements.

Instruction is given mainly in group tutorials and practical courses. Full-time courses last three years.

Courses of higher education are concluded by end of semester or end of year examinations, which act as intermediate examinations for parts of a subject area. Final examinations cover the whole subject area, and consist of both oral and written parts. Exemption can be granted on the basis of grades obtained in independent work.

Student involvement in research is stimulated by competitions which have become an intergral part of academic life. Annual exhibitions take place at every university or college and central exhibitions take place every two or three years, to acquaint the public with the students' best results. Prizes and other distinctions for outstanding achievements are awarded by institutions of higher education and by state bodies.

The proportion of students successfully completing their course is about 85 percent or more. Grades form the basis for allocating jobs to students. In future the system of job distribution to graduates by the state will be replaced by free student choice.

5. Conclusion

Social renewal in the GDR also determines the reform of higher education. Academic work in initial and further education, and in research will have to be intensified by concentrating and recontouring it.

The reorganization of initial and further education for engineers and economists introduced several years ago has to be re-examined, so that a modern method of teaching and studying can be worked out. Progress made in independent study by students should be developed further.

Planned inservice education at graduate level for an increasing number of graduates is an important aspect in preparing for future social change. A considerable potential for education has accumulated.

After 1990 about one worker in four will have a tertiary educational qualification. Such potential ought to be used to increase performance in research and production. The level so far is not satisfactory.

At the universities, university colleges, and technical colleges themselves, the creative capacity of their staff must be made more effective. Democracy in higher education should be allowed to flourish. The revolutionary renewal of society in the GDR, anticipating the twenty-first century, can be realized only when science and academic education function as unlimited factors of growth.

Bibliography

Akademie der Pädagogischen Wissenschaften 1983 *Das Bildungswesen der Deutschen Demokratischen Republik*, 2nd edn. Volk und Wissen Volkseigener Verlag, Berlin

Akademie der Pädagogischen Wissenschaften 1986 *Education 1986*. Report to the 40th Session of the International Conference on Education of UNESCO. Geneva 1986, UNESCO, Berlin

Arbeitsgruppe 1989 Erste Vorstellungen zu einer Reform der Fachschulbildung. *Die Fachschule* 12: 329–32

Bernhardt G 1986 Erfahrungen und Aufgaben in der Leitung der Hochschule in der entwickelten sozialistischen Gesellschaft. *Das Hochschulwesen* 3: 53

The GDR Today 1987 Panorama DDR—Auslandspresseagentur GmbH, Berlin

German Democratic Republic 1988 *Statistisches Jahrbuch der Deutschen Demokratischen Republik*. Staatsverlag der Deutschen Demokratischen Republik, Berlin

Higher Education Conference 1980 *Der Beitrag der Universitäten und Hochschulen zum gesellschaftlichen Fortschritt und zur Stärkung der Leistungskraft unseres Landes in den achtziger Jahren*. Protocol of the 5th Higher Education Conference, Berlin

Ministry of Higher and Technical Education 1988 *Hochschulen und Fachschulen der DDR—Statistischer Überblick 1988*. Ministerium für Hoch- und Fachschulwesen, Berlin

Möhle H 1979 The German Democratic Republic—staff development in a socialist setting. In: Teather D C B (ed.) 1979 *Staff Development in Higher Education*. Kogan Page, London, p. 125

Möhle H 1983 La investigación sobre la enseñanza superior en la República Democrática Alemana. *Revista de Ciencias de la Educación* 12: 105

Möhle H 1985 University adult education in the German Democratic Republic. *Int. J. Univ. Adult Educ.* 24 (1–3): 171

Möhle H 1987 *Initial and Further Education in the GDR Organized as Higher-level Distance Education*. Proceedings of the UNESCO International Consultation of Higher Level Distance Education, Victoria

Möhle H 1988a *La contribution de la R.D.A. dans le domaine de la pédagogie comparée au niveau universitaire*. Université Paris VIII, Paris

Möhle H 1988b *The Future Development of Universities—Its Governance by Rectors and Academic Bodies*. City University of New York Center for European Studies, New York

Möhle H 1988c Social development of the GDR: Consequences for higher-level distance education. In: Sewart D, Daniel J S (eds.) 1988 *Developing Distance Education*. International Council for Distance Education, Oslo, p. 325

Möhle H 1989a *The Development of Creative Personalities in Independent Academic Work*. University of Joensuu, Finland

Möhle, H 1989b The influence of informatics and the use of computers in the content and methodology of higher education. In: Claude C, Chitoran D, Malitza M (eds.) 1989 *New Information Technologies in Higher Education*. CEPES, Bucharest, p. 133

Schulz H J 1983 *Higher Education in the German Democratic Republic*. UNESCO/CEPES, Bucharest

H. Möhle

Germany, Federal Republic of

1. Higher Education and Society

The first German universities were founded in the late fourteenth and the fifteenth century, the oldest being the University of Heidelberg which celebrated its 600th anniversary in 1986. The founding of the University of Berlin in 1810 by Wilhelm von Humboldt was of great importance for the German system of higher education. Humboldt's ideas regarding the unity of research and teaching, the freedom of the arts and sciences, and the autonomy of university research and teaching programs, became, and still are, an integral part of higher education policy, though their realization in practice did not always reflect the original conceptions.

In the late nineteenth century and up to the late 1920s, the German system of higher education expanded and diversified. As well as the traditional university type, comprising the human and natural sciences, new technical universities and teacher-training colleges were founded.

During the time of National Socialism (1933–45), the German institutions of higher education did not only play a discreditable role, submitting in large parts to the Nazi ideology, but suffered a sharp decline because of their subjection to strict political control. Hundreds of scholars were forced to leave the institutions and many emigrated.

In 1949, after the Second World War and the division into East and West Germany, the three western zones under allied control were formed into a new state, the Federal Republic of Germany, and the zone under control of the Soviet Union was formed into the German Democratic Republic. The capital, Berlin, remained under the control of all four allied nations and was divided into an eastern and a western part. East Berlin became the capital of the German Democratic Republic; West Berlin became one of the 11 states or *Länder* of the Federal Republic of Germany. It had a special status, because the three western allies reserved the right of control over certain political questions. Bonn became the new capital of West Germany. Besides Berlin, the Federal Republic of Germany consists of 10 other federal states (*Länder*), two of which, Hamburg and Bremen, are city-states.

Between 1946 and 1974 the population increased in the western zones (later the Federal Republic of Germany) from 46.2 to 62.1 million people. It declined after 1974. In 1986, there were 61.1 million people living in the Federal Republic. The peak of increases in birthrates after the Second World War was in the 1950s and 1960s with over one million births per year. This demographic development led to important changes in educational policies in the late 1960s and early 1970s.

The Federal Republic of Germany is one of the most densely populated countries in Europe, having relatively few raw materials and concentrating therefore on a highly developed and export-oriented industrial sector. In 1984, 41.8 percent of those gainfully employed were working in the manufacturing industries, 18.2 percent were working in commerce and transportation, 34.8 percent in the service sector, and 5.2 percent in agriculture (Führ 1980). Unemployment has seriously increased since the mid-1970s. The average unemployment rate at the start of the 1990s is around 10 percent with peaks up to 15 and 19 percent in some areas.

1.1 Structure of Government and Main Political Goals

The restoration of the higher education system in the Federal Republic of Germany after 1949 was partly concerned with the reconstruction of buildings and working facilities. However, there was also a reorientation toward higher education policies of the pre-1933 era.

Higher education policy in the Federal Republic of Germany had opted for a unitary system. In 1950 there were 31 university-level institutions (18 universities, four institutions specializing in one academic discipline only, and nine technical universities) accommodating more than 80 percent of all students at institutions of higher education. Apart from these, there were 78 teacher-training colleges and 18 art colleges. The responsibility for educational policies and planning rested, and still does, with the *Länder*, whereas the government has limited legislative and financial powers.

The 1950s were a time of growing interest in the coordination of state educational policy, the educational policies of the *Länder*, and the universities themselves in order to generate more efficiency concerning research activities and to accommodate a growing number of students. It was also the time of a boom in economic prosperity which led to a higher demand for university-educated professionals. A Ministry for Research was established, supported by and cooperating with the Standing Conference of the Ministers of Culture of the *Länder* (also being in charge of education), as well as the Science Council (a consultancy board of representatives of the state, the academic institutions, and the public). The Ministry's task was to provide coordination and make recommendations for the quantitative, structural, and functional development of the higher education system.

The 1960s saw the foundation of a number of new universities and the expansion of existing institutions of higher education. In 10 years the number of students increased by more than 75 percent, that of professors more than doubled, and that of other academic staff more than tripled. A higher value was put on education in general because it was feared that the Federal Republic of Germany might fall back economically without expansion, in particular, of the sector of further and higher education. Chances for more and better education were thought to bring about more social equality in general. Parallel to these changes a system of nonrepayable state grants for students was introduced and all fees for learning and studying were abolished.

2. The Institutional Fabric of the Higher Education System

In order to present an up-to-date picture of the structure of the higher education system in the Federal Republic of Germany one has to examine the basic foundations of this structure which were laid in the decade between the mid-1960s and the mid-1970s. Higher education policies in the second half of the 1960s were governed by the aim to raise student numbers and have larger parts of the population participate in more and better education.

The new policies led, first, to a nationwide coordination of educational planning; secondly, to the foundation of new universities with the aim of providing a broad local and regional range of higher education institutions; and thirdly, from 1970 on, to a new diversification of institutional types. Through an upgrading of engineering schools and schools of higher vocational training, a new type of higher education institution was created, called *Fachhochschule*. Apart from this, a number of comprehensive universities were established, merging partially with teacher-training colleges, if the latter had not been granted university status, and combining the more practice-oriented tasks of *Fachhochschulen* with the more theory-oriented tasks of universities.

Before these new conceptions actually started to become effective, the student protests of the late 1960s changed the picture of higher education policies. Students criticized the lack of social and political relevance in the contents of class and course programs, and in teaching and research, as well as the bias in favor of "capitalist interests," and questioned the dominating influence of the professoriate regarding the internal organization of academic life. These protests led to a short but intensive phase of reforms, given additional drive through the change in government from a conservative coalition to a coalition of social democrats and liberals in 1969. The reforms in the higher education system were accompanied by a series of legal acts and organizational changes. The latter included the right of all groups beyond the professoriate (students, non-professorial teaching and research staff, and non-academic technical staff) to represent their interests in the self-governing bodies of the institutions. A closer cooperation between the administrative and the academic sector was achieved, which consequently led to a more influential position for the rector or president. The middle-level, nonprofessorial academic staff was given the right to do independent research and teaching, better counseling facilities for students were established, and more detailed prescriptions for courses of study and examinations were introduced.

In 1972, this phase of experiments and reforms was brought to a halt because of growing political disagreement. A Framework Act for Higher Education was debated and finally passed in 1976 with the aim of guaranteeing the basic unity of the higher education system and prescribing a framework for the higher education policies of the *Länder*. By the mid-1970s, a serious economic depression had led to a reduction in funds for education, including higher education. In addition to this, it was argued that the peak of student enrollment would be over soon and that it was a waste of money to go on with the expansion as before.

In 1982 a change to a conservative coalition government had taken place, and in 1985 the Framework Act for Higher Education was revised, strengthening again the position of the professors in the self-governing bodies of the higher education institutions, restructuring career paths for young academics, introducing and legalizing additional grounds for temporary contracts, and giving up the original goal of combining as many higher education institutions as possible in comprehensive universities.

The Framework Act for Higher Education formulates common tasks for all institutions of higher education:

> According to their specific functions, the institutions of higher education shall contribute to the fostering and development of the sciences and arts through research, teaching, and studies. They shall prepare students for occupations which require the application of scientific findings and scientific methods or creative ability in the artistic fields. (Federal Ministry of Education and Science 1976)

The educational tasks of higher education institutions are defined as follows:

> Teaching and study are to prepare students for a profession in a certain sphere of activity, imparting to them the particular knowledge, skills, and methods required in a way appropriate to each course so as to enable them to perform scientific and artistic work and to act responsibly in a free, democratic, and social state governed by the rule of law. (Federal Ministry of Education and Science 1976)

At the same time, however, the Act acknowledges the right of the individual *Länder* to define different tasks for the institutional types and also emphasizes different curricular thrusts of universities and *Fachhochschulen*.

2.1 Levels of Institution

Table 1 shows the development of the various types of higher education institutions up to the pattern of diversification seen in 1990. This picture is structured on the one hand by a few characteristics which most or all institutional types have in common, and on the other by a rather detailed definition of individual core tasks determining their special function within the system of higher education.

All universities in the Federal Republic of Germany share a strong orientation towards scientific and scholarly research and teaching. The unity of research and teaching is expressed by the fact that university professors as a rule (apart from special research sabbaticals) have to do both, even though their professional reputation is predominantly gained through the publication of their research results. A second characteristic is a certain hierarchy among the various types of institution, balanced by the view that all institutions of one type are equal. This is reflected, for example, by the fact that all potential students can enroll at the institution of their choice (provided they have the required entrance qualification), a relatively homogeneous system of funding, and the selection of candidates for positions on the work market by a variety of criteria rather than by prestige of the institution from which the candidate has graduated. The choice of institution and course of study is limited only in certain disciplines which are in high demand. A third characteristic concerns the structure of courses of study, which is linked to a certain degree with the structure of professional fields in the employment sector. The choice of subject or subjects in a degree program usually determines the professional field in which the student later expects to find employment. The fourth characteristic is that, apart from a relatively high degree of autonomy regarding internal policies, there is a strong influence of the *Länder* governments. This influence concerns large proportions of the funding, control of the administration, the right to approve of or refuse courses of study, a participation in all state

Table 1
Institutions of higher education in the Federal Republic of Germany 1960–88

Type of institution	1960	1965	1970	1975	1980	1985	1988
Universities (including technical universities and special universities)	33	34	41	49	55	59	61
Theological seminaries	17	17	14	11	11	15	16
Teachers colleges	52	54	51	19	13	10	8
Art academies	24	26	26	26	26	26	29
Comprehensive universities	—	—	—	11	9	8	7
Fachhochschulen[a]	—	—	98	97	115	122	122
Total	126	131	230	213	229	241	243

Source: Statistics published by Federal Ministry of Education and Science
a Since 1975 including Verwaltungsfachhochschulen (for public administration)

examinations preparing for the civil service sector, the right to approve of or refuse to acknowledge rectors or presidents having been elected by the self-governing bodies of the institution, and the right to choose the candidate for a professorial chair from a list of three the institution is required to submit. Finally, the state has overall responsibility as regards the general tasks of provision and planning for all higher education institutions.

The main differences between the various types of institution can be described as follows. Universities (including technical and special universities) have a strong research orientation which is reflected not only in the unity of teaching and research and in the definition of the core tasks of the professors and other academic staff, but also in graduate programs with the right to award doctoral degrees and the habilitation requirement for university professors. A large proportion of basic research is done at universities. They also usually offer a broad range of subjects for undergraduate studies.

The *Fachhochschulen*, established in the 1970s with the intention of providing a more practically and vocationally oriented option for qualified school leavers, are considered to serve a complete precareer function (whereas university graduates of all subjects finishing with the state exam have to go through a second phase of practical training in their respective professions), with a strong leaning toward conveying tools and knowledge for applied research and development. The main disciplines covered by *Fachhochschulen* are economics, engineering, and social work. At the end of the 1970s a number of *Fachhochschulen* for administration were established by the federal government and the *Länder*. This institutional type trains for the second rank of public administration and the public service sector in nontechnical fields. Even though course programs are equivalent, this new type features two notable differences as compared to the general *Fachhochschulen*: only persons having been given a contract

by a public agency can enroll and the course program lasts three years, with 18 to 24 months of college and 12 to 18 months of on-the-job training. In 1987, a total of 35,000 students were enrolled at 24 of these institutions.

The range of subjects on offer at *Fachhochschulen* is not, in general, as broad as that at the universities. The degree awarded is a special *Fachhochschule* diploma which does not entitle the graduates to become doctoral candidates, although it enables them to enroll as university students (possibly at an advanced stage) if their previous schooling had not reached the university entrance requirements. Enrollment at a *Fachhochschule* generally requires one year less of upper-secondary education than enrollment at a university. Candidates for the position of *Fachhochschule* professor do not have to go through the habilitation process but are expected to have fulfilled "particular achievements with regard to the application and development of scientific findings and methods in at least five years of professional activity, of which a minimum of three years shall have been spent outside higher education" (Framework Act for Higher Education para. 44). In contrast to university professors, research is not defined as one of the core tasks of *Fachhochschule* professors.

The reform model of the comprehensive universities, which was greeted with much enthusiasm in the 1970s, combines features of universities and *Fachhochschulen* and provides a higher proportion of practical and vocational orientation in its courses of study. Students spend certain periods of time during their courses of study in guided projects of research and with explorations of prospective fields of employment after their graduation. Eleven comprehensive universities were established in the early 1970s, but extension was discontinued in the late 1970s. Since 1985, with the revised Framework Act for Higher Education, this model is no longer considered to be an institutional type for structural development in the future. As Table 1 shows, the number of comprehensive universities has dropped from the original 11 to nine between 1975 and 1988.

The few remaining teacher-training colleges, which have not been upgraded to university status during the period of reforms and expansion, or have not merged with comprehensive universities, mainly serve to train teachers for primary schools or social workers and usually require a shorter period of study than universities and *Fachhochschulen.*

There are several significant indicators which can be taken into account when comparing the prestige of the two types of higher education institution—universities and *Fachhochschulen*—which comprise the largest number of students. Even though it is frequently claimed in the Federal Republic of Germany that study at *Fachhochschulen* has become increasingly popular, figures do not support this view. The quota of new entrant students at *Fachhochschulen* (including the *Fachhochschulen* for administration) compared to all new entrant students for higher education institutions was 27.6 percent in 1971, 26.2 percent in 1975, 28.1 percent in 1980, and 33.2 percent in 1987. A more differentiated view is possible when enrollment quotas in economic and engineering fields offered by both *Fachhochschulen* and universities are compared. In 1976/77 the proportion of new students in economics was 28.9 percent for *Fachhochschulen* and 71.1 percent for universities; in 1986/87 it was 31.5 percent for the former and 68.5 percent for the latter. The reverse picture can be found with regard to the field of engineering. In 1976/77 there was a proportion of 58.9 percent of new entrant students in this field enrolling at *Fachhochschulen* and 41.1 percent enrolling at universities; in 1986/87 the percentages were 60.4 percent for the former and 39.6 percent for the latter.

Another factor which seems to play a role with respect to prestige is the social background of students. Official statistics have shown that there is a larger proportion of students from working-class backgrounds among *Fachhochschule* students. Worsening employment prospects in a range of fields for university graduates might have played an additional role in the choice of the shorter and more practice-oriented courses of study at *Fachhochschulen.* In 1987 unemployment quotas for *Fachhochschule* graduates were 4.0 percent, for university graduates 5.7 percent.

Another survey showed that satisfaction with, and utilization of acquired competencies for, professional work and career paths is higher among university graduates than among *Fachhochschule* graduates of the same field. *Fachhochschule* graduates stated more frequently that they could make little use of their acquired qualifications or even none at all. An additional indicator supporting the higher prestige of universities is that university graduates can expect better career opportunities and a higher income than *Fachhochschule* graduates in the same field. Lifetime earnings of university graduates are estimated to be about 10 to 15 percent higher than those of *Fachhochschule* graduates.

2.2 Admission Policies and Selection

In the Federal Republic of Germany every person who has achieved the entrance requirement has a free choice of subject and institution. The entrance requirement for a *Fachhochschule* is at least 12 years of schooling, the last two of these being at a *Fach-oberschule* which finishes with an exam, or successful completion of the 12th grade at a grammar or comprehensive school. The entrance requirement for a university is 13 years of schooling, nine of them usually done at a grammar or comprehensive school, and passing the final exam, called the *Abitur.* There are some subject-tied certificates entitling the holder to study only within a special field. Exceptions to these requirements are colleges of art and music. They are open to applicants without a higher school certificate if the candidate can prove special artistic talents. There are a number of other possibilities for gaining entrance requirements by consecutive steps through various intermediary schools, further education facilities, and other special courses.

Certain disciplines have admission restrictions because they are in high demand and there are not enough places on offer. Since 1986 a special selection procedure has been in force for human and veterinary medicine and dentistry. Applicants must take a test, and there is a quota system for admission and allocation of study places as well, taking into account particular groups such as foreigners, hardship cases, and so on, grades of higher school certificates and test results, results of personal interviews conducted by the higher education institution, and length of waiting time.

For a few other disciplines, for example, architecture, biology, pharmacy, and psychology, applicants are selected by school grades and waiting time. Applicants for disciplines such as business management, economics, law, and computer sciences are guaranteed a study place but not necessarily at the university of their choice. In order to achieve a more even distribution of students and prevent overcrowding at some institutions, applications must be handed to a Central Office for Admissions which allocates a place. This Central Office handles placement for all disciplines with admission restrictions. Apart from the general entrance qualification all other undergraduate study programs in all other disciplines neither have an admission restriction nor do they subject potential students to selection procedures.

2.3 Quantitative Developments

In 1988 there were 243 institutions of higher education in the Federal Republic of Germany accom-

Table 2
Students at institutions of higher education in the Federal Republic of Germany 1960/61 to 1987/88 (absolute numbers and percentages)

Type of institution	1960/61	1965/66	1970/71	1975/76	1980/81	1985/86	1987/88
Universities, teachers' colleges, and theological seminaries	247,220	302,576	411,951	632,857	749,090	929,161	966,616
	81.3	79.3	78.4	75.6	72.7	69.5	68.5
Comprehensive universities	—	—	—	42,400	69,418	85,044	93,386
				5.1	6.7	6.4	6.6
Fachhochschulen[a]	49,169	70,859	102,804	143,402	195,086	300,726	328,625
	16.2	18.6	19.6	17.5	18.9	22.5	23.3
Art academies	7,761	7,987	10,456	15,343	18,044	21,464	22,162
	2.5	2.1	2.0	1.8	1.7	1.6	1.6
Total	304,150	381,422	525,300	836,002	1,031,500	1,336,395	1,410,789

Source: Wissenschaftsrat 1988 p. 312
a Including predecessor institutions

modating a little over 1.5 million students. The proportion of young people of the age group 20 to 24 years enrolled in higher education institutions has risen to somewhat more than 20 percent. Table 2 shows the quantitative developments of students in the various types of higher education institutions from 1960. The table shows that student numbers in higher education did not only rise continuously—they doubled in intervals of approximately 12 years—but that the proportion of students with regard to the relevant age group (20- to 24-year olds) has increased as well. In 1960 about 9 percent of all people in this age group were enrolled in higher education, whereas in 1986 it was 21 percent. These figures, however, do not make clear certain changes in the structure of the student population itself. For instance, the proportion of female students at universities has risen from 24 percent in 1960 to 41 percent in 1988. There was also a rise in the proportion of university students from working-class backgrounds from 6 percent in 1960 to 16 percent in 1985.

2.4 Structure of Qualifications

One of the main issues being debated in the politics of higher education has been the length of study leading to successful completion of a first degree. Students are older and study longer in the Federal Republic of Germany than in most other European countries. New entrant students at universities are on average 21.3 years old, at *Fachhochschulen* 22.4 years. The average age of those successfully completing university course programs was 27.9 years in 1986, while those successfully completing a *Fachhochschule* course were on average 26.5 years old.

University programs usually take four, sometimes five, or even six years in a few subjects (e.g.,

medicine) plus additional time for examinations. Course programs at *Fachhochschulen* last three years in most cases plus additional time for examinations. The freedom granted by education policies, which include the facts that no fees have to be paid and that quite a few students change university after the first half of their course, have led to individual extensions of study time depending on financial means. It is frequently the case, especially in the humanities and social sciences where study courses are less rigidly structured, that students are enrolled full-time but in fact study only part-time and have a part-time job as well, as part-time study is not formally separated from full-time study. In 1988, the average time spent by successful graduates was 7 years at the university and 4.6 years at the *Fachhochschule*. Another reason for the long duration of study is the fact that many students continue to be enrolled even if they interrupt studies or have already graduated. This is due to the social benefits of being a student as well as to the preferable status of a student in comparison with that of an unemployed or nonemployed person.

There are various degree-awarding procedures at universities (including comprehensive universities). Depending on the course of study, universities award (a) a diploma (by definition more vocationally oriented and awarded in the natural and social sciences and in all fields of engineering); (b) a master's degree (an academic title mostly for the humanities and liberal arts); and (c) nondegree first state examinations for prospective civil servants, such as teachers, lawyers, and medical doctors. These state exams are administered jointly by academic staff responsible for quality and content and by an official of the public examination offices who is responsible for the compliance of the formal organization of studies and the exam with state laws and regulations. Graduates of these study courses usually proceed to a second phase of practical training after which they have to pass a second state exam which finishes their professional training. In addition to these degrees, universities are the only higher education institutions with the right to grant doctoral or professorial degrees. These are awarded after a phase of guided or independent research, published in the form of a thesis, and an oral examination procedure. *Fachhochschulen* award diplomas only, with the additional letters FH (for *Fachhochschule*) in the title in order to distinguish them from a university diploma.

Of the degrees conferred on completion of undergraduate university course programs in 1985, 41 percent were diplomas, 4 percent were master's degrees, 28 percent were state examinations for prospective teachers, 24 percent were other state examinations, and 3 percent were other awards (e.g., art degrees and certificates, church degrees).

2.5 Graduate Training

The pattern of graduate studies at higher education institutions in the Federal Republic of Germany consists basically of two types: those programs offering additional, supplementary, or further education and those leading to a doctorate or to a habilitation, that is, those geared towards the education of academic and research staff.

A large part of the additional, supplementary, and further education studies offers specialized courses designed for the advancement of the professional careers of the participants. The Science Council (Wissenschaftsrat 1988 p. 154) mentions 340 different programs in 1988, of which 50 were offered at *Fachhochschulen*, 40 at teacher-training colleges, and the rest at universities. These programs do not lead to a doctorate, and frequently not even to another degree, but rather cover a range of specialized studies for various fields of employment. Certification is diverse and in some cases also controversial. In the case of quite a few of these programs participants also have to pay a fee.

The doctorate counts as the first stage of qualification of young potential academics. The universities do not only educate candidates for their own future staff needs, however, but also for non-university research institutions, departments for research and development in the industrial sector, and other highly qualified positions on the labor market. The number of doctorates awarded rose from 10,497 in 1975 to 14,535 in 1986 (including medicine), that is, an increase of 39 percent. Excluding the medical fields, the number of doctorates has risen only by about 22 percent between 1975 and 1986. During this time the number of doctorates awarded to women has more than doubled.

Differences in various fields can be seen by comparing the proportion of students successfully completing a doctoral degree with the number of students successfully completing first-degree studies in the same discipline. Here the proportions vary between 50 percent in the medical fields and chemistry and less than 10 percent in theology, psychology, education, law, economics, and architecture. One of the reasons for this divergence is the fact that in some disciplines with high proportions of doctorates, notably the medical fields and chemistry, graduates have few chances of employment without the title.

In some disciplines, mainly the liberal arts and humanities, the quota of doctorates has declined since the mid-1970s, notably because with the end of expansion in higher education academic career prospects stagnated or became almost nonexistent. The general decline in the percentages of those going on to a doctoral degree after having completed their first-degree studies may also be a reflection of the fact that, according to estimated research expenditures, the proportion of research conducted at institutions of higher education has decreased from more than 18 percent of all basic research in 1975 to 13 percent in the late 1980s, whereas there has been immense growth in research and development outside the universities (Krais and Naumann 1991).

The average age upon completion of the doctorate has risen between 1977 and 1986 from 31.0 years to 31.5 years with considerable differences among the various disciplines. In 1986 it was lowest in veterinary medicine (30 years) and human medicine (30.7 years) and highest in the philologies and cultural sciences (34.2 years) and in the engineering sciences (33.7 years).

Upon recommendation of the Science Council, about 70 organized graduate courses were established in 1990. An initial trial phase during the second half of the 1980s, with only a few of these courses, led to the realization that a better organizational framework, more intensive supervision and counseling, and more exchange among candidates of the same field can lead not only to a shorter time for completion of the thesis but to greater efficiency and higher success rates, that is, lower dropout rates, as well. As a rule, universities have to submit applications for the establishment of organized courses on a competitive basis and go through the machinery of the approval system of the German Research Association. On approval, the university, having guaranteed facilities and professorial guidance, can offer research grants for two, or sometimes up to three, years to prospective candidates. The graduate courses consist mainly of doctoral candidates but often also have a few postdoctoral candidates working on their *Habilitation*. However, the courses are not meant to substitute the traditional paths of gaining a doctoral degree through part-time teaching and research positions at the university or through scholarships. Rather, they are meant to supplement these forms.

The traditional means of gaining a doctorate can vary not only according to the field or discipline in which study and research are being done but also to the university where it is done. As a rule, a highly qualified first degree with good grades is a prerequisite. Once a candidate has been accepted by a professor and has a topic agreed upon for the thesis, research or experimental work can start. This lasts between two to three years at least, and often up to five or six years. The candidates do not normally have to fulfill special course requirements. Their work is considered to be guided and supervised, but generally independent, research work. Very often candidates work on a subject in the field of expertise or research of their supervisor. They may also take part in special small group seminars of this supervisor's examination and doctoral candidates where the relevant work is being discussed. Doctoral candidates do their work either on the basis of a part-time and temporary teaching and research assistantship, on the basis of a scholarship, or they have some other kind of part-time work. The need to earn money leads to a lengthening of the time in which a dissertation is finished. There are no data about dropout rates but these are thought to be very high. Exceptions to this pattern are the doctoral degrees in the medical fields. Here the candidates do supervised research work, often during their internship in the hospital, and publish results in a shorter paper for which the doctorate is usually awarded after an additional oral examination.

The universities are usually autonomous in setting up the regulations for their doctoral degrees. Generally, the dissertation has to be submitted for grading to two referees, one of which is the supervisor. If the referees disagree about the grade a third one will be consulted. One of the referees may be a professor from another university. In addition to this, the dissertation has to be laid out publicly at the candidate's university and every professor can comment on it. Once the dissertation has been accepted the candidate has to go through an oral examination consisting in most cases of a public defense of his or her work, and in some cases of an oral examination in at least three disciplines. Candidates are required to publish their dissertation before gaining the right to the title. A doctoral degree usually certifies the ability to do independent research and is one of the main requirements for an academic career.

As with doctoral degrees, a large proportion of habilitations is in the medical fields. In the late 1980s there were between 950 and 1,000 habilitations per year of which 300 to 350 were completed in the medical disciplines. The proportion of women doing habilitations varies depending on the discipline. It is 7 percent on average but it is above average in the philologies, in psychology, and in education. In 1985 about a quarter of those persons having completed a habilitation were employed outside university, mainly in research centers and in business.

A number of scholarships are granted for individual research projects or to research teams, for the promotion and qualification of potential professors. The main path for completing a habilitation is, however, a temporary academic position, called assistantship, of six to eight years at a university. This position is usually linked to a full professorship or chair, the holder of which serves as adviser for the candidate's research work. An assistant has some teaching obligations and is supposed to assist the professor in his or her own research work but devotes at least half of the time to research for the habilitation. The habilitation thesis has to be refereed by three full professors upon completion. In addition to this, there is an oral defense and a public lecture. Upon successful completion of this procedure the right to give public lectures, the *venia legendi*, is granted, but not necessarily a professorship or any other form of employment.

3. Governance, Administration, and Finance

3.1 National Administration

All institutions of higher education are supervised by the education or higher education ministry of the respective *Land*. There are no formal differences in the legal status and the degree of governmental supervision between universities and *Fachhochschulen*. It is the responsibility of the federal government to undertake provision and planning for a certain homogeneity of the system as a whole. However, the institutions are autonomous up to a certain degree with respect to their internal organization and administration.

Policy decisions for the system of higher education as a whole are made by the Standing Conference of the Education Ministers of the *Länder*. This Conference has the task of coordinating the structures, facilities, and patterns of certification of the higher education institutions and of deciding important policy questions in the field. It is supported by a number of more or less formal advisory groups or boards (such as the West German Rectors' Conference and the Science Council) and teams of experts. Amendments to the Basic Law (Constitution) in 1969 granted the federal government certain rights to regularize statutorily the general principles governing higher education and the opportunity to collaborate with the *Länder* in the planning and financing of higher education. The cooperation between the federal government and the *Länder* also concerns the joint promotion of scientific and scholarly research. It is supposed both to guarantee the diversity of the system and to preserve uniform living conditions and equal opportunities, as well as the promotion of mobility.

After the expansion of the higher education system in the 1960s and 1970s sole funding through the *Länder* became too much of a burden and a greater influence of the federal government led to a higher proportion of central financing. Investments in higher education buildings are borne on a 50–50 basis since 1970. There are also joint deliberations on the funding of the German Research Association, the most important body for funding university research (Giesecke 1987 pp. 5–7).

An analysis of the development of decentralization and centralization in the higher education system of the Federal Republic of Germany has reconstructed basically three periods (Peisert and Framhein 1978 pp. 25–84): (a) a period of decentralized reconstruction (1945–56) with limited federal responsibilities but cooperation among the *Länder* through the Standing Conference of the Ministers of Culture as well as the establishment of some advisory organizations on the federal level (the West German Rectors' Conference, the German Academic Exchange Service, and the German Research Association); (b) a period of system-wide initiatives (1957–69) starting nationwide coordination and planning and founding the Science Council for making recommendations on the promotion of research and on the expansion of the system as a whole; (c) a period of cooperative federalism (since 1969) making provisions for common responsibilities with regard to facilities and construction, planning, and funding. A Federal-State Commission for Educational Planning and Research was established in 1970 to submit proposals on long-term planning. In 1976 the Framework Act for Higher Education was enacted and a year later Study Reform Commissions were established to elaborate on guidelines for common elements of curricula in higher education institutions (Peisert and Framhein 1978 pp. 29–49). A fourth period can be added, which started in 1972 with growing political disagreement on general higher education policies and the postponement of the Framework Act for Higher Education. The trend for system-wide coordination was brought to a halt by the refusal of the *Länder* to agree to further state regulations. They began a more intensive cooperation among themselves rather than between themselves and the federal government. A drastic reduction in state expenditure on the expansion of facilities and construction in higher education was not only interpreted by some *Länder* as an indication of the federal government's desire to relinquish its involvement in higher education planning but brought some reform models and newly established universities to a standstill before they had reached their promised range of departments and accommodation facilities. The proportion of the gross national product spent on higher education dropped from 1.32 percent in 1975, to 1.13 percent in 1980, to 1.01 percent in 1986.

Quantitative and structural planning was originally the responsibility of each *Land*. Since the establishment of the Science Council in 1957, however, the federal government has been involved in recommendations. The Science Council sets goals regarding the overall capacity of higher education, its regional distribution, and the quantitative development of certain fields of study. The recommendations of the Science Council are taken up by the governments of the *Länder* according to their budgetary and educational policies. Those decisions not interfering with the existing elements of autonomy of the higher education institutions are put into practice predominantly by decree. The institutions themselves and the rectors or presidents as their representatives can influence decisions by lobbying or by negotiation with the minister. Apart from general supervision by the ministry of the appropriate *Land* there are no formal and established procedures of evaluation and assessment, except at newly founded institutions for the first few years, which rate the institutions' responses to certain goals. Policies of the *Land* are, however, enforced through budgetary means to a relatively high degree. A lot of research is being done on this issue by various means, including university-linked research centers, individual scholars with expertise in this field, and informal teams of experts preparing recommendations for various advisory boards. Apart from the aforementioned forms of financing higher education, a considerable part of the basic research activities at the universities is paid for indirectly by the state in the form of research grants channelled via the German Research Association and other funding through foundations which receive at least part of their money from the state.

3.2 Finance

Every higher education institution has a highly differentiated budget, the block sum of which it receives out of the educational budget of the *Land*. It is one of the tasks of the president or rector to negotiate for more money. Since research was defined as one of the core tasks of the universities but the allocated regular budget only covers a small part of this task, the individual professor with whom it is resting has to compete for grants from the German Research Association and similar institutions or from private sources. A serious debate has been going on about the "emigration" of scientific and scholarly research from the universities, because surveys showed that more and more research and development was being done outside the universities.

Between 1975 and 1986 net public expenditure for higher education decreased in real terms by about 2 percent. In 1986 this expenditure was divided into 80 percent for basic provisions, 9 percent for research grants, and 11 percent for student support and graduate studies. The decrease in real terms was mainly due to substantial cuts in state support for con-

Table 3
Gross National Product and expenditure for higher education in the Federal Republic of Germany 1960–1988 (millions of DM)

	1960	1965	1970	1975	1980	1985	1988
Gross National Product (GNP)	302,710	459,170	675,300	1,026,900	1,478,940	1,830,490	2,110,560
Budget for higher education	—	3,541	6,873	13,585	17,750	21,415	24,592
Federal government	—	—	985	1,339	868	1,071	1,064
Länder	—	—	5,873	12,247	16,882	20,345	23,528

Source: Federal Ministry of Education and Science 1990 Basic and Structural Data 1989–90 p. 12

struction of buildings and for student support and housing. On the other hand, state support for university research increased in real terms.

Table 3 shows the development and the respective proportions in the funding of higher education by the federal government and the *Länder* since 1960. The expenditure by the federal government on higher education went down from 2.02 percent of the whole budget in 1975 to 1.30 percent in 1986. The expenditure of the *Länder* on higher education went down from 5.2 percent of the whole budget in 1980 to 4.9 percent in 1986 (excluding university hospitals). The average figures given here for the *Länder* must, however, be examined at their two levels. Whereas funding of universities stagnated in real terms between 1980 and 1986, it increased for *Fachhochschulen* by about 13 percent. The budgetary distributions for universities, *Fachhochschulen*, and university hospitals are not homogeneous among the various *Länder* (see Krais and Naumann 1991).

3.3 Institutional Administration

The self-governing bodies of higher education institutions in the Federal Republic of Germany were always an important element of the autonomy of these institutions. Originally centered around the full professor only, they became collegiate bodies in the course of reforms during the 1960s and 1970s, including not only nonprofessorial teaching and research staff but student representatives and representatives of the administrative and technical personnel as well.

Higher education institutions are governed by a threefold system: the legal acts of the federal government, those of the relevant *Land*, and their own statutes. A similar threefold system exists for control and supervision within the individual institution itself: the departments or faculties are headed by a dean, and the deans are supervised by the rector or president, who in turn is responsible to the ministry of education or of higher education of the *Land*.

Up to the mid-1960s three characteristics dominated the organization and administration of universities: the mainly representational function of the rector, the negligible influence of the central administration, and the great power of the professoriate. In the second half of the 1960s a series of legal acts of the *Länder* governments prescribed more detailed regulations. Another factor occasioning changes and reforms of the traditional structure was the student protests between 1967 and 1970. The demands for reforms of the formal structure of higher education, voiced by the students, concerned mainly the participation of nonprofessorial groups in the self-governing bodies. In some cases the professors suddenly found themselves in a minority. Finally, in 1976, the Framework Act for Higher Education established certain common elements to be adhered to in the organization of the institutions. The most important changes in this period were:

(a) The short-term (two years) representational office of the rector was replaced by a longer term (four to eight years) office of a rector or president with additional functions in administration and self-governing bodies. Thus, academic and administrative issues were unified and the office of the rector or president took on a more professional character.

(b) The so-called middle-level academic teaching and research staff, students, and nonacademic personnel received between one-quarter and one-third of the votes in the various self-governing bodies at the central level as well as at the departmental level of the institution. A court decision in 1973, however, had guaranteed a majority of 51 percent for the professors with regard to all important issues of research and a 50 percent majority at least concerning issues of teaching. Public representatives were never allowed to be members of these bodies.

(c) In order to strengthen and extend the capabilities of the institution to coordinate issues of research and teaching, the old and rather large faculties were divided into smaller departments. Clear distinctions were established between the management of the block sum budgets and the personal income of full professors. The first of these tasks was the responsibility of the central administration, deciding about the allocation and distribution of personnel and other resources to the various departments and institutes; the second was officially regarded as a point to be negotiated between the individual professor and the department and not, as formerly, the Ministry of Education of the *Land*.

(d) Since the 1960s there had been various reforms concerning the structure of the academic staff. Legal acts in 1985 defined the two categories of professors at universities and *Fachhochschulen*. The highest professorial rank, called C4 after the corresponding level on the pay scale, can be found only at universities. These professors usually hold a chair and are not only tenured lifetime civil servants but are also distinguished by a higher amount of support in the form of junior academic staff, administrative and technical personnel, and a larger proportion of material resources. The two other professorial ranks, called C3 and C2, are normally tenured as well and can be found both at universities and *Fachhochschulen*. There are, however, exceptions in the C2 category because this rank can also include temporary positions. As a consequence of various reforms, professors are forced to seek a higher level of consensus from other members of the department regarding decisions about the distribution and utilization of resources and about teaching and organizational issues.

The senate or council of a higher education institution is the highest and most important body of self-governance. It is headed by the rector or president and consists of the deans of all departments and faculties, and representatives of the professoriate, the other academic staff, the nonacademic staff, and the students. The president or rector is elected by the senate or council and is accountable to this body. After election, however, the ministry of the *Land* has to acknowledge the elected person and officially appoint the new rector or president to his, or rarely, her office. There have been a couple of cases in which the ministry refused to acknowledge and appoint the elected person. The president or rector is supported by a bursar (*Kanzler*), a high level administrator responsible for questions of finance and budgeting. The senate or council deliberates issues of coordination and planning in research and teaching as well as the distribution of the budget.

The regulations for the self-governing body of the departments or faculties vary according to the *Land*. As a rule it is a collegiate body, headed by the dean and consisting of all academic members of the department as well as representatives of the students and nonacademic personnel. The dean is elected by this body for a limited period of time (usually two years) from among the group of academics. In most cases this office is held by a full professor who receives a reduction in his or her teaching load in order to undertake the administrative tasks connected with the office. The professors are guaranteed a majority in this body as well, even though most departments make allowances for the participation of other groups. The dean has intermediating and coordinating functions concerning the organization of departmental work, including course programs and study and examination regulations. The self-governing body on the departmental level deliberates the issues of this work and budgetary questions and establishes search committees if a chair becomes vacant or other regularly budgeted teaching and research positions have to be filled.

4. Faculty and Students: Teaching, Learning, and Research

4.1 Faculty

In spite of substantial changes, the structure of university staff established in the early nineteenth century by the Humboldtian university reforms continues to shape debates in the Federal Republic of Germany. The university staff structure was, and still is to a considerable degree, focused on the position of the full professor, appointed by the minister of education of the *Land* upon recommendation of the university department.

Apart from being the sole and independent representatives of their field, the special status of a civil servant assuring freedom of research and teaching, successful candidates used to be able to negotiate their salary directly with the government and increasingly their staff requirements, equipment, and financial support for teaching and research as well. Furthermore, the traditional university had two other ranks of teaching staff: the "nonregular" professor, a less influential but paid position covering fields which were considered less important than those of the "regular" professor, and the private lecturer or reader, a position for persons having successfully completed the habilitation but not holding a university position as such and whose remuneration came from student fees.

The nineteenth century saw the emergence of a chair structure and an institute structure. The institute was usually headed by a full professor and was in charge of research. The chair might be allocated an assistant, or a laboratory, or a small library. Junior academic staff were badly paid and not allowed to do any teaching.

With the expansion of higher education in the 1960s and 1970s substantial changes in the traditional structure took place. The most important of these were:

(a) An increased number of chairs with various specializations, or more than one chair for the same special field, offering more choices to the growing number of students.

(b) The promotion of cooperation among professors giving way to larger institutes or faculties headed by the professorial members on a rotation basis.

(c) Larger research units incorporating permanent professional staff leading to an increasing diversification of the types of research staff positions.

(d) Improved social positions for all scholars who had successfully completed their habilitation as well as fully paid positions for other permanent teaching staff.

(e) A growing demand for teaching staff to keep up with increasing student numbers. Permanent teaching positions were created for persons without a habilitation and assistants and junior academic staff took over a certain amount of the teaching load, supervised only nominally by full professors.

This growing diversification of academic teaching and research positions led to a high ratio of junior to senior positions so that a secure promotion for the majority of junior staff was no longer guaranteed. In the early 1990s large numbers of junior academic staff are employed on the basis of part-time and temporary contracts with frequent periods of unemployment in between. In 1986 the total number of regularly budgeted positions for academic staff at higher education institutions in the Federal Republic of Germany was around 80,000.

Gradually the reform models of the 1970s, which led to the greater participation and influence of the nonprofessorial personnel in the self-governing bodies of the institutions, were reclaimed or cut back. Since the 1980s, efforts have been made for more direct supervision of junior academic staff, once more linking their positions and tasks more closely to a chair. A greater emphasis was placed on differences among the various ranks of professors in terms of titles, functions, and privileges.

Table 4 provides an overview of staff development over the years as well as the student–staff ratio. The actual number of academic staff employed at higher education institutions is about 10 percent higher than the number of positions. In the early 1960s, academic staff at universities was doubled in order to improve the quality of teaching and research. In fact, the student–academic staff ratio declined from 15 : 1 to 9 : 1 during that period. The subsequent duplication from the mid-1960s to the mid-1970s kept pace with the growing student numbers. Since 1975, hardly any new positions were created for academic staff and in 1986 the student–academic staff ratio was back to the level of 1960. A similar development can be observed in the *Fachhochschule* sector.

4.2 Faculty Career Paths

In a typical academic career a student will acquire the first university degree after about six years of study. Fewer than one in seven graduates will proceed to a doctoral degree. During a period of three to five years, those who do might be doctoral students, possibly supported by a scholarship, hold positions as academic support staff members, or as research staff members financed by external research funds. Upon completion of the doctoral degree, again about one in seven will eventually become a university professor. They might be a university assistant, a member of a research staff financed by external funds, or have been granted one of the relatively few postdoctoral scholarships, and eventually attain the habilitation after about another five years or more. It might take even longer until they finally receive a position as professor. In order to provide better opportunities for this highly qualified group of academics, amendments to the Framework Act for Higher Education in 1985 have created the positions of "senior assistant" and "senior engineer" (*Oberassistent, Oberingenieur*). These are temporary positions in the professorial C2 rank. Prospective *Fachhochschule* teachers might turn to professional activities outside higher education upon completion of a doctoral degree.

The recruitment and appointment procedures are more or less the same at universities and *Fachhochschulen*. Vacancies of professorial positions are publicly announced. The higher education institution in question will, upon hearing of the most qualified candidates, present a list of the three most qualified, and the appropriate ministry will usually appoint the person on top of the list. Sometimes, however, the second or third candidate is appointed, or, in exceptional cases, the ministry might ask for a new list or even appoint someone who had not been proposed.

At universities there are no promotion schemes for the lower professorial ranks (C3 and C2). It is usual to "call" only candidates from other universities. This opens up a mechanism for salary negotiations. If a professor receives a "call" from another university he or she can negotiate salary supplements or other resources in order to stay or as a precondition for accepting the position offered. At *Fachhochschulen* different conditions are established. A person occupying a lower rank professorial position might be promoted to the higher rank position. Members of the highest professorial rank at *Fachhochschulen*, however, are not entitled to negotiate salary supplements or resources.

The teaching load during a semester week is six to eight hours for a university professor and 18 hours for a *Fachhochschule* professor. This difference takes

Table 4
Academic staff at institutions of higher education in the Federal Republic of Germany 1960–1988 (and student–academic staff ratio)

	1960	1965	1970	1975	1980	1985	1988
Universities[a]							
Professors	5,200	8,800	13,300	22,200	24,200	24,600	23,900
	(49:1)	(35:1)	(32:1)	(31:1)	(34:1)	(43:1)	(47:1)
Other academic and	11,700	24,100	34,800	45,700	45,500	46,300	48,100
creative arts staff	(22:1)	(13:1)	(12:1)	(15:1)	(18:1)	(23:1)	(23:1)
Total	16,800	32,900	48,100	67,900	69,700	70,800	71,100
	(15:1)	(9:1)	(9:1)	(10:1)	(12:1)	(15:1)	(16:1)
Fachhochschulen[b]							
Professors	300	600	1,500	8,200	8,600	8,700	8,900
	(164:1)	(118:1)	(69:1)	(18:1)	(23:1)	(36:1)	(39:1)
Other academic and	1,900	3,000	4,000	800	500	500	500
creative arts staff	(26:1)	(24:1)	(26:1)	(182:1)	(391:1)	(625:1)	(686:1)
Total	2,200	3,600	5,500	9,000	9,100	9,200	9,300
	(22:1)	(20:1)	(19:1)	(16:1)	(22:1)	(33:1)	(37:1)

Source: Statistics published by Federal Ministry of Education and Science
a Including comprehensive universities, teachers' colleges, theological seminaries, and art academies b Including predecessor institutions

into account the fact that research is considered to be one of the core tasks of university professors whereas *Fachhochschule* professors might only be granted a reduced teaching load in exceptional cases for conducting applied research. The *Fachhochschulen* do not have any functions with regard to the training of junior academic staff either. They can award neither a doctoral degree nor the *venia legendi*.

Beyond the core tasks of teaching and research, all professors are more or less obligated to take an active interest in departmental activities and policies, taking turns in acting as dean, and taking part in assemblies and committee meetings of the department. In addition to these duties, professors have a certain amount of counseling, supervision, and administration to do which varies according to the number of students attending their seminars, the number of students they have accepted in their role as main examiner for first-degree examinations or as supervisor of a doctoral dissertation, and their research support staff.

More than 95 percent of university and *Fachhochschule* professors are tenured civil servants. In contrast to their relatively secure position more than two-thirds of the other academic staff are temporarily employed or civil servants for a limited period of time. However, there are various ways of extending teaching provisions beyond those provided by academic staff holding tenured positions at higher education institutions. The most frequent ones are the following:

(a) University staff funded by external resources might receive part-time contracts as lecturers.

(b) Practitioners from occupational fields outside the higher education institutions might also be hired as part-time lecturers.

(c) Recent graduates might get short-term contracts permitting them to serve as research and teaching assistants.

(d) Persons of high professional, public, and academic esteem might be appointed as honorary professors with the obligation to teach without remuneration.

A substantial proportion of academic staff is involved in contractual research and development apart from its major functions. University professors have to declare this extra income on their income-tax return only, whereas *Fachhochschule* professors might need approval. Some extra income can also be gained by teaching in the fields of further education and adult education, doing applied research and development for industrial sectors, or engaging in consultancy activities.

Among the nonprofessorial academic staff there are further differences concerning not only income but legal status, rights, and privileges. For example, the right to conduct examinations or to do independent research, the amount of teaching hours per semester week, the type of seminar which can be taught, and the amount of additional resources, including secretarial labor and office space, may all vary.

4.3 Representation of Faculty Interests

There are two main ways in which the academic profession may represent its corporate interests: the more political possibility is to become a member of a union, and the more subject-linked possibility is to become a member of one of the academic associations which exist for almost all disciplines. Apart from these, there are associations of academics, such as the Association for the Freedom of the Sciences, which represent certain political stances in the discussions about policies in higher education and research, but have neither union nor party status.

Unionization in higher education is not homogeneous, even though the principle of "one company, one union" is valid for almost all other sectors in society. The two main unions representing the academic profession are the Union of Public Services, Transportation, and Traffic which also accepts nonacademic staff as members and the Union for Teachers and Scientists, representing only the academic and some of the higher administrative staff as well as students heading for a teaching position. In both of these unions academics only form a minority, although they have more influence in the latter. A small number of academics from the natural sciences and from engineering are represented in the union of the appropriate professional sector, for example, the Union of Metal Workers or the Union of Workers in Chemistry, Paper Production, and Ceramics.

The discipline-linked organizations, such as the German Association of Sociology or the German Association of Education, are concerned mainly with the promotion of new developments in the subject matter. They are often subdivided into standing working groups or sections covering special fields and meeting in between the large biennial conferences. These associations deliberate on issues concerning the standing of their respective disciplines in higher education and society.

4.4 Students

Table 5 shows the development of student numbers in various disciplines for *Fachhochschulen* and universities. The quota of new entrants at all institutions of higher education as a proportion of the corresponding age group (19 to 21 year olds) increased from 7.9 percent in 1960 to 15.4 percent in 1970. The percentage rose to 19.5 percent in 1975 and then stagnated for a decade. From 1985 to 1987 it increased again to 22.9 percent. Because of the nature of the demographic development in the Federal Republic of Germany student numbers are expected to drop by 34 to 48 percent between 1987 and the year 2000.

During the 1970s and 1980s four important changes concerning the transfer from upper secondary to higher education were observable:

(a) The percentage of qualified school leavers ultimately enrolling in higher education institutions decreased from 83 percent in 1976 to an estimated 70 percent in 1986.

(b) The average time span between completion of upper-secondary education and enrollment in higher education increased and so, therefore, did the average age of new entrant students (from 20.8 years in 1975 to 21.7 years in 1987).

(c) Because of improved possibilities of transfer among the various types of upper-secondary schools the school type determined to a lesser extent the likelihood of transfer to higher education. More than half of the students enrolled at *Fachhochschulen* also have the entrance qualification for universities.

(d) The quota of women with university entrance qualifications increased from 42.1 percent in 1973 to 47.5 percent in 1980 and 49.2 percent in 1987. This was not reflected, however, by an equal rise in the number of female students during the 1980s. It was 24 percent in 1960, 26 percent in 1970, 34 percent in 1975, 37 percent in 1980, and 38 percent in 1987.

Between 1972 and 1988 the absolute numbers of new students in most of the disciplines more or less doubled. They increased to a lesser extent in law, agriculture, and the arts, and sharply declined in teacher training. This decline is due mainly to extremely bad employment prospects. In the humanities and social sciences, in particular, hardly any new teaching positions were opened up because of a drop in pupil numbers in upper-secondary schools. However, there are still considerable numbers of students in these disciplines. Students simply opt for the academic degree of MA, rather than heading for teacher training and the state examination in the same discipline.

There are no reliable data on student dropout rates. Long-term comparisons of the number of new students and the number of graduates lead to the conclusion that dropout rates are higher than 20 percent. According to a 1984 survey, the dropout quotas were 16 percent at universities, 18 percent in teacher training, and 14 percent at *Fachhochschulen*. The dropout quota for women enrolled at universities was 25 percent as compared to 11 percent among men. The respective quotas for *Fachhochschulen* were lower.

Table 6 provides an overview of access to higher education and graduation. The expansion of higher education has led to high graduate numbers. It is estimated that the percentage of graduates among the new labor force has increased from about 5 percent in the 1950s to 13–15 percent in 1980. The percentage of higher education-trained persons among the total labor force increased from about 4 percent in 1960 to more than 8 percent in 1980.

Looking at the structure of the student body from the viewpoint of social class origins (Table 7), the proportion of university students from working-class backgrounds has increased from 4 percent in 1952 to

Table 5
Numbers and percentages of students in respective fields of study at universities and *Fachhochschulen* 1960–1988

	1960	1965	1970	1975	1980	1985	1988
Humanities							
Universities	57,700	81,000	169,700	222,600	256,800	289,400	298,300
	(26.8)	(28.8)	(40.3)	(32.0)	(30.5)	(27.9)	(26.5)
Fachhochschulen	—	—	—	2,700	2,800	4,700	5,100
				(1.9)	(1.4)	(1.5)	(1.5)
Social sciences							
Universities	45,100	65,100	81,500	145,900	188,300	250,100	288,800
	(20.9)	(23.2)	(19.3)	(21.0)	(22.4)	(24.1)	(25.6)
Fachhochschulen	—	—	—.	49,000	83,600	109,600	126,600
				(33.8)	(41.4)	(36.4)	(36.9)
Natural sciences							
Universities	31,200	40,000	66,300	136,100	153,800	191,600	214,400
	(14.5)	(14.2)	(15.7)	(19.6)	(18.3)	(18.5)	(19.0)
Fachhochschulen	—	—	—	3,300	6,300	14,400	19,500
				(2.3)	(3.1)	(4.8)	(5.7)
Medical fields							
Universities	35,400	46,600	47,300	56,500	84,000	102,800	106,900
	(16.4)	(16.6)	(11.2)	(8.1)	(10.0)	(9.9)	(9.5)
Engineering							
Universities	36,100	37,000	40,400	85,000	94,800	125,100	139,300
	(16.8)	(13.2)	(9.6)	(12.2)	(11.3)	(12.1)	(12.4)
Fachhochschulen	—	—	—	78,300	92,000	149,300	167,100
			(54.0)	(45.5)	(49.4)	(49.6)	(48.7)
Agricultural fields							
Universities	2,600	3,000	5,500	14,400	21,700	25,200	24,800
	(1.2)	(1.1)	(1.3)	(2.1)	(2.6)	(2.4)	(2.2)
Fachhochschulen	—	—	—	3,800	7,000	10,100	11,100
				(2.6)	(3.5)	(3.5)	(3.2)
Fine arts							
Universities	7,300	8,100	10,500	34,900	42,600	52,100	54,800
	(3.4)	(2.9)	(2.5)	(5.0)	(5.1)	(5.1)	(4.9)
Fachhochschulen	—	—	—	8,000	10,300	13,200	13,600
				(5.5)	(5.1)	(4.4)	(4.0)
Total							
Universities[a]	215,400	280,800	421,200	695,500	842,000	1,036,800	1,127,600
Fachhochschulen	—	—	—	145,100	202,000	301,300	343,100

Source: Statistics published by Federal Ministry of Education and Science
a Including comprehensive universities, teachers' colleges, theological seminaries, and art academies

16 percent in 1985. This is due to campaigns in the 1960s and 1970s promising equal educational opportunities for all social classes and trying to encourage those parents who traditionally kept a certain distance from the educational sector to send their talented children to upper secondary schools. This campaign became known for its motto of "raising all reservoirs of talent."

The total number of foreign students at higher education institutions in the Federal Republic of Germany was 22,000 in 1960, 28,000 in 1970, 58,000 in 1980, and 81,000 in 1987. The proportion of foreign students among all students enrolled in higher education dropped, however, from 7.5 percent in 1960 to 5.6 percent in 1970, after which it remained more or less constant. It was 5.7 percent in 1985 and 5.9 percent in 1988. Of these foreign students 78.6 percent were enrolled at universities, 2.9 percent at art colleges, and 18.5 percent at *Fachhochschulen*. The proportion of women among students has already been discussed. In 1987, the quota of female students was highest at colleges of art and music, at universities and teacher-training colleges; it was lowest at *Fachhochschulen* and comprehensive universities (with the exception of *Fachhochschule* courses in social work). Generally the highest number of women students can be found in the humanities and liberal arts and in teacher training.

Table 6
Participation in higher education and number of graduations in the Federal Republic of Germany
1960–1986

	1960	1965	1970	1975	1980	1986
Secondary-school leavers (in thousands)						
Academic track	55.4	51.7	89.2	125.5	168.0	224.2
Higher vocational track	—	—	—	46.7	50.6	66.6
Total	55.4	51.7	89.2	172.2	218.6	290.8
Secondary school leavers as percentage of corresponding age group[a]						
Academic track	5.6	7.2	10.9	14.7	17.2	21.2
Higher vocational track	—	—	—	5.5	5.2	6.2
Total	5.6	7.2	10.9	20.2	22.4	27.4
New students (in thousands)						
Universities[b]	65.4	63.2	92.2	120.7	138.2	147.3
Fachhochschulen	20.6	26.5	29.2	42.8	51.7	64.4
Total	86.0	89.7	121.4	163.5	189.9	211.7
New students as percentage of corresponding age group[a]						
Universities	6.6	8.8	11.2	14.2	14.2	13.9
Fachhochschulen	2.1	3.7	3.6	5.0	5.3	6.2
Total	8.7	12.5	14.8	19.2	19.5	20.1
Graduates[c] (in thousands)						
Universities	27.9	40.5	47.3	70.7	70.9	80.5
Fachhochschulen	11.3	15.3	22.0	30.6	33.3	48.5
Total	39.2	55.8	69.3	101.3	104.2	129.0
Graduates as percentage of corresponding age group[d]						
Universities	3.4	4.3	7.2	9.6	8.9	8.5
Fachhochschulen	1.4	1.6	3.3	4.1	4.2	5.1
Total	4.8	5.9	10.5	13.7	13.1	13.6

Sources: Wissenschaftsrat 1983 *Zur Lage der Hochschulen Anfang der 80er Jahre. Textteil.* Wissenschaftsrat 1988 *Empfehlungen des Wissenschaftsrates zu den Perspektiven der Hochschulen in den 90er Jahren.*
a 18–21-year olds   b Universities, comprehensive institutions, art academies, etc.   c Total number of examinations excluding those doctoral examinations preceded by previous examinations   d 23–27-year olds

Table 7
Social background of students at universities and *Fachhochschulen* 1952–1985 (percentages)

	1952	1962	1967	1973	1976	1979	1982	1985
University students								
Civil servant	38	33	30	27	25	24	24	25
Salaried employee	23	30	31	33	35	36	37	39
Self-employed	35	28	30	26	24	22	21	20
Manual worker	4	6	7	11	13	14	16	16
Others	0	3	2	3	3	4	2	—
Fachhochschule students								
Civil servant	—	—	—	15	14	14	15	15
Salaried employee	—	—	—	31	31	32	36	38
Self-employed	—	—	—	23	21	19	20	20
Manual worker	—	—	—	27	28	27	28	27
Others	—	—	—	4	6	8	1	—

Source: Regular surveys on "Das soziale Bild der Studentenschaft"

4.5 Representation of Student Interests

The interests of the student body as a whole are represented by the general student board (*Allgemeiner Studentenausschuß*) at each university. Upon enrollment all students automatically become members of the corporate body of the studentship of their university and have to pay a small contribution each semester for the work of the general student board representing this corporate body. Various student political organizations compete for election approximately every two years and might form a coalition in order to gain a majority for the general student board. The board is divided in turn into a main committee and various subcommittees representing the interests of particular groups of students, for example, foreign students or women, or of particular fields of interest, such as culture, social situation of students, international relations. These boards are linked together on the *Länder* level and nationwide. There have been disputes about the political activities of the general student boards, sometimes ending up in court. Two of the *Länder* finally legislated that compulsory membership should end and consequently the general student boards at the universities of these *Länder* ceased to exist. They were replaced by a system of student representation which is not elected by one particular corporate body. Student councils representing the interests of students also usually exist on the departmental level. The Union for Teachers and Scientists offers membership for all students in teacher training, and there are a number of other student organizations and associations of a political, social, artistic, or religious nature. At some universities, mainly the older ones, the traditional student fraternities with their "old boy networks" still exist. These are almost exclusively male organizations with special traditions and rites, some of them even still engaging in dueling (Giesecke 1987 pp. 18–19).

The higher education institutions themselves also offer a broad range of activities with regard to the social and cultural interests of the students. Language courses, a broad range of sports, often dancing, exhibitions, theater, and concerts (choir and orchestra) are on offer for active or passive participation.

Apart from the statutory health insurance scheme for which students over 25 years of age have to pay themselves, social welfare is taken care of by a special organization, called *Studentenwerk*. It receives funding from student contributions, the federal government, and the *Länder* and is located at every higher education institution. The responsibilities of this organization comprise the running of student dining halls, student accommodation in halls of residence, advice services and often an agency for temporary student jobs, some clubs and cultural facilities, and kindergartens. One of the most important surveys on the social situation of students in the Federal Republic of Germany is conducted every three years by the German *Studentenwerk* on a national level. Finally, it has taken over the payment of state loans for students with insufficient personal incomes or assets. Originally devised as nonrepayable state grants in 1971, these grants were later changed to a combination of grants and interest-free loans and, in 1983, became interest-free loans only. The loans are paid for by the federal government (65 percent) and the *Länder* (35 percent) and amounted to DM 2,300 million in 1985. As a rule, the loan has to be repaid within 20 years, beginning five years after graduation (Giesecke 1987 p. 19).

4.6 Learning and Examinations

Curricular innovation at institutions of higher education in the Federal Republic of Germany can take three different routes, according to its source: the department, the *Land*, or nationwide bodies.

The department aiming to revise curricula might propose new study and examination regulations. The senate of the university may then discuss the proposal and comment on it but has no formal power of approval or rejection. The ministry of education or higher education of the *Land* has the power to approve examination regulations. For example, it might reject the proposed examination regulations because it considers them to be incompatible with the diploma framework regulations of the respective field of study. As regards study regulations, the government of the *Land* is only in charge of examining their formal and legal soundness. Until 1985, the *Land* was also in charge of general approval of study regulations.

The Ministry of the *Land* responsible for supervision of higher education could take the initiative regarding curricular reform. It might invite representatives of the respective fields to informal meetings, establish study reform commissions on the level of the *Land* and subsequently establish framework regulations for curricula of the respective fields of study.

Finally, there is the possibility of establishing nationwide framework regulations for course programs. The Standing Conference of the Ministers of Education of the *Länder* and the West German Rectors' Conference jointly form a General Commission for the Coordination of Studies and Examinations. This Commission will decide, among other things, in which fields commissions for individual disciplines should be established. In addition to this, the assembly of the deans is consulted. The commissions for individual disciplines consist of four professors, one junior academic staff member and one student, two representatives of the governments of the *Länder*, and—in advisory capacity only—one representative each of the federal government, the employers, and the unions. They will draw up a curricular framework and might establish subcommissions for universities and *Fachhochschulen* in the process. The regulations eventually recommended will indicate specifications for universities and *Fachhochschulen*. Finally, the Standing Conference of the Ministers of Education and the West German Rectors' Conference will decide on the draft.

From 1978 until the implementation of the 1985 revisions of the Framework Act for Higher Education in the late 1980s, two different mechanisms of national curricular innovation and coordination existed: Study Reform Commissions in charge of innovation on the one hand and the joint commissions of the Standing Conference and the Rectors' Conference in charge of framework regulations for university diploma course programs on the other. These are supposed to merge into a new arrangement which also strengthens the role of the higher education institutions in curricular innovation vis-à-vis the government.

The formal role of the employment system in curricular innovation is weak as far as the private sector of the economy is concerned. Before the establishment of Study Reform Commissions in 1978 its representatives were not formally involved in the decision-making process, although they might have played a strong informal role in fields such as engineering and chemistry. As regards the public sector, governmental influence is very strong. Decisions concerning relatively strict framework regulations for medical education, law, teacher training, public administration, social work, and so on, are carried out by specific formal procedures in which the ministries supervising the respective occupational sector of—mainly—civil servants dominate.

4.7 Models of Undergraduate Courses

Studies are generally divided into two semesters per study year, the winter semester (mid-October to mid-February) lasting four months, the summer semester (mid-April to mid-July) lasting three months. During the times in between, the academic staff are supposed to do research and prepare seminars and lectures, while the students are supposed to write extended essays for credits, carry out independent study, and keep up with their reading. The semesters at *Fachhochschulen* are slightly longer and some institutions have introduced the "academic year" structure.

The main types of classes are:

(a) Lectures: the professor lectures on a given subject while students are expected to listen, take notes, and do additional reading. Attendance is voluntary and examinations are not taken, nor are certificates or credits granted.

(b) Exercise classes: students actively participate in discussing the class's subject matter, preparing papers and hand-outs, or giving short talks about a particular aspect of the subject. Achievement is frequently assessed by a written paper or examination at the end of the semester. Exercise classes often accompany the lectures.

(c) Seminars: these are similar to exercise classes, except that more advanced knowledge is being conveyed and discussed. Achievement will be assessed by extended essays handed in for grading, and possibly by oral contributions. Seminars play an important role in the advanced stages of the course program.

(d) Study groups or tutorials: these might be provided additionally at universities, notably in areas treated by lectures which are attended by large numbers of students. Junior academic staff or senior students are frequently in charge of such classes.

(e) Practical courses or laboratory work: these are common for the natural sciences, engineering, and the medical fields. Students learn experimentation and practical skills in a supervised setting. They receive certificates or credits based on reports submitted.

(f) Field courses: students of agriculture, architecture, geography, and so on, have to participate in these classes exploring special fields of interest for the subject outside the institution. The status of field courses is similar to that of exercise classes.

Apart from these various types of classes *Fachhochschulen* and comprehensive universities require their students to explore prospective professional fields for a certain period of time (up to two semesters). These explorations are often connected with jobs or unpaid practical studies in a company or business or in one sector of the public services and are an obligatory part of the course program.

4.8 Student Assessment

In most of the humanities and social science subjects a maximum of 20 course "hours" per semester week (of 45 minutes each) are recommended. Weekly course hours in the natural sciences, in engineering, and at *Fachhochschulen* are higher. According to a survey conducted in 1984/85, students at universities take on average 17 course hours per week, while students at *Fachhochschulen* take on average 25 course hours per semester week.

Fachhochschule studies, as well as studies in the natural sciences and in engineering, are usually more structured and have a school-type discipline. Attendance is monitored more strictly and assessment is more intensive and continuous. In contrast, course programs in the liberal arts and humanities, as well as in some social sciences, rely more heavily on independent study and grant the student a higher degree of choice in putting together a course of study according to his or her individual interests.

The study and examination regulations usually prescribe in a more or less detailed way how many certificates or credits students have to accumulate and which areas of the chosen discipline or disciplines have to be covered before they can start taking the examinations. Upon first enrollment students usually have to opt for one to three disciplines which they want to study to degree level and for the specific degree program. For example, a diploma degree is granted in only one discipline, for the first state examination students have to enroll in two disciplines, and for the master's degree they are required to have studied three disciplines.

A few universities offer a phase of general studies, called *studium generale*, before or parallel to specialization. These general studies are based on lectures and seminars or exercise classes in the liberal arts and humanities or cultural sciences and try to link a broad range of social and cultural issues to highly specialized subject matters. Generally, however, because university students have one more year of upper-secondary school than students of most other countries, schools are expected to provide the broader outlook so that specialization can start immediately at a higher education institution.

Finally, there is at least some sort of assessment after the first half of the course program. In the case of diploma degree studies it is a document called "pre-diploma" serving only the internal procedures of the system. In some disciplines, for example, engineering or economics, students have to pass a number of written examinations in order to receive this document which entitles them to go on to advanced undergraduate studies. In other disciplines, mainly teacher training in the humanities, the first half of the degree course is completed by a so-called "intermediate examination." This is not necessarily a regular examination but might simply be a person-to-person talk with a professor about achievements and study plans as well as showing proof of enough certificates or credits to be accepted for advanced undergraduate seminars. The "pre-diplomas" or "intermediate examinations" also offer the best opportunity for a change of institution. As achievements and credits from one institution are generally recognized by all other institutions of the same type, students are encouraged to take advantage of a certain degree of mobility. Change of institution is possible at every stage of an undergraduate course program. Surveys have shown, however, that only 15 percent of students actually change institutions and most of them do this after the first half of their course of study has been successfully completed.

5. Conclusion

During the 1980s, the notion spread in the Federal Republic of Germany that various problems of higher education were tending to intensify. Stagnation of personnel and material resources alongside a continuous growth of enrollments as well as a substantial increase in the average duration of studies were the most obvious indicators of this. Both phenomena supported the view that higher education in the Federal Republic faced a decline of quality because the available time for research was reduced and conditions for study had worsened. In addition, experts have agreed that many other issues are pending:

(a) Even though more efforts have been made on the part of the higher education institutions to raise research funds from external sources and to play an active role in the transfer of knowledge to economy and society, these efforts have, in turn, reinforced concern about the role of basic research, the critical function of the university, and the vitality of those disciplines which are not in any position to "sell" their knowledge to society.

(b) As far as academic careers were concerned, young academic staff were discouraged in most disciplines since about the mid-1970s because the number of positions hardly increased and demand for replenishment was low. However, a shortage of candidates for professorial positions is predicted for the second half of the 1990s. Career patterns for academic staff have been restructured and improved about every 10 years without leading to any really satisfactory solution.

(c) Institutional patterns of the higher education system continue to be under discussion. Many debates focus on the role of *Fachhochschulen*; although they are generally assumed to have become a permanent component of the higher education system, their position vis-à-vis the universities has remained controversial. Some of their representatives expect better status for *Fachhochschulen* in the near future because of increased permeability between *Fachhochschulen* and universities; others suggest the establishment of advanced professional programs in order to underscore career prospects within a clearly defined framework. Controversies also focus on the desirability of a diversification of institutions of the same type, on course programs, and on discipline. Undoubtedly, parity of quality and common curricular elements at all universities continue to be held in higher esteem in the Federal Republic of Germany than, for example, in the United Kingdom or in France.

(d) Governance and administration in higher education are generally assumed to be in need of substantial innovation. However, the views on improvements are so diverse that efforts at change are consistently discouraged.

(e) It was generally assumed that the institutions of higher education would take on a more prominent role in lifelong education during the 1980s and 1990s. Increased access for adults without the traditional prerequisites, expansion of continuing education opportunities for professionals, extension of provisions for part-time studies, and the establishment of a broad range of advanced study programs were considered as a matter of course, once the demographic peak of the mid-1960s was channeled through the higher education system. Up to the early 1990s, however, moves in that direction have remained cautious and slow.

Interpreting this state of affairs, one could recall the stereotypical external claims made about the inertia of higher education institutions on the one hand, and on the other the typical justification that dynamic changes take place in the contents of research and studies, whereas formal elements have to be stable to ensure innovation within the disciplines. Neither of these explanations is adequate, however. Rather, three major causes can be named for the reluctance on the part of the Federal Republic of Germany to undertake a substantial reshaping of higher education. First, the experience of a high degree of experimentation in higher education in the late 1960s and the 1970s still reinforces a widespread skepticism in the 1990s with respect to experiments regarding the structures of the system, its governance, and so on. Second, institutions of higher education, government agencies, and most of the political groups concerned agreed in 1977 that the institutions of higher education should accept the substantially increased load of student numbers for about 10 years under the condition that the controversies about the functions, structures, and governance of higher education were more or less frozen during this period. As student numbers continued to grow beyond the years 1986 to 1988, initially predicted to be the peak years of enrollment, the rationale for that freeze is still relevant. Third, the network of federal state and *Länder* tasks, of planning and advisory agencies, of negotiations between institutions of higher education and *Länder* governments, and of formalized decision making within the institutions of higher education, originally designed around 1970 for the purpose of stimulating reforms, turned out to neutralize all efforts at innovation once a minimal consensus on higher education reforms was lost, and controversies increased about scarce resources. All this is taking place in a climate in which some participants see drastic changes in the higher education system as vital to its future, whereas others might claim that the quality of teaching, learning, and research is not in such a bad shape, that popular criticism focuses on marginal phenomena, and that models from other countries are inappropriate.

Debates about the weaknesses of higher education in the Federal Republic of Germany and about the need for improvements have almost completely lost momentum in the course of the unification of the German Democratic Republic and Federal Republic of Germany in 1990. Instead, all attention now focuses on efforts to overcome an outmoded technological standard, overstaffing, segmentation of research and teaching, and political biases of higher education and research. Structural differences in the East, such as 12 years of prior schooling instead of 13 years, as in the West, half the enrollment quotas, lack of institutions equivalent to *Fachhochschulen*, the concentration of research in academies, and so on, are all up for discussion. More or less all Western experts emphasize that some elements of the old system in the East should be preserved, for example 12 years of prior schooling, lower student–staff ratios, and avoidance of a substantial prolongation of studies. Most efforts, however, focus on a rapid transplantation of the rationales of the West into the East, where lack of resources on the one hand and the abundance of staff, many of whom were recruited and promoted for reasons of loyalty to the former regime, are viewed as the crucial obstacles. No matter how detailed the assessment of the situation and activities to redress it, nobody would challenge this general priority. No expert, however, can overlook the danger that would result if efforts for the improvement of higher education in the Western part of Germany are unduly postponed.

Bibliography

Baethge M et al. (eds.) 1986 *Studium und Beruf*. Dreisam, Freiburg

Bargel T et al. 1988 *Studiensituation und studentische Orientierungen an Universitäten und Fachhochschulen*. Bock, Bad Honnef

Bundesminister für Bildung und Wissenschaft 1989 *Studenten an Hochschulen 1975 bis 1988*. Bundesminister für Bildung und Wissenschaft, Bonn

Bundesregierung 1988 *Entwicklungsstand und Perspektiven der Fachhochschulen in der Bundesrepublik Deutschland*. Deutscher Bundestag, Drucksache 11/2603

Deutscher Akademischer Austauschdienst 1988 *Degree Courses at Institutions of Higher Education in the Federal Republic of Germany*. Bock, Bad Honnef

Federal Ministry of Education and Science 1976 *Framework Act for Higher Education*. Bock, Bonn

Federal Ministry of Education and Science 1990 *Basic and Structural Data 1989/90*. Bock, Bonn

Fläming C et al. 1982 *Handbuch des Wissenschaftsrechts*. Springer, Berlin

Führ C 1989 *Schools and Institutions of Higher Education in the Federal Republic of Germany*. Inter Nationes, Bonn

German Academic Exchange Service (ed.) 1982a *Studies at Fachhochschulen*. Bonn

German Academic Exchange Service (ed.) 1982b *Studies at Universities*. Bonn

Giesecke L 1987 *Into the Future by Tradition. Higher Education in the Federal Republic of Germany*. Inter Nationes, Bonn

Goldschmidt D, Hübner-Funk S 1974 Von den Ingenieurschulen zu den Fachhochschulen. In: Deutscher Bildungsrat (ed.) 1974 *Gutachten und Materialien zur Fachhochschule*. Klett, Stuttgart, pp. 11–219

Goldschmidt D, Teichler U, Webler W D (eds.) 1984 *Forschungsgegenstand Hochschule. Überblick und Trendbericht*. Campus, Frankfurt

Helberger C et al. 1988 *Studiendauer und Studienorganisation im interuniversitären Vergleich*. Bock, Bad Honnef

Hermanns H, Teichler U, Wasser H (eds.) 1983 *The Compleat University: Break from Tradition in Germany, Sweden and the U.S.A.* Schenkman, Cambridge, Massachusetts

Holtkamp R, Fischer-Bluhm K, Huber L 1986 *Junge Wissenschaftler in der Hochschule—Bericht der Arbeitsgruppe "Lage und Förderung des wissenschaftlichen Nachwuchses"*. Campus, Frankfurt

Huber L (ed.) 1983 *Ausbildung und Sozialisation in der Hochschule*. Klett-Cotta, Stuttgart

Humboldt W von 1964 *Schriften zur Politik und zum Bildungswesen. Werke Vol. 4*. Flitner A, Giel K (eds.) Wissenschaftliche Buchgesellschaft, Darmstadt

Karpen U 1980 *Access to Higher Education and its Restrictions under the Constitution*. Minerva, Munich

Kluge N, Neusel A 1984 *Studienreform in den Ländern*. Bundesminister für Bildung und Wissenschaft, Bonn

Krais B, Naumann J 1991 Higher education in the Federal Republic of Germany. In: Altbach P G(ed.) 1991 *International Encyclopedia of Comparative Higher Education*. Garland, New York

Kriszio M 1986 Innere Organisation und Personalstruktur der Hochschule. In: Neusel A, Teichler U (eds.) 1986, pp. 93–143

Max Planck Institute for Human Development and Education 1983 *Between Elite and Mass Education*. State University of New York Press, Albany, New York

Mc-Daniel O, Gauye P, Guin J 1989 Government and curriculum innovation in the Federal Republic of Germany. In: Van Vught F (ed.) 1989 *Government Strategies and Innovation in Higher Education*. Kingsley, London, pp. 125–42.

Mönikes W 1988 *More Practice for Future Profession: The Fachhochschulen in the Federal Republic of Germany*. Inter Nationes, Bonn

Naumann J, Köhler H, Roeder P M 1989 Expansion und Wettbewerb im Hochschulsystem. In *Aus Politik und Zeitgeschichte. Beilage zur Wochenzeitung Das Parlament*. No. B 50/89, pp. 3–13

Neusel A, Teichler U 1983 Comprehensive universities—History, implementation process and prospects. In: Hermanns H, Teichler U, Wasser H(eds.) 1983, pp. 175–95

Neusel A, Teichler U (eds.) 1986 *Hochschulentwicklung seit den sechziger Jahren. Kontinuität—Umbrüche—Dynamik?* Beltz, Weinheim and Basel

Oehler C 1989 *Hochschulentwicklung in der Bundesrepublik Deutschland seit 1945*. Campus, Frankfurt

Over A 1988 *Die deutschsprachige Forschung über Hochschulen in der Bundesrepublik. Eine kommentierte Bibliographie 1965–1985*. K G Saur, Munich

Peisert H, Framhein G 1978 *Systems of Higher Education: Federal Republic of Germany*. International Council for Educational Development, New York

Schnitzer K, Isserstedt W, Leszczensky M 1989 *Das soziale Bild der Studentenschaft in der Bundesrepublik Deutschland*. Bock, Bad Honnef

Secretariat of the Standing Conference of Ministers of Education and Cultural Affairs of the Länder 1987 *The Educational System in the Federal Republic of Germany*. Foreign Office, Bonn

Teichler U 1985 The Federal Republic of Germany. In: Clark B R(ed.) 1985 *The School and the University*. University of California Press, Berkeley, California, pp. 45–76

Teichler U 1986 Strukturentwicklung des Hochschulwesens. In: Neusel A, Teichler U (eds.) 1986, pp. 213–55.

Teichler U 1987 *Higher Education in the Federal Republic of Germany. Developments and Recent Issues*, 2nd edn. Center for Graduate Studies Graduate School and University Center of the City University of New York, Wissenschaftliches Zentrum für Berufs- und Hochschulforschung der Gesamthochschule Kassel, New York and Kassel

Teichler U 1988 *Changing Patterns of the Higher Education System*. Kingsley, London

Teichler U 1990a *The First Years of Study and the Role Played by Fachhochschulen in the Federal Republic of Germany*. Wissenschaftliches Zentrum für Berufs- und Hochschulforschung, Kassel

Teichler U (ed.) 1990b *Das Hochschulwesen in der Bundesrepublik Deutschland*. Deutscher Studienverlag, Weinheim

Teichler U 1990c Das Hochschulwesen in der Bundesrepublik Deutschland—Ein Überblick. In: Teichler U(ed.) 1990 *Das Hochschulwesen in der Bundesrepublik Deutschland*. Deutscher Studienverlag, Weinheim, pp. 11–42

Thieme W 1986 *Deutsches Hochschulrecht*, 2nd edn. Heymanns, Cologne

Thieme W 1990 Die Personalstruktur der Hochschule. In: Teichler U(ed.) 1990, pp. 101–22

Westdeutsche Rektorenkonferenz 1988 *Überlegungen für eine zukunftsorientierte Hochschulpolitik*. WRK, Bonn

Westdeutsche Rektorenkonferenz 1990 *Hochschulrahmengesetz. Hochschulgesetze der Länder*. WRK, Bonn

Wissenschaftsrat 1988 *Empfehlungen des Wissenschaftsrates zu den Perspektiven der Hochschulen in den 90er Jahren*. Wissenschaftsrat, Cologne

B. Kehm; U. Teichler

Ghana

1. Higher Education and Society

The system of higher education in Ghana, currently under review, embraces the University of Ghana (1961) in Legon; the University of Science and Technology (1961) in Kumasi; and the University of Cape Coast (1971); the seven diploma-awarding colleges

(Advanced Teacher Training College, Specialist Training College, National Academy of Music, all in Winneba; College of Special Education, Mampong Akwapim; Advanced Technical Training College, Kumasi; St. Andrews College for Agriculture, Mampong Ashanti; and the School of Languages, Ajumako); and the six polytechnics in Accra, Kumasi, Takoradi, Cape Coast, Ho and Tamale. Tertiary education comes under the Ministry of Education, Higher Education Division headed by a Provisional National Defence Council (PNDC) undersecretary, and is funded largely by government. Since it is mostly residential, it caters for a relatively small number of students, some 19,000 out of a total population of over 14 million.

While some university education was available from 1932 in the postsecondary department of Achimota College, founded in 1927, higher education on a more widespread scale was ushered in when the University College of the Gold Coast was established in 1948, under the auspices of the United Kingdom's Inter-University Council for Higher Education Overseas, and in special relationship with the University of London. Following the Asquith and Elliot Commissions and the Bradley Committee, its task was to produce high-level labor force and leadership as the colony of the Gold Coast progressed to Independence achieved in March 1957, adopting the name of Ghana.

Ghana incorporated, as the Volta region, the British mandated territory of Togoland, following the UN plebiscite of 1956. At Independence, the population was estimated at 4·5 million and it has been growing steadily at rates ranging between 2.4 percent and 3 percent, to reach 6. 72 million (urban 23%) in 1960, 8.63 million (urban 29%) in 1970, and 12.39 million (urban 32%) in 1984, and is now around 14.2 million (urban around 35%). The population is densest on the coast and in Ashanti, and least dense in the northern region. The Akan ethnic group, comprising principally Twi and Fanti, constitutes about 44 percent; the Mole-Dagbani 15.9 percent; Ewes 13 percent; and the Ga-Dangbe 8.3 percent.

The problems of multilingualism are partially solved by the use of English as the official language, literacy in English estimated at between 20 to 30 percent. Where religion is concerned the majority of traditional animists co-exist alongside the minority of Christians (Roman Catholics, Protestants, Syncretists) and Moslems. With some 65 to 70 percent living in the rural areas, 61.1 percent of the population work in agriculture and allied activities. Commerce engages 15.1 percent; manufacturing 10.8 percent; with services and transport making up for 8.7 percent and 2.3 percent respectively. The main export is cocoa at 69.9 percent, followed by gold at 18.9 percent. The country has undergone a severe economic crisis, especially since 1975, climaxing in 1982–83. This has been the prime factor causing stagnation in higher education. Fortunately, there are signs of economic recovery, though the country has yet to return to a state of normalcy.

The history of Ghana since Independence has been somewhat chequered. By July 1960, Ghana had become a republic, with Dr Kwame Nkrumah as the first executive president. It was largely through him that the University College of Ghana in Legon and Kumasi College of Technology became independent universities in 1961. However, Nkrumah was overthrown by a military coup in February, 1966. The National Liberation Council (1966–69) then made a smooth transition to the Second Republic—the Busia regime—which lasted from September 1969 to January 1972 and placed emphasis on rural development, until Dr K A Busia was toppled by another military junta. The National Redemption Council, rebaptized the Supreme Military Council (SMC[I]), 1972–78, promoted self-reliance and encouraged agriculture. But eventually personalized government brought about political confrontations, resulting in frequent closing of institutions of higher learning. The Supreme Military Council's second regime (SMC[II]) was short-lived, only to be replaced after yet another coup on June 4, 1979, by the Armed Forces Revolutionary Council (AFRC) with its violent anticorruption campaign, followed by the Third Republic, from September 1979 to December 1987.

The present PNDC government, under Flt Lt Rawlings, is socialist-oriented, laying emphasis on grassroot level development. Government policy, as echoed in the National Program for Economic Development Revised, July 1, 1987, and especially in the report of the University Rationalization Committee (URC) in January 1988, stressed the need to gear university training and research more closely to "actual experiences of Ghanaians," maximizing the use of facilities, reducing costs through a phased removal of institutional feeding and residential subsidies, instituting students' loan schemes, and making higher education more accessible to more people, through part-time and nonformal education.

2. The Institutional Fabric of the Higher Education System

The higher education division of the Ministry of Education looks after the entire system. The three universities constitute the apex of the education setup. Next come the seven diploma-awarding training colleges and finally the six polytechnics.

Research is an integral part of the work of the universities. The other higher education establishments are sporadically engaged in some kind of research and extension work. In addition there are specialized research organizations, outside the system of higher education, such as the Council for Scientific and Industrial Research and its institutes which come under the Ministry of Industry, Science,

Table 1
Enrollment in universities, colleges and polytechnics

	1961	1965	1970	1975	1980	1985	1990
University of Ghana							
Total	682	2,001	2,525	3,620	3,705	3,462	4,017
of which female	62	252	390	609	607	665	925
University of Science and Technology							
Total	708	1,140	1,344	2,354	2,816	3,094	3,582[a]
female numbers unavailable							
University of Cape Coast							
total	—	860	862	1,205	1,430	1,538	2,004
of which female	—	95	132	182	301	281	427
Seven colleges							
total	—	898	879	2,465	1,362	1,332	1,789[a]
of which female	—	—	237	695	218	233	371[a]
Six polytechnics							
total	—	3,285	4,332	5,450	5,948	7,751	7,111[a]
of which female	—	441	1,051	1,110	1,419	2,107	2,024[a]

a Latest figures available

and Technology and the Cocoa Research Institute now with the Cocoa Board, and so on.

Owing to restrictions imposed by limited facilities, especially residential, entry is competitive and based largely on the results of the General Certificate of Education examinations organized by the West African Examinations Council (WAEC). For degree courses the following requirements in Legon have set the pattern: (a) five ordinary level credit passes, including English, of the WAEC or equivalent; (b) three advanced level passes with at least one grade D pass (Kumasi and Cape Coast require only two A levels); and (c) one A-level pass at the general paper, WAEC. In addition, students must satisfy faculty and department requirements. The universities operate individually and they work out a quota system, with efforts being made to have more science and graduate students. Subjects such as medicine, architecture, law, and administration are oversubscribed and have therefore tight quotas. Diploma and certificate courses admit students with five O-level passes and other similar qualifications. There is provision for mature, part-time and occasional students. Diploma-awarding colleges and polytechnics admit students with five O-level passes and other similar qualifications.

Student numbers have gone from well under 9,000 in 1965 to about 19,000 in 1991, with stagnation in the last decade. According to the 1960 census, of the 20–24 age group, only one out of 35 was attending an educational institution. In 1970, one out of four of the 15–24 age group was at school, the males outnumbering the females by two to one, although the proportion of females to males is slowly improving.

The degree course is usually of three years' length with two major examinations: part I after two years, and part II a year later. The degrees, awarded by the individual universities, are designated Bachelor of Arts or Bachelor of Sciences, according to the specialization. Technical subjects such as architecture, engineering, and mining take four years. Medicine takes seven years.

Graduate courses, certificates, diplomas, MA/MSc (one year), MPhil (two years), and PhD (three years) are available to students with appropriate degrees. These courses entail initiation to research training done in the respective departments.

The training colleges offer courses lasting usually three years and award diplomas. The polytechnics lay on a great variety of courses usually taking one or two years and awarding certificates and diplomas.

3. Governance, Administration, and Finance

3.1 National Administration

The Ministry of Education, Higher Education Division headed by a PNDC undersecretary oversees the working of the system of higher education, since the abolition in 1982 of the National Council for Higher Education. The higher education secretariat is nominally the policy-making body. A Board of Accreditation as envisaged will, in conjunction with the ministry, coordinate and decide upon new developments in courses.

Higher education, under firmer government surveillance, will figure even more prominently than in the past in national development plans and in the economic recovery programs. To that end the newly set-up Ministry of Education Planning, Budgeting, Monitoring and Evaluating Division, is being strengthened, with on-going campus seminars on "Program-linked Budgeting and Unified Statistical Management Information Systems for Tertiary Institutions".

3.2 Finance

The central government grants are the principal source of income for both capital and recurrent expenditure. Estimates submitted by the universities are channelled through the Ministry of Education, Higher Education Division, to the Budget Division of the Ministry of Finance and Economic Planning. Pending streamlining, the other tertiary institutions, diploma-awarding colleges and polytechnics, approach the Ministry of Finance via the Ghana Education Service.

While the government is preoccupied with the relatively high cost of higher education, especially expenditure on residential and municipal provision, practically all the tertiary institutions complain about underfunding, even of academic facilities, with chronic uncertainty about the size and time of disbursement of the operational budget allocated. The seminars on "Program-linked Budgeting...," would help determine the real needs of the institutions.

According to a 1991 Ministry of Education memo on Allocation of Resources to and within the Educational Sector in Ghana, the percentage of the Gross Domestic Product (GNP) allocated to education as a whole was 3.2 in 1980, falling to 1.6 in 1983 and rising to 3.4 in 1989. For the present decade, 1991 to 2000, the Ministry is projecting that the percentage will rise to 5.8 percent or even to 8.3 percent, depending on the scenario adopted. Higher education's share of the recurrent budget for education in 1990 was 10.77 percent, while the primary and secondary schools obtained 56.5 percent, thus underscoring the new emphasis on the lower tiers in the current education reform program.

3.3 Institutional Administration

The governing body of each university is the council and according to PNDC Law No. 239 (1990) the composition for Legon is as follows: the chairperson, the vice chancellor, two representatives of convocation, a representative of each of the following: University Teachers Association, undergraduate students, graduate students, Committee for the Defence of the Revolution, Teachers and Education Workers Union, the Education Commission, Conference of Assisted Secondary Schools, Alumni Association, and three other persons including at least one woman. The diploma-awarding colleges and the polytechnics, pending rearrangements, come under the Director-General of education.

The most important body in any institution of higher education is the academic board or equivalent, comprising deans of faculties, directors of schools and institutes, heads of departments, masters of halls of residence, and elected representatives of all departments, schools, institutes, and so on. Its subcommittees include the executive committee, boards for finance, development, appointments, scholarships, research, publications, library, housing, and so forth, with student and nonteaching staff participation where appropriate.

Academic work is organized by heads of departments, on the basis of syllabi approved by the academic board which appoints both internal and external examiners. Departmental heads and deanships normally rotate once every three years. Directors are usually appointed for five years at a time.

4. Faculty and Students: Teaching, Learning, and Research

4.1 Faculty

The mostly British expatriate staff in the early 1960s have now been replaced by Ghanaians. The slump in recruitment in the universities after 1980 was due to the brain drain caused by the economic malaise.

Prospective university teachers should normally hold a graduate qualification before being considered by the appointments board of individual universities. Promotion to the grades of senior lecturer, senior

Table 2
Teaching staff

	1961	1965	1970	1975	1980	1985	1989
Universities	255[a]	628	881	1,126	1,317	1,167	1,160
Diploma Colleges	—	—	77	122	130	174	184
Polytechnics	—	—	152	217	191	268	386

a This figure is made up of staff at the Universities of Ghana, Legon, and Kumasi. The University College of Cape Coast started in 1962, becoming a university in 1971

263

Table 3
University of Ghana student numbers by courses

	1961–71	1971–81	1981–82	1985–86	1990–91
Agriculture	970	2,525	194	245	265
Science	1,963	2,966	343	332	561
Medicine	1,543	3,627	390	282	377
Arts & social studies[a]	9,890	17,957	1,944	2,019	2,382
Law	1,375	1,504	95	50	40
Administration	2,235	3,823	429	509	459

a Arts and social studies are grouped together since their courses often combine

research fellow, associate professor, and full professor, require external assessment of publications. Normally six-year renewable contracts are granted, associate professors and full professors being allowed tenured status. While the nominal employer is the university council, all employees are now considered public servants. Teachers in the diploma-awarding colleges and the polytechnics are appointed by the Ghana Education Service and enjoy a lower status than that of their university counterparts.

Trade-unionist activities are carried on separately by the University Teachers Association of Ghana and by the staff of the other institutions.

There is the likelihood of nationwide patterns being adopted and applied in matters of work load (i.e., teaching hours, administration and research). Previously, the individual academic boards, faculties boards and departments agreed on norms.

4.2 Students

The relatively small numbers of students have been noted. In the University of Ghana, the ratio of numbers in the exact sciences to the liberal studies has improved. There is a noticeable swing towards job-oriented courses. The University of Science and Technology has always been biased in favor of industry and applied science, but the humanities are partially represented. The University of Cape Coast was meant primarily to produce science and education graduates for teaching posts at the secondary schools. Agriculture, commerce and secretarial courses are later additions which have become increasingly sought after owing to their marketability.

Student interests are catered for through the hall

tutorial system, the junior commonrooms and their principal officers who serve on the hall councils. There is a dean of students to take care of areas falling outside the halls. All students in any university constitute the General Assembly which elect the Students Representative Council, officers (president, secretary and treasurer), executive committee, and so on. The nationwide organization is the National Union of Ghana Students (NUGS), embracing the tertiary, secondary, commercial, and vocational schools. The National Executive Committee is made up of the president, secretary, treasurer, editor-in-chief, and coordinating secretary.

The academic boards have so far been responsible for all aspects of academic work in the universities. In the diploma-awarding colleges and the polytechnics, the Ministry of Education is responsible. Any new programs proposed by the universities requiring extra funding need to be discussed with the funding agencies, notably the government. The board of accreditation proposed by the URC will eventually oversee the academic work of the tertiary system, in conjunction with the Ministry of Education.

During the past two decades or so, courses have become less specialized except in the purely professional subjects such as medicine and engineering. Instead of two sets of courses, honors/specialist and general, there is one broad pattern: three subjects in the first year, with a compulsory ancillary in African studies, two in the second, and one or two in the final year. The credit-unit system is in operation in the University of Cape Coast. It is currently being worked out for the other institutions, as well. While the degree examinations are divided into part I and part II, the latter carries more weight. Continuous

Table 4
University of Science and Technology student numbers

	1961	1965	1970	1975	1980	1985	1989
Sciences and agriculture	524	997	839	1,508	1,876	2,219	2,222
Environmental studies & art	106	277	426	619	580	539	608
Social studies	78	118	89	227	360	548	637

Table 5
University of Cape Coast student numbers by courses

	1975–76	1980–81	1985–86	1990–91
Education	124	215	218	494
Science/agriculture	487	367	409	438
Arts/social sciences	637	725	755	743
Commerce/secretarial	—	123	156	329

assessment of course work, essays and projects, contributes about 30 to 40 percent toward the final results.

5. Conclusion

Ghana is in the process of implementing its new education structure: 6:3:3:4 years—primary, junior secondary, senior secondary and university, respectively, instead of the former 9:7:3 years—primary, secondary and university. This will have drastic repercussions in the universities: massive intake of students at a lower academic level, and therefore more preliminary work, as from 1993. Furthermore, the URC recommends new university colleges in Winneba, Tarkwa and the north, and eleven regional colleges of applied arts and science and technology. The future of some of the URC reforms may be open as the country embarks upon the slow but inevitable processes towards a return to a civilian and parliamentary regime.

The challenges facing the universities and other tertiary institutions as we approach the year 2000 are daunting. Increased numbers of students may not be matched by increased financial and other provisions. The beneficiaries of higher education would be called upon to shoulder an increasing proportion of the costs. Fund-raising activities would have to make up for shortfalls in government grants. Residential and municipal facilities would be reduced considerably.

However, with better planning and coordination of changes and improvements in the universities, with government and the higher education institutions in a symbiotic relationship, reaching a consensus about targets and ways of implementation, the quality of the increased output should make an even greater impact on national development in Ghana.

Bibliography

Abban J B 1986 *Prerequisites of Manpower and Educational Planning in Ghana*. Baffour Educational Enterprises Ltd, Accra
Amonoo R F 1987 Higher education in Ghana. In: *Educafrica*. Bulletin of the UNESCO Regional Office for Education in Africa, December, pp. 21–39
Amonoo R F 1991 Stimulating Reflection on the Roles of Higher Education in Society: Identification of Trends in Ghana UNESCO Regional Office for Education in Africa, Dakar
Asquith Commission 1945 *Report of the Commission on Higher Education in the British Colonies*. HMSO, London
Botsio Commission 1961 *Report of the Commission on University Education*. Ministry of Information, Accra
Bradley Committee 1946 *Report of the Committee on Higher Education*. Government Printer, Accra
Central Bureau of Statistics 1964, 1972, 1984 *Reports on Population Census of Ghana* (1960, 1970, 1984). Central Bureau of Statistics, Accra
Elliot Commission 1945 *Report on the Commission on Higher Education in West Africa*. HMSO, London
Ewusi K 1986 *Statistical Tables on the Economy of Ghana. 1950–1985*. ISSER, University of Ghana, Legon
Ministry of Finance and Economic Planning 1985 *Progress of the Economic Recovery Program 1984–1986 and Policy Framework 1986–1988*. Ministry of Finance, Accra
Pandit H N et al. 1989 *Social Demand for Education and Manpower Requirement for Economic Development of Ghana*. Planning, Budgeting, Monitoring and Evaluation Division, Ministry of Education, Accra
PNDC 1990 Laws 239, 240 and 241 on university councils. In: *Gazette*. State Publishing Corporation, Accra
University of Cape Coast *1990–91 Calendar*. University of Cape Coast
University of Cape Coast 1988 *Vice-Chancellor's Report to Congregation* and *Basic Statistics 1962–1987*. University of Cape Coast
University of Ghana *1990–91 Calendar*. University of Ghana, Legon
University of Ghana 1991 *Basic Statistics 1961–1991*. University of Ghana, Accra
University of Ghana 1991 *Vice-Chancellor's Report to Congregation on the Work of the University*, 23 March
University of Science and Technology *1990–91 Calendar*. University of Science and Technology, Kumasi
University of Science and Technology 1990 *Vice-Chancellor's Report to Congregation* and *Basic Statistics 1961–1990*. University of Science and Technology, Kumasi
University Rationalization Committee 1988 *Final Report*. Ministry of Education, Accra

R. F. Amonoo

Greece

1. Higher Education and Society

The first university in Greece was founded in 1837, only seven years after the founding of the modern Greek state, but the development of higher education was slow for a long period of time and the system is still incomplete, despite the acceleration in the rate of growth observable since the mid-1970s. The following major characteristics of the system throughout its history can be identified: geographical and institutional centralism; illogical distribution of institutions and of enrollments among subjects studied; a lack of connection between institutions and economic development; and an increase in the number of Greek students studying abroad, which coincided with growing demand for university studies. Developments in the higher education system, expressed principally in quantitative terms and not always accompanied by qualitative advancements, have improved the geographical distribution of the institutions but have left the problem of statutory centralism untouched; they led to better distribution among the various courses of study but exacerbated the existing confusion between democratization, mass entry, and uniformity.

The borders of Greece were extended slightly in 1947 with the incorporation into the Republic of Greece (by the Treaty of Paris) of the islands of the Dodecanese, which had been under Italian occupation since 1912.

The Second World War and its consequences (occupation, famine, and resistance) interrupted the country's demographic growth and led to significant changes, temporary and permanent, in the geographical distribution of the population. The human lives lost, estimated at seven to eight percent of the population, were not compensated for by the population of the Dodecanese (Kayser 1964). At the end of this period, Greece was subjected to the further misfortune of a civil war (1946–49). The civil war was demographically catalytic, leading to movements of population, political refugees, a massive wave of emigration, and galloping urbanization. The data derived from censuses (1951, 1961, 1971, and 1981) show these trends clearly and paint a picture of a country whose population was seeping away; the regions were emptying while the capital and, to a lesser extent, Thessaloniki in Macedonia, grew at an excessive rate. In 1981 a recovery from these phenomena was noted, but the upturn has been exaggerated, perhaps because of the manner in which the data were collected.

The magnitude of the wave of emigration determined the socioeconomic evolution and physiognomy of the country. For a quarter of a century, emigration was a *"phénomène ubiquiste"* (Kayser 1964) and cannot be associated with one single generative cause such as, for instance, poverty. Cross-checking the official Greek statistics with those of host countries reveals that the Greek side underestimated the numbers of those permanent emigrants, while the number of temporary emigrants contains an unknown proportion of double entries (Emke-Poulopoulos 1986). The growing wave of returning emigrants, which by 1974 had equalled those emigrating permanently in the same year, is a hopeful sign despite the fact that the country's economic structures, the consumer mentality and lack of skilled training of most returning emigrants, and the poor and problematic education of their children do not permit much optimism as regards the dynamic and productive incorporation of returning emigrants into Greek society.

The geographical distribution of the Greek population in 1981 was as follows: urban 58.1 percent (of which 7.2% lived in Thessaloniki and 31.1% in Greater Athens, which by now exceeds one third of the country's total population); semi-urban (2,000–9,999 inhabitants) 11.6 percent; and rural (under 1,999 inhabitants) 30.3 percent.

The official view of the Greek state is that there are no ethnic minorities today, only linguistic and religious minorities for which no data have been collected since 1951. Even the 1951 figures, however, (334,923 non-Greek speakers and 119,135 non-Christians), collected at a time when questions of language and religion were highly charged, both ideologically and politically, seem far from reliable (as can be seen, for example, from the fact that only 121 Greeks stated that they professed no religion). In the case of the largest foreign language group, the Turkish-speaking minority, the Treaty of Lausanne is applied. Instruction is conducted in Turkish, parallel to Greek language education. Freedom of religious belief and worship "in all known religions" is protected by the Constitution (Article 13, which also lays down that "proselytism is forbidden").

Estimates of the true economic and social structure of Greece encounter a number of methodological problems, of which the lack of statistical data and the frequent alteration of the criteria by which they are collected are not the most serious. Theoretical and investigative research has revealed gaps in information and biases regarding underemployment and unemployment along with ignorance of widespread multiple employment, the existence of several sources of income—often from all three sectors on the part of the same person—and frequent moves from one occupation to another (Tsoucalas 1986, Pesmazoglou 1987). Therefore the social structure is flexible and the economy is largely based on the low–medium strata of the population.

The gainfully employed population, according to official statistics (46% of the total population aged 15 years and over in 1981) is low by comparison with other European countries. In addition, the distribution of this population among the three sectors shows the secondary sector has remained at low levels. The rapid reduction in the size of the primary sector has principally benefited the tertiary sector. This development of the tertiary sector has not focused on services which could support productivity in the other two sectors (Pesmazoglou 1987).

The Five-Year Economic and Social Development

Plan 1983–87 set as its fundamental goal the statutory modernization of Greece, with an emphasis on laws which were expected to promote decentralization, participation, social justice, and the fulfillment of a number of basic economic targets: a rise in the rate of growth of the Gross National Product (GNP); a gradual reduction in unemployment and inflation; encouragement of the Greek economy to compete on the domestic market and worldwide; and an improvement in social services and the quality of life. The next Five-Year Plan, for 1988–1992, was drawn up but had still not been published in mid-1989.

The extent to which these targets were achieved is not easy to estimate. It can be said, however, that the specific statutory changes which were promoted with such optimism do not appear to have yielded the expected results, owing to the fact that social practices were formulated in a context of problematic structures and mentalities which were difficult to change.

The Right, victorious in the civil war, maintained for many years, in parallel to a constitutionally protected parliamentary democracy under a monarch, a system of emergency measures which in effect suspended the Constitution as far as fundamental human rights were concerned. The ceaseless struggles, over 15 years, of the people and the political parties led to election victories for the Center in 1963 and 1964. After this "Centrist interlude" (Svoronos 1972), a military coup d'état imposed dictatorship on April 21 1967. Constitutional powers were restored in 1974, the Communist Party was legalized after 27 years of prohibition, and the political life of the country returned to normal. A plebiscite confirmed Greece as a presidential parliamentary republic, and the 5th Constitutional Assembly promulgated the new Constitution in the spring of 1975. Governments under the conservative New Democracy Party succeeded in bringing about a smooth transition from the dictatorship to modern democracy. The 1981 and 1985 elections were won by the Panhellenic Socialist Movement (PASOK) which lost its majority in the elections of June 1989.

Although the political manifestos of both parties claim that their positions on the question of higher education are diametrically opposed, the policies they have implemented in the field of education have been notable for their continuity and lack of radical reforms.

Greek Orthodoxy is the official religion of the state. The president of the republic, the prime minister, the ministers, and the members of parliament take office after being sworn in by the Archbishop of Athens during a religious ceremony; the state's highest representatives are present at major religious feasts; the clergy are paid by the state; and the full title of the Ministry of Education is "Ministry of National Education and Religions." The Minister is responsible for all church issues not dealt with by the Holy Synod. Religious education forms part of the curriculum in both primary and secondary education.

There are faculties of theology at both Athens and Thessaloniki Universities. Graduates are appointed by the Ministry to serve as secondary school teachers. There are also four nonuniversity tertiary level ecclesiastical colleges, over which the Ministry exercises administrative supervision.

2. The Institutional Fabric of the Higher Educational System

Greek higher education consists of two distinct subdivisions: (a) university-level education, lasting between four and six years and available in the universities, the technical universities, and other institutions; and (b) nonuniversity-level education, lasting between one and three years and provided by a variety of types of institution. The former category consists only of public institutions. The ban on the founding and operation of private universities is absolute, vested in the 1975 Constitution. Those private university-level institutions or branches of foreign universities which operate in Greece may not use the title "institution of higher education" and the degrees which they award are not officially recognized. There has been widespread discussion, at both academic and political level, concerning the possibility of a change in this policy, particularly in view of European integration in 1992. The debate has been conducted logically on some occasions and with politically and ideologically charged arguments on others.

At the nonuniversity level, tertiary education can be divided into three categories: (a) teacher-training colleges, (b) technical/technological colleges, and (c) other vocational and ecclesiastical colleges. Here the foundation of private institutions is permitted.

In 1960, there were two universities in Greece and seven other university-level institutions, as follows: The University of Athens (1837); The University of Thessaloniki (1925); The Technical University of Athens (which was reorganized and awarded university status [1914 and 1917] but which constituted a continuation of the Craft School founded even before Athens University, in 1836); The School of Economic and Commercial Sciences (1920); The Athens School of Agriculture (1920); The Panteios School of Political Sciences (1937); The Piraeus School of Industry (1958); The Thessaloniki School of Industrial Studies (1958); and The School of Fine Arts (1930).

In the same year (1960), the nonuniversity-level tertiary education sector included a training college for teachers of physical education, a training college for preschool teachers, and 14 training colleges for primary teachers. Until 1970, other vocational and ecclesiastical colleges which could have been regarded as equivalent in level were included in

267

the figures for vocational education and were not distinguished from the institutions for secondary vocational training.

The universities of Patra and Ioannina were founded in 1964; the universities of Thrace and Crete in 1973; the Technical University of Crete in 1977; and the universities of the Aegean, the Ionian, and Thessaly in 1984. In each case, however, a number of years elapsed between the founding of the university and the entrance of the first students. Presidential Decree 377/14.6.89 stipulated that the School of Economic and Commercial Sciences, the Athens School of Agriculture, the Panteios School of Political Sciences, and the Piraeus School of Industry were to be renamed with the incorporation of "University" into their titles. Thus over 30 years the number of institutions of higher education (IHES) nearly doubled (i.e., 9–17) and, more importantly, the institutions were decentralized.

Since 1983–84, the country's military academies (for army, navy, and air force officers) have been part of the general system of selection for higher education. They are not under the control of the Ministry of Education and are not included in the statistics for education.

In the nonuniversity-level tertiary sector, growth has varied between three categories of institutions. The first, the training of teachers (physical education teachers, preschool teachers, and primary school teachers), has been in process of incorporation into existing universities since 1983–84, with the formation of new departments and the closing of the schools to which they corresponded.

In the second, vocational technical education, a number of attempts have been made to bring about radical reorganization. In 1970, the Centers for Advanced Technical and Vocational Training (KATEE) were founded with the technical and financial assistance of the World Bank. They accepted their first students in 1974 and their growth in terms of enrollments was impressive (see Table 1). However, there was marked discrepancy between the expectations these institutions created and the results they produced. They did not, apparently, convince either employers or prospective students (who placed them last among their choices) of the quality of the studies they offered or the value of the diplomas they awarded. At the same time shortcomings were observed in their infrastructure and operations. Thus it was decided to replace them with other institutions, making an effort to avoid the mistakes of the past. Law 1404/1983 "concerning the structure and operation of the Technical Education Institutions (TEIs)" abolished the KATEEs and established the TEIs in their place. In 1983 11 TEIs were operating, with a total of 23 departments. In the same year, the tertiary technical education sector also contained the Training School for Technical and Vocational Education Instructors (SELETE), and nine schools providing training in electronics and shipbuilding (which are privately owned).

There has been a decline in the third category, which consists of merchant navy training schools, training institutions for the service occupations, art colleges, and ecclesiastical colleges. In 1975 there were 81 institutions in this category, 49 of which were privately owned, and in 1980 there were 65, 28 of which were private. However, despite the drop in the number of institutions between 1975 and 1980 the number of enrollments remained steady. This situation continued during 1981; no data have been published for subsequent years.

Organized research is still a novelty in Greece. The first research centers to receive state assistance were founded during the 1960s. Their slow development was accompanied by consistently low levels of funds for research as a whole. Private funding of research is negligible, and the financial

Table 1
Enrollment and teaching staff by institution 1960–84

	1960	1965	1970	1975	1980	1984
Universities and equivalent institutions	25,658	54,261	72,269	95,385	85,718	111,446
	617	689	3,071	5,810	6,924	6,778
Teacher-training institutions	2,644	3,739	3,929	4,408	6,588	—
	194	139	273	248	205	—
Vocational colleges	—	—	6,026	11,646	22,834	—
	—	—	—	—	2,533	—
Ecclesiastical and other institutions	—	—	3,552	5,811	5,976	—
	—	—	—	—	880	—
Nonuniversity subtotal	—	—	13,507	21,865	35,398	56,511
	—	—	—	—	3,618	4,957
Tertiary level enrollment ratios[a]	3.8	9.8	12.0	17.5	17.4	23.5

a 20–24 years age group

esources for Research and Development (R & D) ran steadily at the exceptionally low figure of 0.2 percent of GNP between 1969 and 1983.

Concern over the situation regarding research has led to specific efforts to deal with it, since 1977. Two significant pieces of legislation (Law 706/1977 and Law 1514/1985) set up a statutory framework for the organization and coordination of scientific and technological research. However, there was no connection between the research centers and universities. This is still the case, and so the development of research continues to be sluggish in the universities (Eliou 1981).

With Presidential Decree 380/14.6.89 "concerning the organization and functioning of graduate studies in the institutions of higher education," which supplemented the relevant articles of Law 1566/85, provision was made, on certain conditions, for collaboration between universities and research centers. There is, therefore, a statutory framework for research and graduate studies. It is impossible to predict the time needed for results to emerge regarding research and development production, the training of research staff, or the utilization of the mechanisms of research for the benefit of the universities themselves.

In the meantime, a number of doctorates are being worked on under the supervision of university teaching staff. These students are not obliged to attend classes or seminars. The number of graduate courses—scattered throughout the universities and the result of individual initiatives—is very small. The number of degrees at doctorate level is very low, and approximately half of these are doctoral theses of medical graduates, for whom the title of MD is indispensible in their professional careers.

2.1 Admissions Policies and Selection

The sole qualification for entrance to higher education is a leaving certificate from an establishment of secondary education. However, since demand is far in excess of the places available, the *numerus clausus* principle applies. Selection takes place at the end of each school year by means of a nationwide competition, strictly governed by laws, decrees, and ministerial decisions frequently introducing individual changes but never touching upon the basic principles of the system. The concept exists that absolute uniformity in examination conditions is the best guarantee of fairness in the selection process.

The principal features of the system are as follows: the total number of candidates for higher education is divided into four large groups, corresponding broadly to the natural, the medical, the human, and the social sciences. These four groups provide entrants to all departments in all university-level and non-university-level institutions of higher education throughout the country. The candidates in each group take written examinations, held simultaneously across the country, in four subjects. The questions are set by a special committee which meets at the Ministry of Education. Marking is also uniform. The following factors, too, are taken into consideration in placing successful candidates in one of the approximately 280 departments of higher education: the list of ranked choices which each candidate has submitted for the departments in the group in which he/she competes; the number of places in the department; and elements of the candidate's grades in senior high school. For certain departments (e.g., architecture, foreign languages, physical education, and fine arts) provision is made for supplementary examinations in the special subjects required.

Between 1960 and 1984, the number of students in higher education rose by a factor of nearly six. The rate of increase in the number of students studying abroad was even greater: it rose by a factor of seven between 1965 and 1984 (see Table 2). UNESCO publications provide interesting data in this respect. The 1988 *Statistical Yearbook* shows that Greece, with 34,267 students abroad, was fourth in absolute terms, behind China, Iran, and Malaysia, and far ahead of any other European country.

The hypotheses which could be advanced to explain this phenomenon may be divided into the historical, structural, and institutional, although it has to be understood that the components themselves are made up of a number of varied and interacting factors (Eliou 1988b).

The first factor to be taken into account is the slow development of higher education in Greece. Comparative international figures (from the UNESCO *Statistical Yearbooks*) show that despite the impressive increase in the number of establishments and students, Greece continues to lag for a European country, both in terms of the number of students per 100,000 inhabitants and in terms of enrollments in the 20–24 year age group (Table 1). Low public expenditure on education in general and higher education in particular has not allowed any progress in making substantive qualitative changes to the educational system. Continuation of the *numerus clausus* practice thus serves to recruit for foreign universities. Although candidates' chances of entering tertiary education rose from 24.5 percent in 1975 to 34.0 percent in 1985, fluctuating between 22.5 percent and 42.2 percent, the increased number of candidates means that the absolute number of these failing to gain entrance rose from 60,726 in 1975 to 98,576 in 1985 (Soumelis 1988).

Greek education is dominated by general studies, with consequent weakness in technical and vocational education. Of the total number of students in secondary education, 79.96 percent were in general education in 1975, rising to 87.35 percent in 1984. No reforms have managed to check this tendency and make technical education a viable alternative. In

Table 2
Number of Greek students at home and abroad 1960–83

	1960	1965	1970	1975	1980	1983
Students abroad	8,516	6,285	9,985	29,480	39,786	44,046
Students in Greece[a]	25,658	54,261	72,269	95,385	85,718	100,254
Percentage of students studying abroad	33.2	11.6	13.8	30.9	46.4	43.9

Sources: Council of Higher Education, Bulletin No. 10; Statistical Yearbooks of Greece
a Universities and equivalent institutions

fact, some reforms have favored general education: the duration of compulsory education has been extended from six to nine years; promotion from one year to another is now unimpeded the end of junior high school; and entrance examinations between junior and senior high school have been abolished. However, the leaving certificate awarded at the end of general secondary education is of very little value in the employment market, and is seen only as a passport to higher education. Furthermore, fluid economic and social patterns give rise to ambitions and expectations whose fulfillment requires a university degree and create the nationwide phenomenon of a university degree forming part of the objective of each family (Tsoucalas 1986). The importance of the public sector in the employment market and the exceptionally large number of graduates in the civil service help to reinforce this trend.

Among the institutional factors which partly explain the large number of Greek students abroad one might mention the following: the competitive admission procedure for admission to IHEs; the importance attached to degrees (regardless of the field of study) in recruitment for the civil service; and the salary increments to which graduates are entitled.

Although regulations governing the competitive process for admission to IHEs have been modified several times since 1964, within the limitation of the number of places available, the following phenomenon has endured: Greek society has created and adhered to the image that failure in university entrance examinations is tantamount to complete social failure, which can only be offset by registration at a foreign university. This is corroborated by the frequently very modest social origins of Greek students abroad.

3. Governance, Administration, and Finance

3.1 National Administration

State supervision of higher education is exercised by the Minister of National Education and Religions. Law 1268/1982 "concerning the structure and operation of the Institutions of Higher Education" (Article 5) set up a Council of Higher Education (SAP) and

laid down its structure and duties. This law, usually referred to in Greece as the "framework law," made substantive reforms to the universities and equivalent institutions, which for fifty years had been governed by a law passed in 1932. Law 1404/83 "concerning the structure and operation of the institutions of Technological Education" (Article 14) set up a Council of Technological Education (STE) and laid down its structure and duties. Provision was also made for the setting up of regional councils of technological education. These laws are imbued with the same spirit and there are many similarities between them. Both the SAP and the STE are advisory bodies, whose decisions take the form of recommendations to the Minister (which are not binding). Both bodies frequently have proposals submitted for discussion by the Minister on their agendas, which are determined by their presidents.

Recommendations issued by both bodies can concern:

(a) the foundation, abolition, amalgamation, organization, and functioning of institutions, faculties, and departments. In the case of the STE, recommendations can also extend to determining or reviewing the content of individual courses;

(b) the number of admissions to each department every year, which is decided partly by vocational orientation questions involving graduates;

(c) the distribution of funds and the creation of teaching posts of all kinds in the appropriate institutions;

(d) the general planning of higher education in conjunction with governmental development planning;

(e) questions of lifelong education, inservice training, and advanced training.

In the case of the SAP provision is made for recommendations on issues relating to "transfers of students and the matriculation of graduates for other degrees." In the case of the STE provision is made for recommendations related to the professional rights of graduates and to ensuring that the TEIs have the necessary material and technical infrastructure.

Both bodies are chaired by the Minister of Education or his/her representative. The SAP meets two or three times a year. It originally had 43 members, this number later rising to 57. The minutes of the meetings are published in the *SAP Bulletin*. This cumbersome body is unable to function particularly effectively. Its significance lies in the introduction, even on a consultative level, of the concepts of transparency and democratic representative and collective decision making, as well as of the coordination and planning of higher education.

It is the Minister of Education's prerogative to act on the recommendations of the SAP. Proposals concerning the number of candidates to be admitted to each department, as assessed by each IHE, are not usually accepted. At the eighth session of the SAP, the rector of the Athens Technical University presented figures showing that in the academic year 1982–83 his institution had proposed the admission of 400 new students; the Ministry fixed the number of 635; and the final numbers, after various legislative arrangements, was 1,323. In 1983–84 the corresponding figures were 405, 720, and 1,323, and in 1984–85 they were 420, 720, and 1,366 (*SAP Bulletin* 8, Athens 1985). The adverse effects of this threefold increase on teaching are clear. The academic community's opposition has repeatedly been expressed in strong terms, both by teaching staff and by rectors.

The resolutions of the Ministry of Education concerning higher education—in the form of simple decisions, decrees, or laws—are sent for implementation directly to the administrative authorities of each university.

The Five-Year Economic and Social Development Plans lay down guidelines for higher education but do not provide detailed figures for each year. The sessions of the SAP have occasionally touched on the questions of formulating criteria for determining the number of new students to be admitted to each department and for the distribution of funds among the universities, but these debates have ended with recommendations of a general nature. In 1987, the Ministry of Education expressed its intention to create a framework for the evaluation of the IHEs and to take the results of that evaluation into account when distributing funds. The centralism of the system may make the separate evaluation of each university difficult.

The funding of higher education is not satisfactory, and total education expenditure continues to be very low (see Table 3). The slight increase in recent years, and the increase in the percentage devoted to tertiary education, has not kept pace with the increases in other spheres, notably that of enrollments. It should also be noted that the existing system of financing depends almost entirely on the general state budget. In a paper (Soumelis 1988) presenting and analyzing the relevant data, it is pointed out that "the present strict financial control, despite its negative effects

Table 3
Expenditure on education 1970–84

	1970	1975	1981	1984
Total educational expenditure as percentage of GNP	2.0	2.0	2.4	2.6
Current educational expenditure as percentage of total	81.6	91.0	95.0	96.0
Tertiary level expenditure as percentage of current educational expenditure	15.5	20.0	20.4	22.3

on the planning and management of the IHEs, will certainly continue for quite a long time, unless 'revolutionary' reforms are introduced."

3.2 Institutional Administration

The articulation and administration of the IHEs are determined by Law 1268/1982. The IHEs consist of faculties divided into departments which may then be divided into sectors. Administration at all levels is collective. Only teaching staff in the two senior grades have the right to be elected to posts of responsibility. Nonuniversity personnel play no part in its administration.

The general pattern is as follows: the sector is administered by a director who is elected by the general assembly (consisting of all the teaching staff, in all four grades [DEP], two students' representatives, and one representative of the postgraduate students [EMY]) and by the general assembly (GA). The department is administered by its president, who is elected by a special electoral college (consisting of all the DEP members, student's representatives equal in number to the DEP members, EMY representatives equal in number to 15% of the DEP, and representatives of the special technical and administrative staff equal in numbers to 5% of the DEP) and by the GA (consisting of all DEP members, students' representatives equal in numbers to 50% of the DEP, and EMY representatives equal in numbers to 15% of the DEP). The faculty is administered by its dean, elected by the assembled electoral colleges which elected the presidents of the departments, by the dean's committee (consisting of the presidents of all the departments, one students' representative for each department, and the dean) and by the GA (consisting of the members of the GAs of all the departments). The university is administered by the rector, the rectorial council and the senate. The rector and two deputy rectors are elected by the assembled electoral colleges which elect the presidents of the departments, with representatives of the administrative staff and other categories of teaching staff equal in numbers to 10 percent of the DEP. The rectorial council consists of the rector, the two deputy rectors, one students' representative, and one representative of the administrative staff. The senate consists of the rector, the deputy rectors, the deans of the faculties, one DEP representative and one representative of the students for each department, one representative of the special teaching staff, one representative of the administrative staff, and five EMY representatives.

The exceptionally high proportion of student participation in the administration of the IHEs and, above all, in the election of the university authorities, is in reality still higher, as one-seventh of the DEP members are absent on sabbatical at any one time. A further undefined number may be absent for various other reasons (sick leave, field trips, etc.). Yet the basis for determining the number of student representatives continues to be the number of DEP positions occupied.

The principal responsibility of these bodies apart from the task of coordinating university activities and dealing with the practical problems of university life, is the implementation of an exceptionally detailed legislative framework and of the decisions from central administration, to which all the relevant documentation, whether financial or academic, is sent: curricula; details of participation in congresses; the election of new DEP members or the promotion of existing members; and so on.

4. Faculty and Students: Teaching, Learning, and Research

4.1 Faculty

The shortage of faculty members in comparison to the rapidly growing student body led in the late 1960s to the recruitment of large numbers of teaching assistants without predetermined qualifications. Ten years later, these teaching assistants, who had an active union organization, exerted considerable pressure in two directions: towards changing the statutory framework for the IHEs (a point on which many more general social and political forces were also agreed); and towards safeguarding the academic careers of the union's members. Many aspects of law 1268/1982, and above all the manner in which it was implemented, testify to the effectiveness of this pressure.

Table 1 shows clearly that the increase in teaching staff did not keep pace with enrollments. Educational statistics for the period 1960–70 do not take into account teaching assistants. For the same decade the table records staff who taught in more than one faculty only once. The problems of identity experienced by other third-level institutions, which were accompanied by problems of transitoriness among their staff, are reflected in the fact that no relevant data are available until 1980, by which time the controversial KATEE colleges had begun to function.

The only data available for the distribution of the teaching staff by rank are those for the period prior

to the implementation of Law 1268/1982 (see Table 4). In the period which followed, the system by which teaching staff were recruited and promoted changed radically. In addition, procedures involved in implementing the law led to high mobility in both vertical (promotion through the grades) and horizontal (movement to other IHEs) terms.

There are only four ranks for the teaching staff in officially recognized posts (DEP)—lecturer, assistant professor, associate professor, and full professor. The criteria for election or promotion to each of these ranks principally concern the candidate's teaching or research experience and publications, with quantitative and qualitative requirements which vary from rank to rank. DEP members are public functionaries. The only tenured staff are those in the two higher ranks and those who had been granted tenure before the implementation of the "framework law."

Interim provisions of the framework law concerned the teaching assistants already serving in the IHEs who did not have the qualifications to occupy the position of lecturer, for which a doctorate is essential. The IHEs have two other categories of teaching staff: the special teaching staff (for instruction in foreign languages, drawing, music, and physical education) and the special academic associates who are responsible for filling temporary gaps in the teaching staff. Academic associates are employed on a contract basis and have no right to participate in the university's administrative bodies. No new recruitments of DEP members or of other categories of teaching staff may take place unless a position falls vacant or the Ministry sets up a new place.

In all cases (recruitment to an official post, promotion of a DEP member, or employment on a contract basis) the responsibility lies with the institution,

Table 4

Total teaching staff and percentage of female staff of universities and equivalent institutions by rank in 1975 and 1980

	1975		1980	
Total professors	747	4.7	1,006	4.9
Full	479	2.3	714	3.5
Associate	110	6.4	236	8.5
Assistant	107	9.3	26	7.7
Other	51	13.7	30	10.0
Readers	127	8.7	199	9.0
Visiting experts and instructors	200	43.5	206	13.6
Total assistant teaching staff	4,436	40.9	5,513	42.6
Lecturers	927	17.5	1,386	23.2
Assistant Lecturers	2,922	39.4	1,780	42.1
Other teaching assistants	587	70.6	2,347	54.4
Total	5,810	35.6	6,924	35.3

but the decision is subject to checking and ratification by the Ministry. The procedures, which are strictly predetermined, take place at department level. In all cases, the decision is the result of a ballot in an electoral college consisting of the department's DEP members who rank at least as high as the candidate under examination (if there are insufficient numbers of such DEP members, they may be made up by co-opting faculty from other departments or universities). The ballot is held after detailed discussion of a report made by a three-member committee.

The legal framework determining all questions of staffing, and whose basic axis is the "framework law," is the same for all the IHEs. There are two organizations which represent the interests of university teaching staff: the union which originally represented the teaching assistants (whose members are now dispersed amongst the various ranks of the staff), which aims to embrace teaching staff of all grades; and the Panhellenic federation of professors, which draws most of its support from the full professors. These organizations, however, are not totally representative of the entire academic community, individually or together.

The legal framework obliges the faculty, in all four grades, to teach for a minimum of five hours per week. However, all teaching staff are supposed to be at the university's disposal throughout all working hours. No provision is made for a balance between teaching, research, and administration. In reality, administration in the form of lengthy general assembly and electoral college meetings occupies much of the faculty's time, as does studying the work of candidates for teaching posts and preparing reports. Research—where and when it takes place—is simply added to other obligations. The specific obligations of each faculty member (which courses he or she will teach, on which committees he or she will serve, etc.) are laid down by the GAs. The Minister of Education and other ministers have acquired the habit of assigning to the faculty—principally to the full professors—work outside the university on various committees and working parties, without, as a rule, relieving them of their university duties or providing them with extra remuneration.

4.2 Students

The overall growth of the student body over the period 1965–84 was impressive. The growth in demand for higher education and the quantitative development in the number of students between 1965 and 1985 were reflected in the evolution of the social composition of the student body. Published statistics do not give a clear picture, while research into and analysis of the subject have rarely been attempted. The earliest projects refer to the years 1963–65 (Lambiri–Dimaki 1974, 1983) and the most recent to no later than 1975–76 (Psacharopoulos and Kazamias 1985).

Two main conclusions can therefore be drawn. First, the democratization of access to higher education altered the social composition of the student body. Thus the application of an index of opportunity by father's occupation shows that in 1956–57 the ratio between the two extreme groups (that group of occupations showing the highest percentage access and the group of occupations showing the lowest percentage access to IHEs) was 20:1, while in 1975–76 it had fallen to 4:1 (detailed findings from Psacharopoulos and Kazamias 1985). The 4:1 ratio between the two extreme groups was also recorded in 1972–73 with relation to access to the Schools of Social and Economic Sciences (Drettakis 1977). Second, there is sharp differentiation/ranking among the IHEs in terms of the origin of their students. The social composition of the student body of each IHE reflects a hidden hierarchy of the IHEs and, to a large extent, determines the social standing of each (Drettakis 1977, Meimaris and Nicolacopoulos 1978).

There are no data concerning access to higher education by ethnic minorities or other population groups, with the exception of breakdowns by sex (see Table 5). The apparently satisfactory figures for the access of women to higher education display, when broken down by subject, faculty, and department, features which give rise to concern. During the years 1975–81 the proportion of women in higher education rose from 34.4 percent to 41.3 percent, but in the field of engineering and technology the increase was only from 8.4 percent to 8.8 percent, while in the

Table 5
Total number of students and female students in the main subject areas 1965–84

	1965		1970		1976		1980		1984	
Humanities	10,990	6,630	13,399	7,842	17,210	11,886	19,783	12,938	40,882	28,334
Social sciences	24,634	7,274	32,175	10,221	49,623	19,682	44,806	20,363	52,306	27,379
Exact sciences	22,376	4,607	30,624	6,216	50,334	12,381	55,449	16,855	74,769	25,468
Other and not specified	—	—	—	—	—	—	1,078	48	—	—
Total	58,000	18,511	76,198	24,279	117,167	43,949	121,116	50,204	167,957	81,181

humanities and theology it was from 71.9 percent to 79.1 percent. Reduction in inequality of access was accompanied by an increase in divergence of orientation. The differing orientations of men and women in their studies and the prospects for utilization of their degrees on the labor market constitute significant elements in evaluating the level of equality between men and women in higher education (Eliou 1987, 1988a).

The interests of the student body are expressed by the students' association of each faculty and institution, while on the national level the student body is represented by the National Union of University Students and the National Union of TEI Students. The management committees of the associations are formed on a proportionally representational basis after elections held each spring, where student political organizations, which are the extension into the student world of the political parties, confront one another. All students are eligible to vote in these elections. The percentage of participants varies from faculty to faculty and also in accordance with the general political atmosphere of the moment. Abstentions, sometimes numerous, are not taken into account when calculating results. The strength of the student political organizations is regarded as being that which is expressed at the elections and not that of their organized nuclei. The students who serve as representatives on the various university bodies are not directly elected, but are appointed by the management committees of the associations on the basis of the strength of each grouping as expressed at the elections of the previous year. This means that the rectorial authorities, in whose election the student body has an overwhelming majority, are in fact chosen by the political parties. Indeed the student elections are to a far greater extent than municipal elections an opportunity for the parties to measure their strength on the national level, and this is how they are treated inside and outside the universities.

Curricula, drawn up by the GAs of the departments on the recommendation of the sectors, are dispatched to the Ministry of Education by the dean of the faculty and come into force after official publication. They may be revised each spring, by the same process. A feature of the Greek system is the statutory obligation for the free distribution to each student of one book per course. Studies are structured into two semesters of at least 13 teaching weeks and two examination weeks each. However, a course may be regarded as having been taught if only nine weeks of classes have been held. The credit unit system is applied. Students are graded for each course at the end of each semester. The manner of assessment is left to the faculty member teaching the course. When their pass marks have allowed them to amass the requisite number of credits, the students are awarded their degrees.

5. Conclusion

Concern over the condition of higher education has been expressed for many years (OECD 1962, 1965, 1980, 1982, 1984), which, however, has not impeded certain developments. A paper published in 1988 recorded problems hampering the internal efficiency of the IHEs as follows: excessive politicization, excessive privileges, indiscriminate distribution of opportunities, curricular rigidity, excessive central regulation, too much student absenteeism, and scantiness of funds for research (Psacharopoulos 1988).

An overall evaluation of Greek higher education might focus on the existence of a network of problems on three levels. First, the existing structure of secondary education, in conjunction with the infrastructural inadequacies of tertiary education, maintains a problematic system of entrance into the IHEs and creates powerful social pressures which, in turn, contribute to the development of excessive central regulation and to student emigration. The delays in developing graduate studies and research confirm the fact that Greek higher education is articulated on only one level. Second, the structural problems have effects on the quality of the education provided, which is marked by its cramping uniformity, the shrinkage of requirements in terms both of learning and of grading, and a type of high-school rationale. Third, problems created by the structure and quality of higher education are expressed in a number of ways—under the statutory cover of the laws—in the day-to-day running of the institutions: in excessive absenteeism among students; in shortcomings in the teaching of faculty members; and in indirect party-political intervention, which distorts the conception of participation, isolates the voice of the academic community, and maintains inertia.

In the extensive and substantive literature concerning higher education which is developing in Greece, two important points stand out: the need for radical intervention in higher education; and the need for this intervention to be prepared with specialized research on the one hand, and consensus procedures, on the other, to ensure the widest possible support from the social and political spectrum.

Bibliography

Dimaras A 1973, 1974 He metarhuthmise pou den egine: tekmeria istorias 1821–1967, 2 vols. Hermes, Athens
Dimaras A 1978 The movement for reform: a historical perspective. *Comp. Educ. Rev.* 22(1):11–20
Dimaras A 1981 A story of frustrated reform. *J. of the Hellenic Diaspora* VIII (1–2): 19–24
Dragonas Th, Kostakis A 1986 Defining educational environments: The case of the Athens Technological Educational Institute (TEI). *Higher Educ.* 15: 651–65
Drettakis M N 1977 Hoi scholes koinonikon, oekonomikon kai politikon epistemon sten anotate ekpaideuse sten Hellada. Papazissis, Athens

Eliou M 1981 Research in higher education. *J. of the Hellenic Diaspora* VIII (1–2): 123–30

Eliou M 1987 Equality of the sexes in education: And now what? *Comp. Educ.* 23 (1): 59–67

Eliou M 1988a Women in the academic profession: Evolution or stagnation? *Higher Educ.* 17: 505–24

Eliou M 1988b Mobility or migration? The case of Greek students abroad. *Higher Educ. In Europe* XIII (3): 60–66

Emke-Poulopoulos I 1986 Problemata metanasteuses palingosteses. IMEO-EDIM, Athens

Fatouros D A 1975 Allage kai Pragmatikoteta sto Panepistemio. Olkos, Athens

Frangos ChP 1978 Hellenika kai Europaika Panepistemia. Papazissis, Athens

Gavroglu K 1981 Certain features of higher education in Greece and the failure of the attempts to reform it. *J. of the Hellenic Diaspora* VIII (1–2): 95–108

Kayser B 1964 *Géographie Humaine de la Grèce*. Presses Universitaires de France, Paris

Kazamias A 1976 The politics of educational reform in Greece: Law 309/1976. *Comp. Educ. Rev.* 22(1): 21–45

Kintis A A 1980 He anotate Paideia sten Hellada. Gutenberg, Athens

Lambiri-Dimaki J 1974 Pros mian helleniken koinoniologian tes Paideias, 2 vols. National Center of Social Research, Athens

Lambiri-Dimaki J 1983 *Social stratification in Greece 1962–1982*. A N Sakkoulas, Athens

Manessis A, Matonitis D, Panou S, Tatakis B, Tsatsos D, Fatouros D, Frangos C 1978 Gia mia demokratike Paideia. Papazissis, Athens

Meimaris M, Nicolacopoulos I 1978 Paragontike analuse dedomenon: Scheseis koinonikoepangelmatikes proeleuses kai scholes phoiteses gia tous spoudastes ton AEI. *The Greek Review of Social Research* 33–34: 225–40

Mouzelis N 1978 *Modern Greece: Facets of Underdevelopment*. Macmillan Press, London

National Statistical Service of Greece 1987 *Educational Statistics 1981/82* National Statistical Service of Greece, Athens

National Statistical Service of Greece 1987 *Statistical Yearbook of Greece, 1986* National Statistical Service of Greece, Athens

Organisation for Economic Co-operation and Development 1962 *Country Reviews: Greece.* OECD, Paris

Organisation for Economic Co-operation and Development 1965 *The Mediterranean Regional Project. Country Reports: Greece.* OECD, Paris

Organisation for Economic Co-operation and Development 1980 *Educational Reform Policies in Greece.* OECD, Paris

Organisation for Economic Co-operation and Development 1982 *Reviews of National Policies for Education: Greece.* OECD, Paris

Organisation for Economic Co-operation and Development 1984 *Reviews of national science policy: Greece.* OECD, Paris

Pesmazoglou S 1981 Some economic aspects of education. *J. of the Hellenic Diaspora* VIII (1–2): 131–60

Pesmazoglou S 1987 Ekpaideuse kai anaptuxe sten Hellada 1948–1985: to asumptoto mias scheses. Themelio, Athens

Polydorides G 1978 Equality of Opportunity in the Greek

higher education system: The impact of reform policies. *Comp. Educ. Rev.* 22(1): 80–93

Psacharopoulos G 1982 Earnings and education in Greece, 1960–1977. *European Econ. Review* 17: 333–47

Psacharopoulos G 1988 Efficiency and equity in Greek higher education. *Minerva* XXVI (2): 119–37

Psacharopoulos G, Soumelis C 1979 A quantitative analysis of the demand for higher education. *Higher Education* 8: 159–77

Psacharopoulos G, Kazamias A 1985 Paideia kai Anaptuxe sten Hellada: koinonike kai oekonomike melete tes tritobathmias ekpaideuses. National Center of Social Research, Athens

Soumelis C 1979 Case study: Greece. In: Härnqvist K (ed.) 1979 *Individual Demand for Education.* OECD, Paris

Soumelis C 1988 *Changing Patterns of Finance in Higher Education. Country Study: Greece.* OECD, Paris

Svoronos N 1972 *Histoire de la Grèce Moderne.* Presses Universitaires de France (Que sais-je?), Paris

Tsoucalas C 1977 Exartese kai anaparagoge: ho koinonikos rolos ton ekpaideutikon mechanismon sten Hellada, 1830–1922. Themelio, Athens

Tsoucalas C 1981 Some aspects of "over-education" in modern Greece. *J. of the Hellenic Diaspora* VIII (1–2): 109–21

Tsoucalas C 1986 Kratos, koinonia, ergasia ste metapolemike Hellada. Themelio, Athens

UNESCO 1988 Statistical Yearbook, 1988. UNESCO, Paris

M. Eliou

Guatemala

1. Higher Education and Society

Higher education in Guatemala began at the University of Santo Thomas Aquino in 1562. It continued at the major colleges and convent schools that operated in the first half of the seventeenth century. In 1676 the University of San Carlos of Borromeo was created. With the political independence of Central America in 1821, San Carlos University acquired a great importance for the country and extended its cultural influence. Since then San Carlos has continued to expand with the impetus of state policies.

Guatemala, with an area of 109,000 square kilometers, has a population of 8.5 million (1988), of which 67 percent reside in the rural areas. In the early 1990s the illiteracy rate is 43 percent. The indigenous groups represent 42 percent of the population and half are monolingual. Some 22 principal languages are spoken.

The situation is further complicated by the cultural underdevelopment, poverty, and acute health, education, housing and public transportation problems from which the majority suffer.

The serious deficiencies in the Guatemalan educational system are exemplified in the following statistics: Only 13 percent of children 4 to 6 years old attend kindergarden; 58.4 percent of 7 to 14 year olds attend primary schools; between the ages of 16 to 20 only 8 percent attend high school. Only 5.7 percent benefit from the system of higher education, which covers the ages 17 to 24, and includes nonuniversity and university education, public and private.

From a qualitative point of view, the educational system has an urban orientation and discriminates against peasants and the rural indigenous population. Informal educational programs are directed towards peasants, workers, and the marginalized sectors; however, they are insufficient and far removed from the real interest and necessity of the rural population and the productive system.

2. The Institutional Fabric of the Higher Education System

During the decade 1961 to 1971, because of the socioeconomic development of the country, four private universities opened as a consequence of the accelerated demand of students and also because of the emergence of an ideological tendency at variance with the state university policies.

Currently the development of higher education has slowed because of the acute economic crisis which afflicts the country and the exhaustion of the existing model of development.

The Guatemalan system of higher education includes nonuniversity and university education. The former includes institutions and programs that do not necessarily lead to an academic degree. Some programs are associated with universities and eventually lead to graduate studies. This category includes the Central American Institute of Business Administration (INCAE); Institute of Nutrition for Central America and Panama (INAP); the Latin American Faculty of Social Sciences (FIACSO); and the Women's Institute of Advanced Studies (IFES). Other nonuniversity programs are government sponsored.

University education is both public and private. The former includes San Carlos University with its central offices and regional centers. The private universities include Rafael Landivar University (1961); Del Valle University (1966); Mariano Galvez University (1966); and Francisco Marroquín University (1971) each with its central offices and extensions.

Research has not reached a high level of development. Its coordination is carried out by a General Council, which is under the control of the Rectorate. There are programs at an intermediate level at San Carlos University and research is conducted in every department, as part of community study programs, during supervised professional exercise and also before presenting a thesis.

The main institutes and research centers include the following: Economical and Social Investigation Institute for the Improvement of Education, Institute for Research in Social and Political Sciences, Institute for the Study of National Literature, Institute for Engineering Research, and the Center of Folklore Studies.

The admission of students in the state university is open, with the only requisite being the high school certificate. In some private universities scholastic examinations may be required, depending upon the space-availability of each department. The distribution of students among the state, private, and nonuniversity institutions is shown in Table 1.

3. Governance, Administration, and Finance

San Carlos University is the oldest and largest of all the universities. According to its by-laws and statutes, San Carlos manages, organizes, and develops the state system of higher education and professional university training. Its stated objectives include the following: cultural diffusion, the promotion of scientific research, and cooperation in the study and resolution of national problems. The internal government comprises the University Superior Council, which includes the rector, the deans of the 10 faculties, one representative of the professional colleges of each faculty, one titular professor and one student from each department.

Financing for San Carlos University is carried out by a private assignment, which according to law, cannot be less than 5 percent of the general budget of state ordinary incomes. It also receives rental income, student fees, and university rights.

The private universities according to law are independent institutions that organize and develop the private higher education of the country and coordinate their activities through the Private Higher Learning Council. Another function is the maintenance of academic standards. They are ruled internally by a board of directors generally composed of the rector, a secretary, and vice-directors, among others. Financing is obtained through donations, subsidies, fiduciary donations, and student fees.

Higher Education, public and private, comprises the following: colleges, schools, departments, institutes and investigation centers and university extensions.

The higher education faculty in Guatemala are

Table 1
Enrollment 1989

San Carlos University	63,919	75%
Rafael Landivar University	7,893	9%
Mariano Galvez University	5,317	6%
Francisco Marroquin University	4,687	6%
Del Valle de Guatemala University	1,457	2%
Nonuniversity higher education institutions	1,727	2%
Total:	85,000	100%

selected through competitive examinations in the state university, and by appointment in the private universities.

5. Conclusion

The development of higher education in Guatemala constitutes a complex problem of both a quantitative and qualitative nature. The policy of the central government is designed to respect the autonomy and independence of the universities, which makes it necessary to maintain a permanent dialogue in order to resolve the problems that arise.

Higher education diversification, its connection with the national reality, as well as its regionalization, must be coordinated accordingly. It must also have financial support from the government agencies in order to promote pertinent research and provide suitable professional education.

The universities and other institutions of higher education are constantly promoting academic quality and diversification in order to meet the demands of the country. Additional efforts are made to coordinate the pedagogical activities within the national education system.

Bibliography

Cuevas Del Cid 1970 *Pensamiento Universitario*. Editorial Universitaria, Guatemala

González O C 1971 *Pedagogía Universitaria*. Editorial Universitaria de El Salvador, El Salvador A.C.

González O C 1987 *Historia de la Educacion en Guatemala*. Editorial Universitaria, Guatemala

Gutiérrez F 1975 *Nuevas Experiencias Pedagogicas en América Central*. Editorial ILPEC, San José, Costa Rica

Instituto de Investigaciones y Mejoramiento Educativo 1982 *El Ejercicio Profesional Supervisado en la Universidad de San Carlos*. Editorial Universitaria, Guatemala

Lemus L A 1963 *Planeamiento Integral de la Educacion*. Editorial Universitaria, Guatemala

Ministerio de Educación 1986 *Plan Quinquenal de Educacion, 1987–1991*. Editorial Pineda Ibarra, Guatemala

Mantovani J 1946 *Mision de la Universidad en Nuestra Epoca*. Facultad de Humanidades, Universidad de San Carlos de Guatemala

Universidad Rafaél Landívar 1989 *Estatutos y Reglamento General. Manual del Estudiante*. Dirección de Asuntos Estudiantiles, Editorial Universitaria, Guatemala

C. G. Orellana

Guinea

1. Higher Education and Society

The following institutions are responsible for higher education in Guinea: the University of Conakry; the University of Kankan; the Normal School of Manéah (in Coyah); the Faculty of Geology and Mines in Boké; and the Faculty of Hydrology and Forestry (in Faranah). The largest and oldest institution is the University of Conakry, founded in October 1962 as the *Institut Polytechnique*. The University is a member of AUPELF (*Association des Universités Partiellement ou Entièrement de Langue Française*)—an association of universities which teach partly or entirely in the French language. It was composed of ten faculties: liberal arts and humanities; science; law and economic sciences; medicine; pharmacy; biology; chemistry; mechanical technology; electronics; and civil engineering. These have now been restructured into five faculties.

In 1984, the Faculties of Agronomy and Animal Husbandry were temporarily suspended due to the high numbers of agronomists and animal husbandry technicians already educated both in foreign universities and in institutions in Guinea including among others Foulaya in Kindia, Bordo in Kankan, Tolo in Mamou, and the National Veterinary School in Mamou.

2. The Institutional Fabric of the Higher Education System

Admission to higher education requires passing two parts of the baccalaureate (the options being in social sciences, experimental sciences and mathematical sciences) and an entrance examination in the field in which the student wishes to specialize.

In 1984, higher education in Guinea was characterized by the training of a relatively large number of upper-level cadres and a small number of middle-level cadres in a country with little schooling. This pyramidal structure of training in higher education has been rectified due largely to the role played by professional schools (both public and private) under the current educational policy.

3. Governance, Administration, and Finance

Higher education is totally financed by the state. The university, especially in Conakry, is seeking government recognition of its autonomy in administration, education, and management of financial resources, as well as the promulgation of special regulations for its teaching and research personnel. The Faculty of Geology and Mines in Boké, originally under the *Institut Polytechnique* in Conakry, was decentralized in order to move it closer to the bauxite mining zone. This faculty receives material and financial assistance from the *Compagnie des Bauxites de Guinée* (CBG)— the bauxite company of Guinea—and professors from the Soviet Union. After the transition period of the educational reform (1984–90), the Normal School in Manéah has been transformed into the Institute of Educational Sciences, to give a practical professional formation to high-school teachers recruited from among university students with an essentially theoretical education.

The length of studies in higher education is usually five years (four years in college plus one year of practical experience, or five years in college, according to the field of study). Medicine is a seven-year program, including an internship in the hospitals in Conakry. In the Engineering Faculty, agreements have been made so that students can undergo their training in firms partially owned by the government, such as the aluminum company FRIGUIA, in their FRIA plant, and the *Compagnie des Bauxites de Guinée* in Boké (in their mine in Sangarédi and in the Port of Kamsar).

4. Faculty and Students: Teaching, Learning, and Research

The teaching faculty is comprised of Guineans, some of whom have studied abroad at the undergraduate and graduate levels and foreigners (Soviets, French, and British). Built with the cooperation of the Soviet Union, the *Institut Polytechnique* in Conakry, which became a university in 1984, has predominately Soviet equipment. In the framework of bilateral cooperation, the English department of the faculty of liberal arts and humanities of the University of Conakry benefits from the support of the British Council, while France aids the French department of the same faculty, and has also given a computer laboratory for the Mathematics department of the science faculty and a recently established Computer Center separate from the faculties of the University of Conakry. Interuniversity cooperation links certain institutions and faculties of higher education with foreign institutions.

During the First Republic (1958–84), all graduating students were automatically hired by the civil service or by companies partially owned by the state. Since 1984, following the liberal policy of less state involvement and a more liberal economy, the students themselves have had to find jobs in the labor market. The structural adjustment program recommended by the International Monetary Fund and the World Bank and the consequent reduction of government posts have created a situation where many students find it difficult to find employment.

5. Conclusion

The people of Guinea, freed from the political and economic restrictions of the previous regime, are enthusiastically constructing schools and health centers in the villages and urban neighborhoods, which have a growing need for teachers and medical and paramedical personnel. This trend, if maintained, should favor in the medium and long term a rise in employment first for middle-level cadres and later for university-level graduates.

A. G. Diallo

Guyana

1. Higher Education and Society

Guyana, the former colony of British Guiana, was ceded to Britain during the early nineteenth century. There was no institution in the country which provided formal postsecondary higher education prior to the establishment of the University of Guyana (UG) in 1963. This was in sharp contrast with Guyana's South American neighbors where universities were often established in the early years of their colonization.

The provision of university education for the Guyanese was historically linked with attempts to establish a university for the entire English-speaking West Indies (Braithwaite 1958) and after many unsuccessful attempts at developing either regional or local centers of higher learning the University College of the West Indies (UCWI), later the University of the West Indies, finally became a reality in 1948. It was originally affiliated to the University of London and was among those higher educational institutions that were established in the British colonial empire, just after the Second World War, as constituent colleges of London University.

UCWI, which was meant to serve the higher education needs of the entire English-speaking Caribbean, including Guyana, was established in 1948 based primarily on the recommendations of the Irvine Commission, appointed by the British government in 1943. It commenced its academic work with a faculty of medicine and later expanded into other fields of study including arts, natural and social sciences, law, agriculture, and engineering. UCWI was originally located in Jamaica which is about 1,000 miles northwest of Guyana and despite the financial support provided by the government of British Guiana, only a small percentage of Guyanese students attended this institution. For example, in 1952 only about 17.5 percent of Guyanese students studying abroad were registered at UCWI. However, as the range of programs on offer increased and local prejudice against a colonial university diminished, the number of students from British Guiana who were registered there increased considerably—from 98 in 1951–53 to 442 in 1960–62, about a fourfold increase in nine years.

With the achievement of self-government in 1960 the government of Guyana began to make provisions to withdraw its support from the University College of the West Indies and establish its own university. There were a number of factors, both educational and political, which contributed to this decision (Bacchus 1980). UCWI was considered to be a "high cost institution," especially when assessed in terms of the average cost of the graduates who came back to Guyana on completion of their studies. A substantial percentage of Guyanese students who studied in Jamaica did not return home, at least not immediately, and this was regarded as a tremendous loss of the country's limited higher-level trained human resources. In 1962 the government estimated that its contribution to the University College of the West Indies represented a cost of about US$40,000 for each university graduate who returned to the country. With local per capita incomes then only about US$650 p.a. this was considered a very high price for the government of Guyana to pay for educating its higher-level personnel. A second reason advanced by the government for its withdrawal from UWI was that, with the achievement of self-government and with Independence on the horizon, there was a need to train an increased "number of high-level professionals to exercise intellectual leadership in Guyana and man positions of highest responsibility [and] to undertake research" (Government of British Guiana 1963).

There were other considerations, some political, which influenced the government's decision to establish a university in Guyana. First, the premier of the country, who was educated in the United States, had a quite different view of university education than that which was offered by the UCWI. He felt that Guyana needed a university which was more directly oriented toward helping to meet the needs of the masses—one which would be somewhat similar in its operations to the original land-grant colleges in the United States. There was considerable dissatisfaction among the government leaders with the political orientation of course programs offered by the UCWI which they felt were dominated by a conservative approach to the analysis of social and economic problems.

The government was hopeful that the proposed University of Guyana would produce educated individuals who would have acquired a socialist perspective which they would use in the analysis and solution of Guyanese social and economic problems. Although this was not often mentioned it was implicit in the first stated goal of the university mentioned in the government's 1963 *Yearbook of Education*. There it was indicated that one of the aims of UG was "to create an intellectual nucleus in Guyana, as a center around which some systematic definition of the national purpose can take place and partly as a defense against the persistent battering from external colonialist and reactionary ideas against which colonial and backward societies are so helpless" (Government of British Guiana 1963).

2. The Institutional Fabric of the Higher Education System

When the University of Guyana was formally opened in 1963 it was not the only institution which provided postsecondary education in the country. In addition there was a teachers' college originally established in 1928 which prepared primary school teachers, a technical institute which was founded in 1951 in the capital city of Georgetown to train craftworkers and technicians, and a School of Agriculture which opened in 1963. Later a second technical institute providing mainly craft training was opened in the country's second city, New Amsterdam. Entry qualifications for these institutions were usually lower than those required by a university and hence they have not been included here as institutions of higher education. However, higher technical, agricultural, and teacher-training programs are now being conducted at the University of Guyana.

3. Governance, Administration, and Finance

The University of Guyana started as an independent university without affiliation to any other existing higher education institution and began by offering only evening classes for degrees in the arts and the social and natural sciences. At the time it was a bold and unusual step for a colonial university and caused the institution to be looked down upon by the local middle class. In order to help boost its prestige, the government appointed an internationally distinguished academician, Dr Lancelot Hogben, as its first principal and vice-chancellor. The institution was given a substantial degree of academic autonomy, largely at the insistence of the vice-chancellor.

The government appoints the chancellor, the pro-chancellor and the board of governors of the university. The chancellor and the pro-chancellor are both ceremonial positions though the pro-chancellor, an educator and a former Minister of Education, continues to play an important advisory role on various aspects of the university's work. The board of governors which is the main policy-making arm of the university is appointed by the government, though an attempt is made to select representatives from various groups in the community. The academic board is responsible for the development of proposals for new academic programs, advising on the need for new faculty members and equipment, and recommending the appointment of new academic staff.

The capital and recurrent costs of the university are met entirely by the government although financial aid and loans are sometimes received from external agencies. All students attending the university must do national service and in view of this they are not required to pay tuition fees. However, consideration is being given to a proposal for students who do not want to do national service to be allowed to enter

UG on a fee-paying basis. There are no private institutions of higher education in the country.

4. Faculty and Students; Teaching, Learning, and Research

The University of Guyana has taken some bold and innovative steps to gear and develop its courses to the development needs of the country. The new university proposed to be actively involved, jointly with various government departments, in the study of local problems. The plan was for all government research units to become research institutes of the university while still maintaining close contact with the relevant government departments. The heads of the particular government departments would be appointed as directors of the advisory boards of the research institutes. The fields that were proposed to be covered included agriculture, forestry, fisheries, geology, education, and social technology (University of Guyana 1962). The objective behind the establishment of these institutes was not only to update the quality and usefulness of the research which was then being undertaken in the country, but also to use the findings to help increase the relevance of the instructional programs. However, with the change of government in 1965 and the resignation of the first principal soon after, these original ideas were not pursued and the university became a more traditional institution. The proclaimed socialist orientation of the government means that some of the original populist concerns of the university continue to be reflected in a number of its innovative programs.

By 1967 UG was admitting full-time students and as confidence in its work increased, partly as a result of the fact that some of its best graduates were accepted for further studies by reputable universities overseas, its enrollment steadily increased too. Between 1963–64 and 1972–73 there was a 114 percent increase in the number of students doing degree courses at UG and if enrollments in the diploma and certificate courses are included the increase between 1963–64 and 1970–71 was about 580 percent. In 1970–71 just over 30 percent of all UG students were registered in full-time nondegree courses. By the 1980s UG was not only teaching for degree courses in arts, social and natural sciences, and law but also for certificate and diploma courses in architectural and building technology, civil engineering, telecommunications, medical technology, radiography, social work, public administration, and education. However, the percentage of the 18–24 age group who attend university in Guyana is still extremely small.

Despite the efforts made to have a balanced enrollment in the arts, social sciences, and natural sciences, in 1972 only 17 percent of graduates were in the natural sciences. This was due not only to the somewhat lower enrollments in this field but also to the greater difficulties which natural science students seemed to face in obtaining their degrees, especially those who were studying part-time. This was reflected in the fact that while about 41.2 percent of the initial group of arts/social science students had completed their degrees after four years only 18 percent of natural science students had done so, over the same period. In addition, the dropout rate among the part-time students was quite high. For example, between 1963–64 and 1970–71 about 35.6 percent of all arts students had dropped out while the figures for the social and natural sciences were even higher, being 54.4 percent and 82.9 percent respectively. This was one of the factors which influenced the university's decision to admit full-time students.

While the financially difficult times of the past decade had an adverse effect on the work of the university, in 1990 a Commonwealth Advisory Group to Guyana noted: "The University has managed over the years to maintain creditable standards of teaching and research, despite having to contend with financial and other hardships in somewhat greater measure than its sister institution, the University of the West Indies" (Commonwealth Advisory Group 1990).

The government of Guyana has increased its ownership of and control over various sectors of the economy between 1964 and 1985. A substantial proportion of the economy (possibly over 80 percent) falls within the public domain. As a result, the majority of graduates from UG have tended to take up, remain in, or return to public sector employment, especially teaching. In 1972 about 51 percent of graduates were teachers, 12.6 percent were in the civil service, 2.2 percent in public corporations and only 4.7 percent in the private sector. With the increased nationalization of the economy since then, this pattern of employment has continued.

For most UG graduates the rate of return on their education has been quite high. It is likely that this was due less to their increased productivity than to the government's policy on pay for graduates and its preference for promoting its own supporters. For example, nearly all students who are employed in the public sector and obtain their degrees are promoted immediately to a new salary scale. Further, it has been shown that Afro-Guyanese graduates, the main supporters of the government, were more likely to experience a faster rate of promotion and larger pay increases than Indo-Guyanese graduates (Baksh A).

One of the major obstacles to the university's development and creativity has been the increasing control exerted by the political party in power. This not only includes control over the type of programs on offer but also the appointment of individuals to various positions within the academic structure. The refusal of the government to allow the Guyanese historian, Dr Walter Rodney, appointed to the Chair of History at UG, to take up the position is an example of political intervention. This type of intervention has been partly reponsible for some of the problems in recruiting and retaining qualified staff. A change in the political leadership, which took place in 1985, has led many academics at UG to hope that rewards and recognition will, in future, be increasingly based on academic competence and performance rather than on ethnicity or political affiliation. This is a crucial factor in the academic rehabilitation of the University of Guyana.

Bibliography

Bacchus M K 1980 *Education for Development or Underdevelopment: Guyana's Educational System and its Implications for the Third World* Wilfrid Laurier University Press, Waterloo, Ontario, pp. 215–216

Baksh A *The Mobility of Degree Level Graduates of the University of Guyana*, University of Guyana Department of Sociology, Georgetown

Braithwaite L 1958 The Development of higher education in the West Indies *Social and Economic Studies* 7 (1)

British Guiana, Ministry of Education 1963, *Yearbook of Education*, 1963, Ministry of Education, p. 19

Commonwealth Advisory Group Report 1990 *Guyana: The Economic Recovery Programme and Beyond.* Commonwealth Secretariat, London

University of Guyana 1962 *Report of the Principal on Research and Research Institutes in the University*, University of Guyana, Georgetown

M. K. Bacchus

H

Haiti

1. Higher Education and Society

The higher education system in Haiti has traditionally been a small, long-time elitist and unbalanced and neglected part of the educational system. Education is said to be mandatory in Haiti since the last century; however, it has not been a priority for the state. In the 1990s Haiti remains a country with around 65 percent illiteracy.

Since the early 1960s, under the Duvalier dictatorship, a number of changes occurred in the structure and in enrollment in education in general and higher education in particular. New faculties were created, but with little regard either to the general structure of the state university (by far the main higher education institution) or the needs for professionals in the country. Meanwhile, a fairly poor private sector developed.

The State University of Haiti started to take shape from the nineteenth century, when the first faculties were organized: the law school in 1860; and the medical school in 1880. The newest faculties were created during the 1970s: social sciences in 1974; and linguistics in 1978. Today, with 11 centers, the State University of Haiti concentrates around 80 percent of total enrollment in higher education.

The total population of Haiti was around 3.3 million in 1950. In 1971 the second general census counted 4.8 million and in 1982 the population had reached 5.119 million, according to the third and latest census. Today it is evaluated at approximately 5.743 million. The urban population remains fairly small (27% of total population) and is concentrated for the most part in the capital area of Port-au-Prince which accounts for more than 75 percent of the total urban population, with 1.6 million people.

Haitian creole, the national language spoken by all Haitians, has only recently been recognized as one of the two official languages; only a 10 percent elite of the population speaks French, the second and long-time single official language in the country.

The occupational structure is dominated by agriculture, which occupies 70 percent of the active population. The industrial sector only employs 11 percent of the occupied labor force. A broad informal sector includes both small commerce and related activities, while the formal service sector is essentially composed of 32,000 public employees in modern commerce and similar. Unemployment and underemployment are always high; recent statistics evaluate it as prevalent as 60 percent in the Port-au-Prince area, and more than 30 percent in the countryside.

In such a context, agricultural development appears to be the number one priority of the newly elected government. The peasantry forms around 75 percent of the population. Industrial growth appears to be essentially dependent on foreign investments, at least for the next decade.

The economy is largely dominated by the agricultural sector which provided around 33 percent of the Gross Domestic Product (GDP) in 1989. Coffee is still the main crop, despite poor and declining production in the last decade. Industry is clearly divided between local manufacturers and export-oriented assembly industries. Altogether, the industrial sector accounts for 22 percent of the GDP. Services have the typical structure of many Third World economies, with a big personal services sector and a large public service.

Haiti has a long history of authoritarian governments. In 1986 the thirty-year dictatorship of the Duvalier family came to an end. During these three decades economic recession was coupled with political repression, until the 1970s saw a short decade of relative economic growth. The past five years are the history of a struggle for a democratic system in the middle of a growing economic crisis. In December 1990, the first democratically chosen government of the country was elected. The main goals of the new political team in education are: a massive literacy campaign as first priority and the extension of the basic school system in general. Higher education is viewed as an instrument to back up the development purposes of the state with technical and academic resources.

2. The Institutional Fabric of the Higher Education System

The public sector consists mainly in the State University of Haiti (UEH), the Technical Center for Planning and Applied Economy (CTPEA), the nursing school, and the National Arts School (ENARTS). Except for two nursing schools in Cap-Haïtien and Les Cayes (two of the largest cities after Port-au-Prince), all public higher education institutions are concentrated in Port-au-Prince. The State University includes eleven faculties and centers which cover some of the main fields from humanities to management. It has been in virtually permanent crisis for the past five years. Budget problems (state allocation remained unchanged since 1987), political trouble (the university never opened at all during 1987–88, after a student strike) combined with severe institutional difficulties (the UEH has had no steady direction since the dismissal of its rector in May 1987) have contributed to confirm such a negative picture.

The private sector has developed virtually without state control. The number of institutions and the level of enrollment are unknown, as most of these centers operate without authorization or legal recognition. Most of the private sector also concentrates in Port-au-Prince, with the exception of three law schools and the University of Les Cayes, largely external to the national system (the courses are taught in English and most of the staff is American). The majority of these private centers offer a technical formation. Academic requirements vary widely from one institution to another.

2.1 Levels of Institution

There is only an elemental hierarchy within the system, between establishments which require complete secondary education, including the two final examinations (*baccalauréat I* and *II*) and those which do not. The State University and the CTPEA for the public sector and Quisqueya University for the private sector, have such requirements. Other centers like the nursing schools, the ENARTS, and most private centers do not require both baccalaureates. Apart from this basic difference, the hierarchy is undetermined.

Higher Education covers essentially one cycle from three to five years. There is only one exception within the UEH, for the career of topography which lasts only two years and does not require both baccalaureates.

Consequently, graduate programs are absent with two exceptions: the faculty of ethnology offers a master's program in sciences of development; and there is a master's program in education under experiment at the *Ecole Normale Supérieure* which educates teachers for the high school level. Research is thus virtually nonexistent at the university except for practical experimentation in agronomy and medicine. Even outside the university no academic research is conducted systematically.

With regard to professional and technical schools, there are three distinguishable categories: teacher-training schools (for elementary schools); agricultural colleges (two in the country); and technical colleges (three recognized ones). Otherwise the many commercial, technological, business administration and computer schools that have multiplied in recent years do not offer, in general, very reliable education.

Table 1 summarizes the main higher educational institutions.

2.2 Admissions Policies and Selection

Both final secondary-level examinations are required to apply for the university. There is, thus, a national legislation. However, admission is not automatic to the UEH because of serious and growing limitations in capacity. The faculties organize an admission examination, with a *numerus clausus* system. Since the early 1960s this was true of the medical school, for instance. But from the late 1970s onwards, it applied to all the centers that conform to the UEH.

There are no figures available for enrollment in higher education as a whole. The following figures for the last decade concern the UEH and indicate a relative tendency to more mass enrollment since the late 1970s: 1972, 2,096 students (UEH); in 1981, 3,945 students; in 1985, 4,701 students; and in 1990, 6,278 students.

3. Governance, Administration, and Finance

3.1 National Administration

Responsibility for the development of higher education lies at present with the Ministry of Education. However, since 1987, this status is in discussion because the new constitution, approved that same year, clearly stipulates that the university should enjoy all the rights and privileges of autonomy. That same year, the rector was dismissed by the military government and ever since the university has lived under a *de facto* status, the Ministry of Education assuming the responsibilities of rector in the meanwhile with no decision so far to officialize autonomy.

Such a situation partly explains why there is no central coordination of the State University, or the higher education system in general. The faculties determine by themselves enrollment, staff recruit-

Table 1
The main higher education institutions 1960–90

Year	1960	1965	1970	1975	1980	1985	1990
Public Sector	State university: 6 faculties, 2 schools	unchanged	7 faculties, 1 school within UEH	9 faculties within UEH	11 faculties within UEH	UEH plus CTPEA	unchanged
Private Sector	4 identified private centers	6 identified private centers	unchanged	unchanged	unchanged	unchanged	13 identified centers

ment, fees, and so on within the limits of an unchanged budget since 1987.

Thus, until recently no clear national plan was elaborated involving definite goals for higher education. The new government has expressed some concern for these problems but they clearly appear to be related to the execution of a number of other priorities. Indeed, autonomy should soon become a reality. But the problem of the role of higher education in the general development policy remains to be discussed and settled.

The State University is financed by the central government. Now and then, foreign cooperation helps in bettering the situation of certain faculties, either material (laboratories, books, etc.) or academic (visiting professors, exchange programs, etc.). In past years this type of cooperation has been increasingly difficult to obtain. State expenditure for higher education represented 1.23 percent of GDP in 1980, 1.13 percent in 1985, and 1.41 percent in 1990.

3.2 Institutional Administration

The dispersion and variety in types and styles of management among the different faculties of the State University make it difficult to talk about models of governance.

In the area of patterns of authority and participation there is a general trend toward an improvement of student participation in the internal life of the faculties: elaboration of new rules, voting power, and so forth. Academic power is poor and rather vertical, since the staff is not full-time.

The academic organization is diverse between the faculties and centers, but all are considered at the same level despite great differences in size, careers offered, and level of specialization. The faculties are internally organized in departments.

4. Faculty and Students: Teaching, Learning, and Research

4.1 Faculty

Only two faculties have a number of full-time professors in their staff: the faculty of sciences (6) and the faculty of agronomy (12). The lack of resources has prevented any improvements in faculty building. Today the State University employs approximately 500 teaching staff, teaching from two to six or eight hours weekly. This academic staff is paid per hour and has virtually no corporate interest represented. Since research does not exist, academic work is reduced to teaching.

4.2 Students

No exact figures are available to trace the evolution of the student body since 1960. For the period 1980–90 these are the figures: in 1980 there were 1,370 students (34.7%) studying exact sciences and 2,575 (65.3%), studying social sciences; in 1990, 1,339

(21.3%) were studying exact sciences and 4,939 (78.7%) studying social sciences. These figures show a clear tendency of predominance of social sciences and law in enrollment. On the contrary, exact sciences have lowered their share, especially in medical and engineering careers.

Because of the general crisis of the university since 1986, graduation is impossible to evaluate: archives were partially destroyed in 1986 and after that most faculties have only produced "candidates" who have completed courses but not the thesis, a requirement until today. Old patterns of evaluation are considered obsolete, particularly the thesis, but no new patterns have been adopted yet.

Middle and upper-middle class students used to be the majority until the early 1960s. Nowadays most students are of lower-middle class extraction.

Students interests have been banned since 1960, when the university was closed down and put under political control. Revival of student associations is quite recent (1986) but these organizations cannot claim a very large membership.

The structure of courses and programs is entirely determined by the faculties and departments. This is part of the difficulty of articulating the university as a whole. It is frequent that one course or a set of courses be repeated in several faculties, while other courses are not provided at all.

In general, undergraduate studies are based on a broad, general content, except for professionally oriented careers (e.g., medicine, agronomy, and dentistry). The programs are based on annual evaluations. The credit system is experimental and only partial, in one faculty.

5. Conclusion

Higher education in Haiti faces a general crisis similar to the general crisis of society itself. Undoubtedly, very serious reforms are required. The new government encourages the tendency to a change but has not enforced measures to make them concrete. Lack of resources is a major obstacle. The State University, which represents the main part and the core of the higher education system, has a number one priority — to reorganize its general structure including revising number of faculties; linking to the central administration; rearticulating curricula and administrative reforms; and organizing proper academic staff. The challenges are serious and the means to face them dramatically scarce.

Bibliography

PNUD/UNESCO 1990 Data are taken from rectorate and financial analysis on higher education in Haiti: Beltramo J. P. *Le sous-secteur de l'éducation supérieure* (mimeo) provisional version. PNUD/UNESCO, Port-au-Prince

S. Manigat

Honduras

1. Higher Education and Society

Agriculture plays a dominant role in Honduran society, contributing 28.4 percent of the Gross National Product and involving 52.4 percent of the economically active population. Exploitation of natural resources is inefficient and there is a growing migration from rural to urban areas.

Postsecondary education was established in 1847 by church initiative; the *Universidad Nacional* (UNAH) became autonomous in 1957. In 1978 the first private university, the *Universidad José Cecilio del Valle* (UJCV), was established. Higher-level training schools have existed since 1941, when the *Escuela Agrícola Panamericana* (EAP) was established.

One of the main objectives of the postsecondary system is the resolution of national problems (Constitución de la República 1982).

2. The Institutional Fabric of the Higher Education System

From 1976 to 1988, the number of institutions doubled: three universities were founded, some existing institutions were upgraded, and there was an expansion of the academic military institutes.

There are presently four universities and ten non-university institutes.

Higher education is offered by four universities, one teacher training college, two agricultural schools, one forestry school, and six military schools. Academic achievement is not an admission criteria, except at the EAP.

In 1972, the UNAH switched to an open admissions policy encompassing all persons who finish secondary school, regardless of academic background. University enrollment increased from 1.9 percent of the 20–24 age group in 1970 to 7.9 percent of the same group in 1980.

Most programs are undergraduate, leading to a *Bachillerato Universitario* (bachelor's degree) or *Licenciatura* as the first degree offered. Intermediate degrees are awarded, such as *técnico* or *diplomado*. Master's programs have only recently begun at the UNAH and the *Universidad Tecnológica Centroamericana* (UNITEC).

Research is conducted at UNAH and EAP only, at the former as a parallel activity, and as part of the curriculum at the latter.

3. Governance, Administration, and Finance

Since 1965, UNAH's prime responsibility has been to organize, oversee, and develop higher education. It is administered by boards of directors where elected

Table 1
Postsecondary institutions by activity

Year	University	Teacher training	Agriculture	Forestry	Military	Total
1960	1	1	2	0	2	6
1965	1	1	2	0	2	6
1970	1	1	2	1	2	7
1975	1	1	2	1	2	7
1880	3	1	2	1	4	11
1985	3	1	2	1	6	13
1988	4	1	2	1	6	14

Table 2
Total enrollment by activity

Year	University	Teacher training	Agriculture	Forestry	Military	Total
1960	1,443	—	234	—	88	1,765
1965	2,112	—	234	—	80	2,426
1970	4,047	981	250	—	81	5,359
1975	10,635	1,207	251	—	129	12,222
1980	24,724	1,058	502	205	237	26,726
1985	30,591	2,889	558	70	422	34,530
1988	34,062	3,518	716	76	188	38,560

Source: Banco Central de Honduras and Survey

Table 3
Enrollment as percentage of population 20–24 years of age

Year	Population	Percentage					
		University	Teacher training	Agriculture	Forestry	Military	Total
1960	165,275	1.0	—	0.1	—	*	1.1
1965	188,257	1.1	—	0.1	—	*	1.3
1970	211,453	1.9	0.4	0.1	—	*	2.5
1975	258,046	4.1	0.5	0.1	—	*	4.7
1980	314,511	7.9	0.3	0.2	0.1	0.1	8.6
1985	387,520	7.9	0.7	0.1	*	0.1	8.9
1988	437,179	7.8	0.8	0.2	*	*	8.8

Source: Estadísticas Centro de Estudios Juan Manuel Galvez and Survey
*<0.1%

Table 4
Graduates from higher education

Year	University	Teacher training	Agriculture	Forestry	Military	Total
1960	46	—	64	—	12	122
1965	112	—	65	—	18	195
1970	118	—	70	—	16	204
1975	211	—	62	—	35	308
1980	705	61	124	42	65	997
1985	1,134	59	141	73	212	1,619
1988	1,295	177	104	22	—	1,598

Source: Banco Central de Honduras and Survey

students and professionals participate in equal number and category.

Degrees, diplomas, and certificates awarded by other institutions, including the military, are recognized by the UNAH on the basis of total credit hours.

Funding for UNAH and other public centers is governmental. The *Universidad Nacional* receives 6 percent of the national revenue (Constitución 1982). Private institutes are financed by student fees and grants. Although elementary education is a top priority in Honduras, in 1985 almost 10 times more was spent on each university student than on each elementary student, namely 2.0 percent of Gross National Product (PIER 1987).

4. Faculty and Students: Teaching, Learning, and Research

In 1988, 84.0 percent of the total faculty taught at the UNAH, 64 percent of those being full-time. At UNAH ranking is based on years of service rather than on academic credentials, as is the case at UJCV and EAP. At UNAH, only 16.5 percent of the faculty hold teaching chairs, a status that requires five years of service or a master's degree.

In 1988, 57 percent of graduates had read exact sciences, 39 percent social sciences, and 4 percent humanities. An average curriculum requires 12 percent general academic courses, and up to 63 percent major courses.

5. Conclusion

Higher education is not related to development; very little effort is made to improve agricultural production and to develop industries incorporating this century's technological advances. There is an urgent need to change admission policies and to coordinate higher learning with other levels of the nation's educational system.

Bibliography

Banco Central de Honduras [annual] *Honduras en Cifras*
PIER 1987 *The Admission and Placement of Students from Central America*. National Association of Foreign Students Affairs, Washington, DC
Universidad Nacional Autónoma de Honduras 1981 *Cronología Histórica de las Unidades Académicas de la Universidad*. Editorial UNAH
Universidad Nacional Autónoma de Honduras 1987 *30 Años de Autonomía*. Editorial UNAH

I. Acosta de Fortin

287

Hong Kong

1. Higher Education and Society

The territory of Hong Kong comprises the island of Hong Kong, a number of other islands, and part of the Chinese mainland. The island of Hong Kong became a British colony in 1842. The territory was subsequently enlarged by addition of sections of the mainland and neighboring islands. The greatest expansion occurred in 1898, when colonial authorities took a 99-year lease on an area known as the New Territories. This lease will expire in 1997, when the whole of Hong Kong (including the island which had been ceded "in perpetuity") will be transferred back to Chinese sovereignty.

Hong Kong has excellent internal communications and a land area of only 1,071 square kilometers. Everybody can easily travel to higher education institutions, so Hong Kong does not have severe regional imbalances in access.

The population of Hong Kong is approximately six million. Almost 98 percent are Chinese, for the majority of whom Cantonese is the mother tongue. Among the remainder, the largest groups are from the Philippines, the United Kingdom, the United States, and the Indian subcontinent.

Its limited natural resources mean that Hong Kong has had to depend on imports for virtually all requirements, including food, fuels, and capital goods. The externally oriented nature of the economy is reflected in the fact that in 1990 the total volume of visible trade (comprising domestic exports, re-exports, and imports) amounted to 235 percent of gross domestic product (GDP). The government has at times been keen to link higher education output to the needs of the economy, though officials have recognized the difficulties of effective labor force planning. The size and shape of higher education has also been determined by historical factors and by social demand.

Although the higher education sector has expanded dramatically, throughout the 1980s competition to enter higher education remained intense. In the middle of the decade, less than 3 percent of the age group in Hong Kong was able to study in local universities, a figure which compared unfavorably with the 5 percent in Singapore and 10 percent in the United Kingdom (Chow 1985 p. 38).

Because of the intense competition many people were forced to study abroad, and in the mid-1980s Hong Kong had as many students abroad as at home. Postiglione (1987 p. 51) reported figures of 12,000 students in the United States, 10,000 in Canada, and 4,000 in the United Kingdom. Some students also went to China and Taiwan. However, these destinations were not popular as the Hong Kong government refused to recognize their qualifications. Extensive overseas study was a drain on the economy, but helped to make Hong Kong an international society.

In the late 1980s, the government embarked on massive expansion of higher education. The policy was devised in the context of substantial emigration in the lead up to reunification with China in 1997. Partly to replace the talent lost through emigration, and partly as a public demonstration of self-confidence, in 1989 the Governor announced that the number of first-year first degree places would expand from about 7,000 in 1990 to about 15,000 in 1995. According to this projection, about 25 percent of the age group would have tertiary education places. By international as well as local standards, this is a significantly high figure.

2. The Institutional Fabric of the Higher Education System

For the purposes of this article, higher education includes all institutions which provide post-sixth-form education. Hong Kong has 13 such institutions, which are described below.

Six institutions receive their main incomes from the University and Polytechnic Grants Committee (UPGC), a semiautonomous body responsible for disbursing government funds.

The oldest institution, founded in 1911, is the University of Hong Kong. In 1990 it had 9,100 undergraduate and graduate students in nine faculties. Competition for entry is intense, and in 1989 19,000 candidates competed for 2,000 places. Official policy has made English the principal language of instruction.

By contrast, the Chinese University of Hong Kong operates mainly in Chinese. The institution was founded in 1963 to provide access to tertiary education for students from Chinese-medium secondary schools. However, English is also required for admission to most courses, and many staff expect their students to read English-language books. The university has five faculties, and in 1989 had 8,400 undergraduate and graduate students. As with the University of Hong Kong, competition for entry is intense.

The youngest institution is the Hong Kong University of Science and Technology. It was incorporated in 1988, and commenced operation in 1991. The university has a general education center, but is principally organized around schools of engineering, science, and business and management. English is the chief medium of instruction. Full-time enrollments are projected to expand to 10,000 by the year 2000.

Two polytechnics offer a wide range of courses to meet the needs of commerce and industry. The Hong Kong Polytechnic was founded in 1972, and in 1990 had 8,040 full-time, 1,870 sandwich, 1,450 mixed-mode, 4,450 part-time day release, and 11,260 part-time evening students. Some courses lead to degrees, but most lead to diplomas or certificates. The City Polytechnic was founded in 1984, and offers similar programs. In 1990 it had 8,800 students, of whom about half were on full-time and sandwich courses.

The Baptist College was founded by the Baptist Church as a private body in 1956. Since 1983, it has been fully funded by the government. In 1990 the College had 2,900 students studying arts, business, science, and social sciences. Nearly 90 percent of first-year students were on externally accredited degree courses. In addition, the Division of Continuing Education offers a broad range of part-time cultural, vocational, and professional courses. In 1990 these courses had an enrollment of 40,000.

Two institutions are registered under the Post-Secondary Colleges Ordinance. The Hong Kong Shue Yan College was founded in 1971. It operates a four-year diploma program without government assistance, and in 1990 had 4,000 students. Lingnan College, founded in 1967, had 1,100 students. Following a 1987 assessment by the United Kingdom Council for National Academic Awards, the College became eligible for greater government financial assistance. Both colleges focus chiefly on arts, social sciences, and business.

The Grantham, Northcote, and Sir Robert Black colleges of education, together with the Hong Kong Technical Teachers' College, train nongraduate teachers for primary and secondary schools. All four colleges are directly financed and staffed by the government. In 1990 they had 2,300 full-time students.

The Open Learning Institute was established in 1989. The Institute is sponsored by the government, though is expected in the long run to become self-financing. The Institute aims to offer a chance to those who were unable to go on to further education after leaving school, opportunities for workers and managers to update their qualifications and skills, and a chance for personal development. It uses chiefly distance teaching courses, and offers programs in science, business, and arts. Enrollments are projected to reach 20,000 in 1995.

3. Governance, Administration, and Finance

Following the tradition seen in the United Kingdom, the universities and polytechnics are permitted to operate with a high degree of autonomy. Individual institutions determine their own policies for recruitment of staff and students, for the nature and length of courses, and for the balance between subject disciplines.

However, the government does exercise some influence through its control of finance. As noted above, the three universities, two polytechnics, and the Baptist College are funded through the University and Polytechnic Grants Committee (UPGC).

This body was established in 1965 on the model of the University Grants Committee of the United Kingdom. Its official role is "to advise the government on the development of, and funding requirements for, higher education in Hong Kong and to administer government grants for the tertiary institutions" (Hong Kong 1990 p. 118). Recurrent funding is normally provided by triennial block grants. Capital grants are considered annually at the same time as the government's annual estimates. Although the UPGC is constituted as an independent body, it pays attention to government priorities when allocating funds.

One clear example of "the power of the purse" arose in the late 1980s. Since its establishment, the Chinese University of Hong Kong had admitted students who had completed Secondary Form 6 into degree programs of which the majority lasted four years. In contrast, the University of Hong Kong admitted students after Secondary Form 7 into degree programs of which the majority lasted three years. It was universally agreed that this lack of uniformity was unsatisfactory and had particularly disruptive implications for the secondary schools. However, it was difficult to find an acceptable solution. The Chinese University wished to retain its degree structures, and the University of Hong Kong was keen to introduce a four-year program. The government, acting on the advice of the Education Commission, wished the Chinese University to move to a three-year program. The ensuing debate raised questions on the balance between institutional autonomy, government control, and public interest. Ultimately it became clear that the command of finance gave the government command of overall structures. The Chinese University was informed that from 1997 it should recruit from Form 7, and that government grants would provide only for three-year basic degree programs.

In 1987/88, expenditure on universities and polytechnics represented 5.3 percent of the total government budget. It seemed inevitable that planned growth of the sector would raise this percentage. However, the Hong Kong government has firmly resisted establishment of private universities on the patterns, for example, of the Philippines and Indonesia. Official policies have been guided by a desire to maintain standards and control.

4. Faculty and Students: Teaching, Learning, and Research

4.1 Faculty

In the past, chiefly because of shortages of qualified local applicants, Hong Kong's institutions of higher education have employed significant numbers of expatriates. The percentage has been reduced, but it remains prominent. The University of Hong Kong, in particular, advertises the majority of its senior

289

posts in overseas periodicals. In 1989, only 55.5 percent of senior staff in the university claimed Hong Kong as their place of permanent residence. The largest number of expatriates (22.3 percent) came from the United Kingdom. Others came from the United States (5.6 percent), Australia (4.8 percent), Canada (3.4 percent), and New Zealand. No staff claimed the People's Republic of China as their place of permanent residence. It must be stressed, however, that the University of Hong Kong was not typical of all institutions. The large number of expatriates reflected both the policy of teaching in English, and deliberate efforts towards international recruitment. Even the local staff tend to have Western orientations. Large proportions gained their higher degrees from universities in Europe and North America. Relatively few have qualifications from the People's Republic of China or Taiwan.

The precise nature of the work of academic staff is determined within the employing institutions rather than by external bodies. Some institutions, especially the universities, also permit strong internal autonomy, allowing most decisions about deployment of staff to be undertaken at departmental level. In general, university staff are expected to undertake research as well as teaching. Hong Kong does have a few independent and specialized research bodies, but it relies on its institutions of higher education for the bulk of research work.

4.2 Students

The vast majority of higher education students are local. For example, in 1989 only 2.6 percent of students at the University of Hong Kong came from outside the territory. The largest group of outsiders came from China. They numbered only 78 students (0.8 percent) in 1989, but this was already a significant increase on the previous year. The other external students came from Macau (0.1 percent), other parts of Asia (0.4 percent), the United Kingdom (0.3 percent), and the United States (0.3 percent).

Over the years, the social base of the student population has widened significantly. Students have to pay fees, but courses are heavily subsidized. In 1987 the government announced plans to reduce the subsidy, but projected that by 1993/94 fees would still cover only 12 percent of the total real cost. This was revised in 1991, but the new projection is still only 18 percent by 1997/98. Moreover, since 1969 the government has operated an efficient student loan scheme. The objective of the scheme is to ensure that "no student who has been offered a place in one of these institutions [of tertiary education] should be unable to accept it because of lack of means" (Bray 1986 p. 344). The scheme seems to achieve this objective, and the high rate of general employment (reaching 98.8 percent in 1989) coupled with high salaries for graduates makes it easy for the majority of students to repay their loans.

Figures on the gender of students show that male have a better chance of proceeding to higher education than do females. Statistics also show sever underrepresentation of women in the sciences. For example, at the University of Hong Kong in 198 women represented only 3.1 percent of undergraduate enrollment in the faculty of engineering and only 17.5 percent in the faculty of dentistry. Women were more numerous in arts, social sciences, law and education, though did not always comprise th majority.

5. Conclusion

Higher education in Hong Kong has expanded dramatically, and is set for further expansion in the future. The establishment of the Open Learning Institute in 1989, and the opening of the Hong Kong University of Science and Technology in 1991, have been particularly notable events. Large numbers of students are still forced to go abroad, but this tendency is likely to become less pronounced when more local opportunities become available in the 1990s.

Hong Kong is also beginning to welcome student from the People's Republic of China. In the 1980 numbers were small, but they seem set to increase further as Hong Kong approaches reunification with China in 1997. However, reunification should no cause Hong Kong models of higher education to be submerged by Chinese ones. The 1984 Sino-British agreement indicated that Hong Kong would retain autonomy to run its own education system at leas until 2047.

Finally, it is worth commenting again on the exten to which higher education is dominated by the public sector. Private institutions are permitted to registe under the Post-Secondary Colleges Ordinance, and two have done so. However, the Hong Kong government has strictly prohibited the establishment of private universities, and despite the high cost of public institutions has been determined to retain its dominance in the sector.

Bibliography

Bray M 1986 Student loans for higher education: The Hong Kong experience in international perspective. *Higher Ed.* 15: 343–54

Bray M 1991 Strategies for Financing Higher Education Perspectives from Hong Kong and Macau *Higher Education* 21: 11–25

Chen J T S 1981 Tertiary education in Hong Kong: Relevance and expansion. In: Jones J (ed.) 1981 *The Common Welfare: Hong Kong's Social Services*. The Chinese University Press, Hong Kong

Chow G 1985 Higher education and the labor market in Hong Kong. *Chinese Univ. Ed. J.* 13: 37–47

Griffiths R C 1984 Hong Kong University and Polytechnic Grants Committee. *Higher Ed.* 13: 545–52

Hong Kong Education Commission 1988 *Education Commission Report No. 3*. Government Printer, Hong Kong

Hong Kong Government [annual] *Hong Kong*. Government Printer, Hong Kong

Luk B H K 1989 Education. In: Tsim T L, Luk B H K (eds.) 1989 *The Other Hong Kong Report*. The Chinese University Press, Hong Kong

Pagliari M, Frost J A 1987 Distance education in Hong Kong. In: *Distance Education in Asia and the Pacific*, Vol. II. Asian Development Bank, Manila

Postiglione G 1987 International higher education and the labor market in Hong Kong: Functions of overseas and local higher education. *Int. Ed.* 17: 48–54

Wilson D 1990 A vision of the future. In: *Hong Kong 1990*. Government Printer, Hong Kong

M. Bray

Hungary

1. Higher Education and Society

The first Hungarian universities, Pecs and Obuda, were established in the fourteenth century, but they began to function permanently only in the seventeenth century. The oldest permanently functioning Hungarian university, was established in 1635 by the Jesuits. Hungarian higher education, particularly university education, started to expand at the end of the nineteenth and at the beginning of the twentieth centuries. Its structure follows the Central European model since Hungary was one of the states forming the then Austro-Hungarian Empire. Hungary's infrastructure, education system, and public administration followed the model developed under the empire.

There was a quantitative development of Hungarian higher education after 1945, in keeping with the prevailing development model of the period. The number of graduates from universities and colleges grew by a factor of six between 1949 and 1984. With new universities and colleges established, the capacity of higher education rose significantly. There were essential changes in the professional and vertical structure of higher education. Nevertheless quantitative development inevitably surpassed qualitative requirements.

1.1 Size and Rate of Growth of Population

In the 40 years since the end of the Second World War, emigration was a significant factor in population trends in two periods: between 1945 and 1948 444,000 Hungarians emigrated; and in the 1950s 160,000 citizens left Hungary (see Table 1).

The total population at the beginning of 1989 was 120,000 lower than that recorded in the census of 1980. The main reason for this is the permanent decline in the birthrate, the high mortality rate among the increasing older population, and an increasing mortality among the middle-aged. Consequently the population can be characterized as aging. The number of the population aged 60 or over in 1941 more than doubled from 997,000 to 1,965,892, while the number of those under 14 has fluctuated significantly—at the end of 1988 it was 200,000 less (almost 8 percent) than in 1941, and 300,000 (12 percent) less compared to 1960 (see Table 2).

In terms of regional distribution the population can be characterized as mainly city dwelling. The number of those living in country towns has increased particularly, as Table 3 shows.

In the 1970s and 1980s the working population gradually decreased, and the number of pensioners increased significantly: 86 percent of the men aged 14 to 59, and 74 percent of the women aged 15 to 54 constitute the working population (see Table 4).

Table 2
Percentage distribution of population according to age

	1941	1949	1960	1970	1980	1984	1989
Age group							
0–4	8.4	8.7	8.3	6.8	8.1	6.0	5.9
5–9	8.5	8.2	9.2	6.3	7.2	8.1	6.6
10–14	9.1	8.0	7.9	8.0	6.6	7.4	8.3
15–19	9.5	8.4	7.6	8.9	6.1	6.7	7.0
20–24	6.2	8.5	6.8	7.5	7.6	5.6	6.4
25–39	24.9	21.9	22.4	20.6	22.0	22.1	22.3
40–59	22.7	24.7	24.0	24.8	25.3	25.7	24.8
60+	10.7	11.6	13.8	17.1	17.1	18.4	18.7
Total	100.0	100.0	100.0	100.0	100.0	100.0	100.0

Table 1
Changes in population 1941–89

	1940	1949	1960	1970	1980	1984	1989
Number of population	9,316,074	9,204,799	9,961,044	10,322,099	10,709,463	10,659,000	10,589,000
Percentage change according to census	100.0	98.8	108.2	103.6	103.8	99.5	99.3

Table 3
Percentage distribution of population according to place of habitation

	1941	1949	1960	1970	1980	1984	1989
Budapest	18.4	17.3	17.9	19.4	19.2	19.4	20.0
Country towns	27.9	27.2	29.6	33.2	37.2	38.7	39.5
Villages	53.7	55.5	52.5	47.4	43.6	41.9	40.5
Total	100.0	100.0	100.0	100.0	100.0	100.0	100.0

1.2 Occupational and Social Class Structure

The number of employed manual workers gradually decreased in the 1970s and 1980s, while the number of nonmanual workers rose (see Table 5). Among manual occupations, skilled workers became more numerous. In the early 1990s, nearly half of manual workers have skilled jobs.

More than half of nonmanual workers are subordinate administrators, one-fourth are in senior positions, and 18 percent are management workers.

Inflow to particular social classes or social strata is the result of the decision made by youths when they have finished their studies and choose their occupation. Their entrance to a certain class or stratum is decisively determined by their education. Mobility between the basic classes is becoming less intensive, while it is becoming more intensive within them.

The number of working-class people has decreased since 1980, mainly as a consequence of the fall in numbers of industrial and building workers. Apart from the trade and services sectors the number of manual workers has also diminished in other areas (see Table 6).

The proportion of peasants working in cooperatives decreased between 1970 and 1980, and has been constant ever since. At this level horizontal restructuring is quite intensive.

The proportion of nonmanual workers is growing permanently, though at a slower pace.

1.3 Structure of the Economy

Until 1970, the number of agricultural workers was permanently decreasing, first rapidly, later at a lower pace. In the industrial sector until 1970 the number of workers was growing, but later it fell in almost all sectors (see Table 7). The proportion of workers in other sectors of the national economy grew.

In nonmaterial sectors the number of white-collar workers engaged in health care, education, and culture increased significantly. The rapid increase in the proportion of technical staff stopped after 1980. The increase in the numbers of workers employed in accountancy, management, administration, and finance slowed down after 1980.

2. The Institutional Fabric of the Higher Education System

Hungary has several universities with only a very small number of students, for example, the University of Horticulture, the University of Veterinary Studies, or the University of Economics. These universities have several faculties, but only in their specialist field. Technical and agricultural higher education were raised to university level after the Second World War. The training of medical doctors was separated from traditional university programs, and was reorganized in specialist universities. The word "university" is not entirely comparable to the term

Table 4
Percentage distribution of economic activity

	1941	1949	1960	1970	1980	1984	1989
Employed	45.1	44.4	47.8	48.3	47.3	46.1	45.5
Pensioner	2.2	2.8	4.4	12.1	18.0	20.8	22.5
Bringing up children age 0–3	—	—	—	1.4	2.6	2.1	2.3
Dependant	52.7	52.8	47.8	38.2	32.1	31.0	29.7
Total	100.0	100.0	100.0	100.0	100.0	100.0	100.0

Table 5

Occupational structure as percentages of the total workforce

	1970	1980	1984	1988
Skilled worker	24.1	28.6	30.8	29.4
Semiskilled worker	24.6	27.6	25.4	24.6
Unskilled worker	21.4	10.1	8.4	9.7
Other manual workers	2.0	1.2	0.4	1.1
Manual workers total	72.1	67.5	65.0	64.8
Nonmanual	24.5	29.7	31.5	29.1
Others	3.4	2.8	3.5	6.1
Total	100.0	100.0	100.0	100.0

as used in Western Europe. It defines a level of higher education lasting from four to six years.

Another feature of Hungarian higher education is that the relatively narrow sphere of university education is supplemented by colleges, which are institutions of higher education independent of the universities, with the exception of agricultural higher education. They do not confer university diplomas. Students graduating from colleges will be "college graduate" engineers, teachers, and so on. Their diplomas differ from those who graduated from universities.

Table 8 indicates the development of institutions of higher education. The increase in 1965 to 1966 indicates the reorganization of technical high schools into colleges. All other changes—apart from the closure of two colleges of agriculture in 1975—involve concentration and reorganization. Changes in 1988 to 1989 are because before that time the table had not contained the data on military institutions and the College of Political Science.

At the start of the 1990s there are 62 institutions of higher education in Hungary, among them 25 universities or university-type colleges. There are four universities of arts and sciences, three technical universities, one university of economics, five medical, and six agricultural universities. There are five

Table 6

Percentage distribution of social classes and strata

	1949	1960	1970	1980	1984
Working class	38.8	51.1	56.5	57.8	55.3
Peasants in cooperatives	0.3	12.0	17.6	12.0	11.8
Nonmanual	8.3	15.7	22.6	27.5	29.6
Private sector	52.6	21.2	3.3	2.7	3.3
Total	100.0	100.0	100.0	100.0	100.0

Table 7

Percentage distribution of occupied workers

	1949	1960	1970	1980	1984
Agriculture	53.8	38.5	24.4	19.0	18.4
Industry	21.6	34.0	43.7	42.1	37.4
Other sectors	24.6	27.5	31.9	38.9	44.2
Total	100.0	100.0	100.0	100.0	100.0

specialized art and physical education colleges working at university level. There are 37 colleges (18 teacher-training colleges, seven technical, three economical and commercial, one agricultural, four military, one college of state administration, and three other institutions). There are 15 church-run higher-education institutes. Diplomas available at these institutions are now accepted in the secular world, which means that students of church institutions (up to 650 persons) supply not only the internal needs of the churches.

Apart from the University of Economics, universities have two or more faculties. University courses and programs last usually for five years (10 semesters), college courses last three or four years (6–8 semesters). There are some exceptions: medical education lasts for twelve semesters, the faculties of law and political sciences for nine.

Apart from some branches of technical studies, college and university teaching is not directly comparable. Those who graduate from colleges have to pass supplementary examinations to pursue studies at university level. The crucial problems in the horizontal structure of higher education are shown in Table 9. As a result of horizontal dispersal of the higher education network, the high number of institutions with small capacities is very significant.

Institutionalized forms of scientific studies developed in autonomous universities in Hungary and, with some delay, followed European development patterns. Until the 1950s, institutions of higher education constituted four-fifths of Hungarian research and development establishment, in terms of institutions, number of research workers, and expenditure. After this period, the permanent reorganization of the Ministry of Culture and Education, the reduction of its governmental functions, scope of activity, and budget, ended its central role in supervising Hungarian scientific life. It was replaced by several central supervisory organizations, such as the Hungarian Academy of Sciences, National Board for Technological Development, and Commissions on Scientific Policy. The 1950s and 1960s were characterized by the extensive development of a network of strongly centralized, independent and professional full-time research institutions; the

Table 8
Number of institutions of higher education

	1937–38	1950–51	1955–56	1960–61	1965–66	1970–71	1975–76	1980–81	1981–82	1982–83	1983–84	1984–85	1985–86	1986–87	1987–88	1988–89
Institutions	16	19	32	43	92	74	56	57	57	56	58	58	58	54	54	58
Faculties	37	43	54	60	111	102	104	95	95	95	97	100	100	98	94	98

294

Table 9
Distribution of higher educational institutions according to number of students

	0–300	300–500	501–1000	1001–2500	2500+	Total
Independent institutes	6	14	16	13	5	54
Percentage	11	26	30	24	9	100
Faculties functioning as part of institutions	21	6	1	—	—	28
Percentage	75	21	4	—	—	100
Total	27	20	17	13	5	82
Percentage	33	24	21	16	6	100

formulation and implementation of research programs and projects reflecting the needs of national economic planning; the central regulation of legal and financial procedures and regulations; and increasing state interference in scientific research. While the basis of Hungarian research and development has been developing dynamically, research in universities declined, and by the end of the 1960s it hardly amounted to 10 percent of Hungarian research capacity.

Today 37.8 percent of those working in research and development, which constitutes one-fifth of all research staff calculated on full-time occupation basis, and more than 50 percent of researchers with scientific degrees work in university or college research institutes in Hungary (see Table 10).

The research basis of higher education is the largest and, geographically as well as disciplinarily, the widest network of research in the country. Research institutes at the universities (university departments, department teams, institutes, and centers) make the most significant contribution both in qualitative and quantitative terms. Institutions of higher education, particularly universities, constitute the main basis of Hungarian theoretical and basic research. They also play a significant supplementary role in research and development through their activities in applied research and experimental developments. Their role in certain academic fields and disciplines (for example, in medicine, law, philosophy, humanities, mathematics, agrobiology, and horticulture, etc.) is authoritative.

2.1 Admissions Policies and Selection

Students prepare themselves for higher education during their secondary-school years. The final examination in secondary schools—which is equivalent to the baccalaureate, and which is taken as a certificate of secondary education under state control—is a prior condition for entry to higher education.

Universities and colleges admit students according to annual quotas based on a plan which sets out the

Table 10
Distribution of staff with scientific degrees in 1985

	Academician	Doctor of sciences	Candidate of sciences	Total number of research and development workers
Totals in higher education institutes				
Technical sciences	13	81	331	758
Natural sciences	45	195	636	1,100
Medical sciences	9	128	624	1,002
Agricultural sciences	9	41	260	566
Social sciences	24	176	755	1,252
Total	100	621	2,606	4,678
Overall totals				
Technical sciences	24	165	842	13,126
Natural sciences	71	297	1,079	2,831
Medical sciences	14	171	794	1,422
Agricultural sciences	15	71	424	1,796
Social sciences	43	269	1,114	3,304
Total	167	973	4,253	22,479

Table 11
Number of first-year students in various sectors of higher education

	1960–61	1965–66	1970–71	1975–76	1980–81	1985–86	1988–89
Courses							
Full-time	8,369	14,154	15,147	17,250	17,886	18,792	20,486
Evening	1,754	3,685	2,215	3,025	2,189	2,061	1,930
Correspondence	5,656	8,081	8,073	14,998	9,249	10,491	9,085
Total	15,779	25,920	25,435	35,273	29,324	31,344	31,501

need for professionals in the national economy. This previously rigid regulation eased to a certain extent in 1989, ensuring greater opportunities for the institutions of higher education to make use of their existing capacities. Students may be admitted to universities or colleges on the basis of having taken their secondary final examination, passed an entrance examination, and met the necessary qualification requirements in certain professional fields. Universities and colleges organize preparatory courses to facilitate admission into higher education for talented school students. Successful completion of these courses qualifies the student for admission.

The number of applicants for full-time courses is twice or two-and-a-half times the average intake, though this differs widely according to faculty. Selection is made under a uniformly regulated procedure based on a point system, which includes the result in point equivalent of both the final secondary-school achievements and the entrance examination. Secondary school leavers take their entrance examination after obtaining their certificate of secondary education. Those who already have a degree in higher education are not required to pass an entrance examination if they wish to pursue further studies.

In summary 13 to 18 percent of 18-year olds enroll in higher education as full-time students. Table 11 shows the number of first-year students in different sectors of higher education. The statistical data bear out the government's aim of increasing enrollment capacity of institutions in 1990 by 20 percent. The government plans a further 50 percent increase in the future. Obviously the quantitative increases have to be connected with reform in the admission system itself. The emphasis in selection would be transferred from the entrance examination to the first semesters of higher education.

The most popular disciplines for full-time students are arts, humanities, and economics. The technical sciences are less popular.

3. Governance, Administration, and Finance

The Act of Education and executive decrees passed by the government in 1985 regulate the system of administration in higher education in the 1990s.

In the Hungarian higher education system administrative powers are highly dispersed. Different agencies and organizations simultaneously have powers over the same institution. Parliament is responsible for regulation by laws and the foundation of new universities. The president is responsible for the appointment of professors and rectors. The government is responsible for regulation by rules, decrees in execution of laws, and the foundation of all faculties. Ministries have at their disposal the widest administrative powers in higher education. Here too the distribution of powers is very significant. The Minister of Culture and Education, as the sectorial supervising ministers coordinates the central allocation of student places, teaching staff, and financial resources. Further to these duties the position entails prime responsibility for the development of higher education. It is also the job of the minister to determine the general rules for the organization and working of institutions of higher education; the scope of admission, education, examination, graduation, and students' support system; the rights and obligations of students; the general conditions of teachers' employment and promotion; and the annual enrollment quota. This list, though incomplete, indicates the complexity of administrative powers.

The supervising ministries (Social Security, Medicine, Agriculture, Commerce, as well as the Ministry of Defense, the Ministry of the Interior, and in regard to some institutions the Ministry of Education itself) supervise the working conditions of individual institutions (teaching staff, financial support) and estab-

Table 12
Expenses of higher education

	1970	1975	1980	1985
Total state funding for education (1,000 Forint)	10,641	16,720	27,516	64,064
Percentage of GNP	3.2	3.5	3.9	6.4
Percentage of total devoted to higher education	22.3	21.4	20.8	20.5

Table 13
Income of institutes 1987 (in thousand Forints)

	Income	Support	Total	Income as percentage of the total
Universities of arts and sciences	461,588	1,903,449	2,365,037	19
Technological universities	1,614,422	1,664,561	3,278,983	49
Agricultural universities	590,458	1,423,584	2,014,042	29
Medical universities	483,504	3,772,756	4,256,260	11
Universities' total income	3,149,972	8,764,350	11,914,322	34
Colleges' and institutes' total income	884,847	3,159,951	4,044,798	21
Total	4,034,819	11,924,301	15,959,120	30

lish the budget system. They approve the undergraduate programs, graduate courses, and the charter of universities and colleges. They decide on the establishment and duration of new courses, programs, and the setting up of new teaching departments, and supervise the working of institutions.

The Hungarian Academy of Sciences exerts influence on higher education chiefly in professional and scientific matters and in the appointment of rectors, deans, and professors. The Academy has the prime responsibility for scientific qualifications. It has an indirect influence on the composition of teaching staff, since the advancement of teachers is strictly connected with scientific degrees.

Institutions of higher education receive direct allocations from the state budget and, in addition, they also derive income from their scientific, vocational, and training services. Around 0.8 percent of gross domestic product is spent on higher education, and its share in the state budget is 2.9 to 3.0 percent (see Table 12). The proportion of their own incomes differs considerably according to type of institution (see Table 13).

The Education Act reaffirmed that financial resources for the development and functioning of higher education in Hungary should be provided from the state budget. Financial conditions must include every material and personal aspect of development and functioning: construction work, renovation, maintenance, and equipment; instruments, books, periodicals, and so forth; scholarship; and salaries at a level to ensure high quality selection of, and creative work by, tutors and other personnel. The level of budget allocation for higher education, however, fails to provide satisfactory financial conditions for development and functioning. As no tuition fees are charged, the main source of finance comes from redistributing the central budget. Control by those using the services rarely influences the service itself.

The autonomy of individual institutions of higher education is a debatable issue: the elements of prac-

tice are constantly changing. Administrative and academic powers are distributed between formal bodies (boards of universities, colleges, faculties, and departments) and responsible leaders (rectors, deans, and heads of departments). Two-thirds of members of boards working in every level and unit of institutions are elected, and one-third of these elected members are student representatives. Non-elected members are appointed leaders, heads of departments, and representatives of teachers' and students' organizations. The number of members is not fixed, so there are many boards with a numerous membership. The administrative powers can be decentralized depending on the extent and structure of the institution.

Self-government of institutions includes—within the legal framework—decisions about the organization and working of institutions, financial, and personnel matters. One guarantee of autonomy is that institutions of higher education have the right to declare their opinion on every question that falls under the jurisdiction of a supervising ministry or other superior authority. The supervising ministries and authorities are legally obliged to ascertain the opinion of institutions before taking decisions and to give them all the necessary information.

Autonomy also embraces professional–scientific issues. It means that institutions of higher education, within the framework of principles determined by supervising ministries, may autonomously validate the courses programs, the examination and graduation system, and study requirements; organize scientific research; take part in international and domestic scientific projects; and have the right to test

Table 14
Number of teachers in higher education

1960–61	1965–66	1970–71	1975–76	1980–81	1985–86
5,635	8,444	9,791	12,135	13,890	14,850

297

new educational models and methods. Under the Education Act, institutions decide independently on admission and intake of students.

4. Faculty and Students: Teaching, Learning, and Research

4.1 Faculty

With the extensive development of higher education, the number of teaching staff grew rapidly from 5,635 to 14,850 in 17 years (see Table 14).

University and college teachers are selected through competition. Some of them enter employment in university education as tutors immediately after their university studies. Others begin their teaching career after a certain amount of time spent in a nonteaching occupation.

Graduate education to obtain an academic degree is the main form of training for young university teachers. This can take the form of a university doctorate, which consists of the writing and defense of a thesis, and oral degree examinations in required subjects.

The Committee of Scientific Qualifications, working under the supervision of the Hungarian Academy of Sciences, is authorized to confer the candidate's degree, that is, the PhD degree. The central part of this process is the preparation of a thesis containing new data in a given academic discipline. The thesis has to be defended publicly. A higher scientific qualification is the doctor of sciences degree. It is awarded on the basis of work that summarizes the results of a whole academic career and can be assessed also in an international context, and is defended in a public debate.

Although it is not laid down in the regulations, university teachers are expected to have the qualifications commensurate with a given position, besides pedagogical and research activity. Principal assistants are normally required to have a university doctorate, although this is not necessary for assistants. Associate professorships require a PhD, while professors are expected to have a doctor of sciences degree. The expectations are somewhat less for colleges and art academies, where only the heads of departments (professors) are expected to have a PhD.

Personnel management, that is, the selection of teachers and research fellows, is mainly handled by the department in universities and colleges. Leading figures in the institutions of higher education and the various committees of the Hungarian National Academy of Sciences play a significant role in the selection of senior staff. The appointment of heads of institutions is determined mainly by the ministries upon proposals from the institutions themselves.

Details of teaching staff according to rank, age, and gender are shown in Table 15.

4.2 Students

The two forms of undergraduate training other than full-time coursework are evening and correspondence courses (see Table 16). The latter, developed only after 1945, played a role of historical significance both from the social and the economic point of view. The importance accorded to them was motivated by political and cultural factors as well as economic demands. In many cases, however, the negative consequences of a lower educational level and the need to make later corrections had to be faced. One might have expected that improved opportunities for traditional study would have reduced the importance of evening and correspondence courses. The opposite occurred. This tendency accelerated in later years. However, with the increase in number of full-time students, the importance of evening courses teaching for first-grade diplomas is gradually diminishing, and correspondence courses cater mainly for graduate studies.

Table 15
Number of teaching staff according to rank 1988–89

	Professors	Associate professors	Principal Assistant	Assistants	Other	Total	Total percentage
Total	1,651	3,219	6,352	3,572	1,448	16,242	100
percentage	10.2	19.8	39.1	22.0	8.9	100.0	
Full-time	1,476	2,941	5,788	3,337	1,332	14,874	91.6
percentage	9.9	19.8	38.9	22.4	8.9	99.9	
Part-time	175	278	564	235	116	1,368	8.4
percentage	12.8	20.3	41.2	17.2	8.4	99.9	
Women	122	601	2,074	1,434	829	5,060	34.0
percentage	2.4	11.9	41.0	28.3	16.4	100.0	
Younger than 30	—	9	50	1,003	156	1,218	8.2
percentage	—	0.7	4.1	82.4	12.8	100.0	

Table 16
Number of students according to type of course

	1960–61	1965–66	1970–71	1975–76	1980–81	1985–86	1986–87	1987–88	1988–89
Course									
Full-time	29,344	51,002	53,821	64,319	64,057	64,190	64,855	66,697	71,689
Evening	1,341	14,721	8,177	8,950	8,035	6,203	6,040	5,851	5,540
Correspondence	13,900	28,279	18,767	34,516	29,074	28,951	27,610	26,477	25,812
Total	44,585	94,002	80,765	107,785	101,166	99,344	98,505	99,025	103,041

Although graduation from evening and correspondence courses is, *de jure*, of a value equal to graduation from regular courses, the level of training in the former is in many respects lower due to lower admission standards, "condensed" curricula, and a lack of specialized methods for training and administering examinations.

Analysis of student numbers according to academic fields (Table 17) shows the high proportion in technological education. One-third of students pursue technical and agricultural studies, another third train for teaching.

Table 18 shows the graduate population in university and colleges from 1960 to 1988. Structurally the undergraduate course formally constitutes an integrated unit. Although there is no rigid distinction, one can still conclude that while essential basic knowledge is taught in the first years, students familiarize themselves with selected specialized themes later in the course. Finally, the preparation of a graduating thesis that represents a typical area of the discipline is compulsory during the last year. Students have an oral examination in their graduating thesis as part of the state examination. If they are successful, they receive their degree.

Full-time students at institutions of higher education receive state support in the form of financial allowances and free facilities. The scholarship grant basically depends on academic achievement, while other types of allowances depend primarily on social circumstances. There is also another element consisting of a fixed sum payable to every student.

Legal regulations lay down only the key principles and parameters of the allowances. Each institution can decide its own system within this framework by taking into account the amount available.

Amongst the free facilities are accommodation in student hostels and meals in student canteens. The availability of places in student hostels are limited; only 70 percent of students can be accommodated.

Table 17
Distribution of students according to fields of study

	1960–61	1965–66	1970–71	1975–76	1980–81	1985–86
Technology	11,985	32,419	29,447	35,373	29,746	24,265
percentage	26.9	34.5	36.5	32.8	29.4	24.4
Agriculture	4,298	11,212	7,966	8,938	5,736	5,837
percentage	9.6	11.9	9.9	8.3	5.7	5.9
Economics	2,390	7,486	8,280	10,415	11,222	11,096
percentage	5.4	8.0	10.2	9.7	11.1	11.2
Law	3,827	3,936	3,544	4,984	6,609	5,836
percentage	8.6	4.2	4.4	4.6	6.5	5.9
Medicine	6,609	7,685	7,378	8,681	9,522	10,202
percentage	14.8	8.2	9.1	8.0	9.4	10.3
Humanities	3,909	7,234	4,274	5,577	6,242	6,477
percentage	8.8	7.7	5.3	5.2	6.2	6.5
Natural Sciences	2,960	5,709	4,545	5,270	4,696	4,467
percentage	6.6	6.1	5.6	4.9	4.6	4.5
Teaching	7,776	17,440	13,988	26,764	25,415	28,848
percentage	17.4	18.5	17.3	24.8	25.1	29.0
Arts	831	858	1,292	1,708	1,889	2,125
percentage	1.9	0.9	1.6	1.6	1.9	2.1
Other	—	23	51	75	89	191
percentage	—	0	0.1	0.1	0.1	0.2

Table 18
Number of graduate population

	1960	1965	1970	1975	1980	1985	1986	1987	1988
University	5,628	7,834	10,010	8,871	10,704	9,813	9,228	9,449	9,469
College	453	6,104	7,804	15,158	16,537	15,323	14,477	14,507	14,236
Total	6,081	13,938	17,814	24,029	27,241	25,136	23,705	23,956	23,705

5. Conclusion

Further development of Hungarian higher education requires a reform process which takes into account the special features and developing tendencies of the Hungarian economy. The reform has to ensure that Hungarian higher education can gradually join the EC unified system from 1992. The principal goals of higher educational policy over this period are the following:

(a) Modernization of the education structure, establishing an integrated two-level higher education system of universities and colleges with a growing proportion of university teaching.

(b) Improved response from higher education to regional needs and characteristics (claims for enrollment to higher education, local labor shortages or unemployment).

(c) Increased role for graduate courses and higher education generally in retraining and further education including lifetime education.

(d) Increased efficiency and economy of higher education, modernization of finance, new tuition, and allowance policies.

(e) Expanding the base of scientific research and development activity in higher education, more effective integration and cooperation between higher education and institutions of scientific research.

(f) Development of autonomy and self-government. Decreasing role of supervising authorities over institutions and more effective representation of higher education interests in the affairs of government.

Bibliography

Andor L 1989 *Mennyiségi fejlődés és strukturális változások; A felsőoktatás útja a felszabadulás után.* Tankönyvkiadó, Budapest

Bakos Í 1991 *A magyar felsőoktatás modernizációjának és hálózatfejlesztésének feladatairól.* Magyar felsőoktatás

Demográfiai Évkönyv. 1987, KSH, Budapest

Évi népszámlálás 1980 *21 Demográfiai Adatok c. kötet.* 1981a, KSH, Budapest

Évi népszámlálás 1980 22 Foglalkozási Adatok c. kötet. 1981b, KSH, Budapest

Polinszky K, Széchy É 1985 *Higher Education in Hungary.* UNESCO/CEPES, Bucharest

Statisztikai Évkönyv. 1988, KSH

Statisztikai Havi Közlemények. 1989, KSH, Budapest

Statisztikai Tájékoztató, Felsőoktatás, Művelődési Minisztérium. 1960–61, 1980–81, 1985–86, 1988–89

Széchy É, Szabó-Pap G 1989 *Higher Education in Hungary.* Ministry of Culture and Education, Budapest

I. Végvári

I

Iceland

1. Higher Education and Society

Until the latter part of the nineteenth century there were no higher education institutions in Iceland. In 1911 the three newly established schools of theology, medicine, and law merged to become the first faculties of the University of Iceland. The University of Iceland, in Reykjavik, represented the only institution of higher learning in Iceland. In the early 1990s, six other institutions also provide university education. The Ministry of Education is the prime administrator of these institutions. All higher education at state-operated institutions is free of charge and courses of study are generally based on a credit–unit system. Table 1 shows the expansion in student numbers since 1960.

Iceland's population of approximately 250,000 is primarily concentrated in the Reykjavik urban area of the country. Since the Second World War there has been a steady migration from rural areas to towns, principally to Reykjavik and its environs.

The language of Iceland is Icelandic, though English and other Scandinavian languages are used in textbooks and lectures at the university level. The official religion is Lutheran.

The Icelandic economy is still strongly concentrated on exports of fish products and fishing equipment. The government since the Second World War has been that of parliamentary coalition parties with strong welfare programs such as medicine, education, and social security.

2. The Institutional Fabric of the Higher Education System

There are seven higher education institutions, five of which are state operated: the University of Iceland; the Technical College of Iceland; the Teachers University of Iceland; the College of Agriculture at Hvanneyri; and the University at Akureyri. The two private colleges are the Commercial College of Iceland and the Cooperative Commercial College.

Table 1
Number of students in higher education in Iceland

	1960	1965	1970	1975	1980	1985	1990
Students	850	1,265	1,972	2,795	3,633	4,722	5,150

Source: Statistical Bureau of Iceland

Admission to university education normally requires the matriculation examination from secondary school.

The University of Iceland is the largest higher education institution (with a student population of approximately 5,000) and has considerable independence, both academically and financially. As shown in Table 2, the university has nine faculties: Theology; Medicine; Law; Economics and Business Administration; Arts; Dentistry; Engineering; Natural Sciences; and Social Sciences. Many of the programs are three-year courses leading to either a BSc or BA degree. The University offers about a thousand different courses each year.

Within the Faculty of Arts, the BA degree may be acquired either by taking a two-year major subject plus one-year minor field (which can be outside the Faculty), or the student may choose to take the entire three years in a single major field. A thesis is required in all major fields. This faculty is the largest in the University and offers the following fields: Icelandic language and literature; comparative literature; history; philosophy; linguistics; Greek; Latin; Danish; Finnish; Norwegian; Swedish; English; French; German; Spanish; and Russian (this last subject can only be taken as a minor subject). Also within this faculty is the three-year program for foreign students leading to the degree of Bacc.phil.Isl. (Icelandic language and literature); and a two- or three-year graduate program (with required dissertation) in Danish, English, History, Icelandic grammar, and Icelandic literature leading to the degree of cand.mag.

The Faculty of Natural Sciences is divided into six departments: mathematics; computer science; physics; chemistry; biology; and geosciences. Each

Table 2
Number of students enrolled at the University of Iceland

	1961	1981	1985	1989
Faculty of theology	23	67	76	64
Faculty of medicine	173	653	792	766
Faculty of dentistry	31	57	70	64
Faculty of law	143	253	408	401
Faculty of business administration	89	563	819	780
Faculty of philosophy	302	895	936	1,013
Faculty of engineering	38	—	259	278
Faculty of science	—	—	591	444
Faculty of social sciences	—	477	519	739

Sources: Gudjonsson 1987 and the University of Iceland Students' Office chart "Toflur um Fjolda Studenta, Studentafjoldi haskolaarid 1989–90"

department offers a three-year program leading to a BSc degree. A thesis is required in geology but is optional in the other fields. In addition, a two-year nondegree program is offered both in chemical engineering and engineering physics for students entering degree programs abroad.

The Faculty of Social Science offers a three-year program leading to a BA degree in psychology, sociology, political science, anthropology, education, library and information science, cultural anthropology, media studies, and social work (the last three can only be taken as minor subjects). The degree may be acquired either by taking a two-year major subject and a one-year minor field (which can be outside the Faculty), or the students may choose to take the whole program in a single major field. Following the BA degree, students may take a one-year program in education, leading to a teacher's certificate (a qualification required for teaching at the secondary school level), or a one-year program in social work, leading to the social worker's certificate.

The Faculty of Medicine has three different four-year programs (three years of preclinical study followed by one year of research) leading to a BSc degree. These programs are in medicine, nursing, and physical therapy. In addition, there is a five-year pharmacy program leading to the degree of cand.pharm., and a six-year program in medicine leading to a cand.med.et chir. degree, which qualifies the holder to practice medicine in Iceland. A competitive examination is held in the first year and the 36 students with the highest scores continue in the medical program. The Faculty of Dentistry offers a six-year program leading to the degree of cand.odont. A competitive examination is held early in the course of study, thereby limiting the number of students allowed to continue.

The Faculty of Law offers a five-year program for the acquisition of the degree of cand.juris., which entitles the holder to practice law in Iceland. A thesis is required for graduation. It is common for graduates to go abroad for further study in some specialized field of law.

The Faculty of Engineering is divided into three departments: civil engineering; mechanical engineering; and electrical engineering. Each department requires a four-year program and a thesis.

The Faculty of Economics and Business Administration offers a three-year program leading to a BSc degree in economics, and a four-year program in business administration leading to a degree of cand.oecon. Theses are required for graduation for both programs. Students in other faculties may take a one-year minor in this faculty.

The Teachers University of Iceland is also located in Reykjavik. It offers a three-year program leading to a BEd degree, which qualifies the holder for teaching in the primary schools. In 1971 the Teacher Training College of Iceland (an upper-secondary school founded in 1907) was reorganized as the Teachers University of Iceland. The Teachers University also offers an advanced two-year program leading to the BA degree in special education. The Teachers University provides inservice training for teachers. According to legislation passed in 1988, the Teachers University may decide to offer advanced programs beyond the degrees of BEd and BA.

The University at Akureyri in the north of Iceland was founded in 1988. Three programs of study have been developed: a two-year program in management studies leading to a diploma in management; a four-year program in nursing leading to a BS degree; and a five-year program in fisheries leading to the degrees of BS/MS.

The Technical College of Iceland was founded in 1964 and is also located in Reykjavik. Certain vocational training, in addition to the completion of a preparatory course equivalent to the matriculation exam in science and physics is required for admission. This college offers two-year programs/diplomas in fishery technology, construction technology, electrical technology, mechanical technology, and industrial technology. It also offers a four-year program leading to the MSc degree in radiologic technology, medical laboratory technology, and civil and constructional engineering.

The College of Agriculture at Hvanneyri was founded in 1889, and is located in the rural western part of Iceland. Entry requirements to the BS program are two years' training in agriculture and the matriculation examination. The college offers a three-year program leading to the degree of BSc in agriculture. The college also offers a one-year additional program in cooperation with other agricultural colleges in Scandinavia. This higher educational institution is administered by the Ministry of Agriculture rather than the Ministry of Education.

The private Commercial College of Iceland was founded in 1904 in Reykjavik. Since 1988 it has offered a two-year program in computer science, leading to a diploma. The college also offers a regular program of study at the secondary school level.

The private Cooperative Commercial College was founded in 1918 and is located in the western part of Iceland, in Bifrost. Since 1988 the college has offered a two-year program in business administration, leading to a diploma. This college also offers a regular program of study at the secondary school level.

3. Governance, Administration, and Finance

The Ministry of Education has primary responsibility for the development of higher education, as well as all other education in Iceland. Certain educational laws have been passed by the Althing (Parliament) and are implemented and enforced by the Ministry of Education through its various departments and agencies. Percentage of gross national product allo-

Table 3
Percentage of GNP for higher education in Iceland

1960	1965	1970	1975	1980	1985	1990
0.1	0.1	0.3	0.3	0.4	0.4	0.5

Source: National Economic Institute

cated to higher education is shown in Table 3. In the University of Iceland, the University Council is the highest governing body. It works to promote the interests and objectives of the University and its research institutes. It also presents matters to the Parliament or to the various government ministries for reform considerations and funding purposes.

The University Council consists of the rector, the executive head of the University and ex officio chair of the council, the deans of the nine faculties, four student representatives, and two representatives of the University Teachers' Union. In addition, the registrar and the dean of studies are nonvoting members of the council. The Rector of the University is elected to a three-year term by the faculty, staff, and students. The deans are elected from among each faculty's professors and serve a two-year term. Students have representatives on the University Council, the Icelandic Student Services Board, the students' Loan Fund Board, the University Cinema Board, and the Federation of Icelandic Youth Organization. The day-to-day management of the University is in the hands of the registrar and the dean of studies.

Approximately 35 organizations or research institutions are affiliated with or directly associated with the University. The principal areas are various aspects of medical research, geology, and Icelandic language/sagas/history research. Also in direct association with the University of Iceland is the Reykjavik Pharmacy and the University Lottery. The Reykjavik Pharmacy is a commercial establishment

Table 4
Number of full-time teaching staff at the University of Iceland

	1961	1981	1985
Faculty of theology	4	8	8
Faculty of medicine	10	78	85
Faculty of dentistry	1	14	17
Faculty of law	4	10	10
Faculty of business administration	3	11	12
Faculty of philosophy	9	40	43
Faculty of engineering and science	5	54	61
Faculty of social sciences	—	11	16
Total	36	226	252

Source: Gudonsson 1987

which also provides training for pharmaceutical students. Until six years ago the capital funds of the University came from the University Lottery, which was established in 1933 by a law giving the University exclusive rights to run a national sweepstake in Iceland. The proceeds of the lottery are used for general capital expenditures. However, the funds have not kept pace with the rapid expansion of student numbers and research activity, so the University obtained capital appropriations from the State. The Icelandic Student Services, a financially separate and autonomous organization, is jointly owned by the Ministry of Education and the University of Iceland.

4. Faculty and Students: Teaching, Learning, and Research

The University of Iceland has an instructional staff of some 300 full-time instructors (see Table 4) in addition to approximately 500 part-time teachers. The permanent teaching staff is divided into three ranks (with their corresponding American/British titles): professor (full professor/professor); *dosent* (associate professor/reader); and *lektor* (assistant professor/lecturer). Nearly all the posts held by permanent teaching staff carry tenure. Permanent staff members are officials of the Icelandic State, and foreign scholars cannot be appointed to permanent academic posts. Formally, the President of Iceland appoints professors, after being advised by the Minister. *Dosents* and *lektors* are appointed directly by the Minister of Education. A committee of three representatives is appointed to determine the eligibility of the applicants to the posts of professor and *dosent*. A person may not be appointed professor unless the majority of the adjudicating committee has voted in favor of his or her eligibility. Also, the opinion of the faculty in question shall be sought regarding the applicants. Student representative groups are often informally formed to determine eligibility of applicants for the posts of lecturers. Each of the faculties is governed by a faculty board, of which all permanent staff on the faculty are members, in addition to representatives of temporary staff and students registered in the faculty.

In the 1980s approximately 1500 new students (about one-third of the 20-year olds in Iceland) have registered at the University. The age of entry has spread, as some students seek employment for several years before commencing their studies. Almost two-thirds of all students at the university level come from urban areas. The difference between enrollment of males and females at the university level is negligible. Males used to slightly outnumber females; however, the entering class for 1989 to 1990 had more females than males, and the current total student enrollment as of October 1989 has 373 more women than men registered. The number of foreign students at the University has been fairly consistent at around one hundred a year. Icelandic students studying abroad for the 1989 to 1990 academic year number 2,784. Almost one-half (1,091) are studying in one of the Nordic countries, with the next largest group in the United States (889). Most of the remaining students are studying in the Continental countries, the United Kingdom, and Canada.

5. Conclusion

An unusual feature of the University of Iceland is its large number of part-time instructors. This is not only due to the difficulty of creating new positions, but also because of increased specialization and the small population of Iceland. The University is looking for ways to get part-time instructors to participate in research to a greater extent. There has been growth in research services and outside contracts. Statistics indicate that the University's role in research is expanding. The increase in opportunities to study at the University has been accompanied by a growth in the student population entering higher education. Yet, most subjects lead only to the BA/BSc degree, and many graduate studies must still be pursued abroad. Many university level subjects are not taught in Iceland since such a small nation does not possess the means to establish courses in specialized subjects with low enrollments. Such subjects which must be studied abroad at undergraduate level are meterology, veterinary medicine, architecture, and archaeology.

High dropout rates (particularly in the first year) of higher education is another concern. Options being considered include a fourth year of study in the programs, to allow the first year to be less specialized.

Bibliography

Gislason I 1981 *University Education in Iceland*. Ministry of Culture and Education, Reykjavik
Gudjonsson H 1987 University education. In: Nordal J, Kristinsson V (eds.) 1987 *Iceland 1986*. The Central Bank of Iceland, Reykjavik, pp. 270–74
Josepsson B 1985 *The Modern Icelandic School System in Historic Perspective*. National Center for Educational Materials, Reykjavik
Josepsson B 1986 *Current Laws on Compulsory Education and School System in Iceland*. Icelandic College of Education, Reykjavik
Josepsson B 1987 Education. In: Nordal J, Kristinsson V (eds.) 1987 *Iceland 1986*. The Central Bank of Iceland, Reykjavik, pp. 258–69
Josepsson B 1988 Iceland. In: Kurian G T (ed.) 1988 *World Education Encyclopedia*, Vol. 2. Facts on File Publications, Oxford, pp. 559–75
Lárusson H 1985 Iceland: System of education. In: Husén T, Postlethwaite T N (eds.) 1985 *International Encyclopedia of Education*, Vol. 5. Pergamon, Oxford, pp. 2379–83
Ministry of Culture and Education 1986 The educational system of Iceland—summary (unpublished report). Ministry of Culture and Education, Reykjavik
Organisation for Economic Co-operation and Development Education Committee 1987 *Review of Educational Policy in Iceland—Examiners' Report and Questions*. Menntamalarathuneytith, Reykjavik
Organisation for Economic Co-operation and Development 1987 *Reviews of National Policies for Education—Iceland*. OECD, Paris
Ragnarsdottir A K, Olafsdottir R 1988 *University of Iceland*. University of Iceland, Reykjavik
Steinsson A 1988 *Curriculum—Industrial Division*. Technical College of Iceland, Reykjavik

B. Josepsson; B. A. Sizemore

India

1. Higher Education and Society

During the Second World War, India was still the jewel in the British Crown and the glory of the empire. On August 15, 1947, however, British rule over the Indian subcontinent ceased. With Partition, two independent countries, India and Pakistan, were created. The administration of small areas under French colonial rule, Pondicherry (293 square kilometers), Karikal (160 square kilometers), Mahe (98 square kilometers), and Yanam (30 square kilometers) was transferred to India on November 1, 1954. They became legally a part of India with the ratification of the Treaty of Cession in 1962. Similarly, Portuguese territories of Dadra and Nagar Haveli (491 square kilometers) joined the Union of India on August 11, 1961 and the remainder—Goa (3,702 square kilometers), Daman (72 square kilometers), and Diu (38 square kilometers)—became part of India four months later. Sikkim (7,298 square kilometers), a protectorate, joined as a fully-fledged state on April 26, 1975. India is the seventh largest country in the world, with an area of 3.29 million square kilometers out of the total world land surface area of 135.79 million square kilometers (Census of India 1991).

1.1 Size and Rate of Growth of Population

Occupying only 2.42 percent of the world landmass, India contains about 16 percent of the world's population and is the second most populous country. Provisional figures of the 1991 census show the population on March 1, 1991 to be 843,930,861. Seven Indian states, if compared with other countries, would rank amongst the 20 most populous. The population and growth rate figures from 1951 to 1991 are given in Fig. 1.

Until 1981, the average annual exponential growth rate rose mainly due to declining mortality rates, while the birthrate continued to be high. The decline in mortality rates may be attributed to absence of natural checks like famines and large-scale

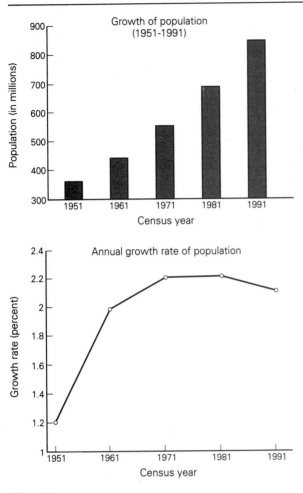

Figure 1
Growth and growth rate of population 1951–91

arashtra, Nagaland, Tripura, West Bengal, and the Union Territories of Daman and Diu, Lakshadweep, and Pondicherry, covering one-third of the total population, saw growth rates increase. In all other states and Union Territories, which together account for 66.2 percent of India's population, growth rates declined. The lowest growth rate of 13.98 percent has been Kerala's, which is also the most literate state.

The percentages of rural and urban population clearly indicate a steady trend towards urbanization. In 1951, 82.7 percent of the total population lived in rural areas, and only 17.3 percent in urban areas, where it increased to 18 percent in 1961, 19.9 percent in 1971, and 23.3 percent in 1981, primarily on account of rural–urban migration.

All major religions in the world have their followers in India. Hindus constitute 82.5 percent of the total population. Muslims account for 11.36 percent, but in terms of numbers, India has the largest Muslim population in the world after Indonesia. Christians (2.43 percent), Sikhs (1.96 percent), Buddhists (0.71 percent), Jains (0.4 percent), and others (0.42 percent) comprise numerically smaller but important minorities.

There are 1,652 languages and dialects which belong to the Indo-Aryan, Munda, Dravidian, and Indo-Chinese language families. These use eight major script-systems, besides Parso-Arabic and Roman scripts, and provide a vast linguistic backdrop. Hindi is the official language but the continued use of English as a link-language has been authorized by parliament. Although 11 languages have their home states, Hindi is the official language of six states whereas Sindhi and Urdu are spread over many states.

While the rigidities of the caste system have loosened considerably in urban areas, it continues to be a very significant feature in rural society. The most deprived castes have been identified for special attention and are referred to as the "scheduled castes." The social discrimination which the scheduled castes suffer from, besides economic deprivation, presents severe barriers in obtaining benefits of any developmental effort including educational opportunities. In 1981, the scheduled castes comprised 15.8 percent of the total population.

About 450 tribal communities in the country, known as "scheduled tribes," constitute 7.8 percent of the population. They have their own rich culture and distinct tradition, social organization, customs, and value systems. The Constitution of India has several provisions for the special protection and development of scheduled castes and tribes, with a number of seats reserved in the state legislatures, parliament, educational institutions, and for employment.

Despite a number of land reform measures including a law limiting land holding, distribution of land

epidemics, and to mass control of diseases, advances in medical sciences, better medical and health facilities, and improvements in food supply. Factors contributing to high birthrates were universality of marriage, early marriage, low standard of living, low level of literacy, traditional customs and habits, and inadequate family planning. During the decade 1981 to 1991, the growth rate fell, though in absolute terms the population increased by 160.6 million—equal almost to the population added during the three decades from 1931 to 1961.

There is considerable regional variation in the growth rate of population. The six most populous states—Uttar Pradesh, Bihar, Maharashtra, West Bengal, Andhra Pradesh, and Madhya Pradesh—which accounted for 59.1 percent of the population in 1981, contributed 62.49 percent of the increase during the decade 1981 to 1991. The states of Andhra Pradesh, Himachal Pradesh, Madhya Pradesh, Mah-

Table 1
Economic classification of main workers: 1981[a]
(Percentage distribution)

Category	Total main workers	Of which			
		Males	Females	Rural	Urban
AGRICULTURAL SECTOR					
Cultivators	41.6	43.7	33.2	51.1	5.1
Agricultural laborers	24.9	19.6	46.2	29.9	6.0
Livestock, forestry, etc.	2.2	2.3	1.8	2.4	1.8
INDUSTRIAL SECTOR					
Mining and quarrying	0.6	0.6	0.4	0.5	1.0
Household industry	3.5	3.2	4.6	3.1	4.9
Other industries	7.8	8.9	3.6	2.4	24.7
Construction	1.6	1.8	0.8	1.0	4.0
SERVICE SECTOR					
Trade and commerce	6.3	7.3	2.0	2.8	19.6
Transport, communication, etc.	2.7	3.3	0.4	1.1	9.0
Other services	8.8	9.2	7.0	4.8	23.9
Total	100.0	100.0	100.0	100.0	100.0

Source: Registrar General India
a Based on 5 percent sample data of the 1981 census excluding Assam

is highly skewed. Some 61.5 percent of the rural population owns only 19.4 percent of the land while 40 percent of land is held by only 7.9 percent of the population.

1.2 Occupational and Social Class Structure

India is a predominantly agricultural country (see Table 1). In 1981, 68.7 percent of the working population was engaged in the agricultural sector, and 13.5 percent in the industrial sector. There is a concentration of infrastructure and tertiary activities in the urban areas to the neglect of the rural sector. Among female workers, 81.2 percent are engaged in agricultural activities. Predominance of agriculture and a judicious mix of private and public sectors in industrial development are important features of the Indian economic structure. Systematic and comprehensive planning for economic development has resulted in the Gross National Product (GNP) registering an annual compound growth rate of about 5.4 percent in the decade 1980 to 1990.

During the entire period of planning through five-year plans, continuing emphasis has been laid on industrialization, particularly on basic and heavy industries, modernization, self-reliance, and use of technology which underlines the importance of higher education in the country's overall planning strategy. The Sixth Five-Year Plan emphasized human resource development as an area for special attention.

1.3 Structure of Government and Main Political Goals

India is the largest democracy in the world. The written Constitution was adopted by the Constituent Assembly on January 26, 1950. It is a union of 25 states, besides 7 union territories directly administered by central government. There is a division of powers between the states and the union government.

Education has been in the concurrent list since January 3, 1977, before which it was in the state list. Since the inception of the Constitution, the subject of "coordination and determination of standards in institutions for higher education, research, and scientific and technical institutions" has been in the union list. Some universities, usually called Central Universities and Institutions of National Importance, have also been in the union list.

Both at federal and state levels, governments are parliamentary in nature. The president of the country and the governors in the states are constitutional heads, obliged to act on the advice of the Councils of Ministers which have real powers and which enjoy the confidence of the parliament/state legislature.

The President of India is the "visitor" of all central universities. He or she appoints their chancellors and vice-chancellors. The state universities do not have visitors. The governors of the states are usually their chancellors.

India has an independent judiciary. High courts in the states and the Supreme Court of India have very wide powers, including the powers of issuing writs and declaring laws or actions of the government as *ultra vires*.

Universities and institutions of higher education have been increasingly involved in litigation, since the powers of the judiciary are invoked by students, teachers, employees, and citizens at large.

Independence was the main political goal in the early 1940s. The preamble of the Constitution and the chapters on fundamental rights and directive principles of state policy articulate clearly the goals and objectives towards which the Indian nation should move. They are:

(a) social, economic, and political justice;

(b) liberty of thought and expression;

(c) equality of status and of opportunities;

(d) secularism;

(e) equitable distribution of ownership and control of the material resources of communities to serve the common good and operation of economic system with emphasis on equity;

(f) right to work, and to education;

(g) provision for free and compulsory education for children up to the age of 14;

(h) promotion of educational and economic interest of weaker sections;

(i) promotion of international peace and security;

(j) minimization of inequalities in income and eliminating inequalities amongst individuals and groups.

The parliament approved a comprehensive National Policy on Education in May 1986, in which the goals of higher education were enunciated as follows:

> Higher Education provides people with an opportunity to reflect on the critical social, economic, cultural, moral, and spiritual issues facing humanity. It contributes to National Development through dissemination of specialized knowledge and skills. It is therefore a crucial factor for survival. . . . The national strategy of education has to ensure the availability of highly educated, trained, and motivated manpower for dealing with the challenges which are inherent in the modernization and globalization of the economy. India has to be able to compete with the most advanced countries in many fields of production to hold its own.

The national policy requires the system of higher education to be socially relevant in terms of the major goals of development, national integration, and equity.

Education in India has an illustrious history. According to Professor F W Thomas, one of the greatest Indologists: "There is no country where the love of learning had so early an origin or has exercised so lasting and powerful an influence. From the simple poets of the Vedic age to the Bengali philosophers of the present day there has been an uninterrupted succession of teachers and scholars" (Dongarkerey 1969).

In the Rig Vedic period, the family of the *guru* (teacher) functioned like an educational institution admitting resident pupils for instruction. A number of *gurus* formed a *Gurukul*, a community of scholars teaching large numbers of students in residential institutions. Religion, philosophy, agriculture, trade, state craft, and military practice were the main components of education.

With the rise of Buddhism, monasteries became centers of education. For the first time in India, educational institutions developed which were comparable to modern universities. Among the well-known places of higher education during this period were Takshashila, Nalanda, Vikramshila, Vallabhi, Banaras, Nav Dweep, and Kanchi (Congiwaram) (Vakil and Natrajan 1966). The international reputation of some spread to Tibet, China, Ceylon, Korea, Japan, Burma, Indonesia, and Turkistan (Vakil and Natrajan 1966).

In addition to the four Vedas, grammar, and philosophy, 18 subjects including medicine, surgery, archery and allied military arts, astronomy, astrology, accountancy, commerce, agriculture, and music, dance, and painting were taught (Mitra 1967).

By the twelfth century AD, *madrasas* had developed as centers of Islamic higher education and learning with a distinctive religious bias, usually teaching grammar, logic, rhetoric, theology, metaphysics, literature, jurisprudence, and science.

With the arrival of the European powers, the modern system of education modeled on the European pattern made its appearance in India. Christian missionaries were the first to establish such institutions. Soon after the Portuguese gained a foothold in India, Franciscan, Dominican, Jesuit, and other Roman Catholic missionaries began to operate and organize institutions in different parts of the Portuguese possessions. In 1575 the Jesuits established The College of St. Annie at Bandra, near Bombay, which continued as a university until 1739 (Vakil and Natrajan 1966).

Indigenous socioreligious reform movements of the late nineteenth century considered education as an important activity. The Mohammeddan–Anglo–Oriental College in Aligarh was founded in 1871, the Dayanand Anglo–Vedic College at Lahore in 1886, and subsequently elsewhere in Punjab and the United Provinces, and a number of Khalsa schools and colleges were established.

The system of higher education in India today has its origins in the Western model of education grafted by the British in the mid-nineteenth century to create, in the words of Lord Macaulay, a class of "Indians in blood and colour but English in tastes, in opinions, in morals and in intellect" (Bhatt and Aggarwal 1977 p. 3) and to secure recruits for the lower ranks of the East India Company's civil service.

The despatch of July 19, 1854 of Sir Charles Wood, President of the Board of Control of the East India Company, stated that the main object of education was to spread Western knowledge and science, although it was desirable to encourage oriental learning at the collegiate stage. Wood further declared that English should be the medium of instruction in higher education, and the bulk of educational institutions organized by private bodies. This despatch drew up a complete organization of education from universities to elementary schools. Subsequently, universities in Calcutta, Bombay, and Madras were established in 1857, modeled on London University, then a purely examining body.

The education system set up by the British was criticized as foreign, irrelevant to the needs of, and incongruent with, the indigenous ethos of India. Gandhi considered the British system of education impractical and destructive of the Indian cultural heritage. He called it an "unmitigated evil," as it ignored the Indian tradition and rich experience of education. He and his colleagues founded a series of national universities between 1920 and 1922. As a synthesis of oriental and Western culture, Rabindranath Tagore founded Vishwa Bharti University in 1921. Annie Besant, with the help of Pandit Madan Mohan Malviya took the first steps in creating the Banaras Hindu University as a model institution fostering Indian values, ancient traditions and the national spirit. These attempts, however, were few and represented inadequate alternatives to the government-sponsored system modeled on the British pattern.

The attainment of Independence in 1947 provided a real opportunity to abolish the colonial system of higher education and to build further upon the rich, varied, and long tradition of learning. The University Education Commission from 1948 to 1949 (headed by Dr S Radhakrishnan, philosopher, educationist and later President of India) and the Education Commission from 1964 to 1966 (headed by Dr D S Kothari) highlighted the inappropriate nature of the colonial system of education in an independent country committed to social transformation and planned economic development. Neither commissions presented alternative models of higher education to build upon Indian cultural and educational heritage. Thus, in the early 1990s, the higher education system is a continuation, with cosmetic changes, of a colonial education system developed by the British to ensure employees for their administration. This lies at the root of many of its ills.

2. The Institutional Fabric of the Higher Education System

At Independence, schooling lasted 10 years (11 years in some states), plus two years each of intermediate and first degree course. Intermediate education was an integral part of higher education.

The Kothari Commission of 1964 to 1966 recommended the 10+2+3 pattern, that is 10 years of general education, 2 years of higher secondary education when students would bifurcate into vocational and academic streams, followed by a degree course of 3 years' duration. This structure was reaffirmed by the National Policy on Education of 1986 and is generally followed.

Higher education is primarily managed by the government. Universities can be established only by an act of parliament or a state legislature. All universities are thus established by government. A privately sponsored institution which achieves excellence is accorded status similar to that of a university, by declaring it as an institution deemed to be a university under Section 3 of the University Grants Commission (UGC) Act. There are 15 privately sponsored institutions out of the 28 that are deemed

universities. They can award degrees and enjoy other privileges of a university.

There are 3,900 privately managed colleges (Vohra and Sharma 1990). Whether government or private, colleges are affiliated to a university and follow the curriculum and the examination pattern determined by it. In academic matters, there are no significant differences between them. Although privately managed institutions have considerable administrative autonomy, the statutes of the universities provide for their structure of management. A board of management or a governing body including representatives of the university and government is responsible for managing private institutions. Almost all that fulfill the eligibility criteria receive maintenance and development grants from the government and the UGC. The universities and the grant-giving authorities lay down norms for private colleges to follow, such as government-prescribed pay scales. Conditions of service differ in the private colleges. A gradual move towards parity with teachers of government colleges in all significant matters is noticeable. This move also calls for appropriate mechanisms to ensure that innovation and excellence are not lost in the process.

Articles 29 and 30 of the Constitution give special protection to institutions established and managed by religious and linguistic minorities. They have greater autonomy in administration and are not required to fully follow the guidelines, regulations, and statutes of the universities and the government.

2.1 Levels of Institution

Universities and colleges form the main institutions of higher education. Most universities are teaching as well as affiliating bodies. A few instruct at undergraduate level, but most university departments teach only graduates and undertake research. Colleges are affiliated to a university. While most colleges provide undergraduate education, some also undertake graduate teaching and research. The affiliating universities oversee the standards of the affiliated colleges, and ensure that management is in keeping with the norms laid down. They hold examinations and award degrees to successful candidates. Some universities have more than 100 affiliated colleges and student enrollments exceed one hundred thousand.

Aligarh, Banaras, Lucknow, Baroda, and Annamalai are unitary universities with no affiliated colleges. They teach at undergraduate and graduate level and also undertake research. Some universities combine the characteristics of unitary as well as teaching and affiliating universities. In such cases, only colleges located within the city are affiliated to the university. Certain colleges are managed by the university and are known as constituent colleges.

There are 26 agricultural universities, 14 engineering and technical universities, 7 medical universities, and one each for law, education, and education of music and fine arts. The professional universities devote themselves to selected disciplines while most other universities provide education in almost all the faculties including professional disciplines like medicine, engineering, and teacher education.

No university is exclusively devoted to research. However, some 28 research institutions have been given the status of a university under Section 3 of the UGC Act 1956. Some prestigious high-quality institutions undertake research whilst offering courses in a limited number of subjects and faculties—the institutes of national importance. Five Indian institutes of technology provide high-quality education in technology and science. The Indian Statistical Institute specializes in statistical techniques. There are three such institutes of medical science and technology and one of Hindi language.

The Indira Gandhi Open University provides distance education throughout the country, and coordinates the activities and funding of the four state open universities.

Three sectors engage in and contribute to research. Research is an important function of all institutions of higher education, and is undertaken in the context of formal degrees of PhD, DLit, DSc, and so forth. They also pursue independent research, sponsored and funded by different organizations and councils. About 200 research laboratories within the purview of major scientific research funding agencies carry out research. The national research laboratories stand at the apex of the parallel research system. Regional research laboratories have been established by the Council of Scientific and Industrial Research. The Atomic Energy Commission, the Defense Research and Standard Organizations, and the Indian Council of Agricultural Research are amongst the organizations which carry out research independent of the universities. Some of them also provide research support to institutions of higher education. This parallel system of research has proved its utility and has contributed significantly to national development and technological progress. Industrial organizations also make a major contribution to research through their R & D activities.

There are several councils and other organizations to promote and fund research in different disciplines. They provide fellowships and study–cum–travel grants for research. The Council of Scientific and Industrial Research and the Atomic Energy Commission provide assistance for scientific and technical research. The Indian Council of Social Sciences Research, the Indian Council of Philosophical Research, and the Indian Council of Historical Research promote and support research in their respective disciplines. Research in medical sciences is supported by the Indian Council of Medical Research while the Indian Council of Agricultural Research assists research in the fields of crop, soil, animal husbandry, and other agricultural and allied matters. The National Council of Educational Research and Training is primarily responsible for carrying out and promoting educational research.

The UGC is a major source of funding research in the institutions of higher education. The UGC set up Interuniversity Centers in different subject areas to provide national research facilities within the university system. Such centers have been set up in nuclear science, astronomy and astrophysics, and regional instrumentation and crystal growth. Information centers in the fields of science, humanities, and social sciences have also been established for common use of the universities and to support research in these areas. Research in high-tech areas has also received increasing support from the UGC.

There has been an impressive growth in the number of institutions of higher learning. The largest growth is seen in the affiliated colleges which increased tenfold during the last four decades. The number of universities has increased by more than 500 percent (see Table 2). The rate of growth in both colleges and universities was low during the 1970s.

Table 2
Growth of universities and affiliated colleges in India

	1950–51	1955–56	1960–61	1965–66	1970–71	1975–76	1980–81	1985–86	1989–90
Universities	27	33	45	68	83	102	112	132	146
Deemed to be universities	—	—	2	7	8	9	11	17	28
Institutes of national importance	—	—	—	—	9	9	11	15	15
Total number of degree awarding bodies	27	33	47	75	100	120	144	164	189
Affiliated colleges	695	1,025	1,542	2,572	3,604	4,395	4,722	5,816	6,949

Source: UGC Reports from 1959 to 1960 to 1985 to 1986 Ministry of Human Resources Development 1987

2.2 Admissions Policies and Selection

No student is eligible for admission to a first degree course unless he or she has successfully completed 12 years of school education. Within the guidelines provided by the UGC, every university determines admission requirements. For professional education, guidelines from the relevant all-India agencies as, for example, the Medical Council, the Bar Council, the All-India Council for Technical Education and the National Council for Teachers' Education, are taken into account.

Any student passing the higher secondary examination of the Boards of Secondary Education (every state has a board which examines students after 12 years of school education) may be admitted to the first degree course, for the degree of Bachelor of Arts (BA) which includes humanities and social sciences. For admission to commerce, most universities require that students have studied commerce or science at the higher secondary level. For science and professional courses, the study of science subjects at the higher secondary level is necessary. In many states, English is also a prerequisite for professional courses.

Admission to general courses is usually determined by the percentage marks obtained at the higher secondary examination, but entrance tests operate for professional courses in most states. A quota, proportionate to the percentage of the group in the total population, is reserved for students of the scheduled castes and the scheduled tribes. In certain states some places for professional courses are also set aside for women.

Students are admitted to graduate courses on the basis of marks obtained in the first degree examination. Admission to MPhil courses is also based on merit. Admission to PhD courses is not regulated or structured. Applicants for PhD courses have to negotiate with their future supervisor and convince them of his or her suitability. Once the candidate is accepted, a Board of Research Studies approves the research topic.

2.3 Quantitative Developments in Higher Education

Independence transformed the psyche of the nation. Large numbers of young people entered higher education to obtain a degree, necessary for a growing number of jobs.

Table 4

Percentage of 19–23 age group enrolled in higher education 1961–90[a]

	1961	1966	1971	1976	1981	1986	1990
Percentage	1.5	2.5	4.2	4.6	4.7	5.7	5.9

a Calculated from population estimates in Census Report (Social and Cultural tables) 1981

During 1960–65, the annual student growth rate was 14 percent. In the 1970s the growth rate slowed (see Table 3). One of the reasons was the switch over to the 10+2+3 pattern which extended school duration by one year. For one year no student entered the first year of college. The impact on total enrollment persisted until the first cohort passing through from the 12th year of school reached its final year of higher education. The growth rate of annual enrollments for the period 1981 to 1990 discloses no definite trend until 1985 to 1986 when it fluctuated, but has remained consistent thereafter. Wide variations exist in the growth rate between different states, ranging from 9.5 percent in Tamil Nadu to only 2.9 percent in Orissa.

In the five years between 1961 to 1966, there was a very substantial increase in the proportion of the 19 to 23 age group enrolled in higher education, almost doubling from 1.4 percent to 2.5 percent. This trend was maintained over the next five years reaching 4.2 percent by 1969 to 1970. Enrollment of the relevant age group during the 1960s outstripped its rate of population growth. In the 1970s the increase is more gradual and steady. In the first half of the 1980s, however, a significant improvement took place, stabilizing towards the second half of the decade. By 1989 to 1990 only 5.9 percent of the relevant age group was enrolled in higher education (see Table 4). Figures from the World Development Report (1989) of the World Bank show that in 1986 low income countries such as Indonesia (7%), Senegal (19%), Morocco (9%), and Egypt (21%) had higher participation rates than India. Compared to developed countries the situation in India is highly unsatisfactory. India has around 10 percent of the enrollment level of countries such as the United States (59%) and Canada (55%), and slightly more than a quarter of that of the United Kingdom (22%).

Table 3

Five-yearly growth rates of student enrollment in higher education

1950–55	1955–60	1960–65	1965–70	1970–75	1975–80	1980–85	1985–89
11.2	13.5	14.0	12.8	4.4	2.6	5.3	—

Source: Moonis R (ed.) 1991 Higher Education in India—Retrospect and Prospect. Association of Indian Universities, New Delhi

Lack of opportunity of higher education for over 94 percent of the age group also implies inability to draw on the full potential of a large pool of untapped talent.

2.4 Structure of Qualifications

Bachelor of arts, bachelor of science, bachelor of law, bachelor of medicine, and bachelor of surgery (MBBS), and bachelor of engineering constitute first degrees. After the first degree, graduate courses lead to the master's degrees including master of arts, master of sciences, master of engineering, and so forth.

In general education, courses leading to the first degree of bachelor of arts, bachelor of science, bachelor of home science, and bachelor of commerce are of three years' duration. Although many universities have separate faculties of social sciences, the bachelor of arts is awarded for the first degree both in social sciences and humanities. Students can combine subjects from social sciences and humanities. In other faculties, a student can offer only subjects included within that faculty. Some subjects like geography, mathematics, and psychology are included in the faculties of both arts and science.

Bachelor of engineering or bachelor of technology is the first degree in engineering and lasts four years. Bachelor of medicine and bachelor of surgery (MBBS), the first degree in medical sciences, lasts five and a half years including one year's internship.

Some professional courses can be taken only after obtaining a first degree. The bachelor of education requires one year after the first degree. The first degree course in law has a duration of three years which follows upon the bachelor's degree. The Bar Council of India, the national body for the legal profession, has recommended a five-year law degree course, but this remains largely a dead letter.

Master's degree courses usually last two years. Only the master's in medicine and surgery requires three years. Master of education is only of one year's duration.

In many subjects, the degree of master of philosophy (MPhil) has also been introduced. Lasting one to one and a half years, its purpose is to train students for high quality research. Wherever it has been introduced, the MPhil is a prerequisite for a doctorate degree. The PhD degree has no fixed duration. The length depends upon the nature of research undertaken. The minimum duration ranges from two to three years, with relaxation by one year in some universities for experienced teachers. There is a maximum length of ten years. If some universities require full-time and exclusive work, most will permit registration for this degree and allow candidates to teach or undertake other assignments, provided they comply with the requirements of residence.

Doctor of Literature, Doctor of Science, and Doctor of Law are the highest research degrees, usually

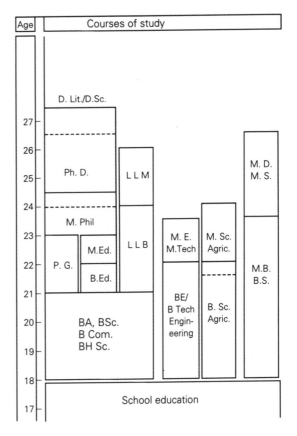

Figure 2
Structure of the higher educational system

obtained only after a PhD. Eminent persons from various walks of life from the country or abroad are conferred the highest research degrees with a view to honor them (see Fig. 2).

3. Governance, Administration, and Finance

3.1 National Administration

Coordination and determination of standards in higher education or research, and scientific and technical institutions is the responsibility of the central government. The development of institutes of national importance, the deemed universities, and ten central universities also comes under central government. Universities and colleges at state level are the responsibility of state governments. Education, including higher education, is a part of the national plan and the planning process. The national plan combines plans of the central ministries and the state. Thus, higher education is a part of the state plan as well as the central plan. The central government and the state governments jointly have responsibility for planning and developing higher education.

At central level, the Ministry of Human Resource Development in conjunction with the Planning Commission is responsible for formulation, implementation, and monitoring the plan. The UGC, a statutory body, is the main instrument of the Ministry in respect of higher education. It is both a grant-giving and a coordinating body. Its major objective is the upkeep, coordination, determination, and maintenance of standards of teaching, examination, and research in universities.

Agricultural education and medical education are taken care of by the Agriculture Ministry and Health Ministry respectively. They are assisted by the Indian Council of Agricultural Research and the Indian Council of Medical Research. The All-India Council of Technical Education, Bar Council of India, Dental Council of India, and the Pharmacy Council of India are some other coordinating bodies in their respective disciplines.

The Central Advisory Board of Education is the apex body providing policy framework and direction to education including higher education in the country. It is chaired by the Minister of Human Resource Development in the central government. Education ministers of the states and union territories are members.

The National Policy on Education (1986) proposed setting up a national body covering higher education in all fields including general, agricultural, medical, technical, and legal training.

At state level, the Departments of Education in the state governments are responsible for planning, development, and management of higher education. Likewise, the National Policy on Education (1986) envisages state-level planning and coordination of higher education through state councils of higher education.

Many states have planning boards, which play a role analogous to the Planning Commission in planning and development of higher education in the states.

The Planning Commission and the central government shape higher education by fixing the priority of allocation to higher education vis-à-vis other sectors both in the Five-Year Plans and in the Annual Plan. The Department of Education in the Ministry of Human Resource Development may issue regulations in consultations with the UGC under the UGC Act of 1956. The regulations have statutory force and play a significant role in setting the pace and direction of the activities in higher education.

The UGC provides grants and funds to universities and colleges, for a number of projects, programs, schemes, and goals set by central agencies including the commission. Selective funding is effective in transmitting goals and obtaining compliance. Direct intervention of the UGC involves expert visiting committees to review progress of the university, examine the five-year plan prepared and programs proposed by the university, and to make appropriate recommendations.

State governments also monitor progress when making grants to universities and colleges. Meetings of the Coordination Committees and the Committee of Vice-Chancellors provide an opportunity to check the progress of various programs and schemes taken up by the universities in the light of goals set by central agencies and state governments.

Respecting the autonomy of the universities, the UGC generally follows an informal approach to monitoring and influencing the policies of universities. For this it has been criticized. It is argued that the UGC should assume a more dynamic, aggressive, and effective stance. Yet, concern also exists at the possible infringement of university autonomy whenever the Commission does act more decisively. On the whole, the Commission has adopted a middle course, and has been largely successful in giving positive direction to the development of higher education.

3.2 Finance

As higher education is the joint responsibility of the central and the state governments, both help to fund it. Central universities receive their grants from the central government and its agencies, such as the UGC. The deemed universities and institutes of national importance are also substantially funded from the center. State universities are primarily financed by state governments. They also receive funds from the UGC. Colleges in the states receive grants from the state government. The government colleges meet their expenditures through budgetary allocations. The amounts allocated usually increase every year by a constant factor, applicable to other government departments included in the budget. In such a system, no room is left for developmental expenditure.

The bulk of private colleges receive grants from the state government, which is substantial. It covers the entire salary expenditure on employees and also has a contingency element. Maintenance grants cover 100 percent of the deficit, so, after taking into account total expenditure and the income of the institution, the gap is covered by the grants. This system provides no incentive to generate additional income, nor rewards for good management and quality education. A few states, however, have adopted differential scales of grant, to promote and reward quality and good management. In a majority of states the trend is to give grants covering salaries of teachers and employees, often the result of pressure from teachers' organizations.

Private colleges also receive state government development grants for buildings, hostels, libraries, and laboratories, depending on the availability of resources.

The maintenance grant to the state universities is also based on the principle of meeting the deficit. It is usually set for a period of four to five years, with provision for an annual fixed increment. Generally, state universities are under severe financial strain as the yearly increase in maintenance grant falls short of needs. Development grants vary from state to state. In most, sufficient funds are not available for development and expansion of state universities, which rely on the UGC for support.

The UGC provides development grants to state universities on the basis of plans the latter submit. The UGC has two basic grant patterns. For some academic programs, the Commission meets the entire cost for a fixed term, usually five years, on condition that state governments finance the activities beyond the period. In the second pattern, usually for infrastructural development, the Commission pays 50 to 75 percent of total costs, the remainder coming from state government. Progressive and financially well-off states are able to take greater advantage of such schemes. Obviously this system of grant is not based on the assessment of the need of the university, but depends on the capacity and willingness of the state government to fulfill the conditions.

Colleges—whether government or private—also receive UGC development grants, provided they are eligible under Section 2(f) of the University Grants Commission Act. In March 1990, 4,115 colleges out of a total of 6,949 colleges were eligible.

The share assigned to different types of institutions in the total UGC grant shows wide diversities and inequities, institutions deemed to be universities receiving substantially higher grants than others. In the first half of the 1980s, central universities received more than twice the per student grant allotted to state universities. Affiliated colleges, lowest in the scale, received only 3 percent of the aid given to central universities, and one-fifth of the UGC's per student assistance given to state universities. Given that 83.4 percent (1989–90) of all students are in the colleges, the elitist nature of this grant system is obvious (Azad 1988 p. 39).

In all, about three-quarters of university expenditure is met by the government—center and state—about 17 percent by fees, and the residual by endowments, donations, and so forth.

Expenditure on higher education as proportion of Gross National Product (GNP) rose from 0.2 percent in 1950 to 1951 to 0.8 percent in 1965 to 1966 (see Table 5). Thereafter it fell in 1970 to 1971 to 0.6 percent, recovering in 1975 to 1976, and reaching once again the high level of 0.8 percent. In 1981 a further decline set in—0.3 percent—only to rise again in 1984 to 1985.

3.3 Institutional Administration

Universities are established by Act of Parliament or by state legislation. All follow broadly the same organizational pattern and structure, although in matters of detail, considerable variations exist. For central universities, the President of India functions as visitor. The state universities have no corresponding office. The visitor appoints the chancellor and the vice-chancellor.

State universities are governed by act of the state legislatures. Some states have a common act for all universities of the state. The governor of the state, barring extremely rare exceptions, is the ex officio chancellor of all universities in the state.

The appointment of a vice-chancellor is usually made from a list submitted by a search committee. The syndicate of the university, the visitor or chancellor, and the UGC each appoint one member to the search committee. In some states there is a state government nominee, and none from the UGC. The tenure of the vice-chancellor is usually between three and five years. In most universities the mandate may be renewed once, but this is uncommon.

The vice-chancellor is the principal executive and academic officer of the university, responsible for ensuring that the provision of the university act, statutes, ordinances, and regulations are duly observed. He or she chairs important committees.

Many universities also have a pro-vice-chancellor or rector, appointed by the chancellor on the recommendations of the vice-chancellor, as chief associ-

Table 5
Expenditure on education and higher education 1950 to 1985

	1950–51	1955–56	1960–61	1965–66	1970–71	1975–76	1980–81	1984–85
Expenditure on education as part of GNP	1.2	2.0	2.5	2.8	3.1	3.2	3.9	4.0
Expenditure on higher education as part of GNP	0.2	0.4	0.6	0.8	0.6	0.8	0.3	0.5

Source: Azad 1975, Shah 1987

ate of the vice-chancellor. He or she exercises the powers and discharges the duties of the vice-chancellor in the latter's absence.

The senate or court is the supreme body of the university. It is primarily deliberative, with more than 100 members representing a variety of interests. A cross section of society, including agriculturists, eminent professionals, artists, and writers, are also represented, usually through nominations by the chancellor. The representatives of teachers and graduates are elected to the senate by their respective constituencies.

The senate or court controls the budget, considers the annual report and accounts, and passes resolution thereon. It confers degrees, and in some cases may modify and repeal the statutes. Its annual meetings in certain universities are characterized by uproar and lack of decorum. Many question its usefulness, consider it outdated, and advocate its abolition. In a few cases this has been attempted. Yet it performs a useful function, provides a forum to discuss the university's affairs, and ensures some degree of accountability to the community at large.

The syndicate or executive council, the principal executive and governing body, meets almost once every month, and is comprised of some 15 to 20 members, government officials, university professors, principals, educationists, and representatives of legislature. Principals, professors, and teachers are either nominated by rotation and seniority or are elected.

The syndicate appoints teaching staff, ensures good management of the colleges, hostels, libraries, laboratories, university teaching departments, and all infrastructural facilities. The vice-chancellor and syndicate together are responsible for the good governance of the university. Within the broad framework of the UGC guidelines, syndicate may grant, suspend, or withdraw affiliation to colleges.

The Academic Council, the main body responsible for the academic activities of the university, usually consists of teachers of the university, teachers and principals of colleges, and government officials concerned with higher education. Students' representatives are also members in many universities. The chancellor or vice-chancellor also nominates some external educationists and experts. The Council prescribes courses, determines curricula, fixes norms and procedure for admission, students' assessment and examinations, and thereby determines academic standards.

The academic activities of a university are performed through faculties and departments. A group of cognate subjects constitutes a typical faculty. In general universities, arts, science, commerce, home science, education, medical science, and engineering are the usual faculties. The head of faculty is a dean. He or she is usually a full professor, the head of department and is usually nominated on the basis of

seniority. There is a system of rotation. In affiliating universities, provisions exist for senior principals and professors of colleges to achieve the position of dean. The dean exercises power vested in him or her by the act or delegated by the vice-chancellor and other authorities.

Every subject has its board of studies, responsible for formulating and updating syllabi. Its representatives serve on committees which select examiners. Teachers of both universities and colleges are represented on the board.

In all teaching universities, the department is the key unit for teaching and research. Some universities appoint the most senior professor as head of department. In others, headship rotates among full professors. In a few, the system of rotation extends to readers too.

Autonomous colleges have bodies similar to academic councils and boards of studies. The representatives of the university are invariably members of these bodies. All colleges also have departments based broadly on similar lines as the university.

Professional universities like agricultural and technical universities follow broadly the same pattern. Deemed universities and institutes of national importance have their own statutes and regulations. They are, however, similar in many respects, with differences reflecting the special nature of the institution.

Academic power lies primarily with the Academic Council. While the situation varies from state to state and university to university, generally, the professors and senior teachers enjoy a disproportionately larger share in the academic power structure.

Many universities have student members in the academic council and boards of studies, nominated on the basis of performance in the preceding examination. Nonacademic staff are usually not represented.

4. Faculty and Students: Teaching, Learning, and Research

4.1 Faculty

Faculty increased rapidly in the 1960s rising by 52 percent during the five years between 1960 and 1965 (see Table 6). Student enrollment and the number of institutions also displayed similar high growth rates.

In keeping with the slowdown in student enrollment and in the number of institutions in the 1970s, the growth rate of faculty in colleges and universities let up. Between 1980 and 1985, college faculty increased partly as a result of attention to improve inadequately staffed colleges and partly because of a rise in the number of institutions.

Clearly, the numbers of faculty have not kept pace with the galloping student enrollment. From the

Table 6
Growth in teaching staff in universities, colleges, and affiliated colleges in percentages

	1960–65	1965–70	1970–75	1975–80	1980–85	1985–89
Increase in university faculty	—	51.28	46.28	26.37	24.01	14.47
Increase in college faculty	—	52.39	26.80	12.78	17.41	10.70
Overall increase	52.68	52.20	30.07	15.34	18.77	11.51

Source: UGC Report 1989–90, Chauhan 1990

1970s onwards, the number of students per teacher in the affiliated colleges was higher than in the universities, mainly because the bulk of the increase in student enrollment took place in undergraduate classes, while universities concentrated on graduate courses and research, both requiring better teacher–student ratios. Moreover, to maintain quality, the universities are more liberal in creating additional posts.

There is no system of part-time teachers in India. Indeed, the statutes and ordinances of many universities prohibit appointment of part-time teachers for colleges. However, provisions exist for temporary appointments in cases of staff shortage. Law colleges in many areas have legal practitioners working as part-time teachers.

Universities and colleges have similar, though not identical structure and ranks in the academic profession. Universities have lecturers, readers, and professors. The position of associate professor also exists in some universities, deemed universities, and institutes of national importance. In the colleges, the bulk of the faculty are lecturers. There are higher grades such as senior scale and selection grade for lecturers. The latter is equivalent to the salary scale of reader without the title. In some states, colleges have teachers equivalent in rank and salary to readers in a university but are designated professors. The rank of assistant professor is found in some institutions.

Currently, qualifications for appointment to the post of lecturer are a master's degree in the relevant subject with at least 55 percent of marks or an equivalent grade and a good academic record. From January 1, 1991, it was decided that only those who have qualified in a test conducted or accredited for the purpose by the UGC may apply for lectureships. Lecturers who at the time of appointment hold an MPhil or a PhD degree are given a higher starting salary.

The post of reader requires: (a) a good academic record with a doctoral degree or equivalent published work; (b) evidence of being actively engaged in research, the innovation of teaching methods, or the production of teaching materials; and (c) five years'

experience of teaching and/or research, provided that at least three of these years were as lecturer or equivalent.

For the position of professor the minimum qualifications are very high. The candidate has to be either: (a) an eminent scholar with published work of high quality, who is actively engaged in research, has ten years' experience of teaching and/or research, and has experience of guiding research at doctoral level; or (b) an outstanding scholar with established reputation who has made significant contribution to knowledge.

India does not have a system of tenure. Teachers, once recruited and confirmed after the satisfactory completion of a probationary period, usually of one or two years, are made permanent in service.

Recruitment to teaching posts in universities is the responsibility of the individual establishment. A selection committee of experts in the subject, interviews or holds discussions with candidates. There is also a provision for appointment to senior positions on the basis of bio-data. Some states have experimented with centralized recruitment, and a few continue to have the Education Service Commission recruit teachers for universities and colleges. The universities usually appoint by direct recruitment through open competition. In addition, lecturers may be promoted internally.

Recruitment for government colleges is centralized on the recommendations of the Public Service Commission or the State Education Service Commission. In private colleges, management recruits, although the selection committee must include representatives of the university and government, which gives a substantial grant.

To encourage research, provision exists for weightage of research degrees for purposes of promotion. Minimum duration may be relaxed by one year for those with an MPhil degree, and by three years for PhD holders.

Performance appraisal of college and university teachers has been a matter of debate and controversy. The UGC with the participation of the All-India Federation of University and College Teachers' Organizations adopted a system on November 4,

1988 to be followed by all colleges and universities. It is based on research contributions, participation in seminars and conferences, performances in extension work, community services, participation in corporate life, innovations, and contributions to teaching.

Two conflicting trends have emerged over the status of faculty in different types of institutions, some favoring parity, uniform pay scales, conditions of service, and opportunities for promotion. Others assert that bearing in mind the level and quality of institutions and the level of talent and achievement they attract, faculty status and conditions of service should also vary. Notwithstanding the formal observation of parity in pay scales and conditions of service, in reality considerable differences exist. The teachers in the Indian Institute of Management, the Indian Institute of Technology, and some renowned universities are more respected than their counterparts in colleges. Many organizations funding and promoting research are criticized for providing disproportionately high support to a limited number of teachers and institutions. Among teachers of affiliated colleges and universities, the latter enjoy higher status.

All states have unions of teachers. In some, separate unions of university teachers, private colleges and government colleges exist, with coordinating bodies for pursuing common interests. In some states and at the all-India level, a number of unions have links with political parties. The code of professional ethics, the system of performance appraisal, and conditions of service and pay scales have been largely determined in consultation with teachers' unions, but many believe that teachers' unions are mainly concerned with trades union activities, and do not adequately meet the role and functions of professional bodies.

Since the UGC is responsible for coordination and

maintenance of standards, it lays down norms for the number of hours of teaching and allocation of time between teaching, research, extension work, and other administrative activities. Within these broad guidelines, workload and the share of different activities are determined by individual states and universities.

4.2 Students

Higher education has not been guided by systematic and comprehensive labor force planning. Table 7 sets out distribution of students by faculty.

In 1950 to 1951, professional courses together accounted for only 10 percent of the total enrollment. By 1989 to 1990, its share increased only to 15 percent. Engineering and technology accounted for 4.3 percent of all enrollments in 1960 to 1961, which reached 4.9 percent in 1965 to 1966, and remained at that level until 1989 to 1990. Medical education gives a similar pattern. Agriculture presents a more disturbing trend in an agriculturally predominant country. It accounted for 1.2 percent of the total enrollment in 1950 to 1951, reached a peak of 3 percent in 1965 to 1966, and thereafter declined to a low of 1.1 percent in 1989 to 1990.

Science, after an initial increase from 28.9 percent in 1960 to 1961 to 32.7 percent in 1965 to 1966, declined to 19.1 percent in 1975 to 1976, and has remained at that level over the subsequent five-year periods. Commerce has continued to improve its share of student enrollment. From 8.6 percent in 1960 to 1961, it crossed the 22.1 percent mark in 1980 to 1981, maintaining this level ever since, with marginal variations. After the mid-1970s, commerce has been drawing in students from other faculties. Its popularity reflects the needs of the economy, growing industrialization, and an increasing share of trade, commerce, and banking services. After banks

Table 7
Enrollment in higher education 1960–89, by faculty in percentages

	1960–61	1965–66	1970–71	1975–76	1980–81	1985–86	1989–90
Arts	44.9	40.9	43.7	44.5	40.5	40.7	40.4
Science	30.0	32.8	31.7	19.1	19.4	19.4	19.6
Commerce	10.2	9.6	11.5	17.1	20.1	21.7	21.9
Engineering/ technology	3.6	4.9	3.0	4.0	4.7	4.9	4.9
Medicine	2.7	4.1	3.3	4.3	4.0	3.4	3.4
Education	1.5	1.9	1.8	3.2	2.6	2.3	2.3
Agriculture	1.3	2.9	1.4	1.2	1.4	1.2	1.1
Law	2.3	2.2	2.3	5.8	6.3	5.4	5.3
Veterinary science	0.5	0.4	0.2	0.3	0.3	0.3	0.3
Others	3.0	0.5	0.4	0.5	0.7	0.7	0.8
Total	100	100	100	100	100	100	100

Source: UGC Report 1989–90, Raza 1991

Table 8
Percentage of scheduled caste enrollment in higher education 1965–80

	1965–66	1970–71	1975–76	1977–78	1979–80
General education	5.5	6.1	7.9	7.7	7.5
Professional education	—	5.5	6.6	6.8	6.9

Source: Chauhan 1990, Raza 1991

were nationalized in July 1969, the demand for commerce graduates rose substantially.

Concern about inequities is not just of moral importance. The strategy of human resource development calls for development and utilization of all segments of the population. Yet, expansion of educational facilities, whilst usually inspired and readily utilized by the better off in society, accentuates disparities, since the deprived do not benefit in proportion to their numbers without affirmative action in their favor. Hence, enrollment levels among scheduled castes, tribes, and women deserve special attention (see Table 8).

Although scheduled castes account for 15.8 percent of the total population, their share in the total enrollment in general education was only 5.5 percent in 1965 to 1966, reached 7.9 percent in 1975 to 1976, and thereafter fell to 7.5 percent in 1979 to 1980. Their share in professional courses, however, while highly unsatisfactory, has continued to rise from 5.5 percent in 1970 to 1971 to 6.9 percent in 1979 to 1980. No satisfaction can be derived from this rising trend, as the pace is not only very slow, but also the gap to be covered is very wide, and at the present rate one cannot see it bridged in the foreseeable future. Systematic figures in time–series of enrollment of the scheduled tribes in higher education are not available.

Female enrollment (see Table 9) has risen continuously. From 16.2 percent in 1960 to 1961, it has reached 32.2 percent in 1989 to 1990. Faculty-wise analysis of women's enrollment, however, shows a disturbing trend. In professional courses, their share is extremely low except in medicine and education. In engineering, it was less than 1 percent in 1960 to

1961, and had only risen to 7.6 percent of the total enrollment by 1989 to 1990. In agriculture, again, their share in 1960 to 1961 was as low as 4.5 percent and had reached the level of 6.9 percent by 1989 to 1990. The medical and teaching professions are considered appropriate for women, and this is reflected in their high participation rate. In medicine they accounted for 21.9 percent of all enrollments in 1960 to 1961 and 31.9 percent in 1989 to 1990. Whilst in education, with 32.8 percent share in 1960–61, they now account for 52.9 percent of all enrollments.

All students belonging to the scheduled castes (SCs) and scheduled tribes (STs) are given fellowships for higher education. Hostels are specially constructed for them, and in the general hostels also, 15 percent of the total accommodation is set aside. The UGC has suggested that 15 percent of places be reserved for SCs and 7.5 percent for those from the STs. Provision for relaxation in the requirements of marks also exists for them. Remedial courses and coaching classes are also organized for the students of the SCs and STs. In the universities, with the assistance of the UGC, a special cell has been set up to ensure effective implementation of various measures to promote education amongst these deprived groups.

To encourage students of these groups to undertake research, junior research fellowships are also reserved for them. Reservations are also made in research fellowships, teacher fellowships, and for teaching posts. The UGC gives special assistance to colleges, with at least 20 percent of enrollments belonging to these groups.

In many states, the education of women is free. In some states for certain professional courses, res-

Table 9
Female enrollment in higher education

	1960–61	1965–66	1970–71	1975–76	1980–81	1985–86	1989–90
Total enrollment	557,000	1,067,000	1,953,700	2,426,109	2,752,437	3,605,029	4,246,878
Female enrollment	90,234	21,980	431,522	595,162	748,525	1,067,485	1,367,495
Percentage of total	16.2	20.6	22.2	24.5	27.2	29.6	32.2

Source: UGC Report 1980–81, 1985–86, 1989–90, Kaul 1974

ervations are made for women, and there are also single-sex colleges for women. In 1980 to 1981, there were 609 of these, and 851 by 1989 to 1990.

The UGC has assisted universities and colleges to establish departments of women's studies, and already 20 universities and 8 colleges have been assisted in this way. Part-time research associateships for women provide opportunities for those women unable to undertake research full-time.

With the rapid growth of higher education, students have emerged as an important pressure group. Consequently, student power has to be reckoned with, and all major political parties have their student organizations.

There are student unions in all institutions of higher education. All students enrolled in an institution are members of the union. Students favor universal membership, but in some states, such as Uttar Pradesh, attempts to make membership of the unions optional brought strong if not violent reactions from the student community.

The student unions vary in their composition, process of election, powers exercised, and scope of activities. Generally, two bodies—a general body and an executive committee—are their basic organization. Political parties take direct interest and provide funds for student elections. Many observers note with concern the growing role of money and muscle power in these elections; violent clashes are not uncommon.

Over the years, the student unions have grown in strength. They take up not only academic, but general issues and do not hesitate to agitate on the slightest provocation, paralyzing both academic life and also life of the community at large. Their influence has gone beyond academia.

The structure of courses and programs is defined and determined by universities, and the affiliated colleges follow. Autonomous colleges, however, are free to evolve their own courses and programs. The UGC, during the Fifth Five-Year Plan, initiated a scheme to make first degree courses more relevant to the environment and developmental needs of the community. Although the UGC has issued guidelines, the final decision rests with the universities. Thus, by March 31, 1990 only 9 universities and 208 colleges had introduced such courses.

The universities and autonomous colleges may introduce new courses and programs, so long as additional grants from the government are not required. Even where funds are required, the grant-giving authority does not interfere in the academic aspects of the program. Except for certain professional courses, no system of accreditation exists. The Medical Council and the All-India Council of Technical Education are responsible for maintenance of certain norms and standards in their respective areas. All courses and programs of medical and technical education and management require approval

of the appropriate body. Proposals for new study programs are sent to the relevant professional body, where experts evaluate and also examine the adequacy of infrastructure and other facilities. On their recommendation, the councils may grant or withhold approval.

Undergraduate courses follow the liberal arts approach. A student is required to study languages and two or three other disciplines in a faculty. The faculty system is very rigid, so subjects from other faculties cannot be studied. There are, however, some subjects like mathematics, anthropology, and psychology which are included in more than one faculty in many universities.

Some universities also have a system of honors courses at the undergraduate level, specializing in a single subject. However, the liberal arts approach within honors courses also requires a general familiarity with two other subjects, usually called minor subjects. The major subject is for in-depth study, and specialization claims roughly 80 percent of the total course component. The credit-unit system is not widespread.

External examinations continue to be the most widely practiced system of student evaluation. Examinations are held at the end of every academic year, which usually extends from July to April. In most universities marks secured in all annual examinations of a course are totaled to arrive at the final result.

In the annual written examination, essay-type questions are most common. Short answer and objective style questions are increasingly used. The written examination is usually of three hours' duration.

In the faculties of science, home science, fine arts, teacher education, professional courses, and in some other subjects, practical examination is an important component. At undergraduate level, the student must obtain a certain percentage in each subject to succeed in the examination and to be eligible to go on to the next year. If he or she fails the course has to be repeated.

Classes of degrees are awarded on the basis of marks obtained. Usually 60 percent and above is considered first division, although for some professional courses 65 percent and above constitute the first division. The second division is attained with 40 percent or over, while 33 to 48 percent is considered third division. Those who do not reach 33 percent have failed.

The examination system is generally held to be highly defective, and a number of measures for reform have been introduced. The general pattern of traditional examination is gradually giving way to more scientific and innovative methods.

5. Conclusion

Consistent with its large size and massive population, India boasts a very large system of higher education, which is vibrant and growing steadily. It is a nation-wide system of education in which all states conform to a broad pattern, with adaptations to take account of regional variations.

After the very fast growth of the 1960s and comparative stagnation in the 1970s, higher education is now growing at a steady and reasonable pace, but is unplanned. It is not aimed at removing regional imbalances, nor providing equitable access. It is unrelated to labor force needs, and is propelled by elitist pressure and political ambitions. It has given rise to alarming levels of unemployment and a mismatch between the skills in demand and those supplied.

In a stratified and traditional society like India, equity must be an important criterion for judging higher education. While increased numbers of colleges have improved the availability of higher education in rural areas, the gap both in quality and quantity between urban and rural areas continues to be very wide. The percentage of women enrolled has increased remarkably, reaching 32.2 percent in 1989 to 1990, but the share of women in science and professional courses remains disturbingly low. A yawning gap remains between the privileged and the deprived groups.

Although the National Policy on Education, successive Five-Year Plans and various education commissions all stressed higher education as an instrument of social transformation and rapid economic development, steps to shape higher education to perform this role were not taken. Its full potential remains unexplored and unexploited.

As befits the largest democracy in the world, democracy in the working of higher education has deep roots. Teachers, students, and employees find appropriate representation, and share power on various bodies in universities and colleges. Because of the nexus with political parties, their organized strength has grown disproportionately at the cost of efficient functioning of universities and colleges. The universities, by and large, function with considerable internal academic autonomy, though glaring examples of blatant interference may be found; mercifully, such cases are few and far between.

Funding is a source of direct control over higher education. All institutions depend primarily on government funds, and the grant-giving authority exercises substantial control, which may in part be necessary in the interest of sound financial management. Grants-in-aid in most states do not provide adequate incentives to good management and quality of performance. Quality is the Achilles' heel of Indian higher education. Measures taken have not substantially improved the situation.

The quality of higher education is subject to wide variation. The few very high quality institutions of international standard coexist with a large number of substandard and nonviable colleges and many ill-equipped universities, while the majority have indifferent standards.

To raise standards in higher education, a Herculean task in itself, initiatives have been taken to develop centers of excellence in a limited number of institutions. There are two major programs as follows:

(a) Certain teaching departments in universities have been singled out for development as centers of excellence, and have been recognized by the UGC as centers of advanced study and departments of special assistance, whilst a third group has been provided with departmental research support. Under all three schemes the UGC provides special grants.

(b) Selected colleges are being helped to develop as autonomous colleges, to innovate and to improve their standards. Similarly, some selected university departments are also being granted autonomy.

Teachers' organizations have in many cases opposed moves towards autonomy for the colleges, fearing arbitrary behavior and exploitation by powerful management. Thus, progress has been uneven.

The future of higher education in India may see some definite trends emerge. With renewed emphasis on universalizing primary education, the pressure of increasing enrollment on secondary and tertiary sectors of education is likely to be stronger. Further expansion, therefore, will be inevitable, and will focus attention on quality, since the experience of the last few decades shows that, unless remedial steps are taken, quantitative growth adversely affects quality. The future strategy of expansion will combine equity and quality. It requires greater financial resources, and given the declining percentage of higher education in the total education budget, this assumes critical dimensions. Growing student power and youth unrest will focus attention on their problems. To avoid large-scale campus disturbances, social unrest, and agitations disrupting community life and public order, the government will have to come up with adequate funds for higher education.

Unemployment amongst educated youth may well be accentuated in the near future, assuming serious proportions and requiring concerted intervention to solve it. Three possibilities seem likely:

(a) a shift away from the liberal arts approach, to include socially useful skill and vocational training. Here, the trend has already been set by the restructuring exercise advocated by the UGC, and a number of vocational programs being introduced by different universities;

(b) the expansion of professional and vocational education turning back the present trend towards general education;

319

(c) a more serious effort to link expansion to labor force planning.

To improve the quality of higher education on a sustained basis, fundamental change in the university–college relationship appears necessary. The pattern of affiliating with a teaching university has an inherent contradiction. Both the university's teaching departments and the colleges offer the same courses, and a growing number of colleges are offering graduate courses. Though universities are supposed to promote excellence in colleges, this situation brings them in competition.Thus, a vested interest exists in the university teaching departments to maintain differences in standards. This contradiction can be resolved only by a complete transformation in their relationship and a radical change in the concept and role of a university. Universities will have increasingly to act as a resource center to develop excellence in the colleges. This implies that university teachers will have to act as the resource support system for the colleges. In this case, faculty and teaching at university level will either become secondary or will concentrate on courses, programs, and specializations different from the colleges.

Planned expansion linked to labor force requirements of the country, greater job-orientation and social relevance, concerted efforts to improve equity for the scheduled castes, the scheduled tribes, and women, greater resource mobilization from non-government sources, systematic and sustained steps for improving quality, and a basic transformation in the relationship between a university and its affiliated colleges are the main components of the agenda for Indian higher education in this decade. Higher education will have to buckle down to the task with all its strength and vitality if it is to deal successfully with this heavy yet crucial agenda.

Bibliography

Adiseshaiah M S 1982 *Remoulding Indian Higher Education*. India International Centre, New Delhi

Agarwal A N, Varma H O, Gupta R C 1991 *India Economic Information Yearbook 1990–91*. National, New Delhi

Association of Indian Universities 1990 Universities Handbook 1989, Association of Indian Universities, New Delhi

Azad J L 1975 *Financing of Higher Education in India*. Sterling Publications, New Delhi

Azad J L 1988 *Higher Education in India: The Deepening Financial Crisis*. Radiant, New Delhi

Azad J L 1989 *Government Support for Higher Education and Research*. Concept, New Delhi

Basu D K, Sisson R 1986 *Social and Economic Development in India*. Sage, New Delhi

Bhandarkar S S 1985 *Association of Indian Universities—A Short History 1925–85*. Association of Indian Universities, New Delhi

Bhatt B D, Aggarwal J C 1977 *Educational Documents in India (1813–1977)*. Arya Book Depot, New Delhi

Bhiday M R 1986 *From Isolation to Mainstream: Higher Education in India*. Radiant, New Delhi

Census of India 1991 Provisional Population Totals Series—1, Paper 1 of 1991, Census Commissioner, New Delhi

Central Statistical Organisation 1988 *Statistical Abstract India 1987*. Central Statistical Organisation, New Delhi

Chaturvedi R N 1989 *Administration of Higher Education in India*. Print Well, Jaipur

Chauhan C P S 1990 *Higher Education in India*. Ashish, New Delhi

Committee on Setting up State Council of Higher Education 1988 *Report*. University Grants Commission, New Delhi

Dash S C 1976 *Problems of Higher Education*. Santosh, Cuttack

DiBona J 1989 *Critical Perspectives on Indian Education*. Bahri, New Delhi

Dongarkerey S R 1969 *University Education in India*. Marnak Talas, Bombay

Ghosh R, Zachariah M 1987 *Education and the Process of Change*. Sage, New Delhi

Gupta L D 1983 *Educational Administration at College Level*. Oxford, New Delhi

Gupta M L 1985 *Indian Economy and Higher Education*. Aalekha, Jaipur

Jalaluddin A K, Behar S C, Aggarwal Y P, Das J P 1990 *Basic Education and National Development: The Indian Scene*. UNICEF, New Delhi

Jha H 1985 *Colonial Context of Higher Education in India*. Usha, New Delhi

Kaul J N 1974 *Higher Education in India, 1957–1971: The Decades of Planned Drift*. Indian Institute of Advanced Study, Simla

Kaur K 1985 *Education in India (1781–1985) Policy, Planning and Implementation*. Centre for Research in Rural and Industrial Development, Chandigarh

Kiranmayi Y S 1989 *Management of Higher Education in India*. Crown, New Delhi

Malik S C 1971 *Management and Organization of Indian Universities*. Indian Institute of Advanced Study, Simla

Mehendiratta P R 1984 *University Administration in India and USA: Approaches, Issues and Implications*. Oxford and IBH, New Delhi

Ministry of Finance 1990 *Economic Survey 1989–90*. Ministry of Finance, New Delhi

Ministry of Human Resource Development 1987 *Handbook of Educational and Allied Statistics*. Department of Education, New Delhi

Ministry of Human Resource Development 1990 *Annual Report 1989–90*. Department of Education, New Delhi

Mitra B 1967 *Education in Ancient India*. Beda Mitra and Sons, New Delhi

Moonis R (ed.) 1991 *Higher Education in India—Retrospect and Prospect*. Association of Indian Universities, New Delhi

Naik J P 1972 *Access Structure and Quality in Higher Education: Some Suggestions for Reorganization (Special Lecturers)*. University of Mysore, Prasarangar

Nair K R R 1986 *Emerging Spectrum Essays on Indian Higher Education*. Himalaya, Bombay

National Institute of Educational Planning and Administration 1987 *Autonomy and Accountability: A Report of Study Visit to Autonomous Colleges*. NIEPA, New Delhi

National Institute of Educational Planning and Administration 1990 *Basic Educational Data, A Complication.* NIEPA, New Delhi

Planning Commission 1985 *The Seventh Five-Year Plan 1985–90*, Vol. I. Planning Commission, New Delhi

Raghavaiah Y, Reddy N Y 1979 *Contemporary Issues in Higher Education.* Osmania University, Hyderabad

Rai N 1990 *Centre State Relations in the Field of Education in India.* Atma Ram and Sons, Delhi

Ramachandran C M 1987 *Problems of Higher Education in India: A Case Study.* Mittal, Delhi

Rao T V 1990 *Planning and Management for Excellence and Efficiency in Higher Education.* Indian Institute of Management, Hyderabad

Raza M 1990 *Education Development and Society.* Vikas, New Delhi

Raza M (ed.) 1991 *Higher Education in India: Retrospect and Prospect.* Association of Indian Universities, New Delhi

Raza M, Malhotra N 1991 *Higher Education in India: A Comprehensive Bibliography.* Concept, New Delhi

Sethi J D 1983 *Crisis and Collapse of Higher Education in India.* Vikas, New Delhi

Shah K R 1987 An ex-post analysis of resource allocation of education in India. *J. Educ. Planning Adm.* NIEPA, New Delhi

Singh A 1985 *Redeeming Higher Education: Essays in Educational Policy.* Ajanta, Delhi

Singh A, Altbach P G 1974 *The Higher Learning in India.* Vikas, New Delhi

Singh A, Sharma G D (eds.) 1988 *The Higher Education in India: The Social Context.* Konark, New Delhi

Singh A, Sharma G D (eds.) 1989 *The Higher Education in India: The Institutional Context.* Konark, New Delhi

Singh B P 1990 *Aims of Education in India.* Ajanta, Delhi

Sobti M L 1987 *Financial Code for University Systems.* NIEPA/Vikas, New Delhi

Sreekumar S S 1990 *Programme Planning in Higher Education.* Vohra, Allahabad

Tata Services Limited 1989 *Statistical Outline of India 1989–90.* Tata Services Limited, Bombay

The Times of India, May 4 1991

University Grants Commission 1986 *Development of Higher Education and Research in the Universities.* UGC, New Delhi

University Grants Commission 1990 *Annual Report for the Year 1988–89.* UGC, New Delhi

University Grants Commission 1991 *Annual Report for the Year 1989–90.* UGC, New Delhi

United Nations Educational Scientific and Cultural Organization 1989 *Statistical Yearbook 1989.* UNESCO, Paris

Vakil K S, Natrajan S 1966 *Education in India.* Allied Publications, Bombay

Varghese A V 1989 *Higher Education and Management.* Ashish, New Delhi

Veeraraghavan J (ed.) 1985 *Higher Education in the Eighties, Opportunities and Objectives.* Lancer International, New Delhi

Verma Y S 1990 *University Management and Administration.* Deep and Deep, New Delhi

Vohra A L, Sharma S 1990 *Management of Higher Education in India.* Anmol, New Delhi

World Bank 1989 *World Development Report 1989.* World Bank, New York

S. C. Behar

Indonesia

1. Higher Education and Society

Although Indonesia is the fifth largest country in the world in terms of its population, reckoned to be 180 million in the early 1990s, it is relatively little known outside the region of South East Asia. One reason for this is that Indonesia is a young nation, having only come into being with the declaration of Independence in 1945, which brought together the territories known at that time as the Dutch East Indies, comprising Sumatra, Java, Borneo, Bali, the Celebes, and a host of other islands. Under its present structure, Indonesia comprises 28 provinces including the disputed territory of East Timor within an archipelago stretching several thousand miles from east to west. The vastness of the area and the difficulty of communications have led to considerable variation within the country with respect to the distribution of population and the cultural heterogeneity of different ethnolinguistic groups.

The island of Java, which contains only a fifteenth of the landmass of the country, is home to over two-thirds of the population. About 12 million people reside in and around the area of the country's capital, Jakarta. The other islands, which are rich in natural resources and considered to have the most potential for development, are considerably less populated. Given this skewing of population, the government has tried to remedy the situation by a program of family planning which has been relatively successful in Java where the growth rate is down to under two percent. Another measure which the government has adopted has been to encourage transmigration from densely populated to less densely populated areas. These transmigration schemes have had mixed success, but the government has always argued that nation building is important and that transmigration should have as one of its aims the construction of a sense of national unity. The problems of welding a nation together out of so many disparate groups continue to be formidable, with the danger that the Javanese will eventually swamp the other groups.

Despite the range of different societies at different levels of development there are various factors which have encouraged the creation of a sense of national identity throughout the archipelago. Foremost among these has been the common experience of colonialism under the Dutch. A further influential factor was the widepread distribution of a common language, Bahasa Indonesia, a language growing out of Malay which became a *lingua franca* for the purposes of trade and government throughout the archipelago and which was adopted as the language of the nationalist movement in 1928. The Japanese occupation of Indonesia between 1942 and 1945 and the subsequent outlawing of Dutch meant that Bahasa Indonesia developed rapidly in those years and by

1950 there were no problems about its introduction as the national language. Thus, although regional dialects continued in use—and indeed still continue—knowledge of Bahasa Indonesia was sufficiently universal to allow for its untroubled introduction as the medium of education from the third grade onwards.

A third factor which assisted the creation of a sense of national unity was religion. Most of the population of Indonesia is Muslim. Indonesian Muslims are of the Sunni faith and follow in general the Syafei school of Islamic law in relation to religious prescriptions. There are, however, sizeable pockets of the country which are Christian, particularly in those areas where Christian missionaries were active: the Batak area in north Sumatra; and the area of Minahasa in north Sulawesi. Another important group which is largely Christian is the Chinese who comprise about three percent of the population. They occupy a commanding position in the country's economy because of their important role in business and commerce.

Although Indonesia's wealth comes principally from oil and mineral resources followed by agricultural export commodities such as coffee, rubber, and palm oil, and although most of the country's population is to be found in rural areas engaged in agricultural production, the government is wholeheartedly committed to developing the country's economic potential in the industrial sector through the introduction of modern technology. The only constraint on such development appears to be the lack of skilled labor. Consequently, planned investment in education has been a feature of Indonesian economic planning since the mid-1970s. It is from that time that a systematic and thorough-going attempt to link development in education with economic planning can be identified. There was a shift away from what has been characterized as random growth to planned expansion, but to put this change in perspective some consideration has to be given to the history of higher education in Indonesia and its organization.

2. *The Institutional Fabric of the Higher Education System*

The Dutch made little effort to develop tertiary education in Indonesia and in 1941, on the eve of the Japanese occupation, the only tertiary institutions were colleges of law, agriculture, medicine, and technology. During the period of the Indonesian revolution, 1945 to 1950, both the government of the Republic of Indonesia and the Dutch occupying forces tried to set up tertiary educational establishments in the areas which they controlled, building on prewar institutions. Out of these early beginnings came the first two Indonesian universities, the *Universitas Gadjah Mada* (UGM), set up in 1949 in Yogyakarta, and *Universitas Indonesia* (UI) set up in

1950 in Jakarta. These two universities, together with the Institute of Technology (ITB) first set up in Bandung in 1920 and the Agricultural College (IPB) in Bogor, remain the premier tertiary educational establishments in the country.

The decade of the 1950s witnessed a remarkable expansion of universities, institutes, and colleges which has been very ably documented by Thomas (1973). The general features of this development were an emphasis on quantity rather than quality, a desire to ensure a measure of equity in terms of access to higher education both in terms of social and regional equality, a vague recognition of the need to match educational priorities to national needs, and a struggle between academics and politicians in relation to the control of the universities.

Most of the early efforts in higher education were put into consolidating UI and UGM, but in 1954 *Universitas Airlangga* was established in Surabaya and this set the stage for rapid expansion. By 1960 there were eight universities established, three of them in the Outer Islands and the rest in Java. Student enrollment increased in the decade from 6,000 in 1950 to about 37,750 in 1960. In addition there were a number of vocational tertiary educational academies set up by various government ministries, and their number increased from 6 in 1950 to 45 in 1959. Also important at this stage was the establishment of five teacher-training colleges both in the Outer Islands and in Java. Paralleling this development in the public sector was private-sector higher education which mirrored what had been set up by the government: universities, teacher-training colleges, academies and—in the case of Christian foundations—seminaries. Many of these private colleges were very small and few of them were comparable to the state institutions. Some of them, however, especially those supported by large Muslim and Christian organizations, did acquire national reputations.

Between 1959 and 1966 the pattern which had been established in the previous five years continued to be the model for accelerated expansion. Several more state universities were set up, many of them in the Outer Islands, in order to promote a more geographically equitable distribution of resources and opportunities. In 1967 student enrollment had reached 103,145 in state institutions. This very rapid development can in large part be attributed to increasing government direction given to higher education. This was the period of so-called "guided democracy" in Indonesia when President Sukarno was attempting to forge greater national unity by dissolving the party political system which had appeared to be such a failure in the 1950s and replacing it with a consensual form of government, representative of broad groupings within the society. A consequence of this direction from above was that, at the ideological level, instruction in the state philosophy, *Pancasila*, was given more prominence in the syllabus of schools and universities. In addition various practical measures were introduced centrally which affected the speed and nature of developments in higher education.

In 1960 an eight-year plan was announced which had immediate consequences for education: a separate Department of Higher Education headed by a minister was set up; a national educational law concerning higher education was passed in 1961; a commitment was made to establish universities in all the then 22 provinces of Indonesia; more stress was placed on the need for education in technology and science; finally some thought was given to the most appropriate manner of instruction in universities, stressing guided rather than free study. All these measures did have a dramatic effect on higher education, but these changes were being initiated at a time when the national economy was in very serious difficulty. Furthermore, there were major political upheavals which occurred between 1965 and 1968: President Sukarno was ousted and replaced by President Suharto, the Communist Party was proscribed, and the government appeared to shift tack very significantly by aligning itself with Western governments, playing down political issues, and then setting its mind to the urgent task of rehabilitating the country's ailing economy. For a number of years higher education was seriously disrupted, so much so that in retrospect one can see the students of those years, 1963 to 1970, as a lost generation in terms of their wasted potential. Nonetheless, numbers of enrolled students increased. One estimate puts the number of state institutions in 1970 at 180 (including academies, colleges, etc.) and the number of private institutions at 200 (Thomas 1973 p. 258).

In the 20 years since 1970 there has been even more rapid expansion as a consequence of the government trying to respond positively to the increasing size of the 19 to 24 age cohort. In 1989 there were reportedly 49 state institutions of higher education and about 720 private institutions, and between them they catered for an estimated 1.6 million students of which 600,000 were in the public sector. This 1.6 million, however, represented only 8.5 percent of the age cohort, and the government has planned to increase that figure to 11 percent or 2,350,000 by 1993–94. Even so, that increase will not keep pace with the number of final grade school leavers, and the percentage of the latter who enter tertiary education is set to decline over the same five-year period from 52 percent to 48 percent (*Repelita* p. 653).

In addition to concerning itself with numbers, the government has tried to ensure a better quality of student by instituting new procedures for university admission which, in terms of ease of access, distinguish between ranked groups of tertiary educational establishments and yet still try to ensure a degree of equity (Watson 1986). These new procedures involving entrance examination scores and

high-school leaving results have only been introduced in the 1980s and are still somewhat experimental. Various criticisms have been made of them, for example, of the deleterious knock-on effect of cramming for multiple-choice entrance exams on the teaching of the senior high school curriculum (Somerset 1984 p. 12). Alongside these new procedures have come attempts since 1979 to streamline the curricula and change academic organization. The former system was based on a Dutch model of five years of university education comprising two stages, three years for the award of *Sarjana Muda*, followed by two years for the *Sarjana*, considered the terminal degree. (In practice it took much longer than five years to obtain the terminal degree and productivity was low.) In place of this there was introduced a four-year program modeled on the United States credit-point system leading to a first degree. Measures were also taken to monitor and give some form of recognition to the degrees awarded by private universities.

While the curriculum structure was being reformed, new diploma programs of one to four years' duration were also introduced into teacher-training colleges, in order to create a multistrata system which would be more productive and efficient. In 1976, with an eye on the labor needs of the country, the first polytechnic was set up in Bandung, soon followed by others, their number now amounting to 27 dispersed throughout the country. An Open University (UT) was set up in 1984.

At the graduate level efforts have been made since 1975 to designate various universities as graduate training centers. There are now ten of these, all but one in Java, which are intended to draw in staff from other universities for training and provide facilities for the award of master's degrees after two years, and doctorates after a further two or three years. A further development in graduate work has been the establishment within a chosen group of five universities of 16 Inter-University Centers (IUC), each with a responsibility for one particular field of research from among the following: engineering; computer science; biotechnology; food and nutrition; life-sciences; microelectronics; economics; and social studies.

3. Government, Administration, and Finance

3.1 The National, Provincial and Regional Level

The responsibility for higher education is now located in the Directorate-General of Higher Education (DGHE) in the Ministry of Education. There is also within the DGHE a Directorate of Private Higher Education, indicating the government's recognition of the need to assist and monitor the performance of the private sector. The Indonesian system of administration is highly centralized and hence, although there are provincial offices of the education department, higher educational establishments throughout the country are directly linked to the central office in Jakarta which controls their budgets and closely monitors their administration. Private institutions have more autonomy, but even they are subject to close government supervision. Islamic universities (IAIN) set up since 1960 are the responsibility of the Ministry of Religion. In addition there are various professional-qualification academies—civil service, accounting, and so forth—which are the responsibility of other ministries.

The goals for higher education are broadly determined by the National Planning Board (BAPPENAS) and are translated into a series of five-year plans (*Repelita* I, II, etc.) the first of which operated between 1969 and 1974. The overall mission of higher education is the *tridharma*, that is, the triple role of education, research, and public service. It is the responsibility of the DGHE to realize these goals in a way congruent with development plans. Effectively, this has been done only since 1974 when a team was set up to draft a blueprint for higher education based on an evaluation of the existing provision and an identification of urgent needs (Amiruddin 1978 p. 14). The blueprint for the long-term development of higher education was eventually brought out in 1977 and continues to guide institutional planning.

Subsequently, the DGHE has also set up policy bodies consisting of various subject consortia, as well as a new National Graduate Education Council, to assist the development of specific programs. In addition the rectors of universities are regularly called to the DGHE for individual consultation or work in committee. The day-to-day administration of research and development is the responsibility of a special division within the department to which foreign consultants are frequently attached. Advice from foreign observers is also available through the monitoring undertaken by the various loan agencies who contribute to developments in higher education: the World Bank; Asian Development Bank; the British Council; Ford Foundation; and so forth.

The budget for higher education is announced in each of the five-year plans as they are brought out, and public universities are almost entirely dependent on this central allocation, which as a portion of government spending has increased dramatically since 1974. Education in general consumes around 13 percent of expenditure and higher education takes about a third of this amount. In absolute figures the government is spending US$350 million on 600,000 students in public higher education and this figure is set to rise to ten times that amount by 1993–94. Private education has its own sources of finance— student fees and charitable bequests—but some government support is available through the establishment of regional coordinating agencies (*Kopertis*)

which share educational resources among private institutions (Craggs and Kennedy 1988 p. 5).

3.2 The Institutional Level

At the apex of the university system is the rector, who has general responsibility for the institution. Under the rector there are three deputy rectors responsible for academic, financial, and administrative affairs. Within the guidelines laid down by the DGHE and the financial constraints of their budgets, these four individuals have considerable control over the administration of universities. They may call people in and seek advice, but they are not responsible to any committees or boards. The rector is appointed directly by central government, and although the university is corporately allowed to suggest names of suitable candidates, the ultimate decision is the government's. With respect to some universities there are boards of trustees, but they do not exercise much control over the day-to-day running of the university.

Each university is divided into academic faculties which are further subdivided into departments. The faculty is headed by a dean who is assisted by a member of the academic staff, and the department by a head who is also assisted by an academic secretary. All these appointments are by election from among the academic staff with positions usually going in rotation to those who are more experienced. Non-academic staff and students will usually have good access to deans who exercise a substantial amount of control.

4. Faculty and Students: Teaching, Learning, and Research

According to official figures there are, in the early 1990s, 58,400 teachers in higher education and this number is expected to grow to 91,000 of which 59,400 will be in the public sector and 31,450 in the private sector by 1993–94 (*Repelita* p. 656). These numbers do not, however, give an accurate impression of the teaching capacity, because of the large number of teachers who are employed part-time. The private sector, for example, draws much of its staff from public sector employees in this way. The government has tried to reduce the amount of part-time teaching and to discourage public employees from engaging in other jobs. However, it recognizes that with the very low salaries paid to lecturers, it is unrealistic to expect total commitment to one institution or one job. The holding of several jobs does affect the quality of teaching. Furthermore, students often find it impossible to meet lecturers, since there are no individual rooms for members of staff, and after teaching, lecturers often leave the campus immediately.

The government has for a long time recognized the need to raise the quality of teaching, the low level of which, as is generally admitted (Amiruddin 1978, Cummings 1981), remains the most serious obstacle to improvements in the educational system. All lecturers are civil servants. Their promotions according to civil service grades used to follow automatically with seniority, but since 1975 the government has introduced a points incentive scheme to encourage self-advancement. Thus points can be earned for research projects undertaken, books written, and further degrees obtained (Hutagaol 1985 pp. 215 ff). The latter is especially encouraged by the DGHE since Indonesian academics are on the whole poorly qualified, few of them holding qualifications beyond first-degree level.

Unfortunately, although this incentive scheme has generated considerable activity, the positive results are slow to percolate through to the system as a whole, and teaching remains poor. Several factors contribute to this: university administration is inefficient and the standard of record-keeping low; there are no proper procedures for monitoring course content and teaching; library facilities are inadequate; knowledge of English, the language in which most of the university text books are still to be found, is abysmal; the nature of classroom instruction is authoritarian and discourages independent thought. All these factors persist through inertia within the system, largely perpetuated by staff being appointed from among graduates of the same institution. Such junior staff tend to follow the practice of their mentors and have no other models to adopt. Thus classroom teaching consists almost entirely of a lecturer reading out notes which are then duplicated for sale to students. Exams, often multiple-choice to avoid the burden of marking, are based simply on these duplicated notes. Not only are students not encouraged to read independently, lecturers themselves rarely read more than a minimum of two or three texts to prepare their courses. What libraries there are in the major universities tend to be underused by staff and students who are reluctant to borrow books in English which they have difficulty understanding.

The credit system introduced in 1975 has certainly streamlined the organization of courses, but there are still difficulties in completing a degree within four years. Students must take 150 credits over eight semesters to graduate. Of these some are made up of compulsory general courses; religion; state philosophy; and so forth. In addition they have to undertake practical work in rural areas, an innovation dating from 1973 designed to introduce students from rural areas to the realities of life for the majority of Indonesians, and to put into effect the notion of service to the community, one of the *tridharma*. The students, therefore, have a very heavy workload and the nature of the teaching they receive is not always inspiring. They are, however, surprisingly docile in relation to the organization of coursework. This con-trasts with their political militancy. Indonesian students have traditionally been heavily involved in political protest and were instrumental in toppling Sukarno (Bachtiar 1968). The New Order Government has tried to curb their political enthusiasm by confining them to the campus with measures adopted in 1978. These were only temporarily effective and students have been demonstrating again over local human rights issues.

5. Conclusion

The expansion in the educational system in general, and higher education in particular, which has been undertaken since 1975 indicates the strength of the government's commitment to raising the quality of life of the people through education. Moreover, the integration of educational planning with overall economic development is being carried out with a seriousness and thoroughness which are commendable. However, the investment in plant—in campus buildings, laboratories, libraries, and equipment—while creating the infrastructure for expansion cannot of itself guarantee improvements. Knowing this, educational reformers have tried to raise the quality of teachers in the universities through programs of graduate instruction, training in university administration, and the sending of staff abroad under various loan-agency schemes. Conditions within universities, however, have not changed as rapidly as had been desired, and educational planners should be considering further strategies to improve the quality of teaching and learning inside and outside the classroom.

Bibliography

Amiruddin A 1978 Pendidikan tinggi kita sekarang. *Prisma* 2: 14–21
Bachtiar H W 1968 Indonesia. In: Emmerson D K (ed.) 1968 *Students and Politics in Developing Nations*. Pall Mall Press, London, pp. 180–214
Craggs P, Kennedy J 1988 *Indonesian Education Market Survey: The Private Sector*. The British Council, London
Cummings W K 1981 Notes on higher education and Indonesian society. *Prisma*. 21: 16–39
Department of Higher Education 1989 *Higher Education Development in Indonesia*. Department of Higher Education, Jakarta
Heneveld W 1979 *Indonesian Education in the Seventies: Problems of Rapid Growth*. Southeast Asian Affairs 1979: 142–154. Institute of Southeast Asian Studies, Singapore
Hutagaol S 1985 The development of higher education in Indonesia, 1920–1979. Unpublished doctoral thesis, University of Pittsburgh
Phillips R P 1990 Higher education in Indonesia: Current issues and future plans. Unpublished document, British Council, Jakarta
Repelita [Five-Year Plan 1989/90–1993/94] Vol. II. State Printing Office, Jakarta

Somerset H C A 1983 *Secondary Education, Selection Examinations and University Recruitment in Indonesia: Some Key Issues.* Institute of Development Commissioned Study No. 3. Institute of Development Studies at the University of Sussex, Brighton

Thomas R M 1973 *A Chronicle of Indonesian Higher Education.* Chopmen Enterprises, Singapore

Watson C W 1986 Higher education in Indonesia. *Indonesia Circle* 41: 39–44

C. W. Watson

Iran

1. Higher Education and Society

Iran is situated in the Middle East region of south west Asia and covers an area of 1,648,193 sq.km. The capital is Tehran and the official name of the country since 1979 has been the Islamic Republic of Iran (IRI).

In 1988 the population of Iran was about 50 million. The majority of the population are Shi'ah Muslims, but there are also Sunni Muslims, Christians, Jews, Zoroastrians, and Baha'is.

The official language of Iran is Farsi (Persian), which is also the medium of instruction. Over the age of four years 61.6 percent of the population are literate, of whom 84 percent are in the school age range. School age literacy is 93.1 percent in the urban districts and 75 percent in the rural areas.

Iran's revolution of 1906 created a constitutional monarchy based on the principle of separation of state powers. In 1925 the Pahlavi Dynasty (1925–79) came to power. There were short periods of genuine parliamentary rule during this period, where the Majlis (The National Consultative Assembly) exercised democratic power without challenge. On the whole, however, both Reza Shah (1925–41) and his son Mohammed Reza Shah (1941–79) ruled more or less as absolute monarchs at the head of a bureaucratic–authoritarian regime.

The Revolution of 1979 finally led to the establishment of the Islamic Republic of Iran (IRI). The principle of the separation of powers remained largely the same as the previous (1906) constitution. The IRI is a theocratic system of government based on Islamic Laws. The constitution stipulates the responsibility of the government for the provision of education for all and the advancement of arts and sciences throughout the country (Article 6, Sect. b, IRI Constitution).

Higher education in Iran, since the Second World War, has undergone considerable qualitative and quantitative change. Up to 1979 it went through a gradual, and at times intensive, secularization phase. This was followed by a religio-political orientation as a result of the 1979 Iranian/Islamic Revolution. There has been a steady movement towards specialization, technological provision, innovation, and even democratization. This process is by no means complete and higher education in Iran is still in a state of flux and experimentation.

The history of higher education in Iran dates back 2,000 years. Famous institutions, such as the Academy of Jundi-Shapur (South West Iran), became intellectual sanctuaries for the learned men of the East and West in early Christian centuries. Later, during the Golden Ages of Islam (9th–13th centuries AD), higher education establishments, such as the Nizamiyyahs, in some Iranian cities, contributed to the advancement of learning and scholarship. Scholars like Avicenna, Farabi, Razi, Biruni, Ghazzali, Khayyam, Hafez, Sa'di, and Mawlana Jalal-al-din and numerous others are a testimony to the great intellectual and scientific philosophical achievements of Iranian culture and civilization.

Notwithstanding these contributions, devastating wars and invasions led to long periods of political and economic instability and thus to the downfall of many excellent centers of higher learning.

Iran's recent history of higher education goes back to the mid-nineteenth century when a renewed process of radicalism and reform engulfed the whole country. This wave of modernization brought political reform and ushered a new era of higher education. Dar-al-Funun (established in the mid-nineteenth century), was Iran's first modern higher technical college with the specific aim of solving Iran's urgent need for trained labor force.

Toward the end of the nineteenth century, the need for a more systematic training program at all levels was felt more strongly than ever. This eventually led to the gradual establishment of separate small colleges affiliated to various government ministries, such as the School of Political Science (1901); the College of Agriculture (1902); the School of Fine Arts (1911); the Boys' Normal School (1918), which was renamed the Teachers' Training College in 1928; and the School of Law (1921). However, a systematic approach to higher education had to wait until the 1930s when the Education Act of 1934 established the University of Tehran which brought all the hitherto small and separate colleges and schools of higher education under a single administration.

Tehran University was virtually the only university in Iran until the end of the Second World War. From this date on higher education became the focus of government concern and gradually the process of expansion, diversification and democratization began.

Throughout Iranian history, religion has been influential in the development of various types of higher education. Before the 1979 Revolution, the Ulama (religious leaders and teachers) were mainly responsible for the administration of religious colleges and seminaries, but since the Revolution, Islamic principles and Shi'ah values have provided the foundation for all educational establishments.

2. The Institutional Fabric of the Higher Education System

Higher education in Iran is a post-Second World War phenomenon. Since the 1940s, higher education has experienced a significant growth in scale and diversity in response to the challenges of modernization and economic development. The government has been mainly responsible for the provision of higher education. However, between 1960 and 1979 private initiative was also instrumental in establishing a wide range of independent and semi-independent institutions of higher education.

In the 1990s almost all institutions are state sponsored and come under the direct jurisdiction of the ministries of Education, Higher Education, and Hygiene and Medical Healthcare. There are a number of institutions affiliated to other ministries or state organizations, but their curricula and academic programs are approved and controlled by the Ministry of Culture and Higher Education.

The cycle of growth and development started immediately after the Second World War and continued at a steady rate until 1960. During this period, five provincial state universities (Tabriz and Mashad 1949, Abwaz 1954, Isfahan 1950, and Shiraz 1956) were established. The Higher Teacher Training College in Tehran became independent in 1955. Tehran Polytechnic and the Police University (1959) were also state owned. A number of small state-sponsored colleges and institutes, in such fields as social sciences, civil aviation, communication, telecommunication, nursing, and finance and accountancy, were also established. Abadan Institute of Technology was affiliated to the National Iranian Oil Company (1934) and was private. Tehran University was the largest and offered the widest range of studies. Most universities had faculties of medicine, letters, and agriculture. Despite urgent need for scientists and technologists only three universities had faculties of science or engineering.

From 1960 to 1979 higher education grew by leaps and bounds. A population explosion and the growing number of secondary-school graduates created a great demand for entry into institutions of higher education. Steady urbanization, industrialization, and economic development increased the need for specialists in all fields. The government, planning authorities, and the private sector came under increasing pressure to meet these demands. New universities and numerous public and private institutions were set up in many modern fields and subjects. The first private university of Iran, the National University, was established in Tehran in 1960. Later, in 1964, the first university of technology (Aryamehr/Sharif), a highly prestigious institution, was founded specifically to train scientists, technologists and engineers.

Westernization and modernization tendencies also prepared the way for the creation of some institutions along Western, particularly United States, lines. Examples of such institutions are the Damavand College for women, and the Tehran Management School. Shiraz University was reorganized and renamed Pahlavi University (1962–79).

There was a further expansion of teacher-training institutions. The Higher Teacher Training College in Tehran became the Teacher Training University in 1973 with several branches in the provinces. Numerous teacher-training colleges, for technical, agricultural, and vocational schools as well as for guidance centers were established. A few private and semiprivate-liberal arts colleges offered professional and specialized teacher-training programs. Many universities at central and provincial levels opened new faculties of education. An interesting innovation was the development of an Open (free) University in Tehran in 1972, with branches in the provinces. By 1976 it was ready to admit students into its teacher-training programs.

Thus, by 1979, Iran had developed a massive system of higher education offering diverse graduate and undergraduate courses. Moreover, the number of Iranian students studying abroad, mostly in medical and engineering fields, had increased from 10,000 in 1960 to over 60,000 by 1979.

In the two decades before 1979, higher education came under the close scrutiny of the government and the intelligentsia. Both parties were critical of the system, albeit for different reasons. Although the state was increasingly involved in the expansion and reform of higher education, the opposition groups did not approve of the system's basic orientation. After the Revolution, in June 1980, all the universities were closed down for a period of over three years. This was done in order to bring the university system under the Islamic code and put an end to the growing influence of the radical student organizations and their Marxist, liberal, or secular views. In line with this the Cultural Revolution Headquarters (CRHQ) was established to plan for the development of an Islamic higher education. This new revolutionary organization introduced some changes at the structural level, aimed at creating more homogeneous and centralized institutions by amalgamating a wide variety of small, independent or semi-independent higher colleges. Some of these institutions were named "higher education complexes." Gradually all the medical faculties, previously part of the universities, also acquired independent status, as medical science universities. The growth and composition of higher education since the Revolution are shown in Table 1.

In 1990, there were also about 131 teacher-training colleges for primary schools, 107 for rural schools, 10 for technical and vocational schools, and 19 institutes of technology. They offer a two-year associate degree (AA) and are all controlled and supervised

Table 1

Growth and composition of higher education since the 1979 Revolution

	1985	1988
Universities	24	26
Medical science universities	16	18
Higher education complexes	13	12
Faculties	4	4
Higher education schools	20	24
Others	—	1
Total	77	85
Total number of students	145,217	204,862
Total number of teachers	15,040	15,950

by the Ministry of Education. The numbers of teachers and students throughout the higher education system is shown in Tables 2 and 3.

An Islamic private Open University was established in 1981 with 73 branches in 70 centers. Entry is not restricted to secondary-school graduates.

There has been a gradual emphasis on research in both pure sciences and humanities in Iran since the late 1950s. The government allocates funds for research to each institution. There are also some centers within universities which are specifically set up for research purposes. Achievement in research centers varies substantially. During the 1970s medical faculties carried out the highest percentage of research, and social sciences, the second highest. Before 1979, a number of national and international agencies provided funds and experts for the purposes of research. However, inadequate research remains one of the great weaknesses of Iran's higher education.

Up to the mid-1960s, each university administered its own entrance examinations. In 1968, a national

scheme was adopted, and this has gradually been refined and standardized by the National Organization for Evaluation of Students attached to the Ministry of Higher Education. Thus, national entrance examinations are held every year in the summer. They have two parts: a general and a specialized test. Gradually, provincial universities introduced a quota system in order to reserve a percentage of their places for "home students." Before 1979 the Ministry of Higher Education also administered separate entrance exams for candidates seeking entry into nonuniversity institutions. However, since 1979, further changes have taken place in admission policies. These include an additional test on Islamic studies and religion, and an investigation into the moral and ideological orientation of the candidates. The quota system has also been reinforced to take into account the veterans of the 1980–88 Iran–Iraq War, and the families of the martyrs of the Revolution and the War.

Female students are not granted equal opportunities of entry into certain higher education programs such as some arts subjects and technological and veterinary courses. The overall number of candidates who take entrance exams increases every year.

Iranian institutions of higher education operate on a credit unit system with two academic semesters in a year. Before the Revolution successful completion of 140 credit units was necessary to obtain a BA degree (i.e., four to five academic years). For an associate (AA) degree, half this amount was required (i.e., two academic years). Since 1979, changes include an increase in the number of credit units from 140 to 160 for a first degree. This is partly owing to the introduction of about 15–20 extra credit units on Islamic culture and learning. At the MA and MSc levels, students are required to complete 45 to 50 credit units as well as submitting a dissertation in a period of two academic years. For a PhD degree, an

Table 2

Total number of teachers and students 1960–88 in all tertiary institutions

	1960	1965	1970	1975	1980	1985	1988
Teaching staff							
Male	—	2,250	5,677	11,561	14,422	12,759	13,296
Female	—	236	797	1,831	2,455	2,281	2,654
Total	—	2,486	6,474	13,392	16,877	15,040	15,950
Students enrolled							
Male	19,815	22,644	55,681	109,116	120,646	100,593	145,933
Female	—	7,039	19,027	42,789	53,571	45,216	58,929
Total	19,815	29,683	74,708	151,905	174,217	145,809	204,862

Table 3
Number of students in the universities and colleges in Iran by field of study

	1956	1962–63	1965	1970	1975	1980	1985
Social sciences	—	3,159	1,993	18,163	32,138	29,399	18,050
Humanities	3,213	7,859	8,268	14,704	22,298	26,350	18,047
Engineering	673	2,637	3,207	14,008	25,848	40,980	31,851
Medicine	4,328	6,180	6,993	10,000	14,965	25,848	32,604
Natural sciences	753	2,264	2,030	9,876	21,996	29,867	24,452
Agriculture	524	898	952	3,162	6,466	6,800	5,992
Fine arts	345	564	899	2,844	4,414	5,352	3,899
Education		1,074	1,062	1,951	4,013	7,033	7,769
Law	2,092	—	3,670	—	3,196	2,588	3,145
Total	11,928	24,635	29,074	74,708	135,334	174,217	145,809

original thesis plus a further 30 to 40 credit units are essential requirements for the course which is expected to take two to three years. All the degrees are awarded by individual universities or institutions. Affiliated institutions award their degrees through their sponsoring ministries.

3. Governance, Administration, and Finance

3.1 National Administration

Up to 1967, the Ministry of Education was responsible for all the universities and various institutions of higher education. However, after the Second World War, developments in higher education gradually created the need for the establishment of central coordination of further development, planning, and evaluation. The Ministry of Education was no longer capable of responding to the increasing pressures for diversification and innovation of tertiary education. Thus, from 1967 to 1968 the Ministry of Science and Higher Education was created. However, what emerged later and has continued ever since with some minor modifications was a system of higher education governed by a number of agencies with often overlapping and sometimes conflicting functions and responsibilities. The Plan and Budget Organization (PBO) determined the budget. The State Organization for Administration and Employment became responsible for employment of non-academic personnel, while the Ministry of Higher Education determined the salary scale of the academic staff. The Ministry of Labor determined some aspects of vocational training in higher education, while the Ministry of Agriculture took the responsibility for agricultural training.

Gradually numerous councils were set up to coordinate the overall activities of various agencies. For example, in the late 1960s the Imperial Council of Education was created to act as cultural coordinating agency defining goals and offering guidelines for budget, management, and evaluation. The Council for Educational Expansion approved the creation of new institutions. The Central Council of Universities and Institutions of Higher Education chaired by the Minister of Higher Education was responsible for all aspects of training and research, student selection, and admissions. Other agencies, for example, the councils for Medical, Nursing, Pharmacy, and Dentistry education, dealt with their respective fields. The Organization for Educational Evaluation controlled student selection and admission. The Institute for Educational Planning and Research was formed to act in collaboration with the PBO and the universities in formulating policies and planning.

During the decade 1968 to 1978 the Annual Educational Evaluation Conferences held in Ramsar acted as a platform for executive agencies, university leaders, and academics in analyzing educational issues and problems, proposing guidelines and suggesting new strategies. After the Revolution, however, the Ministry of Science and Higher Education was renamed the Ministry of Culture and Higher Education. Changes at the sociopolitical level brought about by the Revolution meant a sharp break from the previous administrative procedures and practices.

The Cultural Revolution Headquarters (CRHQ) was set up at the height of 1980 to denounce the objectives of the previous system of higher education and proclaim a radical change. The University Crusade, a radical Islamic student organization, pressed for extreme measures, while the Bureau of Seminaries and Universities was formed to bring secular education under religious examination.

From 1980 to 1984, the CRHQ gradually introduced its plans. During this period differences of opinion among members of CRHQ, the University Crusade and the Ministry of Higher Education became increasingly pronounced. This led to the abolition of CRHQ (1984) and the formation of the Supreme Council of Cultural Revolution (SCCR). This council remains the think tank and the executive body of higher education; all decisions made by it become law even without the approval of parliament.

When the universities gradually resumed their academic activities in late 1983, structural changes were the dominant feature of the new system. The Ministry of Higher Education again emerged as the supreme institution responsible for all the institutions of higher education. Within-system changes included the introduction of 15 credit units on Islamic culture and learning. There was no dramatic change in the content of social science courses and humanities, as had been expected, and the curriculum of many scientific and technological courses remained the same. However, changes in the stated goals and objectives of university education were more pronounced. Islamic philosophy and religious values provide the foundation of the new system.

In 1984, the Charter of the Administration of the Universities and Institutes of Higher Education was approved by the SCCR, and with this, the Iranian tertiary education entered its new phase. The University Crusade confined itself to cultural affairs, while universities have gained some stability in academic and administrative affairs.

All the institutions of higher education receive their entire budget from the central government. Before 1979 certain private institutions charged tuition fees, but even these received contributions from the government. In 1974 the state introduced a student loan system with the cooperation of the banks in order to ease the financial pressures of the students. After 1979, when all private institutions were declared public, tuition fees were also abolished, with the exception of those for the Islamic University.

Each institution of higher education is required to prepare its own budget along with a further development program according to the PBO's regulations. The PBO reviews all the proposed programs and budget requests and finally approves the programs, usually with some modifications. Once approved, each institution receives its allocated budget from the Ministry of Economy and Finance. This ministry has an auditor–treasurer in every higher education institution who controls spendings in accordance with the budget.

3.2 Institutional Administration

Administration of university education in Iran has undergone continuous change. The question of university autonomy has often been raised and attempts have been made to make university administration, and the appointment of chancellors, independent of the Ministry of Education and the political apparatus. There have been certain short-lived periods of autonomy, particularly in the 1950s.

At present, university administration is headed by a chancellor who is appointed by the SCCR, and aided by various councils, committees, and administrative units. In a typical university there are four vice-chancellors, each responsible for a particular unit, such as research, academic affairs, student affairs, and finance and administration. The highest decision-making body is the senate. It consists of all the deans and vice-deans of various faculties as well as the chancellor and his assistants. All the internal regulations, programs, proposals, and changes must have the approval of this body.

Within each university and higher education complex, there are a number of faculties. Each faculty is headed by a dean appointed by the chancellor and approved by the senate. In fact, a similar administrative pattern to that of the university is duplicated on a smaller scale at each faculty level. Each faculty is organized into subject departments led by a departmental head elected through departmental councils.

The director or head of a nonuniversity institution of higher education is usually appointed by the Minister of Higher Education.

4. Faculty and Students: Teaching, Learning, and Research

4.1 Faculty

The academic staff are classified as full professor, associate professor, assistant professor, and instructor. Research institutes and centers have research officers, assistant researchers, and research workers.

To be appointed to the position of an instructor a candidate must hold at least an MA or MSc degree and an adequate command of a foreign language. Since the 1960s regulations stipulate that after four years of successful teaching, instructors are required to complete their professional studies at a higher level. The Ministry of Higher Education is responsible for the provision of adequate funds and scholarships.

The minimum requirements for the position of an assistant professor are a doctorate and mastery of a foreign language. An assistant professor must teach successfully for a period of at least four to five years and also produce research publications before being promoted to the position of an associate professor. A similar procedure is adopted for promotion of an associate professor to the rank of a full professor with an additional emphasis on research and publication of at least one book and several articles in national and international scientific journals.

Applications for promotion are usually subject to the approval of the departmental councils, the faculty councils, and finally the university council upon the recommendations of the promotions committee. All faculties have representatives on the promotions committee. Members are regularly elected by the academic staff of various faculties for a fixed term.

Throughout the 1960s and 1970s, radical changes were made in recruitment, promotion procedures, and conditions of service. These included raising salaries for full-time staff, introducing a more flexible teaching timetable, encouraging research, introducing inservice training, and granting scholarships and study leaves.

After the Revolution, particularly during the Iran–Iraq War (1980–88), higher education experienced no further expansion. During the early years of the Revolution, purge committees had already identified "antirevolutionary" elements. These people faced varying fates: a considerable number of academic staff lost their jobs or were forced into early retirement while others left Iran and some even faced execution and imprisonment. A conservative estimate suggests that higher education lost at least 10 percent of its teaching staff.

During the enforced absence of students (1980–83), CRHQ initiated a scheme to engage the academics in research and publication. A publication committee was set up within the CRHQ with representatives from various institutions to supervise the scheme. Academics could choose either to translate a research work into Persian or work on a research project. The publication committee monitored the progress of the scheme. It was estimated that around 3,000 items were submitted for publication. Some have since been published and the rest are in the process of publication.

As universities resumed their teaching function, new regulations affecting the recruitment of academic staff came into force. Some academics, suspended earlier by Leftist and Mojahedeen Student Staff Committees were reinstated. Since the Revolution all teachers have been expected to be faithful to Islam, the Revolution, and the Islamic Republic.

In Iran, decades of repressive governments have prevented teachers from creating organized unions in order to protect their professional and academic interests. In the months preceding the 1979 Revolution, two faculty associations with somewhat different political orientations were formed which guided the university teachers' action in the revolutionary process. After the Revolution such organizations gradually lost their power and appeal. There are, however, some professional organizations such as the associations of Iranian physicians, architects, and psychologists which promote research through regular meetings, publications, and congresses as do other literary unions.

Since the 1960s a uniform standard has been adopted by many institutions for the number of hours to be devoted to teaching, student supervision, tutorials, research, and administrative work. Full-time academic staff are required to spend at least 40–44 hours per week at the faculty.

4.2 Students

In principle, access to higher education is open to all on the basis of competitive examinations. However,

up to the 1960s higher education was limited to the urban middle classes. The upper classes sent their children to study abroad at an early age. The quantitative expansion of higher education in the 1960s and 1970s broadened the basis of entry into higher education in terms of social class background. Granting scholarships to talented students to continue their higher education abroad has also allowed for upward social mobility.

Since 1979, however, there has been a deliberate attempt to limit study abroad and to encourage graduates to continue their education in Iran. Selection criteria have also been altered to allow a proportion of students from the lower classes who have served the causes of the Islamic Revolution to enter the tertiary level of education. In addition, students who are practicing Muslims have a greater chance of entry into higher education institutions. Some of these attempts have contributed to a breakdown of barriers of class and privilege. Other factors such as those of gender, religion, and political affiliation continue to limit higher education opportunities for certain sections of society.

Student unions representing corporate interests in Iran have been mainly political in nature. Universities and certain institutions of higher education, particularly in the 1960s and 1970s, were centers of dissent and opposition to the government. As freedom of association was limited, many Iranian students joined underground antigovernment organizations. In the 1960s and 1970s student sympathizers inside and outside the campus organized demonstrations, held strikes and meetings, distributed leaflets, and clashed with the police.

These groups, along with other revolutionary forces, played a decisive role in the Revolution of 1979. Soon after the victory of the Revolution and the collapse of the old university administrative structure, a power vacuum was created that was quickly filled with the newly created student/staff councils. Within each university faculty, these so-called "coordinating councils" took control of the academic and administrative affairs of higher education. From February 1979 to June 1980, a number of powerful student organizations whose political affiliations and loyalties ranged from Islamic to Marxist ideologies held university life under a tight grip. The government could no longer tolerate what it saw as the expansion of the Left and Marxism within the universities. Following serious clashes with students, particularly in Tehran University, in the spring of 1980, and the death of a number of students, opposition forces were crushed and the government ordered the closure of universities to students. Meanwhile, the University Crusade, a fundamentalist Islamic organization, and the Association of Students Following Imam Khomeini took control of student affairs. The Islamic Student Associations of the 1990s are strong university student unions which protect Islamic values on the campus and conduct many cultural and religious events.

5. Conclusion

Higher education in Iran has been shaped by socio-political and economic forces in the three decades since 1960. Before 1979, in an attempt to meet the urgent requirements of an ever-expanding administrative, economic, and industrial system, state authorities eagerly followed a policy of expansion, modernization, diversification, and secularization of higher education. Since 1979, Iranian revolutionary leaders have systematically challenged some of the basic assumptions of the previous institutions of higher education. The three-year university closure, damaging as it was for Iran's tertiary education, was justified by the authorities on the grounds of checking the "undesirable" process of "Westoxication" and "Secularization," and creating, in their view, a system of higher education based on Islamic values and norms.

It is too early to assess the educational outcome of the recent changes; a final remark will suffice, though. Iran's higher education has seriously suffered from lack of academic freedom in both pre- and postrevolutionary Iran. No doubt, political stability based on parliamentary democratic principles would enhance and institutionalize the process of intellectual independence and freedom of inquiry vital for Iran's higher education.

Bibliography

Iran Ministry of Science/Culture and Higher Education 1970–88 *Statistics of Higher Education*. Institute for Planning and Research in Education/Center for Educational Planning, Tehran

Manzur C 1971 University reform in Iran: problems and prospects. PhD thesis, Tufts University, Medford, Massachusetts

Parsa M 1989 *Social Origins of Iranian Revolution*. Rutgers University Press, New Brunswick

Samii A H et al. 1978 *Systems of Higher Education: Iran*. International Council for Educational Development, New York

Shamsavary P 1972 A comparative study of the relationship between education and economic development in Iran, Japan, USA. PhD Thesis, Institute of Education, University of London

Sobhi K 1983 Educational planning for engineering schools: a study of Iran between 1962 and 1982. *Higher Educ.* I2: 61–76

Tavassoli G A 1976 *Iran, Social Sciences in Asia (1)*. UNESCO, Reports and Papers in the Social Sciences, Paris

UNESCO 1960–88 *Statistical Yearbooks*. UNESCO Paris

Zonis M 1971 Higher education and social change: problems and prospects. In: Ehsan Yar-Shater (ed.) 1971 *Iran Faces the Seventies*. Praeger, New York, pp. 217–59

P. Shamsavary

Iraq

1. Higher Education and Society

The beginnings of Iraq's modern higher education extend to the early part of the twentieth century when a law school (1919), higher teachers' college (1923), and a medical college (1927), were established. Thereafter, there was a slow expansion in the number of colleges and courses offered, with Baghdad University formally established in 1956. The development of higher education remained slow until the early 1970s, when the education sector began to acquire priority in the developmental goals of the state. In 1974, the goals in the field of education were set as: the eradication of illiteracy; to make primary education a right available to all; to ensure free education to all; to expand higher education; and to coordinate and link education to national development needs. The implementation of these goals resulted in far-reaching changes that affected Iraq's system of higher education.

Though Iraq was under direct British rule for a short period (1914–32), British hegemony continued until 1958, when a revolution brought about a republican regime. The following 10 years were marked by a lack of political stability and economic development. After a new regime came to power in 1968, a break was made with the policies that dominated earlier Iraqi development. The oil industry was nationalized (1972), and agrarian reform, initiated in 1958, was radicalized and implemented. Vast financial resources were injected into the different sectors of the economy. The state became the initiator and arbitrator of societal development.

Iraq's economy has been characterized as agricultural. However, the influx of oil revenues contributed to change the pattern of economic activity and ensured a high annual economic growth. By 1987, the sectoral distribution of gross domestic product showed the share of primary sector was 13.6 percent, secondary sectors 39.8 percent, and tertiary sectors 46.6 percent. The sectoral distribution of the gainfully employed population indicated a different pattern, with 35.5 percent engaged in the primary sector, 25 percent in the secondary sector, and 39.5 percent in tertiary sectors. Those engaged in professional and technical occupations (i.e., requiring a third-level diploma) constituted only 10 percent of the economically active population of the country, hence the required role for higher education institutions in expanding this category of the population.

In 1987, Iraq's total population reached 16,335,199. A number of demographic features relevant to the education sector can be noted. With a high rate of annual population growth of 3.1 percent, the age structure of the population is biased in favor of young age groups (i.e., mainly those of school age). In addition, by 1987 only 29.8 percent of the population lived in rural areas. At the same time the attraction of the capital city, Baghdad, made its share of total population 23.5 percent, requiring a relatively high level of concentration of educational facilities in the city.

2. The Institutional Fabric of the Higher Education System

Since 1968, higher education has undergone a number of changes. One of the more recent has been the reintroduction in 1987 of private sponsored higher education. Within a year there were three such universities, offering between them courses in eight specializations leading to a bachelor's degree. Though this change represents an important factor in the sectoral delineation of higher education, public sponsored institutions remain overwhelmingly dominant.

Higher education is organized around two types of establishments: universities and technical institutes. Between the years 1960 and 1988 the number of universities increased from 1 to 13, and their colleges from 14 to 63, offering four-year courses leading to a bachelor's degree, and graduate courses leading to higher diploma, master's, or doctoral degrees. Except for the University of Technology (established 1975), which specializes in engineering, all other universities are basically multidisciplinary.

In 1985, as a response to an increasing demand for higher education opportunities, there was a positive shift in educational policies and priorities. Accordingly, there were marked increases in the number of universities, colleges, and courses. In addition, greater emphasis was put on research programs, making them an integral part of the universities. These programs are conducted by faculty and research students. Also, a number of ministries have specialized centers for research; however, formal coordination between the two types of research (university and nonuniversity) is somewhat lacking.

Prior to 1972 there were few technical institutes offering two-year postsecondary courses leading to a diploma. The development of this type of education was slow. The formal establishment in 1972 of a Commission within the framework of the Ministry of Higher Education and Scientific Research (MHESR), directly responsible for the development of technical education, signaled a salient change in higher education. By 1988 there were 28 such institutes covering all regions of Iraq, and offering a varied choice in courses. In addition, there are nine institutes established by other ministries (e.g., Education and Oil). These specialized institutes, while offering courses leading to a diploma, require their graduates to work for their respective ministry.

As with most aspects of higher education in Iraq, the processes for admission and selection are centralized and controlled by the MHESR. The Central Admissions Department annually specifies the regulations and size of enrollment for each department and specialization in consultation with the relevant university or technical institute. Though the successful completion of the national secondary school examination is the single most important prerequisite for admission to a bachelor or diploma education, within the last two years greater flexibility was introduced. Educational establishments were allowed to conduct interviews and entrance tests to improve the selection processes. Universities offering graduate degrees, though specifying a bachelor's degree as the basic admission requirement, have made the interview and entrance test an integral part of the selection processes. These innovations give a role to educational establishments in determining the size and quality of their intake; however, the role of MHESR is still dominant.

During the years 1960 to 1988, student enrollment in universities increased from 9,964 to 128,748, while for technical institutes the increase was from 2,296 to 47,018, achieving an annual rate of growth of 9.6 percent and 11.4 percent respectively. The basic trends in the above development can best be outlined through two basic changes. To meet the labor requirements of economic development, policy is to encourage the expansion of technical education. By 1988, out of the total number of students admitted to higher education, the percentage of those admitted to technical education was 45.5. During the above period, as a result of high enrollment, the percentage of higher education students in the population age group 20 to 24, increased from 2.7 to 10.4. This increase contributed to changing the education profile of the population.

3. Governance, Administration, and Finance

With the purpose of giving more power to educational establishments, a law was decreed in 1988 redefining the role of MHESR, its organization, and aims. The main role of MHESR was to be that of a coordinator, though major policy areas remained the domain of state central organs.

The formulation of national development plans, as they relate to the education sector, is an illustration of trends governing the development of higher education. Though the Ministry of Planning is responsible for the formulation of national development plans and the allocation of investment funds, the suggestions that determine projects originally come from the colleges and universities, and are reviewed and approved by MHESR; final consultations regarding project allocations involve universities, MHESR, and the Ministry of Planning.

The financing of higher education is undertaken through two channels. The Ministry of Finance "ordinary budget" covers the expenses of higher education, while the Ministry of Planning "investment budget" covers its capital investment. As a result of the eight-year war between Iraq and Iran, financial constraints affected both budgets. However, it is interesting to note that during the same period higher education witnessed its highest growth rates in enrollment and number of educational establishments.

In aiming to concentrate some power away from MHESR, the reorganization of 1988 stipulated the "department" as the basic unit in higher education structure. Accordingly a council is established for each department, college, and university, with their powers and duties specified by decree; and the higher the council the more authority it has. For major policy issues, final decisions regarding enrollment, curriculum, appointment of faculty, and establishment of new colleges and technical institutes rest with MHESR on the recommendation of university councils. Membership of these councils is by appointment, with representation from teachers unions and students unions.

4. Faculty and Students: Teaching, Learning, and Research

The period 1960 to 1988 saw an increase in the number of university faculty from 728 to 6,928, and technical institute faculty from 88 to 2,530, with a total annual growth rate of 9.1 percent. This growth was achieved through encouraging graduate studies, mainly abroad, and at Iraqi universities as well. While in 1980 around 85 percent of university faculty were Iraqi nationals, by 1988 the percentage had increased to over 96 percent.

The faculty is composed of four grades: professors; assistant professors; lecturers; and assistant lecturers. The MHESR Law of 1988 specified a master's degree as the minimum academic qualification for assistant lecturers, and a doctorate for lecturers and above. Experience in teaching, and research publications, are a prerequisite for promotion.

Due to rapid expansion in enrollment and the increasing need for teaching staff, the distribution structure of university faculty is biased towards junior grades with 39 percent assistant lecturers, and 39 percent lecturers, while assistant professors constitute 18 percent, and professors 3 percent ("others" 1 percent). The result of this distribution is to increase the teaching and research load on faculty. While the ratio of students to faculty is 1:19, the ratio of students to senior faculty (lecturers and above) is 1:30.

Through departmental councils, the faculty exercise their influence in shaping, among other things, the structure and content of degree courses, and exams. However, MHESR has the final decision regarding most aspects of the work of faculty,

whether it is the balance of hours between teaching, research, and administration, or the dates of exams.

The model of undergraduate courses is of the "specialist" single-subject type. Within this context it has a heavy concentration on science programs. During the period 1960 to 1988, the percentage distribution of enrolled students witnessed a shift towards exact sciences (from 29.7 to 45.7 percent), away from social sciences (from 40.2 to 28.5 percent), and humanities (from 17.2 to 13.4 percent), with education maintaining its share (between 12.9 and 12.4 percent).

One of the more remarkable changes affecting the student body has been the positive increase in the participation rate of females. During the above period the percentage share of females to total enrollment increased from 25.5 to 35.8 percent for university students, and from 9.7 to 32.7 percent for technical institute students. Given the trends in secondary education, the above participation rate for women will continue to expand.

5. Conclusion

In the 1970s and 1980s higher education in Iraq witnessed fundamental changes affecting its size, content, and role. Yet as the twentieth century closes, this development has to engage a number of issues; among them is the need for a closer assimilation of the requirements of the technological age. At the same time it has to maintain a balance between high quality education and the provision of educational opportunities that could keep pace with the demand for them. In a manner, such issues might seem contradictory, but in actual fact they all relate to making higher education more relevant to its society.

Bibliography

Al-Dujaili H 1963 *Development of Higher Education in Iraq*. Al-Irshad Press, Baghdad
Alnawwab N 1988a *Strategies and Policies of Education in Iraq*. Ministry of Planning, Baghdad
Alnawwab N 1988b *Supply and Demand for Faculty in Iraqi Universities*. Ministry of Planning, Baghdad
Central Statistical Organization 1989 *Annual Abstract of Statistics*. Ministry of Planning, Baghdad
Ministry of Higher Education and Scientific Research 1989 *Reform of Higher Education in Iraq*. MHESR press, Baghdad

N. Y. Alnawwab

Ireland

1. Higher Education and Society

Higher education in the Republic of Ireland is provided by a network of over forty institutions. In the university sector, some institutions are centuries old like Dublin University and its single college, Trinity, founded in 1592 by Queen Elizabeth of England, while Dublin City University and the University of Limerick were established as late as 1989. Two other university institutions, the National University of Ireland (1908) and the Pontifical University at Maynooth (1886) are federal structures with constituent and associated colleges. The nonuniversity sector has grown rapidly in the 1970s and 1980s and consists of the Dublin Institute of Technology, some specialist national institutions and ten regional technical colleges. This sector now caters for over 40 percent of current total enrollment.

1.1 Geographical Context

The island comprises two states, the Republic of Ireland covering 26 counties and Northern Ireland which covers six. The national frontiers have not changed since the 1920s.

In 1946 the Republic's population of 2.9 million was in the last stages of a demographic decline which began a century earlier and which continued unabated until its lowest point of 2.8 million was reached in 1961. Throughout the 1960s and 1970s net emigration fell dramatically, fuelled by economic expansion, and the rate of natural increase rose. Between 1971 and 1979 the total population grew at a rate in excess of 1.5 percent per year. This produced a demographic pattern which was at variance with the general European model of stability or decline. By 1980 the total population had reached 3.4 million.

The 1980s have witnessed a reversal of the demographic patterns established in the two preceding decades. Natural increase fell from a level of 41,000 in 1980 to 19,000 in 1990. In addition, net emigration levels rose dramatically especially in the years since 1985 and in the three years since 1987, net emigration has totaled 100,000. The outcome of the demographic patterns of the last decade is a decline in population from the peak of 3.5 million in 1987, a decline which is forecast to produce a level of 3.48 million by the year 2,000. The drop in birthrate which began in 1980 has already manifested its educational consequences with primary cohorts falling by 28 percent over the decade. The shrinking cohorts will flow through the postprimary schools and higher education throughout the 1990s.

While the demographic expansion of the 1960s and 1970s has been of general economic benefit, that benefit has not been shared equally among all the regions. While one in three of the population now live in the greater Dublin metropolitan area, which has continously increased its share of national population, all of the other regions, especially those on the western Atlantic coast, have experienced population share decline and the associated infrastructural consequences.

These Atlantic peripheral regions also contain most of the Republic's minority language group, those whose first language is Irish, the original vernacular language of the island, now spoken as a first language in three areas of the west coast. Over 1 million of the population regard themselves as capable of speaking Irish and 40 percent of all households report one member as capable of doing so. These western communities have provision for first and second level education in their vernacular but do not have comprehensive provision for higher education through the medium of Irish.

1.2 Economy

In the period since 1945 agriculture and associated rural economic activity constituted the major element of the economy. Forty years later agriculture is in decline and has been superseded by manufacturing industry and the services which are now the dominant economic sectors. Data on occupational and social class distribution over the 1970s and 1980s show the continued decline of farming and the related rise in the secondary and tertiary sectors. At 14.9 percent skilled manual workers form the largest group while the farmers' group, the third largest group in 1986, is in danger of being overtaken by nonmanual groups, who were much smaller than farmers in 1971. This shift in occupational and social group patterns is accompanied by a sustained high level of urbanization.

A high unemployment rate, 18.2 percent of the civilian labor force in 1991, and a high external debt have remained as stubborn features of the economy for most of the 1980s. However, reductions in public expenditure, a low inflation rate of 3–4 percent and the stable low interest rates of the early 1990s have achieved sustained economic growth with an increase of over 100 percent in GDP since 1980.

This has been catalyzed by a very successful program for national recovery, which produced moderated wage demands and industrial harmony, and a mutually acceptable social reform program. This program is likely to be followed by a similar ten-year program in 1991. Thus the contextual environment would suggest an optimistic medium-term prospect for the economy. A growth rate of 4 percent per year is forecast with inflation at between 3 and 4 percent, a falling rate of unemployment by 1993 being accompanied by a decreased level of net emigration.

1.3 Structure of Government and Main Political Goals

The Republic is a constitutional democracy with the President as head of state, elected by popular franchise and a bicameral parliamentary structure elected by a proportional representation voting system. The present government, in power since 1989, is a coalition of the populist and largest party, Fianna Fáil and the smaller right of center Progressive Democrats. The main political goals pursued by governments since the Second World War include economic stability, the development of indigenous industry and the reversal of net emigration trends. In the more open economic and political environment that European Community membership has brought since 1973 and with national currency tied in to the European Monetary System, social reforms, educational expansion and the promotion of advanced technology have assumed higher political priority.

The expansion and development of higher education has become a major priority since the mid-1970s. The objectives of higher education over the past decade include increasing capacity and output, controlling unit costs, and promoting and developing knowledge, skills and research capacity in economically relevant and strategic disciplines.

1.4 Religious Organizations

Since the foundation of Trinity College in 1592 carried such religious, denominational and political connotations and since throughout most of its history it was not available to the majority Catholic population, it was inevitable that the provision of higher education for Catholics would become a major political question in the nineteenth century. It was also inevitable that such a political quest would be invested with great significance. The Queen's Colleges, founded in 1849 as interdenominational institutions, were not acceptable to Catholic leaders, although attended by many Catholics; since an episcopal decree of 1876 forbade Catholics to enter Trinity College, it was natural that the National University of Ireland, from its establishment in 1908, was perceived as being essentially a Catholic university, though its charter did not permit the public endowment of chairs of theology. This denominational identification of the two major universities has been modified with time, especially as following the lifting of the episcopal ban on Catholic attendance in 1970 Catholic students now form 70 percent of Trinity's student body. All the institutions of higher education in the nonuniversity sector are *de jure* and *de facto* multi-denominational institutions.

2. The Institutional Fabric of the Higher Education System

Higher education became a major policy priority only after access to second level education was considerably expanded by measures introduced in 1967. Accordingly, as the numbers entering second level rose in the early 1970s and the completion rates to leaving certificate also rose, the demand for expansion in higher education grew dramatically. This expansion in higher education involved quantitative and qualitative dimensions, a rapid fourfold increase in full-time students since 1960, a considerable growth in the number and type of institutions, a significant increase in the volume of postgraduate

research and the development of new course modalities and programs.

The anatomy of the system may be formally described as having a binary structure with university and technological sectors; however, such a formulation does not accommodate fully the wide range of institutions or the administrative reality involved. Accuracy and clarity would best be served by using the labels "university" and "nonuniversity" to describe the sectors.

The central political responsibility for policy, funding and development in higher education rests with the Minister for Education and the Department of Education. This responsibility is discharged mainly through the aegis of two statutory bodies, the Higher Education Authority (HEA), which exercises an overall policy and funding role and the National Council for Educational Awards (NCEA), whose policy, course validation and certification remit cover most of the institutions in the nonuniversity sector. Whereas the universities exercise complete internal autonomy in their academic processes, most of the institutions in the nonuniversity sector seek course validation and accreditation from the NCEA.

As to the public/private status of the higher education institutions, the major discriminants relate to the degree to which institutions are funded by voted public funds and the process of student selection and admission. From Table 1 it will be seen that the major portion, 89 percent, of full-time students were catered for in 1987–88 in the universities and in the 18 institutions governed by local education authorities. All are funded from public voted monies and conduct their admission policies according to agreed criteria which are amenable to public sanction. Most rely on state funding for 70–80 percent of their current expenditure and derive the residue from student fees and private benefactions. The other categories of institutions, Colleges of Education and Other Institutions, comprise a wide range of institutions and are mainly private in governance and funding except Thomond College which is fully publicly funded and managed. These other institutions are private foundations, providing various third-level courses and attracting no public fiscal support.

General policy guidelines and fiscal policy are decided by the government, the Minister and the Department of Education. They are implemented by the HEA, which, in consultation with the institutions, determines levels of institutional funding and capacity for each academic year. In the university sector the two larger and older universities, Dublin University and the National University of Ireland, offer undergraduate and postgraduate teaching and research facilities across the full spectrum of academic disciplines. The recently created Dublin City University and the University of Limerick (until 1989 national institutes of higher education) offer a more limited curricular spread and research capacity, with

Table 1
The type and number of higher education institutions, the numbers of full-time students, by gender and total for 1987/1988

| | Institutions | | Students | | | |
Type	Number	Male	Female	Total	Group percentage
Universities	5	16,805	15,949	32,754	54.6
Colleges of education					
Primary	5	315	1,454	1,769	
Home economics	2	—	260	260	
Thomond	1	470	204	674	
Total	6	785	1,918	2,703	5.0
Technological & other colleges	8	4,841	3,575	8,416	14.1
Regional technical colleges	10	7,365	5,046	12,411	20.7
Other institutions	14	2,115	1,482	3,597	6.0
Grand Total	45	31,911	29,970	59,881	100

an intended emphasis on technology, applied science, business studies and engineering. The fifth university, the Pontifical University, is located at Maynooth, sharing a campus with the Catholic National Seminary, offering courses in canon law, theology and philosophy.

In the nonuniversity sector there are designated institutions which are attached to the NCEA and others which offer their own qualifications or are linked to university institutions. The Dublin Institute of Technology, comprising six federated specialist colleges, offers a wide range of courses at degree and diploma level, for some of which it utilizes the NCEA system and for others it uses a link with Dublin University. Numerically, the most significant of the designated institutions are the ten regional technical colleges, short-cycle institutions catering for 20 percent of the total higher education enrollment, which offer a wide range of subdegree and degree courses with an emphasis on the sciences, engineering and technology. In this sector are also included specialist national institutions such as the National College of Art and Design, the Army Cadet College, the College of Industrial Relations and the Institute of Public Administration. Among the other institutions in the nonuniversity sector are many seminaries and religious colleges offering general courses in the humanities to further education students. In the 1980s there has been a rapid growth in the number of small specialist institutions, with enrollments between 200–300, providing courses in professional/vocational disciplines linked to banking, insurance and real estate.

While expansion policies of the 1970s and 1980s have increased rapidly the number of institutions, a countervailing policy movement seeks to rationalize structures and generate more cohesion in the system. This movement towards rationalization has been concerned with: (a) the identification and specification, if not the limitation, of the number of institutions offering degree courses; (b) conferring university status on the national institutes of higher education; and (c) defining the education and research remit of the regional technical colleges and increasing their academic autonomy. The effect of this policy emerges also in the articulation of the colleges of education with the universities, in the sustained "unit cost" studies and the repeated attempts to reduce degree courses to a duration norm of three years.

In addition to the institutions already mentioned, there are also some specialist colleges of music, catering and agriculture which have links to local authorities or to government departments and which offer a wide range of professional and vocational courses.

Research is conducted and promoted both within the higher education system and outside it in specialist research bodies. Within the university sector, research is conducted as an integral and essential part of the dual mission of the university. Funding for such research activity is usually secured from joint university–industry projects or from the state research and development agency, EOLAS. During the recent past a growing and significant part of university research activity has been funded from European Community schemes, conducted jointly with cooperating university institutions in Europe. Recent developments in university–industry links have produced funding for the establishment of specialist research institutes within the universities, institutes which have disciplinary and program orientations towards the sponsoring industries. Within the nonuniversity sector research activity tends to be on a smaller scale and is more usually of an applied nature.

There are also specialist research bodies, established by public statute or by private benefaction, for whom research in specified disciplines is the main function. These bodies cover such disciplines as economics, agriculture and rural development, economic and social policy, physics and the humanities (including Celtic studies). They are funded mainly by the state but may also receive support by means of research contracts.

2.1 Admission and Selection Policies

Selection and admission policy is governed by competition based upon the results of national examinations. For all the institutions of higher education, except the colleges of education, admission procedures are governed by a coherent set of national criteria, administered by an independent national agency, the Central Applications Office (CAO), established by the universities in 1976. The Dublin Institute of Technology established a similar system in 1984 and more recently the regional colleges have harmonized their application procedures and schedules. It is proposed that the colleges of education should join the system without delay.

The dramatic increase in the demand for places over the 1970s and 1980s—there are now on average 2.5 applications per place—has driven the effective entry requirements well above the stated minimum academic entry criteria set by each institution. The selection process begins early in the calendar year when prospective students indicate their preferred institutions and preferred courses and also the subjects they are taking in the June leaving certificate examination. For each applicant the CAO confirms the relevance of the subject choice and its adequacy to the requirements of the institution and courses indicated. Following the publication of examination results, place offers are made on an order of merit basis. This process is continued until the available places and course capacities are filled.

Table 2
The percentage distribution of new entrants to higher education in 1980 and 1986, by level of prior education attainment and the change in the period 1980–86

Attainment[a]	1980[b]	1986[c]	Percentage change 1980–86
0	12.2	7.8	−4.4
1	11.5	10.7	−0.8
2	14.6	12.4	−2.2
3	15.3	13.7	−1.6
4	15.2	14.1	−1.1
5	12.6	13.5	−0.9
6	10.3	13.7	+3.4
7	6.8	11.5	+4.7
8	1.5	2.2	+0.7
9	0.2	0.3	+0.1

a Attainment is measured in terms of the number of subjects in which honors at higher level were secured in the leaving certificate examination   b New entrants in 1980 totaled 12,775   c New entrants in 1986 totaled 16,613

The average ratio (in 1987) of applications per place available was 2.5; in pharmacy, radiography and remedial linguistics, it was over 12.0, while for medicine, physiotherapy, veterinary medicine, law and dentistry it fell between 4.0 and 10.0. This variation in ratio of applicants per place according to discipline is related to the perceived social status and the potential earnings capacity of the resulting professional qualifications. It is also linked to the state policy of *numerus clausus* which operates in those fields of study which are most in demand. The high level of demand and the consequent keen competition have effectively raised the prior academic attainment levels of entrants in the past decade. As indicated in Table 2, the percentage of entrants with 4, 5 or 6 honors in the leaving certificate examination rose from 38 percent in 1980 to 41 percent in 1986, while the percentage with 7 or more honors rose from 8.5 percent to 14 percent in the same period.

Restrictions on access, at the national level, are mainly concerned with the overall capacity of the system and with specific quotas on admission to certain faculties such as medicine, dentistry and veterinary medicine. Such policy restrictions have been in force since the early 1970s. In addition some faculties exercise academic restrictions by requiring specified subjects for some courses in addition to the general admission criteria, for example, mathematics, for engineering, biology for medicine.

Selection and admission procedures to postgraduate courses and to postgraduate research is conducted independently by each institution. It usually involves a minimum requirement of high honors achievement in the relevant disciplines of the student's primary degree course.

2.2 Quantitative Developments in Higher Education

As indicated in Table 3, the period since 1960 has witnessed a sustained increase in full-time student numbers in higher education. Since 1955 the quinquennial growth rate in enrollment has ranged from 26 percent to 39 percent (Clancy 1988). The total enrollment is still rising, due to both demographic and participation factors and is expected to reach its high point of 74,000 in 1999 or 2000; it is projected to fall to 67,000 five years later. Participation by females has increased dramatically from a total of 12,700 in 1975 to over 30,000 in 1989. Although the completion rate to leaving certificate for girls has exceeded that of boys since the mid-1960s, the relative gender enrollment ratio has always favored males and is only now, as indicated in Table 3, approaching parity.

The distribution of new entrants across different institutional types has recently favored the non-university sector; prior to 1980 the universities catered for the majority of new entrants. In the period 1980–86 the university sector enrolled under 45 per-

Table 3
The number of full-time students in higher education, by gender and total for the stated years 1960–90 and projected numbers for the stated years 1992–2006 (in thousands)

	1960–61	1965–66	1970–71	1975–76	1979–80	1980–81	1984–85	1988–89	1989–90	1992–93	1998–99	2005–6
Students	15.4	22.1	26.2	33.1	38.9	41.5	52.1	62.9	66.3	71.4	74.2	67.2
Male				20.4	22.1	23.6	28.3	33.9	35.5			
Female				12.7	16.8	17.9	23.8	29.0	30.8			

cent of new entrants, the nonuniversity institutions between 50 and 53 percent, while new entrants to colleges of education fell from 9 to 5.5 percent (Clancy 1982, 1986). In regional technical colleges growth was particularly strong throughout the 1980s. They now enroll 20 percent of new entrants.

Since 1960 the number of postgraduate students has risen by a factor of 20. Standing now at over 6,000, it represents 10 percent of the total student body in higher education.

The percentage of 20–24 year-olds in full-time education has increased by a factor of two since the 1960s. As indicated in Fig. 1, it has risen from 7.4 percent in the mid-1970s to 12.2 percent in recent years.

2.3 Structure of Qualifications

For most of the system the basic course is the primary degree of three or four year's duration, culminating in the award of a bachelor's degree. At postgraduate level, the master's degrees (MA, MSc, MEd, etc.) are usually gained after a course or a research project over two academic years. The doctorate usually requires a further three years study or research. In the university sector, these degrees are awarded by the individual universities; within the federated

National University (NUI), the senate of the university is the awarding body. One-year postgraduate diplomas are also available.

In the nonuniversity sector, the National Council for Educational Awards (NCEA) is the main certification body, awarding qualifications at sub-degree, degree and postgraduate levels. At the sub-degree level the national certificate relates to a two-year course, the national diploma to a three-year *ab initio* course or a one-year addendum to a national certificate at appropriate performance level. The degree is awarded following a four-year course and the graduate diploma following a one-year course. The other postgraduate qualifications in the NCEA domain follow the normal specifications as detailed for the universities.

2.4 Graduate Training Programs

Normally graduate studies begin immediately after the primary degree has been obtained, except in the case of students of professional or vocational disciplines where some years of vocational experience are usually required before proceeding to a postgraduate course. For admission to a postgraduate course, at master's or doctorate level, the student must hold an honors primary degree at first or upper second class level in the relevant subject. It is also possible, in some disciplines, to gain entry to a postgraduate course by taking a preliminary qualifying course. Most graduate training programs provide relevant research training modules as part of the core content.

3. Governance, Administration, and Finance

3.1 National Administration

The primary responsibility for the development of higher education rests with the Minister for Education and with the Minister's Department, in which an administrative division, under an Assistant Secretary, deals exclusively with higher education policy issues. All voted public funds for higher education are channelled to the institutions by means of the yearly estimates of the Department of Education, following debate and sanction by the Dáil (parliament).

The state's functional relationship with the higher education system is exercised through the Higher

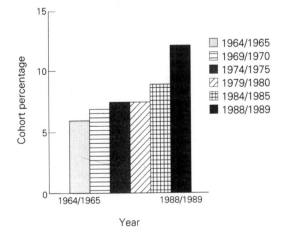

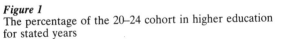

Figure 1
The percentage of the 20–24 cohort in higher education for stated years

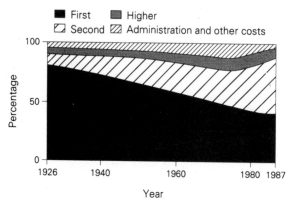

■ First ■ Higher
▨ Second ▨ Administration and other costs

Figure 2
State expenditure by level of education 1926–87

Education Authority (HEA) in a different mode for each of the sectors. The HEA is charged with policy and funding responsibility for all the universities and for the other designated national institutions. In addition the HEA exercises advisory powers over the whole higher education system. The authority also carries out various central research and planning functions related to both university and nonuniversity sectors. They include the development of academic computer networks and the attachment of Irish institutions to such networks, the promotion of research and study projects on aspects of higher education policy, the academic recognition of external qualifications, and the promotion of international exchange schemes principally by acting as the national center for such European Community schemes as ERASMUS and COMETT.

In both sectors umbrella interest groups seek to represent sectional viewpoints and to influence policy, heads of universities, principals of regional technical colleges and the Federation of University Teachers constitute typical examples.

The only subnational agencies which are involved in the administration of higher education are the local authorities, county councils, urban councils, city corporations, and so on, which are usually represented on the governing bodies of universities and colleges. Education committees of county councils are directly responsible for the administration and governance of the regional technical colleges. Legislation is being prepared which will give these colleges a greater degree of academic and administrative autonomy.

Education policy has been a central element of socioeconomic planning since the 1960s and within the recent national development strategies, higher education has been emphasized as an area for investment and as a contributory ingredient of economic growth. In such plans projected levels of expenditure and levels of enrollment are identified for each level of the system. Within higher education, targets are specified for the sectors and the main priorities are identified.

The planning process is frequently assisted by special ad hoc commissions or interdepartmental committees. While the commissions undertake large-scale analysis of policy, the committees are concerned more with specific planning tasks such as projecting capacity needs in a declining demographic scenario, deciding patterns of discipline allocation and associated resources or determining how research activities should be funded.

The response of higher education to such planning exercises is evaluated by means of the normal departmental reporting procedures. Specific issues are occasionally examined by externally commissioned studies, such as the current unit cost exercise which is being conducted in both sectors.

The state provides current and capital funds to the higher education system by means of the estimate votes of the Minister for Education. These votes cover public expenditure at all levels and the associated administrative structures. Figure 2, showing the relative percentage distribution of state funding by level in the period 1926–87, illustrates that as the system expanded and the earlier emphasis on first level declined, the higher education funding allo-

Table 4
The total recurrent income and expenditure of the universities[a] for the stated years 1970–88 (in millions of pounds) and the percentage of income derived from the state and from student fees

	1970–71	1975–76	1980–81	1985–86	1987–88
Expenditure	8.9	24.8	62.8	106.4	123.6
Income	8.4	25.1	62.2	105.7	123.5
Percentage income derived					
State	73.7	84.9	86.5	71.4	70.2
Fees	26.2	13.4	12.2	25.2	26.9

Source: HEA Reports 1970–88
a The institutions involved are the colleges of the National University of Ireland, Trinity College, and St Patrick's College, Maynooth

cation rose from 4 percent to over 11 percent. State expenditure on education as a percentage of all services has varied from a high of 20 percent in the 1920s to a low of 11 percent in the 1950s; in the 1980s it was in the 15–20 percent range.

The funding sources of higher education are threefold: (a) the state; (b) student fees; and (c) benefactions and research earnings. During the past three decades the relative share of institutional funding from these sources has altered appreciably. As indicated in Table 4, the levels of recurrent income and expenditure in the university sector since 1970 have grown by an average factor of 14. This growth has been accompanied by a shift in the relativities between state income and income derived from student fees. The state portion of university income rose from 73 percent to 86 percent during the 1970s but has declined to 70 percent in the 1980s. This decline in state support for the universities has resulted in a severe 9 percent reduction in staff in 1987–88 and a state-imposed pay limit on all institutions. The outcome is that most universities have accumulated deficits on recurrent expenditure in the years since 1970. Most of the institutions derive between 3 percent and 5 percent of their recurrent income from private and corporate sources and some have sought private or corporate funding for capital projects. Table 5 shows the total state expenditure on education and on higher education for the years 1960–90.

3.2 Institutional Administration

Most higher education institutions have a two-tier structure in their governance; a governing body deciding general policy, and an academic body which formulates and implements policy on academic and professional issues. The composition of these bodies and the provenance of their membership may differ as between the older Dublin University and the colleges of the National University of Ireland and the newer universities created in the 1980s. External political representation is likely to be a feature of the newer institutions.

Governing bodies usually have the final and decisive role in appointments, major policy issues and in sanctioning the decisions of the academic councils, which are more concerned with immediate academic issues of daily administration. This is a pattern which is common to both the university and the non-university sectors.

Most institutions, especially the older universities, are organized on a faculty basis, with faculty deans forming an inner academic standing committee within the broader academic council. In the more modern institutions academic power may be exercised through faculty, school or department structures. In either case membership of the effective academic unit is usually confined to all full-time members of the faculty. Students are now represented on most structures from department to institutional levels but are excluded on such bodies from all evaluation and examination processes.

In faculties and departments, deans and professorial heads of department chair committees which determine policy on administrative and organizational matters. Deans are elected for a fixed term and some department headships rotate. These faculty and departmental structures and other base units usually control nonpay budgets, and organize teaching, other duties, and other policy questions at this level. They are also represented on appointment committees and other central policy groups.

4. Faculty and Students: Teaching, Learning, and Research

4.1 Faculty

Table 6 shows the growth in the number of academic and other staff in the HEA institutions in the period 1970–85. In this period staff numbers throughout higher education grew in line with student numbers. This linear expansion pattern was halted by the government restrictions of the 1980s which sought redundancies and early retirements without replacement.

The academic staff structure in higher education may vary in detail according to institutional age and traditions but nowadays there are well-defined grades

Table 5
State current and capital expenditure on education and on higher education (in millions of pounds) and percentage expenditure on higher education, for quinquennial years 1960–90

	1960	1965	1970	1975	1980	1985	1990
State expenditure on higher education	1.00	3.60	9.53	25.10	61.90	116.60	227.00
State expenditure on education	16.72	31.96	75.60	215.70	540.20	1,017.50	1,227.50
Percentage	5.98	11.25	12.61	11.63	11.46	11.46	17.77

Source: Department of Finance

Table 6
The number of full- and part-time academic and other staff in HEA designated higher education institutions for the years 1970–85

	1970	1975	1980	1985
Academic staff	1,907	2,279	2,828	2,759
full-time	1,059	1,291	1,837	1,814
part-time	848	988	991	945
Other staff	2,325	3,025	3,604	3,621
full-time	2,325	2,776	3,363	3,225
part-time		249	241	396

Source: HEA Reports

common to all institutions. These are assistant or junior lecturer, lecturer, senior (statutory) lecturer, associate professor and professor. All of these ranks are attained by open competition or by internal promotion procedures. In addition the titles of research associate or research professor are employed for those who enter the structure outside the normal competitive procedures. Initial appointment is at lecturer or junior lecturer level. Promotion occurs by internal procedures, usually based upon objective assessment of performance in research and teaching, utilizing peer evaluation.

In Irish institutions of higher education faculty are designated as employees of the individual institution in which they are employed; in no sense are they regarded as civil servants even though their institutions are dependent to a large extent upon public funds.

Faculty recruitment and appointment varies by institutions. In universities it is an institutional function, ratified by the ultimate university authority while in the nonuniversity sector it is conducted by the board of the institution.

It is difficult to compare the relative career and status of faculty within different institutions. Older institutions have established reputations and traditions in scholarship and research. The newer institutions, despite their glamorous poses in some fields of technology, have yet to set widely recognized levels of attainment across different fields of scholarship.

The majority of faculty members in the university sector are represented by the Irish Federation of University Teachers, a trade union, affiliated to the national Congress of Trade Unions, which negotiates conditions of employment with management on behalf of its members. In the nonuniversity sector, most of the faculty are members of one or other of the educational trade unions.

Within the higher education system there is no uniform arrangement as to the disposition of faculty time between teaching, research and administration. It is more likely to be an institutional matter than a

sectoral issue in the university sector and within the nonuniversity sector there may be a stated minimum of teaching hours imposed by the board or by the government in the context of negotiations on salary and grading. In the university sector it is usually decided at departmental or school level.

4.2 Students

Over 40 percent of all entrants in 1980 and in 1986 entered fields of study in science and technology. Commerce was second highest at 20 percent in 1980 and 22 percent in 1986, while humanities at 16 percent in 1986 was slightly up on the 14.6 percent of 1980. In general, distribution over fields of study has shown little change during the 1980s but shows a major pattern change from earlier decades; in 1964–65 the sciences enrolled 14 percent of all full-time students while humanities enrolled almost 52 percent.

Gender is a major discriminant in field of study; in 1986 over 40 percent of male students entered technology and only 7.6 percent of females did so, while twice as many females as males entered humanities in that year.

The most reliable data on social class is that contained in the Higher Education Authority studies conducted by Clancy (1982, 1988) and the earlier data in *Investment in Education* (1965). Table 7 shows the economic status of new entrants 1986 and participation by social group for 1980 and 1986. The 1986 data indicate that five social groups (higher professional, salaried employees, lower professional, employers and managers, and farmers) were over-

Table 7
The socioeconomic status of 1986 new entrants to higher education and the participation ratios by socioeconomic group for 1986 and 1980

	Entrants[a] 1986	Participation 1986	Ratios 1980
Farmers	20.8%	1.45	1.04
Other agricultural occupations	1.4%	0.48	0.21
Higher professional	12.0%	3.0	3.93
Lower professional	9.2%	2.14	2.29
Employers & managers	18.2%	1.9	2.75
Salaried employees	6.2%	2.30	2.93
Intermediate non-manual workers	9.8%	0.96	1.11
Other nonmanual workers	5.7%	0.45	0.50
Skilled manual workers	12.9%	0.51	0.51
Semiskilled manual workers	2.5%	0.42	0.49
Unskilled manual workers	1.3%	0.16	0.11

Source: Clancy 1988
a Total numbers of entrants in 1986=14,388

represented and five groups (unskilled manual workers, semiskilled manual workers, other non-manual workers, other agricultural occupations, and skilled workers) were underrepresented among entrants to higher education.

Student support schemes, grants and scholarships, are structured to take account of family income and size, yet the social group disparities persist. In 1986/87 grants were received by over 11,000 students with a total value of over £21 million and over 10,000 students qualified for European Social Fund grants. It has become apparent that the inequalities in participation rates in higher education do not begin at that level but have their origins in the second level in varying completion rates and differential provision in school curricula which vary by school type and size.

All institutions have constituent unions of the Union of Students of Ireland which represents all sectors of the system and has over 95 percent of student affiliation. It is funded by deductions from student fees and from institutional grants, has a full-time officer board and provides various services for students, besides participating in institutional government in all spheres except examination and evaluation.

Course content in the universities is defined at departmental level and sanctioned or coordinated at faculty level. In the nonuniversity sector institutions are regularly evaluated at department, school or course level by the National Council for Educational Awards and all new courses require the prior approval of the Council. The Council employs assessment panels drawn from the higher education system and industry to conduct such assessments.

Undergraduate studies in the universities are generally founded on subject choices within the one faculty; more usually programs are single-subject or two-subject specialist courses. In the newer universities where the academic structures are less rigid, subject combinations are less confined by faculty boundaries and a credit unit system is employed in some institutions.

Students are assessed by formal written examination usually at the end of each year of their course. Some institutions or departments use continuous assessment or assignments on specified topics as additional forms of assessment. Essays are also used as partial instruments of evaluation in some subject areas while laboratory and other practical forms of assessment are regular elements of the process. "Open book" evaluation is also employed.

5. Conclusion

Higher education participation rates have risen dramatically over the 1970s and 1980s and competition for places has become increasingly keen. Demographic changes in the 1980s will result in smaller cohorts passing through second level and entering higher education before the end of the century. Current government policy favors raising productivity within the system by controlling unit costs, increasing throughput without commensurate capacity increases and promoting short-cycle courses. In terms of the sectoral balance, the nonuniversity sector has grown considerably and is likely to increase further over the next 10 years. Due to a high dependency rate it is unlikely that the economy will in the near future be in a position to fund the higher education system at a level which would accommodate all those who are qualified. Seeking higher education in other countries, a practice which developed in the 1980s, is likely to continue and to expand, catalyzed by the various European Community exchange schemes.

Bibliography

Clancy P 1982 *Participation in Higher Education*. HEA, Dublin

Clancy P 1988 *Who Goes to College?* HEA, Dublin

Department of Finance *Estimates for Public Services*. Dublin

Higher Education Authority 1974 *Progress Report 1974*. HEA, Dublin

Higher Education Authority 1985 *General Report 1974–84*. HEA, Dublin

Higher Education Authority 1987 *Women Academics in Ireland*. HEA, Dublin

Higher Education Authority [annuals] *Reports, Accounts and Student Statistics*. HEA, Dublin

National Council for Education Awards *Annual Report*. NCEA, Dublin

O'Buachalla S 1988 *Education Policy in Twentieth Century Ireland*. Wolfhound Press, Dublin

OECD Survey Team 1965 *Investment in Education*. EOCD, Dublin

S. O'Buachalla

Israel

1. Higher Education and Society

Higher education institutions in Israel share goals with similar institutions elsewhere: labor force training; furthering economic development; scientific research; enriching culture; and transmitting and advancing knowledge in general (Clark 1983). In addition to these general goals, Israel's higher education institutions play an important role in the strengthening of Jewish scholarship and the transmission of its culture as well as forging cultural links with the Jewish people in the Diaspora.

Indeed, the sociohistorical roots of higher education in Israel are connected with the Zionist idea of cultural and national revival (Ben-David 1986). Thus, the Hebrew University founded in 1918 and opened in Jerusalem in 1925, was meant to help generate the Jewish cultural revival by becoming an academic center for research in Judaic studies, humanities, and sciences. Its complementary institution, the Technion, Israel Institute of Technology, founded in 1912 and opened in 1924 in Haifa, was devoted toward realization of the Zionist program of providing the pragmatic technological and technical needs of the *Yishuv*, the Jewish community in Palestine, by training engineers and technical personnel (Iram 1983, Ben-David 1986). Thus, the higher education enterprise in Israel was conceived from its beginnings as the responsibility of the Jewish people throughout the world and not only of those in Palestine and later in Israel. Indeed, the supreme authority of these two institutions, the Boards of Governors, were composed of prominent Jewish individuals in the fields of science, arts, management, and economics, and societies of friends of Israel in various parts of the world. Today Diaspora Jewry is represented on the governing bodies of all Israeli universities.

1.1 Geographical Context

The area of Israel within its 1949 armistice borders is 20,700 square kilometers. In addition, Israel controls "administered territories" of about 7,500 square kilometers occupied in the 1967 war from Syria, Jordan, and Egypt. These territories are not dealt with here. They are administered by military government according to regulations in force prior to the occupation. The state is bounded on the north by Lebanon, on the northeast by Syria, on the east by the Hashemite Kingdom of Jordan, and on the southwest by the Gulf of Aqaba/Eilat and the Egyptian Sinai Desert (*The Middle East and North Africa* 1989 p. 505).

Israel's total population in 1988 was 4,476,800 of whom 3,659,000 (81.7 percent) were Jews and 817,800 (18.2 percent) non-Jews. Of the non-Jewish population, 14.2 percent were Moslems, 2.3 percent Christians, 1.7 percent Druze and others (Circassians and Ahmadis) (Israel Central Bureau of Statistics 1989 p. 3).

One of Israel's most striking characteristics is the rapid increase in its population. The main source for growth in Israel's population was immigration, accounting for 30 percent of the yearly increase in the total population and 46.2 percent in the Jewish population between 1948 and 1988 (Israel Central Bureau of Statistics 1989 pp. 39–40). In the early 1990s, Israel remains a migrant society. Of the 2,315,900 Israeli-born Jews only one-third (33.9 percent) were second generation Israelis. Of the total Jewish population only 21.5 percent were second generation Israelis (Israel Central Bureau of Statistics 1989 p. 83).

Israel is also a pluralistic society. Nationally there is a Jewish majority and a non-Jewish, predominantly Arab, minority. Linguistically, there are two official languages: Hebrew and Arabic. As a result of national, religious, and linguistic pluralism, separate educational systems emerged: Jewish; Arab; and Druze (Mar'i 1978).

The Jewish majority is diversified ethnically, religiously, culturally, and educationally. Ethnically, in the sense of country of origin, there are *Ashkenazim*, namely Jews whose origin is in Eastern and Central Europe and *Sephardim* or "Orientals," Jews from the Mediterranean Basin and other Arab and Moslem countries (Patai 1970, Shama and Iris 1977). Israeli Jews are also divided into "religious" and "nonreligious" (Don Yihye 1975). Culturally, diversity arises from the different ethnic groups who brought from their countries of origin different customs, ceremonies, attitudes, values, and ways of life.

The population density of Israel at the end of 1988 was 201 per square kilometer. Three-quarters of the Jewish inhabitants and two-thirds of the non-Jewish population are concentrated in the coastal strip. The northern and particularly the southern district, comprising about two-thirds of Israel's land area, are sparsely populated. More than 88 percent of the population is defined as urban, that is, residents in localities with 2,000 or more inhabitants. However, the rural–urban division in Israel is of small significance, as regards economic status and education provisions.

1.2 Economic and Occupational Structure

Israel's economic development was affected by such objective difficulties as: heavy expenditure on defense (absorbing one-quarter of the budget) as a result of the continuous Arab–Israeli conflict; the need to absorb mass immigration, about half from underdeveloped, semifeudal, traditional societies in the Middle East and North Africa, lacking formal education and skills required by a modern industrial-oriented economy. Israel's economy was adversely affected also by scarcity of water and natural resources. Despite these difficulties, during the years 1951 to 1972 the Gross National Product (GNP), at constant prices, rose by an annual average of 10 percent. From 1973 onward the rate of growth decreased considerably to 1.3 percent in 1976 and 1977, raised to 4.7 percent in 1978, registered no growth in 1982 and increased by less than 1 percent in 1983 (Israel Central Bureau of Statistics 1989). Another significant factor affecting the economy was a rising annual rate of inflation which exceeded 100 percent every year between 1980 and 1983 reaching 190 percent in 1983 and soaring to 444.9 percent in 1984. The current deficit on the balance of payments rose steadily. The sharp rise in inflation and in negative balance of trade have forced the government to adopt austerity programs of reduction in planned governmental expenditure, price and wage freezes, reductions on subsidies on basic food stuffs, public transport, and services including educational services. The economic stabilization program launched in July 1985 restrained the annual inflation rate since then to less than 20 percent in 1986, and 16.1 percent in 1987, the Gross Domestic Product (GDP) resumed growing moderately to 2.2 percent in 1986 and 4 percent in 1987. Unemployment in the civilian labor force reached 7.1 percent in 1986, 6.2 percent in 1987, and 6.4 percent in 1988.

The civilian labor force at the end of 1988 totaled 1,555,000 or 51.4 percent of the population aged 14 years and over, about 39 percent of women, and 61 percent men. An important population characteristic is the relatively high proportion of dependants, with one-third aged 14 years and under. As a result the ratio of the labor force to the total population is less than 35 percent, low by European and American Standards (Israel Central Bureau of Statistics 1989 p. 6, *Middle East and North Africa* 1989 p. 505). Economic development has transformed Israel's occupational structure. Between 1950 and 1988 the proportion of employed persons engaged in the primary sector (agriculture) declined from 17.6 percent to 4.6 percent, that engaged in secondary (production) from 32.8 to 28.4 percent, while the proportion of persons employed in the tertiary sector (services) rose from 49.6 to 67 percent. A concurrent shift has also occurred in the labor force from manual labor and other low-status employment to occupations which require higher level of education and are regarded higher in social prestige (Israel Central Bureau of Statistics 1989 p. 7).

1.3 Structure of Government

Israel's government and politics share basic democratic principles and practices derived from, and associated with, Western parliamentary democracies. National and local elections are strictly proportional, reflecting multiparty competition. No single party has been able so far to secure a majority of seats in the 120-member Knesset (parliament); as a result all governments were formed by coalition between political parties. The Arab and Druze citizens of Israel enjoy full rights of citizenship and formal equality including equal rights in education. However, recognizing the identity of its non-Jewish citizens, the state provides the existence of a separate Arabic system of education with Arabic as the medium of instruction at all levels with the exception of higher education. Unlike other levels of the educational system which are administered directly by the government the higher education system is largely autonomous, in spite of governmental funding of 60 to 80 percent of its budget. Government funding reflects the crucial role accorded to higher education in the nation's development socially, economically, and culturally. This role was indicated by Israel's Council for Higher Education: "Higher Edu-

cation is charged with preparing academic staff in all fields, including basic scientific research, and a major part of applied research" (Council for Higher Education PGC 1985a p. 4).

2. The Institutional Fabric of the Higher Education System

Israeli tertiary education is a multilevel system. It is divided into two main subsystems: postsecondary education and higher education. The term "postsecondary education" refers to vocational or professional training after the completion of secondary school. The postsecondary subsystem includes a variety of 169 small institutions for the training of technical, nursing, paramedical, clerical, and business professionals as well as the bulk of the primary teacher-training colleges. Some of these sectors opt for academization, namely for higher education status.

"Higher education," as defined by The Council for Higher Education Law, 5718 to 1958, "includes teaching, science, and research" which are conducted in universities and other academic degree-granting institutions (Stanner 1963 p. 244). Within the higher education system there is a distinction between universities and other institutions of higher education.

The Council for Higher Education has the authority to grant a license to open a higher education institution. This is followed by accreditation, and in the third stage it authorizes institutions to award degrees (Stanner 1963).

In 1988 higher education in Israel included universities; institutions providing instruction at the bachelor's degree level only in technology, the arts, and teacher training; and courses for which universities are academically responsible. There are eight institutions of university status; seven institutions of higher education which are not universities and are authorized to award only the professional bachelor's degree; seven institutions for the training of teachers that have received either a license or accreditation, either for the entire institution or for certain programs of study; academic courses in eight regional colleges for which universities are academically responsible (Council for Higher Education PGC 1989 pp. 18–20). Only the seven universities (except the Open University) are authorized to award degrees beyond the bachelor in a variety of fields of studies and advanced professional training. The eight "other institutions of higher education" are authorized to award the bachelor's degree only in specified fields of study or training, and the seven teacher-training colleges award the BEd to teachers for primary and junior high schools (K-9).

The most important feature of higher education development in the 1950s and 1960s was the growth of university research in accordance with the long-standing tradition of the unity of research and teach-

Table 1
Students in postsecondary education by course and year of study, sex, and age (including students in Arab institutions)

	Year					First degree students	Year of study				Men	Women	Up to age 24	Aged 25–29	Aged 30 and over	In Arab institutions
	1970/71	1974/75	1979/80	1984/85	1987/88		First	Second	Third	Fourth						
Teacher training for primary and intermediate schools	5,442	11,057	11,770	12,905	11,965	4,979[a]	3,837	3,569	2,848	1,236	1,874	9,616	8,874	2,643	—	475
Practical engineering, technical work, etc.	4,793	7,355	7,857	13,892	23,574	702	7,093	4,738	1,221	367	11,078	2,341	8,192	3,213	2,014	155
Qualified nurses	1,177	1,219	1,961	1,567	1,232	—	480	323	387	42	86	1,146	827	161	244	—
Paramedical occupations	600	607	475	748	728	—	382	206	123	17	255	473	557	116	55	—
Clerical work, administration, banking, economics, and accountancy	1,364	2,353	2,176	2,603	2,946	928[b]	1,775	722	362	87	1,960	986	1,034	884	1,028	—
Arts	876	1,835	1,375	2,028	2,556	1,018	1,091	665	436	374	843	1,723	1,777	559	230	—
Other courses	265	1,801	1,737	874	754	164	556	78	52	68	278	476	180	223	351	—
Total	15,517	26,227	27,351	34,617	33,765	7,791	15,214	10,301	5,429	2,191	17,352	16,067	21,414	7,799	3,922	630

Source: *Statistical Abstracts of Israel* No. 39 1988. Table 22/32 p. 636
a As of 1985/86 includes all first-year through fourth-year students in courses in which the studies were recognized as studies in an institution of higher education   b Includes business administration (as of 1987/88)   c Includes only those Arab students in Arab institutions but not Arabs in other institutions

ing. University teachers were recruited and promoted on the basis of research attainment. The selective character of the Israeli high school, enrolling in the 1950s between 13 to 23 percent of the 15 to 18 age group and providing about 10 percent of the 18-year olds with a matriculation certificate, provided suitable and competent students for the research-oriented universities. Israel's close ties with the international scientific community provided moral support, intellectual stimuli, and research funds to maintain updated research universities.

The government, although covering an increasingly large part of the operating budgets of the universities, did not interfere with the universities' academic autonomy emphasizing research as its supreme goal. This policy continues to guide Israeli higher education and was echoed in the 1986/87 annual report of the Planning and Grants Committee of the Council for Higher Education: "The universities are engaged both in teaching and research. University teaching not accompanied by research cannot maintain a proper academic level for any length of time" (Council for Higher Eduation PGC 1988a p. 62).

About 30 percent of all research and development in Israel (including defense) and about 45 percent of the civilian research and development in the natural sciences, medicine, agriculture, and engineering is carried out in universities. Most of the research in the humanities and social sciences and virtually all the basic research in the country takes place in the universities.

2.1 Admission Policies, Selection, and Qualifications

Admission requirements differ in the three major subsystems of tertiary education: postsecondary, universities, and other institutions of higher education. Further differentiation exists within each of them. A major difference relates to the matriculation certificate (*Bagrut*) which is acquired by success in state leaving examinations and awarded by the Ministry of Education and Culture. While matriculation is a prerequisite for entry to higher education, with the notable exception of the Open University, it is not required by most postsecondary institutions. In addition to an Israeli matriculation certificate or its equivalent from abroad, applicants for undergraduate studies in universities and some other higher education institutions must take the psychometric entrance examination which is administered centrally by the National Institute for Testing and Evaluation. Universities are autonomous in determining their admission policies. Although the language of instruction in all higher education institutions is Hebrew, all applicants to universities must demonstrate an ability to comprehend written English by passing the English placement test of the psychometric entrance examination.

In view of the limited places available, certain faculties and departments such as medicine, dentistry, pharmacy, law, psychology, social work, science, and technology had to restrict the number of entrants by demanding relatively high scores in the 90 percentiles, as well as competitive entrance examinations, personal interviews, and other means. Applicants for admission to graduate studies must hold a bachelor's degree or its equivalent with a final grade of at least "Good" (B/75). Most departments will not admit students to graduate studies unless their undergraduate studies were in the same field, because specialization commences on the undergraduate level. Graduates with a master's degree with at least cumulative "Good" (B) average and a master's thesis grade of at least 80 are eligible to apply for studies toward the PhD or JSD degree.

The duration of the bachelor's degree (BA or BSc) usually extends over a three-year period, in engineering four years and toward the MD for six to seven years. The master's degree requires a minimum of two years' course work. A master's thesis is mandatory in most departments and is usually required for admission to a doctoral program. Doctoral programs in the arts and sciences are individually designed and require an original and significant research dissertation. All university degrees, diplomas, and certificates are awarded by the individual institutions.

2.2 Quantitative Developments in Higher Education

The higher education system between 1950 and 1990 went through several phases, quantitative and qualitative in nature. The 1950s and 1960s were marked by a dramatic quantitative expansion. Four new universities were established, new programs of study were introduced, the number of students grew, and a major structural reform in undergraduate studies was introduced. The 1970s witnessed further expansion and diversification of higher education opportunities within the existing universities and also in the nonuniversity sector, particularly the regional colleges offering academic studies in association with existing universities. Another expression of this diversification was the academization of other nonuniversity institutions particularly for the paramedical professions and primary-school teachers.

In the year 1987/88, 33,765 students attended 172 postsecondary institutions; 11,965 of them were enrolled in 30 teacher-training colleges, and 13,574 in 45 institutions for the training of practical engineers and technicians (see Table 1). It is estimated that an additional 10,000 students attended great *Yeshivot* (rabbinical academies).

Between 1970/80 the number of postsecondary institutions increased from 131 in the year 1970/71 to a peak of 194 in the year 1979/80 However, since 1980/81 this trend has reversed as a result of consolidation of small teacher-training institutions which decreased from 55 in the year 1979/80 to 30 in the year 1987/88. The student population grew from 15,517 in 1970/71 to 26,227 in 1974/75 and to

Table 2
Students at universities, by academic years and growth rate

	1959–60	1964–65	1969–70	1974–75	1979–80	1984–85	1987–88
Growth indexes							
1969–70=100.0	—	—	100.6	143.7	158.7	179.5	187.4
1964–65=100.0	—	100.0	197.3	283.6	313.0	354.1	369.7
Annual percentage of growth	14.8[b]	12.5[b]	14.6[b]	8.2	3.1	0.7	1.1
Total[a]	10,202	18,368	36,239	52,088	57,500	65,050	67,900

Source: Compiled from: Council for Higher Education, Planning and Grants Committee, *Higher Education in Israel—Statistical Abstracts 1983–84; 1986–87. Statistical Abstracts of Israel*, No. 39, 1988.
a Including foreign students and students in special programs b On the assumption of linear growth within the years.

27,351 in 1979/80. The growth accelerated again to 34,617 students in 1984/85 but has decreased slightly since then, in part because of slowing demand in elementary-school teachers and in technical workers (Statistical Abstracts of Israel 1988, Table 22/32, p. 636).

The number of students at the seven university-level institutions reached some 67,900 in 1988, an increase of more than 25 percent over the last 10 years (see Table 2). Some 60 percent are studying humanities, social sciences, and law; 23.3 percent natural sciences, agriculture, and medicine; and 16.7 percent engineering. Some 72 percent are studying for the first degree (bachelor), 21 percent for the second degree (master), 5 percent for the doctorate, and 2 percent for academic diplomas, mainly secondary-school teaching diplomas. At the 13 non-university institutions of higher education there were some 5,800 students. (Statistical Abstracts of Israel 1988, Tables 22/32, 22/33, 22/34, pp. 638–39).

It is difficult to compare the rate of study in Israel with the rate in Western countries, because of variations in the division between university and post-secondary education in different countries. Also, the principal age group attending universities in Israel, 20–29, differs from other countries due to the three years of compulsory military service for men and two years for women. However, given that about 20 percent of the 20 to 29 age cohort received university education and about 33 percent some form of higher education, the rate in Israel is higher than in most developed nations (Israel Ministry of Education and Culture 1989 p. 68).

In 1987 to 1988 and 1988 to 1989 the rate of admission to universities was as follows: about 65 percent of the applicants to departments of humanities were admitted; about 50 percent of the applicants to social sciences departments; but only 20 percent of those applying to law schools, medicine, and engineering.

3. Governance, Administration, and Finance

3.1 National Administration

When the State of Israel was established in 1948, there were two small higher education institutions (the Hebrew University of Jerusalem and the Haifa Technion) and one research institute. They emphasized research and scholarship in very few areas, technological training, and applied research. They were private institutions supported mainly by foreign donors and run like corporations following the model of American private universities. Although they were expected to contribute to "the realization of Jewish culture and the Zionist program of building up the country physically" (Ben David 1986 p. 105), they safeguarded their autonomy from the Zionist organization which created and supported them, and later in the 1950s from the emerging governmental bureaucracy. The universities continued to have full institutional autonomy. Their academic staff enjoyed almost unrestricted, academic freedom of teaching and research similar to the British elitist institutions. Academic staff played a decisive role also in administrative matters of the university.

Between 1955 and 1964 four new universities were founded, the number of students rose from 3,022 in 1950/51 to 18,368 in 1964/65. The academic profession grew from 135 professors and lecturers in 1950/51 to 2,814 in 1968/69. New departments in the social sciences and humanities and professional schools in law and medicine were established both in the old and new universities. This expansion and the increased demand for public and governmental funds have brought to light three interrelated issues: accreditation of new institutions; criteria and means for channeling public funds to the individual institutions; and the issue of governmental control over the system. Indeed, since the Second World War governments tend to intervene in higher education systems in order to democratize access and governance, to make studies more relevant to the economy

348

and careers, and also to augment their influence over the magnitude, the cost, and the future direction of the higher education enterprise (Trow 1984 p. 142, Clark 1983 pp. 119–23). This trend became apparent in Israel in 1958 when the government established the Council for Higher Education (CHE) as a statutory body, serving as "the State institution for matters of higher education in the State" (Stanner 1963 pp. 244–49). The CHE is the sole authority able to recommend to the government the grant of a permit to open a new institution of higher education as well as granting academic recognition, accreditation, and the right to confer academic degrees. In an apparent attempt to safeguard academic freedom, Section 4a states that "at least two thirds of its members must be persons of standing in the field of higher education," namely, full professors.

The continuous quantitative expansion of the higher education system (see Table 2) was accompanied by a massive increase in public expenditure which rose steadily to 45.5 percent in 1959/60 and to almost 80 percent of the ordinary budget in 1974/75 (see Table 3). Increased government involvement in financing higher education intensified the basic issue of how to reconcile the inherent conflict between academic freedom and accountability to the public.

The autonomous governing body of each university decided on its development policy without coordination either with other universities, the Council for Higher Education (CHE), or with the government. There was a need to find both a scheme and a mechanism to make universities more accountable to the public and particularly to work out an equitable system for financing higher education.

In 1974 the Council for Higher Education took charge of planning and appointed the first Planning and Grants Committee (PGC) following the British model of the University Grants Committee (UGC). To safeguard against the intervention of the state, at least four of PGC's six members, including the chairperson, must be full professors appointed *ad personam*. The other two members come from business and industry (Council for Higher Education PGC 1985a p. 95).

The terms of reference of the Planning and Grants Committee (PGC), as set forth in Government Decision No. 666 of June 5, 1977, are as follows: The PGC functions as a central coordination agency of the Council for Higher Education (CHE) in allocating governmental and public funds for higher education. It reviews budgetary proposals, both ordinary and developmental, of each institution, ensuring that they are balanced. The PGC is responsible for coordination between institutions. It reviews and evaluates proposals for opening new institutions, or new programs within existing institutions, having financial implications, and submits its recommendations to the CHE. The PGC reports to the CHE at the end of each academic year. Although the PGC was meant to guarantee academic freedom and institutional autonomy of the universities which may negotiate their budgets only with the PGC, in practice the freedom of the individual institution both in academic and fiscal matters was eroded considerably.

Indeed, during the 1980s the power of government increased, not directly, but through the Planning and Grants Committee. The PGC has become a centralized power in matters of funding, planning, policy initiatives, and evaluation. Thus, the initiatives of the PGC caused it to become a force in the development of certain academic fields and not just an organ for the channeling of governmental funds. During the second term of the PGC (1979–85) its power and status increased further. In times when governmental allocations were cut time and again and research funds, national and international, became scarce (see Table 4) "PGC's authority in the allocation of the higher education budget to the higher education system is, essentially, unlimited" (Council for Higher Education PGC 1985a p. 96).

The principal sources of income for the higher education system are: (a) allocations from the government determined and paid by the PGC; (b) income from current donations; (c) revenue from endowment funds; (d) tuition fees; (e) research contracts and research grants from government and private sources, at home and abroad; (f) sale of services (including teaching services). The share of each is shown in Table 4.

Table 3
Public participation in recurrent budget of higher education

	1959–60	1964–65	1969–70	1974–75
No. of students	10,202	18,368	36,239	52,088
Total recurrent budget (in millions of Israeli pounds)	28.1	78.3	241.3	1,075.0
Public participation[a]	12.8	40.2	162.1	852.0
Percentage	45.5	51.0	67.0	79.8

Sources: Council for Higher Education, Planning and Grants Committee *Report for 1974* (Hebrew), 1988b
a From 1967 to 1968 the Jewish Agency allocated funds to universities for their recurrent budgets.

Table 4
Ordinary budget of the higher education system (N.I.S. thousands at current prices), by sources of income and academic years[a] with percentages shown in parentheses

	1979–80	1980–81	1981–82	1982–83	1983–84	1984–85	1985–86	1986–87
Various[d]	159	450	1,132	3,754	25,763	43,387	43,503	89,179
	(12.1)	(13.2)	(17.2)	(18.0)	(33.6)	(14.4)	(8.2)	(12.5)
Donations from	126	260	505	1,205	5,944	42,199	57,741	80,087
abroad	(9.6)	(7.6)	(7.6)	(5.8)	(7.7)	(14.0)	(10.9)	(11.3)
Tuition fees	64	133	272	1,405	3,290	29,603	99,256	124,085
	(4.8)	(3.9)	(4.1)	(6.7)	(4.3)	(9.8)	(18.7)	(17.4)
PGC Allocations								
Earmarked allocations	52	108	150	569	3,702	24,079	38,629	49,540
and various[c]	(3.9)	(3.2)	(2.3)	(2.7)	(4.8)	(8.0)	(7.3)	(7.0)
Matching allocations[b]	50	225	400	600	1,363	8,820	38,254	43,904
	(3.8)	(6.6)	(6.1)	(2.9)	(1.8)	(3.0)	(7.2)	(6.2)
Direct allocations	867	2,228	4,138	13,326	36,623	153,075	253,037	324,625
	(65.8)	(65.5)	(62.7)	(63.9)	(47.8)	(50.8)	(47.7)	(45.6)
Subtotal	969	2,561	4,688	14,495	41,688	185,974	329,920	418,069
	(73.5)	(75.3)	(71.1)	(69.5)	(54.4)	(61.8)	(62.2)	(58.8)
Ordinary budget	1,318[e]	3,404[e]	6,597[e]	20,859[e]	76,685[f]	301,163[g]	530,420[g]	711,420[g]
	(100.0)	(100.0)	(100.0)	(100.0)	(100.0)	(100.0)	(100.0)	(100.0)

Source: CHE, PGC 1988b p. 56
a From October 1 up to September 30   b To endowment funds at the institutions   c Including allocations for research and for special subjects (earmarked allocations, inter-university activities, aid to students, budgetary transfers, and miscellaneous subjects)   d Including deficits   e According to the balance sheets of the institutions   f According to financial reports received from the institutions   g Final budget at updated prices

The higher education system depends financially on allocation from government. In the 1980s the government, through the PGC, provided 55 to 75 percent of the ordinary budgets of higher education institutions, except for teacher-training institutions and regional colleges, financed directly by the Ministry of Education and Culture.

The PGC operates through five budgetary channels: the direct global allocation; matching allocations; allocations for research; earmarked allocations; and allocations for development. Through each of these channels, and by determining their relative share in the general budget, the PGC exerts influence on higher education. The PGC's increased budgetary control is reflected in its policy in regard to the largest item of the budget, namely, the direct allocations to the budget of the institutions of higher education. This item made up 65.8 percent of the total PGC allocations in 1979/80 and decreased to 45.6 percent in 1986/87 while the share of tuition fees increased in the same period from 4.8 percent to 17.4 percent (see Table 4). In this way the PGC used the budget to support activities in accordance with its own determined priorities. Thus, it increased its earmarked funding for basic research and special projects which suffered severely in the early 1970s (CHE PGC 1985a p. 101).

The method of, and criteria for, apportioning the PGC's direct allocation between the institutions reflects also its increased involvement in the eval-

uation of these institutions. As of 1981/82, budgetary deliberations are conducted in two parallel planes. One team, headed by the PGC's director-general, examines the budgetary proposals submitted by each institution, and the indices on which they are based, such as income, size, and proposed developments. The second team, headed by the chairperson of the PGC, examines data on the "productivity" of each institution: number of students and graduates by degree level and field of study, the value of research grants, and the scope and quality of research in the institution. The PGC has refrained from establishing a binding formula for "institutional productivity" because "a single, predetermined formula gives the omnipotent computer the power of decision rather than the collective balanced judgment of the committee members" (CHE PGC 1985a p. 102, 1988a p. 6, Iram 1987 pp. 155–57).

The range of allocation (not a single amount), determined by the two teams are compared and presented to the PGC for discussion and approval. In this way the PGC determines annually the allocation to each institution, based on its work program, proposed development, and on its research output as well as on its training of highly skilled professionals.

Universities have questioned the validity of this method. The lack of an established definite formula for "productivity" of an institution leaves to the PGC the authority to assess the quality of the universities' performance. This policy no doubt weakened the universities' integrity in Israel, a phenomenon which was observed in many national systems during the 1960s and 1970s (Perkins and Israel 1972, Clark 1983).

The mid-1970s and early 1980s were marked by severe cuts in governmental expenditure on social services, including education, due to slowdown in economic growth and inflation (Kop 1985). Harsh fiscal measures resulted in a major crisis in higher education with long-term implications. While the number of students increased by some 30 percent between 1974 and 1983, academic staff decreased by 3 percent and administrative staff were reduced by 11 percent. A definite trend of substantial disinvestment in higher education was reflected in the share of higher education in the national budget, excluding defense expenditure and debt payment, which fell by some 44 percent (see Table 4).

Indeed, government participation in the ordinary budget of higher education remained unchanged in real terms over the 1980s in relation to the Consumer Price Index; however, it did not compensate universities for the growth in student population by almost 25 percent and for the significant increase in wages and salaries of all employees, including those in higher education (see Tables 2 and 4). In order to reverse the trend of financial deterioration of higher education institutions which might affect negatively academic standards and the quality of professional training, the PGC has submitted to the government a plan for increasing the basic higher education budget by 25 percent in four years (CHE PGC 1988a p. 6). In February 1988, PGC's chairman reported that the Ministry of Finance decided to adopt the principles of the PGC's plan and to make additional funds available to higher education in the years 1987/88 and 1989/90 (CHE PGC 1988a p. 7). Indeed the 1987 to 1988 PGC's apportionment to higher education institutions increased by some 2.5 percent in real terms compared to 1986–87 (CHE PGC 1989 p. 65).

3.2 Institutional Administration

Higher education institutions in Israel are autonomous, and have academic freedom, and academic self-government. Section 15 of The Council for Higher Education Law, 5718–1958 guarantees the autonomy of higher education, not only in its academic conduct but also in its administrative and financial affairs (Stanner 1963 p. 244–49). Although institutions are dependent financially on governmental support and are required to submit to PGC their budgets for approval, "each institution is free to conduct its academic and administrative affairs as it sees fit, within the confines of its approved budget" (CHE PGC 1988a p. 15).

The supreme authority of each university is vested in its board of governors and executive committee, a third of which are drawn from prominent Jewish individuals in science, arts, management, and business outside Israel; another third on the executive committees are academic staff.

The board of governors appoints a president who is the head of the university. However, the president's main responsibility is for the administrative and financial affairs. The president is assisted by a director general or vice-president. The supreme authority in academic matters is the rector, who is a full professor elected for a two–three-year term by the senate, composed of all full professors and representatives from other academic ranks, and a representative of the student body. Faculties, institutes, schools, and departments elect their heads from their ranks. The power of the rector and senate and its committees extends beyond academic affairs to administrative matters as well. The board of governors does not usually interfere in academic matters, thus self-government in academic matters is almost unrestricted.

Because all positions of power are held by temporary academic officials elected by the academic staff from its own ranks, no professional higher education administration has developed in Israel. Constant rotation of academic office holders does not leave time or incentive to staff to become experts in academic administration, politics, and planning. Excessive participatory democracy of faculty assemblies have also prevented the emergence of effective academic leadership. Faculty assemblies attend to both routine business such as appointments, and long-term curricular and research policies, through a complicated system of committees. The support for participatory self-government and opposition to professional administration has been based on the principle that universities should be a loose coalition of self-governing departments (Ben-David 1986 p. 126–27). However, others argue that the lack of academic or administrative authority above the department and faculty levels brings to a deadlock any attempt to relocate resources between departments and units in response to changing financial circumstances, research interests, or shifts in employment prospects which require changes in training priorities.

The rectors and presidents of all universities have formed the Committee of Heads of Universities. It functions as a consultation and coordination organ.

Israeli universities are similar to each other in structure, programs, and aims; they are, or aspire to become, comprehensive research universities. However, three of the institutions established in the 1950s and 1960s, Bar-Ilan, Haifa, and Ben-Gurion universities try to emphasize service to the local community and its vicinity in the north (Haifa) and south (Ben-Gurion), while Bar-Ilan is committed to religious values and religious education.

Academic work is organized in basic units such as departments, which are based on scientific discipline or field of study and research; schools—usually pro-

Table 5
Academic staff in academic institutions

	1948–49[a]	1959–60[a]	1964–65[a]	1969–70[a]	1975–76[a]	1981–82[b]	1985–86[b]
Total academic staff	293	1,531	2,628	5,977	8,148	8,069	7,756
Professors and lecturers	118	511	1,207	3,122	3,988	4,464	4,115

Source: Adapted from: *Statistical Abstracts of Israel* No. 29 1978, Table 22/46 p. 692; No. 38 1987, Table 22/41 p. 618; No. 39 1988, Table 22/41 p. 646
a The number of persons including part-time staff   b The number of full-time equivalent posts.

fessional—and institutes comprising both research and instruction; and programs which are interdisciplinary. Departments are grouped in faculties such as humanities, social sciences, natural sciences, engineering, law, and medicine. Departments are independent in determining their course of study and admission requirements, but are responsible to the dean of the faculty. The academic year extends from late October to June and from September to June in teachers' colleges.

4. Faculty and Students: Teaching, Learning, and Research

4.1 Faculty

The academic profession in Israel has grown very rapidly since the establishment of the state in 1948 and particularly during the periods of expansion of the higher education system in the 1960s and 1970s (see Table 5).

The continuous emphasis on research and on training of researchers at Israeli universities from their inception made it possible to recruit qualified academic teaching staff from among the graduates of the veteran institutions, the Hebrew University, and the Technion. Also, cooperation between Israeli and United States researchers facilitated recruitment of foreign, especially American, academic staff who immigrated to Israel. Because of ample supply of qualified academic staff from these two sources there was no need to reduce standards of teaching and training in spite of the massive expansion of the higher education system (see Table 4). Nevertheless, the growth of the academic staff was slower than enrollments. Between 1956/57 and 1966/67 the aggregate number of students in higher education multiplied by 4.4 while the academic staff multiplied by 3.4. This increased student–teacher ratios. In the 1970s it was estimated that the overall ratio was 9:1 (Bendor 1977 p. 2337). In 1983 the average ratio was about 15:1 in the humanities and social sciences and about 8:1 in the natural sciences, medicine, and engineering. The overall average ratio was about 11.5:1 compared to the desired ratio of 10:1 accepted in England and Wales (Council for Higher Education PGC 1984 p. 37).

The academic staff in the universities consists of assistants "A" and "B," instructors, senior instructors, lecturers, senior lecturers, associate professors, and full professors. Senior instructors and above are required to hold a PhD or another doctorate degree, and only senior lecturers and upward are granted tenure. The academic staff in 1986 numbered the equivalent of some 7,818 full-time positions, with an additional 224 positions in seven nonuniversity institutions of higher education, and a similar number in the seven academic teacher-training institutions.

Higher education institutions are autonomous in appointing, promoting, and granting tenure to their academic staff. However, the procedures and qualifications for appointments and promotions are similar in all universities. These are based almost exclusively on research qualifications demonstrated in publications, evaluated by a committee of professors, and by written evaluations solicited from outside the university and, as a rule, also from foreign referees. This institutionalized procedure in the entire system safeguards the academic standards and research tradition of all seven universities as research universities with research facilities conferring higher degrees in as many fields as possible (Ben-David 1986 pp. 115–17). The teaching load of university teachers is six to eight weekly class hours for about seven months of term time. This leaves them ample time for research and publishing. Moreover, from the rank of lecturer upward, academic staff are entitled every seventh year to full paid leave of absence. Sabbatical leaves are usually spent abroad in a university or research institute. This provides research opportunities in fields for which facilities and funds are not adequate at the home institution, and encourages Israeli researchers to cooperate with the international community of researchers, thus keeping updated in the most recent developments in various disciplines and fields.

4.2 Students

The socioeconomic and geopolitical reality of Israel is responsible for the collective profile of the student body in Israel's higher education system and for some of the distinct characteristics of its students. The majority of students are two-to-three years older than elsewhere because of compulsory military service

Table 6
Distribution of students in universities with percentages shown in parentheses

	1969–70	1974–75	1979–80	1984–85	1986–87
Exact sciences[a]	12,134	19,592	19,987	23,597	25,405
	(36.3)	(39.3)	(36.7)	(38.6)	(40.0)
Social sciences[b]	10,434	18,616	22,071	23,639	23,519
	(31.3)	(37.3)	(40.5)	(38.7)	(37.0)
Humanities	10,815[c]	11,641	12,422	13,914	14,576
	(32.4)	(23.4)	(22.8)	(22.7)	(28.9)
Total	33,383	49,849	54,480	61,155	63,500

Source: Compiled from CHE PGC 1988b Table 8, pp. 9–10
a Including technology, engineering, and medicine   b Including education, teacher training, business and administration, and law   c In 1969 to 1970 education and teacher training are included in the Humanities

without privileges of deferment for academic studies. About half of them are married at the time of their studies. Although tuition fees are relatively low, they are a burden for most students and particularly for those who are married, therefore most of them are working either full-time or part-time (Globerson 1978 pp. 1–18, Silberberg 1987).

Expectations of university students to fill professional and administrative jobs in the expanding economy and administration were met by universities quite successfully between the 1950s and 1970s, both through expansion and transformation of their structure, content, and aims. The major changes were: introduction of the three-year bachelor's degree in 1950 (Iram 1983), followed by the establishment and growth of professional schools such as education, social work, and business administration, as well as changes in disciplinary departments in science, humanities, and social science. These changes also met the aspirations of the students who after their years of military service were eager to acquire a marketable proficiency. Indeed the growth in the number of students in the professional schools and departments and in "practical" fields of study is the most conspicuous feature of expanding opportunities for employment in the professions, as shown in the distribution of students (see Table 6).

Approximately 15 to 18 percent of the relevant age cohort commence higher education, and a further 20 percent of the age cohort enter other post-secondary programs of study. Of an entering class of undergraduate students, approximately two-thirds complete their studies and receive a degree. Four years is the mean length of time needed for completion of an undergraduate course of studies, although the official period of time required is generally three years. This is particularly noticeable in the humanities but is also found in the social and natural sciences.

A large proportion of undergraduate students study the humanities and the social sciences. However, since the beginning of the 1980s the percentage of students studying sciences and technology has risen (see Table 6) (Silberberg 1987 pp. 11–14, CHE PGC 1988a p. 35).

4.3 Social Class Origins

There is a significant difference in the rate of participation in higher education according to socio-economic and ethnic background. Thus, in 1985 the rate among Israeli-born students whose fathers were born in Europe, the United States, or Israel was 3.8 times higher than those of African-Asian (oriental) origin and five times higher than those of non-Jews. However, from 1976 to 1985, the rate of participation of students of oriental origin increased from 19 to 30 percent among undergraduate students, while their percentage in the 20 to 29 age cohort has changed only slightly from 43 to 45 percent (CHE PGC 1988a p. 36, Silberberg 1987 pp. 31–35).

Between 1966 and 1985 the rate of participation of students originating from Asia and Africa has increased two and a half times and the rate of Arab students quadrupled and is close to that of Jewish students of oriental origin. The trend of closing the gap continues (Silberberg 1987 p. 33). There is no significant gender difference in the rate of participation in higher education. In 1986/87, 48.9 percent of the student population and 49.4 percent of the degree recipients were women (Statistical Abstracts of Israel 1988 pp. 640, 644). There are, however, gender differences in fields of studies. About 70 percent of women study humanities while only 13 percent are enrolled in engineering departments (Silberberg 1987 p. 29).

The opening of universities and other higher education institutions, especially regional colleges in the north and the south is probably responsible for the increase in the number of students in peripheral areas, particularly of those sections of the population who were underrepresented. However, there are still differences in rates of participation between the populations in peripheral areas and those in the center of the country.

4.4 Model of Undergraduate Courses

Israel does not have liberal arts colleges specializing in teaching undergraduates, except in the Open University. This function is performed by universities which are research universities and engaged also in training of professionals in law, medicine, engineering, business, and other fields. The typical bachelor's program in the humanities and social sciences is designed for three years of study specializing in one or two disciplinary fields of the student's choice. The two-disciplines system has no stated rationale except for the possible consideration of providing potential school teachers with two school subjects so that they would be able to obtain a full-time job in one school. This possible motive does not apply as much in the natural sciences and social sciences, which are gradually changing in many universities toward majoring in a single discipline department. Professional education in law, medicine, engineering, and the like begins in the first year of studies at the undergraduate level for a duration of three and a half years in engineering, four in law, and five to six years in medicine.

Some alternative models for undergraduate studies have been pioneered such as integrative/interdisciplinary studies in the social sciences, liberal arts courses, general science programs, or general studies.

5. Conclusion

The expansion of higher learning in Israel between the 1950s and 1970s was among the greatest in the world. Access to higher education was not an important political issue, since both the universities and the government were in favor of providing higher education to all qualified applicants. The percentage out of an age cohort attending higher education is comparatively high. As a result, the proportion of college-educated persons in Israel's labor force, whether defined by years of schooling or by occupational classification, is among the world's highest (Klinov 1988 p. 9). However, more effective steps have to be taken to increase the rate of participation in higher education of ethnic and minority groups. The underrepresentation of these groups is inconsistent with Israel's stated social philosophy. In a related development, rising tuition fees and declining employment opportunities have affected a stagnation in attendance rate since 1984. Thus between 1984 and 1986 it remained unchanged in spite of an almost 10 percent increase of recipients of high school matriculation certificates.

The government provided the lion's share in funding expansion in the 1950s and 1960s regardless of real economic demand, while the universities have demonstrated flexibility in adjusting their programs to accommodate the changing expectations of students and the economy by introducing undergraduate and professional bachelor's degrees. However, the basic commitment of the system to research as a hallmark of excellence continued to characterize both the old and new institutions, thus avoiding the utilitarian approach. Worsening economic conditions, with drastic reductions in annual allocations to the universities, by 20 percent in 1982/83 to 1983/84, may affect adversely the delicate balance of institutional autonomy and direct governmental control on the one hand, and between the statutory roles of the Council for Higher Education (CHE) and the authority of the Planning and Grants Committee (PGC) and the universities on the other. Thus, for example, nationally negotiated wage agreements and tuition rates were imposed on the universities by the Ministry of Finance without consulting individual universities and without commensurate provisions for funding. Indeed in his 1988 annual report, PGC's chairman noted "the central and vital question is the higher education system about to lose its independence" (CHE PGC 1988a p. 5).

Another development of far-reaching consequences was the change in the composition of funding higher education: a sharp decline in the government's share, and a rise in both the share of tuition and private funding. The substitution of government funding by private finance resulted in shortages in general-purpose expenditure on basic research infrastructure such as libraries, laboratories, and computers. This trend might affect adversely the quality of instruction and research in the higher education system. To restore the equilibrium of the research infrastructure, additional public funds are required (Israel Academy of Sciences 1986). This demand was echoed in the 1987 PGC's chairman's annual report: "to repeat previous warnings and stress that if higher education does not very soon advance in the national order of priorities, it will no longer be possible to repair the damage that higher education has suffered in recent years" (CHE PGC 1987 p. 5). To halt the risk of deterioration of the system both in academic standards and in its function of labor force training, the PGC has submitted to the government a plan for increasing the basic higher education budget by 25 percent in four years.

On the other hand, demands for accountability proposed that expanding and even existing needs for higher education could be met only by a more efficient and vocationally oriented system. These demands were followed by growing pressure for higher productivity and more efficient or joint utilization of facilities and equipment and interuniversity cooperation in research. University faculties and administrators tended to see some of these demands as a disguised desire for more direct state control at the expense of institutional autonomy.

It seems at this point that Israel's higher education system reached a crossroad. To overcome the crisis, both universities and government will have to explore new ways which will allow effective planning, financing, and policy making at the university and national levels, taking into account both the legitimate public and national interests, academic freedom, and institutional autonomy. However, somewhat more ingenuity will be required by all parties to meet the challenges and exigencies that Israeli higher education institutions will probably continue to face throughout the closing decade of the twentieth century. This is particularly true in the light of increased immigration to Israel from the Soviet Union, which has already resulted in a growing supply of highly skilled professionals such as doctors and engineers, and also in an increased demand for higher education by young immigrants who had left universities and those about to commence further studies.

Bibliography

Academy of Sciences and Humanities 1986 *Scientific Research Activity in Israel. A Blueprint for Basic Research*. Academy of Sciences and Humanities, Jerusalem

Ben-David J 1986 Universities in Israel: Dilemmas of growth, diversification and administration. *Stud. Higher Educ.* 11: 105–30

Bendor Sh 1977 University education in the State of Israel. In: Knowles A S (ed.) 1977 *International Encyclopedia of Higher Education*. Jossey-Bass, San Francisco, California, pp. 2331–41

Central Bureau of Statistics 1989 *Statistical Abstracts of Israel 1989 No. 40*. The Central Bureau of Statistics, Jerusalem

Clark B R 1983 *The Higher Education System: Academic Organization in Cross-National Perspectives*. University of California Press, Berkeley, California

Council for Higher Education, Planning and Grants Committee 1984 *The Higher Education System in Israel: Guidelines on the Development of the System and its Planning for 1988 with a First Glance at 1995*. The Planning and Grants Committee, Jerusalem

Council for Higher Education, Planning and Grants Committee 1985a *Annual Report No. 12, Academic Year 1984/85*. The Planning and Grants Committee, Jerusalem

Council for Higher Education, Planning and Grants Committee 1985b *Higher Education in Israel—Statistical Abstract 1983/84*. The Planning and Grants Committee, Jerusalem

Council for Higher Education 1987 *Report No. 2, The Sixth Council 1981–1986*. The Council for Higher Education, Jerusalem

Council for Higher Education, Planning and Grants Committee 1987 *Annual Report No. 13, Academic Year 1985/86*. The Planning and Grants Committee, Jerusalem

Council for Higher Education, Planning and Grants Committee 1988a *Annual Report No. 14, Academic Year 1986/87*. The Planning and Grants Committee, Jerusalem

Council for Higher Education, Planning and Grants Committee 1988b *Higher Education in Israel—Statistical Abstract 1986/87*. The Planning and Grants Committee, Jerusalem

Council for Higher Education, Planning and Grants Committee 1989 *Annual Report No. 15, Academic Year 1987/88*. The Planning and Grants Committee, Jerusalem

Flexner A 1930 *Universities: American, English, German*. Oxford University Press, New York

Globerson A 1978 *Higher Education and Employment: A Case Study of Israel*. Praeger, Farnborough

Iram Y 1983 Vision and fulfillment: The evolution of the Hebrew University, 1901–1950. *Hist. Higher Educ. Ann.* 3: 123–43

Iram Y 1987 Quality and control in higher education in Israel. *Eur. J. Educ.* 22: 145–59

Klinov R 1988 Allocation of public resource to education. Discussion paper No. 1 in the series *Israel's Educational System: Issue and Options*. The Center for Social Policy Studies, Jerusalem

Kop Y 1985 Social services in the eighties—a turning point? In: Kop Y (ed.) 1985 *Israel's Outlay for Human Services 1984*. The Center for Social Policy Studies, Jerusalem, pp. 7–18

Liebman C S, Don Yehiya E 1984 *Religion and Politics in Israel*. Indiana University Press, Bloomington, Indiana

Mar'i S K 1978 *Arab Education in Israel*. Syracuse University Press, Syracuse, New York

The Middle East and North Africa 1989 1989 Europa Publications, London

Ministry of Education and Culture 1989 *Ministry of Education and Culture 1989*. Publication Department, Jerusalem

Patai R 1970 *Israel Between East and West: A Study in Human Relations*, 2nd edn. Greenwood, Westport, Connecticut

Perkins J A, Israel B B (eds.) 1972 *Higher Education: From Autonomy to Systems*. International Council for Educational Development, New York

Shama A, Iris M 1976 *Immigration Without Integration. Third World Jews in Israel*. Schenkman, Cambridge, Massachusetts

Silberberg R 1987 *Undergraduate Studies in the Higher Education System*. The Planning and Grants Committee, Jerusalem

Stanner R 1963 *The Legal Basis of Education in Israel*. Ministry of Education and Culture, Jerusalem

Trow M A 1984 The analysis of status. In: Clark B R (ed.) 1984 *Perspectives on Higher Education*. University of California Press, Berkeley, California, pp. 132–64

Y. Iram

Italy

1. Higher Education and Society

To understand the status of Italian higher education one must briefly recall some key historical events and summarize the basic social transformations which took place in the decades after the Second World War. Italy is a relatively new state—it was formed in 1861—and a very old nation. Modern Italy was formed out of a variety of smaller states with different sequences of economic growth, types of civil society, and patterns of state administration. Although the Italian people living in the various parts of the country—particulariy the educated upper classes—had for centuries shared a common culture regarding religious and secular beliefs, written language, art and literature, attitudes and behavior, and so on, regional divisions and local and institutional loyalties were powerful obstacles to national cultural integration, once the battle for a unified Italy in the Risorgimento was over. Italian society remained divided and fragmented along traditional lines throughout the Second World War.

The higher education system which emerged from unified Italy was a mixture of continuity and change. The continuity of medieval university traditions had been maintained for centuries in independent and strong institutions like the Universities of Bologna, Padua, and Pavia. The reforms of the new Italian government aimed at creating a system of higher education which would contribute to the political and economic development of the country and to the formation of a new intellectual and scientific atmosphere.

The major task of the higher education system of modern Italy was therefore to form a national elite sharing a homogeneous culture for the liberal professions, the state bureaucracy, and the educational system, through the transformation of many ancient universities scattered around the country into a modern and unified system of academic institutions. This proved to be no easy task, because of strong centrifugal forces, deeply rooted particularistic interests and values, and the role of the Church. The result was a compromise between national bureaucratic control and professorial autonomy.

The Casati Law, which was the first attempt to reorganize the Italian school system, although adopting in principle the German model inspired by Humboldt's learning theory, actually followed more the centralized Napoleonic model. This model had, however, to be adapted to the medieval traditions of university autonomy. The result was a difficult compromise between centralized control of personnel, financial budgets, and curricula, on the one hand, and the safeguard of institutional autonomies—often going back many centuries—and of professorial privileges, on the other. The Ministry of Public Education in Rome, through its special division for university affairs, determined budgets, curricula, and the ways faculties had to be organized. But universities continued to function through their own states, to elect their own rectors and deans, and to decide the distribution of funds among the various faculties and schools.

The Fascist period introduced the Gentile reform of the whole school system, which stressed the elite character of higher education, determined more rigid centralized controls, underplayed the role of scientific and technological research in favor of traditional humanities, banned social sciences and social criticism, and cut off Italian culture from most relevant scientific currents of contemporary thought. After the Second World War, however, with the restoration of democracy, Italian universities rapidly closed the gap existing between themselves and the academic institutions of the major countries of the West through an intense flow of exchanges of people and ideas, and a massive program of translations of foreign works, mostly from the United States, United Kingdom, France, and Germany.

In the four decades after the Second World War Italian society underwent a thorough process of transformation and the higher education system also changed significantly. In the early 1990s, Italy is a modern, advanced industrial country, very different from the predominantly traditional, agricultural society it was 45 years ago. As "modern" and "traditional" are rather ambiguous terms, they must be briefly qualified with reference to the basic processes of change of the last decades and to the fundamental traits of contemporary Italian society.

The Italian population was 47.5 million in 1951 and is 57.5 million at the start of the 1990s, of which 36.5 million are in the north and the center and 21 million are in the south. Population growth is approaching zero in the northern regions and is slightly increasing in the south. Life expectancy at birth is 72 years for men and over 78 for women, while it was around 50 for both men and women in 1920. Whereas in 1951, only 31.1 percent of the population lived in metropolitan areas (i.e., areas with at least 110,000 inhabitants, of which at least 35,000 work in industrial or service sectors of the economy), their number had increased to 54.2 percent in 1981. Among those living in the metropolitan areas in 1981, around 60 percent lived in the north.

The Italian population tends to be homogeneous in ethnic terms. Minorities, speaking languages other than Italian, live in the border regions with Austria, France, and Yugoslavia, and are granted special autonomies and education in their mother tongue. Ethnic heterogeneity is increasing, because there are more than one million foreign workers, most of whom are illegal immigrants. Cultural differences among different Italian regions still exist, but both the diffusion of schooling and the spread of mass media has reduced them significantly. The type of language usually spoken may be taken as an indicator of cultural homogeneity. The percentage of people usually speaking dialect decreases dramatically in the lower age groups.

1.1 Occupational and Economic Structure

Italy has become the fifth greatest industrial power of the world in terms of gross national product (GNP). Only 10 percent of the active population works in agriculture, while more than 57 percent works in the service sector. The rate of activity is 42 percent for men and the participation of women in the labor force is steadily increasing and has reached 30 percent. Only a minority of people work at home and for all others there is a clear-cut distinction between work and residence. Transport and mass media are widespread and favor intense economic, social, and cultural communication within the country and with the rest of the world. Only 3 percent of the population is illiterate. All citizens are entitled to a large and costly network of welfare services.

In the 1950s and 1960s the Italian economy underwent an intense and rapid process of change. Although the process of industrialization started in the nineteenth century, until the Second World War it was almost entirely confined to the triangle defined by the areas of Milan, Turin, and Genoa. It was only in the decades after the Second World War that Italy became a fully industrialized country, as a result of the process of economic development induced by the growth of the domestic market and by European economic integration. Industry spread from the old industrial regions to the northeastern regions, the central areas, and the Adriatic coast. It was followed by the growth of the service sector, both private and public.

After the Second World War there was a dramatic shift of the labor force from agriculture to the industrial and service sectors. People working in agriculture, who in 1951 were still 43 percent of the total labor force, dropped to 10.7 percent in 1985. The industrial labor force rose from 35 percent in 1951 to 42 percent in 1971 and then dropped again to 32.7 percent in 1985, because of labor-saving technological innovations. People employed in the service sector (i.e., trade, communications, banking and finance, professional services, etc.) increased steadily from 15 percent in 1951 to 39.8 percent in 1985. Public administration personnel (including higher education) rose from 7 percent in 1951 to 16.7 percent in 1985.

The "economic miracle" of the late 1950s and early 1960s was accompanied by deep and far-reaching social transformation. Millions of families moved from the countryside to the cities and from the southern regions to the metropolitan areas of north and central Italy. From 1951 to 1961 the population of Milan increased by 24 percent and the population of the towns in the metropolitan area increased by 39 percent, with most of the increase due to migration. Turin and Rome showed similar trends.

The economic miracle deeply changed the country's occupational and social class structure and significantly increased the demand for an educated labor force. Between 1951 and the mid-1980s, the most significant increases were in the professional classes (in particular, teachers, technicians, and intellectual professors) and white collar and service workers, which are all professional roles requiring higher levels of education. Moreover, economic growth and social development raised the expectations of thousands of young people and their families who considered higher education degrees as major channels of social mobility. These raised expectations demanded more than the extent and the timing of economic growth and occupational transformation would allow. The results were, first, that in the late 1960s Italian universities registered a great increase in enrollments, without any comprehensive institutional response by the Italian Parliament and government; and second that the number of young unemployed and underemployed with high educational levels also increased.

Finally, the structural changes of the 1950s and 1960s were followed by the cultural changes in the 1970s and 1980s. The traditional peasant values gave way to an urban, industrial culture.

The influence of the Church diminished and Italian society became more secularized. But religious bodies continue to exert a significant influence on educational institutions. In Milan, Rome, and Piacenza there are campuses of the Catholic University, a significant minority of university professors profess religious beliefs in their teaching, and the most active student group nationwide is nowadays a Catholic group.

As a consequence of major changes in family relations and in the role of women both at home and at the work place, major changes took place also in the attitudes toward children (with a sharp decline of authoritarian patterns), in sexual behavior (two laws making divorce and abortion legal were passed in 1971 and 1975), in attitudes toward work, and in lifestyles and consumption patterns.

All these changes in economic patterns, social relations, values, and attitudes created new needs and challenges for higher education, which were only partially and belatedly met.

1.2 Government and Political Factors

The problems of the modernization of higher education and of the transition from an elite to a mass university system received an unsatisfactory response from the Italian government. A law was passed in 1969, the Codignola Law, which introduced important changes, among which were the abolition of special requirements for entering such faculties as medicine and law, until then reserved to students who had completed the *liceo classico* (i.e., the elite type of secondary school); the granting of more freedom to students in terms of curricula within the different degree-granting faculties; and the attempt to weaken the academic oligarchy by blocking the recruitment of new professors according to the old rules of the national "*concorso*" (without, however, substituting those rules with new, more democratic ones). This law, which was passed under the pressure of a widespread militant student movement, was at the same time a democratic and a demagogic law. It removed unequal and unjust barriers to access to higher learning, which penalized lower- and middle-class students, and allowed greater flexibility in the choice of the curricula, thus contributing to a great increase in the number of students. But it did not modernize the structure of the higher education system, and it did not increase human and financial resources.

What happened is an instance of a partially blocked process of social change which took place repeatedly in modern Italian society and which can be described as follows. Deep structural changes (the processes of industrialization, urbanization, secularization, and so on) develop tensions and contradictions, which in turn foster social protest (such as that of the student movement of the late 1960s and early 1970s). These tensions and this protest, however, do not stimulate thorough and coherent reforms, but only very partial reforms, a multitude of piecemeal adjustments and day-to-day responses, which can quell social unrest and avoid a major crisis, but are unable to modernize the institutional fabric through badly needed innovation.

In Italian universities, institutional innovation and reform took place a decade later, in the 1980s. In July 1980 a law was passed for the reform of academic organization (through the introduction of different institutional levels and of research departments, and the reshaping of the academic career). Also in 1989 a new law was approved which created the new Ministry for the University and for Scientific and Technological Research and set the basic principles of a greater institutional autonomy.

The weak and slow institutional response to change and to social protest can be traced to the specific features of the Italian political system. Italy is a multiparty parliamentary democracy. Emerging from the defeat of an authoritarian regime, the constitution of the Italian Republic stressed the democratic control of parliament over the executive and the electoral law defended the rights of minorities, even tiny minorities.

Political parties hold great power. They have the merit of having institutionalized democratic values and norms, but they also tend to penetrate civil society and to occupy state institutions. The top managers of banks, public firms, many media organizations, and many other institutions are nominated directly or indirectly by political parties through delicate and complex negotiations and partitions. Universities are more independent, but there too political influence is often felt. The Italian party system has been defined as polarized pluralism. There have been on average 8 to 10 parties active at the national level, with the Christian Democratic Party as the majority party always in government, and the Communist Party as the second largest party

always in opposition (except for the short periods of national unity coalitions). Government change proved very difficult in this situation, even if the rise of new parties such as the Greens, the growth of the Socialist Party as a third force, and the reduction of ideological divisions among major parties opens new opportunities for change. Finally, in this context, governments do not last for long and have low decision-making capacity.

Italian politics in the last decades has been a remarkable instance of continuity of the political elite and of instability of governments. Since 1945 Italy has had over 40 governments. The longest lasting was the government headed by the Socialist Party secretary Craxi between 1973 and 1976, but there were also governments which lasted only a few weeks. On the other hand, the Christian Democratic Party was always part of the government coalition and on all but three occasions the prime minister has been a Christian Democrat. The present prime minister Andreotti is a remarkable example of the continuity of the political elite, as he began his government career as undersecretary to the prime minister in 1946. The succession of Italian government coalitions was as follows:

(a) 1944–47—governments of national unity (Socialists, Communists, Christian Democrats, and smaller parties);

(b) 1947–62—center governments (Christian Democrats together with smaller center parties);

(c) 1963–68—center-left governments (Christian democrats, Socialists, and smaller parties);

(d) 1968–76—succession of center and center-left governments;

(e) 1976–79—governments of national unity, led by the Christian democrats with the external backing of the Communist Party;

(f) 1979 to the early 1990s—center-left governments, with the unusual feature of two non-Christian Democrat prime ministers for the first time since 1945.

Governments in the early 1990s put the modernization of higher education and the development of research high on their policy agenda, as is shown by the formation of the new Ministry of the University and Scientific and Technological Research, by the reform laws on institutional autonomy, on the change of the curricula (which are to be discussed in parliament), and by the steady increase of financial resources for research. Reform attempts however, meet the resistance of the central bureaucracy and of segments of the professional body which defend entrenched interests and privileges, and the relative lack of concern of wide sectors of political classes, businesses, and public opinion.

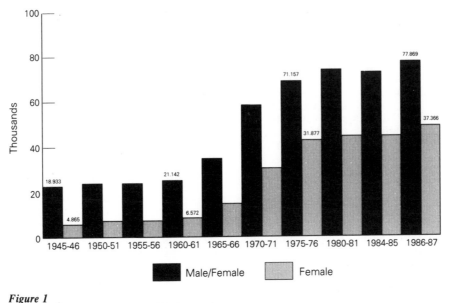

Figure 1
University graduates 1960 to 1987 by gender

2. The Institutional Fabric of the Higher Education System

In the last 30 years Italian higher education expanded dramatically in terms of students enrolled but grew much less in terms of establishments, research facilities, personnel, and finance. As Table 1 shows, between the two academic years of 1960–61 and 1985–86 the number of students enrolled increased more than four times and, as Fig. 1 shows, the number of graduates increased accordingly, with a much higher increase for women. The rate of increase was particularly high until the mid-1970s and then slowed down. The proportion of the age group 20–24 enrolled in the whole higher education system has risen accordingly.

The increase of students was due to a combination of factors: (a) demographic changes (the birthrate's turning point was around 1970 and the effect of demographic decline on university enrollments has started to be noticeable); (b) a growing and varying demand for an educated labor force in different work areas, according to different degrees and patterns of economic growth and social transformation; (c) rising expectations of upward social mobility and changing perceptions of the opportunities for an educated labor force by young people and their families; (d) the increasing participation of women in the labor market as part of a more general process of women's emancipation; and (e) the approval of laws, which, like the Codignola Law of 1969, liberalized access to higher education, or, on the contrary, like the law on medicine, introduced a selective admission policy.

The number of institutions did not grow in a parallel way and caused an overcrowding of universities in the largest cities, primarily in Rome, Milan, and Naples. This, together with significantly differing admission policies, led to an uneven distribution of students in the various institutions. Overcrowding is more serious in Rome (with almost 150,000 students concentrated in one institution plus a few thousands in three smaller ones) than in Milan where a more articulated and diversified system of higher education exists which has five different academic institutions.

The Italian higher education system is predominantly a public system. At present there are 48

Table 1
Students enrolled in the higher education system: universities 1960–86

	1960/61	1965/66	1970/71	1975/76	1980/81	1985/86
Number of student enrollments (000s)	268	403	682	936	1,048	1,113

public universities and 19 private ones. Public and private universities do not differ significantly in terms of quality of teaching and research. But there is a hierarchy of prestige, with the universities of major cities, like Milan, Turin, and Rome, the oldest medieval universities of Bologna, Pavia, Padua and a few first-class campuses, such as Pisa, at the top.

Admission policy is governed by national legislation. According to the Codignola Law, the only requirement is a secondary school diploma. Also since fees are generally low (around US$250 a year on average, for public institutions), access is easy. This however does not mean that graduation is easy. On average, only about 30 percent of the students enrolled graduate, in spite of the fact that there are no requirements for completing courses in a fixed period of time, so that the number of late students (students who have exceeded the lower time limit necessary to obtain a degree) is one and a half times higher than the number of first-year students.

In recent years, a growing number of institutions have been introducing selective admission policies. At first, private universities, like the Bocconi University and the Catholic University of Milan, fixed the number of first-year students to be accepted through an entry exam and charged fees in relation to the student's family revenue (up to US$5,000 in Bocconi). The faculty of dentistry, followed by the much more important faculty of medicine and in 1989 by veterinary medicine, introduced the *numerus clausus* for first-year students through a legislative device: a law was passed which required a fixed number of teaching, laboratory, and training hours for future graduates. On the basis of these requirements and given the size of the teaching staff and of teaching facilities, the maximum number of students to be accepted was calculated. Other faculties, such as engineering, computer sciences, architecture, in large universities like the State University and the Politechnic of Milan, have introduced aptitude tests and have tried to moderate expectations through counseling. The general trend now is toward the introduction of admission policies of some kind, but the process is slow because of fears of student protest. The progressive integration of the higher education systems of European Community countries will favor this process, since completely open access is an Italian peculiarity which can block mutual recognition of degrees with other European universities.

Until the 1980 law, Italian higher education granted one type of academic degree, the *laurea*, which has legal value, that is, is an official requirement for access to the public administration and for participating in the exams which regulate admission to professions such as medicine, law, engineering, architecture, and auditing. Below the *laurea* there are the two-year and three-year diplomas for a variety of professions, from paramedics to statisticians, from musical philologists to primary school assistants,

which are granted by nonuniversity institutes usually attached to universities. Also above it there are the schools of specialization. Qualification for admission to the latter schools is a university first-level degree plus an entry examination. In 1985–86 there were 1,469 schools of specialization, associated with universities, with 67,743 students (among which 21,921 were women) and 16,213 graduates (among which 5,035 were women). Most of the schools (1,191) were and continue to be in the area of medicine, but they are slowly spreading to other sectors as well, such as humanities, business, engineering, and social sciences. The 1980 law introduced a more diversified system, introducing the research doctoral degree (PhD) and strengthened the role of the pre-*laurea* schools, offering two- and three-year diplomas, and the post-*laurea* schools of specialization.

The number of both doctoral programs and students enrolled is planned centrally. Often PhD programs are organized by a consortium of universities. Access is regulated through a competitive examination where the candidate's academic record, knowledge, motivation, and publications are considered. Four years after their introduction in 1983, the total number of PhD programs was 2,309 (318 in physical and life sciences, 228 in humanities and social sciences, and 181 in medicine) and the number of students was 9,158 (1,425 in sciences, 821 in humanities and social sciences, and 625 in medicine).

In Italy, scientific and technological research is undertaken and financed both by public and private institutions, by the public administration and by business corporations. The major research institutions are public: the universities, the National Research Council (CNR) and other national institutions such as the National Institute of Nuclear Physics (INFN), the National Alternative Energy Agency (ENEA), the Higher Health Institute (ISS), the Higher Institute for Work Safety and Prevention (ISPESL), the National Nutrition Institute, the "experimental stations" for various industries, the Institute for Economic Planning (ISPE), the Institute for Workers' Professional Training (ISFOL), and so on. Important research facilities exist in all major corporations, both private, such as the Fiat Research Center, the Montedison Research and Development System, and Olivetti's Computer Science Research Unit, and public, such as Stet's Study Center and Laboratory on Telecommunications (CSELT), the National Agency for Electric Energy (ENEL) Study and Research Division and the state-controled financial holdings of IRI, ENI, and EFIM research centers.

The most important extrauniversity public research agency is the CNR, which comprises 153 permanent institutes, 113 study centers created through conventions with public and private research structures (most of them with universities), and 13 research areas which coordinate the work of the institutes and study centers. In recent years CNR's research activity has been coordinated through so-called "finalized projects" and "strategic projects" dealing with major objectives such as advanced technology, health, the environment, the economy, agricultural resources, infrastructures, and services. "Strategic projects" operate mostly through internal research structures, while "finalized projects" make use of external research structures. Since 1979 the CNR has managed the National Space Plan. The CNR participates in several international research projects with European Community countries and with other countries of the world and has signed 28 bilateral agreements with similar foreign centers.

Alongside the CNR, universities have been the natural loci of research, because of the essential link between teaching and research. With the introduction of the PhD in the 1980 law, basic progress was made in the training of researchers. As Table 2 shows, universities are active primarily in basic research, but also in applied research, while research and development is more the concern of private and public firms. University research has been financed mostly by public sources, in particular by the National Research Council, the national research agencies, the Ministry of Education, and public corporations.

Until recently, research activities were not very well coordinated in spite of the attempts of the CNR. With the 1989 law which created the new Ministry of the University and Scientific and Technological Research, however, the prospects for effective coordination of teaching and research in universities, of different research institutions among themselves, and of research activities and government policies have become better. Every three years the new minister must present to parliament a report on the state of scientific and technological research, together with a report on the state of higher education. The minister decides and promotes scientific and technological plans, with the consultancy of a newly formed body—the National Council of Science and Technology—and, on the basis of those plans, distributes research funds to universities, after having heard the opinion of the faculty's representative bodies, that is, the permanent conference of Italian universities' rectors and the National University Council. The minister also sits permanently with other cabinet members in the committee for economic policy, the committee for industrial policy, and the committee for foreign economic policy.

3. Governance, Administration, and Finance

3.1 National Administration

The governance of Italian higher education does not fit either one of the three basic models of higher education which have developed in other Western countries—the Anglo-American model which is the result of a variety of largely autonomous institutions, the Humboldt model which aims at integrating university teaching and academic research, and the Napoleonic model which aims at building a centralized, uniform, and coordinated system—although it is closest to the Napoleonic model. In fact, the Italian system tried to strike a balance between centralized control of personnel, financial budgets, and curricula and the safeguard of institutional autonomies (often going back many centuries) and of professorial privileges.

On the one hand, the Italian state centralized political authority and control over personnel status and salary, curricula, courses and credits, and budgets for education and research in the special Division on Higher Education affiliated to the State Ministry of Education in Rome. However, the authorities tended to concentrate on specific jurisdictions and agencies with little coordination. Moreover, rules and policies decided in Rome often failed to be accompanied by adequate procedures of enforcement, implementation, and evaluation. There was also little input from below, from the various components of the academic community. On the other hand, professors enjoyed almost complete freedom; not only intellectual freedom, which is an indispensable requirement of the academic profession, and the autonomous power to control the patterns of recruitment of new professors, which is an important corollary of intellectual freedom, but also the freedom to accumulate outside resources and commitments—because of the prestige attached to the academic profession—and to form a professorial oligarchy. This oligarchy lasted through time, and maintained its position even in the face of the complex transformations of Italian higher education from an elite to a mass university system and of the student protest movement of the late 1960s and early 1970s.

As Clark (1977) remarks, the Italian system is a peculiar compromise between a centrally administered bureaucracy and a self-governing professorial body, which also allows for some competitiveness. This compromise has manifest negative aspects, such as institutional rigidity, resistance to innovation, lack of coordination, but also more latent advantages, like its remarkable ability to adjust and to produce high quality research and graduates in several of its institutions. In the last 10 years legislative reforms have been introduced which tried to improve this peculiar compromise between centralized state control and professorial autonomy.

The Italian university system is predominantly public, centralized, and uniform throughout the country. Until May 1989 the Ministry of Education had prime responsibility for higher education through a special administrative division. In May 1989 a law was passed which transferred responsibility to the newly formed Ministry of the University and Scientific and Technological Research. In the

Table 2
University investments by area of financing 1975–80–85 (millions lire)

	1975			1980			1985		
	Basic research	Applied research	Research and development	Basic research	Applied research	Research and development	Basic research	Applied research	Research and development
Public sector:	152,801	99,046	4,009	238,753	192,839	27,549	891,975	720,441	102,920
State	118,080	76,542	3,098	213,616	172,536	24,648	819,808	662,153	94,593
Public corporations	—	—	—	25,137	20,030	2,901	72,167	58,288	8,327
Enterprise:	—	—	—	3,120	2,520	360	13,280	10,727	1,532
Public	—	—	—	1,363	1,100	157	5,783	4,672	667
Private	—	—	—	1,757	1,420	203	7,497	6,055	865
Foreign corporations	—	—	—	1,227	991	141	5,269	4,256	608
Total	152,801	99,046	4,009	243,100	196,350	28,050	910,524	735,424	105,060

Source: Istat-Annuario Statistico dell'Istruzione, 1986

same law the principles of a larger autonomy for academic institutions were also laid out.

The 1989 law pursued two basic goals: (a) a stricter coordination between teaching and research at the higher education level (all the functions related to scientific and technological research which were previously scattered among various ministries are now concentrated in the new one while higher education is separated from education in general); and (b) a satisfying compromise between the two basic needs of centralized planning, coordination, and evaluation and of institutional autonomy. Although maintaining most of the powers of its predecessor, in particular the control of personnel and finance, the new ministry is conceived more as a central coordinating agency, which does not impose central control on the various aspects of university life, but rather guarantees the necessary coordination and implementation. For this reason, the law envisaged a bureaucratic structure of 550 people, organized in departments and services and integrated with a small number of outside experts, who can be hired on a temporary basis.

The national government has primary responsibility for higher education and research. Through the new minister's three-yearly reports which will be prepared on the basis of the reports presented by various universities, after having consulted the representative bodies, it should be possible to assess higher education's response to national plans of economic and social development.

Regional administrations have minor responsibilities, such as student aid. Some regional governments like that of Lombardy are demanding a greater influence in the area of university planning and in the development of diploma courses which are more directly linked to specific labor market needs. Large city councils are increasingly asked by universities to provide resources, mainly land, for university development. However, Italy is still very far from a much needed administrative devolution from central to local government.

The national government shapes higher education by decree and by budgetary control. Since the state legally recognizes university degrees, which are necessary requirements for holding high-level positions in the state bureaucracy, for teaching in post-primary schools, and for entering national competitions for the liberal professions, it is the state that determines the general guidelines for curricula, criteria for admission, examinations, and length of study.

The national government also exercises a thorough budgetary control on universities' expenses. Wages and salaries for university personnel are determined nationally and are the same nationwide. Criteria of recruitment and promotion for professors are also determined by the national government.

The 1989 law has increased institutional autonomy, providing that universities give themselves autonomous statutes and norms with regard to the organization of teaching and research and their administration and finance. A tough conflict between central government and universities can be predicted over the range of autonomy which the law can assure. The law envisages various areas of institutional autonomy for universities, such as curricula, teaching methods, and criteria of evaluation. However, the most important leverages of the university budget, finance and personnel, are still strictly in the hands of the central government. Since university self-financing through students' fees and outside sources, such as contracts and endowments, remains a minor proportion of the university budget, government control through the transfer of funds will continue to be very strong. Besides, the regulation of the other very important form of university autonomy—personnel hiring and management—will not be decided on in the foreseeable future. For the moment, staff resources are still allocated centrally.

Since 1960, a growing percentage of the gross national product has been devoted to higher education, given the dramatic increase in the number of students. However, this has fallen short of the needs of higher education.

3.2 Institutional Administration

Italian higher education is the result of a compromise between centralized government control over finance, personnel, curricula, and so on, and faculty control over conditions of work, content and method of teaching, choice of colleagues, and so on. These issues form the key matters of discussion in the collegial bodies which organize university life.

The basic unit of the system is the university, which is administered by the rector, the academic senate, and the board of administrators. A university is composed of a varying number of faculties, departments, institutes, and research centers where academic work is organized. The faculty is still by far the most important base unit. Faculties can include more than one degree course, each of which grants a degree which is legally recognized. The most important faculties in terms of degrees granted, number of professors and students and quantity of resources, are medicine; mathematical, physical, and natural sciences; engineering; law; literature and philosophy; economics and business; architecture; political sciences.

The rector is the legal representative of the university, a *primus inter pares* among professors, and the head of the university administration. He or she is elected by the whole faculty body of the university for a mandate of three years which can be renewed several times. Rectors must play a variety of roles. They must be mediators in the conflicts of interest among different faculties, different segments of the university, and different components of the academic body. They must know the intricacies of academic legislation, solve problems, and find solutions. They must know how to communicate with the national government, the relevant political parties, the intellectual elite, the business community, and others with a stake in the university. They are guardians of the normal functioning of the academic institution and from time to time must be capable of confronting student protest. They must be good educators and respected scholars to win the consensus of their peers and, according to circumstances, they should also be institution builders, managers, and conflict resolvers. As Riesman remarked with regard to American university presidents, it is amazing that for a role requiring so many different capacities no special training is thought necessary. Rectors are united in the Permanent Conference of the Italian Rectors, which is a lobby for academic demands vis-à-vis the government.

The rector chairs the academic senate, which is formed by the presidents or deans of the various faculties, and the board of administrators, which comprises representatives of the various components of the university—full professors, associate professors, assistant professors, nonteaching personnel—and by the representatives of all the institutions which finance the university. The academic senate is the governing body of the university. It ratifies all important decisions of faculty councils, sets the criteria for distributing resources, and expresses its views on controversial matters. The board of administrators is concerned with the university budget and all financial matters.

The faculty has a collegial self-governing body, the faculty council which is chaired by a dean (*Preside*), who must be a full professor working full-time in the university and who is elected by all full professors and assistant professors for one or more three-year terms. The faculty council and the dean perform at faculty level the functions which are performed by the academic senate and by the rector at the university level. They hold formal responsibilities for selecting teaching personnel at all levels, distributing funds and other resources within the faculty, and organizing teaching activities and academic work in general.

Historically institutes formed themselves around the full professor, and until the 1980 law were the base units of both teaching and research activities within the faculties. The 1980 law introduced a different type of base unit, the department, which was intended to aggregate all professors working in the same research area (also those belonging to different faculties) on a more democratic basis. The underlying idea was that departments would gradually replace institutes, guaranteeing a better coordination among scholars and a more democratic organization of academic work. For this purpose departments were supposed to be favored in the distribution of resources. But the opposition of the more traditional faculties such as medicine and law maintained institutes alongside departments and weakened the innovative character of the proposal.

4. Faculty and Students: Teaching, Learning, and Research

4.1 Faculty

In the last 30 years Italian higher education faced a dramatic increase in the student population and a much lesser increase in the teaching staff. As Table 3 shows, after a significant increase between 1960–61 and 1970–71, there was a decrease in the following decade and then again an increase in the 1980s, which, however, brought the teaching staff only slightly above the level of 1970–71. If this data is broken up by qualification, it can be seen that, although the numbers did not change, a major qualitative change in the composition of the teaching staff took place between 1970 and 1987, involving a process of consolidation and institutionalization of the professorial body. As Table 4 shows, while in 1970–71 there were only 3,472 full professors and the number of temporary teachers of various kinds was more than double that of established professors, in 1987–88 the number of full professors had increased more than three times, up to 11,237, and the total number of full and associate professors now amounted to two-thirds of the entire teaching body. The price for this consolidation of the professorial body was, however, paid by the new generation of teachers who faced a reduced number of new academic positions, as shown by the decrease in the number of faculty members in the 1970s.

According to the 1980 law, the career pattern of teaching staff consists of three levels: assistant professor (*ricercatore*), associate professor, and full professor. The first level, that of *ricercatore* is in

Table 3
University teaching staff 1960–87

	1960–61	1970–71	1980–81	1984–85	1985–86	1986–87
Numbers of faculty	37,976	50,394	43,270	50,154	50,996	51,081

Table 4
University teaching staff by qualification from 1960–88

	1961–62	1965–66	1970–71	1975–76	1980–81	1985–86	1987–88
Full professors	2,091	2,608	3,472	5,209	8,122	8,486	11,237
Associate professors	6,188	7,377	5,542	10,290[a]	13,762[b]	19,577[b]	22,428
Established university lecturers	11,529	16,068	7,673	—	—	—	—
Assistants and other staff	21,205	25,724	33,707	28,150	21,386	22,933	18,919[c]

Source: Istat-Annuario Statistico dell'Istruzione
a Includes assistants with appointment   b Includes professors with annual teaching contract   c Includes researchers, assistants, lecturers, and scholarship-holders

some respects equivalent to assistant professors in the United States, with the notable difference that they cannot have the responsibility of a university course and concentrate on research.

Professors are civil servants with rights and duties equivalent to those of other government employees. However, they enjoy a much higher status than the majority of civil servants, and specific working conditions. All faculty members are granted a tenured status after they win a national competition.

The procedure for appointment is a two-step process. The number of new positions is determined nationally for groups of disciplines by the government on the basis of the demands made by different universities. A complex procedure of national competitions for associate and full professors and local competitions at the university level for assistant professors is then set up. The evaluating commissions are formed exclusively by professors, both elected and chosen from amongst those eligible. Each commission can pass a number of winners not higher than the number of new positions available for each group of disciplines. Finally, the universities which have asked and obtained a given position make their choice among the winners of the national competition. The competition for full professors involves only an evaluation of the research works and of the teaching curricula of the candidates. The competition for associate professors also includes the evaluation of a lecture that each candidate must perform in front of the commission. The competition for the *ricercatori* involves two written essays and an oral colloquium.

No difference exists between the career and formal status of faculty members in different types of institutions. Two professors with extremely different teaching loads and academic responsibilities can draw the same salary. On the other hand, real status can differ very much according to the prestige of different faculties and different universities.

The coming of the mass university, the big increase in the number of full and associate professors, the opening of greater career opportunities, and the introduction of departments, has weakened the traditional model of academic organization which was centered on the chair and the "school." According to that model, university "barons" were able to lead a "school" and to tightly control a number of subordinated pupils since they had the time to train them. Students were loyal to their "*maestro*" since they dedicated time to them and their support was a necessary requisite for getting a chair.

With the advent of the mass university, the strong direct link between full professors and their pupils weakened but did not disappear. There was a proliferation of temporary teaching positions to meet the increasing needs for teaching staff. Uncertainties about their future brought these teachers to rely less on chaired professors and more on trade unionism. In the 1970s, organized unions spread, mostly among lower-level teachers, and also encouraged by the general politicized climate of the country. The three national trade unions—CGIL, CISL, and UIL—entered the university. National teaching staff associations like the CNU were formed and more temporary associations appeared from time to time, like the *Coordinamento docenti precari*. More importantly, several teachers were active in the student movement of the late 1960s and early 1970s and for the whole decade a consistent proportion of the teaching staff participated in strikes. According to the 1972 study made by Giglioli (1979) 89 percent of the assistant and associate professors considered strikes a legitimate means for pursuing their interests and 78 percent said that they had been on strike in the course of the year.

Trade union pressures, together with government parties' attempts to quell political protests in the university, and opposition parties' attempts to win consensus in the teaching staff, contributed both to the opening of new teaching positions, and the filling of these positions through seniority mechanisms rather than on the basis of academic merit. As a consequence, young and brilliant scholars found access to teaching positions much more difficult and the professional model of academic life was weakened in favor of the bureaucratic model. Today, corporate pressure for a bureaucratic seniority system of career advancement is weaker. Scientific capacities are on the whole fairly judged in national competitions. The patronage system in academic careers is still active, although the power of the full professors is not so much expressed by its capacity to guarantee the advancement of their pupils, as to attract outside resources and to distribute them to the members of his group.

Academic work in Italian higher education can vary greatly from one institution to another and from one department to another. The minimum number of hours to be given to academic work is defined at the national level and is rather low: 350 hours a year for teaching and examinations, for assisting students in defining their learning programs and preparing their dissertations, and for administrative tasks of various kinds. The rest of the working time is expected to be devoted to research. The hours are reduced to 250 a year for those full and associate professors who have chosen the "defined time" regime, which allows for professional work outside the university and does not carry an entitlement to a special salary indemnity.

The academic work of assistant professors (*ricercatori*) is also defined at the national level. Strangely enough, it is not the minimum number of hours to be given to teaching activities which are formally laid down, but the maximum number, no more than 250 hours a year. The role of the assistant professor is an ambiguous one. Research activities are correctly stressed, but no substantial evaluation of research work is envisaged, except in national competitions. Since the assistant professor's role is a tenured role, the result is that those people who are not capable or willing to make an academic career have neither incentives to work nor sanctions against failure to do so.

In this situation the Italian system looks like a whirlpool. At the core are those full professors with administrative responsibilities, who teach in the largest and more crowded universities, lead research groups and, often, accumulate roles outside academe. They work very hard and concentrate power and prestige in their hands. Moving toward the periphery of the system of higher education, from the largest cities to the provinces, from the most prestigious and crowded universities to the others, from the most popular subjects to the least popular ones, from the most famous professors to the others, the pace of activity becomes slower and slower, and one finds teachers who work much less, enjoy less academic power and prestige, receive the same salary, but have no outside resources.

4.2 Students

The student population increased greatly from the 1960s onward, because of the various factors mentioned above. Enrollment data tend, however, to overestimate the Italian student population, given the large number of dropouts and the many first-year "phantom students" who do not sit examinations and who do not attend university, for a variety of reasons—from postponing military service to increasing their chances of finding a better job. Although the number of graduates has greatly increased since 1960 (as Table 5 shows, the number of graduates as a percentage of the 23-year old population increased from 2.9 in 1961 to 8.7 in 1986, and the gap between male and female graduates has been greatly reduced), the figures remain below average in comparison with other advanced industrial countries.

Students are also very unevenly distributed among different universities and among various subject areas. It is one of the peculiarities of Italian higher education that in a very centralized system there is no central planning and control of the flow of students. As Table 6 on enrollments and Table 7 on graduates show, this distribution has tended to change significantly over the years: there was a boom in the social sciences and humanities in the early 1970s, then a boom in medicine in the late 1970s and early 1980s, and later a boom in law, business and the physical sciences. Shifts are to some extent more dramatic since undergraduate studies in Italy are not based on a broad, general, liberal arts content, but on rather specialist single-subject courses. The choice made at entry cannot then be reversed without losing one or more academic terms.

After the 1969 law which removed barriers to access for students coming from less prestigious high schools, Italian higher education has become more democratic. However democratization is less than it appears from the social stratification of first-year students. Access is still completely free in many faculties of state universities, but selection which takes place in the university years is severe. Students are assessed through written and/or oral examinations at the end of every course. Given the com-

Table 5

Graduates and 24-year old population by gender (absolute values-thousand)

Total	1961	1971	1981	1986
Graduates	22	61	74	76
24-year old population	762	824	809	871
Graduates as percentage of 24-year old population	2.9	7.4	9.1	8.7
Male				
Graduates	15	34	41	41
24-year old population	384	416	411	441
Graduates as percentage of 24-year old population	3.9	8.3	10.5	9.3
Female				
Graduates	7	26	33	35
24-year old population	378	408	398	429
Graduates as percentage of 24-year old population	1.8	6.5	8.3	8.1

Source: Elaboration on the basis of Istat data

Table 6
Total enrollments (male and female) in the higher education system (university) by main courses of degree

Fields of study	1960–61 Enrolled		1965–66 Enrolled		1970–71 Enrolled		1975–76 Enrolled		1980–81 Enrolled		1984–85 Enrolled		1987–88 Enrolled
	Total	Female	Total	Female	Total	Female	Total	Female	Total	Female	Total	Female	Total
Physical/Life Sciences	26,135	9,608	26,367	12,674	96,377	34,282	124,828	64,044	133,839	72,420	138,713	71,770	93,105
Medicine	17,915	2,181	21,648	3,426	78,973	14,027	168,444	45,388	176,054	60,831	143,234	55,616	65,754
Engineering	23,833	1,030	36,348	2,041	95,603	4,752	143,175	14,682	146,580	20,780	160,744	27,843	126,861
Agriculture	2,831	62	3,571	101	11,406	516	24,306	2,868	41,309	8,815	38,377	9,727	20,716
Economics/Business	47,124	4,826	55,987	11,981	114,453	24,898	126,295	34,158	111,133	33,754	145,815	50,621	130,575
Social/Political sciences									52,210	21,305	62,333	26,524	60,408
Law	31,688	5,564	21,639	4,007	58,747	11,952	114,824	36,310	144,869	59,428	172,267	78,637	130,593
Humanities	36,922	27,557	23,074	68,498	217,218	162,084	220,425	163,390	214,664	162,323	221,938	174,593	147,888
Diplomas	5,342	2,368	3,413	3,008	8,954	3,978	13,498	6,940	24,216	13,169	23,161	12,236	15,305

Source: Istat, Annuario Statistico dell'Istruzione 1988

Table 7
Graduates by subject area

	1960	1965	1970	1975	1980	1985	1987
Physical/Life sciences	3,436	4,536	5,811	10,822	10,783	9,945	10,391
Medicine	2,710	2,857	329	8,590	14,264	13,489	12,603
Engineering	2,462	3,124	4,696	10,237	11,509	9,615	9,845
Agriculture	593	585	512	1,333	1,881	3,034	2,842
Economics/ Business	2,492	4,177	6,022	8,201	3,862	6,834	8,967
Social/ Political[a] sciences					3,548	2,950	3,651
Law	4,969	5,150	4,195	5,441	7,718	8,599	9,959
Humanities	3,961	6,739	16,044	16,100	16,687	14,149	15,827
Diplomas[b]	519	759	1,200	1,623	3,866	3,533	3,784

Source: Istat, Annuario Statistico dell'Istruzione
a Before 1980 the diploma in social and political sciences was assimilated in the economic diploma   b Palaeography and musical philology/statistics/primary-school teaching/gymnastics

plete freedom of professors in setting the criteria of evaluation as well as the content of courses, there can be great differences among courses in the same subject matter. As De Francesto and Trivellato (1978) showed, the proportion of lower-class students in the second year and beyond is lower than among new students, and even more so if "high performance" senior students are considered. This means that there are significant differences in the quality of education given by different types of high school and that the percentage of students with lower-class backgrounds, who enroll without being able to attend, is higher.

The extent and the ways of representing student interests have changed over the years, according to the cycle of student protest. For most of the 1960s, students elected their own representative bodies which were concerned with issues of student life. Student representatives formed university political parties and were related to youth organizations of national parties. Campus politics in the 1950s and in the 1960s mirrored national politics, with some variations, was the training ground for future political leaders, and the site of experimental political solutions which anticipated national politics, such as the coalition between Catholics, socialists, and communists.

The student protest of 1968 and later years denied legitimacy and dismantled this system of representation. It challenged the academic power of full professors and demanded a thorough transformation of university life. A genuine demand for democratization, for antiauthoritarian relations in higher education, and for a closer link with the underprivileged classes was mixed with a good deal of ideological rigidity and demagogic opportunism and in some cases with the harassment of professors.

After the last attempts to build a mass protest movement in 1977, student politics returned to the channels of traditional politics although conditions for a new wave of student unrest are still present.

Student organizations now reflect major political forces. The elected representatives participate in the faculty councils and in the university board of administrators only with consultative, not decision-making, power. Also, because of the little decision-making power which is granted, participation in student elections is very low, under 10 percent on average. Major student organizations are those related to the Catholic movement *Comunione e liberazione* and to the leftist parties' youth movements. The 1989 law provides that student representatives be included in the bodies which universities should form for drafting the new statutes.

5. Conclusion

Higher education in contemporary Italy presents a picture of light and shadow. Many high quality departments and research centers coexist with institutional rigidity and lack of innovation. The good standard of graduates coexists with the high number of dropouts. The long-lasting compromise between centralized control and professorial freedom guarantees the adaptation of the system to changing needs, but it slows down necessary transformations.

Major current difficulties are related to the excessive centralization of the system, the insufficient autonomy of academic institutions; the very uneven distribution of students among universities and subject areas; the problem of access which is still completely open for some faculties and selective for an increasing number of others; the problem of guiding students in their choice of faculty; the great number of dropouts; insufficient numbers of assistant professors; insufficient funding for research; and insufficient development of specialization courses (master's courses) and of predegree nonuniversity sectors.

During the 1990s the most important issues likely to affect higher education are: issues of scientific and technological development related to increasing international competition and to the needs of protecting the environment and of bettering the quality of life; issues of equality of opportunity in university access; issues of closer and more effective relationship between higher education and the labor market; issues of recruitment and training of new professors; and issues of administrative efficiency and institutional autonomy.

In order to cope with these issues it is necessary to proceed with the reform process started by the 1980 law and continued by the 1989 law, accelerating the approval of the law on university autonomy and the law on the reform of teaching curricula and courses of study, and to strike a better balance between the need for centralized coordination, control and evaluation, and institutional autonomy.

Bibliography

Clark B 1977 *Academic Power in Italy.* Chicago University Press, Chicago, Illinois
Clark B 1983 *The Higher Education System.* University of California Press, Berkeley, California
De Francesco C, Trivellato P 1978 *La laurea e il posto.* Il Mulino, Bologna
De Francesco C, Trivellato P 1985 *L'università incontrollata.* Angeli, Milan
De Masi D 1978 *Dentro l'università: studenti, classi, corporazioni.* Angeli, Milan
Giglioli P P 1979 *Baroni e burocrati. Il ceto accademico italiano.* Il Mulino, Bologna
International Council on the Future of the University 1979 *Report on Italian University,* Rome
Martinelli A 1982 *Università e società negli Stati Uniti,* 2nd edn. Einaudi, Turin
Martinelli A 1987 I dilemmi dell'università italiana. *Mondo operaio,* 40 (8–9)
Martinotti G 1969 *Gli studenti universitari.* Marsilio, Padua
Moscati R 1983 *Università: fine o trasformazione del mito?* Il Mulino, Bologna
Presidenza del Consiglio dei ministri 1987 La politica della ricerca in Italia. *Vita italiana* 5
Riesman D 1970 Predicaments in the career of a college president. In: Kruytbosch C E, Messinger S L (eds.) 1970 *The State of the University. Authority and Change.* Sage, Los Angeles, California
Riesman D 1980 *On Higher Education.* Jossey Bass, San Francisco, California
Roveda C, Viale R (eds.) 1989 *Autonomia dell'università e della ricerca.* Fondazione Rosselli, Turin
Statera G 1979 *Il destino sociale dei laureati di massa.* Liguori, Naples
Zuliani A, Multari V, Avallone G 1979 Primi materiali per un quadro quantitativo dell'istruzione universitaria: studenti e personale docente. In: *Economia, istruzione e formazione professionale.* Ceep-La Nuova Italia, p. 5

A. Martinelli

Ivory Coast, The

1. Higher Education and Society

The first institution of higher education in the Ivory Coast, a former French colony, was founded in 1958, two years before Independence. It was established by local political authorities in order to train the cadres the newly independent country would need. This first Center for Higher Studies was a joint initiative of President Felix Houphouet-Boigny and the University of Dakar (Senegal). Ivory Coast students previously studied in France.

The estimated population was 2,525,000 in 1945. At the start of the 1990s it numbers 11,500,000. While still predominantly rural (65% of people live in rural areas), the country is undergoing increasingly rapid urbanization. The native population (82.3% of the total) is divided among the Akan (32.7%), Krou (15.5%), Northern Mandé (12.9%), Southern Mandé (10.7%), and the Voltaiques and the Senoufo (11%). The foreign population (17.2%) is made up of natives of Burkina Faso, Mali, Guinea, Ghana, Lebanon, and other countries. The average growth rate is 4.2 percent and the population density is 35.9 inhabitants per square kilometer (*La Grande Encyclopédie de la Côte d'Ivoire* 1986).

Agricultural concerns remain a priority for the state, which has promoted export agriculture and staple crops as part of its policy of food self-reliance. The state also promotes the development of the livestock and fishing sectors. It has adapted its investment policy to favor small and medium enterprises and create employment in the provinces. The agro-industrial and industrial public sector as well as energy companies have been reformed. Special attention is being given to the energy sector.

The crisis caused by the drop in prices of the main export products has considerably affected the tertiary sector, which has little support.

1.1 Structure of Government and Main Political Goals

The Ivory Coast has a presidential political system. Although formerly a single-party state with one party, the Democratic Party of the Ivory Coast, holding power since 1960, the Ivory Coast has since 1990 had a multiparty system. The main goals since Independence have been to ensure the unity of the nation with a better integration of the distinct ethnic groups, political stability to develop the country, and peace and cooperation with all other countries.

2. The Institutional Fabric of the Higher Education System

The first university-level courses were taught at the Center for Higher Studies in Abidjan in 1958–59, which was the first year of the *licence* (the graduate degree in sciences, humanities, and arts equivalent to a BA degree). The Center for Higher Studies became the Center for Higher Education in 1959, retaining its original structure and having 73 students.

After Independence in 1960, an agreement was signed with France stating that the structure of studies, the ranking of professors, and the degrees given in the Ivory Coast would follow patterns set by French universities.

The University of Abidjan was founded in 1964. It had four schools: sciences, law, humanities, and medicine. They all became faculties between 1966 and 1971. The Faculty of Economic Sciences and the Institute of Odontology and Stomatology were established in 1973, followed by the Faculty of Pharmacy in 1985.

The first University Institute of Technology was founded in 1967. It was initially part of the University, but later became the National Institute of Technical Education (INSET), founded in 1975 and with eight branch campuses.

Various institutions of general and higher technical education were founded between 1961 and 1977 to respond to the pressing need for middle- and upper-level cadres.

Institutions of higher education in the Ivory Coast are either public or private with state subsidies. Of the 34 public institutions, 26 impart general or professional education to future cadres of high-level technicians, while the remaining eight give professional technical training. Technical and technological education includes a large number of specialties.

The ten private institutions provide basic education and updating in different sectors of the economy. The Ministry of Education guarantees the quality of the education in exchange for direct participation by granting subsidies or overviewing part of the teaching faculty. The *grandes écoles* provide general training in public works, administration, postal and telecommunication services, marketing, secretarial skills, public relations, and health care. Besides these public institutions, there are several international institutes providing studies in electricity, oceanography, and continuing education in postal and telecommunication services.

Several schools and institutes are dedicated to training prospective teachers which is a priority in the Ivory Coast. Teachers are required to be trained according to a uniform educational structure. Their training should include a general theoretical background, educational theory, and practice teaching.

Agronomy students study at the National School of Agronomy. Some are selected to continue in a second cycle leading to a degree in agronomy. These are called engineering theoreticians. Practical engineers are trained in other institutes.

Religious educational institutions are limited to the primary and secondary levels. An international center for the education of priests operates in Abidjan (*Institut Catholique de l'Afrique de l'Ouest*).

Research has been promoted by creating research laboratories for professors and researchers in the different university departments. There are also specific research institutes with independent researchers.

To gain admission to the University or *grandes écoles*, a student must have reached a certain standard in the baccalaureate examination, and have been selected and placed by the Interministerial Commission for Secondary and University-level Orientation. This is done according to the country's needs and opportunities, places available for students in the diffferent institutions, the labor market, and the individual student's abilities. Request from foreign students are examined by a ministerial committee after consultation with the various faculties. Ten percent of available places are reserved for foreign students.

After two years of study, the first diploma is granted. The *licence* is given at the end of the third year and the *maîtrise* (master's degree) after the fourth year. A research project is required for certain *licences*. All students are required to do an original research project for the *maîtrise*.

3. Governance, Administration, and Finance

Higher education falls within the competency of three ministries: the Ministry of National Education for Secondary and Higher Education, the Ministry of Technical Education for Professional Training, and the Ministry of Scientific Research. The Office of Higher Education coordinates the activities of the three ministries.

The objective of higher education in the Ivory Coast is "to ensure the transmission of knowledge and its progress. A new direction has been in effect since 1977 to adapt the system of higher education to the society in which it is inserted" (Office of Higher Education).

The 1977 law that reorganized higher education set the framework for the evolution of its structures. This project is being delayed until a decision is made either to found a new university or decentralize the one that already exists.

The state provides most of the funding for higher education. In addition, the government grants scholarships through its Office of Orientation and Scholarships.

The country dedicates 43 percent of its general budget to education. Its main objective is the preparation of men and women capable of contributing to the development of the country. In spite of the crisis, due to falling export prices, funding for higher technical education has not decreased, absorbing close to 80 percent of the public funds allocated to education in the 1980–85 Plan.

The organization of higher education was established by decree in 1966, determining the different councils and commissions and their composition. There are three: the Higher Education Council, the Standing Commission for Higher Education, and the University Council.

The Higher Education Council elaborates development plans. It is presided over by the Head of State, with the Minister of National Education as vice president. This council includes different ministries.

The president of the Standing Commission for Higher Education is the Minister of National Education. Its members are the president of the University and a representative of each of the ministries in charge of institutions associated with the University, the deans of the faculties, the directors of the *grandes écoles*, and the secretary general of the University, who has a say in matters but no vote. The role of the Commission is to pass on budgetary proposals.

The University Council is comprised of the president, the deans of faculties, and the secretary general of the University. In practice, the directors of institutes and the representatives of students and administrative personnel also participate. The Council prepares the budget, disburses funds, defines the curricula and the different types of teaching, and deals with disciplinary problems.

Each faculty is administered by a dean, assisted by an advisor. The faculty assembly is the deliberative body. The basic educational unit is the department, which decides its own academic and scientific questions.

4. Faculty and Students: Teaching, Learning, and Research

To be a professor in higher education, a third-cycle doctorate, a PhD, or a state doctorate is required. The grade received and the theses report are important in selection as an assistant professor. After three years of teaching, those seeking promotion submit their request to CAMES (the African and Malagasy Council for Higher Education), in Quagadougou, Burkina Faso. In certain faculties, those with a state doctorate can apply for the *agrégation* examination, which is the highest competitive examination for teachers.

Professors are recruited by a national committee on the basis of requests from the departments. The number of class hours and the division of time between teaching, research, and administration is established by decree.

Professors, lecturers, and researchers have their own union (SYNARES) to defend their interests.

In the years 1960–89 the number of students enrolled at the institutes of higher education rose from 36 to 5,863 in the sciences, 54 to 5,849 in the social sciences, and 27 to 6,629 in the humanities. Formerly, all students were represented by one national movement, the *Mouvement des Elèves et Etudiants de Côte d'Ivoire* (MEECI). However, MEECI was abolished in 1990 and there are now several unions.

5. Inclusion

Higher education plays a key role in the development of young nations, and this is especially true of the Ivory Coast. In order that it be a driving force for development, the authorities have emphaized scientific and technical education, seeking to adapt education to the workplace. The main problems are finances and the constant concern to adapt the educational system to the context of a developing country. The institutions of higher education are clearly nuclei of progress for the whole society.

Bibliography

*La Grande Encyclopèdie de la Côte d'Ivoire, Editions*NEA 1986, p. 193

Office of Higher Education n.d. *Publication de la Direction de l'Enseignement Supérieur.* Document issued at its 20th anniversary, intro.

B. Tio-Toure

J

Jamaica

1. Higher Education and Society

Jamaica (capital city Kingston) is an island in the western Caribbean, centrally located in the region, with a surface area of 11,396 square kilometers and a population of 2.3 million. Independence was achieved in 1962, though it has remained a member of the British Commonwealth and continues to recognize the Queen. Primary links are now with CARICOM, which is comprised of 13 English-speaking territories in the Caribbean.

1.1 Occupational and Social Class Structure

Noted internationally for its musicians, athletes, bananas, cigars, bauxite, and rum, Jamaica is rich in culture, but less well endowed economically. Overseas earnings—80 percent of which come from tourism, bauxite, alumina, and sugar—have been inadequate throughout the 1970s and 1980s, when large overseas debts have accumulated. In spite of relatively high import levels during this period, about 70 percent of the population remained near or below internationally recognized poverty levels. The average annual Gross Domestic Product (GDP) at factor cost in 1985 was US$858 per person.

A few large agricultural estates exist. There are some large hotels, one or two conglomerates, and a few big specialist production units (such as alumina and cement plants), but small farms and firms predominate. Hundreds of thousands of small peasant farmers are a mainstay of the population. They produce a wide range of tropical crops for local and overseas markets. Trading estates have been developed within a sprawling urban agglomeration around Kingston and along an axis with nearby Spanish Town, which houses almost half of the nation's population. The Kingston and Montego Bay "free-ports" include a textile finishing industry with about 20,000 workers.

1.2 Structure of Government and Main Political Goals

A strong democratic tradition has been established by two strong political parties. Turmoil in the political process arose in consequence of a determined attempt to engineer a just society through the creation of socialist production and distribution mechanisms during the 1970s. This effort failed, and governments of both parties have since turned to divestment, fostering private enterprise, and encouraging overseas investors.

Education, in spite of strong grassroots pressures, has remained on the sidelines. Government policies have not been consistent, and the system has been allowed to run down. However, the government is now committed to the strengthening of provisions, and technical and vocational education have again been earmarked for special treatment. Roles for higher education include the strengthening of management and the achievement of local autonomy in as many professional and technological fields as possible. A number of educational facilities in Jamaica are shared with other CARICOM countries.

1.3 Relationship with Religious Bodies

Churches played a major role in the early stages of the development of education in Jamaica. By 1900, higher education was being provided through four teachers' colleges, two of which were founded by the Moravian Church and two by the Roman Catholic Church. Other forms of higher education were not properly developed until about 1950, although a notable earlier development was the West Indies College (a higher technical institution established by the Adventist Church in 1930). Extensive developments in higher education since the Second World War have been largely independent of the churches, whose initiatives recently have been mostly concerned with education of the clergy.

2. The Institutional Fabric of the Higher Education System

Although the majority of children in Jamaica attend secondary schools, only successful high school children are qualified for admission into higher education. Fewer than 25 percent of the school age population attend high schools, and less than half of them secure examination results which satisfy the entry requirements of the various higher education institutions.

2.1 The Sectoral Organization of Higher Education

Jamaica has a considerable number of specialized control and examining bodies for specific sectors. Sometimes authority is shared between teaching institutions and registration and licensing bodies. For example, in the case of law, it is shared between the University of the West Indies (UWI), the Council of Legal Education, and the General Legal Council. A few other examples are as follows:

(a) Degrees in medicine fall under the academic authority of the UWI senate; programs are accredited for international recognition by the General Medical Council of the United Kingdom; the Medical Council registers doctors in Jamaica.

(b) The Pharmacy Council controls the registration of pharmacists, and the College of Arts, Science, and Technology (CAST) plays a major role in education and training.

(c) The Council of Professions Supplementary to Medicine regulates the training of and registers medical laboratory technologists, radiographers, physiotherapists, and occupational therapists, but curriculum development is shared with CAST and other health training institutions.

(d) The Joint Board of Teacher Education has legal authority over the education and registration of teachers in Jamaica, Belize, and the Bahamas.

(e) The Institute of Chartered Accountants of Jamaica is legally recognized as having authority concerning qualifications for the practice of accountancy.

(f) The Ministry of Public Utilities examines and licenses electricians.

(g) The Architect's Registration Board controls the registration of architects, and the Caribbean School of Architecture is responsible for local education and training programs.

2.2 Levels of Institution

The majority of school leavers in Jamaica are not qualified to enter higher education, so most of the recent government initiatives, such as the seven major vocational training programs, and five new specialist training academies provided by the HEART Trust have been designed for them. There are almost 200 postschool education and training institutions, but fewer than one-third operate programs at the higher education level. The dividing line is obscured since some institutions, such as community colleges, provide training and education at all levels.

The core of higher education is the "tertiary system," a loose hierarchical arrangement of institutions provided by or operated in association with the Ministry of Education. At the top of the hierarchy is the University of the West Indies (UWI), followed by the College of Arts, Science, and Technology (CAST) and the College of Agriculture. Next come the seven teachers' colleges, and the G C Foster College of Physical Education and Sport. Next are the Cultural Training Centre, and schools devoted to the visual arts, drama, dance, and music. The West Indies College and the four community colleges are at the bottom of this hierarchy.

There is a diverse collection of additional higher education institutions. They mostly offer certificate and/or diploma programs, although degrees are available from seven of these. Some are government establishments; others are under the auspices of charities, trusts, or private enterprise; while two others are affiliated to the University of the West Indies. They include business and secretarial colleges, nursing and health colleges, theological colleges, and colleges offering specialist training in finance and management, engineering and technical skills, and for the public service.

2.3 Admissions Policies and Selection

There are six major school examinations, namely:

(a) Jamaica school certificate;

(b) secondary school certificate;

(c) CXC basic;

(d) CXC general;

(e) GCE O level;

(f) GCE A level.

Only in exceptional circumstances are the first three considered for admission into higher education. The lower (subuniversity) higher education programs usually insist on at least three subject passes in CXC and GCE O-level examinations or their equivalent. Tertiary colleges usually require at least four subject passes, while only UWI requires two or three A levels and two or three O levels for normal three-year courses (five years in the case of medicine) while four-year courses require five O levels. Alternative matriculation schemes involve success at other tertiary-level institutions, in some cases with a one-year exemption.

3. Governance, Administration, and Finance

3.1 National Administration

An industrial levy, paid by employers, helps to finance skill training, but this is applied mostly below the higher education level. The Jamaican government applies a tax to students at UWI and CAST, as a contribution towards per capita cost. It also provides student loan services.

Two umbrella organizations for academic administration are in existence. The HEART Trust, established in 1982, administers the industrial levy, and coordinates and oversees all skill training programs. The University Council of Jamaica was set up in 1987 to rationalize the system of higher academic awards.

Higher education provisions are rarely subjected to overall centralized academic control, and there are few national examinations at the postschool level. Traditionally, a great deal of responsibility for curriculum development has been and still is vested with individual teaching institutions, which tend also to award their own certificates and diplomas. Validating procedures make use of external examiners, some from overseas. Additionally, overseas and regional examinations are used where necessary.

Three bodies in Jamaica are vested with legal authority to award degrees. They are: (a) the UWI Senate, under the Royal Charter of Incorporation of 1962; (b) CAST Council, under the Education Act of 1986; and (c) the University Council of Jamaica, under the 1987 Act. The Joint Board of Teacher Education has authority to award teaching certificates and diplomas for primary and secondary education under the 1965 Acts.

3.2 Institutional Administration

The University of the West Indies (UWI) serves, and is supported by, the following 14 territories: Antigua, the Bahamas, Barbados, Belize, the British Virgin Islands, the Cayman Islands, Dominica, Grenada, Jamaica, Montserrat, St Kitts-Nevis-Anguilla, St Lucia, St Vincent, and Trinidad and Tobago.

The University was set up in 1949 as a constituent college of the University of London and became an independent university by a Royal Charter of Incorporation in 1962. Its objectives are to provide education, learning, and research facilities; to advance knowledge; and to extend the arts, sciences, and learning throughout the 14 territories. To these ends it is a teaching and examining body which offers certificate, diploma, and degree programs; provides libraries, research, and advisory services; and prints, publishes and sells books and journals. It has the power to affiliate institutions, and external students can take some examinations through "Challenge" arrangements. It operates on three campuses, the largest of which is in Jamaica at Mona (the others being at St Augustine, Trinidad and Barbados at Cave Hill). There are extramural centers in most of the 14 countries. In addition, teleconferencing facilities administered by UWIDITE (UWI Distance Teaching Experiment) links the three campuses with each other for teaching and other purposes and also provides links with additional centers in Jamaica, St Kitts, Antigua, Dominica, St Lucia, St Vincent, and Grenada. There are special educational arrangements with the University of Guyana, the College of the Bahamas, and the Eastern Caribbean tertiary

institutions. The University is an important regional graduate and research center.

The internal structure of UWI is based upon two majority authorities, the council and the senate. The council is the governing and executive body, vested with power to manage all matters. The senate is the academic authority, with power to regulate and superintend all academic work.

Management functions at campus level are performed by campus councils, and academic supervision rests with academic boards. There is also a guild of graduates, represented on the council, and a students' society on each campus. Discrimination on political, religious, or racial grounds is specifically prohibited as far as admissions or employment are concerned.

The council is presided over by the chancellor. The vice-chancellor exercises general supervision over educational arrangements, supervises the admissions of students, chairs the senate, and is principal of the Jamaica campus.

There are four grants committees: the University Grants Committee for the University Centre, and a Campus Grants Committee for each campus. The greater part of recurrent expenditure is supplied through government grants. Fees are being revised for students from contributing countries. Students from noncontributing countries pay a special higher fee.

The University works to a three-term academic year, but switched to a semester system in September 1990.

Education, learning and research are provided through faculties, departments, special units, and affiliated institutions. Most faculties are represented on all campuses, though with most staff being located in Jamaica. Agriculture and engineering are concentrated in Trinidad, and law in Barbados, while medicine can only be studied in Jamaica (see Table 1 for student numbers at the University of the West Indies).

The College of Arts, Science, and Technology (CAST), founded in 1958, has long been recognized throughout the English-speaking Caribbean as the senior technical educational institution. From the

Table 1
Total student registration, University of the West Indies 1948–89

	1948–89	1953–54	1958–59	1963–64	1968–69	1973–74	1978–79	1983–84	1988–89
Jamaica	33	302	622	1,486	2,564	3,608	4,496	5,188	5,499
Trinidad	—	—	—	583	1,267	2,114	2,661	3,197	4,209
Barbados	—	—	—	118	385	938	1,362	1,641	2,185
Men	23	212	391	465	657	926	477	844	326
Women	10	90	231	722	1,559	2,734	4,042	5,182	6,567
Total	33	302	622	2,187	4,216	6,660	8,519	10,026	11,893

Table 2
Total student registration, CAST 1958–89

	1958–59	1962–63	1968–69	1972–73	1978–79	1988–89
Full-time	56	219	393	758	1,547	1,972
Part-time	—	189	616	842	943	1,053
Evening	—	457	317	428	761	1,065
In-service modules	—	—	—	—	—	810
Total	56	865	1,326	2,028	3,251	4,900

outset it has validated some of its certificates and diplomas, which are widely accepted as full professional qualifications by registration bodies such as the Jamaica Pharmacy Council. The 1986 Education Act gave recognition to the institution's validation expertise, reinforced its structure, strengthened its powers, and facilitated the award of higher programs up to master's degree level. It now provides a parallel track, alongside the UWI, by offering degree programs usually related to specific occupations and professions not dealt with by UWI. Its courses are practically based, work-oriented, scientifically based, and technologically relevant. There is a commitment to responding to national and regional needs.

Authority is vested in the council, a body appointed by the Minister of Education, who provides general direction on matters which affect the public interest. The duties of the council are to maintain the College, manage its financial affairs, determine staff requirements and endowments, hold examinations, and award certificates, diplomas, and degrees.

General authority over staff lies with the president of the College, who is chairman of the academic board, which carries out such duties as are assigned to it by the council. It has power to regulate its own proceedings, and to invite persons who are neither College staff nor members of council. It operates through a series of executive committees (curriculum, examinations, resources, and development). Staff are subject to the education code, and appointed within a hierarchical structure (assistant lecturer, lecturer, senior lecturer, principal lecturer, head of department, vice-president, and president).

The College is divided for administrative and educational purpose into departments (which, it is envisaged, will gradually develop into schools). These in turn subdivide into divisions and sections. There are also two important centers, the Energy Centre and the Entrepreneurial Extension Centre, based at CAST.

A total of 64 major certificate, diploma, and degree programs are currently available, including the MSc in architecture, BSc in environmental design and health sciences, BEng in electronics, and BEd in business and technological subjects. Many short courses are also available (see Table 2 for student numbers at CAST).

The University Council of Jamaica (UCJ) was set up in 1987 to rationalize the system of academic awards in higher education (certificates, diplomas, and degrees). It is a facilitating body, with the power to grant and confer awards at all levels, and functions throughout the following registration and accreditation procedures:

(a) Registration of institutions. Teaching bodies are registered as higher education institutions, but must first comply with established minimum standards.

(b) Accreditation of institutions. Colleges and other institutions may be recognized as "associated institutions," and will then have authority to award UCJ certificates, diplomas, and degrees.

(c) Accreditation of courses. Institutions will be given authority to conduct specific programs for the award of UCJ certificates, diplomas, or degrees.

The University Council of Jamaica aims to expand opportunities through the maximum use of existing facilities, and to coordinate the supply of labor needs. Members of the Council are drawn from public and private sectors, professional bodies and societies,

Table 3
Total student registration in teachers' colleges 1968–89

	1968–69	1972–73	1978–79	1982–83	1988–89
Total number	1,742	1,855	3,512	2,168	2,447

and academic institutions. An international advisory group helps to determine international comparability and authentication.

The Joint Board of Teacher Education is a regional body with its Secretariat on the Mona Campus of UWI. Created by Acts of Parliament in 1965 it covers the Bahamas, Belize, and Jamaica, and deals with curriculum development, staff development, evaluation, and the maintenance of standards for early childhood, primary, special, and secondary education teachers. It also has responsibility for the registration of teachers in all three countries.

Its structure is designed to achieve a partnership in teacher education. (Table 3 sets out student numbers in teachers' colleges 1968–89.) Representatives from the ministries of education, all teachers' colleges, teachers' organizations, and independent members of the community along with the faculty of education of UWI, are brought together in democratic participation in order to achieve flexibility and understanding and the accommodation of diverse needs.

Bibliography

Cropper A, Halliwell J, Sangster A (eds.) 1987 *CARICOM Survey of Technical and Vocational Education and Training.* Report presented to the Council of Ministers, Guyana
Gordon H L A 1985 *Adult and Non-formal Education in the Third World: A Jamaican Perspective.* Centre for Continuing Education, the University of British Columbia, Vancouver, Canada, in cooperation with the International Council for Adult Education
Halliwell J 1986 *Directory of Further Education and Training in Jamaica.* Department of Teacher Education Development, Faculty of Education, University of the West Indies, Mona
Jamaica, Central Planning Unit 1957–72 *Economic Surveys.* Planning Institute, Kingston
Jamaica, Ministry of Education. *Statistical Reviews of the Education Sector.* Ministry of Education Planning Unit, Kingston
Planning Institute of Jamaica 1973–88 *Economic and Social Surveys.* Planning Institute, Kingston
University of the West Indies 1973– *Calenders.* UWI, Mona
University of the West Indies. *Statistics.* UWI, Mona
University of the West Indies 1987 *Teacher Certificate Regulations of the Joint Board of Teacher Education.* Faculty of Education, UWI, Mona

J. Halliwell

Japan

1. Higher Education and Society

Japan consists of four main islands—Honshu, Hokkaidō, Kyushu, and Shikoku—and thousands of smaller islands. The archipelago lies off the north-east coast of the Asian continent, stretching in an arc 3,800 kilometers (2,360 miles) long. The total size of the land area is 377,800 square kilometers (145,945 square miles). The islands lie in the temperate zone and the climate is generally mild.

In 1987 the population was 122 million, and its density was 328 per square kilometer. The population density, however, differs from place to place. In the urban areas, which constitute only 28 percent of the land but are inhabited by 75 percent of the population, the ratio went up to 901 per square kilometer, while in the rural areas it was 105.

As for the age of the population, Japan has undergone a rapid decrease in the number of children and an equally rapid increase in the number of elderly people. In 1987 those under the age of 14 formed 20.2 percent of the total population, while those over 65 formed 10.9 percent. The birthrate has been considerably lowered, in 1987 standing at 11.2 per thousand, in comparison with the figure of 20.9 per thousand in the 1950s. For the aged population it is estimated that this ratio may increase to 15 percent by the year 2000, and 20 percent by 2015.

For the past century Japan has transformed itself from an agricultural to an industrial nation, and is now moving towards a postindustrial state. In 1987 the distribution of the labor force was 8.35 percent, 33.3 percent, and 58.4 percent in the primary, secondary, and tertiary sectors respectively. In the 1980s tendencies were for a rapid decrease in the primary sector, a slow decrease in the secondary sector, and a rapid increase in the tertiary sector.

Japan is almost a mono-ethnic society, the Japanese being the predominant majority. The minority, consisting of less than 0.7 percent of the total population, includes the indigenous Ainu, immigrant Korean and Chinese, and other ethnic groups. The official language is Japanese, which is also the instructional language throughout the whole educational system including higher education.

Historically, Japan has developed as a part of the East Asia Cultural Zone under Chinese influence. Being isolated geographically and having kept political independence, however, Japan was able to develop her own unique culture before her major encounter with the West in the late nineteenth century. The resultant Westernization has enriched Japanese culture yet further.

The major religions are Shintoism which is indigenous and Buddhism which was brought to Japan but has naturalised well. Christianity represents a religious minority. Religion plays an important part in people's private lives in Japan, but it does not form any part of the nation's public life and no part in public education. While public education is secular, there is no restriction on any religious groups or individuals setting up private schools and universities so long as these satisfy the educational standards set by the government.

Japan has a constitutional monarchy, although the emperor is defined only as a symbol of the nation and has no real political power under the still current 1947 Constitution. The constitution establishes the principle of respective independence of the legislature, the executive, and the judicature. The National Diet consists of two houses, the House of Representatives and the House of Councillors. The head of the executive is the prime minister, who is a member of the House of Representatives and the head of the governing majority party. The prime minister and cabinet members oversee the governmental departments including the Ministry of Education, Science, and Culture. The government party has been Conservative since 1947 except for the very short period of a coalition Socialist/Conservative government in 1947 and 1948. The dominant party of that tendency in the 1980s and 1990s is the Liberal-Democratic Party, which is a national party but which finds most of its support in industrial circles and in local interests. The second most important party is the Socialist Party, which is grounded in the support of organized trade unions. Other parties include the Komei, Communists, and Social-Democrats. Thus, since 1946, educational policies have been formulated under Conservative initiatives, while the opposition, above all the Socialists and Communists, have exerted critical power over it either directly in the National Diet or indirectly through the labor unions, in particular the Teachers' Union.

Japanese higher education can be described as an example of mass higher education in a highly industrialized country. It embraces a student population of over two million (in 1989 there were 2,066,962 in universities and 461,849 in junior colleges, in addition to 611,012 in other types of tertiary education institutions). There are 499 universities, 584 junior colleges, 62 technical colleges, and 2,675 special training colleges.

The present system of higher education is governed statutorily by the School of Education Law of 1947 and its subsequent amendments. The 1947 Law was enacted as part of political reforms which took place as the result of the defeat of Imperial Japan. The reforms aimed at democratization not only in the political sphere but also in all other economic, social, and even cultural aspects of Japanese life. Educational reform under the 1947 Law transformed the prewar elitist higher education system to an egalitarian open system accessible to all graduates of unified secondary schools. The attendance rates of the age group in these schools increased from 42.5 percent in 1959 to over 90 percent by 1975, and to 98.1 percent in 1989. The new system of reformed higher education has, in turn, produced a host of well-educated citizens for a stable democratic society as well as a host of human resources for the industrial development of the nation that has been witnessed in the past decades.

The transformation to the mass higher education system was given a framework by 1947 and began to be truly realized by the 1980s. This could not have been achieved, however, without the foundations already laid by the preceding system of higher education. No space can be afforded in this brief historical account for a detailed description of Japan's ancient and medieval heritage of aristocratic higher culture, learning, and refined art. In addition there was the monasterial heritage of Buddhist and Chinese studies, the more pragmatic but still advanced learning and military art of the warrior classes, and the not insignificant zeal among commoners for higher education. It was this complex heritage which laid the foundation for the first Western inspired modern systems of higher education established towards the end of last century and for the transformation of this to the contemporary model in the mid-1980s.

The first attempt to establish a Western-style university was that of Tokyo University by the government in 1877 which followed several Western-style technical and professional colleges set up by the government and private individuals. Tokyo University was transformed in 1886 into the Imperial University of Tokyo and this, with seven other imperial universities founded by 1940, crowned the prewar system of higher education. Under these imperial universities in hierarchical order there were other government universities which were mostly mono-faculty institutions for medicine, engineering, commerce, and education; locally established public universities; private universities; nondegree granting technical and professional colleges; and separate women's colleges.

This hierarchical system was intended to create different social strata through different levels of higher education, although the entire higher education system served only a handful of the population which, during most of the prewar period, did not extend beyond 5 percent of the relevant age group. The graduates of imperial universities dominated the government and politics, and formed the core of the juridical and scholarly world. As Japan's industrialization program took off in the early twentieth century, the expanding private sectors in industry and commerce began to absorb the graduates of the less prestigious government, public, and private universities, and technical and professional colleges, many of which were established at that point to cope with the demands of industrialization.

The democratic reform of higher education introduced by the 1947 Law ended this hierarchical system. All previously established universities and colleges were grouped under the term "*daigaku*" which literally means "grand schools," but is generally translated as university. The intention of this egalitarian policy was both to eliminate social and political stratification among the people by offering a similar kind of higher education and to provide equal opportunities for a broad higher education for young people by introducing a unified pattern of higher education. This policy was well justified from certain social and ideological perspectives at the time when Japan was striving for democratization in all spheres of national life. From it emerged a large mass of enlightened citizens who were then able to help maintain a relatively politically stable society under democratic rules.

On the other hand, enforcement of this policy often sacrificed academic quality, particularly in the immediate postwar reconstruction period. Higher education had to meet growing demands for quality graduates for industry, which by the 1950s began to see a highly qualified workforce and research in higher education as essential for industrial development. Thus, during the 1960s and after, the policy for diversification in higher education progressed by recognizing as a permanent part of the *daigaku* system those two- or three-year junior colleges which had been originally regarded as temporary measures. Progress has continued with the introduction of new colleges of technology and special training colleges as institutions for tertiary education, by centralizing the governmental efforts to develop graduate and research programs at a certain number of universities, and by establishing a few experimental universities under the government's initiatives while allowing individual institutions to develop their own programs, although these must be within a national framework set by the government.

2. The Institutional Fabric of the Higher Education System

Institutions for higher education include universities and junior colleges (see Tables 1 and 2). Other types of institutions such as colleges of technology and special training colleges which offer courses at postsecondary level as well as those at late secondary level, may also be included in the category of higher or tertiary education.

Universities are institutions for higher education, which, as centers of learning, conduct teaching and

Table 1
Number of universities

	1960	1965	1970	1975	1980	1985	1989
National	72	73	75	81	93	95	96
Public	33	35	33	34	34	34	39
Private	140	209	274	305	319	331	364
Total	245	317	382	420	446	460	499

Source: Ministry of Education, Science, and Culture 1990

Table 2
Number of junior colleges

	1960	1965	1970	1975	1980	1985	1989
National	27	28	22	31	35	37	41
Public	39	40	43	48	50	51	53
Private	214	301	414	434	432	455	490
Total	280	369	479	513	517	543	584

Source: Ministry of Education, Science, and Culture 1990

research in depth in specialized academic disciplines and provide students with the opportunities to develop their intellectual, moral, and practical abilities. Universities require the completion of 12 years of schooling for admission (which is in general six years of elementary, three years of middle, and three years of high school education) or its equivalent. Undergraduate courses last for four years, except those in medicine and dentistry which extend to six years. The courses are divided into two elements: general education and specialized education. The former is intended to provide students with a balanced background for their specialized training as well as the necessary qualities for good citizenship.

Junior colleges also conduct education and research and require the completion of 12 years of schooling or its equivalent. They offer two- or three-year courses for general and specialized education.

Colleges of technology admit students from among those completing nine years of schooling and provide them with a five-year semi-professional education in engineering and mercantile marine. Special training colleges offer varied lengths of courses in culture and technical skills to those who have completed 12 years of schooling.

Training for the professions is commonly received through undergraduate programs. Doctors and dentists are given professional licences when they have completed their six-year undergraduate training and have passed the National Qualifying Examination. Other professions, such as teachers, clergy, engineers, and accountants, qualify after completing four-year undergraduate courses and sometimes additional external professional examinations. To qualify as a jurist, an additional two years are required at a national legal training and research institute after candidates have completed a four-year undergraduate program in law and passed a state preliminary examination.

Students seeking entrance to universities and junior colleges sit a competitive entrance examination conducted by the individual institutions. The entrance examination consists of a scholastic achievement test in two to five subjects. School records are also taken into account. In the case of national and public universities the applicants first have to take the National Preliminary Test, which is conducted nationwide by the University Entrance Examination Center under the Ministry of Education, Science, and Culture, and then the entrance examination conducted by the individual universities. The purpose of this national preliminary test is to ensure that the applicants meet the required standard of achievement in five main subjects—Japanese, mathematics, social studies, natural science, and a foreign language—which are taught in high schools. For admission to individual universities, the results of this preliminary test are taken into consideration together with those of the entrance examination specifically designed by individual universities. It has increasingly become the practice of private universities to adopt the National Preliminary Test in their selection of students.

The degree of competition for admission varies according to the popularity of institutions, which is based on a somewhat ambiguous mixture of such various elements as the social prestige of institutions and their graduates, their location and environment, the trends of job markets for graduates, the severity or ease of selection, and so forth. Since each university, faculty, and department sets a quota for the students who will be newly admitted each year, those applicants who are not admitted to the particular institution of their first choice, may either choose their second or third choice by taking a separate entrance examination or may wait for a second chance at their first choice in the following year.

Universities may set up graduate schools. There are two programs. After two years a master's degree may be awarded. After a further three years a doctoral degree can be obtained. The length of doctoral programs may, however, be shortened from the normal five years to three years, depending on the specialization and the candidate's abilities and qualifications. Masters' programs are intended for professional training at a higher level, and in such professions as teaching, engineering, and business studies. There is a tendency, which is not yet prevalent, to value this graduate training. Academic training for researchers is conducted in doctoral programs, or sometimes as a full-time assistantship after finishing undergraduate education or a master's degree.

Research is conducted in universities by most academic staff and with graduate students. Besides faculties and schools, which are subunits of universities for teaching and research, universities may set up research institutes or centers, experimental stations, hospitals, and schools each with full-time research staff. Thirteen of the research institutes attached to national universities and 15 other independent research institutes were designated in 1989 by the national government as joint research institutes at which researchers in other universities are able to participate in the research projects being conducted.

In addition to the universities, about 20 research institutes and museums have been set up by the Ministry of Education, Science, and Culture in the fields of humanities, social sciences, and natural sciences. Other institutes for higher education, such as the Defense College and Defense Medical College are run by the Ministry of Defense, the College of Meteorology by the Meteorological Agency, and the Aeronautical Academy by the Ministry of Transport. There are also a number of institutes for research and development which are run by philanthropic foundations as well as industrial corporations.

Between 1960 and 1989 the student population increased 3.29 times in universities and 5.53 times in junior colleges. Within these figures there was an increase of the female student population; their numbers multiplied by 6.34 in the universities and by 7.47 in junior colleges. In 1989 female students accounted for 26.4 percent of the total student population in universities and 91 percent in junior colleges, compared with 13.7 percent and 67.5 percent respectively in 1960. Another notable expansion is the increase of the student population in the private sector. Between 1960 and 1989 this student population increased 3.72 times and 6.40 times respectively in private universities and junior colleges, while in national universities and junior colleges the figures increased 2.60 times and 2.85 times. Tables 3 and 4 show the growth in student population in private institutions

Table 3
Number of students in universities

	1960	1965	1970	1975	1980	1985	1989
National	194,227	238,380	309,587	357,772	406,644	449,373	504,890
Public	28,569	38,277	50,111	50,880	52,082	54,944	61,264
Private	403,625	660,899	1,046,823	1,325,430	1,376,586	1,344,381	1,500,808
Total	626,421	937,556	1,406,521	1,734,082	1,835,312	1,848,698	2,066,962
Female students	85,966	152,119	252,745	368,258	405,529	434,401	545,241

Source: Ministry of Education, Science, and Culture 1990

Table 4
Number of students in junior colleges

	1960	1965	1970	1975	1980	1985	1989
National	6,652	8,060	9,886	13,143	14,685	17,530	18,988
Public	11,086	13,603	16,136	17,973	19,002	20,767	22,500
Private	65,719	125,900	237,197	322,666	337,437	332,798	420,361
Total	83,457	147,563	263,219	353,782	371,124	371,095	461,849
Female students	56,357	110,388	217,668	305,124	330,468	333,175	420,864

Source: Ministry of Education, Science, and Culture 1990

which in 1989 was 72.6 percent in universities and 91 percent in junior colleges compared with 64.4 percent and 78.7 percent in 1960.

Graduate students also increased their number 5.42 times between 1960 and 1989. However, they accounted for only 4.1 percent of the total student population in 1989. In national universities they represented 10.8 percent in contrast to the 1.8 percent in private universities. In 1989 64 percent of all graduate students were in national universities, 32 percent in private ones, and 4 percent in public ones.

3. Governance, Administration, and Finance

3.1 National Administration

National policies on higher education are generally determined by the Minister for Education, Culture, and Science, who is a cabinet member. In carrying out the responsibilities of this post, the Minister is advised by the university council, composed of both academic and nonacademic members, and by other specially appointed committees. National policies on education, (including higher education) can be set by the prime minister, such as the appointment of an ad hoc Council on Educational Reform in 1984–87. Under the leadership of the prime minister it was then envisaged that this would have an important influence on educational policies in the short-term future.

The Minister of Education, Science, and Culture has the statutory power to charter universities and junior colleges established by local governments and private educational legal entities. National universities and government junior colleges are established by parliamentary enactment. When chartering universities and local junior colleges, the Minister seeks advice from the university chartering council, and the private school council, in the case of private institutions, which review the quality of institutions in the light of the university standards and the junior college standards set by the Minister.

The Ministry of Education, Science, and Culture gives full financial backing to national universities and government junior colleges, and it partially supports the running costs of others by specific items such as equipment, faculty research activities, and student scholarships. In the 1980s the ministry paid some 30 percent of the running costs of private universities and to that extent it exerts its supervising power over private institutions. The expenditure of central government on higher education is detailed in Table 5.

3.2 Institutional Administration

Individual universities and junior colleges are given a high level of autonomy for internal government, including the appointment of academic and executive staff and how they conduct teaching and research. The form of internal government varies according to the nature of the establishment of the institution.

Universities and junior colleges run by the national government are basically faculty-run institutions. Their highest decision-making organization is the senate, consisting of senior representatives of fac-

Table 5
Central government's expenditure for higher education

	1960	1965	1970	1975	1980	1985
Amount (million yen)	55,762	146,912	290,533	714,232	1,332,165	1,432,287
Ratio per GNP percent	0.35	0.45	0.40	0.48	0.55	0.45

Source: Hiroshima University Research Institute for Higher Education 1989

ulties and research institutes and the executive officers. The latter includes the president of the university, elected by the professorial body often from among themselves, and deans of faculties and research institutes who are also elected by and from the professoriat of the particular faculties and institutes. These elected officers, together with the dean of students, who is appointed by the president, and the director-general of the administrative bureau who is appointed by the Minister of Education, Science, and Culture, constitute the executive council which *de facto* runs the institution.

In the case of those universities which consist of several faculties and research institutes, much of the matters for internal decision are left in the hands of the individual faculties and institutes. While the senate and the university executive officers coordinate them from a university-wide point of view, each faculty and institute organizes its own faculty committees to take major decisions on such matters as faculty appointments, curriculum making, student affairs, and research plans. The faculty meeting is attended by full professors, often supported by more junior academic members. Public universities and junior colleges run by the prefecture or municipal authorities have similar internal administrative structures to those of national institutions, and they are also faculty-run institutions.

Private universities and junior colleges are managed by the boards of directors of the educational foundations, which support and run the institutions. In executing its administrative role, each board of directors has to seek advice from the board of trustees, composed of representatives of teaching and administrative staff of the universities and colleges, their graduates, and others appointed by the director-general of the board of directors. The administration of academic matters is entrusted to the president and other academic officers, who, in most cases, are selected and appointed by the board of directors. In not a few cases, these academic executive officers are elected by and from the professoriat of the institution just as in the national institutions. The role of the faculty committee is basically the same as in the national institutions. Depending on the degree of initiative taken by the

board of directors, however, the committee may have a wide range of responsibilities. In some cases the committee has almost full autonomy as do the national institutions, while in other cases it has only a limited role.

In universities the faculty is a unit for both administration, teaching, and research. As all teaching members of the universities belong to some faculty or other, so do students. They are further divided into departments, which may be unidisciplinary or multidisciplinary. The department may function as a subunit of the faculty, but it has no legal power. In the national universities with graduate programs, the department is commonly subdivided into "chairs," each of which is centered around a professor with additional junior faculty members and graduate students. The chair is considered to be a basic unit of research, rather than one of teaching, although its faculty members offer courses to departments.

4. Faculty and Students: Teaching, Learning, and Research

4.1 Faculty

In the 28 years between 1960 and 1988, the total number of academic members of universities and junior colleges multiplied by 2.7 and 3.0 respectively. (The figures are given in more detail in Tables 6 and 7.)

The academic ranks prescribed by the School Education Law are professor, assistant professor, lecturer, and assistant. Their qualifications are also prescribed in the University Standards and the Junior College Standards. A prospective candidate for a professorial appointment must satisfy one of the following conditions: possession of a doctorate or equivalent credentials of academic achievement; successful career experience as an assistant professor; credentials testifying to competence in a specialized field in teaching or research. The qualifications for assistant professorship include: a master's degree, a successful career experience as assistant for over three years, and credentials of competence in teaching or research in a specialized field. Lecturers must have the same qualifications as a professor or assistant professor. Assistants must have a bachelor's

Table 6
Number of academic teaching staff in universities (full-time)

	1960	1965	1970	1975	1980	1985	1989
National	24,410	29,828	36,840	42,020	47,842	51,475	53,188
Public	4,725	5,089	5,342	5,602	5,794	6,053	6,369
Private	15,299	22,528	34,093	42,026	49,353	54,721	61,583
Total	44,434	57,445	76,275	89,648	102,989	112,249	121,140

Source: Ministry of Education, Science, and Culture 1990

Table 7
Number of academic teaching staff in junior colleges (full-time)

	1960	1965	1970	1975	1980	1985	1989
National	211	271	363	654	861	1,121	1,269
Public	927	963	1,248	1,617	1,707	1,898	2,002
Private	5,256	8,087	13,709	13,286	13,804	14,741	16,559
Total	6,394	9,321	15,320	15,557	16,372	17,760	19,830

Source: Ministry of Education, Science, and Culture 1990

degree or its equivalent. It is the right and responsibility of individual universities or faculties and of junior colleges to select and appoint particular candidates under these general standards, although at the time of application for a charter or a subsequent change in the charter and statute caused by the creation of a new faculty or department, the prospective candidates for academic posts must be screened by the credential committees of the University Chartering Council.

Academic personnel in national and public institutions have the status of either national or local public servants, and this is regulated by the National Civil Servant Law and the Local Civil Servant Law. In addition, the Special Law for Educational Civil Servants guarantees the autonomy of universities and junior colleges in appointing and dismissing academic officers and faculty members. For the academic personnel in private institutions, there is no specific law but the Labor Law, by which individual private institutions issue rules for employment to regulate and guarantee the rights of employees. In all higher institutions, national, public or private, the academic personnel, except for those of the rank of assistant, have tenure as a matter of practice. The assistants are usually given fixed terms of appointment. The retirement age for academic personnel is set by individual institutions. In the cases of national and public institutions, the median is 63 years of age, while in private institutions it is over 65.

Table 8
Distribution of students by specialization: graduate students

	1960	1965	1970	1975	1980	1985	1989
Exact sciences	8,072	18,439	28,416	30,483	35,236	47,671	59,825
percent	50.6	64.8	69.4	62.9	65.3	68.4	70.2
Social sciences	3,264	7,766	6,334	6,794	6,480	6,810	8,331
percent	20.7	27.3	15.5	14.0	12.0	9.8	9.8
Humanities	4,398	4,385	7,033	8,440	8,329	8,872	11,385
percent	28.0	15.4	17.2	17.4	15.4	12.7	13.4
Others	—	—	—	—	321	494	796
percent	—	—	—	—	0.6	0.7	0.9

Source: Ministry of Education, Science, and Culture 1990

Table 9
Distribution of students by specialization: undergraduates

	1960	1965	1970	1975	1980	1985	1989
Exact sciences	182,083	299,540	472,997	566,645	597,487	614,878	663,570
percent	30.3	33.5	35.2	34.3	34.3	35.5	34.2
Social sciences	257,979	386,178	562,162	688,667	704,737	671,001	759,636
percent	42.9	43.1	41.8	41.7	40.5	38.7	39.4
Humanities	150,382	199,152	293,248	374,383	417,359	426,967	476,957
percent	25.0	22.2	21.8	22.7	24.0	24.6	24.7
Others	11,020	10,595	21,950	22,308	21,921	21,546	28,974
percent	1.8	1.2	1.6	1.4	1.3	1.2	1.5

Source: Ministry of Education, Science, and Culture 1990

Table 10
Distribution of junior college students by specialization

	1960	1965	1970	1975	1980	1985	1989
Exact sciences	41,226	74,050	116,146	134,900	137,976	140,054	167,040
percent	50.6	50.9	44.7	38.7	37.7	38.2	36.7
Social sciences	16,170	24,409	30,187	37,915	33,499	35,590	55,489
percent	19.8	16.8	11.6	10.9	9.1	9.8	12.1
Humanities	23,633	46,894	113,220	175,940	194,617	187,557	227,649
percent	30.0	32.2	43.6	50.4	53.1	51.2	50.0
Others	189	195	194	167	156	2,979	5,518
percent	0.2	0.1	0.1	0.0	0.0	0.8	1.2
Total	81,528	145,458	259,747	348,922	366,248	366,180	455,696
percent	100	100	100	100	100	100	100

Source: Ministry of Education, Science, and Culture 1990

4.2 Students

The distribution of graduate students across their fields of specialization was as follows: 13.4 percent in humanities, 9.8 percent in social sciences, and 70.2 percent in exact sciences in 1989. Corresponding figures for 1960 were 28, 21, and 51.3 percent in these respective fields. The distribution of undergraduates throughout the fields of specialization was 24.7 percent in humanities, 39.4 percent in social sciences, and 37.7 percent in exact sciences in 1989, compared with 25, 42.9, and 30.3 percent in the respective fields in 1960. The distribution of junior college students was 49.3 percent in humanities, 12 percent in social sciences, and 36.2 percent in exact sciences in 1989, and 28.3, 19.4, and 49.4 percent in these respective fields in 1960. Tables 8, 9, and 10 give a more detailed picture.

In 1985 a total of 847,562 students applied to universities and junior colleges, and 585,496 were admitted. Among these 172,607, or 29.5 percent of their total number, had graduated from high schools a year or more before. Figures for students entering higher education between 1960 and 1985 are given in Table 11.

Students, once admitted, pursue the courses of study prescribed by the individual institutions in accordance with the general guidelines set by the University Standards and the Junior College Standards, which are issued by the Ministry of Education, Science, and Culture. Undergraduate programs consist of courses in general education and specialized education. In addition students are required to take at least one foreign language course and physical education. Courses in general education must cover three areas of humanities, social sciences, and natural sciences. The content of specialized courses varies according to the specialization. At the end of each academic year the work of students is graded and credited by each professor teaching the courses. Accumulation of the minimum of 124 credit units in four years of schooling qualifies students for graduation, which has then to be approved by the faculty.

The majority of graduates find employment. In 1989, out of 376,688 university graduates 25,157 (6.7 percent) continued their education, mostly in graduate schools, while 309,019 (79.6 percent) found work. Among those employed 10 percent went into the teaching profession, 8.8 percent into civil services, 43.1 percent into other service industries, 32.2 percent into manufacturing and construction industries, and 5.8 percent into other spheres. In the same year, out of 174,460 junior college graduates 6,429 (3.2 percent) continued their education, while 174,357 (85.1 percent) found jobs. The kinds of jobs they took were in teaching (7.8 percent), the civil service (3.5 percent), service industries (61.1 percent), manufacturing and construction industries (22.3 percent), and other areas (5.3 percent).

There is little formal participation of students in university administration in either Japanese universities or junior colleges. However, students organize unions through which their voices may be heard by university authorities. Until the early 1970s, the National Federations of Students Unions known as *zengakuren* were active in national politics. Since then, however, students have become apolitical except for some minority militant groups.

5. Conclusion

One of the problems which Japanese higher education will face in the coming decades is the decrease in numbers in the population of college age. In the past, notably in the 1960s and 1970s, the expansion of Japanese higher education owed much to an increase in the number of high school graduates, which was largely the result of the expansion in the population in the age group between 18 and 22 in these periods. It is foreseen, however, that this age group will start to decrease in 1992 and by 2000 it

Table 11
Entrants to universities and colleges

	1960	1965	1970	1975	1980	1985
Population at age 18	2,022,207	1,961,621	1,953,836	1,564,954	1,583,146	1,559,314
Entrants to						
Universities	166,761	249,917	333,037	423,942	412,437	411,993
percent	8.2	12.7	17.0	27.1	26.1	26.4
Junior colleges	42,318	80,563	126,659	174,930	178,215	173,503
percent	2.1	4.1	6.5	11.2	11.3	11.1
Colleges of technology	—	2,781	8,391	10,015	9,539	9,814
percent	—	0.1	0.4	0.6	0.6	0.6
Special training colleges	—	—	—	—	190,570	209,835
percent	—	—	—	—	12.0	13.5

Source: Hiroshima University Research Institute for Higher Education 1989

will fall to about 75 percent of 1990 levels. This population trend will inevitably affect the admissions policy of universities and junior colleges. They will either have to decrease the student intake or, if they wish to maintain the present level of their student population, they will have to cultivate other sources from which new kinds of students may be recruited. A contraction in the number of students would be most difficult, since it directly affects the income of universities and junior colleges, which depend so much on the tuition fees that students pay. The tuition fee is one of the major, or in some private institutions almost the single source of income. The contraction may also meet with objections from faculty members who feel their jobs are threatened.

There is almost no possibility of expanding the number of high school graduates, since its contribution to the age group has already reached well over 90 percent. A small increase in this proportion could not match the decrease of the absolute number of this age group population. One possible way of avoiding decreases may be found in increasing the ratio of the high school graduates admitted as students from the 1989 level of 30.7 percent by making both universities and junior colleges more widely accessible. The question is whether this open door policy can be adopted without also lowering the academic level of the entrants. It would be possible if the number of female students were increased as they still form just over one quarter of the student population in universities. It would also be possible if the admission of more socially and physically handicapped students was encouraged. Though small in number, their opportunity in higher education has so far been limited. Otherwise it would be difficult to maintain the academic standard of the student body, particularly as regards the male student population, if such an open door policy were undertaken.

So far, the vast majority of students in Japanese higher education institutions have been admitted straight, or with a few years preparation, from high schools. As the interest in life-long education has increased for the past decade or so, a number of universities have started to offer special places for adult students. At present the number of adult students is still almost negligible in the total student population. They are, however, a potential, on which some universities or junior colleges may have to depend for filling their deficit in student numbers.

The aforementioned inclusion of new kinds of students, or the increase in numbers of certain kinds of student, such as female, adult, handicapped, or academically less able ones, will challenge not only the present admissions policy, but also the curriculum and teaching methods in universities and junior colleges. The traditional curricula and methods have been severely criticized already since the 1960s, as the increase of student population has brought in a variety of interests and ability among them. In the coming decades, during which the admission of new kinds of students is foreseen, undergraduate education in Japanese universities will inevitably undergo reforms and renovation in its content and method.

Graduate programs in universities will also have to be improved in the coming decades. Universities are facing a crisis which has been caused by the ever increasing burden of undergraduate teaching on the one hand, and by an equally increasing demand to expand research activities both in quality and in quantity on the other hand. The traditional combination of research and teaching has become difficult to maintain in many institutions of mass higher education, unless specific research facilities such as research institutes or graduate schools are attached. In 1989 some 82 out of 96 national universities had one or more attached research institutes. (No figures are available for public and private universities.) As to graduate schools, 94 out of 96 national universities have them, while only 23 out of 39 public universities and 187 out of 364 private universities have them, though the numbers of graduate schools have been increasing yearly. Notable trends are observed in the establishment of two national universities and one private one which offers only graduate programs and in the expansion of interdisciplinary postgraduate programs within the existing graduate schools.

Finally Japanese higher education will have to adjust itself to the society's needs for "internationalization." The Japanese are aware of their increasing role and responsibility in the world. Thus universities and junior colleges are expected to gear their orientation more to the welfare of the world by expanding exchange programs of students, researchers, and professors with other nations, both developed and developing. As to the exchange of students, the Ministry of Education, Science, and Culture has set a target to increase the number of foreign students in Japan up to 100,000 by the year 2000, and has taken measures to encourage and help individual students on the one hand and to strengthen programs and facilities of universities and colleges on the other hand. As a consequence the number of foreign students has been rapidly increasing from 4,703 in 1980 to 33,323 in 1989. As part of their programs for foreign students, some 290 universities and colleges in 1988 offered Japanese language courses and over 40 universities offered courses for training Japanese language teachers. These numbers are expected to increase in the coming years. The Ministry of Education, Science, and Culture and the Japan Society for the Promotion of Sciences encourage the exchange of scholars and researchers by offering fellowships for individuals or grants-in-aid for international cooperative research projects. The exchange of scholars and students is reciprocal, and while inviting foreigners to Japanese universities, the ministry as well as individual universities encourage Japanese students to study at overseas institutions, in cooperation with governments and universities abroad.

It is hoped that through these efforts for exchange programs and by improving curricula relevant to the needs for internationalizing society, universities and colleges will nourish the world-minded citizens and specialists, who are so badly needed.

Bibliography

Amagi I, Keii T (eds.) 1977 *Daigaku Setchi Kijun no Kenkyu.* University of Tokyo Press, Tokyo

Amano I 1980 *Henkakuki no Daigakuzō.* Nihon Recruit Centre, Tokyo

Amano I 1986 *Kōtō Kyoiku no Nihonteki Kōzō.* Tamagawa University Press, Tokyo

Amano I 1989 *Kindai Kōtō Kyoiku Kenkyu.* University of Tokyo Press, Tokyo

Arimoto A 1981 *Daigakujin no Shakaigaku.* Gakubunsha, Tokyo

Aso M 1978 *Eriito Keisei to Kyoiku.* Fukumura Shuppan, Tokyo

Cummings W K, Amano I, Kitamura K (eds.) 1979 *Changes in the Japanese University: A Comparative Perspective.* Praeger, New York

Dore R P 1976 *The Diploma Disease: Education, Qualification, and Development.* University of California, Berkeley, California

Ehara T 1984 *Gendai Kōtō Kyoiku no Kōzō.* University of Tokyo Press, Tokyo

Hiroshima University Research Institute for Higher Education 1978 *Perspective for the Future System of Higher Education: Report of Hiroshima International Seminar on Higher Education.* Hiroshima University Research Institute for Higher Education, Hiroshima

Hiroshima University Research Institute for Higher Education 1980 *Higher Education for the 1980s: Challenges and Responses.* Hiroshima University Research Institute for Higher Education, Hiroshima

Hiroshima University Research Institute for Higher Education 1981a *Innovation in Higher Education: Exchange of Experiences and Ideas in International Perspectives.* Hiroshima University Research Institute for Higher Education, Hiroshima

Hiroshima University Research Institute for Higher Education 1981b *The Internationalization of Higher Education: A Final Summary Report.* Hiroshima University Research Institute for Higher Education, Hiroshima

Hiroshima University Research Institute for Higher Education 1983 *Comparative Approach to Higher Education: Curriculum, Teaching and Innovation in an Age of Financial Difficulties.* Hiroshima University Research Institute for Higher Education, Hiroshima

Hiroshima University Research Institute for Higher Education 1984 *Changing Function of Higher Education: Implication for Innovation.* Hiroshima University Research Institute for Higher Education, Hiroshima

Hiroshima University Research Institute for Higher Education 1989 *Kōtō Kyoiku Tōkei Dētashu.* Hiroshima University Research Institute for Higher Education, Hiroshima

Kaneko M 1987 *Enrollment Expansion in Postwar Japan.* Hiroshima University Research Institute for Higher Education, Hiroshima

Kaneko M 1989 *Financing Higher Education in Japan.* Hiroshima University Research Institute for Higher Education, Hiroshima

Keii T (ed.) 1984 *Daigaku Hyouka no Kenkyu.* University of Tokyo Press, Tokyo

Kitamura K 1986 *Kōtō Kyoiku no Hikakuteki Kōsatu.* Tamagawa University Press, Tokyo

Kitamura K 1987 *Daigaku Kyoiku no Kokusaika.* Tamagawa University Press, Tokyo

Kobayashi T 1976 *Society, Schools and Progress in Japan.* Pergamon Press, Oxford

Ministry of Education, Science and Culture 1986 *The University Research System in Japan.* Ōkurashō Insatsukyoku, Tokyo

Ministry of Education, Science and Culture 1989a *Education in Japan: A Graphic Presentation.* Gyosei, Tokyo

Ministry of Education, Science and Culture 1989b *Outline of Education in Japan.* Asian Cultural Centre for UNESCO, Tokyo

Ministry of Education, Science and Culture 1989c *Wagakuni no Bunkyo Shisaku.* Ōkurashō Insatsukyoku, Tokyo

Ministry of Education, Science and Culture 1989d *Mombu Tōkei Yōran.* Daiichi Hōki Shuppan, Tokyo

Nagai M 1971 *Higher Education in Japan*. University of Tokyo Press, Tokyo

Nakajima N (ed.) 1986 *Sekai no Nyugaku Shiken*. Jiji Tsūshinsha, Tokyo

National Council on Educational Reform 1984 *Reports on Educational Reform*. National Council on Educational Reform, Tokyo

OECD 1971 *Review of National Policies for Education: Japan*. OECD, Paris

Ōsawa M, Ogata K, Terazaki M, Hamabayashi M, Yamaguchi M (eds.) 1982 *Kōza Nihon no Daigaku Kaikaku*, 5 vols. Aoki Shoten, Tokyo

Shimizu Y 1978 *Nyugaku Shiken: Senbatasu kara Kyoiku e*. Daiichi Hōki Shuppan, Tokyo

Shinbori M 1984 *Gakumon no Shakaigaku*. Yūshindo, Tokyo

Terazaki M 1979 *Nihon niokeru Daigaku Jichi Seido no Seiritsu*. Hyoronsha, Tokyo

Ushiogi M 1973 *Gakureki Shakai no Tenkan*. University of Tokyo Press, Tokyo

T. Kobayashi

Jordan

1. Higher Education and Society

The greater part of the State of Jordan, some 97,740 square kilometers, consists of a plateau lying some 700–1,000 meters above sea-level. Jordan has no natural topographical borders with its neighbors—Syria, Iraq, and Saudi Arabia. The River Jordan, which is 251 kilometers long, rises just inside the frontiers with Syria and Lebanon, flows for 96 kilometers in Israel, and lies within Jordanian territory for the remaining 155 kilometers. Jordan's climate is similar to that of its neighbors: summers are hot and winters are fairly cold.

The population numbered about 3.8 million in 1987 with a population density of 38.9 per square kilometer. Some 68 percent of the population is under 19 years and 59.4 percent lives in cities. The principal towns are Amman, the capital (population 972,000), Zarqa (392,000), Irbid (271,000), and Salt (134,000). Life expectancy reaches 62 years, and the crude birthrate per 1,000 persons is 41.7, while infant mortality per 1,000 births is 56.2. The literacy rate is 71 percent. The economically active population is divided as follows: 230,525 people working in social and administrative services; 54,183 in construction; 52,706 in mining and manufacturing; and 49,258 in trade. The number of unemployed totals 42,864, and the employed 492,576, while the total civilian labor force reaches 535,440.

Jordan's economy is based principally on exports and transactions with Iraq. The war between Iraq and Iran has severely curtailed the purchases by Iraq of goods from Jordan, and the situation has now worsened, because of the war between Iraq and the international coalition. It also has to be considered that Jordan's economy has twice been completely disrupted by war between the Arabs and the Israelis, first in 1948 and then in 1967. Jordan exports phosphates, potassium, chemicals, cement, fruit and vegetables, and basic manufacturing goods, and imports food and live animals, raw materials, mineral fuels, machinery and transport equipment. Foreign aid of various kinds accounts for more than 40 percent of budgetary revenues, and workers in the service sector greatly outnumber those in directly productive activities.

Jordan is a constitutional monarchy. The Hashemite Kingdom of Jordan is an independent, indivisible sovereign state. Its official religion is Islam; its official language Arabic. The revised constitution was approved by King Talal I on January 1, 1952. Legislative power is vested in the National Assembly and the king. The National Assembly consists of two houses: the senate and the house of representatives. The throne of the Hashemite Kingdom of Jordan devolves by male descent in the dynasty of King Abdullah bin Al Hussein. On his accession, the king takes an oath to respect and observe the provisions of the constitution and maintain loyalty to the nation.

Over 80 percent of the population are Sunni Muslims, and the King can trace unbroken descent from the prophet Muhammad. There is a Christian minority, living mainly in the towns, and there are smaller numbers of Shi-ite Muslims.

2. The Institutional Fabric of the Higher Education System

Higher education in Jordan is organized on two levels: community colleges and universities. In community colleges the period of study is two years, while in the university it is four years, except for engineering and medicine which takes five to six years. There are about 55 community colleges, 15 of them governmental while the remainder are privately run. All are under the supervision of the Ministry of Higher Education. There are five governmental universities and two private ones. All of these are under the supervision of the Higher Education Council, which is presided over by the Ministry of Higher Education.

The universities are: University of Jordan (founded 1962, Amman, national and autonomous control); Bethlehem University (1973, Bethlehem, private control, Roman Catholic); Birzeit University (1975, Birzeit, private autonomous Arab institution); Hebron University (1971, Hebron, independent national university); Mu'tah University (1981, Mu'tah, state control); An-Najah National University (1977, Nablus, private control); and Yarmouk

University (1976, Irbid, national and autonomous control). All of them teach in Arabic and English.

The University of Jordan was founded by Royal Decree on September 2, 1962 as the country's first institution of higher education. The campus was built some 12 kilometers from the center of Amman. The University of Jordan was established as an independent national institution for higher education, and awards a bachelor's degree in 43 different subjects, a master's degree in 42 subjects, a diploma certificate in 17 subjects, and a PhD in either of the specializations of Arabic language or education.

Admission to higher education is based on an applicant's results in the general secondary examination certificate—the *tawjihi*—which is sat after 12 years schooling. Admission is selective in two ways. First, students choosing a particular faculty may only apply if they have studied the corresponding course of study in school. Thus, for example, entry to the science faculty demands that students have been studying science in upper-secondary school, but they also have the option of applying to other faculties. However, applicants from the arts and literary field can only apply to those faculties which offer arts subjects. Second, university entry is limited to those with a high grade average. For those not admitted, whose total grade is less than 70 percent, the Community College is available. The college intermediate degree (diploma) is considered to be terminal (Badran 1989 p. 22).

Overall student enrollments between 1975 and 1988 rose from 11,837 to 65,979 with university enrollment growing from 5,307 to 34,994 and the community college sector from 6,566 to 30,985 (UNESCO 1990 p. 264).

Jordan has a remarkably high age participation rate in higher education, reckoned to be in the region of some 37.5 percent of the 18 to 19 age group (Badran 1989 p. 21). This development can in part be explained by the high prestige and social standing that is attached to being a degree holder, in part to the fact that, as a country with limited natural resources, an educational qualification is a passport to employment opportunity often outside the country. There are, in addition to student

enrollments within Jordan, some 36,000 Jordanian students studying abroad, most of whom are following courses in medicine and engineering.

3. Governance, Administration, and Finance

The Ministry of Higher Education, which is now separate from the Ministry of Education, exercises a general oversight across both the private and the public sectors of higher education. Formally, it has power to plan higher education institutions, to determine their size and approve their budgets (Ministry of Higher Education 1985 Art. 4 para. 1). It supervises the nonuniversity sector directly, to ensure that it prepares technically trained labor in keeping with national development plans. The Ministry cooperates with other ministerial bodies. The degree of autonomy of the nonuniversity sector is very limited.

By contrast, the universities enjoy a wide degree of autonomy in their internal administration. For the university sector, the main coordinating organ is the Council of Higher Education. Created as part of the same administration restructuring that gave rise to the Ministry of Higher Education in 1985, the Council of Higher Education is chaired by the prime minister. The Council has a very wide remit and span of coordination over the universities. It recommends the appointment of university presidents who are nominated by royal decree. University vice-presidents are appointed by decision of the Council, following the recommendation of the university president. Its weight can be gathered from its membership which, in addition to the prime minister, includes the ministers of higher education, education, planning, all university presidents plus one representative of the public sector community colleges and one representative of their private sector counterparts.

The Council approves the founding of new institutes of higher education and gives its approval of new fields of specialized study, as well as new courses. It gives its assent to abolish established courses. It determines the distribution of the universities' financial resources, their investment policy. It sets the minimum grade requirements for entry to university and evaluates institutional achievement.

State subsidization of higher education in Jordan is considerable, though donations and student fees also have their part to play, the latter constituting a significant proportion. The budgeting system of the university sector in Jordan has one unique aspect to it. It takes the form of the University Tax Law which imposes a tax on goods, and forms a permanent resource in the budget of Jordan's universities. Such a mechanism is held to provide a degree of financial autonomy for higher education, though clearly, since it is directly linked to the state of the economy, the repercussions may well at times be severe.

At the institutional level the principal legislative

Table 1
Student field of study by year

	1980	1987	1988
Education/Teacher training	11,514	17,008	14,211
Humanities	4,342	5,539	14,529
Science	8,251	14,933	19,393
Social science	10,348	16,338	15,327
Other/nonspecified	2,094	2,035	2,234

Source: UNESCO *Statistics* 1990 Table 12 p. 312

body is the university council composed of the president, vice-presidents, deans and elected members of the academic staff. In addition, in the case of the University of Jordan, ex officio membership is extended to the undersecretaries of the Ministries of Education, Agriculture, Public Works and Health as well as the secretary general of the National Council for Planning. Alumni are represented, as well as the student body by one delegate each.

An alternate form, found in certain private foundations, is that of a board of trustees as a layer beyond the university council. Prior to 1985, such boards were also found in public sector universities. However, their powers were transferred to the Council of Higher Education by By-law No. 36 of 1985.

Academic organization rests on the faculty/departmental structure in which the latter acts as the basic unit, with the decision-making body being the department council. Faculty councils are composed of departmental chairpersons, one elected representative from each department and two representatives of external interests. It is chaired by the dean of the Faculty and stands as an intervening layer between department and the council of deans. This latter body, which brings together all deans and vice-presidents, is chaired by the university president. It considers all matters raised by faculty councils and acts as the university's executive body.

4. Faculty and Students: Teaching, Learning, and Research

The total number of teaching staff in the Jordanian higher education system was 797 in 1975, and reached 2,658 in 1988 (UNESCO 1990). Growth in the university sector was especially rapid over the decade from 1975 to 1985, which coincides with the major expansion of that sector. Approximately 20 percent of the teaching staff are women, a figure which has remained stable for some time. Women in academia form a higher proportion in the community colleges than in universities. In 1988, for example, women academic staff constituted 14 percent in the university sector compared with 29 percent in the community colleges.

The structure of academic ranking follows the American pattern of lecturers, instructors, assistant professor, and associate and full professor. Promotion, which is a matter internal to the individual university, follows the usual criteria of holding a higher degree for assistant professors, teaching and publication rates for the two higher ranks. Faculty are employed by the individual university and recruited on the same basis.

Trends in student subject choice are set out in Table 1 for the period 1980 to 1988. Two trends are evident: the first is the considerable rise in student enrollments in the humanities; the second is a steady rise in the numbers studying science. To some extent,

the former can be accounted for by the increase in the number of female enrollments which constituted one third of all students in 1980 and reached 49 percent in 1988. This development, however, is more visible in the community colleges where almost six students out of ten are girls, whereas they represent four students out of ten in the university sector.

The structure of undergraduate and graduate studies follows what is broadly speaking an American pattern based on a system of credit hours, options, electives, and major and minor studies. Examinations take place at the end of each semester and a minimum requirement for students to continue their study is 15 credit hours per semester.

5. Conclusion

The development of the Jordanian higher education system is a remarkable example of a small country which has resolutely embarked on a policy of optimizing its human capital. With participation rates comparable, and in many instances well beyond, the mass higher education systems of Western Europe, and with a unique system of financing higher education, it is one of the major exporters of highly qualified labor force throughout the Middle East. In times of prosperity, what may appear a brain drain is an important source of capital generation in the form of income sent home by those working abroad. In less prosperous times, such a highly developed system serves to show the degree of interdependence on other economies in default of being able to create an economic base sufficient to absorb the skills its higher education system has created.

Bibliography

Badran A 1989 Access to Higher Education in the Arab World. *Higher Education Policy* 2(1): 21–24
Day A 1986 *East Bank, West Bank*. Council of Foreign Relations, New York
Foreign Area Studies 1980 *Jordan: A Country Study*. American University, Washington, DC
Gusber P 1983 *Crossroads of Middle Eastern Events*. Westview Press, Boulder, Colorado
Lunt J 1989 *Hussein of Jordan*. Macmillan, London
Ministry of Higher Education 1985 *Organizing the Ministry of Higher Education: By-law No. 36 of 1985* (mimeo). Amman
Mu'tah University 1987 *Mu'tah University Prospectus*. Department of Cultural and Public Relations, Al-Karak
Shipler D K 1987 *Arab and Jew: Wounded Spirits in a Promised Land*. Bloomsbury Press, London
Shlaim A 1988 *Collusion Across the Jordan*. Oxford University Press, Oxford
UNESCO 1990 *Statistical Yearbook*. UNESCO, Paris
University of Jordan 1982 *The University of Jordan Catalogue 1982–83*. University of Jordan Press, Amman
Yarmouk University 1983 *Yarmouk University Catalogue 1983–84*. Yarmouk University, Irbid

G. Neave; A. Velloso

K

Kenya

1. Higher Education and Society

The first Kenyan higher educational institution, the Royal Technical College, was established in Nairobi in 1956 with the objective of providing technical and commercial education to East Africans preparing for the Advanced Certificate of Education and other professional examinations. When the University of East Africa was established in 1963, the Royal Technical College, which had assumed university college status in 1961, became one of its constituent colleges, the others being Makerere (Uganda) and Dar es Salaam (Tanzania). The demands of divergent political and socioeconomic philosophies forced the three colleges to assume a more national outlook and in 1970 they became fully fledged national universities. Since Independence in 1963, the university has grown into the most dominant higher educational institution in Kenya. Thus, although this article is about higher education in Kenya in general, most emphasis will be placed on university education.

Kenya is located in the eastern part of Africa astride the equator. At the end of the Second World War in 1945, Kenya was still a British colony and remained so until 1963 when, after a protracted struggle between local guerillas and British colonists, it gained independence. It has retained the boundaries which were established by the colonists in 1895 and with only slight modifications in 1902, 1909, 1925, and 1926 (Ochieng 1985 p. 89).

The population of Kenya has grown from roughly 5 million people in 1945 to more than 20 million in 1984 (Republic of Kenya 1984). At the current 4.1 percent growth rate per annum, Kenya has one of the highest population growth rates in the world. As a result about 50 percent of the population are under the age of 15. Some 80 percent of the population live in rural areas. As only about 17 percent of the land is arable, population density in some areas can be extremely high. On average, the population density on the arable land is approximately 232 persons per square kilometer (Ojany and Ogendo 1988).

Urban settlements are characterized by a predominance of small towns with populations ranging between 3,000 and 10,000 inhabitants. Roughly 1 million people in Nairobi the capital city account for more than 60 percent of the total urban population. Two of the four public universities and several private ones are located there.

Kenya is a multi-ethnic society. Asians, Europeans, and Arabs constitute 2 percent of the population, and Africans of some 40 ethnic groups for the rest. Only a very small number of Asians and Europeans enroll in local universities, the majority prefer to study overseas. The African population enjoys varied cultures and languages. The largest African group is the Kikuyu of the Mount Kenya region. This group, along with 10 other ethnic groups, comprise 90 percent of the total African population. There are as many languages as there are groups, but there exists a *lingua franca*, *Kiswahili*, which is spoken by most people in the country. Roughly 20 percent of the population enjoy a reasonably good mastery of English, which is the official language as well as the language of instruction throughout Kenyan education.

Kenya is mainly an agricultural country, and most Kenyans depend on farming for their livelihood. Peasants and pastoralists comprise roughly 90 percent of the population. The majority of the peasants are poor and own very small parcels of land (the average is about one hectare) which are utilized mainly for subsistence farming. Many such peasants supplement their incomes by engaging in waged employment. Unlike the peasants, the pastoral communities living in the drier parts of the country depend on livestock husbandry for their livelihood. As higher education in Kenya has traditionally been subsidized by the state, students of peasant background are the dominant group in Kenyan higher education institutions. However, the rising cost of primary and secondary education is now threatening this dominance.

Less than 20 percent of Kenya's population depend entirely on wage labor for their sustenance. The top positions in government, parastatal organizations, the military and police, and privately owned local and multinational companies go to a small minority of this group. The greater number are employed in low-paying jobs in urban areas; however, the majority work on farms of varying size. It is important to point out that unlike the industrialized West, in Kenya—as indeed is true of most of Africa—a sharp distinction cannot easily be drawn between the wage-earning and farming segments of the population, as many employed Kenyans retain both the rights to their ancestral lands and very strong rural links.

The predominance of the agricultural sector has tended to influence development planning as increasing emphasis is now being placed on the development of the rural areas (Republic of Kenya 1989). Nevertheless, urban centers, and particularly Nairobi, tend to be the main beneficiaries of development efforts.

This uneven development is also reflected in the field of higher education. For example, all the four public universities are located in or very near major urban centers, with Nairobi hosting two of them. The national polytechnics are also based in urban centers while only a few diploma-granting postsecondary institutions (mainly teacher-training colleges) are actually located in rural settings. Likewise students from urban-based schools dominate available places in higher education institutions.

Agriculture and livestock husbandry are the predominant economic activities in Kenya. In 1985, roughly 80 percent of the active labor force was engaged in the agricultural sector, a sector which accounts for 30 percent of Gross Domestic Product (GDP) and roughly 65 percent of all exports (World Bank 1987). The main exports are coffee and tea (Kenya exports more coffee than any other African country). The principal food crops are maize, beans, potatoes, and bananas.

In agriculture, small farms predominate. Currently, large-scale farms cover no more than 30 percent of all arable land as the government has, since Independence, embarked on a policy of redistributing the farms which previously belonged to European settlers, whilst population pressure has increasingly reduced the size of small holdings.

For a developing country, Kenya's industrial and service sectors are relatively well-developed. Between them, they comprise 20 percent and 49 percent of the total GDP respectively (World Bank 1987).

The Kenyan government expects institutions of higher learning to respond to the demands of national development through the production of a highly skilled labor force (Republic of Kenya 1988). However, indiscriminate university expansion, characterized by a duplication of courses offered at the different institutions, has led to an overproduction of labor in areas such as the social sciences where the country may already have satisfied its needs. Graduate unemployment is thus a common feature of university education (Hughes 1987 p. 587).

Kenya is a one-party state. The Kenya African National Union (KANU) has been the ruling party since Jomo Kenyatta led it to power in 1963. The political and social philosophies are based on the principles of a free and open society. Parliamentary elections are held every five years. Although the administrative machinery of government is centralized, at the regional level provincial commissioners appointed by the president enjoy considerable decision-making power. There are eight provinces in Kenya, which are further subdivided into 41 districts. The new development philosophy has increasingly made the districts the focus of important decision making.

The government expects universities and other institutions of higher learning to respond to the dictates of Kenya's political philosophy. This was emphasized before the founding of the second university, with the publication of a government report which stresses that:

> The University must plan its teaching programme in such a way that it is continuously adaptive to Kenyan ideological and pragmatic development aspirations . . . be close to "Wananchi" (the people) and aim at producing graduates who freely interact with people, live comfortably in their own society in the rural areas, are effective in serving all and are innovative, hardworking and committed . . . [and] relate to society in such a way that there is a continuous and positive dialogue and that it addresses itself to relevant national problems. (Republic of Kenya 1981 p. 37)

The extent to which Kenyan higher educational institutions could promote such ideals is, however, limited. The Kenyan university community has on several occasions been critical of many of the government's political goals, seeing itself as representing the more informed sector of society. Neither is it easy for the government to determine or influence what is taught at the universities. Moreover, only a few of the university graduates end up working in the rural areas of Kenya because of the limited employment opportunities. As is true elsewhere, the extent to which universities or other educational institutions can influence any meaningful development is more or less determined by what the wider society can provide by way of either resources or the initiation of development programs.

2. The Institutional Fabric of the Higher Education System

There are a total of four public and 11 private universities operating in Kenya. The majority of the latter are small religious colleges. The University of Nairobi remained the only university in the country until 1983, when Moi University in Eldoret was established. Kenyatta University, which had been a constituent college of the University of Nairobi since 1970, became an independent university in 1985, while Egerton University, previously another constituent college of the University of Nairobi, achieved independence two years later. In addition to the universities and their constituent campuses, higher education in Kenya comprises three national polytechnics, five institutes of science and technology, and six diploma-level teacher-training colleges. However, the four public universities have been the dominant higher education institutions in Kenya.

Several distinguishing factors exist between the public and private universities. Whereas public universities recruit the best academically qualified students and teaching staff available in the country, private institutions base their recruitment on other criteria such as ability to pay fees and religious commitment. Public university education has remained highly subsidized by the state, a factor which has helped promote some form of equity, as many of those unable to pay are not excluded from the system. Public universities are also much bigger than private institutions in terms of available facilities, the number of enrolled students (an estimated 1,400 students are enrolled in the 11 private universities compared to roughly 26,000 in the four public universities), the size of the teaching staff, and the level of research activity taking place. The curriculum of private universities is also much narrower than that of public universities as many of the former specialize in between one and three course offerings on average (theology is the only subject taught in the majority of the private institutions). In contrast, public universities offer a wide range of undergraduate degree courses in addition to graduate degree programs at both master and doctoral levels. Finally, private universities appear more prone to foreign influence than public institutions. This foreign presence manifests itself in the type and length of the degree programs offered, the relatively higher percentage of faculty who are non-Kenyan, and the dominance of external funding.

Universities occupy the top position in Kenya's educational hierarchy with their constituent colleges coming second. Diploma-granting institutions such as national polytechnics and diploma teacher-training colleges come next. Only universities and their constituent colleges grant degrees. Because of the prestige of the degree, most high-school graduates aspire to go to the universities. Diploma-granting institutions and the private universities admit those students who cannot gain places in the national universities.

Although there are a good number of institutions that conduct research in Kenya, the main centers of research activity are the universities. All the public universities, with the exception of Moi University, have established departments that specialize in research in specific fields. The better known of these include: the Institute for Development Studies (IDS) and the Population Research Institute (PSRI) of the University of Nairobi, and the Bureau of Educational Research (BER) at Kenyatta University. Outside the universities, some of the well-known research institutions include the Kenya Medical Research Institute (KEMRI), the Central Bureau of Statistics (CBS) of the Ministry of Economic Planning, and the Kenya Agricultural Research Institute (KARI).

One of the major problems facing university research institutions in Kenya is the scarcity of the research funds available to them. This fact, in addition to the high student enrollments that Kenyan universities have been experiencing, have forced university administrators to give higher priority to teaching than to research needs (Court 1983 p. 178). Research activity is also hampered by the tendency of the government to control the type of research carried out through a mechanism which requires potential researchers to obtain official clearance before embarking on their intended research projects. This mechanism effectively allows the government to censor research, particularly by foreign nationals and in areas perceived as sensitive. In their bid to conduct research which may reflect national needs, Kenyan researchers are further hampered by the relative dominance of external funding in the field of research. Such a dependence has conditioned them to concentrate on areas deemed important by foreign donors (Nkinyangi 1983 p. 190).

Entry into higher education institutions has traditionally been based on performance in the A-level examination, which is taken by students who have completed six years of secondary school education. This examination was replaced as the main selector of university entrants by the Kenyan Certificate of Secondary Education (KCSE) in 1990. This is in accordance with the new 8-4-4 system of education which will comprise eight years of primary, four years of secondary, and four years of university education. This is a reform of the previous system, based on the United Kingdom model, of the 7-4-2-3 cycle (seven years of primary, four of secondary, two of senior secondary, and three of university education).

Recruitment into the public university system is based strictly on merit. In the 7-4-2-3 system, a candidate was required to obtain at least two principal A-level passes to qualify for a university place. However, this was the minimum requirement and many qualified students who attained this grade were left out. For instance, even with the tremendous expansion of university education in 1986 and 1987, no more than 29 percent and 32 percent of the qualified A-level graduates found places in the public universities in these years (Hughes and Mwiria 1990). Since 1990 when the 8-4-4 system took effect at the university level, potential university entrants have been required to obtain a minimum grade of B− in at least 10 subjects including compulsory ones such as mathematics, English, *Kiswahili*, and a physical science.

The emphasis placed by the Kenyan government on the development of the scientific fields of knowledge has inevitably led to the expansion of science-based fields in the institutions of higher learning. This means that students specializing in science subjects at the secondary-school level could enter university with lower grades than their counterparts in the arts fields. This is particularly true in relation to the less competitive generalized fields of arts, science, and education. In the more specialized fields of engineering, medicine, law, and commerce, however, competition for places at the public universities is equally keen for both arts and science-based high school graduates. In all cases recruitment into gradu-

Table 1
Numbers of universities and enrollments 1970–90

	1970–71	1975–76	1980–81	1985–86	1990–91[a]
Universities	1	1	1	2	4
Undergraduate enrollments	3,137	5,589	7,291	7,437	40,000
Graduate enrollments	306	636	1,474	1,710	5,000
Total	3,443	6,225	8,765	9,147	45,000

Sources: Republic of Kenya 1964–1988 *Economic Survey 1964–1988* Government Printer, Nairobi, Republic of Kenya 1966–1987 Statistical Abstracts 1966–1987 Government Printer, Nairobi
a Figures are estimates

ate programs is even more competitive because of the limited number of scholarships available.

As Table 1 shows, Kenyan university education has been characterized by remarkable expansion. In 20 years, university student enrollment has multiplied by more than a factor of 14 from 3,443 in 1970 to approximately 45,000 in 1990.

The main reasons for such an expansion are a pervasive public demand for education in general, a concern with equity aimed at opening up more opportunities to Kenyans, especially those from disadvantaged backgrounds and regions (Hughes 1987 pp. 583–601), and a general belief in the ability of higher education to influence socioeconomic development (Republic of Kenya 1981, 1988).

Additionally, expansion serves to promote a hidden agenda: it legitimizes Kenya's reward structure in the sense that more people are seen as being given the chance for upward mobility. Related to this is the "cooling out" function of such an expansion as it helps to reduce the pressure put on the government by an ever increasing pool of disenchanted high school graduates. In the face of the crisis of graduate unemployment that Kenya has been experiencing, however, such hopes could only be short-lived.

Even with such unprecedented expansion, enrollments in Kenya's institutions of higher learning have never represented more than 1 percent of the relevant age group (20–24). This is because the government cannot commit sufficient funds to education, and because many interested Kenyans are unable to enroll locally in private universities or overseas due to the high cost of education in such institutions.

The successful completion of most degree programs used to require a period of at least three academic years and this has been increased to four years since 1990. Only a few degree programs take slightly longer to complete—pharmacy, veterinary medicine (four years), human medicine (five years). The degrees are awarded by the universities from which the students have graduated. The elitist nature of university education means that much pomp is associated with degree-awarding ceremonies. For public universities, the country's head of state, who is also chancellor of the four institutions, personally presides over the degree-awarding ceremonies. Diploma certificates granted by the universities and other postsecondary training institutions average about two years for successful completion. (Diplomas are the equivalent of associate degrees in the United States.) With the exception of the university diploma certificates, the others are granted by the country's relevant government ministries.

In each degree class the very top students (one or two from each university department) are invited on graduating to rejoin the university for graduate studies. A very limited number of this elite may even obtain overseas scholarships. Graduate fellowships are essentially meant for potential university teachers and researchers. For this reason, research is a major component of graduate training programs.

Ideally, a master's degree should take students no more than two years to complete, while a doctoral degree is expected to take roughly three years. Poor supervision of students by their assigned advisers, however, has at times resulted in students spending up to six years on the master's and ten on the PhD degree programs (Mwiria 1989 pp. 185–86).

3. Governance, Administration, and Finance

3.1 National Administration

Although the recommendations of *The Presidential Working Party on Education and Manpower Training for the Next Decade and Beyond* (Republic of Kenya 1988) suggest an expanded role for the Commission for Higher Education in Kenya's educational planning and development, in reality high level politicians have become a critical part of the decision-making process. The Commission appears to be relegated to a much more peripheral role. The growing involvement of high level politicians was illustrated in May

1988, when at the request of the president, university enrollments were eventually doubled.

However, a number of significant policy changes have also been initiated by presidential working party reports. The *Second University in Kenya: Report of the Presidential Working Party* (Republic of Kenya 1981) paved the way for the creation of Moi University and the establishment of the 8-4-4 system while the *Report of the Presidential Working Party on Education and Manpower Training for the Next Decade and Beyond* (Republic of Kenya 1988) set the stage for the implementation of cost-cutting and cost-sharing measures in the university system.

Because of the weakness of the Commission for Higher Education there is a vacuum in the coordination of tertiary education. Although the vice-chancellors at each of the four universities do work, somewhat informally, to coordinate their efforts, major decisions are more and more likely to be made by the central government. The newest five-year plan (Republic of Kenya 1989), for example, suggests that enrollment should double to 50,000 students by the conclusion of the plan period (1994). This is significantly sooner than the year 2000 goal suggested by the working party report (Republic of Kenya 1988). This target does not reflect significant involvement by the university hierarchy or the Commission for Higher Education.

The central government provides the financial support for the university system. As is clear from Table 2 the rapid expansion that has occurred since 1985 has consumed larger and larger proportions of a recurrent budget of which nearly 38 percent is already allocated to education (Republic of Kenya 1988 p. 117). With the continued exponential growth of higher education, it would appear likely that universities will require greater and greater portions of the education budget.

The only significant prospect for change in this trend lies in the success the government has in implementing cost-sharing and cost-cutting measures. Both the students' loan scheme and students' allowances have been earmarked for revision. In 1987–88, university student allowances accounted for 20 percent of the allocation to higher education.

The ill-fated loan scheme has suffered from a default rate in excess of 90 percent (Republic of Kenya 1988 pp. 173–74). Now, it is not clear whether or not there is significant political will to carry out these steps. Tough proclamations are soon watered down or the sanctions delayed. This was evident in late 1988 when Kenya announced the discontinuation of university student allowances. As a result, 5,000 students rioted at Kenyatta University until it was confirmed that student allowances would continue as before. In early 1989, in the face of protest, President Moi suspended the announced intention to require university students to pay fees.

3.2 Institutional Administration

The internal organization of institutions of higher education in Kenya reflects the influence of the United Kingdom, the dominant colonial power in East Africa. The functional head of each Kenyan university is the vice-chancellor, who is accountable to the President of Kenya. A scholar has always been appointed to fill this role. The university council of each institution, which is composed of staff, students, and lay members, oversees the general administration of the university while the university senate deals with academic affairs, such as examinations and admission of students. Universities are further divided into faculties and departments, headed by deans and professors.

4. Faculty and Students: Teaching, Learning, and Research

4.1 Faculty

Since the 1970 academic year, the size of the university teaching staff has quadrupled, growing from 434 to 1,770 in 1987–88. This represents an increase in the student–teacher ratio from 7.9:1 in 1970 to 10.7:1 in 1987. Although this ratio is still exceedingly favorable, the dramatic rise in student enrollments since 1987 promises to erode this benefit of the Kenyan higher education system.

The increased demand for qualified academic staff has other implications as well. University teaching staff used to be picked only from the very best

Table 2
Budget summary 1970–88

	1970–71	1975–76	1980–81	1985–86	1987–88
Students	2,786	6,225	8,765	9,147	18,881
Percentage budget (KE)	2,880,000	6,490,000	16,750,000	34,250,000	52,200,000
Constant KShs	3,790,000	6,490,000	10,530,000	14,640,000	19,850,000
Percentage of total education budget	13.6	9.7	11.2	11.6	13.5

Source: Hughes and Mwiria 1990

students who joined the extremely competitive University of Nairobi graduate programs or were sent overseas by the university on staff development fellowships. Owing to these initiatives, the proportion of Kenyans on the faculty has grown from 30 percent in 1974 to 80 percent. In more recent years, however, relatively poor remuneration has made it difficult to attract foreign scholars and retain qualified Kenyans. The resulting shortage has been further exacerbated by the current rate of university expansion. In July 1987, the University of Nairobi had 154 vacancies (1,162 total positions) and Moi University had filled less than half of its total number of positions (Republic of Kenya 1988 p. 73). Because of this, universities have been forced to recruit less selectively and to improve faculty pay. For example, before the doubled enrollment of 1987, most university departments required a doctorate for the position of lecturer or research fellow. Now master's degree holders are being recruited into these positions. Competition among the four public universities for qualified staff has also meant that the criteria of experience and publications have largely been ignored in relation to staff promotion. In 1987 the basic monthly salary of a lecturer was increased by two-thirds from about KShs 4,500 (US$250) to about KShs 7,500 (US$416).

Generally the faculty have considerable autonomy in the determination of their academic and research emphasis, even though the shortage of local funds for research has made it possible for external sources to shape research activity in Kenya. The lucrative contract and consultancy market, which had been supported by donor agencies and international organizations, has siphoned off some of higher education's best teaching talent and served to limit the time the existing teaching staff will commit to institutional activity. It has come close to the point where "anticipated fees, rather than peer recognition or a desire to contribute to knowledge, are becoming the mainspring of research activity" (Court 1983 p. 183).

Although the recent surge in enrollment has touched every field of study, growth in the arts and education has been most striking. Neither of these areas of study require specialized facilities, and so it is in these fields that the university system is enabled to expand most rapidly, and as a result, to accommodate the greatest number of new students. Ironically, arts graduates already appear to be in surplus supply in the economy (Hughes 1987).

This growth has also affected the quality of education university students receive and the quality of students admitted to higher education (Hughes and Mwiria 1990). The proliferation of university enrollments without commensurate growth of facilities, qualified faculty, and educational support services and materials threatens to undermine the efforts of Kenyan universities to educate.

4.2 Students

As noted earlier, expansion helps to prevent higher education from becoming a domain of the privileged. In a comparison of the family backgrounds of university students from 1958 (Goldthorpe 1965), 1968 (Van de Berg 1973), and 1975 and 1983 (Hughes 1987), it appears that equity of access may be an important benefit of educational expansion. When the backgrounds of more recent graduates are compared with those of earlier graduates, the more recent graduates tend to come from backgrounds that more closely resemble the Kenyan population as a whole. Expansion has apparently improved equity of access of higher education.

These data may also reflect the efforts that have been made to preserve the basic meritocratic structure of the educational system while improving the primary and secondary training available in the historically disadvantaged arid and rural areas. However, the positive contribution universities have made in remaining accessible to the economically disadvantaged has been partially undermined by the under-representation of women. Women have yet to comprise one-third of the total university enrollment in Kenya. In 1987–88, women constituted 29.8 percent of all students, which represents a proportion that just minimally exceeds the comparable figure at the beginning of the decade (27.8%). Not surprisingly, women university students tend to come from higher socioeconomic backgrounds than do male students (Hughes and Mwiria 1989). The poor representation of women in secondary and higher education is indicative of the subordinate role women tend to occupy in Kenyan society.

The student voice has traditionally been heard through the forum provided by the student representative council (SRC) and groups such as the Student Organization of Nairobi University (SONU). Few student leaders seem to complete their tenure without being expelled, as there is a long tradition of antipathy between such student groups and university authorities. Protests have run the gamut from highly political concerns to anger over the quality of food. Since 1981, when the academic staff union of the University of Nairobi was banned by the government, university faculties have not had any organized representation.

5. Conclusion

Kenya has embarked upon a democratization of higher education that may result in a university system more consistent with the style and flavor of Kenyan society. It is characterized by rapidly expanding student numbers and a proliferation of universities, but a decline in per capita support. It promises to provide more Kenyans with access to higher education. In the process, quality may be compromised, government resources seriously over-taxed, technical training opportunities eroded, and new problems created in the labor market. None-theless, the question is not "if" but "how much" expansion will occur, and not so much whether edu-cational planning and policy will become more poli-ticized but the extent to which this will happen. The final question is less whether higher education will survive in Kenya, and more what shape and form it will ultimately take.

Bibliography

Court D 1983 International research environments in Kenya. In: Shaeffer S, Nkinyangi J A (eds.) 1983, pp. 165–90
Goldthorpe J E 1965 *An African Elite: Makerere College Students 1922–1960.* Oxford University Press, Nairobi
Hughes R 1987 Revisiting the fortunate few: University graduates in the Kenyan labour market. *Comp. Educ. Rev.* 31(4): 583–601
Hughes R, Mwiria K 1989 Kenyan women, higher edu-cation and the labour market. *Comp. Educ.* 25: 177–93
Hughes R, Mwiria K 1990 An essay on the implications of university expansion in Kenya. *Higher Educ.* 19: 215–37
Mwiria K 1989 Major issues in educational research: The Kenya experience. *Kenya J. Educ.* 4(2): 177–93
Nkinyangi J A 1983 Who conducts research in Kenya? In: Shaeffer S, Nkinyangi J A (eds.) 1983, pp. 191–214
Ochieng W 1985 *A History of Kenya.* Macmillan, Nairobi
Republic of Kenya 1981 *Second University in Kenya: Report of the Presidential Working Party.* Government Printer, Nairobi
Republic of Kenya 1984 *1979 Population Census, Vol. 11, Analytical Report.* Government Printer, Nairobi
Republic of Kenya 1988 *Report of the Presidential Working Party on Education and Manpower Training for the Next Decade and Beyond.* Government Printer, Nairobi
Republic of Kenya 1989 *Development Plan 1989–1994.* Government Printer, Nairobi
Shaeffer S, Nkinyangi J A 1983 (eds.) *Educational Research Environments in the Third World.* IDRC, Ottawa
Van de Berge P 1973 An African elite revisited. *Mawazo* 1(4): 57–71
World Bank 1987 *World Development Report.* Oxford Uni-versity Press, Washington

K. Mwiria; R. Hughes

Korea

1. Higher Education and Society

Korea is a peninsula connected by the rivers Yalu and Tumen with mainland China in the north and just touching the Soviet Union in the northeast. Its total area is approximately 220,000 square kilo-meters. It has been divided into two parts, South and North, since the Second World War.

About 45 percent of the total area and nearly 70 percent of the total population, more than 60 million in 1989, are within South Korea (the Republic of Korea). Korea has traditionally been an agricultural society, but it has been rapidly developing its manu-facturing production and industry through the 1960s modernization movement and the impact of higher education.

Korea has a complicated religious structure. Both shamanistic rites and ancestor worship have deep roots in the native folklore and customs of Korean people. Religion has also been shaped by strong Confucian, Buddhist, and Taoist influences; after the nineteenth century, Christian influences were added. The invention of a Korean phonetic alphabet, *Hangul*, and the rich humanist heritage have made Korean culture a unique one.

2. The Institutional Fabric of the Higher Education System

When Korea was liberated at the end of the Second World War, there was only one university and 18 colleges. Higher education was almost nonexistent. For a long time, Korean people had strong aspi-rations towards higher education; however, few of them had the opportunity. Therefore, after liber-ation, they strongly emphasized their education needs to raise the level of knowledge and of civi-lization.

The status of higher education institutions in 1987 is shown in Table 1. There are various types and levels of institutions on the basis of the United States pattern of four years higher education, which was introduced just after the liberation. The total number of higher education institutions in 1987 was 468. Most graduate schools are actually attached to a university; hence, a more realistic total of higher education institutions would be a little over 200. There are a few exceptions. Establishments such as the Graduate School of the Academy of Korean Studies, specializ-ing in research and education in ethics, and the Korean Advanced Institute of Science and Tech-nology, specializing in engineering research, offer a master's or a doctorate degree only. Neither has an undergraduate program. There are also a few special-ized miscellaneous schools, such as a theological seminary.

While some universities and colleges have general graduate schools for academic research, and train for master's or doctorate degrees, many universities have specialized graduate schools awarding a master's degree only, as for example, the Graduate Schools of Public Administration, Education, Social Development, Environmental Studies, and so on. Unlike the university, junior colleges generally emphasize professional and technological training for practical application. All the teachers' colleges,

Table 1
Status of higher education institutions 1987

	Sub total	Institutions						
		Day	Evening	Day & Evening	Men	Women	Co-ed	Departments
Junior College	119	69	—	50	3	26	90	994
National	16	16	—	—	2	4	10	105
Private	103	53	—	50	1	22	80	889
Teachers' College (National)	11	1	—	10	—	—	11	367
Colleges & Universities	103	49	2	52	2	10	91	3,266
National	22	21	—	1	—	—	22	954
Public	1	—	—	1	—	—	1	22
Private	81	28	2	50	2	10	68	2,290
Graduate Schools	209	99	101	9	4	15	190	2,942
National	42	19	19	4	1	—	41	835
Public	2	1	1	—	1	—	1	22
Private	165	79	81	5	2	15	148	2,085
Miscellaneous private colleges	26	15	1	10	—	—	26	84
Grand Total	468	233	104	131	9	51	408	7,653
National	91	51	19	15	3	4	84	2,261
Public	3	1	1	1	1	—	2	44
Private	374	175	84	115	5	47	322	5,348

which were established and operated by central government, train elementary school teachers. Also, there are many noneducational institutions, such as the Korean Educational Development Institute, the National Institute of Educational Evaluation, and the Korean Institute for Research in Behavioral Sciences. The former two were established by government and the latter privately. For many years, these institutions strongly contributed to the development and progress of Korean education.

As shown in Table 2, the number of higher education institutions as well as the number of teachers and students enrolled have increased remarkably since 1960. In the same period, the number of disciplinary specialized fields expanded to more than 450, and the total number of departments by major field of study increased more than three times, as shown in Table 3.

Table 2
Expansion of higher education 1960–87

	1960	1970	1980	1987
Number of institutions	85	168	236	266
Number of teachers	3,808	10,435	20,900	36,916
Number of students	101,041	201,436	601,994	1,467,398

Student enrollment in higher education institutions in the age group 20–24 years amounts to 40 percent of all senior high school graduates in 1989. The enrollment trends of junior vocational colleges and graduate schools during 1977–87 is shown in Figs. 1 and 2, and Tables 4–6 show growth in institutions and students.

An applicant for regular admission to university or other senior colleges must be a graduate of a senior high school or have equivalent qualifications. All applicants must take the qualifying examination prepared by the National Institute of Educational

Table 3
Number of departments by major field of study

	1965	1970	1975	1980	1985
Language and Literature	103	103	119	312	406
Auma	101	67	69	105	137
Social Sciences	200	219	267	574	634
Natural Sciences	108	126	141	290	409
Engineering	130	232	268	478	476
Agriculture and Forestry	83	92	109	145	187
Fishery and Marine	8	11	12	19	21
Arts	50	68	92	141	225
Physical Education	13	16	15	17	57
Medicine and Pharmacy	38	70	79	100	129
Teaching	52	116	256	394	445
Total	886	1,120	1,427	2,575	3,126

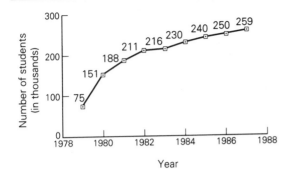

Figure 1
Enrollment trends of junior vocational colleges 1979–87

Evaluation and then pass an entrance examination, interview, or other evaluation procedures which are administered by each institution. For junior colleges, admission is granted to senior high school graduates or to those with an equivalent level of qualifications. From 1988, all applicants have been required to pass the entrance examination which covers five subject areas prepared by the National Institute of Educational Evaluation. In addition, there is a special admission for holders of the National Certificate of Skill, who are specially admitted to particular colleges within the limit, usually 20–50 percent, of the admission quota the college sets. For graduate schools, an applicant must be a graduate of a university or senior college, or have an equivalent qualification. Usually graduate schools expect a grade-point average of upper B in undergraduate course work. A qualified applicant has usually to pass the entrance examination or other evaluation procedures.

Study for the bachelor's degree begins from the freshman stage and normally takes four years. Second degree study for the master's degree begins

Table 4
Number of institutions of education

	1965	1970	1975	1980	1985
Colleges and					
Universities	70	71	72	85	100
National	12	14	14	19	21
Public	2	1	1	1	1
Private	56	56	57	65	78
Graduate					
Schools	37	64	82	121	201
National	12	21	24	32	41
Public					2
Private	25	43	58	89	158
Teachers'					
Colleges					
(National)	13	16	16	11	11
Junior					
Vocational					
Colleges		25	3	128	120
National		5	2	20	17
Public		6		16	
Private		14	1	92	103
Junior					
Colleges	34	14	10		
Public	3				
Private	31	14	10		
Miscellaneous					
Schools	31	16	15	12	24
National	6				
Public	5				
Private	20	16	15	12	24
Total	185	206	198	357	456
National	43	56	56	82	90
Public	10	7	1	17	3
Private	132	143	141	258	363

after graduating and usually takes two to three years. Lastly, work for the doctorate begins after master's degree study and usually needs three to five years or more.

The number of research institutes in colleges and universities are shown in Fig. 3. The expenditures of research institutes attached to colleges and universities are provided by diverse funding sources such as the national treasury, the institution's own source of finance, and private firms.

3. Governance, Administration, and Finance

In 1948, an independent Korean government was established and a new constitution was enacted. This constitution specifically guaranteed equal opportunity for education and free compulsory education at the lower level. At the same time, an education law

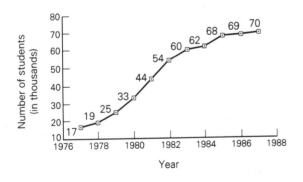

Figure 2
Enrollment trends of graduate schools 1977–87

Table 5
Number of students in higher education institutions

	1965	1970	1975	1980	1985
Colleges and Universities	105,643	146,414	208,986	402,979	931,884
Male	81,882	113,773	153,487	312,345	681,796
Female	23,761	32,641	55,499	90,634	250,088
Graduate Schools	3,842	6,640	13,870	33,939	68,178
Male	3,541	5,833	11,592	28,153	55,726
Female	301	807	2,278	5,786	12,452
Teachers' Colleges	9,920	12,190	8,504	9,425	18,174
Male	7,429	5,571	3,571	1,702	4,927
Female	2,491	6,619	4,933	7,723	13,247
Junior Vocational Schools	—	5,136	579	151,119	242,114
Male	—	22	4	111,236	154,991
Female	—	5,114	575	39,883	87,123
Junior Colleges	15,536	4,907	3,787	394	—
Male	9,052	2,621	1,435	387	—
Female	6,484	2,286	2,352	7	—
Miscellaneous Schools	3,072	2,709	2,993	4,058	17,475
Male	1,064	2,229	2,176	2,849	13,169
Female	2,008	480	817	1,209	4,306
Total	134,013	177,996	238,719	601,994	1,277,825
Male	98,968	130,050	172,325	456,752	910,609
Female	35,045	47,946	66,394	145,242	367,216

was enacted which set down the detailed structure of education, from kindergarten to higher levels, as well as establishing educational administrative organization.

Currently, there are two main bodies of educational administrative organizations in Korea: the Ministry of Education as a central governmental organization, and the Board of Education as a provincial autonomous administrative organization. Almost every board of education has its own offices and some suboffices at county level.

The Ministry of Education supervises higher education institutions directly.

Table 6
Number of students in higher education institutions as a proportion of population

	1965	1970	1975	1980	1985
Population[a]	28,705	31,466	34,707	37,436	40,467
Students[a]	142	178	239	602	1,278
Number of students per 1,000 inhabitants	4.9	5.7	6.9	16.1	31.6

a in thousands

3.1 National Administration

As far as higher education is concerned, governance is fundamentally national, with virtually no provincial or regional level of management. The Ministry of Education, as the central educational administrative body, directly controls university or college policy. In other words, every individual college or university is directly supervised by the Ministry of Education according to the education law. For higher education administration, the Ministry of Education has the University Education and Student Office, which is composed of four branches: the University Education Administrative branch, the University Education Student Affairs branch, the National Education branch, and the Military Education branch. Further, each branch has various divisions. The University Education Administration branch is divided into a University Education Administrative Division, a University Education Finance Division, and a University Education Academic Affairs Division. The University Education Student Affairs branch has three divisions: Student Affairs Management, Academic Research and Promotion, and Student Guidance Officer. Finally, the National Education branch supervises guidance and counselling in general, and the Military Education branch usually supervises a Reserve Officers Training Corps program, and so on. These branches are basically

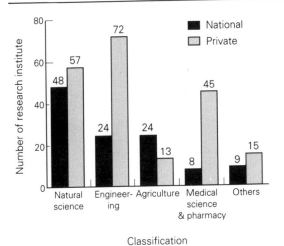

Figure 3
Number of research institutes in colleges and
universities, 1986.

controlled by the Ministry of Education as the central educational administrative entity in the system.

There are a few provincial higher education institutions and many private higher education institutions in Korea, as shown in Table 4. However, all of them are in practice under the control of the Ministry of Education, because they are authorized by the Ministry according to education law. Thus, higher education governance and administration is very different from the European and American models, being essentially a centralized system. However, decisions on detailed matters of policy or management depend on the individual college's or university's authority, even though it has to follow the guidance of the Ministry of Education. In order to encourage new institutions, the provincial or private college and university is given more autonomy in management, except in certain basic issues, involving planning or evaluation at the national level, which are authorized by the Ministry of Education. For instance, the total student enrollment and its depart-

mental allocation of each college and university are strictly controlled and supervised by the Ministry. Any issue related to national administrative plans is formally transmitted through the official channels. If it is considered important, the Minister of Education asks the Central Education Council to organize a workshop to discuss the matter with people from the institution involved. If a reasonable conclusion is reached, the Minister orders the institution to proceed.

The Korean Council for University Education is a seminational and semiprivate organization. It is composed of university and college presidents from the whole country, and is very helpful in the practical development of Korean higher education. On important decisions, the Ministry of Education frequently consults with and relies on the opinion of the Korean Council for University Education. Typical of its interests are: higher education policy, governance, administration, improvement in student quality, staff, and teaching faculty, team organizations and number of teaching staff, and tuition. As mentioned above, education law is strictly enforced. However, the Ministry tries to maintain democratic procedures as much as possible.

Finance for higher education may be classified into three major categories. National institutions and private institutions should be discussed separately, since their source of income is quite different. First, national, public, and provincial higher education institutions are supported mostly from the central or provincial government. In the case of private institutions, the board of trustees is responsible for the institutions' finance. However, the board of trustees are financially not strong enough to support fully the institutions' expenditures. The major source of income in private institutions are student tuition fees. Students in private institutions pay higher tuition fees than those in national institutions. Second, most higher education institutions are partially supported by other central or regional organizations, in the form of donations, research funds, and scholarships. The support from the alumni association is also included in this category. Third, sometimes

Table 7
Ratios of government budget of higher education institutions to other public expenditure (US$ millions)

	1966	1970	1975	1980	1985
GNP (A)	1,500	4,700	15,700	40,600	108,500
Government budget (B)	211.4	666.1	2,368.6	8,662.8	18,321.1
Ministry of Education Budget (C)	37.6	117.1	340.2	1,640.5	3,718.9
Budget for Higher Education Institutes (D)	2.6	8.4	22.3	98.7	252.3
D as percentage of A	0.17	0.21	0.15	0.24	0.23
D as percentage of B	1.23	1.26	0.94	1.14	1.38
D as percentage of C	6.91	7.17	6.55	6.02	6.78
C as percentage of B	17.79	17.58	14.36	18.94	20.30

other sources of income exist: the so-called miscellaneous income. Allocation of funds is dependent on central government decision, which is based on established practice or special cases. In any case, the majority of the institutions' expenditure goes in salaries.

Most finance for national institutions is supported by central government, namely by the Ministry of Education. The source of the Ministry's budget is in turn the national budget, composed of tax and other governmental income. Before the 1960s, when the Korean national per-capita income was below US$100, the financial situation in higher education was precarious, as one may expect. Nowadays with the national per-capita income nearly US$5,000, the budget for higher education has increased considerably and the financial situation greatly improved.

In 1987, the percentage of the education budget in the total government budget was 20.1 percent, second only to the national defense budget. Even though the proportion of the education budget to the total government budget is high, practically, it is limited, given the real need for better education. Many long-term financial problems remain. The major portion, about 67.1 percent in 1987, of the Ministry of Education's budget is spent on salaries, although many teaching staff are not satisfied with their salary. Nor can the budget for buildings and management keep up with the fast growing number of students and schools. Balancing the budget is very difficult, given the high level of aspiration in education. Even if the Ministry of Education is aware of the needs, they simply cannot be met.

Local education expenses, mainly for elementary and secondary education, accounted for 84.4 percent of the Ministry's budget in 1987. The high percentage of local education expenses, while necessary, makes it difficult to allocate more funding for higher educa-

tion. Furthermore, other regional support is hardly expected for national higher education institutions. Progress in the development of higher education has therefore been slow and is far below the level of expectations. Educational expenditure as a proportion of gross national product, and allocations to higher education and research have gradually increased, as shown in Tables 7 and 8. The situation in the private institutions has also gradually improved in parallel with the national situation. Furthermore, the conditions of facilities, salary, and so forth have rapidly improved during the 1980s, boosted by the fast-growing Korean economy.

3.2 Institutional Administration

The basic structure of governance at the institutional level is very similar in different institutions. The structure for administrative organization in higher educational management is similar to that of most democratic countries. Personnel in the national and public higher education institutions are appointed by central government. In the case of private institutions, the president is nominated by the board of trustees. Once the presidential candidate is selected, the board of trustees recommends the candidate to the Minister of Education. Usually the minister approves the board's choice. Other high-ranking administrators, such as deans, section chiefs, and department heads are nominated or appointed by the president. Finally, the university council is usually composed of deans and business managers. Sometimes the presidential candidate is recommended at the general faculty meeting. Department heads are recommended by faculty members in the department. Recently, at certain institutions, business staff or personnel, and even students, are becoming involved in the administrative or appointing procedures.

From a managerial point of view, higher education

Table 8
Academic research funds from the Ministry of Education 1986

	Research items	Researchers	Assisted funds (US$ thousands)
Natural Sciences	516	1,571	3,158
Engineering	496	1,100	3,106
Medicine and Pharmacy	210	502	885
Agriculture, Marine, and Fishery	227	486	876
Humanities	516	1,436	2,258
Social Sciences	754	2,406	3,518
Arts and Physical Education	98	264	348
Others	28	144	648
Total	2,845	7,909	14,797

Table 9
Number of teaching staff

	1965	1970	1975	1980	1985
Colleges and Universities	5,305	7,779	10,080	14,458	26,047
Male	4,701	6,800	8,592	12,192	21,761
Female	604	979	1,488	2,266	4,286
Graduate Schools	165	165	162	238	412
Male	165	159	156	215	380
Female		6	6	23	32
Teachers' Colleges	305	660	791	564	632
Male	285	619	741	524	563
Female	20	41	50	40	69
Junior Vocational Colleges		239	23	5,488	6,406
Male		47	2	4,572	4,893
Female		192	21	916	1,513
Junior Colleges	454	228	160	—	—
Male	367	154	97	—	—
Female	87	74	63	—	—
Miscellaneous Schools	301	194	200	152	407
Male	200	168	180	127	340
Female	101	26	20	25	67
Total	6,530	9,265	11,416	20,900	33,895
Male	5,718	7,947	9,768	17,630	27,928
Female	812	1,318	1,648	3,270	5,967

institutions in Korea operate through two channels: administrative business and academic affairs. Such academic affairs as the development of new curricula and their revision are discussed and decided by specially nominated committees or department faculty meetings. Other administrative processes take a similar course even in special cases, such as research centers, library business, and so forth.

4. Faculty and Students: Teaching, Learning, and Research

4.1 Faculty

Growth in the number of academic teaching staff in higher education was slow from the end of the Second World War to 1960. However, since the 1960s with the five-year economic development plan, the Korean economy has grown steadily and fast. As a result of this, and the emphasis on higher education, the development of the teaching body has been remarkable, as shown in Table 9. The national average student–staff ratio is about 37:1, although it is as low as 8:1 in one particular institution. The high ratio of students to teaching staff is one of the most pressing problems to be solved in Korean higher education.

There is no tenure system in Korea. Once a member of staff is appointed, he or she generally works until retirement age, which is usually 65 years in both national and private institutions. Usually a full-time instructor is appointed about two to three years after completing a master's degree. However, it has become very hard for a master's degree holder to obtain a teaching position, since many PhD holders are also looking for a position. The PhD holder would usually be appointed as an assistant professor, provided he or she is approved by the personnel affairs committee. The personnel affairs committee is usually composed of the president, dean of academic affairs, dean of the appropriate college, the relevant department head, and other nominated faculty members. Again, appointments to either instructor or assistant professor depend on qualification. The usual criteria for promotion depends on the institution's regulations, but generally takes account of the time passed in each position. The normal length of time as instructor, assistant professor, and associate professor is three, four to five, and five to six years, respectively. The top level is full professor.

There are many nationwide, regional, or institutional cooperative organizations for academics. These organizations can be split into two categories: the discipline-based organization and specialized field-related academic associations, councils, and so forth; and the organization for the advancement, protection, and enrichment of its members' professional status, interests, and security.

Teaching and other related workloads in national

and public institutions is laid out in guidelines of the Ministry of Education. In private institutions, the teaching load of the faculty is decided by the president under the guidance of the board of trustees. The balance between teaching, research, and administrative work is usually decided by the president according to a precedent regulation.

4.2 Students

Student organizations or activities are classified into three categories: academic activities related to their major fields of study; the student body, societies and clubs to fulfill personal interests in areas not related to their academic major; and the union organization for improving and protecting their status or power for participating directly or indirectly in related affairs.

Student organizations in Korea have been very active at various times, and sometimes radical. As a representative body for students, usually there is a student union or student association. The number of its active members also depends on their social situation. Since the majority of students are too busy with academic work, they have little interest in student union activities. The numbers of the active and leading members are steady, but not great. The proportion of extremely radical students is estimated to be less than 0.01 percent of the whole student body.

4.3 Model of Undergraduate Courses

The fundamental and philosophical guidelines related to learning and evaluation are the concern of the Ministry of Education. However the practical structures of first degree courses and programs are first defined by the authorities at the individual institutional level. The need of an accreditation body has been discussed for many years, but it has not yet been organized. As second best, the Korean Council for University Education has tried to find an alternative solution, but without success.

In senior colleges and universities, the duration of course work is usually four years, with six years for medical colleges, colleges of oriental medicine, and dental colleges. For a bachelor's degree, students must complete a minimum of 140 academic credit hours in four years. Currently, all establishments in Korea use the two semester per year system. Courses may be classified into general educational courses (about 35%), compulsory courses (about 35%–43%), and elective courses (about 22%–30%). Academic fields may sometimes be classified into two courses of major and minor.

5. Conclusion

In terms of socioeconomic development, mass higher education has accelerated the industrialization process and the economic development of Korea. Highly educated and specialized labor has greatly contri-

buted to the success of the advanced economic development plan since the late 1970s. Mass higher education has also made new generations aware of social conditions in Korea. Many young people believe that equal opportunities should be given to all, and are committed to build a humanized and equal society. At the same time, young people in higher education have pursued cultural reconstruction. They believe that the better life can be realized only by the liberalization of existing social systems and structures. However, sometimes their approach is too idealistic or radical.

Mass higher education in Korea has both positive and negative effects on the challenges to the state in transition. On the negative side, with public awareness increasing, new challenges emerge. Thus, further progress in economic development is retarded, as some advanced countries have already experienced. These challenges must be overcome by the Korean people. The accepted social philosophy has fundamentally changed from a traditional autocratic mode to an equal and democratic one. The general public, children, adults, men and women, believe that all have equal rights, and demand that they should be treated equally. Some think there has been a collapse in the traditional standards of morality. Such fundamental and philosophical conflicts may be settled only by an intellectual consensus. Therefore, the establishment of a relevant educational program is an urgent requirement.

Bibliography

Kim Chong-Chul 1980 *Researches of Korean Higher Education*. Seoul

Kim Chong-Chul 1988 *A Study of Korean Educational Policy*. Seoul

Korean Council for University Education 1982a *Analysis of Problems of the Current College Entrance System and A Study for Its Reform*. Korean Council for University Education, Seoul

Korean Council for University Education 1982b *A Comprehensive Education Research Paper on the Management of Graduate Schools in 1982*. Korean Council for University Education, Seoul

Korean Council for University Education 1982c *An Evaluation Research Paper on Colleges of Engineering in 1982*. Korean Council for University Education, Seoul

Korean Council for University Education 1982d *An Evaluation Research Paper on Colleges of Pure Science in 1982*. Korean Council for University Education, Seoul

Korean Council for University Education 1982e *A Study for the Formation of Ideas and Directions of Korean University Education*. Korean Council for University Education, Seoul

Korean Council for University Education 1983a *An Analytic Study of the Characteristics of Faculty Resources of Korean Colleges*. Korean Council for University Education, Seoul

Korean Council for University Education 1983b *A Research Report on the Seminar for the Improvement of Theo-*

logical College Education. Korean Council for University Education, Seoul

Korean Council for University Education 1983c *A Study on the Contributions of Higher Education to National Development*. Korean Council for University Education, Seoul

Korean Council for University Education 1984a *A Report of Institutional Evaluation on 4-year Colleges and Universities in 1984*. Korean Council for University Education, Seoul

Korean Council for University Education 1984b *A Study for the Analysis of Unit-Cost of College Education Focusing on the Credit-Unit-Based Tuition System*. Korean Council for University Education, Seoul

Korean Council for University Education 1984c *A Study on the Rationalization of University Finance and Management Focusing on the Optional Tuition Fee and Faculty Remuneration in 1984*. Korean Council for University Education, Seoul

Korean Council for University Education 1985a *A Comparative Study on College Curriculum in Major Countries*. Korean Council for University Education, Seoul

Korean Council for University Education 1985b *A Study on the Development of Inter-Institutional Cooperation Models in Korean Universities*. Korean Council for University Education, Seoul

Korean Council for University Education 1985c *A Study on the Model Development of the Departmental Evaluation of Higher Education in Korea*. Korean Council for University Education, Seoul

Korean Council for University Education 1986a *Development of Accreditation System for Medical Colleges and Its Application*. Korean Council for University Education, Seoul

Korean Council for University Education 1986b *A Study on the Improvement of Faculty Recommendation System*. Korean Council for University Education, Seoul

Korean Council for University Education 1986c *A Study on the T.O. Management System for Faculty Members and Administrative Staffs of Colleges and Universities in Korea*. Korean Council for University Education, Seoul

Korean Council for University Education 1987 *A Research Study on the Development of Criteria for Institutional Evaluation of Colleges and Universities*. Korean Council for University Education, Seoul

Ministry of Education 1986 *Statistical Yearbook of Education, 1965–1986*. Ministry of Education, Seoul

Ministry of Education 1988 *Education in Korea, 1987–1988*. Ministry of Education, Seoul

Joon Hee Park

Kuwait

1. Higher Education and Society

Unlike many countries for which higher education is often seen as a means of increasing national wealth, Kuwait's natural resource, oil, has provided the wealth to build up a modern system of higher education, based largely on American inspiration and practices. In short, the development trajectory which the Kuwaiti system of higher education has followed, is a reversal of the usual assumptions that underlie the process of modernization. The degree of destruction wrought by the Gulf War of 1991 was considerable and at the time of writing much has to be done to restore higher education to its former state. It is unlikely, however, that reconstruction will involve major changes to institutional patterns. Rather less clear, however, is whether the press for more participation in the country's affairs, which is often the result of the experience of war, will cause modifications to be introduced in the area of governance and the management of higher education.

The Emirate of Kuwait covers some 17,818 square kilometers. Its northern border is formed by Iraq, with Saudi Arabia to the south and southwest, and its eastern coastline giving on to the Arabian Gulf. Apart from some offshore islands and a neutral zone of 5,700 kilometers inserted between itself and Iraq, it is devoid of major physical features except for low hills, scrub, and desert.

According to the first official census undertaken in 1957, the population numbered 206,000. By 1990, this figure had grown to 2,100,000 of whom 826,586 were Kuwaitis and 1,316,014 were of non-Kuwaiti origin. Population growth rates are higher for the non-Kuwaiti nationals, though clearly this situation has been radically altered by the exodus of foreign workers prior to the declaration of war in January 1991. However, it is certain that the rebuilding of the economy will call for a major injection of foreign labor though whether to the same level or in the same proportions between the different nationalities as before, is a matter for conjecture. In 1990, some 45.5 percent of the population was less than 19 years old and the crude birthrate 32.2 per thousand. Life expectancy is 69 years for men and 74 for women. The main languages are Arabic and English. The literacy rate is held to be 71 percent.

The economy depends almost entirely on the extraction and production of oil and its by-products. In 1986, for example, oil accounted for 86.5 percent of all Kuwaiti exports and brought in a revenue of some KD2,144,000,000 (US$7,352,537,700). In that year imports ran at KD1,698,000,000 (US$5,823,045,200).

Constitutionally and by tradition, Kuwait is an Islamic country. Article 2 of the Constitution states: "The religion of the State is Islam and the Islamic Shari'a shall be the main source of legislation." The country is governed as a hereditary emirate, with legislative authority vested in the Emir and the National Assembly, and executive power being the exclusive responsibility of the Emir, his cabinet, and his ministers. Judicial power is defined in the Constitution and exercised by the courts in the name of the Emir. Though there are officially no political parties, there is nevertheless a tendency which would wish certain of these features to be revised.

2. The Institutional Fabric of the Higher Education System

Kuwait University was founded in 1966, five years after Independence and then numbered some 418 students and 31 academic staff. By 1988, student enrollments were 17,988 and academic staff numbered 1,181. In addition to the University, the Kuwaiti higher education system has a further four establishments of a specialized nature, organized apart from the University and with a very different mission. These are the Colleges of Basic Education, Business Studies, Health Sciences, and Technological Studies respectively (World Handbook of Universities 1990 pp. 747–48). They may be said to constitute the bulk of the nonuniversity sector, though recent documentation claims that the College of Basic Education is a university (ED/BIE/CONFINTED/41/Q/87 1988).

In all, the number of students enrolled in establishments other than the University of Kuwait was 8,092 in 1988 (UNESCO, 1990). The nonuniversity sector trains students for mid-level technician employment with an emphasis on the applied aspects. The nonuniversity sector grew out of the reforms associated with Law No. 63 of 1982 which set up a Public Authority for Applied Education and Training and which involved a policy of upgrading existing provision. For example, the College of Basic Education, as with many other colleges, was upgraded in 1986. Its original foundation, however, was as a teachers' institute dating from 1962. While specialist research establishments do exist, the University of Kuwait is not a doctoral awarding establishment.

Student numbers for both the university and the nonuniversity sector are set out in Table 1 which shows that over the 13 years from 1975, overall enrollments in the university have risen by three and a half times and by four and a third times for the college sector. As a percentage of the age group 20–24, those enrolled in higher education were 9.0 percent in 1975 and 16.7 percent in 1988 (UNESCO 1990, Table 3.2, p. 3).

Admission to university is governed by the applicant's performance in the final general secondary school examination and is differentiated according to the particular faculty in which she or he seeks a place. Thus, admission to study sciences requires

a minimum mark of 62.2 percent, humanities 68.2 percent, engineering 75 percent, and medicine 80 percent. Applicants to the college sector should be holders of the general secondary education certificate and in addition pass a test administered by the college or be interviewed. (ED/BIE/CONFINTED/41/Q/ 87 1988).

The first degree at the University is the bachelor's in arts, science, economics, commerce, political science, law, or Shar'ia law all of which are four-year courses. Engineering sciences require four and a half years and medicine, seven (World Handbook of Universities, 1990). The college sector issues diplomas of varying duration ranging from two to three years. The College of Basic Education also awards a bachelor of arts after four years. It is planned to extend this latter award to other establishments in this sector.

3. Governance, Administration, and Finance

The University comes under the jurisdiction of the Ministry of Education and is regulated according to Law No. 5 which set up a high council of education. The council is chaired by the Minister of Education and its membership is made up of the Undersecretary of Education, the rector of the University and 17 other members representing appropriate interests, appointed by the cabinet.

The "applied education and training" sector, by contrast, comes under the ambit of the Public Authority for Applied Education and Training which has sole control over this sector. The Public Authority, set up according to the Ameral Decree No. 63 of 1982, has an administrative board headed by the Minister of Education with membership composed of the undersecretaries from the Ministries of Education, Planning, and Social Affairs, the Kuwaiti Civil Service Commission, the Secretary General of Kuwait University as well as representatives from labor unions and the Chamber of Commerce.

The nonuniversity sector was set up with the explicit objective to developing mid-range skills. Given the strategic importance of this priority as a means of making Kuwait less dependent on non-nationals, it figures as one element formally included in the Five-Year State Development Plan scheduled to run from 1985–86 until 1989–90 (ED/BIE/ CONFINTED/41/Q/87 1988). Since study content is closely tied to the particular needs of employing authorities, their development, renewal, or discontinuation is a matter of the Public Authority. Thus, as far as the nonuniversity sector is concerned, both the function of validation and evaluation as well as overall coordination are discharged by the Public Authority.

In the General Budget Estimate for 1988, education was second only to water and electricity services in the government's expenditure league.

Table 1
Student numbers by sector 1975–88

Year	1975	1980	1985	1988
Overall	8,104	13,630	23,678	26,080
University	6,246	9,388	16,359	17,988
Nonuniversity	1,858	4,242	7,319	8,092

Source: UNESCO 1990 *Statistical Handbook*. UNESCO, Paris

It took up KD419,600,000 (US$1,438,957,400) or 13.3 percent of the general budget. However, the only statistics available and standardized on an international basis relate to the decade 1976 to 1986. During that period, public expenditure on education in general rose three times from KD113,750,000 (US$390,089,160) to KD343,800,000 (US$1,179,012,300). Current expenditure on all sectors of higher education rose at a slightly faster rate, in absolute figures—from KD18,200,000 (US$62,414,260) to KD57,414,600 (US$196,895,060), that is, by some 315 percent (UNESCO 1990 derived from Table 4.3, p. 4). The amount devoted to higher education in the latter year was 16.7 percent of the total education budget.

Because Kuwait is a higher education system compact in location, the line between national governance and institutional governance insofar as it concerns the University of Kuwait is less evident than it would be in the case of geographically dispersed and multiple institute systems. The University is headed by a rector as academic head with a secretary general subordinate to him, acting as head of administration. Academic work is organized, at the middle layer into Colleges of Arts, Science, Commerce, Education, Engineering, and Petroleum Technology and of Shari'a (Islamic law) which should not be confused with the official name given to establishments in the applied education sector. There are two exceptions in this nomenclature. They are the faculties of medicine and of allied health sciences and nursing. Whether college or faculty, each is headed by a dean who acts as the coordinating administrative head. Within the colleges, the departments act as the basic units in charge of teaching, examinations, and student evaluation and assessment.

Organizational patterns in the nonuniversity sector differ again. If the University is headed by a rector, the applied education colleges are headed by a dean, backed by an administrative deputy. The non-university sector is arranged around departments without the intervening faculty or college layer. Thus, for example, the College of Technological Studies has six departments. Their responsibilities fall into the usual areas of teaching and student evaluation. Unlike the University, however, as has been pointed out earlier, the decision to develop or to abolish courses is not rooted in the individual department and confirmed by the university council, but comes under the direct control of the Public Authority for Applied Education.

4. Faculty and Students: Teaching, Learning, and Research

The teaching body in the university sector grew from 327 in 1975 to 1,181 in 1988 and those in the sector of applied education and training from 269 to 513 between 1975 and 1987. A significant proportion is composed of non-Kuwaiti nationals, particularly in the language departments since the teaching languages are Arabic and English. The academic profession is structured along American lines of instructor, lecturer, assistant professor, and full professor. Advancement to the higher ranks is dependent on holding a research degree PhD equivalent and an appropriate record of publications and academic achievement.

Given the mission of the applied education and training sector, the career path of its teachers is clearly very different from their counterparts in university. Many have a practitioner background.

One interesting trend within the academic body is the small, but nevertheless rising number of women in the University, in contrast to a contrary development in the applied education sector. Thus, between 1975 and 1987, the feminization rate rose from 5 percent to 17 percent in the former, and fell from 55 percent to 20 percent in the latter sector (UNESCO 1990 p. 3). The latter phenomenon can in part be explained by the fact that early in their development colleges which later became part of the applied education sector were closely associated with training of women and girls as kindergarten and primary-school teachers. The change in mission which followed the Law of 1982, plus the wish of the government to extend the provision of vocational training, brought in areas where men were the main exponents.

The student body in the Kuwait higher education system is interesting in several regards, the first of which is its multinational nature. In 1989, for example, almost 6,000 non-Kuwaiti nationals were enrolled (World Handbook on Universities, 1990 pp. 747–48). Clearly, this reflects a demand for higher education amongst skilled immigrant workers, plus the agreement that exists between member states of the Gulf Cooperation Council whereby Kuwait admits their students. An examination of the country of origin of foreign students enrolled between 1987 and 1988 in Kuwaiti higher education shows that 1,683 were from Jordan, 1,031 from unspecified Asian countries, 409 from Iraq, 393 from Bahrain, and 255 from Saudi Arabia (UNESCO 1990 Table 3.15, p. 3 ff).

Yet, Kuwait is also an exporter of students. In the same year, 3,568 Kuwaitis were studying abroad–two thirds of them in the United States (UNESCO 1990 p. 3).

The second point of interest is the gender composition of the student estate. Not only have women formed the majority in the University since 1975, but this majority has grown from 56 percent to 65 percent in the course of thirteen years. Precisely the opposite trend is present in establishments of applied education and training. There, from being the majority of six out of ten in 1975, girls now represent slightly under four out of ten (38 percent).

Undergraduate courses are based on a credit-unit system with the basic requirement to register for 12–16 credit units per semester. Student assessment is based half on continuous evaluation and half on final end of semester examinations. The model of undergraduate study is grounded on a system of core subjects, electives, and options within the faculty the student has chosen. Major and minor subjects are the usual pattern within the undergraduate degree to gain what requires a basic minimum of credit hours accumulated over the stipulated study time. Credit-hour requirements for bachelors' degrees range from 120 for law and economics through to 144 for engineering and petroleum technology. The award of degrees is approved by the University Council on the recommendation of college or faculty councils.

Though registration and tuition fees are levied, they are minimal–KD5 (US$17) for the former and a similar amount for each course. Student facilities are heavily subsidized.

5. Conclusion

Kuwait is an interesting exception in that it is a country with more than sufficient financial resources to have developed a highly modern system of higher education. Yet it is equally a country with insufficient autochthonous human resources to sustain this level of development without labor force being brought in from outside. With one of the highest per capita incomes in the world and a highly developed, if not specialized, industrial infrastructure, it has never theless a form of dependency, above all in the technical fields and at technician level which have obliged the government to seek ways of reducing it. It remains to be seen whether this policy, already under way before the Iraqi invasion of August 1990, will not be pushed forward with greater determination as part of the postwar reconstruction.

Bibliography

Al Sabah Y S F 1981 *The Oil Economy of Kuwait*. Routledge & Kegan Paul, London

Central Statistical Office 1986 *Kuwait in Figures: Twenty-five Years of Independence*. Central Statistical Office, Kuwait

Hakima Abu A M 1983 *The Modern History of Kuwait 1750–1966*. The Westerham Press

Middle East and North Africa 1990, 36th edn. Europa Publications Ltd, London

Ministry of Education n.d. *Education Development in the State of Kuwait*. Ministry of Education, Kuwait

Ministry of Education n.d. *Guide to Education in Kuwait*. Ministry of Education, Kuwait

Ministry of Education 1987a *Education in Kuwait and the Summit Islamic Conference*. Ministry of Education, Kuwait

Ministry of Education 1987b *The Annual Report of the Ministry of Education*. Ministry of Education, Kuwait

National Commission for Education, Science and Culture 1988 Reply to questionnaire on post secondary education and its diversification in relation to employment, ED/BIE/CONFINTED/41/Q/87 (mimeo). Kuwait

Rush A 1987 *Al Sabah: History and Genealogy of Kuwait's Ruling Family 1752–1987*. Ithaca Press, London

UNESCO 1990 *Statistical Yearbook 1990*. UNESCO, Paris

World of Learning 1988. Europa Publications Ltd, London

World Handbook of Universities 1990, 1990 edn. Macmillan Stockton for IAU (2606), London/Paris

G. Neave; A. Velloso

L

Laos

1. Higher Education and Society

Lao People's Democratic Republic (referred to here-after as Lao PDR) is a landlocked country of about four million people with some 236,800 square kilometers of land. It has about 200 kilometers of border with China, 150 kilometers with Burma, 200 kilometers with Cambodia, about 1,800 kilometers with Vietnam (mostly the Phou Louang Mountains) and about 1,000 kilometers with Thailand. It is classified by the United Nations as one of the least developed countries.

Lao PDR became socialist only in 1975, following years of internal conflict, elements of which have not yet been totally resolved, and occupation by foreign powers. Since then, there has been a close relationship with the Soviet Union and other socialist countries including Vietnam, Mongolia, and Hungary, and many Lao have been trained in these countries. The predominant religion in the country is Buddhism, and the leaders of the revolutionary government generally have not tried to suppress the religious hierarchy in the country. Leaders of the Buddhist faith have been consulted in discussions concerning the future of the country, and Lao party leaders make it clear that they are seeking the Lao way to socialism which may differ from the approach of other countries (Spaulding 1990).

Lao PDR has three general populations: those in flatlands (engaged in agriculture); those in remote areas and hills (tribal); and those in between. The several minorities make up the majority of the population, with something of a caste system at work. A UNESCO study carried out in 1984–85, suggests that in the mid-1980s, in 15 largely rural provinces, there were as many as 765,400 illiterates in the 15–45 age group, or roughly 56 percent of the total population in these provinces (UNESCO 1987 p. 12). This is striking in comparison with the estimate of an average of 84 percent literacy nationally. Illiteracy rates are 8 percent for males and 24.2 percent for females (UNESCO 1990 p. 97). In 1987–88, the distribution of enrollment in the 2,100 primary schools by ethnic region was as follows: Lao Theung 23 percent, Lao Soung 4 percent, Lao Loum 73 percent. This disparity is further illustrated by the distribution of enrollment in the first cycle secondary schools: first year: Lao Theung 5 percent, Lao Soung 0.6 percent,

Lao Loum, 95 percent; second year: Lao Theung, 4.2 percent, Lao Soung, 0.7 percent, Lao Lorum 95.1 percent (Commission Nationale Lao 1990 p. 12).

Most of the population lives in fertile plains along the Mekong river. As of 1989, about 79.9 percent of the population worked in agriculture and forestry, about 1 percent in industry, about 0.9 percent in construction, about 0.9 percent in transportation and communications, and about 1.5 percent in other productive enterprises. In the service sector (about 6.6 percent of the economy in 1989, up from 6.1 percent in 1986), about 1.6 percent of the people worked in commerce, 2.2 percent in education and culture, 0.7 percent in health, and 2.1 percent in other service areas. Some 9.4 percent of the population was estimated to be unemployed or working in the private sector in 1989. In all employment categories (other than unemployed), there has been a slight improvement since 1986 (Commission Nationale Lao 1990 p. 3).

The country is rich in mineral resources and has vast agricultural and hydroelectric potential. It is, however, confronted with a number of serious obstacles that prevent it from undisturbed and accelerated development: inadequate physical infrastructure, shortage of technical and managerial skills, and a chronic lack of domestic and foreign savings (Second United Nations Conference 1990).

The government has adopted a new policy and program of action entitled the New Economic Mechanism (NEM). Initially designed to achieve greater reliance on market forces through the improvement of the performance of public enterprises, subsequent measures (since 1986) have included the deregulation of prices, fiscal and financial reforms, removal of trade barriers and investment codes. As of late 1990, the Third Five-Year Development Plan (1991–95) is under preparation.

With an annual population growth rate of about 2.9 percent, the average annual Gross Domestic Product growth rate for the 1980s of 4.6 percent has meant a modest improvement in standard of living. This growth rate is slightly better than the average of one percent growth recorded by less developed countries in the Pacific and Africa. However, the growth is far below the 7 percent targeted in the First Five-Year Development Plan (1981–85) and significantly lower than the 10 percent target of the Second Five-Year Development Plan (1986–90).

Inflation has been persistent in the 1980s, averaging around 50 percent from 1980–86, though it has decelerated since then, and the multiple exchange rate has been eliminated. As of mid-1990, the commercial exchange rate is the same as that of the parallel market (US$1=Kip 720). Exports are accelerating, with forestry an important sector, but with coffee and manufactured goods as potential exports in the future. External debt is high (estimated at US$800 million in 1988, with about 75 percent owed in non-convertible currencies).

Recently, cooperation between Lao PDR and Thailand has become significant, with military and other agreements having led to a relaxation of travel restrictions between the two countries and a lively development of economic cooperation projects. Thailand recently constructed a parade ground in Vientiane as a gift to Lao PDR.

There is a density of only 16 persons per square kilometer in the country making the provision of basic infrastructure such as roads, river ports, telecommunications, water supplies, school and health facilities difficult. In addition, the dependency ratio is high, with about 45 percent of the population under the age of 15.

Education has expanded rapidly since 1975, and it was estimated in the mid-1980s that enrollment ratios reached 81 percent at the primary level, 13 percent at the secondary level, and 1.3 percent at the higher levels.

The social and economic development of the country is severely constrained by critical shortages of trained labor force. The 1986 census showed the proportion of university graduates to total workers was 0.3 percent. In that year, there were only 500 engineers and 1,500 technicians in the entire country. The government, through technical schools attached to the various ministries, has offered in recent years a great variety of training programs for semiskilled, skilled and professional occupations. There are 14 vocational centers in the country, with an average annual output of 1,200 at the skilled level, and 10 lower technical schools with an annual output of 700. All these institutions lack material and equipment and adequately trained teachers. Since 1975, more than 12,000 students have been studying abroad, many in the Soviet Union, Vietnam, Hungary, and other socialist countries, and about 5,000 have completed their studies and returned home. About 60 percent of the students need six or seven years to obtain a higher degree. The remainder stay three to four years and are given technical training.

At the same time, with about 80 percent of the population engaged in agriculture, and only about 7 percent full-time wage and salary earners, there is a question of how much skilled labor is needed. The lack of skilled labor, of course, may be a factor in constraining employment shifts.

2. The Institutional Fabric of the Higher Education System

Higher education in Lao PDR is entirely governmental and no private universities or institutions of higher education exist. As of 1987–88, there were three higher education institutions, plus higher technical schools which function under the various government ministries. These higher technical institutes grew from three in 1984–85 (with 1,324 enrolled and 142 graduated) to seven in 1987–88 (with 1,126 enrolled and 432 graduating). These schools have such specialties as public works (roads and bridges), construction, forestry, post and telecommunications, and electrical engineering and electronics, and admission is on a competitive basis after the first cycle of secondary education (essentially beginning with the ninth year of schooling). The program in these schools may extend for three years (the same as the second cycle of secondary education) or up to three additional years for the higher specialties (UNESCO and ESCAP 1985, Commission Nationale Lao 1990). In addition, there are a number of secondary-level technical and professional schools, including those designed to prepare primary school teachers.

Higher education as generally understood, however, is limited to the University of Medical Sciences (with faculties of medicine, pharmacy, and dentistry), the Sciences and Pedagogy University (with faculties of exact and natural science and of social science, with a foreign language section), and the National Polytechnic Institute (with sections dealing with electrical, civil, and mechanical engineering).

Not much true research can be seen at the universities. The government tends to establish other research institutes under relevant ministries and not attached to the universities. One, for instance, is the *Institute de Recherche Pédagogie*, established in 1982 under the Ministry of Education, which is in charge of curriculum research and the preparation of school curricula and school texts. There is no connection between this institute and the pedagogy faculty at the Sciences and Pedagogy University, though some faculty may be involved on a personal level in both. A Social Science Research Council organizes a variety of research projects (some having to do with the role of the party in development). Under the Third Five-Year Development Plan (1991–95), the Ministry of Science and Technology will transform its Scientific and Technical Council into a true research organization, under its direct authority. It is expected that some 100 researchers will develop around 31 research projects, linked to development goals (Commission Nationale Lao p. 23).

Many projects under the research institutes and councils will be in cooperation with other countries or cooperation agencies. In November 1987, a scientific and technical cooperation agreement was signed with Thailand; in May 1989, such agreements were signed with France; others have been signed with Sweden, Japan, Australia, several socialist countries, the various United Nations funds, the World Bank, the Asian Development Bank (which undertook a major education sector study in 1989), and others. Many of these agreements will ultimately impact on higher education.

Admission requirements to the three higher education institutions are set by the Ministry of Education and are based on examination results at the end of the second cycle of secondary education (11 years of schooling, usually completed at age 17, at which time students receive the *baccalauréat*), supplemented by a system of quotas to assure that there are some students in the three institutions from the educationally disadvantaged provinces. The programs at the University of Medical Sciences are generally of six years duration; those of the Polytechnic, five years; and those of the Sciences and Pedagogy University, four years. The first stage of higher education (generally four years) leads to the *licence*, and the *doctorat* is offered after six years of study.

The Polytechnic is the newest of the institutions, having been created in 1984. It enrolled 126 students in 1984–85 and 399 in 1987–88. The first class of 26 received their diplomas in 1989. Enrollment in the University of Medical Sciences (founded in 1958) totalled 1,012 in 1987–88, with about half (557) the student body female (data provided by Division of Statistics in computer printout November 21, 1990).

The Sciences and Pedagogy University was created as a higher pedagogical institute in 1959, and changed its name to reflect its university status only in 1988. Enrollment grew from 309 in 1975–76 (the first year of the socialist government) to 2,411 in the 1987–88 school year. Degrees offered are those of *professeur de sciences* or *de lettres*, although with new courses of study to be introduced, in keeping with the University's new status, the degrees offered will undoubtedly multiply. There is about a 20 percent dropout rate and many who complete the four years (especially those who do languages) go into positions in the various government ministries and private enterprise (even though they may have been trained as secondary school teachers). The Sciences and Pedagogy University has developed an inservice training program (under a UNDP–UNESCO project) to train secondary school teachers in service. This is an especially important activity given the fact that so many graduates of the University choose to do something other than teach in secondary school (second cycle), for which they have been prepared. Thus, undertrained upper-cycle secondary teachers, who need professionalization, abound.

In 1970, only 16 per 100,000 inhabitants were enrolled in higher education. This number rose to 21 in 1980 and in 1987 there were 27 students in higher education per 100,000 inhabitants (UNESCO 1990 p. 97). About 1.3 percent of the appropriate age group were in higher education in the mid-1980s (Second United Nations Conference 1990 p. 7).

3. Governance, Administration, and Finance

Since 1975 and until the recent liberalization known as the New Economic Mechanism, Lao PDR has followed a socialist system of production, including agricultural collectivism. This involved a highly centralized kind of planning, and resources for higher education were a part of this planning. In spite of many achievements, the rate of growth moderated in the 1980s, state enterprises showed weak performance, and agricultural collectives achieved only insignificant profitability or none at all, even though substantial assistance has been received during the 1980s from such donors as the UNDP, Japan, Sweden, the Asian Development Bank, the World Bank, and Australia.

The Third Five-Year Development Plan (1991–95) will set indicative planning figures, but will rely on a reduced government role in achieving these figures, under the New Economic Mechanism. The use of what appears so far to be a pragmatic approach encourages privatization of state enterprises and foreign investment in the local economy.

Within this context, the government (through its Ministry of Education) appears to be willing to continue the policy of free training for semiskilled, skilled and professional occupations at the higher education level, both at local institutions and abroad. On the basis of government projections it is estimated that by 1995 the country will need annually 140 engineering graduates, 350 high-level technician graduates and an additional 580 high-level staff, not including second-cycle secondary-school teachers who require university training or medical professionals (Second United Nations Conference 1990 pp. 18–19). Clearly, substantial investment is anticipated by the government in higher education and higher-level inservice training in the future, and, although there is a policy to decentralize education at lower levels (including the financing thereof), it is likely that most of the funding of higher education will continue to be from the central government.

At the institutional level, there is a fair degree of decentralization to departments, with fairly weak central control. Departmental faculties under chairpersons develop the curriculum for each program and often develop the teaching materials as well. A university council exists but seems not to be involved in details of program planning once a curriculum area has been approved. There seems to be very limited day-to-day planning and communication between different departmental faculties within the institution.

4. Faculty and Students: Teaching, Learning, and Research

The number of university-level faculty is small, though it has grown from 140 in 1980 to 534 in 1985 to 620 in 1987. There appear to be some differences between the status of university faculty and government employees, though these differences are not pronounced in terms of perquisites and income. The system is structured somewhat along the lines of a French institution of higher education, with department chairs occupying positions of some authority. The rector's role seems to vary from institution to institution, and at the Sciences and Pedagogy University in the late 1980s, the acting rector appeared to be the link with the governing political party with little involvement in the work of the various academic specializations. Clearly, the rector's role in the several institutions will be to introduce changes mandated by the new development goals enunciated by the government.

The complex impact of major involvement of international donors in education can be illustrated by the 1988–89 mix of faculty members at the Sciences and Pedagogy University near Vientiane. Of 261 faculty members, 194 were Lao, and 67 were of other nationalities: 46 were from the Soviet Union; 1 was Czech; 12 Vietnamese; 3 Hungarian; 1 Bulgarian; 1 Mongolian; 1 Indian; 1 Canadian; and 1 French. Fifteen of the foreign faculty—a department which handles pedagogical work as well as ideology—were specialists in Marxism–Leninism (eight Soviets and seven Vietnamese) (Spaulding 1990 p. 119).

In 1987, higher education students were heavily concentrated in the educational sciences and teacher training (3,112 students of a total of 5,322 in higher education). Only 64 students were in the social sciences, 1,012 in the medical sciences, 962 in some form of engineering, 249 in architecture and town planning, and 345 in transportation and communication (data from a computer run by the Division of Statistics, UNESCO, November 21, 1990).

Teaching resources appear adequate at the universities, with much scientific and technical equipment in evidence in the various laboratories (much of it donated under technical assistance schemes). There is some use of modern technological media, for instance, a mobile videocam is used in teacher training to record and play back the performance of student teachers. There are a number of Apple computers at the Sciences and Pedagogy University, but few good programs for them; in the foreign language unit, there are some well-programed computers designed to help in foreign language teaching (provided under a UNDP/UNESCO assistance program). The other two universities also appear to have some computer resources and reasonably good laboratory equipment.

5. Conclusion

The future undoubtedly will offer many changes in higher education in Lao PDR. With more emphasis on a market economy, and with a number of development schemes requiring a high-level labor force, it is likely that the very structure and management of higher education institutions will be altered to take into account the new economic thrusts. At the same time, limited resources will constrain growth unless higher education can continue to acquire substantial assistance from donor agencies outside the country.

Assuming that the trend toward privatization (including joint ventures with those from other countries) accelerates, it is likely that private enterprise will draw off many of the university graduates, thus continuing to create labor shortages in the public enterprises and even within the teaching staff of the universities themselves. Further, the dichotomy between research institutes, under various government ministries and councils, and the university-level institutions may be problematic in the long run considering the limited labor force available for both research and teaching at higher levels.

The disparity in educational opportunity between the various geographic and ethnic groups is recognized by the government and steps are apparently being taken to try to improve the situation. Despite these efforts, the underprivileged groups, especially in relatively isolated rural areas, may continue to be left behind, unless heroic measures are taken to expand educational opportunity for these groups at all levels. At the same time, Lao PDR is a relatively well-endowed country in terms of economic potential, and the spirit of economic and political cooperation in the region should encourage rapid development of that potential in the years ahead.

Bibliography

Commission Nationale Lao pour l'UNESCO 1990 *L'education, la culture, la communication, la science et la technologie dans la stratégie du développement de la République Démocratique Populaire Lao* (May, 1990). UNESCO, Paris

Second United Nations Conference on the Least Developed Countries 1990 *County Presentation by the Government of the Lao People's Democratic Republic, 1990.* Document UNCLDC II/CP.35, Paris, 3–14 September, 1990

Spaulding S 1990 Educational development and reform on the Soviet periphery: Mongolian People's Republic and Lao People's Democratic Republic. *J Asian African Affairs* 2(1): 109–24

UNESCO 1987 *Social Science Research and Women in the Republique Democratique Populaire Lao.* UNESCO, Paris

UNESCO 1990 *Statistical Digest 1990.* Division of Statistics, UNESCO, Paris

UNESCO and ESCAP 1985 *Lao People's Democratic Republic: Country Report.* Fifth Regional Conference of Ministers of Education and those responsible for Economic Planning in Asia and the Pacific, Bangkok, March, 1985 (document UNCLDC II/CP.35, GE.90-51491)

S. Spaulding

Lebanon

1. Higher Education and Society

The Republic of Lebanon, located on the eastern coast of the Mediterranean Sea, became a member of the Arab League and the United Nations after its independence from French mandate in 1943. It is a tiny democratic republic with an area of 10,452 square kilometers. The State of Lebanon was formed by the French around 1920 from Mount Lebanon and four other districts, which were all previously under Ottoman rule.

There have been population fluctuations in Lebanon since 1975, the date of the inception of an unremitting civil war which aborted overall development plans and ultimately brought devastation of the economic social infrastructure, along with an acute devaluation of the Lebanese currency. Traumatized by more than 15 years of atrocious strife in a country that has been called the "Switzerland of the Orient" and the "Paradise of Eden," Lebanese people of all persuasions have migrated internally and emigrated worldwide, much more than ever before. It is estimated that more than 40 percent of the half million workers in the Lebanese private sector are unemployed. There is the continual threat of militias degenerating into armed gangs to rob and loot. Cynically speaking, the overall Lebanese situation is likely to become worse. Table 1 details the density and growth rate of the Lebanese population.

What seems at times to be a religious conflict is underpinned more by economic and political factors on local, regional, and international scales. Religious diversity, which made in part for the glory and prosperity of Lebanon, has been exploited on an ever wider scale. Neither will those responsible for the continuation of the civil war allow the Lebanese people themselves to come to some kind of an internal agreement, as happened once before, in 1943, with the formerly understood "National Pact." If a political compromise was ever reached the high quality workforce that has either been paralyzed or has left the country would come back and reactivate the various productive and supportive sectors, such as the service sector, which has been outstanding even in wartime.

The various religious bodies are still acting and reacting in terms of their parochial interests. The perennial political goal, which is the genuine and just unification of the country under regional and international peace and stability, is still to be fulfilled.

2. The Institutional Fabric of the Higher Education System

Under sporadic daily shelling and various threats and dangers, the Lebanese educational system still works whenever and wherever possible. Cultural activities and higher education especially keep functioning with whatever regularity can be managed under such critical conditions.

There are, in Beirut and its suburbs, five major universities, as well as their extensions and those branches that were established during the war in different parts in the country as separate entities. Nine other colleges or institutes of higher education include: The Lebanese Academy of Fine Arts (established in 1937), *Centre d'Etudes Supérieures* (*Ecole Sup. des Lettres*) (1944), *Centre d'Etudes Mathematiques et Physiques* (1945), Middle East College (1949), Beirut University College (1950), Haigazian College (1955), Al-Hikmah Higher Institute of Law (1961), Imam Ouzai College of Islamic Studies (1979), Islamic College of Business Administration (1986) (AIU 1990). The discussion here will concentrate, however, on the major universities.

Table 1
Population of Lebanon (in thousands)

	1950	1955	1960	1965	1970	1975	1980	1985	1990
Total population	1,443	1,613	1,857	2,151	2,469	2,767	2,669	2,668	2,965
Density per square kilometer	139	155	179	207	237	266	257	257	285
18–23 age cohort (%)	—	—	—	—	—	—	—	12.5	13.5
Percentage growth rate	—	—	—	—	—	—	—	2.24	

Source: UN 1989 pp. 36–437

413

With the exception of the Lebanese State University (1953), all other universities, colleges, and institutions of higher education in Lebanon are private, fee-paying institutions (whether foreign or national). The American University of Beirut (AUB), established as the Syrian Protestant College in 1866 by the Presbyterian Mission, is the oldest. Its language of instruction is English and it is patterned in teaching, research and administration along the United States system. In contrast, *Université Saint Joseph* (USJ) (established in 1875 by the Society of Jesus) has as its principal language of instruction French and it is modeled on the traditional French educational system.

The Lebanese University (LU), the only state university in Lebanon, has operated since 1951 although it was only formally established in 1953. Its foundation, expansion, and development were all influenced by student, faculty, and popular demonstrations, a process which has been suspended since the present war began in 1975.

The Beirut Arab University (BAU), affiliated with the University of Alexandria in Egypt, was established in 1960. It developed and flourished, like the Lebanese University, as a response to the need for national universities. However, BAU helped to meet the need of university entrants living far away from Beirut and Lebanon who register but only show up around examination time. Most of them are not skilled enough in a foreign language to use it to pursue their higher education. The language of instruction at LU and BAU is officially Arabic, although French and English are temporarily used in some courses at some of their faculties. The BAU thus played a major role in increasing equal educational opportunities in the Arab World.

A fifth major institution, the *Université Saint-Esprit de Kaslik* (USE), originally a Maronite (Catholic) seminary, gradually evolved to university status in 1961. However, it is relatively small in size and impact.

Since the establishment of the *Baccalauréat* Part II, the official secondary-school leaving certificate, as the official requirement for university entry, most institutions of higher education have respected it, along with other selective entrance tests and/or competitions held for certain competitive faculties. The *Baccalauréat* Part II for the Lebanese, or its recognized equivalent for the non-Lebanese, is even essential for admission in graduate schools and in government employment to validate all university studies.

In 1979–80, the Lebanese University had the highest enrollment figures (41,684 students), followed in order by Beirut Arab University (28,698), St. Joseph University (5,265), and the American University of Beirut (4,530). Enrollment at other institutions of higher education ranged between 10 and 2,116 students (Jarrar et al. 1988, p. 789). In Table 2, the fluctuations in the enrollment figures clearly show the impact of the civil war.

In all Lebanese institutions of higher education, first degrees require at least three years of study; second degree studies average a further two years, doctorate degrees usually require up to seven years, especially in medicine.

The American University of Beirut, with 4,460 students (IAU 1989, p. 750–52), offers instruction in five faculties, and other schools, institutes and departments, culminating in bachelor's, master's, and PhD degrees and other diplomas and certificates, in two branches. At the USJ (6,009 students) instruction is offered in eight faculties and other schools and institutes, with licenciate, doctoral, and other diplomas and certificates. The LU (24,560 students) has 12 faculties and institutes, along with numerous branches throughout the country, offering licenciate and doctoral degrees, and various diplomas and certificates. The BAU (3,796 students and 33,931 external students) offers instruction in seven colleges, with licenciate, bachelor's and master's degrees. At Kaslik the USE (2,823 students) offers instruction in six faculties and other schools and institutes, with licenciate, doctoral, and other diplomas.

3. Governance, Administration, and Finance

Since the creation of the State of Lebanon, education, particularly higher education has thrived, like other economic and social activities, under an

Table 2
Third-level students in all Lebanese institutions

	1979	1980	1981	1982	1984
Total number of students	85,287[a]	79,073	70,314	73,052	70,510
Female representation	—	28,531	26,284	27,225	27,473
Female students as percentage	—	36	37	37	39

Source: UNESCO 1987 p. 3–266
a In ALECSO 1983 p. 191

414

intended and observed *laissez-faire* policy favoring the private sector.

A 1961 law classified institutions of higher education as universities, colleges, or institutes, and delineated their functions. In 1967 another law established the Higher Advisory Board, to offer advice on standards and to secure cooperation among various higher education institutions. However, this board has had little impact. After student demonstrations and faculty resignations, the government issued a major law in December 1967 for the Lebanese University, which has the largest regular enrollment and is financed completely by the state. Its students pay only nominal fees and the college of education students at LU receive stipends or salaries, whereas at all other institutions of higher education in Lebanon fees are charged and finances basically come from private sources whether foreign or national or a combination of the two. They are governed and administered and planned for by private bodies, with almost no government control.

The Ministry of Education is legally responsible for all education in Lebanon. However, the "Minister of National Education is vested with the right of guardianship over the affairs of the Lebanese University." Nevertheless, the Lebanese University, which falls in the public sector, remains in many respects the unwanted child of the state, and lacks real care and development. Its president, along with an all university council, is responsible for its administration and planning. The total expenditure on education made by the government is shown in Table 3.

The goals of higher education and precollege education have never been spelled out and clarified throughout the history of Lebanon. There has been a constant dualism between certain stated aims and the real aims and inner workings of the Lebanese official institutions.

Table 3
Lebanese Ministry of Education total educational expenditure (including Lebanese University budget)

	1970	1977	1982	1983
Amount in Lebanese Pounds	123,663	298,200	—	—
As percentage of Gross National Product (GNP)	2.5	—	—	—
As percentage of total national government product expenditure	16.8	18.6	15.6	13.8

Source: *UN Statistical Yearbook 1982*, in Jarrar et al. 1988

Each of the private universities, colleges, and institutes has its own board of trustees or directors. Final authority regarding finance, admission, certification, and similar matters resides in such boards, except for the study of law. All faculties of law are officially considered branches of the Lebanese University. Academic work is generally organized by faculties, including departments, and numerous committees. The patterns of authority are not clearly defined.

As the Lebanese University is considered a state unit its faculty and staff are held to be "government employees subject to all laws and regulations pertaining to other employees." The president of the Lebanese University acts on behalf of the Minister of Education in exercising all authority connected with administrative, academic, and financial affairs of the university. The university board or council is composed of the deans of faculties and directors of institutes, one elected faculty member and one student from each faculty or institute. At faculty or institute level, the structure is similar. Final authority in major university affairs is vested with the Council of Ministers, including any faculty move out of the country even in order to attend short scientific conferences.

4. Faculty and Students: Teaching, Learning, and Research

As is shown in Table 4 the number of faculty members has almost doubled in every decade since 1970; the number of students in higher education is dropping, however. This is especially true in regard to the number of foreign students studying in Lebanon, who made half of the student body before the war (there were 25,515 foreign students in 1984).

Part-time contractual employment of faculty members was the norm before the war, especially at the state Lebanese University. For the time being most faculty members are tenured in order to prevent migration. Non-Lebanese faculty members are at an all time minimum.

The ranks of assistant professor, associate professor, full professor, and their equivalents, along

Table 4
Third-level teachers in all Lebanese institutions

	1970	1979	1982	1984
Total number of teachers	2,300[a]	4,500[b]	7,976	7,460
Female representation	—	—	2,478	2,301
Female proportion (%)	—	—	31	31

Source: UNESCO 1987 pp. 3–266
a and b ALESCO 1983 p. 191

Table 5
Third-level students and graduates by field of study

	1980		1984		1984	
	Students				Graduates	
Exact sciences, technical, engineering, and medicine	16,426	[5,228]	15,789	[6,003]	1,729	[564]
Social and behavioral sciences	17,700	[7,617]	10,130	[4,515]	935	[445]
Humanities	44,947	[15,686]	44,591	[16,955]	3,341	[1,382]
Total [and number of females thereof]	79,073	[28,531]	70,510	[27,473]	6,005	[2,391]

Source: UNESCO 1987 pp. 3–314

with a traditional scheme of promotion based on years of experience and research, are well-known in Lebanon. Recruitment, status, and career paths differ from one institution to another according to their by-laws. At the Lebanese University, all full-time ranks ultimately require a decree issued by the President of the Republic. The limits of the hours to be spent in teaching along with other matters of general interest have been predetermined by presidential decrees at LU, whereas such matters are more flexible at the other institutions of higher education, which are all private. It is only at the LU that the faculty has an organized union approved by the Ministry of Interior.

Except for most of the students of the Lebanese University and some of Beirut Arab University, most other higher education students belong to a leisured class. Only the students at the Lebanese University have a recognized union and representation on various councils including the supreme all-university council.

First degree and other degree courses, programs, and examinations are planned for, defined, altered, and carried out by faculties and departments within the universities. Some tend to be based on liberal arts, general contents, others are specialist, professional units according to the nature of various faculties, but a broad "propaedeutic" general education preparation for most specializations is usual in most universities in Lebanon. The numbers of students and graduates in the varying fields of study is shown in Table 5. Private universities and some colleges at the Lebanese University use a credit system. Students are regularly assessed in their undergraduate and graduate careers usually at mid-term or mid-year and at the end of term or year. Traditional marking systems are frequently used.

5. Conclusion

As with all other aspects of economic and social life in Lebanon, higher education has been undergoing a severe crisis during the civil war, most notably in qualitative terms. The state university (LU) has, more than any other, always developed through crises, but the crises it faces in the 1990s may be the worst. As soon as relative peace that is hoped for is established in Lebanon, a huge effort will be needed to reconstruct the fabric of higher and pre-college education in order to remake it as at once larger and much better, a vehicle for nation building and an international center for cultural and educational development.

Bibliography

ALECSO 1983 *Educational Statistics Bulletin for the Arab World*. Arab League Educational Cultural and Scientific Organization, Dept. of Documentation and Information, Tunis
Bashshur M 1984 *The Role of Education in the Fragmentation of the Lebanese Society*. Paper presented at the Ninth Annual Symposium Toward a Viable Lebanon, Center for Contemporary Arab Studies, Georgetown University, Washington, DC
Bashshur M R 1978 Republic of Lebanon. In: Knowles A S (ed.) 1977 *The International Encyclopedia of Higher Education*, Vol. 6. Jossey-Bass, pp. 2459–68
Broum M A M 1989 A Study of the Attitudes Toward Education, Perception of the General Goals of Education, and Educational Behaviors of High School Students in Civil War Setting (Lebanon). PhD thesis, University of Pittsburgh
Dham N S 1988 Schooling and National Development: The Role of Schooling in Building a Sense of Social Integration (Switzerland, Vietnam, Lebanon). PhD thesis, State University of New York at Buffalo
Gilmour D 1988 Lebanon. In: Adams M (ed.) 1988 *The Middle East*. Facts on File, New York, pp. 410–19
Hares A K 1985 Education and National Integration in Lebanon. EdD thesis, Columbia University Teachers College
International Association of Universities 1989 *International Handbook of Universities*. Stockton, New York, pp. 750–53
Jarrar S A, Mikati J F, Massialas B J 1988 Lebanon. In: Kurian G T (ed.) 1988 *World Education Encyclopedia*. Facts on File, New York

Kraïdy M 1985 Lebanon: System of Education. In: Husén T, Postlethwaite T N (eds.) 1985 *The International Encyclopedia of Education*, Vol. 5. Pergamon, Oxford, pp. 2983–87

Kurani H A 1971 Lebanon. In: Deighton L C (ed.) 1971 *The Encyclopedia of Education*. Macmillan/Free Press, New York

United Nations 1989 *World Population Prospects 1988*. Population Studies No. 106. UN, New York

UNESCO 1987 *UNESCO Statistical Yearbook*. UNESCO, Paris

A. A. Sidawi

Lesotho

1. Higher Education and Society

The National University of Lesotho (NUL) is the only institution of higher education in Lesotho. It started in 1945 as a Catholic university college, Pius XII College, and later became an associate college of the University of South Africa. In 1964 the College was replaced by the independent, nondenominational University of Basutoland, Bechuanaland Protectorate and Swaziland (UBBS). In 1966 UBBS became the University of Botswana, Lesotho and Swaziland (UBLS), which was dissolved in 1975 when NUL was established by an Act of Parliament. The National University of Lesotho is an autonomous institution, neither public nor private, but offering its own degree, certificate, and diploma programs.

Lesotho is a small country covering a total land area of 30,355 square kilometers (11,720 square miles). The last five census takings show a steady increase in the population of Lesotho, as indicated in Table 1 (Lesotho 1987b, 1987c), and in 1986 stood at 1,577,000. About 85 percent of the population resides in rural areas. Lesotho has only one ethnic group, and one indigenous language, *Sesotho*, while English is the second official language.

Between 1985 and 1986 the unemployment rate was 34.5 percent of the active population. In the labor market, professional work accounted for 5.75 percent of total modern sector occupations, subprofessional 20.42 percent, skilled 12.83 percent, semiskilled 30.27 percent, and unskilled 30.74 percent. Incomes are unevenly distributed, the ratio of those received by the top 10 percent of the population to that received by the bottom 50 percent being 5:1 (Central Bank of Lesotho 1989).

In 1988 the Gross Domestic Product (GDP) and Gross National Product (GNP) stood at an equivalent of US$143.00 and US$236.23 respectively at the current exchange rate. During the same year the respective GDP and GNP per capita incomes were US$86.15 and US$142.31. The contributions of economic sectors to the GDP were as follows: primary 24 percent, secondary 20 percent, and tertiary 56 percent.

After gaining independence from Britain in 1966, Lesotho adopted a system of constitutional monarchy with a multiparty parliamentary system. In 1986 a military government took over which embraced the essential task of higher education to produce a well-trained labor force, to conduct research, and to service the community.

NUL is a nondenominational institution. However, in line with the agreement reached when UBBS replaced Pius XII College, there are Catholic priests who serve in Council, teach courses and reside within the University premises. Chaplains of other church denominations within the University also teach in the regular programs when necessary. The churches offer scholarships to a limited number of students.

2. The Institutional Fabric of the Higher Education System

The National University of Lesotho is a public institution sponsored primarily by the Lesotho government. A few technical and vocational institutions, offering certificate and diploma programs, are affiliated to it, and are organizationally and administratively separate from the University, being run by the government according to civil service procedures. There are future plans to establish faculties of agriculture, technology, and health sciences (National University of Lesotho 1981, 1988). Research is an integral part of the activities of NUL which all academic staff members are expected to undertake, in particular the staff of the four institutes of the University.

The normal basic entrance requirement for admission is a good pass in the Cambridge Overseas School Certificate. Quotas may be prescribed for some faculties or departments, depending on the labor needs of particular fields (Sebatane 1987). Admissions are governed by senate within the general government guidelines.

Enrollment figures have been increasing progressively in line with the increase in population

Table 1
Lesotho's past population sizes and growth rates

	1946	1956	1966	1976	1986
Population	689,000	794,000	970,000	1,217,000	1,577,000
Annual growth (%)	0.40	1.40	2.00	2.29	2.63

Table 2
Student enrollment 1960–88

	1960	1965	1970	1975	1980	1985	1988
Enrollment	167	220	402	502	995	1,119	1,198

growth and the number of foreign students (see Table 2). From 1975 awards the proportion of the age group 20–24 has ranged from 35–44 percent of the total enrollment.

The first degree programs take four years, leading to a bachelor's degree awarded by the University. Admission for graduate study requires the successful completion of a first degree. Research is an important component of the graduate programs. In practice, enrollment is minimal at the master's level, while none have registered at the doctoral level. This situation is expected to improve when the newly established School of Graduate Studies becomes fully functional.

3. Governance, Administration, and Finance

3.1 National Administration

The government has the prime responsibility for the development of higher education which is accomplished through legislation. It also controls most of the budget for the University. The government defines general objectives for higher education which cover academic programs, finance, and the channeling of students into various programs. The objectives are communicated through national development plans, in which the University is involved, and through direct consultations. NUL also draws up its own development plans, in consultation with the government. The review of the implementation of national plans and regular appraisal commissions are formal mechanisms for assessing and evaluating higher education's response to the goals it has been set.

The main source of finance for higher education is the government. Table 3 shows that between 1960 and 1989 the share of the University's budget constituted between 0 and 23 percent of the Ministry of Education's budget, while its share of the total

national budget ranged from 0 to 5 percent during the same period.

3.2 Institutional Administration

The National University of Lesotho follows a system of management by committees. The council is the supreme governing body whose chancellor and president is the head of state. Administrative, academic and nonacademic staff are represented on the council and most members are either elected or nominated. There are several foreign members and one University graduate. The senate is in charge of all academic matters and is composed of academic and senior administrative staff. Both council and senate have a number of committees and boards.

All teaching staff have representation in the senate. Other bodies responsible for academic affairs are the Academic Planning Committee, faculty boards (or advisory boards in the case of institutes) departments, and course development committees. Academic work is, therefore, organized into departments and faculties, and divisions in the case of institutes.

4. Faculty and Students: Teaching, Learning, and Research

The numbers of academic teaching staff between 1960 and 1988 are presented in Table 4. The majority of part-time staff teach in certificate and diploma programs. The qualification for appointment to positions of lecturer and above is a master's degree.

Table 4
Overall academic teaching staff

	1960	1965	1970	1975[a]	1980	1985	1988
Full-time	39	39	71	226	120	154	175
Part-time	—	—	1	1	78	48	42
Assistants	—	—	—	8	20	24	17
Other	—	—	10	3	2	11	16
Total	39	39	82	238	220	237	250

a Figures for 1975 represent those staff that were operative before the dissolution of UBLS in that year. NUL staff totaled 95 in 1975.

Table 3
Proportion of the higher education budget to the total education and national budgets (in percentages)

	1960	1965	1970	1975	1980	1985	1989
Proportion to education budget	0	4	17	23	22	22	17
Proportion to national budget	0	1	4	5	5	5	4

Table 5
Distribution of students across subject areas

	1960	1965	1970	1975	1980	1985	1988
Exact sciences	58	69	124	135	244	394	431
Social sciences	36	54	139	217	447	495	403
Humanities	73	97	139	150	304	230	364
Total	167	220	402	502	995	1,119	1,198

All positions are advertised and recruitment is the responsibility of the University. Lesotho nationals are granted permanent employment upon the successful completion of a two-year probation, while others are employed on contract terms for specified periods of time. Academic ranks are assistant lecturer, lecturer, senior lecturer, associate professor, and professor. Further qualifications, academic excellence (teaching, research, and publications), and service to the University and the community are the normal criteria for promotion from one rank to another.

Full-time academic staff members are employees of the University, are protected by law against unfair and arbitrary dismissal, and have the right to appeal. The academic profession represents its corporate interests through an association called the National University of Lesotho Academic Staff Association, while nonacademic staff members have their own association called the Non-Academic Staff Association. Senate defines the number of teaching hours and decides, with the approval of council, on the balance between teaching, research, and administration.

The distribution of students across subject areas is shown in Table 5. Enrollments have been increasing progressively in each area; social sciences have produced the highest number of graduates, followed by exact sciences and humanities. Fluctuations are due mainly to changing numbers of certificate and diploma programs and their enrollments. Foreign students constitute 17.5 percent of the total enrollment in line with government policy, while the proportion of male to female students is 50:50. All students belong to the Students Union. Graduation figures have, on the whole, also been going up over the years, as indicated in Table 6.

The structure of the first degree course/program is defined by the senate. The development of new study programs does not require the external approval of accreditation bodies. However, there are usually consultations with the government to win their approval. Undergraduate students are assessed both during and at the end of a semester or year. Formal final examinations and scripts are assessed externally as a quality control to ensure the maintenance of international standards.

5. Conclusion

Higher education in Lesotho is characterized by lack of diversity in program offerings. The National University of Lesotho's "liberal arts" orientation makes it difficult to adequately cater to all disciplines necessary for the socioeconomic development of the country. Recent initiatives likely to enhance the viability and relevance of NUL include plans to establish new faculties, and efforts to articulate its philosophy, restructure academic programs, streamline management machinery, and strengthen functional relationships with other tertiary institutions. Finance constitutes the major problem facing higher education; private means of raising supplementary funds need to be explored. There is also lack of proper linkages between NUL and the lower education levels. The University should be more involved in the moni-

Table 6
Numbers graduating from initial courses

	1960	1965	1970	1975	1980	1985	1988
First degree	28	16	68	123	207	262	179
Higher degree	—	—	1	3	7	21	10
Post-graduate certificate	—	—	3	7	—	7	1
Certificate/diploma	—	—	54	145	141	153	162
Total	28	16	126	278	355	443	352

toring and improvement of primary and secondary education.

Over the coming decade higher education is likely to be affected by the socioeconomic problems that bedevil developing countries, the role of research in providing innovative solutions to burning world issues such as peace and environmental protection, Lesotho's relations with the outside world, and NUL's relations with institutions of higher learning in other countries.

Bibliography

Central Bank of Lesotho 1989 *Central Bank of Lesotho: Annual Report for 1988.* Central Bank of Lesotho, Maseru

Currey J 1987 *University Capacity in Eastern and Southern African Countries.* Heinemann, London

Lesotho 1982 *The Education Sector Survey: Report of the Task Force.* Ministry of Education, Maseru

Lesotho 1987a *Educational Statistics: 1986.* Bureau of Statistics, Maseru

Lesotho 1987b *Fourth Five-Year Development Plan: (1986/ 87—90/91 Fiscal Years).* Ministry of Planning, Economic and Manpower Development, Maseru

Lesotho 1987c *Lesotho Statistical Yearbook: 1987.* Bureau of Statistics, Maseru

National University of Lesotho 1988 *Calendar: 1988–89.* National University of Lesotho, Roma

National University of Lesotho 1981 *National University of Lesotho Second Five-Year Development Plan.* National University of Lesotho, Roma

National University of Lesotho 1988 *National University of Lesotho Third Five-Year Development Plan.* National University of Lesotho, Roma

Pitso P L 1985 Lesotho. In: Tembo L P, Pitso P L, Khalifa M D, Makhurane P M, Dilgassa M(eds.) 1985 *The Development of Higher Education in Eastern and Southern Africa.* Hedaya Educational Books Ltd, Nairobi

Sebatane E M 1987 Educational Selection Procedures and Policies in Lesotho: An Overview. *BOLESWA Educ. Res. J.* 5: 12–22

E. M. Sebatane

Liberia

1. Higher Education and Society

Higher education in Liberia had its genesis in the establishment of Liberia College in 1862 by a private organization in the United States, the Trustees of Donation for Education in Liberia. This was 15 years after the country declared independence from the American Colonization Society (1847) and 40 years after its founding in 1822. The government of Liberia assumed full responsibility for the operation of Liberia College in 1879 and has continued to do so with its successor, the University of Liberia. Over the years, six other institutions of higher learning have been established by religious bodies and one by the government.

Since the mid-1970s other institutions at the tertiary level have developed, particularly two-year and three-year colleges. Meanwhile, enrollment and graduates of higher education have increased greatly in the face of a declining national economy. This has seriously affected the efficiency of these institutions and limited the employment opportunities for their graduates.

1.1 Population

Liberia is located at the southwestern "bulge" of the West African coast. In 1988 the population was estimated to be 2,407,000. This population is relatively young. In 1984 approximately 43 percent of the population was below the age of 15.

There has been a rapid shift of the population from the rural to urban areas. According to the 1962 census, 80 percent of the population lived in rural Liberia; by 1974 the figure had decreased to 70.9 percent, and in 1984 to 61.2 percent.

There are 17 major ethnic groups in Liberia. These include the descendants of the Americo-Liberian settlers who founded the Republic in the nineteenth century. English is the official language used in the schools, in commerce, and for all official government transactions. The local languages, which carry the same names as the indigenous ethnic groups, are part of three major linguistic groups found in West Africa: Krou, Mande, and West Atlantic or Mel.

1.2 Structure of the Economy

The Liberian economy can be said to consist of three sectors: a traditional, agrarian sector where production is predominantly at the subsistence level with minor cash cropping of coffee, cocoa, palm kernels, and so forth; an export-oriented production sector, the principal items of which are rubber, iron ore, logging, cocoa, and coffee; and a domestic-oriented sector consisting of manufacturing, construction and formal services (government service, public corporations, and private companies).

The Liberian economy depends heavily on the export sector for its economic base. The pattern of development created has resulted, however, in a capital and energy-intensive sector: iron ore, rubber, and timber enclaves with few linkages to the rest of the economy. Consequently, it is very vulnerable in terms of the international market. As the demand for these products weakens on the world market, the Liberian economy suffers serious decline. Besides being largely foreign-owned, this sector has been devoid of new investments as the economic picture has become more uncertain.

The mission of higher education, according to the government, can best be explained in the statement of its leader, President Samuel K Doe, to the University of Liberia:

... the activities and undertakings of this institution must be made relevant to the sociocultural and economic realities of the Liberian experience. By this means the subjects taught by the various colleges within the University, and research conducted, should be done with the development needs of our people foremost in mind. (IEES 1988 p. 270)

This thrust is reflected in the curricula of both the University of Liberia and another higher education institution, Cuttington University College, by a growing number of courses relating to the Liberian experience. Depending on the field of specialization, the curriculum has been adjusted in varying degrees to include practical experiences and research, and reflect community orientation and growing involvement in extension, both of which make studies relevant to the Liberian environment and experience.

1.3 Relationship With Religious Bodies

Apart from two public institutions, the University of Liberia and the William V S Tubman Technical College (WVSTTC), higher education in Liberia is provided by various Christian institutions. The oldest and largest is the Cuttington University College (CUC) which was established in 1889 by the Episcopal Church of America. Because the Liberian Church has gained autonomy from the parent Church, Cuttington University is now under the direct jurisdiction of the Liberian Episcopal Diocese, with the Diocesan Bishop as chairperson of the board of trustees.

All of the religious institutions are controlled by independent boards of trustees, constituted in keeping with their respective charters from the Liberian National Legislature. Each institution is headed by a president who is the executive officer of the board. The Minister of Education is generally an ex officio member of the boards of private institutions of higher education, although their charters gave them independence from the Ministry of Education. The Minister often helps to shape policy at board meetings.

2. The Institutional Fabric of the Higher Education System

2.1 The Sectoral Organization of Higher Education

There are two types of institutions in Liberia providing higher education: public and private institutions. Public institutions are those established by, and receiving at least 70 percent of their annual income from, the government; while private institutions are organized by individuals and/or nongovernmental bodies. They may receive substantial income from the government in the form of subsidies or student scholarships; but for the most part they depend on student fees, grants, and gifts for their support.

The University of Liberia, established in 1867, is the larger and older of the two public institutions of higher education in Liberia. It receives about 95 percent of its income from annual appropriations in the government budget, about 3 percent from student fees, and the remaining 2 percent from other sources such as grants, gifts, leases, and agricultural production. The WVS Tubman Technical College (WVSTTC) was established in 1978 in Harper, Maryland County. Only a small proportion of its income is obtained from student fees and agricultural production while almost 98 percent comes from the government budget. There are also two postsecondary teacher-training institutions operated by the government. The Zorzor and Kakata Rural Teacher Training Institutes provide two-year programs for elementary and junior high school teachers leading to the Grade B Teaching Certificate. They, too, receive about 98 percent of their operational cost from the government and 2 percent from student fees.

The oldest private institution in existence is the Cuttington University College in Suacoco, Bong County, established in 1889. It receives a sizeable proportion of its budget from the government. In 1987 student fees accounted for 26 percent and government subsidy 67 percent. Seven percent of

Table 1
Tertiary institutions 1960–89

Level of Program	1960	1965	1970	1975	1980	1985	1989
2-Year (AA degree, teaching and health certificate)	1	1	1	1	6	6	7
3-Year (diploma)	1	1	1	1	3	3	3
4-Year (bachelor's degree)	3	3	3	3	5	6	8
5-Year (LLB degree)	1	1	1	1	1	1	1
6-Year (master's degree)	—	—	—	—	—	1	2
7-Year (BD degree)	1	—	—	1	1	1	1
8-Year (MD degree)	—	—	1	1	1	1	1
Total	7	6	7	8	17	19	23

Table 2
Enrollment in institutions offering four-year courses or longer 1960–89

Year	University[a] of Liberia	Cuttington[b] University College	Our Lady of Fatima College	St. Paul's College-Seminary	Liberia Baptist Theological Seminary	Liberia Assemblies Bible College	Gbarnga[c] School of Theology	Total
1960	384	309	50	—	—	—	—	743
1965	457	370	37	—	—	—	—	864
1970	849	212	18	—	—	—	—	1,079
1975	1,984	387	—	15	—	—	—	2,386
1980	3,400	1,275	—	6	41	10	30	4,762
1985	2,998	1,024	—	14	64	37	52	4,189
1989	4,771[d]	792	—	—	80	62	37	5,742

a From 1975 (in table) includes Business, Medical, and Science Colleges, from 1988 includes the graduate program. Does not include continuing education   b 1980 and 1985 include the Rural Development Institute   c Includes the 3-year diploma students, most of whom returned to complete the BTh degree after one year field service   d Preliminary figures

its income came from grants, gifts, and agricultural production. All other private institutions of higher education depend on grants from their churches or foreign mission boards, and/or student fees for support.

2.2 Levels of Institution

At the apex of the hierarchical structure of higher education in Liberia is the University of Liberia. It is the only institution which offers a doctorate program (in medicine) and master's degree programs (in regional planning and political science). In addition, it offers bachelor's degrees in 26 areas: English, French, geography, history, mass communications, political science, sociology, secondary education, elementary education, agriculture, forestry, wood science and technology, accounting, economics, management, public administration, biology, chemistry, mathematics, physics, civil engineering, electrical engineering, mining engineering, geology, law, and home and community development. The University also offers a two-year Associate of Arts degree in library science and a one-year certificate program in mass communications. Law is studied in a three-year program beyond the bachelor's degree (see Table 1 for level of program).

On the next level down are the bachelor's degree-granting institutions. Of these, Cuttington University College offers degrees in 15 areas, 11 of which are also offered by the University of Liberia.

Next, in terms of duration of program, come two three-year postsecondary institutions. The Tubman National Institute of Medical Arts (TNIMA), established in 1945, offers three-year programs for professional nurses, physician assistants, and medical laboratory technicians. It also offers two-year programs in midwifery, practical nursing, and environmental health. The WVSTCT still carries the three-year Associate of Arts degree program, along with the BSc degree program in engineering. There are three junior colleges which provide two-year

programs leading to the Associate of Arts Degree in business and secretarial science (see Table 3).

There are no higher education research institutions. Research is, however, conducted by the faculties of the University of Liberia and Cuttington University College, when time and resources permit.

2.3 Admissions Policies and Selection

Admission to all tertiary programs in Liberia require a high school diploma and successful pass in the Liberian National Examinations, administered by the West African Examinations Council, or its equivalent, such as the General Certificate of Education examination taken in other English-speaking West African countries. In addition, a placement examination prepared and administered by the individual institution is often required, as well as letters of recommendation from people who can attest to the applicant's academic ability and character. There is no admission requirement determined by a national body or a consortium of tertiary institutions. Each institution sets its own standards.

2.4 Quantitative Development in Higher Education

The social and educational laxity which developed in Liberia after the military coup d'état of 1980 seems to have stimulated the growth of postsecondary institutions. However, the actual increase in enrollment can be traced to the wave of independence of African states in the 1960s. The excitement of seeing people rise from obscurity to prominence overnight encouraged parents of various backgrounds to realize the advantages to be gained from having their children educated. Thus, enrollment increased at all levels of the education system. By 1979–80 the growth in student numbers had reached the senior high school level. In addition, the military government promised when it came to power in 1980 that education would be made free (a goal which was never realized). As a result, the number of students seeking entry to higher education institutions increased beyond the

Table 3
Two-year and three-year institutions

Year	Tubman National Institute of Medical Arts	WVS Tubman Technical College	Zorzor Rural Teacher Training Institute	Kakarta Rural Teacher Training Institute	College of West Africa	AME Zion Community College	Arthur Barclay Technical Institute	University of Liberia Continuing Education Division	Total
1976	NA	—	—	126	—	—	—	—	126
1979	NA	93	—	317	—	—	—	—	410
1982	221	154	222	216	130	—	73	—	1,016
1985	NA	180	69	96	273	—	17	129	764
1988	136	132	115	246	300	408	277	365	1,979

Table 4
Distribution of enrollment in four-year or more degree programs of higher education by main subject areas and institutions, 1960–89

	Exact sciences[a]		Social sciences[b]			Humanities[c]							Totals			
	University of Liberia	Cuttington University College	University of Liberia	Cuttington University College	Our Lady of Fatima College	University of Liberia	Cuttington University College	Our Lady of Fatima College	St. Paul's College Seminary	Liberia Baptist Theological Seminary	Liberia Assemblies of God Bible College	Gbarnga School of Theology	Exact Sciences	Social Sciences	Humanities	Total
1960	97	31	254	256	50	33	22	0	—	—	—	—	128	560	55	743
1965	61	37	357	307	37	39	26	0	—	—	—	—	98	701	65	864
1970	126	21	575	117	78	80	14	0	—	—	—	—	147	770	94	1,011
1975	616	98	1,056	240	—	37	49	—	15	—	—	—	714	1,296	101	2,111
1980	681	574	1,755	676	—	52	25	—	6	41	10	—	1,255	2,431	134	3,820
1985	1,059	461	1,850	542	—	78	21	—	14	64	37	52	1,520	2,392	266	4,178
1989	1,441[d]	356	3,259	420	—	71	16	—	—	80	62	37	1,797	3,679	266	5,742

— Institution not in operation   a Exact sciences include programs in chemistry, physics, mathematics, general science, agriculture, forestry, nursing, medicine, engineering, geology, wood and technology.   b Social sciences include programs in sociology, history, geography, education, mass communications, political science, law, accounting, management, economics, public administration   c Humanities include programs in English, French, religious studies and theology.   The figures for the University do not include the graduate and continuing education programs; similarly those for Cuttington University College do not include the Rural Development Institute   d Preliminary

capacity of the existing institutions to accommodate them. This led to the development of several two- and three-year tertiary institutions to absorb the overflow.

2.5 Structure of Qualifications and Graduate Training Programs

The term "first degree" is usually associated with the bachelor's degree which, under the Liberian education system, requires a four-year university course after high school completion. Over the years a number of two- and three-year associate of arts degree programs or equivalent have been introduced in the system by individual institutions.

Bachelor's degree programs are offered in eight institutions, two of which recently extended their junior college programs to four years and offer both the associate and bachelor degrees concurrently, while others are mainly bible colleges or theological seminaries (see Tables 2 and 3).

The University of Liberia is the only institution which offers graduate programs. There are two-year courses in regional planning and political science, leading to master's degrees; as well as the doctorate in medicine, which is the oldest graduate program in Liberia. The Medical College of the University of Liberia was founded in 1968 as the Monrovia Torino College of Medicine, a cooperative venture between the government of Liberia, the Holy See and the Italian government, and was affiliated with the Faculty of Medicine and Surgery of the University of Turin, Italy. In 1970 the government of Liberia assumed full responsibility for its operation and merged it with the University of Liberia under the name A M Dogliotti College of Medicine.

To qualify for admission to the A M Dogliotti College of Medicine, the applicant must have either successfully completed three years' minimum premedical studies in a recognized college or university or graduated with a bachelor's degree in science or related areas. The duration of the medical course is five years.

The A M Dogliotti College is affiliated with the J F K Memorial Hospital in Monrovia as a teaching hospital. Many of the faculty members of the College also serve on the staff of the hospital. Collaborative research is sometimes conducted by the two institutions for the development of medical science in Liberia.

The graduate program in regional planning, which started in 1983, offers a series of options to applicants. There is the MSc degree program and a graduate diploma program.

3. Governance, Administration, and Finance

3.1 National Administration

There is no agency at the national level that coordinates the activities of higher education. According to law, the Ministry of Education is responsible for education from preschool to the end of the secondary level. Thus, each tertiary institution (except the two rural teacher-training institutes created by the Ministry to train its elementary school teachers) sets its own standard. The degree-granting institutions are chartered by the National Legislature. Each has a separate board of trustees or directors appointed under the terms of its charter to set policies. Generally, the Minister of Education is an ex officio member of each board.

Higher education as a sector has not been given significant consideration in the national development plans, perhaps because of its uncoordinated nature. However, the University of Liberia, as a public institution, was recognized in the Second National Socioeconomic Plan as requiring physical expansion and staff development, and annual provision is made in the government's development budget for this purpose. The national priority placed on agriculture through the government's "Green Revolution Program," means that all students in the College of Agriculture and Forestry of the University of Liberia are given tuition-free scholarships.

3.2 Institutional Administration

All the institutions of higher education have a basically similar administrative structure. Their respective charters provide for a board of trustees, directors, or governors as the policy-making body of the institution. Except in the case of the two public institutions (University of Liberia and WVSTTC), the president, as the chief executive officer, is appointed by the board. In the case of the public institutions the board recommends and the President of Liberia appoints the president of the institution.

The Presidents of the University of Liberia, Cuttington University College, WVSTTC, St. Paul's College Seminary, and the AME Zion Community College are each assisted by two principal administrative officers responsible for academic affairs and administration respectively. These senior officers are generally appointed in the same manner as the president. The only other administrative officer reporting directly to the various presidents is the controller, except in the case of St. Paul's which has a director of field education responsible for apostolic activities.

The University of Liberia is the only higher education institution with an administrative council. It is composed of deans of colleges, coordinators and heads of academic programs, heads of administrative units, and three faculty and two student representatives. Next to the board of trustees, the council is responsible for policy issues relating to administrative and financial matters. St. Paul's has a seminary executive committee which reports to the board of governors. It is composed of the president of the interterritorial conference (representing the three member states which the seminary serves—

Liberia, Sierra Leone, and the Gambia), the president of the institution, who is vice-president of the committee, and the dean of studies, who acts as administrative secretary.

The base unit of the academic organization is the teaching department or division. It is the responsibility of the chairperson of the department or division to organize faculty teaching and other work, prepare course schedules, recommend sabbatical and other leave for department members, monitor and supervise the activities of department staff, and promote their welfare.

4. Faculty and Students: Teaching, Learning, and Research

4.1 Faculty

Appointment to faculty positions at all tertiary institutions is similar, to the extent that the application and curriculum vitae are directed to the head of the department or division, or dean. They are reviewed by a faculty committee which submits its recommendation to the head of the academic program for channeling to the board through the president. In the case of the University of Liberia, the recommendation from the college dean is sent to the faculty Committee on Academic Coordination where the appropriate rank is assigned. It is then channeled through the vice-president for academic affairs to the president for appointment by the board. Academic ranks are also assigned to the faculties of Cuttington University College, and the Gbarnga School of Theology.

The structure of academic ranks at the University of Liberia is as follows:

(a) Professor: must have earned PhD, MD, LLD, JSD, MA, MS, LLM, LLB or equivalents. For holders of the doctorate, at least 10 years' teaching experience at university level plus publications are required. For the other qualifications, at least 15 years' university teaching plus publications are required.

(b) Associate professor: must have earned PhD, MD, JSD, LLM, MA, MS, LLB or equivalents and had work published. For holders of the doctorate, at least 5 years' university teaching experience is required, while for all others at least 10 years' university teaching is required.

(c) Assistant professor: beginning rank for PhD, MD, LLM or equivalents. Those with MA, MS and LLB must have at least 5 years' experience plus publications.

(d) Instructor: beginning rank for MA, MS, LLB, or equivalents.

(e) Research fellow: any academician engaged exclusively in research.

(f) Teaching or research assistant: bachelor's degree holder or equivalent. These positions are specifically to train potential members of the faculty within the context of the institutional staff development program.

The University of Liberia is the only institution that has an organized faculty association. The University of Liberia Faculty Association was established in 1972. Its main purposes are to create social interaction among members, encourage the maintenance of academic standards, and serve as a pressure group in seeking the collective interest of the faculty. It has been instrumental in the harmonization of ranks with salary scale, in urging the systematic promotion of faculty members and demanding the reestablishment of the faculty insurance scheme which lapsed in 1986.

4.2 Students

The distribution of students across the three broad subject areas, as shown in Table 4, shows definite preference for the social sciences, particularly such fields as business and economics, compared to the natural sciences and the humanities. This is especially noticeable at the University of Liberia which offers specialization in such scientific fields as engineering, medicine, and agriculture. At Cuttington University College the program in nursing attracts a large number of female students.

The sharp increase in graduates from higher education institutions in 1980 reflects the growing number of institutions, especially those offering two- and three-year postsecondary programs. Before 1976, the Tubman National Institute of Medical Arts (TNIMA) was the only institution at this level, thus the 739 percent increase in graduates between 1975 and 1980, as shown in Table 6 is actually the result of growth in the number of institutions. On the other hand, at the level of the four-year degree-granting institutions, the increase in output could be attributed mostly to graduates of the University of Liberia and Cuttington University College.

Students in Liberian schools are not classified by ethnicity or social class; however, they are often identified by their county or place of origin during graduation ceremonies. Gender comparison is a common phenomenon. The ratio of male to female students varies from one institution to another. According to current statistics, men constitute 77 percent of the University of Liberia enrollment, 70 percent of Cuttington University College, 85 percent of both the Liberia Baptist Theological Seminary and the Liberia Assemblies of God Bible College, 95 percent of the Gbarnga School of Theology, and 100 percent of St. Paul's College Seminary enrollment. In the case of the two-year and three-year institutions, male students account for 94 percent of the enrollment of the WVS Tubman Technical College, 42 percent of TNIMA, 54 percent of the Arthur Bar-

Table 5
Higher education graduates of institutions offering four-year or longer degree courses, 1960–88

	University[a] of Liberia	Cuttington[b] University College	Our Lady of Fatima College	St. Paul's College-Seminary	Liberia Baptist Theological Seminary	Assemblies of God Bible College	Gbarnga[c] School of Theology	Total
1960	37	16	5	—	—	—	—	58
1965	58	26	5	—	—	—	—	72
1970	86	67	7	—	—	—	—	160
1975	176	59	—	—	—	—	—	235
1980	301	75	—	4	9	—	—	389
1985	373	70	—	26	12	5	4	490
1988	388	109	—	18	20	8	—	543

a From 1975 the University of Liberia figures include the Medical College but exclude continuing education (Library Science) b Cuttington University College figures exclude the Rural Development Institute   c The Gbarnga School of Theology figure excludes the three-year diploma program

clay Technical Institute, 50 percent of the College of West Africa Junior College, 63 percent of the AME Zion Community College, 81 percent of the ZRTTI and 92 per cent of the KRTTI enrollment.

Most tertiary institutions permit their students to organize student leadership teams consisting of elected student representatives from the various classes (or colleges in the case of the University of Liberia), or student political parties. The leadership team usually serves as an intermediary between the student body and the institution administration. It mobilizes student opinions and represents such opinions to the administration for consideration, approval, or action. It also works closely with the administration in coordinating and supervising student activities.

In 1988 the government of Liberia banned student political activities in all institutions. This left a serious gap in the student–administration relationship. Consequently, many institutions sought and received permission from the government to establish provisional student leadership committees to coordinate student affairs. The members of such committees were generally appointed by the administration.

The desired field of specialization for college students is usually specified upon their entry and this becomes the focus around which their program is planned. However, the curricular structure of the four-year bachelor's degree program in all institutions requires certain core courses in the first two years which are general for all students. This is based on the principle that there are certain kinds of educational experience which should be common to all college students, regardless of their career goals. Thus, the prescribed courses aim to provide broad foundations which complement and support specialized training.

5. Conclusions

The growth of higher education institutions in Liberia and their enrollment figures in recent years are indi-
cations of the demand for professional education at this level. However, there are a number of challenging problems which continue to confront higher education and tend to undermine its efficiency. The poor preparation of students at lower levels has caused higher education institutions either to waste scarce resources and valuable faculty ability and time in remediation or refuse them admission and face a rapidly diminishing pool of qualified students.

The second serious problem facing higher education is the dwindling employment opportunities for its graduates. This is a result mainly of the national decline in economic activity. Economic decline has also meant problems associated with limited teaching materials and equipment; poor faculty incentives, inadequate transportation facilities for students and faculty who, in some cases, have to commute several miles for classes or field work; unreliable electricity, water and other basic utilities; poor communication systems; and lack of support or commitment for research.

Subsidies provided to various institutions by the government have either been seriously reduced or cut off, while grants from donor agencies have also declined. It is clear that substantial changes will have to be made in financing higher education in Liberia if the institutions are to cope with such serious problems.

One possibility for increasing the resource base of higher education might be to increase student tuition and fees, which provide less than five percent of the revenue of this level. This option, however, involves certain constraints. Firstly, it depends on family income, which for most Liberians is on the poverty line. Any substantial increase in student fees would therefore encourage elitism in higher education because only the most affluent families would be able to send their children to these institutions.

While awaiting improvement in existing measures of resource provision, it is necessary that the institutions of higher education undertake self-assessment to improve inefficiencies in their operations.

Table 6
Graduates of two- and three-year postsecondary institutions 1960–88

	Tubman National Institute of Medical Arts	WVS Tubman Technical College	Zorzor Rural Teacher Training Institute	Kakartu Rural Teacher Training Institute	College of West Africa	AME Zion Community College	Arthur Barclay Technical Institute	Cuttington University College Rural Development Institute	University of Liberia Library Science	Gbarnga School of Theology	Total
1960	24	—	—	—	—	—	—	—	—	—	24
1965	14	—	—	—	—	—	—	—	—	—	14
1970	34	—	—	—	—	—	—	—	—	—	34
1975	36	—	—	—	—	—	—	—	—	—	36
1980	61	—[a]	—	148	—	—	47	46	—	—	302
1985	70	—	19	49	32	—	11	52	—	4	212
1988	28	33	23	78	30	10	—[b]	52	2	15	271

a No graduation that year   b No figures available

Another significant area to consider in assessing the resource base is the heavy reliance on expatriate staff, which adds as much as US$3,000 to the regular expenses of hiring each faculty member. The institutions of higher education need to develop more viable strategies for attracting and retaining high quality local faculty, such as pension schemes and insurance plans, which are virtually nonexistent.

A nonfinancial problem faced by higher education in Liberia is the lack of coordination and association among the institutions. There is no system of accreditation or program review to establish common standards. Until the enactment of the law creating a Commission on Higher Education, which was submitted by the Ministry of Education to the National Legislature in 1988, this problem will remain a serious one.

Bibliography

The Constitution Advisory Assembly 1983 *Approved Revised Constitution of the Republic of Liberia*. Sabannoh Press, Monrovia
Azango B B 1987 *Higher Education in Liberia*. Prepared for the Regional Symposium on Higher Education in Africa, BREDA, Dakar, Senegal, 4–8 May 1987
Baker C E 1989 Higher Education for National Development. Paper delivered during the Third National Conference on Education in Liberia, Cuttington University College, Suacoco, Bong County, Liberia, February 1989
Brewer D S 1988 *Gbarnga School of Theology Sixth Annual Report of the President to the Board of Governors and Sponsoring Churches.*
Clover R W, Armstrong, R P 1966 *Growth Without Development*. Northwestern University Press, Evanston, Illinois
College of West Africa 1982–1988 *Graduation Programs, 1982–1988*. College of West Africa, Monrovia
Cuttington University College 1952–1983 *Graduates of Cuttington University College, 1952–1983*. Office of Alumni Affairs, Suacoco, Bong County, Liberia
Don Bosco Polytechnic 1989 Prospectus
Government of Liberia 1983–1989 *Annual Budget, 1983–1989*. Bureau of the Budget, Government of Liberia, Monrovia, Liberia
Improving Efficiency of Education System (IEES) 1988 Liberia Education and Human Resources Sector Assessment, USAID, Office of Education, Tallahassee, Florida
Kialain D et al. 1984 Vocational Technical Education and Training in Liberia. Agricultural Council for Vocational Technical Education and Training
Ministry of Education Department of Planning and Development 1984 *Toward the Twenty-First Century. Development-Oriented Policies and Activities in the Liberia Education System*. Institute for International Research, Arlington, Virginia
Ministry of Planning and Economic Affairs 1970 *A Study of the Social Situation in Liberia*. Monrovia
Ministry of Planning and Economic Affairs 1970–1985 *Economic Survey of Liberia*. Monrovia
Ministry of Planning and Economic Affairs 1981 *Population of Liberia: A Planning and Development Prospective*. Monrovia
Ministry of Planning and Economic Affairs 1984 *Indicative Manpower Plan of Liberia for the Period 1972–1982*. Monrovia
Ministry of Planning and Economic Affairs 1985 *Second National Socio-Economic Development Plan, July 1981–June 1985*. Monrovia
National Commission on Territorial Subdivisions of the Republic of Liberia 1962 Report and Recommendations.
Richardson N R 1959 *Liberia's Past and Present*. Diplomatic Press and Publishing Company, London
Tubman National Institute of Medical Arts (School of Health Science) 1980–1988 Commencement Programs
University of Liberia 1980–1988 *Commencement Programs*. University of Liberia, Monrovia
WVS Tubman College of Technology 1990 *Bulletin 1988–1990*. WVS Tubman College of Technology, Harper, Maryland
Yancy E J 1967 *Historical Lights of Liberia's Yesterday and Today*. Around the World Publishing, Tel-Aviv

B. B. Azango

Libya

1. Higher Education and Society

Higher education in the Great Socialist People's Libyan Arab Jamahiriya (official name of the country) has been influenced by various social, cultural, political, and economic factors.

Four years after the country gained its independence in 1951, a great need for qualified leaders, to run government and social institutions, was felt. This led to the development of some sort of higher education institution to produce these skilled personnel.

Prior to the academic year 1955–56, five years after the country had gained its independence, Libya had no secular system or institution of higher education (Bubtana 1976 p. 106). The Libyan University, the nucleus institution of the present system, was established in 1955. This university comprised a single college of arts and education. Its main aim was to produce teachers and government officials.

The establishment of the Faculty of Arts and Education was viewed as a success, and prompted the government to establish new colleges in 1957: the Faculty of Economics and Commerce in Benghazi and the Faculty of Science in Tripoli (Bubtana 1976 pp. 114–15). The latter marked the beginning of the multicampus University of Libya.

The system continued to expand greatly, reaching 11 universities, including an open university and a whole range of postsecondary technical institutes, scattered all over the country. Available statistics indicate that the number of specialized institutions exceeded 15, with various specialties, such as electronics, mechanics, teacher training, agriculture, technology, and so forth (General People's Committee 1988 p. 14). This wide range of teaching institutions was complemented by another range of specialized research centers, in the areas of human sciences, basic sciences, engineering sciences, medical and pharmaceutical sciences, agricultural sciences, and so forth (Al-Hawat 1988 p. 14).

Libya is an Arab country located on the northern part of the African continent. It is bounded on the north by the Mediterranean Sea, on the east by Egypt and Sudan, on the south and southwest by Chad and Niger, on the west by Algeria, and on the northwest by Tunisia. The total area of the country is approximately 1,760,000 square kilometers (680,000 square miles).

Traditionally, the three component areas of Libya are: Tripolitania in the west, with an area of 285,000 square kilometers (110,000 square miles); Cyrenaica in the east, with an area of 905,000 square kilometers (350,000 square miles); and the Fezzan in the south, with an area of 570,000 square kilometers (220,000 square miles) (Fisher 1987 p. 596).

In the wake of the Second World War, Cyrenaica and Tripolitania were occupied, in 1942, by a British military administration and the Fezzan by French forces (Fisher 1987 p. 598). It was only in December 1951 that Libya received its independence, which was granted by the United Nations (Resolution of November 21, 1949). It became, under its constitution, "a free, independent sovereign state," with a hereditary monarchy, and was called the United Kingdom of Libya and consisted of the three major provinces of Cyrenaica, Tripolitania, and Fezzan (Bubtana 1976 p. 60). The revolution of September 1969, led by Colonel Muammar Al-Gaddafi, brought a group of young nationalist army officers to power. The revolutionary government proclaimed the Libyan Arab Republic and renamed the three regions: Tripolitania became known as the Western provinces, Cyrenaica, the Eastern provinces, and the Fezzan, the Southern provinces (Fisher 1987 p. 596).

In 1985 (date of last available statistics), the population was estimated at 3,604,000 people (1,900,000 males and 1,704,000 females), and the natural population growth at 3.5 percent. It is expected that the population will reach 6,072,000 people (3,146,000 males and 2,926,000 females) by the year 2000 (United Nations 1985 pp. 46–51).

As far as regional distribution is concerned, most of the country's population (approximately 88 percent) is concentrated along the Mediterranean coast, particularly around the two main cities of Tripoli and Benghazi. Population density amounts to two persons per square kilometer (United Nations 1985 pp. 46–51). In comparative figures, Libya is considered one of the thinly populated countries of the world. According to the 1964 census, it was estimated that out of every 100 persons enumerated, 79 were settled, 9 were seminomadic, and 12 were nomadic (Bubtana 1976 pp. 57–58).

Since Independence, the country's population structure has been changing, due to a tremendous increase in the rate of migration from rural to urban areas. The two most important factors in increasing the rate of rural migration were the drought that occurred during the years from 1955 to 1959 and the discovery of oil in the early 1960s (Bubtana 1976 pp. 60–61). In 1985, the percentage of urban population was estimated at 64.5 percent of the total population, with a growth rate of 5.85 percent. The rural population was estimated at 35.5 percent of the total population, with a growth rate of 0.05 percent (United Nations 1985 pp. 46–51).

The overwhelming majority of the population are Sunni Muslim Arabs of the Malikite school. They constitute approximately 90 percent of the total population. The rest consists of some minority groups, such as Berbers, Negroes, and Tuaregs (Bubtana 1976 pp. 58–59). The official language in Libya is Arabic. However, there remain a few Berber speaking villages (Fisher 1987 p. 597); English and

Table 1
Employment (official estimates, in thousands)

	1976	1977	1978
Agriculture, forestry, and fishing	141.2	144.9	147.9
Mining and quarrying	18.5	19.2	20.4
Manufacturing	37.4	41.7	47.4
Electricity, gas, and water	13.9	14.7	15.8
Construction	167.8	171.4	164.3
Trade, restaurants, and hotels	52.0	52.3	47.5
Transport, storage, and communication	57.9	63.1	67.5
Financing, insurance, real estate, and business services	8.1	8.5	9.1
Community, social, and personal services	175.8	185.9	191.2
Activities not adequately defined	6.1	63.3	62.1
Total	732.7	765.0	773.2

Italian are sometimes used in trade (Europa Yearbook 1987 p. 1747).

The last available statistics related to employment are shown in Table 1 (Fisher 1987 p. 615). In 1981, the labor force totaled an estimated 800,000 people. The petroleum industry provides direct employment to no more than a small fraction of the population (less than 5 percent of the total labor force in 1980). The percentage of the population employed in agriculture had fallen to 16 percent in 1982, from around 50 percent in the early 1970s (Fisher 1987 pp. 606–07).

According to figures released by the International Labour Organisation, there were 583,900 migrant workers in Libya in July 1985. The United Nations forecast that this number will be about 740,000 by 1990 (Fisher 1987 p. 607).

Agriculture dominated the economy in Libya until the late 1950s. Even now, the present government regards the agricultural sector as being of primary importance. A number of agricultural projects have been implemented, which were meant to provide for the establishment of farms, the building of rural roads, irrigation and drainage facilities and, in some cases, the introduction of agro-industries. Indeed, an important feature of Libya's economic planning in the 1970s was the high priority given to agriculture (in 1976 agricultural development absorbed 30 percent of the total budget expenditure). Nevertheless, despite the money poured into this sector, the percentage of population employed in agriculture has fallen and the contribution of agriculture to the Gross Domestic Product (GDP) has declined slightly during the period 1975–80 (Fisher 1987 p. 607).

Petroleum was discovered in commercial quantities in the late 1950s. From 1955 to 1970, prospecting for petroleum yielded increasing returns (Europa Handbook 1987 p. 1749). Following all the upheavals in the world oil scene, production fell from 159.7 million metric tons in 1970 to 71.5 million metric tons in 1975.

The government revenues from the petroleum sector rose steadily from US$2,300 billion in 1973 to US$15,600 billion in 1981, but declined as from 1980, coming down to US$10,000 billion in 1985 (Houriya 1989). However, it is worth mentioning that in 1983 Libya replaced the United Kingdom as the second largest supplier of oil to the European Community, after Saudi Arabia. Moreover, in 1984, according to estimates by the World Bank, Libya's Gross National Product (GNP) per head, measured at average 1982–84 prices, was US$8,520, the highest level among African countries (Europa Yearbook 1987 p. 1749).

Industry and agriculture, are considered to be the two main economic sectors where the diversification of the Libyan economic base has to be achieved. Within the last few years, a number of industries have developed or are in the process of development: petroleum refining, as well as some petrochemical

activity, iron and steel production, and some light industries (Fisher 1987 p. 597).

Plans were made several years ago for a whole range of factories and efforts were deployed, in successive development plans since the 1970s, to diversify the nonoil sector of industry and to increase its contribution to the GNP. According to the OPEC News Agency, Libya spent US$62,500 million between 1970 and 1983 to develop industry and reduce the country's dependence on the petroleum sector. This resulted in an increase in the value of nonoil production activities from US$1,610 million in 1970 to US$15,280 million in 1983, and their contribution to GNP, from 37 percent to 50 percent, reducing the share of the petroleum sector from 63 percent to 50 percent (Fisher 1987 p. 611).

Since petroleum has been exported, Libya has experienced a considerable trade surplus. In 1971, exports were valued at US$270 million and imports at US$70 million, leaving a trade surplus of US$200 million. The general trend of increasing surplus continued during the 1970s, and in 1980, a trade surplus of US$1,257 million was recorded. However, declining demand and lower prices for petroleum reduced the trade surplus to US$597 million in 1981 and to US$562.5 million in 1982 (Fisher 1987 p. 613). In 1985, there was a trade surplus of US$1,890 million (Europa Yearbook 1987 p. 1749).

Formerly an Italian colony, Libya was occupied in 1942 by British and French troops. Following a UN resolution the country became independent in 1951 as the United Kingdom of Libya, under King Idris.

In September 1969, a military coup was staged in Libya by a group of young nationalist army officers. The officers established a Revolution Command Council (RCC), with Colonel Muammar Al-Gaddafi as Chairman, and proclaimed the Libyan Arab Republic. In June 1971, the Arab Socialist Union (ASU) was established as the country's sole political party (Fisher 1987 p. 600).

Under a decree promulgated by the ruling RCC in November 1975, provision was made for the creation of a 618 member General National Congress of the Arab Socialist Union (ASU). The Congress, which held its first session in January 1976, comprised members of the RCC, leaders of existing "people's congresses" and "popular committees," as well as trade unions and professional organizations. Subsequently, the General National Congress of the ASU became the General People's Congress (GPC), which first met in November 1976. Colonel Muammar Al-Gaddafi announced plans for radical constitutional changes which were endorsed by the GPC in March 1977. The official name of the country was changed to the Socialist People's Libyan Arab Jamahiriya, and power was vested in the people through the GPC, people's congresses, popular committees, trade unions, and vocational syndicates.

In 1973, Colonel Muammar Al-Gaddafi called for

the launching of a cultural revolution and presented his Third International Theory (Fisher 1987 p. 602). Since this new political reform, principles of direct democracy and people's government have been adopted and strengthened. The decision-making processes have been vested in the hands of basic people's congresses and the General People's Congress. All decisions made by these congresses are to be implemented by the various people's committees, under their direct supervision.

No affiliation exists, whatsoever, between higher education institutions and religious organizations. The development of higher education is undertaken through development plans set up by the people's congresses.

2. The Institutional Fabric of the Higher Education System

The higher education system in Libya is composed of four categories of postsecondary teaching and research institutions. All of these institutions are public ones, financed mainly by the state budget. No private higher education institutions exist in Libya, nor has any private finance been provided for the system.

The four main categories of institutions can be listed as follows:

(a) Universities with graduate and research programs. These include the following universities: Garyounis University (Benghazi), Al-Fateh University (Tripoli), Sebha University (Sebha), Nasser University (Tripoli), and the 7th of April University (El-Zawia). All of these institutions provide a mixture of programs in various fields of humanities, social sciences, law, and so on. For this reason, they are categorized differently from specialized universities.

(b) Specialized universities with graduate and research programs. This category includes the Arab Medical University (Tripoli), Omar Muktar University for Agricultural Sciences University (El Beida), Great Al-Fateh for Medical Sciences (Tripoli), Bright Star Technological University (Breiga), and Al Raia Al Khadra University for Engineering Sciences (Tripoli). Some of these institutions were specialized colleges of universities mentioned under the previous category. For example, the Arab Medical University is composed of the College of Medicine and the College of Dentistry, which previously belonged to Garyounis University, before the establishment of the Arab Medical University.

(c) Correspondence higher education institutions. This category includes the proposed Libyan Open University, which is at present located in Tripoli.

(d) Specialized postsecondary technical institutes. This category comprises, according to recent statistics, 15 institutes distributed in various locations throughout the country. These institutes, which are called higher technical institutes, include the following: electronics, mechanics, animal production, electricity, financial and administrative sciences, social services, industrial technology, basic sciences, teacher training (two branches), medical technology (three branches), agricultural sciences, physical education, and the Higher Institute of Technology.

While the first three categories of institutions are four-year universities, with some of them having graduate programs, the fourth category is a mixture of short cycle institutions, with various durations of studies of two and three years.

Research centers in the Libyan Jamahiriya are organized in two main categories: research centers existing within fully fledged graduate universities; and research centers outside the system belonging to various government secretariats.

To coordinate scattered research efforts and programs undertaken on a national level, a reorganization scheme was implemented. This scheme called for the creation of specialized and centralized research units to overlook the implementation of research projects in the various disciplines. Based on the restructuring of the educational system, 11 specialized research centers were established: human sciences (Tripoli); economical sciences (Benghazi); basic sciences (Tripoli); agricultural sciences (Benghazi); health and pharmaceutical sciences (Tripoli); engineering sciences (Tripoli); African studies (Sebha); oceanography (Tripoli); environmental protection (Tripoli); industrial research (Tripoli); and the Center for Development of Desert Communities (Mourzek). All of these centers undertake both teaching and research. All of them, except the Center for Environmental Protection and the Center for Development of Desert Communities, are physically located in the various graduate and research universities. Most of their staff are university professors (Al-Hawat 1988 pp. 25–26).

Table 2 shows the categories and number of insti-

Table 2
Categories and number of institutions

Type of Institution	1960	1970	1980
Multidisciplinary universities	2	2	5
Specialized universities	0	0	5
Open universities	0	0	1
Higher technical institutes	0	4	15
Research centers	0	2	11

Table 3
Number of students enrolled between 1969 and 1987

Year	1969–70	1975–76	1979–80	1986–87
Number of students	3,663	11,234	13,488	38,840

Source: General People's Committee for Education and Scientific Research 1988 pp. 1–25

tutions in 1960, 1970, and 1980. The drastic increase in numbers of institutions, during the 1980s was mainly due to two factors: the restructuring and reform of the educational system, and the increased role of higher education institutions in the sociopolitical life of the country.

The People's Committee (University Council), in coordination with the different colleges, decides the total number of students to be admitted to the institution and to each department within the various colleges. This number is reported to the Central Admission Committee which exists in the General Secretariat of the People's Committee for Higher Education (Ministry of Higher Education), and which, by applying various admission standards and criteria and by utilizing computerized programs, distributes accepted students among the various institutions in the country. Among the general criteria applied are: completion of high school diploma; physical fitness; Libyan citizenship (in order to receive scholarships); and proof of good moral conduct.

In addition to these general requirements, for admission to some professional colleges such as medicine, dentistry, and engineering, a student has to meet additional prerequisites such as passing personal tests and meeting a certain level of high school grades.

For graduate programs, admission of students is left totally to the department and college concerned. Certain requirements have to be met by the applicant such as completion of undergraduate study in the field and maintaining an average "good."

The Libyan system of higher education has witnessed drastic quantitative expansion in student numbers since 1955, when the first institution was established. Enrollment between 1969–70 and 1986–87 has increased tenfold, as shown in Table 3.

From available statistics, the population of Libya in 1984 was estimated at 3.624 million (Fisher 1987 p. 615). The total number of students enrolled in higher education in that year was 35,387, which makes it almost 1,000 per 100,000 of the population.

Available projections indicate that the total population in the age group 18–23 will be about 285,000 by the year 1990 and the projected enrollment, at the third level, for the same year, will be 84,000 students (UNESCO 1980).

The structure of qualifications in Libyan higher education varies according to the category and level of institutions. Higher technical institutes offer both long and short courses and award two types of degrees. For some institutes, such as the Higher Institute of Electronics and the Higher Institute of Mechanics and Electricity, the duration of study is three years. A student will be awarded a BSc upon completion of the program. Other technical institutes, such as the Higher Institute of Management and Finance, have a duration of study of two years and they award a higher diploma in the various branches of study. Universities offer four types of degrees which are BA or BSc, MA or MSc, specialized diploma, and the PhD. Table 4 shows the structure of degrees, type of institution and duration of study required to obtain the degree.

Graduate training in Libyan universities started in the mid-1970s at the Faculty of Education of Al-Fateh University (Al-Hawat 1988). Most of the Libyan universities now provide some kind of graduate program within their specialized centers (departments). Most of the graduate programs offered at the present time lead to the granting of an MA or MSc degree.

Garyounis and Al-Fateh universities are the only two that offer limited programs leading to the PhD degree. Most graduate training has been done through fellowships for study abroad, particularly for obtaining PhD degrees.

Available statistics indicate that in 1989 a total of 305 students are expected to pursue graduate training in foreign universities, most of them in the Eastern Bloc institutions (General People's Committee 1988

Table 4
Length of courses

	Duration of study (years)						
	2	3	4	5	6	7	8
Two-year institution	Diploma						
Three-year institution		BSc					
Universities			BA/BSc	Specialized diploma	MA/MSc		PhD

Source: Al-Hawat 1988 p. 22

pp. 1–25). Graduate training in Libyan universities was encouraged in order to stimulate and promote research programs and activities, particularly projects dealing with solving national problems.

3. Governance, Administration, and Finance

3.1 National Administration

Universities in the Libyan Arab Jamahirya are considered independent autonomous institutions, run mainly by the people's committees (university boards), on the basis of decisions taken by the people's congresses which are composed of a broad base of constituencies from within the institutions, faculties, students, administrators, and nonacademic employees.

The secretariat of the General People's Committee for Universities (Ministry of Higher Education), discharges various supervising and coordinating functions, particularly in three main domains. These are: (a) implementation of decisions taken at the General People's Congress; (b) finance and budgetry allocations for institutions; (c) coordination of admission of students to universities, colleges, and fields of study.

Planning of higher education in Libyan Arab Jamahirya society is not imposed by higher, central government authorities. Necessary procedures should be taken to secure wider popular participation, through People's Congresses, faculty members, parents and all educational institutions, in the formulation of higher education plans and their implementation. (Najm 1989 p. 16)

Like any other social institution in Libya, the goals and objectives of higher education institutions are formulated through the people's congresses and implemented by the people's committees. The people's congresses, which represent wider popular participation, are the main mechanisms for assessing and evaluating higher education's response to the goals and objectives stated initially by them.

All institutions of higher education in Libya are financed from public sources. No private institutions exist nor is any private financing devoted to higher education.

The allocation of financial resources to higher edu-cation institutions is done on the basis of various criteria, such as the nature of institution, specialties offered, size of student body, type of services provided to students, and location.

Although the latest statistics available on the financing of Libyan higher education go back to 1983, these statistics indicate a significant increase in the total budget of higher education for the period 1978–83. Table 5 shows the budget allocation for this period.

Although no figures are available on the percentage of the national administrative and development budgets allocated to higher education, available figures indicate that allocations to the sector of education in 1986 amounted to 37.1 percent of the administrative budget and 7.6 percent of the total national development budget (Busha'la 1988 p. 110).

Table 5 shows that, for the operational budget, steady and continuous increase has been maintained. For the development budget, the greatest increase was achieved in 1981, while in the subsequent years, a slight decrease in the allocations can be noticed. This might be attributed to either slowness in the implementation of development projects or to a success achieved in the development of institutional infrastructures.

3.2 Institutional Administration

The models of governance of Libyan universities differ slightly from traditional models. Universities, colleges and institutions are run by the people's committees, under direct supervision of the people's congresses. The head and members of the secretariat of the General People's Committee for Universities are all elected by the people's congresses of the institutions (consisting of professors, students, nonacademic staff, and workers).

All of the deans and heads of the academic departments are also elected by the constituencies of the institution. Power and decision-making are shared by all of these constituencies, who have representatives in all committees, whether academic or nonacademic. An example of the organizational structure of a typical Libyan university is presented in Fig. 1.

Colleges are organized along the lines of university

Table 5
Budgetary allocations for higher education in million Libyan dinars[a]

	1978	1979	1980	1981	1982	1983	Sub total
Operational budget	34.5	38.5	40.5	43.0	55.0	57.0	269.4
Development budget	46.3	36.7	54.3	71.5	62.0	44.0	314.8
Total	80.8	75.2	94.8	114.5	117.0	101.0	584.2

Source: Busha'la 1988 p. 111
a Libyan Dinar is the equivalent of US$3.30

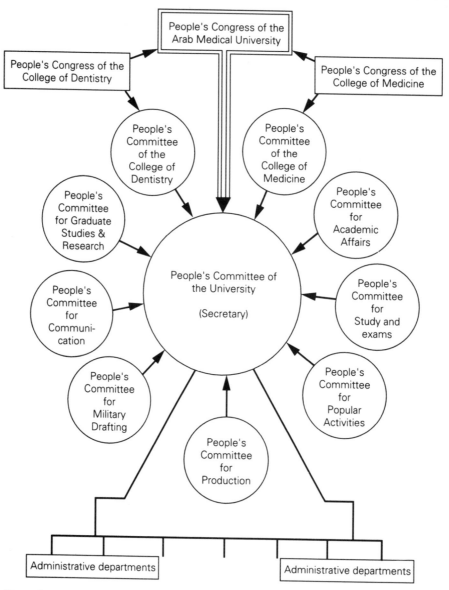

Figure 1
Organizational structure of the Arab Medical University

Source: *Arab Medical University Bulletin for the Year 1985–86*, 1986 p. 17

structures and the people's committees of these colleges are composed of representatives of academic departments, students, and nonacademic staff.

The basic units for academic organizations are the academic departments. These departments, under the supervision of the college people's committee, are responsible for the academic affairs of the institution: curriculum development, teaching, examinations, and appointment of faculty members.

4. Faculty and Students: Teaching, Learning, and Research

4.1 Faculty

The number of academic teaching staff members has increased markedly during the period 1955–88, as shown in Table 6.

For an appointment to a teaching position, an applicant must possess a PhD degree. Nationals who

Table 6
Increase in the number of academic staff members 1955–88

	1955	1969	1972	1982	1988
Academic staff	6	320	820	1,629	2,409

Table 7
Distribution of students 1986–87

Specialties	Number of students
Human and social sciences	7,893
Agricultural sciences	5,762
Basic and natural sciences	7,621
Engineering sciences	7,125
Medical sciences	5,625
Other fields	4,814
Total	38,840

Source: General People's Committee 1988 pp. 13–24

apply for a teaching assistant position must possess at least an MA degree.

The structure of academic ranks in Libyan institutions of higher education is divided into the following categories: teaching assistant; lecturer; assistant professor; associate professor; and professor. Normally promotion from one academic rank to another requires spending a minimum of four years in the previous rank, in addition to publishing research papers in a recognized journal in the field of speciality.

While nationals are all tenured, foreigners are appointed on a contractual basis, renewable every two years. All academic staff members have the same legal status as government employees and receive civil service benefits, such as pensions and social security benefits.

Recruitment, promotion, and dismissal of staff members is the responsibility of the individual institution. No central body is in charge of this aspect.

Faculty members are represented in all committees in charge of the institutions. This body of professors has its own committees through which its representatives are selected.

The workload of professors and teaching hours are defined by basic units and academic departments within the institutions, subject to approval by the people's committees of the college and the university. The balance between teaching, research, and administrative work is also defined by the same procedures and based on stated rules and regulations.

4.2 Students

The distribution of students across subject areas are shown in Table 7.

Available statistics indicate that during the period of 1976–80, a total of 9,294 students graduated from Libyan universities and higher education institutions (Najm 1989 p. 9). Out of this total number, 6,734 graduated from theoretical branches (humanities, social sciences, etc.), while 2,560 graduated from scientific, professional, and technical colleges. The number of graduates in the academic year 1958–59 was 31 (Busha'la 1988 p. 126) and increased in 1970–71 to 597.

Since the Revolution abolished social class in Libyan society, defining the social origins of students on the basis of conventional classes becomes impossible. On the other hand, during the 1980s, a wide geographical distribution of higher education institutions throughout the country reduced the number of students from rural areas who attend institutions located in the urban areas.

In 1957 not more than 5 percent of the total student population was female, while in 1980–81, this percentage reached 22.4 percent (Najm 1989 p. 8). At present, the percentage of women exceeds the 35 percent mark.

After the cultural revolution proclaimed in 1973, the role of university students in sociopolitical life has been strengthened. The role of students in higher education affairs, particularly in running the affairs of institutions, has become dominant. Student committees and representation are the strongest among all constituencies.

Around the mid-1980s, the universities of students were proclaimed, by which the authority and decision-making were equally shared between students, on the one hand, and the rest of the constituencies on the other. A secretary of the People's Committee of Students has been put in charge of running all student affairs in the institutions. This arrangement has increased the role of students in the administration of university affairs, including academic issues.

Learning and examinations are the responsibility of individual institutions represented by the various academic departments. The results of college examinations and the adoption of new courses are subject to the approval of the college people's committee (college council), and the university's people's committee (university board). Professional syndicates express their views on the content of programs of professional colleges, but these views are not binding.

The predominant model of undergraduate courses emphasizes three aspects: university requirements; college requirements; and departmental requirements. The curriculum models adopted by most institutions tend to emphasize the depth of content, particularly in the social and human sciences branches. In professional schools such as engineering, medicine, law, and so on, specialized subjects constitute the greatest percentages of taught courses.

About 50 percent of the colleges follow the academic year cycle and offer prescribed courses, while the rest follow the United States credit and semester systems, through which students are allowed leeway to choose some courses, based on an elective system. In colleges of medicine and dentistry, a premedical year is required.

Due to variations in models of study organization and structure used by various institutions, different assessment and evaluation methods are adopted. For institutions which follow the academic year cycle, two major exams take place, mid-year and finals. The grading systems utilized are composed of five categories: excellent; very good; good; pass; and fail.

For colleges following the United States credit system, assessment is more frequent and includes different methods, exams (midsemester and final), term papers, and frequent tests. The final grade of a student reflects a combination of all of these elements. In this particular system, the grading system utilized is composed of the following categories: A, B, C, D, F, and I for incomplete. Some colleges within this system require that the student maintain a certain grade point average to continue in the program of study.

5. Conclusion

During the development phase (1955–89) of the Libyan system of higher education there have been great increases in the number of institutes, students, faculty members, financial allocations, and graduates. The pace of development, between the 1950s and the 1960s, was balanced. However, during the 1980s, development was dramatic, fast, and striking. There is no doubt that this expansion was a direct response to the pressure of social demand. However, this great quantitative expansion might have negatively affected the qualitative aspect of the system.

In addition to the expansion, a few characteristics have been observed as follows:

(a) the restructuring of the whole system and its impact on higher education;

(b) the greater emphasis on diversification;

(c) the greater emphasis on balanced geographical distribution;

(d) the politicization of the higher education institutions and their increasing role in the social, cultural, and political affairs of the nation.

A noticeable phenomenon which accompanied recent developments in the system is the continued restructuring of academic departments and institutes, in terms of merging or separating some of them from the parent university for the purpose of establishing new institutes. This continued change has caused some confusion in the designation of the institutes and in their names.

In spite of the sharp increase in the number of institutes, there has been a noticeable decrease in the financial allocations for the development budget. This might constrain the future development of the system. In this particular area, Libya, like any other country in which free higher education is provided, must start thinking about tapping and utilizing nongovernmental sources for financing the system.

A shortage of faculty has affected the system and will probably continue to affect it. The ratio of faculty members to students in 1986–87 was about 20:1. However, this ratio is expected to increase by the year 2000. This is attributed to the fast increase in student enrollment and the slow pace by which faculty members are produced. The dependence on training faculty abroad has not changed the situation. This issue must be addressed on a national basis, by increasing the support and development of graduate programs at Libyan universities.

The future prospects for the Libyan system of higher education will not be much different from those of other developing countries, which have a similar increase in population due to high birthrates. The pressure of social demand will continue to increase, and this will force the higher education authorities to continue the efforts deployed at present to deal with the quantitative aspects of higher education. Although some attention will be given to the qualitative aspects of the system, this will not constitute a high priority in future planning.

Perhaps, the most crucial issue facing higher education in the future will be financing. In spite of the high Libyan income from oil revenues, the continued increase in social allocations for higher education will lead to a certain ceiling, after which it has to be halted. However, the increase in the number of students will continue and this will lead to a great dilemma regarding the way to achieve the balance between the ever-increasing demand and the limited financial and human resources available to the system.

Finally, more innovative and non-traditional approaches in the structure, planning, and financing of the Libyan system of higher education have to be adopted, in order to preserve a more healthy and sustainable development.

Bibliography

Al-Hawat A 1988 The new educational structure and university education in the Jamahiriya. Unpublished paper
Arab Medical University Bulletin for the Year 1985–86 1986 University Press
Bubtana A 1976 A comparative study of the perceptions of students, faculty members, administrators and government authorities of the role of the university system in the national development of Libya. EdD dissertation, The George Washington University, Washington, DC

Busha'la M 1988 The structure and development of the educational system in the Libyan Jamahiriya. Unpublished paper

The Europa Yearbook: A World Survey, Vol. II 1987 Europa Publications Ltd, London

First R 1974 *Libya, The Elusive Revolution*. London

Fisher W B 1987 Libya, physical and social geography. In: *The Middle East and North Africa*, 33rd edn, Europa Publications, London

Garyounis University Bulletin 1984 Garyounis University Publications, Benghazi

Garyounis University Statistical Pamphlet for the Academic Year 1983–84 1984 Garyounis University Publications, Benghazi

General People's Committee for Education and Scientific Research 1988 *Progress Report*. Secretariat Press

Habib H 1975 *Politics and Government of Revolutionary Libya*. Le Cercle du Livre de France Ltee, Ottawa

Houriya A 1989 A study on oil revenues in OPEC countries. Unpublished paper, Aleppo

Libyan Ministry of Planning *The Three-Year Economic and Social Development Plan 1973–75*. Ministry of Planning, Tripoli

Libyan Ministry of Planning *A Summary of the Three-Year Social and Economic Development Plan 1973–75*. Ministry of Planning, Tripoli

Libyan Ministry of Planning 1973 *Strategies and Objectives of the Three-Year Economic and Social Development Plan 1973–75*. Ministry of Planning, Tripoli

Najm M 1989 The role of university planning in the popular society. Unpublished paper

Shebani O T 1963 An analytical study of selected aspects of pre-service preparation of prospective Libyan secondary school teachers as provided by the College of Liberal Arts and Education of the Libyan University. EdD dissertation, The George Washington University, Washington, DC

UNESCO 1980 *The Future of Education in the Arab States by the Year 2000*. Main Working Document of Regional Seminar on the Future of Education in the Arab States, Beirut, 7–9 October 1980

United Nations 1985 *World Population Prospects* (estimates and projections as assessed in 1982). UN Population Studies No. 86, New York

A. R. Bubtana; M. Sarakbi

Luxembourg

1. Higher Education and Society

Luxembourg is a small country of 2,600 square kilometers situated between France, Germany, and Belgium. It is a young country as its actual frontiers and independence only date back to the Conference of London in 1839.

Since the Second World War, the population has grown from about 290,000 to 372,000 inhabitants, this growth being due partly to immigration, especially from Italy and later from Portugal. The major part of the population is concentrated in the center and south of the country, whereas the north is the least inhabited area. This distribution is due to the fact that industry is located in the south and the center, and the north is more rural.

The mother tongue of the Luxembourgers is *Letzebuergesch*, a German dialect recognized as the national language since 1984. However, French and German are the official languages. French is the language of legislation and administration, whereas German is used especially in newspapers. In the primary school, German plays the more important part whereas in the secondary schools, and especially in higher education, French predominates. This bilingualism is very useful for a country situated at the crossroads of German and French cultures.

The economy of the country is characterized by the fact that the tertiary sector is by far the most important (65.8 percent of the gross domestic product) followed by the secondary sector (31.4 percent); the primary sector accounts for only 2.8 percent of the gross domestic product. Metallurgy is the predominant industry followed by the chemical industry. In the field of services, trade, tourism and banking play a leading part. The gross national product per head is approximately US\$13,800.

The country is a constitutional monarchy (Grand Duchy) with a parliament, the members of which are elected for five years. All the main parties are in favor of European integration and hope to make the city of Luxembourg one of the capitals of the European Community.

When Luxembourg was created in the last century, no institute of higher education existed in the country. People who intended to undertake university studies went to France or Germany. This tradition, and the smallness of the country, explain why Luxembourg has not developed a complete system of higher education.

Since the beginning of the century, the growing importance of industry and more recently the development of Luxembourg as a banking center have led to major changes in the field of higher education. The government tries to develop the institutions of higher education in the country and to strengthen their links with the universities and nonuniversity institutes of the neighboring countries.

2. The Institutional Fabric of the Higher Education System

Luxembourg has two complete institutes of higher education, a technological institute (*Institut Supérieur de Technologie*) and a teacher training college (*Institut Supérieur d'Etudes et de Recherches Pédagogiques*). Its university (*Centre Universitaire de Luxembourg*) is not complete; it allows only studies of one or two years in a limited range of subjects. Students have to continue their studies abroad.

437

The reasons why the Luxembourg government was for many years not in favor of a complete university are as follows: (a) Luxembourg seemed to be too small to justify the creation of a complete and, hence, expensive university; (b) Luxembourgish students should study in foreign countries in order to integrate their cultural values, to develop an active knowledge of foreign languages, and to avoid narrow-mindedness.

One-year studies at university level in sciences and humanities have existed in Luxembourg since 1848. Those courses were compulsory for all students who wanted to become teachers, lawyers, and doctors. They had to continue their studies in the neighboring countries but were obliged first to pass their examinations in Luxembourg.

By the laws of July 1969 and February 1974, the *Centre Universitaire de Luxembourg* (CU) was created, comprising five departments which integrate all previously existing courses at university level. Three departments (law and economy, humanities, sciences) cover the first year of university studies.

Thanks to arrangements made by the government with several countries (France, Belgium, Federal Republic of Germany, Austria, Switzerland) Luxembourg students' first year of study at the CU is recognized by them, and they are allowed to complete their studies at the universities in those countries. Students are obliged to pass the examinations required in the different countries, and the diplomas of foreign universities are officially confirmed in Luxembourg.

Two departments give a practical professional training to students who have completed their theoretical studies abroad and intend to become lawyers or judges (*Département de Formation Juridique*), or teachers of secondary schools (*Département de Formation Pédagogique*). Since 1976, the department of law and economy has offered a two-year course of studies in management (*enseignement supérieur en gestion*). Luxembourg being an important banking center, the students have no difficulty in finding jobs.

Since 1983, the *Centre Universitaire* contributes to the training of primary school teachers offering them theoretical courses in linguistics, mathematics, computer science, and sciences. The primary school teachers are mainly trained at the teachers' college, the *Institut Supérieur d'Etudes et de Recherches Pédagogiques* (ISERP). This institute comprises two sections, one for primary school teachers and another for kindergarden teachers. Studies take three years. In the first year, programs are identical for students of both sections; in the last two years, there are marked differences in the curriculum.

Students of the primary school section study the methodology of all the primary school branches. The bilingual school system requires a particularly thorough training in foreign language teaching; students must be able to teach German as well as French. Students of the kindergarden section study primarily the psychology and education of children from three to six years of age; much importance is also given to subjects like physical education, art, and music. In order to be able to communicate with the children of the large Portuguese minority, they are also taught Portuguese for one year. Practical training plays a large part; each year, the students must complete seven weeks of practical training in school classrooms.

The third institute of higher education is a technological institute called *Institut Supérieur de Technologie* (IST). It grew out of a secondary technical school which was changed into a technological institute of higher education by a law passed in May 1979. IST consists of four departments: mechanical engineering, electrical engineering, civil engineering, and applied computer science. The institute provides degree courses in order to prepare the future technical staff for industry, public administration and institutions, and for research and development activities.

The courses offered at the IST last for three years and include a comprehensive general education and a thorough training in mathematics, science, and technology. Excessive specialization is avoided. Studies are characterized by numerous practical applications in collaboration with local industries. During their studies, students must complete 16 weeks of practical training and six weeks of specialized training.

For admission to the CU, a General Certificate of Education, advanced level, is required. Candidates to the IST must hold an A-level school leaving certificate of a technical secondary school to be admitted. Holders of a General Certificate of Education are admitted on appraisal of their record by the admission board. Candidates to the ISERP must hold a General Certificate of Education, advanced level. The government decides each year on the number of candidates to be admitted. Selection is based upon the results of the candidates at the national examination leading to the General Certificate of Education, advanced level.

Table 1 shows clearly that between 1960–61 and 1986–87, the number of students at the CU and at foreign universities has more than tripled. In the number of students at the ISERP no clear trend is visible: this number varies from year to year, depending on the number of primary school teachers needed. The IST had about 300 students at the end of the 1980s.

3. Governance, Administration, and Finance

The Ministry of Education has the prime responsibility for the whole system of higher education, which is financed by the government; the latter allocates to

Table 1
Quantitative developments in higher education

Year	1960–61	1965–66	1970–71	1975–76	1980–81	1986–87
Institut Supérieur d'Etudes et de Recherches Pédagogiques (ISERP)	94	255	140	232	180	136
Centre Universitaire (CU)	107	166	157	212	357	397
Students at foreign universities	826	1,069	1,459	2,077	2,290	2,518

the different institutes the necessary funds to achieve their goals.

The structure of the different institutes of higher education varies slightly. Each department of the CU has its council comprising the whole teaching staff except the assistants. It elects for a period of four years an administrator who is in charge of the pedagogical and scientific administration of the department.

The administrators and the delegates of the teaching staff of the different departments constitute the board of directors which elects a president and a vice-president from among its members. This board takes the main decisions which are then executed by the administrators of the various departments. An administrative director is responsible for financial management.

At the head of the ISERP and the IST are directors appointed by the Grand Duke, responsible for both academic and administrative matters.

4. Faculty and Students: Teaching, Learning, and Research

At the CU, professors and lecturers are appointed by the Grand Duke of Luxembourg for a period of five years. The council of the concerned department and the board of directors are asked for their advice regarding the different candidates for a post. The most important criteria of selection are publications and academic degrees.

The procedure of appointment at the ISERP is similar; professors and lecturers are appointed for a period of five years upon proposal by the director of the institute. At both institutes the five-year period of appointment can be renewed. The majority of teachers are teaching only part of their time at the CU or the ISERP, the rest of their task being devoted to research and/or teaching in secondary schools.

The teachers of the IST are granted fixed tenure and most of them are attached to the institute full-time.

All the three institutes of higher education described above conduct research; the CU is especially responsible for theoretical research, the IST for applied research in the field of technology, and the ISERP for the fields of psychology and education.

Besides this research, which is an integral part of the higher education system, special bodies with financial autonomy called Public Research Centers (CRPs) have been created by the government in order to promote research projects in common with private companies or institutions. Two of these CRPs are administratively attached to institutes of higher education: one to the CU and one to the IST.

5. Conclusion

Ideas have changed over the years, as to the benefits of a complete university for the Grand Duchy of Luxembourg. Formerly it was considered obvious that for a small country like Luxembourg such a university was inappropriate and useless. For several years, an increasing number of people have been in favor of a complete university. It is argued that an independent country requires its own university in order to promote the studies and research which it considers of national interest.

Moreover, access to foreign universities is getting more difficult because many of them are overcrowded. Since the foreign universities have gained greater autonomy in organizing their own programs, the CU has increasing problems in providing programs fitting with those of the neighboring universities.

As a first step, the government intends to create a complete first study course lasting two years. Later, it will be decided if further steps towards a full university will be undertaken. Since Luxembourg is well situated in the heart of Europe, a complete bilingual university could be attractive for many students from the surrounding countries.

Bibliography

Kohnen J 1989 Das Hochschulwesen in Luxembourg. Deutscher Hochschulverband 47: 75–80

G. Wirtgen

M

Madagascar

1. Higher Education and Society

Madagascar is an island in the southwest sector of the Indian Ocean. Together with the smaller islands, its total land area is 592,000 square kilometers.

The population was formed by successive migrations of Indonesians, Africans, and Arabs. The Kingdom of Madagascar became a French colony in August 1896. It became independent in June 1960.

The population grew from 4,143,000 in 1950 to 10 million in 1985. The growth rate increased from 1.6 percent in 1955 to 2.9 percent in 1985. Average density is 17 inhabitants per square kilometer, unequally spread throughout the territory, with 80 percent living in rural areas in 1985.

There is one language, Madagascan, of the Malay-Polynesian family.

1.1 Structure of Economy

The socioeconomic structures stem from colonial times. Besides staple crops like rice, the agricultural sector produces export crops such as vanilla, bananas, coffee, and sisal. The mining sector produces graphite, mica, and chromite. The country imports manufactured products.

Besides the service and administration sectors, industrialization is concentrated in textiles and agro-industry. In 1984, 43 percent of the Gross National Product (GNP) was generated by agriculture, 14 percent by industry, 40 percent by services, and 3 percent by import duties.

1.2 Structure of Government and Main Political Goals

From Independence in 1960 until 1972, Madagascar had a liberal regime under the First Republic. After a political crisis, a military transitional regime held power until 1975.

The Democratic Republic of Madagascar was founded in June 1975. This Second Republic adopted a socialist orientation in a referendum on the Charter of the Madagascan Socialist Revolution. In the early 1980s, confronted with domestic problems and the international crisis, the country moved toward a more liberal economy, with the private sector growing and the role of the state decreasing.

The highest authority of the state is the president, elected by universal suffrage. The president presides over the Supreme Council of the Revolution, which orients and controls the government, which carries out state policies.

The legislative branch is the Popular National Assembly, whose members are elected by universal suffrage. Besides these bodies, the Constitution recognizes two institutions as belonging to the central power: the High Constitutional Court, and the Military Committee for Development.

University education is under the technical control of the Ministry of Education and the financial control of the Ministry of Finance.

1.3 Religious Bodies

Madagascar has several religions, both Christian and Moslem. In the nineteenth century, modern education was the work of Christian missionaries. Even today, confessional schools have an important place in the educational system, especially at the primary and secondary levels.

Higher education is completely in the hands of the state, although the Christian religions have their respective theological colleges for the training of their priests and pastors.

2. The Institutional Fabric of the Higher Education System

The first institutions, the Law School and the School of Science, were founded between 1948 and 1952. After the foundation of the School of Liberal Arts in 1959, the Institute of Higher Studies, the direct ancestor of the University, was established in Tananarive.

The University of Madagascar, a public institution, was officially inaugurated in November 1961. It was jointly financed originally by the French and Madagascan governments.

The institutions of higher learning were located both within and outside the University structure. Since they are entirely financed by state funds, they are influenced by political changes. With the change of regime in 1972, higher education was restructured. This reform sought to nationalize the institutions by regrouping them into six institutions according to their specialties: law, economics, management, and sociology; science; liberal arts; health sciences; agronomy; and technology.

In 1976, the structure continued to evolve with the creation of regional university centers (RUCs) in the provincial capitals. In 1977, the University of Madagascar included six RUCs, each with one specialization in each region, except for Tananarive, which had all six specializations, and Tuléar, which had five. The whole system was given a professional orientation. Teacher training colleges and the National School of Computer Science were also founded. Finally, in October 1988, each RUC became a separate university in each provincial capital.

All these measures were part of the official policy to make education more democratic, less centralized, and more Madagascan.

2.1 Admissions Policies

Students are admitted in three different ways: The possession of the baccalaureate gives the student the right to enter three faculties, the school of law, economics, management, and sociology; sciences; and liberal arts.

The files of students with the baccalaureate wishing to enter health sciences and technology are studied by a technical commission. Finally, admission is by competitive examination for entrance to the Third-Level Teacher Training College, the National School of Computer Science, and the School of Dental Surgery.

Higher education has grown enormously, because of the policies of democratization and decentralization. The number of students increased from 723 in 1960 to 73,181 in 1985, with 78.5 percent of these in Tananarive.

2.2 Structure of Qualifications

Programs run in two-year cycles, with a diploma given at the end of each cycle. The licentiate is an intermediate diploma granted at the end of the third year in Liberal Arts and the Sciences. The *maîtrise* is granted at the end of the second cycle (fourth year).

Doctoral studies begin with the DEA (*diplôme d'études approfondies*). There are two levels of doctorates: the specialist or PhD, and the state doctorate.

3. Governance, Administration, and Finance

3.1 National Administration

The Cultural Commission of the Supreme Council of the Revolution gives directives on the national level, and the Ministry of Higher Education implements them through the university structures.

Higher education is part of the general development strategy elaborated by the Charter of the Madagascan Socialist Revolution. This strategy is based on three main principles: democratization, decentralization, and national identity.

Most financing comes from state funds. In 1985, 30 percent of the total state budget was spent on education. The Ministry of Higher Education received 7.8 percent of the total state budget.

3.2 Institutional Administration

There are two forms of administration. In the faculties an administration committee is formed by representatives, in equal numbers, of the professors, students, and administrative personnel. The president of the institution, the equivalent of a dean, is elected by this committee. The heads of departments and programs are also elected by specific committees.

In the schools and institutes, the directors and department heads are appointed by the state.

Students participate in the decision-making as members of academic commissions comprised of elected representatives of professors and students.

4. Faculty and Students: Teaching, Learning, and Research

4.1 Faculty

Originally, most higher education professors were foreigners, especially French. However, local professors became the majority over the years: in 1959–60, 82.4 percent were foreigners, but by 1984–85, 77.5 percent were Madagascans. The number of professors for those same years increased from 51 to 1,059.

The first stage in the recruitment of a professor is for the professors' association of the department concerned to inspect the applicant's file. If approved, the Ministry of Higher Education is informed and proceeds to appoint the professor, if the budget permits.

Academic ranking is according to qualification, in ascending order:

(a) technical collaborator: *maîtrise*

(b) assistant: DEA diploma

(c) teaching assistant: PhD or equivalent

(d) lecturer: state doctorate or equivalent

(e) full professor: on basis of work experience, at least four years as lecturer; appointed by decree.

Professors and researchers are unionized, with an autonomous organization, on the national level. This union has branches in the provincial universities. Also some professors belong to unions affiliated with political parties.

4.2 Students

More than 50 percent of the student body are in social studies or liberal arts. In 1984–85, 37,181 students were distributed according to the following percentages: social sciences 30.3 percent; human sciences 21.7 percent; sciences 25.9 percent; medicine 15 percent; agronomy 0.9 percent; technology 5.9 percent; computer science 0.3 percent.

Many students begin graduate studies with the DEA, but only a few defend their doctoral dissertation.

Democratization and decentralization have favored students of modest social origins. In 1984–85, of a total of 37,181 students, 57.3 percent were on scholarships.

At the beginning of the university, there was only one student federation. The number of student associations grew as the number of institutions increased, organized by institution and home provinces. Political parties and religious groups also have student associations.

The professors at the department level design the program of studies, which must be approved by the Ministry of Higher Education. Each institution organizes its own examinations. The decision to open or close degree programs is within the competency of the government.

Generally, a high percentage of students repeat courses in the first two years, especially in the first year.

5. Conclusion

The university system in Madagascar has grown dramatically since 1975. The present trend is to improve the quality of the educational programs. The six autonomous universities recently established will give more participation to decentralized groups and the private sector.

Bibliography

Hugon P 1976 *Economy and Education in Madagascar.* IIPE, Paris.
Ministry of Higher Education and Scientific Research 1980a *Study of the Projected Development of Higher Education in Madagascar from 1980–2000.* Ministry of Higher Education and Scientific Research, Tananarive
Ministry of Higher Education and Scientific Research 1980b *Account and Overview.* Ministry of Higher Education and Scientific Research, Tananarive
Ministry of Higher Education 1985 *Evolution of Higher Education in Madagascar from 1960–85*
Rajaoson F 1985 *Higher Education and the Development of Madagascan Society: The University/Society dialectic.* EEST/EGS. University of Madagascar, Tananarive
UNESCO 1986 *Democratic Republic of Madagascar: Priorities, Restrictions, and Perspectives of the Development of Education*, Vols 1 and 2. UNESCO, Paris

F. Rajaoson

Malawi

1. Higher Education and Society

Malawi is a small southern African country occupying an area of 119,140 square kilometers of which 20 percent is inland water. The country was formerly the British protectorate of Nyasaland. In 1953 it was linked with two other British dependencies, Northern and Southern Rhodesia, to form the Federation of Rhodesia and Nyasaland. After the dissolution of the federation in December 1963, Malawi went on to achieve Independence in 1964 under the leadership of Dr Hastings Banda. The country became a republic, with Dr Banda as its first president, on July 6, 1966. Under a constitutional amendment, Dr Banda became life president in 1971.

In 1987 the total population stood at 8.0 million with about 49 percent males and 51 percent females. Furthermore, about 46 percent of the total number of persons are aged under 15 years, 50 percent between 15 and 64 years, and 4 percent 65 years and over. From 1977 to 1987 the population increased by 44 percent, representing an intercensal growth rate of 3.7 percent per year. Malawi's population is still largely rural: only 11 percent live in urban areas. There is no dominant ethnic group. The national language is Chichewa. Christianity is the dominant religion, although there is a substantial Moslem minority. The country's population is spread unevenly over three regions. In 1987, the comparative population density figures for the southern, central, and northern regions were 125, 83, and 34 persons per square kilometer respectively. About 11 percent of the total population lived in the northern region, 39 percent in the central region and 50 percent in the southern region.

Under the constitution, executive power is vested in the life president and legislative power in the single-chamber parliament. The 118 constituency representatives are elected every five years by universal adult suffrage. The president is empowered to appoint an unlimited number of nominated members. Cabinet ministers, chosen by the president, are responsible to him personally and to the ruling Malawi Congress Party. Administratively, the country is divided into three regions and 24 districts.

Economic activity is based largely on agriculture, which employs 85 percent of the population and contributes 37 percent of the country's Gross Domestic Product (GDP). Commerce, distribution, and manufacturing depend almost entirely on the handling of agricultural inputs and outputs. Mining and tourism remain relatively undeveloped industries. The service sector is dominated by transport and distribution and by the government, the latter generating 13 percent of GDP.

Although higher education in Malawi is a post-Independence phenomenon, the need for it was felt as far back as the last century, when Dr Robert Laws, Malawi's pioneer missionary, dreamt of developing Livingstonia Mission to university college status. However, that dream was not to become a reality until much later. During the 1953–63 federation decade, for example, Nyasaland students wishing to acquire a university education had either to attend the University College of Rhodesia and Nyasaland in Southern Rhodesia or go to foreign institutions.

Nevertheless, by the early 1960s educated Malawians were already proposing the establishment of a "Nyasa College" and, while in detention in 1959 and 1960, Dr Banda included the proposed university as one of the priorities of an independent Malawi. After Malawi attained self-government in 1963 the American Council on Education conducted a survey of educational needs financed by USAID. Their report recommended the establishment of a national university. The Malawi Parliament passed the University of Malawi (Provisional Council) Act on October 30th and the first vice-chancellor assumed his post in November 1964. Teaching started on the Chichiri campus on September 29, 1965. From the outset, the policy which underpinned higher education was to establish a university that would meet the economic and cultural needs of the country. The primary aim was to give a liberal education leading to a general degree or diploma, and to produce administrators and professionals as well as teachers. University entry was to be at the General Certificate of Education (GCE) O level.

2. The Institutional Fabric of the Higher Education System

The formal education system in Malawi is a conventional primary, secondary, and tertiary structure. The language of instruction is English and the academic calendar runs for three terms from September to July.

In addition to the Polytechnic, a constituent college of the University, technical education is currently offered to students in a range of subjects at three government and two government-aided technical colleges. They offer a four-year apprenticeship followed by three years of alternate institutional and industrial training. Fees are not charged for any basic courses where the student does not receive any income. Primary school teachers are trained at five teacher colleges, three government and two grant aided. Teachers for secondary schools are trained in the faculty of education at the University.

The eleven faculties of the University of Malawi offer courses at the diploma and degree levels with opportunities for graduate studies. Diplomas requiring between three and four years of study respectively are awarded in business studies and nursing. Bachelor's degrees requiring four years of study are offered in agriculture, humanities, social sciences, sciences, and now education. Whereas the original thinking on higher education favored a liberal education, the 1980s saw a definite shift towards specialization as degree level courses in engineering were introduced at the Polytechnic, an honors degree was brought into some subjects at Chancellor College, and increased opportunities were created across the board for higher degrees.

The period also witnessed a greater emphasis on the training of secondary-school teachers in response to the requirements of the Ministry of Education and Culture. Master's and doctoral programs are offered in two to four and three to five years respectively, to suitable candidates in fields of study in which qualified staff are available. Although the University of Malawi establishes its own awards, it maintains, through external examiners and academic consultants, the highest standards in the interest of its own professional and academic reputation.

The University of Malawi has a variety of levels of entrance. Primarily, new students come straight from their secondary schools with the best MSCE results in the whole country. A list of applicants for every program is drawn up by a special committee of the university. The names of all candidates are considered in the descending order of their MSCE aggregate performance, coupled with their career preferences and the marks of the core subjects that have to be taken in the faculty of their choice. There is only one political directive affecting selection at this level: that the annual intake should, as far as practicable, be distributed equally between the 24 districts of the country. The university also admits students with a minimum of three A-level passes. In addition, it readmits a number of mature students with diplomas in agriculture, business studies, or education to take their degrees.

3. Governance, Administration, and Finance

The University of Malawi is closely linked to the government through the chancellor, who is also head of state, and its mother ministry, that of education and culture.

The governing body of the university is the council which, in terms of the University Act of 1974, is responsible for the management and administration of the university. The vice-chancellor is charged with day-to-day decision making as well as the execution of decisions taken by the university council. He is assisted by the officers of the University as well as a number of academic bodies such as the senate, which is the supreme academic authority.

The academic courses committee and the academic assessments and examinations committee, subject to senate approval, in practice define and establish programs of study and curriculum content. They also set academic standards, including degree/diploma requirements and levels of achievement. The academic assessments and examinations committee, subject to the senate's approval, is the degree/diploma granting authority.

The University of Malawi is now composed of five colleges at Bunda College of Agriculture in Lilongwe, at the Polytechnic in Blantyre, at Chancellor College in Zomba, at Kamuzu College of Nursing in Blantyre and Lilongwe, and at the Medical College in Blantyre. All these are under the coordination of a central office, where the vice-chancellor, the university registrar, and the finance officer are based. The activities of the five colleges are coordinated in matters of teaching, research, and administration, including senior staff recruitment.

3.1 Finance

With regard to finance, the University has from its inception depended largely on an annual government subvention. By 1986, it was absorbing 22 percent of the government's education budget. Though this looks generous, one of the University's major problems has in fact been financial stringency. It had for a time, for instance, to budget on the basis of not more than a 5 percent annual increase, despite rising costs. The University's financial worries are perhaps best illustrated by the government's decision to introduce student fees in 1986, prior to when university education had been free. A student loan scheme has also been installed. In 1989–90 the percentage of recurrent government expenditure allocated to all education was 7 percent.

4. Faculty and Students: Teaching, Learning, and Research

4.1 Faculty

The appointments committee deals with policies concerning faculty selection, appointments, promotion, tenure, and other staff matters. There are five teaching ranks: professor, associate professor, senior lecturer, assistant lecturer, and staff associate. The appointments committee, subject to approval by the council, determines salary rates. Expatriate teachers are usually appointed on contract for two years, extendable by mutual agreement. Local staff have tenure after satisfactory completion of a probationary one-year period.

The university research and publications committee has built up an enviable record of encouraging members of staff in their chosen lines of enquiry by the award of carefully determined, generally small grants, always decided on the basis of an interfaculty assessment of what is considered to be viable and relevant. The recent establishment of a research coordinator's office has enhanced the university's work in this area. Its functions are to encourage group research development within departments and faculties, to familiarize staff with the ways of operation of research-supporting agencies at government, private, and international levels, and to advise staff on how to locate suitable donors. For years the university has had the highly esteemed Center for Social Research in Zomba, whose work has influenced government policy in many ways. In 1991 it is launching a Center for Education Research.

4.2 Students

There is no age requirement for university students, although most are between the ages of 17 and 25. The university is multiracial. In 1990–91 students numbered 2,900, the proportion of total enrollment to population being 3.6:10,000. Admittedly, one major problem facing education planners is the perennial imbalance between male and female students. For example, of the 92 students who joined Chancellor College in the first year of the University's existence, only seven were women. The picture in the 1990s is not much different. There are sports and recreational facilities at all the colleges and also facilities for intercollege contests in various sports. Most academic disciplines encourage student societies and clubs in their particular fields. They are organized by students, and provide seminars, debates, and various social activities. Every student is a member of a student union on his campus; the individual unions are affiliated to the University of Malawi Student Union.

5. Conclusion

The main problem facing the higher education system in Malawi is physical expansion to accommodate the fast-growing numbers of suitable Malawi school certificate of education (MSCE) and Cambridge A-level certificate holders. Present plans include an expansion of facilities to permit an increase in enrollment to 4,000 and the introduction of more graduate programs. In addition, all courses below technician level at the Polytechnic are to be transferred to an institute of technical education, thereby creating more space for diploma/degree programs. Another important plan is to start offering some university programs by the distance-learning mode. Eventually, however, the Malawi Government may have to consider developing several of the existing colleges to the level of full-fledged universities.

Bibliography

American Council on Education April 1964 *Education for Development: Report of the Survey Team on Education in Malawi.* American Council on Education
Europa World Year Book 1990 *Vol. II: Kenya-Zimbabwe 1990* Europa Publications, London
International Encyclopedia of Higher Education, Vol. 6 1977, Jossey-Bass, San Francisco, California
Kambalametore A V 1973 The University of Malawi. In: Yesufu T M (ed.) 1973 *Creating the African University: Emerging Issues in the 1970s.* Oxford University Press, Oxford
Macdonald R J 1966 Visit to a New University. *Africa Report II* (2): 38–40
Malawi Population and Housing Census 1987 *Preliminary Report 1987.* Government Printer, Zomba
Maxwell I C M 1980 *Universities in Partnership: The Inter-*

University Council and the Growth of Higher Education in Developing Countries 1946–70. Scottish Academic Press, Edinburgh

Mvalo W E S, Lungu P R 1985 The Historical Development of Higher Education in Malawi. In: Tembo L P, Pitso P L, El Khalifa M D, Makhurane P M, Dilgassa Makhomnen (eds.) 1985 *The Development of Higher Education in Eastern and Southern Africa.* Hidaya Educational Books, Nairobi

Nelson H D et al. 1975 *Area Handbook for Malawi.* American University, Washington, DC

Pachai Bridglal 1967 University Education in Malawi. *Africa Quarterly VI* (4): 343–51

Read F E 1969 *Malawi: Land of Promise.* Ramsay Parker Publications, Blantyre

Statement of Development Policies 1987–1996 n.d. Government Printer, Zomba

A. Nazombe

Malaysia

1. Higher Education and Society

Malaysia, located in South East Asia, was formed on September 16, 1963 as a political entity under the Malaysian Agreement. This was signed on July 9, 1963, by the United Kingdom, the Federation of Malaya (known as Peninsular Malaysia), North Borneo (now known as Sabah), Sarawak, and Singapore. Singapore left the federation on August 9, 1965. The Malaysian Federation consists of two parts: (a) Peninsular Malaysia; and (b) Sabah and Sarawak. In this article, the names Malaysia and Malaya are used synonymously.

The Malaysian higher education system is predominantly publically controlled and financed, and it is formally and substantively differentiated at the institutional level. Despite the implantation of several elitist British-type institutions before Independence, including *Universiti Malaya* (University of Malaya), the accelerated growth and development of higher education is a post-Independence phenomenon in this multiracial society. Since Independence was declared in 1957, Malaysia has made great strides to develop a two-tier higher education system with teacher-training and technical institutions at the first level, and six national universities and the International Islamic University at the second level. The major catalyst was the vigorous affirmative action pursued under the New Economic Policy (NEP) from 1970 to 1990. The higher education system, basically remains as a narrow peak upon a broad-based primary and secondary education system (see Table 1). Tensions and conflicts have arisen because of the higher education system's inability to meet the dramatic rise in demand from its heterogeneous population of 17.58 million, made up of Chinese (32%),

Indians and others (10%), and *Bumiputras* (58%). *Bumiputra* means "son of the soil," a term officially used to cover not only Malays but also all indigenous groups, mainly the Ibans and Kadazans of Sarawak and Sabah.

The British administration's education policy was strictly needs based, with the aim of training essential functionaries, not "unleashing a pool of liberal English-educated malcontents." A limited number of highly functional British-modeled institutions were established. A medical school, later named the King Edward VII College of Medicine, was set up in 1905 in Singapore to train medical and dental graduates. Raffles College, established in 1929 as a science and arts college, provided a three-year higher education diploma for people in Singapore and Malaysia. Most of its graduates went into teaching, while some of the Malay graduates were recruited into the Malay Administrative Service (MAS), the lower echelon of the otherwise exclusively European-staffed Malayan Civil Service (MCS).

The mid-level Technical and Agricultural schools, established in 1925 and 1931 respectively, were upgraded to colleges after the Second World War and offered a three-year diploma. To train teachers for the diverse school systems, a two-year Normal Class teacher-training scheme was introduced, studies being carried out during weekends. Two exclusive residential teacher-training colleges, the Sultan Idris Training College (for men only) and the Malay Women's College, were established in 1922 and 1935 respectively, to train teachers for Malay medium primary schools.

The first residential teacher-training college was established in Sarawak (1948), followed by similar colleges in Kirkby, England (1951), Malaysia (1954), Brinsford Lodge, England (1954), and Sabah (1957). All provided a two-year teacher's certificate course to meet the needs of the rapidly expanding primary and secondary schools.

On the recommendation of the Carr-Saunders Commission the Raffles and Medical colleges were amalgamated to form the nucleus of the first autonomous English-medium residential University of Malaya in Singapore. In this way they bypassed the intermediate stage of a university college which other ex-British colonies like Sri Lanka, Nigeria, Ghana, and the West Indies experienced. The establishment of the University of Malaya as a full-fledged degree-granting institution was hailed as liberal, and in sympathy with the aspirations of the people.

After Independence, the governments of Malaysia and the then colony of Singapore decided in 1958 to maintain the University of Malaya as a single university with autonomous divisions in Singapore and Kuala Lumpur, in line with the Aitken Commission's recommendations. The need for a national university of Malaysia became imperative, however. Effective from January 1, 1962, the Kuala Lumpur

Table 1
Enrollment by level in Malaysian educational institutions 1980–90

	1980			1985			1990			Percentage increase	
	Students	Overall percentage	Level percentage	Students	Overall percentage	Level percentage	Students	Overall percentage	Level percentage	1981–85	1986–90
Level I											
Primary	2,008,587	63.8	100.0	2,191,676	61.2	100.0	2,434,407	59.1	100.0	9.1	11.1
Subtotal	2,008,587	63.8	100.0	2,191,676	61.2	100.0	2,434,407	59.1	100.0		
Level II											
Lower secondary	812,065	25.8	76.6	918,406	25.6	73.4	1,055,756	25.6	71.8	13.1	14.9
Upper secondary	247,889	7.9	23.4	333,401	9.3	26.6	413,866	10.1	28.2	34.4	24.3
Subtotal	1,059,954	33.7	100.0	1,251,447	34.9	100.0	1,469,622	35.7	100.0		
Level III											
Postsecondary	29,484	0.9	36.2	46,638	1.3	33.7	57,882	1.4	27.0	58.2	24.1
Teacher education	13,247	0.4	16.2	16,559	0.5	12.0	19,869	0.5	9.3	25.0	20.0
PI courses[a]	2,014	0.1	2.5	5,280	0.1	3.8	10,005	0.2	4.7	162.2	90.4
Certificate courses	2,603	0.1	3.2	6,878	0.2	5.0	14,353	0.4	6.7	164.2	108.7
Diploma courses	12,262	0.3	15.0	25,046	0.7	18.1	47,226	1.1	22.0	104.3	88.6
Degree courses[b]	21,944	0.7	26.9	37,838	1.1	27.4	65,413	1.6	30.5	72.4	72.9
Subtotal	81,554	2.5	100.0	138,239	3.9	100.0	214,748	5.2	100.0		
Total	3,150,095	100.0		3,581,362	100.0		4,118,777	100.0		13.7	15.0

Source: Ministry of Education
a Preparatory courses at MARA Institute of Technology and all universities, excluding University of Technology Malaysia and foreign students at the International Islamic University. Enrollment in 1985 and 1990 also includes A-level and language courses for students pursuing diploma and degree level courses overseas   b Includes enrollment in graduate courses and at the MARA Institute of Technology, Tunku Abdul Rahman College and off-campus courses at the University of Science Malaysia but excludes foreign students at the International Islamic University

division became the sole multidisciplined national University of Malaysia (*Universiti Malaya*).

Universiti Malaya developed rapidly, establishing an Institute of Advanced Studies in 1979, and thereby moving toward graduate and advanced multidisciplinary research and training relevant to the high-level labor force and development needs of the country. One of its aims was to reduce over-dependence on overseas graduate and research training.

Rapid post-Independence economic growth created an unprecedented increase in demand for a diversified high-level labor force, particularly in science and technology. Demand was amplified by high population growth and the democratization of primary and secondary education. The government set up the Higher Education Planning Committee (HEPC) in 1962 to meet this challenge. The aim of the HEPC was to review the country's higher education system and to chart its future direction. The Committee's substantive recommendation was to create an overall ratio of one university student to four college students to 20 secondary school students. To meet the priorities for the development of agriculture and industry, the Committee further recommended the supply ratio of technological and scientific graduates be distributed such that there were 40 arts to 30 science and 30 technology graduates. These recommendations provided the initial push for expansion and diversification. The New Economic Policy (NEP) boosted the unprecedented expansion of the higher education system.

Malaysia's second university, the *Universiti Sains Malaysia* (University of Science Malaysia),was established in 1969. It adopted a broad-based academic school system, with a curriculum geared to the labor force needs of industry, agriculture, social and welfare services, health, and education. In the following year, the *Bahasa Malaysia*-medium *Universiti Kebangsaan Malaysia* (National University of Malaysia) was established to meet the growing national aspirations for a leading institution which uses the national language as the main medium of instruction. In 1971 and 1972, the Agriculture and Technical colleges were upgraded and named *Universiti Pertanian Malaysia* (University of Agriculture, Malaysia), and *Universiti Teknologi Malaysia* (University of Technology, Malaysia) respectively. The former concentrated on agriculture, forestry, and food technology, while the latter developed science, engineering, architecture, surveying, and related technological fields. Within four years (1969–72), four new universities were established. In 1984 the country's sixth university, *Universiti Utara Malaysia* (University of North Malaysia) was established, focusing on management sciences and information technology. In 1983 the International Islamic University had been established with Arabic and English as the media of instruction. Its main aims are to strengthen cooperation and friendship among Islamic intellectuals, facilitate Islamic studies, and train students in a wide range of modern contemporary disciplines from an Islamic viewpoint.

Attempts were made to spread out the country's higher education institutions through branch campuses, with the aim of increasing communication with the people. Both the *Universiti Malaya* and *Universiti Sains* have established branch campuses in the east coast state of Kelantan in Peninsular Malaysia. The former's branch campus houses the *Akademi Islam* (Academy of Islam), while the latter has the teaching hospital of its School of Medical Sciences in Kota Bahru, the state capital. The schools of civil, electrical and electronic engineering, materials and mineral resources, and mechanical engineering of the *University Sains* are located near Ipoh, the capital of the state of Perak. Both the *Universiti Kebangsaan* and *Universiti Pertanian* have branch campuses in Sabah and Sarawak respectively. The *Universiti Technologi* retains its old campus in Kuala Lumpur as a branch campus.

Within 25 years, Malaysia underwent a rapid expansion in the provision of public university education, and in the number of first-level tertiary institutions (see Tables 2 and 3). The *Institute Teknologi MARA* (MARA Institute of Technology) opened in 1956 to train socially disadvantaged *Bumiputra* youths in mid-level management and technical skills. MARA stands for *Majlis Amanah Rakyat* (the council for the trust for indigenous people.) Since 1960, seven polytechnics and 27 teacher-training colleges have been established. The Malayan Chinese Association established the Tunku Abdul Rahman College in 1969 to meet the growing demand for higher education from students of Chinese origin.

2. Institutional Fabric of the Higher Education System

The May 1969 race riots and their aftermath had a major impact on the structure, institutional arrangement, medium of instruction, and student composition of the higher education institutions within the country. The key to this policy change was the Majid Committee Report and the NEP. The Committee pointed out that the University's meritocratically administered admissions policy perpetuated a racial imbalance in student enrollment. In 1969 the *Bumiputra* enrollment was only 25.4 percent of the total enrollment, compared to 74.6 percent for Chinese, Indians, and others. According to the Committee, this in no way reflected the distribution of the country's main racial groups, where the *Bumiputras* accounted for more than half the population, the Chinese 36 percent, and the Indians 11 percent.

The NEP's major task was to rectify the serious anomalies in income and occupational structure along racial lines. Its strategy was to: (a) eradicate

Table 2
Enrollment in tertiary education by ethnic group and level of education in local and overseas institutions 1980–90

Type of institution	1980					1985					1990 Total[a]	Percentage increase	
	Bumiputra	Chinese	Indian	Others	Total	Bumiputra	Chinese	Indian	Others	Total		1981–85	1986–90
Certificate	2,338	8,287	1,205	128	11,958	13,445	16,995	4,072	476	34,948	14,353	26.8	123.2
Percentage	19.6	69.3	10.1	1.0	100.0	38.5	48.5	11.6	1.4	100.0	11.1		
Polytechnics	1,468	459	93	10	2,030	4,236	907	196	34	5,373	11,995	171.0	93.0
Tunku Abdul Rahman college	—	448	3	—	451	6	1,189	27	—	1,222	2,358	132.0	—
MARA Institute of Technology	122	—	—	—	122	283	—	—	—	283	—	436.6	—
Local private institutions	554	3,029	455	54	4,092	8,694	9,804	3,091	368	21,957	—	16.2	—
Overseas institutions	194	4,351	654	64	5,263	226	5,055	758	74	6,113	—	76.0	—
Diploma	13,809	7,636	1,563	175	23,185	27,151	11,066	2,355	235	40,807	47,226		—
Percentage	59.5	32.9	6.7	0.8	100.0	66.5	27.1	5.8	0.6	100.0			
Polytechnics	148	55	6	—	209	368	104	22	1	495	2,490	136.8	403
Tunku Abdul Rahman college	—	409	3	—	412	—	951	4	—	955	2,004	131.8	109.8
MARA Institute of Technology	7,492	—	—	—	7,492	16,889	—	—	—	16,889	35,062	125.4	107.6
University of Agriculture Malaya	1,566	71	42	2	1,681	2,940	29	34	2	3,005	3,068	78.8	2.1
University of Technology Malaysia	2,215	180	54	19	2,468	3,363	229	96	14	3,702	4,602	50.0	24.3
Local private institutions	577	4,358	943	90	5,968	1,491	6,786	1,602	144	10,023	—	68.0	—
Overseas institutions	1,811	2,563	515	64	4,953	2,100	2,967	597	74	5,738	—	15.8	—
Degree[b]	18,804	18,381	3,928	341	41,454	29,875	24,647	5,581	419	60,522	65,413	46.0	—
Percentage	45.4	44.3	9.5	0.8	100.0	49.4	40.7	9.2	0.7	100.0	100.0		
Tunku Abdul Rahman college[c]	6	1,687	59	—	1,752	3	2,099	42	2	2,146	4,339	19.9	39.9
MARA Institute of Technology[d]	725	—	—	—	725	1,560	—	—	—	1,560	7,363	115.2	372.0
University of Malaya	4,063	3,124	677	181	8,045	5,041	3,374	841	126	9,382	9,544	16.6	1.7
University of Science Malaysia[e]	1,612	1,073	195	17	2,897	3,996	2,509	657	45	7,207	12,576	148.8	74.5
National University of Malaysia	4,896	628	189	13	5,726	6,454	1,914	468	64	8,900	12,794	55.4	43.8
University of Agriculture Malaysia	1,431	221	88	12	1,752	3,652	603	253	17	4,525	9,309	158.3	105.7
University of Technology Malaysia	877	115	44	11	1,047	2,284	567	154	26	3,031	5,616	189.5	85.3
International Islamic University	—	—	—	—	—	363	14	14	—	391	1,740	27.3	269.4
Northern University of Malaysia	—	—	—	—	—	488	161	44	3	696	2,132	42.7	206.3
Overseas institutions	5,194	11,533	2,676	107	19,510	6,034	13,406	3,108	136	22,684	—	5.6	—
Percentage	34,951	34,304	6,696	644		70,471	52,668	12,008		5,130	126,982	77.9	—

Source: Ministry of Education
a Excludes enrollment in local private institutions and institutions overseas   b Includes enrollment in graduate courses   c Degree conferred by the University of Campbell, United States   d Degree conferred by the National University of Malaysia and the University of Ohio, United States   e Includes enrollment in off-campus courses   f Excludes enrollment of foreign students

449

Table 3
Enrollment and graduation of degree and diploma holders by field of study, 1980–90

Field of study	Enrollment				Percentage increase			Number of graduates			
	1970	1980	1985	1990	1970–80	1980–85	1986–90	1971–75	1976–80	1981–85	1986–90
Degree courses											
Arts	4,877	9.727	17,121	27,476	199.5	76.0	60.5	9,033	11,356	14,802	27,779
Percentage	63.5	48.6	49.9	48.75				64.6	58.4	55.2	52.6
Sciences	2,408	8,046	12,505	17,748	334.1	55.4	41.9	4,451	6,513	9,317	17,507
Percentage	31.4	40.2	36.5	31.5				31.8	33.5	34.7	33.1
Technical	392	2,245	4,674	11,134	472.7	108.2	138.2	498	1,566	2,719	7,540
Percentage	5.1	11.2	13.6	19.75				36.0	8.1	10.1	14.3
Total	7,677	20,018	34,300	56,358	260.8	71.3	64.3	13,982	19,435	26,838	52,826
Diploma courses											
Arts	1,368	5,063	13,126	19,744	370.1	159.3	50.4	1,534	6,420	9,808	18,454
Percentage	41.2	41.3	52.4	43.4				33.2	40.7	42.9	50.1
Sciences	889	3,279	5,133	10,167	368.7	56.5	98.1	1,641	4,754	5,636	7,953
Percentage	26.8	26.7	20.5	22.4				35.6	30.2	24.7	21.6
Technical	1,061	3,920	6,787	15,573	369.5	73.1	129.5	1,440	4,593	7,404	10,448
Percentage	32.0	32.0	27.1	34.2				31.2	19.1	32.4	28.3
Total	3,318	12,262	25,046	45,484	369.6	104.3	81.6	4,615	15,767	22,848	36,855

Source: Ministry of Education

poverty by raising the income levels and employment opportunities for all Malaysians; and (b) correct prevailing economic imbalances by associating race with economic function. This strategy aimed at promoting national integration and ensuring greater participation of the people in the life of the nation. The NEP's objective was to be partly achieved through an aggressive policy of affirmative action in higher education.

The government took steps to control and enhance its role in implementing the NEP. The University and University Colleges Act of 1971 (UUCA) and the Constitution (Amendment) Bill of 1971 set a common legislative framework for all universities in Malaysia. No higher educational institution of university status could be established unless the *Yang di-Pertuan Agong* (paramount King) was satisfied of its contribution to the national good.

Under the UUCA, the Minister of Education was responsible for the general policy direction of higher education and the administration of the Act. In 1972, a Higher Education Advisory Council was established to advise the Minister. The university council's previous prerogative to appoint the vice-chancellor and deputy officials was now vested in the *Yang di-Pertuan Agong*. The election of deans was abolished, and instead the vice-chancellor was given the prerogative to appoint them. The Act disallowed the establishment of a new faculty or course within a university without prior approval of the Minister of Education. The 1975 amendments to the UUCA increased the number of heads of government departments on the council. Through the UUCA, the government imposes its political will and closely monitors and coordinates the overall development of the uni-

versities to ensure the NEP's objectives are carried out.

The NEP and its subsequent legislation precipitated major changes within higher education. The universities underwent a process of "indigenization." *Bahasa Malaysia* was introduced as the main medium of instruction in schools from 1970 and in the universities by 1983. Since 1988 all university courses, with the exception of certain technical and language courses, have been conducted in *Bahasa Malaysia*.

Under the Constitution (Amendment) Bill of 1971, university admissions were required to conform to the NEP. The government established the *Pusat Universiti-Universiti* (Central University Admissions Unit) to implement this policy effectively and ensure a substantial increase in the complement of *Bumiputra* students in the universities. This policy dramatically reversed the imbalance in the composition of student population (see Table 2).

Faced with expansion from the 1970s onward (see Table 3), the country's universities lacked the requisite infrastructural capacity, the diverse course specialities, and the local teaching expertise to meet the rapidly increasing demand, particularly in the high-cost science and technologically oriented professional courses. The government's policy to monitor the output of graduates relative to their employability since the mid-1970s contributed to limiting the supply of student places. This was further exacerbated by the NEP's objectives (see Table 2) to correct the underrepresentation of *Bumiputras*, particularly in the professionally oriented science and technology courses in local tertiary institutions.

To overcome the differentials in participation between the *Bumiputra* and non-*Bumiputra* students in professionally oriented science and technology related courses, *Bumiputra* students were admitted into specially designed pre-university (matriculation) courses in science, engineering, and medicine. This scheme intensified the competition among the non-*Bumiputras* to gain entry into the professionally oriented science- and technology-related courses in local universities, and created considerable tension between the *Bumiputra* and non-*Bumiputra* communities.

The majority of the Chinese and Indian students not admitted to a local tertiary institution sought access to overseas institutions or, from the 1980s, to one of the growing number of private tertiary institutions (see Table 2). Under the NEP, the government sponsored a large number of *Bumiputra* students for overseas training. The Ministry of Education estimated in 1987 that more than 68,000 Malaysian students were studying overseas, which is estimated to cost US$1,460 million—seven times the total yearly operational budget of US$220 million for the country's seven universities.

Unmet demand and the cost of overseas education spurred on the development of 27 tertiary institutions which offer more than 60 degree and diploma programs linked with overseas institutions in the United Kingdom, United States, Australia, New Zealand, and Canada. Two are run by MARA and the remainder are managed by private institutions. More than 90 percent of their students are largely Chinese and Indians; and there is an overwhelming emphasis on business studies, computer studies, and law.

3. Governance, Administration, and Finance

The governance of universities has to conform to the rules set by the UCCA. There is no independent overall coordinating or buffer organization between the six national universities and the government. The higher education division of the Ministry of Education acts as a coordinating body. A committee of vice-chancellors chaired by the Minister of Education meets regularly to iron out issues of duplication in expansion and course offerings and any differences between the government and universities, and between the universities themselves.

The administrative machinery of the universities consists of the council, senate, central administration, and faculties and departments. The council oversees the financial and administrative management, while the senate regulates all academic matters. The council and senate have independent powers and ad hoc committees to carry out the various functions of the university. The vice-chancellor is the principal academic and executive officer of the university's central administration and is supported by deputy vice-chancellors for academic affairs, research and development, and student affairs, a registrar for administration, a bursar for finance,

and a librarian. The departments are organized by discipline and are under their respective faculties with the exception of the *Universiti Sains* and the *Universiti Utara*. In these universities, core disciplines are integrated into the broad-based multidisciplinary schools.

Although largely dependent on public funds, universities have considerable autonomy in academic matters and internal administration. The main academic and internal administrative power is located within the university itself, and the diffusion of authority is hierarchical. Each university determines its own course contents, awards its own degrees, and hires and fires its own staff.

In 1986, out of an estimated total of just over 4 billion Malaysian Ringgit (US$1.4 billion) (13.1% of total government expenditure) devoted to education, higher education's share comprised 15.8 percent. The six national universities and the International Islamic University received 77.03 percent of this. The government allocates grants-in-aid to the universities which account for about 90 percent of their total income; student fees account for about 5–10 percent and other revenues may account for about 5 percent. The universities are granted considerable leeway in deciding how they allocate their funds. The first-level institutions, on the other hand, are treated like any government department and enjoy very little freedom in the way they distribute their yearly recurrent expenditure.

4. Faculty and Students: Teaching, Learning, and Research

The ranking system of teaching staff incorporates features of both the British and American systems and is as follows: professors, associate professors, lecturers, and tutors. The rapid expansion of universities has been accompanied by an unprecedented increase in the recruitment of academic staff. This increase in demand coupled with the NEP's affirmative action to correct the racial imbalance of staff within universities have eroded the competitive base for staff recruitment.

Student enrollment and graduate output have substantially increased both at the first (diploma) and the second (degree) levels from the 1970s onward (see Table 3). At the diploma level, enrollments in local institutions have increased from 3,318 students in 1970 to 45,848 in 1990, while at the degree level, from 7,677 in 1970 to 56,358 during the corresponding period (see Table 3). The number of diploma and degree holders graduating also rose dramatically over these two decades (see Table 3). At the diploma level, numbers rose from 4,615 between 1971 and 1975 to 36,855 between 1986 and 1990, and at the degree level from 13,982 to 52,826 during the corresponding period.

Between 1970 and 1980, a huge upsurge in the

numbers and percentages of *Bumiputra* students enrolled took place, rising from 25 percent in 1970 to 72 percent in 1980 and 57 percent in 1990 (see Table 2).

Despite the early emphasis on increasing enrollments and output in science and technology these areas accounted for over 51 percent of total enrollments in 1990. Over 31 percent of this figure were science students and just under 20 percent were technology students (see Table 3). This still fell short of the target set by the HEPC in 1967 for technology student enrollment. The graduate enrollment of 2,394 out of 48,000 students in 1990 (5%) is relatively small for a country with ambitions of becoming highly industrialized by the turn of the twentieth century.

Malaysian universities are basically teaching institutions. Teaching is conducted by the academic staff through lectures, seminars, and tutorials. In the recruitment to academic positions, the emphasis is on academic credentials and quality, rather than teaching skills. The *Universiti Sains* has established a Teaching–Learning Advisory Unit to assist academic staff members in enhancing teaching–learning techniques as well as to advise staff in their preparation of teaching materials.

Research in Malaysian universities has been limited to basic research and donor-assisted ad hoc and short-term research projects or assignments. Research support is given by the government with priority given to projects that propose solutions to national issues and problems. Despite this, Malaysian universities generally have not been able to contribute effectively to the country's technology transfer process. Research grants amounting to about 1.4 percent of the government's total grants to universities may have been a contributory factor. Barriers to Research and Development (R & D) work also exist in the form of a relatively weak industrial base and the unwillingness of industries to support R & D.

In the early 1980s with the Fifth Malaysia Plan (1986–90), the government explicitly spelt out for the first time that a national R & D effort would be utilized to increase productivity and diversity in the country's industrial base so Malaysia might achieve a more competitive edge and penetrate overseas markets. This proactive policy has given an incentive to universities to boost their R & D work, and has resulted in most universities establishing consultancy services.

5. Conclusion

The NEP has given greater priority and weight to eliminating the imbalance in education and occupation between the *Bumiputras* and non-*Bumiputras* than to an overall development of the vital high-level labor force. This policy has created an excess of graduates in the humanities, social sciences, and

natural sciences, with critical shortages in the field of applied technology. Malaysia has embarked upon an export-oriented strategy based on a high value-added manufacturing sector. Malaysia has adopted a two-part strategy to realize this, through its Industrial Master Plan (1986–95) and the Fifth Malaysia Plan (1986–90). This strategy consists of: (a) a human resource development program with an underpinning of science and technology; and (b) a degree of self-sufficiency through an indigenous market-driven technological base.

The prime minister's public announcement (April 1991) that branch campuses of overseas universities may be allowed in the country, and the rising cost of public sector higher education will, in all likelihood, accelerate the growth of private higher education. Higher education in Malaysia would appear to be set for a shift toward greater specialization in professional skills related to applied science and technology and a greater mix between public and private education at the institutional level.

Bibliography

Aziz U A, Chew S B, Lee K H and Sanyal B C (eds.) 1987 *University Education and Employment in Malaysia.* International Institute of Educational Planning, Paris

Carr-Saunders Commission 1948 *Report of The Commission on University Education in Malaya.* The Government Press, Kuala Lumpur

Higher Education Planning Committee 1958 *Report of the Higher Education Planning Committee.* Government Printers, Kuala Lumpur

Majid Committee 1971 *Report of the Committee appointed by the National Operations Council to Study Campus Life of Students of the University of Malaya.* Government Printers, Kuala Lumpur

Selvaratnam V 1986 Dependency, change and continuity in a Western model: The Malaysian case. *Southeast Asian J. Soc. Sc.* 14(2): 29–51

Selvaratnam V 1988 Ethnicity, inequality, and higher education in Malaysia. *Comp. Educ. Rev.* 32(2): 1973–96

Singh J S 1989 Scientific personnel, research environment, and higher education in Malaysia. In: Altbach P G et al. (eds.) 1989 *Scientific Development and Higher Education.* Praeger, New York, pp. 83–136

V. Selvaratnam

Mali

1. Higher Education and Society

The French Sudan became the Republic of Mali in 1960. In the Middle Ages, it was a crossroads of intense commercial and cultural exchange between the Sahara and the Gulf of Guinea. The most active and world famous centers were the cities of Timbuktu (with its famous Sankoré University) and Djénné. Islamic learning developed there in an authentic university system, which reached its high point in the sixteenth-century Sonhoi Empire. The modern history of higher education in Mali begins with the educational reform of 1962. This reform made it possible to provide the young republic with high-level working cadres. However, since the 1980s the educational system in general and higher education in particular have entered a recessive phase that risks being prolonged, given the country's present economic difficulties.

There was no single institution of higher learning in Mali at Independence in September 1960. The present system is the product of the educational reform of October 1962, and is therefore marked by the ideas of the nationalist regime that decolonized the country.

After almost a century of colonization, Mali had only three veterinarians, ten teachers, eight to ten medical doctors, three pharmacists, ten lawyers, and a few engineers, for a population of 4,300,000.

As opposed to the colonial school, which was elitist and sought to assimilate French culture, the 1962 educational reform aimed to promote the political and economic emancipation of the people. It established the following objectives for national education in Mali: (a) to ensure the general and technical training of high-level cadres of the nation and their continuing education; (b) to promote scientific research; (c) to ensure the ongoing adaptation of public education to scientific progress and social change; and (d) to disseminate culture.

2. The Institutional Fabric of the Higher Education System

Higher education in Mali at present is composed of seven multidisciplinary university-level institutions and one specialized institute of higher learning. The University of Mali will be operational soon and will have three faculties and five institutes located in six different cities.

Short-term higher education of two years duration, is at present provided by two institutions: the *Ecole des Hautes Etudes Pratiques* (EHEP), which gives a university-level technician's degree; and the *Ecole Nationale des Postes et Télecommunications* (ENPT), with its section for accounting.

Long-term higher education is provided by four institutions that give degrees equivalent to the French *maîtrise*. They are: the *Ecole Normale Supérieure* (ENsup); the *Ecole Nationale d'Administration* (ENA); the *Ecole Nationale d'Ingénieurs* (ENI); and the *Institut Polytechnique Rural* (IPR).

Graduate Education, lasting six years or more, is at present provided in two institutions: the *Ecole Nationale de Médécine et de Pharmacie*, which trains medical doctors and pharmacists in six-year programs, then organizes special studies programs (CES) after three more years of study; the *Institut Supérieur de Formation et de Recherche Appliquée* (ISFRA) which prepares auditors, chosen for competitive examination after the *maîtrise*, for the *Diplôme d'Etat Approfondi* (DEA)—higher-level state diploma—and then for the specialized doctorate, in addition to its responsibility to apply research to development.

Scientific research is still relatively undeveloped in Mali. It is carried out by the Educational and Research Departments (DER) of the ISFRA and by some specialized institutions not connected with education. Because of insufficient means, research is reduced to some projects at the end of long-term programs, doctoral dissertations, and personal research projects.

The recent establishment of the *Centre de la Recherche Scientifique* and the soon-to-be-operational University of Mali will make it possible to develop research.

Admission to institutions of higher learning is generally by right or by competitive examination, depending on the field of study. No sexual discrimination is allowed.

3. Governance, Administration, and Finance

Higher education and scientific research are run by the state in Mali. In order to carry out efficaciously the mission of higher education, the Ministry of National Education has established a central structure for coordination and supervision, which is the National Office on Higher Education and Scientific Research (DNESRS).

The objectives of the DNESRS are to formulate and implement the national policy for higher education, educational programs, administer scholarships, and promote scientific research.

Generally, the administrative structure of the institutions are composed of a governing board, which includes a director general named by the Ministry. The director general is also on the Teaching and Scientific Council.

There are two sources of financing for higher education: the national budget, by far the most important one; and foreign aid. Although the part of the state budget allocated to education is high in absolute value (29% in 1985), it is still insufficient. Moreover, it has been growing smaller since 1985.

Higher education receives close to 20 percent of the budget, but wages and scholarships take more than half, to the detriment of the infrastructure needed for quality education. The average unit costs of education have increased in the last few years because of a lower student–faculty ratio.

4. Faculty and Students: Teaching, Learning, and Research

The only criterion for joining the faculty is to have a doctorate. The number of faculty members stabilized in the late 1980s. It went from 694 in 1985–86 to 708 in 1989; 293 of these are part-time, and 106 foreigners. Some 85 percent of the faculty are from Mali, recruited by the civil service and placed in an appropriate educational post, according to need. Every professor works at least 10 hours on courses and seminars each week.

Higher education in Mali has been characterized by the rapid growth of student numbers. Growth in the first 10 years after the reform was 2,853 percent, and in the five years from 1969–70 to 1974–75, 270 percent.

The production of diplomas practically followed the same rate, obliging the government to stop automatically hiring all graduates. From 1982–83 to 1986–87, higher education produced 4,797 graduates.

For close to 95 percent of the students whose parents are farmers, the main reason for continuing their higher studies is to be able later to support their family. A higher education is the only means of social mobility.

5. Conclusion

The spectacular development of higher education in Mali did not take place without serious obstacles connected with being a developing country. In spite of achieving unquestionable results and meeting its original objectives, the dropout and expulsion rates are still very high.

Higher education in Mali is also producing a high number of unemployed graduates since the competitive civil service examination began in 1984. Most of the private sector of the economy needed few university graduates. There is certainly an urgent need to rethink higher education in Mali. However, the fourth educational project being prepared with the World Bank, which ratifies the foundation of a decentralized university with the capacity to receive 5,000 to 6,000 students, risks making the situation worse.

Bibliography

Coumare F 1978 *L'enseignement supérieur au Mali: mission, organisations, résultat, problèmes et perspectives.* University of Montreal, Montreal
Diakité D 1988 *Les fondements historiques de l'enseignement islamique au Mali.* Ecole Normale Supérieure
Cuevin S, Orivel F 1988 *Financement et efficacité des enseignements supérieurs et secondaires au Mali.* World Bank, Washington, DC
EDUCAFRICA 1986 *L'enseignement supérieur en Afrique.* UNESCO, Dakar
Guedj P 1988 L'enseignement supérieur en Afrique: le Mali (1960–1985). Doctoral thesis, Université François Rabelais, Tours
Mali, Ministry of National Education 1973 *Contact spécial N°4.* Ministère de l'Education Nationale, Bamako
Mali, Ministry of National Education 1987. *Etude sur la rationalisation de l'enseignement supérieur.* Ministère de l'Education Nationale, Bamako

Y. Diakité

Malta

1. Higher Education and Society

The Maltese Islands are a densely populated archipelago in the central Mediterranean with a geographical area of roughly 300 square kilometers. The postwar 1948 census gave the population figure as 305,991, while the 1988 figures put it at about 346,000. Every official census in between registers a preponderance of females over males, with the 1985 ratio being 967 males for every 1,000 females. After a postwar "baby boom," the birthrate declined steadily and was virtually stable by the end of the 1980s. Although the percentage of the elderly has risen to roughly 10 percent, the Maltese population remains one of the three youngest in Europe. The influences on the demographic figures, besides the drop in the birthrate, include a decrease in infant mortality and improved living and health conditions. An additional factor has been emigration abroad.

After political independence from Britain in 1964, Malta's major socioeconomic challenge was to change its fortress economy and way of life. Thus, subsequent economic policy has focused on four industrial areas: manufacture, tourism, docking and shipbuilding, and services. The primary sector, which includes farming, fishing, construction, and quarrying, accounts for roughly 12 percent of the gainfully employed and contributes 9 percent to the Gross Domestic Product (GDP). The clothing industry, the largest in the labor-intensive secondary sector, employs roughly 29 percent of the labor force (about 75 percent of which are women), and produces about 24 percent of the net output of the sector which also includes docking and shipbuilding, and collectively contributes roughly 30 percent to the GDP. The tertiary servicing sector, which also includes the crucial tourist industry, employs the largest part of the workforce, some 33 percent, with the public sector accounting for 27 percent.

Malta, a republic since 1974, is a parliamentary democracy with one House of Representatives. General elections are held every five years. There are two major political parties: Socialist and Christian Democrat. The head of state, the president, is elected by parliament. Malta has a neutral and nonaligned

Table 1
Academic staff/student numbers

	1960–61	1965–66	1970–71	1975–76	1980–81	1985–86	1988–89
University							
Full-time staff	52	72	115	119	110	110	126
Part-time staff	6	32	46	43	19	46	53
Students	295	624	1,141	877	946	1,474	2,009
Malta College of Arts, Science, and Technology							
Staff		44	109	71			
Students		600	1,302	1,347			
Training colleges							
Staff	29	37	41				
Students	234	390	365				
Faculty of theology							
Staff						14	14
Students						134	147

foreign policy, laid down in its constitution. Socially, increasing economic affluence and the enactment of redistributive social legislation has thawed the former rigid stratification of colonial times. However, a discernable class structure still exists, with a "lower" class made up of the unemployed, the unskilled, and the semiskilled; a small "upper" class made up of persons in the top management grades and the professions, and property owners; and a large "middle" class comprising the bulk of all the other grades of workers and their families. The vast majority of the population is Roman Catholic, and the Church has always exerted a very great influence on the Maltese way of life.

2. The Institutional Fabric of the Higher Education System

Higher education in Malta is provided entirely by the University of Malta, an institution founded by the Jesuits in the sixteenth century. Up to 1978, the Malta College of Arts, Science, and Technology (MCAST), founded in 1963, fulfilled the role of a polytechnic. In 1975 it absorbed the two teachers' colleges, one for men, the other for women, which had hitherto been operated by religious orders. But MCAST ceased to exist by virtue of the 1978 Amendment to the 1974 Education Act, passed by the Socialist government of the time, which radically restructured higher education in Malta. The new "utilitarian" policy was to align higher education totally with the needs of the economy, and to make it more accessible to working-class students by giving them a salary. Its outcome was the "worker–student scheme." The college was first transformed into a "new" university; then fused, by means of the 1978 Act, with the old university, shorn of its liberal faculties, and of its faculty of theology. The University of Malta, as the new institution was called, adopted a system of sponsored admission on a *numerus clausus* basis, a system of alternating work with study, with two student intakes at different times of the year, and dropped all but the vocational and professional courses.

In 1988 the then newly elected Christian Democrat government passed an Education Act which dismantled the worker–student scheme and "refounded" the University by giving it back its old name; reopening and expanding the liberal faculties; and reintegrating the faculty of theology which had, meanwhile, moved to a different campus under the control and sponsorship of the Church, and had been given the power to issue its own degrees and diplomas. The general admission criteria now are three passes at Advanced matriculation level, two at grade C or better, and five at Ordinary level, to include Maltese (for Maltese nationals), English language, mathematics, and another language from French, Italian, German, or Arabic, though there are other conditions specific to some of the courses. The *numerus clausus* system, though dropped as general policy, is retained in some professional courses like medicine and dental surgery which are oversubscribed and have resource limitations. Numbers are controlled in other areas through the device of restricting admission to new courses to alternate years rather than on an annual basis. All first degree courses are at the bachelor's level and general degrees take three years and honors four, except for the five-year MD and LLD courses. The liberal faculties offered a master's and an occasional doctoral program before 1978, and this practice has resumed. Meanwhile the faculty of education continues with its MEd program started in 1987. Apart from these, most doctoral and many other postgraduate studies are pursued abroad, mainly in Commonwealth and European universities.

The other research institution, besides the university, is the Foundation for International Studies, an autonomous institution created by public deed in 1986 with close statutory ties with the University. The Foundation's research is carried out individually, departmentally, and through its interdisciplinary institutes. Student numbers have grown enormously since 1960 (see Table 1), when higher education was provided by the University and the teachers' colleges. The MCAST polytechnic introduced a new kind of student, part-time and short-course. At the turn of the 1970s, both the University and MCAST registered a steep increase in student numbers, mainly through the expansion of the original amenities generated by the economic and sociocultural demands of the newly independent country. The 1980–81 figures, for the first time, show the combined student population for higher education at the University, apart from those attending at the faculty of theology. Those of 1985–86 show a sensible increase over these figures, due mainly to an increase in some *numerus clausus* quotas, and a large expansion of the University's extramural program, while a predictable further rise is also evident in the latest figures available, the first since the "refounding."

3. Governance, Administration, and Finance

The University of Malta is non-feepaying, and is funded mainly by direct grant from the government, which also sets its general policy and orientations. Other minor financial resources derive from matriculation examination fees and nominal fees paid for part-time extramural courses, although a new project called Malta University Services Ltd was launched in 1988 to market the University's research and other resources both locally and abroad. Under Socialist governments after the 1978 reforms, the University's teaching and research activities were almost entirely tied to the country's economic needs and labor force targets identified in the government's plans. Table 2 indicates a very large decline in government expenditure on higher education over the Gross Domestic Product, from 1975 onwards. However, the figures do not include student salaries under the worker–student scheme, which were not paid by the University.

Under the new Act (1988), government-appointed members constitute a theoretical majority of one in the University's council, while the Minister of

Education appoints representatives to the senate and to the different faculty boards, though here they are in a large minority. The president of the republic appoints the University's chancellor on the prime minister's advice after consultation with the leader of the opposition. The rector of the University, who chairs the senate and the faculty boards, is elected by the council. Representatives of the academic staff and of the students are elected to all these bodies by their fellows, but the nonacademic staff are only represented on the council, which is the University's highest body, ultimately responsible for the administration of the University's property; the appointment and dismissal of its academic staff; the setting up of its statutes; the appointment of internal and external examiners; the planning of its academic work; and of interdisciplinary collaboration between its faculties, departments, and institutes.

The heads of faculties, or deans, are elected from among the heads of departments by the academic staff for a two-year period. Heads of department are appointed by the council from among the department's senior members for a period of up to four years after the rector's consultation with the department. Full professors do not hold a "chair"; their appointment is mainly in recognition of their scholarly achievements, and the same is true for all the other academic grades, which include assistant lecturer, lecturer, senior lecturer, and associate professor. The teaching and the administrative work of the department is assigned by the head of department. The deans are the vice-chairs of their respective faculty boards, while the other heads of department are ex officio members, and each department also selects an additional member. The other members of a faculty board are the student representatives and the two representatives of the education minister. Thus, the academic staff have a clear majority on these boards.

4. Faculty and Students: Teaching, Learning, and Research

The academic staff has grown substantially with the University since 1960 (see Table 1), both in numerical terms and in terms of qualifications. Moreover, the tenured staff is almost entirely native. Vacancies, when they occur, are filled after a public call for applications, and upon a selection board's recommendations to the council. Appointments may be to any of the recognized academic grades of the University according to these recommendations and the council's decision. When appointees are given a full-time post this automatically carries full tenure with it and also makes the appointee an employee of the council according to the specifications of his or her contract. Promotions to higher posts are made by the council after annual calls for applications open

Table 2
Expenditure on higher education as percentage of Gross Domestic Product

1960	1965	1970	1975	1980	1985	1987
0.64	1.05	1.12	0.62	0.40	0.33	0.34

to all members of the academic staff, on a special committee's recommendations.

The academic staff of the University do not have their own union. Those who are unionized belong to the Malta Union of Teachers, the island's major teachers' union which caters for all teaching grades. The students have their own union, membership of which is automatic for all students. The University's nonacademic staff are unionized within sections of the two major union organizations on the island: the General Workers Union and the Confederation of Maltese Trade Unions. The respective contracts of the academic staff specify the formal ratio between teaching and research and administrative work according to the different academic grades, with the former decreasing with respect to the latter the higher one's status.

The development of the student body in higher education in Malta is obviously closely tied with its history, especially over the period of change and flux since 1978. There is keen competition to enter medicine, while law and architecture have also long been popular choices. The technical professions, however, have also come into their own since 1978 and attract strong numbers. The liberal faculties, which had ceased to exist for a decade, are struggling to gain their former strength; they are usually considered a path into teaching, though the faculty of education gives a professional BEd degree. There are no available scientific research findings as to the students' social class background, but the statistics show that the ratio of female students has grown considerably since 1960, though some courses continue to be male dominated. The University continues to pay students a salary.

It is impossible to provide a succinct tabular breakdown of how degrees and diplomas have been conferred since 1960 because in many of the courses graduation has been irregular. But the latest figures for 1988 indicate a total of 403 graduates (252 male, 151 female), 340 of these with professional degrees. Most of the courses themselves are organized on the credit unit system, which it is the University's policy to standardize throughout. Undergraduate professional courses are almost entirely specialist, while the first level general arts students all have to do a common course in the history of Mediterranean civilization.

Bibliography

Brigulio L 1988 *The Maltese Economy*. David Moore (Holdings) Ltd, Valletta
Central Office of Statistics *Annual Abstract of Statistics*. Government of Malta
Central Office of Statistics *Census 1985*, Vol. 1. Government of Malta
Central Office of Statistics *Education Statistics*. Government of Malta
Central Office of Statistics *National Accounts of the Maltese Islands* Government of Malta
The Yearbook (formerly *The Malta Yearbook*) De La Salle Brothers Publications, Valletta
University of Malta Annual Calendars Malta University Press, Msida
Zammit E 1984 *A Colonial Inheritance: Maltese Perceptions of Work, Power and Class Structure with Reference to the Labour Movement*, Malta University Press, Msida

K. Wain

Mauritania

1. Higher Education and Society

Mauritania, comprised mostly of desert, is situated between the Atlantic Ocean on its western borders and Mali in the east and southeast. Its northern frontiers are delimited in the northeast by Algeria and the Western Sahara with the Senegal river forming its southern frontiers. Two-thirds of Mauritania forms part of the Western Saharan plain and only in the south, around the strip bordering on the Senegal river is there an exception to the otherwise harsh climatic conditions.

With a surface area of some 1,031,000 square kilometers, the total population was estimated to be in the range of 1.97 million in 1989, an increase of some 72 percent over the 14 years since 1975. Even so, Mauritania must be counted as a sparsely populated nation, with an average density of two persons per square kilometer. The birthrate is 50.1 per thousand. Such demographic pressure is clear from the fact that more than half the population (54.2%) is under 19 years of age. Yet life expectancy is around 44 years for men, and 47 for women.

The Mauritanian population divides into three main groups: the Moorish population, whose roots are essentially Arab or Berber, forms some 30 percent; the Blacks from the Senegal Valley constitute a further 30 percent; and the remaining 40 percent of the population is of mixed origin. Ethnically and historically, Mauritania is the meeting point between the Arab world of North Africa and Black Africa. Successively invaded in the fourteenth and fifteenth centuries by its Arab neighbors to the north, and again in 1855 by the French, the country was incorporated into the French West African possessions in 1920. It became fully independent in 1960, assuming the form of an Islamic Republic. Linguistically diverse—the major language groups are the *Ouloufs, Sarakolés, Toucouleurs, Peuls*, and *Fulas*—the official language is Arabic, though the heritage of having been part of French West Africa means that there is also a French-speaking elite. This ethnic and linguistic diversity is offset, however, by Mauritania's religious homogeneity, 99 percent being Muslim.

The greater part of the population in the south relies on various forms of subsistence farming—millet, sorghum, rice, maize, and dates are the main crops, with cattle breeding and camel raising as an important source of revenue for the nomadic peoples in the center and north. Agricultural production represents some 37 percent of Gross National Product (GNP). Industry, mainly extractive in nature—iron ore around the town of N'Derik, phosphates, gypsum, and processed fish—constitutes some 22 percent of GNP, with the service sector generating a further 41 percent.

Mauritania's economic development has been beset by a number of misfortunes such as the severe and prolonged drought which affected most of the Sahel in the 1970s and decimated the cattle-raising sector, whilst Mauritania's claims to the Western Sahara and its rich phosphate deposits involved the country in a conflict with the guerillas of the Polisario Front, between 1976 and 1979. The war imposed an intolerable strain on the country's resources. It also severely affected the country's communications infrastructure and its industrial development.

The drought forced many nomads into the towns, thus raising the level of urbanization to 34.6 percent of the population. A further feature, though its causality is perhaps best speculated upon, has been the relative volatility of its political regimes. Mauritania's first president after Independence, Moktar Ould Daddah was overthrown by a military coup in 1978 and replaced by Lieutenant Colonel Loully, who in turn was ousted in 1980 by Lieutenant Colonel Ould Haidalla. His successor, Colonel Ould Taya, achieved power by similar means in 1984.

Against such a background of natural disasters and political instability, it is not surprising that economic growth is virtually absent—0.3 percent is a recent estimate—nor that the per capita GNP is low at around US\$434 per year. This situation, when set against a background of illiteracy rates, estimated in 1990 at 66 percent for the whole country (UNESCO 1990 p. 15) and heavily differentiated by gender—the rate among women is held to be 78.6 percent—together with enrollment ratios at primary level of 52 percent in 1987, with a corresponding ratio of 16 percent at secondary level and some 3.4 percent at the tertiary stage, shows the nature of the educational challenge the country faces.

The twin drives towards strengthening education and raising participation rates at all levels, plus the reinforcement of Arabic as a symbol of national unity, have not been accomplished without stress. The resistance of the non-Arabic minorities to the south for whom French is the main second language is an illustration of this.

2. The Institutional Fabric of the Higher Education System

The development of a higher education system *stricto sensu* in Mauritania is recent. The University of Nouakchott, located in the capital city of the same name, was founded in 1981. It is still in 1991 the country's only university, though certain specialized establishments, such as the *Ecole Nationale d'Administration* (National School of Administration) and the *Institut National des Hautes Etudes Economiques* (National Institute of Higher Economic Studies), date from the period immediately after Independence and were founded in 1966 and 1961 respectively. When considering the relatively small number of students in higher education—5,407 in 1987 (UNESCO 1990) it is as well to set this off against the fact that in 1975, the number of secondary school enrollments was around 6,571 (Sonko-Godwin 1988 p. 477). In effect, in the space of a decade and half, such formal progress has been made that the 4 percent enrollment rate that marked secondary education in 1975 is paralleled by the 3.4 percent enrollment rate for higher education in 1987.

The path to higher education lies in a school structure whose terminology and qualifications are based on a model, which has close semblance to the French system as it existed in the late 1960s. Lower secondary schooling lasts three years from 12 to 15 years of age and leads to a *brevet d'études du premier cycle* (First Certificate of Secondary Education), or to an Arabic language equivalent, the *brevet arabe*, a certificate necessary for admission to upper secondary school. Upper secondary schooling since the reforms of 1979 also lasts three years. Successful attendance at the three-year upper secondary school leads on to the *baccalauréat* which is required for entrance to university. A parallel structure at upper secondary schooling of four years duration, and bearing a certain similarity to the French *classes préparatoires aux grandes écoles*, terminates in a competitive examination which governs access to the *Ecole Nationale d'Administration* and to the *Institut National des Hautes Etudes Economiques*.

The structure of higher education in Mauritania has certain specificities that are worth noting. The first is the clear division between the university and other specialized institutions the main task of which is the training of civil service cadres, of high level technical labor force, principally in the area of economics. This pattern, which is a perpetuation of some of the unique features found in French higher education, is, in the case of Mauritania, extended to the science fields as well. The training of future higher civil servants takes place in the *Ecole Nationale d'Administration* which provides first degree courses in administration and politics. Future economists and statisticians are trained in the *Institut National des Hautes Etudes Economiques*. The study of such areas as mathematics, physics, chemistry, biology, and geology is carried out in the *Institut Supérieur Scientifique* (Higher Institute of Science) which as the *École Normale Supérieure* (normal higher school) previously trained teachers for secondary schools. Its transformation in 1987 reflected Mauritania's need to provide training in the basic sciences, rather than relying wholly on foreign universities (Tedga 1988 p. 17). A second characteristic, though by no means unique to Mauritania, is the provision for national training establishments for nursing staff, primary school teachers, and so on which run parallel to upper secondary education.

This segmentation of the higher education system between restricted entry of specialized institutes on the one hand and the university on the other, has resulted in the latter having only partial coverage of disciplines. In effect, the University of Nouakchott has two main faculties—letters and human sciences, and law and economics (IAU 1990 p. 916).

Studies are organized around a pattern of first and second cycle, each of two years and leading respectively to the *diplôme d'études universitaires générales* (similar to a lower first degree) and to the level of the taught master's (*maîtrise*) degree. The university does not have third cycle studies, which in the usual pattern of studies in Francophone Africa, would normally provide the research training base. However, plans drawn up for the development of the *Institut Supérieur Scientifique* do foresee such provision (Tedga 1988 p. 17). Since the Institute's purpose is to develop applied science within the Mauritanian context, its proposed course content is particularly interesting. It is divided into four main subject areas—environment and food resources, conservation and development of natural resources, information on science, and teacher training.

Finally, at the graduate level, the *Institut Supérieur des Sciences et Techniques Halieutiques* (Advanced Institute for Fish Technology and Sciences) was set up in 1988 under the sponsorship of the West African Economic Community and financed by the Organization of Oil Producing and Exporting Countries (OPEC). With institutional links to similar specialist institutes in France, it dispenses advanced training, including research techniques for all the member states of the West African Economic Community as well as for its own nationals, in such fields as the conservation of fish stocks, fish farming, and research. It is located at the port of Nouadhibou.

3. Governance, Administration, and Finance

The University of Nouakchott comes under state control which is exercised through the Ministry of National Education. More precisely, oversight in matters touching on higher education is the responsibility of the Director for Higher Education. The Ministry acts, through the use of laws, decrees, and circulars as the main coordinating and steering body for the higher education system. Formally, it also has responsibility for guaranteeing the quality of state diplomas, be they the *diplôme d'études universitaires générales*, the *licence*, or the *maîtrise*.

Higher education is financed out of central government expenditure. A close examination of the trends in current public expenditure over the period 1975 to 1987 (the latter being the latest data available), shows that the overall level of expenditure on education reached a high point in 1986 when, compared to 1975, public spending based on the local currency—the Ouguiya—had in nominal terms increased almost five times. In 1987, however, reductions were in the order of 11 percent. In absolute terms, current public expenditure on higher education fell from an estimated Ougs784,107,000 (approximately US$7,763,435) in 1986 to Ougs758,160,000 (US$7,506,534) the following year.

This budgetary compression took place precisely at the moment when student numbers rose by approximately 20 percent (UNESCO 1990 p. 45). Though it can, naturally, be argued that fluctuations over one year do not make a trend, it is nevertheless a pointer to a difficult situation, as demographic pressure and demand for higher education build up in line with the expansion of secondary schooling and at the very moment when the nation's economic growth rate is to all intents and purposes flat. In all, higher education absorbs almost one-quarter of public current expenditure on education.

Governance at the institution level is based on the faculty model with the deans of faculty acting as the main coordinating body. The rector is appointed by the Minister of Education. In the specialized institutions, the department structure predominates.

4. Faculty and Students: Teaching, Learning, and Research

As might be expected in view of the rapid growth in higher education, the number of faculty is relatively small being no more than 252 in 1987 for the university sector. Faculty are in effect civil servants and, at the higher ranks, are appointed by the Ministry of Education. The fact that with two exceptions, higher education is concentrated in the capital adds the dimension of proximity to a system already based on the principle of centralization.

If, as has been pointed out student numbers are rising, the feminization of the student body is low at no more than 13 percent in 1987. Given the restricted nature of the disciplines available, student subject choice is equally limited. More than half the student enrollments in 1987 were in the area of social sciences and law, slightly over one-third in the humanities and teacher education (36.7%) with approximately 12.5 percent opting for the natural sciences or engineering. (UNESCO 1990 p. 92). Over and above students enrolled at home, there were some 1,860 studying abroad. The greater part of these students were following courses in Morocco, France, Senegal, Algeria, and Tunisia.

Of all the Francophone African countries, Mauritania's students are, according to a recent investigation, the most costly. In 1983, using as a base US constant dollars, each student was reckoned to cost US\$10,969, the equivalent of 25 times the per capita GNP (IREDU cited in Tedga p. 130). Though it is possible that in the intervening period this figure may have been revised downwards as home-based higher education expanded, nevertheless it is another example of a phenomenon that has inspired certain international agencies to call for governments to switch resources into primary schooling. Higher education in Mauritania both from the concentration of national resources around it, as well as the numbers involved, is very much an elite institution when placed against the broader social and economic backdrop in which it is set.

Bibliography

International Association of Universities (IAU) 1990 *International Handbook of Universities (12th Edition)*. Macmillan, London
Sonko-Godwin P 1988 Mauritania. In: Postlethwaite T N (ed.) 1988 *The Encyclopedia of Comparative Education and National Systems of Education*. Pergamon, Oxford, pp. 476–478
Tedga P J M 1988 *Enseignement Supérieur en Afrique Noire Francophone: la catastrophe?* L'Harmattan, Paris
UNESCO 1990 *Statistical Yearbook 1990*. UNESCO, Paris

M. Herlant

Mauritius

1. Higher Education and Society

The development of higher education in Mauritius, especially after Independence (1968), has been pursued to a large extent in relation to specific labor needs. Prior to Independence there were no infrastructural or institutional bases for higher education in Mauritius, except for the Mauritius Sugar Industry Research Institute (MSIRI) and the College of Agriculture, which provided for research and diploma level teaching directly related to the sugar industry, which was the backbone of the Mauritian economy. Mauritian students had no alternative but to proceed overseas for higher education.

The University of Mauritius was formally set up in 1970. The university was to concentrate essentially on areas with a quick pay-off in terms of growth in the economy. This strictly developmental role of the

university, although desirable for a newly independent small country, limited its effectiveness as an institution for higher learning and research.

A turning point in the history of the university came in 1979, as a result of an increasing level of graduate unemployment. Student unrest and deteriorating economic prospects forced the university to cut down radically the number and range of courses on offer, and virtually abandon degree courses. As from 1985, however, there has been a dramatic uptake of the Mauritian economy which has given a new lease of life to higher education in Mauritius.

2. The Institutional Fabric of the Higher Education System

Responsibility for higher education is shared mainly by the university, the Mauritius Institute of Education (MIE), the Mahatma Gandhi Institute (MGI) and the Mauritius Sugar Industry Research Institute (MSIRI).

The "development" approach had initially led to the establishment of three schools in the University of Mauritius: agriculture, industrial technology, and administration. However, steps are being taken to restructure the university and to phase out certificate courses, to offer more degree courses, and to engage in more research. Instead of three schools, there will be four faculties: agriculture; engineering; science, including a center for medical research and studies; management, social studies, and law.

The university has already started degree courses in law and the natural sciences, besides undertaking training and research in the medical and paramedical fields. Student numbers are expected to increase to 3,000 in 1989 and 4,000 in 1990.

The Mauritius Institute of Education (MIE) was established in 1973 to provide facilities for, and to engage in, education research, curriculum development, and teacher education in order to improve the quality and relevance of education in the country. It also acts as a think-tank and professional arm of the Ministry of Education.

The Mahatma Gandhi Institute (MGI) was founded in 1970 to promote inter alia, Mauritian, Asian, and African studies, with greater emphasis on the study of Indian languages and culture. The MSIRI, founded in 1953, conducts principally sugar-cane research.

Additionally market forces have prompted the mushrooming of private training institutions throughout the country which complement basic and other specialized training needs. None of these can be classified as institutions of higher education.

At the university, and at MIE and MGI, admissions are competitive, except for those students who are specially commissioned and sponsored. Applications for admission far exceed intake, because of control over enrollment.

3. Governance, Administration, and Finance

The University of Mauritius is, in principle, an autonomous body governed by its act and statutes. In practice, the government is adequately represented on its more important boards and committees. Hence the university, while enjoying a great measure of autonomy insofar as the conduct of its academic affairs is concerned, generally functions within the framework of government goals and priorities in close collaboration with the Ministry of Education, which acts as a "parent" ministry.

The other institutions sharing responsibility in teaching, learning, and research at the tertiary level are entrusted with specific responsibilities. They are semiautonomous bodies regulated by an Act of Parliament and responsible to the Minister of Education, who is empowered to give directives of a general nature which these institutions have to implement.

In practice the whole tertiary sector in Mauritius consists of institutions functioning as vocational centers responding to the developmental needs and priorities of the economy and the labor requirements of the public and private sectors. At best, government representation on governing bodies of the university and the other institutions can be reciprocally advantageous to the extent that it makes for greater coordination and harmonization of efforts.

Interinstitutional liaison and cooperation is achieved by joint committees with membership from the university and the respective tertiary institutions, thus ensuring that admission requirements and course content are in conformity with the norms set by the senate of the university.

A development of considerable importance has been the establishment of the Tertiary Education Commission (TEC) set up in May 1988 by Act of Parliament. The Commission addresses questions such as priorities in tertiary education, its infrastructure, and the cost effectiveness of various institutions comprising the tertiary sector: the university, MIE, MGI, and the Mauritius College of the Air (MCA).

The University of Mauritius and the tertiary institutions are almost wholly financed by the government with fees traditionally having contributed a very small percentage of the total cost. Since August 1988, fees have been abolished.

As a proportion of the gross national domestic product, expenditure on higher education peaked at 0.43 percent in 1978, kept decreasing until 1986, and stood in 1988 at about 20 percent higher than it was in 1970, when it amounted to 0.21 percent.

4. Faculty and Students: Teaching, Learning, and Research

4.1 Faculty

In the mid-1970s the university became severely constrained in terms of financial, physical, and human resources. By mid-1985, there existed 25 percent vacancies on all established posts and 35 percent on academic posts. In 1988 the full-time academic staff numbered 67 at the university, 72 at the MIE and 18 at the MGI. It is standard practice to have recourse to part-time lecturers in areas where expertise is limited.

Most of the academic staff have completed master's courses, except for some staff in the creative, practical, and technical areas which are still considered "scarcity areas." There is a pressing need for institutional strengthening in terms of staff development. The university and the tertiary sector in Mauritius, however, do not have sufficient funds to cover training expenses for their staff who have to compete for the occasional scholarship or fellowship.

Staff interests are represented by their respective associations with representatives on council and other important committees. Similarly students are grouped in unions and represented on senate and council. Staff associations are consulted in all matters affecting their interests and well-being.

4.2 Learning and Examinations

At the university, the main organization responsible for preparing courses is currently the school board (which bases its decisions primarily on work carried out by the relevant academic section). The General Purposes Committee (GPC) has the responsibility, on behalf of senate, of ensuring that any new course conforms to the minimum set of criteria already approved by senate (e.g., entry requirements and number of contact hours), that no school poaches on the territory of another, and that there is sufficient understanding between schools whenever more than one school is involved in any new course. Senate generally ratifies the course content, scheme of examinations, and so on, as recommended by the GPC. New courses and examinations are normally moderated by external examiners.

Senate, the supreme academic body, also ratifies the results of all examinations. Except for the odd case, such ratification or approval is a formality, required for legal purposes. These procedures, with minor variations, are followed by other tertiary institutions.

5. Conclusion

Small states are unquestionably disadvantaged in the matter of tertiary education, Mauritius being no exception. Steps are being taken to increase productivity in both the private and the public sectors by ensuring a highly trained labor force and by improving the level and organization of research and consultancy. There is a need to consolidate the tertiary sector in order to: (a) enhance productivity and efficiency, and (b) rationalize research and consultancy. These developments will require the university to invest heavily in both human and physical resources if it is to play its role fully. The outlook appears promising.

There is much ambiguity as to how the tertiary sector is going to address itself to its tasks and as to what organizational structure is most appropriate for the specific context of the country. The setting up of the Tertiary Education Commission (TEC) to bring about more coordination and cost efficiency seems to be no more than a half-way measure. There is a need for a more rational reorganization of the tertiary sector as a whole.

Bibliography

Bhujedhur S 1985 The historical development of higher education: Mauritius. In: Tempo L P et al. (eds.) 1985 *The Development of Higher Education in Eastern and Southern Africa*
Country Paper 1989 *International Symposium on Education*, Government of Mauritius
Leys C 1964 *Development of a University College of Mauritius*. MLA Sessional Paper No. 4
Manrakhan J 1985 *Manraj Visitorial Report*
Manrakhan J 1988 *Human Resources Development at the University of Mauritius*
Ramdoyal R 1977 *The Development of Education in Mauritius*. Mauritius Institute of Education

R. Ramdoyal

Mexico

1. Higher Education and Society

Mexico claims to be the first country in the Americas to have had a university. The Royal and Pontifical University of New Spain was created in 1551. The history of the Mexican university can thus be traced as far back as the sixteenth century, but nineteenth-century positivism and postrevolutionary goals (beginning in 1910 and continuing in the 1990s) constitute the roots of the country's contemporary higher education (Ornelas and Levy 1989).

Since the Mexican Revolution (1910–17), Mexico has formally been a democratic federal republic. Under the rule and control of one "revolutionary" party, the country has had more than five decades of civil government, institutional continuity, and social peace. From 1935 until 1982, it had a sustained economic growth rate, but one based on a dependent model of substitution of imports. Annual per capita Gross National Product (GNP) grew at an average of 3.02 percent (Cordera and Tello 1984 p. 9). Economists have noticed an important change since the 1970s, when the model sponsored proved insufficient

and the country entered a phase of severe foreign indebtedness, which fostered only increasingly shorter periods of economic growth. Since 1982, the country has suffered the most serious recession since the Second World War and growth of GNP was practically nonexistent until the start of the 1990s. Important changes in votecasting favoring the opposition parties during the 1988 presidential election shows the country is at a major turning point.

The country has always had a very high birthrate (4.5% in 1960 and 2.5% in 1985) which, together with better medical care resulting in a decrease in the death rate, produced extraordinary population growth. In 1990 the population had more than tripled in relation to 1950, having grown to 81,140,922 from 25,791,000. The population under 24 years of age still amounted to more than 63 percent of the total, a trend that will continue for years to come.

Urban population constitutes 66.3 percent of the total at the start of the 1990s, but the metropolitan area of Mexico City accounts for about a third of it. There are some 100,000 communities with less than 100 inhabitants.

One of the main characteristics of the Mexican economy is that it is mixed; public and private economic activities coexist and depend on each other in profound and intricate ways. Some of the main resources—oil, mining, electricity, telephones, irrigation, highways, and banking—are controlled by the state. The state has played a major role in development, not only controlling basic economic activities, but promoting and sponsoring huge institutions and programs intended to benefit society (public education and public health, for instance). The state labor market has played a growing role in absorbing up to 20 percent of the employed labor force. Private initiatives accounted for 74.4 percent of GNP in 1983 as well as most of the employment opportunities.

The years 1960–90 witnessed important changes in the general structure of the economy. The proportion of the population engaged in the primary sector diminished from 54.1 percent in 1960 to an estimated 23.6 percent in 1988. The tertiary sector (commerce, services, and government) has shown major growth, and engages 55.4 percent of the total labor force at the start of the 1990s. Since the 1940s the country has been operating an industrial development consolidating important industries: food and beverages, oil, petrochemistry, electricity, household appliances, paper, textiles, and cement and construction are among the main ones.

Occupational structure is extremely unequal and heterogeneous. An important trait is the coexistence of highly sophisticated organizations with traditional household productive units, most of which achieve mere subsistence living conditions. Informal labor markets coexist and interact with formal markets that are often smaller than the former.

Distribution of income also shows extreme inequalities: in 1984 (last available data) the top 10 percent of the population earned 34.6 percent of the country's total income, while the lowest 40 percent earned only 12.4 percent. Around 33 percent of the population did not earn the legal minimum salary, which amounts to some US$3.7 per day (Cortés and Rubalcava in press p. 27).

Public education has been one of the major concerns of postrevolutionary governments. Education has been conceived as the primary means for national integration, and for economic, social, and political development; it is guaranteed by the constitution. Public education is free.

In 1990 there were nearly 26 million students enrolled in the different levels of schooling: 67.8 percent in primary; 19 percent in lower secondary; 8.2 percent in upper secondary, and 5 percent in higher education and graduate studies. More than 90 percent of the school population is enrolled in public institutions. Despite impressive growth, education has been unable to overcome social and geographical inequalities. Illiteracy is still at 5.6 percent of the population and only about 55 percent of first graders complete the six years of primary schooling. The economic crisis of the last decade caused an important decrease in school opportunities, student enrollment, and graduation rates in all levels.

After decades of serious confrontation with the revolutionary government, the University of Mexico was granted autonomus status in 1933 and then national status in 1944. During the early 1920s, several local scientific and literary institutes in the federal states were transformed into universities, and were also granted autonomy. In 1938, the federal government created an institution that was to be its main instrument for the higher education of peasants and workers and the industrialization of the country. This was the National Polytechnic Institute after whose model, in 1948, the first technological institutes were created in other states.

The main private universities have been created since the 1940s, but private higher education began to play an increasingly large role only after 1960. A significant growth of graduate enrollment started in the late 1970s. Teacher training for elementary education was upgraded to higher education level in 1984.

Throughout the twentieth century, there has been important interaction between higher education and society. On the one hand, the state's major development programs were supported by higher education training of the top human resources and sustained the growth of professions that still attract most student enrollment (Cleaves 1987): engineering, involving the construction of highways, irrigation systems, electricity, housing, and, of course, oil; medicine, with the impressive growth of social security; agronomy and veterinary medicine, with the continually renewed efforts to solve the country's agricultural problems; and law, and later accounting and economics, which provide the major cadres of public officials, including the political elite of the country. The development of higher education after the 1970s provided an important academic labor market for all professions. The interaction has been a complex one that includes periods of serious disfunction as regards employment, social mobility, or response to national development needs.

On the other hand, most of the country's important social and political problems have found expression in the universities. During the 1960s, student movements posed the main challenges to economic policies and political control, and were violently repressed by the state in 1968 and 1971. During the 1970s, the major labor movements in the public sector were those organized by university professors to gain legal recognition for their unions and better salaries and fringe benefits from the state. Teachers' movements resulted in violent encounters with the police and even the army.

After 1970, the federal government launched an educational reform that brought about most of the major growth and changes prevailing in higher education in the early 1990s. Political forces found in the institutions of higher education an open space for experimenting with educational projects that would change society: left-wing democratic forces took over most public universities; the state sponsored a large number of directly controlled institutions; and private interests had a wide margin for the growth of private institutions (de Ibarrola 1986, Fuentes 1989a, Ornelas and Levy 1989).

2. The Institutional Fabric of the Higher Education System

An impressive growth of institutions starting in the late 1960s, is one of the basic traits of the fabric of higher education in Mexico in the early 1990s. There were 726 officially registered institutions in 1988, against only 57 in 1960.

Enrollment showed a spectacular growth of 1,415 percent during this period. Nevertheless, the proportion of the 20 to 24 age group enrolled in higher education reached only 17.2 percent in 1985. Data for 1988 clearly show a sharp decrease both in the rate of growth and enrollment in higher education by the cohort generation (see Table 1).

Growth was accompanied by few major changes in the structure of the system, the most important one being the upgrading of elementary teacher training to the status of a higher education degree in 1984. This change explains the sharp increase in the number of teacher-training institutions in 1985 (see Table 2). It

Table 1
Higher education total enrollment

	1960	1965	1970	1975	1980	1985	1988
First-degree studies	77,033	126,380	218,637	543,112	827,881	1,091,620	1,166,674
Percentage: public	90.5	85.6	86.2	88.0	84.4	82.2	82.6
Proportion of the age group 20–24	2.5	3.6	5.2	10.3	13.0	17.2	14.0
Graduate studies	—	—	5,753	—	25,503	37,040	39,505
Percentage: public	—	—	83.9	—	76.3	79.6	79.0

is also important to note the rate of growth and the resulting size of the different sectors of the system.

2.1 The Sectorial Organization of Higher Education

There are two legitimate higher education degree-granting systems in the country: the universities and the state.

The university system, the largest higher education system in the country, still accounts for 70.5 percent of enrollment. Autonomous public universities and a few private ones are authorized by federal congress or state legislatures to grant degrees. They are also authorized to supervise and control the curriculum and teaching staff of private institutions incorporated into the university system.

The state, through federal or state ministries of public education, directly controls a large number of public technological and teacher-training institutes. It also supervises the curricula and teaching staff of private institutions incorporated into this system which has had an accelerated rate of growth since 1970. It controls 86.5 percent of institutions and 29.5 percent of enrollment, including institutions created and operated by a few other federal, state, or municipal agencies authorized to grant degrees in areas of specialized interest to such sectors as the army, navy, agricultural, fine arts, and so on.

Public institutions, by far the most important with 82.6 percent of the total enrollment, are created and sponsored by federal or state governments; financed by public funds, public higher education is free.

After 1970, the growth of public higher education was mainly a federally sponsored endeavor that shows three trends: (a) the creation or strengthening of autonomous universities in most of the state's capital cities (the federal government contributes some 80 percent of the universities' financial allotments); (b) the creation of a large number of technological institutes in a wider range of geographical areas, including rural areas; and (c) the upgrading of normal schools to the higher education level in 1984.

Private institutions are permitted by law, on the condition they receive official endorsement by the state or an autonomous university. Their bigger and faster rate of growth, 2,685 percent during the period 1960–88, meant that they began to play a remarkable role compared to the insignificant one they had played up to the 1960s. The growth of private institutions shows two trends: (a) a small number of the old high-ranking universities, sponsored by monastic orders or powerful local or national business organ-

Table 2
Higher education institutions

	1960	1965	1970	1975	1980	1985	1988
First degree studies	57	75	116	175	269	521	726
Public institutions							
Universities	25	26	28	26	37	43	44
Technological institutes & other	9	17	36	67	81	112	110
Teacher training	5	5	9	16	25	126	240
Private institutions							
Universities	9	13	17		40	42	54
Other higher education institutes	6	10	20		69	136	157
Teacher training	3	4	6	10	17	62	121
Institutions that offer							
Graduate studies	—	—	13	—	102	150	152
Percentage: public	—	—	76.9	—	62.7	63.3	62.5

izations, have been opening branches in most of the important cities of the country (due to their efficiency in incorporating local elites and in strengthening the formation of local cadres, they have a fairly high prestige); and (b) a large number of profit-making small institutions, located mostly in the main cities, found a responsive market as a result of the general growth of education in the country and the expectations of social mobility that higher education creates. This kind of institution shows an absolute decrease in enrollments in 1988.

There are clear differences in the academic nature and scope of all the aforementioned institutions. Statistical classification does not accurately express these differences, as the label "university" is used rather freely to cover many private institutions.

Universities perform the three classic academic functions of higher education: teaching—at both the undergraduate and graduate levels and in most subject areas; research; and the dissemination of culture. Universities are completely autonomous in academic matters. There are some specialized agricultural universities and a National Pedagogic University for teachers.

Public technological institutes depend directly on federal or state departments of education. Curricula and internal authorities are decided at central levels. They were originally intended to include the three academic functions as part of their objectives but most of them reduce activities to professional training and all limit the scope of subject areas to specialized fields, mainly engineering and technological professions, or business administration and accounting. There are some 30 institutes oriented exclusively toward agriculture and forestry.

A large number of private nonuniversity institutions offer only professional training in a very small number of the less costly subject areas such as law, accounting, and business administration.

Research is viewed as part of public higher education in Mexico. In fact, most research, a precarious activity in the country, is carried out in academic institutions. With few exceptions, research has been promoted on a national level only since 1970, but in the early 1990s is suffering from a serious lack of academic consolidation. Since 1982 there has also

been a general lack of financing. No more than 10 private institutions integrate research and cultural dissemination as part of their academic functions.

The proliferation of small public and private establishments, offering only professional training in a small range of subject areas, constitutes a major trait of this institutional growth; 67 percent of them, mainly private technological and teacher-training institutes, have less than 500 students, and 50 percent have less than 200 students. Most public universities and only five private ones reach an enrollment of more than 5,000 students, while only five public universities have more than 50,000 students each.

2.2 Structure of Qualifications and Admissions Policies

The structure of qualifications is general to all institutions, regardless of differences aforementioned.

Higher education in Mexico starts at grade 13, after six years of elementary school, three years of lower-secondary school, and three years of upper-secondary school (*bachilleratos*), curricularly organized around six main subject areas leading to different professions. The official degree granted at the end of this last three-year period is called *bachillerato* (baccalaureate).

A special historical trait of higher education in Mexico is that the *bachilleratos* have been operated academically and administratively by the public sector universities, which explain the impressive size of institutions like the National University (350,000 students—almost 65% at the upper-secondary level) or the National Polytechnic Institute. After 1970, two upper-secondary education systems were created by the state to offer this certificate independently of the universities.

Admission to higher education requires only a baccalaureate certificate in the corresponding subject area and a pass grade in the entrance examination administered by each institution. Student movements during the 1960s obtained an automatic passage for students who had been awarded the baccalaureate certificate by the same university.

Some 80 percent of upper-secondary enrollments are concentrated in schools leading to the bacca-

Table 3
Financing

	1960	1965	1970	1975	1980	1985	1988
Percentage proportion of GNP	0.14	0.20	0.20	0.45	0.71	0.55	0.57
Percentage proportion of federal education expenses	10.7	11.6	10.7	14.9	21.5	18.8	22.5
Gross equivalent number of days at minimum wage per student/per year	234	—	126	143	216	192	210

laureate degree, in spite of opportunities for middle professional training that the federal government has been pushing insistently as a complement to the Educational Reform of the 1970s. There has also been a high continuity from grade 12 to grade 13 (up by 85%). These data show that admission into higher education is the main interest of Mexican students and that opening higher education to this legitimate demand has been a major goal of higher education policy.

Higher education in Mexico leads to specific professional training, requiring an average minimum of four years of course work, usually organized by semesters. (Some professions, mainly medicine, require a six-year curriculum.) Approval of each course depends exclusively on examinations freely applied by the teacher. There are no national or institutional standardized exams. Once the courses are completed, students can obtain an academic certificate of course work, with legal status on the labor market. No more than 60 percent of students achieve this legal status. Those that do become *pasantes* (professional assistants)—a category that has been widely accepted in the labor market.

In order to obtain the first degree, *licenciatura* (licenciate), several other requirements must be fulfilled: a compulsory six-month period of social service has been traditionally required, and is now established by the Federal Law of Education. Other requirements, that may vary among institutions are: thesis; final examination; and an examination proficiency in one or two foreign languages.

There are no nationally available data on rates of graduation (i.e., the number of students actually completing all the aforementioned requirements). Estimations account for some 20 percent of first enrollers.

Licenciate degrees are awarded by the institutions and allow the graduate to obtain from the state a professional patent, professional activities in the country being restricted by law to people with professional training at the higher education level. Once an institution has awarded a degree, there are no further examinations of professional qualifications by any other public or private agency.

Graduate studies offer specialized diplomas in the professions and two academic degrees: master's and doctorate. The degrees are granted in the specific subject area: chemistry; biology; mathematics; engineering; and so forth. Generally, but not always, the previous degree is required for admission to the corresponding level of studies. Admittance is obtained through an entrance examination or a rigorous process of selection administered by each institution. Enrollment in graduate studies starts at grade 17.

Specialized diplomas usually require one year of coursework and a professional thesis; masters' require two years of coursework and a thesis; and

doctorate degrees three additional years and a thesis based on original research.

Only 3.5 percent of the total higher education enrollment corresponds to graduate studies, mostly at the specialty level and with a mere 1,303 students enrolled in doctorate programs. There are no data available before 1970, but the rate of growth since then has been proportionally higher than in first degree studies; and so too has been the growth of private graduate enrollment.

3. Governance, Administration, and Finance

3.1 National Administration

A strong relationship between all higher education and the state shows two main differences: autonomy and dependence.

Autonomy means a formal legal separation between the state and institutions of higher education, and the right and responsibility for self-government; it is granted by a public act of federal congress or state legislature. In addition, public autonomous universities are almost totally financed by the state.

In the early 1990s, out of 726 institutions, 33 public and 6 private universities are autonomous, but they absorb almost 50 percent of total enrollment.

Autonomy has had a long and sometimes violent history in the country. In 1980, as a result of various labor movements among academic personnel, it was incorporated into the nation's constitution as a constitutional guarantee.

Dependence on state authority has different degrees:

(a) Some state universities depend on local government only for the appointment of top authorities but otherwise have freedom in their internal academic decisions.

(b) In contrast, technological institutes and teacher-training institutions depend on the state for all internal government and academic decisions: the appointment of authorities, the approval of teaching staff, and the decision on the curricula.

(c) As already mentioned, most private institutions of higher education must have their academic degrees endorsed by a public authority, which means a high degree of state control over curricula and teaching processes.

Since the late 1960s there has been a sustained effort to plan higher education on a national basis.

In 1970 the National Council for Science and Technology was created. Its main functions have been to promote graduate studies, by means of individual scholarships both within the country and abroad, and sponsor scientific and technological research.

In 1978 a Law for the Coordination of Higher Education was enacted. The prime responsibility for the development of higher education was given to the

Federal Ministry of Education. This top coordinating agency has shaped higher education mainly by budgetary control, political influence, and the initiative for national legislation on higher education matters.

The National Association of Universities and Institutions of Higher Education (ANUIES, created in 1959) has been steadily promoted by the same ministry in order to guarantee the formal democratic participation of all institutions. It constitutes the other main body with responsibility for the shaping of higher education in the country.

Since 1978, both agencies have worked together to produce national higher education plans. They produced a permanent, formal structure for the planning of higher education on a national level that includes a planning office in each institution of higher education, a state council, a regional council, and a national council in a pyramidal organization.

A real conflict exists between long-term academic planning and the strong participation of the federal government. The change of federal authorities every six years produces new plans every time.

Nevertheless, although with different wording and different emphasis, successive national plans have repeatedly set the following national goals:

(a) equality and democratization of higher education opportunities—increased admissions according to "social demand" and geographical redistribution of opportunities;

(b) the establishment of strong links between higher education and the social and economic needs of development—rechanneling of student enrollment toward the subject areas thought to promote development and emphasis on higher education as the moving force for scientific and technological development;

(c) quality of higher education—emphasis on the recruitment of full-time teachers, better on-the-job teacher training, modernization of curricula, and pedagogical innovations;

(d) the optimization of national resources for higher education through an adequate coordination of all institutions;

(e) decentralization of decision making.

National plans are not compulsory; the goals set are supposed to be a frame of reference for each institution. Planning is more a formal exercise in conceptualizing than a strategy that integrates the actual social forces, mechanisms, and negotiations that shape the real development of higher education in the country. Only in the early 1990s has national and institutional evaluation been enforced.

One of the main results of this coordinated planning has been the creation of a National System of Higher Education Information in 1982 that drew up a common format and a degree of continuity in higher education statistical data. However, the lack of information is still a main obstacle in the diagnosis and evaluation of higher education.

3.2 Finance

In 1988, 964,565 students were enrolled in public free institutions. This figure gives an idea of the magnitude of financial requirements.

The prime source of finance for higher education in the country, including graduate studies and research, is the Mexican state, which contributes about 80 percent of all expenses, mainly through the federal government. Private education represents 15 percent, and public institutions themselves contribute no more than 5 percent.

As regards financing, the following main characteristics are noteworthy:

(a) The state has maintained a steady increase in budgetary allotments to higher education, which have been proportionally higher than enrollment and growth of teaching positions. This is shown in the growing proportion of the GNP devoted to higher education and the growing proportion of higher education in the total federal budget for education (Noriega 1985).

(b) Nevertheless, the actual amount assigned to every student per year has always been barely adequate if measured in the equivalent daily minimum wage (see Table 3).

(c) As of 1970, serious thought has been given to alternative ways for financing public higher education. The only one enforced in several institutions was "scholarships on credit." No

Table 4
Higher education teaching staff[a]

	1970	1975	1980	1985	1988
First-degree studies	24,026	47,529	72,958	103,568	113,179
Percentage: full-time	8.1	—	16.5	20.8	22.3
Graduate studies	375	—	1,072	9,046	9,852
Percentage: full-time	46.1	—	52.2	24.1	27.5

a Data available as of 1970

467

evaluation of the success or impact of this measure has been made.

(d) The distribution of resources among institutions, although said to be the result of rational criteria, shows inequalities among institutions that speak of compromises and political influences.

(e) After 1960, privately financed education had a significant growth.

(f) During the last decade, and especially after 1982, the rate of growth of public financial resources dedicated to higher education decreased. At the same time, enrollment and teacher recruitment grew; the equation was solved by restricting salaries and all other institutional expenses. Salaries have been absorbing up to 90 percent of institutional budget in recent years.

3.3 Institutional Administration

Professional training is historically the most important function of all Mexican institutes of higher education, one that absorbs up to 90 percent of the budget and about 70 percent of human resources.

Most universities are organized in professional schools or faculties, the latter authorized to undertake graduate studies and grant master's and doctorate degrees. The academic scope of each is determined by the professional content, and the basic unit of the curriculum is the single-subject course.

Each school or faculty is academically self-sufficient; all the courses established by the curriculum are conceived within the profession's interest and taught within the establishment. In this respect, there are hardly any academic relations among schools or faculties of the same university.

In 1973 there was a national agreement for the use of credits but they have turned out to be more of an administrative measure than a means to academic equivalence and exchange. Although professional curricula always include a small percentage of optional credits, they usually dictate a compulsory and very rigid one-track sequence for all students enrolled.

Research institutes are separated from schools or faculties and organized within the range of academic disciplines. This kind of organizational structure also determines a wide gap between research and teaching, although researchers in research institutes have a small compulsory teaching period per week. In the national university, faculties have established internal research centers to integrate the research function of full-time teachers.

It is important to add that master's and doctorate degrees are generally awarded by faculties. A very small number of institutions is exclusively oriented to both graduate studies and research.

Universities' cultural activities are usually separated from both teaching and research.

Technological and teacher-training institutes are organized by professional careers. Curricula usually include a common body of subjects for the main profession, and a particular body of subjects for the area or speciality. The creation of a large number of new institutions after 1970 hardly changed this pattern of academic organization. Most of the new institutions adopted the professional curriculum and the school/faculty/institute scheme.

Nevertheless, during the early 1970s, the National University, the National Polytechnic Institute, and the federal government created new institutions that introduced important innovations. The innovative principles were both academic and organizational: new professions; interdisciplinary studies; a modular integration of subject courses; integration of research and teaching; a major role assigned to students in the classroom dynamics; departmentalization; inter-institutional links for the optimum use of resources; and a preference for full-time professors. Enrollment in these new institutions amounts to almost 9 percent of total.

The Open University system was also approved in the 1970s, but it was not able to change the rigidity of professional curricula or to benefit from mass media or nonscholastic educational experiences. It had a favorable reception only in a very small number of institutions and has not had an important impact in enrollment, except in the National Pedagogic University for the training of in-service teachers.

3.4 Models of Governance

The relationship of institutions of higher education with the state determines two major differences in internal models of governance.

Universities are governed and administered by internally appointed authorities that include collegiate bodies and individual executives. The hierarchical relationship between them confers formal higher authority on collegiate bodies. The schools, faculties, and research institutes which constitute the basic units of the institutions follow the same model.

The top collegiate body is the university council. In all universities it brings together representatives of authorities, faculty, students, and other employees. Important differences depend on the proportional representation of these institutional actors and the means for their election.

In most cases, teacher and student representatives are elected to the council by individual vote of peers, not by associations or unions. Researchers only very recently acquired a right to be represented at the university council which is responsible for all internal legislation and academic decisions.

Following a model set by the National University some universities have a board of government: a rather small collegiate body of up to 15 prestigious academics usually nominated by the university council, whose main functions are to appoint the internal authorities and solve conflicts unforeseen in the internal legislation.

The different models for the appointment of rectors also reveal differences among universities: by universal and secret vote, or by weighted vote, of teachers, students, and employees; or by internal appointment decided by an internal collegiate body. Nonautonomous universities may have their rector appointed by the state governor, sometimes restricted to a list proposed by the university council.

Public technological and teacher-training institutes have a completely different model of governance. Academic and governance decisions, as well as the appointment of directors, are made at top levels in the Ministry of Education. The law for the Coordination of Higher Education established national councils for each sector. These councils are made up of all the corresponding officials of central ministry offices and by a small number of prestigious academics whose functions are advisory.

These major formal models actually determine the extreme limits of internal governance. Daily operation has been shaped increasingly by internal negotiations between a growing technobureaucratic power, highly versed in budgetary intricacies and educational technology, and teachers' unions.

4. Faculty and Students: Teaching, Learning, and Research

4.1 Faculty

Prior to 1970, teachers of higher education were mainly (90% or more) active professionals who taught one or two single subjects as a means of acquiring academic prestige, rather than added income.

The impressive growth of enrollment and the diversification of institutions brought important quantitative and qualitative changes in the teaching body of higher education. Economic recession also explained the fact that institutions themselves turned into an important labor market for licenciate graduates or even students completing their fourth year of study.

The main changes can be described as follows (de Ibarrola 1986, Kent 1989):

(a) Growth in teacher recruitment meant an annual average of some 4,000 new teachers, most of them drawn from recent leavers without professional experience or academic training. The process still goes on, although at a lower rate.

(b) There has been an intrinsic qualitative change in the functions and identity of higher education teaching, as the number of full-time teachers steadily grew to 22.3 percent. Teaching still relies heavily on single-subject teachers, and for an unidentified number of them, the main pro-

fessional function and source of income is to give classes in different institutions (see Table 4).

Universities and other institutes of higher education now offer paths for a full-time and exclusively academic career. By statute, full-time teachers are expected to give classes for a maximum of an 18-hour period per week each semester. The rest of their time should be dedicated to research. The academic career is formally highly hierarchical, with some nine ranks between the lowest and the highest: teacher's assistant "A" and full professor "D", respectively.

According to the model set by the National University's Faculty Statute, formal recruitment or promotion is the responsibility of each institution and requires a competitive examination evaluated by an appropriate collegiate academic body. The statute establishes the minimum requirements to be met. For instance, an assistant teacher only requires completion of 75 percent of course credits of a professional curriculum. An associate professor requires a licenciate degree or equivalent, plus one year of experience, and one significant contribution to teaching or research. A full professor requires a doctorate or equivalent, six years of experience in teaching or research, academic achievements of a high standard with national or international recognition, and taught students to be established as teachers or researchers.

Teachers in autonomous universities have by statute full teaching freedom. The principle is generally accepted, but the concept seldom applies in universities as teachers are less experienced in academic and professional content and have to teach "by the book."

In almost all institutions, the approval of a competitive examination grants tenure status in the specific rank. However, an unspecified number of teachers have been directly recruited by authorities over a number of years on an annual contract basis.

Due to the accelerated long-term process of teacher recruitment and the power of academic unions during the 1970s, many institutions may have a wide gap between early formal tenure status and actual fulfillment of academic qualifications (Fuentes 1989a). An analysis of teachers' qualifications or of full-time, single-subject teachers' ratio by geographical regions or institutions would show sharp inequalities.

(c) Public university teachers had been regarded as state employees and as such, by law, had certain restrictions in labor rights. During the 1970s and early 1980s, teachers' movements centered on the labor and political aspects of creating institutional unions, defining labor legislation to be applied and unions' participation in academic matters. In 1980, they achieved a major change in the national constitution and in the federal labor law. Autonomy is now a constitutional guarantee and teachers are recognized as workers with specific identity and full labor rights, including the right to strike. Recruitment and promotion are considered academic matters and unions have no intervention in them.

Teachers in state-controlled public higher education institutions are still regulated by state employees' statutes. Most are members of the powerful National Union of Educational Workers and have union intervention in academic matters.

(d) The federal government control of budget allowances and financing of public higher education institutions, forced a bilateral relation between teachers' unions and the federal budget authorities. Negotiations finally resulted in an informal but nevertheless powerful "national model" of higher education salaries and fringe benefits that neglected and restrained quality differences.

(e) Research and graduate studies had a twofold development. In most new small institutions there was hardly any real support apart from salaries for full-time teachers. In the high-ranking graduate centers, principal universities, or technological institutes, the situation was different. Full-time professors, usually with graduate studies in prestigious foreign universities were attached to research institutes. Highly qualified and with due institutional support they were able to construct different, but very selective, internationally prestigious academic networks.

In order to escape the strict salary restrictions set by the higher education salaries "model," the National Academy of Research fostered in 1984 the creation of an additional incomes system—the National Researchers' System—arguing for actual and potential brain drain. This system, financed by the Federal Ministry of Education, may double researchers' income according to merit, evaluated by a national collegiate academic body of highly prestigious academics. In 1988, there were 3,927 national researchers in the country.

4.2 Students

An impressive growth of student enrollment from 1960 onwards has brought important changes in the composition of the student body that can be summarized as follows:

(a) The creation of new institutions in a wider range of geographical areas changed the pattern of opportunities throughout the country. In 1970,

85.7 percent of enrollment was concentrated in the four main cities, Mexico City concentrating 60.7 percent. In 1988 this figure had diminished to 47.1 percent, with Mexico City concentrating only 23.6 percent of total enrollment. Each federal state has at least three institutions of higher education.

(b) As regards social origins, the new opportunities were used in a threefold manner (de Ibarrola 1986, Fuentes 1989a): by most upper-class and by a large percentage of middle-class youth, but also by a significant number of working-class or peasant students who have been able to reach higher education mainly through teacher-training and technological institutes.

(c) In spite of these changes, the different geographical areas of the country still show inequalities clearly correlated to regional socioeconomic development and, on a national basis, enrollment per social class could turn out to be highly correlated to specific institutions.

(d) A large number of students are first generation in higher education, with illiterate parents or parents who hardly had an elementary schooling. This has produced an important change in the cultural environment of higher education, and determines the poor academic demands students can make (Fuentes 1989a, Kent 1989).

(e) The number of different professional curricula, some highly specialized, increased to 443. But almost 50 percent of total enrollment is still in only 10 professions: teaching 11.4 percent; accounting 9.9 percent; law 8.6 percent; medicine 5.1 percent; business administration 3.5 percent; civil engineering 3.4 percent; psychology 2.0 percent; veterinary medicine 1.8 percent; economics 1.7 percent; and mechanical engineering 1.7 percent.

Student enrollment is still concentrated in social sciences and humanities, but there are in fact very modern administrative professions, highly functional to a dependent economic structure. National policies produced changes only in agriculture and medicine enrollments (see Table 5).

(f) Perhaps the most important change in student composition during the period was the increasing participation of women in higher education. In the eighteen-year period, women's participation grew 3,526 percent. They now constitute 40.7 percent of total enrollment. Several researchers have pointed out the "feminization" of enrollment, specially in certain subject areas, but the actual effects this trend has had on higher education are not really known (Fuentes 1989a, Kent 1989) (see Table 6).

Table 5
Percentage of first-degree students across the main subject areas

	1960	1965	1980	1985	1988	Participation of women per area 1988
Exact sciences	4.7	4.9	2.8	2.5	2.4	39.6
Technology/engineering	31.7	27.1	23.2	24.9	26.3	19.6
Medicine	19.7	16.4	19.0	11.6	9.8	53.4
Agriculture	2.5	3.2	8.0	8.1	6.2	14.5
Social sciences	31.7	37.5	32.9	38.8	41.2	48.5
Humanities	9.7	10.9	14.1	14.1	14.1	59.1

(g) The severe economic crisis which started in 1982 brought about a clear decrease in rates of enrollment. In some subject areas, in specific institutions and in women's enrollment, the decrease has been larger.

(h) Growth of higher education opportunities has meant for many little more than the chance to enroll. Severe dropout after the first semesters still limit the percentage of students completing the four-year courses to a decreasing rate of less than 60 percent. In addition, fulfillment of all graduation requirements has been constantly low, about 20 percent. There are important differences in this percentage according to specific professions. It is significantly higher in professions more controlled by law and by guilds (see Table 7).

(i) Although there are no empirical evaluations, there is an impression that quality has been generally low (Fuentes 1986, de Ibarrola 1986). One factor is the hasty planning of curricula or the teaching of new professions where institutions have not been able to find qualified faculty or adapt professional knowledge to significant pedagogic content (Tedesco 1986).

Other factors derive from the usual pattern for undergraduate courses: poor institutional infrastructure as regards libraries and laboratories; poor teachers' qualifications; dialogue between teachers and students based on one textbook or teacher's notes; and abstract classroom work separated from laboratory work or professional practices, the latter always barely sufficient in equipment or frequency. About 50 percent of students work full-time, rarely in activities related to their profession. Frequent absenteeism by both teachers and students has turned into usual practice.

(j) Students' impact on higher education has been due to their informal but very strong political organization at key moments. Opportunities, rather than strict academic matters, have been their aims. Besides protests on all manner of national or international issues, during the 1960s students achieved automatic passage to higher education, changes in examination regulations, and parity participation in universities' internal governance. During the 1970s, the student movement was latent, and political mobilization in higher education was led by new teachers, who had just stopped being students themselves. Only in 1986 did students in the National University once again show an extraordinary capacity for sudden organization and political strength. Their strong movements invalidated measures supposed to improve quality but clearly restricting opportunities.

(k) Achieving a higher education professional training, even if it is just for one or two semesters, still plays a significant role in employment in two ways: (i) it offers a better probability for incorporation into the formal sector of the economy, although on a devalued basis that will vary in time, regions, or subject areas according to employment opportunities. The growth of unemployment rate during the decade has certainly affected higher education students; and (ii) there seem to be clearly segmented tracks to different kinds of employment according to the type of institution.

(l) Graduate enrollment grew mainly at the specialization and master level as a means to upgrading a poorly qualified licenciate degree. The labor market rarely demands a graduate degree but graduate students are achieving the best posi-

Table 6
Percentage participation of women in total enrollment[a]

1970	1975[b]	1980	1985	1988
17.0	26.3	32.1	36.8	40.6

a Data available as of 1970   b Data available for 1977

Table 7
Numbers of students completing initial courses[ab]

	1970	1975	1980	1985	1987
First degree studies	22,722	52,185	69,572	97,496	117,378
Percentage enrollment four years before	—	57.1	48.5	49.0	50.7
Graduate studies	1,126	—	2,334	6,634	7,900

a Teacher training not included   b Data available as of 1970

tions in the formal public and private labor market (de Ibarrola 1986).

5. Conclusion

During the last 30 years, but especially between 1970 and 1982, Mexican higher education witnessed major growth.

It gave rise to a "jostled" creation of institutions, massive enrollment, and faculty recruitment (Kent 1989) that brought a certain democratization of higher education as conceived during the late 1960s in terms of enrollment opportunities. Major changes in the geographical distribution of institutions and access opened to working-class and peasant students, to children of illiterate parents, and to women, all of which accounted for this democratization. At the same time, important geographical and socioeconomic inequalities persist, and the participation of higher education both in all school enrollment and the cohort generation is still rather limited.

Graduation opportunities did not grow at the same rate; about half of the population enrolled are unable to finish the four-year courses and some 80 percent never graduate.

The causal role attributed to higher education in scientific and technological development has not been "visible" in the same scale of time or space (Brunner 1988). On the contrary, during the last 20 years, the growth of higher education was not accompanied by economic growth; a clear recession and unemployment and underemployment have seriously affected students and graduates, thus contributing to a general disappointment in higher education.

Higher education institutions have not been able to change the concentration of student enrollment in certain specific professions, but during the period key institutions and professions were designed and have developed, some to high standards, according to resources available (including curricular and faculty knowledge), students' interests and labor market opportunities.

Consolidation of a "bottom heavy" (Clark cited in Brunner 1988) academic strength in the Mexican higher education system, the only kind that could support superior quality, was held back by different

factors. That many institutions were created mainly by bureaucratic decision or for profits implied that most academic work was pending. The accelerated growth of the teaching corps forced the recruitment of personnel without academic or even professional training. Intense loyalty of new teachers to labor organization set aside academic work. The lack of support by academic authorities to teachers' organizations, that could immediately turn into powerful unions, cut the necessary collective and institutional support for academic creation. The academic emphasis on professional training and single-subject teaching meant that new teachers acquired only very fragmented knowledge on the job. That a large number of students are the first generation enrollments in higher education changed drastically the cultural environment of higher education. It determined the poverty of academic demands placed by the principal actors.

Growth brought along a disintegration of the "decisive units of the system" (Brunner 1988). More than 65 percent of the new institutions have no more than 500 students. An apparently strong central control, led by the federal Ministry of Education, has not been able to integrate an extremely "loosely adjusted" system. This latter has been shaped mainly by political forces that operate through unknown informal organizations and that have been unable to integrate academic content with macrostructural and educational goals.

Financial resources, coming mainly from the federal government, have been barely adequate and since 1982 clearly insufficient, provoking a serious decline in academic working conditions (Fuentes 1989b).

Institutional growth has been extremely unequal as regards resources available for each institution, number, and qualification of teachers, academic infrastructure, and internal organization for fostering fruitful development of academic work. Inequality has produced a clear segmentation among and within institutions, both public and private, as regards the quality of professional and academic training, increasingly related to both the social class origins of students and the degree of acceptance they have in the formal labor market (Fuentes 1986).

As of 1982, this growth seems to have run out.

Actual decrease in enrollment, exhaustion of the main financial source, and decrease in graduation rates in all previous school levels reinforce this impression.

As "disenchantment" turned out to be the corollary to growth so enforced, there is a wide consensus among planners, researchers, but most important, actors themselves, that Mexican higher education has reached a profound turning point (Ornelas and Levy 1989).

The major risk lies in a dual strategy that could enforce selective modernization of a small number of "efficient institutions," leaving the rest of the system to undergo extensive decline (Fuentes 1989b).

The major challenge is the pursuit of both democracy and quality (Tedesco 1986) through the coordinated and collective consolidation of the institutional academic levels that have been so disregarded.

An important human and physical infrastructure is already available and an important historical experience is in the hands of the main actors. These are the main resources to successfully meet this challenge.

Bibliography

ANUIES 1973 *La enseñanza superior en México 1970.* ANUIES, Mexico City
ANUIES 1976 *La enseñanza superior en México 1970–1976.* ANUIES, Mexico City
ANUIES 1977, 1980, 1985, 1988 *Statistical yearbooks*
Banco de México 1989 *Carpeta de indicadores económicos 1989.* Banco de México, Mexico City
Brunner J J 1988 Notas para una teoría del cambio en los sistemas de educación superior. FLACSO, Santiago
Cleaves P S 1987 *Professions and the State: The Mexican Case.* University of Arizona Press, Tucson, Arizona
Cordera R, Tello C (eds.) 1984 La desigualdad en México. *Siglo XXI*, Mexico City
Cortés F, Rubalcava R M in press (*Autoexplotación forzada y equidad por empobrecimiento. La distribución del ingreso familiar en México (1977–1984)*, El Colegio de México, Mexico City, pp. 1–129
de Ibarrola M 1984 El crecimiento de la escolaridad superior en México como expresión de los proyectos socioeducativos del estado y la burguesía. *Revista Mexicana de Sociología* 2: 173–244
de Ibarrola M 1986 *La educación superior en México.* CRESALC-UNESCO, Caracas
Didriksson T A 1987 *La planeación de la éducación en México.* Universidad Autónoma de Sinaloa, Mexico City
Fuentes O 1986 Crecimiento y diferenciación del sistema universitario. El caso de México. *Critica (Revista de la UAP, México)* 26–27
Fuentes O 1989a La educación superior en México y los escenarios de su desarrollo future. *Universidad futura 3.* UAM-A, Mexico City
Fuentes O 1989b *Universidad y democracia en México. La mirada hacia la izquierda.* Contribuciones 59, FLACSO, Santiago
Kent R 1989 *Los profesores de la UNAM en los años setenta:*
Modernización autoritaria y crisis académica. Nueva Imagen, Mexico City
Lajous, V A 1967 *Aspectos de la educación superior y el empleo de profesionistas en México 1959–1967.* ENEP-UNAM, Mexico City
Levy C 1986 *Higher Education and the State in Latin America.* The University of Chicago Press, Chicago, Illinois
Nacional Financiera 1986 *La economía mexicana en cifras, 1986.* Nacional Financiera, Mexico City
Noriega M 1985 *La política educativa a través de la política de financiamiento.* UAS, Mexico City, pp. 34, 53, 75
Ornelas C, Levy D C 1989 Mexico: The challenge of adaptation. In: Altbach P (ed.) 1989 *International Encyclopedia of Comparative Higher Education.* Garland, New York
Padua J N Presiones y resistencias al cambio en la educación superior de México. *Estudios sociológicos de el Colegio de México* 16: 129–78
SEP/ANUIES 1981a National Plan of Higher Education, 1981–1991
SEP/ANUIES 1981b National Program of Higher Education (PRONAES) 1981–1984
SEP/ANUIES 1986 Integrated Program for the Development of Higher Education (PROIDES)
SEP/CONAPO/CELADE *Estimaciones y proyecciones de población 1950–2000.* s.p.i., Mexico City
SEP 1982 *México: Información sobre aspectos geográficos, sociales y económicos*, Vol. 2. Coordinación general de los servicios nacionales de estadística, geografía e informática, Mexico City
SEP 1988 *Compendio estadistico del gasto educativo 1988.* SEP, Mexico City, pp. 49–50
Solana F et al. 1981 *Historia de la educación pública en México.* SEP/FCE, Mexico City
Tedesco J C 1986 Calidad y democracia en la enseñanza superior: un objetivo posible y necesario. *Critica (Revista de la UAP, México)* 26–27: 17–31

M. de Ibarrola

Mongolia

1. Higher Education and Society

From 1690 until the early 1900s, Mongolia was governed by the Manchus who promoted Lamaist teaching and an essentially subsistence economy among the nomadic tribes. Ulan Bator (sometimes spelled Ulaanbaatar, or "red hero"), the capital, was established in 1639 with the foundation of the Da Khure Monastery, the residence of the *bodgo gegen*, or the living Buddha, who ranked third among the dignitaries of the Buddhist Lamaist religion.

A revolutionary struggle culminated with the declaration of the People's Republic in 1924. The Mongolian Constitution, adopted in 1960, states that the country is a socialist state of workers, *arats* organized in cooperatives, and working intellectuals, in the form of a people's democracy (Dash et al. 1990, Spaulding 1990). Since the earliest days of the Republic, the Lamaist religion has been separated from both government and educational activity, although formal freedom of worship exists and there are still elements of a variety of religious practices (Lamaism, Buddhism, Shamanism, Islam, and others) in the country. Until the late 1980s, real political power resided solely in the Mongolian People's Revolutionary Party, but in late 1989 and during 1990, there were nationalist movements culminating in a new multiparty system and a new government, with a legislature and a president with powers similar to those of the former party and its chairman.

Mongolia, home of the Mongols, covers an area of 1,565,000 kilometers—more than twice the size of Turkey and four times that of Japan. Mongolia is landlocked, bordered on the north by the Soviet Union and the south by China. The distance from west to east is as far as from Paris to Moscow. It has an average altitude of about 1,600 meters, and can be divided into roughly three regions: upland steppes, semideserts and deserts. Nearly four-fifths of the country consists of pasture lands which support enormous herds of grazing livestock. The remaining area is divided between forests and barren deserts. An important part of the country is covered by the Gobi Desert and three major mountain ranges which thrust into the country from the north and west.

The population is now in excess of two million, well over half of whom are under 20 years of age, and three-quarters under 40. The average population density (late 1980s) is only 1.22 people per square kilometer. Since the mid-1970s, the average annual rate of population increase has been 2.6 to 2.7 percent, resulting in a doubling of the population. In 1985, 44.8 percent of the population was in the age group 1–15. For every 100 people of working age, there were 112 below that age, including 95 children. About a third of the population is economically active.

Although it is estimated that two-thirds of the economically active population is engaged in rural activity, primarily as farmers and livestock breeders (UNESCO 1990a), there is a tendency to abandon the nomadic life and it is estimated that 53 percent of the population are now settled in cities and towns, 26 percent in the capital, Ulan Bator, alone. Urban dwellers, especially in the larger towns, are increasingly alienated from traditional agricultural occupations, particularly pasturable cattle breeding, while at the same time there is unemployment in the urban areas.

The main agricultural resource is great herds of livestock (which make up about 70% of all agricultural production). These have increased throughout the twentieth century and provide a valuable export commodity. Most livestock is produced by giant cooperatives, mostly organized in the late 1950s, owning an average of 1,700 square miles in area.

Less than one percent of the total land mass is arable and because of short summers, only one annual crop is possible. About four-fifths of the cropland is in grain, and the rest in fodder crops (hay). Potatoes and vegetables occupy only a tiny fraction of the crop area. About four-fifths of the cropland is farmed by state farms (averaging 700 square miles in size), and the rest by cooperatives.

Mongolia is rich in mineral resources (coal, iron, tin, copper, gold, and silver), some of which are exploited. The northern rivers of Mongolia have great potential for hydroelectric development and timber is logged from mountain forests which cover about 10 percent of the land area.

Much of Mongolia's industry is engaged in processing raw materials or meeting basic domestic consumer needs. Processing industries for livestock raw materials, together with food and other light industries, contribute about 40 percent of the aggregate industrial and agricultural output. There is a mining operation at Erdenet which concentrates copper and molybdenum ores and which accounts for about 40 percent of the country's exports. Ulan Bator is the center for light industry, and heavy industry is concentrated in Darhan, where there are a number of projects which have been developed in cooperation with the Soviet Union and Eastern European countries. Forest products are processed in Sukhbaatar. There is a small but well-established tourist industry, attracting visitors worldwide, which concentrates on organizing hunting expeditions into the mountains, where a number of exotic wild animals exist in abundance.

Since 1970, there have been major efforts to reconstruct the economy. From 1970–1985, the proportion of industrial enterprises' contribution to the national income rose from 28.6 percent to 50.9 percent. During this period, the average salary of workers increased by 20.1 percent and material production increased by 23.1 percent. In the early 1990s the economy appears to be growing at somewhere between 3.3 and 3.8 percent a year. Nonetheless, agricultural production was stagnant during most of the 1980s, and sectors of the economy such as construction suffer chronic shortages of materials and delays in the acquisition of necessary machinery.

In the late 1980s, 34.1 percent of social sector funds were allocated to pensions and relief; 8.7 percent to fellowships; 18.6 percent to health services and physical culture training; 24.8 percent to cultural services and 3.8 percent to other allowances and free services.

At its 19th Congress in May 1986, the Mongolian People's Revolutionary Party decided on a national strategy of restructuring the economy and society in general. Subsequently Batmonh, the Secretary General of the Mongolian People's Revolutionary Party, suggested at the country's trade union congress in May 1988, that there was a "lack of dynamism" in carrying out party resolutions and that trade unions should rid themselves of bureaucracy and practice openness, frankness, and democracy. Later, in December 1988, the party's central committee at its fifth plenary meeting, decided that renewal (*shinechiel*) and restructuring of all sectors of the socioeconomic structure should be intensified.

As part of the restructuring, the number of decision-making bodies has been reduced, and a law on the state enterprises was enacted, giving grass-roots organizations and enterprises more decision-making authority. Since the mid-1980s, new management initiatives allow greater flexibility in planning and the use of economic incentives. Since 1988, national planning officials set only a limited number of economic targets. Production enterprises, in turn, plan their own work in the light of contracts and orders received.

Since 1986 there has also been increasing encouragement of private enterprise. The Council of Ministers in the late 1980s announced an ordinance encouraging the formation of private cooperatives for the provision of services or for small-scale manufacturing or processing. In December 1987, there was a relaxation of the limit on privately owned livestock. It is estimated that over 25 percent of Mongolia's livestock is in private hands, and the ratio may increase rapidly if reform efforts and political changes accelerate during the 1990s.

Preliminary projections to 2005, using 1985 as a base, suggest that the gross national product will rise by 230–300 percent, with an annual rate of growth of 7.8 percent. This will require an increase in labor productivity of some 400–500 percent, thus requiring much higher levels of technological inputs into the production processes. The government expects all educational and scientific research institutes to be involved in the process of adapting science and technology to the production needs of the country.

Renewal policies and the winds of *perestroika* and *glasnost* from across the border in the Soviet Union have led to dramatic events during late 1989 through 1990. During this period, the one-party government resigned, a system of government involving multiparty elections was installed, and a new, strongly nationalist government has emerged. The Minister of Education under the new government, Mr N Urtnasan, in a letter of October 13, 1990 to the Assistant Director General of UNESCO, Colin Power, suggested that "thanks to 'winds of change' in political, economic, and social life there are great changes going on in the field of education." Among other changes noted by the Minister in an October 1990 interview with a UNESCO official visiting the country is that Mongolia will no longer blindly copy the "European system" (i.e., the Soviet system) while discarding even the finest parts of local tradition. The Minister called for greater exchange of experience with other Asian nations and indicated that there was to be a better balanced and harmonized development of education in the future, essential for the development of Mongolia as an independent nation. He suggested that, during the 1990s, the rural education system would be reformed to reduce the number of urban boarding schools which cut rural children off from their rural and nomadic roots. This effectively reverses a policy of the former regime which had planned as late as 1989 (Dash et al. 1990) to expand the boarding school scheme to encompass all rural children. Education would be moved closer to the life environment of the children. Further, there would be emphasis on distance education, because of the sparse and thinly spread population. Finally, he suggested, the great emphasis on Russian as a second language would be supplemented by greater emphasis on English as a second language, in order to facilitate the broadening of international relations and cooperation (Kim 1990 pp. 2–5, UNESCO 1990a).

The Minister further indicated (in October 1990) that much of Mongolia's cultural heritage had been abandoned with the adoption of the Cyrillic alphabet in Mongolia in 1950. There is a policy (approved in 1990 by the new legislature which makes decisions instead of the Party) of reintroducing the original Ourgen script in Mongolia, still used in parts of the Inner Mongolian Autonomous Region, just across the border in China. The Minister wishes to reintroduce the Ourgen script into the schools and universities so that, by 1995, all Mongolians, young and old, will again be able to read and write using that alphabet, one of the oldest in the world. The Institute of Mongolian Scripts and the Ministry of Education are discussing with UNESCO and donor agencies the possibility of a major project to train key specialists and teachers in how to reintroduce the script in schools, to develop computer software using the script, to use distance learning in the spread of the use of the script, and to set up a printing facility which can print the many publications and textbooks which will be needed in the traditional script.

The implications of this decision are staggering. Beginning in the 1991–92 academic year, the government wishes to begin reintroducing the Ourgen script at all grade levels through university and by 1995 it hopes that all primary schooling will use that script. Concurrently, a nationwide adult education program, which will include distance education strategies, will teach adults the use of the script, and a comprehensive program to publish classical texts and current textbooks, teachers' manuals, and materials for new readers will begin. The National Institute for Ourgen Script and the *Mongolbichig* or Mongol Script Cooperative will collaborate in developing the resources necessary for the effort.

Dependence on the Soviet Union for policy direction in education appears to be a thing of the past. Most Soviet troops and advisors have left the country, and the current (December 1990) Minister of Education, while acknowledging advances of the past, has indicated that the country is suffering serious side effects from the previous one-sided educational policy. He has asked UNESCO to field a sector study mission in order to further define the nature of desirable changes (UNESCO 1990a pp. 2–4).

2. *The Institutional Fabric of the Higher Education System*

Mongolia has nine higher education institutions (not including a variety of postsecondary technical and vocational institutes): the State University (founded in 1942), the Polytechnic, the Medical Institute, the Agricultural Institute, two State Pedagogical Institutes in Ulan Bator and Khovd, the Military Academy, a Management Institute, and a Russian Language Institute. There are several teacher training institutions at the secondary level for the preparation of primary-level teachers.

The State University has the following faculties: mathematics and physics, natural sciences, social sciences, philology, economics, trade economics, and a preparatory faculty. There is also a department for evening and correspondence courses (International Association of Universities 1990). The two State Pedagogical Institutes have departments of biological and physical sciences, mathematics, literature and languages, and history and are considering the addition of programs in computer sciences and other technological areas. The Agricultural Institute at Ulan Bator has faculties in zoology, veterinary medicine, agronomy, forestry, agricultural engineering, fodder, and so forth. All in all, these, and the other higher education institutions, prepare specialists in over 100 different professions, from physicians to veterinarians, from secondary-school teachers to engineers and research workers.

There is a new attitude to the quality and relevance of higher education. Profound reforms are called for in higher education in order to "radically improve the quality of training and better define the structure of professional disciplines" (Dash et al. 1990). Reforms are envisaged which will put a greater emphasis on polytechnic education, create new specialties which will be needed in such new areas as environmental science, and expand international cooperation in developing and applying the new information and communication technologies in teaching.

Research in Mongolia has generally taken place in research institutes, sometimes but not necessarily connected with the higher education institutions. Already noted are the institutes which deal with the Mongolian language. It is estimated that there are about 60 scientific institutes attached to the Mongolian Academy of Sciences which is the country's

main scientific institution. Estimates in the late 1980s indicated that about 1.1 percent of the work force was engaged in some kind of scientific or technological research activity and that there has been a substantial growth in research activity in recent years in such groups as the Scientific Experimental Center of the Leather and Shoe Industry, the Center of Scientific and Technological Information, the Laboratory of Pasture and Animal Feed, the Experimental Research Center of the Woolen and Food Industries, the Chemical–Technological Laboratory of the Academy of Sciences, and others. A United Fund for Financing Research and Experimental Construction Work was set up at the State Committee for Science and Technology in 1984. In 1985, it was estimated that total research investment was distributed among spheres of activity as follows: 21.7 percent in industry, 8.7 percent in construction, 43.5 percent in agriculture, 4.35 percent in trade and technical material supply, and 17.4 percent in other branches (Dash et al. 1990 pp. 24–26).

Current thinking is also affecting research in the social sciences. It is stated "that sociological research . . . has been dominated by a dogmatic vision, which has led to blind copying and simplification, instead of opening up new vistas as regards development . . ." (Dash et al. 1990 p. 23). The current government has indicated a concern that there be closer linkages between teaching and research in all spheres of activity, thus suggesting that the universities will have a stronger linkage with the various research institutes in the future.

The number of students admitted to the various institutions of higher education has traditionally been controlled by the State Planning Commission, although under the new government, the criteria and standards are being reviewed and perhaps will be revised. Access to higher education is based on the *gerchilgee* (secondary school leaving certificate). Secondary education may take place in general schools of polytechnic education (five years following five years of primary education) which combine together general subjects with those relating to production in a specified sector of agriculture or industry. It is also possible to enter higher education after a three-year vocational course given at the end of eight years of general schooling. Institutions of higher education also have many students who have attended evening classes or secondary schools for adults.

The main stage of higher education leads to the acquisition of a specialist diploma, which may also entitle the holder to exercise a profession, and is awarded after a five-year course (four to five years at the State Pedagogical Institutes and five to six years at the Medical Institute). A further stage may be undertaken, usually by those already teaching in the university. This course lasts at least three years and includes individual research. Final examinations are taken in relevant fields. Candidates also have to submit a thesis.

Higher education enrollment increased from 6,874 students in 1970 to 38,200 in 1981 and 39,072 in 1986, the latest year for which figures are available (UNESCO 1990b p. 115). Around 60 percent of higher education students are female and there are about 2,000 students in higher education per 100,000 inhabitants. About two-thirds of the students are in scientific and technical fields, and this ratio has changed little between 1981 and 1986. Some 8,000 students graduated from higher education institutions in 1981 and 9,978 in 1986. Of the 1986 graduates, 6,533 were female (from a statistical printout provided by the Division of Statistics, November 20, 1990).

The average age of learners in higher education institutions is 25 years and the term of study averages between 5 and 6 years. In 1988 there were 265 higher education graduates per 10,000 of the population (State Committee 1988). In addition, there were, in 1988, over 100 foreign students from more than 10 different countries studying in Mongolian higher education institutions with all tuition and expenses covered by the government.

3. Governance, Administration, and Finance

3.1 National Administration and Finance

All of higher education has traditionally been controlled by the State Committee for Higher and Specialized Education, and all questions of education are regulated by laws governing public education. These laws are administered by the Ministry of Education. Until the change of government in 1990, the policy and strategies for developing higher education were elaborated by the program of the Mongolian People's Revolutionary Party (MPRP), and the enrollment targets of the various higher education institutions were controlled by the State Planning Commission in accordance with predicted demands for trained personnel. In the past, under the one-party system, there were also awards to workers for outstanding service, either in productivity or to the Party, which gave some preference for admission to higher education. Whether these awards and preferences will continue under the new multiparty system is not as yet clear.

Longer-term higher education goals, in the past, have become part of a five-year government plan. At least until 1988, according to the International Bureau of Education questionnaire completed by the Mongolian authorities early that year, the "introduction of the Soviet experience of higher educational training has been given priority in the State Program" (Dash et al. 1990 Part 2 p. 1). Since then, however, with the move to a multiparty system, the emphasis appears to be on the Mongolization of the society and the educational system and on the sharing of experiences with a larger network of countries than before. Further, educational policy appears to be firmly in the hands of the legislature elected under the new multiparty system, although it is expected that ministerial planning commissions and other government bodies will have a professional input into the process and it is likely that five-year planning will continue, but with more decentralization of authority to work out details.

All higher education is free for those who are accepted. The budget is provided by the legislature through the Ministry of Education and each institution is required to provide evaluative reports on its work from time to time.

3.2 Institutional Administration

Each institution is under the direction of a rector who has considerable freedom in managing his or her own institution. A university or institute council of representatives of each specialization usually meets regularly with the rector to discuss policy and budget issues. The rector, in turn, must interface with the Ministry and planning officials and, to some degree, the legislature. Essentially, the rector is the person in the middle, attempting to translate national plans and goals into operating programs and attempting to satisfy both the politicians and his or her own faculty that their interests are paramount.

Department chairs have a reasonable degree of autonomy in setting teaching assignments and in constructing the curriculum in their areas of interest. The chairs have substantial authority, more along the lines of traditional European universities than of those in countries such as the United States. Faculty appointments are similar to government civil service appointments, though there appears to be a sense of tenure within the university institutions, at least after some years of service.

4. Faculty and Students: Teaching, Learning, and Research

4.1 Faculty

In 1975, there were 807 higher education faculties in Mongolia. This number increased to 2,400 (of which 1,100 were female) in 1981 and to 2,712 (of which 1,224 were female) in 1986. (Data from statistical printouts provided by the Division of Statistics, UNESCO, November 20, 1990.) Although figures are not available on numbers of women in administrative roles, the impression of visitors to Mongolia is that administrative posts are heavily weighted in favor of men. Also, although there are sizeable numbers of female teaching faculty, considering the preponderance of female students in most higher education specializations, it is somewhat surprising that there are not more female faculty members.

It would appear that one route to a university appointment has been to study abroad. In the past, this has generally meant study in the Soviet Union or Eastern Europe. Thus, many faculty members have qualifications from institutions in those regions. With the new political changes and the desire to broaden the range of linkages with other countries, it is likely that many young and middle-level higher education faculty and students will have an opportunity for advanced study in Western Europe, the United States, and other countries which have not traditionally had strong links with Mongolia. Some of these people will undoubtedly return to posts in higher education and they will bring with them ideas for structure, process, and content changes which will affect higher education in the long term. At the same time, the new nationalism, with its interest in Mongolization, may, to some extent, encourage greater use of local institutions to prepare faculty members. Certainly, the policy to reintroduce the traditional Ourgen script will require the stepping up of local training of scholars who use that script and who know something of traditional literature written in Ourgen.

In the past, the collective interest of faculty members was expressed largely through participation in Party mechanisms within each institution. With the multiparty system, and the strengthening of the elected legislature and the role of the elected president, it is likely that various forms of independent faculty organizations will emerge.

At the moment, different types of decision on faculty teaching and research roles are taken at various levels. Certain education laws are passed by the legislature; government policy and planning commissions set guidelines and standards and develop five-year plans, based on inputs from the various institutions of higher education; within each institution, in turn, the faculty and administrators decide who will do what to implement the role assigned to the institution and how they will evaluate the progress of the students. Students have periodic examinations and are assessed also on the basis of various kinds of practical work. The rectors and department chairs have considerable authority over the control curriculum and research programs. There appears to be good communication between faculty members and the administration in the various institutions.

4.2 Students

The student body appears to represent all regions of the country, although regional data are not available. It is likely that all regions are represented in the higher education institutions because of the attempts to expand both primary and secondary education throughout the country, and because of the relatively small population of the country, though it is also likely that the students in urban centers, because of the richer intellectual environment, may be more

successful in gaining admittance than those from nonurban environments. The awards for exemplary service to productive enterprises and the Party helped in gaining admittance to higher education until 1990, and these awards may have helped equalize regional disparities to some extent.

In 1986, there were 19,804 students in the natural and exact sciences, including engineering, mathematics, computer science, and medicine, of which 11,369 or 57 percent were female; 4,276 students in the social and behavioral sciences, of which 3,038 (71%) were female; 2,834 students in the humanities (including fine and applied arts and law) of which 1,701 (60%) were female; 5,723 students in educational sciences and teacher training, of which 4,202 (73%) were female; and 5,788 students in agriculture, of which 2,744 (47%) were female.

Numbers of graduates in 1986 were as follows: exact sciences, 5,008 (3,219 or 64% female); social and behavioral sciences, 1,590 (1,184 or 74% female); humanities, 497 (314 or 63% female); educational sciences, 1,394 (1,074 or 77% female); agriculture, 1,417 (742 or 52% female).

The predominance of female students, both among those enrolled and those graduating, is remarkable. Although time studies are not available, the above figures also suggest that there may be higher dropout rates among the male students in that the percentages of female students graduating are higher than those of women in the student population as a whole. This is dramatically illustrated if the engineering figures are extracted from the exact sciences totals. The total student enrollment in 1986 in engineering was 12,803, of which 5,465 were female (42%). Engineering graduates that year totalled 3,203, of which 1,600 (50%) were female. Clearly, there is strong representation of women within higher education. As the new economic initiatives under the liberalization policies mature, it will be interesting to see if these affect the content and enrollment mix within higher education.

5. Conclusion

The implications for higher education of the great changes taking place in the political and social life of Mongolia are difficult to assess. Certainly, the institutions will continue to be asked to accelerate development through the preparation of appropriate labor force for goals expected by public and private enterprises and services to grow and expand during the 1990s and into the twenty-first century.

It is clear that the "winds of change" will affect society and, in turn, higher education dramatically. The Mongolization policies, essentially the expression of a renewed sense of nationalism, seem to progress hand in hand with the new sense of openness toward countries other than those in the traditional socialist bloc. As Mongolian scholars and government officials interact more and more with the international academic community, through exchanges, scholarships, joint research, and joint development projects, it is likely that higher education interests will expand both externally (to explore scholarly ideas in the market economies) and internally (to rediscover historic Mongol traditions and culture). These two trends need not be in conflict.

As in most small countries in the process of rapid change, issues of quantity, quality, and relevance will plague higher education in Mongolia over the coming years as the goals of society change and as the economy develops. Mongolia is on a path designed to draw both on international experience and on its own historic traditions of self reliance as it moves ahead in resolving these issues.

Bibliography

Dash M, Nyamaa D, Damdin D 1990 *Mongolia by the Year 2005*. UNESCO, Paris

International Association of Universities 1990 Mongolia. In: *Country Database*. IAU, UNESCO, Paris

Kim J G 1990 *Mission Report to Geneva, China and Mongolia*. UNESCO, Paris

State Committee for Higher and Specialized Secondary Education (Mongolia) 1988 Postsecondary education and its diversification in relation to employment. Ulan Bator (reply to questionnaire ED/BIE/CONFINTED/41/Q/87), available from UNESCO, Paris, or International Bureau of Education, Geneva, Microfiche SIRE/02239

Spaulding S 1990 Educational development and reform on the Soviet periphery: Mongolian People's Republic and Lao People's Democratic Republic. *J. Asian African Affairs* 2,(1): 109–24

UNESCO 1990a *Mongolia: Reintroduction of the Traditional Ourgen Alphabet*. Draft project proposal, UNESCO, Paris

UNESCO 1990b *Statistical Digest 1990*. UNESCO, Paris

S. Spaulding

Morocco

1. Higher Education and Society

Higher education in Morocco has been in constant change since Independence in 1956. Young and open, the system is still searching for overall coherence and closer links with its industrial and economic environment.

The population of Morocco was estimated to be 22,703,000 in 1986, with a natural growth rate of 2.6 percent. More than 42 percent of the population is less than 15 years old and 53 percent is less than 20. The economically active population was nearly six million in 1982 (the last general census), or some 30 percent of the total population at that time.

Most of the economically active population works in the agricultural sector, an important source of income accounting for close to 17 percent of Gross Domestic Product (GDP). Industry contributes 15 percent of GDP, but only provides 31,000 jobs. Gross Domestic Product at market prices rose from 20 billion dirhams (US$2.3 billion) in 1970 to 134 billion (US$ 15.1 billion) in 1986.

2. The Institutional Fabric of the Higher Education System

Higher education has been a high priority for every government since the 1960s, often in spite of an unstable economic situation. There were 324 *bacheliers* (i.e., those who have passed the baccalaureate) in 1961, 4,701 in 1971, and 54,000 in 1988. The number of students registered in the first two cycles of the university increased 36-fold during the same period, jumping from 4,780 students in 1961–62 to 173,000 in 1988–89.

Morocco had only two universities before the 1960s. In 1990 there are 46 institutions with 37 faculties divided among six universities throughout the kingdom. The number of university graduates has grown constantly, going from 140 in 1961–62 to 12,644 in 1987–88, an annual growth rate of 18.15 percent.

The system of higher education includes six universities and 25 nonuniversity institutions. Both types of educational institutions function with their own logic and relate in their own way to the economic system.

In 1987–88 there were 8,100 students training for public services, 157,484 university students, and a further 11,739 studying at universities abroad, especially in France.

Since the early 1960s several civil service training institutes were established to meet the urgent need for a trained middle and upper level labor force for the economic, government, and social sectors of newly independent Morocco. The length of studies varies from two to six years depending on the field of study and the institution. The number of these training institutions has grown from just three, with 300 students, in 1960–61, to 22 with 8,100 students in 1988.

The ministries have their own institutions for specialized training, in the areas of their competencies. However, despite the high growth in numbers, such training remains elitist, representing only 4 percent of those in higher education. Access to the institutions is carefully regulated by a competitive entrance examination and consideration of the candidates' backgrounds. The number of openings is set at the beginning of each term. Nevertheless, this moderation in student recruitment seems to be insufficient or poorly directed for reaching the desired balance between the number of diplomas and available employment. Job searches are growing longer and some graduates are already unemployed.

An example of the reorganization of universities is the case of *La Quaraouyine*. An historic and famous Moroccan university, and above all a symbol of the cultural identity of the nation, *La Quaraouyine* was in serious decline. It had to be urgently restructured and its courses had to be adapted to the needs of contemporary Morocco, while preserving its original cultural and spiritual dimensions. A slow rehabilitation appears to be under way with the increase in student enrollment (4.4% of university students). *La Quaraouyine*'s courses are given by three specialized faculties (Islamic jurisdiction and law; theological education; and Arab language studies) and a third-cycle school.

Given the growing needs in the different sectors of Moroccan society for personnel with modern training, the foundation of a modern university was considered even more urgent. Thus, the first faculties in Morocco were established as far back as 1957: liberal arts, science, and law. Two years later, the Mohammed V University was founded. At the beginning of the 1960s, an engineering school (EMI) and the Institute of Sociology were established; also the Pedagogical Institute for Secondary Education (*Ecole Nationale Supérieure* [ENS]) was restructured.

By 1977, there were already 53,400 students, an overall growth rate of more than 600 percent. The following decade, however, saw a much more moderate growth rate of some 300 percent, since in 1987–88, there were 169,000 students. Higher dropout rates and failure in the baccalaureate examination helps explain the slower rate of growth.

Scientific research, considered one of the principal missions of the university, is lacking in means and clear objectives. Far from being guided by the Ministry of National Education and public and private enterprises, it is limited to the defense of theses, international colloquia, and research projects connected with French universities. In 1987–88, there were 11,739 graduate students.

3. Governance, Administration, and Finance

3.1 National Administration

University education is the responsibility of the Ministry of National Education which applies the government's education policy and organizes all university programs and teaching. The universities are public institutions with budgetary autonomy. Officially, the objective of higher education is to adapt the content and teaching methods in order to respond to the economic and sociocultural needs. This should be accomplished mainly by improving the quality and productivity of teaching as well as faculty training.

In fact, there is a clear gap between the university and economic life. It was only after 1980 and the unemployment of university graduates that some interesting actions were taken. New presidencies were established in the universities of *La Quaraouyine* and Sidi Mohamed Ben Abdellah in Fez, and Mohamed I in Oujda and Cadi Ayyad in Marrakesh. Several professional institutions were opened: the National School of Applied Engineering in Casablanca; the School of Technology in Fez and Casablanca; the translation school in Tangiers; and the National School of Electricity and Mechanics.

A high percentage of the state's budget is dedicated to higher education, despite a difficult international economic context and internal problems arising from the climate (five years of drought): 20 percent of the investment budget and 17 percent of the operating budget allotted to the Ministry of National Education are reserved for higher education.

The increasingly large number of students and the number of scholarship students (from 1,062 in 1961–62 to 147,600 in 1989) limit the scope of these considerable sums. For example, more than 40 percent of the operating budget goes to scholarships and 51 percent to wages. The institutions receive only 4 percent. This explains the deterioration of the buildings and the mediocrity of the services offered to researchers and students.

Private institutions have the same problems, except for a few famous schools. Small in number (around 15) and inspired more by the profit motive, these schools with their two to three million students have for the moment no real impact on the evolution of higher education.

3.2 Institutional Governance

Each university is under a president who sees that the decisions of the Ministry are implemented. The

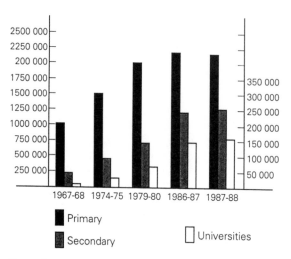

Figure 1

Development in numbers of primary school, secondary school, and university students

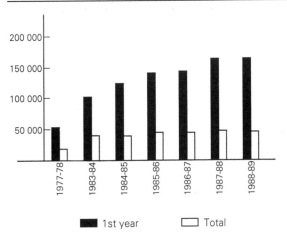

Figure 2
Total number of students in higher education

Ministry also instituted a university council in each university, which rules on important questions related to university life. Each university also has a faculty council, a school or an institute council. These two councils are not very efficacious. They meet two or three times a year to ratify the decisions made by the Ministry. The day-to-day running of the institutions is carried out on the level of the departments, which elect a department head, a board, and a scientific council, who together undertake actions to benefit teaching and research. Professors cannot be recruited without their consent.

The administration and evaluation of technical institutes are the responsibility of the Office of Public Servant Training. The directors are named either by decree or decision of the respective ministries.

These directors are assisted by an internal council and a development council. The first is composed of the director and the director of studies. It must meet at least three times a year to discuss questions related to studies. The second council, presided over by the respective ministry in charge, is composed of representatives of professional sectors interested in the education given by the institution. This council is supposed to guide policy in order to ensure the best conditions for the link between education and the economy, and take an interest in educational programs and methods.

4. Faculty

In the institutes for training public servants the teaching staff is composed of research professors, but with a high percentage of part-time professors (around 50%). The recruitment of both teaching and administrative staff is the responsibility of the supervising ministry, on the basis of proposals by the head of the institution.

In the universities, the teaching staff participates in recruiting colleagues. The important decisions, including recruitment, are made by the scientific council of the department, where all levels are represented, except for the new faculties where such traditions seem to be having difficulty getting established.

The total number of research professors in the universities is increasing constantly. It grew from 3,717 in 1985–86 to 4,641 in 1987–88, an average annual growth rate of 11.74 percent.

The number of foreign professors is strictly limited and is confined to specialized fields, especially in science and technology.

5.1 Conclusion

Higher education in Morocco has grown tremendously from 1960 to 1989. It has grown too quickly in relation to the economy, and needs to be profoundly restructured. It has considerable state funds at its disposition, but neither its content nor its quality is satisfactory. Thus, its capacity to adapt to an unstable international economic environment is also unsatisfactory.

Pushed by strong social pressures and an ideological and paternalistic rationale, the social demand for long-term studies is huge and difficult to manage or avoid. The ideal would be to organize a competitive university entrance examination for *bacheliers* and give scholarships only to those who really merit them. But given social pressure and the unpopularity of this kind of measure, the only possibility is to rearrange the present system somewhat to make it more productive and to adapt it to employment needs.

An intelligent proportioning of long- and short-term programs would also be healthy. Some civil servant institutes have been declining in recent years,

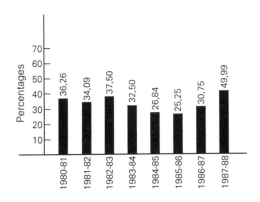

Figure 3
Development of the percentage of successful baccalauréat candidates

confronted with a multitude of participants, which makes it difficult to define programs and directions to follow. Additionally, the top graduates of these institutes cannot find employment.

Finally, scientific research merits more attention and resources. The resources allocated to research is ridiculously small (0.3% of GNP) and the few university research projects that exist are not directed to the development needs of the country. There is an urgent need to establish a system of research in connection with production and corporate objectives. However, as long as research is undervalued and not taken into consideration in evaluating professors in higher education, and as long as professors are promoted from one level to another by receiving state doctorates and by seniority, scientific research in Morocco will not become a serious component of higher education.

Bibliography

Baina A 1984 *Le système de l'enseignement au Maroc.* Editions Maghrébines, Rabat

Bernard C 1984 *La politique de la formation-emploi au Maghreb.* CNRS, Paris

Bulletin Officiel n° 3916 1987 *Réforme du régime des examens du baccalauréat de l'enseignement secondaire.*

Commission Nationale de l'Enseignement Supérieur *Rapport de synthèse.*

Commission Nationale de la Formation Professionnelle et de la Formation des Cadres *Rapport de synthèse*

Morocco, Ministry of National Education *Le mouvement éducatif au Maroc 1986–88. Rapport de synthèse.* Ministère de l'Education Nationale, Rabat

Morocco, Ministry of Planning *Plan d'orientation 1988–1992.* Ministère du Plan, Rabat

Salahdine M 1984 *Composition sociale et aspirations professionnelles des étudiants.* Groupe de recherche Emploi Formation Qualification, University of Fez

Salahdine M 1985a *Caractéristiques Socio-économiques des étudiants Licenciés en Droit et en Economie. Bulletin économique et social*

Salahdine M 1985b *L'Université lieu du savoir ou usine à chômeurs? Revue Lamalif*

Salahdine M 1986 *La formation professionnelle au Maroc.* Fondation Frederick Ebert, Rabat

Salahdine M, Mechkouri 1988 *Le système de l'enseignement post secondaire et l'insertion professionnelle au Maroc.* Colloque, University of Toulouse

Salmi J 1986 *Crise de l'enseignement au Maroc.* Editions Maghrébines, Rabat

Souali M, Merrouni M 1982 *L'enseignement au Maroc Bulletin économique et social*

M. Salahdine

Mozambique

1. Higher Education and Society

Mozambique, formerly a Portuguese colony, gained its independence in 1975. The territory is a long and narrow land, lying on the east coast of Africa. It is bounded by the Indian Ocean on the east; Tanzania on the north; Malawi, Zambia, Zimbabwe, and South Africa on the west; and Swaziland on the south. Mozambique occupies a total area of approximately 780,000 square kilometers, with about half of this area being made up of lowlands stretching inland from the coast. The coast itself extends for some 2,500 kilometers, and includes some good harbors. The north consists of plateaus of medium height. The country is well-watered by a number of important rivers. Mozambique is a relatively fertile tropical and subtropical country with only two seasons: a hot, wet period lasting from October to March, and a dry season from April to September.

The present boundaries were defined by a treaty between British and Portuguese governments in 1891. Portuguese contact with the indigenous inhabitants of Mozambique dates from the time of Vasco da Gama's first voyage to India in 1498. Portuguese settlement began in Sofala, the present-day Beira, in 1505.

In 1965, a guerrilla uprising broke out in the north, resulting in a colonial war which ended in 1974. Negotiations for autonomy followed, and Independence was accorded in 1975. Internally, Independence was not peaceful. A new guerrilla initiative began which was supported by the Republic of South Africa (although this was never admitted) against the new Mozambican regime. In 1991, fighting still continues. Meanwhile, negotiations between the government and the guerrillas are under way.

War has disrupted the Mozambican economy. Severe drought and floods have also damaged agriculture, the main economic source. All this has pushed the rural population into cities which have become overcrowded, with all the related problems, namely food, housing, and sanitation. Famine and disease are widespread throughout the rural areas.

Following the 1980 population census, statistical projections for the present day indicates a population of about 14 million people, most of which is concentrated in the north or in the cities of the south and west. Most of the population is African, but there are also a few thousand foreign experts. The non-African inhabitants also include people of East Indian origin, and some Chinese.

The African population belongs to the Bantu group; within which there are the Shona, who tend to live inland, and the Tonga who live towards the east. The Maravi, living in the north, although not so numerous as the other groups, are also dominant. These groups have their own languages and dialects. Because of this linguistic diversity, Portuguese, the former colonial language, has been adopted as the official and common spoken language.

The Mozambican population is very young and this presents several difficult problems, among them being the demand for education far surpasses the nation's capacity to supply it.

The Mozambican economy is based on agriculture, fishing, and railways and harbor services to neighboring countries. Agriculture and fishing occupy some 85 percent of the population, industry 7 percent, and services 8 percent. A particular feature, which remains from colonial times, is the effect on the economy of foreign currency sent home by the Mozambican migrant workers in the South African mining industry.

Since Independence, Mozambique has been ruled according to the Marxist–Leninist model of one-party Communist regime. Therefore, all social organization is conducted according to the centralized decisions of the political power. Government and administrative actions are subordinated to the Party's political system which is supported by the army. The economy, social services, and home administration are in the control of the state and the state is the Party. More recently, some proposals have been put forward to create a pluralist regime, following on from the political events in Eastern Europe. It is not possible at present to forecast the evolution of this situation.

2. The Institutional Fabric of the Higher Education System

Mozambique has one higher education institution—the university—with its headquarters and most of its schools in Luanda. It is a state university, integrated into the government framework. The university has its origins in the former University of Luanda which was set up in 1962 by the Portuguese Administration. The university used to be attended mainly by White Portuguese students, with the Africans representing less than 10 percent of total enrollments. They reached an enrollment peak of about three thousand in 1974, prior to Independence. Teaching was conducted in Portuguese by Portuguese teachers, and it was also highly supported by local research institutes that were reasonably up-to-date and well-staffed. The exodus of Portuguese settlers in 1974 and 1975 emptied the university of most of its teaching body and students, causing an almost complete breakdown.

Upon Independence, the university was renamed as University Eduardo Mondlane, after the guerrilla leader, and efforts were made to restructure the institution in the spirit of the new political situation. The year 1986 saw the setting up of the Higher Pedagogical Institute, primarily as a means to raise the quality of teacher education—an area in which the country faced desperate shortages. The institute, which is organizationally separate from the university, is essentially a graduate school for the training of secondary school teachers, educational psychologists, and planners.

Admission to the university is open to those who have completed 11 years of secondary studies. Secondary studies can also be achieved through adult education. A particular scheme for workers and combatants has been offered, although with no large success. An additional diagnostic test is required.

Basically, the structure of faculties and courses has remained the same as that of the former colonial university. Nevertheless, some conceptual changes have been introduced. New courses, like law (not allowed before the Independence) and some in the humanities, are planned.

As a broad rule, courses on social sciences and humanities last three years, and are awarded by a bachelor's degree; sciences and technology (apart from medicine) last four years, and are awarded by a licence degree; medicine (also a licence degree) lasts five years. This structure has been undergoing reorganization. One of the proposals is to lengthen all courses to five years and to award only the licence degree (the bachelor's degree is to be abolished). The issue of degrees is underlined by the social esteem attached to different degrees. The bachelor's degree is a short first degree, while the licence degree is a long first degree which is socially more prized and more egalitarian.

Since the late 1980s, the authorities have been concentrating their energies on the Faculty of Engineering, with courses on electricity and electronics, chemistry, mechanics, and civil engineering; the Faculty of Sciences, with courses on chemistry, physics, and geology; the Faculty of Biology; the Faculty of Agriculture and Forestry with both courses; the Veterinary Faculty; the Faculty of Medicine; the Faculty of Economics; and the Faculty of Education, for teacher training on primary and secondary schooling. The Faculty of Humanities, as well as the Faculty of Law, have been closed down for a while.

A particular feature of the university is the existence of a faculty for distinguished workers. Here they are given special training to prepare them for admission to university.

3. Governance, Administration, and Finance

Considering the political nature of the regime, the civil war (1991) and the scarcity of human academic resources, Mozambique, of necessity, has a unique system of governance.

The university is taken as an essential tool of nation building, and therefore is closely ruled by the political power. Officially, both the university and the Higher Pedagogical Institute are state institutions, and as such directly responsible to the Ministry of Education and Culture. The university's internal governing body is the *Conselho Universitario*, composed of the rector and the directors of the faculties. The rector, the university head, and directors of faculties and schools are all appointed by the government. However some academic participation is open through some corporate bodies integrating teacher and student representatives, depending upon the rank and functions of these bodies.

The university is financially supported by public funds and its management follows the public administration pattern. Students do not pay fees; their attendance being a matter of national interest.

4. Faculty and Students: Teaching and Learning

4.1 Faculty

One of the most serious problems of the university, which limits its development, is the composition and academic qualifications of the teaching body. The most important limitation stands on recruitment, origins, and process. Mozambique does not have its own teachers and conditions have not provided autonomy in this particular field, as well as in many others. Therefore, most of the teaching body is recruited from other countries on a cooperative basis. Thus, for example, of the 50 or so academic staff of the Higher Pedagogical Institute, 20 come from such countries as the former German Democratic Republic, Mexico, Norway, Poland, Portugal, and the Soviet Union. The Mozambican staff are young—between 25 and 35 years—and most are trained abroad (ISP 1990 p. 6). This scheme creates different problems: the academic quality is, in general, below some universal academic standards. There is no continuity in the academic staff because of the temporary nature of the postings; the variety of teachers' origins and different academic patterns and languages result in problems of communication. One of the persistent problems is access to higher education. Two-thirds of the students in postsecondary education come from the three southern provinces, which contain some 25 percent of the total population. The need to establish higher education facilities outside the capital, Maputo, led to the establishment of a branch of the Higher Pedagogical Institute in Beira. The government intends to found another branch in Nampula, in the north, by 1993 (ISP 1990 p. 7).

The scarcity of an intellectual and professional elite, and the youth of the state administrative officers (part of them are university students, and even teachers at the same time) means that Mozambicans in the faculty are an extremely diverse group.

4.2 Students

Although detailed statistics are not available, total enrollment figures reveal the fluctuations resulting from the process of Independence and the ensuing difficulties. Most of the students enrolled in 1973 and 1975 were White. The European exodus after independence emptied the university which virtually had to start anew.

Due to the scarcity of "cadres" and youth in the active population, a significant number of students are engaged in occupational activities in addition to

Table 1
University enrollments and graduates

	1973	1975	1980	1985
Enrollments	3,730	2,433	836	1,351
Graduates	—	56	115	54

their studies. This situation causes a lowering in the standards of schooling, including some wastage of successful students, which represents a serious problem.

Progress has been made with regard to the male/female ratio. This was, in 1985, roughly 2.3:1.

5. Conclusion

The fundamental problem facing Mozambique is instability which, obviously, is reflected in university life.

Mozambique is a young country, both in its position as an independent state and through its demographic profile. The problems that arise from this condition are not unknown elsewhere in Africa—the admixture of a colonial past, the power and persistence of its administrative machinery and, despite a marked lack of human resources on the spot, the need, nevertheless, to face the challenge of independent statehood. This challenge has been made no easier by the disaster of a long and bitter civil war. It is clear however, that the government is beginning to set down the basis for a viable system of higher education. The Portuguese-speaking world has its part to play in helping Mozambique's recovery.

Bibliography

ISP 1990 *Introduction to Mozambique's Higher Pedagogical Institute*. ISP, Maputo

E. L. Pires

Myanmar

Known as Burma until 1989, Myanmar is poor, but has a relatively strong educational tradition and university institutions dating from the late nineteenth century. Isolation from the world community since Independence from the United Kingdom was achieved in 1948 has removed the higher education system from international currents of thought and ideas.

1. Higher Education and Society

Geographical conditions dominate the economy, society, and culture of Myanmar. Three river systems, in particular that of the Irrawaddy, create an arable economy, especially in the delta which is one of the great rice-growing areas of the world. The upper reaches of the rivers and the surrounding mountains of the "horseshoe" that dominates the topography of the country are less heavily settled or developed. Between the delta and the mountains are drier arable areas centered on the second city of Mandalay.

The population is mainly rural and agricultural and the capital Yangon (Rangoon), with 2.5 million inhabitants, is the major city (followed by Mandalay with 532,000 and Moulmein (Mawlamyine) with 219,000) in a population of 40 million in 1989. The population growth rate has been moderately high at 2.3 percent per annum between 1965 and 1980 and 2.1 percent between 1980 and 1988.

The population is dominated by Burmans (69%), who are found in the central lowlands. Ethnic minorities including Shan (8.5%), Karen (6.2%) and Rahkine (4.5%) are found mainly in the uplands and so are marginalized geographically, economically, and politically. Burman is the official language and the medium of education though ethnic minorities have their own languages, several of which do not have a developed literary form. Some 90 percent of the population are Buddhist, with 5 percent Christian and 4 percent Muslim.

Measured in terms of Gross Domestic Product (GDP) per capita (US$200 in 1986), Myanmar is one of the ten poorest countries in the world. Most workers are employed in agriculture (67% in 1981). The population is more developed in other ways, however. Historically, literacy rates have been high, even in the nineteenth century, and women have had a more emancipated position at all levels than in other countries of similar levels of socioeconomic development Social class divisions are not acute. Primary education provision is almost universal while 24 percent of the appropriate age group were enrolled in secondary education in 1987. Relatively high levels of participation in postsecondary education, however, have been associated with graduate unemployment since the 1960s as well as with student involvement in political opposition.

The main economic activities in Myanmar are agriculture (predominantly rice production), fishing, and, in the more remote areas, forestry. There is relatively little industrial development. Mining of industrial metals and precious stones developed in the northern areas in the 1970s. The majority of larger industrial and financial enterprises were nationalized in 1962 though it was not until 1973 that foreign investment was again permitted. Economic growth and development have been much more restricted than in neighboring countries to the south and east. The economy was badly disrupted by the Second World War. It was not until 1975 that prewar levels of GDP per capita were regained.

There was a long tradition of powerful monarchies until colonization by the British in 1885. Colonial rule was resisted by a strong nationalist movement which drew upon a Buddhist identity and, after the establishment of a full university in Rangoon, was based upon students. This continuous rebellion was maintained under Japanese occupation (1941–45). Burma became independent in 1948, but, unlike other former colonies, did not join the Commonwealth or maintain links with the United Kingdom.

Military rule began in 1958. A coup d'état in 1962 under Ne Win led to attempts to create a socialist state with one-party government, though in practice military rule persisted. Rebellions also continued among ethnic groups in the north and the mountains and there were attempts to grant greater regional autonomy, including the change of name to Myanmar to symbolize the end of Burman dominance. Despite a pro-democracy movement, which was briefly allowed to develop in the late 1980s then crushed, the major threat to the political unity of Myanmar continues through ethnic groups, especially the Karen, whose armies claim to control half the country.

Buddhist centers of learning existed long before conventional higher education. These institutions continue to have a role, particularly in giving education to young people from poorer social background on entry to religious orders, which they may then continue in the public higher education system.

2. The Institutional Fabric of the Higher Education System

University education in Myanmar began with the foundation of the University of Rangoon in 1920. It had developed from two colleges established in the late nineteenth century, one of which was affiliated to the University of Calcutta in India. Rangoon University, like those of India, developed a number of affiliated colleges.

The University of Rangoon was reorganized from 1958. Two arts and science universities were estab-

Table 1
Student numbers and percentage of the 20–24 age group 1965–87

1965	1970	1975	1981	1987
26,005	46,150	56,086	165,000	—
—	2.2	2.1	—	4.8

lished in Rangoon and Mandalay in 1958 to replace the University of Rangoon. Several faculties including medicine, education, social science, and engineering were detached in 1964 to form separate institutes. The two universities only have faculties of arts and science, therefore. Equivalent level courses are provided in the institutes of agriculture, veterinary science, dentistry, economics, education, medicine (three institutes), technology, and adult education (Workers College).

Lower level, intermediate higher education, similar to American community colleges, exists in the form of seven intermediate and 20 regional colleges. The regional colleges were established from 1977. Several intermediate colleges are specialized engineering or other vocational institutions. There are also teacher-training colleges for middle school teachers which offer one or two years of postsecondary training. Primary school teachers are trained in institutions at upper secondary school level rather than in the higher education system. Students normally complete two-year regional college courses before entering universities. Other students complete three-year terminal technical/vocational qualifications in these colleges. In 1980 half the 32,000 regional college graduates entered the universities of Rangoon or Mandalay. All but three of the regional colleges are outside Rangoon in line with a government policy of geographical dispersal of higher education.

Admission to higher education is on the basis of the certificate of full secondary education. Selection for entry to either regional colleges or terminal intermediate higher education including teacher training is based on performance in the final secondary school examination.

Student enrollments in higher education were substantial in 1960 when seen against socioeconomic levels in the country. The numbers and proportion of the relevant age group expanded particularly in the late 1970s.

Courses at regional colleges lead to intermediate certificates after two years. Further study at universities or specialized institutes leads either to honors (three-year) or pass (two-year) degrees (courses take seven years for medicine, six for engineering, and five for agriculture). Students are allocated to honors or pass degree courses on the basis of their performance in the intermediate certificate. Master's degree courses take one or more years after graduation.

Table 2
Teachers and staff: student ratio 1965–87

1965	1970	1978	1987
1,829	3,509	4,522	9,028
1:14	1:13	1:27	1:22

Table 3
Numbers of students by field of study 1965–72

	1965	1972
Humanities	9,019	7,959
Education	847	3,231
Law	309	834
Social Science	2,156	7,726
Natural Science	5,031	21,873
Engineering	1,910	3,760
Medicine	2,607	5,127
Agriculture	520	1,301

3. Governance, Administration, and Finance

Universities and equivalent institutions are controlled and financed by the Ministry of Education. Since 1977, regional colleges have been controlled and financed jointly by the Ministry of Education and regional State Peoples' Councils. The trend toward regionalization may also be seen in aims to relate the courses in regional colleges to local economic needs.

Information on the proportion of Gross National Product (GNP) spent on higher education has not been made available since the late 1970s. The proportion of GNP spent on education declined from 3.1 percent in 1970 to 1.6 percent in 1977 and the proportion of government expenditure allocated to education declined from 17.9 percent in 1970 to 12.2 percent in 1977. In 1987 13 percent of total government current educational expenditure was devoted to higher education, compared with 10.8 percent in 1975.

The traditional base unit of university organization has been the faculty. Since the reorganization in 1964, the two universities have been limited to general arts and science faculties with the vocational faculties transferred to specialist institutes.

4. Faculty and Students: Teaching, Learning, and Research

The number of teachers in higher education institutions has grown significantly since the 1970s, but less quickly than the number of students, as Table 2 indicates.

The formalization of the two-stage system of higher education (regional colleges followed by universities) has made description of student fields of study by UNESCO categories more difficult. The position before the reorganization was as shown in Table 3.

Information on the social background of students is scarce. There has been a tradition of students from fairly poor backgrounds entering higher education though it is unlikely that ethnic minority students are proportionally represented. Female participation in higher education has always been high in comparison with similar countries. Some 50 percent of students in 1978 were women.

Higher education in Myanmar flourished in the early twentieth century. Its quality until the 1960s was regarded by American universities as higher than that of Indian equivalents. The popularity of higher education among consumers was nonetheless associated with graduate unemployment and student political activism. Governments in the 1960s and 1970s attempted to diversify higher education and to regionalize it, in the process weakening the large universities of Rangoon and Mandalay. The impact of these moves on the quality of higher education in Myanmar is difficult to judge.

Bibliography

Steinberg D I (ed.) 1981 *Burma's Road to Development* Westview Press, Boulder, Colorado
Steinberg D I 1982 *Burma: A Socialist Nation of South-east Asia* Westview Press, Boulder, Colorado

M. McLean

N

Nepal

1. Higher Education and Society

Nepal is situated between Tibet and India in southern Asia. It is a mountainous country, dominated by the Himalayas, with a surface area of 141,000 square kilometers. Transportation and communications are very difficult, because only one-fifth of the 5,000 kilometers of roads are paved. It has few regular contacts with the outside world. The population of some 18 million inhabitants is of Mongol and Indo-European (Gurkha) origin. Some 90 percent live in rural areas.

Nepal is a constitutional monarchy. King Tribhuvan Bir Bikram founded the modern democratic kingdom in 1947. He had a strong desire to provide adequate facilities for the education of the Nepalese people. He was succeeded by his son who was succeeded in 1972 by his son Birendra Bir Bikram Shah Dev.

The economy of the country is based mainly on agriculture (rice, wheat, and corn) and stockbreeding (goats, sheep, and yaks). Industry is based mainly on crafts and agriculture, but the hydroelectric industry is developing. There is also an active tourist industry. The average annual revenue per capita is US$170. Estimates put the number of illiterates at 10 million (Quid 1991).

According to the government's Seventh Plan (1985–1990), higher education must play an important role in training the labor force the country needs. Emphasis has been laid on technical education.

2. The Institutional Fabric of the Higher Education System

Tribhuvan University was founded in 1954 by command of the late King Mahendra Bir Bikram Shah Deva in memory of his father King Tribhuvan. In 1959, the University was incorporated under the Tribhuvan University Act which gave it a legal foundation and authority. Until 1971, it functioned mainly as a teaching and affiliating institution. Under this arrangement, all undergraduate studies were conducted in the affiliated colleges situated throughout the kingdom. It was reorganized in 1972 under the National Education Plan. The Tribhuvan University Act of 1959 was repealed and reenacted. Affiliation was abandoned and all public and private colleges were converted into campuses of the institutes. The University came to have 12 institutes. Two of these were later transformed into research centers. In 1985, four of the ten institutes became technical institutes and the other six were turned into faculties. Today, Tribhuvan University has technical institutes of engineering, medicine, agriculture, animal husbandry, forestry, and science and technology; professional faculties of education, management, and law; and a general faculty of humanities and social sciences. It also has research centers for applied science and technology; for economic development and administration; for educational innovation and development; and for Nepal and Asian studies. The institutes and faculties have 64 colleges in different parts of the country.

The Mahendra Sanskrit University was founded in 1986 to promote higher learning in Sanskrit language and literature and research in Nepalese religious history and culture. It has five campuses across the country. The former Institute of Sanskrit of Tribhuvan University was transferred to Mahendra University.

Departmental training, provided by government ministries and departments, consists of technical inservice training in such fields as telecommunications, civil aviation, surveying, tourism and hotel management, agriculture, hydrology, and nutrition.

Private education is offered by 68 institutions in various parts of the country. According to the Ministry of Education, they cater for some 16,000 students. There are 17 institutions in the eastern region, 28 in the central region, 13 in the western region, six in the midwestern region, and four in the far western region. They offer studies in humanities and social sciences, management, and science, mostly at certificate level.

Access to higher education is based on the school-leaving certificate (SLC), conferred after five years of primary education, followed by two years of lower secondary and three years of secondary education. There is also a competitive entrance examination for entry to technical institutes and to the faculties of engineering and medicine. The first stage of higher education leads to the proficiency certificate and to the technician certificate after two years' study. The proficiency certificate is awarded in humanities, social sciences, management, education, law, and science. The technician certificate is awarded in medicine, engineering, forestry, and agriculture after two to three years' study. The bachelor's degree is usually conferred after four years. In technical fields, it is awarded after three to five years, and in medicine after six and a half years. The master's degree is delivered after a further two years' study and a period of "national development service," which serves to expose students to Nepalese rural life. A doctorate is awarded three years after the master's degree in science and technology, education, social sciences, management, and humanities. This degree was introduced in the 1980s.

New courses have been introduced at Tribhuvan University. At the Institute of Medicine, a bachelor's degree in public health has been created and graduate courses have been established. It has a teaching hospital attached to its main campus.

Most students sit for their secondary school leaving certificate at the age of 16 or 17. They usually enter university between the ages of 17 and 20. Students who undergo training provided by the ministries and departments of the government usually start their studies between the ages of 20 and 25, as this type of training is mostly inservice training. According to statistics provided by the Ministry of Education and Culture, enrollment at the campuses of Tribhuvan University has grown from 8,100 in 1965 to 16,427 in 1975, to 33,450 in 1980, and to 54,355 in 1985. However, despite the growth in enrollments, it is estimated that higher education is available to only 3 percent of the 15 to 24 age group.

3. Governance, Administration, and Finance

3.1 National Administration and Finance

The authorities responsible for policies at the national level are the Ministry of Education and Culture, the National Planning Commission, and the National Education Commission. Policy proposals are also made by the University. Policies of the training institutes run by government departments are established by the ministries concerned in consultation with the National Planning Commission. The design of postsecondary education takes into account the number of students to be enrolled and prospects of employment. The labor force estimates of the National Planning Commission provide the rationale for the expansion of technical education. The Commission considers the fulfillment of labor force needs as one of the primary functions of higher education. There are periodic reviews of programs in which the Ministry of Education and the National Planning Commission play a very important part.

Expenditure on postsecondary school education is shared by the government, the University, local bodies, and private households. According to Ministry of Education statistics, the higher education budget represented 23.4 percent of the total education budget in 1987–88. The budget allocations made to the University consist of grants, foreign aid, and loans negotiated by the Ministry of Finance. The technical institutes receive priority allotment funds. Training centers have a more or less fixed annual budget. Private training centers are run by local management committees and charge heavy fees.

3.2 Institutional Administration

Tribhuvan University is an autonomous institution but its programs are often established by the government. His Majesty the King of Nepal, as the Chancellor of the University, is its head and the chairman of its governing body, the University Council. The Minister of Education is the ex officio pro-vice-chancellor. Those responsible for its administration are the vice-chancellor, the registrar, the deputy registrar, the deans of faculties, the controller of examinations, the chief fiscal officer, and the accounts officer. Those responsible for instruction include the rector and academic staff. The executive director and academic staff are responsible for research.

The University Council consists of 50 voting members. They comprise the chancellor, the pro-vice-chancellor, two Royal Fellows, the vice-chancellor, the rector, the registrar, the deans of the institutes, two elected teacher representatives and five elected graduate representatives, four government officers, and members from outside academia, all nominated by the chancellor. The Council is the highest authority. It supervises, directs, and manages all the functions of the University. The vice-chancellor carries out the Council's decisions and controls all the activities of the University. He or she is appointed by the chancellor for a term of four years upon recommendation of a special committee constituted by the chancellor for this purpose.

The rector is the academic administrator. The appointment is for a term of three years and the rector is member-cum-secretary of the Council. The registrar, who is also appointed by the chancellor for a term of five years, is responsible for the general and financial administration of the University. The registrar prepares the annual budget, keeps the register of students' names, and makes arrangements concerning examinations and diplomas.

Each institute of the University is headed by a dean, who is appointed by the chancellor for a term of three years.

Private campuses have their own admission procedures and fee structures and mostly employ part-time staff. Training centers have a director, trainers, and instructors.

4. Faculty and Students: Teaching, Learning, and Research

4.1 Faculty

Teachers at the University must hold a master's degree. Those at departmental and private training centers must have obtained an advanced degree. Teachers at technical institutes are often trained abroad. The Colombo Plan Staff College in Singapore and the Turin Center of the International Labour Organisation also provide short- and medium-term study fellowships to teachers from technical institutes and departmental training centers. The Nepal Administration Staff College conducts teacher training courses for staff in training centers. A radio education teacher training program catering mainly for inservice teachers is also offered.

Teachers participate in curriculum development, reform, implementation, and management. At Tribhuvan University, this system is widespread. Teachers take part in the work of the Curriculum Development Center of the University, as curriculum development in core content and specialization areas is the responsibility of the institute or faculty. Senior teachers also carry out managerial functions.

In 1963–64, there were 65 teachers at Tribhuvan University. In 1968–69 there were 117, in 1975–76 1,960, in 1982–83 2,130, and in 1986–87 their number had increased to 4,164.

4.2 Students

Nearly 60 percent of university students are enrolled in the humanities, social sciences, and management; about 10 percent are enrolled in the technical institutes; about 7 percent are enrolled in the faculty of education; and about 13 percent are enrolled in the faculty of science and technology. There is a high failure rate, however, and this has caused a great waste of resources. This is mainly due to the facts that students generally come from families with low academic levels and there is a high dropout rate. Examination failure rates, particularly at certificate level, are relatively high in all the institutes of Tribhuvan University. Students tend to find employment, hoping to continue their studies on their own by following evening classes. A greater number of women and students from lower-middle-class families are now entering higher education.

5. Conclusion

Higher education has expanded massively in Nepal. There are now 137 campuses, compared to three in 1951. The setting up of Tribhuvan University has made the development of a national system of higher education more responsive to the needs of the country. It has extended facilities to outlying regions so that students in remote areas can also have access to higher education. Emphasis has been laid on technical education in the Seventh Plan (1985–1990) to meet middle-level technician requirements. Its research centers study the various problems facing Nepal and have provided consultancy services to the ministries.

Outside the University, various government departments are expanding their training facilities. In the private sector, training in computer science is growing and a number of new training centers have been set up to train management personnel in public services.

Diversification of education has also been encour-aged to prepare the labor force for new skills required by the country in fields such as trade, maintenance of electrical equipment, town planning, small industry management, and medicine. Hence it can be seen that the government has tried to keep to its policy of matching educational facilities with labor force requirements, despite the problems arising in a small country where communications are not very developed and economic resources are limited.

Bibliography

Tribhuvan University *Handbook*. Tribhuvan University, Kathmandu

Tribhuvan University Research Center for Educational Innovation and Development 1988 IBE survey on Post-secondary education and its diversification in relation to employment (International Conference on Education, 41st session, Geneva, 1989. Reply to questionnaire ED/BIE/CONFINTED/41/Q/87) Tribhuvan University Research Center for Educational Innovation and Development, Kathmandu

UNESCO 1989 *Statistical Yearbook*. UNESCO, Paris

C. Keyes

Netherlands, The

1. Higher Education and Society

Two main features characterize Dutch higher education: the existence of private (denominational) institutions entirely funded from the central government's budget, and a strict "binary policy" separating university education (*wetenschappelijk onderwijs*, or WO) from the network of higher vocational colleges (*hoger beroepsonderwijs*, or HBO) as two autonomous segments of the higher education system. Both features have historical roots and have often become controversial political issues.

The first university of the (northern) Netherlands was founded at Leiden in 1575, as a reward for the city's courage during the Spanish siege of 1573–74. By the end of the seventeenth century, four other universities with a provincial graduation monopoly had been founded and a dozen so-called illustrious schools or *athenaea*, which were university-level institutions without graduation rights. In 1811, under Napoleonic rule, nearly all the surviving institutions were closed down. The royal decree of 1815 confirmed this first rationalization. Only three state universities (Leiden, Groningen [founded in 1614], Utrecht [founded in 1636]) and the municipal athenaeum of Amsterdam (founded in 1632, and transformed into a full university in 1877) were maintained throughout the nineteenth century and indeed still exist. Their age, size, and prestige, and the full range of arts and sciences they teach, mean they are still regarded as the big four among the Dutch universities, although research has shown that leading entrepreneurs and top ranking civil servants come as often from the younger universities of technology and social sciences.

Two nineteenth-century laws helped to fashion the modern features of the Dutch higher education system. The revised Constitution of 1848 freed the educational sector from a too exclusive state control. Henceforth, private institutions could be founded, albeit under some state supervision. As early as 1880, a private Calvinist university was opened at Amsterdam, followed by a Roman Catholic university at Nijmegen (1923) and business college at Tilburg (1927). A 1905 Act granted civil status to the degrees of private universities, and since 1970 full government funding can be granted to all state-recognized institutions for higher education. Since the Higher Education Act of 1960 civil status may even apply to the degrees of accredited schools such as the theological colleges. At the same time, however, state educational policy and control extends over all these private institutions, and sometimes forces them to reflect upon their denominational identity or at least to define particular strategies of teaching and learning.

The Higher Education Act of 1876 (valid until 1960), was completed by the Academic Statute of 1877, and modified several times before its replacement in 1981–82 by a new statute. The 1876 Act abolished the distinction based on the graduation monopoly between full universities (until then called academies or *hogescholen*) and athenaea or other colleges. But a new distinction between the university-level institutions was created, based on the range of learning: the so-called *universiteiten* had to be institutions for universal learning equipped with a wide range of faculties; while the *hogescholen* (colleges) had only some of them, such as economics, engineering, or theology. The University Education Act of 1960 recognized as universities only those institutions possessing three or more faculties, among which at least one was medicine or sciences, and a central interfaculty with at least one course of philosophy. However, in 1986 two acts of parliament (the revised University Education Act, or WWO, and the Higher Vocational Education Act, or WHBO) thoroughly reformed the general structure of higher education and changed institutional terminology once more. Henceforth, all the university-level institutions, no matter how broad or narrow their range of teaching, were called universities, whereas the colleges for higher vocational training were upgraded and called *hogescholen*. Therefore one should be careful when using the term "*hogeschool*," as very different institutions can be meant according to the period under discussion.

Senior vocational (or professional) training has always remained a separate sector of schooling in the Netherlands, despite the fact that practical forms of civil and military engineering have been taught at Leiden and other Dutch universities since as early as the seventeenth century. The Secondary Education Act of 1863 included all senior vocational education, until in 1905 Delft Royal Polytechnic was elevated by law to university level. With the exception of university-status technology and engineering, higher vocational training remained formally part of secondary education until in 1986 the WHBO made it virtually equivalent to other forms of higher education. It has, however, not been incorporated into the university network. The reasons for maintaining this binary policy are many. Historically, the Humboldtian conception of the university as an institution for general learning, where students are trained in "the independent pursuit of scholarship" (1986 University Education Act) has prevailed in the Netherlands since the nineteenth century. It remains the central focus of the university as defined in the 1986 WWO, whereas higher vocational schools are meant "to give theoretical and practical training for the practice of professions" (1986 Higher Vocational Education Act). In fact, from medicine to business administration, professional training is often as important at the universities as it is in the vocational colleges. The main differences between the two networks are the part played by basic research and applied science, the (historically rooted) social status of their degrees, and the predominantly private character of the higher vocational sector. Finally, the process of "social segmentation" of the educational system (see Ringer 1979 pp. 22–31) may be invoked.

1.1 Size and Rate of Growth of Population

The combined effects of a high birthrate and a low deathrate have produced a considerable increase in the Dutch population since the Second World War (see Table 1). However, from approximately 1965, birthrates have greatly declined. With 1.5 children per adult woman in 1985 (against 3.1 in 1960, the highest rate in Europe), the Netherlands have joined European countries with very low reproduction rates such as the former Federal Republic of Germany and France. Moreover, traditional differences in fertility according to region, socioeconomic position, and religion (Roman Catholics and Neo-Calvinists show much higher rates than others) are fading out. The virtual collapse of the formerly dominant Reformed Church, and the rise of the nondenominational sector diminish the role of religion, once a vital motivation for all social, cultural, and moral choices in pre-1960 Netherlands society. Due to immigration, Islam (0.4% in 1971, 2.6% in 1988) is at present the only growing religion. Higher fertility rates may be assumed among ethnic minorities, mostly originating from Surinam and the Dutch Antilles, Turkey, and Morocco, and amounting together to 6 percent of the

Table 1
Population growth in the Netherlands since the Second World War

	1940	1945	1950	1955	1960	1965	1970	1975	1980	1985	1988
Total population (thousands)	8,834	9,220	10,027	10,680	11,417	12,212	12,958	13,599	14,091	14,454	14,804
Percentage of 0–19-year olds	37.5	36.5	37.3	37.5	37.9	37.9	35.9	34.2	31.5	28.3	26.2
Percentage of population in municipalities											
Less than 20,000 inhabitants	48.3	47.0	43.3	41.5	40.0	38.8	38.2	35.6	35.1	32.5	31.3
20,000–100,000 inhabitants	23.8	23.8	25.0	27.0	26.9	29.7	32.5	36.5	38.1	41.7	43.2
Over 100,000 inhabitants	27.9	28.4	31.4	31.4	33.0	31.5	29.3	27.9	26.8	25.8	25.4

Source: Centraal Bureau voor de Statistiek 1989 pp. 18–20

total population in 1989. The proportion of minority ethnic groups (3% in 1975, 4.6% in 1980) is rapidly increasing, despite the apparent stabilization of immigration.

The birthrate has been rising slightly since the nadir of the early 1980s, but all demographic projections point to an inevitable aging of the population after the year 2000. Children under 20, the proportion of which in 25 years has fallen from 38 percent to 26 percent, will probably continue to decrease rather sharply. The 18–22 years cohort is expected to decrease by 30 percent between 1984 and 2000. At the same time, shifts in the distribution of the population over the country are visible. The eastern and southern provinces share a growing part of the population, at the expense of the highly urbanized western provinces and the north. Ever since the Second World War, people have been concentrated in midsize towns or suburbs having a population of less than 100,000 inhabitants (Table 1). Thus the general picture is of a growing homogeneity between the demographic, social, and cultural parameters, resulting in a greater predictability and an easier control of the educational system on a national scale.

The official language of the Netherlands is Dutch. In the province of Friesland, Dutch is co-official with Frisian, spoken or at least understood by some 400,000 inhabitants. But despite the fact that Frisian has been compulsory at the elementary schools of the province since 1974, there is no Frisian-speaking university. Traditionally the Dutch are inclined to use foreign languages in preference to their own in international relations. Complaints about the decline of French and German (once both compulsory as examination subjects at secondary schools) are counterbalanced by the rise of English. Courses in medicine, engineering, and technology are often taught in English, a measure that the Minister of Education proposed to generalize for all university courses (1989). This proposal has, however, met with much resistance.

1.2 Structure of the Economy

Internationally known as a commercial nation, an important part of the Netherlands' prosperity was built on rationalized farming and oceanwide fishing. They still have a prosperous agro-industry. However, due to their intensive methods, agriculture and fishing employed only 4.8 percent in 1987 (in 1888 30.8%) of the economically active population of roughly 6,000,000 people.

Industrialization came late to the Netherlands and manufacturing never employed more than one-third of the labor force (1960). Ever since, the proportion of manufacturing in employment has been declining. It fell to 18.9 percent in 1987, approximately the same proportion in the active population as the expanding commercial sector (18.1%, against 10.9% in 1899). Almost half of the jobs (48.8%) are to be found in the tertiary sector, including transport and communications (6%), and banking and insurance (3.4%). Building and other activities amount to 9.4 percent. The most important feature of employment is the rapid growth of the service sector: it doubled in 25 years from 18.7 percent in 1960 to 39.4 percent in 1987. This sector is one of the most important segments of the labor market for university trained professionals, and its continuous growth (the quaternary sector alone rose from 20% in 1970 to 29% in 1986) has ensured full employment to growing numbers of graduates for at least two decades. At present, the growth seems to be slowing down. Government services—especially in the sectors of education and welfare work—are confronted with repeated budget cuts. The balance of government revenue and expenditure shows a persistent deficit (−5.5% of national income in 1988) and unemployment rates remain high. Registered unemployment amounted in 1983 to 17.3 percent of the dependent population (14% of total active population) and was still 13.7 percent (and 11%) in 1988. Whereas overall unemployment decreased among graduates of universities it increased by 40 percent and among those of vocational colleges by 20 percent.

2. *The Institutional Fabric of the Higher Education System*

At present, there are three main branches of higher education in the Netherlands: the universities, the vocational colleges, and the Open University. In the 1960 WWO, and again in its 1986 version, the objectives of university education are stated as: (a) training for the independent pursuit of scholarship; (b) preparation for the performance of professional functions; and (c) understanding of the coherence of the whole field of science and scholarship. Universities achieve these objectives through teaching and research, transfer of knowledge for the benefit of the community, graduate teaching, and the promotion of a sense of social responsibility.

The objectives of vocational colleges are defined in the 1986 WHBO as: (a) giving a theoretical and practical training for the practice of professions; and (b) the promotion of the personal development and functioning in society of its students. They achieve these goals through teaching (and eventually a research task), graduate courses, and contributing to the development of the professions for which they provide training.

The founding Act of the Open University however (1981) mentions the following goals: (a) preparation for the independent practice of a profession; (b) training for the performance of functions in which research skills or the application of scholarly insights and methods are required or desirable: and (c) the promotion of personal development and a sense of social responsibility with regard to the practice and application of science and scholarship. It achieves these aims through the "distance teaching" of courses comparable to those provided at the ordinary universities or the vocational colleges, or—if desired— through a combination of both. Its students are also free to compile their own courses.

Thus the main difference between the three types of institution is the status of research, compulsory at the universities, permissible only as a set task at the colleges for applied science, and absent from the Open University. On the other hand, the professions for which they are meant to teach are only defined as those for which the respective kinds of training "are required or desirable." This clause permits any conceivable development in the future, including the integration of the different segments of the higher education system into a single network. The research objective itself is more and more under revision. The automatic allocation of research time to every university teacher is challenged by the "conditional financing" of research programs (continuation of the program being dependent on approval of output) and the new graduate research networks. Important changes in the organization of research and in the individual allocation of research time are expected in the near future.

Three main stages may be distinguished in the development of the university network (see Table 2). The first stage was characterized by a period of state-controlled higher education with traditional curricula and small student numbers. The 1876 Act led to the second stage, a period of expansion and institutional diversification. Denominational universities were founded and professional schools were upgraded to university level (such as Delft Polytechnic in 1905 and Wageningen Agricultural School in 1918). Rotterdam Business College, privately founded in 1913, received formal university status in 1939, while Utrecht Veterinary College had a short-lived autonomy (1917–25) before its incorporation into the university. The third stage, since the Second World War, is marked by a renewed and gradually intensifying state control, the main instrument of which is finance. Universities are now created individually, in order to fill gaps on the geographic or disciplinary map: universities of technology at Eindhoven (1956) and Enschede (Twente, 1961–64), a state University at Rotterdam (Erasmus University, 1973, through a merger of the existing Business College and a state-recognized medical faculty), and Limburg State University at Maastricht (1975). The Open University at Heerlen was inaugurated in 1984, with 18 regional study centers distributed all over the country.

Professional schools are now merely accredited institutions (on the basis of the 1960 WWO), even

Table 2

Number of institutions for higher education 1960–90

	1960	1965	1970	1975	1980	1985	1990
Universities	10	11	11	12	13	13	13
Accredited colleges	3	3	7	8	8	8	9
Vocational colleges	—	—	—	376	353	432	87
Open University	—	—	—	—	—	1	1

when receiving full state support. This is the case with Nijenrode College of Business Administration at Breukelen, privately founded in 1946, accredited in 1960 and state supported since 1971; with seven theological colleges (two Neo-Calvinist colleges at Kampen, 1960, and one at Apeldoorn, 1975; four Roman Catholic colleges at Amsterdam, Utrecht, Tilburg, and Heerlen, 1970); and with a new "University of Humanistics" (upgraded from a training college for humanistic teachers and spiritual advisers) at Utrecht in 1989. Moreover, according to the 1960 WWO special grants are awarded to nine Protestant, Old Catholic, and Jewish religious communities for training courses for ministers that they run in conjunction with the faculties of theology of the public universities (the so-called *duplex ordo*). Some institutes of international education and research in technology or social sciences are state supported as a part of the university network, in particular the International Institute for Aerospace Survey and Earth Sciences at Enschede, the International Institute for Social Studies in the Hague founded in 1952 by the Dutch universities as a graduate school, and the NUFFIC in the Hague, an office for international university relations that itself administers some research institutes. Finally, some privately funded institutions (such as the Dutch branches of Webster or Newport universities, and several small independent theological colleges) depend entirely on the market sector for professional needs. They are not included in government statistics.

During the 1970s and 1980s, new proposals to establish full universities or even complete faculties elsewhere, in particular in the eastern or northern provinces, had not been satisfied. The College of Social Sciences, established in 1976 at Leeuwarden (Friesland) as a branch of Groningen University, appeared to be a failure and has been closed down; university departments have been concentrated at Groningen and vocational colleges at Leeuwarden, the other northern capital. In fact, ever since the 1970s and under the pressure of persisting budgetary deficits, government policy has aimed at a contraction of the network. Cuts in public spending go hand in hand with the desire to make the supply of graduates correspond with the presumed demands of the academic labor market. Generally speaking, the government wants to bring the university into agreement with the market sector by raising efficiency standards in teaching and developing close planning schemes for research. The new idea of the university is of an enterprise that needs professional management and a market orientation; it will have to adapt teaching programs to the market demand and find a large amount of private funding, mainly through contract research and graduate courses.

Government officials legitimize this new policy by invoking the necessary transition from the old Humboldtian university model to Anglo-Saxon (in fact North American) standards: performance supersedes learning. It is true that the new specialized universities grow faster than the old universal ones. Also in 1981 the Two-Stage Structure Act started a process of formal separation between mass university teaching and elite training: widely available four-year initial courses are followed by a phase of restricted access. Research planning increasingly comes under the responsibility of nonuniversity institutions (the Royal Dutch Academy of Sciences, the Netherlands Organization for Scientific Research), whereas graduate teaching is supplied by a variety of superstructures (institutes for professional training, faculty courses, graduate schools, cooperation agreements between universities, and even mixed teaching by universities and vocational colleges together) which are subject to special conditions of access and sometimes demand high tuition fees.

Government policy is also guided by the conviction that the Netherlands is a unified, indeed a uniform country with negligible internal variations; the multiplication of numerous small, similar institutions all over the country is contrary both to the centralizing tendencies of the government's planning departments and to the prevailing "big is beautiful" ideology. Proposals for reorganization occasionally go to the extreme of a single *universitas neerlandica*, of which the existing universities would be mere branches. Consequently, several attempts were made during the 1980s to rationalize the university network as such. Under the programmatic names of Allocation of Tasks and Concentration (TVC, 1982) and Selective Shrinkage and Growth (SKG, 1986–87), two big operations encompassing all the state-supported institutions were set up. Their target was to concentrate teaching tasks by compressing departments (mainly in the humanities, the social sciences, and medicine). Whole faculties (e.g., dentistry) were considered superfluous given the evolution of the academic labor market.

However, an effective rationalization through general measures is politically hampered by the coexistence of public and private universities. Given the virtually unavoidable participation of the Christian Democrats (one-third of the voters) in every governmental coalition, the denominational universities seem untouchable. Educational policy is still guided by the principles of the so-called Pacification Act (1920), which ended the school struggle by putting public and private education on the same footing. This prevents the government, for example, from simply closing down one of the two overlapping universities at Amsterdam. Cooperation between the two Roman Catholic universities is stimulated, and more reallocation of teaching and research may be expected between the six universities (Leiden, Delft, Rotterdam, Utrecht, and the two universities at Amsterdam) in the so-called Randstad, the highly urbanized west of the country. However the TVC and SKG operations have shown that the central administration of the Ministry of Education is not familiar enough with the particular features of teaching tasks and research networks to obtain the legitimation of its decisions by the academic staff, and that it has overestimated the budgetary savings resulting from such operations. As academic resistance has proved successful in several cases, official educational policy appears to have returned to less sweeping measures; particular disciplines are reorganized after a thorough quality control performed by an independent peer review committee (as is the case with theology, under review since 1989). On the other hand, the Association of Cooperating Dutch Universities (VSNU, since 1985 a successor to the former Academic Council) at Utrecht, acknowledged as an interlocutor with the government, may play a growing role in planning and reallocation of teaching and research tasks.

Whereas the university network pertains predominantly to the public sector, most of the vocational colleges have been privately founded, some on a denominational basis, but the majority by professionals with limited educational interests. Whereas in 1986 80 percent of university students were in public institutions, this was the case with only 19 percent of the students at vocational colleges: another 26 percent were in denominational, and 55 percent in private nondenominational schools. This explains the scattered structure of higher vocational education before its reorganization. As late as 1985, more than 430 colleges existed, most of them very small (Table 2). "Private" is a term normally related to the composition of the board and administration, not to funding. Like the universities, and as far as initial courses are concerned, vocational colleges, though privately administered, are entirely financed by the government. Prior to the 1986 WHBO, financing followed a complex set of rules. The WHBO not only placed the vocational colleges on the same institutional level as the universities, but harmonized funding both within the vocational sector and with the universities. At the same time the Student Grants Act of 1986 has entitled every student—whether at a university or at a vocational college—to receive from the government a basic grant that does not have to be paid back and can be supplemented by an extra grant or loan according to the student's situation and parental income.

The structural rationalization of the higher vocational sector started in 1983 with a merger process imposed by the government for the sake of efficiency and better management. It has been accelerated since 1986 under the title Scaling Up, Allocation of Tasks and Concentration (STC). In 1990 the number of vocational colleges had been reduced to 87, established in 40 towns but of a very different size: their capacity ranges from over 10,000 students (Rotterdam, The Hague) to less than 500 (most of the specialized teacher-training colleges). In fact, the 13 largest colleges, providing a wide range of courses, comprise half of the overall student numbers. Generally speaking, the vocational colleges have more internal autonomy than the universities. The WHBO made them more or less free to determine, within the limits of seven sectors previously defined, which programs they offer. A new bill extends this autonomy to the universities, for which nine corresponding sectors have been defined. New degree courses at universities have to be agreed with by the Minister and included in the Academic Statute after a 10-year probationary period. The nine sectors, which constitute a superior level of decision making, will replace the 500-odd different courses offered by the universities and vocational colleges.

2.1 Admissions Policies and Selection

To qualify for admission to universities, students must have a diploma from a secondary school offering a six-year pre-university program (VWO), either in its classical (*gymnasium*) or in its more modern (*atheneum*) form, and with either the linguistic (A) or the scientific (B) variety of both types. Examinations are national, and all VWO graduates are supposed to have achieved a uniform level. Two-thirds of them actually go to university. Since the 1986 Acts, students who have passed the *propaedeutic* (first-year) examination at a vocational college are also eligible for university entrance. In some disciplines, additional tests may be compulsory if certain subjects were not included at the student's VWO. A *colloquium doctum* is required as an admission test for students aged over 21 who do not have such credentials. To qualify for admission to vocational colleges, students must have a diploma from the appropriate kind of general secondary (five-year HAVO or six-year VWO) or senior secondary (MBO) vocational school. For admission to the Open University, no qualifications are required other than a minimum age of 18.

Admission requirements are normally defined by national legislation. They do not operate on the basis of selection according to merit. Such a selection is supposed to take place either at secondary school or during higher education itself, for example, through the propaedeutic examination. From 1972 however, because of accommodation problems and the scarcity of job opportunities, a *numerus clausus* (called *numerus fixus* in the Netherlands) applies to certain degree courses, such as medicine and teacher training (for labor market motives), or business administration (for capacity reasons). The selection of students involves allocation by lottery, weighted by the average marks of the school-leaving examination—a hybrid solution that often causes surprise among foreign observers. However, it reflects perfectly the prevailing Dutch ideology: crude meritocracy (which is in fact favorable to the higher social classes) should be reconciled with equality of educational opportunities for all.

2.2 Structure of Qualifications and Graduate Training Programs

Since the 1986 wwo, all first-degree university courses take four years, but may be extended for two more years, student registration being limited to six years. At the end of the first year of study (or at least before the end of the second year of registration), a preliminary examination (*propaedeuse*) decides whether the student is permitted to continue his or her study at the university. At the end of the fourth year of the study program (not later than the sixth year of registration) the first level of advancement is achieved. Called the *doctoraal*, it is equivalent to a master's degree and should not be confused with the *doctoraat*, roughly equivalent to the PhD. According to the field of study, different (legally protected) titles are used for this first level: the general title is *doctorandus* (abbreviated as drs in front of the name—a source of misunderstanding in other countries, because it means neither a plurality of titles nor a PhD), while *ingenieur* (ir) is used in engineering and *meester* (mr) in law. Some professional qualifications are achieved through a specialized *doctoraal* (e.g., notary), others require graduate training and a special examination (physician, dentist, pharmacist, veterinary surgeon).

The first-level degree is a prerequisite for graduate training programs and for the second-level research degree or *doctoraat* which, obtained during a *promotie* session, entitles one to put dr (*doctor*) in front of one's name. The 1986 wwo abolished specifications of the use of the term "doctorate": the degree of doctor is now awarded regardless of the faculty. At the same time graduates from vocational colleges were authorized to apply for admission to the *doctoraat*. The doctoral dissertation may be completed during a four-year job as assistant researcher at university, at a research institute of a university, or of the Royal Dutch Academy of Sciences (KNAW) or at the Netherlands Organization for Scientific Research (NWO). Students with a research contract are called *assistent* (or *onderzoeker*) *in opleiding*, currently abbreviated as AIO or OIO. They take some courses, do some teaching, and formally belong to the teaching staff. In many fields of study, interuniversity graduate training programs for assistant researchers have been set up, stimulated by the Ministry of Education. In 1990 the Ministry was considering regrouping university research, reorganizing the whole AIO-system into a hundred graduate schools. Virtually independent from single universities, these schools would have coherent research programs with mostly part-time outside teachers and at least 40 graduate students each. To begin with, a dozen top-ranking graduate schools would receive

an important financial incentive. Quality assessments were to be made by the Academy of Sciences. However, every *doctorandus*, even without a formal research contract and a salary, may prepare a doctoral dissertation on his or her own, provided that a full professor is willing to act as a supervisor (*promotor*).

Study programs are predominantly specialist, single-subject degree courses, although there is a tendency to reorganize the propaedeutic year in a general sense. But at some universities large general programs have recently been introduced in the humanities and the social sciences (e.g., at Utrecht). Specialization increases during the course, but so does the student's freedom to choose other subjects. In the fourth year, programs may aim at professional or academic specialization, achieved by practical work, research, didactics, and so on. In order to increase the student's autonomy in compiling his or her own study program, the study load has been standardized in terms of units: one unit requires 40 hours of work; a four-year program (42 weeks or 1680 hours annually) requires 168 units. With the same purpose, some universities have introduced the "module" teaching system (1 module=40 hours), that in past years has been advocated by the Ministry of Education. But since both the students and the teachers are far from unanimous about its merits, it is not quite clear whether future legislation will urge it. The same applies to the voucher system. Cherished by the central administration, it may turn out as a practical instrument of individual development and equality of opportunities; in the hands of market-oriented technocrats it may as easily destroy the cohesion of learning and the conditions of true scholarship.

Like the universities, vocational colleges offer four-year courses beginning with a propaedeutic year during which mainly general subjects are taught. The Harmonizing Act of 1988 established a formal equivalence between the initial courses of the two types of institution. At the same time, registration as a student has been limited to six years for everybody, even for those passing from the vocational to the university sector (for whom shorter degree programs have been developed) or those willing to complete two courses successively. As in the universities, about one-third of the students at vocational colleges do not go beyond propaedeutics. Most of the others complete the whole initial course, whereas at the universities dropout rates after the *propaedeuse* are significantly higher: up to 50 percent in the humanities and in several of the social sciences. Graduates from vocational colleges may use the title *baccalaureus* (abbreviated as B, followed by a specialization) or, in technology and agriculture, *ingenieur* (or "ing", whereas university-trained engineers abbreviate as "ir"). In some cases, degrees automatically involve professional certification. Initial

Table 3
Enrollment in universities and vocational colleges 1960–85

	1960	1965	1970	1975	1980	1985
Universities[a]						
Total enrollment						
(thousands)	40.7	64.4	103.4	122.2	151.2	169.5
Percentage of female						
students	17.9	—	—	25.4	30.9	36.2
Vocational colleges						
Total enrollment						
(thousands)	40.4	52.5	72.1	111.4	131.9	148.8
Percentage of female						
students	—	—	—	39.2	41.5	44.4
As a percentage of age group 18–25 years						
Universities	3.1	4.0	5.6	6.7	7.8	8.4
All	6.9	7.3	9.5	12.8	14.6	15.8

Sources: Centraal Bureau voor de Statistiek 1988 pp. 46–47, 1989 p. 52
a not including the Open University

courses in the vocational colleges can be completed by a wide variety of graduate training programs.

2.3 Quantitative Developments in Higher Education
Since the 1960s, enrollment in both the universities and the vocational colleges has roughly quadrupled (see Table 3). In 1985, it amounted to 15.8 percent of the age group of 18–25 years, in almost equal parts. But since the total population has increased considerably, the proportion of students has only been multiplied by 2.3. The growth rate of recent decades fits in with developments in surrounding countries. Negative long-term effects of the now unfavorable demographic evolution may be counterbalanced by three factors. The proportion of women students (now about 40%) is still much smaller than that of men. Students from ethnic minorities are largely underrepresented. Finally, mature students may increasingly be attracted, given the need for adult education and updating courses, and the increase of leisure: in 1987 more than 40 percent of students were aged over 24. The importance of the enrollment in the newly created Open University (not included in the figures) testifies to the same evolution: in 1988 more than 34,000 students were registered, many of them only for a part of a degree course, and female students being slightly less numerous then elsewhere (35%). Full-time students prefer the full universities: in 1985 only 6 percent of university students were registered on a part-time basis, but 25 percent at the vocational colleges. Less than 2 percent attended the accredited institutions. All in all, student numbers are still growing beyond official prognostics. It is therefore quite uncertain whether the governmental hypothesis of a declining attendance at the end of the century will come true.

3. Governance, Administration, and Finance

3.1 National Administration
In the Netherlands, the provision of higher education is regarded as a duty of the national government. It sets the educational policy framework and allocates annual budgets to the universities and vocational colleges which account for about 90 percent of their income. Outlined by the Policy Document on Autonomy and Quality in Higher Education (HOAK) of 1985, current policy is based on the 1986 WWO and WHBO and the Open University Act (1985), on the Student Grants Act (1986), and on some supplementary laws and regulations. Curriculum requirements still obey the Academic Statute of 1981–82. However, the Statute will be abolished in order to permit a greater variety of courses and increased competition between departments and establishments resulting at length in some national hierarchy. A new Higher Education and Research Act bringing together under one legal system all types of higher education is under preparation. Along with regular contacts between the Ministry and the boards of individual institutions, the goals of higher education policy are discussed and transmitted via umbrella organizations: the VSNU for the universities, the Higher Vocational Education Council for the professional colleges.

Starting with the academic year 1988–89, relations between the institutions and the Ministry of Education and Sciences (or, for agricultural education, the Ministry of Agriculture and Fisheries) are guided by a biennial agreement on the national level, the Higher Education and Research Plan (HOOP), which is meant to leave more autonomy to the institutions than in the past, within the framework defined by law and by the aims of government policy. According to the 1988–89 HOOP, these aims are: (a) to ensure a universal access to higher education (only on the basis of academic aptitude as expressed in formal qualifications); (b) to respect the individual's freedom of choice; and (c) to meet society's demand for higher education, both quantitatively and qualitatively. This is to say that the Dutch government does not want to restrict access to higher education and individual choice for other than market reasons.

The increased autonomy of the establishments should be counterbalanced by the strengthening of quality control, either through regular self-evaluation or through external agencies, such as the inspectorate (with a supervising task) or external review committees (*visitatiecommissies*) assessing a whole discipline every five years. But such forms of assessment may make the largely equal standards between the universities still more uniform.

There is a significant difference between the government funding of the universities and that of the vocational colleges. The latter is almost entirely a function of the number of students, whereas other factors play an important role in the allocation of the annual budget of the university sector, negotiated between the ministries of Education and Finance. The actual funding formula of individual universities, introduced in 1982 (the so-called Places-Funds Model, or PGM), has multiple variables among which are numbers of students (either graduated or not), curriculum profiles, research (partly related to student numbers, partly "conditionally financed" in big five-year programs), and nonacademic staff. Obvious differences in the running costs of courses justify the distinction between several curriculum profiles: annual expenses per student vary from 3,600 (law) to 37,000 guilders (veterinary medicine) at the universities: from 2,400 to 13,000 at the vocational colleges, tuition fees being the same for all students (at present about 1,850 guilders annually). For all the

courses in humanities and social sciences, expenses remain under 10,000 guilders per student; in the exact sciences they mostly exceed 15,000 guilders. However, running costs have been reduced between 1975 and 1983 by 15 percent at the vocational colleges and 30 percent at the universities. At the same time higher education diminished its proportion in the total educational expenditure and the gross national product (see Table 4). Repeated spending cuts (resulting in an increasing workload for the staff), less expansion, and transfer of tasks to other institutions account for this evolution.

3.2 Institutional Administration

The University Administration Reform Act of 1970 (WUB) has transformed the Dutch universities from professorial institutions administrated by an external board of curators and an academic senate presided by the *rector magnificus*, into organizations with a certain degree of self-government on every level. Corporate responsibility has superseded the individual authority of the professor. Both the university and each faculty have an executive board and a council, consisting of academic and nonacademic staff and students in ratios determined by law. Teachers form at least one-third of the university council and half of the faculty council. The councils decide on general policy and the budget, and define biennial development plans. As the financial framework is rather rigidly fixed by existing regulations, real autonomy is, however, very limited. Members from outside the university act on the university council as representatives of society.

The executive board of the university consists of three members appointed by the Minister on recommendation of the council: it is responsible to the council. The chairman of the board is essentially a manager and not necessarily a teacher. The *rector magnificus* of the university represents the academic staff on the board but is not its chairperson. He or

Table 4
Government expenditure on higher education 1960–1990

	1960	1965	1970	1975	1980	1985	1986	1990
Expenditure (millions of guilders)								
Universities	265.2	821.7	1,810.6	3,246.6	4,662.3	4,619.0	4,614.7	—
Vocational colleges	91.2	200.9	445.5	1,071.6	1,731.6	1,937.1	2,043.7	—
Total	356.4	1,022.6	2,256.1	4,318.2	6,393.9	6,556.1	6,658.4	6,539
Percentage of education budget	17.9	23.7	26.4	24.4	24.8	23.8	23.1	22.5
Percentage of total government expenditure[a]	3.43	5.24	6.44	5.65	4.95	3.96	3.92	3.70
Percentage of gross national product (GNP)	0.85	1.51	1.86	1.96	1.90	1.57	1.55	—

Source: Computed from Centraal Bureau voor de Statistiek 1988 pp. 18, 107, 1989 pp. 61–62, 154, 166, National Budget 1990
a Including extraordinary expenditure (capital expenditure and debt service). Rates differ slightly according to the definitions employed

she chairs, however, the council of faculty deans, a relic of the old senate with very limited competency (it grants the doctorates and advises on academic policy). The members of both the university and the faculty council are elected by the whole staff and all the registered students. The executive board of the faculty (including a student member) is appointed by the faculty council: its head, the dean, is a full professor. He or she also chairs the faculty council and represents the faculty outside. With the exception of the chairperson of the university board, none of these positions is permanent. At present, vocational colleges have roughly similar organizational structure, but with more autonomy.

The bottom level of university administration is the *vakgroep* (department), a teaching and research unit roughly equivalent to a discipline or a specialism. The executive committee of the department consists of the whole tenured academic staff and of representatives of other staff and of the (senior) students. It is presided over by a chairperson elected from among the full professors, decides democratically on teaching and research programs, and distributes these tasks among its individual members. As a rule, the individual balance between teaching, research, and administrative duties depends on the specific funding models (some universities or faculties receive much more research time than others) and is the same for all the staff members of the unit, but the department may agree with some individual accommodations (e.g., when graduate courses are not yet accounted for in the funding models). Big departments are sometimes divided into sections, but such more workable base units do not have legal rights. There is a curriculum committee for each degree course (or *studierichting*, defined in the Academic Statute and sometimes equivalent to a department) and each faculty has its research committee; both are consulting and advisory bodies. The extensive qualifications of the university and faculty councils and of the department committee are the outcome of the student movement in the late 1960s. At present, there is an unmistakable tendency to reduce democratic decision making and restore to the professorial hierarchy some of its former authority, but the new motive is efficiency.

4. Faculty and Students: Teaching, Learning, and Research

4.1 Faculty

The Ministry of Education undertook a reorganization of the whole academic staff in 1986. The special Statute (1931) of the full professors who (if at a state university), were appointed by the Queen, was abolished. The teaching positions were renamed and the ratio between full (*hoogleraar*), associate (*universitair hoofddocent* or UHD) and assistant professors (*universitair docent* or UD) was thoroughly changed. In the future, it is meant to approach 1:1.5:2.5, together with about two assistant-researchers (AIO). Moreover, the number of full professors (2,858 in 1986) should decrease. In the Netherlands, only full professors are called "professor" and all titles are used. Highly specialized UHD may obtain a part-time professorship, sometimes sponsored by a private foundation. Staff members are appointed by the individual institutions following a public application procedure that always involves a special selection committe and, in the case of full professors, consultation of the corresponding departments.

At present, all staff members pertain to the civil service regulated by a 1929 Act. Tenure is granted after a four-year probationary period, but it applies only to a specific post. The civil service gives no personal protection. When a faculty member's (even a full professor's) post is removed, he or she cannot claim to be transferred to another one but becomes redundant. During the recent reorganizations, the government has largely used this method: though faculty members cannot be dismissed, they have to disappear with their position. Advancement applies only to salary increase but even then is automatic. Salary scales for both the public and the private institutions are determined by the government and are the same all over the country. Transfer to a higher position requires a formal application and depends on the posts available. The current contraction of the number of higher staff positions leaves little room for career aspirations. There is a growing number of temporary, nontenured posts. Academic staff are slowly aging, whereas graduates are mostly young.

This rigid bureaucratic system is not encouraging for individual scholars, teachers, or other staff members. In some departments (economics, business, computer science) highly qualified faculty members are tempted to switch over to the market sector, where career planning is possible and salaries are better. Therefore the government has recently authorized some financial facilities for scholars with a high market value. This might be the beginning of a thorough change of the system, demanded by many staff members and the institutions themselves.

At the universities, nonacademic staff outnumber academic staff. Because of the numerous part-time appointments, the complexity and frequent changes of the structures, and not least the inconsistency of governmental statistics, it is impossible to present a meaningful range of figures over a long period. In 1985 the universities employed 18,152 full-time equivalents as academic staff (WP) and 21,277 as nonacademic or auxiliary, technical, or clerical staff (NWP). The ratio of NWP to WP was 1:17, one of the highest in Europe. This is at least partially due to the importance of the general services and university bureaucracy. At faculty level there is, however, a

Table 5
Intake of first-year university students, nationwide by sector, 1970–85, and expected intake 1992–2000 (in % of total per annum)

Sectors	1970	1980	1985	1992	2000
Agriculture	2.4	4.0	3.4	3.3	3.3
Engineering	15.6	12.9	14.4	15.1	15.1
Science	11.0	9.1	8.4	7.6	7.6
Health	11.4	10.8	8.3	8.1	8.4
Economics	10.6	9.7	14.7	18.0	18.0
Behavior and society	24.1	18.8	17.1	15.4	15.3
Language and culture	10.7	18.5	17.7	16.7	16.7
Law	14.1	16.1	16.1	15.8	15.7
UNESCO categories					
Exact sciences	40.4	36.8	34.5	34.1	34.4
Social sciences	48.8	44.6	47.9	49.2	49.0
Humanities	10.7	18.5	17.7	16.7	16.7
Total	22,310	26,896	29,529	29,905	28,387

Source: Ministerie van Onderwijs en Wetenschappen 1988 p. 105

considerable imbalance between the sectors: in the exact sciences, the ratio is three or four times higher than in the social sciences and the humanities. About 60 percent of the staff members had a full-time job. The vocational colleges employed in the same year 11,837 full-time equivalents of teaching staff (19,642 persons, two-thirds of whom worked more than 20 hours a week); the ratio of nonteaching to teaching staff in five vocational sectors was 0:31. Finally, nonuniversity research institutes employed 2,069 academic staff and 1,284 nonacademic. As a whole, the combined effects of the various reorganizations mentioned above caused teaching staff to decrease slightly in the 1980s, whereas nonacademic staff increased, but also in small numbers. In spite of official policy, encouraging female employment and sometimes actually using positive discrimination policies (e.g., at the University of Amsterdam), female staff remain scarce, especially in the higher functions: 26 percent at the universities in 1986 (but only 16% of the teaching staff and not more than 3% of the full professors), 28 percent at the vocational colleges (but mainly in the sectors of education, health, and culture). However, rates of female employment are slowly rising on all the levels.

4.2 Students

The distribution of university students across the main subject areas since 1970 (see Table 5) shows a sharp decrease in the exact sciences, in particular of medicine; and, among the social sciences, of the behavioral sector (sociology). The humanities and economics are the most popular sectors and, according to the government's prognosis, will remain so until the end of the century. This applies even to the health sector where traditionally graduation involves larger numbers of students than in other disciplines (see Table 6). As far as engineering and health are concerned, the evolution seems slightly different in the vocational colleges, but even there economics went up by bounds (see Tables 7 and 8). Compared to other countries of Northern Europe, the proportion of students in the social sciences is in the Netherlands 5 to 20 percent higher, whereas that of the exact sciences is significantly lower. This applies equally to the share of the different sectors in the government's research budget. It might be explained by a difference in occupational structure: industry is less important in the Netherlands than elsewhere and the highly developed welfare state with its huge quaternary sector demands high numbers of graduates from behavioral sciences and education, especially among women (Table 8). There is also a certain paradigmatic change: sociology, for instance, has lost its "generalist" outlook and become more empirical, whereas some other social sciences (economics, business) together with contemporary history seem to be considered as new "generalist" studies, aspiring to answer society's major questions or simply to be widely employable on the labor market. Graduation rates are therefore relatively low in these departments.

Nevertheless, employment problems will grow. The steady increase of the proportion of the labor force with higher education (see Table 9) will affect required qualification levels. In 1985 unemployment of graduates was already important in the behavioral sector (14.7%) and the humanities (13%), although the situation seems to have stabilized since then. Anyway, since 88 percent of graduates in the humanities, 89 percent of those in the behavioral sector and 95 percent in the medical sector are employed by

Table 6
University graduates from undergraduate courses, nationwide by sector, 1970–85, and expected numbers 1992–2000 (in % of total per annum)

Sectors	1970	1980	1985	1992	2000
Agriculture	2.8	3.4	4.8	3.8	3.7
Engineering	17.6	13.3	12.2	14.5	14.3
Science	12.7	10.0	9.3	7.3	7.2
Health	20.1	18.7	14.2	8.8	9.7
Economics	10.0	8.1	8.9	18.1	18.4
Behavior and society	12.7	20.4	19.7	16.1	15.7
Language and culture	9.9	12.1	15.9	15.7	15.4
Law	14.3	13.8	15.1	15.8	15.5
UNESCO categories					
Exact sciences	53.2	45.4	40.5	34.4	34.9
Social sciences	37.0	42.3	43.7	50.0	49.6
Humanities	9.9	12.1	15.9	15.7	15.4
Total	7,259	11,146	17,630	21,032	18.473
Graduates as a percentage of intake	32.5	41.4	59.7	70.5	65.1

Source: Ministerie van Onderwijs en Wetenschappen 1988 p. 140

government-funded services (against only one-third of graduates in engineering and economics and half of the graduates in law), the budgetary evolution and general governmental policy remain of vital importance for the future of employment in these sectors, not to forget that of education itself.

It is astonishing that in spite of the prevailing Dutch ideology of equality of educational opportunities, very little is known of students' social class origins. They are no longer mentioned in the government's statistics. The last reliable figures go back to 1974, when 33 percent of university students came from the higher classes, 49 percent were of middle-class origin, and only 18 percent came from the lower classes. However, the share of lower-class students (6% in 1947, 10% in 1964) was rapidly increasing. The same applies, as mentioned before, to female students, responsible for most of the increase of the registered student numbers. However, it has to be noted that female students remain scarce in engineering (8% in 1985) and economics (13%), whereas they form a large majority in the behavioral sciences (60%) and the humanities (64%), especially in pedagogics, psychology, arts and literature; in some vocational health studies and primary teacher training they have got a virtual monopoly. Research remains a male sector: only 9 percent of doctoral dissertations (at PhD level) are written by women.

Foreign students form a small minority in the Netherlands: 2.3 percent of the university student body in 1986, 1.6 percent at the vocational schools. Half of them were Europeans, a quarter came from the former colonies. The Dutch language may be an impediment, although the technical universities (and others) offer many courses in English. More likely, this low rate reflects a certain parochialism. The Netherlands have been marginalized within Europe and often act as a mere appendix of the United States, especially where university policy is concerned. Moreover, the traditional linguistic abilities of the Dutch have suffered from the virtual monopoly of (superficially mastered) English. The solution to this problem might not be found in a forced Anglicization of teaching and learning, as quite recently proposed by the Minister of Education in order to attract foreign students to the Nether-

Table 7
Enrollment in the vocational colleges, nationwide by sector, 1975–85, and expected enrollment 1992 (in % of total per annum)

Sectors	1975	1980	1985	1992
Agriculture	1.9	2.6	3.2	3.5
Engineering	17.9	19.9	21.6	18.1
Health	8.3	10.5	11.6	9.9
Economics	5.0	8.8	16.7	25.5
Behavior and society	12.7	15.1	12.9	10.3
Language and culture	9.0	9.1	9.9	10.9
Education	45.3	34.0	24.2	21.8
Total (1,000s)[a]	142	171	190	212

Source: computed from Ministerie van Onderwijs en Wetenschappen 1988 p. 122
a The totals of this government document are not consistent with those of the Central Bureau of Statistics in Table 3

Table 8

Total number of graduates from vocational colleges aged under 65, by sector, 1981–85 (% of total per annum)

Sector	Total			Women only		
	1981	1983	1985	1981	1983	1985
Agriculture	1.2	1.3	1.5	0.2	0.3	0.3
Engineering	19.2	18.4	17.7	2.4	2.4	2.3
Health	8.6	9.4	9.6	15.7	16.2	16.0
Economics	14.3	14.6	16.3	13.3	14.2	15.1
Behavior and society	8.1	9.4	10.0	10.4	11.6	12.4
Language and culture	4.0	4.0	4.1	3.9	3.7	3.7
Education	41.2	39.7	37.7	52.1	49.4	48.4
Other	3.4	3.2	3.0	2.1	2.2	1.8
Total number (1,000s)	688	743	869	291	330	386

Source: Ministerie van Onderwijs en Wetenschappen 1988 p. 191

lands, but in a new and greater openness of Dutch teachers and students themselves to other cultures, especially academic cultures, and for other than American learning. Naturally the ERASMUS program is vital for this issue.

5. Conclusion

Higher education in the Netherlands has been thoroughly reorganized during the 1980s. The whole system has been streamlined and some bridges have been established between the university and the vocational sector. Both teachers and researchers have become more sensitive to the need for an efficient and productive spending of public money. The institutions have developed a greater sense of responsibility for the students' future employment and the students themselves have been forced to intensify their efforts. The institutions' autonomy,

highly proclaimed by the Ministry of Education, remains, however, largely symbolic. To change the practice of direct government interference would demand a thorough reorganization and thinning out of the central administration, which the current Minister of Education now seems prepared to undertake. There is an evident weariness among the universities' staff members about the structural transformations imposed from above year after year, often without the least apprehension of the realities of education and research or any consultation.

Government policy aims at a reconciliation of university education with the market sector and at a widely accessible and internally flexible higher education system without overlapping institutions. Up to now political considerations prevented government officials from a straightforward attack on private institutions and on the binary system. Ministerial documents show quite clearly however that such a general rationalization of the whole system remains the final objective of at least a part of the responsible officials. A recent (April 1990) OECD report on education in the Netherlands supports this view. In the meantime, both segments should be differentiated by a greater emphasis on their identity: universities ought to be more concerned about science; vocational colleges about professional training.

There are however some major risks. It is not certain that traditional academic culture, the very condition of excellent scholarship, will be able to resist much longer the repeated assaults of the planning bureaucracy both inside and outside the university. The process of scaling up and allocation of tasks between the institutions involves a monopolization of teaching and research by single institutions, which lack henceforth the incentive of competition. The celebration of the market model, of technical skills and management, of crude meritocracy and useful science, of collective research

Table 9

Proportion of the labor force with higher education 1930–85

	1930	1947	1960	1971	1979	1985
Total labor force with higher education (university and vocational)						
Percentage of men	?	?	4.6	9.0	14.2	18.2
Percentage of women	?	?	3.7	6.6	12.6	17.3
Total percentage	?	?	4.4	8.4	13.7	17.9
Labor force with university education						
Percentage of men	0.9	1.2	1.8	2.4	3.9	5.4
Percentage of women	0.2	0.5	1.0	1.1	1.4	2.4
Total percentage	0.7	1.1	1.6	2.1	3.2	4.4

Source: computed from Kouwenaar 1988 p. 97

programs and productive thinking, favors immediate results and applied knowledge above time-consuming and uncertain fundamental science. It favors specialization above a generalist approach, in spite of official ideology. The university could be in danger of losing its function as the think-tank of society, based on academic freedom. New conditions should be created for true scholarship, especially in the humanities and the social sciences, as the Dutch Academy of Sciences has recently brought to the fore, although without much success as yet. But arguably that should be the most vital item under discussion during the coming decade.

Bibliography

Aarts J F M C, Deen N, Giesbers J H G I 1980 *Onderwijs in Nederland*, 4th edn. Wolters–Noordhoff, Groningen

Blume S S, Spaapen J B 1988 External assessment and "conditional financing" of research in Dutch universities. *Minerva* 26(1): 1–30

Centraal Bureau voor de Statistiek 1988 *Zakboek onderwijsstatistieken 1988. Onderwijs cijfergewijs.* SDU Uitgeverij/CBS-Publikaties, The Hague

Centraal Bureau voor de Statistiek 1989 *1899–1989. Negentig jaren statistiek in tijdreeksen.* SDU Uitgeverij/CBS-Publikaties, The Hague

Daalder H 1982 The Netherlands: Universities between the "new democracy" and the "new management". In: Daalder H, Shils E (eds.) 1982 *Universities, Politicians and Bureaucrats.* Cambridge University Press, Cambridge, pp. 173–232

Foppen J W 1988 The interaction of policy style and legislation: Reforms in Dutch universities. *Higher Educ. Policy* 1(3): 18–24

Frijhoff W 1984 The Netherlands. In: Jílek L (ed.) 1984 *Historical Compendium of European Universities.* CRE, Geneva, pp. 43–46

Groen M 1988 *University Education in The Netherlands 1815–1980.* Eindhoven University of Technology, Eindhoven (EUT Report 88-WM-016)

Kouwenaar K, Stannard J 1988 *Higher Education in the Netherlands. Characteristics, Structure, Figures, Facts.* Netherlands Ministry of Education and Science, Zoetermeer

Lock G 1989 The collectivization of the Dutch universities. *Minerva* 27(2–3): 157–76

Luttikholt H W 1986 Universities in the Netherlands: In search of a new understanding. *Eur. J. Educ.* 21(1): 57–66

Mc-Daniël O C 1987 *The Netherlands into the Nineties. Trends in Higher Education Policy.* Netherlands Ministry of Education and Science, Zoetermeer

Ministerie van Onderwijs en Wetenschappen 1988 *Dutch Higher Education and Research. Major Issues, Facts and Figures.* Netherlands Ministry of Education and Science, Zoetermeer

Ringer F K 1979 *Education and Society in Modern Europe*, Indiana University Press, Bloomington, Indiana

Van Steijn F 1990 *The Universities in Society. A Study of Part-time Professors in the Netherlands.* Universiteit van Amsterdam, Amsterdam

W. Frijhoff

New Zealand

1. Higher Education and Society

New Zealand higher education began in Dunedin with a university college in 1869. This created a democratic Scottish influence which has remained prominent in universities, despite some English notions of elitism (Carter 1990). A teacher-training institution followed in 1876, and about 90 years later the first polytechnics were formalized by legislation.

There are now (1990) seven universities, one tribal-based *wananga* (Maori university), six colleges of education and 24 polytechnics (*Education Statistics of New Zealand*). At least two private institutions with international links intend negotiating higher education status. This is possible under important recent legislation (*Education Amendment Act* 1990), covering higher education.

New Zealand lies in the southwest Pacific, comprising two main islands, with an area of 268,675 square kilometers. The population of 3.35 million (1989), includes 12.5 percent indigenous Maori, 3.5 percent from smaller Pacific Islands, and 82 percent of Anglo-Celtic or European origin. The population increased rapidly in 1950–70, but growth has since slowed. Two factors explain this: lower birthrates and emigration, which sometimes exceeded immigration by 10,000.

Most New Zealanders are urban dwellers, with only 5 percent on farms or in small towns. Three-quarters of the population inhabit the North Island, almost half of whom live in Auckland and the capital, Wellington. The rural–urban shift has almost stabilized, but a South–North drift continues.

New Zealand is predominantly English-speaking, although Maori has some legal status. Maori is used in the *wananga*, but all other higher education is in English.

New Zealanders are mainly middle or working class. There is no traditional aristocracy, but there are a few very wealthy people. Some farmers might be considered closest to a "landed gentry." Pacific Island migrants and Maori tend to earn less in mainly working-class occupations.

The economic base has traditionally rested on dairy products, meat, and wool. Forestry, fishing, tourism, and horticulture have contributed more in recent years. Principal imports include metal and petroleum products and manufactured goods. Major trading partners are Japan, Australia, and the United States, all outstripping the traditional British market. Hydroelectric power is significant, while recent discoveries of oil and natural gas have reduced energy imports. New Zealand is nuclear-free.

In 1986, fewer than 6 percent of the 1.34 million full-time workforce were in agriculture, forestry, or fishing. Just over a third worked in mining, manufacturing, and related industries, while almost 60 percent were employed in the tertiary sector. Women make up 37 percent of the full-time workforce, and over three-quarters of part-time workers. Unemployment, a recent phenomenon in New Zealand, has increased sharply since the late 1970s, reaching 7.3 percent in mid-1990.

New Zealand has a democratically elected unicameral parliament of 97 members and universal suffrage. It is an independent constitutional monarchy with a governor-general appointed by the British monarch. Two parties have dominated parliament since the Second World War—a right-of-center National Party and a now center-left Labor Party. The Labor government (1984–90), has recently conducted large-scale reviews of education, including higher education, leading to major changes in education administration (1989–90).

Labor's education policy has had three main thrusts. First, they have legislated greater control of finance, staffing, and administration to local institutions, with increased accountability to central agencies. Important curriculum controls and overall allocation of finance remains centrally determined. A second thrust derives from broader policies on biculturalism and equity, along with greater recognition of the Treaty of Waitangi (1840)—an agreement between Maori and the British Crown. Educational programs and governing bodies are now required to be more representative of the community. Thirdly, they have sought to raise participation rates in postcompulsory education, particularly by Maori, women, and disadvantaged groups. Both major parties aim to increase skill levels in the workforce to improve the economy and international trade. By 1991 a new National government had not altered these policies dramatically, although some strategies have changed.

New Zealand is basically a Protestant country, with a 15 percent Catholic minority and very small groups professing other religions. State education is nonsectarian by law, although Catholic schools are "integrated" into the state system and can teach religion. While religious studies are taught in some universities, organized religion has played no significant part in the development, curriculum or organization of higher education.

2. The Institutional Fabric of the Higher Education System

Higher education in New Zealand is overwhelmingly a state system. Universities, polytechnics, and colleges of education are currently all sponsored and largely financed by the state.

Six of the seven universities are multidisciplinary, teaching arts (social sciences and humanities), science, and commerce. Medicine, engineering, law, and other specialist disciplines are taught at selected universities. Professional degrees in education are offered at most universities, co-taught with a college of education. The seventh university (Lincoln), concentrates on land-related courses and science. All universities teach from undergraduate to doctoral level, and all engage in basic and applied research.

The 24 polytechnics vary greatly in size. Many polytechnics evolved from "senior technical divisions," or from secondary technical schools, while some were planned as community colleges. Polytechnics teach vocational, community, and some higher education programs, such as three-year nondegree courses in nursing, engineering, and accounting. Recent legislation aims to promote greater cross-crediting of such tertiary-level work across institutions.

Most colleges of education offer primary trainees four-year pre-service degree courses with a university, and two-year diploma courses for graduates. Some integrated programs for primary and early childhood trainees are developing. Secondary training generally involves a one-year graduate diploma course, although postschool programs exist. Secondary physical education students at Auckland College of Education, for example, undertake a BEd overseen and awarded by Massey University. Secondary teachers train in Auckland and Christchurch, with smaller groups elsewhere. Occasionally small school-based "outpost" programs are linked to a college.

The numbers of universities and colleges of education has altered only slightly since 1960. Already established, Massey (1961), Waikato (1964), and Lincoln (1990) became full universities, joining Otago, Canterbury, Auckland, and Victoria. The *wananga* at Otaki opened in 1981. Colleges of education have numbered between six and nine. Closures and amalgamations have balanced new colleges, leaving six, one fewer than in 1960. Changes have been due to some course integration and falling school rolls from the mid-1970s.

The polytechnics have expanded dramatically. Prior to legislation formalizing their postschool status (1964), there were three "technical institutes." By 1970 there were eight polytechnics, by 1980, 21; there are now (1990) 24. This expansion comes from government policies both to increase the skilled workforce and to improve advanced training opportunities throughout New Zealand.

Enrollments in higher education have shown interesting variations over the same period, as can be seen in Table 1.

University numbers include extramural students, overwhelmingly studying through Massey University. They represent 21 percent of 1988 enrollments (8% in 1960). Similarly, nearly 40 percent of 1988 polytechnic enrollments were on correspondence. The proportion of "part-time" university students (defined simply on the number of courses taken), has remained constant at 20–25 per-

Table 1
Enrollments in higher education 1960–88

	1960	1965	1970	1975	1980	1985	1988
University	15,809	22,145	34,769	42,436	51,522	59,123	72,313
Colleges of education	3,672	4,790	7,587	7,779	5,919	2,844	4,503
Polytechnics	a	a	a	20,132	26,791	33,875	37,379

a Data unavailable; 1975–88, enrollments in full-year ISCED Level 5 courses

cent. University enrollments rose to 75,900 in 1989, an increase of nearly 30 percent in four years. Polytechnic and university enrollments could continue to rise, because higher retention rates are offsetting lower secondary school intakes. College of education enrollment variations reflect changing government quotas as school rolls decline and more teachers stay in service. This in turn reflects changing economic conditions in New Zealand.

In the age group 20–24, the proportion enrolled in full- and part-time courses in higher education (ISCED levels 5–7) has increased quite slowly reaching 13.4 percent in 1988.

From 1991, all higher education institutions will control their own enrollments, but government funding will be provided for a set number. Overseas students will be charged cost-recovery fees.

University entrance standards will be set by the New Zealand Qualifications Authority (NZQA) after formal consultation with universities. Currently, all students reaching a predetermined level in the final-year national secondary-school examination may enter university as of right, although some courses have restricted entry. This has long applied to specialist courses (e.g., medicine, fine arts), but recent roll increases have forced new restrictions in some universities, notably in commerce, but also in other subjects. Several courses, including law and engineering, require an intermediate year, following which students are selected on merit. Where selection on entry occurs, school examination results usually count, although places are sometimes reserved for Maori and mature entrants who may be admitted provisionally from age 20. Special provisions are also available to unqualified students over 16.

Entry to colleges of education was controlled centrally by the Department of Education. Colleges now control enrollment, and intend generally to require four completed years of secondary schooling, although the current high proportion of mature entrants (over 20) is likely to continue.

Entry requirements to polytechnic courses vary widely, with higher education courses generally requiring at least four years successful secondary schooling. Where course numbers are restricted, higher qualifications or special aptitudes are used to select students.

Degrees are (1990) awarded only by each university, sanctioned and recognized by the state. Under the new law other institutions can (and will) apply to grant degrees for specified courses. The use of the terms "degree," "bachelor," "master," and "doctor" in awards is protected. Most first-level degrees in arts, science, music, and commerce involve three years' full-time study, but law, fine arts, and engineering require four, architecture five, and medicine (a double degree) six. All these are termed "bachelor's degrees." There are a number of university diplomas, both at undergraduate and graduate level (e.g., diploma in clinical psychology).

There are no separate graduate schools for higher degrees. Entry to masters normally requires a first degree with sound passes in a major subject at the final-year undergraduate level. In some cases high enrollments require selection by merit. Masters degrees comprise both course work and research, requiring one to two years full-time study. Many subjects require a research thesis worth up to 45 percent of the total marks. Some universities have BHons degrees, covering master's-level coursework, and a one-year master's program comprising a research thesis.

Entry to doctoral programs is primarily controlled by subject departments. A sound master's qualification and evidence of research skills is usually required. This research degree is normally by thesis only, with a minimum of two years' full-time study.

3. Governance, Administration, and Finance

3.1 National Administration

Higher education is centrally controlled by the state, although individual institutions—especially universities—are largely self-managing. There is no regional control. Under ministerial advice, the governor-general may by order-in-council establish or disestablish a body as a university, *wananga*, college of education, or polytechnic. The 1990 Act protected these names and "established" all present institutions. This also involved substantive definitions of each form, and a guarantee of academic freedom.

Further control exists through NZQA and the Education Review Office (ERO). The New Zealand Qualifications Authority must approve all nationally

Table 2
Expenditure on higher education 1960–88

(To 31 Mar)	1960	1965	1970	1975	1980	1985	1988
US$ 000s	4,686[a]	12,110[a]	42,551	105,308	183,666	275,509	558,451
% of govt expenditure	1.0	2.1	3.4	4.6	3.7	3.1	4.2
% of GNP	0.3	0.6	1.3	1.7			
% of GDP[b]				1.8	1.5	1.2	1.6

a These figures exclude allocations for buildings b Reporting in terms of GNP ceased in 1979

recognized education courses except those in universities, which are approved by the Vice-Chancellors' Committee (VCC). This committee has inherited some functions of the former University Grants Committee, a buffer body between universities and the Ministry. The VCC will approve courses, moderate standards, and administer national scholarships.

The New Zealand Qualifications Authority monitors educational standards and may accredit (or not) public or private institutions to teach nationally recognized courses, including degrees. The Minister has an overriding right to direct a council not to provide a course of study (but not an individual section of a course), where resources could be used inefficiently.

Both NZQA and ERO had rights of entry and other controlling rights removed from the original Bill, following strong national and international opposition to what were serious threats to academic freedom. The Education Review Office's functions are now limited to a three-yearly review of the extent to which higher education institutions are eliminating barriers to disadvantaged groups and actively promoting equity.

Through these agencies, the government can determine directions for higher education, less easily for universities, but quite strongly for polytechnics and colleges of education. Especially potent is the power of NZQA to accredit private institutions and to award degree-granting status.

The government-approved goals of all forms of higher education are implicit in the 1990 legislation, through the definitions of institutions. Universities are concerned with research and "advanced learning"; colleges of education focus on research and teaching relating to institutionalized education; polytechnics deal more with vocational research and teaching; while *wananga* develop and disseminate knowledge particularly regarding *ahuatanga Maori* (Maori tradition), according to *tikanga Maori* (Maori custom). Within that framework, institutions are comparatively free to develop their own goals through an obligatory "charter," approved by the Minister, who can, in certain circumstances, propose (and arguably insist on) amendments.

Finance for higher education comes almost entirely from central government. There are no regional or local education taxes. Government expenditure on higher education is detailed in Table 2.

The figures disguise the fact that expenditure on teacher education fell sharply from about 1975–85, and in constant dollar terms is still less than 50 percent of the 1975 allocation (Goff 1989). Similarly calculated expenditure on polytechnics more than doubled in the same period. This was caused by the increase in the number of institutions and the greater emphasis on postcompulsory vocational education by government. Constant dollar expenditure on universities rose by 26 percent during 1975–88 (student numbers rose by 70%).

From 1991 all higher education institutions will receive bulk grants, determined annually by a common formula based on (approved) numbers of equivalent full-time students. Formerly, universities were funded similarly, but on a rolling quinquennium, and other institutions were funded differently. The Minister can also allocate "supplementary grants," targeted for particular programs proposed by an institution. Institutions can generate finance through research contracts with private (and government) organizations, and student fees, including fully costed fees for overseas (nonassisted) students. But the Minister sets the fees and allowances for domestic students, and enrollment pressures may inhibit institutions from raising large sums through private or overseas students. Most fees rose sharply in 1990, although allowances were also increased.

Institutions will have greater flexibility in how they use centrally allocated finance. This could result in more variety among institutions in the same sector. It will certainly allow more rapid decision-making in polytechnics and colleges of education. Many factors will, however, be indirectly controlled through central provision of finance. Staff numbers and student enrollments, for example, will probably fall largely within financially determined parameters.

Under 1990 legislation, then, central government has given nonuniversity higher education more freedom at the institutional level, but has maintained certain significant controls, and arguably strengthened its grip on the universities.

3.2 Institutional Administration

From 1991, institutions will be governed in the same way irrespective of size or function. The governing body will be a council comprising ministerial appointees, the Chief Executive Officer (CEO), academic and general staff, student representatives, and coopted members where desired. Equity in terms of gender, ethnicity, and the community served is a requirement of final membership. Council appoints the CEO and has responsibility for finance and management; it must develop a charter, have a statement of objectives, and actively promote equity programs.

Each institution is required to establish an academic board, comprising the CEO, staff, and student representatives, with numbers and election criteria determined by each council. This board advises on academic matters and can be delegated various powers by council. In universities the academic board replaces the professorial board or senate, on which full professors generally had the right to sit.

Individual institutions will doubtless continue using a variety of committees and subcommittees, now to be constituted by the council or academic board. Thus, in universities, decisions on leave, promotions, and some research funding will continue to be determined locally. A (national) tertiary research board will administer a contestable research fund and monitor research outputs.

Academically, universities are organized on two main levels: the faculty or school, and the department. Departments, chaired often but not always by a full professor, make academic decisions relating to structure, content, and assessment for individual courses, and progression from one level to the next. Many such decisions are ratified at the faculty level, chaired by a dean. The faculty, normally including student representation, also makes decisions on broader matters, such as the shape of its degree(s) and policies on assessment. Some of these decisions must be ratified by a deans' committee, or by the academic board. Similar patterns of organization are common in polytechnics and colleges of education.

4. Faculty and Students: Teaching, Learning, and Research

4.1 Faculty

Academic staff appointments have lagged behind student enrollments, while the proportion of part-time staff has increased. Women represent under 20 percent of academic staff, and 4.4 percent of full professors (1988). Maori are also underrepresented at all levels. Table 3 traces the development of academic staff since 1960.

All university staff are employed by the CEO. In practice, appointments committees will advise the CEO and departments will advise appointments committees. Contracts will now be determined by individual universities and, with finance less certain,

Table 3
University teaching staff 1960–88

	1960	1965	1970	1975	1980	1985	1988
Full-time	819	1,251	2,211	2,757	3,143	2,936	3,172
Part-time	237	518	862	1,351	1,637	2,148	2,682

more new appointments could be limited-tenure positions. Staff holding tenure in July, 1990 retain previous rights.

Staff are in six categories. Full professors (11% of full-time positions), are normally appointed on the basis of international standing in research and teaching. Associate professors (13%) are frequently appointed internally on similar criteria. Senior lecturer (45%) is considered the "normal" career goal for staff. Usually, new appointments enter at lecturer (23%) level. Assistant lecturers (6%) and various tutor/demonstrator appointments (3%) complete the picture. For appointments to lecturer and above, a doctorate is expected but not mandatory. Promotion is based on research, publications, teaching, and contributions to the university and community.

The Association of University Teachers (AUT) represents staff interests on salaries and conditions. Staff deployment, starting salaries and service conditions are determined institutionally. Salary scales are currently negotiated by the VCC and AUT, and monitored by the State Services Commission. There is still considerable flexibility over conditions such as hours of teaching, but research is expected of all academic staff. New in-service development and appraisal programs may assist staff but could facilitate tighter controls in the future.

A subprofessorial lecturers' association also exists in some universities, but there is no national organization, nor does it have formal negotiating rights. Polytechnics and colleges of education have their own combined teaching staff union.

4.2 Students

While relative proportions have changed slightly since 1960, humanities still account for 34.3 percent of all university students, with 26.6 percent in science and technology and 39 percent in social sciences (1988). Commercial subjects, including business studies and management studies, have experienced large increases in the 1980s, now accounting for 25 percent of undergraduates. Numbers studying education have risen with the introduction of BEd programs. In many other (restricted) vocational and applied courses, proportions have remained relatively constant, with numbers rising mainly when new schools were opened. Law (about 7%), engineering (3%), and medicine (2–3%) are examples of this.

From 1960–88, the number graduating with initial

Table 4
(Internal) university students by ethnic group 1988 (percentages)

	New Zealand residents					Overseas students
	Pakeha[a]	Maori	Pacific Is.	Asian	Other	
University	88.05	4.76	2.01	3.32	1.86	5.99
Total population (approx.)	82.0	12.5	3.5	1.3	1.0	

a "Pakeha" comprises mainly Anglo-Celtic/European ethnic groups

degrees has risen steadily, from 1,231 to 6,781. Proportionate to enrollment, this number represents only a slight improvement, but graduate degree ratios have risen more sharply.

Although the first woman graduated in 1876, enrollments were traditionally dominated by *pakeha* (White) middle-class males. Recently the proportion of women has exceeded 50 percent. In undergraduate degree courses, women hold a substantial majority in education and arts: they have parity in law and medicine; about 40 percent of science and commerce students; but only 12 percent in engineering (1988). Lower proportions take graduate courses.

Evidence from Auckland, the largest university (Jones 1990), shows that 57 percent of all students regularly come from the highest occupation groups of society (18% overall). Only 7 percent come from the lowest groups (18.5%).

Ethnic minority representation has increased in recent years, but several groups, especially the indigenous Maori, are still underrepresented. Table 4 gives 1988 figures.

From 1991 all higher education institutions are required to activate programs removing barriers to ethnic minorities and other disadvantaged groups. Some universities have already appointed Maori or Pacific Island advisers and equal employment officers.

Large numbers of mature students attend university. An amazing 30 percent of first-year students in 1988 were aged over 24. Of these, half enrolled extramurally, and two-thirds were women. Indications from 1990 suggest that fee rises have reduced these enrollments.

University students have a national organization with locally organized unions. Compulsory membership fees assist clubs and societies and social and political campaigns. Students must be represented on both councils and academic boards.

4.3 Learning and Examinations

The structure of first-degree programs is determined principally by individual universities. The VCC is responsible for interuniversity course approvals. The New Zealand Qualifications Authority approves programs in other higher education institutions.

Undergraduate degrees are specialized by faculty, normally comprising four or five subject areas, one or two of which will be a "major," studied each year. Each individual course counts towards the degree, either as a number of credits or as one "paper." For example, success in 21 papers qualifies for an Auckland BA while a BSc requires 96 credits. Mass undergraduate lectures, backed by tutorial and/or laboratory sessions, are still usual, a situation arising from adverse staff–student radios.

Final written examinations are common to all universities, but most courses have credit for on-course work (practicals, tests and/or essays); some have "double chance" systems involving combinations of on-course and examination results. A smaller number have no final examination. Individual universities determine assessment policy. Colleges of education assess mainly through assignments and practical work; a combination of examinations and practical tests is normal at polytechnics.

5. Conclusion

Recent decisions in higher education, culminating in the 1990 legislation, demonstrate the impact of New Right thinking, despite an espoused commitment to equity, which is a required goal for institutions assisted by some targeted funding from government. While polytechnics appear to be relatively favored financially, universities are understaffed and arguably vulnerable, with no buffer organization between themselves and the Ministry. Smaller colleges of education may be at risk, and may find amalgamation with universities an attractive proposition. The new National government (1991) favors this, proposing a Tertiary Education Commission, and is making major changes to tertiary student fees and allowances.

Overall student numbers are projected to continue rising. Whether increases will come in polytechnics, universities, or both is unclear; nor is the effect of degree status for some courses in polytechnics and possibly colleges of education.

Higher education in New Zealand faces a challenging decade. Whether its current high reputation survives, particularly in universities, is likely to be determined mainly by government financial policies over the next few years.

Bibliography

Boston J 1988 *The Future of New Zealand Universities*. VUW/Institute of Policy Studies, Wellington

Carter I (ed.) 1983 *The University and the Community*. AUP, Auckland

Carter I 1990 *Ancient Cultures of Conceit*. Routledge, London

The Education Amendment Act, 1990, No. 60. Government Printer, Wellington

Education Statistics of New Zealand (annual). Ministry of Education, Wellington

Goff P 1989 *Learning for Life Two: Education and Training Beyond the Age of Fifteen*. Government Printer, Wellington

Hawke G R 1988 *Report on Postcompulsory Education and Training in New Zealand*. Government Printer, Wellington

Jones J 1990 *The Socio-economic Background of Students at the University of Auckland*. University of Auckland, Auckland

New Zealand Business Roundtable 1988 *Reforming Tertiary Education in New Zealand*. New Zealand Business Roundtable, Wellington

New Zealand Department of Education 1987 *Alternatives to Universities in Tertiary Education*. Department of Education, Wellington

New Zealand Universities Review Committee 1987 *New Zealand Universities: Partners in National Development*. Report of the New Zealand Universities Review Committee. New Zealand Vice-Chancellors Committee, Wellington

New Zealand Yearbook (annual). Government Printer, Wellington

Parton H 1979 *The University of New Zealand*. Auckland University Press, Auckland

Probine M, Fargher R 1987 *The Management, Funding, and Organization of Continuing Education and Training*. Government Printer, Wellington

Smith, Caldwell Associates 1988 *Higher Education: Our Vision*. New Zealand University Students Association, Wellington

Tombs W, Harman G (eds.) 1988 *Higher Education and Social Goals in Australia and New Zealand*. University of New England, Armidale

R. Peddie

Nicaragua

1. Higher Education and Society

1.1 Development of Higher Education

Historically, Nicaraguan society has entrusted higher education to provide the qualified human resources necessary to satisfy its needs and promote development.

The first establishment of higher education that existed in Nicaragua was the *Seminario Conciliar de San Ramón*, founded in 1680. Before independence from Spain, the Seminary was raised to university status and renamed the *Universidad de León*. Its mission was to prepare the clergy needed by the Church and the public officials for the secondary administrative posts in the Colonial administration.

Higher education did not experience many changes until 1879, when the professionalizing Napoleonic university model was adapted and another institution of higher education was created: *La Universidad de Granada* in the city of Granada. The Liberal Revolution (1893) emphasized the imitation of the French model. In 1898, the university was organized on the basis of professional, independent schools (law, medicine, pharmacy). The School of Civil Engineering was founded in 1941. That same year, a new university was established, *La Universidad Central de Managua*. In 1947, the University of León was raised to the status of the National University of Nicaragua (*Universidad Nacional de Nicaragua*), later becoming the *Universidad Nacional Autónoma de Nicaragua* (UNAN).

1.2 Population and Economy

The estimated population of Nicaragua for 1990 is 3.8 million. The population growth rate was 3.2 between 1950–80 and 3.5 between 1980–90. The population density is 31 inhabitants per square kilometer. Of this population, 2.3 million live in urban areas and 1.5 million in rural areas.

In 1990, the economically active population is estimated to be 1,159,661 people. Its distribution by major areas is as follows: agriculture 41.8 percent; commerce and services 38.2 percent; and industry 15 percent.

Historically, the economy has grown according to demand for primary products such as coffee, timber, gold, rubber, cotton, meat, and sugar. Cotton and coffee exports represent more than half the total exports of the country.

1.3 Government Structure and Main Political Goals

Nicaragua is a democratic and representative republic. The branches of government are the legislative, executive, judicial, and electoral.

The state guarantees the existence of political pluralism, a mixed economy, and nonalignment.

1.4 Relationship with Religious Bodies

As previously mentioned, the first university established in Nicaragua was founded as a conciliar seminary. The influence of the Roman Catholic Church over this university was very powerful until the Liberal Reform of 1893. At present, there are two universities in Nicaragua that are supported by religious congregations: the Central American University founded by Jesuit priests in 1960, and the Polytechnical University of Nicaragua, founded in 1970, under the patronage of the Protestant churches (Baptist and Evangelical). Nearly 30 percent of higher education students attend these two universities.

2. *The Institutional Fabric of the Higher Education System*

In 1980, the *Consejo Nacional de Educación Superior* (CNES) was established to integrate all the institutions of higher education, public and private. Its objective is to harmonize the development of higher education with the needs of the revolutionary process and to formulate the appropriate national policy. In 1982 the president of CNES, nominated by the executive branch of government, was conferred the status of a Minister of State.

As part of the policy of rationalizing higher education, CNES reduced the number of higher education institutions to avoid unnecessary duplications. Presently, and according to the "Law of Autonomy" approved in April 1990, the institutions of higher education in Nicaragua consist of four state and two private universities, as well as two technical centers. The four state universities are the two *Universidad Nacional Autónoma de Nicaragua* (UNAN) at León and Managua, the *Universidad Nacional de Ingeniería* (UNI), and the *Universidad Nacional Agraria* (UNA).

The private universities are the *Universidad Centroamericana* (UCA) and the *Universidad Politécnica de Nicaragua* (UPOLI). The two technical centers of higher education are the *Escuela Internacional de Agricultura y Ganadería de Rivas* (EIAG) and the *Escuela de Agricultura y Ganadería de Estelí* (EAG).

In 1967 a branch campus of the *Instituto Centroamericano de Administración de Empresas* (INCAE) was established in Managua, affiliated with the Harvard Business School, and offering courses in advanced management. With the creation in 1970 of the *Instituto Politécnico de Nicaragua* and the *Centro de Estudios Superiores* (CES), private higher education represented 40 percent of student enrollment. In 1976 another postsecondary institution was created, the *Instituto Técnico de Estudios Superiores de Nicaragua* (ITESNIC), offering short-cycle higher education programs.

Nicaraguan higher education institutions have a public service orientation and enjoy autonomy in relation with the executive branch of government, since it does not depend on the Ministry of Education. The law provides the universities and centers of higher technical education with academic, financial, organic, and administrative autonomy.

Access to higher education institutions is free for all Nicaraguans who have fulfilled the requisite academic conditions. The selection process does not discriminate on the basis of social origin, nationality, political ideology, race, sex, religion, economic, or social condition. A high school diploma or its equivalent is necessary in order to enter higher education institutions.

In 1965 there were 3,343 students enrolled in higher education. This figure rose to 19,062 in 1975 and to 34,710 in 1980. However, in 1985 enrollment dropped to 29,001. This decrease in enrollment is primarily a result of the undeclared war which the country has experienced since 1981. This situation affects, directly and indirectly, the social environment.

In 1960 the percentage of women enrolled in UNAN was 18.2 percent, and in 1976 it reached 40.7 percent. In UCA, in 1961 the percentage of women enrolled was 16.6 percent and increased to 39.0 percent in 1976. In 1985 the female population surpassed the male population in the universities as well as in the technical centers (57.3% and 51.3% respectively).

3. *Governance, Administration, and Finance*

3.1 *National Administration*

The universities and higher technical centers are independent of the Ministry of Education. Because of their autonomy, the National Council of Universities, is in charge of the coordination at this educational level. The function of this Council is to advise and to elaborate general policies. The Council also has the power to authorize the creation of new universities and technical centers. This decision is made considering the needs of the country, available human and material resources, as well as the student population that would be served by the new institution. However, the council does not have authority over the institutions, as its recommendations must be ratified by each university for full validity.

The primary source of financing for higher education, public as well as private, comes from the state, which assigns to it 2 percent of the general budget of the nation. This percentage will be increased to 3 percent in 1990 and will reach 6 percent in the next few years, according to the new university law.

Presently there is not a national plan for the development of higher education. The goals are set by the National Council of Universities on the basis of the proposals formulated by the different institutions.

3.2 *Institutional Administration*

The structure of university governance includes the university council, the rector, the faculty council and faculty dean, the directing council of the school and the director of the school.

The University Council is at the top of the hierarchy of governance. The government and the general administration of the university is in the hands of the rector, who is its supreme academic and executive authority.

The departments are responsible for the teaching

activities, research and social projections of the Faculties and Schools. They also guarantee the quality of the educational process through educational methodology and scientific research.

4. Faculty and Students: Teaching, Learning, and Research

4.1 Faculty

Before 1979, there were few full-time professors. Universities depended on professionals who taught as a secondary or complementary activity and this affected the quality of teaching. In the academic year of 1976–77 the National Autonomous University of Nicaragua (UNAN) had a total of 732 professors, of whom only 22 percent had full-time contracts. That same year, the Central American University (UCA) hired 191 professors of whom 56 percent worked on an hourly basis. However, by 1985 70.5 percent of the total of 2,127 professors were employed on a full-time basis as a means of improving the quality of the educational process.

The recruiting of professors is done individually by each higher education institution. The designations are made by the respective university councils by proposal of the faculty council.

The members of the academic and research staff are classified under the following categories: full professor; assistant professor; associate professor; and adjunct professor.

Professors of public institutions of higher education have the status of public servants and enjoy the rights and privileges set out in the Law of Public Service of 1989. Professors are organized in the *Asociación de Trabajadores Docentes* (Teacher's Union), which on a national level is part of the National Association of Nicaraguan Teachers (ANDEN) and is affiliated with the Central Union of Sandinista Workers (CST).

4.2 Students

Between 1975 and 1985 the distribution of students in the various fields of study has shifted. In the agricultural sciences student enrollment increased from 3.2 percent to 15.4 percent. The medical sciences and education also experienced increased enrollment, from 4.7 to 14.8 percent and from 10.7 to 20.5 percent respectively. The fields with enhanced enrollment have been the priority areas in the national development plans.

In 1965 there were 132 higher education graduates. This figure increased to 693 in 1975 and to 3,296 in 1985.

Students are organized at the faculty or school level in each higher education institution and at a national level in the National Union of Nicaraguan Students (UNEN). The students have representatives in all the organs of the university government, including the University Council, the faculty or school council, and the general university assembly. They also participate in the election of the faculty councils and that of the rector and vice-rector general. Their participation represents 20 percent of the votes.

4.3 Graduate Study

Before the Revolution, educational programs at graduate level were initially nonexistent. The only graduate activities that were accomplished were confined to the brief tenure of the applied ecology program in the UNAN of León from 1971 to 1975.

After the Revolution, it was possible to develop a graduate medical specialization program which has been operational since 1983. This was accomplished through the joint efforts of the Ministry of Health and Higher Education. In the health sector there are also masters' programs in epidemiology, health administration, and public health.

In UNAN at León a master's in biology is offered in the area of integrated pest control and the UNAN at Managua offers a specialized program of international trade. The National University of Engineering has a master's program in environmental engineering.

Some research groups have been able to consolidate, with strong institutional support, international cooperation and high quality advising. The areas chosen have excellent prospects for integrating research projects at a regional level, as is the case with the following topics: contagious diseases, labor medicine, integrated pest control, identification and extraction of active elements of medicinal plants, optimizing and quality control in the local production of medicine, limnology, and agricultural economy.

There are four research institutes with qualified personnel, international participation, foreign financial support, and investigative experience. Although they are part of higher education institutions, their activities are pursued independently, thus reducing their influence on the teaching process. This category includes the following: The *Instituto Juan XXIII*, and the *Instituto de Investigaciones Históricas Centroamericanas* (IIHCA), both affiliated with the Central American University; *Instituto de Investigaciones Económicas y Sociales* (INIES); and the *Centro de Investigaciones y Documentación de la Costa Atlántica* (CIDCA).

5. Conclusion

The Nicaraguan higher education system, starting from the decade of 1970, has experienced a great development in quantity and quality, which has intensified since 1980. As a consequence of the counterrevolutionary war, the enrollment of students decreased greatly and so has the budget assigned to higher education. It is hoped that peace, recently achieved, plus the application of the new "Law of Autonomy" will lead to the improvement of the Nicaraguan higher education process.

Bibliography

Arellano J E 1973 *Historia de la Universidad de León.* Editorial Universitaria, León, Nicaragua

Arnove R F 1986 *Education and Revolution in Nicaragua.* Praeger, New York

Arríen J B 1980 *Nicaragua: Revolutión y Proyecto Educativo.* Publicaciones del Ministerio de Educación, Managua, Nicaragua

Arríen J B, Kauffmann R 1977 *Nicaragua en la Educación.* Ediciones de la Universidad Centroamericana, Managua, Nicaragua

Arríen J B, Matus Lazo R 1989 *Nicaragua: Diez años de Educación en la Revolución.* Claves Latinoamericanas, Mexico, DF

De Castilla Urbina M 1979 *Universidad y Sociedad en Nicaragua.* Editorial Universitaria de la UNAN, León, Nicaragua

Instituto de Estadísticas y Censos, 1989 *Nicaragua en Cifras.* Managua, Nicaragua

Ministerio de Educación 1983 *Fines, Objetivos y Principios de la Nueva Educación.* Editorial del Ministerio de Educación, Managua, Nicaragua

Tunnermann Berhhein C 1958 *Reseña Histórica de la Conquista de la Autonomía Universitaria.* Editorial Universitaria, León, Nicaragua

Tunnermann Bernheim C 1971 *La Universidad: Búsqueda permanente.* Editorial Universitaria de la UNAN, León, Nicaragua

Tunnermann Bernheim C 1980 *Hacia una Nueva Educación en Nicaragua.* Talleres Gráficos "La Salle". León, Nicaragua

C. Tunnermann Bernheim

Niger

1. Higher Education and Society

Until 1971, Niger had only one institution of higher learning, the National School of Administration, which trained upper-, middle-, and lower-level cadres. The upper-level candidates are recruited through a competitive examination among students with the baccalaureate and public administration division heads. This level provides education for civil servants as administrators, tax, customs, and labor inspectors, as well as social security agents, and so on.

2. The Institutional Fabric of the Higher Education System

The Center of Higher Education was founded in September 1971 in Niamey as a public institution with financial autonomy. It is dedicated to scientific research, but also specializes in training upper-level professionals. Originally it was composed of the School of Sciences, the predecessor to the science faculty, and the University Institute for Teacher Training, which became the education faculty of the University of Niamey.

The Center for Higher Education became the University of Niamey in September 1973, adding new faculties throughout the years: liberal arts and humanities (1973); agronomy (1974); health sciences (1974); and economic and legal sciences (1980). In all, the University has six faculties, which grant the *maîtrise* in different liberal arts and scientific disciplines as well as degrees in agronomy and medicine.

The University also has three institutes that are almost exclusively dedicated to research, although most of their researchers also teach in the faculties. The Research Institute in the Humanities (IRSH) was founded in 1974 from the Niger Research Center in the Humanities, which in turn had evolved from the French Institute of Black Africa. In addition to the institute created in Niamey, there are branch campuses in Maradi and Agadez. The IRSH has a rich tradition in the arts, archaeology, and popular customs, as well as economics, geography and the use of space, history, popular traditions, local languages and linguistics, sociology of development, Arab manuscripts, and *ajami*. The IRSH is also responsible for preserving and promoting the national cultural heritage. Finally, it publishes various journals dedicated to the humanities and social sciences in Niger, including *Etudes Nigériennes*.

The Research Institute for the Teaching of Mathematics (IREM) was founded in 1974. The IREM reviews the mathematics programs in schools, writes manuals for the theoretical and practical education of future mathematics professors, and provides continuing education for those currently employed in teaching. The IREM collaborates with similar institutes in the subregion, especially those in Burkina Faso, the Ivory Coast, and Senegal. It is also developing a fruitful collaboration with the IREM of Strasbourg, France.

The Radio-Isotope Institute (IRI) was founded in 1984. Its objective is to apply isotopes to health and agriculture, which leads it to be particularly interested in physics, chemistry, and nuclear medicine on the one hand, and radio-agronomy on the other.

3. Faculty and Students: Teaching, Learning, and Research

Faculty members both teach and carry out research, given the twofold vocation of the university. The faculty includes nationals from Niger, foreigners participating in aid programs, and foreigners contracted by the government of Niger. The total number of professor-researchers has grown from 57 in 1979–80 to 166 in 1989–90. They are reinforced by part-time professors as well as "missionary professors" who have come to Niamey either in the framework of a bilateral aid program or the interuniversity exchange program of the *Association des Universités Partiellement ou Entièrement de Langue Française* (AUP-ELF), headquartered in Montreal.

The University of Niamey has bilateral agreements for interuniversity cooperation with twelve foreign countries, six of which are African (Benin, Burkina Faso, Cameroon, Ivory Coast, Nigeria, and Tunisia), representing 36 university institutions. The non-African countries are: France (24 institutions); the United States (four institutions); Switzerland (two institutions); and Germany and Canada with one institution each.

In 1987–88, the teacher–student ratio at the University of Niamey was one professor for 27 students. However, the situation is complicated by the small percentage of faculty members who have reached the status of professor, which is barely 30 out of 132. More than 75 percent are assistants or teaching assistants, who are obliged to give classes because of the lack of professors. They do as best they can, but often their studies have not prepared them for such a task.

Not only are the faculties underequipped and in a difficult financial situation, but in 1986 professors lost their right to government housing, which has contributed to difficult living conditions. During the 1987–88 school year, the professor-researchers of Niger formed the National Union of University Professors and Researchers (SNECS).

Student enrollment grew from 103 in 1971–72 to 3,960 at the beginning of 1989–90.

Until 1985–86, most students from Niger had state scholarships of between US$100 and $120 a month. Unfortunately, the financial crisis has obliged the authorities to reduce the number of higher education scholarships.

In addition to nationals from Niger, the University of Niamey has students from countries including Benin, Burkina Faso, Cameroon, Congo, Guinea, Ivory Coast, Senegal, Chad, and Togo. Students from Niger belong to the Union of Students from Niger in the University of Niamey (UENUM).

As well as the National School of Administration and the University of Niamey, other institutions of higher learning include:

(a) the African School of Meteorology and Civil Aviation, which since the early 1980s has trained meteorologists, air traffic controllers, and engineers in air-navigation facilities, as well as high-level technicians in the same specialties;

(b) the Islamic University, inaugurated in 1987 in Say (52kms from Niamey). It belongs to the Organization of the Islamic Conference (OCI) and receives Moslem students from West and

Central Africa. The faculty of Islamic law is the only one offering courses;

(c) the School of Mines and Geology (EMIG), opened in January 1990. This school is a member of the West African Economic Community. The EMIG is a *grande école* which recruits its students by competitive examination from among those holding the baccalaureate. It trains high-level technicians and engineers in the fields of geology (prospecting); mines (exploitation and development); electromechanics; treatment of minerals; control and regulation; automation; and electromechanical maintenance.

4. Conclusion

Niger has a population of 7,250,000 and gives scholarships to 4,260 students, 1,760 of whom study abroad. These figures would seem negligible in other contexts. In a country which is among the poorest in the world, however, and with tremendous social and economic problems, and where university graduates cannot be fully absorbed by the labor market, the number of recipients of scholarships is considerable.

A. Salifou

Nigeria

1. Higher Education and Society

The land area known today as Nigeria was a British creation. It was once a conglomeration of tribal nation states that coexisted peacefully among themselves prior to their discovery by enterprising European explorers and subsequently traders in the early nineteenth century. These nation states consisted principally of the Yorubas in the west; the Edos, Urhobos, and Itshekiris in the middle west; the Igbos in the middle east; the Kalabarians, Ibiobios, and Ijaws in the southeast; the Hausa/Fulanis in the northwest and east; and myriads of minority tribes in the middle belt region. These are people who, notwithstanding occasional internecine wars of survival, enjoyed harmonious relationships with one another over the years until the century of British occupation, colonial rule, and influence.

As the British traders engaged in intensive trading activities on the coastal area, Yorubaland was the first to be ceded to the British Crown in 1860. This was achieved by default and not by conquest, but in the 1880s the eastern parts were subdued by British military supremacy to become the Oil-Rivers Protectorate. Although the Fulani Caliphate and its satellites in the middle belt were also conquered and annexed by superior British fire-power in 1903, the entire geographical landmass today known as Nigeria did not become a political entity under the British Colonial Government of Lord Frederick Lugard until 1914.

Apart from the British Cameroons, which broke away from Nigeria in 1954 to join the Republic of Cameroons, Nigeria has remained intact as an entity since the Second World War. This was notwithstanding the events that led to the Nigerian Civil War (1967–71) which could have severed the eastern region from the Republic of Nigeria. Since the Second World War, the internal map of Nigeria has changed dramatically from 23 provinces within three regions (east, west, and north) to 12 states (1967), 19 states (1976), and 21 states with the Federal Capital Territory of Abuja (1987). Along with all these changes 453 local governments replaced the provincial administrations of the pre-Independence (1960) era.

Nigeria is bounded to the north, west, and east respectively by the republics of Niger, Benin, and the Cameroons while the Atlantic Ocean lies to the south. The population has grown from 49 million in 1945, to 54 million in 1952 under the colonial government, and to some 105 million in 1990.

About 53 percent of Nigerians live in the northern areas while the rest live in the south. Approximately 80 percent are rural dwellers with the remaining 20 percent estimated to be living mostly in the towns and cities of southern Nigeria. Factors of history and culture account for the soaring population since a man can take several wives and have many children within a rural lifestyle in which all of them live by tilling the land. There are about 400 languages and/or dialects spoken by both the majority and minority groups with Hausa, Yoruba, and Igbo being the dominant languages already committed to writing for educational, administrative, and commercial purposes as are some dozen other minority languages. The official languages of communication in the elementary schools are the mother-tongue Nigerian languages with English being taught and used alongside, whereas, in the higher educational institutions, English is the official language of communication.

From the time of its origins up to the colonial period, Nigeria was basically an agrarian, self-sufficient society with cocoa, cotton, groundnuts, and palm oil being the main cash crops. There was little ambition for external aggression beyond occasional clashes with its immediate neighbors. Since British occupation in the mid-nineteenth century through to the Independence of 1960, Nigeria was a veritable well spring of raw materials for the growing commercial and industrial concerns of the British Isles. Since Independence, the economy has been, and continues to be, gradually diversified and turned around towards more effective agricultural, industrial, and manufacturing concerns, particularly in relation to the oil industry which accounts for Nigeria's main foreign currency earnings.

The constitutional provision of 1952, which was a British experiment in limited self-government for Nigeria, enabled the nation to attain independence status in 1960. In the 30 years following, up to 1990, Nigerians have lived under six military governments for a total of 20 years with civilian rule only accounting for about 10 years. However, the country is poised for a return to civil rule by 1992 under a presidential parliamentary democracy with the main goals of improving the quality of life, ensuring peaceful coexistence between Nigeria and its neighbors, diversifying the economy, providing education for everyone, and making Nigeria a model democracy in Black Africa.

Prior to British occupation, southern Nigerians in particular were animists and had a variety of different gods and goddesses, while the northerners were predominantly Muslims. Sixty years of intensive Christian missionary activities in southern Nigeria brought Western education to Nigeria, and changed the old situation considerably.

Christian missionaries owned the elementary and secondary schools and the few postelementary teacher–training colleges in Nigeria between 1842 and 1976, with the Nigerian government's control extending only over the quality of the education provided. The government has since then established schools of its own and owns, funds, and controls them along with all postsecondary and higher educational institutions across the country. Even though there are no private higher educational institutions in the country as yet, there are a few private elementary and secondary schools as well as an insignificant number of correspondence institutions geared toward postsecondary institutions.

2. The Institutional Fabric of the Higher Education System

By 1954, in the process of decolonization, Nigeria adopted a federal constitution with three regions (east, west, and north). Higher education was placed on the Concurrent Legislative List which enabled both federal and regional governments to establish and finance their universities and other tertiary institutions.

Although four regional universities were established by and after 1960 (Nsukka 1960, Ife and Zaria 1962, Benin 1970), owing to financial and logistic constraints after the Nigerian Civil War, in 1975 they all became federal universities. However, sections of the 1979 Federal Constitution provided for the establishment of state and private universities. Hence between 1980 and 1983, eight state and six private universities were established in southern Nigeria. These private universities were then shut down by the succeeding Federal Military Government of 1984–85.

The locations of Nigeria's higher education institutions are shown in Fig. 1.

There exist in some universities special research institutes created solely to conduct research into special aspects of national development, for instance, the three nuclear and energy research centers at Zaria, Ife, and Nsukka, and certain academic and research institutes of education, African studies, ecology, health, agriculture, local government, and so forth, that exist in the federal and state universities.

Apart from university research centers and institutes, the federal government created autonomous nonuniversity research centers specifically oriented towards national development. These included the Nigeria Educational Research and Development Council (NERDC), the Nigeria Mathematics Center and the Federal Institute of Industrial Research (FIIRO) at Oshodi, the Institute of Agricultural Research and Training (IART) at Ibadan and in some six other centers around Nigeria.

By law, admissions policies and selection to federal and state universities since the 1977/78 academic year and to polytechnics and colleges of education, since the 1990/91 academic year, have been the provenance of the Joint Admissions and Matriculation Board (JAMB). Each candidate has the choice of three institutions and of two courses. Each sits for four papers relevant to the course(s) of choice and must obtain minimum total marks within the cut-off-points for each course in order to be considered for admission. To redress the characteristic historic imbalance in educational development between the northern and southern states (in which candidates from northern states are handicapped by being late starters), a quota system was decreed for admissions in addition to merit considerations for all federal institutions. Under this system the higher institutions determine the criteria for admission and who to admit while the JAMB is a clearing house. Tables 1 and 2 provide a breakdown of student admissions.

Fourteen federal and six state universities follow the conventional pattern while five federal and three state universities have a technological bias, and two federal universities are mainly agricultural.

The higher educational system in Nigeria has expanded more than ten-fold since the early 1960s in numbers of institutions, enrollments, academic

Table 1

Analysis on student actual admissions (enrollment) by states

	1986/87						1987/88					
	JME[a]	%	DE[b]	%	Total	%	JME	%	DE	%	Total	%
Southern States												
Akwa-Ibom	—	—	—	—	—	—	573	2.6	127	1.2	700	2.1
Anambra	3,442	15.0	544	4.9	3,986	11.7	2,904	13.4	557	5.0	3,461	10.5
Bendel	3,594	15.6	824	7.4	4,418	12.9	3,756	17.3	810	7.3	4,566	13.9
Cross River	1,601	7.0	366	3.3	1,967	5.8	802	3.7	174	1.6	976	3.0
Imo	3,528	15.3	601	5.4	4,129	12.1	3,433	15.8	786	7.1	3,619	12.9
Lagos	1,826	7.9	513	4.6	2,339	6.8	1,686	7.8	567	5.1	2,253	6.9
Ogun	1,350	5.9	449	4.0	1,799	5.3	1,743	8.1	577	5.2	2,320	7.1
Ondo	2,018	8.8	47	5.8	2,065	7.8	1,943	8.9	536	4.8	2,479	7.6
Oyo	2,750	11.9	1,130	10.2	3,880	11.4	2,250	10.3	938	8.5	3,188	9.7
Rivers	917	4.0	194	1.7	1,111	3.3	905	4.2	126	1.1	1,031	3.1
Northern States												
Bauchi	84	0.4	397	3.6	481	1.4	48	0.2	358	3.2	406	1.2
Benue	386	1.7	853	7.7	1,239	3.6	438	2.0	610	5.5	1,048	3.2
Borno	43	0.2	203	1.8	246	0.7	24	0.1	429	3.9	453	1.4
Gongola	40	0.2	355	3.2	395	1.2	56	0.3	386	3.5	442	1.4
Kaduna	59	0.3	1,082	9.7	1,141	3.3	52	0.2	732	6.6	784	2.4
Kano	105	0.5	504	4.5	609	1.8	36	0.2	596	5.4	632	1.9
Katsina	—	—	—	—	—	—	2	0.0	252	2.3	254	0.8
Kwara	638	2.8	1,225	11.0	1,863	5.5	738	3.4	1,211	10.9	1,949	5.9
Niger	154	0.7	326	2.9	480	1.4	32	0.1	408	3.7	440	1.3
Plateau	186	0.8	460	4.1	646	1.9	198	0.9	407	3.7	605	1.8
Sokoto	240	1.0	324	2.9	564	1.7	56	0.3	370	3.3	426	1.3
Foreign	62	0.3	132	1.2	194	0.6	83	0.4	124	1.1	207	0.6
Total	23,023	100	10,529	100	33,552	100	21,758	100	11,081	100	32,239	100

a Joint Matriculation Examination b Direct Entry

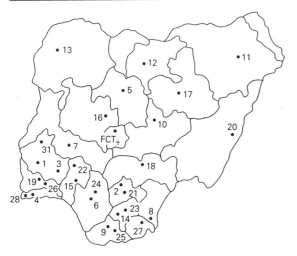

Figure 1
Nigeria, showing locations of higher education institutions

programs, and capabilities. In 1990, there were 51 (19 federal and 32 state) colleges of education in Nigeria of which 46 were traditional in nature, three were technical, and two were special colleges to prepare qualified teachers for the nation's elementary schools. The polytechnics are responsible for preparing middle-level technical manpower for the nation. There were also 10 federal and 17 state polytechnics.

Candidates for undergraduate degree courses must have successfully fulfilled their time in the national secondary school system.

Throughout the Nigerian university system, eight semesters of study are then necessary before a bach-

elor of arts degree in the humanities, administration, or education is completed. Bachelor's degrees in science (in both basic and health sciences), education, and law are also eight semesters long whereas diploma courses run for only two semesters in each of the disciplines whether at undergraduate or postgraduate levels.

In the professional disciplines, it takes 10 semesters to complete bachelor's degrees in agriculture (BSc), pharmacy (BPharm), engineering and technology (BSc) and 13 semesters in medicine (MBBS).

Each university awards its own degrees under its own laws. To ensure comparability, there is an external moderation of the examinations by academic colleagues from sister institutions appointed on individual merits on a rotational basis. The reports of these external examiners are crucial. Experience over the years has stabilized the system as a valuable check.

The three-tier higher education system now runs the semester and course credit systems (CCS) spanning two semesters of each academic year. The CCS takes care of resource requirements, definition of course credits, number of credit units, staff/student workloads, grade point averages, and the place of continuous assessments. It deals with conditions for student withdrawals and probation as well as duration of degree courses and examination fees.

Since July 1989, the National Universities Commission (NUC) approved the implementation of minimum academic standards in all Nigerian universities in the following academic disciplines: arts, administration, management and management technology, education, law, social sciences, agriculture, forestry, fisheries and home economics, dentistry, engineering and technology, environmental sciences, pharmaceutical sciences, medicine, nursing, physio-

Table 2
Analysis on student actual admission (enrollment) by faculty

	1986/87						1987/88					
	JME[a]	%	DE[b]	%	Total	%	JME	%	DE	%	Total	%
Agriculture	1,127	4.9	363	3.3	1,490	4.4	1,028	4.7	443	4.0	1,471	4.5
Arts	3,357	14.6	1,638	14.7	4,995	14.6	3,594	16.5	1,741	15.7	5,335	16.3
Business administration	1,348	5.9	847	7.6	2,195	6.4	1,235	5.7	900	8.1	2,135	6.5
Education	2,520	10.9	3,918	35.2	6,438	18.9	2,442	11.2	3,507	31.7	5,949	18.1
Engineering technology and environmental studies	3,264	14.2	957	8.6	4,221	12.4	3,386	15.6	872	7.9	4,258	13.0
Law	1,429	6.2	895	8.0	2,324	6.9	1,146	5.3	889	8.0	2,035	6.3
Medical science	1,532	6.7	754	6.8	2,286	6.7	1,662	7.6	802	7.2	2,464	7.5
Science	5,952	25.9	666	6.0	6,618	19.4	4,492	20.7	934	8.4	5,426	16.5
Social science	2,494	10.8	1,091	9.8	3,585	10.5	2,773	12.7	993	9.0	3,766	11.5
Total	23,023	100	11,129	100	34,152	100	21,758	100	11,081	100	32,839	100

a Joint Matriculation Examination   b Direct entry

therapy, physiology and anatomy, sciences, and veterinary medicine. Different minimum academic standards are being worked out for the polytechnics and colleges of education through the NBTE and the NCCE respectively. Institutions planning to open must meet the established minimum academic standards or they will not be permitted to do so, nor will existing institutions be allowed to continue any courses or programs in which they are found deficient.

The minimum academic standards deal with the philosophy and objectives of a discipline, its academic contents, the course requirements and synopses, course evaluation and/or continuous assessment, personnel, equipment, physical facilities, and general conditions for ensuring excellence. In 1990, the minimum academic standards panels were already in the universities to monitor and assess the degree of compliance with the above conditions and to apply sanctions as they became necessary. The application of minimum academic standards has implications for the adequate funding and judicious use of money, materials, and human resources in the nation's higher educational institutions.

In the Nigerian higher education system graduate training programs generally begin after a student has obtained a minimum of a second-class lower honors university degree or the national diploma from a polytechnic at the lower (and increasingly at the upper) credit level.

Quite a number of graduate degree courses emphasize knowledge and practice whereas some are research training oriented and require the submission of a supervised thesis for master's or doctoral degrees in such fields, whether at university or polytechnic level. The colleges of education, which are basically concerned with diploma courses, do not offer graduate training or research work. Some of them, however, offer first degrees of the universities to which they are constituents or affiliates.

There are variations in the content of both first and graduate degrees of the universities as is true of the polytechnics, which do not offer degrees of any type apart from their traditional ordinary and higher diplomas (OD and HD).

3. Governance, Administration, and Finance

By 1957 it was becoming clear that if the central federal government was to play a coordinating role and avoid an imbalanced development and costly and wasteful duplication then some central planning and purposeful direction must be given to higher education throughout the country. Thus, the Ashby Commission Report (1960) recommended among other things that all universities must be national in outlook and subject to some central planning and direction with the bulk of capital grants and a proportion of recurrent funds coming from the federal government. Tables 3 and 4 outline the capital and recurrent appropriations in Nigeria's universities. The Government's White Paper on the Ashby Report reiterated that while each federal or regional university should be autonomous, the overall national interest should be safeguarded through the establishment by law of an interregional workforce board, an all-Nigeria academic council, and a National Universities Commission (NUC).

The NUC, established in 1962, was responsible for the following duties: advising the government on the recurrent and capital financial needs of universities; consulting universities in their balanced and coordinated planning and development; receiving block grants and allocating them to universities with such conditions as necessary; channeling external aids to the universities; collating, analyzing, and publishing information about universities; and making recommendations to universities or to government on matters of national interest. It was also to have access to records of universities seeking federal grants.

The takeover of government by the armed forces in January, 1966, the transition from four regions to 21 states plus the federal capital territory of Abuja by 1987, along with the civil war of 1967 to 1970 had important consequences for the fortunes and planning of higher education in Nigeria as both the federal and state higher education depended on the federally generated oil revenues.

Meanwhile, the Committee of Vice-Chancellors of Nigerian Universities (CVC) emerged in 1962. It was intended as an informal but effective coordinating body whose members would consult jointly and facilitate a common approach on the part of the universities in tackling mutual problems including staff and student welfare.

The different national commissions on education seemed to have justified their corporate existence with respect to the orderly planning, implementation, and evaluation of higher education programs and functions in Nigeria. Through these commissions, it is now possible to maintain the orderly development of every institution while a depressed economy makes dwindling financial resources available to the higher education sector. The Joint Admissions and Matriculations Board (JAMB), a central organization created by government to organize admissions to universities and lately to other tertiary institutions, has succeeded in eliminating delays and wastes that used to plague admission processes when these were handled by the individual institutions.

The economic problems that started to become manifest in the late 1970s and which were aggravated in the early 1980s did not spare the higher education sector. Since the federal and state governments were the sole financiers of all the higher education institutions, the fall in revenue accruable to government from every source caused serious fluctuations in both

Table 3
Capital appropriations of Nigeria's federal universities 1976–87

	Grants						
	1976/77	1978/79	1980	1982	1984	1986	1988
Ibadan	3,866,500	5,000,000	1,800,000	14,855,082	14,138,601	5,525,000	3,621,327
Lagos	8,182,650	6,050,000	16,999,999	7,973,662	1,305,086	5,525,000	3,621,327
Nsukka	7,001,036	8,750,000	16,538,007	13,938,901	1,413,860	5,525,000	3,621,327
Zaria	7,621,000	1,470,000	21,499,999	8,268,304	1,413,860	5,525,000	3,621,327
Ife	10,344,500	33,800,000	16,499,999	7,973,662	1,413,860	7,416,668	3,621,327
Benin	10,858,009	10,500,000	179,999,999	10,963,785	1,413,860	6,863,542	5,026,054
Jos	1,784,900	1,024,000	13,949,999	12,957,200	1,915,660	6,550,390	5,026,054
Sokoto	1,383,850	10,870,000	14,500,000	11,960,492	1,915,660	6,550,390	526,054
Calabar	1,784,900	10,030,000	1,376,001	10,027,077	1,915,660	14,571,407	5,026,054
Kano	2,214,500	10,450,000	14,130,000	9,967,077	1,915,660	6,550,390	5,226,054
Maiduguri	1,383,850	10,870,000	14,500,000	9,967,077	2,046,660	6,550,390	5,026,054
Ilorin	1,383,850	10,030,000	15,760,001	9,967,077	2,095,660	803,924	5,026,054
Port Harcourt	1,383,850	9,610,000	1,440,000	11,960,492	2,315,661	6,550,390	4,705,689
Bauchi	—	—	2,000,000	13,463,785	2,000,000	6,318,269	4,705,689
Makurdi	—	—	—	10,963,785	20,000,000	6,318,269	4,705,689
Owerri	—	—	—	10,963,785	2,000,000	9,979,324	4,705,689
Akure	—	—	—	10,963,785	2,000,000	6,730,918	4,705,689
Yola	—	—	—	19,963,785	2,000,000	6,318,269	4,705,689
Abeokuta	—	—	—	199,425	2,500,000	3,700,000	29,823,384
Minna	—	—	—	2,400,000	2,000,000	6,730,918	4,705,699
Abuja	—	—	—	—	—	—	2,000,000
Adeyemi College of Education, Ondo	—	—	—	2,392,098	1,657,620	850,001	514,631
Advanced Teachers College, Kano	—	—	—	2,392,098	1,474,500	850,001	514,631
Advanced Teachers College, Zaria	—	—	—	2,392,098	1,474,500	850,001	514,631
Open University	—	—	—	500,000	—	—	—
Nigeria Defence Academy	—	—	—	—	—	—	—
Total	59,193,395	128,454,000	330,994,004	208,374,532	72,325,368	133,153,461	114,726,292

Table 4
Recurrent appropriations of Nigeria's federal universities 1976/88

	Grants						
	1976/77	1978/79	1980	1982	1984	1986	1988
Ibadan	21,447,500	25,725,000	28,638,199	40,232,619	48,618,605	42,009,553	47,705,000
Lagos	19,331,100	18,487,000	25,562,498	37,532,866	45,730,871	38,480,519	43,788,000
Nsukka	19,559,100	22,299,000	27,036,849	40,358,500	46,060,000	30,043,331	44,197,000
Zaria	21,164,700	23,407,000	29,753,549	41,635,671	51,940,723	44,116,101	50,128,000
Ife	160,010,800	18,275,000	27,528,798	35,635,563	45,041,986	38,063,983	43,140,000
Benin	9,816,800	11,741,950	21,013,150	26,019,816	28,401,000	21,316,000	31,181,000
Jos	2,528,200	51,160,001	11,159,550	17,291,381	21,929,022	20,107,946	22,709,000
Sokoto	813,333	2,727,000	6,399,949	10,021,516	12,931,803	120,951	13,554,000
Calabar	3,025,200	5,438,000	10,492,299	15,441,605	19,526,003	179,874,800	20,335,000
Kano	3,294,400	6,350,000	9,599,698	13,696,154	18,066,019	16,101,439	18,245,099
Maiduguri	2,713,200	6,974,000	8,817,249	15,594,626	20,283,759	19,547,561	22,067,000
Ilorin	1,513,000	4,083,000	8,382,248	15,137,732	19,141,132	18,473,339	20,747,000
Port Harcourt	9,130,000	2,850,000	7,068,406	12,189,535	16,312,019	15,674,606	16,409,000
Bauchi	—	—	2,000,000	4,162,593	6,217,115	6,212,367	6,497,000
Makurdi	—	—	100,000	4,616,601	6,343,115	6,368,794	6,703,000
Owerri	—	—	—	4,067,998	5,634,422	6,975,561	7,652,000
Akure	—	—	—	2,481,245	3,010,805	4,742,556	5,557,000
Yola	—	—	—	2,420,828	3,017,211	3,840,684	39,270,000
Abeokuta	—	—	—	2,000,000	4,163,750	3,700,972	3,740,000
Minna	—	—	—	—	—	—	2,000,000
Abuja	—	—	—	2,000,000	4,163,750	3,700,972	3,748,000
Adeyemi College of Education, Ondo	3,333,235	1,528,000	1,675,225	2,160,000	2,721,468	2,543,973	2,365,000
Advanced Teachers College, Kano & Zaria	15,142,110	64,027,200	7,924,775	6,663,000	5,728,840	5,399,852	5,595,000
Nigeria Defence Academy	—	—	—	—	2,577,926	2,453,493	2,319,000
IAL	—	—	—	260,000	500,000	—	—
Open University	—	—	—	—	250,000	—	—
Total	148,822,678	265,072,151	233,155,442	351,618,849	436,310,244	529,869,353	485,951,099

capital and recurrent grant allocations to these institutions. (There were shortfalls of 25 to 60% in recurrent expenditures and 30 to 84% in capital expenditures from the late 1970s to the 1990s.) To compound the problems, the economic doldrums of that period coincided with the start of an era of high demand for university education as total student enrollments in all institutions increased by 50 percent between 1982 and 1989. The effect has been to create an inadequacy of lecture rooms, workshops and laboratories, and library books and journals and a breakdown of existing research and teaching equipment as fresh supplies of laboratory consumables have been unavailable. The overall result has been an apparent fall in the quality of university education.

In addition to these constraints, academic salaries are low in comparison with earnings from the private sector of the Nigerian economy. The overall picture of academic life has not been conducive to retaining staff in the higher educational institutions. In a developing country like Nigeria, such staff and institutions play a vital role. It is not only necessary to train qualified graduates but also to conduct research in order to solve the multifarious problems of survival, and constraints on maintaining let alone developing the higher educational system are of national importance.

By 1985 it was becoming obvious that, in respect of higher education, the philosophy should be one of consolidating existing institutions and programs. The aim of this would be to strengthen existing facilities to make them relevant and responsive to national growth and development; to rationalize growth and development in order to avoid waste and unnecessary duplications within and among the institutions; and to turn them into centers of excellence in the areas of their individual specializations and competencies. Meanwhile in respect of the younger and new institutions, such a policy would afford an opportunity for growth and development to justify the investment in them. It would allow them the chance to develop into centers of excellence for the nation's labor requirements and for the scientific and technological future of the country. Consolidation would answer the fundamental need for institutions to respond adequately and with relevance to national needs.

There is provision in the regulations (edicts/decrees) of each higher institution for a "visitor." In federal institutions, the visitor is the head of state or the president, while in the state institutions it is the governor. The visitor is expected to be eager for the progress, welfare, and happiness of the institutions and its members.

The visitor does not, and is not expected to, interfere in the day-to-day administration of the institution. Apart from the visitor, there is a chancellor, who is the titular head of the university—a type of constitutional monarch whose actions are based on the recommendations of the council and senate or academic board of the institution.

In the actual governance of each institution, there is provision for a council comprised of laymen and representatives of the institution who are all appointed by the government to act as trustees in the interest of the nation. The property, finances, and public relations of the institutions are under the council's control. Subject to any limitations in the relevant laws, councils are expected to be autonomous. Senates or academic boards have authority in all academic matters. The chief executive (who may be known as the vice-chancellor, rector, or provost) of each institution is expected to act not only in accordance with the provisions of the laws and the decisions of the council and senate or academic board, but also is required at all times to act justly, fairly, and in the national interest.

The "visitation" is a feature of the management of Nigerian higher education institutions. It is an inspection routinely ordered by the visitor towards the close of a five-year period (known as a quinquennium) to assess the achievement of the current quinquennium. In the light of the investigation the visitor and the university are advised on the direction in which growth and development as well as investment should go in the ensuing five years. It serves not only to make account to the public and clients of the university of the competence of the institution, but also acts as a pointer to future trends and goals.

The academic organization of higher education in Nigeria closely follows the British model. British academics initiated the processes toward the establishment of all higher educational institutions but one (the University of Nigeria, by Americans) in Nigeria and so it is understandable that Nigeria should follow the British system almost exactly with the introduction of departments, institutes, faculties, and senates or academic boards as the vehicles for instruction and research. Likewise the same system is followed in the awarding of certificates, diplomas, and degrees. Recommendations on appointments are passed from the most basic unit concerned to the highest academic policy-making body for approval, again following the British model.

4. Faculty and Students: Teaching, Learning, and Research

4.1 Faculty

There are five ways of appointing teachers to Nigerian higher educational institutions: temporary appointments which depend on interviews and ratification; direct appointments following interviews; appointments for one year on sabbatical leave; annually renewable invitations made on retirement until the age of 65; and, with respect to newly established institutions, appointments on probation. These latter are for first degree holders registered with the appointing university or elsewhere for graduate degrees in specified areas of need. On completion of their graduate degree they will assume office as regular academic teachers.

Figures for academic staff in the higher educational system are not immediately available. However, for the 1973/74, 1977/78, and 1978/82 academic years, there were 3,459, 5,190, and 7,980 academic staff in the universities of which 28 percent, 22 percent, and 20 percent were expatriates recruited under a special scheme for each of the periods.

After a successful interview in response to an advertised position, a candidate is offered the appointment. To be appointed to the position of Lecturer Grade Two a PhD in the relevant field is necessary. A candidate with a master's degree can hold an assistant lectureship.

Progression beyond grade two lectureships is only possible if the candidate has published journal articles and books that are referenced by at least three colleagues of professorial rank and adjudged in quantity and quality to deserve promotion to the grades of lecturer one, senior lecturer, reader/associate professor, or professor respectively at intervals of at least two or three years from one promotion to the other. Staff of the federal and state higher education system are employees of the individual governing councils of the institutions they belong to; they are in the public service and are *not* civil servants. The NUC, NBTE, and NCCE could, if required to, assist in placing advertisements for overseas recruitment on behalf of these institutions although they have no power to impose any candidate on them.

The career and status of academic staff of polytechnics and colleges of education differ considerably from those of the universities even though, in 1990, the categories of academics were placed on the same university salary scales (USS) as their counterparts in the universities. The system of recruitment for those in the tertiary institutions is the same, although conditions for promotion or appointment to the higher grades differ enormously with emphasis on materials production rather than on research publications.

The Academic Staff Unions of Universities (ASUU), the registered umbrella union of academic staff in all Nigerian universities, caters for the interests of academics either at the individual university level or at the national level. Likewise the Senior Administrative and Technical Staff Unions (SATSU) and the Non-Academic Staff Union (NASU) take care of their senior administrative and technical staff and junior staff respectively. Equivalent organizations and unions exist under different names in the polytechnics and the colleges of education. In cases where such unions have seemingly run foul of the law, the government has put a ban on their activities on university and other higher educational campuses (and later lifted that ban). A parallel organization, the National Association of Nigerian Students

(already mentioned in this article), advocates collective students' interests in respect of all higher educational institutions in Nigeria. These organizations become involved in the day-to-day management of their respective institutions.

To ensure the achievement of minimum academic standards in all the higher educational institutions in Nigeria, the NUC, NBTE, and NCCE have been mandated to formulate guidelines for these institutions. The guidelines are to provide a basic statement for each institution of what should constitute their philosophy and objectives in each course; the resource requirements for a course credit system; and the number of credit units needed by each student in each of the two semesters in an academic year in each course/subject. They also indicate the appropriate staff/student workload per semester, divided into contact hours per week and the modalities for semester examinations and continuous assessments by staff on each student. They approve guidelines for fail/resit/repeat examinations, probations, withdrawals, and duration of degree courses. Equally they determine credit hours for teaching, tutorials, and laboratory work. Students take courses leading to general and specialist degrees classified as first, second upper and lower, third class, and pass.

4.2 Students

Since the mid 1960s, it has been the policy of the government and university authorities to admit students into universities and colleges of education in a ratio of three to two between the sciences (including engineering, medicine, pharmacy, and technology) and the humanities (arts, administration, education, and social sciences). It has been a daunting task to achieve this ratio. Thus, most universities deliberately admitted fresh school leavers to predegree courses for a year's preliminary science. A number of basic schools or colleges of arts and science, mostly those in the sciences, were created at federal and state levels to cope with the demand for scientific and technological orientations. This was done to the extent that in the 1990 academic year, such colleges were being phased out again as they had outgrown their usefulness. In addition, a number of polytechnics and technical colleges had been opened at federal and state levels to cope with the demand for technological education. Figures are hard to come by to illustrate these developments which would also include the social class and gender breakdown of the students in the entire system.

5. Conclusion

The higher education system in Nigeria faces a number of growing pains. It is suffering a brain drain as its most talented academics seek greener pastures abroad, while loyalty among the remaining academics is divided in the wake of enforced early retirements. Salaries are low as compared with earnings from the private and public sectors of the economy; teaching and research facilities are inadequate and obsolete; and financial resources available for recurrent and capital expenditures are dwindling, making expansion as well as maintenance of minimum academic standards difficult to achieve. There has been growing student and staff unrest on various campuses which has resulted in temporary and long-term closures of the institutions involved. The different statutory powers of the organs of government (NUC, NBTE, NCCE, JAMB) have come into conflict with those of the ministries of education and the councils of the higher institutions of learning. Finally, the appointments, quality, management skills and job performance of the academic and administrative heads of the institutions is in itself a matter of some difficulty.

Without doubt the Nigerian higher education system has come a long way since 1948 when the Yaba Higher College (1932) and the University College, Ibadan (1948) were the only extant higher education institutions. The system has benefited tremendously over the years from both the British and American systems. Since 1960 it has been the American system particularly as this was the date when the University of Nigeria made its debut on the American land grant college pattern. Information and documentation retrieval opportunities continue to be the bane of all systems in Nigeria, even with the growing demands for computer education and computer hard and software. Other pernicious problems plaguing the management and internal relationships of the higher education system include the need for rapprochement between the government and its agencies on the one hand and the authorities, staff, and students of the system on the other hand.

There is no doubt at all that both the government and the institutions mean well. These and other issues will be addressed by a new Commission (similar to the Ashby Commission of 1960), now in place to review and recommend as appropriate the continued development and progress of higher education for the next two decades.

There is a dire need for a better mutual understanding and appreciation among authorities and functionaries of higher educational institutions, statutory agencies of government, and national and state governments. They must appreciate one another's conventions, roles, and procedures in order to avoid the pitfalls of strife, discords, and wasteful confrontations which are capable of deterring each and everyone from attaining the corporate set goals.

Bibliography

Aboyade O 1978 Memorandum submitted by the Vice-Chancellor, University of Ife to the Universities Crisis Commission of Inquiry sitting at the University on Monday, 22nd May, 1978

Adaralegbe A (ed.) 1972 *A Philosophy for Nigerian Education.* Heinemann Educational Books (Nigeria), Ibadan

Adaralegbe A 1985 Report of the NUC Working Party on the 5th National Development Plan, 1986–1990

Ade Ajayi J F 1983 Planning and co-ordination in a federal system: the evolution of the Nigerian university system. In: *20 Years of University Education in Nigeria.* National Universities Commission, Lagos

Aminu J 1983 The factor of centralisation in two decades of Nigerian university development. In: *20 Years of University Education in Nigeria*, National Universities Commission, Lagos

Ashby E 1960 *Investment in Education: Report of the Commission on Post-School Certificate and Higher Education in Nigeria.* Federal Ministry of Information, Lagos

Economic Commission for Africa 1966 Manpower Requirements for African Development. Memorandum submitted by ECA to the Second Conference of Heads of African Universities, Zaria

Eke A Y 1974 Government and university relationships in Nigeria. *The Quarterly Journal of Administration* 8(4): July 1974

Fafunwa A B 1967 *New Perspectives in African Education.* Macmillan, London and Lagos

Fafunwa A B 1969a *Over a Hundred Years of Higher Education for Nigerians* N.B.C. October Lectures (1968). Federal Government Printer

Fafunwa A B 1969b Philosophy of education and manpower development in Nigeria. In: Yesufu T M (ed.) 1989 *Manpower Problems and Economic Development in Nigeria.* Oxford University Press, Ibadan

Fafunwa A B 1971 *A History of Higher Education in Nigeria.* Macmillan, London and Lagos

Fafunwa A B 1972 The purpose of teacher education. In: Adaralegbe A (ed.) 1972 *A Philosophy of Education for Nigerian Education.* Heinemann Educational Books, Ibadan

Fafunwa A B, Adaralegbe A 1973 The University of Ife case study. In: Yesufu T M (ed.) 1973 *Creating the African University.* Oxford University Press, Ibadan

Fafunwa A B 1974a *History of Education in Nigeria.* George Allen and Unwin, London

Fafunwa A B 1974b *Growth and Development of Nigeria Universities* Overseas. Liaison Committee Paper No. 4, Washington DC

Fafunwa A B, Hanson J W 1974 The post-independence Nigeria universities. In: Altbach P G (ed.) 1974 *University Reform.* Schenkman, Cambridge, Massachusetts

Fafunwa A B *The Universities of Nigeria: An Introduction to the Commonwealth Universities Yearbook*, 1973–1978 editions. Commonwealth Secretariat, London

Fafunwa A B, Aisiku J U 1982 (eds.) *African Education: A Comparative Survey.* George Allen & Unwin, London

Federal Ministry of Information 1977. *Federal Republic of Nigeria National Policy on Education.* FMI, Lagos. Republished 1981

Ike V C 1976 *University Development in Africa: The Nigerian Experience, 1976.* Oxford University Press, Ibadan

Ikejiani O et al. 1964 *Nigerian Education.* Longmans, Lagos

National Manpower Board 1978 Current Manpower Demand and Supply Situation. Background Paper for the National Conference on Manpower Constraints to Nigeria's Economic Development, September 1978

Okafor N 1971 *The Development of Universities in Nigeria.* Longman, London

Onushkin V G et al. 1973. *Planning the Development of Universities II.* UNESCO/IIEP, Paris

Perkins J A 1976 The university and society: Is the university an agent for social reform? *Dialogue* 9(2)

Thompson K W, Fogel, B F (eds.) 1976 *Higher Education and Social Change: Promising Experiments in Developing Countries*, Vol. 1. Praeger, New York

UNESCO 1966 Conference on the Development of Higher Education in Africa, UNESCO

Yesufu T M (ed.) 1973 *Creating the African University: Emerging Issues on the 1970s.* The University of Ibadan Press, Ibadan

A. B. Fafunwa

Norway

1. Higher Education and Society

Compared to other European countries, the history of higher education in Norway is short. The first university in Norway, the University of Oslo, was founded in 1811 by the king of Denmark and Norway, as a response to the increasing demand of Norwegian citizens for national and cultural independence from the long union with Denmark. At the end of the Napoleonic wars in 1814, the union with Denmark was dissolved and a union with Sweden was established. However, before entering the new union, which lasted until 1905, Norway drafted its own constitution based on ideas from the French Revolution and the American Constitution and established its own parliament in 1814.

In the years that followed, the new university played an important role in the development of the young Norwegian state and made a considerable contribution to the formation of national identity in the nineteenth century. The next university, the University of Bergen, was not established until 1946. However, as the economy of the country developed, specialized institutions with university status were established in the early part of the twentieth century.

Schools for the education of the semiprofessions (teachers, nurses, etc.) were originally institutions on a secondary level. The oldest were founded in the nineteenth century. After the Second World War, an increasing proportion of students entering these schools had completed secondary school ("gymnasium"). Consequently, most of these institutions were upgraded as institutions of higher education from the 1960s to the 1980s.

During these years, two new universities and several regional colleges were established to provide opportunites for the increasing number of secondary-school graduates applying for higher education, and to stimulate development in peripheral areas of the country.

There has been no change in the political geography of Norway for more than two hundred years, except for the inclusion of the Spitzbergen islands in the Arctic Ocean in 1920. In the 1960s, Norway gained sovereignty over a large part of the continental shelf off its western and northern coastline. This has been of enormous importance for the Norwegian economy due to the abundance of oil and gas discovered.

The population of Norway grew from 3,280,000 in 1950 to 4,221,000 in 1989. The annual increase in population was reduced from about 30,000 in the 1960s to 20,000 in the 1970s, and further to about 13,000 in the 1980s. Net immigration increased from zero in the 1960s to 4,000–5,000 annually in the 1970s and 1980s. The total population is expected to grow slightly during the coming decades.

The number of people in the 20 to 24 year old age group increased by about 50 percent from 1960 to 1970. Growth continued during the 1980s, but will fall by 20 to 30 percent in the 1990s.

In all regions, people have moved to cities and towns from rural areas. As for distribution between regions, there has been a small tendency for the population in the northern part of Norway to diminish and some concentration in the Oslo region.

There are some thousand Sami, the indigenous population of the north, who speak their own language. A Sami institution of higher education was established in 1989.

1.1 Occupational and Social Class Structure

Equality between men and women is an important issue in Norwegian politics. There are still considerable differences betwen sexes with reference to occupational level, unemployment, wages, and educational level.

There are considerable salary differences between occupations. None the less, the political goals of wage equity between sectors must, according to the government, be evaluated in relation to the competitive ability of the different branches of industry.

1.2 Structure of the Economy

Almost two-thirds of those employed work in the private and public service sectors. A general development of prosperity related to income from oil has resulted in increased employment within the service sector at the expense of other branches.

An expansive economic policy to keep unemployment low, income from oil, and the liberalization of the credit market were the main reasons that growth in domestic prices, wages, and salaries was greater in Norway during most of the 1980s than in countries which are her most important economic partners within the Organisation for Economic Co-operation and Development (OECD).

In 1986, Norway was affected by a sudden fall in oil income due to lower oil prices. The result was a strong deterioration in Norway's balance of payments.

In the long run this could lead to a serious crisis in the country's economy. However, governmental economic initiatives have been successful in reducing growth in domestic prices, salaries, and wages. The rate of inflation in 1989 was on the same level as in other OECD countries. On the whole, the balance of payments has improved. Concurrently, unemployment has reached an unusually high level for Norway, about 4 percent. Even though this is low by international comparison, the government in its long-term program for 1990–93 nevertheless gives high priority to reducing unemployment.

1.3 Structure of Government and Main Political Goals

Norway is a parliamentary democracy with a monarch as the formal head of state.

The main political goals after the Second World War can be summarized as follows: (a) rebuilding the Norwegian economy and the parts of the country destroyed in the war; (b) developing the welfare state based on economic growth, full employment, fair distribution of income, and high social security standards. Governments have also attempted to develop the more remote and less developed regions and to maintain a dispersed population pattern.

Higher education policy has been an integral part of general Norwegian policy and has been used to a great extent as a means to obtain desirable societal goals. The governments have particularly stressed two aspects: (a) the development of the economy and the welfare state should not be hampered by a shortage of professional work force; (b) the explosive growth in demand for higher education from the baby boom generation after the Second World War should be met.

In addition to increasing the number of institutions and their capacities, the government in the early postwar years took measures to secure a more equitable social balance in recruitment to higher education as well as greater equity between sexes and regions. This was done through the State Educational Loan Fund, established in 1947, which administers low interest loans and scholarships.

1.4 Relationship with Religious Bodies

Church-affiliated organizations have formerly run several teachers colleges, however today they only administer a couple which receive substantial state funding. Some nursing colleges are run by churches or church organizations but are funded by the state.

A free faculty of theology was established in Oslo in 1907. For several decades this faculty has educated far more ministers for the Evangelical Lutheran State Church than the University of Oslo and has for the last 15 to 20 years received state support.

2. The Institutional Fabric of the Higher Education System

2.1 The Sectoral Organization of Higher Education

Norway has three groups of public institutions of higher education: (a) the university sector—four universities and six specialized institutions with university status in fields such as business administration, agricultural sciences, and so forth; (b) the college sector with approximately 110 institutions organized under 17 regional boards—regional colleges and institutions specializing in a particular field, for example, nursing, social work, teacher training, engineering, and so forth; (c) institutions in the arts and the performing arts.

In addition to these groups, there are a few private institutions, mainly institutions with religious affiliations and schools of economics and business administration.

The universities provide programs at all levels and in a wide range of fields of study, depending on the size of the institution. The specialized institutions with university status concentrate on their particular fields, but also offer more general courses. Two universities have been established since 1960, in Tromsø in northern Norway and in Trondheim, both in 1968. However, the latter is not a new institution, but was founded by merging the Technical University (established in 1910) with another institution of higher education.

The regional colleges, a particular group of institutions in the college sector, generally offer courses below the master's level in several fields. In a few cases, they also train engineers and business administrators up to a master's level. These colleges, at present 14 in number, were established in the 1970s and 1980s as part of the expansion and decentralization of the higher education system. Originally, they were supposed to provide alternatives to universities by concentrating on shorter professional programs, for example, two- to three-year programs in business administration. However, they soon took over and developed the general university courses already being offered in the regions. Concerning research, these institutions were supposed to focus on applied Research and Development (R & D) of relevance to the local region. Increasingly, as they began offering university courses, the regional colleges also began to carry out more basic research. The main difference between these institutions and the universities is that they generally do not offer advanced courses. Only two of these colleges have more than 1,000 students. Thus, most of them cover a rather limited number of fields. The 14 regional colleges make up the bulk of the institutions established after 1960.

The rest of the institutions in the college sector (teachers colleges, nursing colleges, colleges of engineering, etc.) are typically older and specialized institutions, which were organized under regional boards of higher education in the 1970s and 1980s. With the exception of two engineering colleges with more than a thousand students, these institutions are typically small. In most of these institutions research activity is limited.

In general, courses from the regional system are accredited by the universities. Thus, some students start their higher education at a local college, and complete it at a university.

The number of graduates from public institutions is insufficient to meet both labor market demands for graduate workforce and student demands for higher education in certain fields, in particular in economics and business administration. Thus, private institutions fill a gap in the public system of higher education.

Norwegian Research and development may be classified into three sectors: the higher education sector; the institute sector; and the industrial sector. In 1987, the distribution of research by sector was as follows: higher education (21 percent); independent institutes (35 percent); and the industrial sector (44 percent). Norway differs from most other European countries by having a relatively large sector of research institutes not affiliated with the higher education system, and comparatively limited research activity in the industrial sector.

Most basic research (75 percent) is performed in the higher education sector. About half of the Research and development in this sector is classified as basic research, the other as applied Research and development. Research and teaching are closely tied together in the university sector—most staff have both a right and an obligation to do research.

2.2 Admissions Policies and University Expansion

Generally, the prerequisite for admittance to higher education is the completion of secondary school. For university matriculation, students are normally required to have completed the academic stream of secondary school, but in some cases they may take other streams in conjunction with certain academic subjects. Some fields have open admission, but in general, admission is competitive. Secondary-school grades are normally the basis for selection, but in some cases work experience gives extra credit.

The number of university students increased by more than 300 percent between 1960 and 1975. In the period 1975–85, the number of university students was fairly stable, but the number has increased substantially since then, partly as a result of higher unemployment.

From 1975 until 1988 the college sector grew by about 145 percent, partly due to the expansion of programs (e.g., teacher education from two to three years in the 1970s), upgrading (see Table 1) and the establishment of new institutions (regional colleges).

Traditionally, there have been large numbers of Norwegian students abroad, formerly mainly in medicine, now mainly in business administration and engineering. The number of foreign students in Norway is about 5,000.

Table 2 gives figures for the percentage of persons in the age group 20–24 enrolled in postsecondary institutions. The percentage of persons in this group enrolled in higher education diminished from 12.1 percent in 1975 to 11.7 percent in 1980. In 1985, the percentage increased to 14.3. However, this is partly a result of the upgrading of education from secondary to higher education mentioned above. Of the age group 20–24, 8 percent were in secondary education. Thus, in total, 22.3 percent of this age group were in either secondary or postsecondary education in 1985. This percentage has increased in the last five years.

In 1985, 45 percent of all students enrolled in universities and colleges were older than 24. The percentage of older students is increasing. As seen in Table 2, the total number of students enrolled in postsecondary education amount to 29.3 percent of the age group 20–24.

2.3 Structure of Qualifications

University programs in the professions (theology, law, medicine, dentistry, psychology, etc.) typically take five to seven years. In the humanities and social sciences, universities offer courses of different length. The most common units are:

(a) *grunnfag* (GF) = 1 year

(b) *mellomfag* (MF) = GF + 1/2 year,

(c) *hovedfag* (HF) = MF + 2 years.

A lower degree in these fields (cand. mag.) is normally composed of 2 GF plus 1 MF. A higher degree (master's) is composed of 2 GF plus 1 HF (5.5 years). As all students are required to take preparatory courses in the history of philosophy and logic (1/2 year), the length of time for a lower degree is a minimum 4 years; for a higher degree, minimum 6 years. The faculties of science have a credit system— 10 credits per half year. A lower degree requires 65 credits plus philosophy, a higher degree, two further years. The length of these programs is thus only a little shorter than in the humanities and social sciences. The titles of higher degrees are cand. (*candidatus*) and a Latin abbreviation of the field, for example, cand. scient. for the natural sciences. A higher degree always includes a thesis.

The specialized institutions of university status offer programs which last four to five years. The typical length of study in institutions under the regional college boards is two to three years. In some cases regional colleges offer four- or five-year programs. The lower degree (cand. mag.) may be granted by regional institutions.

The highest degree awarded by Norwegian uni-

Table 1
Students by type of university or college 1960–1988/90

	1960	1965	1970	1975	1980	1985	1988
Norwegian students abroad	—	—	—	—	4,417	6,841	7,015
Students, University and Colleges	—	33,438	50,132	66,628	73,856	93,984	111,605
Total	—	33,438	50,132	66,628	78,273	100,825	118,620
University sector	9,609	19,638	30,165	40,774	40,620	42,083	47,884[c]
College sector	—	13,800	19,967	25,854	33,236	51,901	63,721
Regional Colleges	—	—	477	3,194	4,902	6,806	10,461
Colleges of education	—	—	—	11,070	13,696	12,391	12,299
Colleges of engineering	—	—	—	6,652	6,249	7,775	7,936
Colleges of health education	—	—	—	340	411	7,919[a]	9,106
Other colleges of higher education	—	—	—	4,598	7,978	17,030[b]	23,341

Source: Institute for Studies in Research and Higher Education. Notat 9/87. Students and Graduates Table 1987
a Nursing education upgraded to college education   b including 6,000 students (estimate) from a private School of Management   c 57,231 in 1990

versities is the doctoral degree. In recent years, several new doctoral degrees, modelled after the PhD at English and American universities, have been introduced to promote structured and efficient doctoral training programs. The older degrees, which have not been abolished, are generally taken quite late in a research career and are based on independent study without any advisory system. The new degrees emphasize compulsory courses and an advisory system, and are scheduled to be completed in three to four years after taking a higher degree or graduating from a professional school.

3. Governance, Administration, and Finance

3.1 National Administration

The Ministry of Cultural and Scientific Affairs, hereafter called the Ministry, has responsibility for higher education and research. There is no general law governing all institutions of higher education, and most universities and institutions with university status were governed by individual laws. In 1989, the Norwegian parliament passed a law covering the four universities and the six institutions with university status, but not covering the college sector. Within this sector, only teachers colleges are regulated by law, through the Teacher Education Act of 1973. Institutions not covered by law are guided by cabinet or ministry regulations.

General trends toward decentralization in public administration affect higher education. Institutions are being given more autonomy and greater budgetary flexibility within the limits established by par-

liament or the Ministry. The new university law formalizes and extends this.

In Norway, there is no common governing board to act as a "buffer" between universities and the Ministry, though representatives from institutions with university status meet twice a year in an informal forum called "The University Council."

Colleges and schools in the college sector are governed by regional boards in which representatives of the county have a majority. Institutions in this sector are also influenced by central agencies which may exert influence on curricula, examinations, etc. The trend toward decentralization affects the function of these agencies by giving them more of an advisory role.

Table 2
Students enrolled in postsecondary education (universities and colleges) as percentage of persons in the 20–24 year old age group

	1970	1975	1980	1985
Percentage of the age group 20–24 years old in universities and colleges	—	12.1	11.7	14.3
All students enrolled in postsecondary education as percentage of total age group 20–24	14.8	22.1	23.9	29.3

Source: Based on Central Bureau of Statistics of Norway
Population Statistics and Educational Statistics Universities and Colleges

3.2 Planning, Implementation, and Evaluation

One of the main guidelines of higher educational policy has been to make higher education more accessible by distributing institutions over a wider geographical area. Improving the quality and efficiency of the institutions has recently become a focus of policy. In 1988, a royal commission on higher education recommended a series of proposals including some radical changes in the system of higher education. The main points are:

(a) Stimulating research by an annual increase in government appropriations of 5 percent in real terms in the period 1990–93.

(b) Encouraging students to take graduate degrees with more generous financial student aid and a considerable increase in the number of scholarships for research training.

(c) Encouraging the universities to make their contributions to society more visible and to establish a regular system of evaluation of performance in research and teaching.

(d) Recommending the amalgamation of smaller institutions and departments into larger ones and also recommending more cooperation between units, thus promoting sustainable units for research and higher education.

(e) Recommending that the universities become more internationally oriented.

The less costly of these recommendations have found support in a Cabinet white paper on research (1989) and on higher education (1991).

3.3 Finance

Table 3 illustrates main traits in the development of the financing of higher education in Norway since 1966. Higher education is mainly financed through the state budget. None the less, the table shows a growth of private funding in the 1980s. During the period 1981 to 1987, public support for private schools diminished considerably, mainly because some of these schools changed status from private to public institutions.

Expenditure on higher education as a percentage of the Gross National Product (GNP) increased until 1974, then began to stagnate, then increased again from 1985. These fluctuations are in part due to variations in oil income and government economic policies.

The total cost of higher education is somewhat higher than indicated in the table since there is a loss in GNP caused by students withdrawing from full

Table 3
Financing of higher education in Norway. Fixed prices based on 1979 NKr. mill.[a]

	1966	1970	1974	1977	1981	1985	1987
Public Institutions[b]							
Total expenditure	1,369	1,628	2,030	2,635	2,588	2,812	3,082
Of which expenditure on educational functions, etc.	747	902	1,021	1,365	1,381	1,495	1,726
Private institutions							
Public subsidy	30	38	48	68	172	166	89
Private financing	15	26	38	57	120	178	172
Total private expenditure	46	65	87	126	292	345	262
Of which educational functions, etc.	46	65	82	121	286	339	254
Scholarships, grants, etc.	327	343	740	777	1,042	894	1,079
Total higher education expenditure	1,743	2,036	2,857	3,539	3,923	4,052	4,424
Of which educational functions, scholarships grants, etc.	1,121	1,310	1,843	2,263	2,719	2,728	3,060
Educational functions and scholarships, grants, etc. in percent of the gross national product	0.7	0.8	0.9	1.2	1.1	0.9	1.1

a Figures estimated on the basis of budget figures for higher education in Propositions to Parliament from 1968–89. Figures for research are based on the research statistics of the Institute for Studies in Research and Higher Education b The university sector, the college sector, and other state colleges

activity in the labor force. This economic loss is shared by the private sector (students' loss of income) and the government (less tax income). The private contribution to the financing of higher education is considerable, even though tuition at all public and many private institutions is free.

3.4 Institutional Administration

At the universities, the general model of governance is a structure with three levels: university; faculty/school; and department. Each level has a council with about 20 to 50 representatives, a board with fewer members, 5 to 15, and a chairperson.

The chairperson (rector, dean, or department head) is elected among academic staff, usually among professors elected to the council, for a period of two to three years with re-election limited to one term of office. Students and other staff participate in these elections. Until 1989 only full professors could be elected rector, but since then all offices are open to all types of professors.

In the councils and boards, elected for a period of two to three years, professors have a majority of the seats, staff in recruitment positions 0–10 percent, students 15–25 percent, and administrative and technical staff 5–25 percent. Less important matters are decided by the board, daily business by chairpersons or administrators.

Under the new law of 1989, a board with 9 or 13 members chaired by the rector with a majority of the members elected from among the professoriate is the highest governing body of the university. Under this system the university council acts as an advisory body to the board. On the faculty/school and department level, the council is still the highest body.

In addition to councils and boards, permanent committees exist on all three levels, traditionally in areas of budgeting, planning, and education. Increas-ingly, institutions have also established committees for research policy.

Though not mandatory, most faculties/schools are divided into departments and large departments have subdivisions. Their main task is to organize teaching and related activities. Research is often left to the individual or a research group applying for additional support from research councils and other agencies outside the university. The question of academic leadership in departments with elected chairpersons has become a topic for discussion.

In the college sector, many institutions are headed by a rector who is appointed by the Ministry upon the recommendation of the college and the regional board. Regional colleges all have elected rectors as do some other schools in this sector. In the college sector, the system of boards and councils is less complex than in the universities.

4. Faculty and Students: Teaching, Learning, and Research

The expansion of higher education in the 1960s and 1970s is illustrated in Table 4. Since the late 1970s, growth has leveled off. The number and proportion of women has been increasing in some fields, possibly due to special regulations favoring female applicants. Statistics for the other institutions in the college sector are less readily available due to the reclassification of these institutions.

4.1 Faculty

Faculty members at universities and similar institutions are classified as *amanuensis* (assistant professor), first *amanuensis* (associate professor), and professor (full professor). These are generally tenured positions. In addition, there are temporary recruitment positions (usually for three to five years)

Table 4
Tenured faculty including professor II (PII, part-time positions) in the university and college sector for the period 1961–87

	1961	1966	1970	1974	1977	1981	1985[ab]	1987
University sector	927 (7)[c]	1,570 (8)	1,999 (10)	2,736 (11)	3,156 (12)	3,393 (12)	3,557 (13)	3,641 (14)
hereof PII	43	64	77	118	191	242	283	305
State colleges hereof	—	—	—	—	—	—	2,754.5	
Regional colleges	(—)	(—)	(—)	188 (5)	281 (9)	370 (11)	414 (13)	445 (12)
hereof PII								4
Engineering colleges	—	—	—	—	—	—	492	—
Teachers colleges	—	—	—	—	—	—	1,054	—
Schools of nursing	—	—	—	—	—	—	560	—
Other colleges	—	—	—	—	—	—	234.5	—
Private colleges, estimate	—	—	—	—	—	—	220	—

Source: Institute for Studies in Research and Higher Education   a For 1985 tenured teaching positions at other colleges have been included   b In addition to these figures there are an estimated 50 positions at county municipality maritime colleges   c Figures in parentheses show the percentage of women (no figures available in engineering etc.)

Table 5
Higher degree graduates from Norwegian universities, 1960–84

	1960–64	1965–69	1970–74	1975–79	1980–84
Exact sciences	3,859	5,418	8,015	8,435	9,699
Social sciences	940	1,670	3,075	4,034	4,124
Humanities	556	1,226	2,189	2,750	2,464
Other[a]	429	596	823	795	1,019
Total	5,784	8,910	14,102	16,014	17,306

Source: Institute for Studies in Research and Higher Education. Academic Register
a Other: graduates in agriculture, forestry, and fish

with minimal teaching load. Many of these positions are financed by the research councils.

Until 1989 the government appointed full professors upon recommendations from department, faculty/school, and university. Under the new law, full professors are appointed by the board of the university. Appointment committees hire other professors and technical and administrative staff. All professors are appointed after the qualifications of applicants are reviewed by ad hoc committees. Faculty members are civil servants and have the same rights and protection as other civil servants.

Promotion to the rank of full professor is in principle dependent upon vacant positions and competition with other applicants.

There are differences in the career structure and status of faculty at the universities and the six institutions with university status versus the institutions in the college sector. In general, the universities require higher qualifications, and they have a full range of academic positions. Only a few institutions in the college sector have full professors, they usually do not have recruitment positions, and few staff have completed a doctoral degree.

The academic profession represents its corporate interests mainly through two organized unions which cover the university and college sectors. Thus, in addition to having a majority in councils, boards, and so on, faculty can also exert influence through a system of negotiations inside the institutions.

In the university sector, the teaching hours are decided by the institutions themselves within frameworks set by the Ministry. Traditionally, full professors teach five hours a week. When assistant professorships were established in the 1960s, these professors were expected to teach up to twelve hours a week, but over time their teaching load has been reduced, and is in many institutions often identical to that of a full professor.

In the college sector, regional colleges have developed norms similar to the universities. The other institutions in this sector themselves decide upon the number of teaching hours on the basis of general guidelines negotiated between the Ministry and the unions, local negotiations, and traditions in the particular type of institution.

4.2 Students

Within the university sector, the number of students increased far more in the social sciences and the humanities than in the exact sciences during the period of expansion in this sector (1960–75). Since then, moderate growth has continued, except in the humanities where student numbers decreased by more than 40 percent since the early 1980s. These trends are of course reflected in the number of graduates (see Table 5). Similar trends can be seen in the college sector.

During the period of strong growth in the universities, from 1960 to 1975, the influx of female students and those from lower social class origins increased. None the less, in 1975 students from higher social strata continued to be strongly over-represented at the universities. The colleges had considerably less uneven social recruitment. After 1975 the systematic registration of student social class origins was discontinued. A few individual studies clearly show that the tendency for greater equality in recruitment to the universities has stagnated after 1975. A study of 1980 secondary-school graduates shows that 50 percent of the girls and 44 percent of the boys from higher strata (upper-middle class and professionals) had begun university or college studies by 1985 versus 11 percent of the girls and 8 percent of the boys from lower strata (unskilled workers, etc.).

Table 6 shows the number of female students in different sectors and fields. As late as 1975, men were clearly dominant in both universities and colleges. In 1985, there are still more men than women at universities, but considering all higher education, women are a majority. As shown, women increasingly are taking subjects which traditionally have been male-dominated. However, they complete higher degrees less frequently than men.

There are three types of student organizations in

Table 6
Students in Norwegian universities and colleges. By sex and field 1960–85

	1960	1965	1970	1975	1980	1985
University students						
Exact sciences	5,142	8,399	10,488	12,718	14,094	15,184
Social sciences	1,288	3,465	6,761	9,969	10,736	13,034
Humanities	2,821	6,746	8,721	13,593	10,480	7,808
Other and not specified	335	918	4,195	4,494	5,310	5,632
Total	9,586	19,528	30,165	40,774	40,620	41,658
Of which female	—	4,775	8,618	14,695	16,642	19,533
Exact sciences	—	1,122	1,360	2,403	3,437	5,067
Social sciences	—	498	1,345	2,972	4,233	6,487
Humanities	—	2,870	3,729	6,816	5,740	4,629
Other and not specified	—	285	2,184	2,504	3,232	3,350
College students						
Exact sciences	—	—	—	8,226	8,955	18,196
Social sciences	—	—	—	4,514	6,853	16,774
Humanities	—	—	—	12,438	16,550	15,061
Other and not specified	—	—	—	676	878	1,870
Total	—	13,800	19,967	25,854	33,236	51,901
Of which female	—	5,594	6,505	10,393	16,145	27,586
Exact sciences	—	—	—	1,206	2,311	9,134
Social sciences	—	—	—	1,248	2,378	7,066
Humanities	—	—	—	7,863	11,375	10,907
Other and not specified	—	—	—	76	81	479
Total students	—	33,328	50,132	66,628	73,856	93,559
Of which female students	—	10,369	15,123	25,088	32,787	47,119

Source: Institute for Studies in Research and Higher Education. Notat 9/87. Students and Graduates Tables 1987.
Central Bureau of Statistics of Norway. Educational Statistics, Survey October

Norway. Most students are members of a student union, of which there are several—one for university students, one for students at teachers colleges, and so on. Various political groups compete for power and influence within these organizations. The unions are engaged in debates about educational policies, conditions for loans and scholarships, and student welfare; they are also requested to comment on proposals from central authorities.

University and college students may establish their own committees at different levels in the institutions. These committees are intended to be liaison units between the institutions and students.

Student welfare organizations, with compulsory membership, can be regarded as interest organizations. Through their professional staff these organizations administer student housing and cafeterias, some of them also administer bookstores, kindergartens, health services, sports, travel agencies and other welfare services. These welfare organizations, where students traditionally have considerable influence, are mainly financed through membership fees and the sale of goods and services, but they also receive government grants.

The Cabinet makes decisions concerning which academic degrees the institutions may offer, and the number of years a program should take. On the basis of suggestions from the institutions, the Ministry decides which subjects and topics shall be included in a degree. Within this framework, the university board makes decisions concerning examinations, whereas the faculty/school makes most decisions concerning the content of the curriculum.

In the college sector, local government or regional boards have little influence on curricula, but may try to influence the institutions and the Ministry about what programs to offer at a given institution. The regional colleges which offer courses similar to university courses will be influenced by the universities, as universities decide whether or not a regional college course will be accredited as a basis for taking a higher degree.

Institutions of higher education generally offer specialist or professional courses. The general or "liberal arts" component is supposedly completed during secondary school. However, universities require a first semester course in the history of philosophy and logic (*examen philosophicum*) of all students.

The typical method of assessment is the written

examination at the end of a course. This is graded anonymously by external examiners and teachers from the institution. A written examination is often combined with an oral examination, the latter normally has less weight than the former. Take-home exams have been introduced in some fields. At some institutions group examinations, written and/or oral, are used. Grading scales vary considerably.

5. Conclusion

The Norwegian system of higher education has undergone rapid development and expansion since the Second World War, especially during the 1960s. In the early 1990s, the most important problems seem to be the following:

(a) The administration of higher education has been somewhat inflexible and centralized.

(b) The number of 19-year olds will decrease by 25 percent during the period 1988 to 1996. Authorities have been worried about a possible scarcity of a highly qualified workforce, including university faculties where staff hired during the expansion period will reach retirement age around the turn of the century.

(c) Resources for higher education have perhaps been spread too widely across too many small institutions, without sufficient attention being given to the quality of research and higher education.

(d) Statistics and surveys of higher education are not sufficiently updated.

Norwegian authorities seem to be aware of these problems and have taken deliberate measures to solve them:

(a) In 1989, parliament passed a law which transfers more decision-making authority from central agencies to the universities themselves.

(b) An increase in appropriations for university research in real terms for 1990 to 1993 has been announced in the government's Long-Term Program. Similar statements have also been made about improving financial aid to students who take higher degrees. However, these statements have not been followed up in budget proposals.

(c) Both the Ministry and the research councils support "research priority areas" considered to be highly relevant for the development of science and society. Authorities are also eagerly recommending the amalgamation and integration of small research units, and are concerned with evaluation of higher education and research.

(d) The Ministry is negotiating with units which collect statistics to improve and update statistics on higher education.

During the 1990s, in addition to the problems already mentioned, others are likely to occur or grow in importance. The international integration of Norway—both economically and politically—will probably gain new momentum and pose challenges to the Norwegian economy and to society at large. In order to keep up with partners and competitors in other countries, Norway needs to improve her expertise in industry and foreign trade. A special problem will occur for the Norwegian economy: the exploitation of offshore oil resources is probably nearing its peak and mainland industry will have to compensate for the loss in export income.

In this context, the qualifications and expertise of the workforce will be of great importance. This indicates that education in general, and particularly higher education, will be high on the political agenda for the years to come.

More international cooperation is necessary to avoid the consequences of pollution threatening the environment. This necessitates an increase in the supply of research experts and the implementation of proposals to protect the environment.

The need for better and more extensive cooperation with developing countries, in order to bring about sustainable development on a global basis, also necessitates cooperation between institutions of higher education in Norway and the Third World.

Bibliography

Aamodt P O 1990 A New Deal for Norwegian Higher Education? *Eur. J. Educ.* 25: 171–85
Aamodt P O, Skoie H, Kyvik S 1991 Norway—Towards a more indirect model of governance? In: Neave G, van Vught F A (eds.) *Prometheus Bound: The Changing Relationship Between Government And Higher Education*. Pergamon, Oxford, pp. 129–44
Bie K N 1981 *Creating a New University. The Establishment and Development of the University of Tromsø*. Institute for Studies in Research and Higher Education. Report 1981: 3, Oslo
Eeg-Henriksen F 1985 *The Role of Women in Higher Education. The Case of Norway*. Institute for Studies in Research and Higher Education. Report 8: 85, Oslo
Gundem B B 1983 Trends in research on higher education in Norway—a tentative outline and some examples. *Higher Educ. Eur.* 8 (1): 12–18
Gundem B B 1987 The case of Norway: State-of-the-art in ten selected areas of research on higher education. *Higher Educ. Eur.* 12 (7): 83–90
Kyvik S 1981 *The Norwegian Regional College. A Study of the Establishment and Implementation of a Reform in Higher Education*. Institute for Studies in Research and Higher Education. Report 1981: 1, Oslo
Kyvik S 1986 Postgraduate education in Norway. *Eur. J. Educ.* 21: 251–60
Kyvik S, Skoie H 1982 Recent trends in Norwegian higher education. *Eur. J. Educ.* 17: 183–92
March J G, Olsen J P (eds.) 1976 *Ambiguity and Choice*

in Organizations. Universitetsforlaget, Oslo, Chapters 7, 10, 13, and 14

Med viten og vilje 1988 *Report of the Norwegian Royal Commission on Higher Education*. Norwegian Official Reports 28. NOU, Oslo

Midgaard K 1982 Norway. The interplay of local and central decisions. In: Dalder H, Shils E (eds.) 1982 *Universities, Politicians and Bureaucrats*. Cambridge University Press, Cambridge, pp. 275–328

Norway, Central Bureau of Statistics (annual) *Educational Statistics, Universities and Colleges*. Central Bureau of Statistics, Oslo

Norway, Central Bureau of Statistics (annual) *Statistical Yearbooks*. Central Bureau of Statistics, Oslo

Norway, Ministry of Finance Report No. 4 to the Storting 1988–89. Norwegian Long-Term Programme 1990–93. Ministry of Finance, Oslo

Norway 1984–85 *White Paper on Scientific Research in Norway*. Government Office, Oslo

Organisation for Economic Co-operation and Development 1988 *Review of National Policies of Education, Norway*. OECD, Paris

S. Vangsnes; K. Jordell

O

Oman

1. Higher Education and Society

The history of Omani education, both in its general and higher forms goes back as far as the rise of Islam in the mid-seventh century AD. Omanis, unlike many other Arabs and non-Arabs who converted to Islam, have accepted this religion without any violent resistance. The main purpose of learning which started in mosques and Koranic schools was to understand Islamic beliefs. These came through revelation and were preserved in the writings of the Koran (the Muslim's Holy Book). The Koran which all learners studied represented the core curriculum. The interpretation of the verses of the Koran and the sayings of the Prophet Muhammad (and, later, his Caliphs) constituted essential knowledge for Muslims. Different locations and mosques in Oman served as teaching centers, such as the Grand Mosque in Nizwa, Su'al, Samad, Farq, and Aqar. Similar centers existed in the cities of Bahla, Sarh, Al-Hamra, Al-Mudhaibi, Al-Qabel, Izki, Manh, Nakhel, Dhophar, and Matrah.

It is well-known that hundreds of scholars have graduated from these higher education centers in the last fourteen centuries, including Jaber Bin Zaid Al-Azdi—an outstanding scholar and religious leader; Hesham Bin Muhammad Al-Kalbi—the author of *Jamharat al-Ansab*; Abu al-Munther Salamah bin Muslem al-Owtabi—the author of *Ansab Al-Arab* (AD100–1200); and Abu al-Munther al-Nizwani—one of Oman's most highly respected scholars. Broadly known in Omani Islamic circles also is Al-Khalil Bin Ahmad Al-Frahidi Al-Azdi, whose famous book *Al Ain* is still taught and considered to be an important resource in Arabic language and literature. Still other important scholars and educational leaders were Abu Bakr Ahmad Bin Muhammad bin Duraid Al-Azdi—author of the well-known book *Al-Jamharah*; and Abu-Al-Abbas Al-Mubarad—author of the equally well-known book *Al Kamel*.

Prior to 1970 there was almost no formal system of education in Oman. The beginning of modern education was initiated under the leadership of His Majesty Sultan Quaboos Bin Said, the Sultan of Oman. He initiated the development of a nationwide system of education. From 1970 to 1986, graduates who wanted a college education had to go outside the Sultanate.

Within 18 years, Oman has moved from a country which offered its people limited educational opportunities to a country which now provides a full range of educational experiences and opportunities for men and women. There are seven institutions for teacher training at junior college level (three for males, four for females); one secondary commercial school; one industrial secondary school and one agricultural secondary school; and two special education schools (one for the hearing and speech impaired; one for the mentally handicapped). In the late 1980s there were 13,250 teachers employed in the Ministry's educational institutions as well as 1,228 administrators.

A new ten-year educational plan was initiated in 1978–88 which called for an increase in the number of students enrolled at teacher-training colleges. From 1986–89, 1,031 teachers graduated from the institutes of teacher training. Three more teacher-training colleges opened in the 1990–91 academic year in the interior regions of the country. A fifth college for women will be added in time for the 1992–93 academic year.

2. The Institutional Fabric of the Higher Education System

Modern higher education in Oman started with the opening of Sultan Qaboos University on November 9, 1986. Five colleges were developed: the College of Education and Islamic Sciences; the College of Sciences; the College of Engineering; the College of Agriculture; and the College of Medicine. A sixth, the College of Arts, was added on November 9, 1987, and a College of Commerce and Economics will be opened by September 1992.

2.1 Levels of Institution

(a) The College of Education and Islamic Sciences offers a four-year Bachelor of Arts (BA) degree in educational and Islamic sciences. The Islamic science program is designed to prepare specialists in Islamic religion for positions in courts, schools, and mosques. The education programs are designed to train teachers in the following disciplines: Islamic science, Arabic, English, geography, history, home economics, mathematics, philosophy, science, social sciences, and humanities. In addition, this college offers one-year advanced diploma programs in Islamic sciences and education.

(b) The College of Sciences offers a five-year Bachelor of Science (BSc) degree with specializations in biology, chemistry, earth sciences, mathematics and computing, and physics.

(c) The College of Engineering offers a five-year program leading to the Bachelor of Science (BSc) degree. Students can elect to major in various branches of engineering: civil, electrical and electronics, mechanical or petroleum, and mining.

(d) The College of Agriculture offers a five-year program leading to the Bachelor of Science (BSc) degree in plant science, animal science, fisheries science, and agricultural engineering. Other areas of specialization are fisheries technology, soil and water management, and agricultural mechanization.

(e) The College of Medicine offers a four-year program leading to the Bachelor of Medical Science (BMedSc) degree. Students who complete this degree can elect to continue in a three-year study program in clinical medicine followed by a one-year internship which leads to the Bachelor of Medicine and Bachelor of Surgery (BM and BS) degrees. These programs are designed to take advantage of the 500-bed teaching hospital and medical library located on campus. The University teaching hospital provides treatment to individuals living throughout the Sultanate in such specialisms as medical psychology and pediatrics to traumatic and orthopedic surgery.

The language of instruction is English, except in the College of Education and Islamic Sciences, and in the College of Arts.

2.2 Admissions Policies and Selection

The ultimate decision to admit any student rests with the academic council. Selection of students for admission to the University is made from those applicants who have received their secondary-school national certificate or its equivalent less than one year prior to their application. Students are usually Omani nationals and must score above a certain minimum level in examinations in both English and Arabic. Textbooks are provided free. The University also provides transportation and meals to those students who need such assistance, and other forms of aid are available. In addition, the students are not charged tuition or any other fees. The current capacity of Sultan Qaboos University is about 3,500 students. Within the next ten years, the capacity of the university could be doubled.

3. Governance and Administration

The University organization consists of a university council, the president, assistant president for academic affairs, the academic council, deans of the various colleges, the dean of student affairs, and heads of the departments. In addition there are directors for the Research Center, the Language Center Library, the Computer Center, and the Teaching Hospital. In addition to the University entrance requirement, each college has its own individual requirements for admission to a program. The academic year is divided into two semesters of 16 weeks each, followed by an examination week. The undergraduate programs of the University, except for the College of Medicine, are organized on a credit-unit system.

4. Teaching, Learning, and Research

In addition to the various colleges of Sultan Qaboos University, there are a number of specialized centers and facilities which assist faculty, staff, students, and the Sultanate in general. The library is a state-of-the-art facility which provides access to over 1,000 databases. The Educational Research Center participates in and provides services to theoretical as well as applied educational research projects. A modern Language Center exists to teach English to students as part of their science foundation courses. The media service, institutional design, and education planning departments provide support services to the University community through the Center for Educational Technology. The Computer Center is equipped with the latest in computer hardware technology, database packages, and software programs, and supports the University community through a broad network of cabling and data transmission equipment. Three agricultural facilities are provided for faculty, staff, and students in order to gain practical experience and to complete research projects. The Campus Farm (55 hectare), University Research Farm (110 hectare), and the Botany Garden allow students and faculty to conduct basic and advanced, long- and short-term research on agronomic and horticultural crops, soil and water management, pest management, livestock, and crop processing. The Islamic Research Center is connected to the Mosque, its main objective being to encourage research in various Islamic fields with special emphasis on the relationship between various Islamic sects.

Bibliography

Al-Dhahabi n.d. *Tathkerat al-Hufadh*
Al-Durgini A Al-S S n.d. *Tabaqat al-Mashaikh bil-Maghreb*. In: Talal (ed.)
Al-Harthy S H n.d. *Al-Uqoud al-Fedhiyah Fi Usool al-Abadhiva*, 1st edn. Dar-al-Yagdhah
Al-Salmiy A H n.d. *Tuhfat al-A'aian be Seerat ahl-Oman*. Oriental Press. Mattrah
Ismail S J 1985 Higher education in Oman. Unpublished paper. Muscat
Ministry of Education 1989 *Educational Statistics for the Academic year 1988–89*. Education Planning Department, Muscat
1988 Foundation Committee Final Report
Wilkenson F C 1980 *Oman, History and Scholars*. Abdulla M A (trans.). Segel Al-Arab Printings, Cairo

S. J. Ismail

P

Pakistan

1. Higher Education and Society

Pakistan emerged in 1947 as a result of the partition of India to constitute two far-flung wings of East and West Pakistan, separated by a thousand miles of Indian territory. Its coming into being marked the culmination of a 100 years' struggle by the Muslims of India, who having ruled over the subcontinent for 800 years, had found themselves reduced, during the Raj, to the position of a backward, minority community (Qureshi 1961). In 1971, however, East Pakistan seceded to become the independent state of Bangladesh.

The basic urge among Indian Muslims, at the end of the colonial rule, was to eradicate their chronic backwardness, poverty, and stagnation. Pakistanis chose to achieve these objectives within the framework of an Islamic polity. Higher education in Pakistan aimed therefore, apart from meeting the social and economic needs and aspirations of its people, at the evolution of a viable and modern Islamic social order.

Pakistan occupies a strategic geographical position bounded on the east and south by India, on the northwest by Afghanistan, on the west by Iran and to the south by the Arabian Sea. It has a common border with China alongside Gilgit and Baltistan.

The country consists of four physical regions: the western offshoot of the Himalayas which covers its northern and northwestern parts of which the highest peak, the famous K-2, rises to a height of 28,250 feet above sea level; the vast, arid plateau of Baluchistan with altitudes varying from 10,000 to 25,000 feet above sea level lying to the west of the mountain-wall; the Potowar plateau and the Salt range in the northwest; and the expansive plains of the Indus basin stretching from the foothills of the Himalayas in the northeast and Salt range in the northwest to the Arabian Sea. Fed by the River Indus and its five tributaries, the Indus basin plains constitute the very fertile and densely populated provinces of the Punjab and Sind.

Pakistan is both an ancient and a new country. Its ancient history goes back some 5,000 years when it formed the seat of a flourishing Indus Valley civilization. The rich, fertile lands and congenial climate of the region have throughout history attracted invaders, mainly from the northwestern mountain passes, especially the famous Khyber Pass. Therefore, the people of Pakistan constitute a sturdy mixture of various migrant races, the Aryans, Persians, Greeks, Arabs, Afghans, Mongols, and Turks. During the eight centuries of Muslim rule, different middle-eastern racial groups migrated and settled in these lands to become the ruling classes. Most of the landowning upper-class families in Pakistan today descended from these early migrants. Following the upheavals of partition in 1947, millions of Muslims migrated from India and settled in cities and towns of the Punjab and Sind to be known as the Muhajirs or migrants.

The ethnic population of Pakistan in the early 1990s consists of about 55 percent Punjabis, 22 percent Sindhis, 12 percent Pathans, 6 percent Baluchis and 6 percent others. The languages spoken as mother tongues constitute 48.17 percent Punjabi, 9.84 percent Saraiki (which is considered to be a dialect of Punjabi), 11.77 percent Sindi, 13.5 percent Pushto, 1.21 percent Brahavi, 2.43 percent Hindko, 7.6 percent Urdu and 2.81 percent others. About 1.5 percent people speak English as an additional language (adapted from the 1981 census).

West Pakistan's population, according to the 1951 census, amounted to 33.34 million. According to the 1981 census, it had risen to 84.25 million; an increase, in 30 years, of 51 million people. There has been a constant growth rate of 3.1 percent per year among the highest for developing countries and higher than Pakistan's neighbors. At the time of Independence, over 70 percent of the population lived in villages. Since the 1960s, however, there has been a massive urbanization, with the number of towns over 500,000 inhabitants increasing from two to seven. Karachi, the largest city, which in 1947 was only a backwater port city of some 360,000 inhabitants, could, in 1982, boast a population of some seven million people. Obviously, the high population growth rate and unchecked urbanization had serious repercussions for the country's ecology, economy, and society. The educational system was bound to become seriously affected by such demographic changes.

Pakistan inherited an extremely restricted type of occupational structure. In 1947, about 85 percent of the total workforce was engaged in agriculture as the country did not inherit any worthwhile industrial base. With the launch in 1955 of a series of five-year development plans, a considerable shift took place in the sectoral distribution of employment from agriculture to other sectors. In 1988–89, only 51.15 percent of employees aged ten and over were engaged in agriculture while 12.84 percent were engaged in manufacturing and 11.93 percent in trade (Ministry of Finance 1989).

The social class structure in Pakistan is changing. Migration overseas and the wealth returning migrants have acquired give clear signs of upward social mobility, yet the traditional urban and rural upper classes have also become more entrenched. Among the urban upper class are landlords, senior civil servants, high-ranking military officers, industrial and commercial business families, and the tribal elites. Rural society is dominated by the Zamindars (landlords) and their dependent share-croppers. Between them, these upper classes have monopolized economic and political power in the country while the urban middle and working class and peasants remain powerless. The gap between the very rich and poor has widened during the past decades. Inequality in income distribution between the highest and the lowest 20 percent income households showed a ratio of 44:7.6 respectively in the year 1985 to 1986 (Ministry of Finance 1989).

During British rule Pakistan's economy was predominantly agricultural: over 90 percent of its exports consisted of primary commodities. Manufacturing was mainly of elementary-type small-scale units contributing only seven to eight percent of the Gross Domestic Product (GDP). Over 60 percent of the total imports consisted of consumer goods. Since the economic take-off of the mid-1950s and 1960s, (the "Development Decade") under the Ayub Khan regime, the annual growth of the Gross National Product (GNP) doubled from 3.4 percent to 6.7 percent in the 1960s, slowing down to 4.2 percent in the 1970s but reaccelerating to 6.8 percent in the 1980s (Burki and Laporte 1985 pp. 15–41). The latest available growth rate (for 1988 to 1989) stands at 10.6 percent (Ministry of Finance 1989). However growth in the GNP is offset by the heavy debt the country has incurred in recent decades. Pakistan's external debt was estimated to stand at US$14.4 billion by the middle of 1989 and its debt servicing payment amounted to US$1,193 million (Ministry of Finance 1989). This enormously heavy debt has reduced the country to dependency, made it vulnerable to foreign interference in decision making besides raising prices and the level of inflation. This economic crisis had adverse effects on educational finance.

The Islamic Republic of Pakistan has a federal parliament and four provincial legislatures. The Federal Legislature is bicameral, consisting of the Lower House called the National Assembly and the Upper House called the Senate. The four provinces, Baluchistan, North Western Frontier Province (NWFP), the Punjab, and Sind are not merely administrative or geographic divisions but may be identified by clearly distinguishable ethnic and linguistic characteristics. They have their own provincial assemblies and governments. The Federal Capital Area and the Federally Administered Tribal Areas (FATA) are also under the Federal Legislature. The Federal and Provincial legislatures have authority respectively over their own legislative lists, while under the concurrent list, both are empowered to legislate on certain crucial subjects. Certain aspects of higher education fall under the concurrent list and are thus controlled both by the federal and the provincial governments. As embedded in the Constitution the main political goals of Pakistan as a nation are: (a) to uphold the principles of democracy, freedom, equality, tolerance, and social justice as enshrined in Islam; (b) to guarantee fundamental rights of equality, freedom of thought, speech, worship, assembly, association, and publication. Pakistan being an Islamic state, no law shall be enacted to contravene the injunctions of the Holy Quran and Sunnah (Teachings) of Prophet Muhammad. In keeping with these national norms, higher education in Pakistan has the tasks of inculcating a deep understanding of the Islamic faith, guiding Muslims to order their lives, in their individual and collective spheres in accordance with the teachings of Islam; and forging unity among the various ethnic, linguistic, and religious groups in the country. To achieve these goals, Islamization of education was taken up as the national policy by the government of Zulfiqar Ali Bhutto in 1973 and then intensified by Muhammad Zia-ul-Haq (Hayes 1987 pp. 99–100).

The overwhelming majority of Pakistanis—97.6 percent—are Muslims and belong to the Sunni belief. There is no centrally established religious body in Islam analogous to the Christian Church. A number of Islamic organizations have, however, consolidated themselves as political parties and contest elections. The most prominent of such organizations are the *Jamaat-i-Islami* (Islamic Party), the *Jamiat-i-Ulema* (Organization of the Islamic Scholars) of Pakistan, and various other smaller groups. These religious bodies collectively aim to bring about an Islamic social order and to prevent secularism or any other anti-Islamic ideology to gain supremacy in the country.

2. The Institutional Fabric of the Higher Education System

Pakistan inherited two parallel systems of higher education: the modern, Western system that was introduced by the British in 1859 with the opening of the universities of Bombay, Calcutta, and Madras; and the traditional Islamic system in vogue in Muslim India, in the form of Madrassahs, before the advent of the Raj. Following Lord Macaulay's edict of 1832, the Raj undertook to sponsor only the former type of education. The latter type was left to fend for itself. Consequently, for over a century, Indian Muslims faced a diarchy in their higher education: their youth learned and lived in two different worlds (Hussain and Ashraf 1979 pp. 51–73). After Independence, therefore, one of the major policy objectives in Pakistan was to integrate the two systems.

Tertiary-level education in Pakistan starts after the school leaving/matriculation certificate at the intermediate or degree college and extends from grades 11 to 14 in two tiers of two-year duration. Whereas the first two-year intermediate colleges are controlled by the Boards of Secondary and Intermediate Education, degree colleges are administered by the university.

The larger number of degree colleges are colleges of liberal arts. Originally established during the British Raj as government colleges at selected towns, their numbers proliferated in the beginning of the century when Lord Curzon encouraged community participation in higher education. Most of them remained autonomous, private sector institutions until 1972 when the government nationalized them (Hayes 1987 p. 52).

For postsecondary technical and vocational education, a network of 24 polytechnics has been created to meet the growing demand, at home and abroad, for a skilled labor force (*International Handbook* pp. 317–18).

In addition, a variety of professional colleges offer a wide range of courses for various specializations in first and graduate degrees. These include: colleges of agriculture; business administration; commerce and management; home economics; education; engineering and technology; law; medicine and pharmacology; dentistry; animal husbandry; forestry and so forth.

The traditional Islamic colleges still remain, by and large, outside the state-sponsored system. Some are affiliated to the Islamic universities, others remain autonomous. Most are housed in large, central mosques in towns and cities.

Universities form the apex of the institutional structure of higher education. There was one functioning university in Pakistan at the time of Independence; now Pakistan has 22 universities of which nine are general universities, three agricultural, four engineering, two Islamic, one medical, one open, and one for women. (For the women's university see Ahmad and Sajid 1982.)

There was no research facility at all at the only inherited University of the Punjab. The need to promote research was first emphasized in the Report of the Commission on National Education in 1959 and reinforced by all development plans. As a result, there are three levels of research institutions, all integrated within the higher education system: (a) research centers; (b) centers of excellence; and (c) national research institutes. Research centers were created by upgrading certain university departments to supervise research leading to the award of MPhil and PhD degrees (Hayes 1987 p. 74). Centers of excellence were developed by assigning to various general universities the responsibility of sponsoring and supervising research in major specializations as well as in certain global regions. National research institutes were set up at different universities to pro-

Table 1
Expansion in higher education: number of institutions and enrollments by kind, level, and sex

		1947–48	1960–61	1965–66	1970–71	1975–76	1980–81	1985–86	1988–89
Numbers									
Arts and science colleges									
	Total	40	131	228	314	404	433	528	599
	F	5	33	63	87	107	119	167	182
Professional colleges									
	Total	—	42	48	73	98	99	100	99
	F	—	5	5	6	8	8	8	8
Universities									
	Total	2	4	6	7	12	19	21	21
	F	—	—	—	—	—	—	—	1
Enrollments									
Arts and science colleges[a]									
	Total	14	43	139	199	211	270	400	439
	F	1	6	28	50	53	87	126	140
Professional colleges									
	Total	4,368	8,082	19,061	37,245	56,140	55,897	68,317	80,316
	F	327	833	2,919	4,612	8,785	8,519	13,817	19,799
Universities									
	Total	664	1,998	13,420	17,507	22,772	42,688	59,891	609,361
	F	55	49	2,979	3,703	5,121	7,113	8,801	10,048

Source: Pakistan Economic Survey 1988–89
a These figures are in thousands

mote research concerned with crucial Pakistani cultural, ideological, and national areas (Zaki 1975 pp. 53–141).

Pakistan's legacy from the colonial rule was the "sponsorship" model of selection policy whereby the dominant elites specify rules, procedures, and criteria of selection for higher education. For reasons of democratization, Islamization, and national cohesion, however, it had to adopt an open, "contest" model, based more on competition and merit (see Turner 1971). The prestige attached to English as the medium of instruction and Urdu as the national language helps the upper class elites and hinders the commoners in gaining access to higher education.

Higher education in Pakistan has expanded in terms of number and diversity of institutions, enrollments, and graduate output since 1950. Table 1 indicates the progressive expansion of the system with numbers and types of institutions. The number of arts and science colleges has risen from 40 to 600 (from 5 to 182 female colleges). College enrollment has gone up from 14,000 to 439,000 students (1,000 to 140,000 female students). The number of professional colleges increased from 19 to 99 and their enrollment grew from 4,368 to 80,316 (from 327 to 19,800 females) (Ministry of Finance 1989). Universities expanded from 2 to 22 and university enrollment from 644 to 69,361. The increase of female enrollment has been more dramatic. In 1948, there were only 56 female students at university while in 1988 to 1989, their number stood at 10,048 (Ministry of Finance 1989).

The participation rate measured in terms of the age group 20 to 24 attending higher education institutions, has not improved—it has been largely offset by the high rate of population increase. The percentage increase has only gone up from 0.16 percent to 0.87 percent in the past decades.

The colleges of arts and science offer two-year programs leading to the award of a BA/BSc degree: but certain colleges also offer a three-year honors program for bright students. Some polytechnics offer a condensed one-year course leading to the award of a BTech degree/Diploma. Medical colleges offer a five-year program for the MBBS or a four-year program in pharmacy. Agricultural and engineering colleges offer a three-year program for the award of a BSc Agr or BSc Eng degree (Hussain et al. 1987 pp. 81–82). Colleges of education offer a one-year, graduate course leading to the award of a BEd degree.

3. Governance, Administration, and Finance

3.1 National Administration

Historically higher education was the responsibility of the provincial governments. In 1973, however, the National Assembly assigned responsibility for policy formulation on issues of nationwide importance to the central government. The present system of administration of higher education is a combination of centralized and decentralized control whereby the central and provincial legislatures enact laws on the basis of a concurrent list on areas of common interest. The central legislature, however, has exclusive authority for policy formulation on subjects like the libraries, museums, and the national research institutes. With regard to the universities, the central legislature formulates policies in conjunction with the University Grants Commission which was established in 1974 to coordinate policies and maintain national standards (Hayes 1987 pp. 47–49).

Higher educational planning is built into the overall economic development planning. The National Planning Commission defines, translates, and transmits goals of educational planning which are then assigned priorities and rationalized for financial allocations in the five-year development plans. National goals are also formulated by commissions set up by the government and each government has had its own policy emphases articulated in the form of a National Educational Document or an Education Commission Report.

Implementation of national policies on higher education rests, in the main, on the Federal Ministry of Education which has a special wing for higher

Table 2
Government expenditure in higher education by level (in million rupees)

	1960	1965	1970	1975	1980	1985	1989 (Estimated)
Total expenditure	163.8	450.9	578.7	1,744.5	4,153.5	10,224.3	21,425.1
College education	17.7	33.1	49.6	162.3	387.5	1,034.0	1,950.0
University education	15.2	47.9	44.7	124.0	426.2	936.5	1,832.0
Total higher education	32.9	81.0	94.3	286.3	813.7	1,970.5	3,782.0
Percentage of budget	20.0	17.9	16.2	16.3	22.0	19.3	17.6
Percentage of GNP	0.97	1.11	1.73	1.79	1.98	2.1	—

Source: Pakistan Economic Survey 1988–89

education and the universities. Similarly, the provincial ministries of education have departments responsible for the administration of colleges.

Provincial revenues are the main source of funding for all tertiary-level education except the universities. However, central government also contributes large sums to the provincial budgets in the form of grant-in-aid. The universities, since 1978, receive their finance from the central government through the University Grants Commission. The International Islamic University in Islamabad is financed by Saudi Arabia and the Agha Khan Medical University in Karachi by the Agha Khan Trust.

As indicated in Table 2, the government budget on education has increased hugely since 1947 from Rs30.4 million (US$1.24m) to Rs21,425 million (US$873m). Higher education always received a larger proportion of the budget though most of the expenditure on higher education was incurred in development costs. The total expenditure on education stands at 1.5 percent of GNP (Husain et al. 1987 p. 87), which is lower than a number of other developing countries in the region: Indonesia 2.17 percent; Thailand 2.97 percent; Burma 3.11 percent; Sri Lanka 4.9 percent; and Malaysia 4.99 percent (World Bank Staff Report No. 246, 1976).

3.2 Institutional Administration

The chief governing authority of the university is the chancellor who, by convention, is the provincial governor. The Chancellor of the Quaid-e-Azam University in Islamabad is the President of Pakistan. The political and administrative engagements of these high-ranking chancellors have made it necessary, though, to appoint pro-chancellors to act on their behalf.

The day-to-day administration of the universities devolves on the vice-chancellor who is the Chief Administrative Officer and academic head. To assist the vice-chancellor in policy formulation and implementation, there are two organs, the Syndicate and the Senate, as well as various subsidiary boards, committees, and councils. The Registrar and the Treasurer are respectively responsible for academic and financial matters.

At the college level, the principal of the college is the chief authority who is advised and assisted by the College Council composed of the senior members of faculty. Similarly, there are departmental boards to advise the head of the department on various policies related to admissions, discipline, hostels, sports, and so on.

Each university has its Academic Council to advise the Syndicate and the Senate on academic matters concerned with teaching, examination, and research. Members of the Academic Council may be appointed, nominated, or elected and hold office for three years. Boards of Studies at the universities and colleges consisting of departmental chairs, professors, associate professors, and college teachers, as well as other experts appointed by the vice-chancellor are responsible for the actual academic functions within institutions. Boards of Advanced Studies and Research, which consist of the vice-chancellor, the dean, and three university professors other than the dean, and are appointed by the Syndicate, along with university teachers with research qualifications and experience, appointed by the Academic Council, advise the Council on promotion of advanced studies and research at the universities.

4. Faculty and Students: Teaching, Learning, and Research

4.1 Faculty

Development of the teaching body started haphazardly. Emphasis was placed on quantitative development. However, the inadequacy of suitably qualified teachers remains a problem. Special incentives such as scholarships for study abroad and additional increments at the start, have failed to attract young talent to the academic profession; many

Table 3
Number of teachers in institutions of higher education by kind, level, and sex

		1960	1965	1970	1975	1980	1985	1989 (Estimated)
Arts and science colleges								
	Total	—	5,711	8,823	11,313	12,384	25,599	34,295
	F	—	1,522	2,695	3,167	3,544	10,408	15,094
Professional colleges								
	Total	—	1,370	1,868	3,087	3,343	3,925	3,989
	F	—	180	255	472	463	762	968
Universities								
	Total	452	1,264	1,568	2,726	3,183	3,740	4,162
	F	40	85	137	296	395	541	619

Source: Pakistan Economic Survey 1988–89

leave the country after obtaining higher qualifications to work abroad. Table 3 indicates the progressive increase in the number of teachers in the universities and colleges.

The minimum qualification required for appointment as lecturer in a college faculty is an MA or MSc degree and for an assistant professor (faculty cadres have been modelled on the American pattern: assistant professor; associate professor; and professor) a PhD. Promotion to higher ranks was initially based on seniority. By the early 1990s research publications have become the essential requirement. Contract of employment and tenure are offered after the successful completion of two/three years probation. The work of the professor is evaluated by a special committee of the Selection Board which is appointed by the vice-chancellor from a standing list of experts and approved by the Syndicate (Rahman 1988).

Faculty interests are represented at all levels of university administration: the Syndicate; the Senate; the UGC (University Grants Commission); the Academic Council; and various boards and committees by the presence on regular basis of the members of faculty. Similar representation of the college faculty prevails at college level administration. Unionization of Teachers of Higher Education began originally in 1950 and in 1968, the Professor's Association came into existence to safeguard the rights of the faculty and to articulate the viewpoints and demands of the academics in general. By mobilizing and organizing their profession, these associations were able to have the salary scales of all teachers of higher education regularized in 1968 on the basis of a nationwide pay scale (Kalim 1978 pp. 18–19)

4.2 Students

A reasonably large and viable student body has developed within the last decades. Though the traditional predominance of male students remains, yet female enrollments have increased more rapidly. Increases in scientific, technological, and professional subjects correspond to priorities in the National Plans and to opportunities for work at home and abroad. The preponderance of enrollments in

Table 4
Distribution of students by sex and subject of study

		1960[a]	1965[b]	1970[c]	1975[d]	1980[e]	1985[f]
Humanities	Total	9,912	22,368	44,569	41,664	46,886	9,577
	F	—	8,654	12,383	17,738	22,259	2,959
Education	Total	1,402	3,027	3,933	4,861	5,675	1,975
	F	—	871	1,179	2,461	2,211	684
Law	Total	882	1,567	5,528	12,632	10,299	4,221
	F	—	17	45	211	248	177
Social sciences	Total	1,517	3,752	11,350	12,070	11,909	4,175
	F	—	50	2,147	494	2,022[g]	430
Natural sciences	Total	3,163	7,100	16,672	18,294	23,681	11,928
	F	—	1,208	2,663	3,496	7,146	2,793
Engineering	Total	472	738	7,334	13,867	18,221	14,502
	F	—	—	26	58	108	466
Medical sciences	Total	794	790	5,210	16,919	24,427	1,614
	F	—	146	1,217	3,664	6,067	456
Agriculture	Total	416	829	8,498	5,675	6,137	6,362
	F	—	—	204	71	454	62
Others	Total	—	—	5,054	83	8,047	5,537
	F	—	—	—	36	1,531	774

a UNESCO Yearbook 1971   b UNESCO Yearbook 1971   c UNESCO Yearbook 1975   d UNESCO Yearbook 1980
e UNESCO Yearbook 1985   f UNESCO Yearbook 1987   g Including 1,316 Home Economics

general arts and science subjects is yielding to more career-oriented subjects. Table 4 shows the distribution of students by sex and types of institution. As regards regional participation, the two comparatively backward provinces of Baluchistan and Sind have steadily increased their rate of participation while the Punjab and NWFP provinces have a trend of relative decline in the participation rate (Husain et al. 1987 p. 90).

Students always had the freedom to organize into unions at all levels and represent their interests at various forums and administrative systems. Originally expressing their interest in academic and cultural pursuits, student's unions and organizations have been exploited by political parties and religious factions, for their own vested interests. Backed by these groups, students have openly clashed with each other and with the authorities on campuses, using firearms and killing both their fellows and some officials (Hayes 1987 chap. 9).

Undergraduate programs are generally based on clusters of courses in liberal arts and general sciences. Apart from the two nationwide, compulsory subjects of Islamiyat (for Muslin students) and Pakistan studies for all, there are four compulsory subjects and three elective but related subjects in a particular specialization. The introduction of the semester system has remained, ever since its introduction by the federal government in 1975, a hotly debated question. The choice has since been left to individual institutions so there is no uniformity. The government is, however, determined to make it compulsory in due course.

Closely associated with the semester system is the question of assessment of students at internal and terminal examinations. The 1959 Commission originally recommended that 25 percent weightage in each paper should be attached to teachers' own assessments. Students must pass in both the internal and external tests. Pass marks are fixed at 40 percent in each subject and 50 percent in the aggregate and 60 percent to obtain a Second Division and 70 percent for First Class. Honors and master's degree candidates also submit to a viva voce. The assessment systems have been beset with a host of corrupt practices. Students and influential relatives have been able to secure more favorable grades.

5. Conclusion

Pakistan has, within a relatively short period of time, made significant achievements in higher education. It developed an elaborate network of institutions—22 universities, 600 colleges, 24 polytechnics, 100 professional colleges, 1,200 Islamic institutions and a variety of research institutes. All in all, some two million students are enrolled at different levels and in various specializations. Pakistani qualified professionals, technicians, and skilled labor force are employed in many African, Middle-Eastern, European, and American countries.

Two main historical factors have acted as the driving force for Pakistan's accomplishments: (a) centuries of Islamic educational and cultural traditions; and (b) the modernizing zeal unleashed during the British rule. Yet, these same traditions crystallized into rival ideological polarities. The traditionalist versus the modernist and the religious versus the secularist, are proving to be stumbling blocks in Pakistan's quest for national unity which is a prerequisite for progress in higher education.

The most daunting problem the country faces is the alarming growth of population. Population projections for the year 2000 range from 118.5 millions to 151 millions while estimates show it to have been 107 millions in 1989. With such constant pressure, Pakistan could never provide even basic educational facilities for its teeming millions. Yet, failure to do so, especially in the less developed regions, is bound to produce even more divisive tendencies and political crises. Already, the monopolization of economic, political power in the country by the elites and their control of higher education, coupled with regional disparities, has given rise to parochialism and provincial nationalism. The Islamization movement has also become politicized and university campuses witness almost daily disruption and violence.

Solutions to these problems are not easy. Nations and their educational systems do not mature overnight. Additionally, Pakistan has resolved to gear its higher education towards a modern, Islamic social order. This demands even more dedication, sense of purpose, and the will to achieve. Once a representative leadership and a democratic pattern of life is established, Pakistan will hopefully succeed in evolving a viable system of higher education suited to the needs and aspirations of its people.

Bibliography

Ahmad A, Sajid M 1982 *Muslim Women and Higher Education: A Case for Separate Institutions and a Workplan for Womens' Universities.* Islamabad
Ahmad V, Amjad R 1984 *The Management of Pakistani Economy (1972–82).* Oxford University Press, Karachi
Burki S J, Laporte R Jr 1984 *Pakistan's Development Priorities—Choices for the Future.* Oxford University Press, Karachi
Cowan R, McLean M (eds.) 1984 *International Handbook of Educational Systems. Vol. IV: Pakistan.* Wiley, London, pp. 301–31
Hayes, L D 1987 *The Crisis of Education in Pakistan.* Vanguard, Lahore
Hussain S S, Ashraf S A 1979 *Crisis in Muslim Education.* Hodder and Stoughton, London
Husain T, Sanyal B, Abbas M H, Khan S R (eds.) 1987 *Higher Education and Employment Opportunities in Pakistan.* International Institute of Educational Planning (IIEP), Paris

Kalim M S 1978 *Pakistan: An Educational Spectrum.* Arsalan Publications, Lahore

Kraan J D 1984 *Religious Education in Islam with Special References to Pakistan.* Christian Study Centre, Rawalpindi

Mellor W L, Khan M A (eds.) 1983 *Priorities in Educational Development in Pakistan—Projects and Training Programme.* Centre for International Education and Development, University of Alberta, Edmonton

Pakistan, Ministry of Education 1959 *Report of the National Commission on Education.* Ministry of Education, Karachi

Pakistan, Government Planning Commission 1983 *The Sixth Five-Year Development Plan, 1983–88.* Government Planning Commission, Islamabad

Pakistan, Ministry of Finance 1989 *Economic Survey (Pakistan) 1988–89.* Ministry of Finance, Islamabad

Qureshi I H 1961 *The Muslim Community of the Indo-Pakistan Sub-Continent.* Mouton, The Hague

Qureshi I H 1975 *Education in Pakistan.* Ma'aref, Karachi

Rahman T 1988 Pakistani universities: Actual, ideal, possible. In: University Grants Commission 1988 *Higher Educ. Rev.* UGC, Vol. 5, No. 1, Islamabad, pp. 7–18.

Salam A 1983 A note on the structural changes in Pakistan's educational system. In: University Grants Commission 1983 *Higher Educ. Rev.* UGC, Vol. 1, No. 2, Islamabad, pp. 1–9

Saqeb G N 1983 *Modernisation of Muslim Education in Egypt, Pakistan and Turkey.* Islamic Book Service, Lahore

Saqeb G N 1985 The effects of tension between nationalism and provincialism in educational administration in Pakistan. In: Lauglo J, McLean M(eds.) 1985 *Control of Education: International Perspectives on Centralisation and Decentralisation Debate.* Heinemann Educational for Institute of Education, London, pp. 33–44

Shami P A 1988 Higher education in Pakistan—A case for change. In: University Grants Commission 1988 *Higher Educ. Rev.* UGC, Vol. 5, No. 1, Islamabad, pp. 65–70

Tikmani P A 1987 Re-shaping the style of teaching at the college/university level. In: University Grants Commission 1987 *Higher Educ. Rev.* UGC, Vol. 4. No. 1, Islamabad, pp. 49–58

Turner R E 1971 Modes of social ascent through education. In: Hopper E(ed.) 1971 *Readings in the Theory of Education Systems.* Hutchinsons, London, pp. 71–90

University Grants Commission 1975 *Report of Study Group on Improvement of Education and Research in Universities.* UGC, Islamabad

Zaki W M 1975 *Education of the People.* People's Open University, Islamabad

G. N. Saqeb

Panama

1. Higher Education and Society

Panama is the least populated of the Latin American countries, with a population of only 2.4 million (est. 1990), although a high rate of growth characterized the post-Second World War period. Panama is also the youngest Latin American republic, having gained formal independence in 1903 after cutting its historical ties to Colombia. Panama is located on an isthmus that barely separates the largest oceans of the world; at one point only 80 kilometers of rugged terrain separate the Pacific from the Atlantic. It was here that the Panama Canal was built during the early years of the twentieth century.

Ever since Panama linked up with Europe in the early sixteenth century, its dominant activity has been related to servicing commerce and financial endeavors between the Pacific basin and the growing North Atlantic economies. As a consequence, internal development of its own agriculture and industry was traditionally overlooked. After the Second World War a strategy aimed at promoting economic development—based on import substitution industrialization—demanded a more sophisticated labor force and generated a more labor intensive economy. The consequences of these changes brought forth political transformations that are still being felt. Economic growth, social reform, and US military bases resulted in political instability and a military regime was installed from 1968 to 1989.

Panama has been forced to deal directly with the leading international powers throughout its history. In the twentieth century it has had a special association with the United States. In 1904 Panama conceded territorial rights to the United States in order to accommodate its expanding economy. Since then the United States has been a political factor in the day-to-day life of Panama. In recent years Japan has also played an important role, using the isthmus of Panama as a stepping stone in its thrust toward the rich Atlantic markets. Panama's social and economic structures changed significantly after the Second World War. The population at the beginning of the 1990s is mainly urban, an important internal market has developed, and new relations with the United States have ensued. Panama still has a relatively high rate of population growth, but it also enjoys a higher per capita income (US$2,100) than its Latin American neighbors. The illiteracy rate has fallen sharply in recent decades to only 11 percent, but the economy has a serious structural unemployment problem.

2. The Institutional Fabric of the Higher Education System

Higher education was first established in Panama during the eighteenth century by Jesuit priests. The University of San Francisco was disestablished, however, when the Jesuit order was expelled from the Spanish American empire. In 1935 the University of Panama (*Universidad de Panamá*) was established by the state. Since then the University has grown and changed, keeping pace with the country's development.

At present the University of Panama is governed by a charter that provides it with autonomy in its academic activities and financial matters. It is also responsible for supervising the country's other institutions of higher education.

The University's authorities are elected by a body of 80 representatives—the General Council—comprised of professors, students, and administrative members. They elect the top administrative officers of the university.

In 1965 the first private university was founded by the Catholic Church: *Universidad Santa Maria la Antigua* (USMA). In 1982 another private university was established, the *Universidad del Istmo (*UI). That same year the *Universidad Tecnólogica de Panamá* (UTP) was created by separating the engineering faculty from the university of Panama.

The four universities concentrate their activities in Panama City. In compliance with a constitutional mandate the University of Panama has six campuses in the provincial capitals.

The four universities have a total student enrollment of 55,000. The University of Panama is by far the largest with 40,000 students. The University Santa Maria la Antigua follows with 8,000; the Technological University has (6,000); and the University of the Isthmus (1,000).

In order to gain admission to a university a student must complete a secondary education. In 1989 there were 17,000 applications for admission to first-degree courses.

3. Governance, Administration, and Finance

The University of Panama is governed by a general council that elects its own authorities. Students represent 20 percent of the council's membership, while employees have 10 percent. The remaining 70 percent is given over to faculty.

In recent years the economic crisis, compounded by the conflict with the United States, has weakened the University's ability to promote its academic programs. Its future is closely linked to economic growth and social change. The demand for professionals and technical experts will depend on the country's capacity to stabilize its international relations and promote internal development. According to Panama's Constitution, the University of Panama is an autonomous public institution. The conflict with the United States has resulted in an extremely curtailed budget of only US$40 million. This has meant that the University has had to cut most of its research, cultural, and editorial programs. The allocation barely covers teachers' salaries.

Because of state financial support student registration fees are very low (US$26 per semester), which permits the University to open its classrooms to all high school graduates. There is also a national scholarship system. Although the private universities are also subsidized by the state, these institutions have to finance most of their expenditures through student registration fees. The average students pays $700 per semester at the USMA.

The rector is the presiding officer of the higher education institutions. In order to fulfill his duties, he is assisted by one or more deputies (vice-rectors), a secretary general, and an auditor. The state-financed universities are also audited by the Central Comptroller's Office.

4. Faculty and Students: Teaching, Learning, and Research

At present the University of Panama has 2,100 professors, distributed throughout 14 faculties. Half of the faculty members have gained tenure through due process.

A large majority of students at the University of Panama are from low-income working-class families. More than half the student body is female. The USMA and UI students are mainly from middle-class backgrounds. A large segment of upper and middle-class families send their children to universities abroad. (Mexico and Brazil are among the most favored countries.) Owing to the limited number of graduate programs, students also travel abroad in order to specialize.

When the University of Panama opened its doors in 1935 its objective was to create the professionals needed in an expanding society. Three faculties were created: law, pharmacy, and public administration. Training professionals assumed a higher priority over the years than investing in research. The research which was going on was not conducted at the Panamanian institutions of higher learning. Research projects have been developed on a regular basis by the United States armed forces and institutions such as the Smithsonian in Washington; however, there are no formal relations between Panama's establishments of higher learning and these institutions.

Table 1
Panama: higher education student enrollment and budget

	1964	1966	1971	1976	1981	1986	1989
Students	6,972	9,904	15,074	30,642	43,382	56,413	52,000
Budget (US$)	2,162,000	2,636,000	5,978,000	14,780,000	31,896,000	50,870,000	40,000,000

Source: Contraloría General de la República (Panama)

Table 2
Registration at the University of Panama (1st term 1988)

	Registration					
	Total	Percent	Male	Female	Day-shift	Night-shift
Campus: Faculties	24,946	67.2	9,144	15,802	13,657	11,289
Business administration	6,560	17.7	2,244	4,316	2,802	3,758
Public administration	1,932	5.2	585	1,347	903	1,029
Architecture	1,783	4.8	947	836	949	834
Agro-sciences	196	0.5	4	192	94	102
Natural sciences	1,092	2.9	559	533	686	406
Journalism	1,843	5.0	662	1,181	863	980
Law	1,991	5.4	1,154	837	1,335	656
Economy	1,370	3.7	670	700	755	615
Education	2,097	5.6	472	1,625	902	1,195
Nursing	1,281	3.4	33	1,248	1,232	49
Pharmacy	613	1.7	217	396	418	195
Arts and sciences	3,072	8.3	1,064	2,008	1,602	1,470
Medicine	866	2.3	448	418	866	—
Odontology	250	0.7	85	165	250	—
Agro-sciences (chiriqui)	293	0.8	179	114	244	49
Regional university centers	10,538	28.4	3,273	7,265	2,894	7,644
Azuero	1,603	4.3	427	1,176	220	1,383
Coclé	814	2.2	251	563	98	716
Colón	1,612	4.3	529	1,083	142	1,470
Chiriqui	3,916	10.6	1,093	2,823	1,649	2,267
Los Santos	502	1.4	183	319	—	502
Veraguas	2,091	5.6	790	1,301	785	1,306
Extensions	1,348	3.6	341	1,007	—	1,348
Bocas del Toro	229	0.6	46	183	—	229
La Chorrera	1,119	3.0	295	824	—	1,119
Percent	100		34.2	65.2	45.2	54.8
Total	37,125	100.0	12,937	24,188	16,795	20,330

Source: Boletin de Estadistica No. 32, Universidad de Panama 1989 p. 2

Several efforts have been made to link higher education in Panama to research. However, resources have not been available. Small, but significant steps have been taken in natural and social sciences. The results of these efforts can be measured by the number of publications coming from the higher education institutions. As of 1990 there were about a dozen scientific journals edited by the universities.

5. Conclusion

In a recent statement, the President of the *Universidad de Panamá*, Abdiel J Adames, said that the university was "the source of knowledge and the country's guide towards historical change." Since its creation in 1935, the University has been considered the nation's intellectual center and its "critical conscience." The University played a crucial role in two different periods of modern history. In the 1935–55 period it prepared a host of new professionals for the growing commercial and service economy, and then between 1955 and 1975 gave priority to the technological areas in order to promote the agricultural and industrial economy. The Panamanian institutions of higher education as a whole have been closely related to the country's quest for economic development. They have, for the most part, supplied professionals rather than research breakthroughs contributing strongly to Panama's struggle towards development promoting upward social mobility. The University has also been able to remain free from the influence of either the military or the church.

The institutions of higher education, especially the University of Panama, have played a historical role in molding a strong national identity. The student bodies of the University of Panama have had extraordinary influence over broad issues that have shaped the country's development in the past half century. Its alumni have reached the highest positions both in government and private enterprise. In the last 20 years, 12 out of Panama's 14 vice-presidents and presidents were graduates of higher education institutions and eight were graduates of the University of Panama.

Bibliography

Adames 1988 *Perspectivas de la institución universitaria,* University of Panama, Panama City
Adames 1990 *La Universidad ante la crisis.* University of Panama, Panama City
Bernal 1988 La alternativas de la crisis educativa. *Liberación* 1: 11–13
Castillo de M 1988 La Universidad de hoy: Una visión hacia el futuro. *Liberación* 1: 5–9
Castillo F D 1985 La Universidad de Panamá. Un Proyecto de la nación *Boletin* ORPE 3: 67–86
Castro N 1978 La reforma ahora. *Revista Nacional de Cultura* 9/10: 5–21
Ceneño Cenci 1979 *La Universidad profunda.* University of Panama, Panama City
Escobar B r 1974. *Sentado pautas en la política académica universitaria.* University of Panama, Panama City
Garrido C 1989 La Universidad y el desarrollo científico-tecnológico. *Cuadernos Nacionales* 3: 5–10
Ho C, Ho T S 1983 Génesis de la Universidad de Panama. *Lotería* 331: 5–18
Méndez Pereira O 1953 La Universidad de Panama. en *Panamá. 50 años de República.* Ed. de la Junta Nacional del Cincuentenario, Panama City
Pereira M N de 1989 Las ruinas de la Universidad de San Javier. *Panorama Católico* 173: 10–11
Pinzón R M 990 *La educación universitaria en la región de Azuero.* Centro Regional de Azuero, dos Santos
Pizzurno-Gelós P 1985 Génesis y fundación de la Universidad de Panama. *Boletin* ORPE 3: 9–36
Salas D E 1977 *Desplegando banderas de ciencia e investigación.* University of Panama, Panama City
Sánchez C 1981 *La nueva ley de la Universidad de Panamá.* University of Panama, Panama City

M. A. Gandásegui

Papua New Guinea

1. *Higher Education and Society*

Higher education is defined very broadly in Papua New Guinea (PNG) as all education after completion of year 10, with the exception of the years 11 and 12 programs of the national senior high schools (PNG 1983). Most of the institutions were established during a period of rapid expansion of the system in the 1960s by the Australian administration, prior to Independence on 16 September 1975. The earliest were designed for primary teacher and nursing training, followed by many other types, including the establishment of the University of PNG (UPNG) and the Institute of Higher Technical Education in 1965.

The latter became the PNG University of Technology (PNGUT) in 1973.

The 1980 census estimated the PNG population at approximately three million and growing annually at a rate of about 2.3 percent, with about 87 percent rural and engaged mainly in subsistence agriculture (Department of Finance and Planning 1986). English was adopted at an early stage as the official medium of instruction in both schools and higher education institutions, as some 750 indigenous languages existed, with no single dominant linguistic group. The PNG economy has an agrarian base complemented by a small but growing number of enclave mineral developments. The country is heavily dependent on export of primary commodities including gold, copper, coffee, timber, copra, cocoa, and palm oil. In addition, Australian budgetary aid constitutes about one-fifth of government revenue.

In the 1980s there were frequent changes of government in a democratic system based on ruling coalitions made up of a number of smaller parties. A major political development was the creation in 1978 of 19 provincial governments and their associated bureaucracies.

The main mission laid upon higher education by successive governments was the production of highly trained human resources to meet the needs (particularly the economic needs) of the nation. Religious organizations played a significant part in the development of higher education (particularly primary teacher and nursing education) as well as in the education system in general.

2. *The Institutional Fabric of the Higher Education System*

In 1988 the higher education institutions fell into the following eight main groups: universities (2); technical colleges (7); primary teachers' colleges (9); nursing schools (13); paramedical colleges (2); primary industry training colleges (7); miscellaneous institutions (12); and privately funded institutions (10). Church agencies operated nine of the nursing schools and eight of the primary teachers' colleges with at least partial government funding. The universities, technical colleges, paramedical colleges, six primary industry colleges, and eight miscellaneous colleges were wholly government funded. Two others were funded by commercially operating statutory authorities. Two of the ten privately funded institutions were funded by commercial enterprise and eight by church agencies.

The two universities are responsible for all degree- and graduate-level education, as well as secondary and technical teacher training, and undergraduate and graduate diplomas. (The only other degree level education is offered by the theological colleges.) The paramedical colleges and nursing schools provide postbasic training and basic nursing training respectively. Certificate-level training is provided through the primary teachers and primary industry colleges, while the technical colleges offer a range of basic, trade, apprenticeship, and technician-level training. Most of the miscellaneous colleges confine themselves to vocationally oriented programs. Research is an integral part of the universities, but there are also several research institutes separate from the higher education system, notably the National Research Institute and the Institute of Medical Research.

Admission to the universities normally requires successful completion of Year 12 (or equivalent) with passes at specific levels for particular study programs. Most of the remaining higher education institutions require successful completion of Year 10 with passes at specific levels in particular subjects, although a number also require Year 12, particularly those offering postbasic programs.

Comprehensive data on higher education as a whole exists only from 1983 onwards when the Commission for Higher Education (CHE) was created and undertook its first annual survey of institutions of higher education. In 1985 enrollments in programs of one academic year or more by level of institution were: universities 3,555 (subdegree 1,318, degree 2,290, postgraduate 28); technical colleges 1,578; primary teachers' colleges 1,771; nursing schools 666; paramedical colleges 129; primary industry colleges 533; miscellaneous colleges 557; privately funded (religious) institutions 835 (subdegree 796, degree 39), totalling 9,624. In addition there were approximately 5,500 enrollments in programs of less than one academic year. The proportion of the age group 20 to 24 years enrolled in the whole higher education system in 1985 was (very approximately) 1 percent (1980 National Census figures adjusted for 2.3 percent per annum population growth and CHE 1986).

First degrees normally require four years for completion, except medicine which requires five years followed by two years of professional experience for registration, and architecture which requires six years including professional experience. Degrees are awarded by the universities themselves.

3. Governance, Administration, and Finance

Although higher education institutions are distributed between 17 of the 19 provinces, higher education is a national (as compared to a provincial) function. The main responsibility for the development of higher education lies with the Ministry of Education. Despite this, a considerable number of institutions and enrollments fall outside the education portfolio. Fifteen institutions (representing about 8 percent of total higher education enrollments) come under the Health Ministry, and seven (representing about 6 percent of the total) under the Ministries of Agriculture and Livestock,

and of Forests. Another 12 are distributed between a further 11 ministries. The CHE (the designated coordinating agency) attempts to shape higher education by three main means: advice on institutional funding to the Minister and the (national) Resource Management Committee; the award of national tertiary scholarships; and the preparation of a national plan for higher education.

Since the creation of the CHE in 1983 its main goals were to reduce higher education costs to government while maintaining approximately the same quantity and quality of output, and to reorient that output more toward the human resource development needs of the economy. These goals were transmitted to the CHE by the cabinet. The first formal national higher education plan entitled "Higher Education Plan: A Strategy for Rationalisation 1986 to 1990" was presented to the cabinet in 1986, and approved for implementation in late 1987. This plan presented basic indicators for evaluating higher education's response to the rationalization goal, and provided for the improvement of those indicators over the plan period. The CHE also administers a central selection unit for processing admissions to the majority of institutions, and for the administration of the national tertiary scholarship scheme through which most students are financed.

By far the largest source of finance for higher education is the national budget. All government monies for higher education are appropriated through the National Departments and the CHE, with the exception of the universities, the Legal Training Institute, and the PNG Maritime College which have direct appropriations. In 1983 appropriations to higher education accounted for approximately 6.5 percent of total appropriations (CHE 1984).

The two universities were established as autonomous institutions by separate parliamentary acts. They are each governed by their own council with membership drawn from a variety of sources, including members of parliament as specified in the acts. Some members are ex officio, others appointed by the minister for education, others representing private enterprise and the lay community, and others are elected representatives of the staff and student bodies. Each has a number of standing committees, including an academic board. In the nonuniversity sectors, the CHE has encouraged the establishment of governing councils, but many institutions have very little autonomy. The major policy and resource allocation decisions are made by their parent departments, which perform the role of coordinating authorities for these sectors.

Academic power in both universities is collegial, particularly in UPNG, although there are differences of structure and emphasis between the two. Nonacademic staff and students have elected representatives on the key committees including the council.

The basic units in both universities are departments, with faculties existing at the UPNG. The formal responsibilities of the departments are primarily the teaching of undergraduate programs in their own disciplines, and secondarily, research. The PNGUT also has a National Testing Laboratory and an Appropriate Technology Development Institute. The UPNG has a Marine Sciences Research Department and a Teaching Methods and Materials Center. Its former Education Research Unit was amalgamated in 1988 into the National Research Institute.

4. Faculty and Students: Teaching, Learning, and Research

In 1985 there were 1,376 full-time teaching staff in higher education, with 379 of these in the universities. Of these 767 (310 in the universities) were noncitizens.

Noncitizens were by definition ineligible for tenure. The majority of citizen academics were appointed initially on three-year contract terms, renewable for periods not exceeding five years at a time. The academic ranks were tutor, senior tutor (1 and 2)/technical instructor (1 and 2)/lecturer (1 and 2), senior lecturer, associate professor, professor. These were directly linked to citizen and noncitizen public service salary scales, and generally subject to similar conditions of service, which were tightly controlled by cabinet's Salaries and Conditions Monitoring Committee. Promotion between these grades within the universities was subject to university criteria and generally based on performance in teaching, research, and publication, except in the case of senior tutors and technical instructors of whom research and publication was not a requirement.

Responsibility for recruitment of university staff lies with the universities, whereas recruitment to institutions of the Department of Education, Health, Agriculture and Livestock, and so on is through the public service. Teaching staff in all institutions (except staff funded from solely private sources) are linked to the same public service salary scale, but considerable differences existed between the career and status of teaching staff in different types of institutions compared to the universities.

Within the universities separate citizen and noncitizen staff associations exist, whereas in the nonuniversity sector, staff interests are represented mainly through the Public Service Association and the Overseas Staffing Assistance Group.

The universities are funded by government on a staffing formula related to student load and notional

Table 1
Preservice output from selected institutions of higher education by level of program and field of study 1980

Field of Study	Certificate	Diploma	Degree	All levels
Agriculture, forestry and fisheries	320	24	29	373
Architecture and town planning	—	—	10	10
Arts	—	—	43	43
Commercial, business administration and secretarial	584	9	57	650
Education and teacher training	786	135	58	979
Engineering and technical trades	830	14	76	920
Law	—	—	37	37
Mass communication, documentation and journalism	—	15	—	15
Medical science and health related (nursing)	89	—	27	116
Natural sciences	—	—	15	15
Social and behavioral sciences	—	—	30	30
Other and not specified (land studies)	23	30	—	53

Source: Commission for Higher Education 1984

standard staff contact hours. However, the actual allocation of teaching hours between individual staff members is decided at departmental level. The staff contact hours formula includes the assumption that a proportion of noncontact hours will be spent on research.

The distribution of students across the main subject areas is reflected in Table 1 showing the output of preservice programs in 1980 classified according to UNESCO categories.

In 1985 almost 30 percent of the total higher education student body were female. The breakdown by sectors was as follows: universities 16 percent; technical (including secretarial) colleges 38 percent; primary teachers' colleges 40 percent; nursing schools 74 percent; paramedical colleges 35 percent; primary industry colleges 5 percent; miscellaneous colleges 15 percent; and religious institutions 19 percent.

5. Conclusion

Despite attempts since the mid-1980s to rationalize higher education, it continued to be characterized by a large number of very small institutions. This was attributable chiefly to the deconcentrated distribution of power in higher education, which grew up prior to Independence, in response to urgent human resource development needs, and the fact that the creation of the state fixed this distribution in place in the post-Independence period. Cabinet was unsuccessful in bringing about a significant redistribution. Consequently the high cost of higher education to the government was likely to remain a major issue. A related issue upon which considerable emphasis was focused in the late 1980s was the high cost to government of student financing. Higher education policy tended to ignore the social demand factor, but it was likely that demand would increasingly be felt, particularly from provincial populations. This might result in greater attention to distance education in the future.

Bibliography

Commission for Higher Education 1984 *Higher Education—A Review of Trends in Papua New Guinea.* Higher Education Commission, Waigani
Commission for Higher Education 1986 *Annual Survey of Institutions of Higher Education in Papua New Guinea 1985 Part A: Enrollments in Programmes of at least One Academic Year or more.* Report AS-85/1.1, Higher Education Commission, Waigani
Department of Finance and Planning 1986 *National Development Plan,* Vol. 1 (unapproved draft)
Papua New Guinea, Independent State of 1983 *Higher Education Act,* Section 2

P. S. Murphy

Paraguay

1. Higher Education and Society

Paraguay is an independent republic located in the heart of South America. To fully understand the characteristics of the current education system, it is necessary to consider the political context present until 1989 along with the restrictions in civil liberties, freedom of the press, social rights and the persecution of those opposing the military regime.

The origin of the current university system and the first Paraguayan institution of higher education was the National University of Asunción (UNA) founded in 1889. Initially it offered programs in law, medicine, and engineering. In 1960, the Catholic University (UC) *Nuestra Señora de Asunción* was established by the Paraguayan Episcopal Conference. Since its creation, the UC has been an "oasis of liberty," that is to say the authorities and students have resisted most of the pressure exercised by the structure of power.

In 1954, General Alfredo Stroessner assumed the presidency of the republic. A process of consolidation of power was initiated and sustained by the triumvirate of the government, armed forces and the governing Colorado Party, which lasted until February 1989. From the beginning of his rule, the policies implemented by Stroessner had a "national security doctrine" orientation, which emphasized internal defense against the communist "threat." In 1989, there was a military coup d'état with a democratic orientation which gave way to the free election of new governmental authorities.

2. The Institutional Fabric of the Higher Education System

In addition to UNA, there are other institutes of higher learning, including the Higher Education Institute (ISE) for teacher training, and two schools for the preparation of physical education teachers (one is affiliated with ISE and the other with the armed forces).

The most important private institution is the Catholic University *Nuestra Señora de La Asunción* (UC). This institution comprises the faculties of philosophy and social sciences, accounting and administration, physics and mathematics, medicine, and the Institute of Theology. The Center for Anthropological Studies (CEADUC) has also been part of the institution since 1950.

There are two other small private institutions of higher learning in the areas of business administration and computer science, the *Escuela Superior de Administración de Empresas* and the *Universidad Privada "Columbia."* Degree programs are offered in the fields of accounting, systems analysis, international commerce, and business administration. These institutions have gained popularity in the last few years, although a limiting factor has been the tuition fees, which are prohibitive for young people with few resources.

The primary function of higher education has been and continues to be professional development, while research and university extension are undertaken in a parallel and isolated manner by private institutions outside of the official higher education system through the initiative of a faculty, department, or professor. These activities are generally considered secondary and normally do not receive sufficient human or financial resources. There is a substantial disequilibrium between professional development and research and university extension. This has resulted from the limited financial resources and lack of impetus in the university environment for the promotion of research and extension.

Academic organization in the diverse fields is determined largely by the same administrative structure of the university. In general, each institution offers yearly regular courses which correspond to the academic calendar. However, admissions, evaluation, and advancement is not standardized. The system also tends to be academically rigid, limiting the possibilities for students to choose programs on a credit basis which include required courses and electives. A few faculties and institutes, including chemistry, architecture, and the Institute of Sciences, among others, have introduced semester courses taught by full-time and part-time professors, which has led to improvement.

3. Governance, Administration, and Finance

3.1 National Administration

All levels of education in Paraguay, including higher education, are monitored by the Ministry of Education and Religion (MEC). In the case of higher education, the MEC collaborates closely with the president of the UNA and has a supervisory role with the UC.

Annually a percentage of the national budget is allocated for higher education. Additionally each university (UNA and UC) attempts to self-finance part of its operations. These funds are obtained principally from tuition fees and other charges. Some faculties have also implemented a fee system to cover the cost of laboratories and the maintenance of equipment.

Periodically, the government designates to higher education certain donated funds received through the international agencies promoting development. For example, US$300,000 was designated for the expansion of UNA infrastructure from the Interamerican Development Bank (BID) funds. The UC, on the other hand, does not receive any state support; its services are funded by student fees.

In the 1954–1989 period, the average percentage of the national budget assigned to education was 10 percent, while defense (armed forces and police) received 25 percent. This meager budget allotment was one of the causes of the stagnation in higher education evidenced during the harsh military dictatorship. It also impeded the initiative and development of a dynamic and modern system capable of contributing significantly to the development of the country.

3.2 Institutional Administration

The organization and functioning of the UNA is governed by the Higher University Council, which has ample facilities to decide the general orientation and specific institutional development. The executive functions are exercised by the president of the University, who is named by the National Executive. The president is the legal representative of the University and manages the administration and academic matters. The Higher University Council and the president have the authority to study, define, and implement the University policies through the different educational institutions. Each faculty is headed by a dean. Currently the faculties include philosophy and letters, law and social sciences, economic sciences, natural sciences, mathematics, chemistry and pharmacy, medical sciences, odontology, agricultural engineering, veterinary sciences, polytechnology, architecture, and basic sciences.

The UC is governed by the University Council, the head of which is a rector named directly by the Paraguayan Episcopal Conference (CEP).

4. Faculty and Students: Teaching, Learning, and Research

4.1 Faculty

The categories of faculty established by university law are assistant, adjunct, titular, and honorary professor. All of these categories require the appropriate degrees, merit, and aptitude verified by open competitive examination. However, this type of competitive examination is not regulated by the university and in practice promotions are given on the basis of seniority. As a result of this practice the university does not have a homogeneous and standardized selection process according to merit and aptitude. Each faculty and school develops procedures in this area.

The number of professors increased 211 percent in the period from 1956 to 1969, which represents an accumulated annual rate of 5.9 percent. Nevertheless, the student–professor ratio rose from 7.2 in 1960 to 8.3 at the end of 1969. In the 1969 to 1982 period, there was a 268 percent increase in the number of professors. However, during this same period, the professor–student ratio also rose significantly, reaching 11 students per professor in 1982.

4.2 Students

During the period from 1960 to 1969, the two universities in Paraguay faced serious problems due to their limited capacity to adapt education facilities to the demographic, economic, social, and cultural demands of the country. The pressure increased as the intensive flow of students entering the university reached unprecedented levels, generating distortion in the capacity to absorb the students in educational institutions in all areas and levels.

The absence of coordination between secondary schools and the university in plans and programs, the insufficient laboratory and classroom space, and the dispersed locations of the institutions have been factors limiting the capacity to absorb all registered university students. The response has been the introduction of an entrance examination or limiting the number of entering students, notwithstanding the justified policy of training the human resources necessary for the development of the country.

In addition to the entrance examination, there are tests at the termination of university studies. In order to decide who enters, each faculty individually establishes the minimum score in the examinations that correspond to their institution.

In 1983, the two universities jointly received 11,924 students. Five years later (1988), the normal period required to complete university studies, 2,304 professionals graduated. This figure represents only 19 percent of the 1983 entering class.

5. Conclusion

University research and extension are scarce and the small amount of experience that has developed has occurred outside of the university institutions. Access to public facilities is obstructed by entrance examinations, which are not clearly regulated. Private universities are formally easier to gain access to; however, access to these is becoming more difficult for students with few resources because of the rising costs.

The new government intends to strengthen the education system in general, and higher education in particular, with the goal of reaching an efficient system which will be able to train appropriate professionals in order significantly to support the development of the country. The challenge that higher education faces in the coming years will be converted into an instrument for the consolidation of the process of democratic transition and into a leading role in the road to development.

Bibliography

Ministerio de Educación y Culto 1984 *Diagnóstico del Sistema Educativo*. Asunción
Ministerio de Hacienda. Dirección General de Estadisticas y Censo 1987 *Encuesta de Hogares 1989*. Asunción
Morínigo J N 1981 Hacia una cuantificación de la población probre en Asunción. *Separata de Estudios Paraguayos*. 19(1)
Morínigo J N n.d El proceso de cambio en la estructura de la PEA. *Estudios Paraguayos*. 6(2)
Rivarola D 1970 *Población, Urbanización y Recursos Humanos en el Paraguay*. G Heiseke, Asunción
Economía Paraguaya, 1986 1987 *Vol. 1: Análisis y Debates*. Centro Paraguayo de Estudios Sociológicos (CPES), Asunción
Plan de Desarrollo Nacional 1965 1965 Presidencia de la República, Secretaria Técnica de Planificación, Asunción
Salcedo E, Ortiz de Salcedo M 1970 *Perfiles de la Educación Paraguaya*. Asunción
Elitización, Disyuntiva del Movimiento Estudiantil 1985 *Nueva Linea*

V. Caballero

Peru

1. Higher Education and Society

Higher education in Peru has developed predominantly at the university level, with a strong wave of expansion since the 1960s that far supersedes the high rate of demographic growth of the country. This development is related to the major social changes undergone during this same period; changes that have given the educational sector an increasingly important social and political significance. The expansion of the educational system however, especially at the university level, has occurred under precarious circumstances, with respect both to material resources and teaching personnel, thus seriously affecting the quality and results of the educational process. This is owing to the fact that the evolution of the Peruvian economy has suffered long periods of stagnation and recession, causing the country to persist in a state of underdevelopment. It is within this general perspective that an overview of the development of higher education in Peru is offered.

Peruvian society in the 1990s is the result of a long historical process which includes three centuries of Spanish colonial dominance extending from 1533, when the Inca Atahualpa was captured, to 1824, when the capitulation of the Spanish army was signed. Independence did not bring substantive changes in the social structure; the same system of subordination and exploitation of the indigenous population continued for a long time.

Until the middle of the twentieth century, Peru was an extremely rural country, with a multicultural and very diverse population, an economy based on the exploitation and export of traditional raw materials, and an oligarchic political regime based upon the control of agricultural lands and mining rights, with political–administrative centralization in the capital city, and a rigid social structure in which inequality of property was linked to ethnic inequality and educational exclusion. The entirety of political and social life was organized around and developed through a complex structure of patron–client relationships and patrimonialism that to a certain extent still exists in the 1990s.

It is primarily in the second half of the twentieth century that the processes of social and political change in Peru, which are significantly modifying the social structure and organization of the country, have been intensified. These changes are occurring in conditions of economic stagnation and deterioration, however, combined with growing demographic pressure, producing a climate of marked social deviance and political violence.

The demographic evolution of the population has been characterized by intense growth, migratory mobility, the transformation of an intensely rural society into a predominantly urban one, the concentration of this society in the capital, and the prevalence of the younger age groups in its makeup. Census information broadly reflects this evolution.

The Peruvian economy has traditionally been linked to the international market in raw materials, with the advantage of having a very diversified range of products. The industrial manufacturing sector has had a troubled development. In the 1960s, there was an attempt to install a model of substitution of imports, based on private enterprise and promoted by tax motivations and importation barriers. In the following decade, under a military dictatorship, an integral model of industrialization was attempted, with the direct intervention of the state in the economy. Both attempts failed.

Until 1986 agricultural activity continued to be the principal occupational field, employing about 36 percent of the labor force. Urban growth has been based on the expansion of commerce and services, above all. In 1983 the "informal urban sector" represented 34 percent of the labor force in metropolitan Lima, consisting basically of retail commerce activities, preparation and sale of food, and services (Carbonetto et al. 1988).

The Gross Domestic Product (GDP) has been characterized by cyclical alternations of expansion and recession (Figueroa 1989). In 1991 Peru's economy is undergoing the greatest crisis in its history: a negative growth of the GDP, high inflation, a huge external debt (over US$20,000 million), and a significant influence of cocaine production and traffic.

As a result the structure of Peruvian society is not clearly defined. However, there is still a marked stratification with a pyramidal tendency, expressed in a definite correlation between the major occupational categories and educational inequalities.

1.1 Higher Education Within the Context of Peruvian Society

Up to the middle of the twentieth century, the formal education system has been largely restricted to the major urban centers, and university education to the dominant social elite. Given the multicultural nature of the country, exclusion from the formal educational system implies an impediment to the learning of Spanish, the official language.

In 1940, the proportion of native-language speakers in the population was considerable (35% monolingual Quechua and Aymara and 15% bilingual). The majority of the population (58%) had no formal education, and a significant part (20%) had only reached the first years of primary schooling. This situation had changed considerably by 1981, with a marked decrease in the native language population (reduced to 8% monolingual and 16% bilingual), and a diminution in the proportion of the population with no formal education to 16 percent. There was still a significant proportion who had attained only initial grades of primary schooling (25%) (Pozzi-Escot 1987).

Formal education has played an important role in Peru; its importance, beyond the practical aspect (occupational opportunity and social mobility), lies in the fact that it has become the principal institutional means of access to citizenship. For this reason, a considerable portion of the population has found itself obliged to suffer the trauma of Castilianization, with the resulting loss of its own

Table 1
Population (in thousands) with regard to higher education in Peru 1960–85

	1960	1965	1970	1975	1980	1985
General population[a]						
20–24 years	847	942	1,106	1,337	1,578	1,867
20–29 years	1,582	1,767	2,026	2,423	2,894	3,422
Enrolled population						
Total advanced	38	80	130	223	319	457
University	30	65	109	182	257	355

a Two age groups have been used to facilitate international comparisons. In Peru, the more relevant group is the one from 20 to 29 years

language. The right to vote was only extended to the illiterate population with the Constitution of 1979.

Despite this fundamental advance in civic rights the problem of social status still exists in Peruvian society, owing to discrimination which forces the ethnic minorities to work at the inferior occupational levels. This has resulted in the demand from the general population for entry into the university as a means of resolving or transcending this problem of social status. Admission is thus imbued with a socio-political significance. This would explain, to a great extent, the growth in the university system since the 1960s.

2. The Institutional Fabric of the Higher Education System

Higher education in Peru has traditionally been limited almost entirely to university education. Only in the 1960s did a clear differentiation appear between university and nonuniversity higher education, and the latter is still in its initial stages. In 1960, university enrollment accounted for almost 80 percent of the total enrollment in higher education. This level has been maintained, with slight variations, until 1985, as shown in Table 2 and through to the start of the 1990s.

The university system in Peru dates back to 1535 when the University of San Marcos was founded in Lima, making it the oldest university in America. Towards the end of the seventeenth century, the University San Cristobal in Huamanga (1677) and that of San Antonio Abad in Cuzco (1692)—the two most important cities of the high Southern Andes—

were created. Later, towards the beginning of the Republican era, the universities of Santo Tomas and Santa Rosa were founded in Trujillo (1824) and that of San Augustin in Arequipa (1925). These are both on the coast, in the north and south, respectively. Lastly, the *Pontificia Universidad Catolica* was founded in 1917, under the auspices of the Catholic Church, the first private university in the country. The University of Huamanga, closed in 1876, reopened in 1957.

The first nonuniversity institution of higher education specialized in teacher education. The *Escuela de Preceptores* (School for Preceptors), was founded in 1822 in Lima; and subsequently became the Teaching University Enrique Guzman y Valle. In 1876, the *Escuela Normal de Mujeres* (Normal School for Women) was established, also in Lima.

In the first half of the twentieth century, there was a growth in normal schooling, both in urban and rural areas. Thus, in 1950 there were two national pedagogical institutes, six urban normal schools, and eight rural normal schools, giving a total of sixteen higher education institutions for the preparation of teachers. In the late nineteenth and early twentieth centuries, there was also a new growth in non-university higher education: in Lima, the *Escuela de Construccion Civil y Minas* (School for Civil Engineering and Mining) was created in 1875, the *Escuela de Agricultura y Veterinaria* (School for Agriculture and Veterinary Medicine) in 1902, and the *Escuela de Bellas Artes* (School of Fine Arts) in 1918. The first two became the *Universidad Nacional de Ingenieria* (National University of Engineering) in 1965 and the *Universidad Nacional Agraria* (Agricultural National University) in 1960 respectively.

Table 2
Enrollment in national and private institutions of higher education 1960–85

	1960	1965	1970	1975	1980	1985
University level						
National	27,040	54,170	81,486	127,819	183,317	228,490
Private	3,207	10,506	27,744	53,852	73,903	126,398
Total	30,247	64,676	109,230	181,671	257,220	354,888
Advanced nonuniversity level						
National	6,725	9,311	15,886	26,629	38,348	65,941
Private	696	6,007	5,209	15,174	237,224	36,017
Total	7,421	15,318	21,095	41,803	62,072	101,958
Total advanced level						
National	33,765	63,481	97,372	154,448	221,665	294,431
Private	3,903	16,513	32,953	69,026	97,627	162,415
Total	37,668	79,994	130,325	223,474	319,292	456,846
Gender relationship (women/men)						
National	0.34	0.39	0.43	0.49	0.53	0.57

Sources: Asamblea Nacional de Rectores, Boletin Estadistico 10, unpublished data collected from the Department of Statistics of the Asamblea Nacional de Rectores

The demands made of higher education in Peru were thus answered by this group of five universities, 16 centers for the preparation of teachers, two professional schools, and one school of fine arts, until the middle of the twentieth century. (For a general history of education in Peru see Valcarcel 1975.) At the start of the 1990s higher education comprises university education, which is dominant, and three nonuniversity areas given over principally to the training of teachers, that of technicians, and that of various other professionals (diplomats, military officers, religious personnel, etc.). Table 2 shows the enrollment in university and nonuniversity institutions between 1960 and 1985.

2.1 Preparation of Teachers

Until the 1970s, nonuniversity higher education was almost exclusively limited to the preparation of teachers principally at the primary level. It was mainly in the universities that teacher-training for the secondary level was carried out, a situation which continued to the 1990s. In the 1970s the training of intermediate level technicians for production capacities and administrative, economic, and social services began. Under the "Revolutionary military government," this new area was prioritized and the preparation of teachers was reduced drastically. During the 1980s, under a new government, there was a renewed growth in the preparation of teachers. This did not, however, reach its previous predominant position.

Throughout the 1960s, especially under the administration of the first presidency of Fernando Belaunde (1963–68), considerable encouragement was given to educational development and the preparation of teachers, with extensive establishment of normal schools. There were thus 130 institutions by 1968 dedicated to the preparation of teachers, 83 percent of which were state schools. The total number at all the institutions was 21,768 students (Zúñiga 1988).

The military regime of General Velasco (1968–75) began a widespread educational reform. A diagnosis of the situation revealed the existence of a marked unemployment rate for teachers, and a very limited level of professional preparation in the technical–production areas. The new regime prioritized technical education, and hence established the *Escuela Superior de Educación Profesional* (Superior School for Professional Education) or ESEP. Teacher training colleges were in large part predominantly closed, with only 32 remaining in 1976.

The subsequent governments of Morales Bermudez (1975–80, this being the second phase of the military government) and Belaunde (1980–85) overturned the reforms initiated by Velasco, giving renewed support to teacher training. The number of normal schools reached a total of 91 in 1985, and were now called *Instituto Superior Pedagógico* (Superior

Education Institute) or ISP. Enrollment decreased to 5,849 students in 1979, then rose progressively to reach 26,211 in 1985, a figure slightly higher than that in 1968.

The ISP are oriented mainly toward primary school teacher training. In 1985, university enrollment in the field of education as a whole reached 38,205 students, with 79 percent concentrated in the area of secondary education (Campos 1985).

2.2 Technical Training

In addition to teacher training, a stimulus toward nonuniversity higher education was provided by the policies of the Velasco military government oriented toward developing working and professional skills, and giving priority to technician training. Educational reform integrated primary and secondary levels into a single cycle of basic education. Upon completion of the ninth grade (equivalent to the third grade in secondary school), children could begin their professional training in the ESEP. This was organized into two tracks: basic regular and basic labor. The latter received the principal emphasis, offering the population the opportunity to be trained at an early age, with a correspondingly rapid entry into the labor force.

The ESEP divided professional education into two cycles. The first cycle offered general preparation in areas related to industrial activities and economic and social services, and lasted for six academic semesters. The second cycle lasted for five semesters, and offered a specialized professional education, awarding the title of Specialized Professional upon graduation.

The reform affected the levels corresponding to basic education and the first cycle at the ESEP. It was interrupted owing to the change in direction of the military government of the "second phase," under the leadership of General Bermudez, and later, because of the reversion to the earlier educational system under the second administration of Belaunde. In 1982, there were 104 ESEPs, of which 53 were national and 51 private, schools.

The 1982 law defined advanced technical education as a postsecondary educational subsystem, turning the ESEP into the new establishment of the *Instituto Superior Tecnológico* (Superior Technological Institute) or IST. By July 1985, there were 161 ISTs of which 84 were government run and 77 private, with 21 superior schools of which 15 were national and 6 private—in all 182 higher educational institutions specialized in technical-production and economical, administrative, and social service fields (Franco 1985).

A series of specialized institutions may be added to this conglomerate of ISP and IST, in the field of advanced nonuniversity education. These include the following: training schools for military and police officers; national schools for public health, public administration, the diplomatic academy, fine arts, and music; the *Escuela Superior de Negocios para Graduados* (ESAN); and the *Facultad de Teologia Pontificia y Civil de Lima*.

2.3 University Education

Until 1950 there were only five universities in Peru. Between then and 1990 there was intense growth in this area. In 1985, Peru already had 46 universities, 26 of them national and 20 private; of these, 15 were located in Lima and 31 in the rest of the country (see Table 3). This expansion of the university establishment took place mainly during the 1960s and 1980s, with government leadership in the first period, and private primacy in the second. It also signalled a move from the capital, Lima, to the provinces. Lima nonetheless contained 40 percent of the universities in 1985.

During the 1970s, the limited growth in the university sector can be explained by the global reform of the educational system under the Velasco military dictatorship. Under the new standards governing university activity, founding persons and bodies were excluded from university government. Universities were the exclusive responsibility of representatives of the three university communities: faculty, students, and nonacademic personnel.

The growth of universities in the provinces is due to two basic demands: first, for greater access to university-level education; and second, for decentralization. In all departmental capitals and cities over 100,000 inhabitants, pressure built up for the establishment of a local university. This is very strong, and has become, for the representatives of congress, difficult to evade. Hence it is probable that expansion will continue.

Demand for access to university is being reflected in a growing expansion in university enrollment. Consequently, a larger proportion of the overall population in the postsecondary age group have been able to become students at university.

Information concerning the age structure of this population is not available, but the relationship may be examined between the whole of the university population and the totals that correspond to the age groups of 20–24 and 20–29 years. In developed countries, it is considered that the majority of students enrolled at university come from the first of these two age groups, but in the case of Peru the second group is more appropriate. The vast majority of Peruvian university students work and study at the same time, and thus require more time to finish their studies. Another factor is that university politics are characterized by frequent strikes, especially in the national universities, leading to a considerable prolongation of the time required to complete a course of study.

In 1960 the percentage of students in the 20–24 years age group was 0.04, and 0.02 in the 20–29 years group. These proportions have grown continually, reaching the levels of 0.19 and 0.10 respectively in 1985. This expansion has occurred under precarious conditions, however, both as regards human, financial, and equipment resources. The quality of university education, with the exception of a few institutions, both national and private, has declined.

3. Governance, Administration, and Finance

3.1 National Administration

Education has suffered greatly from lack of stability in its legislation, because of its high social and political significance. Higher education is regulated by the Constitution of 1979, the General Law of Education of 1982, and the University Law of 1983. (For a historical review of university legislation, see Sánchez 1961 Chap. 2, and for the more recent periods, MacGregor 1981 Chap. 1). Universities are recognized as fully autonomous, and their creation must be approved by the National Congress of the Republic. Institutes and nonuniversity schools for higher education are authorized and supervised by the Ministry of Education. In all of these, titles and degrees are granted in the name of the nation.

Despite the fact that research is one of the functions of the university system, legislative and practical emphasis has been placed on professional training. According to the figures of the *Concejo Nacional de Ciencia y Tecnologia* (National Council of Science and Technology), of the total national investment budgeted in 1970 for scientific and technological research, 43 percent went to the university sector. This proportion had been reduced to 7 percent by 1980, and this marked diminishing tendency is still continuing (Soberón 1988a).

Table 3
Number of universities in Lima and the rest of the country 1950–85

	1950	1955	1960	1965	1970	1975	1980	1985
Lima								
National	1	2	3	5	7	7	7	7
Private	1	1	1	6	7	7	7	8
Total	2	3	4	11	14	14	14	15
Rest of the country								
National	3	4	5	14[a]	14	16	17	19
Private	0	0	0[a]	3	5[b]	5	4[b]	12
Total	3	4	6	17	19	21	21	31
Total country								
National	4	6	8	19[a]	21	23	24	26
Private	1	1	2[a]	9	12[b]	12	11[b]	20
Total	5	7	10	28	33	35	35	46

Source: Asamblea Nacional de Rectores 1988
a One private university established in 1959 was nationalized in 1962 b One private university established in 1968 was closed in 1977

3.2 Funding

Higher education in Peru is, for the most part, publicly funded. This is the case with state universities, and subsidies are given to private universities, teaching institutes, and some technological institutes. Statistical information, especially for the period from 1970 to 1988, indicates a systematic decline in the resources allocated for education, both as a proportion of GDP and of total central government expenditure. University funding, however, has shown a relative increase, indicating a greater protection of this level in the face of the general recessive tendency. Funding assigned to higher education is predominantly at the university level, in a ratio of approximately 8:1 with relation to nonuniversity higher education.

The decrease in educational funding has been accompanied by a sustained growth in enrollment at both levels of higher education. The consequence has been a drastic decline in the average funding per student, representing a reduction in real terms of 50 percent of the initial value in the case of university education and of 85 percent in the case of nonuniversity education. The expansion of the Peruvian university system, in terms of the number of universities and institutes for higher education and the proportion of the population served, has occurred under conditions of declining resources. This has caused a marked deterioration in the quality of preparation of human resources at this level, resulting in very limited scientific and intellectual production. This situation has been aggravated in the period 1988–90 by the growing recession in the Peruvian economy and the increasing fiscal deficit.

3.3 Institutional Administration

The faculties constitute the basic units of operation, and their organization is determined by each individual university. The faculties offer professional training in one or more related specializations, granting the academic degree of bachelor and the professional title of licenciate. Programs of study are structured around a system of credits, with between 160 and 180 credits required to complete the licenciate; this takes approximately 10 academic semesters.

To be admitted to the university, candidates must pass an examination, to determine academic knowledge and aptitude. The contents of this examination and its application are established independently by each university. The number of vacancies and the order of placement in the results of the examination form the basis for entry into the university; previous academic standing is not taken into account. The students immediately begin their chosen course of professional studies, except in the case of two private universities, which have an initial period of general education that lasts four semesters.

Graduate school is the administrative body for studies towards the master's and doctorate degrees, though these studies are carried out within the respective faculties. The development of this advanced level is still quite precarious, especially given the lack of highly qualified teaching staff. Scholarships for graduate studies outside Peru have provided for the development of highly qualified professionals and scholars. These graduates seem to account for the vast majority of the authors of specialized articles and books (Soberón 1988b).

In 1987, of the 46 universities in operation, 16 offered studies towards master's degrees and seven towards doctorates. Master's degrees are available in 61 fields and doctorates in 27; most of these are offered in only one university (Asamblea Nacional de Rectores 1988a). In 1988, there were 1,119 master's and doctoral students, constituting 0.3 percent of the total university enrollment (Asamblea Nacional de Rectores 1988b).

Each university has a university assembly comprised of the rector, the vice-rectors, the deans of the faculties, the director of the graduate school, and representatives from teaching and student groups. The assembly is the ultimate authority, and the body that elects the rector and the vice-rectors (for a five-year period). University administration is the responsibility of the executive committee, presided over by the rector and comprised of the vice-rectors, the deans, and a representative from the student body. In general, the authorities and representatives are universally elected by the members of the university community, a system that extends to the faculties as well.

Lastly, there is a National Assembly of Rectors, which serves as an interuniversity coordinating body and as the organ of relations with the state.

4. Faculty and Students: Teaching, Learning, and Research

This section will deal exclusively with higher education at the university level. As has been mentioned, Peruvian universities concentrate on teaching and learning, with very limited research activity.

4.1 Faculty

In the period from 1960 to 1990, the number of teachers in both public and private universities has greatly increased, growing from a combined total of 3,544 in 1960 to 27,405 in 1990 (see Table 4). In the public universities, only about half of the teaching personnel work full-time; in the private universities, this is only true of about 20 percent. In the public universities, there has been a significant increase in the number of appointed personnel, reaching a level of 80 percent; in the private universities, fluctuation has been minimal, and they have maintained a figure of about 35 percent.

Table 4
Teaching personnel in universities

	1960	1965	1970	1975	1980	1985	1990
Teaching personnel[a]							
Total	3,544	7,125	7,736	11,132	14,782	20,123	27,405
Gender relationship (women/men)	1:14	1:13	1:8	1:7	1:5	1:4	
Public universities	3,176	5,884	5,979	8,140	10,936	14,035	18,247
Private universities	368	1,241	1,757	2,992	3,846	6,088	9,158
Percentage of full-time teachers							
Total	—	—	39.3	40.7	47.1	47.6[b]	—
Public universities	—	—	46.5	50.2	57.8	58.3[b]	—
Private universities	—	—	14.7	15.3	16.2	19.6[b]	—
Professors							
Total	—	—	6,556[c]	9,476	13,006[d]	14,722	21,399[e]
Public universities	—	—	4,841[c]	6,897	9,742[d]	10,695	14,880[e]
Private universities	—	—	1,715[c]	2,579	3,264[d]	4,027	6,519[e]
Percentage of appointed professors							
Total	—	—	56.1	52.3	68.1	68.3	66.9
Public universities	—	—	62.0	61.7	79.3	80.6	80.5
Private universities	—	—	39.6	27.3	34.7	35.8	35.8

Sources: Asamblea Nacional de Rectores. *Boletin Estadistico* 10, Asamblea Nacional de Rectores 1991, GRADE 1990
a Teaching personnel include professors and assistants   b Figures are for 1983   c Figures are for 1969   d Figures are for 1981   e Figures are for 1989

The ratio between nonteaching and teaching personnel has undergone a sustained increase, from 1:3 in 1960 to 2:3 in 1990. Taking into account professorial staff only (excluding teaching assistants), the relationship increases, reaching in 1990 a ratio of almost 1:1. Owing to the lack of available information, it is impossible to differentiate between public and private universities. This is also true for the following point.

Where teaching personnel are concerned, the ratio between the sexes has increased from 1:14 in 1960 to 1:5 in 1985. There is no significant variation in the nonteaching personnel, remaining at about 1:2. Both teaching, in particular, and nonteaching, personnel thus continue to be predominantly male. At the student level the ratio increased from 1:3 in 1960 to 1:2 in 1985.

The teaching ladder comprises three levels of academic staff/faculty: auxiliary, associate, and principal professor. In general, they begin as contracted appointments. Their appointment to one of the professional categories occurs through open competitions conducted by the educational councils of each university. The time of tenure in each category and the promotion to a higher level varies; there is no standard policy. However, a common tendency is as follows: an academic evaluation is conducted every three years for auxiliary professors, four years for associate professors, and six years for principal professors. On the basis of this a confirmation of appointment or promotion to a higher category is made.

The regular professors' regime is defined by the distribution of their responsibilities. Most important is that their semester teaching load must not exceed ten credits (three to four courses), and that they include in their activities time dedicated to research. Most contracted professors are obliged to assume teaching loads that surpass twenty credits in order to assure an income equivalent to that of an ordinary professor. Severe financial limitations have led to the maintenance of a high percentage of professors at the contract level, and also teaching part-time.

In the universities, as a general rule, the various teaching categories are represented in the councils of the university government, which is periodically renewed and elected by universal vote within each category. Both teaching and nonteaching personnel, especially in the public universities have also tended to form associations and unions, which are concerned principally with matters relating to wages.

4.2 Students

The expansion in university enrollment has already been described. A high percentage of students are male, though by 1990 a relation of 0.57 women to men had been reached. There is insufficient statistical information available to deduce tendencies or a precise profile of the social background of students. A study based on a sampling survey at the national level carried out in 1985–86 leads to the conclusion that higher education, especially at university level, shows appreciable social divergency insofar as accessibility and student recruitment are concerned. In the case of heads of household with university education, for example, 4.5 percent of their parents had no formal education, and 45.6 percent only primary education.

Table 5
University enrollment in scientific and professional fields of licentiate level 1960 to 1985 (percentage)

	1960	1965	1970	1975	1980	1985
Natural sciences	1.1	0.8	0.6	1.2	1.7	1.4
Life sciences	7.2	3.1	2.4	2.6	3.4	2.7
Social sciences	3.8	7.2	12.5	15.6	12.6	10.2
Mathematical and statistics	1.0	1.1	1.0	1.1	1.4	1.1
Arts and humanities	1.3	0.8	2.2	4.5	2.9	3.5
Engineering	19.0	17.1	18.6	29.0	29.3	26.4
Health professions	16.0	8.2	9.1	9.7	9.7	10.9
Teaching professions	18.6	39.2	25.6	9.7	7.7	10.9
Legal professions	13.2	7.9	8.2	5.9	6.6	9.4
Administrative professions	17.2	13.1	16.5	17.5	21.4	20.4
Other professions	1.5	1.6	3.4	3.5	3.9	4.0

Source: Asamblea Nacional de Rectores, *Boletin Estadistico* 10

In the case of heads of household with nonuniversity higher education the figures were even higher, at 7.6 percent and 62.9 percent respectively. When the occupational categories of the parents were examined, it was found that the heads of household with university-educated parents were 54.2 percent laborers, while those whose parents had attended nonuniversity higher education were 69.4 percent laborers (Muelle 1990).

In the evolution of university enrollment in scientific and professional fields, Table 5 demonstrates that between 1960 and 1985 the greatest variation

Table 6
Licentiate-level courses with the highest enrollment 1985

Course	Scientific or professional field	Number of enrollments	Percentage within field	Percentage within total enrollment
Accounting	Accounting	41,633	58.4	11.9
Law	Law	32,846	100.0	9.4
Secondary education	Education	30,105	78.8	8.6
Administration	Administration	25,837	36.2	7.4
Economy	Social sciences	24,443	68.4	7.0
Industrial engineering	Engineering	15,479	17.2	4.4
Civil engineering	Engineering	13,327	14.8	3.8
Human medicine	Health professions	12,206	31.9	3.5
Psychology	Humanities	10,489	85.4	3.0
Nursing	Health professions	9,799	25.6	2.8
Chemical engineering	Engineering	7,370	8.2	2.1
Social work	Other professions	7,075	50.8	2.0
Agronomy	Engineering	6,813	7.6	1.9
Obstetrics	Health professions	6,228	16.3	1.8
Architecture	Engineering	5,527	6.2	1.6
Biological sciences	Life sciences	5,384	57.3	1.5
Sociology	Social sciences	4,727	13.2	1.3
Dentistry	Health professions	4,413	11.5	1.2
Mechanical engineering	Engineering	4,083	4.5	1.2
Pharmaceutics and biochemistry	Life sciences	3,795	40.4	1.1
Mining engineering	Engineering	3,916	4.4	1.1
Mechanical and electrical engineering	Engineering	3,757	4.2	1.1
Metallurgical engineering	Engineering	3,568	4.0	1.0
Journalism	Other professions	3,434	24.6	1.0
Electrical engineering	Engineering	3,101	3.5	0.9
Total		289,355		82.6

Source: Asamblea Nacional de Rectores, *Boletin Estadistico* 10

has occurred within the fields that occupy the first five positions. Engineering continues to occupy first place, but with a greater margin between itself and the rest. Administration has risen from third to second place. Some way behind are health and education, followed by social science and law. The rest of the fields remain at an even lower level.

Despite these fluctuations, accounting (within the administration field), law, and education are still among the main courses, as can be seen in Table 6, which shows the 25 most popular courses. These account for 83 percent of university enrollment. Despite engineering's primacy in enrollment as a whole the various courses that this field comprises occupy positions from the sixth place down, a situation which results from the great diversification occurring within this area of specialization.

The different patterns of development are found to be associated to a large extent with the major political changes undergone by Peru. In the 1960s, civil politics were development oriented, with stress being placed on the educational factor as a basic instrument for development. In the 1970s, especially the first half, politics were oriented towards a vast organizational reform of society and the economy, with an emphasis on the direct intervention of the state aimed at intensifying the process of industrialization. In the second half of the 1970s and the first half of the 1980s, governmental politics were oriented toward containing and dismantling, as far as politically possible, the reforms of Velasco, and toward promoting the reprivatization of the economy. To these political changes can be associated, more or less directly, the evolution of the fields of education, engineering, administration, and social sciences, as well as the resulting impact on the rest of the scientific and professional fields.

5. Conclusion

Education, and especially the area of higher university education, is very significant from the point of view of the democratization of Peruvian society. Its real effects, especially since the start of the 1970s, have nonetheless been drastically reduced by the decreasing allocation of resources, resulting in poor production and training. The fields of specialization have grown and diversified, representing a relative modernization, but within the context of an economy that is stagnant and in recession. The Peruvian universities need profound changes which must be given priority, within a general framework of policies for economic revival and growth.

Bibliography

Aramburú C E, Brito P F, Fernández H, González-Vigil J E, Wendorff C 1983 *Población y políticas de desarrollo en el Perú*. Instituto Andino de Estudios en Población y Desarrollo, Lima

Asamblea Nacional de Rectores 1988a *Universidad del Perú*. Departamento de Informática y Documentación, Lima

Asamblea Nacional de Rectores 1988b *Perú: Estadísticas universitarias 1960–1986. Boletín Estadístico* 10. Assemblea Nacional de Rectores, Lima

Asamblea Nacional de Rectores 1991 *Universidad Peruana y desarrollo nacional*. Editorial Universitaria, Lima

Campos A 1985 Formacion magisterial. Paper presented to the Seminar on Analysis and Perspectives on Higher Education in Peru. Centro de Investigaciones y Servicios Educativos, Pontificia Universidad Católica del Perú, Lima

Carbonetto D, Hoyle J, Tueros M 1988 *Lima: Sector informal*. Centro de Estudios para el Desarrollo y la Participación, Lima

Consejo Nacional de Población 1986 *Perú: Hechos y cifras demográficas*, 2nd edn. Consejo Nacional de Población, Lima

Fernández H 1985 Aspectos cuantitativos de la educación en el Perú. Paper presented to a seminar on Education and Society. FOMCIENCIAS, Lima

Figueroa A 1989 Integración de las políticas a corto y largo plazo. *Economía*. 23: 225–47

Franco G 1985 Inventario e informe de la educación superior tecnológica (1980–1985). Paper presented to the Seminar on Analysis and Perspectives on Higher Education in Peru. Centro de Investigaciones y Servicios Educativos, Pontificia Universidad Católica del Perú, Lima

Grupo de Análisis para del Desarrollo 1990 *Educación Superior en el Perú: Datos para el análisis. Documento de Trabajo*. GRADE, Lima

Instituto Nacional de Estadística e Informática, Dirección de Cuentas Nacionales 1990 *Perú: Compendio estadístico 1989–1990*, Vol. 1. INEI, Lima

MacGregor F S J 1981 *Sociedad. Ley y Universidad Peruana*. Fondo Editorial de la Pontificia Universidad Católica del Perú, Lima

Muelle L 1990 Desigualdad social y desigualdad educativa: un análisis intergeneracional. *Revista Peruana de Ciencias Sociales* (RPCS). 2(2): 31–60

Pozzi-Escot I 1987 La incomunicación verbal en el Perú. *Allpanchis*. 29/30: 45–63

Sánchez L A 1961 *La universidad no es una isla* . . . Ediciones Perú, Lima

Soberón L 1988a Niveles de actividad y logro en la investigación científica y tecnológica. (Unpublished paper) Grupo de Análisis para el Desarrollo (GRADE), Lima

Soberón L 1988b Características, comportamientos y percepciones de los científicos peruanos. (Unpublished paper) Grupo de Análisis para el Desarrollo (GRADE), Lima

Sobrevilla L A, Chu M V 1989 *Perú 2005. El desafío demográfico*. Universidad Peruana Cayetano Heredia, Instituto de Estudios de Población IEPO, Lima

Valcárcel C D 1975 *Breve historia de la educación Peruana*. Editorial Educación, Colección Ciencias Histórico-Sociales, Lima

Zúñiga M 1988 La formación magisterial de los docentes de la Sierra. Documento de Trabajo 1, Proyecto Escuela, Ecología y Comunidad Campesina, Lima

L. Soberón

Philippines, The

1. Higher Education and Society

The Philippine school system has its roots in the sixteenth century when the country became a Spanish colony. It remained under Spanish rule for three and a half centuries, from 1565 to 1898. The Spanish–American War which ended in 1898 resulted in the takeover of the Philippines by the United States whose policy of colonization included the establishment of a public school system, the continuation of the religious Catholic schools created during Spanish times, and the establishment of new private religious and nondenominational schools.

The outbreak of the Second World War in the Pacific region in 1942 interrupted this educational expansion. The Philippines became an independent republic in 1946, and much attention was given to education. During the period 1950–60, education was getting almost one-third of the country's annual budget. By the late 1960s, the school-age participation rates in the Philippines, particularly in the tertiary level, ranked among the highest in the world.

Increasing demand for higher education arose mainly from the massive expansion of the lower levels of the school system, the traditional social and economic prestige of possessing a college diploma, and the job entry requirements of minor supervisory and clerical positions in the government bureaucracy, as well as in the emerging technological sector of the country's economy. The resulting unrestrained and unsystematic expansion of tertiary-level institutions finally reached the point when the country experienced deteriorating quality of education, proliferation of low-cost degree programs, and acute surpluses and shortages of professional labor force in some specialized fields. This situation poses a great challenge to the future of tertiary level education in the Philippines.

1.1 Geographical Context

The Philippines is an archipelago of some 7,100 islands extending over 1,000 miles north and south and approximately 660 miles east and west with a total land area of 300,000 square kilometers. The three biggest islands are Luzon with a total area of 141,395 square kilometers, followed by Mindanao with 101,999 square kilometers and the Visayan Islands with 56,606 square kilometers. North of Luzon are the Republic of Taiwan and the Peoples' Republic of China, to the northeast is Japan, and to the south and southwest are the other South East Asian nations of Thailand, Kampuchea, South Vietnam, Laos, Malaysia, Singapore, and Indonesia. At its extreme southeast are Papua New Guinea, Australia, and New Zealand.

The country is classified into geographical administrative regions; provinces, 60 cities, 1,505 municipalities, and 40,162 barangays comprise the thirteen regions (NCSO 1982).

The population of the Philippines is one of the fastest growing in the world, averaging 2.7 percent annually, and increasing from 19.2 million in 1948 to 27.1 million in 1960. In 1980, the reported population was 48.1 million and in 1985, it was estimated to have reached 54 million (NCSO 1987 p. 117). The annual growth rate of the urban population was 5.02 percent from 1975 to 1980. The urban population comprised 37.23 percent of the total in 1980 (NCSO 1984 p. 14).

There are 87 known languages in the country. The ten leading languages spoken in private households in 1980 were: Tagalog, 29.6 percent; Cebuano, 24.2 percent; Ilocano, 10.3 percent; Hiligaynon/Ilonggo, 9.6 percent; Bicol, 5.57 percent; Lineyte/Samarnon, 3.98 percent; Pampango, 2.77 percent; Pangasinan, 1.84 percent; Maranao, 1.06 percent; and Maguindanao, 1.0 percent (NCSO 1982). The predominance of Tagalog speakers may be due to the fact that the emerging *lingua franca*, officially known as Filipino, is originally Tagalog based.

1.2 Occupational and Social Class Structure

Filipinos are a product of the mixture of East and West, culturally and racially. The people are predominantly Christian with the Roman Catholics comprising 85 percent of the total population. Other Christian sects are: Aglipayan, 3.9 percent; Protestant, 3.06 percent; and Iglesia ni Kristo, 1.3 percent. Islam accounts for 4.3 percent and Buddhism, 0.9 percent (NCSO 1987).

The social class structure may be described as a pyramid with a very broad base representing almost 70 percent of the population who are poor and live in rural areas, and a narrow tip corresponding to the 10 percent of very rich people who account for about 37 percent of the total household income in the country. The average income of the richest families is about twenty times that of the poorest (Cortes 1987 p. 14).

The proportion of gainfully employed 15-year olds and over engaged in agriculture in 1975 was 53.38 percent, decreasing to 51.4 percent in 1980. The second highest percentage of gainfully employed workers for the same age group were those in community, social, and personal services, comprising 17.12 percent in 1975, and 16.85 percent in 1980. Manufacturing accounted for the third highest percentage of gainfully employed workers, with 10.9 percent in 1975 and 9.66 percent in 1980 (NEDA 1983).

Distribution by major occupation group shows that agricultural, animal husbandry, and forestry workers, fishermen, and hunters comprised the biggest group of workers (51.8 percent in 1970, 53 percent in 1975, and 49.2 percent in 1980). The second biggest group is the production and related workers, transport and equipment operators, and laborers (21.8 percent in 1972, 19.7 percent in 1975, and 20.6 percent in 1980). Sales and service workers ranked as the third biggest group (13.9 percent in 1970, 15.6 percent in 1975, and 15.9 percent in 1980). The professional and technical and related workers ranked fourth (6.8 percent in 1970, 5.4 percent in 1976, and 6.6 percent in 1980), while the clerical workers comprised only 3.2 percent of the total gainfully employed workers in 1970, 4.1 percent in 1975, and 4.7 percent in 1980 (NEDA 1983).

In 1986, the country's labor force was estimated at 22.06 million. Of this number, 1.472 million or 6.7 percent were unemployed. Unemployment was higher for females. Waged and salaried workers accounted for 42.27 percent of the total employed, 40.4 percent were self-employed, and the remaining 17.29 percent comprised the unpaid family workers. Furthermore, 25.03 percent of the employed were elementary school graduates, 15.25 percent were high school graduates, and 9.56 percent, college graduates, while 4.89 percent had no qualifications (NSO 1987).

1.3 Structure of the Economy

The Philippine economy is supported by its agricultural sector. The agricultural sector accounted for 30.61 percent of the country's Gross Domestic Product (GDP) in 1986, the industry sector contributed 31.33 percent, and the manufacturing sector contributed 24.63 percent (NSO 1987).

The country's 10 leading exports in 1985 were copra, sugar, bananas, logs and lumber, desiccated coconut and coconut oil, canned pineapples, gold, abaca, and copper concentrates. Other nontraditional exports were manufactured electrical equipment and components, handicrafts, chemicals and chemical products, furniture, and so on. Its major imports were capital goods (e.g., machinery, electrical apparatus and appliances, and transport equipment), raw materials and intermediate goods (e.g., textile fiber, mineral fuels, lubricants, chemical elements, and feeding stuff for animals), and consumer goods, mostly foodstuffs and dairy products. The value of imports has been consistently greater than that of exports. The United States and Japan are the Philippines' top trading partners (NEDA 1986, NCSO 1982).

1.4 Structure of Government and Main Political Goals

In 1935, under United States rule, a transitory form of government aimed towards self-rule was introduced when the Commonwealth of the Philippines was established, as a republican form of government. With the outbreak of the Second World War and the occupation of the country by the Japanese, the Commonwealth Government, headed by President Manuel L Quezon, went into exile to Washington, DC.

On July 4, 1946, the Philippines became a fullfledged independent republic with the 1935 Philippine Constitution as the fundamental law of the land. This continued until 1971 when Ferdinand Marcos placed the country under martial rule. In 1973, a new constitution was proclaimed by Marcos. It provided for a modified parliamentary system similar in some respects to the British system. However, the 1973 Constitution was amended in 1981 and 1985 to return to the presidential system but with parliamentary features. Under this system, the president was the head of state and chief executive of the Republic of the Philippines. The prime minister was the nominee of the president, although elected by a majority of the members of the Batasang Pambansa, the legislative body. The president also appointed the ministers who composed his cabinet. The authoritarian and repressive rule of Ferdinand Marcos ended with the "people power" revolution of 1986 and the assumption of Corazon C Aquino as president of the Philippines.

The government of President Aquino is organized around the principles and policies set out in the constitution adopted on February 2, 1987. It declares the Philippines be a democratic and republican state. As such, "sovereignty resides in the people and all government authority emanates from them." Under the 1987 constitution, the legislative power is vested in the congress of the Philippines which consists of a senate and a house of representatives; the judicial power is vested in one supreme court and in such lower courts as may be established by law; and the executive power is vested in the president of the Philippines.

2. The Institutional Fabric of The Higher Education System

The Philippine school system consists of six years of elementary education (age 7 to 12 years old), four years of secondary education (age 13 to 16 years old), and at least four years to complete a first degree. First degree programs are available in agriculture, chemistry, commerce and business administration, engineering, food and nutrition, law, liberal arts, nursing, teacher education, mathematics, science, social science, and other fields. Master's and doctoral degrees are also available in these fields.

Institutions of higher education in the Philippines are predominantly privately owned. The Bureau of Higher Education of the Department of Education, Culture, and Sports formulates standards and minimum requirements for the operation of private schools. Once given permission to operate by the bureau, a private college or university is required to register with the Securities and Exchange Commission under the Corporation Law. It may be organized either as a stock or nonstock corporation with a board of trustees as its governing body. Most stock colleges and universities are family-owned or controlled. The government has been encouraging their conversion into nonstock, nonprofit making educational foundations so they can benefit from tax exemptions and long-term, low-interest loans from public lending institutions. Private colleges and universities are also classified as denominational or nondenominational. Denominational institutions are owned by religious groups. The country's oldest university is the Catholic University of St Tomas which sets its foundation as occurring in 1611.

Public institutions of higher education are classified into chartered and nonchartered institutions. Chartered state colleges and universities are autonomous, with no intervention from the Department of Education, Culture, and Sports, and are governed according to their respective charters. The oldest and the most prestigious chartered state university is the University of the Philippines (UP) founded in 1908. At present, the UP is a system with four autonomous campuses at Diliman, Los Baños, Manila, and the Visayas. Each campus specializes in specific fields of study: UP Diliman in basic natural science and social science disciplines and in some professional courses, UP Los Baños in agriculture and related fields, UP Manila in medical and health sciences, and UP Visayas in marine sciences.

Nonchartered public tertiary level institutions include vocational and technical institutions and community colleges that are directly supervised by the Department of Education, Culture, and Sports, schools of nursing associated with government hospitals, which are supervised by the Department of Health, and the Philippine Military Academy which is directly under the supervision of the Department of National Defense.

2.1 Admissions Policies and Selection

Admission to tertiary level education requires completion of ten years' elementary and secondary education, qualifying in the National College Entrance Examination (NCEE) and passing a college admission or entrance test administered by individual colleges and universities. The NCEE is given annually by the National Educational Testing and Research Center (NETRC) to high-school graduates seeking admission to first-year college. It was introduced in 1973 to regulate enrollment in academic degree programs and to minimize the observed mismatches between the supply and demand of professional labor force in the country. Since 1974, an average of 65 percent of candidates qualify in the NCEE.

State universities and colleges impose their own quota of first year students and have additional requirements for admission approved by their respective boards of trustees or boards of regents. On the whole, chartered colleges and universities have stricter admission policies than the nonchartered institutions. Similarly, nonstock denom-

inational private universities and colleges have stricter admission requirements than the stock, nondenominational private institutions.

Admission to some professional degree programs, for example, Bachelor of Laws, Doctor of Medicine, are governed by academic requirements prescribed by their respective professional board of examiners. For example, a bachelor's degree in a social science, humanities, or a related field is required of a student seeking admission to the Bachelor of Laws degree program. Admission to a College of Medicine requires that a student has a Bachelor of Science diploma. A Certificate of Eligibility for entrance to a medical school, issued by the Board of Medical Education, is also required. Colleges of Medicine run by private schools are also given a quota of first year students. The quota in 1986 was less than 4,500 (Task Force on State Higher Education Report, Vol. 3, 1987).

Many universities and colleges also give priority to first year applicants who belong to the upper 25 percent of their graduating class in high school and whose high-school grade point average is at least 85 percent.

In general, admission to graduate programs requires completion of an undergraduate degree program with concentration in a relevant discipline. In addition, a grade point average of at least 85 percent or its equivalent is required. Additional requirements such as proficiency in the English language, recommendations from former professors, and certification of good moral character are asked of the applicant for admission to graduate studies.

2.2 Quantitative Developments

The Presidential Commission to Survey Philippine Education reported in 1970 that the Philippines ranked second only to the United States based on the number enrolled in college per 10,000 of the population. The phenomenal growth of enrollment at collegiate level is indicated by these data: 300,752 in 1960; 628,798 in 1970; and 1,127,968 in 1985. Between 1960 and 1985, the size of the collegiate enrollment more than trebled.

Table 1 shows the percentage of state colleges and universities in relation to the total number of institutions of higher education in the country from 1960 to 1985. The data indicate that public universities and colleges assumed an expanded role in higher education. In 1985, 30.5 percent of higher educational institutions were state owned compared to only about 6 percent in 1970. This may be explained by the increasing demand for government support to collegiate courses in science, engineering, and technology, areas of study not offered in most private universities and colleges.

The geographical distribution of these universities and colleges in 1982 is shown in Table 2. Almost 56 percent of these institutions are located in Luzon,

Table 1
Number and percentage of public and private colleges and universities 1960–85

	1959–60	1964–65	1969–70	1974–75	1979–80	1984–85
Public	41	36	37	85	290	360
Percentage of total	10.0	7.2	6.0	12.3	29.1	30.5
Private	366	463	584	606	707	818
Percentage of total	90.0	92.8	94.0	87.3	70.9	69.4
Total	407	499	621	691	997	1,178

Sources: NEDA 1984, pp. 488–89, MECS 1984–85, NEDA 1986, pp. 446–47

specifically, Regions 1, 2, 3, 4, 5 and in the National Capital Region (NCR). Approximately 54 percent of the country's population reside in Luzon. The data also show that in 1982, there were 70 universities, 19 public, and 51 private. Twenty of these universities are in Metro Manila.

The share of the public universities and colleges of the total collegiate enrollment has also increased over the years as shown in Table 3. In 1985, enrollment in state-owned institutions was 15.3 percent of the total compared to only 10 percent in 1970.

The participation rate of the relevant college population (17–20 year-olds) in the Philippines is 24 percent.

2.3 Structure of Qualifications

The undergraduate or bachelor's degree program generally requires four years to complete. Engineering and dentistry each take five years; veterinary medicine, six years; law, eight years; and medicine, nine years. Law and medicine require that students have a bachelor's degree before they can be admitted to the degree program in these fields of study.

The master's degree generally requires four semesters of regular course work, a comprehensive written examination, a thesis, and defense of the thesis. In some state institutions, for example, in the University of the Philippines, the master's degrees in education and in public administration are of two types: Plan A and Plan B. The latter does not require a thesis but the student has to earn as much as 10 more academic units than the total academic units required under Plan A, which is from 30 to 34 units. Plan A requires a thesis.

A doctoral degree is a combination of course work for at least four semesters equivalent to approximately 42–48 academic units in addition to the master's degree, and research for the doctoral dissertation equivalent to 12 academic units. The candidate must successfully defend this before a panel of five to seven members who are recognized specialists or experts in the subject of the dissertation.

Table 2
Public and private tertiary level institutions by region 1982[a]

Region	Public			Private			Total
	Universities	Colleges	Subtotal	Universities	Colleges	Subtotal	
I[c]	3	25	28	4	54	58	86
II[d]	2	15	17	1	23	24	41
III[e]	1	24	25	4	60	64	89
IV[f]	1	34	35	2	102	104	139
V[g]	1	21	22	4	56	60	82
VI[h]	1	53	54	4	57	61	115
VII[j]	0	22	22	7	32	39	61
VIII[k]	1	40	41	1	14	15	56
IX[l]	1	20	21	0	24	24	45
X[m]	1	18	19	2	48	50	69
XI[n]	1	14	15	5	59	64	79
XII[o]	2	8	10	1	31	32	42
NCR[b]	4	6	10	16	131	147	157
Total	19[a]	300	319	51	691	742	1,061

Source: MECS 1981–82. PASUC *Profiles of Philippine State Universities and Colleges in the 80s*
a Includes the two autonomous units of the UP system (UPLB, UP in Visayas) and Pamantasan ng Lungsod ng Maynila
b NCR—National Capital Region (Manila) c I—Ilocos d II—Cagayan e III—Central duzon f IV—Southern Tagalog g V—Bicol h —Western Visayas j VII—Central Visayas h VIII—Eastern Visayas l IX—Western Mindanao m X—Northern Mindanao n XI—Southern Mindanao o XII—Central Mindanao

Table 3
Enrollment in tertiary education 1965–66 to 1984–85 (in thousands)

	1965–66	1966–67	1967–68	1968–69	1969–70	1970–71	1971–72	1972–73	1973–74	1974–75	1975–76	1976–77	1977–78	1978–79	1979–80	1980–81	1981–82	1982–83	1983–84	1984–85
Public	59	61	62	62	65	67	72	76	89	98	106	114	123	152	184	185	179	194	211	230
Private	468	493	539	565	573	584	614	667	702	614	666	685	710	997	1,025	1,069	1,128	1,155	1,180	1,274
Total	527	554	601	627	638	651	686	743	791	712	772	799	833	1,129	1,209	1,254	1,307	1,349	1,391	1,504

Source: MECS 1985, p. 17

3. Governance, Administration, and Finance

3.1 National Administration

By a constitutional mandate, all educational institutions are under the supervision of and subject to regulation by the state. Authority to supervise and regulate educational institutions is exercized by the Department of Education, Culture, and Sports. Higher education institutions, however, enjoy academic freedom (Art. 14, Sect. 4 (2), 1987 Constitution). Academic freedom is specified in the Education Code of 1982 as "the right of institutions of higher learning to determine on academic grounds who shall be admitted to study, who may teach, and what shall be the subjects of study and research" (Para. 2, Sect. 13, Chap. 2).

The 1987 Constitution further provides that "the State recognizes the complementary roles of public and private institutions in the educational system . . ." (Sect. 4 (1) Art. 14) and that "the control and administration of educational institutions shall be vested in the citizens of the Philippines" (Sect. 4 (2) Art. 14).

The Education Act of 1982 provides for the organization of a board of higher education whose main functions are: (a) to make policy recommendations regarding the planning and management of the integrated system of higher education and the continuing evaluation thereof; (b) to recommend to the Minister (now Secretary) of Education, Culture, and Sports that the governance of the various components of the higher education system at the national and regional levels be improved; and (c) to assist the Minister (Secretary) of Education, Culture, and Sports and make recommendations relating to the generation of resources and their allocation for higher education (Sect. 61, Chap. 2).

The Bureau of Higher Education should provide staff assistance to the Board of Higher Education in its policy formulation and advisory functions and technical assistance to encourage institutional development projects. So far, however, the Bureau of Higher Education has concentrated on the regulation and supervision of private colleges and universities.

3.2 Institutional Administration

The governance of a chartered college or university at the institutional level is in accordance with the charter or law that created or established it. This system makes a chartered institution a state corporation and therefore covered by the Corporation Code of the Philippines. Besides the charter and Corporation Code, a state college or university is also governed by laws promulgated on various aspects of its governance, programs, and operations. In addition, the Philippine legislature processes and approves laws and policies on education.

Each chartered college or university has a governing board whose members are called trustees for colleges and regents for universities, appointed by the president of the Philippines subject to the confirmation of the Commission on Appointments. The Secretary of Education, Culture, and Sports or a delegated representative sits as ex officio chairperson of the board with the president or head of the institution as vice-chairperson. Governing boards have the power to approve programs, curricula, budgets, and appointments, and to hire or fire school heads (Task Force to Study State Higher Education, Vol. 3, 1987).

Except for the University of the Philippines, Mindanao State University, and Mariano Marcos State University which exercize fiscal autonomy, all state colleges and universities are virtually controlled by the Office of Budget and Management through the budgetary mechanism.

Nonchartered state colleges are directly supervised and controlled by the Department of Education, Culture, and Sports and their annual budgets are integrated in the department's annual budget.

Private colleges and universities, as earlier mentioned, are governed by their respective boards of trustees according to the Corporation Law. They are supervised and subject to the regulation of the Bureau of Higher Education which formulates the minimum standards for the operation of private schools and maintenance of quality education.

3.3 Finance

Private colleges and universities are largely dependent on tuition fees for their operations. Other sources of income are capital contributions of stockholders, loans from institutional lenders, investment income, and donations. Student and other fees account for as high as 96 percent of the total income of stock corporations and about 86.5 percent of educational nonstock corporations (Zwaenepoel 1975 pp. 326–27). The rising cost of education and the corresponding increase in tuition fees have caused yearly mass protests against tuition fee increases by students and other groups.

The heavy dependence on tuition fees among private colleges and universities has resulted in inadequate funding which in turn has led to the proliferation of low-cost curricular offerings, for example, teacher education, business and commerce, and liberal arts; the absence of research activities; and the poor quality of education in most private institutions of higher education.

Between 80 and 90 percent of the total budget of state colleges and universities is provided by the government. The remaining 10–20 percent comes from tuition fees. The share of the state system of higher education in the annual national budget for education averages approximately 16 percent. This amount is shared by 78 state colleges and universities. The University of the Philippines gets a substantial share of the budget for higher education.

4. Faculty and Students: Teaching, Learning, and Research

4.1 Faculty

The total number of teachers in both public and private colleges and universities increased from 26,708 in 1970 to 41,690 in 1980 and to 54,691 in 1985. The proportion of teachers to the total in the state-owned tertiary institutions rose from 13 percent in 1970 to 16.4 percent in 1985 (MECS 1985 p. 26). However, state-owned institutions have more faculty members with master's and doctoral degrees (44 percent) compared to only 24 percent among the faculty members of private colleges and universities (FAPE 1975, Pada 1988).

By field of specialization, approximately 25 percent of the faculty are in teacher education, 15 percent in business administration and commerce, and 12 percent in engineering and technology. Faculty members with specializations in physical sciences, mathematics, and biological sciences represent less than 12 percent of the total collegiate faculty (HERC 1971).

The salaries for faculty members of tertiary institutions are not competitive with the salaries offered by business/industrial establishments and government corporations. With the exception of a few private colleges and universities, salaries are higher for teachers in state-owned tertiary institutions. In addition, there is greater stability, security of tenure, and opportunity for career advancement for teachers in public colleges and universities.

Recruitment policies and procedures governing tertiary level teachers differ from institution to institution. However, the most common recruitment practices are by oral or written invitation, formal application, and encouraging the institution's outstanding graduates to join its faculty.

The criteria for recruiting a faculty member include academic qualifications, experience and training, grades obtained in college, and personality. Religious affiliation is an important consideration in denominational schools. In state colleges and universities the recommendation of an influential person in government and/or the community is also important in the selection of an applicant for a teaching position (Zwaenepoel 1975).

The formal appointment to a faculty position in state-owned tertiary institutions is made by the institution's board of regents or board of trustees upon the recommendation of the president or head of the institution, in consultation with the appropriate lower level academic officials, starting with the department chairperson. The same pattern exists in private tertiary institutions. Appointments may be either temporary or permanent. An initial appointment to a faculty position is usually temporary and lasts for three years, after which, if the individual meets the criteria such as appropriate educational qualifications and marked scholarly performance in teaching, research, and extension work, he or she is issued a permanent appointment.

Faculty ranking in state colleges and universities is determined by a set of criteria for each rank. By and large, the system provides four ranks; in ascending order these are instructor; assistant professor; associate professor; and professor. Within each rank is a range of steps for salary promotion. Promotion is determined by a markedly higher level of academic performance, academic growth, and moral integrity. A promotion requires the approval of the institution's board of regents or board of trustees.

In the private sector, the Manual of Regulations for Private Schools provides a ranking system similar to that of state colleges and universities, and the suggested criteria for the ranking of faculty members, for example, a master's degree for assistant professor and preferably a doctoral degree for associate professor and above. Years of experience, teaching efficiency, scholarship, and character, are other criteria suggested. However, this ranking system is not implemented in all private tertiary institutions (PSCPE 1970). This may be due to the inadequacy of funds available especially among schools classified as stock corporations.

In state colleges and universities academic load includes teaching, research, and extension work. The regular teaching load ranges from 9 to 12 hours per week. The load for graduate courses is one and a half times that for undergraduate courses. Teaching beyond the regular teaching load merits additional pay according to the rate for overtime fixed by the board. Salaries of teachers in state-owned tertiary institutions are computed on a monthly basis; full-time faculty members have to spend 40 hours a week in the institution, 10 hours of which must be available for consultation with students.

The teaching load in private colleges and universities is regulated by the Manual of Regulations for Private Schools which considers 18–24 hours of teaching per week as the normal teaching load (Zwaenepoel 1975). As teachers in private tertiary institutions are paid according to the actual number of hours taught, it is not surprising that the regular teaching load in private colleges and universities is much higher than in state-owned institutions. It is not unusual to find a teacher in a private college or university assigned to teach different subjects requiring three or more preparations.

Faculty members of public colleges and universities are, under the Civil Service Law, entitled to sick leave, retirement benefits, and life and health insurance. They are insured with the Government Service Insurance System (GSIS). They are also entitled to a living allowance and yearly bonuses. In addition and in accordance with policies and rules approved by their respective institution's board of trustees or board of regents, the faculty members are provided such professional advancement benefits as study grants, scholarships, tuition fee discounts for their dependants, sabbatical leave, and financial assistance for attendance at national and international conferences. Reduced teaching load is also enjoyed by a faculty member who engages in research/creative work and extension service. Some state universities and colleges like the University of the Philippines, Mindanao State University, and Central Luzon State University provide housing to the faculty based on certain criteria.

In the better funded private tertiary institutions, the faculty enjoy the same benefits as those granted to faculty members of public tertiary institutions. Under the Medicare Act of 1969, faculty members of private colleges and universities, as members of the Social Security System (SSS)—the insurance system for employees in the private sector, are automatically entitled to hospital beds if necessary. A few private colleges and universities, mainly denominational institutions, provide housing for faculty members. Housing loans are, however, available to SSS members.

No permanent appointment of a faculty member in a state college or university can be terminated without strong cause and only then after strict procedures. The same rule applies to faculty members of private schools. Temporary faculty members who are under probation can be dismissed without such procedures. A faculty member, whether temporary or permanent, can always terminate a contract after its expiration in a private college or university.

The Education Act of 1982 specifically states that in addition to other rights provided by law, all school personnel shall "enjoy the right to free expression of opinion and suggestions, and effective channels of communication with appropriate academic and administrative bodies of the school or institution . . . and the right to establish, join and maintain labor and/or professional and self-regulating organizations of their choice to promote their welfare and defend their interests" (Chap. 2, Sect. 10). Faculty members of most colleges and universities have their respective organizations to assert and protect their rights. The Association of Concerned Teachers (ACT) with membership from teachers of all levels of the formal school system is the most militant teacher organization in the country. It not only works for teachers' rights and welfare but also takes an advisory position on national issues which do not concern education.

4.2 Students

Colleges and universities continue to register an extremely uneven distribution of enrollment among the different disciplines. During the school year 1968–69, teacher training, business administration and commerce, and arts and humanities attracted the biggest number of students, absorbing 80 percent of the collegiate enrollment for that year. In 1980–81, the three most popular academic degree programs, accounting for 64 percent of the total enrollment, were business administration and commerce, engineering and technology, and the medical sciences. Teacher education, which registered 33.6 percent of the enrollment in 1969, dropped to 7.4 percent of the enrollment in 1980–81. The physical sciences continued to be the least popular, accounting for an average of 0.4 percent of the total enrollment during the same period. Agriculture and related fields averaged 0.5 percent of the total collegiate enrollment (see Table 4).

The data on college graduates from both the public and private institutions are, unfortunately, not available. However, data on graduates for 1969–70 from the private colleges and universities appear to reflect

Table 4
Undergraduate enrollment in government and private tertiary institutions by major field of study

Program/major field of study	1968–69	Percentage	1978–79	Percentage	1980–81	Percentage
Agriculture and related fields	3,190	0.5	63,871	7.0	54,553	4.4
Arts, social science, humanities	114,877	19.0	107,977	12.0	85,978	7.0
Commerce and business administration	164,228	27.3	321,541	35.0	442,581	35.6
Engineering and technology	57,517	9.5	170,816	19.0	225,404	18.1
Fine arts/music	7,616	1.2	15,208	1.4	9,612	0.7
Home economics, food, nutrition	3,263	0.5	13,150	1.4	13,899	1.1
Law and foreign service	16,120	2.7	23,374	2.6	24,451	2.0
Medicine and related medical science	27,384	4.5	95,294	10.5	123,367	10.0
Physical science/maths, science	2,453	0.4	4,068	0.4	5,119	0.4
Teacher training and education	202,463	33.6	63,543	7.0	92,359	7.4
Other courses (technical, vocational, nautical science)	2,798	0.4	29,743	3.3	166,146	13.3
Total	601,989	100.0	906,585	100.0	1,243,469	100.0

Source: MECS 1982

Table 5
Number of students by field of study in private schools
1969–70

Major field of study	Male	Female	Total
Agriculture	551	38	589
Chemistry	56	164	220
Commerce and business administration	12,191	15,511	27,702
Engineering and technology	5,151	314	5,465
Food, Nutrition, and Dietetics	1	871	872
Law and foreign service	1,382	261	1,643
Music and fine arts	550	174	724
Liberal arts	5,606	8,219	13,825
Medical science	614	3,142	3,756
Nautical studies	693	2	695
Teacher training	8,112	33,039	41,151
Graduate level	262	432	694
Undergraduate level	34,907	61,735	96,642
Total	35,169	62,167	97,336

Source: Zwaenepoel 1975 p. 654

the pattern of enrollment by field of study. The largest number of graduates occurred in business administration and commerce, teacher education, and liberal arts (see Table 5). The popularity of these course programs may be attributed to the fact that they are low-cost academic degree programs that do not require heavy capital investment in laboratories, scientific apparatus, and salaries for qualified faculty that are in short supply. This situation has led to imbalances in the supply and demand for college graduates and the twin problem of "educated unemployed" and the "brain drain."

Research has shown that children of the upper socioeconomic classes are the least likely to drop out of school and the most likely to proceed to college. An empirical analysis of the scores in the National College Entrance Examination revealed that in general, for the Philippines as a whole and for each province, scores in the NCEE increased with the socioeconomic variables of parental education and family income (Tan 1976). This finding is corroborated by other studies (MECS–EDPITAF 1976, Tan 1975, Manlapaz 1976, Ibe 1985).

A random survey of students enrolled in 12 private universities from eight regions of the country in 1975 showed that 27.3 percent of college students belonged to the upper class, 37.3 percent to the upper-middle class, 24.3 percent to the middle class, 9.1 percent to the lower-middle class and 1.9 percent to the lower class. The social classification was based on three variables: income; education; and occupation of parents (Sanyal et al. 1981 p. 101).

Most colleges and universities have organizations such as a student council which provides the forum for students' opinions and concerns. Chapter 2, Section 9 of the Education Act of 1982 stipulates that students and pupils in all schools have "the right to form, establish, join and participate in organizations and societies recognized by the school to foster their intellectual, cultural, spiritual, and physical growth and development, or to form, establish, join, and maintain organizations and societies for purposes not contrary to law." Furthermore, students have the right to "publish a student newspaper and similar publications." The board of regents of the University of the Philippines has a student regent representing the student body of the university.

Assessment of the academic performance of a student is exercized exclusively by the teacher in whose subject the student is enrolled. The most common forms of assessment other than class participation and attendance are: quizzes; midterm examination; final examination at the end of the term; and a term paper.

Every college or university has its policies and rules governing scholastic standards and delinquency which every member of the faculty observes in evaluating student performance. Academic progress is likewise covered by rules and policies adopted by the faculty of the university. The same is true of the academic requirements for graduation or completion of a degree.

5. Conclusion

Higher education in the Philippines faces serious problems concerning equity and quality. The notion of equity relates to fairness in the distribution of access to the nation's educational resources and services, while quality implies the satisfaction of a set of standards or criteria of relevance and excellence in the inputs, process, and outcomes of education.

The Philippines have one of the most expanded systems of tertiary level education in the world with the participation rate of its relevant college-age population exceeding those of Great Britain and the Soviet Union. Competing claims on the nation's resources from equally important national concerns mean that the Philippine school system is perennially beset by the problem of inadequate funding. Under the state policy of making available free public education at the elementary and secondary levels, tertiary level education necessarily receives a small share of the country's annual budget for education. Higher education has to rely on the private sector for financing.

Two-thirds of the nation's colleges and universities are privately owned. Many are nondenominational stock corporations largely dependent on private investment and tuition fees. Private colleges and universities patronized by children of the rich and upper-class families are fortunate. They can charge fees which make possible the hiring of better qualified teachers, maintenance, and improvement of their physical and library facilities, and better quality instruction. The remaining private colleges and universities have to adjust their tuition fees to the socio-economic origins of their students, otherwise these institutions will face the possibility of closure due to lack of students.

The law granting a subsidy to students enrolled in private colleges and universities charging moderate tuition fee rates is the government's response to this problem. The subsidy is intended to absorb any increase in tuition fees that may otherwise be charged by the private institutions. Whether this law will help foster equity and quality in higher education in the Philippines remains to be seen. Attaining quality and equity is by no means dependent only on tertiary institutions' increasing tuition fee rates, but on how much of the tuition fees is used to benefit the faculty and improve library and school facilities. Moreover, to achieve the goals of equity and quality at the tertiary level the same goals must be attained in elementary and secondary education.

Bibliography

Arcelo A 1988 Financing education in the Philippines. Paper presented at the First Round Table Discussion on a Legislative Agenda for Educational Development in the Next Decade. Congress of the Philippines, Department of Education, Culture and Sports, Makati

The 1935 Philippine Constitution. In: Mendoza V V (ed.) 1978 *From McKinley's Instruction to the New Constitution.* Central Lawbook Publishing Co., Quezon City, pp. 183–220

The 1973 Philippine Constitution. In: Mendoza V V (ed.) 1978 pp. 211–54

Cortes J R 1987 *Education and National Development: The Philippine Experience and Future Possibilities.* Publishers Printing Press, Quezon City

Fund for Assistance to Private Education (FAPE) 1975 *The Philippine Atlas*, Vols. 1 and 2. Manila

Higher Education Research Council (HERC) 1971 Higher education in the Philippines. A report to the Senate Committee on Education. Manila (mimeo)

Manlapaz R 1976 Democratization of the University's admission policies. *UP Newsletter.* Quezon City, September 20

Ministry of Education and Culture 1976 *Survey of Outcomes of Elementary Education.* Educational Development of Implementing Task Force (EDPITAF), Ministry of Education, Culture and Sports, Makati

Ministry of Education, Culture, and Sports (MECS), Bureau of Higher Education 1982 Tertiary education in the Philippines, Schoolyear 1981–82 (mimeo)

Ministry of Education, Culture, and Sports 1985 *Philippine Indicators, 1965–85.* Ministry of Education, Culture and Sports, Manila

Ministry of Education, Culture, and Sports 1985 *Statistical Bulletin, SY 1984–85.* Ministry of Education, Culture and Sports, Manila

Ministry of Education, Culture, and Sports, Task Force on State Higher Education 1987 Report on State Universities and Colleges in The Philippines, 3 vols. (mimeo)

National Census and Statistics Office (NCSO) 1982 *Journal of Philippine Statistics.* Manila, 3rd Quarter

National Census and Statistics Office 1984 *Statistical Handbook of the Philippines.* Manila

National Census and Statistics Office (NCSO) 1987 *Philippine Yearbook, 1987.* Manila

National Statistics Office (NSO) 1987 *Philippine Yearbook, 1987.* Manila

National Economic and Development Authority (NEDA) 1984 *Philippine Statistical Yearbook, 1984.* Manila

National Economic and Development Authority 1986 *Philippine Statistical Yearbook, 1986.* Manila

National Economic and Development Authority 1983 *1980 Census of Population and Housing*, Vol. 2. Manila

Pada F S 1988 The State Colleges and Universities: Problems and prospects. Paper presented in a Round Table Discussion on a Legislative Agenda for Educational Development. Congress of the Philippines and DECS, Makati

Presidential Commission to Study Philippine Education (PCSPE) 1970 *Education For National Development: New Patterns, New Directions.* PCSPE, Manila

Philippine Association of State Colleges and Universities Profiles of Philippine State Universities and Colleges in the 80s

Sanyal B, Perfecto W S, Arcelo A 1981 *Higher Education and the Labour Market in the Philippines.* UNESCO, Paris

Tan E 1975 UP Admission and tuition policy. Paper presented to the University of the Philippines Program Development Staff. December 1975

Tan E 1976 Income distribution in the Philippines. In: Encarnacion J et al. (eds.) 1976 *Philippine Economic Problems in Perspective.* UP Institute of Economic Development, School of Economics, pp. 214–61, Quezon City

Zwaenepoel P P 1975 *Tertiary Education in the Philippines, 1611–1972.* Alemar-Phoenix Publishing House, Manila

Batas Pambansa Blg. 232 (The Education Act of 1982) In: Ministry of Education, Culture and Sports *Journal Supplement*, February 1983, pp. 20–54

The 1987 Constitution of the Philippines. Supreme Court of the Philippines, Manila 1987

J. R. Cortes

Poland

1. Higher Education and Society

Poland is situated exactly in the geographical center of Europe and is bordered by the Soviet Union to the east, Germany to the west, and Czechoslovakia to the south. Its territory covers 120,350 square miles. The Second World War brought about a shift in Polish boundaries. As a consequence of agreements made at Teheran, Yalta, and Potsdam, Poland lost 69,290 square miles of territory in the east and gained 39,587 square miles in the west. Millions of Poles were moved from the eastern to the western territories. As a result, mass migrations brought almost every third Polish family into a new geographical setting, and it was many years before the new communities became integrated social systems.

Of the 35 million prewar citizens of Poland, over 6 million perished in the Second World War—i.e., 220 out of every 1,000 people. However, the postwar natural population increase was rapid. In 1938 it had been 10.7 per thousand, it rose to 14.9 in 1947, and in 1953 reached the postwar peak of 19.5. Only in 1958 did it begin to drop, decreasing to 17.9, after which it steadily went down, reaching 6.0 per thousand in 1987. As a consequence the population in 1989 was almost 38 million.

It is a homogeneous population with only about 5 percent from ethnic minorities. About 95 percent of the people are Roman Catholic. It is also a relatively young population: in 1987, out of a population of 37,571,000, 12,187,700 were under 19 years (over 32 percent). Taking into consideration that school education is free, the numerous age groups are a lasting pressure on the state education system. In 1987, 60.9 percent of the population were city dwellers. Although the rural population is still high, about 40 percent of those in rural areas are employed outside agriculture.

1.1 Economic and Social Class Structure

In 1987, over 17 million Poles were employed: over 71 percent (12.3 million) in the public sector, with the remainder in the private sector. The nationalization of important sections of the economy was a major factor in efforts to transform Poland into a socialist society, in keeping with the Soviet model. The Second World War destroyed the fabric of interwar society, but that society would still have been capable of resurrection. However, in 45 years of postwar history the macrostructure of Polish society has been changed by two essential processes: the transformation of the traditional social classes and the emergence of a new differentiation and stratification due to the workings of a socialized economy, a new political order, and technological progress. The existing socialist society has become industrialized, with a complex economy and centralized political institutions requiring highly structured hierarchical organization. As a result functional differentiation has developed.

The transformation of the traditional social classes resulted first in the disappearance of some of the traditional upper class groups: the land-owning class, the aristocracy and the landed gentry. A similar fate met the second-ranked upper class: the Polish business class. The remaining four traditional classes: the intelligentsia, the workers, the peasants, and the class of urban small producers also changed in composition, structure, and functions. The intelligentsia and the workers were slowly transformed into a complex of institutionalized occupational categories. The peasantry, steadily decreasing in numbers under the impact of industrialization and urbanization, mass media, and so on, was transformed into farmers and worker-peasants—that is, farmers simultaneously employed in industry or other branches of the economy outside agriculture. The Marxist–Leninist dream of a classless society did not come true. Property, income, level of education, prestige, position in the hierarchy of political power, and occupation still remain the important factors of social differentiation and stratification.

In such a stratified society, education has been a major factor in social mobility, although in the 1980s diplomas of higher education lost their value as factors of upward mobility due to economic crisis and a pronounced slowdown in economic growth. However, an examination of the social and occupational composition of the labor force still reveals categories requiring higher education. Although most senior posts require higher education, not every higher education diploma leads to high social position. As in every society, education is not the only factor affecting upward mobility.

The Polish society established after the Second World War has been a "political society," where the political institutions were the generating forces of social processes. The most important creation of this political system has been the socialized economy. All of the numerous revolts in Poland have been caused by economic shortcomings. The Marxist ideological model made clear that the main objective of the socialist economy is to provide the satisfaction of the needs and wants of every section of the population. The chief traits of such a socialized economy are: collective ownership of the means of production; central planning and management; limited autonomy of enterprises; free choice of occupation, place of work, and consumer goods, within the limits of state-assured supply.

One can distinguish several periods in the postwar development of the Polish economy: (a) reconstruction, (b) basic industrialization aimed at construction of heavy industry, (c) complementary industrialization with some emphasis on consumer goods, and (d) a period of permanent reform. In all these periods, however, some major economic problems remained unsolved. The first is organization; that is, finding effective methods of planning and ensuring that the management and the labor force is capable of achieving the planned targets. The second unsolved problem is that of work motivation and the third, following on from this, has been low productivity. The fourth problem has been how to ensure the flexibility and continuing modernization necessary to keep up with technological and scientific progress. Out of 17,244,600 employed Poles, 4,860,000 are in agriculture, 4,916,000 in industry (559,600 in the extractive industries), 1,338,800 are in construction, and 6,130,000 in other branches of the economy. The main problem of the Polish economy is still low productivity and the low quality of products, high foreign debts, and discontent among the labor force. In the period 1987–89 the relatively high level of inflation was seen as the main factor in the economic crisis. Such a state of the economy had an important impact on the educational system and on higher education as well. To recapitulate, East European socialist societies are political societies, which means that political criteria are foremost in the evaluation of every aspect of social life, public or private.

1.2 Structure of Government and Main Political Goals

Poland was ruled by the communist Polish United Workers Party (PUWP) until the election in June 1989. These elections consolidated the powerful movement for political reform, and changed the nature of the established order. The opposition won a strong position in the lower chamber of the parliament and an absolute majority in the senate. Thus, for the first time in postwar Polish history, the government was a coalition of many political forces, without a power monopoly of the Communist Party. Since the 1989 election, several political parties have been involved in government: Christian Democrats, Social Democrats, Liberals and others. In all these new political movements teachers and students of higher education have played an important role.

1.3 Relationships with Religious Bodies

Relations between higher education and religious bodies were under the control of the ruling party, and as a result there was little formal interaction between them. However, the Roman Catholic Church has always played a powerful role and religion is important to many students. There is one private Roman Catholic university in Lublin and two state-supported theological academies. In its resistance to Marxist atheism and ideology the Roman Catholic Church gained the support of the masses. Even if not directly engaged in politics, the great movement of Solidarity in the 1980s would never have gained such an influence in political life and such a victory in the 1989 elections, without the able and far-seeing support of the Church.

At the end of the 1980s, Polish society was in transition from the unfinished political and economic order of Soviet socialism, towards a new, as yet undefined form. The Communist Party had to recognize the power of the Christian faith and feelings of national identity, the power of political opposition, and the form of parliamentary democracy emerging from the various strivings of diverse social and political groups, organizations and unorganized forces. As educational institutions are linked with society by various ties, so the impact of changes in society are also felt in educational processes, as the following analysis will show.

2. The Institutional Fabric of the Higher Education System

The first Polish university was founded in Krakow in 1364, the second in Vilna in 1578, and the third in Lwów in 1661. Between the two world wars, 32 institutions were organized with 49,500 students enrolled in 1938. Those institutions employed 2,460 professors and teaching assistants, and 3,409 auxiliary nonacademic teachers. This system of higher education was destroyed during the Second World War and the Occupation. All institutions of higher education were closed, the teaching staff dispersed and about 750 members of Polish academia died on the battlefields, in prisons, and in concentration camps.

In 1944, with the liberation of the Polish territories, there also began the process of reconstruction and development of a new system of higher education. This system is now an integral part of the state school system. The educational doctrine forming the model of that system was based on the following principles:

(a) There is continuity of teaching on all levels of the system.

(b) The system tries to secure equal opportunity of admission to secondary and postsecondary levels.

(c) All types of schools, vocational or professional, must provide elements of general education enabling leavers to participate in cultural, social, and political activities.

(d) Admission to secondary, vocational, and higher education is in principle a guarantee of employment.

(e) Graduates from all schools of a given type have the same rights, and all diplomas of a given type are equal by law.

(f) Curricula are established to secure a similar scope of knowledge and skills required in a given vocation or profession.

(g) It must be possible for graduates of any level to enroll in the next highest level, up to higher education.

(h) Educational planning in the whole system is based on a consideration of labor force needs.

(i) Education in the schools is based on principles of socialist ideology.

These principles were applied with varying degrees of stringency in the educational policy of the government departments responsible for the education of youth, training of adults, and the supply of labor to the economy. However, the everyday reality was also determined by the aspirations and expectations of parents and pupils which often produced modifications in the model.

2.1 Levels of Institution

In 1990, the system of higher education in Poland comprises: 11 universities, 18 technical universites and colleges, 9 agricultural academies, 5 economic academies, 10 teacher training colleges, 11 medical academies, 2 naval colleges, 6 colleges of fine arts, 8 colleges for music, 3 colleges for theater and film, 6 colleges for gymnastics and sport, 1 social science academy, 2 theological academies. Out of these 92 institutions only two are in private hands: the Roman Catholic University in Lublin, and the Social Science Academy run by the Central Committee of the PUWP. All others are state institutions financed by the government from public funds. This does not include the military schools run by the Ministry of Defense.

The difference between secondary education and institutions of higher education is defined clearly: secondary education transmits knowledge to students; higher education additionally creates knowledge through research. Higher education faculty are under an obligation to conduct research because they are expected to use the results of their own research in their teaching. The institutions of higher education are divided into two categories. Those engaged in basic research continue the tradition of general education, theoretical sciences, and training researchers. The second category is that of colleges giving professional training and diplomas, and conducting mostly applied research. The dividing line is not always clear. Of course universities, the oldest and most prestigious type of higher education, stand at the top of the hierarchy, but in a socialist society polytechnics and other institutions directly linked with the economy are the most appreciated.

Research is regarded as an essential and integral part of higher education, although there are research institutions outside higher education. The Polish Academy of Sciences has a system of research institutions, and there is a system of research linked with ministries, working directly for various governmental agencies. Institutes of higher education receive some funds for contract research from various sources. However, their importance is in basic research and in the training of research personnel. The quality of that training decides the quality of the research personnel in the Academy of Sciences and all other research institutions. Every institute of higher education has its own projects financed by budget or by contracts with various firms. Both sources usually involve public funding. The participation of higher education in the entire research and development outlay in 1987 was over 21 percent. Universities and colleges have engaged a considerable portion of their research potential in the so-called major research program, which are government sponsored, or so-called key problems, regarded as essential for development of theory in all branches of sciences, including the humanities and social science. Higher education employs about 75 percent of higher qualified research personnel working in all research institutions in the country. There were 85 institutes of higher education in 1970, 91 in 1980, and in 1989 the number increased to 92. The number of institutions tends to be stable, but the number of students is more volatile.

2.2 Admissions Policies

The rules for admission to higher education are uniform throughout the country. A precondition for applying is the certified completion of secondary school. The basic criterion for admission is the entrance examination, but the winners of special contests and competitions in given subjects in secondary schools can be admitted to higher education without having to take the entrance examinations. Enrollment is based on the so-called points system. The conversion of examination marks into points, with their scale being expanded, permits more precise differentiation regarding qualification for particular studies. The total sum of points is awarded for the entry examination, good marks in secondary school, preuniversity periods of employment, and sometimes for social background and various other, more transient, criteria. The aim is both to select talented students, and to ensure a more equal composition of the student body. There is a continual search for better predictive criteria for selection which will also ensure recruitment of students from all social strata in Polish society. Graduation from an institute of higher education not only signifies the acquisition of professional skills and the right to a profession, but also involves a kind of social "ennoblement," a crossing over into a higher social stratum. Therefore admission to higher education opens the possibility not only of a professional career but also of social mobility.

Total enrollment rose steadily in the 1960s and 1970s and dropped in the years of economic crisis in

Table 1
Changes in enrollment figures in higher education

	1960	1965	1970	1975	1980	1987
Enrollment	166,000	252,000	331,000	468,129	489,300	339,144
Per 10,000 population	55.6	79.8	101.3	136.9	126.9	90.7

Table 2
Distribution of students in higher education institutions 1987–88

Institutions	Total	Daytime	Evening	Extra-mural	Extension
Universities	119,069	88,035	302	29,651	1,081
Technical	63,809	55,699	905	7,067	138
Agricultural	34,760	26,190	—	8,285	285
Teacher training	40,651	24,901	—	15,991	59
Economic	18,770	14,043	105	46,622	—
Medical	34,765	34,508	—	258	—
Naval	2,379	2,039	77	256	7
Arts	7,473	6,296	793	384	—
Sport	13,163	9,009	—	4,107	47
Social Science	2,086	263	—	966	733
Theological	2,219	1,268	—	951	—
Total	339,144	261,951	2,182	73,394	1,617

the 1980s. The changes are shown in Table 1. The distribution of students in institutions in the 1987–88 academic year is shown in Table 2.

Some additional information is necessary. One noticeable trait is the high percentage of women in the student body—about 50 percent. The highest percentage of women (73.8 percent) were in teacher training colleges, 63 percent were in universities, 62 percent in medical academies, 59 percent in economic academies, and 53 percent in arts colleges. The second trait is the relatively high percentage of adults: 23 percent of the total enrollment of evening courses, and extramural and extension courses is made up of students gainfully employed. In the years just after the Second World War that percentage was considerably higher. The admission of working persons as students has had important consequences in bringing higher education closer into contact with firms employing graduates. It is difficult to give the exact percentage of the 19–24 age group because of the unknown percentage of adults in the full-time group of students, but in 1970 it was approximately 9 percent, in 1980 it had risen to about 12 percent, and in 1987–88 was about 11 percent.

2.3 Structure of Qualifications

Higher education courses, depending on type of institution and discipline, last on the average of four to six years. An academic year has two semesters, at the end of which credits are awarded for courses taken and examinations passed. After having passed all compulsory examinations, students prepare theses which, along with the final examination, are the bases for graduation and the award of the diplomas indicating various specializations. Medical studies last six years terminating in a cycle of final examinations, but not requiring theses. A doctoral degree is awarded to graduates after they have submitted their doctoral theses, and passed a viva, and the

requisite examination. A higher doctoral degree is necessary for appointment to a full professorship, and requires another thesis. All diplomas are awarded by institutions of higher education. There is no clear-cut division between undergraduate and graduate studies. Some colleges can confer a so-called "professional" diploma which is different from the title of Magister which is regarded as the lowest "scientific" title. In principle, most students try to obtain the title of Magister, permitting them to go on to obtain a doctoral degree.

What do society and the state expect to get from higher education? What are the purposes and functions of higher education in the life of society? The Higher Education Act, passed by parliament in November 1958, and amended several times since, defines the following purposes for every institute of higher education:

(a) Instruction of qualified personnel for all jobs in the economy, culture, and all sectors of public life;

(b) education of scientific labor for all research and development institutes, and the education of academic teachers;

(c) advancement and dissemination of research by publications and application;

(d) political and civic education to prepare students for political activity, voluntary associations, and community life;

(e) preparation for participation in culture and promotion of the cultural heritage of the nation;

(f) education for self-fulfillment; and

(g) the rendering of services for communities where the institutions are located. The leading principle governing activities in the institutions is to fulfill these purposes with "unity of teaching, education, and research." Priority is given to teaching, and the effectiveness of higher education is basically evaluated by the numbers and quality of graduates and their professional performance.

3. Governance, Administration, and Finance

Institutes of higher education in Poland, with two exceptions—the Roman Catholic University in Lublin and the Academy of Social Sciences in Warsaw—are state institutions supervised by the government ministry of education. Institutions of higher education are established, dissolved, and transformed by act of parliament. The Minister of Education is responsible for the implementation of state policy in higher education, coordinating, supervising, and controlling the activities of all institutions. Schools operate according to their statutes, adopted by the senate after prior consultation with the official university committees operating in the given school. The general principles for management of higher education are determined by the fact that education is an integral part of a planned economy society and must therefore meet labor force targets and ensure congruence between education and projected employment. Since admission to any institution of higher education is also a guarantee of employment, the government must try to match admissions with the demands for graduate employment. Up to 1989, there existed a strictly organized system of higher education management and the planning of enrollment and teaching was part of economic planning. Since the events of 1989, the system has begun to be radically changed and the Higher Education Act reshaped to meet the demands of the newly elected pluralistic parliament. Higher education will certainly be given greater autonomy, although institutions of higher education will remain state units, financed by the state budget, and consequently the government will still "call the tune." The parliament will determine the budget of higher education, which will be free, as is the case in the whole of the school system, but institutions will have more say on the curricula and content of teaching.

Institutions of higher education are headed by rectors, who are elected for three years by their respective senates from among two to four candidates approved by the education minister. Normally only a professor can be a rector but, in exceptional circumstances, an assistant professor holding a higher doctoral degree can qualify for the post. Thus, a rector must be a research worker and have proven research achievements.

Every institution is divided into branches called in Poland *facultet* or *wydział* which is, on occasions, somewhat more comprehensive than a department in an American university—for example, a *wydział* of social sciences might include departments of sociology, anthropology, social psychology and so on,

each of which in the United States would form separate departments. *Facultets* are headed by deans elected by the *facultet* council for a three-year term. Only professors or assistant professors can be candidates. The candidates are approved by the rector, in consultation with the Minister. *Facultets* are composed of specialized institutes, headed by directors elected by their institute councils, and of chairs, divisions, and sometimes other auxiliary units. Senates and *facultets* councils make up the self-government of schools. Their members are selected from professors and assistant professors, teaching assistants, students organizations, and representatives of school administration employees. Senates and councils perform advisory functions for the rectors and deans. With the progressive democratization of higher education, these bodies are taking over larger decision-making functions. Student associations are also growing in importance and influence.

The law on higher education provides for the setting up of the Council of Science and Higher Education, an elected organ representing all the institutions of higher education in the country. It establishes the main lines of research and training of academic staff; advises on the preparation of draft plans of higher education development, plans of study and curricula; and contributes to the elaboration of state policy in the field of higher education.

4. Faculty and Students: Teaching, Learning, and Research

4.1 Faculty

An academic career in Polish higher education involves many steps: Usually it begins after obtaining the MA degree, with a job as a junior teaching assistant. The assistant is engaged by and under the direction of a professor, who, after one or two years, may propose advancement to senior teaching assistant. This post carries some teaching duties and the obligation to participate in research. When assistants get their PhDs, they become "adjuncts" and have greater teaching and research duties. Usually within six years, they must prepare new theses for *Habilitation* which conveys the title of "docent" which is the first professorial rank. After having taught successfully and had work published, a docent may be promoted to the rank of associate professor, and then, after several years, become a full professor. The adjuncts who do not complete their *Habilitation* thesis may become lecturers or senior lecturers, which are not professorial posts. In the academic year 1987–88 Polish institutions of higher education granted 2,380 PhD degrees (of which 654 went to women) and 624 degrees of *Habilitation* (of which 124 were women).

Between the 1960s and 1980s academic staff expanded rapidly, as shown in Table 3.

Table 3
Development of teachers in higher education

	1960–61	1965–66	1970–71	1975–76	1980–81	1985–86	1987–88
Full professor	587	653	656	721	871	1,063	1,135
Associate professor	1,001	1,072	1,194	1,688	2,067	2,403	2,577
Docents	1,461	1,944	4,099	5,345	5,391	5,769	6,170
Adjuncts	4,067	5,968	6,690	11,706	18,143	22,451	22,636
Senior assistants	6,677	6,258	9,252	14,090	13,700	10,318	9,468
Assistants	2,389	2,824	3,752	5,368	4,648	4,264	3,956
Lecturers	1,277	1,960	3,301	4,383	5,342	11,137	12,426
Total[a]	18,600	22,486	31,320	48,837	54,681	57,280	58,398

a Auxiliary teachers included in total are not enumerated separately

In 1987–88 the average ratio in all institutions of assistants to professors was 3.9 assistants and adjuncts for each professor and docent. The ratio of students and teachers at the same time was 33.6 students for each professor and docent, and 8.6 for each adjunct and assistant.

The procedure of advancement for professorial rank is initiated by the *facultets* council. Three full professors must present positive evaluations of the candidate. The motion, approved by senate and the rector, is sent to a special Central Qualifying Commission which approves the proposals and transmits them upwards to government. Finally, the State Council nominates the new professor. It is thus not a university but a state nomination. Once nominated professors are irremovable, except on the decision of a court of justice. However, the State Council can refuse the nomination. The new Higher Education Act passed in September 1990 will introduce some changes in the process of nomination. It should be stressed that in the lengthy process to become a professor, candidates are required less to prove their teaching abilities and skills than their abilities and skills in research work.

The teaching load of academic faculty is in principle defined in the Higher Education Act, but senates and *facultets* councils tend to decide otherwise. The load changes depending on type of school and discipline. Teachers doing some administration work, such as deans, have their teaching load reduced. There are also some research only posts. A teacher engaged in important research can have his or her teaching load reduced by the dean of *facultet*.

4.2 Students

In Polish higher education, some methods of planning seek to match the real needs of society and the economy with a supply of properly trained graduates. But before 1989 no such effective method had been found. As can be seen from Table 4 the stress has been on technical sciences, economics, and medical sciences rather than on agriculture and humanities, social sciences. Only in the 1980s under pressure from social demand, were large numbers of students admitted to courses in the humanities. The labor force approach to planning in higher education has been steadily changing under the impact of unforeseen developments. Plans for socioeconomic growth were changed after the previously projected number of students were already enrolled. There may also be changes in investments and so on. Also, factors indicating the anticipated number of graduates in any given period, once taken into consideration, often proved false.

In 1987, 55,267 students graduated from all institutes of higher education. Of these, 15,558 were from technical universities and colleges, 4,203 from agricultural institutions, 5,964 from economic institutions, 3,116 from law and administration institutions, 12,953 from humanities and social sciences institutions, 4,702 from science institutions, 5,094

Table 4
Number of students in the main disciplines of study[a]

	1960–61	1965–66	1980–81	1985–86
Technical	55,945	92,080	145,900	84,900
Agricultural	10,934	18,325	40,500	23,300
Economics	21,477	31,827	54,500	34,800
Law/administration	10,234	17,973	32,000	19,900
Humanities/social science	21,428	34,185	84,100	87,100
Science	15,160	26,528	36,600	32,700
Medicine	23,728	22,121	35,100	34,200
Sports	1,877	2,841	13,500	12,300
Arts	3,712	4,570	7,800	7,600
Total	165,687	251,864	453,700	340,700

a Some disciplines have not been separately enumerated (e.g., theology), but they are represented in the total

from medical institutions, 1,898 from sports institutions, and 1,263 from arts institutions.

In each year of study students must attend the requisite courses, participate in seminars, and pass the required examinations in order to progress to the next year. Certain courses are compulsory, others are elective. Curricula are established by a commission composed of professors and approved by the appropriate ministry. Teaching is under the supervision of deans and examinations are administered by those who teach the subjects. Different concepts of curricula are under ongoing discussions. One calls for encyclopedic, formal, and utilitarian education. A second stresses general education, basic professional knowledge, and leaves specialized knowledge for systematic adult education linked with employment. The concept of lifelong education is regarded as the solution for many problems. The Higher Education Act provided for institutes of higher education to offer special courses for adults, including refresher courses. Such graduate studies constitute an integral part of higher education programs. They are organized as extramural, evening, and full-time courses. The majority of adult students enroll in two-semester courses. However in the 1980s the number of courses and students decreased considerably, as a consequence of the economic crisis.

An important field of activity is research on higher education. The first institute set up to conduct research into higher education was the research group at the University of Łódź. Its task was to study sociopedagogical problems connected with the adaptation of students and schools, to social life, graduate employment, and so on. In 1962 it was reorganized as an institute in its own right and moved to Warsaw. In 1973 it was reorganized again as an Institute for Science Policy and Higher Education. The main fields of research were: improvement of teaching and learning processes, organization and management of higher education, relations between institutions and their environment, financial and material bases of higher education, employment of graduates, the use of the educated cadres, and international and comparative studies. In the 1980s more attention was given to the modernization of higher education. Research is carried out by the staff of the Institute in cooperation with teams from other institutions of higher education. The Institute publishes several series of monographs and studies, two periodicals and a bibliography of higher education.

5. Conclusion

Like the whole of Polish society, higher education at the end of the 1980s was in turmoil due to the political reforms which were changing established structures of political life. In the election of June 1989 many professors presented themselves as candidates for the senate and the parliament and (20 for senate, 20 for sejm) were elected, mostly as members of the opposition. Students have been occupied with organizing new independent unions and demonstrations, and struggling for more institutional autonomy. The new Higher Education Bill aims to increase self-government, and give more votes to students and assistants in *facultets*, councils, and senates. It represents a strong reaction to the domination of the Communist Party in higher education, although this domination has eroded since the workers' revolt in 1980. However, the political upheaval is linked with the economic slump, and the considerable diminution of the budget for higher education, with a resulting slowdown in research, the limitation of contacts with educational institutions abroad, and a growing unrest in institutions.

The changes in the political system, the return to parliamentary democracy, brings with it the hope for new trends in the development of higher education, although the economic situation of the country will cause considerable hardship in that process. However, the general evaluation of the performance of the system must be positive. In 1987 the nationalized sector of the economy employed 1,078,000 graduates of higher education, and the census has shown 1,679,000 citizens with higher education qualifications. The system of a planned economy did not always permit full use to be made of their skills and knowledge, but in the process of political and economic reform they are playing an essential role.

Note: All statistical data quoted in this article are taken from the official *Statistical Yearbooks of Poland*, published every year by the Central Statistical Office.

Bibliography

Adamski W 1983 *Education and Careers in Today's Poland.* European Institute of Education and Social Policy, Paris

Januszkiewicz F 1985 Poland: System of Education. In: Husen, T, Postlethwaite T N(eds.) 1985 *The International Encyclopedia of Education.* Pergamon, Oxford, p. 3951–54

Józefowicz A 1982 *Manpower and Education Planning.* UNESCO, Paris

Józefowicz A, Kluczyński J 1980 *Determinants and Options in the Development of Higher Education in Poland.* UNESCO, Paris

Kluczyński J 1979 *Educational Trends and Prospects in Poland.* UNESCO IIEP. Paris

Kluczyński J 1987 *Higher Education in Poland.* CEPES, Bucharest

Kluczyński J, Sanyal B C 1985 *Education and Work in Poland.* UNESCO, Paris

Sanyal B C, Józefowicz A 1978 *Graduate Employment and Planning of Higher Education in Poland.* UNESCO, Paris

Słomczyński K, Krauze T 1978 *Class Structure and Social Mobility in Poland.* M E Sharpe, White Plains, New York

Szczepański J 1978 *Systems of Higher Education: Poland.* ICED, Paris

J. Szczepański

Portugal

1. Higher Education and Society

Higher education in Portugal began in 1289, when the *Studium Generali* was set up, in Lisbon, which contained the *universitas* of master and students. This university was founded on the initiative of the King of Portugal and the bishops, and approved in a papal bull by Pope Nicolaus IV in 1290. The university followed the usual course pattern of medieval universities in Europe at that time. It was moved to Coimbra in 1308, came back to Lisbon in 1338, and then definitively settled down in Coimbra in 1537. Meanwhile, several colleges were opened, closed or transferred. In 1559 a new university was set up in Évora which was run by Jesuits only to be closed in 1759.

With the advent of the Enlightenment and liberal ideals during the eighteenth century, several schools of higher education were established initially according to the French Napoleonic model, and later taking over many of the concepts of the German university.

On the eve of the Republican Revolution (1910) there were already enough schools in Lisbon and Porto to enable them to merge and form two new universities. An almost explosive expansion of higher education began in the 1970s.

1.1 Geographical Context

Portugal is an old country located on the extreme periphery of Western Europe. Its existence, as an independent country, goes back to 1142, and the present borders have remained almost unchanged since 1251. The continental part of Portugal has borders on the north and east with Spain, and the west and south with the Atlantic Ocean. Also part of Portugal are the Madeira and Azores archipelagos, both on the Atlantic.

From the fifteenth century, Portugal established a large colonial empire, which, at its greatest included parts of India, the Far East, Africa, and Brazil in South America. Part of her Far East possessions were taken over by the Netherlands and the United Kingdom during the last centuries, and Brazil became independent in 1822. The remains of this vast colonial empire became independent this century: Goa (India) in 1961, and five territories in Africa in 1975. There still is one non-colonial territory under Portuguese administration: Macao, in China, which will be restituted in the year 2000. The Portuguese educational system still works there. To date, the territorial extension of Portugal represents 91,631 square kilometers, with the state capital in Lisbon.

1.2 Population and Economy

During the second half of the twentieth century, the Portuguese population moved towards the coastal areas and the main urban areas. In the early 1990s, almost one-quarter of the entire population is located in and around Lisbon. Nevertheless, the major population concentration and density remains in the north west part, where Porto City is the regional pole.

The population has grown since the Second World War, although only slightly. Two main population movements caused some irregularities: the flux emigration towards Europe, Africa, and America in the 1960s, and the return of half a million European residents from the former Portuguese colonial territories in Africa.

The evolution of the population was as follows (figures in thousands): 8,065.4 in 1945; 8,479.9 in 1950; 8,727.4 in 1955; 9,076.7 in 1960; 8,979.6 in 1965; 8,863 in 1970; 9,093.4 in 1975; 9,766.3 in 1980; and 10,157.0 in 1985.

Of the entire population in 1981 (last population census) 29.7 percent were residents in towns of 10,000 inhabitants or more. Population ageing in Portugal follows the European patterns, though slower, mainly because of the rural population still present. Portugal is rather homogeneous as regards ethnicity and language. Ethnically it is European. The original stock of Iberians has been added to for centuries in different but significant proportions, of Celts, Phoenicians, Romans, Moors, Goths, and Jews. During the colonial empire, some Hindus and Africans were also absorbed though despite this variety there remains a very broad homogeneity.

In the early 1990s, there are still some minuscule minorities, including Gypsies, and Africans.

In 1988 the occupational structure of 4,372,700 working people, showed 19.8 percent in the primary sector, 34.9 percent in the secondary sector (including extractive industries), and 45.3 percent in the tertiary sector. In this latter sector, compared to the entire working population, 6.5 percent were in public administration, and 4.8 percent in education. Most of this sector also belong to public administration.

Although the population involved in the primary sector is still large, compared with other European countries, by the end of the Second World War,

Table 1
The distribution of the occupational structure

	Percent
Executives and higher administrative staff	1.69
Professional and scientific occupations	8.04
Administrative and commercial staff	21.98
Qualified workers	34.20
Personnel, home, and security services	12.16
Agricultural workers	19.56
Nonqualified workers	1.97
Others	0.39
Total	99.99

this sector covered about half the entire working population. The decline in this sector is continuing; transfers go to the tertiary sector, the secondary sector being almost stationary. The distribution of the occupational structure is given in Table 1.

The balance of the Gross Domestic Product (GDP) in 1986 shows a broad picture of the economic structure: 10 percent for the primary sector; 37 percent for the secondary sector; and 53 percent for the tertiary sector.

1.3 Structure of Government and Main Political Goals

The "Pink Revolution" of April 25, 1974, overthrew the authoritarian regime established after 1933, ruled for years by Salazar. This was a one-party regime, inspired by Italian corporative fascism, but also very close to the Christian Roman Catholic tradition.

The revolution led to the loss of the remaining colonial empire in Africa. This, and the return of the Portuguese expatriate population from there, also brought to Portugal a large scientific and academic labor force, working in two universities and several research institutions. This staff, qualified and experienced, provided most of the human resources for the development of the new universities and polytechnics set up at that time.

When the dust of the revolution settled, a new democratic regime emerged, and is still in place. The three usual powers, legislative, executive, and judicial, sit in the *Assembleia de República* (parliament), the Government, and the Courts.

The parliament is elected every four years, and today includes five political parties from the right to left. The government consists of a Prime Minister and several ministers, state secretaries, and under secretaries. The Prime Minister is appointed by the *Presidente da República* (Head of the State) who is elected in a general election every five years. The Ministry of Education which has a State Secretary for Higher Education supervises the entire educational system, both public and private.

Table 2
Number of higher education institutions

	1960	1965	1970	1975	1980	1985
Universities	4	4	4	7	11	12
University schools and faculties	19	22	22	31	41	44
Nonuniversity schools[a]	1	1	2	15	13	19
Arts schools[b]	6	6	6	4	4	3
Private schools	5	7	9	10	13	17
Total	31	36	39	50	71	83

Source: *Estatísticas da Educação*, Lisboa
a Includes polytechnic schools after 1973   b They have been integrated into polytechnic system

After an increase in the number of state universities during the 1970s, since stabilized, policies have emphasized the development of the polytechnic system of higher education, and selective support to private higher education. A further trend is to compensate the centripetal concentration of population by setting up new institutions of a polytechnic nature, everywhere, to promote regional development and to lessen regional imbalance. The same applies to the Atlantic islands where there is one university in the Azores, and another in Madeira.

2. The Institutional Fabric of the Higher Education System

Portugal has been a secular state since the Republican Revolution (1910), which overthrew the monarchy when the Roman Catholic Church formed part of the state apparatus. Nevertheless, after the first republic, which ended in 1926, the "new state" had close ties and an explicit alliance with the Church. In spite of this binding relationship, the state never allowed the Church to have its own university. Only by the end of the regime was the Catholic University permitted to open its doors. Although this situation was never clear, it was after the leftist Revolution in 1974 that the Catholic University expanded, under privileged conditions which were set out in the former *Concordata* years before. The Catholic University is today a rather large network spread across the nation, with several schools located in different places, but all under the authority of the University Rector, in Lisbon. Such a privileged situation is not found in any other religious group, or in any other part of the private sector in higher education.

After the 1974 Revolution, the private higher education system gradually emerged and developed. In the early 1990s, private higher education represents about one fifth of schools, and one tenth of students (see Table 2).

Different types of higher education developed after the Second World War in three distinct periods: from 1945 until the 1973 reform; from 1973 to the 1986 reform; and from 1986 onwards. The first period drew a net distinction between the university sector and the nonuniversity. Parallel to higher education were several institutions in the middle range, between secondary and higher education—technical college (industrial, commercial, and agricultural) and teacher-training college—types which in time merged into the higher education system.

The reform of 1973 introduced a new type of higher education institution: the polytechnic. Inspired by the British model of the same name, these short-cycle institutions were to be strongly involved with their region and of the ten envisaged only two were set up. At the same time, some new universities were established. The 1974 Revolution retained this

Table 3
Proportion of students aged 20 to 24 receiving higher education

Students	1960	1965	1970	1975	1980	1985
University sector	19,522	26,647	43,627	52,681	64,978	62,914[b]
Nonuniversity sector[a]	239	278	394	12,471	7,605	10,850
Fine arts schools	1,140	1,109	1,658	2,561	2,733	1,607
Private sector	378	653	2,225	2,673	8,219	12,871
Total	21,279	28,687	47,904	70,386	83,535	88,242
Proportion of the age group 20 to 24 years (percentage)	3.23	—	7.63	—	10.87	—

Source: *Estatísticas de Educação*, Lisboa
a Includes polytechnic schools after 1973   b Data from University of Porto not provided

solution, but immediately upgraded the technical colleges (*escolas, institutos médios*) to higher education status, similar to the polytechnic model, despite students claiming university status. Much later, and following recommendation and support from the World Bank, teacher-training colleges were closed and new "schools of education" were set up, inserted into the polytechnic system.

The 1986 reform clarified the entire system which now includes just two types of higher education: university institutions (universities or university schools nonintegrated into universities); and polytechnic institutions bringing together several different schools. Apart from the more professional/vocational nature of the polytechnic school, the main difference lies in the prerogative of the university to award higher degrees (master's and doctorates), which the polytechnic is not entitled to do.

In general, polytechnics include teacher-training schools, technological and management/accountancy schools, agricultural schools, and arts schools (drama, cinema, dance). Fine arts have university status. Universities include sciences, medicine, pharmacy, agriculture and veterinary sciences, physical education, engineering, architecture, law, economics, social sciences, psychology, philosophy, and the humanities. Fine arts are in the process of being integrated into universities.

New universities also include teacher-training schools, for all levels of teaching, according to the university model (secondary teaching) and to the polytechnic model (primary and infant teaching). Research is done in universities as well as in separate institutes. There are some major independent institutions which work under ministries other than the Ministry of Education. These cover fields like agriculture (including animal husbandry, veterinary science, and food technology), fishing and fisheries, civil engineering, and technology. Other minor independent institutions also exist in several fields.

Due to the existence of the former colonial empire, a specialized institution devoted to overseas studies is kept on. This is the Tropical Medicine and Ethnology Institute. Most of these studies are carried out in cooperation with other research institutions and universities.

2.1 Admissions Policies and Selection

In terms of control, admission policies, since the Second World War have been shared between higher education institutions and the secondary education system. Until the 1974 Revolution, admissions to all higher education faculties, which defined their own criteria, were open to all whose complete upper-secondary course corresponded to the requirements of the university course. In certain cases, high marks in secondary education permitted free entrance into higher education. Since 1975 two radical changes have taken place. First, the *numerus clausus* has been introduced, with restrictions on entrants. This meant that some candidates were not given places in higher education. Second, a national agency was set up to coordinate all admission policies. The criteria for selection were based on secondary education results ordinarily complemented by a national examination, which has undergone some variations.

In 1989 a new system was introduced which combined the marks attained in secondary education, with a national examination on general culture and mastery of the Portuguese language, and some specific examinations at institutional level, if desired. This system has been changed over the following years. To summarize, admissions policies have been unstable, and it seems they will remain so for some years to come. The Comprehensive Law on the Education System (1986) laid down the main criteria based on a disciplinary match between secondary education options and a particular university or polytechnic course. It stated that any secondary course can provide access to any higher education course,

Table 4
The development of the student body

Students/Graduates		1960	1965	1970	1975	1980	1985[c]
Exact sciences[a]	Students	11,035	13,223	20,490	31,878	37,042	33,687
	Graduates	895	1,032	1,679	5,302	4,944	2,724
Social sciences	Students	5,040	7,507	12,959	21,763	27,622	38,262
	Graduates	304	522	762	2,870	2,706	3,270
Humanities[b]	Students	5,240	7,957	14,455	16,745	18,871	16,772
	Graduates	317	570	260	1,435	3,131	2,265
Totals	Students	21,279	28,687	47,904	70,386	83,535	88,721
	Graduates	1,516	2,124	2,701	9,607	10,781	8,259

Source: *Estatísticas da Educação*, Lisboa
a Including technology/engineering, and medical sciences b Including fine arts c Data from University of Porto not provided

provided the candidate submits to a specific examination on entry to higher education. The reformed system, just referred to, answers this policy.

Development of the student body by broad specialized fields is shown in Table 4 as well as the corresponding outputs in terms of graduates.

Since the nineteenth century a dual system has existed with two first degrees, of different lengths and with different social standing. In the early 1990s, the first and lower degree, called the *bacharel* (bachelor), lasts three years, and the higher first degree, called the *licenciado* (licenciate), lasts four to six years, depending on the course.

The *bacharel* degree is awarded by polytechnics, and can also be awarded by universities for teacher-training courses. The *licenciado* degree is the usual first university degree. Polytechnics and universities can also award a diploma, called *diploma de estudos superiores especializados* (diploma on specialized higher studies) which is equivalent, for academic and professional purposes, to the *licenciado* degree. This diploma requires a previous *bacharel* degree.

All degrees are awarded by the university institutions themselves, but the studies which leads to those degrees needs to be validated by the Ministry of Education and published in the *Diário da República* (the official journal). Private schools are also entitled to award diplomas and degrees in accordance with the degree system described, but they also need to be officially validated.

Until the early 1990s graduate programs were exclusively based on preparation for the doctorate.

Applicants for a PhD have to present a thesis before an examination committee. The thesis is based on original research carried out under the supervision of a university professor. The doctorate was, and still is, essentially required for an academic career. Doctorate training is a typically closed scheme inside the university for internal purposes.

Since the 1980s new graduate training has been introduced based on the *mestrado* (master's degree).

This model combines course work with a final dissertation. It takes two to three semester courses, and although specialized, also has options which are linked to the field in which the main subject belongs (e.g., education, engineering, economics, etc.); it involves the presentation of a dissertation at the same time. The *mestrado* combines research initiation with depth of subject and professional specialization.

This program, which is still under development, has opened up and enlarged graduate training, and is demanded mainly from outside the university. It acts as an important reinforcement to the scientific and technological human resources needed for national development. Also it has been determinant in enlarging the polytechnic system of higher education.

3. Governance, Administration, and Finance

3.1 National Administration

Both public and private sectors of higher education are under the strict supervision and control of the Ministry of Education. Portugal is a unitary country, strongly centralized; hence, decisions on higher education are in the hands of the state. Usually, higher education institutions have been founded by government decree. Courses and study programs also depend on Ministry authorization. In 1989 a new law was published, the *Lei da Autonomia Universitária* (law on university autonomy), which ensures more autonomy to the universities in these and other matters. Private schools also require authorization to open and operate.

Planning higher education has varied with time, though it has been done exclusively inside the Ministry of Education. The so-called "new" universities were planned at the beginning of the 1970s as a national plan. However, most of the more recent development has been a result of a combination of central political decisions and regional claims.

The polytechnic network was also planned alongside the new universities in the same way. The development of higher education was stopped after the 1974 Revolution, and restarted and replanned after the normalization period: that is, from 1976 onwards. The development of the polytechnic network has been more technical/economic than political, in contrast with the university network. Even this national program was stimulated and partially supported by the World Bank.

The reasons for negotiation, in both cases, came from both sides. In spite of it, there is a special consensus, a sort of corporative consensus, about university goals, and the system runs by itself. In formulating ministry or parliament policies about higher education, in general, and university education, in particular, the university is never absent, either through explicit claims or the lobby. In the polytechnic system, weaker and younger compared to the university, the policies applied are more firmly dictated by the Ministry.

Most of the financing of public institutions of higher education comes from the State Budget each year. Varying from institution to institution, some work is done from external requests and provides additional money. A rough estimate is that such a financial inducement accounts for no more than 10 percent of the institutional budget.

3.2 Institutional Administration

Although there are similarities between university and polytechnic, the differences are important enough to be noted.

Typically, any university has at the top the *reitor* (rector), with large administrative powers, assisted by some *vice-reitores*, and, in a few cases and for particular matters, by *pro-reitores*. The main decisions on scientific and academic matters are taken within the main influential body, the *Conselho Científico* (Scientific Council). A doctorate is essential for belonging to this council.

The council has the power to approve study programs, the recruitment and advancement of teaching staff inter alia. Alongside, there is also the *Conselho Pedagógico* (Pedagogic Council) which mainly runs the routine implementation of educational policies passed down from the scientific council. In financial and administrative matters, the *reitor* is assisted by the *Conselho Administrativo* (Administrative Council). The *reitor* was traditionally appointed by the Minister of Education. In the late twentieth century election is the general rule, though. The electoral system varies from university to university, but a common feature is an electoral body, including representatives from teaching staff (doctors and nondoctors), students, and administrative staff, with different weighting for each particular corps. The *reitor* is elected for three years. He appoints the *vice-reitores* and the *pro-reitores*.

In both faculties/schools or departments, there are elected bodies of directors, the chairperson being elected from their ranks.

The polytechnic system is still under the steering committee, and all academic authorities are appointed by the Ministry. A similar law of autonomy is under study.

There is no common pattern of academic organization and there are also differences between the two systems of higher education, universities and polytechnics. Traditionally, universities are groups of schools, a more traditional designation being the faculty. In the twentieth century, names like institute, or even school, are employed with the same meaning as faculty.

Changes in the 1970s created pressures for the acceptance of the department structure, following the Anglo-Saxon pattern. This policy has succeeded in the new universities. However, even in these universities a tendency to revert to the traditional model of organization based on the school, is discernible. In the faculty model, the responsibility of running academic life belongs to a Directive Council (*Conselho Directivo*), elected within the faculty itself, composed predominantly or even exclusively by staff with doctorates. In the departmental model a similar body of academic administration exists, but with less formal powers. The polytechnic system lacks as yet a coherent model of organization, which is still undergoing study and experimentation.

4. Faculty and Students: Teaching, Learning, and Research

4.1 Faculty

Table 5 gives the evolution of the number of faculty teaching staff. In both systems, university and polytechnic, assistants and professors are civil servants. However, at the beginning of their career, appointment is on a one-year contract. At a more advanced stage it is on a two-year contract. Tenure is reserved only for the top ranks. To start a career in both systems, one must hold a licenciate degree with good marks (14/20 as minimum). The development of careers is differentiated between the two sectors.

In the university, the career ladder is as follows. For *assistente* advancement requires a probationary period of a minimum of three years, and a candi-

Table 5
Development of faculty teaching staff

Teaching staff	1960	1965	1970	1975	1980	1985[a]
Full-time	1,093	1,450	2,337	6,561	8,865	7,208
Part-time	—	—	—	—	—	3,290

Source: *Estatísticas da Educação*, Lisboa
a Data from University of Porto not provided

582

dature which requires either a master's degree or a public examination plus a dissertation at the same master's level. Access to the rank of professor starts with the rank of *professor auxiliar* which requires a doctorate. Advancement to *professor associado* depends on a competition based on a nonpublic examination of the candidate's curriculum vitae. Finally, the *professor catedrático* (full professor) requires a public examination, called *Agregação* (aggregation).

For the polytechnic system promotion for assistants is based on evaluation of work done every three years. Access to the rank of *professor adjunto* requires in general a master's degree, but in some cases a holder of the *licenciado* degree and qualified professional experience can be appointed. Access to the rank of *professor coordenador B* requires a competition via public examination. *Professor coordenador A* requires the *agregação* like the university full professor. Recruitments are the responsibility of individual institutions, but need to have administrative confirmation from the *Tribunal de Contas* (the Audit Court) (a special national court which judges the legality of formal and financial government procedures).

In general, corporate interests of the academic body are expressed through the university lobby, though some teaching staff are affiliated to teachers' trade unions. Such unions are of a vertical nature, and represent all levels of teaching, for primary school to higher education. They are distinguished by their ideological and political affinities. This is the reason why the lobby itself is more influential and powerful than trade unions. The *reitores* of all universities are assembled in a *Conselho de Reitores* (Rectors' Council). It has no executive powers, but its influence is considerable and its opinions are listened to by the Ministry. Sometimes the council also serves as a vehicle for academic staff interests.

The polytechnic system is less venerable and has not yet developed a similar scheme, and therefore trade unions are more influential. There is also a *Conselho Coordenador do Ensino Politécnico* (Coordinating Council for Polytechnic Education) with similar functions to the Rectors' Council, though much less influential.

Time allocation for teaching is under Ministry regulation, on a national basis. Individuals teach between six and twelve hours weekly. The average is nine to ten. Also, as a national rule, any individual has to work a 35-hour week in the institution, like any other civil servant. In practice, the difference between the total working time and time assigned for teaching, is split between research, institutional duties, and a varying amount of external institutional services. This does not necessitate a strictly physical presence on site. Research and external services are a matter of personal initiative and departmental leadership. Research is also stimulated by the *Instituto*

Nacional de Investigação Científica (National Institute for Scientific Research)—a special department within the Ministry of Education, which finances investments in equipment, distributes individual grants for research and study visits abroad, and helps authors to publish their research. In the early 1990s links with the economy (industry, business, and even government departments) have been increasing, and provide funds for research and development (R & D) work. Academies, foundations, and so forth, afford opportunities and some support for research work, namely in the social sciences and humanities. A new policy based on setting up some interface institutions, with higher education and other public bodies (enterprises and government departments) for joint work in some particular fields, is under development.

4.2 Students

The few systematic studies about social class origins of students reveal the dominant social class origin to be the lower-middle class, including the technical and management classes. Given the relative proportion of the different social classes within the whole population, the upper- and lower-middle classes are overrepresented in the student world while the working class is underrepresented.

Before the 1970s the dominance of the ruling class was much more marked. The expansion of other social classes, namely those of lower status, began from the 1970s onwards. It is still proceeding, and coincides with higher education expansion. Another feature is the rise of female attendance in higher education (see Table 6).

Student associations have developed in two different periods: before the 1974 Revolution; and after. Before 1974, only a few student associations were tolerated, and these were generally school-based. The old Coimbra University retained student association across the whole university. Permission to create new associations was not given. Thus some unrecognized pro-associations undertook national meetings, under different forms and denominations, which eventually mobilized students into mass movements, explicitly critical of the government and the regime.

After the 1974 Revolution, support to all emergent student associations was given, but the legal frame-

Table 6
Percentage growth of female participation in higher education

	1960	1965	1970	1975	1980	1985[a]
Students	33.5	39.6	46.2	41.7	45.3	52.1
Graduates	37.2	44.6	39.6	46.4	50.3	55.8

Source: *Estatísticas de Educação*, Lisboa
a Data from University of Porto not provided

work came out only in 1987. However, even without this legal framework, there was plenty of financial support from the state, or through different political groups and parties, or even from some minor groups, ranging from the extreme left to the extreme right. Universities also encouraged student associations and supported their running; this political cycle ended in 1979 to 1980. Since then, the larger group has been linked to government and the major political parties. The struggles to politically control the student associations is an open and a fierce one. A few associations began to seek greater independence, a movement which is still developing.

In the early 1990s, there are about 70 to 75 student associations, generally one per school, with the exception of Coimbra University. At the same time, there is a trend towards regionally based associated federalism. The focus of association interest is changing from the institutional policies (participation, access to higher education, and national welfare) to more general societal concerns: employment; European integration in 1992; and corporative interests in sectoral terms. The economic dimension prevails over the political dimension. With the support of the industrial and business sectors, student associations tend to operate in accordance with the enterprise model. Student passivity and conformism are flourishing.

4.3 Courses, Learning, and Assessment

First-degree courses are the responsibility of individual establishments whose Scientific Council is the only authority entitled to pronounce on and approve of every course scheme. Notwithstanding, a sort of Ministry ratification will be necessary to implement it. However, the recent law on university autonomy devolves them full authority on this matter.

The internal design or redesign of all courses may be initiated by any department, or even by the controlling bodies of the establishment. It is currently a matter of bargaining between all interested parties.

The university has recently implemented a credit system. Yet, the long tradition of fixed and unified course design, the free or quasi-free choice of subjects has little in common with such a system. Polytechnics still maintain the policy of unified courses, and the credit system does not apply.

Assessment rules are the responsibility of the institution. The *Conselho Pedagógico* at universities and Scientific Councils in polytechnics, are the authoritative decision-making bodies. However, slight variations are accepted, and individual professors can adapt general rules, providing they are in accordance with the principles laid down. Continuing assessment for small classes, written tests, personal essays, group work, final examinations, either written or oral, are common forms of assessment. Marks are numeric; a scale of 0 to 20 is used. A mark of less than 10 means fail, 14 is good, and 16 and above is excellent.

Every single subject course is assessed. At present (1991), there is no final examination at the end of the course, and its final mark depends on subject course marks, whether assessed or not.

5. Conclusion

Higher education is seven centuries old. However, the expansion of higher education which began in the 1970s can be summarized as follows:

(a) the consolidation of the "new" universities and their expansion;

(b) the enlargement of state universities' autonomy;

(c) the expansion of the polytechnic system;

(d) the creation of the *Universidade Aberta* (the Open University);

(e) the rapid expansion of the private sector of higher education, both university and polytechnic;

(f) the trend for a regional balance of the higher education network;

(g) growing secondary education enrollment, and therefore rising numbers of applicants to higher education;

(h) the recent expansion of postgraduate studies, especially at the master's degree level.

In spite of the development of higher education, whether qualitative or quantitative, some problems remain to be solved. Foremost among them is the tension between increasing numbers of new applicants to higher education and the difficulty in accommodating them and finding teaching staff and resources to meet the demand. The second challenge is the capacity of the classic or old universities to adapt to new social and economic needs. The final challenge comes with full integration of Portugal into the European Community (EC), the free circulation of labor within the Community, and competition bearing down on Portuguese higher education.

Bibliography

Braga C L, Grilo E M 1981 Ensino Superior. In: Silva M, Tamen M T 1981 *Sistema de Ensino em Portugal.* Fundação Calouste Gulbenkian, Lisbon, pp. 223–57

Carvalho R 1986 *História de Educação em Portugal.* Fundação Calouste Gulbenkian, Lisbon

Pires E L 1986 *Lei de Bases do Sistema Educativo, Apresentação e Comentários.* Edições ASA, Porto

Ministry of Education and Culture 1987 *Comprehensive Law on the Educational System: Law 46/86.* Planning and Research Bureau, Lisbon

Ministério de Educação 1988 *A Investigação Científica Nacional no Quadro do Ensino Superior.* Comissão de Reforma do Sistema Educativo, Ministério da Educação, Lisbon

Ministério da Educação 1988 *Cursos de Mestrado nas Universidades Portuguesas*. Direcção Geral do Ensino Superior, Lisbon

Ministério da Educação 1989 *Ensino Superior: Guia 1989*. Direcção Geral do Ensino Superior, Lisbon

Ministério da Educação 1988 *Ensino Superior Politécnico: legislação*. Gabinete de Estudos e Planeamento, Lisbon

Ministério da Educação 1988 *Oportunidades de Educação Pós-secundária*. Direcção Geral do Ensino Superior, Lisbon

Revista Crítica de Ciências Sociais 1989 Vol 27/28; June (issue devoted to the 700 years of the University of Coimbra)

Stoer S 1981 Democracy and socialism in Portugal. In: Dale R (eds.) 1981 *Education and the State. Vol. 1: Schooling and the National Interest*. The Falmer Press, Lewes, Sussex, pp. 335–55

E. L. Pires

Puerto Rico

1. Higher Education and Society

1.1 Geographical Context and Population

Puerto Rico is an island with an area of 5,600 square kilometers, the smallest of the major Antilles located in the northern part of the Caribbean archipelago. Its current population of 3.5 million makes it one of the most densely populated areas in the world (625 per square mile). The population mix coalesced an Afro-Antillean culture, a blend of the Spanish and the African, with residual vestiges of the Amerindian. Under the colonial domination of Spain from 1508 to 1898 Puerto Rico was under an authoritarian political regime, and integrated into a mercantile economy. The attempts by the local Creole population to establish a center of higher learning were foiled by the Spanish government.

In 1898, as a result of the Spanish–American War, Puerto Rico was ceded to the United States. It remains under the sovereignty of the United States as a nonincorporated territory. Since 1952, it has had a constitutional form of elected self-government within the framework of the constitution and laws of the United States. As American citizens, Puerto Ricans can move freely to the United States and enjoy its rights and privileges. There are two million Puerto Ricans residing in the United States.

Average yearly increases in the population have been 1.5 percent, due to the net effect of decreasing birthrates (44.8 per 1,000 in 1940 to 19.4 in 1984), and the continuous net migratory outflow of the population. These processes together with the increase of life expectancy (from 46 years in 1940 to 74 in 1982) is changing the age structure of the population: there are fewer under 24 years of age and an increasing absolute and relative number of mature and elderly people.

1.2 Occupational and Economic Structure

From 1900 to 1940 the economy was based predominantly on sugar plantation and factories dominated by United States corporations. A social and economic transformation carried out between 1940 and 1990 achieved a dependent accelerated industrialization, urbanization, and modernization in all spheres of social life. From being a predominantly agricultural economy and agrarian rural society Puerto Rico has undergone an economic restructuring where the dynamic and leading sectors have been, first, labor-intensive manufacturing industry, and thereafter heavy capital industry, mostly subsidiaries of United States corporations. In the 1980s the dominant sector was the high-tech manufacturing industry, pharmaceuticals, chemicals, and electronics which are attracted by tax shelters in Puerto Rico.

The most recent data on income distribution (1977) shows that the lowest 20 percent receive 5.5 percent of family income while the upper 20 percent received 38.7 percent (Corrada 1987 p. 86). Unemployment is about 14 percent. Fifty percent of the population benefits from the economic assistance of transfer funds from United States federal government.

2. The Institutional Fabric of the Higher Education System

The first institution of higher education, the University of Puerto Rico, was founded by the United States colonial government in 1903 as a teacher training institute. It was intended to educate the teachers required by the public schools, whose main goal was the assimilation of Puerto Ricans to United States culture and political values. By 1920 it had developed a College of Agriculture and Mechanical Arts to train professionals and technicians for the growing sugar plantation and factory economy; as well as professional programs in law and pharmacy, and liberal arts, mostly for the teacher training program.

By 1940, there were two campuses of the University of Puerto Rico with a total of 5,426 students, which was 1.8 percent of the 18 to 24 age group. Also there were two church-supported liberal arts colleges, Catholic and Protestant, with 439 students (Rodríguez-Fraticelli 1985).

The period from 1940 to 1975 is characterized by the accelerated growth of student enrollment and the establishment of new programs and institutional units. The University prepared professionals for the new demands of a merit-based civil service, state-run utilities, manufacturing, and the modern services industries.

During this period the University of Puerto Rico expanded into a complex hierarchical system of 11 units. It included research and graduate-level campuses in the arts, sciences, and professions; four-year liberal arts colleges; and two-year technical community colleges spread throughout the country. The state university, particularly its three research campuses, has the highest academic standards.

The three research and graduate campuses are specialized in a cluster of related disciplines: (a) arts, humanities, sciences, education, and law; (b) the field of medicine and careers in health services; and (c) engineering and agriculture. They have major research laboratories, faculty with the highest degrees and research and publications record, and students with the highest academic achievement.

The University's expansion and growth has levelled to 56,993, which accounts for 36 percent of higher education. However, it has twice the number of graduate students in the master's and doctoral programs than the private sector. There are graduate programs in the social and natural sciences, humanities and arts, medicine, and engineering.

During the decade of the 1970s, the high rate of unemployment and the transfer of financial and scholarship funds from the United States federal government to individuals, which amounted to $350 million in 1988, increased the effective demand for higher education. This was absorbed by the private universities. The older four institutions expanded their programs and facilities, and a total of 29 new institutions of different levels, including four-year colleges, business and technical institutes, and graduate level specialized schools were created.

The programs are low-cost career programs oriented to the labor market and social demand. They span all levels, from nondegree short courses to doctoral programs. The graduate programs are mostly in education, business, and applied social sciences. There has been a rapid increase in enrollment that reached a peak of 98,402 in 1985–86, and in 1988 levelled to 96,337 (61 percent of the

Table 1
Total enrollments in higher education by level of institution public and private

	1960–61	1965–66	1970–71	1975–76	1980–81	1985–86	1988–89
Public sector							
State university system	—	—	—	—	—	—	—
Research university and graduate level	18,893	25,539	36,801	37,139	34,752	35,013	35,176
Four-year colleges	—	—	3,817	5,452	6,529	7,064	7,182
Community colleges	—	945	1,898	8,470	11,399	13,303	14,635
Total	18,893	26,484	42,516	51,061	52,680	55,380	56,993
Other public institutions							
Schools of art, music, and culture	—	—	—	1,396	3,246	3,036	3,573
Subtotal	18,893	26,484	42,516	52,457	55,926	58,416	60,566
Percentage of total enrollments	56	61	66	51	41	37	39
Private Sector							
Older major universities with graduate programs	14,752	16,730	21,933	46,199	63,355	79,570	75,264
Four-year colleges	—	—	—	4,777	11,896	11,619	14,050
Technical and business institutes (two- and four-year levels)	—	—	—	—	3,634	5,301	5,257
Graduate professional schools	—	—	—	—	348	1,912	1,766
Subtotal	14,752	16,730	21,933	50,976	79,233	98,402	96,337
Percentage of total enrollments	44	39	34	49	59	63	61
Total enrollments	33,645	43,214	64,449	103,433	135,159	156,818	156,903

Source: Consejo de Educación Superior de Puerto Rico. *Estadísticas de las instituciones de educación superior en Puerto Rico 1971–1988.*
Junta de Planificación de Puerto Rico. *Informe de recursos humanos.* 1973. Vol. 2 p. 520. Tabla I

Table 2
Number of graduates of higher education

	1965–66	1970–71	1975–76	1980–81	1985–86
University of Puerto Rico	4,115	5,582	8,411	8,173	8,459
Other public institutions	—	—	266	239	691
Private	1,630	3,135	5,357	8,970	10,825
Total	5,745	8,717	14,034	17,382	19,975

Source: Consejo de Educación Superior. *Estadísticas de las instituciones de educación superior en Puerto Rico 1973–1985.*

total). There is aggressive competition among private universities for the postsecondary education age group (18 to 24 years), which will decrease in the 1990s.

There is also a dynamic, postsecondary nonuniversity sector which offers short careers programs in business, services, and technology. At present there are 479 institutes.

The expansion of the private sector during the 1980s, spurred by the federal government's scholarships, drove the enrollment ratios to 44 percent of the 18 to 21 age group, and 16.5 percent of the 22 to 24 age group.

Research in arts and sciences, theoretical and applied, is concentrated in the public university system. There is very little research and development in technology, except in the agricultural experimental stations of the state university.

Admissions policies and selection is determined by the universities. In general the state university requires a minimum grade point average from secondary school and tests scores of the College Entrance Examination Board or other specialized upper-level tests for graduate programs. Each faculty or department unit establishes the specific requirements for their academic programs.

The college level offers a two-year associate degree for career courses, and four-year bachelor degrees, which are awarded by the institution.

Graduate studies consist of master's and doctoral programs which require a bachelor's degree. Research training is emphasized in the arts and sciences.

3. Governance, Administration, and Finance

3.1 National Administration

The Council of Higher Education, a nine-member autonomous body appointed by the governor, functions as the board of trustees of the state university system. It appoints the public university high officials, and approves academic programs and budget allocations submitted by the units and the University Board.

It also serves as a regulatory board that licenses private institutions. It sets the standards to evaluate periodically every institution and renews licences. Every new academic program requires the approval of the Council.

3.2 Finance

By law the financing of the public university system is through the allocation of 9 percent of the government revenues, and other specific allocations approved by the legislature and the executive branches of government. The University of Puerto Rico's total budget in 1987–88 was $406.2 million. Its sources were: state government 67 percent, tuition fees 9 percent, United States federal government 18 percent, and other sources 6 percent.

The private institutions are entirely dependent on tuition fees paid by its students. These are supported

Table 3
Number of graduates of higher education by degree

	Certificate and others	Associate degree	Bachelor's degree	Master's and professional degrees	Doctorate	Total
University of Puerto Rico	25	1,826	5,345	967	31	8,194
Other public institutions	121	645	219	10	—	995
Private	616	3,289	6,648	1,219	27	11,799
Total	762	5,760	12,212	2,196	58	20,988

Source: Consejo de Educación Superior. *Estadísticas de las instituciones de educación superior en Puerto Rico 1988–89*

by United States federal government scholarships and loans. Scholarship grants have increased steadily from \$23.3 million in 1975 to 253.7 million in 1988. In this year, other financial aid and loans amounted to a total of \$350.3 million, which benefits over 80 percent of students enrolled in private institutions. (Consejo de Educación Superior 1989 pp. 42–68, Crespo 1988 p. 29).

3.3 Institutional Administration

The Council on Higher Education is the ultimate seat of authority which appoints the president and campus chancellors of the University of Puerto Rico and can veto the chancellor's appointment of deans. It approves the rules and procedures proposed by the units and the University Board. The Board is constituted by the six chancellors, the academic senate, and student representatives of each unit which coordinates the administrative and academic operations of the system.

At each campus the faculty in each department and college participates through elected committees and unit meetings in decisions concerning curriculum (new programs and revisions), courses, schedule of classes and assignment of faculty tasks, recruitment, tenure, and promotion. The academic norms, standards, and programs, campuswide, are revised and approved by the academic senate, a body of deans and elected faculty and students. Nonacademic staff do not have representation. They channel their participation through collective bargaining processes.

Private corporate type universities are governed by boards of trustees. They have limited faculty participation in governance. Proprietary colleges and institutes' governance and academic direction is managerial and centralized without any governance role by the faculty or students. There are no collective bargaining agreements with faculty or nonacademic staff.

4. Faculty and Students: Teaching, Learning, and Research

4.1 Faculty

In the University of Puerto Rico recruitment is carried out at the base units, the campus department or college, though the final decision rests on the campus head. The General Rules stipulate minimum academic degrees, the time period for tenure and promotion, and general criteria. The departments and colleges establish specific requirements according to the program needs and orientation, whether its emphasis is on teaching or research, and the nature of the discipline. Elected faculty committees mediate peer review for tenure and promotion.

In the major private universities there is some degree of peer review in the decision making on recruitment, retention, and promotion. It is non-

Table 4
Faculty in higher education by academic degree

	University of Puerto Rico (Systemwide)		Private universities	
		%		%
Bachelor's	139	3	454	8
Master's	2,240	56	3,766	68
Doctorate	1,093	27	859	15
Other	551	14	531	9
Total	4,023		5,610	

Sources: Consejo de Educación Superior. *Estadísticas de las instituciones de Educación Superior de Puerto Rico 1988–89*

existent in proprietary institutions, where decisions are made solely by management.

4.2 Students

Student enrollment in the public university system has been increasingly shifting from arts and sciences to career occupation programs. The 44 programs in the arts, humanities, social and natural sciences constitute only 23 percent of all academic programs of the public system. In 1984 the 1,798 graduates (of all levels) of these programs comprised 21 percent of the total graduates. The other 79 percent have graduated from technical, business, teacher training, and professional programs. In the private sector 90 percent of the students are enrolled in career programs. The other 10 percent in arts and sciences are mostly oriented to teacher training. (Irizarry 1986 pp. 114–16).

4.3 Student Characteristics

The public university attracts the higher academic achievers, which is directly correlated with the socioeconomic level of their families, who are mostly from the upper and middle classes. The private universities draw lower income students, 95 percent of whom are recipients of financial aid and scholarships. Students of the higher income and social elite groups enroll in colleges in the United States.

In both the public and private universities around 62 percent of the students are women and 38 percent are males.

4.4 Representation of Student Interests

In the University of Puerto Rico there are elected student representatives in faculty decision-making bodies in departments and colleges, campus academic senates and administrative boards (comprising the deans and the chancellor), and in the system's university board. Students have their own voluntary organizations to pursue political, cultural, religious, social, and professional interests. Some private universities have student councils and voluntary organizations, but few have representatives in their governance organisms.

4.5 *Learning and Assessment*

In the state university, the curriculum program, which defines learning objectives, degree requirements, the sequence and content of courses, and the methodologies for teaching and assessment is formulated in the first instance by the departments and colleges within the general norms and requirements established by the academic senate for the campus. New programs, revisions and elimination of established ones require the approval of the academic senate and the university board. Final approval is granted by the Council of Higher Education. Programs in collegiate and regulated professions require accreditation by the professional associations, but this is not a condition for approval by the Council.

5. *Conclusion*

Higher education is at a critical stage due to a reduction in revenues allocated by the state government, and an expected decrease in financial aid from the federal government. The private sector is facing a saturated and constrained market as the college age population decreases. The liberal arts programs face a shortage in demand, even at the graduate level, which places the humanistic mission of the University in jeopardy.

Technical and scientific programs are not abreast with advances in technology, and therefore are not able to provide a competitive base for a national economy and industry.

The public university will need to set priorities in the research and graduate levels, reduce its undergraduate course offerings, and establish a separate system of community college for career programs. There has to be a coordinated effort between the private and public universities to define different and complementary missions and roles, avoid duplication, and pool resources for joint programs and projects.

Bibliography

Consejo de Educación Superior 1973–88 *Estadísticas de las instituciones de educación superior en Puerto Rico*
Consejo de Educación Superior 1989 *Informe sobre el financiamiento de la educación en Puerto Rico*
Corrada Guerrero R 1987 Las desigualdades del ingreso familiar en Puerto Rico. *Revista Ciencias Soc.* 26(1–4): 73–101
Crespo J 1988 *Sistema de apoyo decisional para el fortalecimiento de la Universidad Metropolitana a través de la aplicación de escenarios para la proyección de matrícula e ingresos.* Proyecto Tesis Maestría en Planificación, Universidad de Puerto Rico
Departamento del Trabajo de Puerto Rico 1988 *Empleo y salarios cubiertos por municipio e industria*
Irizarry R L 1986 La evolución de la estructura ocupacional y su impacto en los programas académicos de la Universidad. *Revista Admin. Pública* 18(2): 109–20
Irizarry R L 1987 La inflación educativa y los recursos humanos redundantes en Puerto Rico. *Revista Ciencias Soc.* 26(1–4): 141–66
Junta de Planificación de Puerto Rico 1970 *Informe de recursos humanos al Gobernador 1970*
Junta de Planificación de Puerto Rico 1984 *Compendio de estadísticas sociales 1984*
Junta de Planificación de Puerto Rico 1985 *Serie histórica del empleo, desempleo y grupo trabajador en Puerto Rico*
Junta de Planificación de Puerto Rico 1986 *Informe de recursos humanos 1986*
Junta de Planificación de Puerto Rico 1988 *Informe económico al Gobernador 1988*
Rodríguez-Fraticelli C 1986 *Education and Imperialism: The Puerto Rican Experience in Higher Education.* (mimeo) Centro de Estudios Puertorriqueños, Hunter College of the City University of New York
Universidad de Puerto Rico 1981 *Reglamento General*
US Census Bureau 1960 and 1980 *General Characteristics of the Population*

R. L. Irizarry

Q

Qatar

1. Higher Education and Society

Qatar realized its national independence on September 3, 1971. On February 22, 1972 His Highness Sheikh Khalifa bin Hamad Al-Thani assumed the reins of power. The occasion inaugurated a new era during which the need for change and renovation was formulated, and achieved in the creation of various fields of progress and modernization covering all aspects of life and reflected in the dignified status of the country in the international field.

Before 1956 there was no official education in Qatar. The late beginning of governmental education was followed by a rapid increase in the number of schools and pupils. These were needed to meet the country's pressing demand for educated citizens, who would face the challenges of the political, economic, and social growth of their country, while abiding by its original traditions, helping to renovate its society, and realizing its hopes and ambitions in a bright future. (For the development of general education during the last three years see Table 1.)

Having achieved its economic and political independence, and having gained full control over its economic wealth, it was necessary for the state to establish higher education.

2. The Institutional Fabric of the Higher Education System

Higher education was conducted abroad in Arab universities until 1973 when the Faculty of Education was established and the Ministry of Education laid down plans to make full use of its facilities.

Table 1
Quantitative development of the number of university students 1973/1974–1988/1989

	1973/1974	1977/1978	1983/1984	1988/1989
Qatari				
Male	48	276	801	1,078
Female	72	443	1,929	3,335
Non-Qatari				
Male	9	189	781	758
Female	21	326	554	737
Total	150	1,234	4,065	5,888

As most teachers proved to be holders of degrees nonoriented for teaching, a plan was set up to improve this situation in a radical way. Access to the Faculty of Education was provided to all teachers to obtain special diplomas in education.

2.1 University of Qatar

The University of Qatar requires full-time attendance and follows a credit hours system. Its academic year is divided mainly into two study seasons: spring and autumn each of 16 weeks' duration with an optional intensive summer course of 8 weeks' duration, decided by the University Council.

Students must gain at least 144 credit hours to obtain the first university degree (BA) from the Faculty of Education, Faculty of Humanities and Social Sciences, Faculty of Islamic Jurisprudence and Islamic Studies, and Faculty of Sciences. To obtain the BSc degree from the Faculty of Engineering, 156 credit hours are required. In all cases the accumulative average of the student must be not less than 2.0 (grade D).

The University has the following faculties established at the dates indicated:

(a) The Faculty of Education—established in 1973 as the nucleus of the University. It is both the oldest and largest.

(b) Faculty of Humanities and Social Sciences (1977).

(c) Faculty of Science (1977).

(d) Faculty of Islamic Jurisprudence and Islamic Studies (1977).

(e) Faculty of Engineering (for men only) (1980).

(f) Faculty of Administrative Sciences and Economics (1985).

The University also has the following Research Centers established at the dates indicated:

(a) Scientific and Applied Research Center (1980);

(b) The Prophet's Biography and Sunna (doings and sayings) Research Center (1980);

(c) Educational Research Center (1980);

(d) Documentation and Humanities Research Center (1980);

(e) Arab Gulf States Development Studies Project;

The University has the following Units:

(a) Arabic Language Teaching Unit;

(b) English Language Teaching Unit;

(c) Environmental Studies Unit.

The University's library contains approximately 250,000 volumes and 2,000 periodicals in Arabic, English, and other languages, 15,000 microfiche, 2,800 theses, and over 2,000 Arabic manuscripts.

The Department of Educational Technology is the University's central agency for acquiring, producing, circulating, and maintaining different forms of instructional media and audio-visual equipment for classroom use.

3. Governance, Administration, and Finance

His Highness, the Emir of the State of Qatar, Sheikh Khalifa Bin Hamad Al-Thani, is the supreme head of the University.

The University governing bodies include:

(a) The University Council—established in 1981. This is the highest governing body on all academic, administrative, and financial matters relating to the University.

(b) The Higher Council of Education—established in 1975.

(c) The University Consultative Board of Regents.

(d) The President of the University.

(e) The Assistant President of the University.

(f) The Undersecretary of the University.

(g) The Secretary General of the University.

The organizational structure of each faculty consists of Faculty Council, responsible for formulating its policy concerning research and other academic activities within the framework of the University policy.

Education in the State of Qatar, financed by the government, is entirely free, except in the Civil Aviation College. Moreover the state supplies students with all materials required for their academic work, free of charge plus transport, sportswear, and financial support to encourage them in some educational stages.

4. Faculty and Students: Teaching, Learning, and Research

The recruitment of academic staff is the responsibility of the Academic Staff Recruitment Committee. The members of the Committee are the President, Vice-President, and Secretary General. A bachelor's degree (BA or BSc) is required of the applicants for a first appointment. (For a breakdown of teaching staff in the years 1988–89 see Table 2.)

Qatari students should obtain a general (or religious) secondary certificate or a joint certificate averaged out at 55 percent or above (for science students) and 60 percent or above (for arts students).

Science students who obtain only 50 percent and arts students who obtain only 55 percent should successfully complete a two-season formative course before admission to programs of University standard.

For entry into the Faculty of Engineering a student should obtain either a general or religious secondary certificate (Sciences) averaged at 60 percent or above or a diploma of industrial secondary school averaged out at 75 percent or above.

For admission to the Faculty of Administration and Economy, a student must hold a general secondary certificate (Arts) or an equivalent certificate averaged out at 65 percent or above or at 70 percent or above (Sciences) provided that the number of admitted students (Sciences) does not exceed five.

The top three Qatari students from among those

Table 2
Teaching staff 1988/1989 at the University of Qatar

Title	Qatari		Non-Qatari		Total		Grand total
	M	W	M	W	M	W	
Professor	1	—	62	10	63	10	73
Assistant professor	4	2	96	3	100	5	105
Lecturer	19	14	47	15	66	29	95
Assistant lecturer/ demonstrator	23	48	—	—	23	48	71
Graduate assistant	25	20	—	—	25	20	45
Expert	—	—	2	2	2	2	4
Instructor	—	2	15	10	15	12	27
Teaching practice supervisor	—	10	7	20	7	30	37
Field work supervisor	—	7	1	—	1	7	8
Grand totals	72	103	230	60	302	163	465

gaining the commercial secondary certificate may be admitted if their certificates averaged out at not less than 70 percent. Children of non-Qatari residents are eligible for admission if they have completed all educational stages in Qatar, or if their guardian has resided in Qatar for 15 unbroken years, or if their guardian is one of the employees of any ministry or government affiliate.

To meet admission criteria a non-Qatari student should obtain a general (or religious) secondary certificate or a joint certificate averaged out at 65 percent or above (Sciences) and 70 percent (Arts). Fur-

thermore, graduation should be in the same year in which he or she applies for enrollment. In general, the number of such students accepted for enrollment in the University is limited to 10 percent with some exceptions of the total enrolled Qatari students. In the Faculty of Engineering, equal numbers of Qatari and non-Qatari students are admitted. (For a break-down of graduates in the years 1987–88 see Table 3.) There are special terms for admission to some sections and faculties.

In nonuniversity institutes, the Institute of Administration is the sole organ that undertakes

Table 3
University of Qatar graduates 1987/1988

Faculties	Men		Women		Qatari	NonQ
	Qatari	NonQ	Qatari	NonQ	Total	Total
Education						
Autumn 1987	27	30	79	21	106	51
Spring 1988	33	48	190	62	223	110
Summer 1988	—	3	14	2	14	5
Total education	60	81	283	85	343	166
Humanities						
Autumn 1987	16	8	8	2	24	10
Spring 1988	21	9	34	6	55	15
Summer 1988	6	1	1	1	7	2
Total humanities	43	18	43	9	86	27
Science						
Autumn 1987	3	5	11	2	14	7
Spring 1988	2	15	17	24	19	39
Summer 1988	—	2	2	—	2	2
Total science	5	22	30	26	35	48
Islamic Studies						
Autumn 1987	13	5	22	1	35	6
Spring 1988	7	5	46	7	53	12
Summer 1988	—	1	1	—	1	1
Total Islamic studies	20	11	69	8	89	19
Engineering						
Autumn 1987	2	2	—	—	2	2
Spring 1988	5	4	—	—	5	4
Summer 1988	—	1	—	—	—	1
Total engineering	7	7	—	—	7	7
Total Autumn 1987	61	50	120	26	181	76
Total Spring 1988	68	81	287	99	355	180
Total Summer 1988	6	8	18	3	24	11
Totals 1987/1988	135	139	425	128	560	267
Grand total 1987/1988					827	

national long-term training courses. It was established in 1964 to qualify students for administrative posts in the government and private sector. To gain admission, applicants should be of Qatar nationality, have a secondary education certificate, or an equivalent qualification, a governmental post, and have the written approval of the applicant's employment unit. Graduates obtain the diploma of the Institute of Administration after the successful completion of its two-year duration course.

The teaching staff, in addition to their eight years, experience in administrative, legislative, and economic fields also have a PhD degree and/or an MA degree.

The Civil Aviation College also offers special admission terms. It was established by the Arabian Gulf States in 1977, as a regional institution to train nationals in the various fields of aviation. Entry is open only to students from Arab countries as well as from the four participating states. Courses are offered in Air Traffic Services; Aviation Electronics; and Aeronautical Meteorology.

5. Conclusion

The vital achievements recorded by higher education in Qatar can be confidently taken as excellent predictors for productive innovation in the country's future. These achievements will be enhanced by reforms which aim to improve the quality of work undertaken by academic staff, administrators, and students. These include: the raising of the standard required for admission to the University; continuing research to prepare the introduction of technical and applied education programs as areas essential for the country's internal development; an ongoing re-evaluation of the curricula in each faculty; the establishment of new programs to meet the student's needs and suit their future employment; new English language programs recently introduced into the Faculty of Engineering and the Faculty of Administration, Science, and Economics; progressive studies on the introduction of a BSc in computer science and in nursing.

Moreover research is being undertaken into the problems specific to Qatar and the region in general, problems considered of prime importance both for interaction with society and for developing and improving the quality of life.

Bibliography

Abdulla A M 1988 Education in Qatar. MA thesis, University of Bradford

Kazem M I, Subaih N A 1984 *Considerations in the policies of student admission to Universities of Gulf Arab States in the light of development policies.* Qatar University Data

Mursi M M 1987 *Contemporary University Education: its issues and attitudes.* Dar Al Thagafa Doha

Jawad N A D M A 1983 *A Comparative Study in Administration and Organization of the Continuous Education Programmes in the Universities of Egypt and Some Foreign Countries.* Dar Al-Uloom Printing and Publishing Organization, Riyadh

Al-Misned Sheikh A 1984 The development of modern education in Bahrain, Kuwait and Qatar. PhD thesis, University of Durham

The Educational Research Center, University of Qatar, *Studies in University Education and its Organization,* Vol. 5

Ministry of Education, State of Qatar, *Development of Education in Qatar 1986, 1987, 1988.* Ministry of Education, Doha

A. A. T. Al-Sobaie

R

Romania

1. Higher Education and Society

Romania lies in southeastern Central Europe, and covers 237,500 square kilometers. It is divided by the Carpathian Mountains, and by the river Danube which constitutes most of its southern frontier. Romania is bordered by the Black Sea on the east side. Its frontiers have not changed since the Second World War.

The population of Romania was 15,872,524 in 1948, 18 million in 1960, over 20 million in 1970, 22 million in 1980, and 22,940,430 in 1987. The estimated population in 1991 is over 23.1 million. The average annual growth rate over the post-War period has been 13 per thousand people. According to official statistics, life expectancy increased from 65 years in 1956 to almost 70 in 1984.

Urbanization has been a major trend. At the end of the Second World War, only one fifth of the population lived in towns. During the following decades, the proportion of urban dwellers (including those in suburban areas) grew, to 32 percent in 1960, over 41 percent in 1970, almost 50 percent in 1980, and over 54 percent in 1987. The latest population census (January 1977) showed the ethnic distribution to be as follows: 89.1 percent Romanians and 10.9 percent other nationalities (7.7% Magyars, 1.5% Germans, 0.2% Ukrainians, 0.2% Serbians, 0.1% Jews, 0.1% Tartars, 0.1% Russians, Bulgarians, Croatians, etc.).

The active population has evolved from over nine and a half million (roughly 51% of the population) in 1960 to eleven million, one hundred thousand (46.7%) in 1987. These figures, the only ones available, must be treated with caution, as they were aimed to prove two merits of the socialist system: providing employment for women and its incompatibility with the phenomenon of unemployment. The occupational structure of the population has undergone important changes. In 1950, 74.3 percent of the employed population worked in agriculture. This figure has dropped to 28.6 percent in 1987. By contrast, the proportion of people employed in industry and construction rose from 14.2 percent in 1950, to 44.8 percent in 1987. Increases also occurred in the service industries (including transport and telecommunications, trade, education, research, culture, the arts, health, administration, etc.). Those working in this sector constituted 14.4 percent of the total working population in 1960, and 26.6 percent in 1987.

The economic changes occurring after the December 1989 revolution meant that the occupational structure of the population would undergo important modifications. A decrease in the number of industrial workers will take place, the service sector will diversify, and with individual land ownership being reinstated some of the workers without jobs may be able to return to the land.

1.1 Structure of the Economy

Throughout the post-War period, Romania's economic development followed the dogmatic course set for the "construction of socialism." This involved socialist ownership of the means of production, highly centralized planning, allocation of a large share of the national income for the development of favored sectors of industry, and so on. Romania applied the tenets of socialist construction with greater force than its neighbors. As a result, the private sector was virtually nonexistent and the production of consumer goods was neglected, as were services. In agriculture, despite the quality of the land, productivity was low.

During the 1970s and 1980s, about 70 percent of the national income has been earmarked for consumption and 30 percent for investments in economic development. The distribution of investments is illustrated by the data available for 1987: 47.1 percent went to industry (expansion of energy and raw material resources, and development of key branches—machine-building, metallurgy, and chemistry); 16.7 percent to agriculture; 4.7 percent to construction; 9.8 percent to transport and telecommunications; and 2.3 percent to other branches. According to official figures, in 1987 the three economic sectors held the following shares in the Gross Net Product: the primary sector 15.9 percent; the secondary sector 69.9 percent, and the tertiary sector 14.2 percent.

The socialist economic system failed dramatically in Romania, particularly after Nicolae Ceausescu assumed unlimited dictatorial powers in the 1960s and embarked upon plans which defied all economic laws. As a result, living standards in Romania plummeted.

The new government formed after the elections of 20 May 1990, emphasized the drive toward a market economy. Despite the fact that Romania is the only country in Eastern Europe to have paid off its foreign debts, this transition will not be easy.

1.2 Structure of Government and Main Political Goals

Throughout the post-War period (more precisely from 6 March 1945 when a communist-dominated government came to power, until 22 December 1989) Romania followed the political and economic goals typical of the socialist states in Central and Eastern Europe. There were several changes in the structure of government, the monarchy was abolished in December 1947, and the People's Republic of Romania was proclaimed. The last constitution adopted under the communist regime by the Romanian parliament (Grand National Assembly) in 1985 proclaimed the Socialist Republic of Romania "a sovereign, independent, and unitary state of the working people," with the dominant political power being the Romanian Communist Party. Power was exercised through the Grand National Assembly and the people's councils (as the state-empowered local bodies). The state council was the supreme body of state power, subordinated to parliament. The president of the Republic was head of state. The president, in the person of Nicolae Ceausescu, assumed absolute dictatorial powers. The council of ministers (the government) was in charge of state administration and overall management of state activities. Bodies subordinated to both party and state were created to carry out combined political and executive tasks (e.g., the National Council of Science and Education was meant to organize, manage, guide, and control activity in the fields of education and science).

All political, legislative, and executive bodies created during the Ceausescu dictatorship were dissolved on 22 December 1989, and power assumed by the self-proclaimed Council of the National Salvation Front. There was reason, particularly because of a certain reluctance to disclose all the details of the overthrow of Ceausescu, to call into doubt the sincerity and genuinely democratic convictions of those who came to power after the events of December 1989. The date set for free elections (20 May 1990) was thought by some to be too soon, while others were pressing for an end to the provisional nature of the authorities in power, dominated by the National Salvation Front. Political parties multiplied (there were 77 parties registered for the May elections and their number has since grown to 100). The opposition parties were highly fragmented, with no common platform. The National Salvation Front, profiting by its role in the December 1989 revolution and the popular measures, both political and economic, adopted subsequently, won the elections by a large majority. Its recognized leader, Ion Illiescu, became the president of the country, now called Romania. The newly elected parliament is bicameral, being made up of the senate and of the chamber of representatives. Both are dominated by the National Salvation Front. Legislative and executive powers are separated and so is the judiciary. One of the major tasks of the chamber and of the senate is to devise a new constitution.

The consequences of all the political changes

described above for higher education are self-evident and highly complex.

1.3 Historical background

Higher education in Romania has followed a development pattern shared by several countries in southeastern Europe: it was formally established at a relatively late stage in the country's history (19th century), knew a period of very fast development in an effort to catch up with the rest of Europe, particularly during the period between the two world wars, and experienced traumatic changes after the Second World War, when its role and functions were radically readjusted to comply with new political, social, and economic conditions of the communist regime.

The first schools in Romania date back to the Middle Ages. Education at the higher level was first offered at the Princely Academies of Bucharest (1694) and Iasi (1714). Universities were founded in Iasi (1860) and Bucharest (1864). A Hungarian university was established at Cluj, then part of the Austro-Hungarian empire, in 1872. Following the union of Transylvania with the rest of Romania in 1918, the University of Cluj became a Romanian university in 1921. New universities were established after the First World War, at Kisinau, in Bessarabia, and Cernautzi, in Bukovina. By 1938 there were 16 higher education establishments in the country, with a total enrollment of 26,500 students.

Following the Vienna Diktat imposed by Hitler and Mussolini in 1940, under whose terms Northern Transylvania was taken over by Hungary, the University of Cluj moved temporarily to Sibiu. The universities of Kisinau and Cernautzi also ceased to function as Romanian universities in 1940, when, following the Molotov-Ribbentrop Pact, Bessarabia and Northern Bukovina became part of the Soviet Union.

After the Second World War, Romania fell completely under Soviet influence and underwent sociopolitical and economic changes, in pursuance of the goal of building up a socialist society. Higher education felt the full impact of these changes. Three reforms (in 1948, 1968, and 1978) changed its organizational structure and system of governance and management as well as the principles and practices underlying course contents and methods of teaching, to bring it in line with the policy of the Romanian Communist Party, which was constitutionally defined as the sole political force in control of the country. Higher education was completely state controlled and centrally planned. Emphasis was laid on the teaching of Marxism–Leninism, the dominant ideology in all spheres of activity.

The role of the party and the state in decision-making was much more direct and forceful than in any of the other socialist countries of central and eastern Europe. The direct involvement of Nicolae

Ceausescu, party secretary and president of the country, and his wife, Elena Ceausescu was an important feature of the system. They had special responsibilities for higher education and science. Romanian higher education was almost completely cut off from the rest of the world.

In December 1989 the Ceausescu dictatorship fell. Fundamental changes were set under way which included higher education among their top priorities. Measures were taken to depoliticize and deideologize programs. Academic freedom and university autonomy became a primary concern for both students and staff. Students, radicalized during the December revolution (they were among its chief protagonists), now have a stronger say in the shaping of changes in the system. New universities and other institutions were created.

2. The Institutional Fabric of the Higher Education System

Higher (postsecondary) education in Romania is provided in state institutions only. There has, however, been heated debate about establishing private institutions. Over 20 private institutions were established in 1990, with an enrollment of more than 10,000 students in Bucharest alone. A new Law of Higher Education is in the offing. It provides for the setting up of private and other types of higher education institutions. Another development concerns the inclusion of the Institute of Theology as a faculty within the University of Bucharest in 1990. In the past, such institutions, although offering courses and degrees at higher education level, were not considered to be part of the system. Military higher education establishments depend directly on the Ministry of Defense. However, curricula for general subjects and admission procedures are formulated in cooperation with the Ministry of Education and Science.

The system of higher education is regarded as being unitary, that is to say, there is no distinction per se between university and nonuniversity types of institutions. From the organizational point of view, however, it is very complex. In the academic year 1989/1990 it included 43 institutions, located in 20 university centers. They can be grouped into the following categories:

(a) Universities: there are eleven universities. The four principal and oldest ones (Bucharest, Iasi, Cluj, and Timisoara) provide teaching, training, and research in the exact and natural sciences, the humanities, economics, and law. The universities of Brasov, Galatzi, and Craiova, which acquired university status in the 1960s, offer programs in other fields as well (technical fields and medicine). Four universities (Constantza, Oradea, Sibiu, and Suceava) were created in

1990, by reinforcing the programs offered previously in existing technical higher education institutions and adding teacher training to them.

(b) Polytechnics: there are four polytechnics (Bucharest, Iasi, Clug, and Timisoara) which train engineers in diverse technological fields. They all have full university status and are larger than the universities in their respective cities, in terms of both students and staff.

(c) Specialized institutes of higher education: included in this broad category are 23 establishments which offer programs by specific subjects. These comprise five institutes of medicine and pharmacy (Bucharest, Iasi, Cluj–Napoca, Timisoara, and Tirgu Mures, the latter with a special section in which the language of instruction is Hungarian), four institutes of agronomy (Bucharest, Iasi, Cluj-Napoca, and Timisoara), one institute of civil engineering and one of architecture (both in Bucharest), one institute of naval transport (Constantza), one institute of mining engineering (Petrosani), one institute of oil engineering (Ploiesti), three conservatories of music (Bucharest, Iasi, and Cluj-Napoca), three fine arts schools (Bucharest, Iasi, and Cluj-Napoca), two drama and film institutes (Bucharest and Tirgu Mures), and one institute of physical education and sports (Bucharest).

(d) *Institute de Invatamint superior:* a fourth category includes five institutions—*Institute de invatamint superior*, which translates literally as Institutes of higher education—created recently, like the new universities mentioned above, in Arad, Bacau, Baia Mare, Pilesti, and Tirgu Mures by transforming short-cycle technical colleges which had functioned in the past as extentions of the polytechnics. They train mid-level technical specialists (under engineers).

All higher education institutions enjoy equal status with the universities. They function outside the universities for purely organizational reasons, not as a reflection of difference in status. Differences in excellence may exist among them, however. No higher education institution is designed solely for research.

The institutional organization of higher education has been restructured several times over the post-War period. The number of institutions grew from 16 in 1938 to 54 in 1950. There were two reasons for this: new institutes were created, in both old and new university centers, and previous faculties and departments (in medicine, economics, the arts, etc.) branched off from the universities to become independent institutions. Their number has fluctuated from 47 institutions in 1965 to 42 in 1975 to 43 in 1990.

The changes in the number of faculties (the basic

institutional structures of instruction and research) further illustrate the trend of establishing manageably sized units. In 1938 the number of faculties was 33; it increased to 136 in 1950; decreased slightly to 127 in 1955; rose to 131 in 1960 and increased substantially to 195 in 1970. Subsequently, during the worst period for higher education in post-War Romania, their number decreased dangerously from 137 faculties in 1975 to 134 in 1980, and 101 in 1989.

2.1 Admission policy and selection

Admission to all forms of higher education in Romania is determined by competitive entrance examination. Before 1989, quotas were established in line with the national plan for economic and social development. They were supposed to reflect the demand for highly trained personnel in various branches of the economy, science, and culture (following labor force forecasts). Major mistakes in planning had disastrous results: by 1985, Romania had the lowest number of students per 100,000 inhabitants (694) in Europe. This was less than Albania (721) and Hungary (921).

The entrance examinations are written. In the past they were standard across the country, being established and administered by the Ministry of Education. Institutions of higher education were awarded a degree of autonomy in administering admissions for the coming academic year. Preliminary oral tests must be passed for admission to foreign language courses. Aptitude tests are taken for certain courses such as fine arts, music, drama, film, and physical education. A medical examination is a prerequisite for admission to courses in other fields such as mining and oil engineering.

Any person who holds a secondary school leaving certificate (the baccalaureate) is eligible for the entrance examination. There are no restrictions other than the quota system for any faculty or department. Persons wishing to pursue evening or extramural courses are employed in a related area to the chosen field of study.

2.2 Quantitative Developments in Higher Education

Enrollment in higher education grew steadily over the post-War period, as a result of economic, social, and demographic factors. Throughout the 1960s and 1970s, growth was remarkable: numbers rose from 72,000 students in 1960 to 131,000 in 1965, 152,000 in 1970, 165,000 in 1975, and 193,000 in 1980. There followed a period of decline (160,000 students in 1985 and 157,000 in 1988). These figures include foreign students. There were 897 in 1960, 503 in 1965, 1,766 in 1970, 4,971 in 1975, 15,888 in 1980, 10,744 in 1985, and 7,062 in 1989. In the late 1970s, Romania had one of the highest percentages of foreign students to local students (over 16% of students in 1980 were foreign).

Student enrollment in short-cycle studies fluc-

tuated, sometimes showing great variation over a short space of time, reflecting their principal aim, namely to meet immediate demands for specific levels of training. Thus, following the extension of compulsory education, there was a significant increase in enrollments in three-year teacher-training colleges which prepared teachers for first-level secondary education (forms 5 to 8). After saturation of this demand, the institutes were either discontinued or restructured into mixed technical and pedagogical institutions. During the 1970s and the 1980s, short-term studies were represented mainly by the *subingineri* (under-engineer) sections of polytechnics.

Evening and correspondence courses, created in the 1950s, were given particular, sometimes disproportionate attention; they accounted for 21 percent of total student enrollments in 1985. Correspondence courses had a large share in the mid-1960s (22.7% of total enrollments), but declined afterwards, accounting for only 5 percent of the total number of students in the mid-1980s, when evening courses came to be favored. There were heated discussions throughout the spring of 1990 concerning short-cycle and part-time studies. Both forms of studies were said to have been promoted artificially (one reason being to hide the dramatic drop in the number of full-time students) and to have led to a marked deterioration in the quality of higher education. Consequently, in 1990/1991 the short-term cycles were discontinued and admission figures showed much lower percentages for both correspondence courses (2,000 students, or 4.5%) and evening courses (4,000 students, or 9%) of the total intake figure of 43,000. This represents a 30 percent increase on figures for 1988/1989.

2.3 Structure of Qualifications

First-degree courses in Romania last from three to six years, depending on institutions and fields of study. Evening and extramural (correspondence) courses last one year longer. Course programs comprise a first period of basic training, standard for all students in a given study discipline, followed by a period of specialized training (the 2–3 final years of a course) which includes compulsory and optional specialist subjects.

First-degree studies lead to a diploma, conferred upon successful completion of course requirements and the diploma examination (*examen de diploma*) for which the submission of a diploma dissertation (*teza de diploma*) or the defense of a diploma project (*proiect de diploma*) is the main requirement. Two principal categories of first-degree diplomas were awarded: (a) *diploma de subinginer* (the engineering technician diploma), awarded after a three-year study course and on successful defense of a diploma project (discontinued as of the 1990/1991 academic year); (b) *diploma de licenta* (the first-level, higher education diploma), awarded after four to six years of study and defense of a dissertation, before an examining board (*comisia de examen de licenta*). The *diploma de licenta* is roughly equivalent to a Master of Arts degree.

First-level degree courses in Romania are considered self-contained. This gives graduate training courses (*cursuri postuniversitare*) a specialized nature. Traditionally, their function was to update and perfect the professional in-service training of specialists working in economic, scientific, technological, and cultural fields. Courses were open to holders of a first-level diploma. The Ministry of Education, after consultation with other bodies involved, submitted annual proposals regarding field of specialization, enrollment figures, and forms of courses (short duration, evening, nonattendance, etc.) to the state council for approval. Institutions of higher education are now being awarded full autonomy in organizing graduate courses.

The position of the doctorate (*doctoratul*) as the highest academic degree and the principal form of graduate advanced research became unstable. By 1989, the number of doctoral candidates for all fields of scholarship in the whole country, had fallen to 652. The conditions for admission to doctoral studies (principally possession of a first-level higher education degree and the passing of an entrance examination), the number of places available, and the procedures for the award of the doctor's degree were approved by degree of the state council. Doctoral research topics had to be approved by the Ministry of Education and by the National Council for Science and Technology.

The first measure to reenhance the doctorate included the designation of some 1,500 supervisors. The number of doctoral candidates will be increased substantially and doctoral studies reorganized. Requirements for the doctorate extend over a four-year study period (*stagiu de doctorat*) and include a number of examinations, the presentation of scientific papers for approval by the university departments or research units concerned, and the public defense of the doctoral dissertation (*teza de doctorat*).

3. Governance, Administration, and Finance

3.1 National Administration

The relationship between higher education and the state in post-War communist Romania was one of subordination and control. Academic freedom and university autonomy, which had acquired some substance before the Second World War, were replaced by a system of close political, ideological, and administrative supervision.

Higher education institutions were required to train highly qualified specialists, to inculcate into them the ideas of socialism, and to provide "scientific" legitimation of the superiority of the socialist

system and party policy. This latter function became the primary objective of scientific research in a number of sciences, especially the economic, political, and social sciences. The others were not completely exempt from this ideologizing process. In the person of Elena Ceausescu, self-appointed "scholar of world renown," Romania presented a case of scientific fraud surpassing even the notorious Lysenko case in Soviet biology.

National higher education policy (aims, functions, and tasks) were defined in accordance with the overall objectives set by the Communist Party for the country's development. General directives were initially drawn up by the party congress, by its central committee, and the executive political committee. Education laws were adopted by the national assembly. Measures to be enacted were decreed by the state council and through regulations of the Ministry of Education. A congress of science and education was instituted in 1985 as a propagandistic form of "participatory" democracy in the field of education and science. It elected a national council, to which the Ministry of Education was subordinated. There was also a commission on higher education and manpower further training. In practice neither the congress nor any of the bodies it created played any significant role.

Direct responsibility for the organization, content, and implementation of all educational, teaching, and research activities rested with the Ministry of Education, to which all higher education institutions and affiliated research units were strictly subordinated. The Ministry drew up normative acts which were submitted for deliberation to the National Council of Science and Education. These were consequently revised and submitted for approval to the council of ministers, the state council or to the Grand National Assembly. These formal provisions were often bypassed or served simply to rubber stamp decisions already taken by Nicolae or Elena Ceausescu.

Planning implementation and evaluation were recognized as playing an important role in economic and social development, and featured very high in national planning. Planning included projections for enrollment figures, the creation of new types of institutions and forms of higher education, budgetary allocations, projections for graduate employment, and so on. With the deterioration of the economy in the late 1970s and the 1980s, planning for higher education lost any valid basis and became a travesty, consisting of ad hoc measures meant to solve crisis situations.

Assessment and evaluation of higher education, with the aim of fulfilling established goals, was assured by the council of ministers, which supervised the activity of the Ministry of Education and Instruction, as well as by other specialist ministries and central bodies, which monitored areas under their competence (the State Planning Committee, the

Ministry of Finance, the National Council for Science and Technology, etc.). The Congress of Science and Education reviewed achievements with regard to higher education, while the National Council for Science and Education supervised the implementation of decisions.

The government is (until private institutions come into being) the primary source of finance for higher education. The education budget, allocated by the national assembly, accounted for 6 percent of public expenditure in 1960, rising to 6.7 percent in 1980. This figure was preserved throughout the 1980s. The proportion of expenditure for higher education in the total public expenditure on education varied between 13 and 15 percent between 1965 and 1989.

Other sources of funding included free transfer of equipment and installations from industry, funds from research contracts, and income from production units functioning within higher education institutions. Such funds, administered by the institutions themselves, were more substantial in the technical fields. According to available statistics, public expenditure per student per year was US$237, the lowest in Europe, in 1985. One of the first measures adopted after December 1989 was to increase the budget for education considerably, with higher education and science being given high priority.

3.2 Institutional Administration

Given the complete control exercised by party and state authorities over higher education, there was no real system of governance at the institutional level. The function of institutional administrative bodies was almost exclusively to implement decisions transmitted from the Ministry of Education or from higher party echelons. Officially, the principle of "collective management" was supposed to operate. The leading body was the senate, composed of appointed members: the rector (as chairperson), vice-rectors, and deans, as well as representatives of the Communist Party, and student and trade union organizations. Nonappointed members were elected from among professors holding chairs and other staff and students (junior staff and students had a low representation).

Day-to-day management was the responsibility of the bureau of the senate, consisting of the rector, the vice-rectors, the scientific secretary of the senate, and the secretaries of the Communist Party organization, the communist student association, and the trade union. The rector, as administrative head, was appointed by the Ministry of Education from among three candidates submitted by the senate. Candidates for vice-rectors and for the scientific secretary were submitted to the senate by the rector, but subsequently had to be confirmed by the Ministry.

Faculties were managed by an academic board or professorial council (*consiliu profesoral*), made up of the dean (as chairperson), vice-deans, heads of departments and elected professors and students. Its bureau carried out the day-to-day management of the faculty. Proposals for deans and vice-deans were submitted by the professorial councils to the senate (as the next highest body), which decided upon the best candidates who were then confirmed by the Ministry of Education. Heads of departments were proposed by members of the respective department and seconded by the professorial councils, the final decision resting with the senate and subsequently confirmed by the Ministry. Specialists from industry, research, and other sectors were elected to university senates and professorial councils.

Following the December 1989 revolution the principle of full autonomy in the election of administrative bodies was reinstated: rectors, deans, heads of departments, and members of the senate and professorial councils are elected by direct vote by the staff and students. They are no longer confirmed at the ministerial level. The appointed members of these bodies (representatives of the party and the student and trade union organizations) were ousted. Student representation has been raised to 30 percent. Students insist on veto rights on all matters that affect them directly.

Teaching, training, and research in higher education is organized by broad disciplines, or profiles (*profile de invatamint*). Within each profile, several specializations (*specializari*) are established. Their number may vary considerably from one profile to another. For instance, there are only two specializations for the physics profile (theoretical physics and technological physics) but more than ten for the mechanical engineering one (machine building, precision mechanics, thermal mechanics, railway engineering, aeronautical engineering, naval engineering, agricultural engineering, etc.). Programs of study for related profiles (sometimes a single profile) are offered within a particular establishment of higher education (*Institut de invatamint superior*). For instance, universities unite, as a rule, programs in mathematics, physics, biology, chemistry, geology, geography, history, economics, philosophy, psychology, pedagogy, sociology, political science, philology, and law. The polytechnics bring together profiles of a technological and engineering nature. Academic activity is organized by faculties, sections of studies within a given faculty, and departments. The faculty constitutes the main institutional structure as far as academic activity is concerned. It comprises several departments, the basic organizational units of teaching and research. They bring together teaching, research, and service personnel working in one or several closely related disciplines. Their members may sometimes teach in several faculties.

Curricular matters are discussed at departmental level; course contents and proposals for the allocation of teaching hours in specific disciplines are delegated to higher academic authorites (the professorial council and the senate). Teaching materials prepared by departmental members are examined by these authorities before publication. Teams exist which are responsible for the implementation of the departmental research plan, a high priority. The department is empowered to accept or reject doctoral assignments. Other departmental tasks include work in associated research laboratories; various service activities (design and expert services provided to industry on a contractual basis), and the organization of students' practical training.

4. Faculty and Students: Teaching, Learning, and Research

4.1 Faculty

The number of academic staff in higher education in Romania has been a matter of grave concern. It has evolved from: 13,038 in 1965, to 14,592 in 1980, when it then fell to 12,961 in 1985 and 12,036 in 1988. This dangerous decrease was accompanied by an increase in the average age of staff, with devastating effects on quality. There were departments whose youngest members were around their mid-forties. In some of them, no new staff has been admitted since before the start of the 1980s. The proposal to increase higher education staff to 14,363, made in January 1990 was therefore a significant step towards redressing the situation. The number of part-time staff is insignificant. They are mainly employed in the polytechnics, on short-cycle programs.

The university teaching hierarchy in Romania is as follows: assistant (*asistent*), lecturer (*lector* or *sef de lucrari*), reader (*conferentiar*), and professor (*profesor universitar*). The general prerequisite for appointment to a university teaching post is the diploma of higher education; for readers' or professorial appointments it is the doctor's degree. However, even candidates for assistants' and lecturers' posts tend to hold a doctorate. Candidates for an assistant's post take oral and written tests, and have to undertake a period of probationary teaching, while for a lectureship, a curriculum vitae and publications are submitted for examination. The board recommends one candidate to the professorial council, which takes votes and proposes the candidate. The senate makes the final decision. Where appointment to a readership or professorship is concerned, the recommendation of the examining board is voted upon by the professorial council and the senate. The appointee gains academic tenure; promotion does not depend on length of service.

In theory, all appointments used to be open to competition. In practice, party and state authorities intervened directly and had the final say in the process. Over the last fifteen years of communist rule a drastic policy of freezing posts (or discontinuing them upon the retirement of the incumbent) was adopted under the pretext of reducing costs. No promotions (or very few, politically motivated ones) were made since around 1975. This placed Romania in a singular position, with no young aspiring scholars retained as university teachers, and those holding junior positions not being promoted, despite the fact that they had all the necessary qualifications and were actually discharging the functions incumbent on higher posts. One of the first demands of university staff after the December revolution, in addition to bringing in new staff to the departments, was that the normal process of promotion be resumed. About 30 percent of the teaching posts (i.e., some 4,300 posts) were opened for promotion on a competitive basis during the academic year 1989/1990. The institutions of higher education have full autonomy in the selection and promotion of new staff members. Women account for 29 percent of all academic staff, and many of them occupy high positions, including administrative posts.

There are no significant differences between faculty careers and status enjoyed by types of institution, or by region. This partly explains why there has been little mobility of personnel. With the opening of new institutions in provincial towns, mobility is expected to increase rapidly.

The principle of collective management supposedly allowed staff members to express their interests directly or to have them expressed by delegated representatives. In practice, however, although grievances were sometimes raised in the monthly meetings of the departments, in the faculty councils, or in the senates, little attention, if any, was paid to them. Party and official trade union organizations played an influential role in the life of institutions, but this role had little to do with the real interests of the staff. After December 1989, autonomous trade unions and professional and academic organizations were created.

4.2 Students

The distribution of students by fields of study over the 1960–1988 period is shown in Table 1.

Technical higher education (including all forms of technological engineering, civil engineering, architecture, agronomy, and veterinary science) was clearly favored at the expense of the humanities and the social sciences. The proportion of students enrolled in these fields was 42.4 percent in 1960, 40 percent in 1965, 68 percent in 1980, and 79.1 percent in 1988. Student enrollments grew by almost 400 percent in oil engineering, machine building, and metallurgy, 450 percent in the fields of transport and telecommunications, and 210 percent in electrical engineering and electrotechnics, between 1965 and 1985. This sort of growth was also evident in other fields.

The number of higher education graduates closely resembles the intake figures, because of the low dropout rate (5–7%). The number of higher edu-

Table 1
Evolution of student enrollments in higher education by fields of study

	1960/1961	1965/1966	1970/1971	1975/1976	1980/1981	1985/1986	1987/1988
Technical and medical programs	38,321	61,610	63,490	93,058	147,387	125,617	124,240
Economic science	5,085	12,866	21,016	22,857	21,919	16,485	14,924
Law	3,101	4,534	5,901	6,820	3,863	2,380	2,368
Exact and social sciences	23,752	49,185	58,108	39,055	17,393	14,417	14,594
Fine arts, drama, and music	1,730	2,419	3,370	2,780	2,207	899	915

cation graduates has evolved as shown in Table 2, since 1960.

Immediately after the Second World War various incentives, including special quotas for working-class students, were created in order to enhance equality in higher education. Soon however, these measures began to be used by members of the working class for preferential access. Their discontinuation in the mid-1960s was therefore received with satisfaction. There are no special incentives to increase the representation of students from ethnic minorities or any other categories of the population. Admission depends on merit alone.

Access of young people from all social strata is facilitated by the fact that higher education is free. However, certain fields display unequal opportunities of access. Candidates from educated families stand a better chance of admission to certain programs (medicine, the exact sciences, architecture, electronics, aeronautical engineering, etc.). Candidates from rural areas and the smaller provincial towns feel handicapped by the less competitive training they acquired in secondary school.

Progress has been made in assuring equal access to higher education for girls and women, as illustrated in Table 3.

While the percentage of women is higher in certain subject areas (philology, economics, certain branches of medicine, etc.) their representation has also grown steadily in science and technology.

Under the communist regime, students enrolled in regular courses automatically became members of the Union of Communist Student Associations of Romania (UASCR). Many of the best students also became members of the Communist Party. The president of the student association of a faculty and university was nominally a member of the professorial council, and the senate. Student opposition to the disastrous situation of the country and in particular to the lack of openings for themselves emerged in their participation in the revolution of 22 December 1989, in which many of them were killed. The students, now highly radicalized (1991), are strongly represented in all governing bodies of the faculties and universities (30%). Their organizations forcefully present student views both inside and outside the higher education establishments.

Teaching and training programs (*planuri de invatamint*) used to be standard throughout the national system. Drawn up by the Ministry of Education, study programs/courses included subjects to be taught, and their phasing over the study period; the number of hours scheduled for teaching, for seminar work, and for other requirements; the verification procedure (examination or other forms) for each discipline; and the hours devoted to practical activi-

Table 2
Numbers and percentages of graduates by field of study

	1960/1961	1965/1966	1970/1971	1975/1976	1980/1981	1985/1986	1986/1987
Technical and medical programs	5,910	9,536	12,003	16,899	26,442	23,323	20,740
	57.4%	42.2%	41.6%	54.1%	68.5%	76.1%	73.3%
Economics	967	1,275	4,408	4,111	4,779	3,471	3,443
	9.4%	5.6%	15.3%	13.3%	12.4%	11.3%	12.2%
Law	893	553	1,072	1,309	1,270	493	497
	8.7%	2.4%	3.7%	4.2%	3.3%	1.6%	1.8%
Exact and natural sciences, humanities, teacher training	12,273	10,809	10,783	8,022	5,265	3,159	3,241
	22.1%	47.9%	37.4%	26.0%	13.6%	10.3%	11.5%
Fine arts, drama, and music	253	416	574	708	859	187	201
	2.5%	1.8%	2.0%	2.3%	2.2%	0.6%	0.7%
Total	10,296	22,589	28,840	30,839	38,615	30,643	28,122

Table 3
Numbers and percentages of male and female students

	1960/1961	1965/1966	1970/1971	1975/1976	1980/1981	1985/1986	1987/1988
Male	47,883	79,254	86,254	90,877	110.656	88,140	84,017
	66.5%	60.7%	57.0%	55.2%	57.4%	55.4%	53.5%
Female	24,106	51,360	65,353	73,690	82,113	71,658	73,024
	33.5%	39.3%	43.0%	44.8%	42.6%	44.6%	46.5%

ties and research. Higher education specialists were consulted in relation to curricula and programs, but their views were systematically disregarded whenever they differed from those of the authorities concerned.

Departments, faculties, and institutions of higher education played a more substantial role in establishing the contents (*programa de studiu*) for each discipline set out in the study programs, although the ideological side of the contents was imposed and controlled from above. In principle, study programs were supposed to provide an equilibrium between general and specialist training. Thus, the first two to three years were based on a common core program of study for the various fields of specialization within the same profile or group of profiles. The concluding years were devoted to specialization through compulsory and optional subjects and specified research requirements.

The trend under the communist regime was to increase the percentage of applied, practical training (50–70% of activities in a program of study). Students spent two to three months annually, during the first three years of study, carrying out practical activities (*stagii de practica*) as a prerequisite training for their future professions. During the final years, they were engaged in research, culminating in the diploma thesis.

The academic year is divided into two semesters varying from 12 to 17 weeks in length (not including the periods of practical activity) and ending in an examination session (winter and summer). A number of examinations and other requirements are set for each academic year. Students who fail in up to three examinations may resit in a special session, held in autumn. Certain subjects are evaluated by continuous assessment or special assignments. Promotion to the next year of study is dependent upon success in all examinations and other course requirements. Students who fail can repeat a given year only once, otherwise they are expelled from higher education.

Until December 1989 attendance of seminars, lectures and so on was compulsory. It could go up to 36–40 hours per week for regular day courses and 20 hours for evening courses, which last one year longer. These numbers have been reduced considerably and attendance is no longer compulsory, except for certain laboratory classes and other specialized requirements. Instruction is organized in each faculty by profile and field of specialization into years of study and groups of students. Groups of 15–30 students are created for seminar work and for other practical activities. Smaller groups, of 7 to 15 students, may be established for practical activities, depending on specialization, year of study, and discipline.

No credit system operates. The minimum pass mark in examinations is 5; the maximum is 10. Students wishing to change institution, faculty, profile, or field of specialization can apply for transfer. Once approved, previous work is recognized if it corresponds to the requirements in the new study program.

5. Conclusion

Urgent measures are called for to deal with the legacy left by the totalitarian regime to Romanian higher education. The higher education system's quality has been considerably affected by excessive politization and ideologization; excessive control and subordination to state and party; centralized planning, based on invalid criteria; inappropriate resources (financial and otherwise); and almost complete international isolation.

Some of the main problems facing higher education in Romania today are:

(a) Adoption of a new law on higher education: this may only be achieved after the adoption of the new constitution. This will take time. A law on academic freedom and university autonomy has been laid before parliament in 1991, as the necessary prerequisite for real change.

(b) Access to higher education: Pressure for admission by secondary school leavers is considerable. The 20 percent increase in the intake figure for the academic year 1990/1991 over 1989/1990, is insufficient. However, the provision of jobs upon graduation, which in the past was an obligation of the state, can no longer be maintained. The interface between secondary and higher education on the one hand and between these two levels of education and the world of work on the other, will be a central issue in Romanian education for a number of years to come.

(c) Diversification of higher education: Part-time higher education (evening or extramural courses) and short-cycle programs (the "under-engineer" studies) have been substantially reduced. The duration of studies has been extended (in most cases from four to five years). Most institutions of a nonuniversity level have obtained university status. In the long run, however, faced with the need to increase student numbers under external pressures, a diversification of institutions, programs, types and forms of study, as well as of levels of degrees is a likely scenario.

(d) Graduate studies: These need reorganizing. Changes since the end of 1989 have tended to reinstate the French traditional model in the organization of studies up to the level of the *maitrise* (*licenta*). Doctoral studies continue to follow a pattern tailored after the Soviet *aspirantura* model after 1945. This hybrid situation cannot endure.

No evaluation of the prospects of Romanian higher education can be complete without making reference to the confused political situation. The students in particular and the young intellectuals in general are pressing for more radical and rapid measures to install genuine democracy and remove the structures of the old totalitarian regime. Unless the new authorities can come to terms with the students, they will continue to be a major source of social and political unrest, with important repercussions on the situation of the country in general and, implicitly, on higher education.

Bibliography

Burloiu P 1983 *Higher Education and Economic Development in Europe 1975–1980.* UNESCO–CEPES, Bucharest

Directia Centrala de Statistica 1988 *Anuarul Statistic al Republicii Socialiste Romania.* Directia Centrala de Statistica, Bucharest

Higher Education Act 1991 Law of University Autonomy 1991 (Draft submitted to Romanian Parliament)

Matei H, Brindus I (eds.) 1988 *Romania Yearbook 1988.* Editura Stiintifica si Enciclopedica, Bucharest

Ministry of Education and Instruction 1978 *The Education and Instruction Act.* Editura Didactica si Pedagogica, Bucharest

Ministry of Education and Instruction 1986 *Education in the Socialist Republic of Romania.* Editura Didactica si Pedagogica, Bucharest

Nicolae V, Smulders R H M, Korka M 1989 *Higher Education and Research in Countries of the Europe Region, 1980–1985.* CEPES, Bucharest

Pagahagi M 1990 Interview with Deputy Minister for Higher Education in Romania, *Opinia Studenteasca* Year VII, 28

Sadlak J 1988 Planning of Higher Education in Countries with a Centrally Planned Socioeconomic System: Case Study of Poland and Romania. PhD thesis, SUNY, Buffalo

Sadlak J 1990 Higher Education in Romania, 1860–1990: Between Academic Mission, Economic Demands, and Political Control. *Special Studies in Comparative Education 27*, Graduate School of Education Publications, SUNY, Buffalo, New York

D. Chitoran

Rwanda

1. Higher Education and Society

Rwanda is a small mountainous country situated in Central Africa which has frontiers with Uganda to the north, Tanzania to the east, Burundi to the south, and Zaire to the west. It has a surface area of 26,400 square kilometers and a population of 7.1 million, divided into several ethnic groups, the main ones being the Tutsis and the Hutus. It has the highest population density in Africa, with 257 people per square kilometer (UNESCO 1990), living mainly in isolated communities due to the geography of the country. More than 70 percent of the population are under 25 years of age. Initially a part of the Ruanda-Urundi kingdom, Rwanda was administered by Belgium after the First World War until 1923, then came under the mandate of the United Nations and became a Republic in 1961. It obtained full Independence in 1962. In 1973, a military coup overthrew President G Kayibanda and brought General Habyarimana, a Hutu, to power. Social and economic development made Rwanda a truly developing country, unlike many Third World countries. It is one of the five Third World countries with the lowest debt. Tensions that existed between the main ethnic groups lessened during the 1980s but struggles have placed strains on the country since October 1990.

Essentially agricultural, Rwanda's economy depends primarily on coffee, cotton, crops, and tobacco, which in normal circumstances ensure self-sufficiency. Major industries include textiles, plastics, and mining. Rwanda was badly hit by the fall in the price of coffee in 1989. Moreover, natural and climatic catastrophes in 1990 led to a famine when torrential rains destroyed the crops. Rwanda's worst problem is its very high birthrate, increasing at the rate of 3.7 percent per year, which is much higher than the increase in food production (2.5% per year).

Great emphasis has been laid on education since Independence. Current estimates suggest that some 50 percent of the population are illiterate (UNESCO

1990). Total educational expenditure amounts to 22.3 percent of total governmental expenditure. A reform of the education system was adopted in 1977, beginning in 1979 at the primary education level and in 1981 at the secondary and higher education levels. Secondary education became more vocational to train the middle-level cadres and access to education was broadened. The first reforms in higher education began in 1981 with the merger of the *Institut pédagogique national* and the *Université nationale du Rwanda*. The objects of the reform of higher education were to train the cadres the country needs, promote scientific research, preserve and enrich the cultural heritage, and serve the community. Higher education was called to participate in social, economic, and cultural development through teaching and research, while preserving the cultural heritage.

2. The Institutional Fabric of the Higher Education System

The main national institution of higher education is the *Université nationale du Rwanda* which was founded in 1963. Its initial organization and direction were entrusted to the Dominican Order of Canada. It was reorganized in 1981 when the *Institut pédagogique national* was incorporated. It has two campuses, at Ruhengeri (Nyakinama) and Butare, and comprises faculties of letters, agriculture, law, medicine, applied sciences, economics, social sciences and management, education, and science. It also comprises centers of modern technology, applied research, energy research and pharmacopeia, and traditional medicine research. A reform was initiated at the University in October 1987 which created new programs and curricula adapted to those of secondary education, and reduced the length of study in certain courses from three years to two years for the first stage and two years for the second stage, giving a total length of four years for the first and second stages instead of five years. Courses last six years in medicine and five years in agriculture.

Other institutions of higher education include the following: first, the *Université adventiste d'Afrique centrale*, Gisenyi, founded in 1984. It is an international private institution of higher education open to candidates from Sub-Saharan Africa and the Indian Ocean. It includes faculties of education, theology, science, arts, technology, and administration and management. It confers the *baccalauréat*. The *Institut supérieur des finances publiques*, Kigali, was founded in 1986 and offers specialized courses in budgeting and public accountancy, tax systems, customs, and financial control. The *Institut Africain et Mauricien de Statistiques et d'Economie appliquée*, Kigali, was founded in 1975 by the *Organisation Commune Africaine et Mauricienne* (OCAM). It is an international public institution of higher education open to candidates from Francophone countries in Africa and the Indian Ocean such as Madagascar and La Réunion.

Private institutions include the *Ecole supérieure de Gestion et d'Informatique (Institut Fidèle)*, Kigali, which was founded in 1985. It provides courses in computer sciences, management, accountancy, and secretarial studies. The *Institut supérieur catholique de Pédagogie appliquée* was founded in 1986 and provides courses in education.

In order to have access to higher education, students must hold the *certificat* or *diplôme de fin d'études secondaires*, obtained after 14 years of primary and secondary schooling. Qualifications awarded in higher education tend to follow the Belgian model. The first stage of higher education leads to the *baccalauréat* in law, science, letters, economics, social sciences, human biology, management, agriculture, education, nutrition, public health, and pharmacy after two years; or to the *diplôme d'ingénieur technicien*, or the *diplôme de technicien supérieur*, obtained after two to four years of study. A second stage leads to the degrees of *licence, ingénieur agronome, ingénieur civil, ingénieur économiste*, or *docteur en médecine*, the only doctorate conferred in the country, after two to four years' study following on from the first stage or after three years of the only existing cycle at the *Institut Africain et Mauricien de Statistiques et d'Economie appliquée*, which leads to the award of the *diplôme d'ingénieur des Travaux statistiques*.

Nonuniversity-level postsecondary education is provided by the *Institut supérieur des Finances publiques*, the *Ecole supérieure de gestion et d'informatique*, and the *Institut Africain et Mauricien de Statistiques et d'Economie appliquée*, which offer short-term technical and professional courses in public accountancy, public finance, management, computer science, and statistics.

3. Governance, Administration, and Finance

Most institutions of higher education come under the jurisdiction of the *Ministère de l'Enseignement supérieur et de la Recherche scientifique*. The *Université nationale du Rwanda* is an autonomous institution, governed by the *Conseil universitaire* which is made up of a representative of the president of the republic, the Minister of Education, the rector, vice-rector and deans, the secretary-general, the treasurer, and the administrator. The Council is the highest academic body of the University. It proposes the creation of faculties, institutes, centers of research, and university extension. It establishes the budget of the University and approves the grants, as well as donations made by foreign countries, international organizations, and public and private institutions. It is responsible for the governance of the University. The *sénat académique* coordinates academic activities. Members of the senate include the vice-rector, the deans of faculties, the heads of institutes, tenured professors, and student representatives. The president of the republic is honorary president of the University. The rector of the University is nominated by the president of the republic for a three-year term, which can be renewed. The secretary-general of the University is also nominated by the president of the republic, as is the treasurer. The *Institut Africain et Mauricien de Statistiques et d'Economie appliquée* is governed by a *Conseil d'Administration* which comprises ministers (or their representatives) of OCAM member states.

Educational policies are included in the manifesto of the *Mouvement Révolutionnaire national pour le Développement* (MNDP), the country's ruling party; in the president's speeches; in the Third National Plan for Economic, Social, and Cultural Development (1982–86); in the Fourth National Plan (1987–91); and in resolutions adopted at the MRND's congresses. The Second Congress recommended a reform of the University; the Third Congress a study of objective criteria for access to higher education and the rationalization of institutional development; the Fourth Congress an increase in the number of students, and a study of how to introduce third-cycle studies and lifelong education for civil servants and those who wished to upgrade their education and obtain certificates and diplomas; and the Fifth Congress a study of how to set up third-cycle studies.

Public institutions are financed mainly by the state. Students also pay registration fees which at the *Université nationale du Rwanda* amounted to 100 Rwandan francs (US$1), plus 4,000 Rwandan francs (US$36) for tuition in 1989–90. At the *Institut Africain et Mauricien de Statistiques et d'Economie appliquée* fees amounted to 80,000 Rwandan francs or US$727 during the same period.

4. Faculty and Students: Teaching, Learning, and Research

Academic staff is divided into *professeurs titulaires, professeurs associés, maîtres de recherche, chargés de cours, chargés de recherche, chargés de cours associés, chargés de recherche associés*, and *assistants* and *assistants de recherche*. Higher education teachers are trained at the University and often go abroad to complete their training. Emphasis was laid in the Third National Plan of Economic, Social, and Cultural Development (1982–86) on increasing the number of teachers nationally and encouraging able students to become teachers.

The academic staff at the *Université nationale du Rwanda* has developed considerably. In 1969–70, there was a total academic staff of 90, dropping to 70 in 1975–76, but then rising again to 80 in 1980–81. In 1984–85, with the incorporation of the *Institut pédagogique national*, their number rose to 130 and in 1989–90 it stood at 315. The student population at the University was 287 in 1969–70, 530 in 1975–76, and 903 in 1980–81. In 1984–85, the figure reached 1,567 through the incorporation of the *Institut pédagogique national* and in 1989–90 there were 1,886 students enrolled at the University.

The president has always attached great importance to research. In a speech broadcast in 1986, he recommended that teachers should encourage their students to undertake research linked to development. Research is carried out at university level in the fields of energy, pharmacy and traditional medicine, education and lifelong education, and modern technology. Efforts should be made to improve the dissemination of research results to the community at large.

5. Conclusion

Problems facing higher education include the high costs of education, the need to develop higher education in relation to national needs, and broadening access for female students. Higher education should not be cut off from society. It should take part in technological innovations and in the preservation of national culture. Language studies should be developed to facilitate communication but emphasis should also be laid on the national language. Planning of educational development should also promote new types of services. Administrative, academic, and research structures should optimize resources. Emphasis should also be laid on a better student–teacher ratio.

Resources are limited, and the government is therefore trying to involve the private sector more actively. The industrial and commercial sectors are also being encouraged to set up new institutions. External studies should be developed to broaden access to education and limit government costs on accommodation and services. Grants for students to study abroad are being limited to fields of study that are not offered in the country. The private sector and the Church have opened several institutions in the last few years that offer education in subjects promoting national development (e.g., finance, administration, computer science, and technical research). Moreover, the national education policy stresses the importance of nonformal education for all. International cooperation is being encouraged and agreements with universities in Africa, Europe, Canada, and the United States have been reached.

The total number of students and teachers in Rwanda's institutions of higher education seem relatively low when compared to other countries. Rwanda is a small country, however, where communication is difficult, and it only has one national university which has expanded considerably in the course of its thirty-year history.

Bibliography

Ministére de l'enseignement supérieur et de la recherche scientifique 1987 *Les grandes orientations de la réforme de l'enseignement supérieur au Rwanda*. Ministére de l'enseignement supérieur et de la recherche scientifique

Rossel H 1991 Rwanda-Afrique des Grands Lacs: des problémes politiques et économiques, mais surfont sociaux. In *Afrique Annales* 1991 (3) Jan–March

UNESCO 1991 *Statistical Yearbook 1990*. UNESCO, Paris

National University of Rwanda 1986 *Textes légaux et réglementaires de l'Université nationale du Rwanda de 1963 à 1985*. National University of Rwanda, Butare

C. Keyes

S

Saudi Arabia

1. Higher Education and Society

Education in general, and higher education in particular, is relatively new in Saudi Arabia. The origin of this modern type of education coincides with the foundation of the kingdom five decades ago. General and higher education in their bygone formative years were, by and large, strongly influenced by Islamic teachings and principles. The speedy development of higher education and its sustained spread throughout the country resulted inevitably from interaction of varied but closely related factors which assumed geographical, demographic, socioeconomic, and political dimensions.

Geographically, the kingdom occupies an area of 2,250,000 square kilometers in the Arabian Peninsula. Major urban centers are located along the Red Sea, the Gulf, and in certain parts of the country. Semiurban formations and diminishing nomadic groupings are scattered all over the kingdom.

According to published international reports and surveys, Saudi population has grown from 3.6 million persons in 1955 to 11 million in 1986, a growth rate equivalent to 3.8 percent annually. Twenty-three percent of all inhabitants are non-Saudis. All Saudis are Muslim and Arabic is their mother language.

Estimated educational enrollments are around 70 percent, 40 percent, and 15 percent for primary, secondary, and higher levels of education respectively. However in 1986 one source put these figures as 103 percent, 62 percent, and 37 percent for the same three categories (United Nations Economic and Social Commission for West Asia [UNESCWA] 1987.)

The Gross Domestic Product (GDP) in 1985 approximated SR284,115 million (US$75,764 million) generated sector-wise as follows: (a) agriculture 2.5 percent; (b) industry and related activities 19.5 percent; (c) services 38 percent; (d) oil 40 percent. The oil sector contributes on average 90 percent of state revenues. The remaining part comes from custom duties, services fees and charges, and so on.

In 1985 total civilian employment equaled 4,446,000 persons of whom 37.2 percent were Saudis. Female participation accounted for 3 percent of the labor force. In the same year, 15.8 percent, 32 percent, and 40 percent of the economically active population were employed in the primary, secondary, and tertiary sectors of the national economy, respectively. Percentage-wise, employees were classified in the following occupational groups:

(a) 12.7 percent in professional, semiprofessional, technical, and semitechnical groups;
(c) 23 percent in office workers groups;
(c) 32.6 percent in skilled and semiskilled labor groups and;
(d) 31.7 percent in unskilled labor groups (UNESCWA, 1987, and Ministry of Planning, 1985).

Major national development objectives are many-sided but in 1989 the primary focus tended to be on: (a) completing uncompleted infrastructural projects; (b) diversifying and broadening the base of the national economy; (c) developing human resources; and (d) improving social, health, and educational services.

The crucial role assigned to higher education in achieving strongly cherished and officially declared national objectives and aspirations is a well-established reality that can hardly be disputed or minimized.

2. The Institutional Fabric of the Higher Education System

In the early 1990s, the seats of advanced learning and training which constitute the higher education system are composed of six comprehensive universities, one specialized university, and 60 different educational and training establishments (see Table 1). All these bodies are exclusively state-managed both administratively and academically. Private participation in such management is virtually nonexistent.

Most universities and other institutions of higher schooling were established after 1973 when massive capital accumulations began to generate in their aftermath enormous expansionary forces in every sector of the economy. The fundamental functions of universities are oriented, in the first instance, towards inculcation of knowledge and promotion of scientific research activities. Thus it has become a major concern of every university to establish a research center (or centers) affiliated to it and to be involved in a wide range of theoretical as well as applied research works. However, the rapid emergence of such centers within a short time span (1973–83) coupled with their unabated multiplicity have

Table 1
Development of higher education institutions in Saudi Arabia 1960–89

	1960	1965	1970	1975	1980	1989
Comprehensive universities	1	1	2	4	5	5
Specialized university in Islamic studies	—	1	1	1	1	1
Specialized university in humanities and social sciences	—	—	—	1	1	1
Girls colleges (education + sciences + arts)	—	—	1	4	7	12
Teachers' training junior colleges (female)	—	—	—	—	3	14
Teachers' training junior colleges (male)	—	—	—	1	9	18
Polytechnic	—	—	—	1	1	1
Commercial institutes	—	—	—	1	2	2
Military and security academies	1	1	4	4	5	6
Specialized schools, centers, and institutes offering training in public administration, civil aviation, passports, traffic control, diplomatic work, and telecommunication	—	—	—	—	—	8

Source: Ministry of Higher Education, Riyadh 1987. *Higher Education Directory in Saudi Arabia.*

prevented most of them from making positive, if not rich, contributions to the cause of research at large. In particular, some centers engaged in research associated mainly with humanities and/or social sciences and their related domains have failed to survive or to develop for one reason or another. Nevertheless, the successful experience of the National Institute for Science and Technology (recently renamed King Abdul Aziz City for Science and Technology—KACST) is worth mentioning. KACST encourages universities and their staff members to participate in implementing research projects submitted by KACST or other government departments and agencies. Conversely, KACST sponsors, finances, and evaluates relevant research proposals submitted by universities or individual researchers.

As a general rule, all seats of higher education require candidates to attain the secondary-school certificate as a minimum condition for entry. Each institution devises its own internal admission policies and procedures. Entry to higher education was almost fully guaranteed to every secondary-school graduate, but in face of the massive growth in number of graduates plus relative stagnation in further expansion of educational facilities, universities imposed tougher admission requirements. For example, to secure entry to the faculty of medicine or engineering an applicant must score a total pass mark not less than 90 percent.

The university student population increased substantially from 6,942 students in 1970 to 107,528 students in 1987 greatly exceeding the targets set by the Fourth Development Plan.

Usually, students registered for bachelor degrees undergo four years of academic study except for engineering (five years) and medicine (seven years). Some universities award masters' and doctoral degrees in certain fields of study especially in Arabic and Islamic studies. Diplomas, offered by nonuniversity institutes, are conferred after successful completion of prescribed study or training courses whose duration ranges from one to three years depending upon the kind of diploma to be awarded.

3. Governance, Administration, and Finance

3.1 National Administration

The task of supervising higher education is shared by different government organizations. Universities are supervised by the Ministry of Higher Education, while nonuniversity teachers' training colleges came under the Ministry of Education and the General Presidency for Girls' Education. Polytechnic and commercial institutes are supervised by the General Organization for Technical Education and Vocational Training. Military academies, security colleges, specialized schools, centers, and institutes are the responsibility of the appropriate government ministry or department.

Social demand for higher education coupled with the ambitions of the institutions themselves exert clearer effects on higher education than the supervising agencies. However, certain bodies outside the educational system exercise powerful domination and regulatory control over the pace, direction, and pattern of higher education. They are legally empowered, among other things, to allocate financial resources, and decide on the creation of new educational opportunities or facilities. Apart from the Ministry of Finance, which allocates the budgets, and the Ministry of Planning, which is entrusted with the overall responsibility for incorporating higher education plans into national development plans, two other official agencies are directly involved in steering and directing higher education. They are the Higher Committee for Educational Policies and the

Manpower Council. The committee chairman is the king, while the council is under the presidency of the Second Deputy Premier. From the practical point of view, the extent of influence exercised by these two bodies remains limited unless they formally oblige specific units to implement particular policy decisions issued by them. Such a course of action is rarely taken.

Until the early 1990s no unified approach or mechanism has been adopted by the government to identify, measure, and evaluate the degree of receptiveness of higher education, nationwide, to avowed national objectives. Exercises of this kind are conventionally confined to databased reports issued annually by the Ministry of Higher Education. Included in the reports are comparative series of results actually achieved in relation to planned targets especially in the field of student enrollment.

Multipurpose activities undertaken by institutions of higher schooling are funded entirely from government budgets. In 1987 budgetary appropriation earmarked for higher education totalled SR6,003 million (US$1,600 million) compared with SR11,079 million (US$2,954 million) in 1985 and only SR80 million (US$21 million) in 1970. In this respect, it is only fair to mention that students annual cost per capita in higher education is exorbitantly high by any standard.

Taking such facts into consideration, the Fourth National Plan has explicitly underscored two major challenges that will eventually confront higher education namely: (a) how to boost productivity and reduce drop-out rates; and (b) how to improve quality and standards of educational programs as well as to raise their general operational efficiency (Ministry of Planning 1985).

3.2 Institutional Administration

Directors of universities and their assistants are directly appointed via ministerial decrees. They discharge the prescribed administrative and financial affairs of their universities. On the other hand, academic matters such as pedagogical activities, distribution of students among various fields of specialization, appointment, and promotion of staff members, deans of faculties, and heads of departments, etc. are decided by each university senate. The director presides over senate meetings. The highest decision-making organ in the university power-sharing hierarchy is represented in the Higher University Council. Its membership includes the director and faculty deans together with other dignitaries appointed by royal decrees. The Minister of Higher Education chairs the council. The Council is authorized to approve internal rules or propose their alterations or modifications. It also recommends establishment of new rules, faculties, or departments (Ministry of Higher Education 1985).

At the faculty level, there is a board composed of department heads who collectively nominate the faculty dean. The board handles academic matters which comprise, among other things, appointment and promotion of staff members.

Insofar as departments are concerned, staff members of each department (full professors, associate, and assistant professors) form the Department Council which nominates the head of department and vets all subjects of an academic nature.

4. Faculty and Students: Teaching, Learning, and Research

4.1 Faculty

A heavy dependence on foreign staff members (especially Arabs) in the early stages of the development of higher education was an understandable inevitability. With the passage of time, the recruitment of Saudis in teaching positions began to experience steady and marked expansion arising from 159 staff members (28 percent of the recorded total staff) in 1970 to 4,225 members (45 percent of total) in 1987 out of whom 24 percent were females.

Staff membership requires a PhD. Saudi PhD holders, appointed officially to teaching bodies, are granted permanent tenured status. New recruits join the academic workforce as lecturers or teaching assistants. Non-PhDs remain as teaching assistants or lecturers or may assume administrative responsibilities (within the university or outside) in accordance with civil service rules and ordinances. All Saudi higher education staff are state employees on a virtually permanent basis.

Non-Saudi staff members are appointed by faculties either through secondment or by direct contract for a four-year period. This period is renewable or may be terminated before expiry with due compensation. Advancement to senior posts on the academic ladder is conditioned by clearly defined and

Table 2
Total number of staff members in higher education 1970–87

	1970	1975	1980	1985	1987
Overall staff numbers					
Males	556	1,496	3,761	7,032	6,976
Females	17	245	1,030	2,237	2,297
Total	573	1,741	4,791	9,269	9,273
Saudi staff					
Males	152	507	1,301	2,999	3,210
Females	7	31	309	941	1,015
Total	159	538	1,610	3,940	4,225
Saudi percentage of total	28	31	34	42	45

Sources: Ministry of Higher Education 1989 *Statistical Indicators on Development of Higher Education*. Ministry of Higher Education, Riyadh, 18

well-stipulated performance criteria. Included among the criteria are efficient teaching, core research contribution, demonstrated ability to shoulder administrative work, and completion of four working years between one rank and the next. Research contributions are subjected to internal and external assessments. Advancement nomination emanates first from Department Council, then goes to Faculty Council, before being submitted to the Academic Board which sets advancement conditions and ensures their proper implementation and observance. The final decision on promotion is then issued by the Senate.

Recruitment procedures, pay scales, and allowances are standardized with respect to all institutions constituting the higher education system.

Members of the academic profession represent their corporate interests through active participation in department, faculty, and university councils. Organized unions or national staff associations do not exist either on an institutional or countrywide basis.

The teaching load, measured in terms of weekly hours, is fixed according to semiunified procedural systems applicable throughout the country. Thus 12, 8 to 10, and 6 to 8 teaching hours per week are the respective norms undertaken by assistant, associate, and full professors.

4.2 Students

Graduate output equalled 13,023 graduates in 1986 compared with only 808 graduates in 1970. Tables 3 and 4 indicate a relative improvement in the balance between various subject areas although the majority of students and graduates alike are schooled in social sciences and humanities. Despite the fact that this article has not attempted to measure educational waste, the student–graduate ratio pinpoints high wastage rates.

Each institution constructs its own study courses and a related syllabus leading to the award of the first degree. In this context, the balance of requirements needed to qualify for graduation is centered around 55 percent for specialization, 30 percent for general education and liberal arts, and 15 percent for Islamic culture and Arabic language.

Students come from all walks of life; their social and economic class origins represent all community stratas. Differentiation or discrimination among students on the basis of their origin is totally unknown. By virtue of being free and because all students are granted equal financial hand-outs, higher education is accessible to all eligible candidates irrespective of social or economic background. It could, however, be rightly ascertained that the majority of the student body belong to the broad-based middle class.

The absence of institutions of higher education in certain populated areas has denied some students (girls in particular) the benefits of higher learning. It is worth noting that in 1989 the government started to conduct a strenuous nationwide drive, aimed at widely dispersing seats of higher schooling among all areas and locations.

Student interests are safeguarded through the student affairs unit established in every institution. The unit caters for student welfare in general, including provision of housing facilities and medical care, social and academic guidance. Moreover, faculties and departments in collaboration with admission and registration units provide academic guidance besides looking into student complaints and petitions with respect to studies or exams.

4.3 Learning, Examinations, and Assessment

Most universities and higher education establishments model their learning systems on accredited hours. However, an alternative model based on the academic year or semesters, is operative in girls'

Table 3
Total number of students at higher education level according to fields of study 1970–87

	1970	1975	1980	1985	1987	%
Islamic studies	2,122	3,736	8,805	14,872	15,010	14.0
Humanities and social sciences	1,651	4,478	13,064	28,277	31,066	28.9
Administrative and financial sciences	1,037	3,263	7,742	9,947	8,200	7.6
Education	578	3,168	6,999	17,330	22,329	20.7
Natural sciences	405	1,045	2,735	9,461	13,770	12.8
Engineering	847	2,263	5,359	7,191	7,461	6.9
Medicine	200	617	2,130	5,317	6,841	6.4
Agriculture	102	523	1,156	2,361	2,851	2.7
Total	6,942	19,093	47,990	94,756	107,528	100

Source: Ministry of Higher Education 1989 *Statistical Indicators on Development of Higher Education*, Riyadh

Table 4
Total number of higher education graduates according to field of study 1970–86[a]

	1970	1975	1980	1986
Islamic studies, humanities and social sciences	676	1,060	2,779	7,755
Education	48	469	849	2,924
Exact sciences, medicine, engineering, and agriculture	84	380	1,014	2,344
Total	808	1,909	4,642	13,023

Source: Ministry of Higher Education 1989 *Statistical Indicators on Development of Higher Education*. Riyadh

university colleges, the Islamic university, and the Imam Mohammed University. In this model, specific timetabled subjects form part of the instruction of all students and failure in some majors may entail overall repetition.

Students, in their undergraduate career, are assessed through regular testing or final examinations duly arranged and set for every class. Assessment mechanisms are either directly masterminded by the teaching staff concerned or by a committee composed of several members who teach the same subject matter. Some colleges and institutes host committees to supervise final examinations whose questions are drafted, subject-wise, by a group of teaching staff.

As regards institutions directly responsible to certain government units, their pass requirements follow the same marking specifications but are subject to final approval by the relevant government unit. Although there is no central national accrediting body, and no formal relation with outside accrediting agencies, so far no problem has arisen with respect to their due recognition on the part of Arab or foreign authorities. All educational programs developed through this methodological device are recognized domestically.

5. Conclusion

Higher education in Saudi Arabia may be characterized by its supremacy in rapid quantitative expansion in response to the social demand for higher education. This expansion is also characterized by a deep-rooted trend visible in Third World countries which tend to accord high priority to liberal arts, social sciences, and humanities. This tendency is due to the relative ease with which these programs are set in motion with limited prerequisites or resources—be they human or otherwise.

Eventually, a two-way mismatch has emerged between higher education and the realities and needs of society. The first aspect can be visualized in the weak link between higher education output and actual labor market requirements. The second aspect pertains to the need to alter goals, modes, and contents of the educational system to keep pace with the ongoing economic, cultural, social, and political developments of society and its imperative goals.

One indicator of mismatch is the fact that most teacher-training institutions and all vocational, technical and specialized institutions and programs have been founded outside universities by concerned authorities, thus pinpointing a lack of awareness and response in universities to the issues and needs of society at large.

Due to the seemingly weak functional relationship between society and universities, higher educational programs have, bizarrely, been heavily biased in favor of social disciplines and humanities. As a consequence, the country has become saturated with certain specializations in different fields of the social sciences. By contrast, the need for "specialist" output in exact sciences has been and still is constantly growing. With a view to accelerating the output of science graduates, universities have belatedly begun to orchestrate their activities in that direction. Another implication arising from the relationship at issue is made manifest by constant complaints against appallingly low standards of basic skills and technical competency on the part of certain higher education graduates.

These features depicting the state of higher education are by no means unique to the kingdom of Saudi Arabia alone. However, there are other problems peculiar to and typical of the country. The major difficulties facing higher education in Saudi Arabia could be summarized as follows:

(a) An acute shortage of higher education programs catering for technological, technical, and vocational needs of developing society.

(b) A heavy concentration of higher education facilities and hence opportunities in big urban centers at the expense of other disadvantaged geographical areas and locations.

(c) Overstaffing of administrative and teaching posts in certain institutions which thereby inflate educational costs generally and generate unwarrantable disparities between institutions.

(d) Limited female participation in higher education pursuits especially in areas with an underrepresentation of higher education institutions. This is due to the prevalence of conservative norms and values which disapprove of female mobility in search of schooling and of boarding outside close family boundaries. Moreover, employment for female graduates is relatively scarce.

(e) Insufficient attention to the active development

of syllabi and teaching methods as well as internal and external evaluation of educational programs.

(f) Disillusionment and lack of interest among some staff members who eschew specializing, training, and research, in a specific subject area. Instead, they seek energetically highly placed administrative postings, which are considered to be the road to power and repute. The security of employment offered to Saudis and the power accorded to administrative posts may partly explain this disinterest in formal specialization development be it in teaching, creative work, or research.

(g) A multiplicity of higher education sponsoring agencies coupled with weak interagency coordination has unearthed the very real issues of duplication, lopsided growth, and cost escalation.

Bibliography

Al-Jallal A 1985 *Education of Affluence and the Backwardness of Development*. The National Council for Culture, Literature and Arts, Kuwait

Al-Mania M A 1988 *Analytical Study of University Graduates vis-à-vis the Developmental needs in the Arab States of the Gulf*. Annals of the College of Education, University of Qatar, Doha

Al-Qublan Y 1985 *Coordinating Educational Services in Saudi Arabia*. Institute of Public Administration, Riyadh

Arab Bureau of Education for the Gulf States 1982 *Proceedings of the First Seminar of the Rectors of the Universities of the Gulf States*. Arab Bureau of Education for the Gulf States, Riyadh

Birks J S, Rimmer J A 1984 *Developing Education System in the Oil States of Arabia: Conflicts of Purpose and Focus*. University of Durham, Durham

Ministry of Higher Education 1985 *Higher Education in Saudi Arabia*. Ministry of Higher Education, Riyadh

Ministry of Higher Education 1987 *Higher Education Directory in Saudi Arabia*. Ministry of Higher Education, Riyadh

Ministry of Higher Education 1989 *Statistical Indicators on Development of Higher Education*. Ministry of Higher Education, Riyadh

Ministry of Planning 1985 *Fourth Development Plan*. Ministry of Planning, Riyadh

Rahmah A 1985 *Issues of Planning Higher Education in the Arab World*. UNESCO Regional Office of Education for the Arab Countries, Amman

Sochnat J A 1983 Progress and problems in the development and utilization of human resources in the Arab Gulf States. Unpublished typescript. Washington, DC

Sonbol A A, Khateeb M S, Motwally M M, Abdljawad N 1987 *Educational System in Saudi Arabia*. Riyadh

United Nations Economic and Social Commission for West Asia 1987 *Demographic and Related Socio-Economic Data Sheets*, No. 5. UNESCWA, Baghdad

UNESCO 1980 *Future of Education in the Arab World 1981–2000*. UNESCO Regional Office of Education for the Arab Countries, Beirut

UNESCO 1982 *Development of Education in the Arab Countries*. UNESCO Regional Office of Education for the Arab Countries, Beirut

Yamani M A 1974 *Universities of Saudi Arabia: Case Study*. Paper presented to the Seminar of the University Mission in Developing Countries. University of King Saud, Riyadh

A. A. Al-Jallal

Senegal

1. Higher Education and Society

Senegal's system of higher education is of relatively recent formation, beginning in 1948 with the foundation of a medical school by the colonial power, France. It provided the basis for a university, founded in 1956 with four autonomous facilities: medicine and pharmacology, law and economics, liberal arts and social sciences, natural sciences. After Independence in 1960, Senegal sought to complete this system by creating new structures and institutions of higher learning.

The University of Dakar benefited from French aid throughout the first decade after Independence for financing its equipment and development, as well as for the salaries of its personnel, scholarships, and subsidies. This financial aid was gradually reduced throughout the second decade (1970–1980) and came to an end in 1981–1982. During this time, the government of Senegal had to take over the development of the University and see to it that it was effectively rooted in Senegalese and African reality. France continued throughout the period to provide technical assistance to the University in the form of scientific and technical personnel, aid projects, and so forth.

From the beginning, the University had a regional and subregional focus, educating students from throughout what was formerly French West Africa, and recruiting scientific and technical personnel from the same countries.

1.1 Geographical Context and Population

Senegal is a small country located on the western extreme of Sub-Saharan Africa. Its land area covers 196,000 square kilometers. The Bureau of Statistics put the population at 6,881,919 in 1988, with an average density of 35 inhabitants per square kilometer. The World Bank estimated that the population grew at a rate of 2.9 percent between 1970 and 1980, and projects the population growth rate for the period 1980–2000 to be 3.2 percent. Between 60 and 70 percent of the population lives in rural areas, and 53 percent of the population is under 21 years of age. The school-age population (7–12 years old) was estimated to be 135,000 in 1988, giving rise to a strong but problematic demand for education, given the country's limited resources and the economic crisis in effect since 1979.

1.2 Structure of the Economy

The main economic activity is the cultivation of peanuts, introduced in colonial times, followed by fishing which is becoming more and more industrialized. Tourism is the third most important source of wealth.

Primary sector activities (agriculture, fishing, stock-raising) remain dominant, in spite of the fact that, during the first decade after Independence, several mining operations (phosphates) were started, along with canneries, breweries, textile factories, and so forth. Industry was further diversified by setting up a duty-free industrial zone in Dakar and industrial parks in all of the regional capitals.

Per capita gross domestic product was $380 per annum in 1984.

1.3 Social, Political, and Religious Organization

Economically, socially, politically, and religiously, Senegal is characterized essentially by a rich and fruitful pluralism. Tolerance and respect for differences are key values cultivated by everyone: Senegal is a society in which the basic freedoms are recognized, guaranteed, and defended.

In the pluralistic religious context, public schools (including higher education) are secular and free. Religious groups however, both Christian and Muslim, have the right and the possibility of contributing to the state's educational efforts by maintaining their own institutions at the preschool, elementary, middle, and secondary levels.

2. The Institutional Fabric of the Higher Education System

2.1 Sectoral Organization of Higher Education

The system of higher education was developed gradually by the state following France's initiative. The state finances, manages, administers and controls the system. Higher education is open to all citizens free of charge, without discrimination. There is no private institution of higher education, since the law allows for private education only on lower levels.

The system of higher education comprises the University of Dakar (with its component, dependent and associate institutions), renamed in 1987 the University Sheik Anta Diop after the famous Senegalese Egyptologist who died the previous year; as well as the schools of higher learning attached to different government ministries, including the Ministry of Higher Education.

The president of the University, the president of the University Assembly and the Director of Higher Education all have authority over the University. The Directorate of Higher Education also coordinates the system of higher education on a national level.

2.2 Levels of Institutions

The core of the University comprises four independent faculties, a basic research institute, an engineering and technical school, and two teacher training schools. Other institutions have been added to this core, as components, dependents, or associates. They are called university institutes or faculty institutes.

The four autonomous faculties are classical university institutions, providing general education and granting the classical university degrees: the licentiate, the *maîtrise*, the *agrégation*, third-cycle and state doctorates.

The institutes are largely financially, administratively, and organizationally independent of the faculties, while having ample opportunity to collaborate with them, especially on the scientific and instructional level. Faculty institutes are attached to specific faculties and depend on them scientifically and pedagogically, as well as for their governance, administration, and management.

There are various institutions dependent on the Ministry of Higher Education found throughout the country. These institutions are not located on the University campus and are largely independent on the scientific, instructional, financial, administrative, and governance levels.

Other institutions are dependent on other ministries and provide training in a wide variety of specializations: administration, customs, military health care, technology, officers' training, architecture, plastic arts, theater, music, hotel management, seamanship, telecommunications, and physical education.

Three other institutions of higher education located in Senegal are organized on an international level and are independent of the state. They provide graduate studies to high-ranking officials of the subregion. The *Centre d'Études Supérieures Africain de Gestion* (CESAG), founded by the West African Economic Community, provides higher studies in management. The *Centre Africain d'Études Monétaires* (CAEM) was founded by the West African Monetary Union, as was the third institution, the *École Multinationale des Postes et Télécommunications* (EMPT).

2.3 Admissions Policies and Selection

The *baccalauréat* or a recognized equivalent is required for entrance into the system of higher education. Adults and others without secondary schooling are accepted if they pass an entrance examination set once a year. Foreign students, whether or not they have the baccalaureate, must be approved by a committee set up by the University president's office before being accepted. This committee judges whether or not their previous studies comprise the equivalent of what is demanded for entrance in Senegal.

Three kinds of institutions of higher learning can be distinguished, according to the type of degree they grant. The classical university structures (faculties) have the admission requirements mentioned above. They provide a general education, leading to a licentiate after three years, a *maîtrise* after five, a third-cycle doctorate after eight; a state doctorate (in liberal arts, social and natural sciences) and the *agrégation* (in law, economics, medicine and pharmacology) are the last and highest degrees granted in Senegal, with no time limit being placed on fulfilling all the requirements.

National and teacher training schools provide professional training. Besides the above-mentioned entrance requirements, students must take an entrance examination, owing to the high number of applicants and limited number that can be accepted.

Research institutes recruit researchers, especially on the third-cycle level (further studies diploma and third-cycle doctorate). Students are introduced to research during the second cycle, while preparing their *maîtrise* dissertations, and continue to do research throughout the third cycle.

3. Governance, Administration, and Finance

3.1 National Administration

Senegal's system of higher education was founded by the state and is completely dependent on the state for financing its functioning, equipment, and development. The state provides an annual budget, which is managed and administered under its control and by university organizations (assemblies and councils).

The organization and governance of the University were determined by a decree of October 1970.

The state and the government exercise their authority and their attributions with respect to the system through the Ministry of Higher Education (or the Ministry of Education); other ministries with their own educational institutions; the president of the University, the president of the University Assembly and the Director of Higher Education, named by the president of the republic for a three-year period.

The president of the University, a member of the system of higher education and possessor of a state doctorate, directs the institutions of higher learning and their administrative services, oversees their budgets and controls their functioning with the aid of a University Secretary General (a civil administrator) in charge of administration.

3.2 Institutional Administration

The University Assembly is established by the statutes of the University. It is composed of the president (who presides over the assembly); deans and their assistants; directors of institutes, university schools, and institutions; elected representatives of professors, researchers, and students; the Director

Table 1
Public expenditures per student (in 1983 dollars)

	1975	1980	1983
Higher Education	2,006	1,849	—

Source: World Bank 1988 pp. 147–9

of the Center for University Activities; the Secretary General of the University (who serves as secretary of the Assembly); representatives of the government, congress, the supreme court; worker representatives, designated by the most representative union; and representatives of the Chamber of Commerce and Industry of Dakar.

The Assembly deliberates on every aspect of University life: teaching (courses, programs, schedules, examinations, holidays); financial (budget, goods, registration fees); and functioning (personnel, recruitment, assignments), etc.

On a lower level are deans and their assistants, faculty assemblies, department heads, and department assemblies in the faculties. The institutes, centers, and schools have directors, assisted by assemblies or councils (scientific or administrative), department heads and department assemblies.

3.3 Finance

Projects, teaching and research programs, schedules and courses, examinations and budgets, rules and regulations, and so forth, are all conceived and elaborated by lower-level structures and the academic authorities, and are then passed up the line to government authorities who normally ratify them by adopting and promulgating the rules, decrees, or orders.

Every year the state assigns to all of its structures (including the University and higher education) a precise budgetary limit which they are not allowed to go beyond. The Ministry of Higher Education sees to it that the annual budget allotment conforms with the needs expressed by the lower level University structures and other institutions of higher learning.

This state budget, the main source of financing, is complemented by financial support from France, aid programs from several other countries, and the financial contribution of African countries that sent students to the University of Dakar. Nevertheless, financing from foreign sources, despite their number, is still very small in relation to that given by the state and in relation to needs.

The state has faced serious economic crisis for more than a decade and also budgetary constraints. The financial dependence on the state is beginning to produce effects on the current situation and functioning of the educational system and its students. The state's budget evolves very slowly. In any case, it

Table 2
Student enrollment 1959–1976

	1959–60	1960–61	1961–62	1962–63	1963–64	1964–65	1965–66	1966–67	1967–68	1968–69	1969–70	1970–71	1971–72	1972–73	1973–74	1974–75	1975–76
Type of institution																	
Faculties	4	4	4	4	4	4	4	4	5	6	8	9	9	9	9	9	9
Institutes	—	—	—	—	—	—	—	—	2	3	4	5	5	5	5	5	5
Enrollment	1,012	1,018	1,260	1,476	1,799	1,822	2,139	2,814	3,109	2,502	3,054	4,285	4,690	5,376	5,898	6,688	7,312
Nationality as a percentage																	
Senegalese	33	39	34	28	28	31	28	26	32	50	53	55	60	62	65	70	71
French African	—	—	—	—	—	—	—	38	38	32	28	31	25	25	23	20	22
French	67	61	66	72	72	69	72	36	27	17	15	11	9	7	6	5	4
Others	—	—	—	—	—	—	—	—	3	1	4	3	6	6	6	5	3

Source: Office of the President of the University of Dakar

increases nowhere near as quickly as do the financial needs and charges, still less the number of students. The quality of education is deteriorating. Since recourse to private financing (agreements between the educational system and corporations) is prohibited by law, the financial situation is in danger of deteriorating even further if lasting solutions are not found.

4. Faculty and Students: Teaching, Learning, and Research

4.1 Faculty

The professors in the different university structures come from a variety of countries. The University of Dakar has always had a regional focus. The professors are divided into three categories: (a) Senegalese, already the largest group; (b) Africans from the subregion (Mali, Guinea, Burkina Faso, Togo, Benin, etc.); (c) French technical assistants, still numerous. The latter two groups are growing smaller, to the extent that Senegalese are taking over teaching positions in higher education and there are rapidly increasing numbers of upper-level Senegalese officials.

The changing composition of teaching and research personnel over the 1980s shows a continuous and rapid Africanization. The process should be completed some time during the 1990s. The number of women teaching in higher education is also increasing.

Professors and researchers at the University of Dakar can be divided according to the different kinds of degrees required for recruitment. Their appointments, salaries, promotions, and benefits (housing, travel, grants) are set by decree of the president of the republic.

All recruits are required to have the degree necessary for their position (diploma of further studies, third-cycle doctorate, *agrégation*, state doctorate, etc.).

The recruitment, appointment, and promotion of personnel falls to the competency of the state. The process is similar to that of elaborating the budget. Needs (vacancies, new positions open, new positions needed) are determined on the lower levels (departments, assemblies, department heads). These needs are centralized and discussed on the level of the department assembly which sets priorites. Then the department head communicates the decisions to the dean and the faculty assembly, which in turn examines them and sets priorities according to the needs of all the faculty departments and the real possibilities of the state. The president of the university finally presents these needs and demands to the University Assembly, which takes into account all the needs expressed by all of the structures of the University, as well as the number of positions created by the state. After that, the candidates are recruited and appointed by decree of the president of the University or the Minister of Higher Education, or by decree of the president of the republic.

The different teaching and research faculties are organized on the academic level into assemblies in different colleges according to categories and rank. On the union level, their interests are represented and defended by different unions.

Table 3
Student enrollment 1984–1989, University Sheik Anta Diop of Dakar

	1983–84	1984–85	1985–86	1986–87	1987–88	1988–89
Law and economics	2,490	3,418	3,770	4,364	4,419	4,284
Medicine and pharmacy	1,748	2,435	2,486	2,718	2,803	2,502
Liberal art and social science	1,473	2,137	2,672	3,321	4,141	3,522
Science and technology	1,350	2,218	2,348	2,940	3,257	2,960
ENSUT	510	432	378	377	403	343
ENS	175	527	429	419	380	327
EBAD	188	137	203	214	192	167
CESTI	84	85	91	87	76	63
EISMV	201	237	258	264	289	243
IFE	55	52	76	85	88	122
Total	8,274	11,678	12,711	14,789	16,048	14,833
Senegalese					13,592	12,871

Source: Office of the President of the University of Dakar

4.2 Students

At the time of its founding by France, the University could accommodate 5,000 students. Only 1,000 of these were Senegalese. The rest were from France or the subregion. Today, the student body numbers between 15,000 and 20,000, about three-fourths of whom are Senegalese.

Table 2 shows the continual growth of the student body and its changing composition from predominately foreign to predominantly local.

Table 3 presents the distribution of students among the major fields of study and the more important university structures for the period 1983–1989.

4.3 Representation of Student Interests

Students elect their representatives on the academic level for determined periods of time and in proportions set by official regulations. These representatives function in the various university structures for consultation, administration, and governance.

On the union level, different unions represent students from each country. The Student Coordinating Body of Dakar (CED) coordinates all these unions and their activities and demands.

5. Conclusion

The World Bank (1988) notes that African education in general and Senegalese education in particular suffers from four weaknesses that threaten to vitiate its contribution to development:

(a) it graduates too many students, of doubtful quality and usefulness;

(b) the quality of the education imparted has deteriorated;

(c) the cost is too high;

(d) the way in which it is financed is socially inequitable and economically inefficient.

This gives rise to an urgent need to reform African higher education, along the lines of the following objectives: improving the quality and efficiency of teaching, modifying the degree programs, and alleviating the financial burden of the state. The World Bank suggests that these objectives be achieved by adjustment, revitalization, and selective expansion.

In addition to these weaknesses of African higher education in general, Senegal has structural weakness flowing from the multiplicity of small educational units and their dispersion, unemployed graduates, an education poorly adapted to the job market, an imbalance between social sciences and natural sciences, inadequate management, and so forth.

Senegal began to face these weaknesses and difficulties in 1981 by holding the Estates-General of Education and Training (EGEF) and by appointing a national committee to reform education and training (CNREF 1982–1984), to achieve an overall and systematic reform of the educational system. The conditions for carrying out the reform were examined and the necessary means (material and financial, technical and human) were listed. The reform began to be put into effect in 1985.

The reform aims to make the Senegalese educational system national, democratic, secular, and popular. It is a challenge that Senegal and its teachers hope to take up and win.

Bibliography

Le Soleil 1989 30 May 1989, no. 5708

National Committee for the Reform of Education and Training (CNREF) 1982–84 *General Report and Supplements*, Vol. 1–6

Sylla A 1987 *L'école future: Pour quoi?* ENDA, Dakar

World Bank 1988 *L'éducation en Afrique subsaharienne: Pour une stratégie d'adjustement de revitalisation et d'expansion.* World Bank, Washington, DC

A. Sylla

Sierra Leone

1. Higher Education and Society

Higher education in Sierra Leone is still in the process of developing its own distinctive national character, after 163 years of university experience in the country. Developments involving training in the applied disciplines may have signaled the start of change, but many educationists still doubt whether the style, character, and scope of higher education in the country are as relevant as they should be. In society as a whole, the effectiveness of the present higher educational institutions is continually being questioned by impatient citizens yearning for a miraculous transformation of their poor economic and social conditions.

While it has been found difficult to make these changes at the highest level of the system, that is, at the University, it has perhaps not been so in the case of institutions at the lower tertiary level. New courses have been introduced, with the support of the government and UNESCO, at teachers' colleges training primary school teachers. These courses focus on the training of the polyvalent teacher, that is one who can teach in the formal and nonformal sectors.

Graduates of these courses are expected to become active both within their school walls and without, where they will function as community developers. These and other less radical changes taking place elsewhere in the higher education system, do not seem to have lessened criticism of the system. It is felt that higher education should rid itself of the remaining vestiges of imported traditions which still restrict development of an indigenous and more relevant system.

2. *The Institutional Fabric of the Higher Education System*

The first higher educational institution, Fourah Bay College, was founded by the Church Missionary Society of London in 1827. Courses were initially provided for training Africans as schoolmasters, catechists, and clergymen. In 1876, however, the scope of training was expanded, following the affiliation of the college to the University of Durham. This allowed the introduction of a more liberal education, including the study of Latin, Greek, Hebrew, Arabic, history, geography, comparative philosophy, some branches of the natural sciences, French, and German. It was not until 1954 that further development took place in the broadening of course options. More branches of the natural sciences were included in the curriculum, and courses in civil, electrical, and mechanical engineering introduced. Later, disciplines in education and agriculture were added, with the establishment of a second university college, Njala University College, in 1964. The idea behind establishing this college was to apply the land grant philosophy of some universities in the United States to the Sierra Leone higher educational system to give what post-Independence planners felt was the desired focus for national development. The University of Sierra Leone came into being as an autonomous university when the two colleges, Fourah Bay College and Njala University College were brought under one authority in 1967 by the University of Sierra Leone Act. That Act introduced a federal arrangement and provided for the vice-chancellor's position to be rotated biennially between the principals of the two colleges. However, five years later the Act was repealed and replaced by the University of Sierra Leone Act 1972 which transformed the federal structure into a unitary one with a full-time vice-chancellor. Academic boards and councils of the constituent colleges were abolished and a standing committee was established in each of the colleges. Principals were retained as academic and administrative heads of their colleges but made responsible to the vice-chancellor, the chief academic and administrative officer of the University. The new Act also provided for a single senate, a single court and a central planning and budgetary control for the con-

stituent colleges and institutes of the University. Sixteen years after the new Act came into effect, the third constituent college of the University was established. This college, the College of Medicine and Allied Health Sciences, had been under consideration since 1961. Its realization in 1988 was a significant step forward in creating a more reliable mechanism for maintaining a constant supply of personnel for the country's health sector than the previously tried method of training such personnel overseas. The constituent colleges, particularly the older ones, have developed certain specialized programs within separate institutes. In addition to these campus-based institutes, there are three off-campus institutes.

Outside the university system, there are six teacher-training colleges and four technical institutes which, with the university colleges and off-campus institutes, constitute the framework of the nation's higher educational system, generally referred to in the country as the tertiary educational system.

At the University, both general and honors degrees are offered in all faculties. There are also graduate programs in selected subjects leading to masters and doctorate degrees. In addition, there are under-graduate and graduate diploma and certificate programs, offered in specialized units and institutes. Important among these are programs in marine biology and oceanography, adult education, cultural studies, business studies, public administration, accountancy, and banking.

Programs at the teacher-training colleges are all coordinated. They lead to the award of certificates at two levels, namely, the ordinary and higher teacher certificates. At the technical institutes, programs cover technical, secretarial, and business studies, and lead also to the award of certificates and diplomas at the ordinary and higher levels.

3. *Governance, Administration, and Finance*

The University of Sierra Leone is composed of three constituent colleges and three off-campus institutes. The University body, however, also comprises members of the University court, the supreme authority of the University, the senate, faculty boards, staff, and students registered for degrees, diplomas, and certificates. The system is managed from a central secretariat, headed by the secretary and registrar, acting under the supervision of the vice-chancellor, who is the chief academic and administrative officer of the University. The constituent colleges are headed by principals and the institutes by directors. Heads of all these organs of the University are responsible to the vice-chancellor.

The operations of the various organs of the University are quite intricate. The University of Sierra Leone, like other universities, has had to deal with the overlapping responsibilities and interactions between various officers, committees, and boards. It is through these channels that lines of authority pass. Authority may run in parallel lines, or branch out from a central policy body. The authority of individual officers in fact devolves from those committees for which the officers or individuals may act. University bodies operate in two broad areas, one dealing with academic affairs and the other with academic support. Academic affairs refer to all matters concerned with courses of study, research, and those services to the community which are directly related to these aspects of university activity. Academic support functions relate to activities which promote the smooth operations of the educational, research, and service objectives of the University. The central university administration takes responsibility for ensuring that all academic and academic support functions are carried out satisfactorily according to policy guidelines laid down by senate. Administrative matters relating to colleges and institutes are handled through departments at the colleges and institutes, which are answerable to college committees and relevant boards of faculties and institutes. This reporting system is long-established and has always been closely followed.

At the operational level, the tasks of teaching and research are carried out within departments or specialized units, with heads responsible for all activities. With the exception of the off-campus institutes, departments and specialized units at the University are constituted into faculties headed by deans. There are ten faculties, five at Fourah Bay College, three at Njala University College and two at the College of Medicine and Allied Health Sciences. At Fourah Bay College are: (a) the faculty of arts, consisting of the departments of classics and philosophy, education, English, linguistics, history, modern languages and theology; (b) the faculty of economic and social studies, consisting of the departments of accounting, economics, political science, and sociology; (c) the faculty of engineering, consisting of the departments of civil, electrical, and mechanical engineering; (d) the faculty of law, with only one department; and (e) the faculty of pure and applied science, consisting of the departments of botany, chemistry, geography, geology, mathematics, physics, and zoology.

Njala University College contains: (a) the faculty of agriculture, consisting of the departments of agricultural economics and extension, agricultural engineering, animal science, crop protection, crop science, home economics, and soil science; (b) the faculty of education, consisting of the departments of agricultural education, English, physical education, and teacher education; and (c) the faculty of environmental sciences, consisting of the departments of biological sciences, chemistry, geography, mathematics, and urban and regional planning.

The two faculties at the College of Medicine and Allied Health Science are: (a) the faculty of basic medical sciences, consisting of the divisions of human biology and behavior, and science of pathology; and (b) the faculty of clinical sciences, consisting of the divisions of community health care, dental care, and hospital care.

3.1 Finance

The prime source of university finance is the government, which allocates an annual block grant through the Ministry of Education, Cultural Affairs, and Sports. The block grant is intended to defray recurrent expenses. Grants for research and institutional development are normally channeled through the Ministry of Development and Economic Planning. However, because of the low level of the grants received from the government under these two categories, many of the University's research activities and some of its campus development are funded from other sources, including international organizations, and friendly governments offering bilateral aid. Funding received from these additional sources still has to be supplemented by the University's own fundraising effort, to keep the University functioning above minimum accepted levels. Three independent organs for generating income have been established since the mid-1980s. The first of these is the University Research and Development Services Bureau. This bureau is responsible for identifying and competing for commissioned research, and for developing research findings which have market potential. The second is the Department of Commercial and Industrial Enterprises. This department commercially exploits scholars' inventions, undertakes consultancies, and carries out any other commercial activity from which the University can honorably earn profit. The third, the University of Sierra Leone Development Fund, is the agency through which direct appeals are made to the public for donations in cash and kind.

3.2 Other Higher Education Institutions

Colleges outside the university system are governed, in general, by councils, appointed by the Minister of Education, Cultural Affairs, and Sports. Each council works under the direction of the Ministry of Education, Cultural Affairs, and Sports on matters relating to staffing and funding for recurrent and capital expenditures. On matters relating to academic programs, including examining and certifying overall standards, teachers' colleges are controlled by the university senate. Technical institutes, however, are governed by boards appointed by the Ministry of Education, Cultural Affairs, and Sports, which is responsible for the welfare and development of these institutes. The nonuniversity institutions receive funds from the government in much the same way as the University does, through a block grant.

They also attract supplementary funds in the form of assistance from local and international bodies.

4. Faculty and Students: Teaching, Learning, and Research

There has been a tradition of high standards of recruitment into the academic staff of all higher educational institutions. Staff numbers vary from institution to institution. The total number of senior academic staff at the University is 450. The number in the other, nonuniversity institutions is slightly smaller. It has been extremely difficult to fill vacancies, or to recruit for newly established positions. This is no doubt a consequence of the deteriorating economic situation in the country, which has had an adverse effect upon the quality of life of staff. There is now a growing tendency for staff to seek better employment opportunities elsewhere. In order to reverse this trend, urgent action is being demanded by all concerned to improve all aspects of the academic environment, and make conditions more competitive with other, nonacademic careers.

Institutions are extremely worried about the high attrition rate and difficulties over retention of staff, especially when the quality of students admitted into higher educational institutions has been reasonably good, and in certain cases has tended to rise. The selection procedures seem to have assured the maintenance of quality. Students enter the various institutions after passing the General Certificate of Education Ordinary and Advanced (O and A) level examinations, conducted by the West African Examinations Council. University entrants are expected to have attained prescribed grades in a minimum of five subjects at O level, for admission into the preliminary year (first year) of study, and in a minimum of two subjects at A level, for admission into the intermediate year (second year) of study. The duration of the general degree is four and three years for students entering at the preliminary and intermediate stages respectively. In both cases, honors programs last a year longer. It has been found that there is no difference in ultimate attainment of students entering at the preliminary or intermediate stage.

There are about 3,000 students enrolled at the University, and about 5,000 at the other institutions. The labor force needs of the country require more students to be enrolled. Expansion is restricted, however, because of the cost of implementing any such program. There is a significantly smaller proportion of students undertaking science-based courses than other courses. There is a plan by the Ministry of Education, Cultural Affairs, and Sports to restructure the secondary school system with a view to introducing more diversity and more science-based courses in these schools. It is anticipated that this plan will result in a shift towards the sciences by students leaving the secondary school system.

All higher educational institutions in the country make use of the lecture system as the basic method of instruction. Seminars, tutorials, and laboratory and workshop sessions are other methods utilized in most institutions. Teaching aids of various kinds are employed to facilitate learning. These are proving progressively more expensive to acquire and maintain, but the trend of modern teaching methods compels their use. Despite meager resources, institutions have had to find funds for such items. This means that students are given the opportunity to learn more effectively and to be exposed more readily to the vast amount of new knowledge available in their areas of study.

In order to enhance the learning process, it is a policy of most institutions, particularly the University, to provide teaching and learning programs for staff willing to participate in them. These programs aim at increasing the frequency of course renewals, the use of up-to-date equipment, the improvement of teaching, and the acquisition of administrative and management skills.

5. Conclusion

Higher education faces serious challenges. At the start of the 1990s society is being forced to adjust under pressure to the prevailing economic constraints. These constraints have reduced what were once respectable standards of livelihood and behavior, to levels which tend to undermine the fabric of society. Society is gradually being encouraged to adopt a quaint system of values, and accept an assessment pattern which regularly recognizes and rewards the less capable, less competent and less productive elements in the society. The adoption of that system has the effect of rendering higher education, of whatever type, suspect. This system and its entrenched values must be changed. Society should also be made to appreciate that higher education is vital for development and can indeed respond to its needs, as well as contribute to the overall improvement of the quality of life of its people. Unless society itself desires and motivates that change in the near future, the future of higher education in the country will be bleak indeed.

Higher educational institutions are conscious of the lead the country has in higher education in this part of the world, and so are endeavoring to maintain the aura of dignity and achieve the standards expected of them in the pursuit of their objectives, even though they are often confronted by economic and other problems outside their control. There is no doubt that willingness to succeed in these difficult times exists, and that all the institutions involved in higher education in the country are determined to protect the legacy of excellence and respectability inherited from their rich historic past.

Bibliography

All Our Futures 1974 *The Sierra Leone Educational Review*
Koso-Thomas O 1991 *"NOT WORDS ALONE" Selected Speeches of Kosonike Koso-Thomas.* Stockwell
Porter A T 1976 *Factors Limiting the University's Contribution to Development.* Centenary Symposium on the University and Development. Fourah Bay College, December
UNESCO 1986 *Case Studies on Higher Education — The University of Sierra Leone.* Educafrica, Dakar

K. Koso-Thomas

Singapore

1. Higher Education and Society

Singapore, a small island state of 616 square kilometers, has a multiracial population of 3.0 million, made up of 78 percent Chinese, 14 percent Malays, 7 percent Indians, and 1 percent others. It obtained internal/self-government from the United Kingdom in 1959. On 9 July 1963, the Malaysian Federation was formed. Singapore became a member state on 8 September 1963; and left the Federation on August 9, 1965 to become the independent Republic of Singapore.

Singapore's higher education system is based on the British system. In the 1960s a two-tier higher education system was developed which is state-managed and financed: the first tier consists of the two national universities, the National University of Singapore (NUS) and the Nanyang Technological University (NTU); the second is made up of3three polytechnics, the Singapore Polytechnic, the Ngee Ann Polytechnic, and the Temasek Polytechnic. The primary function of the first tier is to meet the country's high-level labor force needs including professional requirements. The second tier provides workers at the middle level with technical skills. These institutions come under the direct purview of the Ministry of Education. However, their enrollments, course orientation, and output are orchestrated by the Ministry of Trade and Industry's Council for Professional and Technical Education (CPTE).

The vocational and technological institutions were either restructured or newly created from the 1960s. They were initiated to meet the anticipated demand for middle- and high-level skilled labor forces during the 1970s industrialization program and to launch Singapore towards high-tech industries and services in the 1980s. These outward-oriented policies were necessary to ensure growth in a country of small size lacking natural resources. Singapore's economy is dominated by manufacturing, trade, and services. To maintain a competitive edge in a highly market-oriented global economy, Singapore has to sustain economic activities with high value-added content, achieved through constantly upgrading technologically-driven and high-productivity manufacturing and service activities. This in turn requires a human resource development program of a high quality. Singapore places a premium on human resource development, investing approximately 5 percent of its Gross Domestic Product (GDP) in high quality education and training.

Until the late 1950s, the mid-level labor needs of Singapore's public and predominantly European owned and managed private sectors were met by specialized colleges established by the British in Peninsular Malaysia. The Technical and Agriculture Colleges set up in 1925 and 1931 respectively met the needs of Singapore's public and private sectors.

A big boost was given to tertiary education in Singapore in 1948 when the Carr-Saunders Commission recommended the establishment of the University of Malaya. The Commission recommended the amalgamation of the Medical and the Raffles Colleges to form the nucleus of a degree-granting English-medium residential University of Malaya, within the territory of Singapore. Because of the exceptionally high academic standards of both the Medical and Raffles Colleges, the University of Malaya was made a degree granting university, without undergoing a probationary period as a University College of the University of London. On 8 October 1949 the University of Malaya was founded with modest beginnings to serve the needs of both Singapore and Malaysia. It had three faculties with 645 students (395 in medicine, 168 in arts, and 82 in science) from Singapore and Malaysia. Faculties of education, engineering, law, and agriculture were added in 1950, 1955, 1957, and 1960, respectively. At the second tier, a teacher-training college (TTC) was established in 1950, to meet the growing demand of the rapidly expanding primary and lower-secondary school system.

After the political independence of Peninsular Malaysia on 31 August 1957, the governments of the then Colony of Singapore and the Federation of Malaya, following the recommendations of the Aitken Commission, voted in November 1958 to continue the University of Malaya as a single university system for both countries. In January 1959, an autonomous division of the University was established in each country, while the University as a whole was administered by a vice-chancellor and the Central Council with a common court and guild of graduates. To ensure cost-effectiveness, medicine (including dentistry and pharmacy), law, philosophy, social studies, and Chinese language and literature were offered in Singapore. Engineering, Malay studies, Indian studies, and geology were offered in Kuala Lumpur. Core courses in arts and sciences were offered in both places.

Running costs of the University as a whole were met by both governments on a triennial basis. However, each division of the University had a large measure of administrative and academic autonomy, which enabled Singapore to pursue an independent policy to meet its own requirements for a high-level labor force. This arrangement was short-lived. The high-level labor needs of both countries diverged more rapidly than anticipated. The advantage of a national tertiary system for each became both politically and economically imperative. From 1 January 1962, the Singapore division of the University became known as the University of Singapore. The Kuala Lumpur division retained its original name of University of Malaya. Still, a high percentage of Malaysian students continue to pursue their studies in the University of Singapore and subsequently in the NUS and NTU.

The University of Malaya, as an English-medium institution, was open only to those who could satisfy the highly competitive entrance examination held in English. This effectively excluded from higher education the large and growing Mandarin-educated pool of Chinese school leavers from Singapore and Malaysia. Before the Communist takeover in 1949, these students had access to universities on mainland China. In 1956, to meet the demand from Chinese-medium school leavers for higher education, to preserve Chinese culture, and to keep Chinese education independent, the Chinese community in Singapore and Malaysia established the Chinese-medium Nanyang University. The University adapted the American credit system of course offerings and concentrated on low unit-cost subjects in the humanities, social sciences, and sciences. In 1959, the Nanyang University Ordinance was passed, and in 1964 the government partially funded the University. Nearly another decade passed before the government fully recognized its degrees. The Singapore and Nanyang universities in 1974 had established a common admissions system and in July 1978, a joint campus was established. Students from both universities in arts, social sciences, sciences, accountancy, and business administration underwent a unified teaching and examination system.

2. The Institutional Fabric of the Higher Education System

If the colonial state determined the structure, institutional arrangement, medium of instruction, and student composition of the tertiary institutions in Singapore before 1959, afterwards, the dominant government of the People's Action Party (PAP) molded the institutional fabric of the higher education system. At every stage of the country's political and economic development, the government, through a constant interventionist policy, directed higher education institutions to respond and adapt. Control over the first-tier institutions, the University of Singapore and the Nanyang University, evolved through a series of confrontations between government and universities. Since the second-tier institutions came directly under the Ministry of Education, the government's directives were implemented without any overt dissent and tensions.

The University of Singapore, though fully state-supported, enjoyed a considerable amount of autonomy till the mid-1960s. This was gradually eroded. Three incidents between the University and government brought this about. The first was the "Enright affair." In November 1960, Professor D J Enright, Professor of English and an expatriate, gave his inaugural lecture on "Robert Graves and the Decline of Modernism," during which he made critical comments on the PAP Government's attempt to clean up Singapore society of "yellow culture." The government accused Professor Enright of meddling in the country's internal affairs and gave a stern warning that further allusions would lead to the cancellation of his professional visitor's pass. Both the Academic Staff Association and the student body saw the government's action as an attempt to curtail the University's autonomy.

The second incident in the mid-1960s revolved around the introduction of the Suitability Certificate in 1964. The year before its introduction, the government requested the vice-chancellor to remove from the list of candidates admitted for the next academic session those whom the government suspected of being subversive. The government sought to prevent the enrollment of highly politicized left-wing Chinese middle-school students into the University thus keeping the campus free of disruptive activities. The vice-chancellor refused on the grounds that this was political interference and an infringement of university autonomy. He pointed out that university tradition admitted on merit not on the basis of political belief, gender, race, and so on. The government then threatened to cut off financial support, the vice-chancellor was forced to resign, and in 1964 the Suitability Certificate was introduced through an amendment to the Internal Security Act. The new vice-chancellor was neither a "government man" nor willing to stick his neck out against the government's interference into the affairs of the University.

The third incident occurred in 1966. Four final-year Malaysian law students were expelled for allegedly meddling in the internal affairs of the country. Since the students had not violated any university regulation, the dean of the law faculty proposed they should sit their final examinations in absentia in Malaysia. The senate refused on grounds that the government might withhold the University's grant.

Its decision to bar these students for strictly non-academic reasons, was a further blow to university autonomy.

The relationship between the PAP, the government, and tertiary institutions have become blurred because of constant government intervention. Tertiary institutions in Singapore are an instrument of the state. Since Singapore's survival rested upon the maximum development of its human resources, the government may subscribe to the view that higher education is too important to be left entirely in the hands of vice-chancellors, deans, professors, lecturers, and university administrators. Maybe this view has helped Singapore attain the right mix of high- and mid-level labor forces necessary for rapid modernization and the high level of its economic success in the world market.

2.1 Levels of Institution

The University of Singapore developed into a high-quality, multifaculty and multidisciplinary institution. It also pursued a highly performance-oriented admission policy, largely because the government did not respond to popular demand for higher education. Thus Singapore did not expand university and other tertiary places to satisfy individual demands. Access is highly selective, and, with exceptions in certain courses, is based exclusively on performance in the Cambridge O- and A-level examinations. The official view is that university and other tertiary level enrollments should be strictly linked to development planning. Though this policy is strictly adhered to, enrollments and course offerings in the university and other existing tertiary institutions expanded as new institutions opened. Two other critical factors contributed to the expansion of higher education. First, in the highly achievement-oriented society of Singapore, educational credentials are an important passport to high-income employment and rapid socioeconomic mobility. This has focused aspirations of students and parents on higher education. Second, democratization and participation in high quality primary and secondary education by every school-going child increased the pool of qualified candidates able to benefit from higher education, faster than foreseen.

The university and other publicly funded tertiary institutions continue to use English as the medium of instruction, for functional reasons, as English is a universal language and is dominant in the areas of science, technology, and commerce. Apart from courses in the humanities, social sciences and sciences, the NUS offers courses in medicine, law, dentistry, engineering, architecture, building sciences, accountancy, and business administration. The university, responding to Singapore's drive to modernization and industrialization, gives priority to engineering, economics, accountancy, business administration, medicine, and law. Through the Department of Extramural Studies it conducts short courses.

To meet the growing technical and vocational needs at the middle level, Singapore Polytechnic was established in 1958 with departments of engineering, architecture and building, accountancy, and nautical studies. In 1963, the Polytechnic was upgraded to a status similar to an advanced college of technology. Craft courses were transferred to the vocational and technical institute. A second independent technical institution, the Ngee Ann College, was set up in 1963 for Chinese-medium school leavers to acquire a vocationally-oriented postsecondary education. In 1967, it became a public institution and was named the Ngee Ann Technical College. Statutory boards and professional groups established the National Productivity Centre, the Singapore Institute of Management, the Institute of Banking and Finance, and the Singapore Institute of Marketing, which may offer various certificates, diplomas, and, in some instances, external degrees on a full-time and part-time basis. In April 1973 the Teacher Training College was upgraded to become an Institute of Education with responsibility for all teacher training and research in education.

In 1979, Singapore embarked on its second industrial revolution, restructuring the economy to high technology manufacturing and services activities. To meet the anticipated high-quality, skilled labor demand, the government took radical measures to expand engineering and technology training facilities at all levels. Marked differences in the quality in the medium of instruction and in the employability of graduates between the University of Singapore and Nanyang University, became apparent. Tensions mounted between the Chinese- and English-educated as the role of the Chinese-educated declined. Seemingly Nanyang University and its graduates, could not "survive the test of the market." The government merged the two universities in August 1980 to form the NUS. The merger followed the recommendations of Sir Frederick Dainton's *Report on University Education in Singapore*, which stressed the need for a single strong university.

In 1981, the Nanyang Technological Institute (NTI) was established at the campus of the defunct Nanyang University with three schools—mechanical and production engineering, civil and structural engineering, and electrical and electronic engineering. Later two more schools were added—applied science, and accounts and business. The main thrust of NTI was to train practice-oriented engineers, to complement the output of the more academically biased engineers of NUS, more suited for research, development, and corporate management. Administratively and financially independent of NUS, in academic matters the NTI was part of the NUS, and its graduates were awarded NUS degrees. The Ngee Ann Technical College was upgraded in 1982 to polytechnic status.

A third polytechnic, the Temasek Polytechnic, was established in 1990 to meet the rapidly growing requirements for middle-level labor force in the various fields of technical education. The three polytechnics offer a variety of full-time and part-time diploma courses. In June 1991, NTI was upgraded to full university status and named the Nanyang Technological University (NTU). The Institute of Education and the College of Physical Education were formed into a single National Institute of Education (NIE), linked to NTU. The Nanyang Technological University will award its own degrees from 1992 and its degree structure will be based on an American–British hybrid. The two universities will become comprehensive universities, encouraged to compete and offer as many courses as required by the country.

3. Governance, Administration, and Finance

Tertiary institutions in Singapore come under the direct purview of the Ministry of Education. There is no buffer organization between them and the government. The governance of the NUS and NTU consist of the council, senate, central administration, faculties, various departments, and specialized institutes and centers. The council overseas the financial and administrative managements, while the senate determines all academic issues of the universities. Within the broad policy guidelines laid down by the government, the universities have considerable latitude in student admissions, course design and content, examination policy, staff selection and promotion, and financial management.

The NUS, in keeping with its British traditions, has a chancellor as the ceremonial head. The vice-chancellor is the chief academic and executive officer of the university's central administration. The NTU has a president as the chief executive officer, assisted by a deputy president, registrar, bursar, librarian, and directors of personnel and student affairs. The NIE has a director who reports to the president of the NTU.

Each polytechnic is governed by a board of governors or council appointed by the minister-in-charge in accordance with the relevant statutes of the Polytechnic Act. The board of governors or council is composed of prominent persons from business and industry, employers, trade unions, the army, and the government. The principal, who is also the chief academic and executive officer, is a member of the board or council, and is assisted by one or more deputies.

Given its emphasis on human resource development, Singapore has singled out education as a major item of public expenditure. The tertiary education system gets a substantially large and progressively increasing portion of this expenditure. It ranged from s$86.5 (US$52.9) million (15.5%) in 1979–80 to s$471.6 (US$288.4) million (25.5%) in 1989–90 of the education budget (see Table 1). In the mid-1980s the government's direct grant covered approximately 90 percent of the operating cost of the tertiary institutions. However, since then the government's policy has been to reduce their overwhelming dependence on government funding. Since 1986 tertiary institutions have progressively increased student fees and other user charges as well as establishing endowment funds. Student fees vary according to the course of study chosen. Subsidies for accounting and business administration, arts and social sciences, and law are 80.5 percent; 81.55 percent for architecture and building, engineering, and science or computer science; and medicine and dentistry 84.78 percent. Foreign students from the ASEAN (Association of Southeast Asian Nations) pay 50 percent more than home students, while other foreign students are charged 100 percent more. The government has established a s$100 (US$61.2) million tuition loan fund. Students can borrow up to 65 percent of their fees at an interest which is an average of the prime interest rate charged by Singapore's four big banks. The loans are to be repaid within a period of 20 years and repayment starts two years after graduation. The aim is to reduce institutional dependence on government funding from 90 percent to 60 percent of their operational budget. Currently they stand at 74.5 percent of the operating budget.

4. Faculty and Students: Teaching, Learning, and Research

4.1 Faculty

The faculty nomenclature at both the NUS and NTU unites both American and British systems. The staff are ranked as professors, associate professors, senior lecturers, lecturers, and tutors. This system allows a more flexible multichair composition of senior staff within each of the teaching departments, which has attracted and retained talents, particularly within the high priority teaching and research departments. The polytechnic staff are ranked as principal lecturers, senior lecturers, and lecturers.

Despite a dramatic rise in demand for academic staff and the objective of the government to have Singaporeans form the majority, Singapore's tertiary institution are highly competitive in their staff recruitment. They have a high proportion of expatriate academic staff, and are prepared to pay this cost to maintain the objective of becoming centers of excellence for teaching and research. The proportion of expatriates varies, from 5 percent in science and business administration to about 25 percent in computer science, electrical engineering, and so on. The majority of expatriates are from the United States, the United Kingdom, Australia, Canada, New Zealand, Sri Lanka, India, Hong Kong, and Taiwan.

Since 1969, the minimum academic qualification

Table 1
Government expenditure on education (in Singapore dollars) 1979–80 to 1989–90

	1979–80	1980–81	1981–82	1982–83	1983–84	1984–85	1985–86	1986–87	1987–88	1988–89	1989–90
Recurrent expenditure	503,149	589,431	712,745	983,751	1,107,126	1,272,574	1,388,341	1,277,304	1,352,570	1,461,875	1,648,384
(percent)	90.2	85.6	75.6	72.4	68.7	71.9	78.2	77.9	81.8	91.1	89.2
Vocational and Industrial Training Board[a]	25,000	29,694	38,900	47,401	55,121	65,662	80,294	68,966	64,191	72,857	79,042
(percent)	4.5	4.3	4.1	3.5	3.4	3.7	4.5	4.2	3.9	4.5	4.3
Tertiary	86,544	109,662	156,118	229,057	291,795	350,167	387,240	362,829	413,560	393,315	471,638
(percent)	15.5	15.9	16.6	16.9	18.1	19.8	21.8	22.1	25.0	24.5	25.5
National University of Singapore and Nanyang Technological Institute[b]	58,185	74,557	108,527	156,435	197,947	240,448	253,811	240,805	293,443	259,014	314,716
(percent)	10.4	10.8	11.5	11.5	12.3	13.6	14.3	14.7	17.7	16.1	17.0
Institute of Education and College of Physical Education[c]	7,831	11,089	13,955	17,746	18,817	21,268	22,979	19,883	20,843	21,072	28,093
(percent)	1.4	1.6	1.5	1.3	1.2	1.2	1.3	1.2	1.3	1.3	1.5
Polytechnics	20,516	24,004	33,623	54,876	75,018	88,436	110,434	102,125	99,255	113,212	128,810
(percent)	3.7	3.5	3.6	4.0	4.7	5.0	6.2	6.2	6.0	7.1	7.0
Others[d]	23,794	28,092	31,423	46,791	54,761	60,443	66,135	59,069	57,613	62,764	77,657
(percent)	4.3	4.1	3.3	3.4	3.4	3.4	3.7	3.6	3.5	3.9	4.2
Development expenditure	54,391	98,910	229,785	374,679	504,534	497,169	387,255	361,479	301,405	142,444	200,344
(percent)	9.8	14.4	24.4	27.6	31.3	28.1	21.8	22.1	18.2	8.9	10.8
Total	557,540	688,341	942,530	1,358,430	1,611,660	1,769,743	1,775,596	1,638,783	1,653,975	1,604,319	1,848,728
(percent)	100	100	100	100	100	100	100	100	100	100	100

Source: Ministry of Education   a Prior to 1980–81, figures include expenditure of Adult Education Board   b From 1981–82, figures include expenditure of Nanyang Technological Institute   c From 1984–85, figures include expenditure of College of Physical Education   d Include Curriculum Development Institute of Singapore, Extra Curricular Activities Centre, Institute of Southeast Asian Studies, Science Centre Board, and headquarters expenditure

Table 2
Tertiary level enrollments for selected years

Institution	1960 Male	1960 Female	1960 Total	1965 Male	1965 Female	1965 Total	1970 Male	1970 Female	1970 Total	1975 Male	1975 Female	1975 Total	1980 Male	1980 Female	1980 Total	1985 Male	1985 Female	1985 Total	1990 Male	1990 Female	1990 Total
First tier																					
Singapore University and National University of Singapore	1,215	426	1,641	2,035	835	2,870	3,167	1,513	4,680	3,399	2,718	6,117	5,162	4,038	9,200	7,299	7,694	14,993	9,696	8,646	18,342
(percent)	74	26	100	71	29	100	68	32	100	56	44	100	56	44	100	49	51	100	53	47	100
Manyang University	1,483	378	1,861	1,559	567	2,126	1,392	918	2,310	1,373	1,056	2,429									
(percent)	80	20	100	73	27	100	60	40	100	57	43	100									
Manyang Technical Institute and Manyang Technical University																1,825	253	2,078	4,265	2,700	6,965
(percent)																88	12	100	61	39	100
Subtotal	2,698	804	3,502	3,594	1,402	4,996	4,559	2,431	6,990	4,772	3,774	8,546	5,162	4,038	9,200	9,124	7,947	17,071	13,961	11,346	25,307
(percent)	77	23	100	72	28	100	65	35	100	56	44	100	56	44	100	53	47	100	55	45	100
Second tier																					
Singapore Polytechnic	2,287	55	2,342	2,255	80	2,335	3,877	217	4,094	6,293	1,331	7,624	6,562	1,712	8,274	9,965	2,880	12,845	10,864	4,583	15,447
(percent)	98	2	100	97	3	100	95	5	100	83	17	100	79	21	100	78	22	100	70	30	100
Ngee Ann College and Polytechnic				634	239	873	437	161	598	1,243	409	1,652	2,049	782	2,831	5,718	3,047	8,765	8,180	5,111	13,291
(percent)				73	27	100	73	27	100	75	25	100	72	28	100	65	35	100	62	38	100
Temasek Polytechnic																			185	561	746
(percent)																			25	75	100
Teachers Technical College and Institute of Education	1,125	1,202	2,327	2,804	3,440	6,244	611	1,390	2,001	141	544	685	351	1,977	2,328	216	909	1,125	347	1,284	1,631
(percent)	48	52	100	45	55	100	31	69	100	21	79	100	15	85	100	19	81	100	21	79	100
College of Physical Education																52	55	107	85	65	150
(percent)																49	51	100	57	43	100
Subtotal	3,412	1,257	4,669	5,693	3,759	9,452	4,925	1,768	6,693	7,677	2,284	9,961	8,962	4,471	13,433	15,951	6,891	22,842	19,661	11,604	31,265
(percent)	73	27	100	60	40	100	74	26	100	77	23	100	67	33	100	70	30	100	63	37	100
Total	6,110	2,061	8,171	9,287	5,161	14,448	9,484	4,199	13,683	12,449	6,058	18,507	14,124	8,509	22,633	25,075	14,838	30,913	33,622	22,950	56,572
(percent)	75	25	100	64	36	100	69	31	100	67	33	100	62	38	100	63	37	100	59	41	100

for nonprofessional disciplines is a PhD. Practically every suitably qualified local staff member is sent to an overseas university in the United States, the United Kingdom, Australia, Canada, or New Zealand for PhD training.

4.2 Students

Despite highly selective admissions, overall tertiary student enrollments have increased dramatically: from 8,171 in 1960 to 56,572 in 1990, a sixfold increase (see Table 2). At the first-tier (degree level) student enrollments increased from 3,502 in 1960 to 25,307 in 1990. At the second-tier (diploma level), enrollments rose from 5,216 students in 1960 to 31,265 in 1990 (see Table 2). The overwhelming majority of students in the first-tier are enrolled at the NUS: in 1990, 18,342 students with one-third living in residential halls. In 1990 the NTI had 6,965 students, with approximately two-thirds in residential halls. It is envisaged that the NTU, in its opening session in the academic year 1991–92, will raise its student enrollment to 9,800 including students from the NIE. Female enrollment at both levels of the tertiary system has increased substantially, from 2,061 (25.22 percent) in 1960 to 22,950 (40.57 percent) in 1990 (see Table 2). The overall age cohort participation rate in tertiary education was 35 percent in 1991.

Stringent selection and increasing private demand has led to a growing unmet demand—nearly half the eligible students who applied to the NUS and NTI in 1986 and 1987 were rejected. Current estimates reckon there are approximately 9,000 students studying overseas: the majority in North America, the United Kingdom, Australia, and New Zealand, with a smaller number in Taiwan and Japan.

Despite the intense pressure for university places from home students, Singapore sets aside between 15 and 17 percent of its tertiary education places for foreign students. To gain admission into Singapore's tertiary institutions, foreign students must have better scores than their Singapore counterparts and before entry into public-funded tertiary institutions must sign a bond to work in the Republic for three years after graduation and to pay differential tuition fees.

4.3 Research

Singapore's tertiary institutions attach considerable emphasis to excellence in teaching. Teaching is conducted during the two semesters of the academic year, through lectures, seminars, and tutorials. In the recruitment of academic staff, emphasis is given both to all round high academic credentials and quality, and also to teaching ability. All new teaching staff are inducted through a short teaching–learning program and attend regular seminars on teaching methodology.

Increasing attention is being given to upgrading

the quality of education, to enhance students' analytical and creative skills, independent learning skills, and skills in human relations and teamwork. Thus, the universities in particular have opted for a low staff–student ratio of 1:10. The tertiary institutions have developed a comprehensive method of recording and summarizing the performance of each student at every level by grade-point average.

Research is expected of all tertiary institutions and their staff. In the universities, considerable weight is given to research and publication in promotion. In particular, the NUS has a large library with a collection of 1.5 million volumes including some research collections. Currently 2 percent of the GNP is committed to research and development (R & D) activities. Since Singapore does not have a comparative advantage in fundamental research, it judiciously pursues an R & D policy, concentrating on incremental technology—that is, improving product design, development capability, and upgrading the productivity of those technologies critical to its economy.

Under this strategy, both the NUS and NTU have embarked upon graduate education and research. It is targeted at improving the technical proficiency of the country's industries, management skills, business offerings as well as supporting high technology and R & D activities. In 1990 the government upgraded the Singapore Science Council into a Science and Technology Board with the remit to identify promising new fields of research and to strengthen existing R & D activities. The NUS has established three selected centers of excellence—the Institute of Molecular and Cell Biology; the Institute of Systems Science; and the Clinical Research Centre for the Faculty of Medicine—which focus on high priority fields of research. In 1990, NUS had about 1,900 graduate students, of whom 630 were engaged in supervised research for higher degrees.

Both NUS and NTU have links with foreign universities, particularly with leading research universities in the United Kingdom, Europe, and the United States. For example, NTU has a research link with the Massachusetts Institute of Technology's Sloan School of Management in areas involving global and regional issues. Closer university–industry links have been developed. A large number of staff are engaged in consultancy work with the public and private sectors. Since 1985, with the initiation of the Technology Associate Scheme, industry participation in university research has been growing. The NTU established an Institute of Manufacturing Technology and developed an on-campus technology park, called The Innovation Centre. A number of local and multinational companies have anchored their R & D activities within this center. The new university plans to raise its graduate training and research through increasing student enrollment from 43 in 1990 to 1,000 by 1995, and by attractive graduate scholarships and fellowships open to international competition, irrespective of nationality.

5. Conclusion

For the future, Singapore's objectives for tertiary institutions are threefold: (a) to keep abreast of the growing internationalization of Singapore; (b) to cater for the country's fast changing industrial structure in which workers must learn new skills and even change jobs to meet new economic demands; and (c) maximize the opportunities for those Singaporeans yearning for a higher education. To meet these objectives, Singapore has studied various options. Among them are: (a) expanding part-time and evening courses at the NUS and NTU; (b) establishing a third university, possibly private, by converting the Singapore Institute of Management (SIM) into a university; (c) establishing an open university, to cater mainly for mature students; (d) establishing a fourth or even a fifth polytechnic; and (e) allowing foreign universities to run courses in Singapore.

When a third university is established, the government will encourage it to link with Japanese tertiary institutions, thus complementing the NUS's ties with Europe and NTU's with the United States. These networks, according to the Minister of Education "will provide Singapore with very valuable links to the three main economic power-houses which will predominate in the world in the coming decades."

Singapore, in its moves to expand higher education, takes a "cautious and calculated approach." The government is deeply committed to seeing that current and future courses and the student intake are relevant to the country's economic success. There is also equal commitment to avoiding graduate overproduction, which would lead to a pool of unemployed graduates.

Bibliography

Asher M G 1984 *Financing The Development of Higher Education in Singapore*. The Regional Institute of Higher Education and Development, Singapore

Islam I 1987 Manpower and educational planning in Singapore. In: Amjad R (ed.) 1987 *Human Resource Planning: The Asian Experience*. International Labour Organisation Asian Employment Programme, New Delhi, pp. 114–50

Pang E F, Gopinathan S 1989 Public policy, research environment and higher education in Singapore. In: Altbach P G et al. (eds.) 1989 *Scientific Development and Higher Education*. Praeger, New York, pp. 137–76

Puccetti R 1972 Authoritarian government and academic subservice. *Minerva* 10(2): 223–41

Tregonning K G 1990 Tertiary education in Malaya: Policy and practice 1905–1962. *Journal of the Malaysian Branch of the Royal Asiatic Society* 63: 1–14

V. Selvaratnam

Somalia

1. Higher Education and Society

The Somali Democratic Republic was created on July 1, 1960 by uniting the former British and Italian Somalilands and thus the culturally homogeneous Somalis. Somalia lies in the Horn of Africa and covers an area of 638,000 square kilometers. It borders with Ethiopia in the west, the Gulf of Aden in the north, Kenya in the south and the recently created Republic of the Afars and Issas in the northwest. Its coastline of 3,300 kilometers—the longest in Africa—stretches from the Indian Ocean in the east to the Red Sea in the north.

In October 1970 Somalia was declared a socialist state by the former president, General Siad Barre, who executed a bloodless coup in order to "eliminate corruption and tribalism." He ruled the country for 20 years, and was overthrown after plunging the country into a bloody tribal war which prompted the former British Protectorate to secede in April 1991.

The Somalis comprise over 80 tribes, divided into major groups known as Hawiye, Darod, Dir, Isahaq, Rahanwein, and Digil. Most Somalis are Sunni (orthodox) Muslims and Islam is kept very much alive by the teachings of the "Wadad"—the itinerant preacher.

The population of Somalia is estimated to have grown from 3.67 million in 1970 to 7.11 million in 1988 (UNESCO 1990). This gives a density of 11 inhabitants per square kilometer and an annual growth rate of about 3 percent. Life expectancy at birth is about 43 years which is among the lowest in the world. About 25 percent of the Somalis live in urban centers. Of the remaining 75 percent who live in the rural areas where 1,700 persons are served by one physician, about 60 percent are pastoralists. About 44 percent of the population is under 15 years of age.

The terrain is mostly semi-desert, except for the vast and fertile territory between the Wabe-Shebelli and Juba rivers. The economy is essentially based on subsistence farming and livestock raising. The industrial sector is still in its infancy. Major export items include livestock, fish, hides and skins, and bananas. Imports consist mainly of food, textiles, oil, and manufactured products. In the early 1980s agriculture accounted for about 60 percent, industry 11 percent and services 29 percent of the total Gross Domestic Product (GDP).

Somalia has had a succession of five national plans since the 1969 revolution, which improved access to primary health care in the rural areas. The Somali economy suffered a series of setbacks during the 1970s and 1980s. These were caused by the OPEC oil crisis, severe droughts, a costly war with Ethiopia, the withdrawal of Soviet financial support, and the civil war which has left the country devastated and divided. The depressed economic situation limits educational development at both the lower and higher levels.

2. *The Institutional Fabric of the Higher Education System*

Higher education in Somalia is 30 years old and is still being developed. It is provided by the *Jaamaccada Ummadda Soomaaliyeed* (National University of Somalia), its six constituent colleges, and at least seven other specialized postsecondary institutes. These are all sponsored by the state and use Italian, English, Arabic, and Somali as their media of instruction.

Access to higher education in Somalia is based on the secondary school leaving certificate, awarded after 12 years of study, and in some cases after passing a special entrance examination. Somalization of higher education staff is underway, although its progress seems faster in some institutions or faculties than others. The duration of courses varies from one to about five years and many courses are organized for persons already in employment.

If all higher education institutions are financed by the government, they are not all under the purview of the Ministry of Higher Education and Culture. Indeed, they seem to be operated by a plethora of ministries (e.g., Education, Posts and Telecommunication, National Planning, and Labor) making the coordination of their programs and activities rather difficult, Moreover, lack of space and paucity of data due to the current crisis in Somalia make it mandatory to briefly identify only some of the characteristics of these institutions.

2.1 *Levels of Institution*

Colleges or schools in Somalia include the following: the School of Industrial Studies with departments of carpentry, mechanics, building construction, electronics, and radio; the School of Islamic Disciplines with a faculty of law; the School of Public Health; the School of Seamanship and Fishing; and the Veterinary College with a student–staff ratio of 3:1 (all at Mogadishu); and the Technical College at Burgo, running four-year courses.

Postsecondary institutes in Somalia include the following:

(a) the Civil Aviation Training Institute at Mogadishu offers one to two-year courses in air traffic control and radio.

(b) the National Institute of Telecommunications at Mogadishu offers three and a half-year courses in transmission and related technology. The course consists of two years of basic study, half a year of English language upgrading and one year in a specialization. The program of training is super-

vised by the Ministry of Posts and Telecommunications.

(c) the Institute of Statistics and Applied Economics offers a two-year part-time course of study for civil servants and is maintained by the Ministry of National Planning.

(d) the Institute of Commerce.

(e) the Somali Institute of Development, Administration and Management (SIDAM) in Mogadishu was created to coordinate the training needs of the diverse ministries and to rectify the shortage of middle-level management skills identified by the 1982–86 Five-Year Plan. Its programs include general management, industrial management, accountancy, development administration, and in-service courses in commercial, clerical, and secretarial skills. It uses English as a medium of instruction and is one of the few institutions in Somalia which offer a small graduate program. (In 1983, it had 31 graduates and 140 undergraduates.)

(f) the Technical Teacher Training College (TTTC) in Mogadishu, was created in 1978, with UNESCO funding, to prepare teachers for vocational and technical education. Its courses, now of three-years duration include general mechanics, auto-mechanics, electronics, civil construction, marine engineering, and commercial studies. Entrants to the TTTC are selected from among those who have completed three and four years technical secondary education. In the mid-1980s, there were about 50 members of staff of whom five were UNESCO experts. Graduates from the TTTC (about 150 per year) are, theoretically, expected to serve as vocational and/or technical teachers for five years.

Interestingly, this institution, administered by the Ministry of Education, is responsible for developing its own curriculum and examination procedures. This responsibility (accompanied by the more recent task of preparing instructional materials) is entrusted to a Technical Board consisting of the dean of the college, department heads and UNESCO experts.

(g) the Lafole College of Education was established in 1963 in the Afgoi district about 40 kilometers from Mogadishu to produce secondary school teachers. In the late 1960s the duration of its training was three years, later reduced to two years and one summer in the 1970s and subsequently increased to three years in the mid-1980s.

Admission to this college is via three separate routes. The first which produces about 50 percent of the entrants meets the requirements of teachers who graduated from Halane Primary Teacher Training Institute and who have taught for at least three years. The second is for those who wish to become secondary-school teachers after completing their secondary education and national service. These, coming straight from school, account for about 46 percent of the college entrants. The last route involving a special entrance examination, is for a small number of civil servants wanting to become teachers.

Though those who complete this three-year course are expected to teach in Somali, and their competence in English is limited, the medium of instruction in the college is English.

Student enrollment in 1982–83, the year when the latest data was available, was 1,014. There were 111 full-time staff (of whom 21 were expatriates) and 42 part-timers. This appears to give a staff-student ratio of about 1:8 which is indeed very low by African standards. This ratio does not, however, seem to have a positive impact on the quality of output from the College even though these are estimated at 1,194 by 1991. Lafole College of Education is a part of the National University.

The National University of Somalia (NUS) is administered by the Ministry of Higher Education and Culture. With its origins in the Institute of Law, Economics and Social Studies, established in 1954, NUS became a University Institute offering (in 1964) two years of study in Somalia followed by two final years in Italy. It began operations as the National University in 1969 and was authorized by the government to offer its first degrees in 1971.

The NUS was created to meet the professional labor force needs of Somalia, laid out in the 1982–86 Five-Year Plan which highlights two key goals of higher education; one was to increase the provision of higher education in the northern and southern parts of the country; the other, more difficult to achieve, was to expand intake to 25 percent of secondary-school graduates.

The National University of Somalia is the major provider of higher education in Somalia, hence we will concentrate on items such as organizational structure, administrative committees, teaching staff, students, courses and equity, in relation to NUS (and where applicable to higher education).

2.2 Admissions Policies and Selection

Admission is based on the Somali school-leaving certificate, the University entrance examination, and completion of national youth service for one year. Intake of new students is determined by quotas set by the Ministry of Higher Education in the light of national labor force needs and also the available space within a faculty, for example. University entrance exams are given every year and are assessed by the instructional staff of the NUS. Those students who obtain very high marks are often allowed to

select the faculty of their choice, usually medicine or engineering. Low achievers are assigned to faculties that are not their first choice and seem to find their way into education, the least favored faculty.

2.3 Structure of Qualifications

The National University of Somalia has started providing its own master's degrees (e.g., at SIDAM). The 15 or so faculties of NUS offer programs varying from two to four and a half years in duration. A two-year course in education qualifies the student to teach the first phase of the secondary studies. In law, economics, medicine, and engineering, studies last for four years leading to the awards of LLB, BSc or B(Med), The BEd or BSc(Ed) is obtained after three years. All awards (ranging from the two-year teaching diploma to the *laurea* (equivalent to BA/BSc) and the more recent master's degrees are recognized by the University.

3. Governance, Administration, and Finance

3.1 National Administration

Although some postsecondary institutions are administered by different ministries, the overwhelming majority come under the purview of the Ministry of Higher Education by decree and budgetary control. There are two semi-autonomous units within the Ministry of Higher Education. One of these is the NUS and the other the National Academy of Science and Art. Both of these are directly responsible to the Assistant Minister. The organizational chart of the Ministry of Higher Education also includes a department of higher education under the supervision of a director general, responsible for the management of scholarship programs and research activities. The government being the major supplier of funds and the major consumer of the products of higher education, has a lot of say both in how money is spent and on what is taught. Government planners fix intake quotas and assign students to specific fields of study. Representatives of the government and the ruling political party are members of the University Council. Thus, although the nature of relationship between the government and higher education in general and the NUS in particular can vary from cooperation to domination, one can argue that NUS does not stand apart from the government in Somalia.

3.2 Finance

Total public expenditure on education rose by 470 percent from 1975 to 1986. The 1986 total education budget represented 0.4 percent of the GNP and 2.8 percent of the national budget, both among the lowest in Africa (UNESCO 1990). The shares of the primary, secondary, and tertiary levels of education are about 62.4 percent, 25.8 percent and 11.8 percent respectively.

The prime source of finance for higher education in general and NUS in particular is the government. However, the NUS obtains substantial financial assistance from Italy and other donors including Saudi Arabia and the European Community. The unit cost of higher education in Somalia in 1980 was equivalent to US$895. On average the starting salary of a graduate (employment is still more or less guaranteed) was about 10 times per capita income. This, coupled with the subsidization of instructional costs and boarding and lodging facilities, makes the private rate of return (33.2%) much higher than the social one (19.9%). As a result the social demand for higher education in Somalia is likely to remain high, even in the absence of subsidization. Given the limited economic base of the country and the difficulty of justifying the subsidies on equity and efficiency bases, the only way the growing demand for higher education can be met is by devising a carefully studied loan system and tuition fees.

3.3 Institutional Administration

The chancellor, who is the head of state, is also the statutory head of the University. His functions are ceremonial.

The rector is the chief executive officer of the NUS. He is assisted by two vice-rectors responsible for administrative and academic affairs respectively (IEES 1984). Until the early 1980s the rector was appointed by the Central Committee of the Revolutionary Socialist Party on the recommendations of the Minister of Higher Education. Recently, however, it appears he is chosen "from among the academic members of the staff" and is expected to carry out his teaching activities to which he will return when his term of office expires (ESAURP 1987). This pattern of authority in the NUS is collegial rather than

Table 1
Third-level students by field of study and gender (1987)

Field of study	Male and Female	Female
Exact sciences (including medicine, engineering, agriculture, forestry, and fishery)	4,055	550
Social sciences (including law, social and behavioural science, and commercial and business administration)	2,540	550
Humanities (including education, religion and theology, and fine and applied arts)	8,751	1,993
Other not specified	326	
Total	15,672	3,093

Source: Adapted from UNESCO (1990) Statistical Yearbook

concentrated around the full professors, of whom there are very few anyway.

The two main administrative committees of the University are the University Council and the senate. The Chairman of Council, the highest decision- and policy-making body, by decree is the Minister for Higher Education. The ruling political party, unlike the student body, has its own representative in council. The senate committee is chaired by the rector and includes two academic staff members selected by their deans from each of the faculties. The academic staff in each faculty are responsible for the design and implementation of the curriculum for their students.

Each faculty is headed by a dean who acts as its chief academic and administrative officer. The dean, who reports both to the vice-rector and the rector, provides leadership for the faculty in drawing up regulations pertaining to research and the admission, registration, teaching, and examination of students.

4. Faculty and Students: Teaching, Learning, and Research

4.1 Faculty

The total number of teaching staff at the NUS and other third-level institutions rose from 324 in 1975 to 817 in 1986. Of these, only about 12 percent taught at other third-level institutions in 1975, the year for which data are available (UNESCO 1990). Given the fact that there were 657 academic staff at NUS by the mid-1980s, it is safe to assume that the proportion of staff at other third-level institutions has risen from 12 percent in 1975 to about 18 percent in 1986. This makes the NUS the major provider of higher education.

As of July 1983, the total number of academic staff at the NUS was 579 (IEES 1984). Of these, 471 were Somalis. About 72 percent of the total taught on a full-time basis while the rest (28%) were part-timers. Women represented about 11 percent of the full-time Somali academics. When analyzed on the basis of academic rank, the picture which emerges is: 54 percent of the Somali academic staff (i.e., full- and part-time, male and female, but excluding the expatriates) were assistant lecturers; about 44 percent lecturers; 2 percent senior lecturers; and zero professors. The 108 expatriate staff were concentrated in the science-based disciplines. In terms of staff numbers, education and medicine appeared to be the largest faculties. The minimum requirements for the rank of lecturer are a master's degree and a minimum of three years' teaching experience. The rank of professor, however, requires a PhD, scholarly publications, and a minimum of five years' service at the University.

For the 1984–85 academic year the salary scale of a lecturer at the NUS was fixed at the equivalent of

US$1,020 and that of a professor at US$1,875, both among the lowest in Africa. The pay structure for the full-time academic staff is categorized into a base salary, a housing allowance, and a responsibility allowance.

According to the latest data available (see ESAURP 1987) the overall number of the academic staff appears to have risen from 579 in 1983 to 657 in the late 1980s. Viewed against a total student population of 3,101, this gives a staff–student ratio of 1:5, which is half the 1:10 ratio accepted as the standard by many African universities.

4.2 Students

The total number of students in all types of higher education institutions rose from 1,936 in 1975 to 15,672 in 1986 (UNESCO 1990). The percentage of females for the same period rose from 11 percent to 20 percent. The distribution of higher education students by field of study and gender for 1987, is shown in Table 1.

The humanities are by far the most popular fields of study with education and teacher training alone accounting for 7,538 out of the total entrants of 8,751 (or 86%). The highest number of degree graduates are bound to come from the faculties of education, political science, medicine, and veterinary science of the NUS, in that order. However, only 5 out of the 11 faculties managed to graduate on time 70 percent or more of their original intake in 1982 (IEES 1984). There is a rather high attrition rate. One anomaly which characterizes the University student population is the problem of equity between those from rural and urban backgrounds, more specifically from the Banaadir and non-Banaadir secondary schools (Banaadir being one of the 16 administrative regions in the country). Thus, in 1983 of the 910 university entrants 540 came from the Banaadir region. Furthermore, these students seem to be overrepresented in the highly preferred faculties of medicine, economics, and law (IEES 1984). Agriculture and veterinary science seem the only two faculties where the Banaadirs are not in the majority.

On balance the undergraduate courses at the NUS are "specialist" (single subject) rather than broad based in content and orientation. Each faculty is responsible for the design and implementation of the curriculum it teaches and for the assessment of students.

Assessment of student progress at the NUS seems to employ a combination of at least three methods in varying degrees: continuous assessment of course work, the formal and comprehensive final examinations, and assessment of the practical work or fieldwork experience. In the faculty of education greater weight is placed on the examination (60%) rather than the coursework (40%) component of the evaluation. But equal weight is given to examination (50%) and coursework (50%) in the science-based courses. On the other hand, in the faculties of medicine and veterinary science, the three methods of assessment (exam 33%, coursework 33%, and fieldwork 34%) seem to be given equal weighting (ESAURP 1987).

These assessment methods do not throw light on a major problem associated with the four media of instruction used at the NUS. Whatever the merits of using Italian as the medium in about a dozen faculties, English in one (faculty of education) and Somali in another (political science), there is a fundamental educational policy at stake here. To expect a student to follow a degree-level course after only a term's presessional Italian or English, does not seem to be realistic.

5. Conclusion

During the last three decades, the higher education institutions in Somalia have made remarkable contributions towards meeting the skilled labor force demands of the nation. They are producing enough teachers for the secondary schools, and are also "exporting" some technically trained labor force to neighboring Gulf states. They have also started offering graduate courses in selected disciplines. On the other hand, a critical assessment of the current condition of higher education suggests that the system is bedevilled with a number of difficulties. These, among other things, include:

(a) heavy dependency on expatriate staff and aid;

(b) curricula heavily skewed towards the arts and humanities;

(c) potential mismatch between output and demands of the labor market;

(d) equity problem between the sexes and the urban and rural areas;

(e) excessively low staff–student ratio;

(f) limited involvement in research.

These six issues are likely to affect higher education in Somalia over the coming decade. Meanwhile, considering the following five proposals may help improve the internal and external efficiencies. First, it is necessary to carry out a systematic tracer study of all the higher education graduates. Second, there is a need for coordination between the institutions (and the ministries administering them) responsible for the training of teachers. The pros and cons of using four media of instruction is also a matter to be discussed. Fourth, there is the need to organize staff development programs to improve teaching and research skills. Finally, although a close relationship between the government and the NUS is in a sense indispensable for development, one should beware of the danger of reducing the latter to a mere service agency.

Bibliography

ESAURP (Eastern and Southern African Universities Research Programme) 1987 *University Capacity in Eastern and Southern African Countries*. J. Currey, London

Hinchliffe K 1987 *Higher Education in Sub-Saharan Africa*. Croom Helm, London

IEES Somalia: Improving the Efficiency of Educational Systems 1984 *Education and Human Resources Sector Assessment*. State Printing Agency, Mogadishu

Laitin D D and Samatar S S 1987 Somalia: Nation in Search of a State. Westview Press, Boulder, Colorado

Lewis I M 1988 *A Modern History of Somalia*. Westview Press, Boulder, Colorado

Metra Consulting 1986 *Handbook of National Development Plans*. Graham and Trotman, London

Psacharopoulos G and Woodhall M 1987 *Education for Development: An Analysis of Investment Choices*. Oxford University Press, Oxford

The Weekly Review January 11 1991 (lead article: Somalia in Flames). Nairobi

Todaro M 1989 *Economic Development in the Third World*. Longman, London

UNESCO 1990 *Statistical Year Book*. UNESCO, Paris

T. Mebrahtu

South Africa

1. Higher Education and Society

Higher education in South Africa started in the nineteenth century with the training of teachers, ministers, and missionaries at different religious institutions. By the second half of the century a number of secondary schools in the Cape Colony provided advanced study that enabled some students to take the higher examinations of the University of London. Consequently, the University of Good Hope was founded in 1873. At the time of the formation of the Union of South Africa in 1910, eight institutions were affiliated as constituent colleges of the University of Cape of Good Hope.

Nowadays South African universities provide degree and diploma courses with the basic goal of providing scientific training, which prepares students for high-level occupations. The technikons provide postsecondary technical and vocational education while the teacher training colleges are responsible for the training of teachers, mainly for primary (elementary) schools. Other examples of postsecondary education include institutions that prepare students for specific occupations, including the colleges of nursing, agriculture, mining and the police colleges.

1.1 Geographical Context

The Republic of South Africa is an independent country on the southern tip of Africa with an area of 1,124,100 square kilometers. The country is rich in raw materials and is agriculturally self-sufficient.

The political borders of South Africa were set in 1910 with the unification of the former British colonies into the Union of South Africa. Since the independence of the Republic of South Africa in 1961 four areas, originally part of the Republic of South Africa, have become independent national states; namely the Republics of Transkei, Bophuthatswana, Venda, and Ciskei. Although these republics are not officially recognized by the world community, they organize their own educational systems and therefore their activities in the field of higher education will not be included in this article.

1.2 Size and Rate of Population Growth

South Africa is both multicultural and multilingual. The official languages, Afrikaans and English, are those which are used in most of the state and state-supported schools and institutions.

The current growth rate of the population is 0.65 percent for Whites, 1.64 percent for Coloreds, 1.56 percent for Asians and 2.72 percent for Blacks. Of the total population, 56.9 percent live in urban areas, with 89.6 percent of Whites, 77.8 percent of Coloreds, 93.4 percent of Asians and 39.6 percent of Blacks living in urban areas (RSA 1988 p. 1.10).

Table 1
Size of population 1960–87 (in thousands)[a]

	1960	1965	1970	1975	1980	1985	1987
Asians	476	548	642	735	824	905	913
Blacks	12,077	13,869	15,918	17,995	18,003	18,748	20,132
Coloreds	1,500	1,782	2,074	2,357	2,626	2,922	3,069
Whites	3,069	3,409	3,835	4,256	4,538	4,901	4,911
Total	17,122	19,607	22,469	25,343	24,986	27,476	29,025

Source: RSA, 1971, 1988
a The population is given in race groups, because this is the commonly accepted way of dividing the population in South Africa

635

1.3 Structure of Government and Main Political Goals

Since the major changes affecting the structure of the South African government in 1984, the legislative power has been vested in the parliament which consists of three houses, namely the House of Assembly (Whites), the House of Representatives (Coloreds) and the House of Delegates (Asians). The executive power is vested in the state president who is assisted by the cabinet for general affairs with the ministers' council for each house being responsible for its own affairs. The execution of government is based on the principle of general and own specific affairs. For example, "own affairs" refers to welfare, education, art, health, community development, local authorities, and certain aspects of agriculture, finances, and elections. "General affairs" refers to all the other responsibilities of the government. Aspects concerning the preservation of the identity of the different cultural groups come under the auspices of the legislative and executive powers and are the responsibility of the respective houses and ministers' councils.

With regard to education, provision is also made for general and own affairs. The Minister of National Education, a member of the cabinet, is responsible for general affairs which includes formulating general policy on the financing of education, salaries, and conditions of service of the teaching personnel; the professional registration of teachers; and the standards of syllabus and evaluation of education. A minister of the different ministers' councils, namely the Minister of Education and Culture, is responsible for the implementation of the general policy with regard to the different cultural groups in order to satisfy their individual needs (Steyn and Steyn 1988 p. 9). Certain aspects of higher education are therefore handled as part of general affairs, while other aspects are handled as own affairs.

1.4 Relationship with Religious Bodies

Although several facilities in higher education have developed as a result of the direct involvement of religious institutions, there is no real, direct involvement in the 1990s of religious bodies in the provision of higher education. The only exception to this rule is the training of their own functionaries by the different religious institutions.

2. The Institutional Fabric of the Higher Education System

Postsecondary education is expected to fulfill the following functions (CUP 1987 pp. 17–18):

(a) to provide the state with a high-level labor force as well as leadership in the scientific, cultural, political, economic, and social spheres;

(b) to provide the private sector with scientifically literate and occupationally prepared individuals;

(c) to provide professional societies with university-trained members;

(d) to provide parents and students with adequate training to pursue a successful occupation; and

(e) to meet the general expectation that the institutions for higher education should contribute to the acquisition and dissemination of knowledge.

These objectives should be realized through the teaching/training and research activities of the agents for higher education of which, in the case of South Africa, the universities, the technikons and the colleges for teachers training are the most common.

The Committee of University Principals accepted the following guidelines to determine the place and role of universities in South Africa (CUP 1987, pp. 1–2):

(a) The university should obey the demand of relevancy in teaching and research activities with regard to the social, economic, and cultural needs of the community without sacrificing the aim of academic expertise and intellectual creativity.

(b) As agent for cultural development, the university should associate with the social and cultural values of its specific target group.

(c) Universities should execute their autonomy with responsibility and self-discipline.

(d) Entrance to university should be available to everyone with the required ability, aptitude, and interest in consideration of the financial position of the university and the labor needs of the country.

(e) As a legal entity, the university should recognize its interdependence on and liability to the state.

The aims of the university with regard to teaching are (CUP 1987 pp. 18–20):

(a) that university courses cover the range of the arts, humanities, natural sciences, and applied sciences.

(b) that university teaching is directed at the development of the intellectual abilities of the student in order to stimulate new insight and independent thinking.

(c) that the university will prepare students to fill high-level positions and to contribute to the development of scientific knowledge in their field of study.

(d) that the university will exercise leadership in higher education as well as in secondary education, especially with regard to the admissions requirements of higher education.

(e) that the university will serve as agent for innovation in the educational system.

It is believed that the university should widen the intellectual and cultural horizon of the student through teaching and research as well as through its extracurricular activities.

The medium of instruction at each of the universities is either or both official languages. Ten residential universities primarily serve the White community, four residential universities serve the Black community, one residential university primarily serves the Colored community, one residential university serves the Asian community, and the one correspondence university serves the total community. The growth in the number of universities since 1960 has been as follows: 1960—14; 1965—15; 1970—16; 1965—16; 1980—17; 1985—18; 1987—17 (RSA 1988, p. 5.39).

The technikon prepares students for specific occupations and all its programs must be directed to this end. These programs are of postsecondary nature and not only include training in the technical field but also, for example, training in the field of the economic and management sciences, health care, the fine and performing arts, and the commercial arts. The technikon is seen as the leader in the field of vocational training and technology. Students' training therefore includes problem solving and innovation.

At present there are 12 technikons in South Africa. Seven of these residential technikons primarily serve the White community, two serve the Black community, one serves the Coloreds, and one the Asians. One technikon offers correspondence courses and serves the whole community. The growth in the number of technikons since 1970 has been as follows: 1970—10; 1980—12; 1987—12 (RSA 1988 p. 5.58).

Teachers training colleges train teachers for the primary (elementary) school in cooperation with the universities, which are responsible for training secondary school teachers. However, some of the students who graduate from the colleges are also appointed to the junior secondary schools.

Examples of other institutions for higher education are:

(a) The nursing colleges, which have the objective of training and developing students on a personal and professional level. These colleges were previously attached only to hospitals, but have been autonomous institutions affiliated with universities since 1982.

(b) The colleges for agriculture, which have the objective of training farmers in practical farming skills.

Table 2
Number of teachers colleges

	1960	1965	1970	1975	1980	1985	1987
Whites	14	18	15	16	17	16	18
Coloreds	12	13	12	14	14	12	13
Asians	2	2	2	2	2	2	2
Blacks	44	35	33	41	40	33	37

Source: RSA, 1988 pp. 5.47–5.48

(c) The police colleges, which have the objective of training the police force in functional police work and assisting students in bettering their academic qualifications.

2.1 Admissions Policies

The minimum entrance requirement to higher education is the school-leaving certificate. The Joint Matriculation Board moderates the official examinations of the recognized examining bodies and issues an exemption certificate to those candidates who have passed at a standard acceptable to the Board. Individual institutions may, however, set their own requirements as is generally done in the case of certain degrees; for example, mathematics at the higher level is required for admission to the bachelor's degree in natural sciences.

Enrollments in higher education from 1960 are given in Table 3. The major feature is the high growth in the total number of students in higher education.

2.2 Structure of Qualifications

The structure of qualifications in universities is primarily the responsibility of the individual university but consensus between the individual universities and the educational authorities is necessary to ensure the recognition of different qualifications with regard to character and standard. This consensus on qualifications allows for the horizontal movement of students between different institutions for higher education.

The universities award degrees and diplomas as qualifications. Degrees include the following (DNE 1986 pp. 5.59–5.62):

(a) First baccalaureus degree: the general degree takes three years to complete and the vocationally directed degree takes four years.

(b) Second baccalaureus degree: an example of which is the Baccalaureus Education which has a first degree as a prerequisite.

(c) Honors baccalaureus degree: the honors degree implies a greater depth of study in an academic subject or discipline. The duration of the course is one year for full-time study and two years for part-time study.

Table 3
Enrollments in higher education

	1960	1965	1970	1975	1980	1985	1987
Universities	42,363	58,819	82,909	116,168	152,346	211,756	247,694
Technikons	—	—	—	43,813	46,706	59,118	53,636
Teachers colleges	14,304	16,477	22,350	31,227	31,757	36,480	

Source: RSA, 1988 p. 5.41; Committee of University Principals, 1987

(d) Magister degrees: the magister degree follows on from the second baccalaureus degree or the honors degree and the course can be of one year full-time or two years' part-time duration. It represents the achievement of a greater depth in a specific subject or discipline which has been studied previously.

(e) Doctoral degree: although no general rules exist, it is recommended that the first doctoral degree which is awarded on the basis of original research under the supervision of a promoter, will be the PhD. Higher doctorates may be awarded to scholars producing exceptionally high quality original research over a sustained period.

There are three levels of diplomas available which include the first diploma, the advanced university diploma, and the postdegree diploma.

The technikons award diplomas and certificates with standards evaluated by the Certification Board (Technikons). The awards are as follows: (DNE 1988, pp. 6, 12–13):

(a) National Certificate and National Higher Certificate: a school-leaving certificate is the minimum entrance requirement and the courses are one and two years in duration respectively.

(b) First National Diploma: the course is three years in duration with a minimum entrance requirement of a school-leaving certificate.

(c) National Postdiploma Certificate: this diploma requires prior completion of the First National Diploma. The aim is not a vertical addition of knowledge but a horizontal broadening of knowledge and skills aimed at a specific occupation. The diploma is a one-year course.

(d) National Higher Diploma: the course is of one year's duration, and requires prior completion of a First National Diploma. The aim is a vertical development and deepening of knowledge and skills in a specific field of knowledge.

(e) Master's Diploma in Technology: this advanced course requires a National Higher Diploma as the requirement for entry and is of one year's duration. This diploma is awarded on the basis of theoretical study and a research report.

(f) Laureatus in Technology: the Laureatus course is of a minimum duration of one year and is awarded on the basis of a scientific report on a research project to prove an individual's abilities in research.

The teachers training colleges are responsible for the training of teachers for the primary schools and award the Higher Education Diploma (Primary). The course, which is of four years' duration, includes academic as well as professional content and makes provision for specialization in either preprimary, junior primary or senior primary education. As an exception, some colleges still train teachers for the secondary school and award the Secondary Education Diploma after four years of study.

3. Governance, Administration, and Finance

3.1 National Administration

According to the political structure, the Minister of National Education is responsible for the general policy of higher education. This includes the general aims and functions of the different institutions for higher education. The political liability of the different institutions, however, is vested in the hands of the ministers of the four departments responsible for the education of the different cultural groups. According to the general policy these ministers are responsible for the financing of higher education and for the approval of certain developments on the academic and physical level—for example, the introduction of new academic departments, degrees, or subjects, or the building of new facilities.

In drawing up policy, the Minister of National Education, as well as the other ministers, is advised by the Universities and Technikons Advisory Council especially in those matters concerning universities and technikons. The Advisory Council serves as a buffer between the political authority and the universities and provides a knowledgeable basis for policy formulation.

On issues directly concerning universities, the ministers as well as the Universities and Technikons Advisory Council are in turn advised by the Committee of University Principals. The committee is also empowered to prepare and execute general statutes and regulations for the more effective functioning of the universities. The committee therefore serves as a body to promote the interests of the universities. Similarly, the Committee of Technikon Principals acts to promote the interests of the technikons. It must be kept in mind that each university was founded by its own legislative act while the technikons were founded by several acts making provision for the establishment of the different technikons (DNE 1987 pp. 8–12, 1988 pp. 2–3).

The other institutions for higher education—for example, teachers training, nursing, and agricultural colleges—are more closely controlled by the different departments responsible for the various institutions. They are therefore less autonomous than the universities and technikons, although they strive to become academically accredited by those institutions.

Government expenditure on higher education as a percentage of the Gross National Product at current prices has been as follows since 1960: 1960—0.29 percent; 1965—0.32 percent; 1970—0.51 percent; 1975—0.70 percent; 1980—0.61 percent and 1983—0.69 percent (Dreijmanis 1988 pp. 130, 134).

3.2 Institutional Administration

As the universities and technikons are autonomous institutions, there are no general rules for their governance at the institutional level. Some general characteristics can, however, be described.

For the university, final executive responsibility is vested in the university council. The council administers the property of the university and controls all the functions of the university. It appoints the personnel and determines and receives the fees payable by the students. Although the senate is responsible for all academic aspects of the university, the decisions of the senate are always subject to the approval of the university council. The university council usually consists of the vice-chancellor, some representatives from the community, elected representatives of the senate and the convocation, and representatives of donors and other interest groups (DNE 1987 pp. 10–11).

The authority over academic work is vested in the university senate. The senate usually consists of all full professors and all heads of departments and academic institutes as determined by the university council. It is responsible for the organization of and supervision over all lecturing and examination activities, as well as for the standard and requirements of all degrees and other qualifications awarded by the university. The university is usually organized in faculties and, as a result, the various faculty councils advise the senate on academic matters pertaining to their faculty. The different departments are the operational units for the academic responsibilities of the senate. The personnel of each department are responsible for the highest level of research and best possible teaching and evaluation of students. The responsibilities of the convocation of the university are stipulated in the university statutes. The convocation elects a certain number of people to the university council and gives its opinion on any matter concerning the university. Usually the convocation has no academic authority. Day-to-day administration of the university is the responsibility of the management committee, usually consisting of representatives of the academic staff—for example, the rector and the deans of the different faculties—and some administrative personnel.

4. Faculty and Students: Teaching, Learning, and Research

4.1 Faculty

The personnel of the institutions for higher education can generally be divided into three categories, namely the faculty (teaching staff), the research personnel, and the administration staff. The final responsibility for recruitment and appointment of these personnel is that of the institution itself. Although no rigid criteria exist, the following guidelines represent the career path, legal status, and promotion criteria for faculty at universities.

(a) Junior lectureship: the minimum academic qualification for appointment is a relevant honors degree or second baccalaureus degree.

(b) Lectureship: the minimum academic qualification for appointment is a relevant magister degree.

Table 4
Numbers of faculty of universities and technikons

	1960	1965	1970	1975	1980	1985	1987
Universities	3,228	4,594	6,195	8,388	6,762	8,919	9,432
Technikons	—	—	2,130	2,034	2,414	2,415	2,668

Source: RSA, 1988 pp. 5.39, 5.58

(c) Senior lectureship: the minimum qualification for appointment is a relevant doctoral degree and experience in research.

(d) Associate professor: the minimum qualification is a doctoral degree with extensive experience in research.

(e) Full professor: the minimum qualification is a doctoral degree with proven experience in research and an established professional reputation among academic colleagues at national and even at international level.

Although differences exist, the career paths of the other institutions for higher education follow those of the universities. The highest levels of the academic posts of the other institutions are deemed to be of lower status than that of a full professor. The balance between teaching, research, and administration responsibilities of the teaching personnel is decided at the institutional level.

The faculty has no official representation at government level. The different faculty associations of the individual universities must therefore promote their interests through their universities and the Committee of University Principals (CUP). The Committee of University Teachers' Associations represents the corporate interests of all the associations at the CUP. Numbers of personnel are given in Table 4.

4.2 Students

One of the major characteristics with regard to the student body is the growth in student numbers in higher education up to the point that the university numbers alone represent 7.7 per 1,000 of the total population. It is generally accepted that the economy cannot handle a higher figure.

Another characteristic is the growth of the economic and related sciences at the expense of the natural sciences. The division between undergraduate and graduate students at the universities is given in Table 5. This represents an annual percentage growth over the period 1965 to 1985 of 6.4 percent with regard to undergraduate students and of 8.1 percent with regard to graduate students. The percentage of male and female students at universities, technikons, and teachers training colleges was as follows:

1970—66.3 percent male and 33.7 percent female; 1975—64.7 percent male and 35.3 percent female; 1980—63 percent male and 37 percent female; 1985—59.1 percent male and 40.9 percent female; 1987—55.6 percent male and 44.4 percent female.

5. Conclusion

Although relatively new, higher education in South Africa has already achieved much. The challenges which are at present being focused on, include the following:

(a) Economic and financial restraints are being attended to in order to improve educational services and the holding power on qualified personnel.

(b) Rationalization of activities and services in higher education in order to reduce the per unit cost and the duplication in and between the different institutions in higher education has been set in motion.

(c) Attempts are continuously being made to reduce the gap between secondary and higher education.

(d) Measures to be taken to ensure a more balanced distribution of students between universities and technikons need to be considered.

(e) A national research policy and especially the financing of research should be formulated.

Bibliography

Committee of University Principals (CUP) 1987a Report of the main committee of the CUP investigation into macro-aspects of the university within the context of tertiary education in the Republic of South Africa. CUP, Pretoria

Committee of University Principals 1987b Tendencies of Tertiary Education in the RSA. CUP, Pretoria

Department of National Education 1982 An Investigation of Government Financing of Universities. DNE, Pretoria

Department of National Education 1986a Qualification Structure for Universities in South Africa. DNE, Pretoria

Department of National Education 1986b Syllabi for Technikons in the RSA (Sanso 176). DNE, Pretoria

Department of National Education 1987 Academic Standards of Universities in South Africa. DNE, Pretoria

Department of National Education 1988 Vereistes vir nasionale onderrigprogramme aan technikons. DNE, Pretoria

Department of National Education 1989 Nasionale beleid vir algemene onderwyssake. DNE, Pretoria

Dreijmanis J 1988 The Role of the South African Government in Tertiary Education. South African Institute of Race Relations, Johannesburg

Republic of South Africa 1971 South African Statistics. Government Printer, Pretoria

Republic of South Africa 1988 South African Statistics. Government Printer, Pretoria

Table 5
Proportion of undergraduate and graduate students at universities

	1965	1975	1985
Undergraduate	50,277	103,301	174,326
Graduate	8,686	19,134	40,913

Source: Committee of University Principals, 1987, p. 17

Rossouw J P W 1987 *The South African Population: 1985–2035, Newsletter 176.* HSRC, Pretoria
Steyn H J, Steyn E S 1988 *Die Suid-Afrikaanse Onderwysstelsel.* Pro Rege, Potchefstroom
Van Schalkwyk O J 1988 *Die onderwysstelsel: Teorie en praktyk.* Alkanto, Alkantrant

H. J. Steyn

South Pacific, Islands of the

1. Higher Education and Society

The South Pacific is not a country, but an ocean. This article arbitrarily restricts itself to the 11 English-speaking island countries which together set up the University of the South Pacific (USP) in 1968 and the one which joined it in 1991; it will use South Pacific in that sense. Nine of these countries are fully independent states: Fiji, Kiribati, the Marshall Islands, Nauru, the Solomon Islands, Tonga, Tuvalu, Vanuatu, and Western Samoa. The other three are self-governing dependencies of New Zealand: the Cook Islands, Niue, and Tokelau. All had, until the late 1960s, some kind of dependent relationship with the United Kingdom, the United States or New Zealand, and, in the case of Vanuatu, with France as well. The region of the South Pacific spreads over 1.5 million square kilometers of ocean, the size of Africa or four times the size of Western Europe. The total land mass is equal to the size of Denmark. The distance from the Solomon Islands in the west to the Cook Islands in the east is about equal to that of New York to Los Angeles. The combined population of the countries concerned is about 1.5 million: Fiji is the largest with 720,000 and four of the countries have populations under 10,000. The average annual rate of increase is about 2 percent.

The dominant economic activity is agriculture (largely subsistence but with some important export crops, such as sugar in Fiji) with increasing importance attached to tourism in one or two countries. There are few reliable national income statistics, but the average Gross Domestic Product (GDP) per head has been estimated at around US$1,600 in Fiji and perhaps US$450 in the other countries. All are in great economic difficulty, struggling to increase and diversify export earnings, and in some cases very heavily dependent upon remittances from emigrants.

The countries are culturally and linguistically diverse, including people of Melanesian, Micronesian, Polynesian, Indian, Chinese, and European origin among their populations. English is the common second language, taught in all secondary schools except for some in Vanuatu where French is the second language; there are some 235 languages spoken in all. All the governments are elected through variations of parliamentary democracy, though the constitution in Fiji was suspended following a military coup in 1987, and has not (to date) been restored.

2. The Institutional Fabric of the Higher Education System

There was no university education in the South Pacific, other than courses in theology, and, to a lesser extent, medicine, until the foundation of USP. Since the Second World War increasing numbers of students have gone overseas for first and higher degrees, and there are probably almost as many abroad as there are full-time students at USP.

The USP is the only university in its region providing internationally accredited university education to undergraduate and graduate level. It is a research university, in that all academic staff are expected to carry out research as part of their duties, and its charter defines its objects as "the maintenance, advancement, and dissemination of knowledge by teaching, consultancy, and research." It has two main residential campuses, in Fiji and in Western Samoa, where its School of Agriculture is located. In addition, it has centers employing academic staff in eight other countries of the region; their purpose is to organize enrollments for distance education courses, with supplementary tutorial support for their students (the main teaching being done by staff based in Suva), and continuing education programs.

The University offers three-year bachelor's degree programs, to which admission is obtained by achieving a prescribed standard in either the University's own foundation (predegree) year, or a comparable school-leaving qualification. The University sets its own admission requirements for the foundation year, which are a high level of achievement in the relevant sixth form (12 years of schooling) secondary school leaving examination of the country concerned. Science degree programs require science and mathematics entry qualifications and all require English Language. There are no government requirements for admission, but the overwhelming majority of students are supported by scholarships, the award of which is determined by governments. The University's charter forbids it to discriminate in the admission of students (or the appointment of staff) on religious, ethnic, or political grounds.

In the early 1990s enrollments at USP total about 8,000 on credit courses, including just under 2,000 full-time residential students, and a further 6,000 studying part-time, mostly through the distance education mode at the centers in countries throughout the region. The number of full-time students has been fairly stable since 1983, but there have been dramatic increases in the number of distance education students, which amount to nearly 40 percent of all the full-time equivalents (FTEs). Some two-thirds of the total FTEs are from Fiji, the next largest contingents being from Tonga and the Solomon Islands. The largest enrollment per 1,000 of the population is from the very small countries, Tuvalu and the Cook Islands; the lowest figure (under 1 per 1,000) being in the Solomon Islands, which is the second largest country in the region. There is a small but growing number of students from outside the region, including significant groups from the Maldive Islands and the Federated States of Micronesia, and a few also from the United States, Australia, Canada, South Korea, Japan, and Finland.

After three years of study at university, it is possible to attain a BA or BSc degree after which the opportunity exists to go on to a master's program, consisting of a one-year course leading to a graduate diploma followed by a year's supervised research and thesis; and thence to a PhD—a three-year program of supervised research. In 1989 there were only about 60 graduate students, as most study at this level was being undertaken overseas.

3. Governance, Administration, and Finance

The governing body of the University is its council, consisting of representatives (in most cases ministers of education) from the 12 member countries, with Fiji having five members, Western Samoa, two, and the rest, one each. The chairperson (the pro-chancellor of the University) is appointed by the council; the chancellorship is an honorific role appointed in three-yearly rotation to each head of state of the member countries. There are also academic and student members of the university council, and some appointed by outside bodies, including the governments of Australia, New Zealand, and the United Kingdom.

The council carries out the University's policy-making, while in each constituent country the Ministry of Education is responsible for higher education, including the distribution of students between USP and overseas universities, and the establishment of other national tertiary institutions. The University is formally autonomous, being established as a corporation by charter. It is, however, virtually entirely dependent for funding upon its member governments.

The University budget is established every three years by the ministers of finance of the member countries, in response to detailed advice from a University Grants Committee established by the member governments, but with three outside members from Australia, New Zealand, and the United Kingdom. This committee recommends the total funds to be

allocated to the University over the next triennium, and the manner in which these are to be divided between the member countries. The formula is a complex one, two-thirds being allocated in proportion to past student numbers from each country, and one-third in proportion to the University's payroll expenditure in each country. The result is that some two-thirds of the total comes from Fiji, the rest being divided among the other countries. In addition, the governments of Australia and New Zealand contribute about 10 percent of the total recurrent budget, as part of their overseas aid programs. The recurrent budget in 1991 is about US$14 million.

Capital development has been almost entirely funded from overseas aid sources, and these donors also contribute substantially to the University by funding short-term projects, by topping up the salaries of some of their nationals working for the university, by contributing books and equipment, and in other ways. The major donors have been Australia, New Zealand, the United Kingdom, the United States, the European Community, Canada, France, Japan, United Nations agencies, and the Commonwealth Fund for Technical Cooperation.

Within the University, academic policy is the responsibility of the senate, consisting of some 40, mostly senior, academic staff, and chaired by the vice-chancellor, who is the chief academic and administrative officer of the University. There are a range of committees, usually chaired by the vice-chancellor or by one of the two pro-vice-chancellors, with participation by students but not by nonacademic staff.

The University is organized into four schools, (agriculture, humanities, pure and applied sciences, and social and economic development) each of which has several departments. Each department is headed by the senior staff member, usually a full professor. Each school has a head appointed by the senate (schools are equivalent to faculties, and their heads to deans). There are also eight institutes responsible for applied research and for short noncredit courses; these are intended to be funded outside the regular academic budget, and to earn their own costs. The library, computer services, extension services, and media unit are separate organizations serving the whole University and reporting direct to the vice-chancellor.

4. Faculty and Students: Teaching, Learning, and Research

4.1 Faculty

There are some 200 members of the academic teaching staff, plus a further 90 in comparable professional grades in the library, research institutes, administration, and extension services. Some 70 percent of the staff are nationals of the 12 member countries, the rest coming from about 20 other countries. All posts are advertised worldwide. Appointment is by the University, with no involvement of the governments. There is no tenure, all appointments being for renewable three-year contracts.

There are four main academic grades: professor (14); reader (14); senior lecturer (40); and lecturer (90). Promotion is by academic merit alone. The staff are employees of the University, and are not civil servants: they are free to engage in political activity as long as this does not interfere with their university duties.

Duties of staff are allocated by heads of department; no hours are specified, and all staff are expected to teach, on-campus and by extension, write distance education courses, and undertake research and consultancy work and administration as required. There are no set hours, and staff are entitled to six weeks' leave each year.

4.2 Students

About two-thirds of the degree-level students are in the social sciences and humanities faculties and about one-third in science. A third of all FTE students are in predegree courses. Ninety percent of full-time students are on full government scholarships, providing for full tuition and maintenance, and there are no fees for these students. Of the two-thirds of the students who come from Fiji, about half are ethnic Indians while half are Fijian. The Fiji Government discriminates positively in favor of the latter when awarding scholarships. Forty percent of the internal students are female. There is a student association for full-time students on the two main campuses; it elects its own officers and controls its own funds, and membership is compulsory.

The undergraduate course structure is determined by the University, and involves choosing a major and a minor study focus with limited electives—the model is a modified liberal arts one, on a credit-unit system with prerequisites for some courses. Students are assessed continuously for each course and at end of semester examinations: there are two semesters a year. The final transcript shows grades for each course completed.

5. Conclusion

The main problems confronting the system are economic—the difficulty of providing sufficient resources to staff adequately a university which will be able to respond to increasing demands from the countries of the region—and educational—the increasing difficulty of national secondary school systems in producing qualified school-leavers, and the consequent need for the University to take on more subdegree-level work. It is hoped that national postsecondary institutions will develop, which will then permit countries to leave to the University that work

(undergraduate and graduate education, research, and consultancy) which can only economically be done by a regional, international institution with a larger resource base. However, the economic situation of the South Pacific countries, which is not improving, is a serious obstacle.

Bibliography

Crocombe R, Meleisea M 1988 *Pacific Universities: Achievements, Problems, Prospects.* Institute of Pacific Studies, University of the South Pacific, Suva

G. Caston

Soviet Union

1. Higher Education and Society

In 1986, the process of *perestroika* (restructuring) of the political and economic structures started in the Soviet Union, entailing the reformation of the education system as a whole, and higher education in particular, as a main level in the national strategy of the development of the country. In connection with this, some of the latest data given below will, to a certain extent, describe the situation of the transition period.

The foundation of the first higher education institutions in the Soviet Union began in what is now Armenia and Georgia in the fourteenth century AD (the Colchis Academy). In the fifteenth and sixteenth centuries Gelatia, Ikatei, and Germ academies were founded. These were mainly centers of theological education. However, Gelatia Academy, not far from Kutaisi in Georgia was also the center of secular education, offering courses in arithmetic, geometry, astronomy, grammar, philosophy, rhetoric, and music.

The Vilnius Academy in Lithuania serving mainly the interests of the Catholic Church, was founded in 1579, but enjoyed the rights and privileges of a university. It was reorganized into Vilen University in 1803. In 1632, the Gustavian Academy was founded in Tartu, Estonia, functioning intermittently until 1710, and later reopening as Derpt University in 1802, Yuriev University in 1893, and—after 1918—Tartu University.

The first Slavonic academy—the Kiev-Mogilyan Academy—was founded in 1632. It offered courses in the Slavonic languages, Greek, and Latin, and seven liberal arts (grammar, arithmetic, geometry, astronomy, rhetoric, dialectics, music), and also theology. The Slavonic Greek–Latin Academy was founded in 1687 in Moscow. It was both a secondary

Table 1
Growth of the number of higher education institutions

Year	1915	1927	1937	1940	1950	1960	1970	1975	1980	1985	1990
Number of institutions	34	148	683	817	880	739	805	856	883	894	904

Table 2
Population of the Soviet Union

	1940	1959	1970	1979	1987	1990
Population in millions of people	194.1	208.8	241.7	262.4	281.6	288.6
Urban	63.1	99.9	136.0	163.6	186.0	190.6
Rural	131.0	108.9	105.7	98.8	95.6	98.0
RSFSR	110.1	117.5	130.1	137.5	145.3	148.0
Urban	37.9	61.6	81.0	95.3	106.9	
Rural	72.2	55.9	49.1	42.2	38.4	
Ukranian SSR	41.3	41.8	47.1	49.7	51.2	51.8
Urban	14.0	19.1	25.7	30.5	34.2	
Rural	27.3	22.7	21.4	19.2	17.0	
Byelorussian SSR	9.0	8.0	9.0	9.5	10.0	10.2
Urban	1.9	2.4	3.9	5.2	6.4	
Rural	7.1	5.6	5.1	4.3	3.6	
Uzbek SSR	6.5	8.1	11.7	15.3	19.0	20.3
Urban	1.6	2.7	4.3	6.3	7.9	
Rural	4.9	5.4	7.4	9.0	11.1	
Kazakh SSR	6.1	9.2	13.0	14.6	16.2	16.7
Urban	1.8	4.0	6.5	7.9	9.4	
Rural	4.3	5.2	6.5	6.7	6.8	
Georgian SSR	3.6	4.0	4.6	5.0	5.2	5.4
Urban	1.1	1.7	2.2	2.6	2.8	
Rural	2.5	2.3	2.4	2.4	2.4	
Azerbaijan SSR	3.2	3.6	5.1	6.0	6.8	7.1
Urban	1.2	1.7	2.5	3.2	3.7	
Rural	2.0	1.9	2.6	2.8	3.1	
Lithuanian SSR	2.9	2.7	3.1	3.3	3.6	3.7
Urban	0.7	1.0	1.5	2.0	2.4	
Rural	2.2	1.7	1.6	1.3	1.2	
Moldavian SSR	2.4	2.8	3.5	3.9	4.1	4.3
Urban	0.3	0.6	1.1	1.5	1.9	
Rural	2.1	2.2	2.4	2.4	2.2	
Latvian SSR	1.8	2.0	2.3	2.5	2.6	2.6
Urban	0.6	1.1	1.4	1.7	1.9	
Rural	1.2	0.9	0.9	0.8	0.7	
Kirghiz SSR	1.5	2.0	2.9	3.5	4.1	4.3
Urban	0.3	0.7	1.1	1.3	1.6	
Rural	1.2	1.3	1.8	2.2	2.5	
Tadzhik SSR	1.5	1.9	2.9	3.8	4.8	5.2
Urban	0.3	0.6	1.1	1.3	1.6	
Rural	1.2	1.3	1.8	2.5	3.2	
Armenian SSR	1.3	1.7	2.4	3.0	3.4	3.3
Urban	0.4	0.4	1.4	2.0	2.3	
Rural	0.9	0.9	1.0	1.0	1.1	
Turkmen SSR	1.3	1.5	2.1	2.7	3.3	3.6
Urban	0.5	0.7	1.0	1.3	1.6	
Rural	0.8	0.8	1.1	1.4	1.7	
Estonian SSR	1.0	1.1	1.3	1.4	1.5	1.58
Urban	0.3	0.6	0.8	1.0	1.1	
Rural	0.7	0.5	0.5	0.4	0.4	

and higher education establishment and offered courses in the same subjects.

Researchers have different opinions concerning the date of the foundation of the first secular higher education institution in Russia. Some think that higher education in Russia has its roots in the School of Mathematics and Navigation—established in 1701 in Moscow, and removed to St. Petersburg in 1715, before being reorganized into the Naval Academy. Other authors refer to the foundation of Moscow University in 1755. In any case, this period marked an obvious separation of religious and secular education in the humanities in Russia. Young people wishing to take exclusively theological courses entered the Slavonic Greek–Latin Academy, which had moved to the Trinity-St. Sergy Lavra near Moscow and where it still functions as the Moscow Theological Academy.

For almost 50 years, Moscow University was the only university in the country. Prerequisites for the growth of university education were created only at the beginning of the eighteenth century under the relatively liberal period during the reign of Alexander I. At this time Derpt (1802), Vilen (1803), Kazan (1804), Kharkov (1805), and St. Petersburg (1819) universities were successively established. Only one university—St. Vladimir University in Kiev (1834)—was founded under the reign of Nikolas I. During the second half of the eighteenth century a number of universities were founded including Novorossisk in Odessa (1865), Russian Warsaw (1869), Tomsk (1888), Saratov (1909), and Perm (1916) universities.

The dynamics of growth in the number of higher education institutions in the Russian empire from 1914–15 and later in the Soviet Union is presented in Table 1.

1.1 Geographical Context

The Union of Soviet Socialist Republics was founded at the first All-Union Congress of the Soviets on December 30, 1922 and originally comprised 16 Union Republics. Later one of the union republics, the Karelo-Finnish Soviet Socialist Republic (SSR) was transformed into Karelian Autonomous SSR becoming a member of the Russian Soviet Federative Socialist Republic (RSFSR), and the number of union republics was reduced to 15 (see Table 2). In 1940, the western Ukraine and Byelorussia, Bessarabia, and the Baltic Republics of Lithuania, Latvia, and Estonia became member states of the Soviet Union. In 1991 the Soviet Union covered an area of 22.4 million square kilometers.

In 1914, the population of the Russian empire was 159.2 million, with the majority of people living in rural areas (130.7 million).

Between 1917 and 1939 rates of growth of the population of the Soviet Union were rather moderate for such a large country and increased at an average of 0.47 million people per year. Undoubtedly, the Civil War and the Second World War influenced such a low average growth. By 1939 the population of the Soviet Union was 170.5 million, including a rural population of 114.7 million. The rate of growth of the urban population exceeded that of the rural one (28.5 million in 1914 and 55.8 million in 1939). This was caused in the first instance by the industrialization of the Soviet Union in the 1930s. In 1940 the population of the country reached 194.1 million. After the Second World War the territory of the Soviet Union increased as a result of the annexation of the Kaliningrad region (formerly East Prussia) and the southern part of Sakhalin and Kuril Islands, but the total incorporation of the population reduced drastically as a result of the losses in the war. There were 178.5 million people in 1950, comprised of an urban population of 69.4 million and a rural population of 109.1 million.

The dynamics of change of the population of the country across the republics and the rural/urban balance is shown in Table 2.

The social structure of the population of the Soviet Union and average annual number of industrial, clerical, and agricultural workers is presented in Tables 3 and 4 respectively. The number of specialists with higher education qualifications, employed in the national economy on the whole and their distribution across specialties is shown in Tables 5 and 6 respectively.

The structure of the economy of the Soviet Union is expressed through the structure of the Gross National Product (GNP), main constituents of which are given in Table 7.

Table 8 gives the distribution of absolute magnitudes of the basic indices of the socioeconomic development of the Soviet Union's GNP, the Gross Social Product (GSP), and the national income, across the main constituents.

Table 3
The percentage social structure of the population

	1939	1959	1970	1979	1989
Total population (including unemployed members of families)	100	100	100	100	100
Office workers	16.5	18.1	22.1	25.1	29.3
Industrial workers	33.7	50.2	57.4	60.0	58.8
Agricultural workers	42.7	31.4	20.5	14.9	11.7
Persons engaged in individual productive activity, priests, and those who have not indicated their social group[a]	2.6	0.3	0.0	0.0	0.2

a In 1959, 1970, 1979—individual peasants, handicraftsmen working by themselves, and priests

Table 4
The average annual number of industrial, office, and agricultural workers (in millions)

	1940	1960	1970	1980	1985	1986
Total industrial, office, agricultural workers	62.9	83.8	106.5	125.6	130.3	130.9
Office workers	10.0	15.8	25.3	33.7	36.1	36.4
Industrial workers (including junior operating personnel)	23.9	46.2	64.9	78.8	81.7	82.1
Agricultural workers[a]	29.0	21.8	16.6	13.1	12.5	12.4

a Excluding students working in agricultural sector and workers of state enterprises and organizations

1.2 Structure of Government and Main Political Goals

It is generally known that higher education is one of the main factors of a nation's progress because its development affects to a great extent the scientific–technical and cultural potential of society. Modern scientific–technical revolution converts the intellectualization of productive activity into the main factor of the development of the productive forces in society. For that reason the government of the Soviet Union has always paid special attention to the general education and specialized training of the population.

The peculiarities of the historical development of the Soviet Union successively determined a number of specific goals, i.e., raising the literacy level of the population after the October Revolution and the Civil War, providing personnel for the industrialization and collectivization of the country, and reconstructing the national economy after the Second World War. However, these have resulted in certain distortions in the functions of the higher education system.

Higher education, directed primarily at satisfying the needs of the national economy, took the path of increasing the number of specialities—a pragmatic approach to the satisfaction of the momentary demands of branches of industry—which has resulted in the decline of the fundamental and general cultural level of specialists. Planned assignment of higher education graduates under conditions of an expanding economy did not promote an increase in the quality of education. The economic infrastructure did not stimulate and support the desire for better education.

Present radical change in the concept of higher education, directed primarily at the satisfaction of educational needs of the individual, is a result of those transformations in society which have been formulated at the stage of reconstruction of the political and economic structures of the Soviet Union.

The following principles form the basis of the new state policy:

(a) autonomy—higher education, forming the intellectual core of society, should be free from political and economic pressure.

(b) freedom in academic and research activities—this principle should be fundamental to the functioning of higher education and should be ensured for all participants. Each educational institution should, with regard to concrete conditions, guarantee students the freedom of choice in implementing their cognitive and creative needs.

Table 5
Number of specialists with higher and specialized secondary education qualifications (in thousands)

	1941	1960	1970	1980	1987	1989
All specialists	2,401	8,784	16,841	28,612	35,693	36,484
Those with higher education qualifications	909	3,545	6,853	12,073	15,531	15,870
Those with specialized secondary education qualifications	1,492	5,239	9,988	16,539	20,162	20,614

Table 6
The distribution of specialists with higher education qualifications employed in the national economy across their specialties (in thousands)

	1980	1985	1987	1989
Engineers	4,914.2	6,057.6	6,490.6	6,593.5
Agronomists, livestock experts, veterinaries	618.2	701.7	716.1	729.3
Economists	1,091.8	1,396.7	1,480.5	1,601.1
Experts on merchandise	143.1	175.4	229.0	198.1
Lawyers	187.2	217.9	230.3	237.8
Teachers and cultural organizers	3,803.0	4,418.4	4,649.8	4,557.8
Doctors of different specialities	997.0	1,170.0	1,231.0	1,278.0
Others	318.7	347.2	503.6	6,742
Total specialists with higher education qualifications	12,073.2	14,484.9	15,530.9	15,869.8

(c) humanization of education—the missions and perspectives of higher education should be connected with the humane, cultural aspects of education, striving for the noble goals of strengthening international cooperation, peace, the protection of human rights, and the preservation and enrichment of national cultures. Higher education, developing human potential harmoniously, should take part in molding human dignity, and in preserving and strengthening its rights.

The principles mentioned above are already in action within the higher education system of the Soviet Union, manifesting themselves in granting higher education institutions much broader rights to decide both curricula and programs, the content of courses, and methods of educational process organ-

ization. But all new things require time for their implementation, especially in such an inert structure as higher education. For these reasons, existing structures and methods characterizing higher education activities in the Soviet Union will be described, without reference to recent innovations.

In accordance with the program of public education developed after the October Revolution, the following principles have been laid as an ideological and organizational basis of the Soviet higher education system: the secular character of education; the separation of the school from the Church; and the recognition of the scientific character of education and its link to life and productive labor.

2. The Institutional Fabric of the Higher Education System

2.1 Levels of Institution

There is a state system of public education in the Soviet Union. All institutions of higher education are funded by the state. There are no private higher education establishments.

All higher education institutions are legally and functionally equal throughout the Soviet Union. On successful completion of a course of study their graduates are awarded diplomas of similar status. There is no formal hierarchy of higher education establishments.

Fig. 1 shows the structure of the modern higher education system with data on the forms (on a full-time basis and a part-time basis without interruption of employment) and duration of study in higher education institutions of different types, and also graduate studies.

The system of higher education in the Soviet Union is a powerful academic and scientific complex,

Table 7
The percentage structure of the Gross National Product

	1980	1985	1988
Gross National Product including that produced by the branches:	100	100	100
Primary			
Agriculture	13	17	18
Secondary			
Industry	42	37	34
Construction	8	8	10
Tertiary			
Transport and communication	16	6	6
Trade	13	14	12
Paid services	18	18	20

Table 8
Basic indices of the socioeconomic development of the Soviet Union 1980–88 (actual prices—from thousand million rubles)

	1980	1985	1987	1989
1. Gross National Product including:	619.0	777.0	825.0	924.1
Consumption of the material values and services by the population	—	421.5	444.7	508.5
Gross accumulation (capital investments and increase in the material current assets)	—	248.4	264.8	287.6
Administrative, defense, research expenditures, etc.	—	107.1	115.5	128.0
2. Gross Social Product including that produced by the branches of industry:	1,078.5	1,383.6	1,464.5	1,568.6
Agriculture	152.6	219.5	234.9	270.1
Industry	685.5	844.6	892.3	930.7
Construction transport and communication	103.4	136.3	155.9	168.6
Transport and communication	47.6	66.0	70.3	75.4
Trade, provision, state purchases, and other kinds of services	89.4	117.2	111.1	123.8
3. National income including that produced by the branches of industry:	462.2	578.5	599.6	656.8
Agriculture	68.9	112.8	122.6	150.0
Industry	238.1	263.1	268.6	277.1
Construction	47.6	62.3	74.7	83.0
Transport and communication	27.0	35.0	36.6	39.5
Trade, provision, state purchases, and other kinds of services	80.6	105.3	97.1	107.2

deployed throughout the country, and serves practically all levels of production, science, culture, and ways of life. It has a flexible organizational structure based on a unity of branch and interbranch principles.

The branch principle is a result of the structure of the Soviet economy being a system of interconnected branches. It is the main principle when determining the type of higher education institutions and the content of specialized training of personnel. The interbranch principle is a result of the fact that higher education is a specific field of public activity with social functions that go beyond the limits of branch demands and interests.

Table 9 shows the categories of higher education institutions according to type and branch principle:

Data on the growth in the number of higher education institutions in the Soviet Union from 1960 onward are presented in Table 10.

Despite the fact that there is no formal hierarchy of higher education institutions in the Soviet Union, the university sector is the leading sector of Soviet higher education. This is because university education has rich historical traditions and the foundation and development of higher education in Russia is connected with the functioning of universities. Hence, during the first 10 years after the October Revolution much attention was devoted to the development of university education. In 1914 there were 12 universities in the Russian empire with a total of 40,000 students, and by 1926 this had risen to 18 universities and 53,000 students. The foundation of universities in Byelorussia, Transcaucasus, and Central Asia, where there had been no higher education institutions prior to the Revolution, was an important stage.

The social and class structure of the student body has changed. In 1914, 4.5 percent of children of

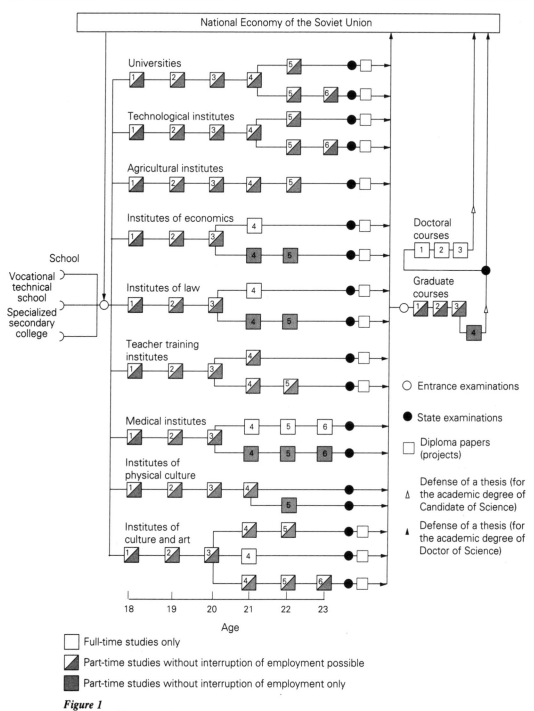

Figure 1
Structure of the system of higher education in the Soviet Union

peasants, workers, and working intelligentsia were enrolled in eight Russian universities, and in 1926 their quota increased to 48.5 percent.

In 1988, 69 universities contained 538,716 students

and university graduates made up about 12 percent (90,520 students) of all higher education graduates.

The leading role of universities emerged in the 1930s during the implementation of the indus-

Table 9
Type and branch groups of higher education institutions
in the Soviet Union

Types of higher education institutions	Branch groups of higher education institutions
Universities	Public education
Teacher training institutes	
Technological institutes (polytechnical and branch)	Industry and construction; transport and communication
Agricultural institutes	Agriculture
Specialized institutes (offering courses in the humanities— economics and law)	Economics and law
Medical institutes	Public health, physical culture, and sport
Institutes of physical culture	
Institutes of culture and art	Art and cinematography

trialization of the Soviet Union and collectivization
of the agricultural sector. Within this framework
higher education was directed toward strengthening
the link with industry and the improvement of practical study on the part of personnel. It was considered
necessary to establish higher education institutions
of a branch type, which would be under the authority
of the corresponding branch administrative bodies of
the national economy. Such higher education institutions were established first of all on the basis of
the departments of multisectoral higher education

Table 10
The distribution of higher education institutions across the
branch groups of educational establishments at the
beginning of the academic year

	1960	1970	1975	1980	1985	1988
All institutions	739	805	856	883	894	898
Publication education	241	268	283	287	289	287
(of which universities)	40	51	63	68	69	69
Industry and construction	169	201	219	228	233	235
Transport and communication	37	37	43	46	46	45
Agriculture	96	98	100	103	104	106
Economics and law	51	50	54	57	56	57
Public health, physical culture and sport	98	99	102	104	106	106
Art and cinematography	47	52	55	58	60	62

institutions and universities. For example, industrial,
agricultural, medical, irrigational, financial and economic, teacher-training, and veterinary institutes were
founded on the basis of the departments of the Central Asian University. The Byelorussian University
served as a basis for the establishment of polytechnical, medical, teacher-training, economic, and
legal institutes.

Of course, such roles of universities in the foundation of specialized higher education institutions
required the revision of the specific character of
university education and a more accurate definition
of the profile of university graduates. It was decided
that the main task of universities was to train
researchers, lecturers for higher education, and
secondary-school teachers. To a considerable extent,
universities upheld this role even in the early 1990s.
The fact that recently a number of leading technological and specialized higher education institutions have been made into universities may serve
as an illustration of the leading role played by universities in the higher education system of the Soviet
Union. For example, the Moscow Higher Technological School has become the Moscow State University
of Technology, and the Moscow State Historical-
Archive Institute is now the Moscow Humanitarian
University.

This does not mean, however, that technological
and other specialized higher education institutions
have been established exclusively on the basis of
universities. In the Russian empire in 1915, 18 technological and 14 agricultural higher education institutions existed with 25,000 and 4,600 students
respectively. In addition, there was a military medical
academy in St. Petersburg, five commercial educational establishments, 167 teacher-training seminaries, and 47 teacher-training institutes, which
together formed the basis for the development of
applied specialized training.

In particular the first polytechnical institute in the
Russian empire was founded in 1862 in Riga, and
in 1895 11 higher technological institutes, enrolling
5,500 students functioned in the country. Polytechnical institutes were founded as universities of
technology to provide training for a wide spectrum
of specialists in applied sciences.

In 1928 there were 32 industrial institutes in the
Soviet Union, but particularly rapid growth in the
number of technological higher education institutions could be observed by the 1930s. In 1940 there
were already 164 technological higher education
institutions, with a total enrollment of 204,600 students. The growth of higher technological education
was also observed after the Second World War.
Between 1950 and 1960 the number of students
enrolled in technological higher education institutions increased from 320,700 to 1,019,800. In the
first half of the 1950s, 26 technological institutes were
founded in the Urals, Siberia, and the far east. The

share of engineers in the total number of specialists increased and made up 36 percent between 1961 and 1965, 38 percent between 1966 and 1970, 42.6 percent between 1971 and 1975, and 43.5 percent in 1980. Up to 1980 polytechnical institutes could be found in 61 cities.

Recently a new type of higher technological education has been established in the Soviet Union. This is in the training of research engineers, which has been implemented at the Moscow Physico-Technological Institute, with an indepth program of study including theory and experimental methods of basic sciences.

Higher agricultural, medical, and teacher-training education has also been developed intensively in the Soviet Union. In 1914 agricultural higher education institutions enrolled 4,600 students. There was only one forestry institute (in St. Petersburg) in a country which possessed one-third of the world's forestry resources. In 1923 there were already about 30 agricultural and veterinary institutes with some 20,000 students. Sixteen agricultural institutes were founded in 1930. Agricultural education developed on an extensive scale after the Second World War. In 1955, agricultural institutes enrolled 196,000 students, almost four times more than in 1945. The institutes trained students in new specialities, such as the mechanization of agriculture. In 1975, 103,000 students were enrolled in this specialty. At the beginning of the 1980s there were 102 institutes and 10 branch institutes within the system of agricultural education. In 1979, 100,000 students were enrolled in agricultural institutes. Graduates of agricultural institutes made up 9 percent of the total number of graduates.

Medical education has been developing on an extensive scale in the Soviet Union. The first medical institute—the School of Military Doctors—was founded in Russia in 1654. In 1707 Moscow Hospital School was founded, marking the beginning of the foundation of such schools in St. Petersburg and other cities. Before 1917, 17 higher education institutions and faculties of universities trained doctors, but the scale did not meet the needs of the country. There were 20,000 doctors in the Russian empire, and most of them worked in the central provinces of Russia. In Tadzhikistan there were only 13 doctors; in Kirghizia 15 doctors; and in Azerbaijan 33 doctors. For that reason the Soviet government took urgent measures to accelerate medical education: in the universities 16 new faculties were founded in 1918. Between 1929 and 1935 specialized medical institutes were established in 24 cities, and in 1935, 55 higher medical institutes and faculties of universities trained Soviet doctors.

At the beginning of the 1980s, 82 medical stomatological and pharmaceutical institutes and a number of medical faculties of universities trained doctors. Medical graduates made up 6 percent of the total number of graduates and there were 36 doctors per 10,000 inhabitants.

The Soviet government has always regarded the higher teacher-training institutes as playing an important role in the implementation of the cultural policy and spread of education in society.

Before the October Revolution a system of secondary and higher pedagogical education had been established, but researchers considered it to be extremely unsatisfactory. The system of teacher-training institutes was inadequate; there were no teacher-training establishments, and, in particular, no higher institutions in the outlying and more remote districts which led, according to Lenin's definition, to the situation that the way to education was blocked for 90 percent of the population. Therefore, in 1918 the program for the development of teacher training was elaborated and adopted. During the implementation of the program three state universities and nine teacher-training institutes were founded in Petrograd (St. Petersburg) at the beginning of the 1920s. Teacher-training faculties were founded in all the universities, which were reorganized into independent educational establishments during 1930 and 1931. The number of teachers with higher education qualifications was constantly increased. Between 1951 and 1955 the share of teachers of general education schools with higher education qualifications increased from 15.8 percent to 23.5 percent, compared with 2 percent of teachers in prerevolutionary Russia.

In 1988, 199 teacher-training institutes with 822,800 students were in operation. In 1979, 148,500 students, 18.8 percent of the total number of graduates, graduated from teacher-training institutes.

From the first years of Soviet power, the government considered higher education institutions as important research centers, and an important part of training for life a highly skilled labor force. The foundation in 1925 of graduate courses attached to higher education institutions contributing to the formation of scientific schools serves as an illustration of such a policy.

However, during the first decades of the Soviet regime the main goal of higher education was to eliminate the shortage of a skilled labor force, which could not help adversely affecting research work, the latter being practically relegated to the background. The existing system of teacher's pay on an hourly basis contributed to the situation and prevented development of research work in higher education institutions.

In 1936 the government tried again to solve the problem of intensifying research in higher education institutions, considering it to be the primary factor which ensured the quality of specialist training and growth in the qualification of the academic staff. The system of permanent appointments was introduced into higher education which envisaged both teaching and research to be a teacher's role. However, the efficiency of research in higher education fell behind that in the specialized branch research establishments which had been formed by that time.

Measures to strengthen research work in higher education institutions were undertaken in 1944, 1956, and 1978. Research departments and sectors were founded in most higher education institutions, and the post of Prorector for Research Affairs was introduced. Funding of research in higher education institutions was regulated, and funds were also allocated from nonbudgetary sources, such as industry. The progress in research conducted by higher education institutions was observed as resulting from these decisions. For example, in 1967, the volume of research taking place in higher education institutions, in cost indices, exceeded by eight times the level of that in 1957. The further increase in the amount of research costs without capital investments of higher education institutions within the authority of the Ministry of Higher and Specialized Secondary Education of the Soviet Union is characterized by the following data: the index of work, including contractual work, was 100 in 1970; increasing to 183.5, or 195.8 including contractual work, in 1975; and 251.5, or 275.3 percent including contractual work, in 1980.

The most recent reforms by the government on the development of research in higher education institutions were in 1987. These promoted the increase in the number of institutes, including research into the teaching process. Up to 30 percent of full-time students participate in different forms of research work and the tendency to expand research activities in higher education institutions is strengthening. Nevertheless the share of higher education in the amount of current research expenditures made up only 7 percent in 1989, and 47.5 percent of Doctors of Science and 47.4 percent of Candidates of Science were working in the higher education sector.

2.2 Admission Policies and Selection

The Constitution of the Soviet Union and the Fundamentals of Legislation of the Soviet Union and Union Republics on public education guarantee the right to higher education for all citizens irrespective of sex, race, nationality, religion, social origin, and property status. Education in the Soviet Union is free of charge.

These constitutional and legislative guarantees serve as a basis for admission regulations valid for all higher education institutions, which are approved annually by the Soviet Union's State Committee for Public Education.

The basic level of education and age of the applicant, and a transcript of entrance examinations form some of the admission requirements. In addition, peculiarities of certain specialties and forms of study, procedure and date of submission of applications,

procedure of enrollment, and so forth are included in the admission regulations.

Recently, the right of higher education institutions to organize the admission process has been considerably expanded. In 1991, standard regulations of admission to higher education institutions were elaborated, detailing only basic stages in the organization of admission, educational level of applicants, date of admission, and so on, leaving it to the institute to determine the rest of the conditions, such as the number of competitive examinations, language, firms, system of evaluation of entrance examinations, procedure of enrollment, and so forth.

The main condition for entering a higher education institution, however, is to pass competitive entrance examinations whose main goal is the selection of the most suitable young people with a school leaving certificate. It is interesting to note that according to the Decree of the Council of People's Commissars of the RSFSR, approved on August 2, 1918, applicants were not required to have a preliminary educational level, and all those who wished to study and had reached the age of 16 were enrolled in universities and institutes.

Certain groups of applicants enjoy privileges. For example, according to regulations approved in 1991, those applicants who finish school with gold (silver) medals, or come from specialized secondary institutions, or leave vocational technical schools with honors certificates need only pass one examination with a high grade (excellent mark) in order to be released from other examinations. Restrictions on admission to some faculties and fields of study are determined only by an unsatisfactory health certificate.

2.3 Quantitative Developments in Higher Education

The distinctive feature of higher education development during the Soviet regime is the constant and systematic increase in the number of students. However, recently it has slowed down and, in a number of branches of the economy, has even reduced. This is not connected with deviation from the extensive development of higher education and the increase in the requirements for quality of specialist training. Concrete figures are given in Table 11.

2.4 Structure of Qualifications

In the Soviet Union, graduates are awarded a national diploma, which gives details of the subject taken and the qualification achieved. The diploma is awarded by the State Examination Board, a branch of which can be found at each higher education institution and includes experts from the national government. The diploma is awarded on the basis of state examination results and defense of the diploma project. At the institutes of physical culture and a number of other institutions offering courses in the humanities, the award is based on the results of

Table 11
The distribution of students across the branch groups of educational institutions (in thousands)

	1960	1970	1975	1980	1985	1988
All students	2,396.1	4,580.6	4,854.0	5,235.2	5,147.2	4,999.2
Public education (including	769.6	1,375.7	1,415.3	1,509.0	1,519.6	1,611.8
universities)	248.9	503.5	565.9	609.4	590.1	593.7
Industry and construction	873.1	1,825.7	1,950.0	2,088.2	1,996.8	1,835.6
Transport and communication	146.7	251.7	277.6	300.5	290.5	264.4
Agriculture	264.5	423.9	460.0	533.8	532.8	513.3
Economics and law	161.9	314.4	354.7	377.0	383.2	355.1
Public health, physical culture, and sport	188.9	321.0	351.6	378.7	376.0	368.5
Art and cinematography	19.4	41.2	44.8	48.0	48.3	50.5

state examinations only. Duration of study varies according to the type of institute as follows (see also Fig. 1):

(a) Universities—5–6 years;

(b) Technological institutes—5–6 years;

(c) Agricultural institutes—5 years;

(d) Institutes of economics—4–5 years;

(e) Institutes of Law—4–5 years;

(f) Teacher-training institutes—4–5 years;

(g) Medical institutes—5–6 years;

(h) Institutes of physical culture—4–5 years;

(i) Institutes of culture and art—4–6 years.

2.5 Graduate Training Programs

Graduate courses were founded in 1925 to train highly skilled personnel for basic and applied research. Graduate courses may be found at higher education institutions and also at branch research institutes and institutes under the Academy of Sciences of the Soviet Union. The main criterion for introducing graduate courses in higher education or research institutions is a sufficient number of highly skilled specialists in a particular field of research activity with a scientific background (the degree of Doctor of Science is obligatory).

Those who have the diploma of higher education and have successfully passed a competitive entrance examination are enrolled in graduate courses. Duration of studies depends on the form that studies will take (with or without interruption of employment) and is either three or four years in length (see Fig. 1). The data characterizing quantitative aspects of the training of graduate students in the Soviet Union are presented in Table 12.

Thus, in 1988 only 60 percent of graduate students were trained within the system of higher education of

Table 12
Number of graduate students

	1960	1965	1970	1975	1980	1985	1988
All graduate students	36,754	90,294	99,427	95,675	96,820	97,352	97,569
All graduates in research institutes with interrupted employment	16,348	36,882	42,518	39,969	38,767	39,417	38,645
	9,515	17,765	18,725	13,052	11,376	13,120	14,620
All graduates in higher education institutions with interrupted employment	20,406	53,412	56,909	55,706	58,053	57,935	58,924
	13,463	33,344	36,299	28,805	28,290	33,119	35,806

the Soviet Union. There is also extramural graduate study where a candidate for the degree of Candidate of Science presents and defends a thesis, having successfully passed examinations to a suitable level.

The next level of training for highly skilled research workers are doctoral courses which have functioned since 1987. In doctoral courses students are trained on a full-time basis, with interruption of employment; the duration of studies is three years (see Fig. 1). The number of doctoral courses in higher education and research institutions is considerably lower than graduate courses because of the very high entry requirements for doctoral courses; consequently, the number of doctoral students is lower than that of graduate students.

3. Governance, Administration, and Finance

3.1 National Administration

Questions of governance are crucial for solving problems in higher education. Higher education is a social system, where governance of people prevails over governance of material subjects and resources, and has the intellectual and spiritual life of society as its aim, object, and result.

The organizational and management peculiarities of higher education are a problem connected on the one hand with historical institutions with academic freedom, and on the other with the necessity for the state-monopoly regulation of child-rearing and education, both from the standpoint of satisfying the needs of the development of the productive forces of society under conditions of scientific–technological revolution, and from the point of view of the responsibility of higher education institutions for the realization of social order put out by the government.

Traditional academia with its traditional set of freedoms and privileges has at the same time both positive functions and some serious drawbacks. These manifest themselves in the striving for corporativeness and academic seclusion which puts an appreciable brake on social progress as the interaction between education, science, and socioeconomic bases is strengthened.

The Soviet government, realistically appraising the irreconcilability of the alternatives of academic freedom and state-administrative centralized governance of higher education, has refused to reconstruct these freedoms in the traditional and classical sense in higher education institutions. It should be noted that such an approach preserved, to a certain extent, the historical continuity of governance in higher education. In progressive European and American countries, the institution of academic freedom found stable forms, and only slowly evolved under the influence of new circumstances. The bureaucratic machinery of autocratic power in Russia only allowed the insertion of separate elements of these freedoms into higher education institutions.

In the Soviet Union, the path of employing the advantages of self-governance of educational institutions free from academic seclusion and corporativeness became the starting principle for designing organizational structures of higher education from basic levels of higher education institutions to governance at the level of higher education as a whole, which in the 1930s was singled out as an independent sector of the national economy.

The most important stages of the development of the governing system of higher education can be presented in the following order.

First, there was a stage of reconstruction of the national economy of the country after the Civil War, when two interconnected tasks had been solved—concentrating and revising the functional content of state management of educational establishments including higher education institutions, and developing and implementing forms of higher educational institutional activities and self-governance of academic and student bodies. All educational establishments were put under the authority of the People's Commissariat on Education (1918).

Second, there was a staged industrialization of the national economy and the collectivization of agriculture (1929–30). In order to strengthen the link between the system of specialist training, industry, and agriculture, to intensify the professional orientation of their training, and the development of a system of planning and assignment of graduates, specialization of higher education institutions was implemented and the right to govern their activities was passed to branch economic bodies of the state government. The general organizational—methodological governance of the higher education system was retained within the People's Commissariat on Education, and from 1936 onwards within a specially established All-Union body—the All-Union Committee on Higher Education under the authority of the Council of People's Commissars of the Soviet Union. Since that time the interconnection of branch and interbranch planning principles has been established in the higher education system.

Third, there was a stage of development of technological progress into scientific–technological revolution (mid-1960s). The productive branch approach to specialist training resulted in the training of "ready" specialists, whose knowledge and skills were formed on a recipe basis, that is, as a set of ready solutions. The question of professional mobility of specialists and improvement of their education in basic science has deepened. The Union–Republic Ministry of Higher and Specialized Secondary Education became an executive state body of higher education governance. It performed the following functions: general organizational–methodological governance of all higher education institutions irrespective of their departmental subordination; governance of higher education institutions within the authority of the ministries of higher and specialized secondary education of the republics; and direct governance of universities and higher education institutions within its authority. They are, as a rule, multisectoral, multibranch institutions—universities, polytechnical institutes, institutes of public economy, and so forth—which carry the functions of basic scientific–methodological centers, concerned with problems of finding ways of increasing the quality of specialists training.

The foundation of the Ministry of Higher and Specialized Secondary Education of the Soviet Union within the subordinate corresponding ministries of the republics, practically resulted in the establishment of a higher and specialized secondary education system, considered to be a separate branch of the nonproductive sphere of the national economy. Governing research in higher education was a new direction in the activities of the Ministry. For that purpose, the Research Institute for Higher Education (1974) was founded within the direct authority of the Ministry. Nevertheless, a considerable number of higher education institutions remained under the branch governing bodies despite growing tendencies towards strengthening the leading role of the Union–Republic and republic ministries of higher and specialized secondary education.

Fourth, there was a stage of reorganization of the system of public education in the Soviet Union resulting from the reorganizing of political and economic structures in the country. In order to simplify the governing structure and to abolish unnecessary levels in the public education system, the State Committee of the Soviet Union for Public Education was established in 1988. It exercises governance over all organizations and establishments, formerly under the Ministry of Higher and Specialized Secondary Education of the Soviet Union, the Ministry of Education of the Soviet Union, and the State Committee of the Soviet Union for Vocational and Technical Training, that is, all levels of education in the country, including higher education. The State Committee of the Soviet Union for Public Education is entrusted with the following main tasks:

(a) the development of strategy and uniform state policy in public education;

(b) the establishment of the system of continuing education;

(c) the comprehensive democratization of public education, thereby increasing independence of educational establishments;

(d) the development of training and employment of academic staff;

(e) the systematic renewal of education content, improvement of forms and methods of teaching, taking into account present-day requirements;

(f) the maintenance of the high quality of professional training of specialists, and the general adoption of effective forms of integration of education institutions with industry and science;

(g) the upholding of the effective use of the research potential of higher education in accelerating scientific–technological progress;

(h) the development and implementation of measures for technical re-equipment of the technical base of public education;

(i) the evaluation of quality of the education process and specialist training and the classification of education institutions by the state;

(j) the development of international cooperation in education and research;

(k) the coordination of the activity of ministries and agencies in the Soviet Union, plus coordination with the councils of ministries of the republics in the development of public education.

Thus, despite certain changes in the development of governing structures of higher education, the basic principle—centralized governance of the system—remains fundamental up to the early 1990s. At the same time, two basic tendencies are being developed simultaneously. These are: a tendency towards concentration of higher education institutions within the authority of the Union–Republic Ministry and the ministries of higher and specialized secondary education of the republics; and a tendency towards governing higher education, taking due account of certain branches of the national economy for a number of specialized higher education institutions.

Within the first tendency, the principle of organizing the activity by the Union body through the ministries of the republics and branch governing bodies is carried out by issuing orders and instructions adopted usually in a collective form, which are binding on all the aforementioned governing bodies. At the same time, the Union governing body enjoys an exclusive right in dealing with issues of Union significance: adoption of uniform admission regulations, standard curricula and programs, international cooperation, and so on in their turn, the ministries of the republics enjoy an exclusive right in dealing with those issues specific to the national language and culture. They also have independent budget funds from the Council of Ministries of the Republics. The Union body allocates funds only for institutions coming under its direct authority.

Within the context of the second trend, branch governing bodies also enjoy full rights to exercise functions of operational governance. But their terms of reference are restricted as a rule to matters associated with teaching specialized subjects and the organization of students' field practice.

The system of control over the activity of education institutions is based on the present governing system, in which each level of governance has its specific control functions. In 1966, the Ministry of Higher and Specialized Secondary Education was entrusted with functions of state inspection over all higher education institutions, irrespective of their departmental subordination, to improve the system of control. The State Inspectorate was established for that purpose.

3.2 Planning, Implementation, and Evaluation

The Union governing body (at present (1991) the State Committee of the USSR for Public Education) occupies the leading place in higher education planning. It carries out the following functions:

(a) determination of basic guidelines of higher education development;

(b) determination of current and long-range demand of the national economy for specialists;

(c) the rational distribution of higher education institutions in economic regions of the country;

(d) design and presentation of annual and long-range plans of specialist training to the government of the Soviet Union;

(e) determination and approval of the list of specialties.

The Union governing body is responsible for the organization and implementation of assignments and plans by governing bodies and higher education institutions. The monitoring of the execution of assignments and plan targets is carried out at each governing level according to its terms of reference and at the upper level by the Union governing body and the Cabinet of Ministers of the Soviet Union.

3.3 Finance

The basic source of finance for higher education is the state budget of the Soviet Union, comprising the Union budget and the budgets of the republics, both of which finance higher education institutions within the direct authority of the Union governing body and

within the authority of branch bodies—according to the branches. Main figures on finance of higher education are given in Table 13.

In 1990, 5,671 billion rubles (US$3,415 billion) were allocated for higher education. On the whole, as can be seen in Table 13, the share of Gross National Product (GNP) allocated for higher education is about 5 percent.

3.4 Institutional Administration

All types of higher education institutions in the Soviet Union, despite the difference in historically developed names—universities, institutes, academies, schools, conservatoires—take guidance from common norms and carry them out in similar ways.

Despite the fundamental variety of educational establishments and the complexity of their organizational structure, the basis of the structure is very simple and includes three levels: rector's office, department, and faculty.

The rector's office is practically the only administrative unit in a higher education institution. It is headed by a rector, who is appointed by the body under the authority of which a higher education institution, is located. He or she is selected from the most authoritative and highly skilled members of the academic staff. In accordance with the principle of one-person management, he or she bears full responsibility for the work of a higher education institution. The rector's office also includes deputies in the form of prorectors for academic and economic affairs, research, and administration.

The central task of the rector's office is to control the curricula and programs and research plans, and to guide educational activities. Additionally, the rector's office deals with applicants and graduate students. It bears responsibility for the establishment of working conditions and the improvement of academic and material facilities of the institute.

Thus, the rector's office carries out mostly control functions but not those of a direct administration. Such a role follows from the implementation of institutional self-governance where the leading role is played by the Academic Council.

The following are members of the Academic Council: prorectors, deans of faculty, holders of a chair, representatives of the academic staff, and, recently,

Table 13
State budget expenditure on higher education (in US$ billion)

	1960	1970	1980	1985	1989
Gross national product	—	—	372,753	467,899	556,420
State budget expenditure (including higher education)	44,020	93,098	177,404	232,143	290,615
	648	1,316	2,259	2,448	2,930
Percentage of GNP	—	—	5.1%	5.1%	5.2%

representatives of students. The following matters are within the authority of the Academic Council:

(a) control of the quality of specialist training;

(b) approval of list and programs of elective subjects;

(c) assessment of student performance;

(d) staffing of the institution; and

(e) elaboration of research, educational, and economic plans.

The Academic Council is chaired by the rector. As a collective and democratic governing body the Academic Council plays a very important role in the everyday activity of the institution.

The department is a basic educational and research unit within a higher education institution. The following members are included in a department: full professors, professors in an advisory capacity, associate professors, assistant lecturers, assistant professors, lecturers, and researchers at different levels. A department is headed by a holder of a chair.

Within the authority of a department all types of academic activities are conducted including field practice for students and guidance of course and diploma projects. Departments are responsible for the development of curricula and the preparation of teaching aids while organization of scientific research is another important role. Specialized research units, such as problem and branch research laboratories are attached to many departments, and they are also responsible for cooperation with industrial organizations and research institutions outside the system of higher education.

The faculty is the next organizational level above a department. The faculty forms a research and administrative unit comprising all departments and laboratories concerned with a particular specialty or group of specialties. A faculty is headed by a dean, elected by the Faculty Council from the most experienced full professors or associate professors for a period of three years. The dean is responsible for the control of the academic process, the design of the curriculum, the supervision of examinations and credits, and the control of the process of transfer of students from one year of studies to another. The dean also permits students to take state examinations and credits, and grants students scholarships. He or she is a permanent member of the state examination board, and a member of the commission on admission. The dean is guided by the Faculty Council, to which he or she is answerable.

The faculty council is a very important level of institutional self-governance. One of the activities of a faculty council is to work with staff, which includes the consideration of records of personal performance, competing to obtain the title of full professor, associate professor, and assistant lecturer. It also has responsibility for candidates in the competitive selection of researchers. The council is also responsible for graduate course enrollment and design of the plans of activities in a faculty.

4. Faculty and Students: Teaching, Learning, and Research

4.1 Faculty

As higher education institutions carry out both teaching and research, and in a number of leading higher education institutions research is an element of the education process, Table 14 presents data on both research and academic staff. It can be seen from Table 14 that the share of employees engaged purely in research does not exceed 21 percent (in 1990). However, it should be noted that certain members of the academic staff are engaged in research work and teaching on a regular basis.

4.2 Career Paths

In accordance with the concept of development of the Soviet higher education system, teaching staff play an important role in the implementation of cultural policy and the strengthening of the intellectual development of society. Under the Soviet form of government, a uniform system of work with academic staff has been created. This is based on state methods of control of recruitment of academic staff which envisage centralized and planned training and employment. The approach is characterized by common principles and standards of selection, recruitment and employment of academic staff, methods of classification, and control of their qualifications.

Table 14
Research and teaching staff of the higher education system in the Soviet Union (in thousands)

	1960	1965	1970	1975	1981	1986	1990
All research and teaching staff	146.9	221.8	348.8	427.7	506.6	516.5	539.5
Doctors of science	5.9	7.3	11.6	15.5	18.4	20.9	23.6
Candidate of science	51.9	66.4	111.1	153.3	194.3	219.4	236.8

Such a system of state oversight for staff recruitment is unique in historical practice. But its principles were laid down with the foundation of the St. Petersburg teacher-training institution (later the chief teacher-training institute) at the beginning of the twentieth century as a specialized center for the training of teachers. These principles were established because Russian higher education institutions did not possess their own historical traditions of organizing the activity of the professorial collegium and the resulting reproduction of academic staff with elements of corporativeness and seclusion. Therefore, side by side with the invitation of foreign academics, the tsarist government of imperial Russia centralized training of teaching staff and recruited them for the newly founded educational institutions. At the same time the system of degrees and titles in Russia, which remained broadly similar to that adopted in the European countries, differed greatly by the more strict and logical conditions for their conferment and by the more severe requirements demanded from applicants.

In the 1870s, the state system of academic staff training for higher education institutions was established in imperial Russia.

Organizational principles of selection and recruitment of academic staff for Soviet higher education were approved by the Council of People's Commissars in 1921. Academic staff were grouped into three categories: full professors teaching separate courses who were elected by the State Academic Council of the People's Commissariat for Education of the RSFSR for a ten-year period; lecturers teaching auxiliary courses and classes under the guidance of full professors who were elected by the board of a higher education institution for a seven-year period; and researchers who assisted professors and lecturers. The period up to 1925 was the most important stage in the formation of the Soviet system of recruiting academic staff through the institution of the Red Professorate, faculties of social sciences in universities, communist higher education institutions, and through a number of other specialized educational institutions. In 1925, "Regulations on training researchers within the higher education institutions and scientific–research establishments" were adopted, in which a new form of training—three-year graduate courses, attached to the leading institutions of the country—was approved. The titles of lecturer or researcher were awarded on completion of graduate courses and defense of research work on a topic decided beforehand. General guidance of academic staff was entrusted to the special commission of the State Academic Council responsible for organization, control, and coordination of selection and classification of academic staff.

Between 1932 and 1934 the system of classification of academic staff was improved. The degrees of Candidate and Doctor of Science and also the academic titles of assistant lecturer, associate professor, and full professor were introduced. The degree of Candidate of Science was awarded by the Academic Councils of higher education institutions. In 1937 the right to award the degree of Doctor of Science was passed to the Degree Awarding Commission under the All-Union Committee for higher education. In the late 1950s and the early 1960s the rights of the Degree Awarding Commission were extended. It received the right not only to award the degree of Doctor of Science, but also to confirm the award of the degree of Candidate of Science, which increased effectiveness of centralized government and control for the classification of academic staff.

Two alternative forms leading to the award of the degree of Doctor of Science exist in the form of independent work on a doctoral thesis by way of a system of doctoral courses. Doctoral courses attached to higher education and research institutions were established at the end of the 1940s and functioned up to 1956. Doctoral studies, as the upper level in the system of continuing education, were revived again in 1987. Organizational forms of doctoral courses are similar to that of graduate courses. Duration of studies is no more than three years.

As far as the personal aspect is concerned, the training of research and teaching staff starts in undergraduate courses. Despite the fact that according to the general concept of Soviet higher education there are no differences in organizational and stimulation forms of training of the research and teaching staff in higher education institutions of different types, universities, multisectoral, and specialized institutes play a special role. It is typical for these institutions to insert elements of research into the teaching process, to draw students into all forms of research, carried out in the department, to develop students' independent scientific and technical creativity, and to allow advanced students to study according to the individual curricula. The best students are attracted and kept at the department as laboratory assistants. They receive recommendations to graduate courses. At the same time, it is often envisaged that receiving degrees, they will teach and do research work at the same department.

Posts of probationary researcher and probationary teacher were introduced for the most gifted students—entrants to a profession, capable of research and teaching work. Probationary teachers, upon receiving a recommendation after a year's probationary period, are recruited as assistant lecturers or lecturers without competitive selection. Under the supervision of highly skilled members of the academic staff, probationers take the candidate's examinations, which are one of the compulsory elements for successful completion of graduate courses, and confer the right to defend a thesis.

Nevertheless, graduate courses are the main form of graduate training for academic staff. They are attached to large higher education and research institutions which have the necessary conditions for successful studies. The Degree Awarding Commission of the Soviet Union grants the right to establish graduate courses in a higher education and research institution. At the beginning of the 1980s graduate courses were established in more than 600 higher education institutions and 1,300 research institutes in the Soviet Union.

A list of courses for study is determined according to the present list of specialties of researchers approved by the Degree Awarding Commission. Candidates are required to pass examinations as a guarantee of the quality of selection. There are two forms of graduate courses: full-time and extramural. The latter provides training in teaching and research with part-time employment; the former runs without interruption. Most of the specialists in the field of basic knowledge—that is, physico–mathematical, chemistry–biological, psychological, philosophical, and philological—take full-time courses, and specialists in applied fields of knowledge are distributed equally between the two forms of training. Students are trained for three years on a full-time basis, and four years on an extramural basis. There are common regulations for the attestation and assessment of graduate students' knowledge, including examination of a candidate's minimum standard.

Pedagogical training is carried out during the whole period of graduate studies. The main element of the system is the course in the basic principles of higher education pedagogics, delivered during the second year of study. Teaching practice is obligatory for a graduate student of a higher education institution. Studies are finished with the preparation and defense of a thesis at the session of the academic council of the higher education institution, or with a presentation of a thesis for the academic degree of Candidate of Science.

One of the widespread organizational forms of graduate studies are the fixed-target graduate courses, training specialists for establishments which cannot provide such training on their own. After completion of studies, graduate students return to their places of employment.

One-year graduate courses are one of the specific forms of fixed-target graduate courses, being an effective form for highly skilled academic staff. Members of the teaching staff of higher education institutions and other educational establishments, having considerable teaching and research experience and having achieved certain results in research, are accepted on the courses.

The last form of extramural graduate studies is the independent study of specialists, who are assigned to higher education or research institutions for passing examinations and consultations. Some 20,000 graduate students were enrolled in this form of training in 1980.

More than 1,500 specialized academic councils, one-third of which were attached to higher education institutions, were engaged in practical work concerned with the classification of researchers and teaching staff. They have common organizational principles and regulations for research and academic staff selection.

Thus, a typical career path of a specialist in the higher education system of the Soviet Union can be presented as a sequence of the following stages: undergraduate studies (four to six years); probationary teacher or researcher (one year); graduate studies (three to four years) leading to a Candidate of Science degree (for associate professor); doctoral studies or independent work on a thesis (no less than three years); and a Doctor of Science degree (for full professor).

No differences exist in the legal status of academic staff or that of other citizens of the Soviet Union. They are employees of the state establishments of the Soviet Union. All advantages received during one's academic career (i.e., high salary, and access to higher research and administrative posts) are usually granted on the basis of the level of qualification and professional training. There are no differences between the career and status of faculty in different types of institutions.

4.3 Representation of Faculty Interests

Up to 1990 all researchers and lecturers of higher education institutions were members of the Trade Union of Employees of Public Education and Science of the Soviet Union, established according to the multilevel principle, with departments in the republics and regions throughout the country. This was a centralized structure for the professional defense of members of the faculty and was similar to the system of centralized governance of higher education in the Soviet Union. Recently there have been changes in the Soviet trade union movement, and reorganization is still taking place. Independent trade unions were established with regional organizational structures analogous to the previous structure of the trade union. In particular, the Independent Trade Union of Employees of Science and Education has been established in Moscow. It is a member of the branch of the federation of Moscow independent trade unions.

There are also various associations of faculty members, but they are not concerned with the legal and social defense of their members and include employees of higher education and research institutions on a professional basis.

4.4 Academic Work

Planning of academic work in higher education institutions is based on "Standard Regulations of Planning the Academic Workload of Faculty," approved

Table 15
The distribution of students of higher education institutions across branch groups (in thousands)

	1960	1965	1970	1975	1981	1986	1990
All students	2,396.1	3,890.6	4,580.6	4,854.0	5,284.5	5,088.4	5,161.6
Public education including	769.6	1,198.7	1,375.7	1,415.3	1,521.4	1,547.8	1,726.5
universities	249.0	401.2	503.5	565.9	609.8	586.7	658.1
Industry and construction	873.1	1,528.3	1,825.7	1,950.0	2,102.8	1,934.9	1,844.5
Transport and communication	146.7	221.6	251.7	277.6	300.5	281.0	268.3
Agriculture	264.5	377.1	423.9	460.0	545.2	523.1	525.3
Economics and law	161.9	264.1	314.4	354.7	380.3	384.9	336.1
Public health		215.3	284.8	308.8	338.3	319.4	346.2
Physical culture and sport	188.9	23.5	36.2	42.8	47.0	48.1	63.1
Art and cinematography	19.4	32.0	41.2	44.8	49.0	49.2	51.6

by the union body, governing the system of higher education in the Soviet Union. The academic workload of the faculty is determined by the rector on the basis of the total number of employees and the type of work to be done.

The total volume of teaching and other types of activities per lecturer per academic year is calculated on the basis of a six-hour working day and a total of 1,536 hours. Included are: lectures; laboratory practice; practical work and seminars; credits and examinations; assessment of test papers; supervision of field and prediploma practice of students; consultation of undergraduate and graduate students; participation in the State Examination Board; and so forth. The head of department is granted the right to consider individually the volume of different types of academic work performed by a lecturer during a six-hour working day.

The academic workload of a full-time lecturer is 450–1,000 hours per year, including (for full professors and associate professors) not less than 150 hours per year for lectures and seminars (practical work), examinations, and credits.

Rectors are responsible for the balance between teaching, research, and administration for faculty members on the basis of the aforementioned norms.

4.5 Students

The distribution of students and graduates from higher education institutions in the Soviet Union

Table 16
The distribution of graduates from higher education institutions across the branch groups (in thousands)

	1960	1965	1970	1975	1981	1986	1990
All graduates	343.3	403.9	630.8	713.7	831.2	839.9	765.0
Public education including	139.1	142.1	219.2	245.3	265.4	264.4	276.4
universities	38.4	—	69.1	—	101.5	101.5	98.1
Industry and construction	95.2	139.9	214.2	260.0	308.5	310.3	246.4
Transport and communication	16.1	19.3	28.2	333.3	41.8	42.0	30.8
Agriculture	34.7	36.0	68.7	62.6	78.7	84.0	72.6
Economics and law	25.0	32.1	50.9	60.5	67.1	68.1	67.6
Public health	—	27.3	—	—	51.9	55.4	43.1
Physical culture and sport	30.7	3.3	42.9	54.2	9.2	6.3	9.6
Art and cinematography	2.5	3.9	6.7	7.8	8.6	9.0	9.5

Table 17
The distribution of students among the native nationalities in the republics at the beginning of the 1984–85 academic year (in thousands)

RSFSR (Russians)	2,463.3	81%
Ukranian SSR (Ukrainians)	576.3	66%
Byelorus.SSR (Byelorussians)	130.3	70%
Uzbek SSR (Uzbeks)	195.1	67%
Kazakh SS (Kazakhs)	152.5	54%
Georgian SSR (Georgians)	78.0	88%
Azerbaijan SSR (Azerbaijanians)	91.1	84%
Lithuanian SSR (Lithuanians)	59.2	86%
Moldavian SSR (Moldavians)	34.1	64%
Latvian SSR (Letts)	23.3	51%
Kirghiz SSR (Kirghizs)	37.4	63%
Tajik SSR (Tajiks)	35.9	61%
Armenian SSR (Armenians)	56.6	98%
Turkmen SSR (Turkmen)	30.3	78%
Estonian SSR (Estonians)	18.0	73%

across branch groups of specialties is given in Tables 15 and 16.

In the Soviet Union, society is divided into the worker and peasant classes, and also into the considerable stratum of office workers. The higher education level for urban and rural population per 1,000 inhabitants of age 10 and older describing the social and class origin of students is as follows: 126 per 1,000 urban; and 41 per 1,000 rural (see Table 17). The same data, in the case of men and women were as follows in 1989: 102 per 1,000 men; and 94 per 1,000 women (see Table 18 for the percentage of women studying in higher education institutions from 1988–89).

The right to education in the Soviet Union is guaranteed by the availability of education free of charge of all types of educational institution. Also in accordance with the law, nationality cannot be an advantage or a disadvantage.

Table 18
The percentage of women studying in higher education institutions and their distribution across the Union Republics in the 1988–89 academic year[a]

USSR	52	Lithuanian SSR	62
RSFSR	53	Moldavian SSR	59
Ukranian SSR	54	Latvian SSR	64
Byelorus.SSR	59	Kirghiz SSR	46
Uzbek SSR	44	Tajik SSR	43
Kazakh SSR	48	Armenian SSR	39
Georgian SSR	49	Turkmen SSR	36
Azerbaijan SSR	33	Estonian SSR	56

a RSFSR—Russian Soviet Federative Socialist Republic; SSR—Soviet Socialist Republic

4.6 Representation of Student Interest

In accordance with the general concept of Soviet higher education, a student has special status as a citizen of the country, resulting from the need to study in a higher educational institution, that is, to be engaged in a special activity.

The legal status of students is embodied in legal acts based on the Constitution of the Soviet Union. The most important rights and responsibilities of students are determined by the "Fundamental Legislation of the USSR on Public Education" and "Regulations on Higher Education Institutions of the USSR." More specific rules on student status are defined in the decisions of the Council of Ministers of the Soviet Union and that of the Republics, in orders, regulations, and other acts of the Ministry of Higher and Specialized Secondary Education and the State Committee of the Soviet Union for Public Education. These are, for example, "Regulations on the Order of Granting and Payment of Student Grants," "Institutional Regulations and Rules," and so forth. Finally, certain questions on the legal status of students are defined in the rector's orders. The legal status of a student is regulated by different norms of law: financial (granting scholarships and grants, tax privileges, etc.); civil (rent and transport privileges and preservation of lodgings for the duration of a period of study); labor (conditions of labor and payment); and administrative (admission regulations, appeals against administration, etc.).

On the whole, students enjoy the following legally stipulated rights:

(a) the right to use laboratories, libraries, and other facilities free of charge, that is, the necessary guarantees of the right to higher education;

(b) the right to participate in state administration; recently, the right to take part in the governance of higher education institutions through participation in academic councils and in organizing student self-governance has been considerably broadened;

(c) the right to security for the period of studies (grants, pay and tax privileges, additional paid leave for students, training without interruption of employment, etc.).

The All-Union Leninist Young Communist League of the Soviet Union (LYCLSU) is the most numerous mass sociopolitical union of students in the Soviet Union. Recently, the mass movement for the establishment of amateur unions of students has grown. They are called nonformal unions or groups. The participants in these nonformal unions are often also the members of the *Komsomol* (Communist youth movement). On the whole the following typology of these nonformal groups can be given: sociopolitical; sociocultural, creative; of applied character (housing complexes of youth, clubs of amateur initiatives); social aid clubs; religious and semireligious; ecological and socio-ecological, environmental; groups and units for protection of rights, social justice fighters; sport, healthy living; ethically (or sociopsychologically) directed; nationalistic; and historico-patriotic, and so on.

At present it is impossible to define the exact number of students participating in these groups as they are in a state of flux, and most of them are not formally registered.

4.7 Learning and Examinations

Since higher education governance is centralized, the Union and Republic (branch) governing bodies enjoy the right to define the structures and content of curricula within their terms of reference. However, the academic councils and unions enjoy the right to develop programs in basic and specialized subjects. Unions are established within the leading universities and specialized higher education institutions, provided they have specialists and educators with the required qualification.

The profile of specialist training serves as a basis for the development of a generalized scheme of curriculum. The main task of this stage is to determine the list and balance of disciplines of general scientific, professional, and specialist cycles. General scientific disciplines provide knowledge in the field of basic (social and natural) sciences. General professional subjects introduce the field of the future specialty to a student. Specialist subjects impart knowledge and skills, directly related to the professional functions of a highly skilled specialist and make it possible for a graduate to quickly settle down to practical activity.

The curriculum is contained in a state document, determining general direction and content of specialist training. It sets out the methods of academic work, forms, and date of knowledge assessment. The curriculum ensures common requirements for training specialists of the same specialty in different higher education institutions of the same specialty in different higher education institutions of the country, regulates procedures, the duration of studies, and the scheduling of the education process on the whole.

The study program—determining content, logical structure, succession of studies, types and forms of academic work, and the required level of acquisition of material—is also an important normative document.

In practice, curricula determine the strategy, and study programs the tactics of the education process. Curricula and study programs are revised at five-yearly intervals, and, if necessary, more often.

The following types of classes are used in the education process: lectures; practical classes (seminars and laboratory practice); training out of classes (independent study) to intensify the education process; and field practice in order to bring students closer to their areas of study.

Other important types of academic work are course and diploma projects. The study of a certain general technical or general professional subject ends with a course project. A diploma project, apart from being the final paper, is the basis for awarding a qualification and diploma of higher education once it has been successfully defended.

Each academic year is divided into two semesters—autumn and spring. At the end of each semester student performance is assessed at an examination session. On the whole, the types of evaluation used in higher education are credits, examinations, and defense of course and diploma papers.

The second semester of the final year of studies is devoted to the preparation of the diploma project (for technical institutions) or to the graduate paper (in universities and institutes offering courses in the humanities). In some institutes studies terminate with the state examination (teacher-training institutes).

In technical institutes the final semester is usually devoted to prediploma practice in industry and the diploma project is often directly connected with the solution of practical problems.

Defense of a diploma project as well as the state examinations are assessed by system of marks (excellent—5, good—4, satisfactory—3). There is a supplement to a diploma with marks in all the subjects undertaken by a student. These marks should not be lower than satisfactory. Only students receiving excellent marks are awarded diplomas with honors.

Bibliography

Agranovich B L, Valentinov V V, Kovalenko V E 1988 *Tipovye sredstva avtomatizatsii upravleniya VUZom.* Tomsk State University, Tomsk, p. 190

Arakelov A A, Kazakova R A 1990 *Perestroika vysshego obrazovaniya v 1989: Ezhegodnyi doklad o razvitii vysshego i srednego spetsialnogo obrazoyaniya* SSSR. State Committee of the USSR for Public Education, SRIHE, Moscow, p. 172

Bezrukova V S, Malshtein L K, Zeer E F 1990 *Soderzhanie i perspektivy razvitiya inzhenernopedagogicheskogo obrazovaniya.* Sverdlovsk Engineering Pedagogical Institute, Sverdlovsk, p. 128

Buga P G 1987 *Vuzovskii uchebnik: Sozdanie, vypusk, rasprostranenie.* Moscow, p. 158

Bulleteni Gosudarstvennogo komiteta SSSR po narodnomu obrazovaniu, seriya 1987, 1988, 1989, 1990 *"Vysshee i srednee spetsialnoe obrazovanie".* Nos. 1–12, 1987, 1988, 1989, 1990

Butenko N U 1990 *Vosproizvodstvo spetsialistov s vysshim obrazovaniem.* Kiev State University, Kiev, p. 122

Chugaev A A *Vysshavya shkola i proizvodstvo (Vzaimodeistvie. Planovo-ekonomicheskie metody upravleniya).* Vishcha shkola, Kiev, p. 147

Chuprunov D I, Zhiltsov E N 1988 *Ekonomika, organizatsiya i planirovanie vysshego obrazovaniya.* Vysschaya shkola, Moscow, p. 175

Dmitrienko V A, Lurya N A 1989 *Obrazovanie kak sotsialnyi institut: Tendentsii i perspektivy razvitiya.* Krasnoyarsk State University, Krasnoyarsk, p. 184

Dneprov E D, Lazarev V S, Sobkin V S (eds.) 1991 *Rossiiskoe obrazovanie v perekhodnyi period: Programm stabilizatsii i razvitiya (Proekt doklada Pravitelstvy RSFSR).* Moscow, p. 334

Dolzhenko O V, Shatunovski V P 1990 *Sovremennye metody i tekhnologiya obucheniya v tekhnicheskom VUZe.* Vysshaya shkola, Moscow, p. 191

Elutin V P 1980 *Vysshaya shkola obshchestva razvitogo cotsializma.* Vysshaya shkola, Moscow

Finansy i statistica 1987 *Narodnoe khozyaistvo SSSR za 70 let, statisticheskii zbornik.* Finansy i statistika, Moscow

Finansy i statistica 1988 *Narodnoe khozyaistvo SSSR v 1987 g., statisticheskii zbornik.* Finansy i statistika, Moscow

Finansy i statistica 1988 *Trud v SSSR, statisticheskii zbornik.* Finansy i statistika, Moscow

Finansy i statistica 1989a *Narodnoe khozyaistvo SSSR v 1988 g., statisticheskii zbornik.* Finansy i statistika, Moscow

Finansy i statistica 1989b *Narodnoe obrazovanie i kultura v SSSR, statisticheskii zbornik.* Finansy i statistika, Moscow

Finansy i statistica 1990 *Narodnoe khozyaistvo SSSR v 1989 g., statisticheskii zbornik.* Finansy i statistika, Moscow

Gabai T V 1988 *Uchebnaya deyatelnost i ee sredstva.* Moscow, p. 255

Gartung U A, Kaidarov K K 1989 *Programmno-tselevoi metod upravleniya kachestvom uchebnogo protsessa.* Alma-Ata, p. 144

Gerchikova V V 1986 *Sovremennoe vysshee obrazovanie: funktsii, realizatsiya, perspektivy.* Tomsk State University, Tomsk, p. 164

Gershunskii B S 1987 *Komputerizatsiya v sfere obrazovaniya: problemy i perspektivy.* Pedagogika, Moscow, p. 264

Gershunskii B S (ed.) 1990 *Perspektivy razvitiya sistemy nepreryvnogo obrazovaniya.* Pedagogika, Moscow, p. 224

Kalinkin E A 1990 *Vysshaya shkola v sisteme nepreryvnogo obrazovaniya.* Vysshaya shkola, Moscow, p. 144

Krokinskaya O K, Smirnova E E (eds.) 1989 *Stanovlenie spetsialista.* Leningrad State University, Leningrad, p. 136

Ladatko A A 1991 *Neformalnye molodezhnye ob'edineniya.* Vysshaya shkola, Moscow, p. 50

Lednev V S 1981 *Nepreryvnoe obrazovanie: Struktura i Soderzhanie.* APN USSR, Moscow, p. 282

Lisovskii V T 1990 *Sovetskoe studenchestvo. Sotsiologicheskie ocherki.* Vysshaya shkola, Moscow

Litvinova N P 1989 *Obrazovanie v usloviyakh intensificatsii ekonomiki.* Moscow, p. 192

Maizel I A, Mozelov A P, Fedorov B I (eds.) 1990 *Inzhenerfilosofiya-VUZ.* Leningrad State University, Leningrad, p. 128

Mashbits E I 1988 *Psikhologo-pedagogicheskie problemy komputerizatsii obucheniya.* Pedagogika, Moscow, p. 260

Mechtova I I 1990 *Sotsialno-ekonomicheskie problemy perestroiki vysshego obrazovaniya.* Alma-Ata, p. 189

Minko E V 1989 *Organizatsionno-ekonomicheskaya podgotovka ingenernov-issledovatelei v sisteme TsIPS.* Moscow Polytechnical Institute, Moscow, p. 180

Nechaev N N 1988 *Psikhologo-pedagogicheskie osnovy formirovaniya professionalnoi deyatelnosti.* Moscow State University, Moscow, p. 210

Osnovnye kharakteristiki rasvitiya i razmeshcheniya nauchno-tekhnicheskogo potentsiala VUZov strany, Gosobrasovanie SSSR, MAI 1990. Moscow

Ovsyannikov A A (ed.) 1988 *Vysshaya shkola v zerkale obshchestvennogo mneniya (Obzor sotsiologicheskikh issledovanii 1987–1988).* SRIHE, Moscow, p. 148

Ovsyannikov A A, Ryazantsev V V 1991 *Studenchestvo SSSR: Ekzamen perestroike.* Moscow, p. 56 (System of Education in Higher Education: Analytical Review/ SRIHE, No. 3)

Peregudov F I, Tarasenko V P, Ugorelov S N 1988 *Tomskii mezhvyzovski eksperimentalno-proizvodstvennyi kompleks.* Tomsk State University, Tomsk, p. 178

Savelyev A Ya (ed.) 1990 *Osnovnye rezultaty issledovanii NII vysshego obrazovaniya v 1989.* State Committee of the USSR for Public Education, Academy of Pedagogical Sciences of the USSR, SRIHE, Moscow, p. 442

Savelyev A Y, Zuev V M, Galagan A I 1990 *Vyschee obrazovanie v SSSR.* G A Yagodin (ed.)—SRIHE, Moscow, p. 112

Sotsialisticheskii obraz zhizni i problemy obrazovaniya. 1988, Sverdlovsk

Statistika 1977 *Narodnoe obrazovanie, nauka i kultura v SSSR, statisticheskii zbornik.* Statistika, Moscow

Topchii L V 1990 *Novyi oblik sovetskogo studenta.* Saratov State University, Saratov

Topchii L V 1990 *Novyi oblik sovetskogo studenta: Tyeoriya i praktika politicheskogo razvitiya.* Saratov State University, Saratov, p. 142

Verbitskii A A 1991 *Aktivnoe obuchenie v vysshei shkole: Kontekstnyi podkhod.* Vysshaya shkola, Moscow, p. 210

Vetoshkin A P 1990 *Studencheskoe samoupravlenie v VUZe.* Omsk Institute of Railway Transport Engineers, Omsk, p. 56

Voronov E P 1987 *Khozraschet v ekonomike vysshego uchebnogo zavedeniya.* Saratov State University, Saratov, p. 120

Yampolski V Z, Petrov O M, Chudinova I L, Valentinov V V *Avtomatizatsiya upravleniya vysshei sckoloi.* Voronezh State University, Voronezh, p. 176

Zaitsev G P, Bezlipkin V V, Tavologin N A, Lipanov A M, Lukoshin A I (eds.) 1987 *Tselevaya intensivnaya podgotovka spetsialistov.* Leningrad State University, Leningrad, p. 184

Zeer Z F 1988 *Professionalnoe stanovlenie lichnosti inzhenera-pedagoga.* Ural State University, Sverdlovsk, p. 120

V. N. Afanassiev

Spain

1. Higher Education and Society

Spain boasts a long tradition of higher education. The University of Salamanca, in part a continuation of earlier initiatives, dates back to the early thirteenth century. Other universities were subsequently formed at Valladolid, Toledo, Alcalá, Valencia, Seville, and elsewhere. The fifteenth and sixteenth centuries are thought of as periods of splendor for university studies and the acquisition of knowledge in

Spain. In the seventeenth century an air of decadence began to set in, even though the number of universities—mostly church-run—continued to grow, finally numbering 40. The Spanish Enlightenment in its early years did little to counter this decline, as the institutions behind educational and cultural reform fell mainly outside the university system. A period of reform commenced in the reign of Carlos III, following the expulsion of the Jesuits in 1767, but nothing remarkable was to come of it (Alvarez de Morales 1972). The first winds of reform brought a tendency for growing state intervention in the universities, to the detriment of ecclesiastical power and of the autonomy hitherto enjoyed by the universities. The same period saw the beginning of a slow, laborious reform of syllabuses, consisting in the introduction of a number of new or revised fields of learning (e.g., greater emphasis on Spanish law and less on Roman, introduction of some experimental sciences, etc.).

These hesitant beginnings were to become more firmly established in the nineteenth century. The Constitution of 1812, marking the advent of the Liberal state in Spain, ushered in (though not without fierce resistance and periods of reaction) the concept of the university as an institution of the state, which now succeeded to the monopoly once wielded by the church in this field. An ordinance of 1821 created a Central University in the Spanish capital, to provide both example and driving force for the universities as a whole. In mid-century (1857) a statute was issued which more than any other was to affect the Spanish university system, and indeed the structure and working of the entire education system: the *Ley Moyano* of 1857 (named after Claudio Moyano, the Minister responsible). This Act provided for the first-ever structuring of higher education in Spain, which was divided into three distinct sectors: the "university" sector, comprising the traditional faculties; the "higher education" sector, bringing together new subjects in technical areas (e.g., engineering) and in training for senior civil service posts; and lastly, "professional instruction," including such intermediate-grade subjects as veterinary studies, construction, surveying, primary schoolteaching, and so on. According to the Act, all institutions entering these three categories "shall be maintained by the State." The Act provided for 10 recognized universities—the "Central University" at Madrid and nine others—each endowed with a university district.

Despite a wealth of movements for change and conflicts of varying kinds (prominent among them those surrounding "teaching freedom"), the structure with which the *Ley Moyano* endowed higher education lasted for more than a century, practically until the promulgation of the *Ley General de Educación* (General Education Act) of 1970 in the closing years of the Franco regime. There were in fact movements for modernization, promoted above all by the

Institución Libre de Enseñanza (an institution for liberal education) in the late nineteenth and early twentieth centuries; the Second Republic (1931–36), in the formation of whose education policy former disciples of the *Institución Libre* were prominent, drew up an ambitious reform program which was only partially implemented. The basic structure, however, remained intact, and although the church once more gained a large say in education under Franco, higher education continued to be the exclusive preserve of the state.

The 1960s saw a major increase in the numbers of university students. In only eight years (from 1961 to 1968), these rose from 81,721 to 176,428—in other words matriculation more than doubled. As in other countries during these years, Spanish universities underwent a process of massive intake and overcrowding, which here, in a context of restricted freedoms under a dictatorial regime, prompted frequent outbreaks of student unrest (for more details on the Franco years, Garcia Garrido 1988 and both titles in print, Montoro 1981). The opening of more universities and university faculties, which had already begun by 1968, combined with measures of other kinds, constituted the immediate lead-up to the reform of 1970 which, while in many ways was excessively timid, was definitely a major step forward. It was at this time that the principle of university autonomy became finally established while the number and type of institutions multiplied considerably and the structure largely existing in the early 1990s was finally adopted. In this period there was another spectacular increase in student numbers, so that by 1980, 10 years after the promulgation of the Act, over 450,000 students were matriculated at Spanish universities. Since then, there has been a further comparable increase, which means that in each of the last three decades the number of university students has more than doubled.

Such major growth, coinciding with far-reaching political developments in the country, has necessitated a fresh series of political and legal measures, the outstanding manifestation of which is the *Ley de Reforma Universitaria* (University Reform Act) of 1983 and the Royal Decrees subsequently promulgated in the instrumentation thereof. It must be pointed out, nonetheless, that for all the important modifications introduced, and for all that it finally establishes, the principle of university autonomy within the new Spanish regional government structure, the *Ley de Reforma Universitaria* (LRU) has wrought no structural changes of any importance on the higher education system. The institutional structure of the Spanish university system remains essentially that which was introduced by the *Ley General de Educación* of 1970, which even at the time, be it said, was criticized as being too continuist. The most important changes introduced by the LRU affect the structure and selection of university teaching staff, define the meaning of "university autonomy" more precisely, and provide for democratic participation in university governing bodies.

1.1 Geographical Context

After this brief introduction to higher education in Spain, it will be useful to take a rapid look at a number of background aspects which will help provide a fuller understanding of the present situation.

Perhaps because it is practically surrounded by seas and hemmed in by mountains, Spain's frontiers have suffered no major change since the single nation-state was formed in the fourteenth century. In the early 1990s, Spain covers 503,432 square kilometers, with a population numbering 39 million. On the whole this is a sparsely-populated territory (72 inhabitants per square kilometer) compared to other European countries, although there are more densely-populated nuclei in Madrid, the Basque Country, and the Mediterranean littoral. The bulk of the populaion has become steadily more urbanized, so that almost half the population live in cities of over 50,000 inhabitants. Although the population is relatively uniform in ethnic terms as a result of centuries of intermarriage and internal migration, the same cannot be said of language, since Castilian (or Spanish) is the language of the overwhelming majority. Of the other native tongues, Catalan is well-established in Mediterranean provinces, where, together with Castilian, it is the day-to-day language of some five million people. The other two languages in use (Gallego and Basque or Euskera) are spoken by a far smaller proportion of the population. Like the Catalans, their speakers are (with the very odd exception) bilingual, being equally grounded in Castilian.

The birthrate, which had showed a mild tendency to drop since the beginning of the century, has fallen sharply since 1980. From 21.6 per thousand inhabitants in 1960, it had slipped to 13.44 per thousand by 1982, a figure very similar to those of other developed countries. This has decidedly affected the population distribution by age-groups, with a constant increase in the proportion of persons over 65 and a marked decline in the under-14 group (little more than 20 percent of the total population).

1.2 Structure of the Economy

Barely one-third of the Spanish population is classified as active. This proportion has been shrinking steadily since 1960 and is one of the smallest of all OECD member countries. The causes of this development are manifold and include the raising of the minimum working age (from 14 to 16), extended schooling, larger numbers of retired persons, the economic crisis of the 1970s, and others. At the same time, more and more women have been entering the labor market.

Practically 50 percent of the active population

work in the tertiary or services sector while 30 percent are employed in the secondary sector (industry and manufacturing) and only 20 percent in agriculture.

The active population rate is low in comparison with other developed countries, but the situation is yet worse if we consider that a sizeable proportion of this number are unemployed. Despite the improvement in Spanish economic performance since 1986, the unemployment rate is still close to 20 percent. The group worst hit by unemployment are the 16 to 19-year olds, over half of whom are without work. Next come the 20 to 24-year olds, with almost 40 percent unemployed. Even among those aged from 25 to 29, the number lacking paid employment is still large, somewhat in excess of 21 percent.

It is interesting to see how these figures relate to those for students and graduates of higher education institutions. In fact, the universities have almost become a byword for "dole-queue factories" (Martin Moreno and de Miguel 1979); particularly during the 1980s, Spanish higher education institutions have ceased to offer their graduates the prospect of "guaranteed employment" which they once assured. Above all in certain professional fields, university graduates have encountered great difficulties in finding a steady job. Large numbers of these have been forced to set aside their original aspirations and accept jobs which have little or nothing to do with their training.

Nevertheless, higher education is still an attractive option for many young Spanish people, for the prospects of subsequent employment and social enhancement are still significantly greater than those offered by other types of instruction which are vocationally oriented or pursue lower academic levels. As mentioned above, the unemployment rate in Spain has been acquiring alarming proportions for some years now and is the highest in the European Community (EC). As regards graduates of higher education specifically, in 1986 the unemployment rate (i.e., with respect to the total number of such graduates) stood at 15.6 percent, a significantly large proportion. It must be pointed out, however, that the bulk of those unemployed were aged between 20 and 29, within which group the total unemployment rate for graduates was 36.5 percent; in the following age group (30 to 44) this rate fell to 8.6 percent, and was tiny in the 45 to 54 age range (1.7 percent), rising slightly among those over 54 (2.9 percent). Briefly then, what these figures highlight is that the really difficult thing is to find work soon after completion of higher education, especially for graduates in the humanities or social sciences. It is quite common for such graduates to take two or even more years to find a relatively stable job.

These figures show, then, that one of the toughest problems facing Spanish society is the marked lack of phasing between the spheres of higher education and work, the upshot of which is a high rate of

665

unemployment among university graduates (particularly in the period immediately following the completion of their studies). "In the long term," according to the ICED Report:

> The solution to the problem of unemployment in Spain lies in the reformation both of the economic structure and of the system or model of higher education. If Spain decides to pursue higher levels of industrialization while developing a more rational system of agriculture and a more dynamic services industry, including tourism, it will find it essential to introduce a more solid and wide-reaching technical education system . . . . However, if Spain sets itself a higher goal and decides to try and become one of the more advanced societies in the fields of information, communication and high technology, all its universities must place full emphasis on basic research and advanced technology. (ICED 1988 p. 161)

1.3 Structure of Government and Main Political Goals

Throughout the long years of Franco, the administration of the Spanish education system intensified its tendency towards centralization, already a well-marked feature resulting largely from its development over the last two centuries. However, under persistent regionalist pressure in favor of greater autonomy, the democracy newly restored in 1978 was forced to set the groundwork for a new political and administrative structure which would allow the regions a greater say in political affairs. The 1978 Constitution did not confine itself to satisfying the long-voiced demands of the historical regions—Catalonia and the Basque Country—but went on to reorganize the entire political fabric of the country, creating 17 regions or "autonomous communities." Later on the extent to which regionalization has affected the governance and working of higher education will be analyzed. It will suffice for the moment to note the importance to the country of a measure which brought it more or less in a single step from total centralism in matters of government to out-and-out regionalism.

The Constitution of 1978 confirmed the form of the Spanish state as a monarchy, in the terms laid down by General Franco, with a system of multiparty democracy on the lines of other Western countries. With reference to education, article 27 of the Constitution affirms the universal right to basic education, the right to free choice in teaching (in the dual dimension of "teaching freedom" and "freedom to create educational institutions") and the autonomy of universities, while calling for regulations to give concrete form to these constitutional precepts. The response of the Socialist Party, which came to power in 1982, was the *Ley de Reforma Universitaria* of 1983 mentioned earlier. The Act's stated objectives amount to the updating of Spanish higher education (by definition, university education), the main thrust being to reorganize teaching staff and set guidelines

for the democratic running of institutions. At the end of this article this subject is examined to see to what extent the reforms introduced are actually helping to improve the working of higher education institutions at a crucial moment for the future of Spain.

As has already been noted, the Spanish tradition in higher education has been at once centralizing and state-oriented; that is to say that there has been little room for social or private initiative in the creation and furtherance of institutions in this sphere. Although at other educational levels private initiative—particularly that inspired by the Catholic Church—has been afforded freedom to act within the limits set by the political situation at any time, from the nineteenth century and for much of this one, the principle of higher education as a state monopoly held firm. This was true for the Franco regime until the Concordat signed with the Vatican in 1951 which obliged it to contemplate the possibility of church participation. Even so, until 1965 there was no explicit recognition of any private university, despite the fact that two years earlier the Vatican had awarded the status of Church University to the University of Navarra, an institution run by the lay religious organization, *Opus Dei*. The terms of the Concordat obliged the regime to officially validate qualifications from the University of Navarra—a process only completed with great difficulty in the face of extremely stringent academic requirements—and later on, to a lesser extent, those issued by other institutions likewise enjoying the status of "Church Universities," which we shall examine in due course. The upshot of all this is that at present the Catholic Church maintains a stable, well-founded relationship with the state in connection with these religious universities, which have not, however, grown in number or in the state assistance received since the restoration of democracy.

2. The Institutional Fabric of the Higher Education System

In Spain, the terms "higher education" and "university education" have come to mean exactly the same in theory as in practice. This similitude developed gradually, but attained full legal status in the *Ley General de Educación* of 1970 and has undergone no alteration since. The first article of the *Ley de Reforma Universitaria* states quite plainly that "higher education is provided by the universities through teaching, study and research." In a word, there is no "nonuniversity" sector within higher education. It might be argued that a number of areas yet remain outside the university domain, for example, military or ecclesiastical instruction, or certain musical and artistic subjects. But even in these few exceptional cases, there is a move to have them considered "university level" or brought under university aegis.

There are 30 public universities and four private ones (belonging to the Catholic Church). This overall list encompasses centers of different types:

(a) *Facultades universitarias* (university faculties) offering all three university levels; the first two levels lead to the *licenciado* (similar to the master's) qualification and the third to the doctorate. University faculties are entitled to offer studies in all branches of knowledge (health sciences, physical, and natural sciences, social sciences, humanities, etc.) with the exception of technologies.

(b) *Escuelas técnicas superiores* (higher technical schools) also offering all three university levels, but confined to the sphere of technology. These are in fact engineering (with various branches) and architectural schools. Thus, graduates of the first two levels do not receive the degree of *licenciado* but of engineer or architect. As in the faculties, the third level leads to the doctorate.

(c) *Escuelas universitarias* (university schools) offering only the first level of university studies (normally lasting three years) on completion of which graduates receive the degrees of *diplomado*, *ingeniero técnico*, or *arquitecto técnico* (similar to the bachelor level). The studies undertaken at these colleges are largely vocational (primary teaching, various types of technical engineering, nursing, business studies, etc.). Some of these centers may be privately run even though they are linked to public universities.

(d) *Colegios universitarios* (university colleges) offering only the first level of university studies corresponding to *facultades universitarias* (physical/natural sciences, social sciences, humanities, etc.). Each center is registered under a specific university, which students will attend to continue their studies (in the corresponding faculties). As with the *escuelas universitarias*, these may be public or private and in the latter case may be linked to public universities.

The 30 public universities include four *universidades politécnicas* (polytechnic universities) (in Madrid, Barcelona, Valencia, and Las Palmas de Gran Canaria) combining *escuelas técnicas superiores* and technical *escuelas universitarias*. There are also schools of this type which form part of other public and private universities. The *Universidad Nacional de Educación a Distancia*, whose headquarters are in Madrid, is also part of the public university network. Other public universities are in the process of formation in Madrid, Barcelona, and Pamplona. The four existing private universities are Deusto (in Bilbao), Navarra, *Pontificia de Comillas* (in Madrid), and *Pontificia de Salamanca*, but more are expected to open in the coming years.

Table 1 shows how the numbers of institutions have developed since 1960. If these figures are taken in conjunction with those for Table 2 (on numbers of students) it will be seen that the *facultades universitarias* have grown far more than both the higher and first-level technical schools. There has also been a marked decline in primary teacher-training schools. In interpreting the table it should be borne in mind that until 1970 the *escuelas universitarias* did not exist as such; the figures appearing in these rows refer to intermediate-grade professional schools (secondary level).

All public and private universities carry out a large amount of research, a task which is performed through both university departments and university institutes; whereas all the former are required to provide teaching and conduct research, the latter are devoted exclusively to research. But even so, a major proportion of Spanish research is carried on outside the universities, through the *Consejo Superior de Investigaciones Científicas* (CSIC). This is a state-run organization enjoying a certain degree of autonomy, which controls many institutes devoted to the various fields of scientific knowledge and employs its own research staff. Generally speaking, there is a great deal of collaboration between the university departments and institutes and the institutes and research centers run by the CSIC. Moreover, there has been

Table 1
Growth of numbers of university centers

	1960	1965	1970	1975	1980	1985
Public universities	12	12	19	25	29	30
Private universities	1	3	3	3	4	4
Faculties	130	132	148	175	208	255
Escuelas técnicas superiores	25	26	26	30	39	41
Escuelas universitarias (total)	—	—	—	—	309	362
Teachers	176	147	129	81	88	88
Technical	48	52	67	86	90	92
Others (nontechnical)	—	—	—	—	125	182

Table 2
Growth of student numbers (in thousands)

	1960	1965	1970	1975	1980	1985
Public universities[a]	76.4	120.9	232.1	518.6	629.6	825.3
Private universities[a]	—	4.9	7.5	13.2	19.4	28.8
Faculties and *colegios universitarios*	62.1	89.4	170.4	346.7	423.9	578.5
Escuelas tecnicas superiores	14.3	30.4	44.5	48.5	46.1	52.5
Escuelas universitarias (total)	—	—	115.7	136.5	180.0	223.0
Teachers	43.1	63.1	47.5	70.5	86.5	75.4
Technical	39.9	62.4	60.9	50.7	52.0	64.0
Others (nontechnical)	—	—	7.2	15.2	40.5	83.6

a The total numbers of students at public and private universities for the years 1960 and 1965 *do not include students attending escuelas universitarias*. Such students are, however, included in the figures for subsequent years

growing collaboration between the universities and productive industry in basic and applied research.

2.1 Admissions Policies

Students may not commence higher or university education at less than 18 years of age, generally speaking after completing 12 years of primary and secondary studies in two basic stages. The first stage comprises *educación general básica* (basic general education), an obligatory period of eight years (from 6 to 14 years of age). The second stage comprises the *bachillerato* (equivalent to high school and lasting three years) and a one-year period known as the *curso de orientación universitaria* (university orientation course). This educational structure, introduced under the *Ley General de Educación* (1970), is now under review.

In principle, higher education is open to all students who possess the *bachillerato* (certificate awarded on completion of secondary studies), have subsequently completed the *curso de orientación universitaria*, and finally have passed a general entrance test commonly known as the *prueba de selectividad* (selectivity test). The *curso de orientación universitaria* (COU) was an innovation introduced under the *Ley General de Educación* of 1970, an interesting idea in principle but one which was devalued practically from the outset, becoming little more than an extra year of secondary studies with virtually no real orientation in terms of higher education. As for the "selectivity test," this was brought in some years later as a means of placing barriers to university entrance in the path of students considered to lack sufficient grounding and/or motivation; like COU, this test has not properly fulfilled its intended function, but so far no better alternative has been suggested.

However, even a pass in the "selectivity test" does not suffice to ensure entrance to the center of the student's choice. All higher education centers are entitled to limit admission numbers in accordance with their physical capacity and the resources available to them. In fact an increasing number of centers are applying this limitation on numbers, to the extent that in the early 1990s the majority do so (many *escuelas técnicas superiores*, faculties of medicine and other health sciences, *escuelas universitarias*, etc.).

The *Ley General de Educación* also provided that all persons aged over 25 could enter university directly without even presenting certificates of primary or secondary studies, provided that they passed a special entrance test designed for this specific purpose. All public universities run such tests, although the *Universidad Nacional de Educación a Distancia* (UNED) has done so more systematically than any other and with the largest number of candidates. In the 1988–89 academic year, this university had over 25,000 student matriculations in its Access Course for persons aged over 25.

2.2 Quantitative Developments in Higher Education

The university student population has undergone spectacular growth since 1970 and in the early 1990s stands at almost one million, of whom approximately 50 percent are women (although less evenly distributed among the different types of university center).

The sizeable Spanish student population is distributed unevenly among the universities, the largest numbers of matriculations being at the *Universidad Complutense de Madrid* and the *Universidad Nacional de Educación a Distancia* (each with over 100,000 students registered), the *Universidad Central de Barcelona* (around 80,000), and the *Universidad de Valencia* (over 50,000). There are, besides, 10 universities with over 25,000 students (Universities of the País Vasco, *Politécnica de Madrid*, Santiago de Compostela, Seville, Granada, *Autónoma de Barcelona*, *Autónoma de Madrid*, Zaragoza, Valladolid, and Oviedo). A further 11 have more than 10,000 students: *Politécnica de Barcelona*; Salamanca; La Laguna (Canary Islands); Málaga; Murcia;

Extremadura; *Politécnica de Valencia*; Córdoba; Alcalá de Henares; Cádiz; and Alicante. There are five public universities with less than 10,000 students: León; Cantabria; Baleares; Castilla-La Mancha; and *Politécnica de Las Palmas* (Canary Islands). As for the private universities, the two most populous are Deusto and Navarra, each of which have rather more than 10,000 students; the other two have some 6,000 (*Pontificia de Comillas*) and 2,000 students (*Pontificia de Salamanca*). This means that the private university sector caters for only about 7 percent of all university students, although the portion is clearly growing.

2.3 Structure of Qualifications and Graduate Training Programs

Since the 1970 Act, higher education is divided into three levels, leading respectively to the qualifications *diplomado*, *licenciado*, and doctor. In the technical schools these are denominated respectively *arquitecto técnico* or *ingeniero técnico* (equivalent to *diplomado*), *arquitecto* or *ingeniero* (equivalent to *licenciado*) and doctor. The first level has always lasted three years and since 1970 the policy has been to try and ensure that large numbers of students completing this level receive a practically oriented certificate qualifying them for some profession. However, the attempt has failed time and again with the result that (except in the case of *escuelas universitarias*) it serves as little more than an obligatory first step prior to entry into the second level (lasting two years) and study for the *licenciado* degree—the one really required for entry to a profession. Neave has written extensively about the possible reasons for this failure, which has affected Spain in a similar way to other countries (Neave 1989 pp. 107–9). In the Spanish case, the reality is that university studies last five years (six in the case of medicine and some higher technical subjects), at the end of which the student may opt to enter the third level leading to the doctorate; this has a minimum duration of two years but is more normally three or four.

As regards the structure of higher education, although the 1983 Act largely maintains the structure already existing, major efforts are being made to finally achieve the end which has hitherto proved so elusive: to interest the majority of students in first-level studies (of two to three years) which will really offer some professional future. The *Consejo de Universidades* (Universities Council) is busy preparing new plans and syllabuses which will free the system from the straitjacket of overly traditional degrees and qualifications which generally afflicts Spanish universities, and offer students a grounding in new and revitalized professions along the lines being developed by higher education in other industrialized countries, above all in Europe. Indeed, from 1992 the European Community plans to introduce free circulation of professionals and university teachers and students, which means that all member states will be forced to adopt if not similar, at least homogeneous criteria governing graduation and qualification. In Spain, the traditional structure still persisting makes the pursuit of homogeneity as difficult as it is necessary.

Another aspect in urgent need of reform is that of graduate studies. As mentioned, the third level of university studies consists of neither more nor less than the doctorate, the basic purpose of which is to equip students for research and university teaching. Excepting a small number of fields (e.g., medical specialities) there are practically no really vocational studies. However, the universities have been organizing increasing numbers of graduate programs leading to the master's degree in specific subjects, and these are growing fast in popularity.

3. Governance, Administration, and Finance

3.1 National Administration

The transition from dictatorship to democracy which culminated in the Constitution of 1978 undoubtedly brought about thorough-going changes in the governance and administration of higher education. The governmental reorganization of the country has been accompanied by the transfer of many universities from the central to the new regional authorities. Spain is divided into 17 autonomous regions (*comunidades autónomas*), six of which have been invested with full authority in matters of higher education.

Although the Spanish Constitution of 1978 awards explicit recognition to the principle of university autonomy, this does not mean that the universities are now totally independent of political and governmental bodies. Article 6 of the *Ley de Reforma Universitaria* clearly states that "under this Act, the Universities shall be governed by such regulations as the State and the Autonomous Communities shall establish by virtue of the powers invested in them, and by their statutes." To begin with, the 1983 *Ley de Reforma Universitaria* itself sets forth a large body of regulations which, in certain areas (engagement of teaching staff, internal university government, general structure of courses, types of center, etc.) is fairly exhaustive, or in other words, allows very little room for autonomous action by the universities. In addition to this, both the central government and the regional governments concerned can issue (and in fact have done so) further regulations governing the organization and working of the universities under those terms of the Act referring to staffing, university departments, and so on. Above all else, there is the fact that the public universities are entirely dependent on state funding. University autonomy, then, is subject to certain restrictions.

At central government level, in the Ministry of Education and Science there is a department headed by a Secretary of State for Universities and Research which, through its various General Directorates, is the supreme authority in higher education. However, there is also a *Consejo de Universidades* manned chiefly (but not exclusively) by university rectors and this is basically dependent on the initiative of the state, which appoints many of the members (including the general secretary and his assistants). Then again, the *Consejo de Universidades* does not simply advise but, as the Act provides (article 23), "organizes, coordinates, plans, proposes and advises." The *consejo* is then an instrument of government controlled by the central authority, although it is also undeniably a forum where common problems are openly discussed and examined.

As was noted earlier, to date the central government has transferred responsibility for higher education to six regions (Catalonia, Basque Country, Galicia, Andalusia, Valencia, and the Canary Islands). In these regions both parliament and government can therefore lay down certain guidelines and coordinate action in the universities falling within their territorial bounds. The political-administrative structure clearly mirrors that of the central government: under the *Consejero de Enseñanza* (equivalent to Minister of Education) there is a Director General of Higher Education commanding a number of services and officials. Although the duties and responsibilites of such regional politicians have a tendency to grow, it must be recognized that these specific duties are not at all easy to discharge, given on the one hand the major limitations entailed by the regulations and central government funding, and on the other the desire of the universities themselves to enjoy without interference the autonomy which is their legal right.

In the sphere of higher education, and others in Spain, there is no planning as such either of staffing requirements or of demand, and there is only a limited amount of planning of human resources and material requirements. The central government and some of the regions see a need to create new universities and other higher education centers to cater for the ever-growing demand for places. However, it seems that in creating such institutions they are heeding only the vaguest considerations of general demand.

Nor is there any systematically organized assessment of higher education institutions in terms of their results or how well or badly they employ their resources. All public universities are financed by the state in accordance with a number of variables (number of institutions, number of students, buildings, laboratories, etc.) but not in accordance with their results (number and quality of graduates, research completed, etc.).

Most of the income received by public universities comes from the central budget, although tuition fees are also an important source of revenue, which has

Table 3
Proportion of the gross national product allocated to higher education as a percentage

1980	1981	1982	1983	1984	1985
3.32	3.49	4.89	4.39	4.23	4.19

been growing in the last few years. On average, some 70 percent of public university income is furnished by the state, but within a wide margin of difference. Thus for example, while in 1987 the *Universidad de Extremadura* received 80.96 percent of its income from the state (and the remaining 19 percent from fees), the *Universidad Autónoma de Madrid* received only 61.2 percent. The public university which has received least state aid to date is the *Universidad Nacional de Educación a Distancia*, of whose 1987 budget, only 37 percent came from the state, the remaining 67 percent deriving from academic fees and other sources.

As it is, the government determines the fees to be charged to students at all universities, which are allowed no discretion in the matter. For the 1989–90 academic year, the matriculation fee for all the subjects included in a one-year course at experimenting *facultades universitarias* and at *escuelas técnicas superiores* was 58,150 pesetas (approx. US$500), while at nonexperimenting faculties and centers it was 41,050 pesetas (approx. US$350). It is not hard to deduce that the amount paid by the student covers only a fraction of the real cost of his or her place.

Finally, the private universities do not receive any direct funding from the state. However, students there may be entitled to the general grants and subsidies provided by the state.

3.2 Institutional Administration

Article 3 of the 1983 *Ley de Reforma Universitaria* sets forth a long list of aspects in which the universities could theoretically exercise the autonomy attributed to them by the Constitution. Nevertheless, in reality many of these aspects are heavily dependent upon central government decisions. The universities do in fact have complete autonomy as regards the drafting of "their Statutes and other regulations governing internal running" and in "the election, appointment and dismissal of their organs of government and administration"; they are also empowered to establish relations with other Spanish and foreign institutions. However, in all other areas considered by the Act to be encompassed by university autonomy, discretionary power can only be exercised partially, heavily bounded as it is by provisions laid down by the central government. Such is the case in the "drafting, approval and administration of their budgets," in the "formation and modification of their workforces" (academic and nonacademic), in the "selection, training and promotion of staff," in the "drafting and approval of syllabuses," and so on. In all these (and other) aspects the state lays down operational guidelines which obviously reduce the scope of university autonomy. Then again, the largely nonacademic Social Council (referred to farther on) existing in all universities is, in the eyes of many at the universities, yet another obstacle to the full exercise of autonomy.

Article 20 of the 1978 Constitution expressly recognizes and calls for the protection of teaching freedom. The 1983 Act for its part, in article 2 provides that "both the activity and the autonomy of the universities obey the basic principle of academic freedom, in the concrete form of freedom in teaching, research and study." As far as teachers are concerned, this academic freedom must be seen in the light of article 33 of the Act, which states that all permanent university teachers are "fully capacitated for the purpose of teaching and research" (the latter subject to possession of a doctoral degree). Thus, all university teachers can and do claim the right of teaching freedom as guaranteed by the Constitution. Both the regular courts and the Constitutional Tribunal have had occasion since then to reaffirm the importance of this right, which encompasses not only the free expression of ideas in spoken and written form, but the freedom to adopt syllabuses, methodologies, texts, and so on.

The multipersonal bodies and individual offices comprising their governing structures must be identical in all public universities. The former include the *consejo social*, the *claustro universitario*, the *junta de gobierno*, the *juntas de facultad* or *juntas de escuela*, and the *consejos de departamento* or *consejos de instituto*.

The *consejo social*, defined in the Act as "the organ through which society participates in the University" (article 14), comprises a three-fifths part "in representation of the interests of society," legally determined by the pertinent autonomous region; it is expressly stated that none of these representatives may be a member of the university community. The remaining two-fifths are composed of "representatives of the *junta de gobierno*, elected by the latter from among its own members and necessarily including the rector, the general secretary, and the administrator." The *consejo social* is presided over not by the rector but by an appointee of the autonomous region concerned. The *consejo social* may thus be seen to some extent as an organ of external control, exercising as it does such essential functions as approval of the university's budget and supra-annual programming or "supervision of economic business" and "supervision of performance."

The *claustro universitario*, or senate, is on the other hand a strictly university-staffed organ, at least three-fifths of whose members must be teachers, although it also contains a significant body of students and nonacademic staff. Its three basic duties are to draw up the university statutes, to elect the rector, and to approve the general lines of university action, besides other functions as may be determined by the statutes of each university. The rector presides over the claustro.

The *junta de gobierno*, or governing board, defined by the Act as "the body in charge of the normal running of the University," is also presided over by the rector. Besides the directorate (vice-rectors, general secretary, and administrator), this board is staffed by representatives of structural components of the university (deans, department heads, etc.) and by members of the different bodies (teachers, students, and nonacademic staff). Each of the institutions or centers comprising the university (faculties, schools, departments, and institutes) has its own board or council, whose functions always include that of electing the person who is to preside (dean or director as the case may be).

As far as unipersonal offices are concerned, the head of the university is the rector, who must be elected by the *claustro* in accordance with the statutes of each university, from among the *catedráticos* (professors) of that institution. Upon the appointment, the rector in turn appoints the members of his staff (vice-rectors, general secretary, and administrator).

The principal centers (faculties, schools, university colleges, etc.) which go to make up the university were described at the beginning of this article and may also include *institutos universitarios*, devoted exclusively to research. It must be added, however, that under the 1983 Act the chief university organs "responsible for the organization and furtherance of research and teaching" are the departments, structured around the various areas of scientific, technical, or artistic knowledge. Since the promulgation of the 1983 Act and under its provisions, the government has issued a fairly comprehensive body of regulations governing the organization and running of university departments, which are now seen as basic elements in the university structure.

As regards the organization of university teaching, the methodology followed in most Spanish universities is still highly traditional, with little or no use made of the new technologies. Nevertheless, the universities' material infrastructure has improved considerably and most are equipped with quite advanced physical and technological resources; these are, however, more widely used in research than in teaching. The *Universidad Nacional de Educación a Distancia* (UNED) itself, despite the fact that it gives no direct classes and despite a major effort to introduce more technologically advanced methods, still has too much of a tendency to cling to a traditional concept of teaching.

4. Faculty and Students: Teaching, Learning, and Research

4.1 Faculty

The number of teaching staff at the universities has grown considerably over the last two decades, although less than the numbers of students. There are (in the early 1990s) about 48,000 teachers, 28 percent of them women, and most work in university faculties. Only 10 percent of teachers work in private as opposed to public universities. Finally, the average student–teacher ratio in Spanish universities is 18:1, although ratios do in fact differ widely from one university to another and, within individual universities, from one center to another. For example, whereas the ratio in *faculties* is in the region of 20:1, in *escuelas técnicas superiores* it is only slightly over 10:1, while at *escuelas universitarias* it is roughly 17:1. As for differences between universities, those with the highest ratios are Valencia (26:1), Barcelona (24:1), and Santiago de Compostela (24:1), (the UNED, with a ratio of 95:1, is a case apart owing to its special nature). There are public universities with extremely low ratios, such as the *Universidades Politécnicas* in the Canaries (10.2:1) and Barcelona (11.8:1), the *Universidad de Cantabria* (12.8:1), the *Universidad de Córdoba*, and others. Ratios also differ considerably among the private universities; while at three of them (Navarra, Comillas, and Salamanca) ratios are below 10:1, the *Universidad de Deusto* has the highest of all Spanish universities (27.8:1).

The bulk of Spanish university teaching staff work full-time, although there are centers where part-time work is more common, as in the case of *escuelas técnicas superiores* and certain faculties (medicine, law, economics, and business in particular).

As mentioned earlier, the most innovative part of the 1983 *Ley de Reforma Universitaria* was the change provided in the structure and recruiting of university teaching staff. Indeed, the situation prior to that time left much to be desired, as only a part—sometimes a small part—of the teaching staff (those classified as *profesores numerarios*, that is, teachers having tenured status) enjoyed stable employment. A large proportion of teachers (in many universities a

majority), on the contrary, enjoyed no such stability, working under annually renewable contracts. The latter were known by the initials PNN, that is, *profesores no numerarios* (teachers without tenure). Despite the fact that after 1970 the number of teachers with tenured status rose steadily, this was insufficient to cover the needs of an equally expansive student body and as a consequence large-scale recruitment of nontenured teachers continued to be necessary. There was thus a need for a law to regulate the precarious status of these teachers, most of whom had been engaged without any kind of selection process, through the patronage of professors or other tenured staff.

In the first place, the 1983 Act introduced a major simplification of the categories existing hitherto, all of which were reduced to four basic ones: *catedráticos de universidad* (university professors); *profesores titulares de universidad* (tenured university teachers); *catedráticos de escuela universitaria* (university school professors); and *profesores titulares de escuela universitaria* (tenured university school teachers). All such teachers have civil servant status although they are assigned to specific universities. The Act further permits recruitment (for periods of two to three years) of a number of nonpermanent teachers (associate professors, visiting professors, and assistants), which in any case does not form more than a small proportion of total academic staff.

Such structural renewal was not, however, enough in itself. A procedure was also needed to afford stability to those nontenured teachers so wishing, and able in some way, to demonstrate sufficient capacity. The procedure chosen in the Act was to award all teachers already possessing a doctorate the status of *profesor titular de universidad* (tenured university teacher); for this purpose, aptitude tests (*pruebas de idoneidad*) were organized and sat by a large number of PNNs. Aptitude tests were also arranged for those working in *escuelas universitarias* without possessing a doctoral degree. As the tests were extremely simple, this turned out in fact to be an easy means of converting many PNNs to civil servant status. Those not possessing a doctoral degree were given time and various kinds of facilities to enable them to complete their theses and attend further test sessions. Briefly, then, in a very few years the situation has been completely reversed, so that by the early 1990s, teachers with tenured status comprise the vast majority in all universities.

The 1983 Act has also greatly simplified the competitive examination for aspiring university teachers (known in Spain as *oposiciones*). Candidates (except for the lower teaching posts in *escuelas universitarias*) must possess a doctor's degree and successfully complete a test administered by a board comprising five members, two of whom are designated by the university offering the post, and three chosen by lot from among all the teachers of the speciality or field

Table 4
Growth in numbers of teachers (thousands)

	1970	1975	1980	1985
Faculties and colegios universitarias	12.8	16.4	22.9	27.2
Escuelas técnicas superiores	4.5	4.4	5.0	5.1
Escuelas universitarias	5.6	6.8	10.3	12.9
Total	22.9	27.6	38.2	45.2

Table 5

Growth of student numbers at facultades and escuelas tecnicas superiores, classified under broad fields of study (thousands)

	1960	1965	1970	1975	1980	1985
Sciences	46.3	80.0	120.6	174.9	198.0	306.9
Social sciences	20.3	27.1	44.3	96.2	156.9	171.4
Humanities	8.6	17.3	45.3	78.3	109.3	152.7
Total	76.4	125.8	213.1	386.6	470.0	631.0

of learning concerned. The new tests introduced under the 1983 Act came under heavy criticism on the grounds both of the scant discrimination afforded by the tests and the pressures put on the boards to select the local candidate. A survey (1989) conducted by the *Consejo de Universidades* has shown that in fact approximately 90 percent of posts offered are awarded to the local candidates. This is evidence of an endogamous tendency which many prominent teachers do not hesitate to classify as local isolationism, confirming the fears expressed by the International Council for Educational Development in its report, thus:

> What concerns us is that this propensity of Universities to close in upon themselves may be exacerbated by the new system of university autonomy, whereunder they have even greater freedom in the selection and engagement of new academic staff members. This tendency stands in sharp contrast to the practice current in the more prominent universities in other OECD countries . . . (ICED 1988 p. 121)

Teaching staff at Spanish universities have hitherto shown little eagerness to join unions and similar associations for the defense of their professional interests. However, interest has been growing gradually with perception of the need to negotiate with the government on pay and working conditions. The

association which enjoys the greatest amount of support and votes is the *Unión Sindical Independiente de Funcionarios* (USIF), which aspires to independent representation of the university sector although still a part of the wider-based CSIF (*Confederación Sindical Independiente de Funcionarios*). There are also two other associations with significant support among university teachers: FETE-UGT (*Federación Española de Trabajadores de la Enseñanza*, part of the socialist *Unión General de Trabajadores)*; and the university section of CCOO (the communist union, *Comisiones Obreras*). Within each university the various bodies (professors, tenured-status teachers, etc.) are represented on all the collective organs of government (senate, faculty committees, etc.).

Working conditions for university teaching staff are set by the government, which establishes the numbers of hours to be devoted to teaching business, student guidance, and research. Those discharging specific executive or administrative duties generally receive a pay supplement.

4.2 Students

The absence of higher education outside the university system in Spain has done much to restrict the range of subjects theoretically open to students. Equally detrimental and also the object of criticism in the past has been the lack of an effective guidance system during secondary education. Together, these two factors prompt major imbalances in the distribution of students among the various specialist fields, as can be seen from Table 5.

Table 5 shows only students, matriculated at public and private university faculties and higher technical schools, who are undertaking studies of at least five years' duration leading to the degree of *licenciado* or the equivalent. The figures therefore do not include students undertaking three-year courses either technical or otherwise, at *escuelas universitarias*. The "sciences" heading encompasses the exact and physical–natural sciences, health sciences, and technologies. "Social sciences" include law, economic and

Table 6

Growth of numbers of graduates classified by type of center (thousands)

	1960	1965	1970	1975	1980	1985
Public university[a]	5.7	4.5	9.0	16.9	35.2	82.6
Private university[a]	—	0.2	0.7	1.2	2.7	3.4
Faculties	5.0	4.7	9.5	17.9	37.7	47.5
Escuelas técnicas superiores	0.7	1.8	2.5	3.3	2.8	3.0
Escuelas universitarias	—	—	—	—	33.3	35.7
Teachers	8.9	8.9	11.0	11.0	23.7	21.5
Technical	2.6	5.2	5.5	5.1	4.6	5.4
Others (nontechnical)	—	—	—	—	5.0	8.8

a The total numbers of students at public and private universities for the years 1960, 1965, 1970 and 1975 *do not include students attending escuelas universitarias*. Such students are included in the figures for 1980 and 1985

business studies, political science, sociology, psychology, and studies in social communication. Lastly, the "humanities" heading covers both humanities per se and also fine art, theology, and educational sciences (but not primary teacher training).

The figures in Table 6 reveal a lot about some important questions, such as the levelling-off of numbers of graduates from technically oriented *escuelas universitarias* after 1965 (when they were still intermediate-grade technical schools), or how there has been very little growth in *escuelas técnicas superiores*.

A detailed analysis of these and the figures for previous years will bring out clearly how little suited higher education is either to the labor market or to the foreseeable economic development of the country. A total of 90,393 students graduated from higher education institutions in 1986 (*Consejo de Universidades* 1989: 192). Of this number, 57 percent (52,343 students) did so from *facultades universitarias* (humanities, science, law, medicine, etc.) after five years or more of study and 3.3 percent (3,031 students) completed long-term studies at *escuelas técnicas superiores* (architecture and the various branches of engineering). The technical *escuelas universitarias* (3-year courses) produced 5,516 graduates (6 percent); and finally, the nontechnical *escuelas universitarias* (also short courses, in primary teaching, data processing, nursing, business management, etc.) produced 29,503 graduates, that is, 32 percent of the total.

Two important conclusions emerge from this preliminary analysis: first, there is a bias in Spain in favor of long-term university studies (five years or more)—the choice of 60 percent of students graduating in 1986; and second, there is very little interest in technical studies of either long or short duration—completed by only 9 percent of all graduates.

Looking again at the high proportion of graduates from university faculties, it can be seen that a majority studied humanities and social sciences. Arts faculty (humanities) graduates numbered 15,378, that is, 17 percent of all Spanish graduates that year. There were 8,947 law graduates, almost 10 percent of the total and more than all the graduates in long- and short-term technical studies put together. Similarly high figures for graduates are seen in other fields of social science (economics, psychology, etc.). Health sciences—and specifically medicine—were another popular field; in 1986 there were over 7,000 medical graduates, that is almost 8 percent of all graduates for that year. In the experimental sciences and mathematics, 1986 produced rather more than 6,000 graduates (almost 7 percent).

In short-course nontechnical studies, the largest single group were the graduates from teacher-training schools, who numbered 19,667 in 1986, that is over 21 percent of all Spanish graduates.

All these data highlight a major gulf separating higher education from the world of work and Spanish requirements for balanced economic development. For example, Spanish universities produce more lawyers than engineers. Almost one-half of graduates from higher education eventually turn to teaching at one level or another, and this at a time when there is a surplus of teachers while pupil numbers decline in the wake of a falling birthrate. Again, more doctors, psychologists, journalists, and other professionals are produced than are really needed, while there is a shortage of technical people, and courses of study leading to much-needed new professions are not even being organized.

However, there is at least growing awareness of the need to remedy this breakdown between higher education and employment, a feeling of concern which is giving rise to some interesting experiments and innovations in both the public and the private sectors.

The bulk of Spanish university students come from the upper and middle strata of society. Since 1970 there has been a gradual increase in the numbers of youngsters from working-class families in the big cities, while the offspring of agricultural workers are as scarce as ever on the campuses. In the context of the democratization pursued by higher education institutions, a major step has been the "second chance" offered by the *Universidad Nacional de Educación a Distancia* (UNED).

Like the teachers, students nowadays take little part in union associations and movements. In the wake of the highly-charged political atmosphere prior to and immediately after the death of Franco, interest in politics has tended increasingly to decline among Spanish students, even in those union groupings directly affiliated to specific parties (UGT, *Comisiones Obreras*, etc.) which in times past enjoyed a great deal of support from, and influence, over the student body. However, as interest in politics has declined, so the presence and strength of students in university senates has grown.

5. Conclusion

Higher education in Spain is going through one of the most fraught periods in its long history. Among the numerous manifestations illustrating this situation are the following: (a) the massive increase in the number of students matriculated in higher education; (b) the transformation of the country's political and administrative structure; (c) the pursuit of up-to-date models of structural and functional autonomy; (d) the effects of the 1983 Act, particularly on the selection of academic staff and university governance; (e) the need for effective integration in the body of European higher education; and (f) the need for an adequate response to the economic, social, and cultural challenges facing a country in the process of rapid evolution. In the course of this article specific reference has been made to all of these aspects, but it would perhaps be useful at this point to return to some of them.

To begin with, Spanish higher education institutions must clearly undergo a major process of adjustment in pursuit of integration with Europe and, more generally, an international dimension in their structures and activities. In this respect, for instance, the pressure being brought to bear on syllabuses by teachers and students hardly seems destined to favor the homologation of courses, degrees, and diplomas with those of other EC countries. However, there are also other obstacles in the path of such homologation. As the ICED Report quoted earlier rightly states, the first of the tasks facing Spain on EC entry is "to inject a strong international dimension into hitherto relatively provincial syllabuses, as an integral part of the general education of each and every student" (ICED 1988 p. 48).

We have already noted the significance in Spain of the lack of postsecondary (or higher) education outside the university system. It seems clear that this has led young people to see the university as the only possible avenue to cultural, social, and economic advancement; yet, as Diez-Hochleitner aptly puts it, "the university itself must know when to give up trying to provide the whole gamut of professional and specialized instruction" (Diez-Hochleitner 1989 p. 16). The creation of a prestigious sector of the kind envisaged here—which moreover exists already in most developed countries—would be of great assistance in clarifying the situation and ensuring the success of attempts at a qualitative reform of the entire body of higher education institutions.

It is obviously not enough that there be a variety of nonuniversity options in higher education; the students must feel motivated towards them and society at large must learn their true value. Hence the endemic lack of systems of vocational guidance in Spanish secondary education is one of the problems most affecting higher education. The reform of the education system at an advanced study stage addresses this defect, but it will not be an easy problem to tackle unless abundant human and material resources are made available. At the same time, selection procedures will have to be better defined in order to ensure that those entering higher education are properly grounded and can be guaranteed instruction of sufficient quality.

It is also extremely important to find the right point of equilibrium for the autonomy of the universities within the new Spanish territorial structure. So far, although some progress has been made, the centralist mentality still prevails so that most university decisions are subjected to a great deal of interference or pressure from central government agencies. This time-honored "Napoleonic" tradition can also be felt in the behavior of the new regions or "autonomous communities," which frequently display a tendency to reproduce centralist conduct within their own boundaries. Internal university authorities often yield to the temptation to leave the state to solve even the most minor problems rather than make a real effort to address them in a spirit of responsible autonomy.

Partly as a result of the inadequacy of previous policies regarding selection and recruitment of teaching staff, the 1983 Act opted to try out new formulas. These, however, are coming in for strong criticism on the grounds that they lead to indiscriminate recruitment, endogamy, and lack of prospects for younger people with talent, who, for the present at least, will have very little chance of obtaining a teaching post at a university. While there are many excellent teachers, since the 1983 Act the universities have been inundated by permanent teachers many of whom leave much to be desired and cannot easily be replaced for some time.

More attention has also been paid to the need to reinforce research at universities. On this point, Spanish universities still compare badly with their European counterparts and there is some awareness that Spain has only a few years in which to achieve better resources and more commitment from academic staff in order to have any chance of competing with other industrialized countries in Europe and elsewhere. In the light of this need, a number of legal and financial provisions are in place or being prepared to help attain an objective which is vital for the entire body of higher education.

Bibliography

Alvarez de Morales A 1972 *Génesis de la Universidad española contemporánea.* Instituto de Estudios Administrativos, Madrid

Cacho Viu V 1962 *La Institución Libre de Enseñanza.* Rialp, Madrid

Consejo de Universidades 1986 *Legislación Universitaria 1: Normativa general y autonómica*, 2nd edn. Tecnos, Madrid

Consejo de Universidades 1986 *Legislación Universitaria 2: Estatutos de las Universidades*, 2nd edn. Tecnos, Madrid

Consejo de Universidades 1987 *La reforma de la enseñanza universitaria.* Ministerio de Educación y Ciencia, Madrid

Consejo de Universidades 1988a *Anuario de Estadística Universitaria 1988.* Ministerio de Educación y Ciencia, Madrid

Consejo de Universidades 1988b *Guía de la Universidad.* Ministerio de Educación y Ciencia, Madrid

Diez-Hochleitner R 1989 La educación postsecundaria ante la sociedad del conocimiento y de las comunicaciones: documento de trabajo básico. In: Fundación Santillana 1989 *La educación postsecundaria: documentos de un debate.* Madrid, pp. 9–17

D'Ors A 1961 *Papeles del oficio universitario.* EUNSA, Pamplona

García Garrido J L 1987 *Sistemas educativos de hoy*, 2nd edn. Dykinson, Madrid

García Garrido J L La educación en España durante la etapa franquista. In: *Historia General de España*, Vol. 20. Rialp, Madrid (in print)

García Garrido J L Universidades durante el franquismo. In: Delgado B (ed.) *Historia de la Educación en España y América*. Fundación Santamaría, Madrid (in print)

International Council for Educational Development (ICED) 1988 La reforma universitaria española: evaluación e informe. In: Fundación Santillana 1988 *La educación postsecundaria*, ICED, Madrid, pp. 33–166

Jiménez Frau A 1971 *Historia de la Universidad española*. Alianza, Madrid

Laín Entralgo P 1984 *El problema de la Universidad*. Edicusa, Madrid

Maravall J M 1984 *La reforma de la enseñanza*. Laia, Barcelona

Martín Moreno J, de Miguel A 1979 *Universidad, fábrica de parados*. Vicens Vives, Barcelona

De Miguel A *Reformar la Universidad* 1976. Barcelona

McNair J M 1983 *Education for a Changing Spain*. Manchester University Press, Manchester

Montoro Romero R 1981 *La Universidad en la España de Franco (1939–70)*. Centro de Investigaciones Sociologicas, Madrid

Neave G 1989 ¿Ave Fénix o locomotora? Algunas reflexiones extraídas de "La reforma universitaria española: evaluación e informe." In: Fundación Santillana 1989 *La educación postsecundaria: documentos de debate*. Madrid, pp. 105–117

Ortega y Gasset J 1960 *Misión de la Universidad*. Revista de Occidente, Madrid

Puelles Benítez M 1980 *Educación e ideología en la España contemporánea*. Labor, Madrid

Vilar S 1987 *La Universidad, entre el fraude y la irracionalidad*. Plaza y Janés, Barcelona

J. L. Garcia-Garrido

Sri Lanka

1. Higher Education and Society

Sri Lanka is an island of 65,000 square kilometers. Although national frontiers have not changed, the population has grown from 6.657 million to 16.507 million during the last four decades with a corresponding rapid increase in the population of school-going age. With the introduction of universal free education in 1945 and the gradual switch-over of media of instruction to national languages in schools as from 1947, there occurred an unprecedented rise in school enrollment from 1.490 million in 1952 to 3.638 million in 1985.

Sri Lanka is a multiracial and multireligious society, with Sinhalese accounting for 74 percent, Tamils, Moors, and others comprising 18 percent, 7 percent, and 1 percent respectively, while Buddhism is practiced by 69.3 percent, with Hindus (15.5 percent), Muslims (7.6 percent), and Christians (7.5 percent) accounting for the rest.

The population is heavily dependent upon agriculture. The primary sector accounts for nearly 30 percent of Gross Domestic Product and provides nearly 50 percent of the total employment. The secondary and the tertiary sectors account for the other 15 percent and 55 percent respectively. The fortunes of the economy are significantly tied with the vagaries of trade as the export income contributes nearly 25 percent of the gross national product (GNP). The funds for education coming mainly from the government exchequer are intimately linked with fluctuations in the economy.

2. The Institutional Fabric of the Higher Education System

In colonial times, education was mainly in the vernacular and education in English was confined to the elite. Until about the middle of the twentieth century, higher education was identified with university education, itself dating from 1942, when the first University of Ceylon was established.

There was one Ministry of Education until 1978. In higher education little privatization took place. During the two decades from 1958 to 1977, university education in Sri Lanka underwent several changes. Hitherto independent it was placed in the charge of the Ministry of Education by Act No. 20, passed in 1966. In 1972, the government introduced a new Act, the University of Ceylon Act No. 1, which converted the five existing universities as well as the Institute of Practical Technology at Moratuwa into six campuses to form one monolithic university. Several alterations were made in the period from 1966 to 1978 to university admissions policy and entry requirements to universities and other institutions of higher learning.

Major changes in higher education occurred in 1978. The Ministry of Higher Education was established to take charge of all university, higher technical, and vocational education, with teacher training still left to the Ministry of Education. The Universities Act No. 16 of 1978 created a University Grants Commission (UGC) to plan and coordinate the activities of all universities so as to conform to national policy.

With the passing of the new Act and the establishment of the UGC, not only the six separate campuses were each restored to independent university status, but within seven years of its operation, two new universities were established in the south and the east, an Open University in Colombo, and several university institutes.

Now, in the late twentieth century, there are nine fully fledged universities including the Open University, and nine institutes at graduate and other levels. There are two graduate schools attached to the two oldest universities of Peradeniya and Colombo. Several University Centers of Excellence have now come of age.

Undergraduate courses take three years while special courses take four years except for medicine which takes five years. There are graduate courses in all fields, leading to either a diploma, a master's degree, or a doctorate. Normally, except in the field of medicine, a first degree with a good class (first or upper second) is required to be admitted to a master's or a doctorate course. In the case of medicine, those with two years' experience in a teaching hospital after the first degree can register for a doctor of medicine (MD) or master of surgery (MS) at the Postgraduate Institute of Medicine.

The network of technical institutes under the Ministry of Higher Education comprises 13 Grade 1 and 12 Grade 2 colleges and five affiliated units. They conduct two four-year courses in accountancy and commerce, three three-year courses in civil, mechanical, and electrical engineering respectively, leading to a Higher National Diploma (HND) and three two-year courses in business studies (available also as a three-year part-time course), home economics and English (available also as a three-year part-time course) leading to a National Diploma. The requirements for HND courses are the same as for university entry. The total enrollment (1988) in higher technical education is 3,600.

Other ministries also act for higher education in the technical and commercial areas. Teacher training remains the responsibility of the Ministry of Education although the universities of Colombo, Peradeniya, and Jaffna and the Open University continue to provide postgraduate diploma courses in education. In 1985, the National Institute of Education was set up, with five colleges of education for teacher training, the total enrollment being 6,200.

Higher education is also provided in certain areas by other government and government-approved institutions and private-sector organizations. The only two private degree-awarding institutions, the North Colombo Medical College (vested in the government since June 1989), and the Institute of Technological Studies have a total student enrollment of around 1,000. The enrollment in higher education within the Ministry of Higher Education is 34,000 while the total enrollment in higher education in Sri Lanka is around 60,000 (1988). This is about 2.5 percent of the total 18 to 24 age group and is less than 0.4 percent of the total population.

3. Governance, Administration, and Finance

Higher education was once considered a public good in Sri Lanka and was not only provided almost entirely by the central government and state-sponsored institutions, but also almost entirely financed by it.

The budgetary resources received by education in 1956 were 3.6 percent of the GNP. This increased to 4.3 percent in 1966 but declined thereafter until 1984/85 when there was a reversal. In 1988 it was slightly above 3 percent. The total resources diverted from the education budget to higher education have also consistently risen since the establishment of the Ministry of Higher Education. The 12 percent of the education budget then diverted to higher education has risen to 20 percent.

4. Faculty and Students: Teaching, Learning, and Research

4.1 Faculty

The total approved teaching cadre of all universities (at the end of 1987) including the Open University was 2,450, of whom only 1,962 or 80 percent had been filled. In addition to these tenured posts, there were 477 temporary posts of which 379 or 80 percent had been filled. The number of part-time appointments is not significant. The recruiting grade to the tenured posts is assistant lecturer (or lecturer as very often is the case in the medical faculties). A good first degree in the relevant field (i.e., with a first or upper-second class) is a normal minimum requirement for appointment to this grade.

Of the total tenured posts, 10.8 percent are professors, 3.6 percent associate professors, 21.9 percent senior lecturers, 25.9 percent lecturers (including medical registrars) and the largest, 37.8 percent, assistant lecturers. Of this tenured cadre 30 percent are in arts, social sciences, and humanities, 3.0 percent in commerce and management, 2.4 percent in law and education, 25.4 percent in physical and biological sciences, 16.8 percent in medicine and dentistry, 1.2 percent in veterinary medicine, 6.6 percent in agriculture, 13.3 percent in engineering, and 0.5 percent in architecture. Of the permanent staff nearly one-third are females.

University teachers are represented on all university bodies, such as the council, the senate, and the faculty board. There are no rules governing the work load of teachers, although the unweighted average weekly teaching load is 10 to 15 hours. The average weekly hours devoted to research is less than three hours.

Universities in Sri Lanka have traditionally developed as undergraduate teaching institutions, but an effort has been made to shift this emphasis from undergraduate teaching to graduate study and research (Corporate Plans of 1984 to 88, 1986 to 90 and 1988 to 92). The government does not allocate separate funds for university research. Other local institutions funding university research are also very limited.

Universities and university institutes in Sri Lanka have more than twice as many nonteaching as teaching staff. Of them, administrative/executive grades comprised 6.0 percent and females 25 percent.

4.2 Students

Table 1 gives the composition of total enrollment of tertiary students in universities and university institutes and the Open University. The output of graduates is classified in Table 2 according to institution, academic stream, and sex.

The University Act of 1972 gave adequate representation to university students on all university bodies. This was done away with by the Act of 1978. However, university students could make representations to university authorities on matters concerning them through the students' unions. The Amending Act of 1985 abolished these unions, but they have now been restored.

The curricula of universities, university institutions, and technical institutes are varied and are spelt out in the Statistical Handbook on Higher Education. They are decided by the respective academic bodies. Although the government can give directives with regard to any matter of national interest, universities are generally left to themselves to plan their curricula in relation to changing socioeconomic needs of the country.

The institutions of higher education have several methods of evaluation built into them at least in the state sector. The annual reports of the higher education institutions and the UGC is one such method.

These reports are placed before parliament and may come for scrutiny during budget debates. They may also come for scrutiny before its Committee of Public Enterprises and Higher Education Consultative Committee.

There has been, however, a certain lacuna in the evaluation of teachers and courses offered. The practice of evaluation of courses by students themselves has so far not gained currency in Sri Lanka.

The most regular element of evaluation in higher education institutions is the assessment of students by their teachers. This is done mainly by comprehensive end-of-year written examinations. A few departments do practice continuous assessment of coursework and give some weightage to this in final evaluation. It too has, however, gained little currency. On the basis of final marks allotted, students are graded into first class, upper-second, lower-second, or pass categories. The system of student assessments seems to have won general acceptance judged by the rarity of student protests about examination results. On the basis of the whole performance, distinctions and merit passes are also given in diploma and master's courses while subject distinctions are also awarded in the case of medical degrees.

5. Conclusion

Many changes have occurred in the field of higher education since Independence. The key feature of

Table 1
Composition of enrollment

Stream	Universities and university institutions	Open University	Universities and university institutions			Open University			Total
			D[a]	M[b]	P[c]	D	M	P	
Arts	6,484		105	374	62				7,025
Fine art	808								808
Commercial and management studies	3,807		46	194	12				4,059
Education			102	125	11	3,510			3,748
Law	571	1,356		93	20				2,040
Science	3,462	1,843	75	207	13				5,600
Medicine and dental science	2,656		48	117	109				2,930
Indigenous medicine	373								373
Agriculture and veterinary science	1,009		6	247	19				1,281
Engineering	1,914		33	28	1				1,976
Architecture	152		12	61	1				226
Total	21,236	3,199	427	1,446	248	3,510			30,066

Source: Division of Planning & Research, UGC.
a D=diploma   b M=master's degree   c P=doctorate

Table 2
Total output of graduates from universities according to academic stream and sex: 1976, 1981, 1986 (academic years of 1975/76, 1980/81, 1985/86)

University and Year	Arts	Commerce	Management studies	Law	Science	Medicine	Dental science	Veterinary medicine	Agriculture	Engineering	Architecture	Education	Total
CMB[c] 1976	256 (92)[a]			32 (11)	131 (48)	162 (83)						653 (433)	1,234 (667)
1981	354 (158)			49 (29)	158 (52)	148 (74)						128 (67)	837 (380)
1986	278 (149)	88 (32)		61 (30)	180 (75)	145 (76)						—	752 (362)
PDN[b] 1976	626 (307)				179 (57)	87 (37)	50 —	25 —	92 (30)	115 (15)			1,174 (446)[b]
1981	537 (230)				173 (43)	89 (43)	32 (18)	28 (11)	103 (28)	85 (03)			1,047 (376)
1986	392 (181)	54 (26)			120 (44)	81 (42)	63 (22)	20 (07)	94 (42)	124 (09)			948 (373)
SJP[e] 1976	—	169 (39)			49 (23)								218 (62)
1981	257 (130)	201 (59)			119 (34)								577 (223)
1986	316 (173)	82 (39)	247 (96)		129 (50)								774 (358)
KLN[f] 1976	395 (195)	—			48 (17)								443 (212)
1981	400 (196)	234 (84)			83 (34)								717 (314)
1986	467 (242)	96 (36)			117 (49)								680 (327)
MOR[g] 1976	—									99 (08)	09 (03)		108 (11)
1981	—									102 (15)	11 (04)		113 (19)
1986	—									162 (26)	28 (03)		190 (29)
JAF[h] 1976	—				—	—							—
1981	125 (70)				104 (36)	—							229 (106)
1986	202 (148)	74 (30)	40 (20)		124 (42)	44 (27)							484 (267)
RHN[i] 1976	—				—								—
1981	26 (15)				28 (13)								54 (28)
1986	109 (67)	37 (12)			60 (32)	68 (27)			34 (12)				308 (150)
EUSL[j] 1976	—	—			—								—
1981	—	—			—								—
1986	—	—			29 (12)				14 (04)				43 (16)
Total 1976	1,277 (594)	169 (39)		32 (11)	407 (145)	249 (120)	50 (N.A.)	25 (N.A.)	92 (30)	214 (23)	09 (03)	653 (433)	3,177 (1,398)
1981	1,699 (799)	435 (143)		49 (29)	665 (212)	237 (117)	32 (18)	28 (11)	103 (28)	187 (18)	11 (04)	128 (67)	3,574 (1,446)
1986	1,764 (960)	431 (175)	287 (116)	61 (30)	759 (304)	338 (172)	63 (22)	20 (07)	142 (58)	286 (35)	28 (03)	—	4,179 (1,882)

Source: Division of Planning and Research, UGC.
a Figures within brackets denote female data   b does not include female data on Dental and Veterinary Science.   c Colombo   d Peradeniya   e Sri Jayewardenephra   f Kelaniya   g Mortatuwa   h Jaffna   i Ruhuna   j Eastern University of Sri Lanka

these has been a movement towards equity and greater access. There also has been a relatively fast expansion in higher technical and vocational education thereby removing the synonymity of higher education with university education which long existed.

Sri Lanka is facing problems of slow economic growth and increasing unemployment. Higher education has a crucial role to play in human resource development to remedy these trends. To this end, higher education has to be diversified in the context of the employment situation. The changed emphasis must continue from arts-based courses to science-based courses, and undergraduate teaching to graduate studies and research, in universities; adult and continuing education both through face-to-face teaching and distance learning must be promoted to continuously upgrade skills and also to form part of life-long education. Higher education at the same time should not lose sight of its broader objectives. It has a crucial role to play in shaping the society and influencing the environment for a better quality of life.

The greatest constraint for higher education planning is the inadequacy of financial resources. Therefore, both public and private sectors have to be included in the planning process. The private sector has not only to supplement the limited resources of the public sector but also, by establishing links between the employers and the higher education institutions, make higher education planning socially and economically more meaningful and purposive. It is recognized that an important function of higher education planning is human resource development. It should, however, not ignore its broader socio-cultural aims. While promoting equity, efficiency, excellence, and relevance, higher education has also to promote the growth of such qualities as creativity, critical thinking, intellectual stimulation, and social responsibility. Higher education therefore cannot be planned in isolation. It must be an integral part of an education plan built into the country's overall socioeconomic plan.

Bibliography

Central Bank of Sri Lanka 1988 *Annual Report 1987.* Central Bank, Colombo

Central Bank of Sri Lanka 1989 *Sri Lanka Socio-Economic Data 1988.* Statistics Department-Central Bank of Sri Lanka, Colombo

Department of Census and Statistics, Sri Lanka 1984 *Statistical Pocket Book of the Democratic Socialist Republic of Sri Lanka 1984.* Ministry of Plan Implementation, Colombo

Indraratna A D V de S, de Silva C R, Jayaweera S, Peiris G L 1986 *Case Study in Higher Education Sri Lanka: Report Submitted to* UNESCO, *Bangkok.* University Grants Commission, Colombo

Indraratna A D V de S (ed.) 1988 *Increasing Efficiency of Management of Higher Education Resources.* University Grants Commission, Colombo

Sri Lanka, Ministry of Higher Education 1979 *Report of the Committee on Technical Education.* Mimeograph Ministry of Higher Education, Colombo

Sri Lanka, Ministry of Higher Education, 1989 *Directory of Technical Education, 1988–89.* Ministry of Higher Education, Colombo

University Grants Commission 1982 *Basic Statistics on Higher Education in Sri Lanka 1981.* University Grants Commission, Colombo

University Grants Commission 1983 *Basic Statistics on Higher Education in Sri Lanka 1982.* University Grants Commission, Colombo

University Grants Commission 1984 *Corporate Plan for University Education 1984–1988.* University Grants Commission, Colombo

University Grants Commission 1987a *Corporate Plan for University Education 1986–1990.* University Grants Commission, Colombo

University Grants Commission 1987b *Report of the Committee Appointed to Review University Admissions Policy.* University Grants Commission, Colombo

University Grants Commission 1988 *Capacity for Research Supervision in Higher Educational Institutions.* University Grants Commission, Colombo

University Grants Commission 1989 *Corporate Plan for University Education 1988–1992.* University Grants Commission, Colombo

University Grants Commission *Statistical Hand Books 1983, 1984, 1985, 1986 and 1987.* Statistics on Higher Education in Sri Lanka, Colombo

A. D. V. de S. Indraratna

Sudan

1. Higher Education and Society

The Sudan is the largest country in Africa (2,505,812 square kilometers) with a population of 23.80 million (1989 estimate) of whom 2.2 million are nomadic. The Sudan's ethnic density is reflected in its 19 major ethnic groups and 597 subgroups. Sixty percent of the population is Muslim. Southern Sudan is predominantly animist and 15 percent Christian.

There are over 115 tribal languages of which 26 are spoken by more than 100,000 people. While Arabic is spoken by about 60 percent of the population, and as such is the major language of communication, English is spoken by a small urban elite and is used mainly for commercial purposes and in teaching in universities and institutes of higher education.

The Sudan economy is dependent on agriculture and especially on cotton, oil seeds, and gum arabic as its principal cash crops. Like most African countries, it has suffered from famine, desertification, and the civil war and therefore little economic progress has been achieved. The country lives in perpetual economic crisis and in a state of political instability. It had been ruled, since it became independent in January 1956, by a series of civilian coalition governments and three military regimes.

The burden of a public external debt (US$9.1 million in 1987) has reached serious proportions and further crippled the economy. Other problems include mismanagement, corruption, and the paucity of infrastructure. All this has direct harmful effects on the educational system and the training of a higher-level labor force. The outlook for the future of education seems gloomy unless some drastic measures and major reforms are undertaken.

About 70 percent of the Sudanese population is illiterate. The system of education comprises three levels—primary, secondary, where instruction is in Arabic and English is introduced as a subject, and higher. English is the language of instruction in the universities and higher education institutes, except in the Islamic University in Omdurman. The adoption of Arabic as the language of instruction in secondary schools and the lack of adequate opportunities to learn English have had a negative effect on the ability of students to assimilate knowledge in institutions of higher learning.

2. The Institutional Fabric of the Higher Education System

The Sudanese university and higher education system owes much of its present state to the establishment of the early institutions including: the Gordon Memorial College in 1902; the Islamic Institute in 1912; the Kitchener School of Medicine in 1924; the Khartoum School of Law in 1936; the higher schools in 1938, and the University College (affiliated with the University of London) in 1951. The University of Khartoum, incorporating all the post-1924 institutions of higher education, and awarding its own degrees, came into being in July 1956—six months after the Sudan's independence from Britain and Egypt. Most teaching staff except a few, until 20 years ago, were British. The few Sudanese to be found were in administration. The first Sudanese vice-chancellor was appointed in 1958 and from then on, a new phase in university and higher education began.

In 1956, the Egyptian Government and the Sudanese Government established a branch of Cairo University in Khartoum. In the same year, three other institutions of higher education were established following reports of experts commissioned by the first Sudanese Minister of Education including: the Khartoum Technical Institute; Shambat Agricultural Institute; and the Higher Institute of Nursing. The total number of students in these institutes at the time of Independence was 1,333 of whom 700 were in the University of Khartoum and only 5 percent of the total were female. Khartoum Tech-

Table 1
Student numbers in universities according to sex 1975–76, 1986–87

	1975–76	1986–87
Male	16,509	21,033
Female	3,020	12,900
Total	19,529	33,933

nical Institute had the highest number and percentage of females. The education of women has lagged behind that of men, especially in the rural areas.

Two new nonuniversity institutes of higher learning were established during the years 1963 to 1969 in addition to the already existing three. The Higher Institute of Education in Omdurman and the High Technical College in Khartoum were established to meet the increasing demand for qualified teachers for the expanding secondary-school system and for middle-level technicians.

There was further expansion in university and higher education during the years 1971 to 1978 as a result of the establishment of the Ministry of Higher Education (1972) which is responsible for administering all educational institutions except universities. The University of Juba admitted its first 199 (19 female) students in 1977 and the University of Gezira 202 (28 female) students in 1978. Both universities are located outside of Khartoum with a view to serving the regional interests.

Other new institutions established included: the Atbara Mechanical Engineering College (1976); the Institute of Physical Education (1976); the Institute of Music and Drama (1976); the Higher Institute of Radiography (1977–78); the Abu Nama Agricultural College (1977–78); and the Abu Haraz Agricultural College (1978–79). Tables 1 and 2 provide the details regarding students admitted and total number during the 1976 to 1987 period. The emphasis in higher education in the Sudan was carefully planned to satisfy the need and the demand for well-trained personnel by the public and private sector. However, graduates from the Khartoum Branch of the Cairo University and from universities and institutes out-

Table 2
Student numbers in the institutes of higher education, nonuniversities, according to sex 1975–76, 1986–87

	1975–76	1986–87
Male	1,937	1,219
Female	335	368
Total	2,272	1,587

side of Sudan have contributed to the growing numbers of unemployed graduates, which totalled 36,000 in 1986/87. In 1987 20,000 undergraduate students studied abroad.

The Ahfad University for Women (1974) and the Omdurman Ahlia University (1986) provide higher education at degree and diploma levels for those seeking education relevant to the needs of Sudanese society. Both are job-oriented, self-supporting institutions functioning outside the official and government systems. They are governed by Boards of Trustees drawn from the community, professionals, academics, and business people.

Before the graduate college was established in 1974, the majority of students pursuing graduate studies did so abroad.

The graduate college was established in order to provide and coordinate the already existing degrees in the various faculties. The numbers of students registered for higher degrees has increased from 387 in 1975/76 to nearly 1,206 students in 1987 covering all disciplines.

The college has a general council responsible for its administrative affairs and special councils and committees responsible for academic affairs. The council for medical graduate studies was established in order to ensure that the requirements in the areas of medical studies are provided. In the meantime, special graduate institutes and centers were established with the purpose of providing research and training facilities in particular areas and disciplines. They include: (a) the Institute of African and Asian Studies; (b) the Development Studies and Research Centre; (c) the Building Research Centre; (d) the Institute of Animal Studies; and (e) the Institute of Environmental Studies.

3. Governance, Administration, and Finance

3.1 National Administration

The universities and institutes of higher education provide free education and residence and are financed by the Sudanese Government. The allocation of funds is made annually within the national budget of the government and the development budget.

The funds approved are allocated to each university and institute by the grants committee of the National Council of Higher Education. Universities and institutes have limited additional financial resources obtained from students' fees and donations from internal and external bodies concerned with higher education.

The universities' and institutes' need for books and equipment is provided by the government from foreign currencies when available. This total dependence on government resources and foreign currencies has hampered the development of disciplines relevant to the needs of society.

3.2 Institutional Administration

The administration of higher education has been entrusted since 1975 to a National Council of Higher Education which has the responsibility of planning, supervision, and development. The Council is responsible for defining the role of each institution of higher learning.

Each university and institution of higher education has its own council or Board of Governors. The universities, unlike the other institutions, enjoy autonomy of their administration especially in the areas of staff appointments and promotion and curriculum development. The fast growth in the number of students and in the number of institutions has created management problems. The absence of sound national economic policies, and the inability of universities and institutes of higher education to generate new and additional resources, made it difficult, if not impossible, for them to fulfill their objectives. The financial constraints have adversely affected graduate and undergraduate programs, facilities, and equipment. There are serious shortages in laboratory equipment and text books.

4. Faculty and Students: Teaching, Learning, and Research

The majority of the academic staff in the University of Khartoum at the time of Independence in 1956 were expatriates drawn mainly through the then Inter-University Council in the United Kingdom, from the United Kingdom, and afterwards from European countries. The appointment of the first Sudanese vice-chancellor in 1958 was followed by the appointment of qualified Sudanese to senior administrative posts and to leading academic posts in the various faculties. A scheme for training qualified and outstanding graduates for future academic and administrative posts was started in 1960. About 20 to 30 graduates carefully selected were sent to the United Kingdom and other countries to pursue graduate degrees. Financial support for the scheme came from the universities' own budgets and from the British Government and bodies such as the Ford Foundation and the German exchange scholarships scheme. No less than 60 members of staff were trained every year through the schemes. By 1978 70 percent of the staff of the University of Khartoum were Sudanese. The rest came from different countries.

While the dependence on the outside world in the case of staff ended, dependence in the area of books and equipment continued. The lack of books and equipment threatens the continuity of the university life. It is not unusual to learn about book famine in academic quarters. Imaginative schemes, similar to that developed for staff training, have to be found. This area and the provision of equipment for teaching and research purposes are fields where the international community can actively be involved and helpful.

5. Conclusion

There is no doubt that the universities and institutes of higher education have contributed extensively to the limited change and development in the Sudan. Since its Independence in 1956 constructive and positive aspects of these institutions have, due to disjointed policies and bad management, been very limited, and in some cases, negative. The universities and higher education institutes continue to suffer from a lack of adequate resources. The civil war, the debt burden, famine and desertification have resulted in the reduction and reallocation of available resources away from the education sector.

The Sudan, in common with all African countries, will be left behind by the beginning of the twenty-first century unless it succeeds in rebuilding its economy and ensures a situation of sustainable growth and development.

The universities and institutions of higher education have a major role to play in this process. They should evolve within their walls disciplines and research programs which would provide the skills and concepts relevant to positive change and development.

It is suggested that the higher education institutions' slow and cautious way of handling change is no longer relevant to the general situation in the world. They have no choice but to venture into new, nontraditional fields of learning, for example, management studies, engineering and technology, information and communication systems, regional studies and planning, transport and telecommunication systems, and environmental studies. They need to modify their teaching practices and provide opportunities for students to learn by doing. To keep students for eight hours a day in a classroom or library and not expose them to the farm, the factory, or the shop is bad education. Modern techniques need to be adopted in the university systems of administration, that is, computers, and data systems.

The willingness, ability, and success of the universities and institutions of higher education to adapt and change along these lines will, to a great extent, determine the position of the Sudan in the twenty-first century.

Assistance and support to the universities and higher institutes from the international community is a prerequisite in order to overcome their serious problems and start the rebuilding and reconstruction of what they have lost as the result of the catastrophes referred to. Hence the appeal to the international community, and especially the universities abroad in the developed world, to urgently come to the rescue of the universities and institutes of higher education in the Sudan.

Bibliography

Advisory Committee on Education in the Colonies *Report*. HMSO, London

Ali M A 1980 University Education and Employment in the Sudan 1969–1979 (MSc thesis) University of Khartoum, Khartoum

Ali M A 1984 Manpower Forecasting: Approach to Planning of Higher Education. *The Sudan Economic and Social Research Council Bulletin* 1984: 116

Ali N A H 1981 Aspects of Higher Education in Sudan. In: Al Tom M A A (ed.) 1981 *The Development of the University of Khartoum and Issues in Higher Education*. Khartoum University Press, Khartoum, pp. 19–32

Ali N A H 1962 *Higher Education in the Sudan*. Sudan Philosophical Society Conference. (mimeo)

Al Mubarak K 1985 *Higher Education in Sudan*. Dar Al Bahar, Beirut

Ashby E 1966 *Universities: British, Indian, African*. Harvard University Press, Cambridge, Massachusetts

Asquith Commission Report on Higher Education in the Colonies. HMSO (Cmnd 6647), London

Bakneit G M A 1965 British Administration and Sudanese Nationalization 1919–39. (PhD thesis) Cambridge University

Beshir M O 1969 *Educational Development in the Sudan*. Clarendon Press, Oxford

Beshir M O 1981 The University of Khartoum—History and Development 1956–81. In: Al Tom M A A (ed.) 1981 *The Development of the University of Khartoum and Issues in Higher Education*. Khartoum University Pres, Khartoum

Beshir M O 1977 *Employment Profession in the Sudan*. Khartoum

Bowles et al 1967 *Access to Higher Education Vol J*. UNESCO, Paris

Dafalla A N 1981 Philosophy of Higher Education in Sudan. In: Al Tom M A A (ed.) 1981 *The Development of the University of Khartoum and Issues in Higher Education*. Khartoum University Press, Khartoum, pp 1–10

El Tayib S 1963 *The Student Movement in the Sudan*. Khartoum University Press, Khartoum

Gordon Memorial College 1901–1946 Report

Hamid G M 1970 *Economics of Higher Education in the Sudan*. (MSc thesis) University of Khartoum

Lord de la Warre's Commission 1937 *Report*. Khartoum

International Labour Organisation 1976 *Growth, Employment and Equality—a Comprehensive Strategy for the Sudan*. International Labour Organisation, Geneva

Mills L R 1973 *Population and Manpower in the Southern Sudan*. International Labor Organization, Geneva

Passmore L, Sanderson N 1981 *Education, Religion and Politics in Southern Sudan 1899–1964*. Ithaca Press, London

Philosophical Society of Sudan 1963 *Education in the Sudan* (Proceedings of the annual conference, January 1963). Khartoum. (mimeo)

Reports of the Governor General on Finance, Administration and Conditions of The Sudan 1921–1952.

University of Khartoum *Calendar 1952–53*

University of Khartoum *Calendar 1977–78*

University of Khartoum *Vice chancellor's report 1958*

University of Khartoum *Vice chancellor's report 1963*

M. O. Beshir

Swaziland

1. Higher Education and Society

Swaziland is a small, landlocked country surrounded on three sides by the Republic of South Africa and by Mozambique on its eastern border. The relationship with its immediate neighbors is somewhat uneasy. The country has considerable natural resources and enjoys an excellent climate, which has enabled the development of the agricultural sector (Booth 1983).

The population is under one million (681,059 at the 1986 census) and, like many other Third World countries, half the population is under 15 years of age. According to the Central Statistical Office the population growth rate is 3.3 percent, which poses considerable problems for economic planning in general and for education in particular (Swaziland, Economic Planning Section 1989).

A former British High Commission Territory, Swaziland achieved Independence in 1968 and has remained a member of the British Commonwealth.

The expansion of education has received considerable attention in the post-Independence period. King Mswati III, who came to the throne in 1986 (having previously studied in an English public school) has given new impetus to development and education. His Majesty is the chancellor of the University.

2. The Institutional Fabric of the Higher Education System

Little attention was paid to higher education during the colonial era. Indeed, the education officer reporting to the colonial office in London in 1955 could go so far as to say: "There are no universities in Swaziland, nor can any development in this direction be contemplated because of the smallness of the Territory and its population" (Swaziland 1955). The need for technical education had been recognized, however, and the Trades School for Africans was built in 1946 with the support of the Colonial Development and Welfare Fund, as the same colonial officer was pleased to report.

It was possible for Swazi students to attend the Fort Hare University College up until 1958; the closure of its doors lent some urgency to the need to provide for the most able students from the three territories of Basutoland, Bechuanaland, and Swaziland.

As early as 1945 a move had been made to provide for higher education in what was then Basutoland (now Lesotho) when the small Pope Pius XII College was established by the Roman Catholic Mission. The college had very humble beginnings when a group of four priest-lecturers taught five students in a converted schoolroom. This staff–student ratio was not maintained! The college grew slowly but surely, and soon the original plan to prepare students for a Bachelor of Arts degree only, was widened to include courses leading to Bachelor of Commerce, Bachelor of Science, and Diploma in Education. The validating body was the University of South Africa. When discussions began on the provision of higher education for the three territories, the college was an obvious focal point. By 1963, the college property had been made over (with certain guarantees to the Roman Catholic Church) and on January 1, 1964 the University of Basutoland, Bechuanaland, and Swaziland came into being. There were 31 academic staff members and 188 students.

In 1966 Bechuanaland and Basutoland gained Independence and accordingly the institution was renamed the University of Botswana, Lesotho, and Swaziland (UBLS), conferring its first degrees in April 1967. Although the UBLS was equally funded by the governments of the three countries it had comparatively little presence in either Botswana or Swaziland in the period between 1964 and 1970, except for the Swaziland Agricultural College and University Centre (SACUC). This college opened in 1966. In 1970 the government of Swaziland decided to hand over the college and an associated research station, to the University. From 1972 onwards, these institutions constituted a new faculty of agriculture.

With Independence came a close questioning of the colonial inheritance of education and a recognition of the need to identify the role of the University in the training of higher- and middle-level personnel. Consultations and a series of reports ensued; the most significant of these being the second Alexander Report of 1970, which concurred with "the major recommendations of previous reports for the development of university campuses in each country and the unified development of higher education and vocational and technical training" (Alexander 1970). Consequently teaching of part 1 studies began in Swaziland in 1971 and the new campus at Kwaluseni became fully operational in 1973. The two existing teacher-training colleges became affiliated with the University. In 1975 Lesotho withdrew somewhat precipitately from the joint venture and constituted the National University of Lesotho. The

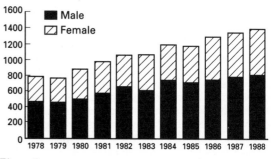

Figure 1
University enrollment 1978–88, males and females

appropriation of all the property and buildings by the Lesotho authorities resulted in the withdrawal of all Swazi and Botswana students and a swift reorganization of teaching and courses took place at the two constituent colleges of the new University of Botswana and Swaziland. It was now inevitable—and, indeed, desirable—that two separate universities be developed and in 1982 the planned separation was completed on schedule.

The Fourth National Development Plan for Swaziland, dealing with the period 1983 to 1988, envisaged the goal of higher education as fulfilling the nation's need for a professional and highly-skilled labor force. By 1989, in addition to the University, there were three teacher-training colleges, two for primary-school teachers and one for secondary-school teachers. The Trades School referred to earlier, founded in 1946, has now developed into the Swaziland College of Technology (SCOT). The Institute of Health Sciences (SIHS), opened in January 1980, training nurses, midwives, health inspectors, and dental hygienists.

The University offers bachelor's degrees in five faculties, namely agriculture, education, humanities, science, and social sciences. There are plans to introduce master's programs in the near future, but such studies are all undertaken overseas. The teacher-training colleges offer a diploma program and students who obtain a credit or better are allowed to transfer to year 2 of the degree program in the University. The College of Technology admits students to two different levels—craft level and technical courses. The Institute of Health Sciences offers diploma courses.

Research is an integral part of the work of the University and there is also a commendable commitment to research in both teacher-training colleges and the College of Technology. Additionally, the National Research Council (with subcommittees for agriculture, education, social and economic studies, humanities, science and technology, and health and population) seeks to coordinate and facilitate research for development. This council relies heavily upon the University for its personnel and general functioning.

2.1 Admissions Policies and Selection

The colonial legacy of education in Swaziland has been examined and adapted at many levels but in the area of high-school curriculum and examinations it retains a strangle-hold. A British system developed several decades ago is still in place in this one-time protectorate. At the end of five years of primary schooling children sit a public examination (set and marked locally) on the basis of which they are selected/rejected for secondary schools. After three years of secondary schooling another local examination is given (the Junior Certificate) and a further selection is made for high schools. Two years of high

Table 1
Student enrollment in university and teacher-training colleges

	1968	1973	1978	1983	1988
University	—[a]	270	782	1,107	1,357
Teacher-training colleges	78	164	233	558	—[a]

Source: Ministry of Education and University Registry
a Data unavailable

school precede yet another public examination—the Cambridge Overseas School Certificate—which, as the name implies, is set and marked by the Cambridge Examination Syndicate in the United Kingdom.

Selection for university and college courses is made on the basis of performance in this school-certificate examination. The minimum requirement for university entrance is a first- or second-class certificate with a credit in English language; the faculties have additional special regulations. Some O-level passes/credits are also required for entry to teacher training, the Institute of Health Sciences and the technical courses at the College of Technology. The ultimate decisions about admissions are made by the authorities of the individual institutions but there is a good deal of political pressure to admit ever-increasing numbers from the rapidly expanding pool of applicants.

2.2 Quantitative Developments in Higher Education

The post-Independence period (since 1968) has seen an enormous expansion in the provision of secondary-school places from a little over six thousand in 1968 to more than thirty-one thousand 20 years later—with a consequent increase in the number of those qualifying for, and expecting to have, tertiary-level training. The actual numbers of those admitted to the University and teacher-training colleges are shown in Table 1.

These figures reflect the national commitment to the development of the local university and the awareness of the need for more trained primary school teachers, which led to the opening of a third teacher-training college in 1983.

3. Governance, Administration, and Finance

3.1 National Administration

The ultimate responsibility for higher education rests with the Ministry of Education. There is considerable control of teacher education with a Ministry Inspector designated for that area. The University enjoys a semiautonomy with the senate and administrative officers being free to make and implement some decisions in the academic area. However, any move to change the admissions policy, for example, would require approval from the Minister and Principal Secretary. There are definite expectations with regard to the University's role in producing high-level personnel and thus contributing to the goal of national self-sufficiency. This role is carefully spelled out in the National Development Plans.

For the period 1978 to 1983, education consumed 24.4 percent of the average recurrent spending per annum and 16.7 percent of the average capital spending per annum (Government of Swaziland 1984). Of this recurrent figure 11 percent was allocated to higher education and 3 percent to teacher training; the proportions of the capital spending are 6.7 percent on higher education and 4.7 percent on teacher training. In addition to this, the government makes a considerable investment in the University by means of the Scholarship Secretariat, which provides grants to all Swazi students regardless of their financial circumstances. Almost all building developments at the University have been, and continue to be, done with donor funding.

3.2 Institutional Administration

As mentioned above, the University has some degree of autonomy to manage its own affairs. All matters of academic and day-to-day interest are dealt with by faculty boards, which in turn refer to the senate. All teaching staff are members of their respective boards and each faculty elects a professor and one other member to the senate; deans are ex officio members of the senate. The University also exercises some responsibility for the other colleges through the Board of Affiliated Institutions. The University also moderates their examinations and validates their diplomas.

4. Faculty and Students: Teaching, Learning, and Research

4.1 Faculty

The data in Table 2 reflect the development of the independent University in Swaziland, which had its beginnings in the joint venture originally located in Lesotho. In addition to the growth of overall numbers of staff, there has been a concurrent move to increase the proportion of Swazi citizens among the academic staff and, in particular, women.

The University is free to advertise for and appoint its own staff. The Ministry of Education has some say in appointments at the other institutions. The need to localize the academic posts at the University led to the establishment of a thorough scheme for the professional development of Swazi staff, enabling qualified graduates to undertake study programs overseas leading to master's and/or doctoral degrees and thus equipping them to move from teaching assistant's posts to lectureships. Permanent, pensionable posts are granted to citizens only. All expatriate staff are employed on short-term contracts with the same salary and a gratuity paid upon completion of contract. However, there is no bar to expatriates holding high office.

Promotion through the ranks of lecturer, senior lecturer, associate professor, and full professor is determined by a special committee and based upon research and publication record, teaching ability, and general commitment to the academic life. There is a trade union, which represents the interests of academic staff. It has a fairly wide membership but excludes those holding administrative positions (deans, registry staff, etc.).

4.2 Students

The University has only five faculties—agriculture, education, humanities, science, and social science (including law and commerce). Students wishing to study such subjects as medicine or engineering usually complete part 1 of their degree in Swaziland and then transfer to an institute in another country.

As with enrollments, graduate production has risen steadily since the separation of the national elements of the former University of Botswana, Lesotho, and Swaziland (see Table 3). Most students are Swazis, though there is a significant proportion of students from Botswana as a result of an agreement between the governments of Swaziland and Botswana, and a very small percentage are political refugees from other African countries. At the present

Table 2
University of Swaziland: academic staffing (Library and Division of Extra-Mural Studies excluded)

	1974–75	1979–80	1984–85	1989–90
Professors	1	8	10	17
Senior lecturers	6	16	13	22
Readers/lecturers	25	54	92	90
Assistants/study leave	3	10	34	56
Total	35	88	149	185

Source: University Registry

Table 3
Student enrollment by year and area of study (diploma and degree courses)

	1975	1980	1985	1990
Science (including agriculture)	—	433	515	595
Social sciences	—	304	444	768
Humanities	—	148	182	353
Total	387	885	1,141	1,716

Table 4
Graduate production (degrees only) by year and area of study

	1970	1975	1980	1985	1990
Science	21[a]	16[a]	10[b]	70	65
Social science	21[a]	36[a]	25[b]	58	114
Humanities	34[a]	45[a]	30[b]	39	55
Total	76[a]	97[a]	65[b]	167[c]	234[c]

a University of Botswana, Lesotho and Swaziland b University College of Swaziland—first stage of creation of national university c University of Swaziland

time 44 percent of all students are female; this percentage has risen slowly but has never been less than 36 percent of enrollment.

There is a system of continuous assessment coupled with end-of-year examinations operating in all departments. These are weighted equally in some subjects while in others they are evaluated on a 40:60 proportional basis. It is necessary to obtain an aggregate pass mark for the whole program before being allowed to proceed further. Examinations are moderated by external examiners, most of whom are drawn from other universities in the region.

There is a students' representative council which looks after students' interests in all spheres and liaises with the central administration through a dean of student affairs. There is student representation on both the senate and university council.

Conclusion

The overriding constraint on the development and expansion of university programs is financial. There is need for much physical development and the University has recently launched a huge fundraising campaign. This has been well covered by the media and general public and has served to highlight the role of the University in national development; it is receiving a generous response from the public and private sector.

The University's stated aim is to produce a high level laborforce to meet the nation's needs and it must, therefore, respond to felt needs in the economy. Such a response has led to plans to create a separate faculty of commerce (formerly part of the social sciences) and to upgrade the professional training it gives to undergraduates. The faculty of humanities has recently introduced courses in modern languages. It is likely that future developments will include the introduction of some engineering courses, possibly in conjunction with the College of Technology which offers diploma level programs at present. Another useful area of cooperation would be in the field of nursing and paramedical training.

Diploma level courses are currently offered at the Institute of Health Sciences.

In such a small country it is not feasible for the University to stand alone and expect to meet all the diversified needs for trained personnel. Cooperation with other institutions in the country and with similar bodies in neighboring countries should mark out the path ahead. The future course of events in the Republic of South Africa could be significant in this regard.

Bibliography

Alexander N 1970 *Second Report of the Academic Planner to UBLS.* University Registry
Bonner P 1983 *Kings, Commoners and Concessionaires.* Raven Press, Johannesburg
Booth A R 1983 *Swaziland, Tradition and Change in a Southern African Kingdom.* Gower, Westview
Davies R H et al. 1985 *The Kingdom of Swaziland—a Profile.* Zed Books, London
Hailey (Lord) 1953 *Native Administration in the British African Territories.* Pt. 5. Stationery Office, London
Hailey (Lord) 1963 *The Republic of South Africa and the High Commission Territories.* Oxford University Press, Oxford
Matsebula J S M 1988 *A History of Swaziland*, 3rd edn. Longman, London
Swaziland 1955 *Annual Report of the Principal Education Officer.* Colonial Office, London
Swaziland 1984 *Fourth National Development Plan—1983/84–1987/88.* Government of Swaziland
Swaziland 1989 *Development Plan—1989–92*, Economic Planning Section, Government of Swaziland

A. C. Smith

Sweden

1. Higher Education and Society

The Swedish system of higher education is basically a public system, as there is only one major private institution. The higher education system consists of a dominant state sector and a small local government sector. Its present condition is the outcome of unintended processes of institutional development as well as of changes brought about by means of comprehensive policymaking. In all aspects the higher education institutions have developed tremendously since the Second World War.

The strong organizational expansion of the higher education system after the Second World War is only partly a function of the overall social transformation. The institutional growth reflects not only the advent of a postindustrial society, but also the attempts which were made to govern the process of higher education change by outlining specific goals.

Sweden is a unitary state. As a neutral member of the world community of nation-states it stayed out

Table 1
Population data 1900–88

	1900	1920	1940	1960	1980	1988
Total	5,136,441	5,904,489	6,371,432	7,497,967	8,317,937	8,458,888
Number of women per thousand men	1,049	1,037	1,016	1,004	1,019	1,026

Source: Statistical Abstract of Sweden, Table 18, 1990

of the major wars of the twentieth century, which means that its borders have remained unchanged since 1809 when Finland was lost to Russia.

Table 1 has data on the size of the population. There has for many years been a small increase in the size of the Swedish population, partly due to immigration after the Second World War.

Swedish politics has to a considerable extent reflected the class divisions in industrial society, as the division of the population in social strata had organizational implications for the structure of interest groups. Tables 2 and 3 present an overview of the major transformation of the social structure since 1930. Blue collar workers increased their share of the workforce up until roughly 1950; then a post-industrial society began to emerge in which the white collar workers and the civil servants constitute the bulk of the working force.

The overall international impression of Swedish politics has been one of stability, coherence, and accomplishment, confirming the practicality of the so-called "Swedish model." The Swedish model is a regulative notion comprising a set of concepts and ideas about what is good government in a wide sense as well as about the proper way of structuring the public sector and connecting the public and private lives of the population. For the first time since the end of the Second World War it meets with extensive uncertainty and hesitance.

The Swedish model has been perpetuated by a center-dominated party system, itself actively supported by a large Social Democratic Party and generally speaking by two of the three major nonsocialist parties, the Liberals and the Center Party. Against the Social Democrats three bourgeois parties have competed for the nonsocialist vote. The balance between the socialist and nonsocialist camps has been a delicate one. The vote of the three nonsocialist parties has wavered considerably. The spread in voter support for the various bourgeois parties is most extensive: from 29 percent to 11 percent for the Conservative Party, from 10 percent to 25 percent for the Agrarians or the Center Party, and from 6 percent to 24 percent for the Liberals.

The Swedish model recommends strong governments, which has meant that governments have been either large minority or bare majority ones except during the war when there was a grand coalition. If the tacit support of the Communist Party for the Social Democrat government is recognized, then most governments have been minimum-winning and minimum-sized. However, in the 1980s the Community Party or *Vänsterpartiet* showed reluctance to support the Social Democrat government. Some look upon the politics of the 1980s as a return to the committee parliamentarianism typical of the interwar years before the Social Democratic government hegemony initiated in 1933. The competition between the two blocs in the party system, the socialist versus the bourgeoisie, has at times been replaced by cooperation that has been issue-oriented and confined to separate deals on concrete questions negotiated in the Riksdag (parliament). Between 1976 and 1982 there were three nonsocialist governments.

The Swedish model impressed an international audience because it seemed so successful in stimulating a high rate of growth in the economy. Political consensus was paralleled by a social consensus between the trade unions and the employers' association to avoid industrial conflict and jointly reap the

Table 2
Estimates of Swedish class structure as percentages

	1930	1950	1965	1975	1985
Working class	57	56	54	54	51
Middle class	12	22	31	38	38
Owners	31	22	15	8	11

Source: Ahrne et al. 1985 pp. 34 and 62

Table 3
Swedish occupational structure as percentages

	1940	1945	1950	1960	1970	1980
Agriculture	28.8	24.5	20.3	13.7	8.1	5.5
Industry	35.7	38.2	40.8	45.1	40.3	33.5
Commerce	13.6	14.4	16.0	13.5	19.3	20.3
Transport	6.7	7.3	8.0	7.4	7.2	7.2
Services	12.7	15.5	14.7	19.8	24.8	33.4

Source: Lane and Löfqvist 1985 p. 98

benefits from sustained economic growth. In 1938 an agreement was signed by the trade union group (LO) and the Swedish Employers' Federation (SAF) to cooperate as extensively as possible and work out their differences of opinion in various institutions.

The so-called *Saltsjöbaden* compromise lasted for about 30 years reinforced by other agreements and by vigorous Keynesian economic policy-making intended to enhance full employment and economic growth. This was the golden era of the Swedish model in terms of the average economic growth rate which was as follows: 1950–60, 3.4; 1960–70, 4.7; 1970–80, 2.0; and 1980–87, 1.8.

In the 1970s the practicality of the Swedish model began to dwindle as social consensus was replaced by trade union assertiveness and a reorientation of the employers' association towards market values. The development of the industrial climate is not only reflected in the growth figures for the period but also in strike data. The growth in public expenditure made it possible to meet a number of demands from large citizen groups without fundamentally restructuring the economy or the system of private ownership of the means of production. The public sector was rather small in Sweden after the Second World War in comparison with other West European countries. However, in 1982, when the seminal public sector growth process came to an end, Sweden had been transformed to a public-oriented society with the largest public sector of all the OECD countries.

2. *The Institutional Fabric of the Higher Education System*

Swedish universities and colleges have never had a legally autonomous status in the nature of Anglo-Saxon universities. Members of the Swedish academic profession are regarded as state employees rather than as an independent professional group, although the position of full professor (or *Ordinarius*) carries extensive liberties. The structure in place at the beginning of the 1990s is the outcome of two processes, the organizational growth of the 1960s and the political reforms of the 1970s (Lane 1989). The

Table 4
Structure of the Swedish higher education system in 1991

	State principal	Private principal	Local government counties
Units with permanent research	11	1	—
Units without permanent research	24	—	42

Table 5
Structure of the higher education system in 1977

	State principal	Private principal	Local government principal
Universities	6	—	—
Professional schools with research	10	1	—
Professional schools without research	80	7	41

standard elements of the higher education system are universities and colleges structured according to the scheme in Table 4.

Before the decade of organizational reform in the 1970s the Swedish system was quite heterogeneous, including as it did a large number of different institutions (see Table 5).

Coping with the sudden and drastic increase in student enrollment in the late 1950s and early 1960s involved enlarging already existing institutions and founding new ones (see Table 6).

Although after the extensive political reforms of the 1970s the Swedish higher system is an almost exclusively public system, there is complexity and variation. Table 7 presents data that indicate the manifold nature of the Swedish postsecondary education system.

The state sector of the higher education system consists of 35 universities and colleges. The bulk of the student body is enrolled within the state sector, but a considerable portion of the new entrants go to the local government sector where shorter vocationally oriented courses in health care training are given.

The formal institutional structure is based upon a distinction between research and graduate instruction on the one hand and undergraduate training on the other. The division into faculties follows the traditional international model. Education is divided into five basic sectors comprising five vocational

Table 6
Structure of the higher education system in 1950

	State principal	Private principal	Local government principal
Universities	2	—	—
Professional schools with research	9	3	—
Professional schools without research	12	2	19

Table 7
The state higher education sector in 1987

Unit	Number of undergraduates	Number of employees	Number of faculties	Number of educational sectors
Stockholm University	20,385	3,545	4	5
Royal Technological Institute	6,880	2,895	1	1
Caroline Medical Institute	2,370	3,165	1	2
Stockholm Teacher Institute	3,750	635	1	1
Uppsala University	14,370	4,825	8	5
Linköping University	10,140	2,220	3	5
Lund University	22,740	7,135	8	5
Gothenburg University	18,000	4,910	6	5
Chalmers'	6,255	2,335	1	1
Umeå University	7,790	3,155	5	5
Agricultural University	2,530	3,600	1	1
Luleå College	3,625	895	1	3
Eskilstuna/Västerås	1,680	140	—	3
Falun/Borlänge	1,320	145	—	3
Gävle/Sandviken	1,690	215	—	2
Örebro	4,450	450	—	4
Jönköping	1,740	140	—	3
Halmstad	705	70	—	1
Kalmar	1,380	310	—	—
Kristiansstad	1,450	125	—	3
Växjö	3,825	337	—	4
Borås	1,545	160	—	3
Karlstad	3,380	355	—	4
Skövde	820	60	—	1
Sundsvall/Härnösand	1,710	250	—	3
Östersund	1,180	105	—	1
Schools of Artistic Training (8 units)	1,695	810	—	1
Other	—	575	—	—
Total	147,405	43,562		

Source: Statistics Sweden 1988: 8, 1988: 13. A new college Karlskrona/Ronneby was added in 1989

areas: technical; administrative, economic, and social; health care; and educational. Cultural and informational vocations are also provided for.

The state sector is composed of 11 institutions that have both research and educational programs, the universities and the technological institutes, and the Caroline Medical Institute. The remaining colleges, with the exception of the Stockholm Teacher Training School at which there are permanent professorships, provide in principle only for undergraduate training programs. However, at the colleges that lack both permanent resources for research and a graduate training program there is academic drift as they search eagerly for ways to obtain those resources and advanced training as well as nonpermanent professorships.

The small schools for artistic training in Stockholm are special as they are very small and most of them have professors. The number of students enrolled ranges from 35 at the Opera School to 500 at the School for Music in the capital. The private Stock-

holm School of Commerce has about 1,600 students enrolled. The universities of Uppsala and Lund have a more comprehensive program structure than the other universities. Of nine possible faculties and five possible educational sectors these universities cover eight faculties and all of the educational sectors.

Undergraduate training is conducted in terms of educational lines and single courses. A line of training or a program is a set of courses lasting between 1 to 5.5 years and oriented towards vocational preparation in some form. There are three types of educational programs: general lines (120), local lines (45), and additional lines (25). The system of single courses identifies a liberal arts type of education. These courses vary considerably in length, from one week to one semester.

2.1 Admissions Policies and Selection

There is screened admission to all types of higher education. Before 1969 there was a large free sector which was open to any competent applicant.

However, the system now excludes some 10,000–15,000 applicants each year as the provision for higher education training does not meet student demand any longer. Actually, there has been no increase in the total number of higher education opportunities since 1977, meaning that Swedish higher education enrolls about 2,000 per 100,000 inhabitants whereas the United States higher education system enrolls about twice the amount. All Swedish youngsters pass through a nine-year primary school. Of the relevant age cohort 90 percent go on to some kind of secondary training with about 80 percent pursuing it to the end. Roughly 40 percent start some type of higher education training.

The admission rules, introduced in 1977 were changed in 1991. They received much international attention due to the so-called "25/4 rule" which resulted in a high average age of the new entrants into higher education (i.e., 22–23 years of age). The rule allowed for entrance into higher education of applicants of 25 years of age with at least four years of occupational activity. It was about general competency and it governed the entrance into the higher education system along with special competency rules specified for some lines and courses. General competence was given as either a gymnasium-leaving certificate or, under the 25/4 rule, work experience. Students who met the general and special competency regulations were divided into three groups for selection: 33 percent were selected on the basis of their gymnasium certificate, about 60 percent were selected by means of their certificates and their experience from working life, and about 7 percent were selected from the group of students with 25/4 competence with reference to their working life experience and a national higher education test (Kim 1982, Cerych and Sabatier 1986).

The new system will provide all those who leave the three-year gymnasium with a general competency for higher education training. Students will be selected on the basis of their certificates or with reference to their score on the national higher education test combined with work experience. The relative proportion of students entering on the basis of these two distinct criteria will vary from one training program to another as will the special competency rules. However, although at least one-third of the students must be selected on the basis of their gymnasium certificates, a much stronger emphasis will be placed on the national higher education test.

The selection of students for entry to the general education programs is handled by a central agency, the National Swedish Board for Higher Education (NBUC), whereas the universities and colleges select students for the local educational programs and single courses. The relevance of single courses has increased at the same time as the gulf between educational lines and single courses has narrowed. About 40 percent of the new entrants go to single courses, which is a rather high figure considering the 1977 reform attempt to push most of the students into vocationally oriented lines of education. However, several students attend both general educational programs and single courses.

2.2 Quantitative Developments in Higher Education

The number of students increased very rapidly in the 1960s before reaching a steady state in the 1970s. Under the amalgamation reform of 1977 certain training programs that used to be regarded as outside of the proper higher education sector were upgraded with the result that the number of students enrolled in higher education increased. In the 1980s there was a gradual increase in both the number of undergraduates and graduates (see Table 8).

Among the beginners, the relative proportion of older students, that is, students of more than 25 years of age, has been larger than the proportion of young students. However, in 1982 it was decided to narrow down one-third of the beginners to students under 25 years of age. Females outnumber males with a proportion of 60 percent to 40 percent. However, study preferences are very different between the two sexes as men dominate the technically oriented lines and courses whereas women are more numerous in nursing and in teacher education. Women take a greater number of basic degrees than men. The number of degrees per year within both the health care and teacher education sectors is far higher than that of any other sector, and in these two sectors women dominate. Among the new entrants 22 percent go to train in technical vocations; 20 percent in administrative, economic, and social vocations; 27 percent in health care vocations; 24 percent in educational

Table 8
Number of students enrolled in higher education 1960–88 in undergraduate and graduate education

	1960	1965	1970	1975	1980[a]	1985	1988
Total number	36,909	66,413	120,200	110,012	167,000[b]	176,400	179,100
Women	—	24,573	45,847	43,679	90,000[b]	95,716	98,862

Source: *Fickskolan 1988*
a The sharp increase between 1975 and 1980 is mainly due to the comprehensive amalgamation reform in 1977 upgrading local government training into higher education   b Exact numbers are not available

vocations; and 7 percent in cultural and informational vocations.

2.3 Graduate Training Programs

Graduate training attracts roughly 2,500 beginners each year. The total number of graduate students is about 13,000, most of whom are males (roughly 70 percent). A graduate program formally lasts for four years, but few are able to reach examination standard within that time. In order to increase the number of graduate examinations a version of an old short-term type of graduate degree was reintroduced in 1981 which would take only two years to complete; its predecessor was abolished in 1969 when a new kind of PhD degree was introduced. The number of doctoral degrees attained each year is about 1,000, of which 18 percent are the work of women. Of those who receive a PhD from the technical and natural science faculties two-thirds are less than 35 years of age whereas the opposite holds true of those that obtain a PhD in the other faculties. Graduate students may receive either a grant or a special position as a means to financing their studies.

3. Governance, Administration, and Finance

3.1 National and Institutional Administration

Until the 1975–77 reform the typical system of higher education was collegial, focusing the administrative and political power on full professors. Swedish universities and professional schools with permanent research were run by the tenured staff from which the governing board and its chair, the rector, were drawn. Academics recruited the decision-making boards in accordance with professional criteria. The colleges without permanent research resources were run by a rector or a board appointed by the government.

However, academic internal governance was offset by a low level of institutional autonomy with provision for recognition of the principle of *Lehrfreiheit*. The government and its central agencies made decisions in a large number of crucial domains including the appointment of tenured staff on the basis of proposals from the university, the orientation of the curriculum, the construction of physical facilities, and student enrollment into lines of training with screened admission.

The Swedish higher education system is a public administration system in which centrally placed public bodies coordinate the activities of the local units. Above the local institutions, which are primarily state universities and colleges, there is a national agency— the National Swedish Board of Universities and Colleges—with roughly 190 employees. Within the Ministry of Education there are two units, one for higher education and one for research policy that have about 20 employees altogether. During the 1980s the NBUC

has emphasized evaluation more than planning. It monitors the overall development of the local institutions and coordinates budgetary requests from the universities and colleges. However, its control over the higher education system has decreased.

Although the NBUC is involved in the planning and development of educational programs and single courses, the universities and colleges may introduce courses on their own. The basic thrust of the present policy is to decentralize the education system, meaning that decision-making power is transferred from the national level to the local level. Two important policies introduced in the major institutional reform of 1977 involved extensive decentralization and the introduction of external participation in the decision-making bodies, and the decentralization theme remained relevant in the policies of the 1980s.

The organizational expansion of the 1960s and 1970s was managed by means of a comprehensive higher education reform policy that involved most aspects of the higher education institutions. The U 68 Commission initiated the attempt at a major institutional reform in 1973 which led to the 1975–77 reform decisions. They were implemented in a carefully designed process which was monitored through a series of evaluation studies. The policy performance was mixed: some objectives achieved their outcomes whereas others met with unintended results and failed. The higher education policy of the 1980s was different to that of the 1970s, aiming at institutional consolidation after the academic profession had acquiesced in the major political reforms.

The 1975–77 higher education reforms decentralized major functions including the allocation of money which was granted in broadly specified budgetary appropriations, certain decisions about the curriculum, the right to offer a graduate degree, the creation of non-permanent professorships, and the structure of departments and basic units. An investigation in 1979 called for a "decentralized higher education system," resulting in changes in the composition of central and regional bodies. Decentralization was enhanced by the 1983 reform which gave the universities and colleges more autonomy to determine their internal decision-making structure. This has allowed for greater variation locally in the number and types of intermediate level bodies both within institutions and at the basic departmental level.

The faculty boards are responsible for planning gradaute training and research. Educational boards handle the undergraduate training. Each board is recruited on the basis of representative criteria providing various groups with a legitimate voice: teachers and researchers, students, the trade unions, and those with related external interests.

Finally, the structural reform of the academic profession introduced in 1984 and implemented in 1986 was in part concerned with decentralization. The policy of decentralizing higher education was continued in the reforms of 1987 and 1988, particularly in regard to financial decisions. The appropriations system used to be highly centralized, consisting of narrow line item expenditures, but it now takes the form of program budgeting comprising broad program functions depending greatly upon local discretion as to the use of the resources.

Increased external participation in universities and colleges has been the counterweight to increased autonomy. The 1977 reform abolished academic self-governance in the sense that members of various boards of the institutions were forthwith to be recruited from among all kinds of staff. Moreover, instead of rectors being recruited from within academia, the government was to appoint them on the basis of proposals submitted from the local governing board. The 1983 reform strengthened this development still further. Roughly one-third of the eighteen-member local governing boards would be nonacademics, appointed by the government (instead of by the local governments as in the reform of 1977) to represent external interests.

There is also external participation in the so-called line committees at the intermediate level. The 1983 reform implied that external participation at this level was to be extended to one-fourth of the committee who could represent occupational life. A university or a college may set up a comprehensive board for both education and research at the intermediate level, on which no less than one-fourth of the members must be external participants. Typically such regulations only apply to line committees, whereas the faculty committees that deal with research and graduate instruction include only internal representatives. Finally, the 1987 reform changed the overall composition of the institutional board so that of the eleven board members six are drawn from outside academia.

Recent higher education policy has reflected deep concern about the complex nature of internal higher education planning. The government stated in the 1983 reform that organizational complexity had to be reduced and the relative scale of the administrative element decreased as they held that enhanced local discretion would be conducive to greater flexibility and adaptation in the system. Thus, a strictly regulated system was to be transformed into one with fewer rules and a greater degree of latitude in local decision making. This principle has applied both to the structure of the decision-making system within the universities and colleges and to the new structure of the academic profession itself.

An important part of the antibureaucracy policy conducted since 1979 was the decision in 1986 to abolish the entire system of regional coordinating bodies, six in all. The 1975 decision to introduce a totally new regional level of higher education planning was severely criticized from the beginning and the outcomes never matched the ambitions.

3.2 Finance

The state universities and colleges receive three basic types of resources: a state grant for education; a state grant for research; and variable amounts for research projects from the national research councils among other public or private bodies. Whereas the first two items are allocated in the yearly budgetary process, the size of the last item depends on how proposals for research projects are handled by various research councils or how much research public authorities or private companies will commission. There are a variety of national research councils or agencies for commissioned research providing the universities and colleges with the soft money that is crucial to complement the faculty appropriations on the national government budget. Local government education receives a small state grant but is mostly paid for by the municipalities and county councils.

The overall development of resources in Swedish higher education cannot be described as one of fiscal stress. In real money terms there has not been a retrenchment as all the political parties generally consider higher education a promising area in which money invested will somehow pay off in the distant future. At the institutions with permanent resources for research, soft money usually makes up about 30 percent of the total whereas the units that lack such facilities have to manage with a smaller share, roughly 10 percent. It should be pointed out that academic drift makes it hard to distinguish between the two types of units, but the attempts of the colleges without permanent research resources to attract soft money are on a far lesser scale than those of the universities. The higher education sector now spends roughly 12 billion Swedish Crowns (US$2 billion) of which more than one-third goes to undergraduate instruction, one-third to permanent research, and somewhat less than one-third is soft money.

Whereas the grant for undergraduate education has shrunk in real money terms, the grant for permanent research has increased considerably, indicating the political trust in benefits from advanced research. New professorships are being added each year as well as new junior research positions, while the amount of soft money for commissioned research remains static. There is a strong commitment to joint ventures between academia and various external interests.

The formal development of the higher education budgetary system reflects the new emphasis on decentralization and evaluation. Thus, since 1990 a budgetary cycle of three years has been in operation for higher education funding. This means that the entire grant will be up for reconsideration triennially on the basis of extensive evaluation data on various aspects of system performance. In between there will be a yearly appropriation decided upon by means of standard operating procedures. The budgetary process is basically a negotiation procedure in which the local institutions submit budgetary requests to the government. Although these requests employ various allocative formulas including unit cost data, budgeting for higher education is not strictly based on any such formulas.

The single most expensive item on the higher education budget is salaries. Since salary increases showed a persistent tendency to be high during the 1980s, it is all the more obvious that the higher education sector has not suffered from any fiscal retrenchment. The budget of each institution has kept up with the inflationary pressure.

Universities and colleges with advanced research are of key importance in the total research effort of the Swedish society. In the early 1990s roughly 34 billion Swedish Crowns (US$5.6 billion) are being spent on research and development activities, of which 8.5 billion end up with the universities and colleges. More than half of this money is allocated in terms of stable faculty appropriations on the yearly national budget whereas the rest of the money is soft money for special research projects funded by a variety of research councils and foundations. The system of several councils for pure (natural science, medicine, arts, and social sciences) as well as applied research (technology, construction, ecology, energy, agriculture, and forestry) is mainly a public one, but it is truly heterogeneous involving multiplicity and redundance rather than coordination. On a yearly basis, Swedish society spends three percent of its total resources on research and development activities.

4. Faculty and Students: Teaching, Learning, and Research

4.1 Faculty

From about 1970, when the higher education system moved towards a steady state, the number of staff has grown at a more rapid rate than the number of students. Table 9 presents data about the overall development in the state sector. The total number of people employed in the system increased from 18,550 in 1969 to 34,186 in 1984. In terms of full-time equivalents the growth between 1975 and 1985 was not as striking. Table 10 has the information about the full-time equivalents.

There was a substantial growth in the number of administrators both locally and centrally. Thus, the number of employees in the central coordinating bodies grew from 197 to 419 between 1968 and 1980. The growth in administrative personnel within the universities and colleges was sufficient to start a debate about the level of bureaucracy in the entire system. As the number of supervisors rose by almost 100 percent it was feared that the basic functions

of academia—research and instruction—would be swamped in various administrative systems for planning and evaluating performance and decisions. However, the process of bureaucratization was halted in the mid-1980s, partly due to a policy reversal on the part of the government. An emphasis on administration and planning *ex ante* gave way to greater values being put on the performance of training and research and *ex post* evaluation. The administrative estate is no longer expanding in absolute or relative terms within the higher education system (Högskolan 1989).

The male dominance among teachers and researchers is overwhelming: 95 percent of full professors are male; 85 percent of associate professors; 84 percent of university lecturers; 79 percent of assistant professors; 72 percent of university teachers; and 54 percent of other teachers. This pattern is in strong contrast to recruitment figures for positions other than those of teachers and researchers where women dominate.

Since 1986 there have been four types of academic position, namely full professor and associate professor, which are tenured posts, and lecturer and assistant professor, which are not. Full and assistant professorships are research posts whereas the other two positions are oriented toward teaching. The government still appoints full professors on the basis of proposals submitted from the institutions, while the university or college board of the higher education unit makes the other appointments. The claim that the 1986 reform of the academic profession impinges upon the decentralization of higher education is clear in the case of local planning of workforce resources.

The reform has meant that universities and colleges introduce all levels of posts except full professorships. Various decision-making bodies within the local units also use their own discretion more to plan workforce resources; for instance, associate professors may receive a grant to carry on full-time research for an extended period. Planning the labor resources of the department is a task for the departmental head.

4.2 Government Influences

The Riksdag decides on the overall size of the higher education system, controlling the number of entrants into the general educational programs as well as the total number of students enrolled at the universities and colleges in local educational programs and single courses. It also decides on the structure of the general educational programs and the general outline of the system of single courses. However, the continuing decentralization of both the financial system and educational planning has meant that universities and colleges exercise an increasing amount of real power in relation to both finances and educational planning. Although the government still appoints full pro-

Table 9

Occupational structure of the higher education system 1969–84: various occupational groups in percentages of the total number of employees[a]

	1969	1977	1978	1980	1981	1984
Teachers	18.1	17.8	21.3	20.6	22.4	23.8
Researchers	11.6	10.1	8.8	9.2	9.3	10.7
Academic Assistants	18.7	18.6	15.4	16.8	15.1	13.8
Engineers	3.7	4.8	4.7	5.6	5.8	5.9
Administrators	2.6	5.1	4.6	8.3	8.7	9.9
Secretaries	8.3	11.5	10.2	8.8	8.9	8.1
Technicians	15.2	13.8	11.8	11.5	11.9	11.3
Librarians	2.5	2.3	2.3	2.6	2.7	2.6
Other personnel	19.2	16.1	20.9	16.7	15.1	15.0
Total	18,500	26,400	30,900	30,900	32,300	34,100

Source: Lane 1989
a The total number of employees includes full-time and part-time staff divided by two

fessors, defines their subject areas and allocates a large share of the money in the state budget, considerable steps have been taken to increase local discretion and initiative. In 1990 a new budgetary system involving three-year budgetary frames besides the ordinary annual budget appropriation was introduced. These budgetary frames will be evaluated after each three-year period, but they are very broadly defined leaving a great deal of discretion to the universities and colleges. There will be one single appropriation for undergraduate training and one appropriation for the graduate training and research at each faculty. There is a real recognition among the central authorities of the value of decentralization, both as an end in itself and as a means to other ends.

The ideology of decentralization derives its support from various sources. First, it may be regarded as a reaction against the expansion of the public sector in combination with the typical centralized model of Swedish planning and administration. It is no longer believed that the best solutions to all kinds of problems come from the center. It is argued that local initiative should be encouraged more and that local adaptation is desirable. There is more confidence in what the market may accomplish and it is believed that public sector performance would be greatly improved if decision making was devolved structurally. Secondly, there is the fiscal aspect. According to one view, the state is using decentralization in order to relieve itself of extensive financial obligations by allowing local institutions more discretion. The central authorities maintain fewer and less conspicuous mechanisms of control such as central evaluation of the performance of local operations.

Table 10
Full-time equivalents

	1975	Percentage	1984	Percentage	1985	Percentage
Teachers	4,732	17.8	6,114	18.4	5,937	19.1
Researchers	2,645	10.0	3,631	10.9	3,808	12.2
Academic assistants	4,140	15.6	4,357	13.1	4,232	13.6
Administrators	1,551	5.9	3,193	9.6	3,270	10.5
Secretaries	3,246	12.2	3,229	9.7	3,163	10.2
Engineers	1,056	4.0	2,061	6.2	2,067	6.6
Technicians	3,626	13.7	4,015	12.1	4,016	12.9
Librarians	589	2.2	932	2.8	945	3.0
Cleaners	1,290	4.9	1,524	4.6	1,463	4.7
Porters	425	1.6	505	1.5	481	1.5
Other	3,216	12.1	3,714	11.2	1,747	5.6
Total	26,516	100	33,275	100	31,129	100

Source: Lane 1989

Thirdly, the growing importance of regional and local identities in general is bound to have an impact on the structure and functions of the higher education system. If, previously, the regional and local environment served the universities and colleges, the ideology of decentralization has reoriented this relationship. Higher education institutions are now considered to be crucial resources for regional development. These educational resources are held to be a local asset, and it is felt that they should be employed to serve regional and local needs.

The relevance of the decentralization model must also be interpreted in a perspective of political power. The expansion of the public sector at the local government level means that municipalities and county councils are powerful enough to be successful in demanding that the onus of decision-making be moved away from the center. The ideology of decentralization reflects the weakening of the state and the strong expansion of local government organizations. It also reflects a resurrection of a professionalism that is highly critical of central administration in educational and research matters. It is increasingly difficult for central planners and administrators to claim that they know enough about the internal life of the higher education institutions to allow them to regulate in detail what is going on at a local level.

Efficiency in higher education refers to quality on the one hand and productivity on the other hand. The role of the central authorities has been redefined, from planning *ex ante* to evaluation *ex post*. The internal functions of universities and colleges are considered more important than the external tasks of academia. Gone is the ambition to govern education and research in terms of comprehensive social goals. The prevailing trend is for the universities and colleges to identify their own means for accomplishing their basic tasks of education and research. The traditional academic degree, the Bachelor of Arts (*filosofie kandidat-examen*), has been partly reestablished as has the *filosofie licentiat-examen* in graduate studies.

The combination of organizational decentral-

ization and an emphasis on quality means that there is a larger scope for planning and decision making at each university and college in order to enhance its attractiveness and status. Thus, there is much activity going on locally to develop various educational lines and research projects that are adapted to regional needs including the creation of non-permanent professorships on the basis of the external funding which is additional to the state budget. The ivory tower characteristics of Swedish academia have been done away with in a number of joint efforts between universities and colleges on the one hand and industry and local governments on the other. There now exist several development centers for cooperation between academia and society in a broad sense.

4.3 Students

Student achievement is not altogether easy to measure. There has been a long and sustained debate in Swedish educational planning about how to interpret data about student performance. It is now considered vital to make a distinction between capacity utilization and the passing of tests. Whereas the first measure relates to how the educational opportunities are used by the students, the second measure taps how they score on tests within a certain time limit. The basic lesson is that capacity utilization measured by the actual number of students versus the planned number of seats and test scoring measured as the proportion of students taking a certain number of points in one year vary according to the educational line.

In some educational lines all seats are utilized and more than 90 percent of the students pass their tests in due time: musicians, librarians, doctors, civil engineers. In other educational lines less than 70 percent of the seats are utilized and about two-thirds of the students make it on time: public administration, law, social studies. On the other hand, for single courses in general, for example, journalism, and systems science there is a low of 50 percent of the students taking their tests even where capacity utilization is a high 90 percent.

Table 11
Proportion of students with an examination

	After 3 years		After 5 years		After 7 years	
	Men	Women	Men	Women	Men	Women
Technical sector	5	7	30	37	42	46
Administrative and economic sector	10	9	42	57	53	65
Health care sector	43	45	71	88	—	—
Educational sector	85	78	93	90	—	—
Culture and information sector	12	10	27	30	38	35

Source: NBUC report 1987: 12

Table 12
Productivity changes in higher education 1960–80

	1965–70	1970–75	1975–80	1965–80
Overall productivity development	−10.8	−3.8	+0.7	−4.5
Adjusted productivity measure (part-time students)	−13.0	−2.11	−4.5	−4.5
Productivity with regard to undergraduate examinations	−3.8	−4.7	+2.3	−2.1
Productivity with regard to graduate examinations	−5.4	−5.9	−11.3	−7.8

Source: Stenkula 1986

The standard measure of student performance, however, is the frequency of examinations. The data on examinations shows that at least with regard to certain educational sectors, student performance is a problem. Table 11 illustrates the proportion of students who have passed an examination on an educational line intended to take 3–3.5 years after certain time intervals.

These figures have not changed much over the years, but what they actually mean has been much debated. To some it indicates poor student performance, particularly within technology, social science, and arts. Others interpret the data differently as they argue that there are valid causes for study interruptions: students may change to other training, leave higher education, or start graduate training without passing an examination. These changes, moreover, may not indicate poor performance. In any case, there is now much more sensitivity about student performance than there was in the 1970s.

The measurement of productivity in the higher education sector proceeds from a model that relates output measures to the costs for the input of resources. The difficulty is in identifying quality improvements on the output side. The focus in the Swedish debate has been on yearly productivity comparisons over longer time intervals (see Table 12 for the result).

There was, therefore, a negative productivity development in the higher education system, costs outpacing the number of students taught or the number of degrees passed. In a sense it costs more each year to produce the "same" output in the system of higher education. The productivity measurements have resulted in a search for measures that would reverse the seminal development since 1965. Attempts are made to cut back on redundant seats in some educational lines moving the resources to meet certain types of student demand. Positive productivity changes have been reported for the late 1980s. Moreover, per capita costs are compared between various institutions in order to hold costs back. Basically, however, the budgetary system for higher education

is not an advanced one as it is very much based on negotiations within the institutions and thereafter with the central authorities.

5. Conclusion

In addition to the traditional tasks of higher education and research there is, in the early 1990s, an emphasis on local adaptation to the needs of the environment of the university or college. Planning functions have been moved from the national level to the local level (Wittrock and Lindström 1984, Premfors 1986). Decentralization combined with concern over quality means that the initiative has come to rest with the local institutions. Higher education engages in innovative activities in both the supply of training and the structuring of research. A number of new local educational lines have been introduced with the effect that the centrally governed system of general educational lines has been complemented by locally defined educational needs. Several centers for various kinds of research have been created by local initiative. Each university and college may introduce life or temporary professorships from its own budget, in particular six-year professorships in order to attract people who are not normally involved in higher education but who have some special competence beneficial to academia. In order to enhance the interaction between the community at large and academic research and training, special research villages have been built up: Ideon (Lund), Stuns (Uppsala), Teknikhöjden (Stockholm), Uminova (Umeå), Centek (Luleå), and Teknikbyn (Linköping). At the regional level the universities and colleges have entered various research and development councils in order to promote the development of regional areas.

The creation of new tenured and nontenured professorships has rested with the institutions themselves since 1982 and it has become very important as local planning has taken over from central planning. One may speak of a new enterpreneurship at the local level where various interests have joined forces in order to develop the vicinity through higher education activities (Richardsson 1989). A large number of new professorships, extra permanent ones as well as time-limited adjunct professorships, have been created, mainly in engineering, the natural sciences, and medicine. The developments at the local level were rapid once central coordination gave way to decentralized planning: the number of new professorships created by the institutions themselves far outnumbering the number of professorships introduced by the central authorities. Both the policies brought into effect in the 1980s and the locally initiated developments have moved the Swedish system of higher education away from the integration model that dominated the U 68 attempts at a major institutional reform and towards a diversified model as it is envisioned in the United States system of higher education (Teichler 1988). Most probably, the future path will be one of further diversification and decentralization.

Bibliography

Ahrne G (ed.) 1985 *Bok om den svenska klasstrukturen.* Arkiv, Stockholm

Cerych L, Sabatier P 1986 *Great Expectations and Mixed Performance: The Implementation of Higher Education Reforms in Europe.* Trentham Books, Stoke-on-Trent

Fickskolan 1988. Statistics Sweden, Stockholm

Högskolan 1989. Statistics Sweden, Stockholm

Kim L 1982 *Widened Admission to Higher Education in Sweden: the 25/5 scheme: A study of the implementation process.* UHÄ, Stockholm

Lane J-E 1989 *Institutional Reform.* Dartmouth, Aldershot

Lane J-E 1991 (ed.) The Swedish Model. *Western European Politics* 14(3) (special issue)

Lane J-E, Löfquist S 1985 Klasser och klasskillnader i administrationssamhället. In Berntson L, Skogh G, Söderqvist T (eds.) *Klassamhälle i förvandling.* Liber, Stockholm: 98

Lindensjö B 1981 *Högskolereformen.* Stockholm University Press, Stockholm

Premfors R, Östergren B 1978 *Systems of Higher Education.* International Council for Educational Development, New York

Premfors R 1986 *Svensk forskningspolitik.* Studentlitteratur, Lund

Richardsson G 1989 Den frigjorda högskolan—ett oberäkneligt inslag i den statliga forskningspolitiken. *Forskning om utbildning* 16

Statistical Abstracts of Sweden 1990. Statistics Sweden, Stockholm

Statskontoret 1986 *Högskolans administration.* Statskontoret, Stockholm

Stenkula P 1986 *Produktions-, kostnads- och produktivitetsutvecklingen inom den offentlig finansierade utbildningssektorn 1960–1980.* Ds Fi, 1986: 17, Stockholm

Ström G (ed.) 1985 *Erövra universiteten åter.* Liber, Stockholm

Teichler U 1988 *Changing Patterns of the Higher Education System.* Jessica Kingsley, London

UHÄ materials: *Året som gick* (1982/83–88/89); *Petita* (1978–88); *Reports 1983: 6, 1984: 1, 1984: 2.*

Utbildningsstatistisk Årsbok 1978. Statistics Sweden, Stockholm

Wittrock B, Lindström S 1984 *De stora programmens.* Akademilitteratur, Stockholm

J-E. Lane

Switzerland

1. Higher Education and Society

Swiss education before 1800 developed along much the same lines as that of Central Europe, that is to say: education was first the task of the monasteries, before municipal schools were founded. In 1460 the first university was founded by the city of Basel, while elementary education remained in private hands for still some centuries.

In connection with the political changes brought about by the French Revolution, education was developed on a broader basis. Pedagogists like Pestalozzi gave a decisive impetus to education by opening up primary schooling for wider strata of the population.

A new stimulus to develop higher education manifested itself in the nineteenth century, at the same time as the political, liberal forces gathered in order to create the Swiss Confederation. At that time most Swiss universities were founded, although some of them (e.g., Geneva, Zurich) originate in the theological academies founded during the Reformation.

In the second half of the nineteenth century and also in the twentieth century the secondary schools, the vocational schools, and the universities underwent important reforms. Since the Second World War and the ensuing structural changes in society and industry, the Swiss educational system has continued to experience some alteration.

In the 1960s and early 1970s secondary and higher education enjoyed top priority at the national and the cantonal levels as well as in public opinion, inducing a phase of quantitative expansion. This phase of growth has come to an end, mainly—but not exclusively—due to the prevailing financial and economic regression around 1974. Similarly, the endeavors of several cantons to create new institutes of higher education have been dimmed.

The late 1970s and early 1980s have been characterized by budgetary difficulties, in particular at the federal level. The universities, most of which are partially or entirely financed by the central government, have consequently suffered. The second half of the 1980s had to come to terms with two main phenomena: first, the strong valorization of research, in particular of applied research in industry;

secondly, the urgent need, partially unsatisfied, for a highly qualified labor force (e.g., engineers, computer specialists, economists, etc.).

With 6.62 million inhabitants (1988 figures), Switzerland is a small country situated in the heart of Europe (boundaries with the Federal Republic of Germany, France, Italy, and Austria). Its population is relatively stable, composed of a growing number of elderly people (14.5 percent over 65 years) and a decreasing number of young people (23.8 percent of young people between 0 and 19 years). Foreigners account for about 15.6 percent (circa 1.03 million) of the population.

Switzerland comprises four linguistic regions. The resident population can be distributed according to mother-tongue as follows: German 73.5 percent, French 20.1 percent, Italian 4.5 percent, Romansch 0.9 percent, and others 1 percent. Urban regions of the country account for about 3.9 million inhabitants against about 2.5 million in rural regions (1980 figures). The largest Swiss city is Zurich (about 370,000 inhabitants in 1980). Only four other cities have more than 100,000 inhabitants (Basel, Geneva, Bern, Lausanne).

The active population (53.1 percent in 1989) can be distributed according to sectors as follows: (a) primary sector (agriculture) 5.6 percent, (b) secondary sector (industries) 35.1 percent, (c) tertiary sector (services) 59.3 percent. In the last few years, the unemployment rate has been very low: about 0.7 percent in 1988.

Politically, Switzerland is a confederation of 26 states (cantons). The central government is practically solely competent in such fields as foreign policy and defense. In other fields, competences are shared. Yet others (e.g., compulsory education) are devolved only in the cantons which sometimes share their competences with the municipalities (in Switzerland, the smallest political entity). Whether on the central or on the cantonal level, democratic rights are considered very important (initiative and referendum).

1.1 The Educational System

As the 26 cantonal school systems differ greatly, a cursory description of the outstanding features of the main stages is the most that can be attempted here.

Children enter kindergarten at ages varying from four to six according to the canton and the local district; they attend it until they are six or seven. Preschool education is optional but nonetheless state-run.

According to the canton, compulsory schooling begins at the age of six or seven and extends over a period of usually nine years. Pupils who leave school at the age of 16 usually move on to a practical apprenticeship with a firm, post office, the local administration, or similar, attending compulsory vocational schools part-time (on average one or two days a week). Those who do not take up an apprenticeship can enter a full-time vocational school leading for example to a commercial diploma, or in various cantons enter a teacher-training college for infant or primary teachers. The courses at these schools last some four years.

Grammar school courses last some four years, bringing the leaving-age of their pupils up to about 19. In order to obtain the leaving certificate (maturity), the candidates have to succeed in 11 subjects. The Swiss Maturity Regulations distinguish five main types of grammar school training: type 1 stressing Latin/Greek (plus mother-tongue, one or two modern languages, mathematics, natural sciences, history, geography, art); type 2 offering Latin and modern languages (instead of Greek); type 3 which emphasizes mathematics and natural sciences, and, since 1973, type 4 (modern languages) and 5 (economics). The "maturity" certificates are at the same time the leaving certificates of the grammar schools and certificates giving access to the universities.

2. The Institutional Fabric of the Higher Education System

Switzerland ranks among those countries having the highest university density, with one university for every 650,000 inhabitants. There are 10 institutions of higher learning. Three of the cantonal universities (Basel, Zurich, and Bern), one cantonal institution at university level (the Graduate School of Economics in St. Gall) and one Federal Institute of Technology (FIT, Zurich) are situated in the German-speaking part of Switzerland, which has 19 cantons and about three-quarters of the population; the other four universities (Lausanne, Geneva, Neuchâtel, and Fribourg, the last being bilingual, i.e., offering courses in French and German, and having a mainly Catholic character) and the second Federal Institute of Technology (Lausanne) are situated in the French-speaking part, which has six cantons and about one-fifth of the population—that is, one university for every 330,000 inhabitants. Italian-speaking Switzerland (about one-twentieth of the population) does not have a complete university of its own. This wealth of universities is the consequence of the historical evolution of Switzerland.

Furthermore, there are a few institutions, modest in size, with a limited curriculum in the field of higher education (e.g., the Faculty of Theology in Lucerne, the Pedagogical College in St. Gall) which award diplomas equivalent to university diplomas. There are also several graduate institutions, as a rule associated with a traditional university, such as the *Institut universitaire de hautes études internationales* (Geneva), the *Institut de hautes études en administration publique* (Lausanne), and so forth.

The private sector, so far of little importance on

the academic level, is limited to a few graduate study institutions, specializing mainly in management.

Nonuniversity training institutions, and there are many of them, offer a vocational rather than an academic education in a wide range of subjects (technical, agricultural, commercial, administrative schools, teacher-training colleges, paramedical, and social work training schools, arts and crafts colleges, etc.). Their educational spectrum is very wide: younger and less institutionalized, they are also more difficult to assess. In many other countries such vocational training is offered by the universities. This is why in Switzerland the proportion of university education is one of the lowest of Europe, that of postsecondary education (including the vocational schools) supersedes the average in OECD countries. A "bridge" system makes it possible, under certain conditions, to step over from postsecondary to university studies.

Domestic expenditures for Research and Development (R & D) amounted to 7.1 billion Swiss francs in 1986 (i.e., at an average exchange rate of 1.796 SF to $1 in 1986, $4 billion or $615 per inhabitant). This amount corresponds to 2.9 percent of the Gross National Product (GNP); Switzerland ranks with the countries which devote the highest share of their (GNP) to R & D costs (United States, Japan, FRG, and Sweden), not to forget the 3.1 billion SF ($1.73

billion) spent by Swiss enterprises for R & D work carried out abroad.

Figure 1 shows the distribution of the total amount according to sources of financing and responsible bodies: the share of private industry is enormous (78 percent), and as a consequence that of the public sector modest (22 percent). According to the Frascati Handbook, private industry spends 90 percent of its budget on development against 20 percent only for the public sector. Total research expenditure may be estimated at 3 billion SF ($1.67 bn). The chemical industry is an exception in that 60 percent of its expenditure is for research, and only 40 percent for development.

In 1986, R & D staff represented 45,000 full-time equivalents (FTEQ), of whom three-quarters were employed in the private industry, about a sixth in universities (including the FIT), the rest in the federal administration (Confederation). The public sector (universities included) occupies about 6,000 FETQ staff with a university education against 9,000 in the private sector. In Switzerland, 45 out of 10,000 active persons are engaged in R & D work.

The financing of university R & D (R & D) carried out in the eight cantonal institutions and the two FITs) represented 900 million SF ($500 million) in 1986, or 13 percent of total R & D expenditures and 56 percent of public expenditure in this field. Figure

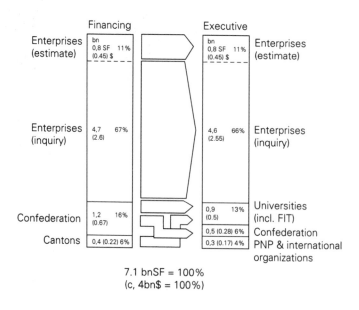

Figure 1
Financial flows of R & D in Switzerland 1986 (in billions US dollars and Swiss Francs)

Source: Federal Office of Statistics 1989
a Not including the financial resources devoted by the private economy for R & D work carried out abroad (3.1bnSF)
b Financial flows representing less than 5 percent of total R & D financing are not accounted for (mandates and contributions of private enterprises to high schools and ISBL; mandates of the Confederation commissioned to the private economy)

1 gives the detailed distribution of this sum according to institutional and functional criteria: the Confederation finances 52 percent of the total; the cantons 45 percent, the rest comes from other sources.

The universities' own funds allocated to R & D represent about a quarter of total public resources of the universities (approx. 2.6 billion SF, or US$1.45 billion): 55 percent of this sum for personnel costs (not including the university-hospital staff) and 40 percent for operational costs (purchase of machines, equipment, documentation and other material). The labor force involved in university research and development represents 7,100 full-time equivalents, of whom 2,300 are remunerated by the Swiss National Science Foundation (SNSF).

Swiss universities are rather elitist and restrictive. Students entering university must be at least 18 years old and have a secondary education leaving certificate ("maturity") or a foreign certificate considered equivalent (sometimes the requirements are higher than those of the foreign country). A "maturity" remains an absolute essential for studying medicine. This certificate is awarded in most cases by the canton but it is recognized by the Confederation which decrees relevant provisions and organizes its own secondary-leaving examinations (often for candidates coming from private schools).

Other ways of access to higher education remain as yet exceptional: entrance examinations (in specific faculties); working candidates without a school-leaving certificate, candidates stepping over from the nonuniversity postsecondary sector (primary school teachers, engineers from the higher technical schools, etc.). However, in fact, conditions of access may vary from one university to another, some being very restrictive, others more liberal. Of course anyone can enroll as an *auditeur* (an unregistered student who attends lectures).

The conditions for admission to nonuniversity higher education are extraordinarily varied. These institutions are often, but not uniformly, involved in the secondary and postsecondary sectors. For admittance to Advanced Technical Colleges an apprenticeship is usually required; here as elsewhere, admission may also be granted on dossiers or on examination, and the number of places may be limited. A secondary education leaving certificate may also be requested, formally or *de facto*.

As access to university studies is *de facto* restricted, there has not been as yet any *numerus clausus* in Swiss universities, although the percentage of maturity holders among the 19-year old age group has practically doubled since 1970. It is true, the idea of a *numerus clausus* crops up regularly (especially for medicine), but the difficulty of implementing such a measure and the genuine injustices this would generate, together with the firm policy of refusing such a scheme on the federal level, have always defeated such attempts.

Although each university has its own characteristics, they are all basically the same in structure. Most of them are divided into faculties: theology; law; economics and social science; arts; natural sciences; and medicine. Fribourg and Neuchâtel offer the basic medical courses only, and St. Gall specializes in economics and law. The two Federal Institutes of Technology produce highly qualified engineers, architects, and natural scientists.

The teaching at Swiss universities consists of basic studies leading to specialization and graduate studies. Considerable differences exist between the various universities and between the fields of study themselves as far as the length of study, the structure of the course, and the selection and combination of subjects, are concerned. The basic study, which as a rule stretches over at least four years (=8 semesters) leads to a first academic degree, a *licence* or a diploma. Its completion allows further specialization in the chosen field of study leading up to a doctorate.

A *licence* or diploma with good grades is a condition for access to graduate studies. Promotion to the doctoral degree is achieved at the end of a piece of work of academic research (the thesis), carried out independently and having an original quality, as well as after an oral examination. The topic of a thesis is determined in coordination with the professor who directs and follows the research work. The thesis must be published. The duration of graduate studies is not regulated but depends on the chosen topic, the accessibility of sources and documents, laboratory experiences, and the individual's methods. As a rule, a thesis requires three to five years' work.

As in all other countries, the number of university students has strongly increased in the postwar period (20,000 in 1960, 80,000 in 1980, 86,000 in 1990). Nonetheless, the rate of university training has not reached the high level of other countries. Only 12 percent of the 20–24 age group attends university, which is modest compared with other OECD countries but the frequentation rate of the nonuniversity, postsecondary sector is one of the highest in Europe. As a result of a drop in the birthrate since 1965, the number of students has been more or less stable.

3. Governance, Administration, and Finance

In education as in other fields, the decision-making process in Switzerland is strongly marked by federalism.

The responsibility for education lies, in very general terms, with the cantons or sometimes even with the municipalities. The Confederation interferes relatively little in postsecondary education, for example, to help support the costs of higher education, to coordinate and organize certain sectors or independent activities (such as medical studies), also with a view to guarantee to a certain extent equal access for all.

According to article 27, paragraph 1, of the Federal Constitution, "The Confederation is authorized to found, apart from the already existing Federal Institute of Technology, a federal university and other higher education establishments, or to subsidize such institutions."

The creation of the Federal Institute of Technology (Zurich) in the mid-nineteenth century and the take-over of a faculty of Lausanne University to found the *Ecole polytechnique fédérale* (Lausanne) are two examples of the federal government's intervention in higher education. Since 1968, a federal act concerning the financial assistance to the universities has set off the intervention of the Confederation in the financing of cantonal universities (about 20 percent of total expenditure plus contributions to investments). The decision-making power remains essentially with the cantons, but the federal government endeavors to link its financial contributions to prerequisites or to general recommendations on the functioning of the universities (planning, coordination, etc.). The cantonal governments try to confine federal intervention to financing. The Confederation also influences university matters, though indirectly, through the financing of public research (where it plays an essential role).

Thus postsecondary education is essentially the responsibility of the education departments of the cantonal governments which share this responsibility with the university institutions themselves, but on different levels and in different ways from canton to canton. The autonomy of the institutions is relatively strong in the university sector. Though the universities are also supported by a minor financial contribution from the cantons without a university (they pay a certain yearly amount per student) there is no transfer of power outside the actual canton in charge.

Federal authority with regard to science, research, and higher education lies essentially with the Federal Department of Home Affairs (Federal Office for Education and Science), whereas the Federal Department of Public Economy is responsible for technical and other higher vocational training (e.g., Advanced Technical Colleges).

Various bodies assist the cantonal and federal governments in their tasks (Conference of the Directors of the Cantonal Education Departments, Conference of the Swiss University Rectors, Swiss University Conference, the Swiss Science Council, etc.).

The two Federal Institutes of Technology are financed entirely by the Confederation; as for the cantonal universities, approximately 70 percent of their operational costs are met by the cantons in charge, 20 percent by the Confederation, and the remaining 10 percent by other sources of income (other cantons, consultancy and other services, study fees, donations, etc.). This cost-sharing may vary considerably from one university to another as the Confederation varies its financial assistance among other things according to the means of each canton. For the university sector as a whole (cantonal universities and Federal Institutes of Technology), the participation of the Confederation amounts to 37 percent against 58 percent for the cantons (1985 figures).

If this may seem complex to the outsider, the responsible bodies for the nonuniversity postsecondary sector describe the university sector as being of a "geometrical clarity" as compared to their own. Let it be said that the institutes of the latter sector are usually the concern of one or several cantons, that private economy is also involved, and that the Confederation sets the rules for and supervises higher vocational training.

University planning in Switzerland was implemented on the basis of the Federal Act on assistance to universities at the end of the 1970s, that is to say once its utility was acknowledged by all in a context of restricted finances. Usually, this planning is built from the bottom upwards. The only exceptions to this process are the input given at the beginning of the preparation of a planning period (about four years beforehand); the "objectives of the research policy" proposed by the Swiss Science Council and decided upon by the Federal Council (i.e., the government); and the "Prospects of University Development" worked out by the Swiss Science Council and intended for the Swiss University Conference and the universities.

So it is actually the latter Conference which sets the planning process in motion at the university level: the units express their needs which are then transferred to a higher level and so on. This bottom upwards process leads as a matter of course to a refitting and shifting of priorities up to a manageable project.

Negotiations can start: between the universities and the cantonal authorities (concerning the global budget for the four-year period), between the cantonal and the federal authorities (concerning the participation of the Confederation in the financing of universities), the Swiss University Conference—a semicantonal semifederal body—the Swiss Science Council, the Federal Department of Home Affairs, the Federal Department of Finance, the Federal Government, and eventually the two chambers making up parliament, all intervening in turn.

3.1 Institutional Administration

The organization of the universities may take different forms from one university to another. Universities situated in the French-speaking part of Switzerland seem to have on the whole a larger share of autonomy than the "German-speaking universities"; the influence of the cantonal ministries in university matters is thus weaker in the former than in the latter, as is approximately, that of the faculties.

Though each university has a fair margin of freedom in many fields and is anxious to keep it, the necessity of coordinating different spheres of activity without the intervention of the central government has made itself increasingly felt. Among all Swiss universities, arrangements were passed with a view to coordinate education in general and its certain disciplines. This was especially true at graduate level at French-speaking universities. Medicine (ruled by a federal act but taught on a cantonal level) and technical science studies are organized on a federal scale.

As for the administration of the university sector—invariably rated too heavy by the professors—it also differs from canton to canton. The participation of the junior staff and of the students greatly varies too: quite important in Geneva for example, it balances between poor and zero in other universities. The executive power of the university is entrusted to a rector or rectorate, supported by the internal administration; the internal legislative power is devolved on an assembly, varying in size, of representatives of the various groups within the university. Each university usually has one or several "bridging bodies," consulting only, which represent the interests of the outside world.

4. Faculty and Students: Teaching, Learning, and Research

4.1 Faculty

The university staff is divided for statistical reasons into 17 categories to cover the extreme diversity of tasks to be performed in the university sector. Since within these categories functions may vary from one university to another, the following scheme has been adopted to facilitate the reading of the data:

Category A: professors (*ordinarii* and *extraordinarii*, assistant professors, associate professors); a higher doctorate (usually) or doctorate and professional experience; comprehensive or specialized teaching or research activity; ability to conduct projects in the fields of teaching, research or services, or to head an institute; medium to long-term (rarely for life) appointment. Peak of the academic hierarchy.

Category B: teacher or researcher with lesser responsibilities than the former category (assistant lecturer, visiting professors, lecturers, etc.); a higher doctorate or doctorate, sometimes only degree or diploma; medium or long-term, also temporary engagement (visiting professors); practical experience (also employed in economy, administration, or the private sector).

Category C: junior staff; teacher or researcher on a lower level, scientific staff, assistant teachers, senior assistants, student assistants; doctorate or degree or (for student assistants) on their way to obtaining one; mostly limited (at the most to four to six years).

Category D: administrative or technical staff (libraries, laboratories, caretaking, etc.).

Categories A, B, and C form the academic staff; categories A and B are sometimes labelled the "teaching body."

The distribution in functions (FCT) and in full-time equivalents (FTEQ) of the staff of the Swiss universities is as shown in Table 1.

Ratio FTEQ/FCT (reference year 1984) is especially high in the professorial (teaching) body; this rate varies quite considerably from one university to another, from 0.73 (Basel) to 0.98 (Zurich University and FIT). The same goes for category B, less committed to academic life as the staff of this category are often meant to bring practical experience; here the rate is 0.18 in Basel and 0.44 in Bern. These variations may be at least partly justified by the fact that members of category B may expect to be or may be on the verge of entering category A. The FTEQ/FCT ratio is more homogeneous in the two lower categories.

The ratio of junior staff (category C) to professorial body (category A) expressed in FTEQ averages 2.9. In other words, each professor is on average assisted by three members of the junior staff. But,

Table 1
Swiss university staff in 1984, according to functions (FCT) and full-time equivalents (FTEQ)

	Category A Professors	Category B Other Teachers and Researchers	Category C Junior Staff	Category D Administrative and Technical Staff
FCT	2,229	3,600	8,089	7,181[a]
FTEQ	1,990	1,121	5,795	5,981[a]
Ratio FTEQ/FCT	0.89	0.31	0.72	0.83[a]

Source: Federal Office of Statistics
a Not including figures for Basel University (not available)

Table 2
Ratio students–academic staff and professors (per function) in the different faculties 1985

	Humanities + Social Sc.	Exact + Nat. Sciences	Medicine Pharmacy	Engineering Sciences	Total
Students (%)	56.5	16.3	16.5	10.7	100
Academic staff (%)	37	30	16.5	16.5	100
Students/ Acad. Staff	7.2	2.6	4.0	3.0	4.6
Professors (%)	42	29	19	10	100
Students/ Professors	45.3	19.4	24.9	34.8	32.9

Source: Federal Office of Statistics and Swiss Science Council

of course, such figures are never realistic: in fact, this rates varies from 1.05 (Basel) to 6.21 (FIT Zurich), the latter being atypical as the second highest rate is 3.33 (Bern).

The university structures are so diverse, the available figures so unsatisfactory, and the academic staff changes so often that the student–teacher ratio in Swiss universities is very difficult to assess, all the more so as it encompasses aspects that are hard to quantify (e.g., quality of teaching or research). Table 2 nevertheless gives some figures which only have an indicative value.

It is to be noted that the student–professor ratio varies considerably from one faculty to another (from 1 to 2 between exact and natural sciences and humanities and social sciences) and from one university to another. Thus, at Zurich University, there are 54 students per professor (full-time equivalent) against 26 only at Lausanne University or Zurich FIT.

In 1984, 25 percent of the 2,278 professors (category A), that is to say 570, were foreigners (but only 2 percent women). This percentage of foreign staff varies among faculties. In exact and natural sciences as well as in technical sciences it corresponds to the Swiss average; in medicine, it is 17.5 percent and 29 percent in humanities and social sciences; it reaches 33 percent in psychology and educational sciences, peaking with 42 percent in philosophy, languages, and literature. The differences are also considerable between the universities: 12 and 15 percent respectively in Neuchâtel and St. Gall, 32 percent in Geneva, and 42 percent in Fribourg.

4.2 Students

Two out of three students of the postsecondary sector are enrolled in university level institutions (cantonal universities and Federal Institutes of Technology), a third in a nonuniversity institution. Table 3 shows the distribution of the 121,683 students registered in 1987 (about 10 percent of all persons enrolled in teaching establishments at that time) in greater

detail; Table 4 shows the distribution of university students according to disciplines and universities.

In 1985, the Swiss universities awarded 6,300 degrees or diplomas and more than 1,800 doctorates (this academic level being more frequent compared to the student ratio in German-speaking than in French-speaking Switzerland). The Advanced Technical Schools award more than 2,000 diplomas per year (not including architecture). The number of entrants in the nonuniversity sector is proportionally much higher than in the university sector; this may be explained by the shorter duration of studies in and easier access to the former. Whereas the total number of university students is still noticeably increasing (+1.5 percent annually over the last six years), that of entrants is stable, if not actually decreasing (medicine, −4 percent), except in such fields as economics (+10 percent), technical sciences—including computer sciences—as well as in psychology and pedagogy (+4 percent). Despite a strong increase in the percentage of women students—from 20 to 37 percent over the last 20 years—Switzerland lags behind other OECD countries. The age of entrants is increasing. As for the number of foreign students, it has remained stable at around 19 percent between 1981 and 1990.

5. Conclusion

Only a cursory description of the Swiss higher education system has been given: the relevant data have been summarized to a high degree and simplified. The not always compatible university diplomas have scarcely been mentioned which makes it difficult for students to change from one university to another. Neither have the procedures, contents, and value of the different works to be accomplished in order to obtain a doctor's degree been touched upon. The fact that some degrees (e.g., the ones necessary for secondary education) are not yet fully recognized in all cantons has not been commented upon; neither have the important differences in salary between

Table 3
Distribution of the students of the postsecondary sector in 1987 according to institutions, sex and origin

	Total	Of whom females (percentage)	Of whom foreigners (percentage)
University	78,473	28,534 (36.4)	13,814 (17.6)
Humanities and Social Sciences	45,608	19,796 (43.4)	8,769 (19.2)
Exact and Natural Sciences	13,238	2,964 (22.4)	2,406 (18.2)
Medicine	10,640	4,458 (41.9)	1,027 (9.7)
Engineering Sciences	8,987	1,316 (14.6)	1,612 (17.9)
Nonuniversity	43,220	10,081 (23.3)	4,711 (10.9)
Advanced Technical Studies	9,819	301 (3.1)	962 (9.8)
Technical Colleges	3,253	107 (3.3)	302 (9.3)
Social Workers, Children Home Staff Training Institutes	1,635	1,021 (62.4)	156 (9.5)
Higher College of Business & Administration	1,339	167 (12.5)	46 (6.1)
Teachers Training Colleges	2,900	1,885 (64.0)	141 (4.1)
Other[a]	24,274	6,630 (27.3)	3,104 (12.8)
Total postsecondary	121,693	38,615 (31.7)	18,525 (15.2)
Total pupils and students	1,272,666	586,455 (46.1)	209,497 (16.5)
Population[b]	6,366,000	3,251,100 (51.1)	945,000 (14.8)

Source: Federal Office Statistics and Swiss Science Council
a Preparation for higher vocational examinations, vocational examinations, paramedical schools, graphic arts, etc.   b Figures for 1980 (estimation 1987: 6.619m). Foreigners = resident population

equally qualified teachers in the different universities, or the organizational differences (sabbatical leaves, research, or service contracts with outsiders, etc.) been discussed.

All these differences are the result of decentralization of the decision-making power, as well as of political federalism. If they bear positive witness to the real autonomy of the tertiary education institutions, they are at the same time an obstacle to the smooth functioning of the global higher education system. As a matter of fact, they greatly hamper the mobility of students, teachers, and scientists, they lead to stress (imbalanced student/teacher ratio) and other such situations.

Some recent trends and developments of the Swiss higher education system include movements at the legislative, administrative, and financing levels; the operational level; and the international level.

The Federal Act concerning financial assistance to the universities, in force since 1968, is being revised with a view to simplifying the financing modalities of the central government, confining the latter's conceptual role to planning tasks and giving financial impulses in fields of national interest. The Federal Institutes of Technology, under a transitory regime since the takeover of the Lausanne FIT, will soon be given a new organization law. The federal administration in the field of science, research, and further

Table 4
Distribution of students (S) and beginners (B) according to disciplines and universities

		Humanities + Social Sc.	Exact + Nat. Sciences	Medicine Pharmacy	Engineering Sciences	Total
Uni Basel	S	3,568	1,336	1,807	—	6,711
	B	650	237	227	—	1,014
Uni Bern	S	5,625	1,668	1,765	—	9,058
	B	785	220	258	—	1,263
Uni Fribourg	S	4,656	490	192	—	5,338
	B	1,027	85	60	—	1,172
Uni Geneva	S	7,878	1,695	1,480	301	11,354
	B	1,870	271	211	67	2,419
Uni Lausanne	S	4,152	882	1,460	—	6,494
	B	1,147	141	180	—	1,468
Uni Neuchâtel	S	1,716	504	58	73	2,351
	B	456	62	38	21	577
Gr. Sch. St Gall	S	3,507	—	—	—	3,507
	B	790	—	—	—	790
Uni Zurich	S	13,907	2,105	3,324	—	19,336
	B	2,034	303	370	—	2,707
FIT Lausanne	S	—	809	—	2,425	3,234
	B	—	133	—	593	726
FIT Zurich	S	279	3,682	555	6,188	10,704
	B	71	739	86	1,134	2,070
Théol. Lucerne	S	211	—	—	—	211
	B	55	—	—	—	55
Pédag. St Gall	S	108	67	—	—	175
	B	22	15	—	—	37
Total	S	45,607	13,238	10,641	8,987	78,473
	B	8,807	2,206	1,430	1,855	14,298

Source: Federal Office for Statistics and Swiss University Information System (SUIS)

education is being restructured in order to be headed by a State Secretary.

As a consequence of the public finance problems in the late 1970s, the universities increased their service function and tightened their links with the private economy and the public services in order to increase their income. The Confederation took special measures in the field of computer science to help the universities and other institutions to catch up. Other federal measures were decided in order to promote recurrent education, both academic and vocational as well as academic mobility.

Two main factors—the end of the increase in students number as well as the lack of highly qualified staff in our economy—coincide with the true concern of guaranteeing a better access for all groups of the population to higher education. The development of further education, a cautious but real opening of the universities to the hitherto not admitted (e.g., to candidates without a school-leaving certificate, candidates earning their living, etc.) is gradually taking place. An improvement of the sometimes quite strenuous conditions of learning and teaching (especially in the humanities) is also called for. Last

but not least, there is the problem of recruitment of academic staff.

The contacts and exchanges which are fairly frequent between the Swiss and many other foreign universities. Especially with German universities, organizational and structural similarities, e.g., due to the federal systems, can be found. Negotiations are taking place with neighboring countries regarding the mutual recognition of higher education diplomas.

It should also be mentioned that even if Switzerland maintains a certain distance with respect to the construction of Europe, it will and cannot remain indifferent to it. There is a positive feature for the field of higher education: the necessity to open up toward Europe, to coordinate activities with those of the European Community or, simply, to offer a unified front, will encourage Switzerland to become more flexible, especially regarding certain excessive particularities.

As the Swiss government promotes the mobility of students, teachers, researchers, and to the recognition of diplomas, universities are intensifying their efforts in these fields. Switzerland is preparing for participation in international programs of mobility; it is also a party to numerous other conventions established on a multilateral, bilateral or intergovernmental level (e.g., Council of Europe, UNESCO), between universities, or even (in many cases) between faculties or academies.

The Swiss tertiary system is being confronted with numerous challenges (e.g., European integration, growing demand of the industry for applied research). It is also torn between opposite tendencies: sectorialization versus interdisciplinarity; basic versus applied research; elitism versus "education for all"; expanding know-how versus ethics, etc.

With regard to these problems, a certain number of priorities arise (e.g., the ones raised by the Swiss Council of Science) and can be summarized as follows:

(a) to increase the financial commitment of the Confederation in this field;

(b) to strengthen the management structures of the cantonal universities, and thereby foster their initiative;

(c) to encourage the coordination between tertiary institutions;

(d) to improve teaching conditions;

(e) to adjust the higher education system to the requirements of economy and society;

(f) to better prepare the junior staff;

(g) to pass the "entrance examination" in the European university space;

(h) to remain the main buttress of public research.

This is a critical time for the Swiss higher education system, but it is also a time of challenge, change, innovation, and opening up towards the future.

Bibliography

Dällenbach J F 1989 *Comparison of Higher Education Policies in Small Countries of the European Region: Switzerland.* Swiss Science Council, Bern
Garke E 1990 Switzerland. In: Wickremasinghe W (ed.) 1990 *Handbook of Educational Systems of the World.* Houston, Texas
Swiss Science Council 1989a *La place scientifique Suisse: Horizon 1995. Objectifs de la politique Suisse en matière de recherche: pour la période 1992–1995.* Swiss Science Council, Bern
Swiss Science Council 1989b *La place universitaire suisse: Horizon 1995. Perspectives du développement universitaire suisse pour la période 1992–1995.* Swiss Science Council, Bern
Switzerland, Federal Office of Statistics 1986 *Recherche et développement en Suisse 1986.* Federal Office of Statistics, Bern
Switzerland, Federal Office of Statistics 1987 *Formation Professionnelle 1986/87.* Federal Office of Statistics, Bern
Switzerland, Federal Office of Statistics 1989 *Diplômes des Hautes Ecoles Suisses.* Federal Office of Statistics, Bern
Switzerland, Federal Office of Statistics 1990 *Annuaire statistique de la Suisse 1990.* Federal Office of Statistics, Bern

E. Poglia; J-F. Dällenbach; E. Garke

Syria

1. Higher Education and Society

Historically, Syria has witnessed a succession of civilizations such as the Canaanites (known as Phoenicians), Amorrites, Assyrians, and Aramaens. These and other peoples of Syria left traces that display the beginnings of civilized life in settled agriculture, animal husbandry, pottery, ceramics and glass works, textile industry, and the growth and spread of commerce on land and sea. Syrian archaeological findings illustrate original art in city building, sculpture, and ornaments. Tens of thousands of clay tablets, engraved with cuneiform script, have been discovered and are now classified in libraries and archives at Mari, Ugarit, and Ebla. The first alphabet was found at Ugarit.

With the advent of Islam, the religion that sprung from Arabia in the middle of the seventh century, Syria was to experience the greatest revolution it has ever seen. It transformed social relations and affected the behavior, culture, values, and attitudes of the Syrians. It encouraged people to acquire knowledge so as to help them understand the religion and to organize their life better. Mosques became learning centers somehow resembling universities. This led to a flourishing movement in various disciplines: language, grammar, philosophy, mathematics, astrology, medicine, and music. Caliphs (prophet Muhammed's successors) urged and supported scholars and translators to render their books and to translate Greek and Latin scientific texts into Arabic.

With the rising of the Turkish civilization, Syria became a province of the Ottoman Empire. Arts and literature were encouraged at the beginning. But Syria (*Bilad ash Sham*), which then comprised Lebanon, Jordan, and Palestine, began to feel the occupation becoming increasingly oppressive. In the early years of the twentieth century, the beginnings of a new development grew from the contact made by members of some of the well-to-do families, close to, or descending from, the ruling classes, with European countries or with the cultural transformations going on in Egypt at that time.

Under the Treaty of Sèvres (August 10, 1920) Syria, with its present frontiers, was officially placed under French control. In 1946 a sovereign and independent Syria saw the existing national frontiers take shape, undergoing many changes before the Baath Arab Socialist Party took power on March 8, 1963.

After Independence Syria witnessed several governments. All of them faced almost the same problems, but in particular, socioeconomic orientation and the liberation of occupied Arab territories of Palestine. With the Baath Arab Socialist Party in power, fundamental reforms were initiated in the economic, political and constitutional spheres. An agrarian reform promulgated in 1963 redistributed the vast land ownerships, limited private agriculture in terms of fertility and location, and encouraged the formation of cooperatives. Developments in several industries naturally followed all under a system in which the state played the dominant role. The remainder of the Gross National Product (GNP) is made up of cooperatives and individual enterprises. Finding a just solution to the Palestinian cause, developing agriculture and extractive and manufacturing industries, and improving public health and education were always questions of prime importance.

The size and rate of growth of population has increased considerably since the Second World War, today standing at 3.4 percent, which is one of the highest rates in the world. The obvious economic development and the improvement of social and health conditions in the 1970s and 1980s were the main reasons. The infant mortality rate has decreased appreciably due to perinatal medical care. The number of inhabitants was three million in 1945. The most recent statistics put that number at 12 million. In 1960, 37 percent of the population lived in the cities, and 63 percent in rural areas. However, in 1990, 50 percent of the population were urban, due to the emergence of different industries, the emigration of peasants, and the expansion of towns to include nearby villages. More than 90 percent of the inhabitants of Syria are Arabs in origin, the rest are ethnic minorites, including Kurds, Armenians, Turkmen, or Circassians. Arabic is the official language, and all citizens speak and write it. The middle class is the largest socioeconomic group in the country. Class distinction and disparity in the standards of living on a wide scale do not exist. Thirty-five percent of the population work in governmental departments and 65 percent in the private sector. However, with regards to labor force, the proportion of agricultural workers is 23 percent, professional and technical workers 31 percent, and people working in the services sector 47 percent.

A limited number of schools were set up in large Syrian cities. The establishment of the Arab Medical Institute in 1903 marked the inception of university teaching in Syria. The Institute taught such subjects as medicine, dentistry, and pharmacology. Syrian as well as Arab students were enrolled, but only students coming from wealthy families were able to join the Institute. Founded in 1923, the Law Institute

graduated students who were to occupy governmental and political posts and who went on to become lawyers and judges. Students from Arab countries also entered the Institute, though their number was very small.

The state, at present, has concentrated efforts on higher education and given it priority in order to attain the following objectives:

(a) To secure technical and qualified cadres to work in different production centers;

(b) to undertake research in applied sciences in the light of the plans for social and economic development;

(c) to undertake research in basic sciences so as to make contributions to knowledge;

(d) to disseminate culture and education amongst the public at large.

The significance the state attaches to the development of higher education is great. Thus it assumes control of the universities academically, administratively, and financially. Religious organizations and societies, Moslem or Christian, do not play any role in modern Syrian academic life.

2. The Institutional Fabric of the Higher Education System

Both the Arab Medical Institute and the Institute of Law remained attached to the Syrian Ministry of Education as independent bodies until 1923 when they were merged under the name of the Syrian University. In 1946 four new faculties were established: science, arts, education (formally the Teachers Higher Training College) and engineering in Aleppo. Additionally, in 1955 a faculty of Islamic law was opened. In 1958 the Syrian University became the University of Damascus. Today, the University has 14 faculties in addition to the Higher Institute of Administrative Development. In 1959, Aleppo University was inaugurated to include 10 faculties together with the Higher Institute of Arab Scientific Heritage and a faculty of agriculture in Deir Azor later. Tishreen University was founded in Lattakia in 1971, and it now comprises eight faculties and the Center of Marine Science. In 1979 Al Baath University was founded in Homs. It now has 11 faculties, two of them being dentistry and veterinary science which are situated in Hama. The differences among the universities lie chiefly in the specializations which their departments and faculties offer.

In 1966, the Ministry of Higher Education was set up to supervise and coordinate the universities as well as intermediate institutes. Teaching in intermediate institutes began in 1958 when eight were attached to the Ministry of Public Works. Their number has now increased to 94; a good number belong to the

Table 1

Number of universities and intermediate institutes 1960–90

	1960	1965	1970	1975	1980	1990
Universities	2	2	2	3	4	4
Intermediate institutes	9	10	18	37	88	94

Ministry of Higher Education and the rest to different ministries. Intermediate institutes qualify assistants in the fields of health, agriculture, industry, and tourism. Thus, all higher education institutions belong to the state with no private sector involvement.

Scientific research forms an important part of university work, either through higher studies, independent research carried out by members of staff, or contracts universities sometimes make with firms and companies. There are, however, specialized research centers associated with the different governmental departments, but their main purpose has nothing to do with teaching.

Table 1 shows the number of universities and intermediate institutes in Syria from 1960 to 1990.

During the 1970s, the number of higher education institutions increased remarkably, and President Assad's government vigorously pursued the policy of democratic education. All holders of the baccalaureate certificates are admitted to universities and institutes taking into consideration geographical and demographical factors. Students wishing to apply to the humanities faculties are required to hold the baccalaureate certificate in literary specialization, while those applying to the technical faculties must hold the baccalaureate certificate in scientific specialization. The required grade average differs from faculty to faculty and from year to year. The five top students who hold the baccalaureate certificate in technical, industrial, agricultural, or commercial specializations can apply to the faculties that correspond with their disciplines.

The university council recommends the number of students to be admitted the following academic year. The recommendations are usually discussed by the council of higher education. A decision is taken by a committee chaired by the prime minister in the presence of the appropriate ministers and rectors. Those admitted are chosen from among those who have already obtained the baccalaureate certificate or high school diploma in the last examination preceding their admission. Since 1985, this process has been computerized. Students may apply to several departments simultaneously. Their acceptance depends on the marks obtained in the baccalaureate examination. Applicants to the faculties of architectural engineering and fine arts sit an exam in drawing which determines their admission. This was introduced in 1983. In the same year, admission to the faculty of education also depended upon interviews. The latter arrangement has been used in the departments of journalism since 1987.

The number of students in the universities and intermediate institutes is set out in Table 2.

The number of students has increased since 1975 as a result of the policy of democratization and the wish of many students, particularly women, to pursue their study in the universities. Also, the rise in the number of students in institutes is clearly due to the founding of a large number of institutes after 1985 following the five-year governmental plan to increase the number of graduates of these institutes.

The minimum residence requirement for the first degree in medicine is six years; five years for engineering, pharmacy, veterinary science, and dentistry; and finally, four years for science, arts, law, and education. The first university degree is the bachelor's degree and is granted by the university council and signed by the Minister of Higher Education. To be eligible for admission to a graduate course of study, a student must hold a bachelor's degree with an average of "good," the grade given to students who get a score of 60–69 in a subject. Admission to a master's degree course requires a student to hold the graduate diploma with an average of "good," the grade given to a student who gets a score of 65–74 in a graduate course. The minimum residence requirement for the graduate diploma is one year, for a master's degree two years and usually ending with the submission of a thesis, examined orally by a three-person committee nominated by the council of scientific affairs in the university. A student registering for a doctorate degree should get a gradu-

Table 2

Number of students in the universities and intermediate institutes 1960–90

	1960	1965	1970	1975	1980	1985	1990
Universities	10,116	33,733	36,761	61,156	94,794	131,224	169,139
Intermediate institutes	—	—	419	2,747	6,589	8,992	22,404

ate diploma and a master's degree with an average of "good" in both, and carry out research for two years minimum, though extension can be granted when necessary. The main requirement for this degree is to submit a dissertation to be examined orally by a committee of five members nominated by the university council.

3. Governance, Administration, and Finance

3.1 National Administration

In Syria, the Ministry of Higher Education is primarily responsible for the development of higher education. It supervises and coordinates higher education institutions. Higher education is organized and run through ministerial decisions or the higher education council chaired by the minister.

The congresses of the Baath Socialist Party draw higher education general policy such as opening new universities and institutes, orienting students towards specializations needed for development, and directing scientific research and university activities and other issues pertinent to higher education. A bureau in the party regional leadership, responsible for higher education and student affairs, supervises the execution of the party decisions in this respect and keeps in touch with the prime minister, who, in turn, presides over a committee which allocates student numbers, to every discipline, and decides on higher education programs to be carried out by the ministry and universities.

Universities enjoy financial as well as administrative independence. The main source of income is the government grants. Each university receives a subsidy, as an ordinary budget, directly from the Ministry of Finance, and a fund, as an investment budget, from the Ministry of Planning, after submitting its own budget proposals on a yearly basis or five-year plan. Subsidizing intermediate institutes is the responsibility of the ministries concerned. The proportions dedicated to higher education of GNP is not known. It can be stated that the proportions devoted to higher education institutions from the budget were as follows: 2 percent in 1970, increasing to 2.25 percent, 2.3 percent, and 3.58 percent in 1980, 1985, and 1990 respectively. This shows a slight increase in the sums set aside for the aforementioned institutions.

3.2 Institutional Administration

The department is the basic unit in higher education, around which revolve most academic activities, such as designing the curricula, holding lectures, seminars, and practical training sessions, and undertaking research. The chairperson, who administers departmental work, is appointed by ministerial decision in accordance with a recommendation from the rector. There is, in addition, the departmental general board which meets three times a year. This board, including all members of the teaching staff, members of the technical staff, and two students, a graduate, and an undergraduate, represent the student's union. It is presided over by the chairperson. Its function is to plan improvements to the academic and professional standards in the department. It discusses scientific research, sending assistant lecturers abroad to pursue graduate study, departmental requirements for premises and equipment, and the previous year's activities.

Departments, and their related specializations, constitute a faculty. Each faculty has a dean, assisted by two vice deans, one for scientific affairs and the other for administrative and student affairs. All are appointed by ministerial decision often with recommendations from the rector. The deans administer the academic, financial, and administrative affairs of their faculties, complying with the rules and regulations of the university. They are responsible for fulfilling the decisions of the council of higher education and the three university councils, as well as the faculty council. Each faculty has a faculty council which coordinates departmental activities, organizes examinations, recommends the conferring of degrees, regulates internal affairs, considers participation in scientific conferences, suggests a training program for faculty employees, and reports its decisions to the university council. Each faculty has a committee for student affairs which is consulted in all matters relevant to the cultural, social, and academic interests as well as student health. It also considers rules for transferring students from one faculty to a similar one in another Syrian university.

The university is administered by the rector, two vice rectors, a general secretary, and three councils: the university council, the council of scientific affairs, and the council of students affairs. The rector governs and directs the academic, administrative, and financial affairs of the university. He or she is responsible for enforcing the laws and regulations of the university as well as the decisions of the council of higher education. The rector has the same administrative powers held by the minister with regard to government officials. These powers, however, apply only to university employees and workers. The rector is appointed by presidential decree on a three year mandate. The two vice-rectors assist the rector in discharging the duties of his office, and one of them acts for him in absentia. In administrative matters, the rector is assisted by the secretary of the university who, under the supervision of the rector, is responsible for the implementation of the university's laws and regulations.

The university council suggests the appointment and promotion of academic staff, confers academic degrees, decides on matters related to scholarships, grants, and research programs, draws up financial and administrative regulations, prepares a construction plan for building of new premises, such as hospitals, farms, printing houses, and so on, and fixes the dates of the academic calendar for examinations and vacations. The university council is assisted by two other councils: the council of scientific affairs and the council of students affairs. The first council organizes, finances, and supervises all matters related to scientific activities and research within the university. It puts forward internal regulations for faculties, rules for scholarships and participation in scientific conferences, supervises publications of the university's specialized journals and textbooks, and establishes academic and cultural relationships with other universities and international organizations.

The council of student affairs is taken up with such matters as the regulations of student admission, transfer of students from one university to another, disciplinary actions, scientific trips, as well as running sociocultural activities, accommodation and health services, and all matters relating to the academic welfare of students.

Coordination of all Syrian universities is carried out via the council of higher education, chaired by the minister of higher education. Its membership is as follows:

(a) the minister of higher education as president;

(b) the rectors of the four Syrian universities—Damascus, Aleppo, Tishreen, and Al Baath;

(c) the vice-rectors for scientific affairs in the four Syrian universities and one vice-rector for administrative and student affairs nominated by the minister;

(d) three vice-ministers from the ministries of Education, Planning, and Higher Education;

(e) the director of the departments of scientific research and planning in the Ministry of Higher Education;

(f) three specialists from the ministries of Industry, Agriculture, and Health;

(g) two members representing the teachers' union;

(h) two students representing the students' union;

(i) the general secretary of the council.

Among the council of higher education's main functions are the following:

(a) to take the necessary measures to carry out the higher educational policy and to facilitate the fulfillment of scientific, cultural, social, economical, and national aims of the state;

(b) to suggest higher educational policy on all levels;

(c) to suggest the general policy of scientific research at the university level;

(d) to set down general rules for student admissions;

(e) to coordinate educational programs and scientific

research and publication of books in the universities and institutes attached to the Ministry of Higher Education;

(f) to advise on other matters related to the council's functions.

This council brings several committees together. The most important are: the committee of higher education policy which recommends the general educational programs; the committee of qualifications and workers' affairs which is concerned with appointing, promoting, training, and developing the technical skills of the working people in the universities, and which nominates committees to evaluate the scientific work of the teaching staff; the committee for assessing academic degrees obtained from Arab and foreign universities and which draws up the rules of this process; the committee of research and higher studies which distributes the higher study branches and coordinates research areas in the universities; and finally, the committee of educational programs and curricula which deals with the study plans across similar departments and faculties.

4. Faculty and Students: Teaching, Learning, and Research

4.1 Faculty

The number of teaching staff in the Syrian universities has noticeably increased between 1960 and 1990. This can be seen in the following figures given for five-yearly intervals: 280, 567, 630, 919, 881, 1,200, 1,862. Statistics for staff in the intermediate institutes or part-timers on contract who change a lot during the same academic year, are not available.

Members are appointed either as graduate assistants through a contest supervised by the Ministry of Higher Education according to the needs of each university. Graduate assistants must hold at least a bachelor's degree with an average of "good." They are usually sent abroad for four years after being appointed to prepare for a doctorate in his or her field. Alternatively, the Ministry of Higher Education announces university needs for PhD holders who have obtained the degree at their own expense. However, in both cases, a doctorate holder should submit the necessary documents together with a copy of his or her dissertation to the committee which assesses academic degrees within the council of higher education. This committee validates the degree of the appointee in keeping with the University Regulation Ordinance, and according to special principles available for qualifying any degree from any university and in any field. The department concerned then forms a three-member committee to examine the scientific content of the candidate's dissertation. The committee of qualifications and workers' affairs in the higher education council grants its final decision as regards the three-member committee. The dissertation, however, is sent confidentially to the latter committee to prepare a final assessment. This report is passed on to the council of higher education which, in turn, sends it to be approved by the specialist department, the faculty council, scientific affairs council, and the university council respectively. The minister eventually issues a decision appointing the doctorate holder a lecturer in the department. Through this process the candidate is interviewed for his or her competence in the Arabic language. The candidate should also deliver a lecture through which his or her eligibility as a lecturer is considered.

The newly appointed lecturer spends at least five years before being promoted to the rank of an assistant professor (senior lecturer). Assistant professors spend five further years before becoming full professors. In both cases, the individual submits his or her scientific publications for the five years that have ensued: to a committee which recommends the work before it is processed through the department, faculty, and university councils. The candidate is eventually promoted to a higher rank by ministerial decision.

All members of staff are subject to the University Regulation Ordinance, which differs from the general law governing civil servants. This ordinance has its own articles for the appointment, promotion, vacations, and bonuses connected with full-time university staff.

A member of staff works 39 hours per week, while the teaching load is regulated by the executive rules of the University Regulation Ordinance. The teaching load differs according to rank of lecturer, assistant professor, and professor, and his or her administrative or scientific responsibilities. The remaining teaching hours may be distributed among the fields of teaching, research, and professional duties by a decision from the university council.

All teaching staff, lecturers, laboratory assistants, officials, and workers are members of the teachers' union, which has a branch in each university. The teachers' union, in Syria, includes all the universities' employees together with those working in schools and institutions of the Ministry of Education.

4.2 Students

Students are classified by the universities into two groups: first, basic science, that is, medicine, engineering, science, agriculture, and so on; and second, social science and the humanities. Table 3 illustrates this.

Science students were 25 percent of all students in 1960, and 50 percent in 1990. This increase comes through the ambitious development programs in agriculture, industry, construction, and the social and health services.

The number of university graduates began to develop from 1960 onward. The following figures display the increase at five-yearly intervals: 670, 2,409, 3,409, 3,926, 10,105, 9,950, 13,508. A big leap can be noticed in the numbers of graduates between 1975 and 1985, due to the rising number of university students, on the one hand, and the change of the one-semester study system into a bi-semester one. The proportion of graduates compared with the tremendous number of students is small indeed, due in part to the fact that a student may stay registered in the faculty for a period double the minimum residency period required to get a bachelor's degree. This leads to accumulations in the number of undergraduate students.

The bi-semester system is based on two semesters in one academic year, and it is not the same as the credit hours system. At the end of each semester, the students sit a written, oral, or practical exam. Students are examined in all courses at the end of every semester. If a student fails in more than four courses, he or she can still proceed to the following year, provided that the student sits an exam in these courses together with the following year's courses. The bachelor's degree is generally granted in a single field, like Arabic, English, mathematics, or civil engineering, and so on.

Higher education in Syria is free. Syrian students pay only nominal tuition fees; almost the same applies to university accommodation charges; even the textbooks are supplied through the university at very low prices.

5. Conclusion

This enables virtually all students, especially those from less well off families, to go to university. Students from outlying areas, such as the border areas, or under-developed regions are encouraged to enter the faculties of medicine, pharmacy, and dentistry; they are accepted with two scores less in the grade

Table 3
Number of students in the universities classified into groups 1960–90

	1960	1965	1970	1975	1980	1985	1990
Basic science	2,056	8,635	10,618	29,639	48,876	67,246	81,383
Social sciences and humanities	8,060	25,098	26,143	31,514	45,918	63,978	81,937

average in comparison to ordinary students in order to secure specialists for these areas.

There is only one student organization in Syria which is called the National Union of Syrian Students. This organization comprises all students in the universities and institutes, and it has branches and committees representing students in Syrian as well as foreign universities. The percentage of the student members of the union inside the country is 79 percent. The union plays an important role in supervising the sociocultural activities, sports and tours, as well as the health and accommodation services. It represents the students in the university councils and participates in scientific and administrative work.

Higher education institutions in Syria are well-organized, have several decades' experience with high-level teaching, and are governed by advanced laws and regulations. The policy of democratic teaching provides good opportunities for youth to enter the universities and institutes on a wide scale. Of course, some young people who do not wish to pursue university studies naturally go to different production sectors, while other students go abroad, usually to study medicine and engineering, either because they can finance their own studies in foreign universities, or because the scores they got in the baccalaureate examination debar them from the faculty of their choice.

Institutes make their contribution by qualifying large numbers of students for which governmental departments are badly in need, thus reducing the pressure which the universities are exposed to in admitting large numbers of students.

However, the economic difficulties which confronted Syria during the 1980s affected it in two main areas. First, they reduced employment opportunities and gave rise to a graduate surplus, some of which was absorbed by the job market in wealthy Arab countries, while others went into private enterprises. Moreover, governmental establishments in Syria should employ all graduates of engineering and some of intermediate institutes. Second, there is a lack of equipment and other necessary means that can be used to perform the teaching process adequately. Most departments, especially in the humanities, are understaffed and overcrowded. Together with heavy teaching loads, examinations and related duties have reflected negatively on scientific research output of teaching staff.

Some research is conducted by graduate students, mainly in literature and humanities, but research is limited with regard to the scientific and technological fields. It only exists to fulfill the requirements of academic degrees, irrespective of their practical benefits. Contracts which production centers pass with the universities to undertake research can be described as mere services and serve mainly to increase the income of teaching staff with no real scientific value and without leading to any publication. Nevertheless, some measures have been taken to improve the conditions of the teaching process.

Another step was made by the governmental authorities to appoint 3,452 graduate assistants to be sent abroad for five years to prepare for doctoral degrees. Many are back now and work in the different higher education institutions. This has considerably increased the number of teaching staff and improved graduate studies and research. Preparations are now in hand to improve the conditions of the premises, laboratories, libraries, and so on.

The following points represent the essentials of the government's policies for higher education:

(a) considering geographical distribution of universities with regard to the population and the area. This applies to intermediate institutes;

(b) completing construction works of the buildings of existing universities;

(c) providing the needs and necessities to equip laboratories used at undergraduate level, to improve the circumstances of practical work and promote its quality, so as to train students to deal with apparatus, and to extend training inside the workshops to include smithery, carpentry, and electricity as part of the syllabus;

(d) qualifying cadres of specialized laboratorians for the operation and maintenance of modern equipment;

(e) working in accordance with flexible financial systems to equip and maintain these laboratories;

(f) financing the process of securing reference books and specialized journals, updating work in university libraries, acquiring memberships in databanks, and establishing printing houses in all universities;

(g) encouraging newly appointed members of staff to follow educational courses and to acquaint them with teaching methodologies;

(h) constantly sending members of staff on sabbaticals for limited periods to technologically advanced countries to enable them to study recent achievements in their own fields;

(i) improving the standard of living and the financial conditions of people working in the universities and institutes;

(j) concentrating on scientific research conducted through graduate studies in different fields and at all levels particularly in applied science, and granting financial rewards for supervisors;

(k) undertaking applied research through the contracts made with production centers to solve particular problems, with the aim of supporting research and improving the financial status of the working people concerned;

(l) facilitating the publication of research works;

(m) enhancing the relation between faculty and students through seminars and discussions;

(n) combining the teaching process with practical affairs through the application of theories and results of research in the production centers;

(o) collaborating with production centers to train and qualify graduates and to exchange experience.

Democratic teaching remains the cornerstone of higher education in Syria at all levels: social, cultural, health, and production. In the light of development programs in agriculture, industry, and services, it is necessary every five years to reconsider the plan of directing students to work in different specializations.

Bibliography

The University Regulation Ordinance in Syria 1975
Executive Regulations of the University Regulation Ordinance 1982
Statistical Data in Syria Since 1960. Central Bureau of Statistics
Higher Education in Syria. Ministry of Higher Education
Intermediate Teaching in Syria. Ministry of Higher Education
The World Almanac 1990. St. Martin's Press, New York
Symposium on Higher Education in the Arab World 1985. Arab Organization for Education, Culture, and Science

A. M. S. Hussein

T

Tanzania

1. Higher Education and Society

The public momentum that spearheaded the support of Tanzanian higher education in the 1960s and less so in the 1970s has shrunk, making the pictorial representation of the education system even more pyramidic. The growth of tertiary education had previously been encouraged by the need to develop a strong local labor base to replace the British Administration and to occupy public/private institutions of the then-healthy economy. The institution building heat of the post-Independence era that witnessed the mushrooming of the University of Dar es Salaam and other tertiary institutions, cooled off in the mid-1970s and came to a complete stop in the 1980s to give way to social demands for universal primary education and adult literacy/education, but also because of the economic difficulties. However, the Tanzanian education system has inculcated and maintained a high degree of political awareness and participation.

The 1988 census revealed that Tanzania's growth rate has contracted from 3.2 percent to 2.8 percent since 1978. Other sources put the growth rate at 3.1 percent. There are 23.2 million people in Tanzania. There is widespread rural–urban migration.

Tanzania is basically an agricultural country. Agriculture earns 80 percent of the country's foreign exchange earnings and accounts for 40 percent of the Gross National Product (GNP).

Major constraints on the development of the agricultural sector include: low levels of technology; poor distribution of inputs; inadequate rural credit; late payment of peasants by crop authorities; poor marketing organization; erratic pricing policies; dependability on the rains; wastages; and inadequate storage facilities. As a result a large potential for expanding crop production remains unexploited.

The structure of government and main political goals became clear after the Arusha Declaration (1967) which put the nation on the path to socialism and self-reliance. The major means of production were nationalized including financial institutions, local and foreign firms, buildings, hospitals, and schools.

The first seven years of exchange of flags exhibited no fundamental differences from the colonial administrative strategy of divide and rule, commodity production, lack of industrialization, and racial discrimination creating artificial divisions. Thus, during the colonial era a tripartite schooling system existed for the majority Black, Asians, and Whites.

The system was funded by the state, which favored the Whites (Msekwa and Maliyamkono 1979). Per capita spending was 1.9 percent for Blacks compared to 3.9 percent for Whites of all government recurrent expenditure at Independence. In addition, the colonial government designed a system of job discrimination such that the majority of Black people ended up with jobs and positions of inferior levels in order to reserve technical and managerial jobs for the White minority and some to Asians. Such injustices forced the Asians to go into commerce and trade as an alternative. Thus, education for self-reliance, a system introduced to serve the major social objectives of socialism and self-reliance, was clearly a policy to reject the previous discriminating educational policies. Schools, including tertiary education, were open to all and paid for by the state. The education sector not only expanded but also diversified the fields of study in order to fill employment gaps and to increase labor productivity.

Other actions taken to rectify the ill-conceived colonial education system included changing the curriculum to provide more Tanzanian content. Some textbooks were written to replace those which reflected colonial mentality. Ways and means were introduced to prepare the student for the service of an egalitarian society.

Agriculture as a subject (theory and practice) was emphasized in schools, and national service where students spend time as militia before employment was introduced.

All this was meant to change the old colonial attitudes and prepared students for the challenge of an independent socialist state. The new values would be inculcated while young men and women were still in school, but they would continue to observe the new values at places of work and at home while living in *Ujamaa* villages (i.e., communal villages of the 1970s Tanzanian style).

In the early 1990s, Tanzania seems to have postponed some of the policies declared in 1967; although the main goals of socialism and self-reliance remain basically the same, some of the earlier methods adopted have been at least temporarily abandoned following the economic crisis. Liberalization, for example, is part and parcel of the newly adopted means. Education, still paid for largely by the state, is receiving subsidy from individual beneficiaries and the state total recurrent spending has dropped from nearly 20 percent in 1967 to less than 5 percent in

1988. As a result there has been a reduction in the percentage of students benefiting from the education system for instance, primary enrollment dropped from over 95 percent in 1977/78 to about 70 percent in 1988. The nonsalary inputs at all levels of education have disappeared to an embarrassing level.

Religious bodies have not been quite as active in higher education as they were for primary, secondary and specialized centers such as schools for the deaf. However, there are centers covering such disciplines as health, journalism, and community development organized and funded by religious groups.

2. The Institutional Fabric of the Higher Education System

The organization of higher education takes the shape of the British system and subject concentration begins while in secondary school. All tertiary institutions including the University of Dar es Salaam and Sokoine University of Agriculture are publicly owned.

Three main categories of higher education exist. The University of Dar es Salaam and Sokoine University of Agriculture are the only degree-granting bodies. They offer undergraduate degrees, master's degrees, doctoral degrees, and a few certificates and diplomas on their own and sometimes under sandwich arrangements, especially at the graduate level, where students may do courses in overseas universities and conduct fieldwork or experiments at home or vice versa. The second function of the two universities is to conduct both basic and applied research. Findings suggest that most of the research conducted in universities is applied (ESAURP 1987). A third function is to provide service to the general public. This is done by advice and consultancy. Consultancy has been on the increase due to changing attitudes regarding local expertise and income poten-

tial. The Economic Research Bureau, the Institute of Resource Assessment, the Institute of Development Studies, the Institute of Production Innovation, and the Faculty of Engineering are some of the most active participants.

Diplomas and advanced diplomas are offered by nondegree-offering institutions for areas such as water resources, land surveying and town planning, animal husbandry, and finance management, just to mention a few. There are three leading technical institutions in the country distributed evenly to the southern, northern, and Dar es Salaam zones. Other institutions offering diplomas are those specializing in agriculture, teacher training, and natural resources.

A number of institutions exist in similar areas of study, and some specialize in other disciplines at certificate level. This forms the third category.

Available data on enrollment into the higher education system given in Table 1 indicates that out of every 1,000 competing postsecondary school students between 20 and 24 years of age, less than 10 (i.e., less than 1 percent) are accorded opportunities for higher education, either locally or through overseas scholarship awards.

Over the 20-year period (1967/88) those selected have remained between the range of 0.3 percent (1967) and 0.7 percent (1983) of the entire 20 to 24-year-old population.

Qualifications at degree, diploma, and certificate levels, the nature and content of the program, and the length of time needed to attain a given certification are determined by the examining institution. Degrees are offered only by the two universities, but each of the tertiary institutions examines their own students and their governing councils offer diplomas or certificates. For the nonuniversity tertiary institutions relevant or parent ministries must participate as well. However, institutes

Table 1
Proportion of the age group 20–24 years enrolled in the higher education system in Tanzania at five-year intervals

Year	Enrollment (No) (10–24 yrs)	Total Population (20–24 yrs)	Enrollment as a percentage of total population 20–24 yrs
1967	5,290	1,841,848	0.3
1972	8,496	2,142,550[a]	0.4
1978	13,360	2,659,114	0.5
1983	20,348	2,988,276[a]	0.7
1988	18,000[b]	3,476,150	0.5

Sources: 1. Ministry of Education: Basic Education Statistics of Tanzania (BEST) 1981–85, June 1986 and 1983–87, June, 1988 2. Annual Manpower Report to the President 1968, 1974, 1975 ... 1983 3. Economic Surveys 1967–72, 1972–76 and 1982 4. Population Censuses 1967, 1978 and 1988 a Figures have been estimated using the average growth rate of about 3.1 percent for the period 1967/88 b The figure has been estimated from the observed trend

are becoming more autonomous every day, though at the university level examinations are regulated by the external examiners from other universities who must be approved by the university senate and council.

Graduate programs are offered to students with first class and upper-second class pass levels at their undergraduate programs. This is universal to all faculties at Sokoine University of Agriculture and at the University of Dar es Salaam.

3. Governance, Administration, and Finance

3.1 National Administration

Higher education is centrally administered by the state through relevant ministries. Because there is a tendency for each ministry to have its own institutions, coordinating higher education is sometimes problematic. Individual institutions have their own boards and councils which are semiautonomous, but these bodies simply translate central government plans. Evaluation is done collectively.

The Ministry of Labour and Manpower Development allocates students at colleges to employers usually on their first or second choices.

3.2 Finance

Higher Education is virtually paid for by the state (92 percent). Other sources are tuition and fees (6 percent) and the university's own services to the community (2 percent) (ESAURP 1987 p. 201). Because of the financial support, naturally the state, through the ministries of Education and Labor and Manpower Development, controls the system.

An Education Board has been formed to advise the minister on matters of education. Among other duties the Board will seek less costly ways of providing higher education, which already consumes 35 percent of the total recurrent budget for education. Distance learning is being considered.

As is shown in Table 2, the share allocated to higher education relative to the Ministry of Educa-

tion's annual recurrent expenditure budget has been growing significantly over the last 10 years. It has clearly risen to slightly over 36 percent in 1987/88 from about 9 percent of the ministry's recurrent budget in 1977/78.

In terms of the Gross National Product (GNP), however, the proportion allocated to higher education has remained relatively small and somewhat constant at slightly above 0.4 percent between 1982 and 1987. This is, perhaps, partly due to the shockingly sharp decline in the proportion of the respective ministry's budget to the national budget which has dropped from 19.6 percent in 1962/63 to a merely 5.4 percent in 1987/88.

The Chief Executive Officer at the two universities is the vice-chancellor whose powers are shared by the senate and faculty boards. There are students, academic and nonacademic members of staff represented on virtually all the major committees.

3.3 Institutional Administration

The style of governing higher education institutions is the same across the board with minor differences between universities and tertiary institutions. They have executives, appointed by the state. They are responsible to the council presided over by an independent chairperson approved by a relevant minister or the president in the case of universities. The councils are made up of committees, of which the most important is the senate. Council members are professionals and politicians, both nominated and elected.

4. Faculty and Students: Teaching, Learning, and Research

4.1 Faculty

Available figures on the strength of teaching staff at the two universities are shown in Table 3. Of the University of Dar es Salaam's senior academic members of staff (including senior lecturers, associate professors, and professors) only 35 percent are

Table 2
Recurrent expenditure on the higher education system in Tanzania (in millions)

Year	Allocated amount (1)	Ministry's Recurrent Budget (2)	(1) as a % of (2) (3)	GNP (current market prices) (4)	(1) as a % of (4) (5)
1977/78	38.92	440.00	8.8	28,780	0.14
1982/83	254.42	913.14	27.9	57,995	0.44
1987/88	1,194.04	3,289.05	36.3	271,716[a]	0.44

Sources: 1. Ministry of Education—Annual Budget Estimates for 1977/78, 1982/83 and 1987/88 2. The Planning Commission—The Economic Survey 1988 3. ERB and Ministry of Planning & Economic Affairs and Planning—Tanzania Economic Trends, A Quarterly Review of the Economy, Vol. 1 No 4, January 1989
a Figure given for 1987 is the country's GDP (and not GNP) at factor cost using current market prices.

Table 3
Teaching staff at the universities of Dar es Salaam and Sokoine

	1983	1984	1985	1986	1987
Total Teaching Staff	963	877	1,025	1,136	1,087
Teacher/Student Ratio	1:3.2	1:3.8	1:3.3	1:3.0	1:3.1
DSM University					
Teaching Staff	963	877	1,025	910	879
Teacher/Student Ratio	1:3.2	1:3.8	1:3.3	1:3.3	1:3.3
Sokoine University					
Teaching Staff	—	—	—	226	208
Teacher/Student Ratio	—	—	—	1:2.1	1:2.4

localized, compared to 49 percent for Mauritius and just 14 percent for Swaziland.

Prospective university teaching staff are recruited after the first degree in all faculties and usually these are first-class graduates and in a few cases have upper-second class degrees. Most of them receive scholarships to study overseas for master's degrees initially and PhDs later. Ordinarily, they do their courses in an overseas institution and return home for a short period of time to collect data and conduct surveys or experiments. With master's degrees they are appointed assistant lecturers and become lecturers after obtaining a PhD. There must be a minimum of three years before going to the next rank, and other conditions include acceptable levels of teaching and publication. Research and nonteaching academic staff must publish nearly double that of the teaching staff, for promotion.

Members of staff, both academic and nonacademic, have their own professional bodies mainly concerned with terms of service, although the University of Dar es Salaam Academic Staff Association has voiced its concern on human rights issues when academic staff members in Tanzania and in other countries were politically harrassed. Nonuniversity institutions have student and staff associations too.

Research is conducted by the research bureaus and institutes, although during the long university break teaching staff may get time off to do field research.

4.2 Students

Table 4 presents a picture of student enrollment for the years where figures were available. Until 1984 Sokoine University of Agriculture was a faculty of the University of Dar es Salaam.

Issues of social class origin are not as significant as they were 30 years ago. However, women continue to be underrepresented in science, engineering, medicine, and agriculture. By 1984 total female enrollment in the universities was only 19 percent. A new law requires that an equal number of girls be admitted to the first year of secondary school in all public schools. Also, women enter the university directly after national service, so they do not have to have two years of practical working experience. Of course these advancement programs have their own problems.

Degree programs are decided upon by the National Planning Commission based on employment needs. Generally, universities are requested to establish faculties, bureaus, and institutions or departments. The internal arrangements and details on courses such as

Table 4
University education statistics: total enrollment at the two universities

	1970		1975		1980		1987	
	FRG	TZN	FRG	TZN	FRG	TZN	FRG	TZN
Law and Commerce	—	96	—	107	—	483	114	591
Arts and Social Science	—	739	—	764	—	525	214	961
Natural Sciences	—	307	—	426	—	399	46	403
Agriculture, Veterinary Medicine and Forestry	—	61	—	251	—	184	61	504
Engineering	—	—	—	243	—	535	32	628
Medical Sciences	—	113	—	250	—	273	45	267
Total	350	1,316	165	2,041	92	2,399	512	3,354
	1,666		2,206		2,491		3,866	

who the instructors should be, or how students should be assessed, are matters within the autonomy of the universities. All examinations are matters of the faculty, and the state does not interfere at all.

5. Conclusion

The Tanzania system of education has been hailed by a significant number of observers, although it is facing critical resource problems. State recurrent spending and capital development on education has dropped sharply and little has gone into other education infrastructures and nonsalary inputs. Parent or beneficiary contributions in the nature of fees and so forth will discourage the poor, and if this happens, issues of equity and care for the minority groups and women will obviously be affected. A more serious political problem will emerge. National economic planning, at least the labor sector, will be affected adversely as students make their own decisions based on private rates of return. On the one hand, for example, who will take courses leading to secondary-school teaching when teachers are so poorly paid? On the other hand student contributions through fees, be it through loans or direct cash payment, may encourage efficiency in the provision of quality university education.

With the growing population at the rate of 3.1 percent per annum, the nation is going to need new universities or additional space within the existing facilities. Money by means of fees, grants, consultancy, and university services will have to be raised. Additionally, employer/industry input in the institutional training programs should be enhanced.

These two major adjustments: resource raising, and creating a healthy relationship between institutions of higher learning and the employing agencies or industry, will undoubtedly require a different kind of administration to face up to those challenges. These and many others are the problems facing higher education in Tanzania.

Bibliography

Eastern and Southern African Universities Research Program (ESAURP) 1987 *University Capacity in Eastern and Southern African Countries*. James Currey, London
Kahama C G et al. 1986 *The Challenge for Tanzania's Economy*. James Currey, London
Maliyamkono T L 1982 *The Unproductive School*. African Publishers, Dar es Salaam
Ministry of Finance, Economic Affairs and Planning, 1988 *1988 Population Census Preliminary Report*. Bureau of Statistics, Ministry of Finance, Economic Affairs and Planning, Dar es Salaam
Msekwa P, Maliyamkono T L 1979 *The Experiments: Education Policy Formation Before and After the Arusha Declaration*. Black Star Agencies, Dar es Salaam

T. L. Maliyamkono

Thailand

1. Higher Education and Society

The establishment in 1899 of the specialized school named "The Royal Pages School" to educate skilled government officials, practically marked the origin of Thai higher education. However, the formal organization began when higher education was declared as postsecondary education in the National Education Scheme in 1902. Since then the provision of higher education was revised and reorganized from specialized education to a standard contemporary system. The transition was made by the implementation of several Educational Schemes and a series of National Education Plans corresponding to the National Social and Economic Development Plans initiated in 1961 (Nathalang 1970). Subsequently, the present higher education system has been shaped by Western influences combined with the physical, social, economic, and political factors, from which it has emerged.

Thailand occupies an area of 513,115 square kilometers on the Indo-Chinese Peninsula of South East Asia, stretching from 5°30′ to 20° north latitude and from 97°30′ to 105°30′ east longitude. It is surrounded by China, Laos, Cambodia, Vietnam, Malaysia, and Burma. Geographically, there are four regions: the rich and fertile central plain; the mountainous and forested north; the semi-arid northeast, and the sandy and wet south. In spite of her long history of wars with her immediate neighbors, the civil wars and coups, and the colonial rivalry period, Thailand remains one of the few developing countries never to have been under Western control. Her national frontiers have never changed over 150 years.

The population of Thailand was 27.2 and 51.8 million as of the years 1960 and 1985. There was a rapid growth of 3.6 percent per annum during the 1960s, and a remarkable slowdown in growth of 3.0 percent and 2.8 percent during the 1970s and in 1985 respectively as a result of an intensive family planning campaign. The population density per square kilometer increased from 51.1 in 1960 to 100.9 in 1985, ranging from 61.2 in the north to 439.1 in the central plain. Of the total population, approximately 88 percent resided in rural areas in 1960. The proportion decreased to 80 percent in 1985 mainly because of urbanization and rural-to-urban migration.

Although Thai nationals contributed to 98 percent of total population in 1960, only 80 percent were indigenous Thai. The remainder was made up of minority ethnic groups composed of the important Chinese immigrants, the native Lao, Khmer, Malay, and several hill tribes. It has been the policy of the Thai government for decades to blend these groups to the Thai way of life and culture. As a result, there is a growing trend of nationalization and at present almost 99 percent of the population are Thai nationals.

The dominant language is Thai which has four major dialects: official Thai; northern Thai; Isarn; and southern dialect. At least 80 percent of the total population speak and understand Thai which is mainly used as an official language. To eliminate minority problems, great emphasis is laid on weakening the languages of the minority groups and on promoting Thai. English is usually the second language taught in secondary schools and universities by government decree.

The occupational and social class structure consisted of the urban class-conscious group in Bangkok and big towns and the rural classless group in the villages and small up-country towns. Whereas the village society seems to have a single basic culture pattern and have no real hierarchical class structure, urban society indicates the class stratification where wealth, social position, political power, and government appointment are the key to success in social mobility (Watson 1980).

The series of Five-Year National Social and Economic Development Plans initiated in 1961 has not made much difference to the poor. The first two Plans emphasized the provision of basic infra-structure for economic development. The next two Plans were oriented towards social and cultural development and labor force production in the fields required by market demand and necessary for national development. It was the Fifth Plan (1982–86) which was the first to place emphasis on rural development, together with social services and income distribution.

Thailand has had a predominantly agricultural subsistence economy, but it is already envisaged that during the Sixth Plan (1987–91), it will become an agro-industrialized country. Hence, there are noteworthy changes in the structure of the economy. Agriculture which accounted for 39 percent of Gross Domestic Product (GDP) and employed 84 percent of the total labor force in 1960, decreased to 17 percent and 68 percent in 1985 respectively. Manufacturing industry, services, and trades increased. In 1985, they contributed to GDP for 29.8, 20.2, and 26.8 percent as compared to 15.9, 16.2, and 19.6 percent in 1960, and employed 14.1, 10.3, and 13.1 percent of total labor force respectively. Responding to the structural changes of the economy, institutions of higher education have been developed and become academic manufacturing institutions.

The stable factors in the Thai political system have remained the monarchy, the bureaucracy, and the centralized military-dominated polity. After the abolition of absolute monarchy in 1932, Thailand became a Western-style constitutional monarchy. The king exercises legislative power through the National Assembly, executive power through the cabinet, and judicial power through the Courts of Law. The cabinet, headed by the prime minister, forms the supreme governing body. Its structure is divided into three levels: central; provincial; and local. Central administration consists of ministries, each of which is divided into departments, divisions, and sections. The provincial administrative units covering 74 provinces in four geographical regions and the local government units in each province, are directly under the Ministry of Interior and the governor (Xuto 1987). As the government, through different ministries, has prime responsibility for the Thai educational system, the political structure and stance of the government are other factors influencing higher education.

Approximately 95 percent of the total population are Buddhists and the Buddhist monastery functions as a social and cultural center of the community. Despite its close connection with traditional education for the masses before the Second World War, in the early 1990s, the religious sector accounts for only a little in the development of higher education. Its main function is to provide postsecondary education for the monks.

In sum, higher education institutions are called upon as a central agent responding to an accelerating national development and the increasing social demand for higher education. The system originally produced elites and slowly developed prior to 1960. During the 1960s, rapid population growth and the requirement to accelerate the national growth led to the expansion in enrollment and programs. During the 1970s, the policy to lessen the rural–urban disparity led to the establishment of regional universities. The 1980s saw higher education as a means of transforming the country to become agro-industrially oriented.

2. The Institutional Fabric of the Higher Education System

All higher education institutions in Thailand are under government supervision and control. In 1989, they consisted of 13 traditional government universities and institutions, 1 open-admission and distance-teaching university, and 21 privately sponsored universities and colleges under the jurisdiction of the Ministry of University Affairs (MUA). Except the private ones, all institutions provide a full range of programs and university functions. In addition, there are 117 government teachers' colleges, vocational, technical, and other specialized colleges under the supervision and control of the Ministry of Education (MOE), plus 24 government colleges under several other ministries. These colleges offer specialized education relevant to the requirement of their ministries.

The first university, Chulalongkorn University, established in 1917, was a consolidation of the Royal Pages School and other specialized training schools. The second university was set up in 1933 offering programs in law, economics, and political sciences. In the early 1940s, three more universities specializ-

Table 1
Number of institutions by types

Types of support	Control	1960	1965	1970	1975	1980	1985
Government	MUA	5	7	12	13	14	14
	MOE	69	71	75	98	109	117
	Teacher training	27	29	29	36	36	36
	Vocational education	42	42	46	62	73	81
	Other ministries	18	22	22	24	24	24
Private	MUA	—	—	1	10	11	17

ing in medicine, agriculture, and fine arts were established in quick succession. Hence, in 1960, there were five universities, all located in Bangkok. The number of the universities increased, as shown in Table 1, by the late 1960s when the regional universities were established and the private sectors were allowed to operate higher education colleges (Srisa-an 1983). The MUA, instead of combining specialized universities to form a complete and efficient one, allows each university to grow from the existing system. In the 1980s, most of the government specialist universities expanded their programs to cover all fields of study.

As a consequence of the demand for qualified teachers, the first teacher-training school was set up in 1982 to provide a two-year training after primary education. Only in 1903 was a one-year program after secondary education created. The beginning of the twentieth century saw the establishment of teacher-training schools in the areas of agriculture, arts and crafts, commerce, and physical education, as well as the other specialized schools to meet the government need. The implementation of the first Five-Year National Plan in 1961, in addition to the recommendation from a Thai-USOM Joint Study Group to improve vocational schools established several teachers' colleges and vocational and technical institutes (Suntornpithug 1979). The late 1960s onward witness the increasing number of institutions under the MOE following government support and foreign assistance to develop agricultural, technological, industrial, and teacher training.

There are 156 research offices in the government higher education institutions, 23 of which are research institutes and the remainder organized on departmental and faculty levels. Research in private institutions is still in the planning stage (UNESCO 1988). In addition, there is the Office of National Research Council which promotes research dissemination and application for national development. Moreover, the MUA, in the early 1980s encouraged university staff to do research especially in areas for the improvement of national development.

The admission policies of all higher education institutions are the government's legitimate concern. The National Education Commission (NEC) and later, the MUA assumed the task of coordination and formed the central committee on joint entrance examination comprising representatives from the higher institutions involved, since 1963. Candidates have to be secondary-school graduates or equivalent. Those who pass the written test, the interview, and the medical examination are enrolled in the institutions under the MUA control. The Open University requires no entrance examination. For all other specialized colleges, the MOE and other related ministries determine the admission policies, the number of students to be admitted, and allows each college to administer its own entrance examination. In addition, quotas have regularly been set by all institutions to reserve places for abler and talented students, and to expand educational opportunity for regional students.

Total enrollment in higher education, shown in Table 2, had increased more than 10 times and the percentages of the age groups rose by more than five times in the period of 25 years. The decrease in enrollment from 1960 to 1965 was due to the reduction of part-time enrollment at the colleges under the MOE and at Thammasat University which changed its status from nonselective to selective university. The increases from 1970 to 1975 and from 1975 to 1980 were due to the establishment of two open universities in 1971 and 1979 respectively, which provided broader educational opportunities and accelerate the production of a high-level labor force.

Each of the government selective universities offers a six-year course for a bachelor's degree in medicine, a four-year course for a bachelor's degree in health sciences, natural and computer sciences, social and behavioral sciences, political sciences, law, humanities, arts, education, communication, commercial and business administration, agriculture, economics, engineering, and architecture, and a three-year course for a diploma in almost all fields of study at undergraduate level. It provides a two-year master's degree program, a one-year program for a specialized higher certificate and a three-year program for a doctor's degree and PhD degree in almost all fields of study. The Open University offers

Table 2
Enrollments (in thousands) and percentages of the age-group

Types of support	Control	1960	1965	1970	1975	1980	1985
Government	MUA Graduate	}51.3	}34.8	4.1	7.4	10.1	15.6
	Undergraduate			55.3	123.6	561.4	661.9
	MOE Teacher training	6.8	6.4	21.2	51.9	58.6	61.0
	Vocational education	20.9	17.3	28.7	37.6	69.7	189.2
Private	MUA	—	—	—	13.2	27.8	46.2
Total		79.0	58.5	105.2	226.3	717.5	958.3
Percentages of age group		3.3	2.3	3.9	5.5	15.8	18.8

a four-year course leading to a bachelor's degree in social sciences, humanities, law, and education. Private universities offer a four-year course leading to a bachelor's degree in law, commercial and business administration, engineering, social and behavioral sciences, humanities, communication, nursing, agriculture, and natural and computer sciences.

The teachers' colleges, technical colleges, agricultural colleges, colleges of physical education, colleges of fine arts and drama under the MOE and other specialized colleges under other ministries provide a two-year program leading to a certificate equivalent to upper-secondary education, a two- to three-year program leading to a higher certificate and a four-year program leading to a bachelor's degree.

The first master's degree program was offered at Chulalongkorn University in 1942, but it was 1962 when the first graduate school was established in that university. All government selective universities have graduate schools, the main functions of which are to coordinate with academic departments to offer graduate education. They are administrative centers controlling and promoting the standards of the graduate programs and activities. Graduate programs may differ among universities, but they have to meet the minimum requirements set by the MUA. To be admitted to the graduate programs one requires a bachelor's degree or equivalent and to successfully pass the medical and the entrance examination administered by the university. Every program is research oriented, but students can choose to study either plan A: writing a master's degree thesis; or plan B: studying extra courses equivalent to the thesis and writing a qualifying paper.

3. Governance, Administration, and Finance

3.1 National Administration

The prime responsibility to provide Thai higher education belongs to the national government. The government concern, expressed in terms of legislation, funding and quality control, is divided mainly among three ministries. Within the Office of the Prime Minister, the National Education Commission (NEC) is responsible for the overall policy and planning; the Budget Bureau is in charge of funding, and the Civil Service Commission (CSC) takes care of staffing. Established in 1972, the MUA is responsible for all government universities and colleges. The MOE is left with vocational and technical higher education and teacher training. The MUA and the MOE are top-level policy-making and planning agencies. They set standards and approve curricula, allocate staff, recommend budget allocation and control accreditation.

Higher education planning is an integral part of a Five-Year National Social and Economic Development Plan. The NEC is responsible for the overall coordination of planning and development of educational policies. The major goals of higher education are to train the qualified labor force required for national development, to give equal educational opportunity, and to promote social betterment. These goals are transmitted to each university, college, and institution through the central allocation of student places, staff, and resources. Although the National Educational Plans have been implemented, there is, despite systematic follow-up procedures, an overproduction in the areas of education, social sciences, law, and humanities. The reason is because the higher education systems are tied to and affected by the social, economic, and political aspects of the country.

The government bears more than half of the total cost for all higher education programs. Students pay only a small tuition fee. The increase in higher education expenditure by sectors from 1960 to 1985 is shown in Table 3. Total expenditure rose from 274.1 to 8,587.2 million Bahts, an approximate rate of 100 percent at five-year intervals. A major rise in expenditure between 1960 and 1970 reflected an emphasis on the development of vocational education, teacher training, and the establishment of regional universities. The implementation of the Fourth and the Fifth National Education Plans resulted in a slowdown of teacher-training expen-

Table 3
Distribution of the national higher education expenditure (in million Bahts) by sectors

Sectors	1960	1965	1970	1975	1980	1985
NEC	0.6	25.8	31.5	19.3	31.3	49.0
NRC	0.1	7.2	18.5	36.1	42.2	66.7
MUA Universities	120.0	284.5	619.7	1,453.6	3,526.8	5,212.8
MOE Teacher training	85.9	80.9	231.6	452.0	492.9	694.2
Vocational education	67.5	149.0	334.6	468.1	1,467.7	2,834.5
Total	274.1	547.4	1,235.9	2,429.1	5,560.9	8,857.2
Percentages of GNP	0.5	0.7	0.9	0.8	0.8	0.9
Percentages of national budget	3.6	4.4	4.7	5.4	5.0	4.7

diture and a sharp increase of university and vocational expenditure between 1975 and 1985.

3.2 Institutional Administration

In each university, the supreme governing body is a university council which consists of the administrators, the academic staff, and the qualified independent outsiders, the number of which may vary. The term of membership in the council lasts two years while the term of office of most university administrators lasts four years. The council is concerned with policy matters, general supervision, and final approval of the degrees awarded. Day-to-day business is run by the administrators and the faculty members. In the MOE, some departments act as a governing body responsible for the operation of colleges under its supervision and control. In each college, as well as university, there are faculties, schools, institutes, centers, an office of the president/rector, and other affiliate institutions. However, the status of the university and institution under the MUA is equivalent to that of the departments under the MOE, while the status of each faculty in the university is equivalent to that of each college under the MOE.

Under the University Act and the College Act, the formal pattern of authority is a hierarchical network comprising the president/rector, vice-presidents, deans and directors, associate and assistant deans and directors, department heads, academic staff, academic supporting staff, and administrative and clerical staff. In addition, there are some functional specialists for services such as legal services and construction. The decision-making structure includes several committees. The administrative board consists of all administrators at and above the faculty level, chaired by the president. It runs the university in accordance with the policy set by the university council. Authorized by the president, the academic board, which consists of all deans and directors and is chaired by the vice-president for academic affairs, oversees all academic affairs run by the faculties and schools. In each faculty and institute, the dean and the director appoint and chair the board consisting of the department heads and a number of academic staff to be responsible for financial allocation, academic standards, and curriculum development of the faculty.

4. Faculty and Students: Teaching, Learning, and Research

4.1 Faculty

The rapid growth of higher education personnel has been caused by the need to keep pace with the great educational demand. However, despite the tenfold increase in university enrollment over the past 25 years, staff increased by only sixfold, as shown in Table 4, because the establishment of the open-admission, distance-teaching university does not require many staff members. Under the MOE, with an initial staff of 4,679 in 1960, it expanded to 22,634 in 1985.

There are four groups of staff members, a great number of academic staff, academic support staff, administrative staff, and a small number of clerical staff. The personnel in the first three groups are academically qualified and can be elected or appointed to assume responsibility in any group. Excluding staff in private institutions, all personnel are governed by the Civil Service Act. They are paid according to civil service salary scales, have security of tenure, and a pension for life after at least 30 years of service. They are eligible to receive welfare allowance and free medical treatment from the government hospital.

Recruitment and promotion of personnel are generally uniform in both government and private institutions. Each university, and the Department of Vocational Education and the Department of Teacher Training alike, has direct responsibility to select, appoint, and promote personnel. Usually when there is a vacant position, the university appoints an ad hoc committee to select a candidate qualified for that position. The president then appoints the selected candidate for a six-month pro-

Table 4
Distribution of staff members

Types of support	Control		1960	1965	1970	1975	1980	1985
Government	MUA		2,475	3,788	7,193	11,406	11,520	13,807
	MOE[a] Teacher training	} 4,679		1,836	3,069	4,588	5,317	5,789
	Vocational			5,484	6,010	7,452	11,240	16,845
Private	MUA		—	—	—	1,018	1,743	2,763

a These members are responsible for teaching at both upper-secondary and higher education levels

bation period. If his or her performance is qualified, the university, through the president, will grant permanent lecturer status. Promotion, involves the university appointing an Academic Evaluation Committee. The university, after its recommendation, will grant all academic ranks except the rank of full professor and a special promotion which requries the approval of and appointment by, the Civil Service Commission at the university level. The criteria used for promotion are academic qualifications, amount of salary, length of services, research work, teaching load, and other services. The career pattern of the bachelor's degree holders and the master's degree holders normally requires not less than three and six years as lecturer, three years as assistant professor, two years as associate professor, and then a full professorship.

By the Teacher Act of 1945—the main legislation relating to the teaching profession—all public and private teachers must belong and subscribe to the government sponsored *Kuru Sapa* (Teachers' Union). The union protects the interests of teachers and promotes the teaching profession. The executive committee is chaired by the Minister of Education and consists of the directors-general of various departments and nine senior experienced teachers. Besides *Kuru Sapa*, by regulation of each university and college, all staff members have to be members of the Staff Council. The executive committee of the council consists of a number of nonadministrators as representatives from each constituency. The council plays an important role promoting staff security and welfare. All staff councils are quite uniform because the National Staff Council acts as a consolidating organization. There are in addition, several professional organizations—the National Education Society, the National Social Sciences Research Association, and so on, to which staff members can apply for membership.

Some academic staff have sole responsibility for teaching. Others may not teach but are concerned with student affairs, though such cases are rare. Generally, every staff member is required to teach and besides teaching they are free to undertake all other types of work. Department staff members decide how much teaching each member will do. The teaching load can range from 0 to 3 hours a week to as much as 30 to 39 hours a week. Those with small teaching loads may already have or acquire other responsibilities. According to the Civil Service Act, staff members are required to work 35 official hours a week.

4.2 Students

There was a rapid growth of total enrollment between 1960 and 1985, but the growth in the social sciences exceeded that of exact sciences (including technology, engineering, and medical sciences) and humanities in the government universities. Table 5 shows that the student body consisted of 63.79 per-

Table 5
Distribution of enrollments (in thousands)

Types of support	Control	Fields	1960	1965	1970	1975	1980	1985
Government	MUA[a]	Exact science	na	na	17.5	27.9	42.4	69.7
		Social science	na	na	37.9	92.3	511.2	581.7
		Humanities	na	na	4.0	10.7	17.9	26.1
		Total	51.3	34.8	59.4	130.9	571.5	677.5
Private	MUA	Exact science	—	—	—	2.2	4.5	8.0
		Social science	—	—	—	10.4	22.0	36.1
		Humanities	—	—	—	0.6	1.3	2.1
		Total	—	—	—	13.2	27.8	46.2

Table 6
Distribution of graduates (in thousands)

Types of support	Control	Fields	1960	1965	1970	1975	1980	1985
Government	MUA	Exact science	0.8	1.4	3.1	5.9	8.3	9.9
		Social science	1.3	5.6	6.7	15.8	24.4	39.0
		Humanities	0.1	0.2	0.9	1.7	3.1	4.7
		Total	2.2	7.2	10.7	23.4	35.8	53.6
Private	MUA	Exact science	—	—	—	—	0.9	2.4
		Social science	—	—	—	—	3.0	5.6
		Humanities	—	—	—	—	0.1	0.3
		Total	—	—	—	—	4.0	8.3

cent of social sciences students in 1970 as compared to 85.80 percent in 1985, a fifteenfold increase in 20 years. Growth in exact sciences and humanities was only four and six times respectively. On the contrary, the composition of the student body in private universities remained the same between 1975 and 1985. It implies that the growth rate of enrollment in each of the three areas is about the same—about fourfold in 10 years. The distribution of enrollments in Table 5 reflects expansion of higher education in the social sciences which was in accordance with the establishment of open-admission universities.

The distribution of graduates in Table 6 shows a similar overproduction of social scientists in government universities. In addition, a significant number of social sciences students admitted to the open-admission universities did not graduate.

Higher education in Thailand historically has been and still is for the advantaged. The student body in the closed admission universities in 1985, broken down by gender and parental occupation, consisted of 52 percent males and 48 percent females; 25 percent civil services and state enterprises, 55 percent self-employed, 10 percent agriculture, and 10 percent employees and others. The composition showed that there was no sex discrimination but there was inequality of educational opportunity among youth from different social classes. The establishment of regional universities, open-admission universities and quotas helped to increase educational opportunites for the disadvantaged.

In each higher education institution students have organized and formed a council of university/college students, the committee of which is annually elected from each faculty. Student councils organized extra-curricular, recreational and sporting activities in the campuses. They also actively participate in the social, economic, and political affairs of the country. The National Student Center of Thailand (NSCT), initiated in 1972, brought close cooperation and consolidation to student councils in different campuses. Representing more than 100,000 students throughout

the country, the NSCT held a number of demonstrations against the government in 1972 to 1973 forcing the resignation of the military government and the formation of a civilian government. After their victory, the committee resigned because of internal conflicts and later the rival student organization, the Federation of Independent Students of Thailand (FIST) developed (Watson 1980). In the early 1990s the FIST revolves more around social and academic events than political ones.

4.3 Learning and Examinations
Under central control of government, standards and the final approval of the program structure and curriculum are made at the ministry level. University curricula and programs are designed, revised, and developed by individual departments, with the approval from the faculty board, the academic administrative board, and the university council, and the final approval from the MUA. College curricula are developed by ad hoc committees consisting of representatives from the relevant colleges, and approved by the relevant department at the MOE. When universities and colleges develop a new study program, they require the approval of the curriculum, then apply for permission to operate the program from the MUA and the MOE. Finally, they submit the program to the Civil Service Commission (CSC) to set a salary scale for the graduates of that program.

Historically, most universities and colleges offer narrow professional courses and produce specialized graduates. Students have very little knowledge of liberal and general education. Much attention has been paid to Western concepts and principles, but little to the requirements for rural development. In the early 1990s, an attempt to integrate local and Western intellectual traditions and to apply them to real life is being made by senior scholars and disseminated to every higher education institution.

All courses are generally offered on the credit system. Normally, undergraduate students have to study for about four years and earn approximately

130 credits to get a bachelor's degree. Graduate students have to study two years and earn 25 to 60 credits to get a master's degree. They continue for another three years covering 45 to 90 credits to get a doctoral degree.

Under the credit system, the assessment procedure is an internal and summative one, not an end-of-year evaluation. The course grade is the summative result of several tests, course participation, term papers, final test, and other activities. If the student fails any course, he has to repeat to obtain the grade. At the end of the program, the cumulative grade point average is obtained. The student is entitled to receive a degree if his or her performance meets the criteria. In the early 1990s, assessment procedures make the attainment rate greater than it was previously and reduces educational wastage due to repetition or withdrawal.

5. Conclusion

During the past decades, Thai higher education has achieved the quantitative rather than the qualitative objectives of the National Education Development Plans producing qualified graduates needed for national development. In quantitative terms, the need to reduce regional disparities is effectively fulfilled by the establishment of regional universities and the expansion of specialized colleges under the MOE, with the trade-off of a reduced investment in the existing universities. The need to increase educational opportunity for the disadvantaged is achieved by adult programs at open universities and a quota admission procedure. The increase in quantity of enrollments and graduates, however, is unbalanced among the fields of study. There seems to be an overproduction in social sciences, education, and law rather than medical sciences, exact sciences, and technology. The unbalanced proportion may be due to the fact that responsibilities for operating higher education are divided among the MUA and the MOE. There is no active consolidating agency to coordinate and monitor the operation. Another aspect is the quality of graduates. Teaching emphasizes the narrow, specialized and theoretical experiences rather than practical and up-to-date knowledge. This problem derives from the historical origin of higher education institutions as specialized training institutions. They do not fully function as a university, even though university status is granted to them.

Since Thailand aims to be an agro-industrialized country in the near future, Thai higher education institutions have to play a significant role and be leaders in the development of human resources, especially the development of the qualified teachers, to encourage and promote change. All four functions of the higher education institutions: teaching; research; community services; and the promotion and preservation of national culture, should be inte-grated and comprehensively performed in order to let the theoretical and practical intellectuals be integrated with the communities. All institutions should initiate and expand effective relationships among institutions, both in and out of the country, and other productive sectors to utilize optimally human and physical resources. They should be, not just a center of high-level labor force production, but a services and resource center for national development. They should be a leader in introducing high technology and innovations to better and upgrade the communities. The government should develop a coordinating organization and find ways to promote a quantitative and qualitative expansion of higher education with minimum wastage and maximum cooperation. It is important that higher education should commit itself to performing its role and function even more effectively than before, otherwise the objectives of the national development will not be accomplished fully.

Bibliography

Bureau of Budget 1981 *Thailand's Budget in Brief, Fiscal Year 1981.* Bureau of Budget, Bangkok
Chomchai P 1980 *Thailand: Chulalongkorn University. The Role of the University in National Development: Four Asian Case Studies.* Vikas House, New Delhi
Eurich N P 1981 *Systems of Higher Education in Twelve Countries: A Comparative View.* Praeger, New York
Hayden H 1967 *Higher Education and Development in South-East Asia, Vol. 2: Country Profiles.* UNESCO and IAU, Paris
Nathalang E (ed.) 1970 *Education in Thailand: A Century of Experiences.* Ministry of Education, Bangkok
National Statistical Office 1960–85 *Statistical Yearbook.* National Statistical Office, Bangkok
National Education Commission 1983 *Thailand: Education Sector Survey.* Office of the National Education Commission, Bangkok
Setamanit S 1981 Thailand. *RIHED Research Series: Staff and Faculty Development in Southeast Asian Universities.* Maruzen Asia, Singapore
Singh R R 1986 *Education in Asia and the Pacific, Retrospect: Prospect.* UNESCO, Bangkok
Srisa-an W 1982 *Innovations in Higher Education for Development in Thailand* RIHED Occasional Paper No. 8. Maruzen, Singapore
Srisa-an W 1983 Thailand. *Bulletin of the UNESCO Regional Office for Education in Asia and the Pacific: Higher Education in Asia and the Pacific.* 24: 86–94
Suntornpithug N 1979 *A Study of the Evolution of Teacher Training in Thailand: Towards a Model for Development.* Ministry of Education, Bangkok
Thailand, Ministry of Education 1975–85 *Educational Statistics in Brief.* Ministry of Education, Bangkok
Thailand, Ministry of Education 1981 *Thai Education in Brief.* Ministry of Education, Bangkok
Thailand, Ministry of University Affairs 1984 *Introducing Public and Private Institutions of Higher Education in Thailand.* Ministry of University Affairs, Bangkok
UNESCO 1976 *Thailand, Education: Towards Equalization and Reform.* UNESCO, Paris
UNESCO 1988 *Higher Education and National Development*

in Four Countries: India, Bangladesh, Thailand, and the
Philippines. UNESCO, Bangkok

United Nations, ESCAP 1985 *Statistical Yearbook for Asia
and the Pacific*. ESCAP, Bangkok

Virasai B (ed.) 1977 *Higher Education in Southeast Asia in
the Next Decade*. RIHED, Singapore

Watson K 1980 *Educational Development in Thailand*.
Heinemann, Hong Kong

World Bank 1988 *Educational Development in Thailand:
The Role of World Bank Lending*. World Bank, Washington, DC

Xuto S (ed.) 1987 *Government and Politics of Thailand*.
Oxford University Press, New York

Xuto S, Prasithrathsint S, Nakata T, Yongkittikul T 1981
*Thailand in the 1980s: Significant Issues, Problems and
Prospects*. TURA Institute, Bangkok

N. Wiratchai

Togo

1. Higher Education and Society

The present Republic of Togo, bordered by Burkina
Faso to the north, Ghana to the west, and Benin to
the east, was a German colony in the late nineteenth
century, and after the First World War came under
French and British influence. Subsequently, part of
Togo merged with an independent Ghana and French
Togo became fully independent in 1960.

In 1988 the population of Togo was estimated by
the United Nations to be something over three million within a geographic area of 56,785 square kilometers. Given the approximate nature of these
statistics, the population density would be around 53
persons per square kilometer. Population increase in
the 1980s was around an annual average of 3.5
percent, and the consequences include an extreme
imbalance in the age structure (with over half the
population being under 20 years of age) which poses
problems for the provision of basic education and
basic literacy.

Of the working population, industry employs
approximately 10 percent. However, although a
small industrial base has been developed—in mining,
manufacturing, construction, and the power industry—about 70 percent of the population works in
subsistence agriculture, which contributed 34 percent
of Gross Domestic Product (GDP) in 1988. Industrial
production declined slightly during the 1980s, and
agricultural production rose at less than 1 percent
per annum. A series of droughts has made reliable
agricultural production difficult and agricultural
renovation remains one of the government's top
priorities, not least because agriculture (especially
coffee, cocoa, and ginned cotton) is a major source
of cash and exports. Other exports, and those in the
future, look likely to be dependent on the exploitation of local deposits of a variety of minerals (such
as iron ore, manganese, chromite, and perhaps petroleum and uranium) which may add to the current
exports of calcium phosphates.

Partly as a consequence of this economic base,
Togo, in international statistical terms, can be termed
an economically poor country. Togo's GNP, in 1988,
according to estimates by the World Bank was
US$1,240 million, equivalent to about US$400 per
head. There have been difficulties in balancing the
national budget, and in servicing the national debt
(of over 1 billion US dollars). The pattern of solutions
has included IMF involvement, wage freezes in the
public sector, the creation of Lomé as a free economic zone, and the sale of unprofitable public enterprises. The results of this, now classic and typical,
economic situation have included difficulties in the
provision of education and social welfare. For
example, medical services are provided by the
government, and in the 1989 budget, it was intended
that 5.5 percent of the total expenditure by the central government be allocated to the public health
sector. However, this was in the context in which the
country has only one doctor per 20,000 inhabitants
and less than 5,000 hospital beds (Department of
Statistics, Lomé).

The occupational and class structure implicit in
this economic division of labor, with a small political
and industrial entrepreneurial elite and a large
peasantry, is confirmed and made more complex by
linguistic diversity. Kabiye in the north and Ewe
in the south are the main indigenous languages,
although there are over 15 other major ethnic groups
(and many minor ones) with their own languages.
The European languages were introduced into the
country through a variety of colonial and neocolonial
experiences. The official language of instruction in
the schools is French, and French is the normal
language of government and of international
business, although it is spoken well by only a small
proportion of the population. Because of Togo's
history as a German colony, some German is spoken,
and English also, not least because of British intervention in the area and British colonial influence
on neighboring Ghana. A small proportion of the
population is Muslim (about 15%), and approximately 30 percent are Christians, mainly Catholic.
The majority of the population follows a variety of
local animist religions.

Although mission schools are important and educate almost one-half of all pupils, the effort being
made by the government to improve the state provision of education is considerable: budget estimates
for 1989 allocated about one-fifth of total expenditure
by the central government to education. However,
the ability of the Togolese government since Independence in 1960 to sustain investment in education
was affected not only by the economic base of Togo,
but by political factors. There was some political

instability and a pattern of authoritarian regimes. After the new Constitution of 1979, there has been one political party—the *Rassemblement du Peuple Togolais*—and the political system is dominated by the president, who is elected for seven years through universal adult suffrage. The president has power of appointment over ministers and he or she can dissolve the National Assembly, whose members are directly elected for a five-year term (*World of Learning* 1990).

2. The Institutional Fabric of the Higher Education System

The higher education system is affected by the educational base which precedes it. Both the school system generally, and higher education in particular have until a recent indigenization movement followed French institutional patterns and epistemological assumptions, with the exception of some interesting experiments in the German colonial period and aspects of missionary education.

General schooling is formally compulsory from six to twelve years of age, with primary education beginning at the age of six, and lasting six years. Secondary education begins at the age of twelve and lasts for seven years, with a first cycle of four years and a second cycle of three years. In 1987 enrollment in primary schools included 73 percent of children in the relevant age group, and 24 percent of the relevant age group were in secondary school—totals which measure considerable progress since Independence and which in their African context are impressive. Proficiency in the two main indigenous national languages, Ewe and Kabiye, is expected. However, in 1981, estimates of the adult illiteracy rate were in the order of 70 percent. Thus there is a considerable backlog of educational activity which is needed, and which is being undertaken by a variety of formal and nonformal techniques including distance education for adults.

Against this general educational background it may be expected that the higher education base is narrow both in its institutional format and in access to it.

The centerpiece of higher education in Togo is the University of Benin in Lomé, and its associated colleges or schools. The University of Benin was founded in 1970, building on an earlier joint venture with the governments of Dahomey and Benin in 1962, which saw the creation of a Center of Higher Education (*Centre d'Enseignement Supérieur*) on a split-site basis. The schools of the University include: a school of Medical Sciences, Letters, Natural Sciences, Administration and Law, Agriculture, and Industrial Engineering; the Technical Institute of Health and Biological Sciences; the National Institute of Education; the Institute of Management and Business Studies; and a Medical Training School (which prepares medical assistantships) (*World of Learning* 1990).

In addition there are a number of colleges, of varying status and sometimes outside of Lomé, which mainly concentrate on preparation for, or retraining of, particular professions or high-status occupational groups, such as the Tiove Center of Professional Agricultural Training (*Centre de Formation Professionelle Agricole de Tiove*), in Kpalime, founded in 1901; the African and Mauritian School of Architecture and Urbanism (*Ecole Africaine et Mauricienne d'Architecture et d'Urbanisme*) in Lomé, founded in 1975, with specialist courses in architecture and town planning and in-service courses for trained architects; the National School of Administration (*Ecole Nationale d'Administration*) in Lomé, founded in 1958, which provides training for Togolese civil servants.

Overall, the system is aimed at serving national needs, including those of modernization and development, but the domestic system of higher education is supplemented by a strong tradition of studying abroad. By the late 1970s, over 3,000 Togolese students were studying abroad, particularly in France, the United States, and Canada, but also Ghana and other African countries. In this sense the relatively narrow domestic base of higher education is broadened, but selection for higher education is still made from the relatively small group of those who have survived the examination systems of primary and secondary schooling. In fact about 2 percent of the age cohort are admitted to higher education.

Admission to higher education is via the long cycle of secondary education, which itself is divided into phases on the traditional French model. The first phase, after four years, leads to the BEPC (*brevet d'études du premier cycle*) a diploma obtained after completion of the first four years of secondary schooling. After a further two years students take a probationary examination (*examen probatoire*). Success gives access to a final year leading to the *baccalauréat* examination, which is divided into classical, modern, or technological fields. In turn the choice of specialization within the *baccalauréat* limits the range of faculties in the university to which application may be made (Michel 1988).

The available statistical estimates of the numbers of students enrolled in higher education suggest the following dimensions to the admissions group. According to the Department of Statistics in Togo, students in 1987–88 numbered 6,724 at university level, and in other higher education institutions, 116. The UNESCO Statistical Yearbook, for the year 1988, indicates 7,348 students at university level and 118 students in other higher education institutions. However, those numbers should also be understood against a background of expansion in university student numbers; in 1972, 1975, 1979, and 1982 there were 1,370, 2,353, 3,638, and 4,034 students respectively (Michel 1988).

The pattern and naming of qualifications available within the university also follows the traditional French pattern. A first cycle of two years produces a first diploma of higher education (*diplôme de fin des études du premier cycle*) with minor variations in nomenclature depending on the faculty within which the diploma is awarded. The second cycle after one more year's work leads to a bachelor's degree (*license*); and a further year's study leads to a master's degree (*maîtrise*). Because the system until recently so closely resembled that of metropolitan France, the qualifications are recognized there. Alternatively, qualifications gained in France itself have high status and it has been suggested that the possession of a doctorate (*doctorat d'état*) awarded from France is likely to lead to an excellent academic career in Togo (Michel 1988).

3. Governance, Administration, and Finance

Nationally, the system of education in terms of its governance, is centralized, through the Ministry of National Education with, as appropriate, consultation and coordination with other ministries, notably the Ministry of Finance and Planning. Within education the minister is in overall charge, and works through four directorates, one of which takes particular responsibility for higher education, including the university.

At the institutional level of the university itself, the form of governance is through the rector and a university council composed of members of the university and assisted by a secretary who is in charge of general administration. However, senior appointments within the university, including the rector, are handled by the minister, either in making the appointment directly, or in approving a proposal if the nomination is from staff of the university.

4. Faculty and Students: Teaching, Learning and Research

Although there has been a steady increase in the amount of resources devoted to education in the last two decades—a doubling of the proportion of Gross National Product (GNP) devoted to education—the financial situation of the university is difficult and teaching in the university is rarely a full-time and permanent career. Where possible, the university takes in appropriate professionals from outside. Full-time staff are organized in a considerable hierarchy, at the head of which is the full professor (*professeur titulaire de chaire*) moving down through various ranks of lecturer (*maître: maître de conférences, maître assistant, maître assistant délégué*) to assistants. This embryonic academic profession of about 300 people has two central characteristics. Until recently a very high proportion of teachers—over half—in the university were foreigners, mainly French; and teachers (and students) were predominantly male. Efforts have been made to redress both imbalances, with some success since the mid-1970s in the Africanization of the academic profession. However, with a university student population that contains less than 20 percent female members, increased feminization of the academic profession will necessarily be a slow business.

Research is mainly linked to the country's development plans. It is carried out in specific institutions, such as the institutes for research on cotton and exotic textiles, on coffee and cocoa; and on tropical agriculture. In addition there is a National Institute for Scientific Research and the Togolese Institute of Human Sciences.

5. Conclusion

The higher education system can be construed along four dimensions. Firstly, until the indigenization movement in the educational system, generally, in the last couple of decades, it was a French higher education system, with French style examinations, epistemological assumptions and the French academic hierarchy, inserted into an African context and a socioeconomic structure which posed most of the classical development problems. Secondly, major efforts have been made to invest heavily in the whole education system, including the university, under conditions of great economic stringency and some political difficulty. Measurable progress has been made, particularly in numerical expansion, though there are notable difficulties especially in the inequality of educational provision for girls, including female students in higher education. Thirdly, the simultaneous demands to provide an economically relevant higher education system, that is, one which will in some fashion contribute directly and immediately to the economic development of Togo, is in some tension with the needs of a culturally relevant higher education system, which takes more account of local languages, reduces the numbers of foreign teachers, and begins to redress regional imbalances in the provision of higher education. Finally, the cultural messages and practical success which follow from education overseas together with access to European languages and elite positions are likely to contribute to tensions implicit in Togolese socioeconomic and cultural structures.

Bibliography

Europa World Yearbook 1990, 31st edn. Europa Publications, London
Husen T, Postlethwaite T N (eds.) 1985 *The International Encyclopedia of Education*. Pergamon Press, Oxford
Michel C 1988 *World Education Encyclopedia, Togo*. Facts on File, Oxford

République Togolese, Ministère de l'Education Nationale
et de la Recherche Scientifique 1988 *Statistiques Scolaires
1987–88*
UNESCO *Statistical Yearbook 1988*. UNESCO, Paris
World of Learning 1990, 40th edn. Europa Publications,
London

R. Cowen

Trinidad and Tobago

1. Higher Education and Society

Higher education in Trinidad and Tobago typifies
the struggle for decolonization and nation-building
of a newly independent country.

Trinidad and Tobago became an independent state
within the British Commonwealth of Nations in 1962.
In 1976 the state adopted the status of a republic
within the Commonwealth. The 1987 estimate of the
population is 1,217,139, which reflects an increase
since the 1960s when the population grew by an
average of 2.0 percent as a result of high birthrates
and declining deathrates. However, the effect of
natural increases in the population has historically
been offset by migration, largely motivated by the
quest for higher education and employment. In 1987,
it was estimated that 54 percent of the population
was aged 24 and under, 31 percent fell between the
ages of 25 and 49, 9 percent between the ages 50
and 64, and 6 percent were 65 and older. The age
distribution of youth represents a slight decline from
the late 1970s, when 58 percent of the population
was younger than 24 (Central Statistical Office 1988).

The twin-island nation-state has inherited a complex racial, ethnic, and religious diversity from its
colonial past: enslaved Africans, who gained emancipation in 1838; indentured East Indians, who came
as migrant labor in 1845; immigrant laborers from
Madeira; and some Chinese immigrants who
remained and intermarried after unsuccessful
attempts to introduce large-scale Chinese labor. Syrians and Lebanese entered as traders and remain as
a numerical minority. Ancestors of the early Spanish,
British, and French colonists still remain, and they,
too, represent a numerical minority. The earliest
Amerindian settlers were decimated during the
invasion of Columbus. Africans and East Indians
comprise the majority of the population (some 45
percent each), while the other ethnic groups represent the remaining 10 percent. The society has
retained its pyramidical structure which places Whites and those of White descent ("Trinidad Whites")
at the top, in spite of their numerical paucity. English
is the official language, but a local dialect is pervasive.

During the colonial period, the trend of higher
education in Trinidad and Tobago was for the co-

lonial power to cater only for their own citizens and
to exclude those in the colonies. In fact, it was only
during the period of the world wars, when citizens
of the colonial power could not be spared for administration in the colonies, that the need for higher
education for locals was recognized (Williams and
Harvey 1984). Thus education became an important
tool in maintaining the social stratification that
characterized colonial Trinidad and Tobago, and
which has continued in its postindependence history.
For, as Braithwaite (1975) has noted, it was "the
ladder thus established by the educational system
that became one of the most important methods by
which members of the middle and lower classes could
improve their position on the occupational scale and
come to play an important role in public affairs." It
is because of this historical role that education
remains the critical mechanism for instilling egalitarian values and ensuring equality in the society, a
factor that must be taken into consideration in any
examination of higher education in Trinidad and
Tobago.

1.1 Structure of the Economy

Until 1982, Trinidad and Tobago experienced long-
term economic stability, based primarily on revenues
from its petroleum sector. The economy sustained
"an average annual growth rate of 3.1 percent over
the period 1967–1973. In the succeeding period of
1973–1983, it grew at the accelerated annual rate of
5.8 percent" (National Planning Commission 1988).
The oil boom years of 1975–1982 pushed the standard
of living to the level of one of the highest of the
newly industrialized countries. However, between
1982 and 1987 the economy suffered a severe economic contraction, with six consecutive years of negative economic growth. The economic decline
continued through 1988, with an unemployment rate
of 22.3 percent by the end of the first quarter of
1988, which is more than double the 10 percent
unemployment rate of 1982.

1.2 Political Goals

Education was clearly a national priority for the
government which took the country from self-
government to independence. It has retained its
priority status, and at the end of the 1980s roughly
one-fifth of the recurrent budget was allocated to
education annually, making it the largest single item
of government expenditure. Primarily the challenge
was to eradicate the elitist function and perception
of education, and instead use education as a social
leveller and a mechanism for correcting inherited
structural inequalities. The provision of free secondary education was a critical step in ensuring that
education, and consequently certain prestige occupations, did not remain the sole domain of the elite.
Yet the view of education as a mechanism for achieving social mobility continues to linger in the national

psyche. The challenge remains that of reorienting national thinking to the more functional aspect of the contribution of education to national development through the mobilizing of skills for national goals, and specifically for eliminating an inherently hierarchical structure, and achieving egalitarianism and harmony in a small complex society. The current economic crisis also demands the urgent matching of education with labor market needs.

Higher education in Trinidad and Tobago was initially part of a regional focus, both because of the regional structure for the administration of the colonies, and the corresponding regional character of the struggle for self-government and independence. This historical inclination was enforced by the fervor of nationalism and regionalism of the 1930, and gave rise in 1948 to the establishment of the University of the West Indies, designed to serve the Anglophone Caribbean community. In 1984, however, the University embarked upon a restructuring course in order to achieve greater autonomy and to emphasize territorial rather than regional input. The restructuring process of the University of the West Indies (UWI) and the establishment of the National Institute of Higher Education, Research, Science, and Technology (NIHERST) in 1984 are the high points of the period of transition which currently characterizes higher education in Trinidad and Tobago.

2. The Institutional Fabric of the Higher Education System

Interpretations of higher education are subject to the historical developments and/or orientations of the societies which they are designed to serve. Hence, the term higher education in Trinidad and Tobago is defined as postsecondary formal education, leading to certificates, diplomas, or degrees. Two major institutions are currently responsible for higher education: The University of the West Indies (UWI), which falls under the purview of the Ministry of Education; and the National Institute of Higher Education, Research, Science, and Technology (NIHERST), under the Ministry of Planning and Mobilization.

Because of the regional focus of the University of the West Indies, it is located on three campuses, based in different territories. The first campus was established in Mona, Jamaica, in 1948; the second campus was established in 1960 in St. Augustine, Trinidad and Tobago; and the third campus in Cave Hill, Barbados, in 1963. The other noncampus territories are: Antigua, The Bahamas, Belize, The British Virgin Islands, The Cayman Islands, Dominica, Grenada, Montserrat, St. Kitts/Nevis, Anguilla, St. Lucia, and St. Vincent. Prior to the establishment of the campus in Trinidad and Tobago in 1960, students were forced to leave the country to seek higher education, primarily in Jamaica, or to enroll in external programs of foreign universities.

In fact, extra-regional arrangements for higher education are still necessary, either because of the nonavailability of a program at the UWI, or because of the higher prestige still accorded foreign university degrees. The United Kingdom, the United States, and Canada are the most popular destinations for study abroad, although the current economic downturn has minimized this activity.

The late 1960s and early 1970s in the Caribbean were characterized by periods of "economic crises, political upheavals, and cultural assertiveness, which brought the University to a period of heightened political awareness" (Williams and Harvey 1984). The introspection which followed provided the catalyst for the restructuring of higher education in general, and the University in particular, with the aim of placing greater emphasis on national goals and objectives, without losing its regional perspective. One specific objective is to establish more effective two-way communication links between the University and the wider community. This period coincided with the mid-1970s economic oil boom, which stimulated an increasing concern about science and technology. This concern culminated in the conception of the National Institute of Higher Education, Research, Science, and Technology (NIHERST), to coordinate the national effort in science, technology, higher education, specialized training, and extension services. However, NIHERST was not legally constituted until 1983, when the country was in the grip of an economic contraction. While the thrust towards technological development might have decelerated, NIHERST has been executing its coordinating and implementing mandate, particularly with respect to instructional and research programs.

In carrying out this function, NIHERST has thus become the main coordinating body for the diverse institutions of higher education, located outside of the UWI, and scattered throughout the system under various ministries. It also executes an instructional function for the schools within its network.

Tertiary-level institutions in the country which now offer academic and training programs include the University of the West Indies Extra-mural Unit, and various colleges and institutions providing training in the following areas: teacher education; agriculture, forestry, and fishery; technical and information technology; management and banking; languages; nursing and health care; and theological education.

A current major development is the grouping of extra-UWI higher education institutions into a Community College. The NIHERST Schools of Information Technology, Banking, Allied Health Services, and Languages are scheduled for immediate incorporation into the Community College. Two technical institutes and a hotel management school will be incorporated during the second phase of the project. Final policy guidelines to determine fee structure, validation procedures, and so forth are currently being developed. However, the Community College is expected to start by September 1991. It is viewed as a viable mechanism for educating and training students over 15 years of age with an emphasis on production rather than consumption, and for preparing students for admission to institutions of higher learning through the provision of transfer curricula. The Community College is intended to serve as the umbrella organization, under which will be grouped all postsecondary government-financed educational institutions offering technical/middle-level training.

In addition, the Eric Williams Medical Sciences Complex which will become operational at the end of 1989 will comprise: a teaching hospital; a medical school with an annual intake of 65 students; a dental school and hospital, with an annual intake of 25 students; a veterinary school and hospital, with an annual intake of 20 students; and schools of pharmacy and advanced nursing, with an annual intake of 12 students each.

The Extra-mural unit of the UWI was established in 1949–50, initially to serve the noncampus territories, and later to meet the continuing education needs of adult learners in campus territories. The Extra-mural unit is divided into diploma and certificate programs in various disciplines: allied health sciences, mass media and communication, pharmacology, social behavior and survey methods, public relations, and so on. Conferences, seminars, workshops, and general and special public lecture series also offer continuing education opportunities.

University education represents only a small part of the higher education and training required for national development, and indeed it is often impossible for university-trained academics and professionals to function effectively without the support from paraprofessional staff. It is in this vein that a national system of Tertiary Education, Training, Research, and Development (TETRAD) has been formulated, with the specific mission of effecting greater articulation between the national system and the University.

2.1 Admissions Policy

Matriculation requirements vary from one faculty, institute, or school of the University to the other. Every student, however, is required to have an Ordinary Level pass or its equivalent in English language. There are two levels of admission to the UWI: Normal Matriculation (higher level); and Ordinary Matriculation (lower level). Normal Matriculation is obtained by possession of two Advanced Level GCE passes and three Ordinary Level passes; or three Advanced Level and one Ordinary Level in different subjects. Holders of certain certificates or diplomas from other postsecondary and professional institutions are also accepted, but this process needs to be regularized. Ordinary Matriculation allows entry

to the preliminary (4-year) course in natural sciences, to evening classes in both arts and sciences, and the pre-agriculture course in the faculty of agriculture. Programs of study lead to the degrees of BSc, MPhil, and PhD in most programs. Diplomas are also awarded in most areas. Programs for first degrees are conducted over a period of three academic years.

3. Governance, Administration, and Finance

The University of the West Indies is organized into three categories of personnel: academic staff, administrative and other support staff, and students. The vice-chancellor is the top full-time officer of UWI, as the academic and executive head of the university, and the ex officio chairperson of the senate, the UWI's highest academic board. The "committee structure" is the basic functional unit of governance, particularly in the pre-1984 regional context, and serves as a matrix for simultaneous decision making. The standing committees of the senate include committees for academic affairs, planning, examinations, and awards.

Restructuring agreements have now led to the process of decentralization of decision making, particularly with respect to funding and academic needs. The new structure includes campus bodies, which comprise a campus council; academic board; single and cross-campus faculties; and campus appointment committees. There are also central bodies, with continuing regional responsibilities, which include: the university council; the senate; the advisory council on education; and the central appointments committee (with joint assessment and promotions committee). In addition, these councils service noncampus territories through university programs and outreach educational activities. There continues to be central committees with ministerial representation of all member countries, specifically for the seeking and management of funds, and the sharing of the cost of activities of the central university.

The University is financed through contributions from participating governments, grants from private corporations and individuals, and of course, fees from students. Various faculties also receive research grants from international agencies and governments. The development of a decentralized system for funding and financial management is a core restructuring issue, and each campus seeks funding and programming for its own specific needs.

4. Faculty and Students: Teaching, Learning, and Research

The UWI is made up of the following faculties, each of which executes its own research and development activities: arts and general studies, social sciences, education, agriculture, engineering, law, medical sciences, and natural sciences, as well as the Institute

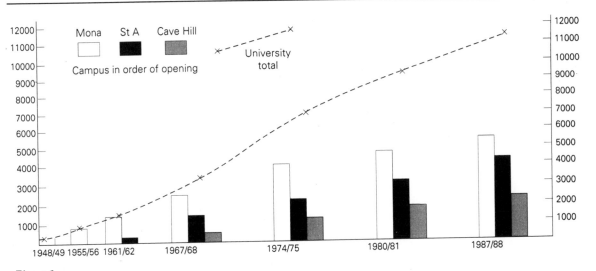

Figure 1
Growth of total student registration 1948/49–1987/88

of Social and Economic Research, the Institute of International Relations, the Unit of Extra-mural Studies, and the Creative Arts Center. Table 1 shows a departmental breakdown of faculty, indicating representation of the various Caribbean countries.

The University of the West Indies has enjoyed a steady increase since its inception in 1948. Figure 1 charts the growth in student registration from 33 in 1948 to 11,494 in 1988 for the regional body, and from 67 in 1960 to 4,156 in 1988 for the St. Augustine campus in Trinidad.

The 1987–88 figures in Table 2 show the total student registration at the St. Augustine campus. For the period 1952 to 1983, the highest number of first degree graduates came from the faculty of arts and general studies (2,109) and natural sciences (1,251). The highest number of graduates from professional faculties were from engineering (823) at the first degree level, and education (817) at the diploma level (Williams and Harvey 1984).

The high participation in engineering in part reflects the increased level of government financial and other support during the economic boom, which led to a policy of industrialization. The program in education receives special interest and funding from the government, and this is reflected in the high number of diplomas in education (Williams and Harvey 1984). There were also a huge number of graduates in agriculture, which, like engineering, is located in Trinidad, and receives high levels of financial support. There is great pressure for entry into the faculty of law. For example, in 1982–1983, more than 600 applicants competed for 100 available places for new entrants. The overall percentage of Trinidad and Tobago graduates from 1952 to 1983 is approximately 30 percent, reflecting a relatively high level

of access. For 1980 to 1983, participation of males outnumbered participation of females. However, the margin has been narrowing in recent years, with women showing a distinct preference for arts and general studies. Male participation is still far greater in medicine and engineering, but the ranks are closing in the faculty of natural sciences, where female participation is steadily increasing. Other faculties reflected smaller differences in the male/female student population, particularly the faculties of law and agriculture, where male registration traditionally far outnumbered female registration.

Figures for 1987–1988 first-degree admissions are shown in Table 3. At the certificate and diploma level, education continued to reflect high interest in new admissions: of the total of 118, an overwhelming 86 were women. Of the total 332 new admissions for certificates and diplomas, 195 were women.

5. Conclusion

A fundamental question for higher education in Trinidad and Tobago is the purpose of education, as experts grapple with two conflicting views: knowledge for its own intrinsic value, and the utilitarian function of education and research. This is a particularly critical issue, given the imperatives of nation-building and decolonization for a newly independent society.

The prevailing direction is the bridging of these two diametrically opposed views by maintaining the excellence of academic scholarship teaching and research, while at the same time acknowledging responsibility for the community which supports it. More importantly, the specific mission of institutions of higher education to chart the direction of the

Table 1
Staffing by departments (as at November 1, 1988) St Augustine

Country of origin spans the columns from Antigua to Australia and New Zealand.

Faculties/departments/units	Budgeted	Numbers	Numbers West Indians	Antigua	Barbados	Bahamas	Dominica	Grenada	Jamaica	Montserrat	St Kitts/Nevis	St Lucia	St Vincent	Trinidad and Tobago	Guyana	South America	Canada	USA	United Kingdom	European/Asian	India	Africa	Australia and New Zealand
Administration	30	22	22	—	1	—	—	1	2	1	—	—	—	16	1	—	—	—	—	—	—	—	—
Library	21	18	17	—	1	—	—	—	3	—	—	—	—	11	2	—	—	—	—	—	1	—	—
Computer centre	4	4	3	—	—	—	—	—	—	—	—	—	—	2	1	—	—	—	1	—	—	—	—
Extra mural studies	1	1	1	—	—	—	—	—	—	—	—	—	—	1	—	—	—	—	—	—	—	—	—
Sub-total	56	45	43	—	2	—	—	1	5	1	—	—	—	30	4	—	—	—	1	—	1	—	—
Faculty of agriculture																							
Departments																							
Agricultural Economy and Farm Management	5	5	4	—	—	—	—	—	1	—	—	—	—	2	1	—	—	—	—	—	1	—	—
Agricultural Extension	4	4	4	—	—	—	—	1	—	—	—	—	—	2	1	—	—	—	—	—	—	—	—
Crop Science	7	6	5	—	1	—	—	1	—	—	—	—	—	3	—	—	—	—	—	—	—	1	—
Livestock Science	4	3	2	—	—	—	—	—	—	—	—	—	—	2	—	—	—	—	—	—	—	1	—
Plant Science and Biochemistry	14	14	8	—	—	—	—	—	—	—	—	—	1	6	1	—	1	1	1	2	—	1	—
Soil Science	5[a]	4	3	—	—	—	—	—	—	—	—	—	—	3	—	—	1	—	—	—	—	—	—
Cocoa Research Unit	4	1	—	—	—	—	—	—	—	—	—	—	—	—	—	—	—	—	—	—	1	—	—
Dean's Office	2	2	2	—	1	—	—	—	1	—	—	—	—	—	—	—	—	—	—	—	—	—	—
Sub-total	45	39	28	—	2	—	—	2	2	—	—	—	1	18	3	—	2	1	1	2	2	3	—
Faculty of Arts and General Studies																							
Departments																							
English	6	5	5	—	—	—	—	—	—	—	—	1	—	3	1	—	—	—	—	—	—	—	—
French & Spanish Literature	8[b]	5	5	—	1	—	—	—	—	—	—	—	—	4	—	—	—	—	—	—	—	—	—
Language & linguistics	7	6	6	—	—	—	—	—	2	—	—	—	—	4	—	—	—	—	—	—	—	—	—
History	11	8	7	—	—	—	—	1	—	—	—	—	—	6	—	—	—	—	1	—	—	—	—
Sub-total (Arts & General Studies)	32	24	23	—	1	—	—	1	2	—	—	1	—	17	1	—	—	—	1	—	—	—	—

Faculty of Education																							
Departments																							
Education foundations and teacher education	19[c]	12[f]	10	—	—	—	—	—	—	—	—	—	—	8	2	—	—	1	1	—	—	—	—
Educational research and development	8	4	4	—	—	—	—	—	—	—	—	—	—	4	—	—	—	—	—	—	—	—	—
Sub-total (Education)	27	16	14	—	—	—	—	—	—	—	—	—	—	12	2	—	—	1	1	—	—	—	—
Faculty of engineering																							
Departments																							
Chemical engineering	20[d]	13	10	—	2	—	1	—	1	—	—	—	—	6	—	—	—	—	1	2	—	—	—
Civil engineering	22[e]	17	10	—	—	—	1	—	—	—	—	—	—	9	—	—	—	—	1	2	4	—	—
Electrical and Computer engineering	17	15	10	—	—	—	—	—	1	—	—	—	—	9	—	—	—	—	1	1	2	1	—
Mechanical engineering	24	18	13	—	—	—	—	—	1	—	—	—	—	9	2	—	—	—	—	1	4	—	—
Land surveying	7	5	2	—	—	—	—	—	1	—	—	—	—	2	—	—	—	—	2	1	—	—	—
Faculty office	2	1	1	—	—	—	—	—	—	—	—	—	—	1	—	—	—	—	—	—	—	—	—
Sub-total (Engineering)	92	69	46	—	2	—	2	—	4	—	—	—	—	36	2	—	—	—	5	7	10	1	—
Faculty of law	2	1	1	—	—	—	—	—	—	—	—	—	—	1	—	—	—	—	—	—	—	—	—
Faculty of medical sciences																							
Departments																							
Medicine	7	5	5	—	—	—	—	—	—	—	—	—	—	5	—	—	—	—	—	—	—	—	—
Surgery	10	9	8	—	—	—	—	—	—	—	—	—	—	8	—	—	—	—	1	—	—	—	—
Faculty office	1	1	1	—	—	—	—	—	—	—	—	—	—	1	—	—	—	—	—	—	—	—	—
Health library	5	3	1	—	—	—	—	—	—	—	—	—	—	1	—	—	—	1	—	—	—	1	—
Sub-total (Medical sciences)	23	18	15	—	—	—	—	—	—	—	—	—	—	15	—	—	—	1	1	—	—	1	—
Faculty of natural sciences																							
Departments																							
Chemistry	12	11	11	—	—	—	—	—	1	—	—	—	—	9	1	—	—	—	—	—	—	—	—
Mathematics	12	10	7	—	—	—	—	—	—	—	—	—	—	7	—	—	—	—	—	1	2	—	—
Physics	10	10	7	—	—	—	—	—	—	—	—	—	—	5	2	—	—	—	1	—	2	—	—
Zoology[g]	6	4	4	—	—	—	—	—	—	—	—	—	—	4	—	—	—	—	—	—	—	—	—
Computer science	5	4	4	—	—	—	—	—	—	—	—	—	—	2	2	—	—	—	—	—	—	—	—
Seismic research unit	5	3	2	—	—	—	—	—	1	—	—	—	—	1	—	—	—	—	1	—	—	—	—
Sub-total (Natural sciences)	50	42	35	—	—	—	—	—	2	—	—	—	—	28	5	—	—	—	2	1	4	—	—

Table 1 (*contd*)
Staffing by departments (as at November 1, 1988) St Augustine

Faculties/departments/units	Budgeted Numbers	Numbers	Numbers West Indians	Antigua	Barbados	Bahamas	Dominica	Grenada	Jamaica	Montserrat	St Kitts/Nevis	St Lucia	St Vincent	Trinidad and Tobago	Guyana	South America	Canada	USA	United Kingdom	European/Asian	India	Africa	Australia and New Zealand
Faculty of social sciences																							
Departments																							
Economics	10	10	10	—	—	—	—	—	—	—	—	—	—	9	1	—	—	—	—	—	—	—	—
Government	5	5	2	—	1	—	—	—	—	—	—	—	—	1	—	—	1	—	—	1	1	—	—
Management studies	11	8	6	—	—	—	—	—	—	—	—	—	—	6	—	—	—	—	—	1	—	1	—
Sociology	6	5	3	—	—	—	—	—	—	—	—	—	—	3	—	—	—	—	1	—	—	1	—
Institute of social and economic research	4	4	4	—	—	—	—	—	—	—	—	1	—	3	—	—	—	—	—	—	—	—	—
Sub-total (Social sciences)	36	32	25	—	1	—	—	—	—	—	—	1	—	22	1	—	1	—	1	2	1	2	—
(St Augustine)	363	286	230	—	7	—	2	5	15	—	—	2	2	179	18	—	3	3	13	12	18	7	—
Percentage of numbers on staff	100	78.2																					

a 1 post frozen b 2 posts frozen c Includes 1 post of Librarian/Documentalist d 3 posts frozen e 2 posts frozen f Includes Librarian/Documentalist g 1 post frozen

Table 2
Total student registration—St Augustine 1987–88

	Full-time		Part-time		Total first		Full-time certificates		Part-time certificates		Total certificates		Full-time diplomas		Part-time diplomas		Total diplomas		Full-time higher degrees		Part-time higher degrees		Total higher degrees		Total registration	
	M	W	M	W	M	W	M	W	M	W	M	W	M	W	M	W	M	W	M	W	M	W	M	W	M	W
Anguilla	1	—	—	—	1	—	—	—	—	—	—	—	1	—	—	—	1	—	—	—	—	—	—	—	2	—
Antigua	6	—	—	—	6	—	—	—	—	—	—	—	—	—	—	—	—	—	—	—	—	—	—	—	6	—
Bahamas	3	—	—	—	3	—	—	—	—	—	—	—	—	—	—	—	—	—	—	—	—	—	—	—	3	—
Barbados	31	9	—	—	31	9	—	—	—	—	—	—	—	—	—	—	—	—	3	1	—	1	3	2	34	11
Belize	4	—	—	—	4	—	—	—	—	—	—	—	—	—	—	—	—	—	—	—	—	—	—	—	4	—
British Virgin Isles	—	—	—	—	—	—	—	—	—	—	—	—	—	—	—	—	—	—	—	—	—	—	—	—	—	—
Cayman Islands	—	—	—	—	—	—	—	—	—	—	—	—	—	—	—	—	—	—	—	—	—	—	—	—	—	—
Dominica	7	2	—	—	7	2	—	—	—	—	—	—	2	—	—	—	2	—	—	—	—	—	—	—	9	2
Grenada	12	5	—	—	12	5	—	—	—	—	—	—	1	—	—	—	1	—	—	—	—	1	—	1	13	6
Jamaica	161	23	—	2	161	25	—	—	—	—	—	—	—	—	1	—	1	—	7	5	2	2	9	7	171	32
Montserrat	4	1	—	—	4	1	—	—	—	—	—	—	—	—	—	—	—	—	—	—	—	—	—	—	4	1
St Kitts/Nevis	11	—	—	—	11	—	—	—	—	—	—	—	—	—	—	—	—	—	—	—	—	—	—	—	11	—
St Lucia	9	3	—	—	9	3	—	—	—	—	—	—	2	—	—	—	2	—	—	—	1	1	1	1	12	4
St Vincent	12	1	—	—	12	1	—	—	—	—	—	—	—	—	—	—	—	—	2	—	—	—	2	—	14	1
Trinidad and Tobago	1,169	1,157	132	253	1,301	1,410	7	11	101	111	108	122	19	8	109	140	128	148	111	79	235	136	346	215	1,883	1,895
Turks	—	—	—	—	—	—	—	—	—	1	—	1	—	—	—	—	—	—	—	—	—	—	—	—	—	1
Guyana	2	2	—	—	2	2	—	—	—	—	—	—	—	—	—	—	—	—	4	—	3	—	7	—	9	2
Other	4	—	—	—	4	—	—	—	—	—	—	—	—	—	—	—	—	—	17	3	1	1	18	4	22	4
Total	1,436	1,203	132	255	1,568	1,458	7	11	101	112	108	123	25	8	110	140	135	148	144	90	242	140	386	230	2,197	1,959

Source: University of the West Indies Statistics 1987–88

Table 3
New university admissions to first degrees St Augustine 1987–88

	Full-time first degrees																Part-time first degrees							
	Arts and general studies		Agriculture Preagricultural degree		Agriculture degree		Engineering		Natural science		Social science		Law		Total full-time first degrees		Arts and general studies		Social science		Total part-time first degrees		Total full and part-time first degrees	
	M	W	M	W	M	W	M	W	M	W	M	W	M	W	M	W	M	W	M	W	M	W	M	W
Anguilla	—	—	—	—	—	—	—	—	—	—	—	—	—	—	—	—	—	—	—	—	—	—	—	—
Antigua	—	—	—	—	—	—	2	—	—	—	—	—	—	—	2	—	—	—	—	—	—	—	2	—
Bahamas	—	—	—	—	—	—	1	—	—	—	—	—	—	—	1	—	—	—	—	—	—	—	1	—
Barbados	—	—	—	—	—	—	7	5	—	—	—	—	—	—	7	5	—	—	—	—	—	—	7	5
Belize	—	—	—	—	—	—	1	—	—	—	—	—	—	—	1	—	—	—	—	—	—	—	1	—
British Virgin Isles	—	—	—	—	—	—	—	—	—	—	—	—	—	—	—	—	—	—	—	—	—	—	—	—
Cayman Islands	—	—	—	—	—	—	—	—	—	—	—	—	—	—	—	—	—	—	—	—	—	—	—	—
Dominica	—	—	—	—	—	1	2	—	1	—	—	—	—	—	3	1	—	—	—	—	—	—	3	1
Grenada	—	—	—	—	1	—	2	—	—	1	—	—	—	—	3	3	—	—	—	—	—	—	3	3
Jamaica	—	—	—	—	11	4	35	4	—	—	—	—	—	—	46	9	—	—	—	1	—	1	46	9
Montserrat	—	—	—	—	—	—	1	—	—	—	—	—	—	—	1	—	—	—	—	—	—	—	1	1
St Kitts/Nevis	—	—	1	—	—	—	—	—	—	—	—	—	—	—	1	—	—	—	—	—	—	—	1	—
St Lucia	—	—	1	—	—	—	2	1	—	—	1	—	—	—	4	1	—	—	—	—	—	—	4	—
St Vincent	—	—	—	—	—	—	1	—	1	—	—	—	—	—	2	—	—	—	—	—	—	—	2	1
Trinidad and Tobago	37	109	35	34	10	11	97	15	111	126	63	75	9	19	372	389	19	45	21	30	40	75	412	464
Turks	—	—	—	—	—	—	—	—	—	—	—	1	—	—	—	1	—	—	—	—	—	—	—	—
Guyana	—	—	1	—	—	—	—	—	—	1	—	—	—	—	1	2	—	—	—	—	—	—	1	—
Other	1	—	—	—	—	—	—	—	—	—	—	—	—	—	1	—	—	—	—	—	—	—	1	2
Total	38	109	38	34	22	16	151	25	113	128	64	76	9	19	445	410	19	45	21	31	40	76	485	485

Source: University of the West Indies Statistics 1987–88

society cannot be abrogated, and must be given special emphasis in this transition phase.

In this context two issues come to the forefront. First is the need to prioritize technical/vocational training and paraprofessional programs, and to eradicate the lingering stigma attached to these programs, as opposed to the more prestigious academic degrees. The second is the need to target education to meet the specific labor market and other needs and goals of the society; but more importantly, to educate the nation to its responsibility in this direction, as opposed to narrow individualistic goals which reinforce stratification.

> Education cannot be neutral; the educational process cannot consist of mere techniques for transmitting knowledge. If we are to attempt to overtake our expectations and engage our resources, we must transform both the focus of our attitudes and the nature of our skills. Hence education is the key to what must be an act of self-transformation. (Manley 1974)

Self-transformation as a means to societal transformation, especially for a young society such as Trinidad and Tobago, remains the ultimate goal.

Bibliography

Braithwaite L 1975 *Social Stratification in Trinidad.* Institute of Social and Economic Research, University of the West Indies, Kingston

Central Statistical Office 1988 *Review of the Economy 1987.* The Central Statistical Office Printing Unit, Port-of-Spain

James-Bryan M 1986 *Youth in the Anglophone Caribbean: The High Cost of Dependent Development.* CEPAL Review 29 United Nations Economic Commission for Latin America and the Caribbean (UNECLAC), Santiago de Chile

Manley M 1974 *The Politics of Change: A Jamaican Testament.* André Deutsch, London

National Institute of Higher Education, Research, Science and Technology (NIHERST) 1988 *Report of the Community College Task Force.* NIHERST Port-of-Spain

National Planning Commission 1988 *Draft Medium Term Macro Planning Framework 1989–95.* National Planning Commission, Ministry of Planning and Mobilization, Port-of-Spain

Oxaal I 1968 *Black Intellectuals Come to Power: The Rise of Creole Nationalism in Trinidad and Tobago.* Schenkman, Cambridge, Massachusetts

Ryan S D 1972 *Race and Nationalism in Trinidad and Tobago: A Study of Decolonization in a Multiracial Society.* University of Toronto Press, Toronto

University of the West Indies 1988 *Guidelines for Participation in the UWI Public Consultation on Long-Term Development Needs for Tertiary Education, Training, Research, and Development (TETRAD) in Trinidad and Tobago.* UWI St. Augustine

University of the West Indies 1987 *Final Report of the Academic Board Committee on Restructuring.* UWI St. Augustine

University of the West Indies 1989 *The University of the West Indies Statistics 1987/88.* University School of Printing, Mona

Williams G, Harvey C 1984 *Higher Education in Trinidad and Tobago: A Focus on Organizational Development and Change.* Centro Regional para la Educación Superior en America Latina y el Caribe (CRESALC), Caracas

Wilson L A 1988 *Coordination of Training in Science and Technology in the National Institutional System in Trinidad and Tobago.* University of the West Indies, St. Augustine

M. James-Bryan

Tunisia

1. Higher Education and Society

The history of higher education in what is present-day Tunisia may be traced back to the Middle Ages when the Beit Al Hikma, located in the city of Kairouan, served as a major center of learning for the whole of the Maghreb—the region of North Africa running West to Morocco and bordering the Mediterranean. The origins of Tunisia's contemporary system of higher education, however, are associated with the French occupation of the country, first as a Protectorate in 1881 and subsequently, until Independence in 1956, as part of the French North African possessions. Higher education remained vestigial until the end of the Second World War and consisted of various specialized training establishments such as the Colonial School of Agriculture, the School of Fine Arts and the Tunis School of Public Administration. The common assumption was that students wishing to pursue higher learning would attend universities abroad, predominantly in mainland France. At the end of the Second World War, an Institute for Advanced Studies was set up, though restricted in the range of disciplines taught and limited in level, to studies up to first-degree level.

Though cultural and economic ties with France remain strong—Tunisian students represent the third largest foreign country in French higher education—Tunisia achieved Independence in 1956 under the leadership of Habib Bourgiba, whose presidency continued until 1987 when he retired from the political scene. French influence, though less strong than in earlier times, is nevertheless substantial in the intellectual, administrative, and political life of the country. And this is reflected to a certain degree in the structure and development of Tunisia's system of higher education.

As with many countries gaining independence, considerable emphasis was laid upon the role of higher education in economic development, in the formation and training of political and technical elites, as too in the reaffirmation of the national culture. There are today some six universities and 21 other institutions of higher education, mainly of a specialized nature, all of which grew out of the establishment of the University of Tunis in 1960.

Tunisia is a relatively small country of some 145,610 square kilometers, situated between Algeria to the west, and Libya to the southeast with its northern and eastern coastline bordering on to the Mediterranean Sea. Essentially an agricultural country, Tunisia enjoys a relatively mild climate except in the south which borders on to the Sahara Desert and the Great Western Erg. The last two decades have seen considerable demographic growth. With a total population of some 8,000,000, just over half (51 percent in 1989) are under the age of 19 years. This development has placed considerable pressure upon the education system at all levels and despite major attempts to restructure industry and to develop a modern service sector, large numbers of young Tunisians migrate abroad in search of better prospects, either in the Arab-speaking world or in France. The crude birthrate per thousand in 1989 was 31.1 and the life expectancy for males 61 years. Estimates as to the overall literacy rate are in the region of 62 percent of the population.

In the decades since Independence, urbanization has accelerated so that today 53 percent of the population live in urban areas.

Tunisia's economy relies principally on the export of crude oil, phosphates, fertilizers, textiles, and olive oil. Its industrial structure is characterized by the predominance of the extractive industries with some degree of diversification into the manufacturing sector, primarily in food processing, footware, and construction. The country has considerable reserves of iron ore, lead, zinc, and salt. In recent times, the development of the tourist industry has provided an additional source of income generation. The annual average growth rate of the Gross National Product is estimated around 3.5 percent and GNP per capita is reckoned to be around US$1,200 per year.

The population of Tunisia is 98 percent Arab with some 2 percent of European origin. The official language is Arabic, though French is widely used. There is, however, a small Berber-speaking minority. Although formally a secular state, Tunisia has a high degree of religious homogeneity—some 98 percent of the population is of the Islamic faith.

The Tunisian Republic was officially created on July 25, 1957 and led to Independence under the guidance of the Neo-Destour Party. In 1965, after some dissent within this organization, the party changed its name to the Destourian Socialist Party and embarked on a wide-ranging series of economic reforms of a centralized nature designed to accelerate development above all in the agricultural, industrial, and tertiary sectors. The success of these reforms was partial and lead to further debates within the government. The upshot of these exchanges was the appointment of Habib Bourgiba as president for life in 1974.

The issue of which path the country should hew to in pursuing the goal of economic and social modernization has been an ongoing issue. Initially following the model of a single party centrally planned government, pressure for parties other than the Destourian Socialist Party to be recognized, as too the right to form trade unions, were recognized in 1981. However, the difficulties associated with demographic pressure on the one hand and an economy dependent on agricultural exports on the other have provided fertile ground for alternative models, put forward by Islamic fundamentalists, and often drawing strength from occasional outbursts of popular unrest. Bread riots in 1983–84 and confrontations with Islamic radicals in 1987 were instrumental in causing President Bourgiba to step down in November 1987. He was replaced by the then prime minister, General Ben Ali.

2. The Institutional Fabric of the Higher Education System

Prior to the reorganization of the university sector in 1988 Tunisia counted three universities—one in the capital, Tunis to the north of the country, a second in Monastir in the center and a third at Sfax to the south. The reform of 1988 which may be seen as having certain similarities with the French reform of 1968, involved a fundamental regrouping of faculties and the creation of three further universities around basic administrative units known as "establishments of higher education and research" (*Etablissements d'Enseignement Supérieur et de Recherche*). There are currently (1991) 74 of these entities which may be seen as not dissimilar to the French administrative unit known as the *Unité de Formation et de Recherche*. Their recombination has given rise to six universities, three of which are in the nation's capital— the University of Tunis I, bringing together the humanities, Tunis II which specializes in science, technical studies, engineering, and medicine, and the University of Tunis III, given over to economics, political science, legal studies, and management. The University of Monastir may be seen as a "comprehensive university" in the sense that it covers the full range of disciplines in addition to textile technology and advanced teacher training. The study of religion and theology is undertaken at the Islamic University of Ezzitouna.

The nonuniversity sector offers training in such applied areas as food technology, agriculture, veterinary medicine, drama, music, and public administration. If distinguished from the university sector by the practical and applied nature of its specialization, the nonuniversity sector is also distinguished by coming under the oversight of ministries other than the Ministry of Education, Higher Education and

Research which exercises overall responsibility for the universities. Amongst such ministries are the Ministry of Agriculture, the Ministry of Social Affairs, and the Ministry of Culture and Information.

Admission to higher education is based on the *baccalauréat*, sat after seven years of general secondary schooling. There is, however, a further qualifying and competitive examination, set by the Ministry of Higher Education and Research. Termed the *Orientation universitaire*, this further selective device permits the government some degree of control over the number of places available in the university sector as well as providing leverage for ensuring that the economic and manpower requirements of the country are given cognizance.

First degree studies divide into two types, the first being essentially a short-cycle program of a terminal nature, lasting two years. It leads to qualifications of a vocational and technical nature. The second type—a long-course program—also lasts two years and in the humanities leads to the *Diplôme universitaire d'études littéraires* (DUEL) and in the sciences to the *Diplôme universitaire d'études scientifiques* (DUES). The second stage of the long-cycle program involves a further two years' study and results in the award of the master's degree (*maîtrise*). For humanities studies, an additional qualification may be had, after a further year's study and the defense of a short thesis. This is the *certificate à l'aptitude à la recherche*. Prior to their incorporation into the university as part of the 1988 reforms, teacher-training colleges (*Ecoles normales supérieures*) also awarded a *maîtrise* after four years' study.

Research training begins with third cycle studies—that is, four years after admission and results in the *diplome d'études approfondies* and eventually to the *Doctorat troisième cycle*—a species of shorter doctorate—or to the monumental *Doctorat d'état* which may require upwards of eight to ten years' study. It is perhaps not entirely coincidental that this structure closely resembles its French counterpart prior to the latter's reforms introduced in 1986.

In 1989–90, approximately 7 percent of the age group 19–24 years was enrolled in higher education, a figure which the Tunisian authorities regard as insufficient when compared to countries with a comparable level of economic development (République Tunisienne 1990 p. 14).

3. Governance, Administration, and Finance

Though the reforms of 1988 were introduced to give greater institutional autonomy and latitude, the Tunisian system of higher education comes under the overall control of the Ministry of Education, Higher Education and Research. National objectives for higher education are set out in successive national plans for which the Ministry has responsibility for implementing in the educational domain. A new

consultative agency—the Upper Council for Education (*Conseil Supérieur de l'Education*) presided over by the prime minister and composed of all ministers having an interest in education—including higher education—was set up in October 1988. It is called upon to give its opinion on all major matters including financial policy.

If one of the objectives of the 1988 reforms was to pave the way for the development of private sector higher education, the fact remains that the overwhelming majority of higher education is a state service, obtains its finance from central government, and is steered by ministerial circulars and decrees. Steps are now being taken to develop a greater degree of self-government in the area of pedagogy and management. Universities are being encouraged to seek other sources of finance and to take charge of setting institutional goals.

Hitherto, nominations to posts of major responsibility in academia have come under the purlieu of the Ministry of Education. Provisions in the New Guideline Law of 1988 have opened new possibilities for participation and consultative procedures at institutional level to recommend nominations to leadership posts. Elections for such posts as dean of faculty and head of department are also undertaken.

4. Faculty and Students: Teaching, Learning, and Research

Faculty of Tunisian universities are civil servants, their conditions of employment and scales of remuneration set out nationally by central administration. Nomination to post is subject to Ministry approval and in the case of rectors, they are nominated by the president of the republic for a three-year term of office. Formally speaking, the number of hours to be taught and the qualifications required for each level of academic rank are also set out in national legislation which, naturally, applies across the land.

Current student enrollments in the university sector amount to 62,700 in 1989–90 and pressure for places resulting from demographic growth has been considerable. At the start of the 1980s, the average growth rate in student numbers per annum was of the order of 4 percent. Since 1988, this has reached around 10 percent per year. Over the coming decade, if such growth is sustained, student enrollments will reach 149,000—two and a half times their present level.

Such pressures have created a highly volatile student body in which different political viewpoints and organizations are hotly discussed, discussions which sometimes go beyond the university. As has been pointed out earlier, the structure of first-degree studies tends to follow a broad general curriculum in the first two years and to becoming increasingly specialized later. Assessment is on a 0–20 point grading scheme and based on formal written examinations. Finally, it should be noted that higher education in Tunisia does not charge admission or enrollment fees.

Bibliography

République Tunisienne 1986 *Développement de l'Education en Tunisie 1984–1986.* Commission Nationale Tunisienne pour l'Education, la Science et la Culture, Tunis

République Tunisienne 1990 *Développement de l'Education en Tunisie 1988–1990.* Commission Nationale Tunisienne pour l'Education, la Science et la Culture, Tunis

G. Neave

Turkey

1. Higher Education and Society

The Republic of Turkey was founded in 1923 and the present system of higher education is a product of new Turkey. Yet, the country has an old civilization and a centuries long tradition of higher learning, with its heritage being deeply embedded in its Ottoman past. After the Ottoman Empire collapsed at the beginning of the twentieth century, a series of sweeping reforms were introduced by Ataturk who founded the new Republic on strictly modernist, westernized, and secular lines.

The forerunners of Turkish institutions of higher learning can be traced back to two key schools in Ottoman history, the *enderun* and *medrese*, which had organic ties with their related social classes, namely the military and the clergy. The former was educated in special institutions, most distinguished of which is the *enderun*, an elitist school supported by the palace clique; the latter received its education and training at the *medrese* which may be traced back as early as the fourteenth century. Both institutions were deeply rooted in the Islamic tradition.

Since our concern is higher education in the present secular Republic of Turkey, two later institutions based on Western models will be of greater significance: namely, the *Mühendishane-i Bahri-i Hümayun* (the Imperial Navy Engineering School) established in 1773 and the *Darülfünun-u Osmani* (the Ottoman Imperial University), first established in 1846 and acquiring its definitive body in 1900. The origins of the Ottoman Imperial University can be traced back to *Medaris-i Semaniye* (the eight most prestigious *medreses*) established by Mehmet the Conqueror in the environs of the great Istanbul mosque bearing his name. The social background of these institutions was class-oriented. The *Mühendishane-i Bahri-i Hümayun* was set up after the Ottomans suffered a series of military defeats and the rulers then thought that certain reforms should have priority in the military field. Likewise, the social significance of the clergy as a dominant class in the administrative or judicial circles declined drastically, particularly during the nineteenth century. Thus, the need for a new bureaucrat class gave rise to a modern and Western-style education, through which the newly emergent group received its training. One would hardly expect the *medreses*, during their last years deeply immersed in the scholastic mentality of the Middle Ages, to provide this.

During the nineteenth century an overt dualism prevailed in the Ottoman state apparatus in the secular and the antisecular mode of thinking. Only after the proclamation of the Republic was a national, democratic, and secular system of education introduced. This was a Herculean task. Change in the educational field went hand in hand with social reformations enforced by Ataturk, such as the abolition of the Sultanate and Caliphate, the prohibition of polygamy, the suppression of religious schools and subsequent adoption of laicism, the European legal system, Latin script, the Western calendar, and the metric system. In the beginning, however, the young Republic devoted much of its efforts to modernizing elementary and secondary education. Nevertheless, during Ataturk's presidency, a higher education law passed by parliament in 1933 led to the founding of Istanbul University (the earlier *Darülfünun*). Three other laws were enacted in 1946, 1973, and 1981, all of which, within different contexts of academic freedom, introduced an overall system of centralized control over financial sources; the recruitment, assignment and promotion of academic staff; the elaboration of curricula and distribution of courses; and the selection of undergraduates.

1.1 Geographical Context

Geographically, Turkey is roughly a rectangular peninsula between the Black Sea and the Mediterranean linking two continental portions of Europe and Asia. Of the total area (780,576 sq kms), a small part lies in Europe (Thrace), and the larger part in Asia (Anatolia). A mountainous country with an average altitude of 1,000 meters it has a climate of severe, cold winters particularly in the east bordering the Soviet Union and Iran and in the southeast bordering Iraq and Syria, and hot, dry summers in the central regions. The coastal regions surrounded by the Mediterranean and the Aegean seas and including Thrace which borders with Bulgaria and Greece have milder weather. Turkey's borders have undergone practically no change since the proclamation of the Republic in 1923, following the War of Independence and the international recognition of the Republic by the Treaty of Lausanne.

1.2 Size and Rate of Growth of Population

Basic demographic data drawn from the 1990 census results give the total population as 56.9 million of which 59 percent live in urban areas and 41 percent in rural areas and villages. The annual population growth rate is around 2.4 percent. The 14 and under age group comprises 35.8 percent (i.e., 20.4 million) of the total population. The fertility rate and infancy deathrate have steadily declined since the early 1970s: the former was around 6 percent in the 1960s and 3.5 percent from 1985–90; the latter was 208 per thousand in the 1960s dropping to 65.2 per thousand from 1985–90.

The rate of population growth is high, and approximately every 25 years the total population doubles. The projection for the year 2000 is estimated to be around 70 million according to World Bank and Turkish State Planning Organization data. This imposes a very heavy burden on education. Moreover, that the under-14 age group is close to half the size of the total population (the 5–24 age group is about 46 percent of the total) is obviously another pressing demand for the education system. The rural–urban balance sees a steady migration toward urban centers. A typical example in this respect is the case of Istanbul which, as a sizable metropolitan center, has an annual population growth of 5.4 percent (according to the State Planning Organization figures). Fertility and infancy deathrates, however, display a steady decline. There exists a massive difference between the eastern and western provinces, due to literacy and birth control rates among the female adult population. In the metropolitan centers of Western Anatolia, lettered women graduates on average give birth to 1.4 children. Of these 2.2 percent die before the end of their first year; however, in Eastern Anatolia unlettered women give birth to an average of 5.1 children of whom 21 percent die before their first birthday. Ethnically, Turkey is of uniform and homogenous constitution with negligible percentages of minority groups. The preponderantly spoken official language belongs to the Altaic language family; the Ottoman intelligentsia in their zeal to associate themselves with Islamic civilization imported Arabic and Persian elements and transformed their tongue into a composite language—so-called "Ottoman Turkish." However, the Republic of Turkey, through the language reform of 1928 (in effect, the Romanization of the Arabic script) made great strides in reorienting and re-educating its people. In other words, the language reform had pedagogical, cultural, nationalistic, and religious implications. Arabic was the language of the Koran and the Arabic script symbolized the people's attachment to Islam. To the revolutionaries it was a powerful medium chaining the minds of the people to the old order, superstition, alien beliefs, and reactionary inclinations. The change in the alphabet was followed by a systematic attempt to expurgate the language of all Arabic and Persian accretions and to develop a purely Turkish medium of communication. The purification of the language and the laicization of religion were part and parcel of the general process of modernization, developing a sense of belonging on nationalistic terms in the post-1923 Republican period.

1.3 Relationship with Religious Bodies

In the Ottoman era, Islam was a unifying element in society and the bedrock upon which the Ottoman state rested. Accordingly, religious schools and religious instruction in schools were unquestioned premises in the Ottoman theocratic ideology. Moreover, Ataturk considered this type of education to be a stumbling block in modernizing the new nation and an integral part of the old order that should be stamped out. In 1923, the Ministry of Education assumed control and administration of all religious schools along with their means of support (endowments and funds). Teaching of religion was prohibited in all state schools. The abolition of the Caliphate in 1924 was followed by the closing of the *medreses*, the closing down of the august office of the *Sheik-ul-Islam*, and by the replacement of the Ministry of Religious Law with a Presidency of Religious Affairs under the prime minister. In 1928, Article 2 of the Republican Constitution was amended, disestablishing Islam as the state religion. In 1937 the principle of secularism was incorporated into the Constitution. In the meantime, the jurisdiction of the Sheriat courts was replaced by lay Western-style courts. The Turkish Civil Code, virtually modeled on the Swiss Civil Code, replaced the orthodox private Mohammedan laws. Finally in 1933, the foundering Faculty of Theology of Istanbul University was abolished.

These changes were dramatic and took place almost overnight. Yet, to what extent Ataturk had succeeded is today not as clear as it seemed during the heyday of religious reform. The issue of religion or the role of Islam in the new state lay dormant until the 1940s. With Turkey's transition from a one-party to a multi-party system (1946–50) religion again emerged as a cultural and political issue. The process of liberalizing restrictions on religion, imposed during the Ataturk regime through positivistic secularist policies, has always been a controversial issue. Turkey has always been groping with the problem of readjusting its democratic ideology and policies to the pressing demands for a more accommodating attitude to Islam as an educational and social institution. Within this framework, little wonder that the liberalization of religion became a political slogan for vote hunting especially in the remote rural areas where religion plays a very important part in the lives of a great number of people. In a society with deep roots in Islam, it was natural for open criticism of the restrictions imposed by government to be voiced once the lid was lifted or a more pluralistic approach to politics was introduced.

Two significant developments in religious education took place in Republican Turkey. In 1949 a Faculty of Divinity was established at the University of Ankara, under the supervision and control of the Ministry of Education. At about the same time, six-year secondary schools for the training of religious employees (i.e., *imams*) were re-established. By the 1960s the number of students enrolled at these secondary-level schools were around 7,000 with an additional 300 at the higher level (i.e., Faculty of Divinity in Ankara and the Higher Islamic Institute in Istanbul). However, after the passing of the Bill in 1965 granting local directorates permission to open Koranic study courses the student number reached 155,000. Some 10 higher Islamic institutes were opened, later changing their names to faculties of divinity. In 1989, 6,029 undergraduates were enrolled at these higher institutions. The boom remains an open question since the principle, laicism and secularist education is safeguarded by Article 2 of the 1982 Constitution. Yet Turkey still seems to maintain a balance between the secular state and the traditionally Muslim population.

1.4 Structure of Government and the Economy

The Republic of Turkey today enjoys a democratic system, based on pluralism, free elections, and constitutionally secured rights and freedoms. Until 1946 a one-party system prevailed and after the transition to a multi-party system, Turks experienced a highly sophisticated political phenomenon in the form of a change of government through free elections: a unique experience in a part of the world where undemocratic political regimes predominated. There were three interruptions to the Turkish practice of democracy due to internal instabilities in 1960, 1972, and 1980. Nevertheless, the country recovered quickly and today has good grounds to be proud of its democratic institutions. The composition of the government is as follows: a unicameral legislature of 450 deputies, a council of ministers headed by the Prime Minister, and the President of the Republican State. According to the 1982 Constitution, a constitutional court passes rulings on the constitutionality of the legislations, and the supremacy of the executive power is highly emphasized by the establishment of a council of state directly answerable to the president. This institution has the power of judicial review regarding the decrees issued by all the state and executive organizations.

Turkey is a founding member of the United Nations and a long-standing NATO ally, and currently seeking full membership of the European Community. The administrative structure is centralized with 73 provinces with Ankara as the capital.

According to the latest statistics, the shares of Gross Domestic Product (GDP) of the main economic sectors are: agriculture providing 19.2 percent; industry making up 26.1 percent; and services, the largest sector, providing 54.7 percent of the aggregate output. In contrast, employment among the main sectors is distributed rather differently than the output shares. In 1989 agriculture provided 50 percent of employment, industry, 15 percent, and services, only 35 percent of the labor force. Nevertheless, this is a very large improvement from 1962 when agriculture employed 77 percent of the labor force while industry absorbed 8 percent, and services provided 15 percent of employment. Since 1962–89 the population increased from 28.9 million to 56.9 million, a 92 percent growth in 27 years. In contrast, the labor force increased from 12.6 million to 16.7 million, only a 32 percent increase—the employment rate has lagged 60 percent behind the population growth.

The share of the educational sector as a percentage of Gross National Product (GNP) has declined constantly from a high 4.44 in 1971, reaching a low level of 2.77 in 1989. These figures include the Ministry of Education as well as the Higher Education Council shares (1989). A different picture emerges when one looks at the share of the educational expenditures in the total government budget. While the total education budget as a percentage of the total governmental budget was 12.2 in 1971 and still has the same share of 12.2 percent in 1989, the share of the educational sector investments as a percentage of total investments in the government budget increased from a low 7.1 in 1971 to a level of 14.7 in 1989. The share of higher education investments as a percentage of total government investments has stood relatively fixed at a level of 4.6 in 1970 compared to a level of 4.9 in 1989. On the other hand, the share of the Ministry of Education investments as a percentage of the general government investment budget increased dramatically from 2.5 percent in 1970 to 9.8 percent in 1989. That the schooling ratio in higher education increased from 4.1 percent in 1964 to 12.6 percent in 1989 while the shares in budgetary allocations and government investments in higher education remained relatively low is one aspect of the current problems of the system.

2. The Institutional Fabric of the Higher Education System

The current structure of higher education stems from the Higher Education Law No. 2547 that went into effect on 6 November 1981 and the subsequent establishment of the Higher Education Council, or properly known with its Turkish acronym (YÖK) in December 1981. The provisions made in this law and the articles 130 and 131 of the Turkish Constitution state that the supreme authority for the regulation of higher education is the Higher Education Council, composed of 24 members. Seven of these 24 members are appointed by the President of the Republic, seven by the Council of Ministers, one by the Office of Chief of the General Staff, two by the Ministry of Education, and seven by the Interuniversity Board from among nonboard-member university professors. The terms of office are four years and the appointment of all members is to be approved by the President of the Republic.

Apart from the current Higher Education Law there have been three attempts in the past (in 1933, 1946, and 1973) to reorganize and restructure the higher education system. The first was the 1933 reform through which the only full-fledged university in the country—the *Darülfünun* of Istanbul—was renamed Istanbul University. This paved the way for the establishment of genuinely reformist higher education centers all over Turkey. Several new independent faculties were established in Ankara (in addition to the old Higher School for Civil Servants—*Mülkiye Mektebi*) which were amalgamated later to form Ankara University. During the same period, the Higher School of Engineering in Istanbul was granted university status as the Istanbul Technical University in 1944.

The 1933 reform of Istanbul University scored a definite success over its previous Ottoman constitution and contributed tremendously to the improvement of academic standards. This reformist spirit came to fruition in 1946 when Law No. 4936 came into effect. This law granted universities a comparatively high degree of administrative autonomy and academic freedom.

From 1946 onward the Turkish Republic experienced a boom in the establishment of new universities, faculties, higher education institutions, and academies in different parts of the country. This phenomenon was the response to increasing demand for higher education by the younger generation. Within this context an interesting experience was the founding of private higher education centers after 1965. More than 40 of these centers came into being by the early 1970s; nevertheless, they were closed down after a constitutional court ruling that the state alone may found universities.

The 1970s marked the period when higher education problems were always at the top of the agenda on national issues. Access to higher education and academic and administrative autonomy of the universities were the most fiery topics. In 1964, for the first time, students had to sit for centrally organized matriculation examinations instead of examinations set by individual university bodies. This practice led to the establishment of the Interuniversity Student Selection and Placement Center in 1974. In 1973, Law No. 1790, the third significant university law

(prior to the 1981 Law) came into force establishing a central governing body—the Higher Education Council—for all universities. However, in 1975 the Constitutional Court ruled that the composition and powers of this Council were contrary to the principles of the academic and administrative autonomy. Under the 1981 Law a delicate balance was maintained between centralization and individual autonomy on administrative and academic matters. For this purpose, the objectives of higher education institutions and the principles of the Higher Education Council were set by articles 131 and 132 of the 1982 Constitution, respectively.

2.1 The Sectoral Organization of Higher Education and Levels of Institution

Turkish higher education institutions, after the reorganization enforced by the 1981 Law, can be categorized into: (a) 29 universities and (b) nonuniversity higher education institutes, such as military colleges and academies, police academies, and health education institutes. The 1981 Law incorporated teacher-training colleges and institutes of higher education, which had earlier been affiliated with the Ministry of National Education, into the university system. Similarly, metropolitan and rural academies of Economics and Commercial Sciences, dating back to the early 1960s and state academies of Architecture and Engineering, first set up in 1969, were also incorporated into the university system.

The current number of state-financed universities is 28. There is only one privately funded university—Bilkent University—located in Ankara and established through the joint endowment of the Hacettepe University Foundation, the Hacettepe Medical Center Foundation, and the Hacettepe Institute of Child Health Foundation. In 1991, through an amendment to the Higher Education Law, foundations were granted the right to establish privately funded universities. Being financed by the state does not hinder Turkish universities from establishing a fruitful liaison with industry. They undertake not only research projects for industry and government agencies but also provide services (such as medical consultation, etc.) thus creating extra resources for their own use. This income is channeled into the so-called revolving funds of individual universities and is used for funding all kinds of educational expenses.

The research system in the Turkish Republic has primarily been associated with higher education institutions. This steady trend has changed considerably since the 1960s and nonuniversity units of research have gradually been established on a nationwide scale. The Scientific and Technical Council of Turkey (TÜBITAK), a state organization founded in 1963, is a center well-known for developing, encouraging, and organizing research in the basic and applied sciences. The center not only offers training programs, research grants, and scholarships for students and faculty, but also presents awards annually to researchers from university or nonuniversity circles alike. Research institutions can be categorized as: (a) those directly linked to the office of the prime minister and certain ministries; (b) state-subsidized agricultural, forestry, veterinary, and zoological institutions; and (c) private sector research institutions. Higher education institutions still maintain a major position in this spectrum, because numerous measures have been taken to better the quality of research. For example, institutes of universities which had the sole purpose of offering graduate courses have been reorganized into centers of scientific research covering a vast number of fields from nuclear science to demographic studies and earthquake research to the history of Turkish reforms. Furthermore, within the university structure, research funds have been created as distinct from teaching and administrative expenses to support and encourage original research.

Another significant boost to scientific inquiry comes through the criteria for promoting university teaching staff. The Higher Education Law stipulates that only those who have undertaken and published original research can be granted the title of associate professor. Promotion to full professorial rank requires published research deemed original by international standards. The rise in the number of articles appearing in foreign journals (371 in 1982 to 1,451 in 1987) may be interpreted as a positive response to the measures taken.

2.2 Admissions Policies and Selection

Admission procedures in Turkish universities ran smoothly until the 1950s when, faced with a large increase in the student population, they proved inadequate. The need for objective assessment brought about a centralized university entrance examination system. The practice began in the 1964–65 academic year. In 1974 the Interuniversity Board established the Interuniversity Student Selection and Placement Center. According to the 1981 Higher Education Law the Center was taken over by the Higher Education Council and changed its name to Student Selection and Placement Center. To qualify for admission to a Turkish university as an undergraduate, demands a valid *lycée* diploma or its equivalent, to sit for a central matriculation examination set by the Student Selection and Placement Center (Turkish acronym, ÖSYM), and score the minimum points demanded by the particular faculty or school of one's choice. Since 1981, this central examination has two stages. All candidates scoring specified minimum points at the first stage may either (a) take the second-stage exam; or (b) be considered for placement into a two-year vocational or four-year part-time Open University education program. Candidates who wish to sit for both stages may be placed in any of the higher education programs on the basis

of their scores in both stages and their personal preferences. Applications are made in November for the first stage which consists of a multiple-choice test of two parts, namely verbal and quantitative. In 1990 a minimum composite score of 105,000 was required to sit for the second stage. After the results of the first stage in May, qualified candidates make their application and sit for the second stage in mid-June. An applicant may sit for both stages of the examination in all provincial centers of the country. There are 927 programs in 29 different universities (according to 1990 figures) and a maximum of 18 choices can be listed in preferential order. In the second stage, the examination comprises five individual tests, namely on natural sciences, mathematics, Turkish language and literature, social sciences, and a foreign language. The composite scores are calculated in the same way as for the first stage results. The higher education institutions are notified about the candidates placed in their programs. Registration takes place at the beginning of the academic year, which is some time around mid-September (see Table 1).

Since 1981, foreign students who wish to pursue their higher education in Turkish universities have had to take a separate matriculation examination (YÖS) conducted by the Student Selection and Placement Center. The main center for the YÖS examination is in Ankara but it is also held in various cities in the Middle East, Africa, and Asia. The examination, which is of multiple-choice format, has two parts: the first a basic learning skills test in English; and the second part a Turkish proficiency test. For the placement procedure, only the standard score of the first part is taken into consideration. No student with a standard score below 40 can be admitted to any program. The Turkish proficiency test plays no part in the placement of foreign students; however, those not proficient in Turkish are required to take Turkish language courses during the course of their higher education. From among 4,512 candidates, 2,047 were admitted to undergraduate programs in 1985; 1,544 out of 3,560 candidates were admitted in 1990.

All students have to pay nominal tuition fees which vary according to their field of study. There are several state-backed bodies granting loans and scholarships to eligible students. The Institution for Student Loans and Dormitories gives monthly allowances to students which can be used for board and meals and pays the tuition fees of needy students.

2.3 Structure of Qualifications

The granting of degrees or diplomas for undergraduate programs are defined in individual university regulations within the framework of the basic ordinances given by the Higher Education Council (HEC). In Turkish terminology the French word *licence* is appropriated and popularly used synonymously both with a degree and a diploma. The

Table 1
Student enrollment in higher education institutions

	1990–91 Number of students			1988–89 Number of students		
	Male	Female	Total	Male	Female	Total
Universities						
Vocational schools	50,156	21,243	71,399	46,412	20,373	66,785
Undergraduate	228,336	135,013	363,349	195,098	115,124	310,222
Open University	80,886	80,076	260,962	122,060	52,651	174,711
Graduate—master's	5,855	9,151	25,006	11,647	6,524	18,171
Graduate—PhD	7,555	4,150	11,705	5,772	3,115	8,887
Medical internship	3,144	1,196	4,340	3,041	1,156	4,197
Nonuniversities						
Vocational schools	264	544	808	69	118	187
Undergraduate	8,764	127	8,891	9,395	146	8,541
Graduate—master's	4	7	11	4	11	15
Graduate PhD	35	7	43	31	3	34
Medical internship	2,435	972	3,407	2,152	760	2,912

award of diplomas and degrees can be grouped as follows:

(a) pre-baccalaureate diploma—awarded to students who initially enrolled in a four-year course but who do not wish to pursue their studies, provided that they successfully completed all requirements of the first two years' work, or at least half the credits of the four-year program with a "C" average;

(b) vocational college diploma (associate degree)—awarded to graduates of vocational schools upon the completion of a two-year prescribed program;

(c) diploma of a higher school of education—awarded to graduates of prescribed four-year courses (such as the School of Journalism and Mass Communication, or the School of Home Economics, etc., usually affiliated with a full-fledged university). The diploma is acceptable for admission to a graduate program;

(d) bachelor's degree—awarded to graduates of various departments upon completion of a four-year prescribed course of study. In the case of medicine (i.e., qualifying as an MD) and dentistry and veterinary sciences the prescribed course of study is six years for the former and five for the latter two.

In the pre-1981 period the organization and supervision of all graduate studies were realized on a departmental or faculty basis. In 1982, the stipulations set up by the Higher Education Law gave way to a massive reorganization of these studies and institutes within the university functioning as graduate schools were established. Graduate degrees are grouped into four categories as defined by Article 3 of the Higher Education Law:

(a) master's degree (higher *licence*)—the applicant must hold a bachelor's degree and pass a qualifying exam for candidacy. The normal length of a master's program is two years, the first of which is usually devoted to course work and the second to the writing of a thesis.

(b) doctoral degree (PhD)—the applicant must hold a master's degree and pass a qualification exam after completion of the prescribed course work, normally lasting for two years. Then upon the approval of a proposed research project by the candidate's committee, the candidate can carry on with the writing of his or her PhD thesis, usually supervised by a committee member. The thesis is ultimately defended by a viva voce exam before a committee of three examiners.

(c) specialization in medicine—a graduate program of study conforming to the regulations set up by the Ministry of Health. The basic aim is the training of medical doctors so that they acquire special skills and expertise in higher specialized aspects of the medical sciences.

(d) proficiency in fine arts—a program which may run for six terms for those candidates holding a bachelor's degree, and four terms for those holding a master's degree. Generally speaking, the presentation of an original work of art or of an outstanding performance in theatrical arts or music are the basic requirements.

3. Governance, Administration, and Finance

3.1 National Administration

The HEC is the sole coordinating, planning, and policy-making body for higher education on a general scale in Turkey. There are four more affiliated organizations with advisory functions. These are:

(a) The Higher Education Supervisory Board—a ten-member body supervising the universities, their units, and teaching staff and acting on behalf of the HEC.

(b) The Student Selection and Placement Center (ÖSYM)—first established in 1974 and then affiliated to the HEC in 1991 which has been involved not only in selection and placement of students in higher education programs but also in offering services to higher education institutions for administering large-scale and interuniversity examinations. The ÖSYM also collects and processes statistical data on teaching staff and students of higher education establishments. It offers services to public organizations in preparing and conducting examinations for recruitment and promotion of their personnel. The Center's president is appointed by the president of the HEC.

(c) The Turkish University Rector's Committee—exclusively an advisory body with no executive power. The president of the HEC serves as the president of this committee as well, and the rectors currently in office together with five former rectors comprise the membership.

(d) The Interuniversity Board—coordinates academic activities and prescribes the basic standards to be appropriated by individual universities. The membership comprises all the university rectors and representatives of universities (a full professor from each university), with the chairmanship rotating among member rectors. The Board may pass rules concerning research activities, publications, higher degrees, equivalences of titles and doctoral degrees obtained abroad, academic procedures for the promotion of senior faculty members, and final regulations on the minimum period of required instruction. Furthermore, the Board also selects seven members of the HEC.

As for the HEC, Article 131 of the Constitution states that the Higher Education Council is established to plan, organize, administer, and supervise the activities of different institutions of higher education; to coordinate teaching and scientific research, to ensure the establishment and development of higher education institutions as determined by law; to ensure the effective use of resources alloted to universities; and to take measures for the recruitment and training of the teaching staff. In practice, the following are some of the major functions undertaken by the HEC:

(a) to determine the enrollment capacities of universities, setting the general principles of admission;

(b) to convey to the Minister of Education, for proposal to the Council of Ministers and parliament, recommendations for the annual higher education budget based on budgetary proposals made by individual universities;

(c) to propose four candidates to the President of the Republic for each vacant rectorate;

(d) to appoint deans of faculties, taking into consideration the recommendation of the rectors;

(e) to determine the teaching load of the faculty and the length of the curricular programs, in the light of recommendations made by the Interuniversity Board;

(f) to set regulations to enable the transfer of students from one university to another;

(g) to propose to the Council of Ministers the amount of tuition fees for each academic year. According to the most recent amendments in the Higher Education Law, the HEC also assumes a consultative role in determining the particular status (such as the newly created "special status") of a university.

These functions may indicate a very strict practice of centralized governance. However, it is possible to think of a certain degree of administrative autonomy since each higher education institution has its own governing body and can make its own curricular regulations. What is important to note here is the fact that the individual bodies are absolutely free to set up their own academic standards and policies as long as they are in conformity with the guidelines prepared by the HEC.

3.2 Finance

Although universities may create extrabudgetary resources (through contracts, research projects, and consulting services with industry which are channeled into the revolving fund), 28 universities are for the most part financed by the state except for the Bilkent University in Ankara, which is on the whole privately funded. The major source of income for the universities and their affiliated institutions is a state subsidy. The allocation mechanism operates thus: the HEC, by taking into consideration individual budgetary demands of all the universities, submits through the Council of Ministers a budget proposal (in the form of a lump sum demand) to parliament. Every fiscal year, the budget thus allocated for each university usually consists of capital investments and recurrent expenditures. Capital investments are endorsed and coordinated by the State Planning Organization. Three basic categories constitute the recurrent expenditures: staff salaries; conference, research, or study visit expenditure; and other recurrent expenditures such as services, office stationery, and so on. The tuition fees fund, first set up in 1985, constitutes a very small part of the total source of income for the university. Funds gathered through this channel are spent for social, cultural, and sporting activities by each university. Individual universities administer and control the utilization of this source, just like they do with revolving funds.

In 1983 the higher education budget was separated from the Ministry of National Education budget and, thereafter, the HEC assumed the role of an autonomous body to coordinate university budgets in the country. In this respect, only post-1984 figures are available for the proportion of gross national product devoted exclusively to higher education expenditure, because earlier figures in the consolidated state budget are inclusively Ministry of National Education allocations on general education. In 1984, HEC's proportion of GNP is 0.64 (Ministry of Education has a proportion of 1.85). The ratios underwent a steady decline thereafter, recovering in 1988, and finally reaching 0.94 (coupled by Ministry of National Education share of 1.83) in 1989. Given the high rate of population increase, currently about 2.4 percent, the proportion of GNP devoted to higher education in Turkey is indeed very low. This is a burning issue, or a bottleneck, because demographic developments in Turkey display a very young profile of Turks between the 5–24 age group which accounts for 46 percent of the total population, thus putting a heavy burden on education at all levels.

3.3 Institutional Administration

University governance at the institutional level presents a uniform picture, with the exception of Bilkent University which is governed by a board of trustees. Each university has two supreme governing bodies: the Senate acting in a legislative capacity and the University Council which mainly has executive powers. The rector presides over the Senate which has the following membership: vice-rectors, faculty deans, institute or higher school directors, and senior faculty members (usually a full professor from each faculty) elected for a term of three years by the board of their own faculty. Apart from preparing draft regulations and bylaws, the senate concerns itself with curricular procedures and academic matters, research activities, scientific publications, the academic calendar, the conferment of honorary degrees, and finally the appointment of the members of the university administrative council. The University Council, as an executive body, deals with the implementation and enforcement of the Senate's rulings, statutes, and bylaws, as well as controlling and managing budgetary and administrative matters. Members include the rector (as the president), faculty deans, and three full professors elected by the senate. The administrative services of every university is headed by a secretary-general.

Faculties also have a board and an administrative council as their governing bodies. The Faculty Board which generally deals with academic problems has the dean (as the president), together with chairpersons of the departments, directors of institutes or affiliated schools, three full professors, two associate professors, and one assistant professor elected by their respective peers. The Administrative Council has, likewise, the dean (as the president), three full, two associate, and two assistant professors, again elected by their respective peers. Duties of the Administrative Council include the implementation of the rulings and academic programs passed by the Faculty Board, and any other administrative matters. The Council is also concerned with budget proposals and capital investment plans.

Undergraduates and graduates alike together with administrative personnel are not represented in any council or board, and thus assume no responsibility in the decision-making process of the universities. The sole channel they have is the submission of a petition through which they can bring to the attention of the governing body concerned any personal or academic problem relating to them.

4. Faculty and Students: Teaching, Learning, and Research

4.1 Faculty

Article 130 of the Constitution stipulates the general principles regarding the status of university teaching staff, such as, basic rights and duties, liberty to engage in scientific research; tenure status, and so on. It is explicitly stated in the Constitution that the detailed procedures concerning these are to be regulated by law, hence the Higher Education Law of 1981. According to the provisions of this law, full, associate (*dozent*), and assistant professors, instructors, lecturers, and ancillary staff (research assistants, translators, and educational and training planners) are designated as teaching staff. Among the staff, seniority falls on professors who are particularly concerned with teaching at both undergraduate and graduate levels, supervising dissertations, conducting seminars, and undertaking research. In addition, they may also assume administrative duties in their own units. The title of an assistant professor may be granted to PhD holders or those who have completed their specialization in medicine or proficiency in the fine arts, and who have passed a required foreign language examination. Associate and full professors are tenured university teaching staff. Promotion to associate professorship

Table 2
Number of faculties in higher education institutions 1990–91

	Universities				Non-universities		
	Vocational schools	Undergraduate programs	Graduate schools	Research centers	Vocational schools	Undergraduate programs	Institutes
Professor	23	4,548	102	5	—	89	8
Associate Professor	19	2,306	33	1	1	66	7
Assistant Professor	70	3,584	27	2	—	166	13
Instructor	1,144	3,724	41	5	24	231	—
Lecturer	147	2,639	17	31	—	61	—
Specialist	71	935	16	22	10	90	1
Research Assistant	40	13,212	854	11	—	39	—
Translator	—	3	—	—	—	1	—
Educational planner	—	10	—	—	5	5	—

goes through the following path: PhD holders, or those who have earned specialist status in medicine or proficiency in the fine arts, initially pass a foreign language examination, and provided that the academic jury set up by the Interuniversity Board deems their work the result of original scientific research, they take a further examination conducted viva voce, and if necessary, also a practical test. Successful candidates then become associate professors. After receiving this title, those who have worked in their field for at least five years may be promoted to the rank of full professor if their published research is judged as being of an international standard.

As for other teaching staff, instructors are expected to lecture and supervise practical studies at special instances where there is no appointed senior staff or when special expertise is needed for a particular sort of course. Lecturers teach standard compulsory courses (such as Turkish language, foreign language, and history of Turkish reforms) in different universities or other higher education institutes. Ancillary staff members undertake specific duties assigned by their seniors in their pertinent fields and are usually employed on a contractual basis and, where viable, part-time basis (see Table 2).

Teaching load for full, associate, and assistant professors is at least 10 hours or its equivalent per week, and may be part-time (with the exception of assistant professors, who may be employed full-time). Rectors, deans, and directors of institutes and higher schools of education are exempted from the minimum teaching load. For instructors and lecturers working on a full-time basis, the teaching load is at least 12 hours per week.

Appointment procedures for senior staff (full, associate, and assistant professors) is of a uniform nature across the country. In the case of assistant professors, it is the rector who appoints from a group of candidates applying for vacant positions. It goes without saying that the recommendations of academic juries on each applicant are of great importance. Assistant professors have no tenure and work on a contractual basis for a maximum of 12 years on two- or three-year terms, and they may be dismissed at the end of each term. Associate professors are appointed in a similar way, but they have tenured status just like full professors who have a slightly different appointment procedure. Previously the HEC used to appoint them to vacant positions at different universities. However, a recent amendment to the Higher Education Law has the rector ratify the recommendation made by the University Council.

Article 35 of the Higher Education Law stipulates that the higher education institutions are themselves responsible for the training of their own academic staff. The trend in staff development from the late 1980s has been sponsoring teaching assistants for graduate studies abroad. (The figures for 1987 and 1988 were 157 and 345 respectively.) Upon termination of their graduate studies, they are expected to return and join the teaching staff of their base universities.

4.2 Students

In 1990 Turkish higher education institutions had a total of 635,828 students. This enrollment figure indicates a boom when one compares it with a pre-HEC figure of 177,281 in 1974 and a post-HEC one of 398,185 in 1985. However, there is a grim picture in the figures provided by the Student Selection and Placement Center concerning the number of applicants for the centralized matriculation examination and the number of students who are actually admitted to undergraduate programs. These figures for the year in which the center was first founded (i.e., 1974) are 37,271 admissions from among 229,906 applications; for 1985, 156,065 admissions from among 480,633 applications; and for 1990, 196,253 admissions from among 892,975 applications. This dramatic rise in the demand for higher education is indeed a burning issue. One particular cause that can be cited among many is the lack of an organic tie between the objectives of second- and third-stage (university level) education systems in Turkey. In so far as the schooling process is concerned, Turkey has experienced a boom in the number of technical and vocational high schools from the early 1980s. Almost all the graduates of these schools initially preferred to apply to four-year course programs rather than applying to education programs in two-year vocational schools corresponding to their particular fields of training. The sole reason for such a preference is the fact that industry accommodates the degree holders from four-year programs on a better scale than the graduates of two-year vocational schools.

5. Conclusion

To propose a remedy is outside the scope of this article. It may suffice to reiterate here the most important issue, namely centralization in the Turkish higher education system. In Republican Turkish history there are four major attempts at systematization of higher education. The laws passed in 1933, 1946, 1973, and 1981 all display different degrees of centralization measures adopted by the authorities. With the most recent law, this trend culminated in a strictly centralized control of the higher education system with respect to the following areas: recruitment; appointment and promotion of the teaching staff; general structure of the curricula and approval of course offerings; selection and placement of students; and above all, finances. Centralization in all these areas was very carefully designed so as not to clash with the immaculately preserved academic autonomy of individual universities.

Bibliography

Akyol A 1990 *1991 National Education Report to Parliament*. Ministry of National Education, Ankara

Akyüz Y 1985 *Türk Eğitim Tarihi*. Ankara Üniversitesi Eğitim Bilimleri Fakültesi, Ankara

Baloğlu Z 1990 *Türkiye'de Eğitim*. Publications of Turkish Industrialists' and Businessmen's Association (TÜSIAD), Istanbul

Doğramacı I 1989 *Higher Education in Turkey: Developments since November 1981*. Ministry of National Education, Ankara

DPT 1990 *1980'den 1990'a Makroekonomik Politikalar*. DPT, Ankara

Koçer H A 1970 *Türkiye'de Modern Eğitimin Doğuşu ve Gelişimi* Universitesi Yayıaları, Ankara. Ankara

Organisation for Economic Co-operation and Development 1990 *Education in OECD Countries 1987–88 (A Compendium of Statistical Information)*. OECD, Paris

ÖSYM 1990 *Monograph on Higher Education in Turkey 1990*. UNESCO/CEPES, Ankara

ÖSYM 1991 *1990–1991 Öğretim Yılı Yükseköğretim Istatistikleri*. ÖSYM, Ankara

Parla T 191 *Türkiye'de Anayasalar*. iletişim Yayınları, Istanbul

Shaw, S 1977 *History of the Ottoman Empire and Modern Turkey*, Vols. 1 and 2. Cambridge University Press, Cambridge

Tekeli I 1980 *Toplumsal Dönüşüm ve Eğitim Tarihi Üzerine Konuşmalar*. Mimarlar Odası Yayınları, Ankara

Toğrol E 1976 *iTÜ İnşaat Fakültes: Cumhuriyetin Ellinci Yılı Kitabi*. iTÜ Yayınları, Istanbul

Turkish Industrialists' and Businessmen's Association (TUSIAD) 1991 The Turkish Economy '91. TÜSIAD, Istanbul

Umunç H 1986 Higher Education in Turkey. Paper prepared for the Turkish University Rectors' Committee, Ankara

1990 Yıllık Hükümet Programı. Resmi Gazete, 30 October 1989, No. 20327, Ankara

E. E. Taylan; C. Taylan

U

Uganda

1. Higher Education and Society

Uganda, a landlocked country, is one of the riverain states of Lake Victoria in central Africa. With the Sudan on its northern border, Zaire to the west, Kenya to the east and with Rwanda and Tanzania abutting onto its southern frontier, it was a focal center for the development of higher education during the period when, under British administration, it formed part of the Kenya, Tanganyika and Nyasaland federation.

With a surface area of 243,410 square kilometers, Uganda has an estimated population of 17,567,000 (1990), of which almost half (48 percent) are under the age of 15 years. With a high crude birthrate of 50.2 per thousand, the demographic pressures are considerable. Since 1975, the population has risen by approximately one-third. Against this, however, life expectancy is tragically short, being some 48 years for men and 50 for women. The country remains overwhelmingly agricultural, both as regards the distribution of the population and its economy. Less than 10 percent live in urban areas. The Gross National Product (GNP) per capita is low at around US$242 per year, and the growth in GNP is of a corresponding level, around 2.6 percent. Three-quarters of the active population is employed in agriculture and some 5 percent in industry, with services accounting for 19 percent. Clearly, the economic development of the country has suffered immeasurably from the tyrannous regime of Idi Amin, who seized power in 1971, and from the sequels of intercommunity tension which remained after his overthrow in 1979 by the opposition supported by the Tanzanian Army.

Apart from English, some four major language groups are found in Uganda: Luganda, Swahili, the Bantu languages, and those spoken by the Niolotic peoples in the northern regions, bordering on the Sudan. This ethnic diversity is not foreign to the problems of political instability with which Uganda has been beset for a good part of the last two decades. The religious composition shows a similar diversity. Catholics and Protestants each account for one-third of the population, with Muslims forming some 16 percent. The remainder subscribe to indigenous beliefs.

The main natural resources of Uganda are copper, cobalt, limestone and salt, though they have yet to give rise to industry of any significant dimension. The major exports are agricultural produce, like coffee, tea and cotton, but these are commodities which undergo considerable fluctuations on the world market, a situation which, in the quasi absence of an industrial infrastructure, serves to underscore Uganda's economic fragility.

Though multiparty politics have returned, there now being three main political groupings: the Uganda People's Congress, the Democratic Party and the Uganda Patriotic Movement, government is assured by a transitional military regime.

2. The Institutional Fabric of the Higher Education System

Uganda's main center of academic learning is Makerere University, first founded in 1922 as a government technical school. The De la Warr Commission, sitting in 1937, recommended that it be upgraded to a university college. The Second World War delayed its realization until 1949, when Makerere entered into a special relationship with the University of London. By 1950, courses which led to general degrees in arts and sciences were put in place. In 1963, Makerere became one of the three constituent colleges of the University of East Africa. On the breakup of the East African Federation in 1970, the college was upgraded to full university status and, five years later, was assigned the name of Makerere University.

The University sits atop a system of higher education which numbers ten relatively specialized institutes ranging from the Uganda Polytechnic at Kyambogo to the National Teachers' College, the Veterinary Training Institute and the Kigumba Cooperative Colleges. There is, in addition, the recent establishment of an Islamic University which offers degree courses in Islamic studies and education (Uganda National Commission for UNESCO 1988 p. 3). The nonuniversity sector provides courses of some two years' duration with the exception of the Veterinary Training Institute, where the length of program varies from two to three years and the Kigumba Cooperative College which puts on courses of a three year duration. Their awards, however, take the form of diplomas or certificates. They are not degree courses. The number of students in higher education has more than doubled in the twelve years from 1975 to 1987, rising from 5,474 to 12,531 (UNESCO 1990 pp. 3–253).

To be admitted to a degree course, a student is required to have passed at least six approved subjects in the Uganda Certificate of Education plus at least two passes in the Uganda Advanced Certificate of

Education. These examinations are conducted by the Uganda National Examinations Board which is a nongovernmental body. Following the British model, students apply to enter a particular department and certain departments may demand that applicants have passes in specific school subjects related to the course they wish to follow. For example, to study for the Bachelor of Commerce requires passes in mathematics and economics. The average age of entry is between 19 and 20 years, though provision is made for mature entrants who ceased education at least five years prior to their application.

The typical degree course is of three years' duration, with exceptions for engineering and veterinary medicine (four years) and dentistry and medicine (five years). First degrees conform to the British model of classification, that is, first class degree, upper second class, lower second class or pass degree. The first degree is the Bachelor of Arts, of Science, of Veterinary Medicine or of Medicine. First degrees, as well as higher awards and PhDs, are awarded by the University of Makerere.

Graduate research begins after the first degree and requires a minimum qualification of a second class honors degree. Masters degrees are awarded on the basis either of a thesis presented after research, by course work fulfillment, or both. Residence requirements are officially 18 months. The PhD degree has a minimum two years full time residence qualification and is awarded on the basis of a dissertation presented in fulfillment of an approved theme.

3. Governance, Administration, and Finance

The Makerere University Act of 1970 conferred both academic and administrative autonomy upon the University. However, it is wholly dependent on public monies for its financing which are paid in monthly installments through the Ministry of Education (UNESCO 1990 pp. 2, 11). The planning of postsecondary education is the responsibility of several ministries. The Ministry of Education exercises oversight for teacher training, technical and commercial education, whilst the Ministry of Agriculture and the Ministry of Health, Animal Resources, Marketing and Cooperatives have a similar responsibility for agricultural education, and for paramedical, veterinary and cooperative education. Their responsibilities are exercised in consultation with the ministries of Planning and Economic Development, Finance and Public Service. There is, in short, no single coordinating agency for postsecondary education, though it should be noted that the nonuniversity sector enjoys only limited independence. Many of the decisions affecting their functioning are taken within the appropriate ministry.

The key body which assumes a similar responsibility for planning university education is the university council in consultation with the appropriate government agencies such as the ministries of Education, Health, Planning and Economic Development and Finance. The university council bears considerable similarity to its counterpart in British civic universities. It acts as the main governing body of the University and has a joint membership of both academic staff and representatives of external society, sometimes known as lay members. In planning the University's development, the council is assisted by a senate which is responsible for all academic concerns.

The model of academic governance is based on the faculty with departments forming the basic units. There are ten faculties in the University, each headed by a dean. Departments have the responsibility for undergraduate teaching within their own disciplinary area. They also exercise responsibility for graduate study. Coordination at faculty level is performed by deans of faculties. The vice-chancellor fulfills the role of chief campus executive for both administrative and academic affairs. He or she is backed by a secretary and an academic registrar who are in charge of the administration of the university. The chancellor, as with many universities founded on the British model, is a honorific post, held by the head of state.

The University also includes a number of specialized research institutes among which are the Institute of Statistics and Applied Economics and the Makerere Institute of Social Research. The former is jointly financed by the Uganda government and the United Nations Development Program. It provides a three-year training for future economic planners for the English-speaking East African region. The latter undertakes research in the areas of anthropology, sociology, public administration, law, and linguistics.

4. Faculty and Students: Teaching, Learning, and Research

Estimations for 1989 suggest that Makerere counted approximately 7,000 students and 700 academic staff (ACU 1990). Staff numbers have risen from some 444 in 1975, and during the ensuing decade, rose slowly to approximately 500 ten years later. The subsequent rapid growth can, in part, be attributed to the effort of the government not merely to meet increased demand but also to remedy the difficulties of the intervening years. Recruitment and nomination to posts are the responsibility of the University alone, as well as promotion up the academic ladder. The structure of academic posts is a combination of the British and the American system and consists of junior lecturer, lecturer, senior lecturer, associate professor and full professor. The 1970 Act set upon the University the right to determine what the qualifications of those who teach shall be, and what may be taught.

Over the same period, overall student numbers in all sectors of higher education rose from 5,474 in 1975 to 12,531 in 1987 (UNESCO 1990). This growth, however, is not evenly distributed across the different sectors. In effect, by far the greater part of the increase in student numbers took place in the nonuniversity sector. Student numbers over the 12 years from 1975 increased by more than four times in the nonuniversity sector, that is, from 1,560 to 6,797 compared to a rise of slightly under 50 percent for the University, and in absolute numbers from 3,914 to 5,734 (UNESCO 1990). The participation of female students in the University rose from 16 percent in 1975 to 22 percent in 1987.

As has been intimated earlier, the structure of first degree courses is determined by the University itself, though from an operational level this task is located and defined by the department. The development of new study programs are, therefore, a matter internal to the University, and ultimately of the senate as the highest academic body. Undergraduate degree courses tend to be specialized and single subject which is evident by the often specific admissions requirements linked to particular departments.

Postsecondary education in Uganda is free to the extent that the government pays tuition fees and, in certain instances, pays transport costs and some educational facilities. However, students are required to pay caution money and also to assume their personal expenses (Uganda National Commission for UNESCO 1986 p. 16).

5. Conclusion

Though the government has set itself the goal of diversifying postsecondary education further, a number of limitations have prevented this policy from being implemented. The first is the lack of financial resources. The second is a shortage of people with the appropriate qualifications necessary for the development of additional disciplinary fields. This, in a country with a fragile infrastructure and with a tendency for graduate unemployment, although well below that of unqualified school leavers, illustrates some of the difficulties faced by a country which, while eager to modernize, does not have the self-generated capacity to do so.

Bibliography

Association of Commonwealth Universities 1990 *Handbook of Commonwealth Universities*. ACU, London
Uganda National Commission for UNESCO 1988 *Response to the International Bureau of Education Questionnaire.* (ED/BIE/CONFINTED/41/Q/87) Ministry of Education, Kampala
Uganda National Commission for UNESCO 1984 *Development of Education in Uganda 1981–1983*. Ministry of Education, Kampala
UNESCO 1990 *Statistical Yearbook*. UNESCO, Paris

G. Neave

United Arab Emirates

1. Higher Education and Society

The United Arab Emirates (UAE) federated on December 2, 1971 comprises the seven following states: Abu Dhabi, Dubai, Sharjah, Ajman, Umm Al-Qiwain, Ras Al-Khaima, and Fujeira. The UAE lies within an area of 77,000 square kilometers bordered to the north by the Arabian Gulf, to the west by the state of Qatar and Saudi Arabia, to the south by the sultanate of Oman and Saudi Arabia, and to the east by the Gulf of Oman and the sultanate of Oman. It is a relatively new country.

Population growth is shown in Table 1. Population distribution by religion, sex, urban and rural areas, and emirate is shown in Table 2. The last published government census was for 1980.

United Arab Emirates nationals comprise approximately 30 percent of the total population while the remaining 70 percent are expatriates residing in the UAE on work permits. Language and religion vary among expatriates, but the formal religion in the UAE is Islam, and the formal language is Arabic. English is considered the second language for most nationals, yet the Persian and Indian languages play a big role, due to the large numbers of residents in the UAE from Iran, India, and Pakistan.

Table 3 shows numbers of the population actively employed in the federal and local government sectors for the year 1985. The majority of the labor force in the country still consists of expatriates, as mentioned earlier under population growth.

Although the UAE is considered to be desert land, several agricultural areas are to be found. The successful efforts of the federal and local governments in implementing modern irrigation and cultivation projects has rendered barren land fit for farming.

Oil and oil revenues are the main source of income for the UAE. It was first exploited on a commercial scale in 1962 in Abu Dhabi, then in 1969 in Dubai, 1974 in Sharjah, and 1985 in Ras Al-Khaima. There are also promising gas resources in most emirates. The second half of the twentieth century has witnessed a substantial increase in the role of the government in economic and social development, supported by this natural wealth. Crude oil income rose from 18,025 thousand million dirhams (US$4,938,000) in 1975 to 52,000 thousand million in 1980, then dropped to 20,670 thousand million (US$5,663,000) in

Table 1
Population growth in the UAE 1975–85

1975	1980	1985
558,000	1,042,099	1,622,464

Table 2
Total population by religion, sex, and emirate (urban/rural) 1975–89

	1975 Muslim Male	1975 Muslim Female	1975 Others Male	1975 Others Female	1975 Total Male	1975 Total Female	1975 Total	1980 Muslim Male	1980 Muslim Female	1980 Others Male	1980 Others Female	1980 Total Male	1980 Total Female	1980 Total
Abu Dhabi														
Urban	117,479	42,641	12,990	5,357	130,469	47,998	178,457	204,682	84,630	40,770	15,504	245,452	100,134	345,586
Rural	22,113	8,724	2,416	32	24,589	8,756	33,345	56,914	19,778	29,322	248	86,236	20,026	106,262
Total	139,592	51,365	15,406	5,389	155,058	56,754	211,802	261,596	104,408	70,092	15,752	511,688	120,160	451,848
Dubai														
Urban	103,861	46,060	22,852	7,152	126,713	53,212	179,926	128,884	67,459	48,148	18,958	177,032	86,417	263,449
Rural	1,905	1,153	203	—	2,108	1,153	3,261	5,511	1,826	5,171	344	10,682	2,170	12,852
Total	105,766	47,213	23,055	7,152	128,821	54,365	183,187	134,395	69,285	53,319	19,302	187,714	88,587	276,301
Sharjah														
Urban	37,073	20,107	5,618	1,270	42,691	21,377	64,068	66,262	40,566	22,652	6,503	88,915	47,068	135,983
Rural	7,619	6,150	945	8	8,564	6,158	14,722	12,824	9,313	1,046	151	13,870	9,464	23,334
Total	44,692	26,257	6,563	1,278	51,255	27,535	78,790	79,086	49,879	23,698	6,654	102,785	56,532	159,317
Ajman														
Urban	8,019	5,491	710	131	8,729	5,622	14,351	17,614	12,111	3,113	813	20,727	12,924	33,651
Rural	1,751	546	40	2	1,791	548	2,339	1,284	906	234	26	1,517	932	2,449
Total	9,770	6,037	750	133	10,520	6,170	16,690	18,898	13,917	3,347	839	22,244	13,856	36,100
Umm Al-Qiwain														
Urban	3,096	2,149	365	32	3,461	2,181	5,642	4,806	3,358	1,287	201	6,093	3,559	9,652
Rural	729	464	73	—	802	464	1,266	1,321	891	446	16	1,867	907	2,774
Total	3,825	2,613	438	32	4,263	2,645	6,908	6,227	4,249	1,733	217	7,960	4,466	12,426
Ras Al-Khaima														
Urban	12,851	8,361	1,829	283	14,680	8,644	23,324	22,269	14,035	3,924	1,207	26,193	15,242	41,435
Rural	11,737	8,607	521	56	12,258	8,663	20,921	16,547	11,950	3,785	201	20,332	12,151	32,483
Total	24,588	16,968	2,350	339	26,938	17,307	44,245	38,815	25,985	7,709	1,408	46,525	27,393	73,918
Rujeira														
Urban	1,796	1,001	97	15	1,893	1,016	2,909	6,272	3,829	2,267	291	8,539	4,120	12,659
Rural	7,202	5,640	877	27	8,079	5,687	13,766	9,394	7,180	2,863	93	12,257	7,273	19,530
Total	8,998	6,641	974	42	9,972	6,703	16,675	15,666	11,009	5,130	384	20,796	11,393	32,189
Total														
Urban	284,175	125,810	44,461	14,240	328,636	140,051	478,666	450,789	225,988	122,161	33,477	572,950	269,464	842,415
Rural	47,650	31,284	5,075	125	58,191	31,429	89,620	103,895	51,844	42,867	1,079	146,761	52,923	199,684
Total	331,825	157,094	49,536	14,365	386,827	171,480	568,286	554,684	277,832	165,028	34,556	719,712	322,387	1,042,099

Sources: Ministry of Planning 1980, UAE 1976, 1982

Table 3
Federal and local government employment 1985

	Rural	Urban	Total
Federal government	23,091	97,282	120,373
Local government	18,741	72,242	90,983
Total	41,832	169,524	211,356

Source: Ministry of Planning 1987a

1985. Industry, agriculture, and livestock breeding represent an innovation in the UAE. The boom is evident through the various industries spread throughout the UAE, such as mining and quarrying, the manufacture of petrochemicals, aluminum, cement, ceramics, food and beverages, textiles, wood and wood products, and several other industries. The UAE also has important underground and desalination water industries, the latter being associated with electricity production (Ministry of Planning 1987a).

1.1 Structure of Government and Main Political Goals

The UAE is ruled by a federal government, presided over by the head of state, Sheikh Zayed Bin Sultan Al-Nahayan. Each emirate is ruled over by a sheikh, but is a member of the federation, under the umbrella of the UAE. The welfare of each emirate is the welfare of the rest. The UAE is a member of the Gulf Cooperative Council (GCC) and the Arab League.

The federal government, guided by the wishes of the president of the UAE, lays great emphasis on all affairs that create wealth, advancement, and prosperity for the nation. Special attention is paid to general and higher education, which are highly valued tools for the nation's continuous progress and development. It is maintained that only an educated society is capable of achieving success in the fulfillment of projected objectives, and preserving the heritage, values, and identity of the nation.

There is no affiliation or influence existing between religious organizations or theological groups and institutions of higher education. The federal government is solely responsible for the development of higher education, with the exception of the private institutes of higher education. These are individually governed, but again have no affiliation with religious bodies.

2. The Institutional Fabric of the Higher Education System

It was in 1977–78 that the first state institute of higher education was created. This was the UAE University. In 1988–89 a number of State Higher Colleges of Technology were established in the various emirates.

A variety of other institutes also contribute to higher education; most of these are local or private.

All institutes of higher education, public or private, adopt the credit hour semester system. They offer free open-door education, and provide free teaching facilities, books, full accommodation, and transport.

There are several levels of institution in the UAE. The first of these is the research university exemplified by the UAE University, the first public institute of higher education in the country. This offers programs in various fields of humanities, social sciences, and basic and applied sciences. The university comprises eight faculties: arts, science, education, Islamic religion and law, economics and administration, engineering, agriculture, and medicine and medical sciences. The main goals of the university are teaching, research, and community service. The university now encompasses six research institutes affiliated to different colleges. The medium of education is Arabic in all faculties except those of medicine and engineering, where it is English.

The second level is that of the specialized university. Under this category falls the Ajman University College of Science and Technology, a private institute partly subsidized by the local government of Ajman. Established in 1988–89, it offers specific scientific fields such as electronic engineering, management and computer sciences, and education and foreign languages. It also offers masters' degrees in business and administration (MBA) and education (MEd). The medium of education is English.

The next level comprises four-year colleges, an example of which is the Dubai College of Medicine, a private college established in 1986–87 offering a Bachelor of Medicine and Surgery (MBBS) degree. Other four-year colleges are the Dubai College of Islamic and Arabic Studies, and the Dubai Police College.

Technical colleges form the fourth level of institution. The Higher Colleges of Technology, established in 1988–89 and offering programs for a postsecondary higher diploma, are mainly oriented toward vocational training, and offer three-year programs in business office administration, and technology.

The final level of institution are those open university institutions which offer external tutorial studies. These are an extension of the UAE University, established in 1982, consisting of seven centers, one in each emirate. They were established with the aim of providing opportunities in higher education to citizens unable to receive a university degree, due to their distance from the UAE University.

2.1 Admissions Policies and Selection

Admissions policies show little variation between public and private higher education institutes. They cater solely for UAE nationals, with the exclusion of GCC members, faculty members' children, and children of expatriates working for the federal government. The exceptions are Ajman University College of Science and Technology and Dubai Medical College, which provide for all nationalities.

All public higher education institutes are coordinated by the federal and local government. The various ministries, in coordination with the higher education institutes, determine their needs with regard to numbers and fields of specialization. Thus, for example, as there is an urgent need for teachers, the majority of students are enrolled in the Faculty of Education. Where graduate programs are concerned, admission is left totally to the college. Certain requirements have to be met by the applicant, such as having an undergraduate degree and maintaining the minimum academic requirements in his or her field.

2.2 Quantitative Development and Structure of Qualifications

In 1977–78 the first institute for higher education (UAE University) enrolled 502 students. By 1989–90, enrollment had soared to a total of 13,833 students, in public and private institutes, as shown in Table 4.

The structure of qualifications varies according to category and level of institution. The structure may be summarized as follows:

(a) Universities and specialized four-year colleges—These offer five types of degree, which are the BA or BSc, MA and MBA, MBBS diploma for higher studies, and a two-year diploma degree offered by Ajman University. Degree courses for the BA and BSc last for four years, MA, MBA, and graduate higher diploma courses for five years, and MBBS courses for seven years.

(b) Higher colleges of technology—These offer three-year higher diploma and a two-year core diploma which is awarded after a high-school diploma.

(c) Postsecondary teacher training colleges—These run a two-year program offering a certificate for teacher training.

Graduate programs are offered in only two faculties at the UAE University in the form of graduate higher diploma, established at the Faculty of Education in 1977–78 and at the College of Literature in 1978–79. Programs for MEd and MBA are offered to students at Ajman University College of Science and Technology. The first students with a master's degree obtained from a local university are estimated to graduate by the academic year of 1990–91.

3. Governance, Administration, and Finance

Public higher education institutions have a direct relationship with the federal government legislation. The chancellor, appointed by decree by the government, has prime responsibility for the institutions and is directly responsible to the federal government. They operate as independent corporate bodies and do not report to any ministry. Private institutions are individually governed through the board of trustees of each institution.

An interview with the vice-chancellor of the UAE University in May 1990 provided the following information: public higher educational goals are physically and organically oriented towards the effective fulfillment of national plans. The institutional plan is geared toward the adoption of admissions policies, educational plans, and curricula in its various disciplines, which will help meet labor force requirements of different sectors. A ten-year plan has been laid down to provide the University with its requirement of national faculty members and researchers, thus aiming to meet the goals of the labor force nationalization policies in the sectors of higher education and research.

The University has adopted a system for evaluation and assessment of its educational plans and curricula, research activities, and administrative and managerial procedures, with emphasis on their response

Table 4
Student enrollment from 1977–90

	1977–78	1980–81	1985–86	1989–90
Research university tutorial extension studies				
Male	317	1,397	3,132	2,701
Female	189	1,029	4,064	6,730
Total	502	2,606	7,196	9,431
All public and private institutions				
Male	317	1,397	3,291	4,190
Female	189	1,029	4,998	9,643
Total	502	2,606	8,289	13,833

to national goals. The Civil Service Council and the Supreme National Council contribute to the evaluation of higher educational bodies with relation to their response to national goals.

All public institutions are financed by the federal government. Decisions concerning the budget are made at university council level and submitted to the federal Ministry of Finance. Budget requirements are set at the beginning of each academic year. Private institutions are funded through private organizations, tuition, and donations. Dubai Police College is financed and governed by the state of Dubai.

The budget allocation for the UAE University rose from 39,291,638 UAE dirhams in 1977–78 (US$10,764,832), to 328,293,983 (US$89,943,556) in 1980–81, 337,284,799 (US$92,406,791) in 1986–87, and 433,800,000 (US$118,849,310) in 1989–90. The board of trustees (regents) is responsible for finance, student admission policies, appointment of high-ranking academic positions, and the overall welfare of the institution. Private institutes' boards of trustees are solely responsible for all matters concerning their institute. Public institutes' trustees are appointed by decree of the president of the UAE upon the recommendation of the chancellor of the University.

The bodies of authority, within academic institutions include: (a) department council, (b) college board, (c) council for academic and scientific affairs, and (d) board of trustees or regents.

Academic ranks are recognized within these bodies; usually a professor is entitled to more privileges and a greater role in decision making than lower ranks. Nonacademic staff take part in administrative decisions only. The student body may be considered a pressure group, represented by the students union, but no chair is appointed for them in any of the councils.

Primary decisions begin at the base unit (department) level and then move up to the higher councils. They are finally approved by the council for academic and scientific affairs.

Table 5
Numbers of academic staff from 1977–78 to 1989–90

	1977–78	1980–81	1985–86	1989–90
Public institutions				
Full-time	54	207	258	591
External faculty	14	49	89	143
Teaching assistants	2	16	105	123
Total	70	272	452	857
Private institutions				
Full-time	—	—	—	137
External faculty	—	—	—	15
Teaching assistants	—	—	—	—
Total	—	—	—	152

4. Faculty and Students: Teaching, Learning, and Research

4.1 Faculty

The number of full-time academic teaching staff has dramatically increased from a total of 54 in 1977–78 to 728 in 1989–90. These figures are for public and private institutions together. Table 5 shows the increase in staff numbers in more detail.

Candidates for a full-time teaching position at an institute of higher education must possess a minimum of a PhD degree. External faculty applicants should possess a minimum of an MA degree, and nationals applying for a teaching assistant position must possess a minimum of a BA degree as well as being required to obtain a PhD degree abroad through scholarships from the University. The structure of academic ranks at the UAE institutions of higher education is as follows: teaching assistant (demonstrator); assistant lecturer; lecturer; assistant professor; professor. The criteria for advancement from lecturer to assistant professor are five years work experience, with a minimum of three published research papers in recognized journals or its equivalent, plus recommendations from the department and dean. The same applies to advancement from assistant professor to professor, except the requirement is a minimum of five published papers.

Each department is responsible for the recruitment of its own faculty, who are recommended according to the requirements set by each institution. An appointment is finally made after a personal interview. Expatriate faculty members are appointed on a contract basis and nationals on a permanent contract (tenure). Teaching load, research, and other duties are incorporated through internal regulations within each individual institution. Decisions on these matters are made by the highest administrative body at the institute.

4.2 Students

The majority of students, as shown in Table 6, are enrolled in the social sciences. Humanities enrollment numbers have dropped since 1985–86 and an increase is evident in the exact sciences, which is credited to some of the private colleges.

Institutes of higher education are attended mainly by nationals with a small percentage of students from GCC States and other Arab countries, between roughly 8 and 10 percent of the total student body. The body of native students is basically homogeneous (Muslims).

Each establishment is responsible for the structure of first-degree programs, which are designed at department level and then approved by the Council of Academic and Scientific Affairs, or whichever body has the highest authority within each establishment. Most private colleges are geared towards specialized single-subject fields, for example the Col-

Table 6
Total number of students and number of graduates in main subject areas from 1977–78 to 1989–90

	1978–79	1980–81	1985–86	1989–90
Exact sciences				
Total	—	54	373	1,427
Graduates	—	—	55	36[a]
Social sciences				
Total	695	1,782	3,415	7,480
Graduates	—	316	670	709[a]
Humanities				
Total	334	810	2,927	1,553
Graduates	—	156	550	556[a]

a Approximate figures

lege for Islamic Studies and Arabic; and the Dubai Police College, which graduates students in police law. In the case of the higher colleges, specialized programs exist in particular career areas (e.g., civil engineering) with supporting general studies. The UAE University program is divided into two parts: (a) general studies program; and (b) specialized program, organized according to the credit unit system, with compulsory and optional courses, and supplementary courses taken from other departments. Students are assessed at the end of each semester, after the completion of course requirements, to determine whether they can proceed to the next semester in their program.

5. Conclusion

The University has accomplished a notable standard in undergraduate teaching, fairly competing with the credited standards of well-developed international universities. On the other hand, one should admit that the educational pattern of the UAE University is still deficient in graduate studies, which are not well-integrated with undergraduate studies and research. Coordination of research work between faculties and research centers is seen to be necessary. The relationship between the University and the different spheres of activity in the country, such as industry, agriculture, trade, and so on, should be substantially consolidated, so that the University may play the role of a center of excellence in society. As the University stands at the top of the educational system, more effective cooperation should be adopted between the university and preuniversity levels (general and technical education), to procure continuity and integrity.

Finally, as the national faculty members at the UAE University comprise only an approximate 5 percent of the total, nationalization of the faculty body is of crucial importance. It can be carried out only through self-generation via graduate studies.

Bibliography

Ajman University College of Science and Technology 1989a *Establishment and Education Policies*. Ajman

Ajman University College of Science and Technology 1989b *MBA Program*. Ajman

Dubai College of Islamic and Arabic Studies 1989 *Student Guide*. Dubai

Dubai Police College 1989 *An Informative Book on the Occasion of the Official Opening of Dubai Police College*. Dubai

Higher College of Technology 1988a *Business Programs for National Women*. Abu Dhabi

Higher College of Technology 1988b *Health Science Program*. Abu Dhabi

Ministry of Information and Culture 1986 *The United Arab Emirates: 15 Years On The Road To Development, 1971– 1986*. Abu Dhabi

Ministry of Planning 1982 *General Population Statistics for 1980*, Pt. 3. Central Statistical Department, Abu Dhabi

Ministry of Planning 1987a *Annual Statistical Abstract*, 12th edn. Central Statistical Dept, Abu Dhabi

Ministry of Planning 1987b. *Socio-Economic Development in the UAE: 1975–1985*. Dept. of Planning, Modern Printing Press, Dubai

Ministry of Planning 1989 Central Statistical Department

UAE University years 1982–86 *Tutorial External Studies: Bulletins*. Abu Dhabi

UAE University 1985 *Statistical Abstract: 1984–85*. Al-Ain

UAE University 1988a *Annual Statistical Abstract: 1987/88*. Al-Ain

UAE University 1988b *Guide for Higher Education Diplomas*. Al-Ain

UAE University 1989 *Executive By-Laws of The UAE University*. Al-Ain

UAE University 1989 *Year Book of Graduates for 1988/89*. Al-Ain

S. E. Abbas

United Kingdom

1. Higher Education and Society

Provision of higher education in the United Kingdom has never fully merited the description of "system." It has always had one margin well defined by the ancient universities of Oxford and Cambridge ("Oxbridge"). The other margin has, since the mid-nineteenth century, been a ragged frontier advancing as it were into territory in much of which other forms of tertiary education, known as "further education" already flourish. The definition became sharper in the Education Act in 1988, but it remains somewhat vague. Little attempt will be made here to discuss provision beyond that frontier.

The characteristics of British higher education may still briefly be encapsulated thus: (a) public funding; (b) institutional autonomy; (c) small units tending to develop into the same style; (d) high national standards; (e) selectivity and an exclusive stance; (f) close teaching of undergraduates; and (g) success in research. These characteristics apply especially to the universities but also more broadly to all the institutions in higher education. These institutions fall into three main categories, all of which would in many countries be called universities:

(a) universities—of diverse origins, treated officially (until 1991) as equals, and seen as more academic than other higher education institutions;

(b) polytechnics—formed in the late 1960s from diverse bodies and seen as more vocationally oriented;

(c) colleges and institutes—mainly local and some more specialized than others.

These categories and characteristics, that in the early 1990s are in a considerable state of flux, are described in more detail later in this article.

The British government claims that enrollment in these institutions of higher education will total one and a quarter million students in 1991. (There are also over three million students enrolled in other types of public tertiary education.)

If national higher education systems are a product of a society's history, then this factor should be especially important in the United Kingdom. England has the oldest surviving institutions of higher education which although not originally defined as universities, gradually emerged as such. The background is thus steeped in history, symbolized by the enormous architectural inheritance of both Oxford and Cambridge (whereas the universities in Bologna and Paris have so little to show). Much more remarkable is the institutional continuity of Oxbridge. Whereas the university system in Paris was abolished for a century, and that of Bologna virtually so more than once, Oxford and Cambridge have been active and powerfully autonomous since before 1215. Something as remarkable may be said of Scotland, where the continuities are as striking. However, this ancient history does tend to obscure the importance of more recent history, much of which has also proved seminal.

Higher education in the United Kingdom has thus for an exceptionally long time grown alongside British society. The last century and a half has seen great change: a constant welling up of uncoordinated initiatives by different interests whose diverse social needs created a mass of constantly changing institutions which the state has made sporadic attempts to rationalize. (This has not excluded the state initiatives which are noted below.) A second characteristic in the modern period has been a continuous state interest in standards, seen most clearly in its jealous control of validation, that is, the right to grant degrees. It is hard therefore to understand either the system's relationship to society, or its nature, without

reference to its history, to which attention will be paid in the next section.

1.1 Occupational and Social Class Structure

Throughout the twentieth century, the United Kingdom has been building a welfare state at both the local and national levels. The socialist elements were largely privatized in the 1980s, but despite the image of the government in the 1980s the commitment of the country to major social services—health, education, pensions, unemployment pay—remains great. In the 1980s the government attempted to reduce costs by seeking more efficient management, including management in higher education. It has tried to reduce the extent to which higher education is driven by academic imperatives and the needs of research, and has sought more instrumental goals by cheaper methods.

The government has been alarmed by the open-ended implications of expansion and has doubted if academics can manage the great enterprises that the institutions have become. It has increased enrollment—by 22 percent in 10 years—and contained costs, with considerable immediate damage to research and to morale in the traditional sectors, while perhaps raising spirits elsewhere. It has stressed the goals of direct service to the economy, and to technology and business in particular.

The dissolution of the Empire has not affected the internal organization of the country, though British higher education has lost some of its (never great) involvement with Third World universities. The economy has lost a large part of its heavy industrial base. Mining, steelmaking, docks, textile mills, and the like have shed manual workers wholesale, while white-collar industries and the proportion of professionals have grown. An urban tenant population is being suburbanized in its owner-occupied houses. The population has expanded by one-fifth to 56 million since 1945, and women are about to overtake men in gaining the grades to enter higher education. Applications to enter higher education in 1989 were up by 10 percent on 1988. Since nearly 70 percent of university students are from social classes 1 and 2, and 3 percent from class 5 (figures for polytechnics are not dissimilar), and since the over 30 percent fall (to 1996) in the 18–24 age group is concentrated in the manual classes 4 and 5, demography is of limited relevance to selective higher education institutions. However, the rate of staying on at school was static in the five years to 1986–87.

Staying-on rates are significantly lower in the working-class north than in the nonmanual and suburban south. However, the inner cities have received an inflow of mainly manual Black and Asian immigrants, who have as yet sought higher education on much the same limited scale as the native manual groups. The system is under some, mainly unofficial, pressure to draw more of these ethnic groups, and desires to do so; but so far many see the problem as lying more in class and culture than color barriers. There are some recent indications that immigrants from nonmanual backgrounds, especially Asians, are overtaking native Britons in school achievement, and it may follow that they will then seek freer access to higher education. Determined and fairly large-scale attempts to improve access routes, so far resulting mostly in increased adult participation, are gathering strength.

1.2 Religious Bodies

The established Church was paramount until the end of the nineteenth century and may still contribute to the atmosphere of Oxbridge, but its academic influence in the 1990s is small. At Oxford an endowment for the defense of Anglicanism from heresy (The Bampton Lectures) was opened in 1989 to non-believers. Elsewhere, a handful of former teacher training colleges have sectarian links.

2. The Institutional Fabric of the Higher Education System

The institutions of higher education fall into two separately funded groups: the universities who have been funded since 1989 by the Universities Founding Council (UFC) on the one side, and the polytechnics, colleges and central institutions funded by the Polytechnic and Colleges Founding Council (PCFC) on the other.

There are 50 bodies with the right to grant degrees (including doctorates). All but four of these are called universities. Of the four, two are specialist institutions, one is the Archbishopric of Canterbury, and the fourth is the Council for National Academic Awards (CNAA), validating the higher education teaching of most of those bodies in higher education which do not have the right to grant degrees. These include 33 polytechnics; 16 Scottish central institutions; and 133 other colleges, 51 of which are funded by the PCFC and so are formally included in higher education.

Of the 46 universities, 44 are publicly funded. There are some 15 major multifaculty teaching institutions, such as the London School of Economics. Some have their own separate campuses, but their teaching is validated by universities. (There is also a group, at present rapidly changing, of smaller colleges validated by universities.)

The right to confer degrees is awarded by the state, normally after much consideration and usually by royal charter. (The colleges of Oxbridge have never had this right.) In the nineteenth century, university colleges were required to teach to degree level for awards by the universities of London or Manchester. In the twentieth century institutions have had to teach for CNAA degrees or for a local university's degree. In addition, even those with the right to grant degrees have in effect to appoint outside assessors, known as "external examiners." The Committee of Vice-Chancellors and Principals (CVCP) set up a body in 1987 to extend and reinforce this assessment (the Sutherland Committee). Since the CNAA is required by its charter to demand standards comparable with the universities, there is a national "gold standard" of first degrees, maintained by the CNAA and external examiners.

2.1 The Sectoral Organization of Higher Education and Levels of Institution

The institutions fall within the three main divisions mentioned earlier into historically determined groups with their own characteristics and contributions that are best understood in their historical context. However, it must be borne in mind that, important as the differences may appear to the native Briton, to the outside observer these will appear as less striking than the broad similarities mentioned before. But it must also be borne in mind that the effects of the 1988 Education Act appear likely, in 1989, to increase considerably the diversity of higher education institutes in both sectors.

Cambridge and Oxford enroll over 12,000 students each, around 3 percent of all degree students in Britain (see Table 1); their influences have been great, and they hold worldwide acclaim. In the research league table prepared in 1989 by the University Funding Council (UFC), they took first and second place respectively.

They began, like the university in Paris, as unitary and primarily undergraduate universities (unlike that in Bologna, which started as a graduate university). Like Paris, they acquired specialized and mostly graduate colleges. By the sixteenth century, these colleges became responsible for all students and the university organization emerged in a special form as validator of college teaching.

Two important traditions eventually flowed into mainstream English, and indeed British, higher education from this. First, a pastoral and cultural style of education, a style that is today often associated with Cardinal Newman but of which he was as much a product as a progenitor. The style has been steadily eroded, partly by the reorganization of knowledge and the introduction of research (against Newman's prescription). Research also brought with it the strong specialization that has been so characteristic of all English higher education. Nonetheless, the style remains vigorous and adaptable; it is highly visible to the observer, and remains a powerful influence on English, and indeed British, ideals and practice. It is a factor influencing, for instance, the small size of universities with their broad academic spread, in contrast to, say, the French system. (For example, the University of Sheffield, with 8,154 students enrolled in 1987, listed 72 departments in 1983.)

Table 1
Percentage student enrollment 1953–88

	1953–54	1965–66	1970–71	1975–76	1980–81	1985–86	1987–88
Universities							
Oxbridge	17.9	11.6	9.6	—	—	—	7.0[a]
London	21.9	15.6	14.5	—	—	—	12.6[a]
Overseas	11.0	9.5	—	12.2	10.0	12.0	16.8
Resident in halls	—	33.4	38.7	—	—	—	—
Advanced further education							
Overseas	—	—	—	—	—	1.8	4.9
All higher education							
Overseas	—	—	—	—	—	—	10.7
Universities—subjects							
Exact sciences	—	58.3	55.5	53.0	53.0	51.9	—
Social sciences	—	20.9	21.6	23.8	24.7	29.6	—
Humanities	—	20.8	22.9	23.1	21.5	18.5	—
Advanced further education							
Exact sciences	—	—	50.1	—	—	41.1	—
Social sciences	—	—	41.2	—	—	46.4	—
Humanities	—	—	7.8	—	—	12.6	—
All higher education							
Exact sciences	—	—	—	—	56.0	—	48.0
Social sciences	—	—	—	—	29.0	—	36.0
Humanities	—	—	—	—	14.0	—	16.0

a Full-time only. This means that Oxbridge enrolls about 3 percent of all degree students, and London about 6 percent
Sources: Department of Education and Science *Statistics of Education for the UK*. HMSO, London; Department of Education and Science *Statistical Bulletin*; Department of Education and Science (to 1979) *Statistics of Education, Vol. 6*. University Grants Committee. HMSO, London; Department of Education and Science (from 1980) UGC *University Statistics, Vol. 1*. University Statistical Record, Gloucester

The second tradition that flowed from the history of Oxbridge as a validating mechanism was the separation of teaching from examination. There is, as a consequence, a limit to the teacher's autonomy in curriculum development and in validation that is familiar enough on the European continent, but foreign to the United States. This tradition, called by Rothblatt (1987) "the Cambridge Principle," has been central to the spread of higher education, together with its more modern form, the "external examiner."

Except for the University of Durham, founded in 1832, and three of the "new universities," no further colleges on the Oxbridge model have appeared.

The second great influence is found in London. The need for nonsectarian and modern education, borrowing much from Scotland and emulating Prussian reforms, led to the foundation in 1826 of the first University of London (now University College), which was intended as a self-validating unitary institution organized professorially with the subject department as the academic unit. The right to confer degrees was withheld however. In 1836 the government set up an examining body with explicit instructions to use the "Cambridge Principle," and conferred the name "university." This 1836 University of London made possible the creation of a countrywide system of "university colleges." These institutions were organized professorially in the Ger-

man—and Scottish—manner, but their teaching was validated in the Cambridge manner, by London. The examining body still remains, serving more than 25,000 "external students" who do not have to be enrolled in any institution, and do not generally appear in the university statistics.

In 1900 parliament attempted to set up a continental-type organization with teaching delivered in large units based on subjects. Some progress was made towards this objective, of which there remains the Imperial College of Science and Technology, the London School of Economics, and the School of Oriental and African Studies. But though the older multifaculty London colleges, King's and University, surrendered their charters to undergo rationalization by the new teaching university, they were in fact little changed. (University College and King's, still multifaculty institutions, regained their royal charters in 1977 and 1980 respectively.)

Alongside, and in harness with, the old examining body, a second rather similar body emerged. It overarched a collection of teaching institutions and specialist institutes—known as schools—which included, in addition to the five bodies mentioned, a growing number of sometimes small multifaculty teaching units, teaching "internal students" whose degrees are validated by the central body. Several drastic reorganizations have amalgamated most of the smaller multifaculty units with the larger, though without materially altering the main features just described. There are now four major multifaculty units, all with royal charters, which have also absorbed many specialist units, notably many of the 12 formerly separate medical schools. With the "great faculties," they form a set of institutions larger than many of the independent universities (the UFC research table gave London schools the three places after Oxbridge). The central organization, known as Senate House, has, apart from validation, major financial functions and acts as an umbrella body to numbers of specialized units such as the part-time Birkbeck College, the Institute of Historical Research, or a major computer center. This double anomaly in the British scene, which continually bedevils generalizations and statistics, occupies a large space: the "internal students" amounted in 1987–88 to some 12 percent of all university first-degree students and 18.7 percent of all research students.

The next major group is the foundations, mostly Victorian and civic, that today form the backbone or infantry of the system. They are often referred to as "redbrick" and, with the London schools and the Scottish universities, provide the group comparable to the mainstream European, African, or Indian universities, or to the flagships of the American state systems. They are professorially organized, self-validating and, in principle, unitary. They passed the threshold of self-validation between 1900 and 1957, two of them after more than 50 years of teaching for London degrees. Bristol with 7,294 students won ninth place in the 1989 research table. The largest, Manchester, enrolls over 11,000 students.

In the 1950s two institutions with long university connections were chartered: Strathclyde as self-validating, and the University of Manchester Institute of Science and Technology (UMIST) as validated by Manchester University. After the Robbins Report of 1963, and in one of the government's campaigns to shift the academic balance away from the arts and social sciences, nine colleges of advanced technology (CATs), or the Scottish equivalent, became self-validating universities, while another joined London and another Wales. They have also stayed small and many suffered badly in the cuts of 1981. Two took opposite routes to recovery. Salford became entrepreneurial and diversified, while Aston took the traditional British ground and concentrated on standards by raising its admission grades for students and by losing almost half of its staff, and leaving the resultant posts vacant. In the UFC 1989 research table UMIST with 4,201 students took eighth place.

The "new universities" were intended to be innovatory and were so in that they granted their own degrees from the start. The earliest of them (Keele in 1949) attempted to redress the already serious over-specialization in schools with an extra, fourth, "foundation year"—something that cost has pre-

cluded elsewhere. Eight new universities (one in Scotland, and one in Northern Ireland) appeared in the 1960s: Warwick, by far the largest, with 6,285 enrolled students, took sixth place in the research table; Essex with 3,222 took seventh place; and York with 3,746, tenth place. They are highly selective in their enrollment.

The four ancient universities of Scotland were vigorous while Oxbridge slept, and their professorial organization and their curriculum were as important to English—and to American and Australian—development as that of the German universities. They dominate the other four Scottish institutions, which are made up of the two technological universities, one redbrick, and one new university.

The Scottish system is still distinctive. It employs many Scottish graduates and is closely bound into national culture. It resembles the system in the United States in that it starts from a lower school level and teaches a four-year course, though it then awards a master's degree in arts and humanities. Glasgow serves its local manual working class to a greater extent than any other British university. With Edinburgh it enrolls 10,000 students. Edinburgh was fourteenth in the research table and, along with St Andrews, has become popular with the English middle class.

In Wales, late Victorian nationalism and a belief in the value of education to underdeveloped countries produced five small colleges and a college of technology (now merged with the Cardiff college) which are virtually independent, the central validating university being essentially a political centerpiece. The largest college, since the merger, now has over 8,000 students.

Northern Ireland has a "redbrick" type of university, Queen's University in Belfast, founded in 1845 in a government attempt to provide Ireland with a system comparable to London's. Recently, one of the eight "new universities" was amalgamated with Ulster Polytechnic to form Ulster University.

The term "direct funded" means that an institution receives its money from the minister (Secretary of State for Education) who is directly answerable in Parliament and cannot therefore attribute responsibility for decisions to a buffer body. This position can make some difference: one reason for it was fear that the elitist and conventional University Grants Committee (UGC) would not devote funds to such innovative or marginal activities. Though self-validating, these bodies are thus not related to the binary line.

The Open University, like the Council for National Academic Awards (CNAA) and the "new universities," is a direct creation of government. It is devoted to distance teaching of part-time mature students and is thus free from the Oxbridge pastoral tradition mentioned above, which has no doubt been a factor in its powers of methodological innovation. It has concurrently achieved a very reasonable academic reputation, and an unprecedented nontuition income from its teaching materials. British higher education has been able to add to its high international reputation the lead in distance education. As with the polytechnics, the Open University has been unable to fulfill the hopes of its left-wing founders that it would enroll "the people," and it is firmly middle class.

Cranfield Institute of Technology was founded after the Second World War as an aeronautical college. It has expanded to cover sciences, technology, and agriculture, and validates the military university at Shrivenham (funded by the Ministry of Defence). It has called on direct government funding for only 30 percent of its income, less than half the average for the universities.

The Royal College of Art is a small fine arts college that in recent years has been firmly, if not violently, realigned towards more commercial objectives.

So far the discussion has been of universities. At this point the binary line is crossed.

The Council for National Academic Awards (CNAA) was set up in 1964, by royal charter. This council is comparable to the 1836 University of London in that it does not teach but confers degrees. There were two innovations underlying its creation. Firstly, CNAA has accreditation power: it has accredited not only institutions, but also each course within the institutions. This power has, since 1987, been largely delegated to the polytechnics and some colleges, which are called "accredited institutions." Secondly, in validating degrees it associates the teachers with a local examination. Since 1989, despite much hesitation by the government, the polytechnics and some colleges have been virtually franchised to award CNAA degrees (using external examiners).

By the mid-1960s there was a mass of colleges in further education—mostly technical, fine arts, or teacher-training colleges, some whose roots extended back to the nineteenth century, others with the title "polytechnic"—which offered tuition for degrees (much of it for London degrees) or diplomas. After the Robbins Report (though against its advice) the Labour Government in 1967 grouped the more advanced Welsh and English colleges into 30 polytechnics run by local government (plus one in Northern Ireland). They teach for CNAA degrees, though a fifth of their enrollment in 1987 was for diplomas.

The sector referred to here as "the colleges," is made up of institutions not grouped into polytechnics in 1967. They are often former teacher-training colleges, some Church-related, which diversified their offerings, usually into the humanities, and started to teach for degrees. Some (6–10 in England) have wider origins. The Scottish central institutions escaped being grouped in 1967, and are generally stronger than the English colleges. There are fine arts and professional and technical colleges (e.g.,

agricultural). Some of them work for degrees of universities other than London, the rest for CNAA degrees for which they take only limited responsibility. In 1989 they faced much rationalization; some becoming polytechnics. This sector of higher education which in 1986 enrolled up to a quarter of students in the nonuniversity sector may therefore largely disappear.

What distinguishes polytechnics and higher education colleges from universities? The differences may seem marginal, but they have always been more vocational with no facilities for pure research. They award in effect the same degrees as universities, and have been funded for some applied research. Many attempted in the 1970s to assimilate to the national tradition, notably by increasing their academic spread, offering courses in humanities and so on, by seeking to extend their teaching to doctoral level, and by adopting more collegiate styles of internal governance. This atavism has been partly checked and in the 1980s their curricula have been innovative, certainly by all appearances; alternatively, the universities have begun to be more managerial and vocational, and some will do little research.

Other colleges fall outside higher education and consist of large numbers of further education colleges mainly engaged in professional, business or technical training and cultural work. Some students are under 18, many are in adult and continuing education, but a few sit London and CNAA degrees or professional diplomas. The White Paper of 1987 enumerated 376 of these colleges. It appears to be the intention to run down the small amount of degree work as an administrative rationalization. Nevertheless, drives for increased access, especially for part-time and mature students, will call for local centers.

Until the Second World War, nonuniversity tertiary teaching was referred to as "further education." There was in fact a useful amount of degree work in further education, mostly teaching external students of the University of London and students working for roughly comparable qualifications, mainly professional (often validated by bodies without the right to confer degrees) called "diplomas." This work was called "advanced further education" and is still designated as such in the statistics (up to 1989).

By the 1980s, advanced further education (mostly the polytechnics and colleges on the other side of the "binary line," and sometimes referred to as "local authority higher education") was enrolling more students than the universities. A significant number of these were diploma students (28.8 percent of advanced further education in 1988). Accordingly, "higher education" had come, in common parlance, to describe the work of advanced further education and of universities taken together, as in the 1987 White Paper. The Act of 1988 made this statutory, defining higher education in terms related to the level of a basic entry qualification for entry to higher education: the A-level General Certificate of Education, taken typically at the end of secondary school. What have been referred to in this article as "institutions"—universities and their major units, polytechnics, colleges, and so on—are coming to be referred to as higher education institutions.

Buckingham University which falls within the private sector is small, even by British standards, though its enrollment of 700 would, until well after the Second World War, have been quite normal. It was required to pass the threshold by teaching for CNAA degrees before gaining the right to validate its own degrees by royal charter in 1983. It receives no direct governmental grants or tuition fees (though its students are eligible for state subsidies for maintenance).

There is also a profit-making sector mostly concerned with providing professional qualifications—for example, in law—sometimes by distance teaching; and also courses for London degrees. Some of the professions, like insurance, run colleges for their own qualifications.

Foreign universities in the United Kingdom, both American and Japanese, cater for foreign qualifications; but some have considered petitioning for the right to grant local degrees. With new ideas welling up and with the spread of modularization of British degrees and of alternative entry routes, these bodies may exert more influence if they start to compete for local students.

2.2 Admissions Policies

To enter higher education, application has to be made to the institution. This is organized through two agencies, the Universities Central Council for Admissions (UCCA), which had 195,000 applications in 1989, and the Polytechnics and Colleges Admissions Council (PCAS) which had 150,000. Applications to some of the smaller specialized institutions are best made direct.

2.3 Quantitative Developments in Higher Education

Statistics of the universities are generally for the United Kingdom; and reasonable time-series can be readily found, though they seldom include the directly funded higher education institutes (e.g., the Open University) nor the private or military ones (the agricultural schools, for example, or Buckingham University).

For the rest of higher education the figures may include nonadvanced further education, and those that appear in debate are seldom for the United Kingdom. There are exclusions (e.g., of students supported by ministries other than DES, such as paramedicals); but staff figures are difficult to find, and so on. Quite large differences between, and within, series subsist. This will improve when the PCFC statistics are in place, though they will be for England

only, and will exclude the higher education still provided by local governments.

In any event, since the mid-1960s many professions have moved or are moving from qualifications typically validated by professional bodies to degrees: lawyers, accountants, the paramedicals, for instance. The largest group, teachers, formed a major element in the public figures before moving from two-year courses which were not comparable to degrees, to three-year courses which are (indeed teacher training is no longer a recognizable sector). At the graduate level, teacher training, and such, is seldom distinguished from degree work.

The complexities may be gauged from the DES *Statistics of Education* 1987. This lists under "advanced courses" full-time, short full-time, sandwich, block released, day released, other part-time day and evening. Table 1, relating to England, gives an idea of the magnitudes in the nonuniversity sector. It gives the distribution of full-time and sandwich students in advanced further education in November 1986:

(a) Polytechnics—166,450

(b) Large colleges with significant advanced further education—45,213

(c) Large colleges with some advanced further education—8,986

(d) Large colleges with nonadvanced further education only—172

(e) Small colleges with significant advanced further education—7,205

(f) Small colleges with some advanced further education—920

(g) Small colleges with nonadvanced further education only—92

"Large" means a total enrollment of more than 1,000 in full-time education *or* an advanced further education enrollment of more than 500 in full-time education. The first two categories plus a few of the "small" category include the (English) institutions funded by the PCFC.

It appears from advance figures that in 1990–91 total enrollment in higher education reached some 1.25 million including 90,000 at the Open University, and some 425,000 at the Universities Funding Council's institutions. That would leave some 650,000 students at the Polytechnics and Colleges Funding Council's institutions (listed in the tables as "advanced further education"). To this 1.25 million might be added 90,000 paramedics and a few students of UFC institutions not funded by the Council, plus perhaps 5,000 home students studying for London degrees externally, and rather less working for CNAA degrees and equivalent professional qualifications in nonadvanced further education, making a total of over 1.3 million in 1990–91. This would exclude some nonstate professional education, continuing education, private education (e.g., law schools), and the local government further education sector now (1991) about to be nationalized (see Table 3).

Despite the considerable variety discussed in this section, the key to British higher education remains its academic unity, held together by a rigorous system of degrees policed directly by central validating bodies; indirectly by the interlocking system of external examiners; and by the emulation and ambition of teachers, institutions, and students. To this is added the aversion of government and its agencies to spending money on anything which does not appear to be of high standard

3. Governance, Administration, and Finance

3.1 National Administration

For the purposes of education, the United Kingdom has separate administrations for England, Scotland, Wales, and Northern Ireland. These produce important differences—outside the universities—and confuse the statistics. However, the English system has 75 percent of the students.

Since 1989, only national-level government has had a significant hand in higher education as local government has seen its powers in this area eroded. Government has exercised its unlimited, if immanent, powers over British universities in every century (except the thirteenth). The control has seldom been academic and its exercise usually rare: it is a tenet of academic thought that it should be more so. Apart from legal power there is financial power, and as the state has taken greater financial responsibility in the twentieth century, fears of interference have been continually present.

The state has been shy of using Parliament to regulate provision outside Oxbridge, London, and Scotland. It has more usually made use of the royal prerogative, which enables the Queen in Council to grant charters by her "especial grace, certain knowledge and mere motion" and so to insulate universities from the democracy. The charters confer powers (which may include the power to confer degrees), and regulate internal governance: they may on occasion, as with the technological universities, indicate academic priorities. Parliament has, however, in the 1988 Act appointed commissioners to revise any charters which appeared to grant tenure to staff.

Central government has historically preferred, on academic and ideological grounds, to deal financially with the universities "at arm's length" through a buffer, namely the University Grants Committee (UGC) and to respect institutional autonomy. Local government has not, and has generally administered its institutions very directly and taken substantive interest in academic provision. Although charters need not confer the power to grant degrees, the state

conspicuously chose not to employ charters when releasing the polytechnics and some colleges from the control of local government in 1989. They have instead been incorporated under the Companies Act. (The London School of Economics has been so incorporated since 1895.) This grant of institutional autonomy represents a major change; one which brings half the higher education system formally within an immensely long tradition.

The Act of 1988 made the immanent powers of the British government explicit; it gives greater powers to new agencies (see below) than to the old. Its general remit to the institutions might be encapsulated as relevance, standards, accountability for public money and efficiency in financial terms. It has yet to be seen whether the "arm's length" tradition will be maintained, but it would be logical if the remit to the state were at the most to provide means, and to enable the market to plan.

3.2 Planning, Implementation, Evaluation, and Finance

The Department of Education and Science (DES) appeared in 1964, after the Robbins Report. Till then the Ministry of Education had no responsibility for the universities (while the rest of education was, and is, primarily the responsibility of local or Scottish government). Its capability for planning higher education has been limited to general policy. Apart from the Open University, state funds are distributed mainly through the separate, and significantly autonomous, streams discussed below.

The notion of central planning arrived in the United Kingdom late (if indeed it has arrived with a government ideologically committed to the market). The universities on the one hand were autonomous; and the colleges on the other hand were run by the local governments. Between the First and Second World Wars the University Grants Committee (UGC) offered discreet advice, in its capacity as distributor to all the universities of the subsidies which it received, not through the Ministry of Education, but direct from the Treasury. The grants were unconditional ("block grants"). After 1946, the UGC gave some consideration to "national needs." In 1964, it was transferred to the DES, which thus acquired a limited responsibility for all higher education. In the 1970s the UGC began to attach conditions to its grants and to attempt minor rationalizations. In the 1980s it began to issue directives and attempted to evaluate the quality of research. To its functions as a buffer between the academy and the state, it added those of a coupling.

However, the UGC was only one stream from which public money flowed: there was "dual support" for the research effort in universities of which the UGC provided the basic half, while the research councils provided the other, selective, half.

In the advanced local government sector—the

polytechnics and major colleges—there was little financial control of the sector as a whole, which had access to an open-ended funding source composed of all local authority contributions. The sector took its opportunity to grow. In 1981, an organization was set up to centralize budgeted grants (the "capped advanced further education pool") to the sector. The National Advisory Body (NAB) included strong representation of the local governments. It attempted a considerable measure of central planning, but for England only, and in the face of local government reluctance. A reason for the overall size of the polytechnics in the early 1990s lies therefore in an administrative breakdown in the 1970s, in the light of which the Conservative governments since 1979 have shown up well, realizing that student numbers could be substantially increased without corresponding expense.

Under the 1988 Act a first element of planning continued to be the division of higher education down the "binary line." Money for each division flows from its own funding council. The reason for this is not clear. It may be an example of the traditional skepticism of British governments about academic standards seen first in the 1836 University of London, and of a more explicit emphasis on economical and vocational first degrees.

The two new funding councils that took over effectively from January 1989 are not informal and advisory like the former UGC. They are legal corporations with powers to make, or not make, payments and to attach conditions to them. The Secretary of State for Education may give both bodies directions. Many fear that the greater political ease with which statutory powers can be used will encourage interference, and will do so when the growing size and public cost of higher education have made it more prominent. Some key issues already illustrate the fear. The government itself insisted that the 1989 pay increases depend on changes that many see as being at the core of the academic process: the appraisal of teachers. It seems, however, as likely that the legal position will become irrelevant. The real pressures on tradition will come from increased research selectivity, and from direct competition for funding.

Though there was much talk of introducing business drive into planning, the new Universities Funding Council (UFC) has only four members out of 15 without academic experience. Its two chief officers have held chairs in the top five research institutions. Nonetheless, its first actions have broken new ground. It funds, in effect, the whole of the United Kingdom, but not the directly funded higher education institutions. The new Polytechnics and Colleges Funding Council (PCFC) funds 83 higher education institutions in England, including 32 polytechnics. In 1989, the first year in which the PCFC's new consolidated advanced further education figures appeared, projected central government spending on higher education was 2.03 percent of projected total spending of US\$275 billion.

The new funding councils are instructed to be "proactive." Their titles illustrate this, for they are to disburse not "grants" like the old UGC but "funds," with the implication that they are purchasers rather than charities, and are to make formal contracts for specified services. The idea represents the new thinking. Bidding for a form of contract for the funding of student places is already being called for by both councils: the winners being those who bid the lowest cost. The UFC is extending its predecessor's attack on the block cover for research time and the "well-found laboratory." The watchword is now "selectivity." Only certain activities get support for research, chosen on the basis of the 1989 national research league table or on the basis of new internal appraisals. The implications for the traditional university from this alone are profound. Both councils are interested in the training of staff and, much more, in its appraisal. They are also interested in the appraisal of teaching, though the means are not yet available to them.

If the funding councils provide one half of the "dual support," the five research councils provide most of the other. They disposed of £607m (US\$1,000m) in 1986–87 (DES 1987a p. 67). The councils cover most academic fields. Certain public moneys may flow through bodies like the British Academy (supplying in part the lack of a council for the humanities) and the Royal Society. Some more flows through individual ministries' research budgets. There are also the charitable foundations. All operate largely by peer-review, but draw heavily on the universities.

The research councils are thus largely extensions of the academic community. The Economic and Social Research Council (ESRC) has penalized universities for poor supervision of graduate students and expressed interest in encouraging research training courses mounted jointly between institutions. All the councils have intervened in a fundamental prerogative of autonomy, that is, the selection of staff, which together with other such matters would have been regarded as interference previously.

The research councils are to some extent coordinated by the Advisory Board for the Research Councils (ABRC) which advises government on common issues. In the face of cuts in public money and the escalation of the costs of "big science" there has been pressure to merge the councils into a single body.

The research councils have for long been highly selective, and exempt from the rule that all universities are equal in the sight of government. Two developments, not yet fully implemented, bid to make that exemption highly important. First, the government has begun to move some of the allowance for basic research that had been built into university block grants over to the research council budgets. There is then a further possibility. Tuition fees have always existed, but as little more than an administrative device. They have now been raised and the total transferred from the two funding councils to the research councils. There is no administrative reason why the whole of the subsidies to universities should not be provided through these fees.

In the mid-1970s the then Manpower Services Agency started to provide vocational further education for the 16–19 age group. It acquired a very large budget from the Department of Trade and Industry and in the 1980s began to fund some courses in higher education. In 1987 it offered funds to those willing to orient courses ideologically, including universities: "the Enterprise Initiative" is perhaps the most radical change in the approach of government to the organization of higher education.

In 1980–81, universities received 76 percent of their income in UGC grant and publicly paid tuition fees. Awards by the research councils and industrial contracts totalled 13 percent.

In 1986–87, universities received the following:

(a) UGC ("Exchequer grants") 55.6 percent

(b) Research councils 19.0 percent

(c) Other government 1.2 percent

(d) Student fees (mainly government) 12.3 percent

(e) Endowments 1.3 percent

(f) Services 6.1 percent

(g) General income 3.6 percent

This represented about 65 percent from grants and public fees.

Government continues to press higher education to raise a greater proportion of its income from nonstate sources, pointing out that this would reduce dependence on the funding councils and hence their power. A chief potential source—industry—has rejected any large responsibility, but is having to pay, for instance, greater overheads on its research grants.

3.3 Institutional Administration

It is generally said that at Oxbridge the scholars govern the university as equals in a democratic community and without lay interference, while in the other universities laypersons have power. Though technically almost correct, this often gives a misleading impression. At Oxbridge there have always been nonscholars who had votes (such as some heads of the colleges), and since 1945 there has been a steady accretion of bureaucrats with votes to whose ranks the vice-chancellor may be said to have transferred.

In the rest of the system the charters give large formal power to the lay members of governing bodies (usually "Council"). The charters are not, however, managerial, nor do they give formal powers to the vice-chancellor: over years the formal powers of the laypeople have been much eroded and those of staff democracy increased. These tendencies were not merely approved by government, but actively encouraged, as the Privy Council's Model Charter of 1963 shows. Informally, these tendencies have been more pronounced, though at the same time the growing amount of business increased the size and influence of the bureaucracy (which is a civil service without votes). This applies still more to the vice-chancellors whose power derives from key chairmanships and a position at the center of internal and external communications. (They are still almost all good-to-distinguished scholars and their deputies are part-time and temporary academics.) One important movement in the Oxbridge direction was an increasing representation of nonprofessors on the academic side of the council and on the senate, in some cases depriving professors of seats ex officio. Headships of departments began to rotate or even be elected.

By the 1970s it was reasonable to say that in all universities academic staff as a whole had an important degree of democratic control including financial control, effectively an overriding one, and that nowhere was this more so than at Oxbridge.

The democratic inheritance of scholars' self-governance did not reach the sector run by local government from which the modern polytechnics and the colleges emerged. There, the tradition was strongly managerial. Nonetheless, there were keen aspirations to participative government, supported by governments of the day. The new polytechnics were given significantly democratic instruments of government by the Weaver Report (Department of Education and Science 1966). The spirit in which many polytechnics were run began to approximate to university ideals.

The direction of these developments was deplored by the Conservative Government elected in 1979. Higher education—and especially the universities—was described (by some senior academics as well as by politicians) as unmanageable. There was the traditional distrust of academics, mentioned in the discussion of validation; there was also in part a belief in the superiority of businesspeople to academics as managers, and in part a desire for more decisive internal management irrespective of the value of the decisions; there was also a belief in the validity of the market, rather than of "wise persons" operating monopolies. As much can be inferred from assaults on other professionals, notably financiers, insurers, lawyers, and doctors.

This atmosphere and, more important, financial pressure, forced university administrations into a more managerial stance. Some now speak of "management." (In 1989 Imperial College dropped the traditional title of "secretary" for the chief administrator in favor of "managing director.") Financial pressure, indeed, had started in the mid-1970s, when finance officers seldom knew what their income was even for the previous year. In 1981 the government imposed, for the first time in history, absolute cuts in its grants. Oxbridge suffered cuts approaching 5 percent, and two former colleges of advanced technology suffered cuts approaching 45 percent. These exigencies showed up some of the limitations of collegiate governance when times were bad, such as the difficulty of imposing selective cuts on peers, and of evaluating relative merits and priorities.

A result was that the only disinterested persons available, officials and above all the vice-chancellors, gained greater influence; indeed, they were often accorded it. Calls were even made on laypersons in governing bodies. The Committee of Vice-Chancellors and Principals (CVCP) and the UGC invited an industrialist to chair a study of administration. The Jarratt Committee reported in 1985 that it found no quantifiable inefficiency. However, it called for more executive vice-chancellors (but not for their recruitment from among businesspeople), more streamlined procedures, responsible officials, and academic leaders (especially a return to old-fashioned departmental headships), and for greater use of laypersons. The Report did not, however, call for a revision of charters to make these things mandatory or indeed possible.

Before new methods came in, the governmental structures grouped academic subjects into faculties, each with a board, still occasionally composed of heads but normally elected, sometimes on an open franchise. Subject departments are still the norm at the beginning of the 1990s, commonly run by elected boards, usually with a formal constitution and rights. However, much departmental reorganization is taking place, with many mergers and transfers designed for administrative rather than academic reasons, in response to transfers of whole subjects between universities, and to the creation of research concentrations. These bodies, from senate down, have,

or have had, full responsibility for curriculum, courses, organization, teaching, examinations, and research.

The polytechnics were run much more managerially under the aegis of local government. Their independence, as they were incorporated by virtue of the Act of 1988, did not affect that (the Welsh Polytechnic is still with local government). They assumed their responsibilities in April 1989 under Articles of Government which must comply with the Secretary of State's wishes. These define the powers of the subordinate bodies, and strengthen the American-style managerial position of a director flanked by full-time professional and permanent deputies (as well as a bureaucracy). The director has, for instance, powers of dismissal without a hearing greater than those of the local governments. Directors are generally less strongly academic than vice-chancellors.

A board of governors with a strong lay ("independent" and local government) majority has a preponderant role in later cooptions. Academic staff have a maximum of 25 percent of the seats and a minimum of 4 percent (in universities the figures are often nearer 45 percent and 30 percent). There is one student member. Staff and student members may not sit on the finance or employment committees. The government appointed the first independent members, and made a major effort to discover business and professional people able to contribute. The board has final powers over all aspects of the polytechnic's life and work subject to the 1989 Articles.

There is normally an academic board on which directors, heads of faculties and departments are represented and on which more junior staff have sometimes half the seats. This board has power to recommend on any academic matter and on some general policy matters.

There are faculty boards in the larger higher education institutions with powers to recommend to the academic board. Nearly all subject departments have

Table 2
Percentage teaching staff 1953–89

	1953–54	1960–61	1965–66	1970–71	1976–77	1981–82	1986–87	1988–89
Universities	10.7[a]	11.4[a]	18.8[a]	28.6[a]	33.1[a]	34.0[a]	47.0[b]	54.6[b]
			21.5[b]	35.0[b]	40.8[b]	45.6[b]		
Advanced further education	—	—	—	—	11.5[c]	—	29.4[c]	29.7[d]

a Paid entirely by the university
b Includes all faculty. Of the full-time staff in 1976–77, 12 percent were women; in 1981–82, 13.8 percent were women; and in 1988–89, 20 percent were women when there were 4,175 part-time staff, a higher proportion of whom were women
c Full-time equivalents in England at polytechnics and "large colleges with significant advanced further education," that is, not all were teaching higher education. Total number of teachers in further education in 1986–87 were 94,000. The figures for "polytechnic only" teaching and research faculty in England were in 1982–83, 17,630; and in 1987–88, 17,743 including 1,162 part-time
d In 1987–88 in England only, there were 17,743 teachers at polytechnics, 11,992 at "large significant higher education colleges," and 1,454 at "small significant higher education colleges." Not all of these were teaching higher education
Sources: Department of Education and Science (to 1979) *Statistics of Education, Vol. 6*. University Grants Committee, HMSO, London; Department of Education and Science (from 1980) *UGC University Statistics, Vol. 1*. Universities Statistical Record, Gloucester; Department of Education and Science 1988 *Statistics of Further Education Nov 1987*. HMSO, London

permanent heads, and often have formal boards on which staff are variously represented. The duties of these bodies are similar to those in universities, but reorganization and innovation are creating a different landscape.

Many of the governmental demands made by the student movement of the late 1960s were met by the award of places on governing bodies at every level (not all with full voting powers). Much of this remains in place, if little used, in the universities. In the polytechnics similar if weaker provision is made. In 1989 it can be said that while student power is not wholly negligible, it is not a factor in the running of the system, if only because students do not make it so.

Institutional autonomy means that all higher education institutes have formal control of their own finances. They have the status of charities, and in addition to the normal restrictions on charitable finance, have, since the late 1960s been subject to scrutiny of their use of public money by the—parliamentary, not government—comptroller and auditor general. There was much concern among universities that this would erode autonomy: in practice it has been no more than an extra chore, and possibly some defense against intrusion by the Department of Education and Science. Under the 1988 Act, higher education institutions are also subject to direct accountability to the government, through the funding councils. It is not clear whether this will change reality. In any case, the smaller the proportion of income from government, the less the prospect of interference, and so too in principle with the transfer of public moneys from "block" funding to research contracts or to direct support of students. That is not to say that autonomy must result in academic-driven decisions.

Nonetheless, it is in the management of finances that autonomy has always resided, as the government has noted when disbarring polytechnic staff from finance committees. This is more so in the early 1990s because government has made clear that the old implied safety net is no longer there. When University College Cardiff ran out of money in 1987 it had to be taken over by the University of Wales Institute of Science and Technology. It has always been in the management (as opposed to the disposal) of finance that laypeople have played their chief part, a part that will become more important.

4. Faculty and Students: Teaching, Learning, and Research

4.1 Faculty

In the universities, the main ranks are professor, reader, senior lecturer (not at Oxbridge), and lecturer. Some heads, usually of a unit outside the normal teaching departments, may be termed "director." There are minor grades, not uniform through-

out the country, such as tutor, fellow, and so on. (At Oxbridge the fellowship of a college is a career grade normally carrying membership of the governing body.) Many vice-chancellors now hold the title "professor." All four ranks (except clinical) have been paid on national scales; in 1991 government is anxious to see salaries more personal.

The polytechnics now increasingly award the title of professor, sometimes to their directors. The other ranks are principal lecturer and lecturer. Some colleges are talking of awarding professorships. The shift from further to higher education since 1960 has distorted direct comparisons, and in any case staff have been employees of many local governments (see Table 2). The figures for university staff mask a rise in short-term appointments funded by research grants and contracts. The university figures for staff–student ratio are distorted by the rise in outside-funded staff. The government claims that in 1988 the figure was 10.7:1.

With a few exceptions at Oxbridge and in Scotland, mainly "regius" chairs, the state plays no part in making appointments. (It is normal, however, for the institution to select external advisors for senior appointments.) One of the main formal changes made when the polytechnics were incorporated in April 1989 was that local governments lost the right of appointment to the academic body. This one change lifted half the academic staff of the country into an ancient category.

The status of staff is closely tied in to the status of their institution. This has been a powerful factor in the homogenization of the system, and one that has been backed by the equal treatment of all universities.

Traces of the old Oxford pastoral tradition can be seen in an indifference to research training in American or Continental European terms. Substantial numbers of tenured staff hold a single earned degree. This is most evident among senior staff at Oxbridge (where the present chief executive of the UFC held a chair with one earned degree). At most universities cases can be found in many subjects and at all ranks. The ordering of research training and the absence of graduate schools has caused considerable comment in the post-Second World War years. The research councils made efforts to improve matters in the 1980s, especially the Economic and Social Research Council (ESRC), which removed accreditation from several universities, including Cambridge. Staff are not typically trained at the major research universities. Also, there has long been a need for training in teaching, the small and patchy provision for which suffered early in the 1981 cuts. The government's doctrine that public money should reward measured performance (and its covert belief that many teachers are incompetent) appears to be defeating the fears of "staff developers" that training and appraisal are incompatible. The Committee of Vice-Chancellors

Table 3
Number of students (in thousands) with degrees awarded including percentage number of women 1953–90

	1953–54	1960–61	1965–66	1970–71	1975–76	1980–81	1985–86	1987–88	1988–89	1989–90
Universities										
Full- and part-time undergraduate	67.7	92.9	149.0	197.0	222.0	263.0	265.0	274.0[cc]	285.0[kk]	300.0[s]
All full-time	82.7	111.0	175.0	235.0	269.0	307.0	310.0	320.0	334.0	351.0
% Women	24.0	24.0	23.0	35.0	33.8	37.8	40.3	41.3	42.2	43.1
Total	98.8	129.0	186.0	258.0	295.0	340.0	352.0	367.0	384.0	405.0[tt]
% Women	23.0	23.0	26.0	28.6	33.2	34.4	40.1	41.4	42.1	43.2
First degrees awarded	16.8	23.0	32.6	52.7	57.0[i]	68.1	72.3	71.9	74.9	—
Honors	10.1	15.5	23.8	40.7	46.3	56.4	68.0	62.5	66.2	—
Higher degrees awarded	—	—	6.4	13.1	16.4[j]	19.5[o]	24.6[v]	26.5[dd]	30.2[ll]	—
Advanced further education										
Full- and part-time undergraduate	—	—	246.0[b]	342.0[d]	383.0	419.0	507.0[w]	539.0[ee]	562.0[mm]	—
All full-time	—	—	136.0	221.0	246.0	208.0[p]	290.0	305.0	311.0[mm]	—
% Women	—	—	51.4	51.5	50.0	46.2	46.9	48.2	48.9	—
Total	—	—	246.0[b]	342.0[b]	383.0	419.0	507.0	539.0	633.0	650.0[uu]
% Women	—	—	46.5	36.8	37.6	35.1	40.6	42.6	43.6	—
First degrees awarded	—	—	—	3.9[e]	13.0[k]	34.6[q]	49.4[x]	53.1[ff]	56.2[nn]	—
Honors	—	—	—	0.8	9.9[k]	24.7[q]	35.2[y]	36.7[gg]	41.3[oo]	—
Higher degrees awarded	—	—	—	0.17[f]	0.6[l]	1.4[r]	2.4[z]	2.8[hh]	3.1[pp]	—
All higher education										
Full- and part-time undergraduate	—	—	395.0	539.0	605.0	682.0	772.0	814.0	847.0	—
All full-time	—	—	309.0	454.8	514.0	535.0	600.0	626.0	645.0	670.0
% Women	—	—	38.1	40.1	41.5	40.6	43.6	44.7	45.2	46.5
Total	—	—	433.0	621.0[g]	734.0[m]	827.0[s]	937.0[aa]	992.0[ii]	1,102.0[qq]	1,150.0[vv]
% Women	—	25.3	28.7	33.0	36.0	36.6	41.0	42.6	43.5	—
First degrees awarded	—	—	34.6	56.6	73.5[n]	107.2[t]	125.0[bb]	133.0[jj]	137.0[rr]	—
Honors	—	—	—	—	—	—	—	—	—	—
Higher degrees awarded	—	10.1[a]	15.2[c]	13.3[h]	—	20.3	27.0	29.3	33.3	—

772

a Includes higher diplomas
b Mainly two-year nondegree courses
c Includes higher diplomas
d Mainly two-year nondegree courses
e CNAA degrees. In addition there were London External and other university-validated degrees
f CNAA degrees including 79 PhDs
g Includes Open University: 20,000 (25% women)
h In addition, 11,000 other higher diplomas were awarded
i In addition, 1,940 first diplomas were awarded
j In addition, 11,591 higher diplomas were awarded
k CNAA degrees. In addition, 115 diplomas and 11,148 Higher National Diplomas were awarded
l Includes 143 PhDs
m Includes Open University: 56,000 (35.7% women)
n Includes 3,552 Open University ordinary degrees
o In addition, 5,894 higher diplomas were awarded
p Includes full-time nondegree students (42,000 first years in 1979–80)
q CNAA only
r Includes 219 PhDs. In addition, 5,703 higher diplomas were awarded
s Includes Open University: 68,000 (44.1% women)
t Includes 6,500 Open University ordinary degrees
u Includes 4,000 first-year subdegrees
v Includes 6,492 PhDs. In addition, 10,613 higher diplomas were awarded
w Includes 54,700 first-year subdegrees
x Includes 43,900 CNAA degrees
y CNAA only
z Includes 352 PhDs. In addition, 3,600 higher diplomas were awarded
aa Includes Open University: 78,000 (46.2% women)
bb Includes 6,700 Open University ordinary degrees; excludes 1,387 honors
cc Includes 9,927 part-time
dd Includes 6,839 PhDs. In addition 11,000 higher diplomas were awarded
ee Includes 55,100 full-time first-year subdegrees
ff Of these 45,800 were CNAA degrees, 7,300 degrees of universities other than Buckingham and London external degrees
gg CNAA degrees
hh Includes 428 PhDs. In addition, 4,200 CNAA higher diplomas were awarded
ii Includes Open University: 86,000 (46.5% women)
jj Includes 6,500 Open University ordinary degrees; excludes 1,542 O.U. honors graduates
kk Includes 10,000 part-time, and 6,300 students on subdegree courses
ll Includes 7,801 PhDs. In addition, 13,139 higher diplomas were awarded
mm Includes 54,900 full-time first-year students on subdegree courses
nn Includes Cranfield etc. and 49,600 CNAA degrees. In addition, 6,344 CNAA diplomas were awarded
oo CNAA degrees
pp Includes 491 PhDs. In addition, 9,061 higher diplomas were awarded
qq Includes Open University: 85,000 (47% women); also 1,941 full-time and 342 part-time students at Cranfield; 584 full-time and 16 part-time at the Royal College of Art; 721 full-time at Buckingham University; and 84,000 paramedics
rr Includes 6,500 Open University ordinary degrees; excludes 1,681 honors
ss Includes 10,558 part-time and 6,300 first-year subdegree students
tt Includes 53,850 part-time, excluding over 650,000 "continuing education" part-time students
uu Includes Cranfield and 57,400 full-time first-year subdegree students, excluding N. Ireland
vv Includes 89,000 students in Open University; 145.7 graduate, 604,100 first degree, and 316,800 subdegree students. Excluding 84,000 paramedical students

Sources: Council for National Academic Awards Annual Report. CNAA, London; Department of Education and Science (to 1979) Statistics of Education, Vol. 6. University Grants Committee. HMSO, London; Department of Education and Science (from 1980) UGC University Statistics, Vol. 1. Universities Statistical Record, Gloucester; Department of Education and Science Statistical Bulletin; Department of Education and Science 1989 Social Trends. HMSO, London; Department of Education and Science Statistics of Education for the UK. HMSO, London

and Principals set up a development unit at the University of Sheffield in 1988, and have found it politic to issue one of their new codes of practice (CVCP 1987–89).

Few criteria for the promotion of staff are published, and fewer for initial appointment. The procedure relies on peer review and personal judgment in which the preliminary review of peers by the institution is sometimes important. Reasons if given at all are general; research performance is generally believed to be the main ingredient. There is much confidence in the procedure.

The national salary scales established after the Second World War chimed well with the academic beliefs in the equality of scholars noted in the approach to governance, and that helped to explain, for instance, the absence of the "senior lecturer" grade at Oxbridge.

The degree of professional control within the universities meant that little need for unionization was seen. Indeed, a main object of the lecturers' association after the First World War was to share the power being won by the professoriate. By the beginning of the 1970s, the Association of University Teachers (AUT) had become very interested in pay, while reliance on public money meant that government had taken on the major characteristics of an employer. The Association decided to become a trades union in 1971 hoping at the same time to upstage the students, who had been affected by the student riots that broke out throughout Europe, starting in 1968. A chief effect has come to be to make rough treatment of scholars politically more practicable; status as a union soon lost its emotive value, and reduced the AUT's public authority as a professional body.

In the polytechnics and colleges open union attitudes came more naturally. A broader-based union including technical and administrative staff emerged with traditional trade union concerns and politicization. The National Association of Teachers in Further and Higher Education (NATFHE) was well fitted to its constituency when the local governments were the main employers and managers. There were, however, divergences of interests between advanced and nonadvanced further education, which must be increased by the grant of autonomy throughout higher education. In the mid-1970s divergencies led to the formation of the nonunion Association of Polytechnic Teachers (APT) which is not politicized. It has now approached substantial parity with NATFHE in the higher education sector.

4.2 Students

Given institutional autonomy, the number of students in Britain depends normally on what the managers of institutions decide they can accommodate. There are no rights to places and demand has always enabled many institutions to be selective.

Despite this *numerus clausus* there has been no denial of places. Before 1979, governments provided institutions much as required, and in the sciences more than required, with free maintenance for all but the richer students, and free tuition. It has been in this managed context that "student demand" has been understood; and within it numbers were in effect dependent on demand. Since 1979 expansion has continued, mainly in the (cheaper) polytechnics and colleges (though not, it is claimed, at the expense of real funding per student) to a total of 22 percent by 1989, when the age-participation index of full-time English 18–21-year olds would approach 16 percent. The index in the other countries might have been higher: in Northern Ireland it was 19.6 percent in 1985.

The 1987 White Paper assumed that this managed demand would fall after 1989 back to the 1985 figure as the age-group declined (it bottoms out in 1996). By mid-1989 it had been conceded that the selective institutions would be unaffected—the universities took in 6 percent more in 1989, and the polytechnics similarly—and that total demand is unlikely to fall. This, even though some of the instruments of management are being weakened, not least public funding. The Secretary of State for Education in 1989 expected the age participation to rise to 23 percent by 1999, and talked of doubling enrollment in 25 years. It was made clear, however, that no extra public funding could be expected, and no planning for increases was initiated. Meanwhile, there is a general campaign to increase the intake of mature and minority students. Against these influences is that of loans, discussed below.

The rate of participation of women has increased throughout the twentieth century. A large proportion went into teacher training, which contracted sharply in the 1970s, masking the rise elsewhere; but women are now clearly approaching parity, even at Oxbridge. Indeed they are now overtaking men at the basic qualifying level—A level—and may therefore soon form a majority in higher education.

Though some ethnic minority children are beginning to perform well at A level, they are not yet applying strongly for higher education. They, and other minority children who do not stay on at school, now form a substantial pool of potential applicants. The largest such pool is found among children from White manual homes: as the numbers of these shrink, they will become the largest of the minorities.

Student union membership has been compulsory in the sense that the state has in effect paid membership fees on behalf of all full-time students in each institution. (Part-time and many mature students are not covered by government money.) The local union is run by students elected by the local membership; and may affiliate to the National Union of Students (NUS), or to the Scottish union, and pay the affiliation fee. Most local unions are run by students who receive maintenance grants while working full-time for the union. In 1989 all these features are under scrutiny. The word "union" derives from the Oxbridge debating and social clubs which are unions of all colleges, and the unions are mainly active in social, sporting, and welfare areas. The word came to be confused with trade unions and since the mid-1960s the national unions have been well politicized, to the left or the far left but with a sprinkling on the farther right, as are most local unions. Only the more violent political activities have been of interest to the media, and as that interest has declined, so has the violence; nonetheless some disruption has continued.

Home students are entitled to a maintenance grant that in principle is sufficient to live on, but has not been so for much of the 1980s. The grant is progressively reduced if parental income is above a lower-middle manager's salary, and children of the rich have lost all benefit. Full grant is, however, payable if the student is over the normal age and, for instance, has worked for some time. Tuition is free for all European Community students. Many students work in the vacations and for some time students who must live on the grant have done so with the help of personal bank loans.

The fear that free maintenance and tuition distorts demand while benefiting the better off has led to a search for a loans system. However, the scheme suggested in early 1989 is to cover only half the cost of maintenance, the rest continuing to come from the state. It is not proposed to charge students fees for tuition, but the vice-chancellors see that as a way forward. Since full maintenance and free tuition has attracted from manual (largely skilled) homes a participation of under 20 percent of university students, proponents of loans find the access arguments of limited force. Effective objections have come from the beneficiaries, that is, middle-class parents who are largely the government's own supporters, and from those objecting to the great administrative cost.

4.3 Model of Undergraduate Courses

All degree conditions are laid down by bodies authorized by charter, without any input from government. Official influence can only penetrate through the persuasive power of the purse. Since the professional bodies have power to refuse to recognize a degree for professional accreditation, their views are in practice taken into account. Some major industries, notably telecommunications, have a form of influence through their subsidies.

After the Second World War the trend was to greater specialization, and the three-year single honors degree in an "academic" subject became the main type, with an extended essay-based examination at the end of the course. (For numbers of degrees awarded, see Table 3.) The CNAA awarded 37,000 honors degrees, of various sorts, out of 43,900 in 1986. Attempts have been made to move away to more general courses, such as "joint honors" degrees in two subjects; but general education or culture has not featured. Continuous or course assessment, and modular courses, are becoming common. There are now many less academic and more vocational courses, especially in the polytechnics. Credit transfer modular schemes have now become established on a small scale.

5. Conclusion

The United Kingdom in the early 1990s is in the middle of what appears likely to prove a major restructuring of its higher education system after two decades of rapid and often incoherent evolution. A positive drive that had been gathering pace for some years was given a formal basis and a new thrust in 1989 when the new funding councils were put in place. Some of the important issues have been noted, but others may prove more potent.

The main concept to have finally fallen is that of the equality before the state of all universities; a concept built up in the nineteenth century, and that has since 1919 included Oxbridge. It grew from the assumptions that the definition of a university was known, and that the implied mission could best be served by providing the equivalent of an endowment for use at the discretion of a highly autonomous collegium. The endowment should be large enough to cover both intensive teaching and substantial but unspecified research. Those assumptions have been under question for some time; they appear no longer to hold in the United Kingdom.

This naturally produced a strong tendency to similarity of institutions, a tendency reinforced by a major feature of the system. Despite the autonomy of the units, the administration was highly centralized, with national levels of salaries, senior–junior staff ratios, student–staff ratios, and so on. The feature was being duplicated in the nonuniversity sector. The general aim has become decentralization and reliance on the market to produce diversity. Where higher education institutes competed for students by offering equally resourced courses, they are already in 1989 competing by tender for the resources. Autonomy is being turned from an honor into a lever.

The universities have been most bruised by this. Whatever the financial statistics may say, they have suffered continuous reductions: from being straitened, their finances have often become desperate. The new world has terrible implications for the values and missions they thought permanent and sacred. Reshaping is no longer driven by primarily academic needs, but often by economic and even cosmetic ones. The system was built on a cooperative ethos; that ethos is now expected to make competition work. Perhaps most of all they feel that they are not esteemed and their remarkable record not noticed.

In the polytechnics it is different. They have ceased to be municipal parks and become national estates. Their grievance over the automatic funding of academic research has been rectified, if cruelly. They can no longer be overlooked. If the colleges remain a separate sector, they should have a bright future as a favored means of increasing access, fears about a dearth of candidates proving wrong.

In general, things may not turn out quite as the signs now suggest. University morale is not down everywhere. There are signs that the worst of the disparagement is over. Scientists are bypassing the national research councils for better grazing in the European Community.

At all events two new concepts may be noted: first that of higher education as an entity going beyond the universities, although it may merely be that the frontier of higher education has made one of its biggest advances (much greater than when it overran the colleges of advanced technology in the mid-1960s). In either case, the acceptable curricular range of higher education and its social purposes have widened sharply. The second concept that seems bound to emerge is that of the nonresearch university, perhaps harking back to the mid-nineteenth century and to Newman.

Meanwhile, there remains at least as large a tertiary sector, proportionately, beyond the frontier as there was between the First and Second World Wars. It is here that the main moves towards mass higher education are likely to take place, probably unplanned.

It is possible that the system as a whole, whatever the punishment that vital parts like superb research have suffered, will present a firmer and broader base for expansion, especially in its lower reaches, than it did at the beginning of the 1980s. The reorganizations now taking place should at least mean that public policy and the roles of institutions will be more clearly articulated.

Bibliography

Allen M 1988 *The Goals of Universities*. Society for Research into Higher Education (SRHE) and Open University Press, Milton Keynes

Becher A (ed.) 1987 *British Higher Education*. Allen and Unwin, London

Becher A, Kogan M 1980 *Process and Structure in Higher Education*. Heinemann, London

Berrill K et al. 1983 *Excellence in Diversity*. Society for Research into Higher Education (SRHE), Guildford

Cantor L R, Roberts I F 1986 *Further Education Today*. Routledge and Kegan Paul, London

Church C 1988 The qualities of validation. *Stud. Higher Educ.* 13(1): 27–43

Cobban A B 1988 *The Medieval English Universities*. Scolar Press, Aldershot

Committee of Vice-Chancellors and Principals (CVCP) 1987–89 *Codes of Practice*. Committee of Vice-Chancellors and Principals

Department of Education and Science 1966 *Report of the Study Group on the Government of Colleges of Education (Weaver Report)*. Her Majesty's Stationery Office, London

Department of Education and Science 1987a *Annual Report 1986–87*. Her Majesty's Stationery Office, London

Department of Education and Science 1987b *Statistics of Education for the UK*. Her Majesty's Stationery Office, London

Eggins H (ed.) 1988 *Restructuring Higher Education*. Society for Research into Higher Education (SRHE) and Open University Press, Milton Keynes

Eustace R 1987 The English ideal of university governance. *Stud. Higher Educ.* 12(1): 7–22

Eustace R 1991a The audit of teaching: A British historical accident? In: Moodie G, Berdahl R, Spitzberg I (eds.) 1991 *Quality and Access in Higher Education*. SRHE and Open University Press, Buckingham

Eustace R 1991b Gold, silver, copper: Standards of first degrees. In: Moodie G, Berdahl R, Spitzberg I (eds.) 1991 *Quality and Access in Higher Education*. SRHE and Open University Press, Buckingham

Flexner A 1930 *Universities: American, English, German*. Oxford University Press, New York

Halsey A H, Trow M 1971 *The British Academics*. Faber and Faber, London

Jarratt Report 1985 Steering Committee for Efficiency Studies in Universities. *Report*. Committee of Vice-Chancellors and Principals

Lindop Report 1985 *Academic Validation in Public Sector Higher Education*. Her Majesty's Stationery Office, London

Matterson A 1981 *Polytechnics and Colleges*. Longmans, Harlow

Merrison Report 1982 Joint ABRC/UGC Working Party on Support of University Scientific Research. *Report*. Her Majesty's Stationery Office, London

Moodie G C, Eustace R 1974 *Power and Authority in British Universities*. Allen and Unwin, London

Perkin H J 1987 The academic profession in the United Kingdom. In: Clark B R (ed.) 1987 *The Academic Profession*. University of California Press, Berkeley, California, pp. 13–59

Pratt J, Silverman S 1988 *Responding to Constraint*. Society for Research into Higher Education (SRHE) and Open University Press, Milton Keynes

Robbins Report 1963 Committee on Higher Education. *Report*. Her Majesty's Stationery Office, London

Rothblatt S 1987 Historical and comparative remarks on the federal principle in higher education. *Hist. Educ.* 16(3): 151–80

Scott P 1984 *The Crisis of the University*. Croom Helm, London

Shinn C H 1986 *Paying the Piper*. Falmer Press, Lewes

Stewart W A C 1989 *Higher Education in Postwar Britain*. Macmillan, London

Swinnerton–Dyer Report 1982 Working Party on Postgraduate Education. *Report*. Her Majesty's Stationery Office, London

Trow M 1987 Academic standards and mass higher education. *Higher Educ. Q.* 41(3): 268–91

Trow M 1988 Comparative perspectives on higher education policy in the UK and the US. *Oxf. Rev. Educ.* 14(2): 79–94

Trow M 1989 The Robbins trap: British attitudes and the limits to expansion. *Higher Educ. Q.* 43(1): 55–75

Wagner L (ed.) 1982 *Agenda for Institutional Change.* Society for Research into Higher Education (SRHE), Guildford

White Paper 1987 *Higher Education—Meeting the Challenge.* Her Majesty's Stationery Office, London

Williams G L, Blackstone T 1983 *Response to Adversity.* Society for Research into Higher Education (SRHE), Guildford

R. Eustace

United States

1. Higher Education and Society

In 1636, 16 years after English Puritans settled on what is now the East Coast of the United States of America, Harvard College was established in Cambridge, Massachusetts. Its announced purposes were to advance learning and perpetuate it to posterity, to train ministers for the churches in the American colonies, and to educate both English and Indian youth in knowledge and godliness (Cremin 1970 pp. 211, 219–22).

Early American college building was not planned. It was essentially a private enterprise undertaken in response to uncoordinated impulses within a developing society. One of these impulses was to provide for the perpetuation and expansion of a religious ministry for both the European settlers and the natives in the new world. Another was to bring to the American settlements the civilizing influence of older cultures. Another, was to accommodate within the American education enterprise new knowledge and the promising potential of developing scientific inquiry.

There was also the land itself, vast and undeveloped, stretching from the Atlantic coast to the Pacific Ocean, and eventually to the Hawaiian Islands and to Alaska on the northwest corner of the continent.

After the American Revolution, Great Britain ceded the "northwest territory" (now occupied by five states: Ohio, Indiana, Illinois, Michigan, Wisconsin, and part of Minnesota) to the United States. To acquire statehood, developing territories in this area were required by national legislation to acknowledge that "Religion, morality and knowledge, being necessary to good government and the happiness of mankind, schools and the means of education shall forever be encouraged" (Cremin 1980 p. 10). The young nation's commitment to education could not have been clearer.

Additional government encouragement for the westward expansion of American higher education was provided by the Land Grant Act passed by Congress in 1862. This measure (also known as the Morrill Act to recognize its author, Congressman Justin Morrill), permitted the sale of public lands to obtain funds the states could use for:

> . . . the endowment, support, and maintenance of at least one college where the leading object shall be, without excluding other scientific and classical studies, and including military tactics, to teach such branches of learning as are related to agriculture and the mechanical arts . . . (and) to promote the liberal and practical education in the industrial classes in the several pursuits and professions of life. (Levine 1978 p. 556–59)

Some of the colleges developed under this legislation were new free-standing technical institutions in which agriculture and engineering education, applied research, and public agricultural information services became the principal activities. Others were existing institutions that incorporated teaching and research in agriculture and technology into their liberal arts programs in order to qualify for land grant college status.

In 1989, the population of the United States reached 247,732,000. In that same year, 66.5 percent of all adults had completed at least four years of high school; 31.9 percent had completed one to three years of college; and 16.2 percent had completed at least four years of college (US Bureau of the Census 1987 as cited by *The Chronicle of Higher Education* 1989 p. 3).

Between 1940 and 1980, the population of the United States increased from 131,669,275 to 226,545,305, with particularly large increases in each of the last two decades of that period. The 1989 figure also represented an increase in population over the previous decade, but a small one. In fact it marked the fifth consecutive year that the annual population growth rate in the United States was less than 1 percent a year. One of the possible consequences of the declining population growth rate could be decreasing demand for higher education among future members of the traditional college-age group.

1.1 Structure of the Economy

In 1988, the Gross National Product (GNP) of the United States was nearly $4 trillion in constant dollars, setting a record for the number of consecutive years (16) the country has achieved peacetime economic expansion.

The United States has a free enterprise or capitalist economy that involves the voluntary interaction of the production of goods and services with consumers' needs and ability to pay for what the system makes available to them. In such a system, decentralized day-to-day decision making by large numbers of organizations and individuals is essential, and educational attainment makes a significant difference in the ability of managers of both public and private enterprises to function effectively.

The percentage of employees in the service sector of the economy—which includes government, education, communication, banking, and health care, is particularly impressive. By 1980, 69 percent of all employees worked in this sector.

1.2 Structure of Government and Political Goals

The government of the United States of America has three branches. The executive branch is responsible to the President who is chosen by a popular national election every four years. Cabinet members, who hold their offices by presidential appointment and confirmation by the US Senate, include secretaries of such federal departments as State, Defense, and Treasury.

Education was first recognized as a cabinet-level concern in 1953 when a department of Health, Education, and Welfare was created. In 1979, education was given still greater national recognition when a Department of Education was created. It monitors educational developments; administers federal financial assistance to institutions and students; collects, maintains, and disseminates information concerning educational progress and development; and encourages programs that might improve education in the country.

The Department of Education has had four Secretaries: Shirley Mount Hufstedler, from 1979 to 1981; Terrel Bell, from 1981 to 1985; William Bennett from 1985 to 1989; Lauro F. Cavazos from 1989–91; and Lamar Alexander who assumed the office in 1991.

In the Congress of the United States, there is a Committee on Education in the House of Representatives, and a subcommittee on Education, Arts, and Humanities of the Labor and Human Resources Committee in the Senate.

Federal concern for higher education has increased significantly since the Second World War. One reason is the national encouragement of research and technological development that was intensified in the postwar era and continues to be a major concern. Another has been the steady and, at times, dramatic growth in the demand for postsecondary education that began with the return of servicemen to civilian life after the Second World War and continued through the years when children born during the baby boom of the 1940s and 1950s reached college age. Such programs generated a substantially enlarged demand for higher education in the 1960s and 1970s.

1.3 Relationship with Religious Bodies

Throughout the seventeenth, eighteenth, and early nineteenth centuries, many of the colleges in the United States were founded by religious denominations. Among them are some of the best known Ivy League colleges (Harvard and Princeton are examples), and such other well-known institutions as the University of Notre Dame in Indiana.

Some of these institutions were established to educate the ministers of religious denominations. Others were founded to provide education with a denominational perspective. Regular chapel attendance may be required at such institutions.

Over the years, many of the institutions founded by religious denominations have deemphasized formal religious activities on the campus, and enroll students with diverse religious convictions.

Still, although many of them are small, church-related colleges continue to constitute the majority of higher education institutions in the United States and, in 1987, they enrolled 2,844,000 students.

2. The Institutional Fabric of the Higher Education System

Americans often talk about a "system" of United States higher education in order to acknowledge that it consists of many parts and serves a variety of clientele and functions. Higher education has not been centrally planned as a system, however, and its development reflects many interests and concerns.

Numbers and enrollment figures for both private and public institutions are given in Table 1. By 1987 there were 1,841 privately supported colleges and universities in the United States, enrolling 3,844,000 students (Carnegie Foundation for the Advancement of Teaching 1987 p. 5). Many are church-related, although they conform to broad standards of operation imposed by the states in which they are located. Their own governing boards have authority in the management of their financial resources, general operating procedures, personnel, maintenance of campuses and equipment, and the creation or termination of academic programs. Private institutions include 94 percent of the nation's liberal arts colleges, 72 percent of its specialized institutions, and about 38 percent of its two-year colleges (Carnegie Foun-

Table 1
Number and enrollment of institutions of higher education in the United States (Fall 1987)

Institutions	Enrollment
599 Public four-year	5,434,010
1,536 Private four-year	2,558,075
992 Public two-year	4,541,054
460 Private two-year	235,168
All undergraduates	11,047,902
First-time freshmen	2,246,352
Graduate schools	1,451,936
Professional	268,467
Total	12,768,307

Source: US Department of Education, as published in *The Almanac of Higher Education* 1989–90, Chicago University Press, 1989, p. 4

dation for the Advancement of Teaching 1987 p. 5). They are heavily dependent on tuition income and private contributions for the support of their programs.

In the early 1990s, the College Entrance Examination Board estimated that the average cost of attending a private four-year colleges is $14,326 for resident students and $12,321 for students who commute. For students attending private two-year colleges, the average cost is estimated to be $9,650 for resident students and $7,862 for commuters.

Academically able students with limited financial resources may receive scholarships or other financial assistance at these institutions.

One attractive characteristic of many private colleges and universities is that they are small. Half of the public research universities in the United States have enrollments larger than 20,000, but only 5 percent of the private research universities are that big.

Students interested in attending single-sex colleges also have to turn to the private sector. Although the number of single-sex colleges started to decline soon after the Civil War, and by 1900 71.6 percent of American colleges and universities were coeducational (Brubacher and Rudy 1976 p. 68), there are still 99 colleges for men and 102 colleges for women in the United States. There are also 13 "coordinated" institutions with separate programs for men and women (National Center for Education Statistics, *The Digest of Educational Statistics, 1988*).

Higher education for women started relatively late in the United States. Georgia Female College was chartered in 1837 and conferred its first degrees in 1840 (Carnegie Commission on Higher Education 1973 p. 15). Oberlin accepted women in its college department in 1837 but, according to one account, they "were given a watered-down course and expected to serve the men students at table and remain silent in mixed classes" (Bird and Briller 1972 p. 22).

By 1870, educational opportunities for women began to improve. In that year, out of 570 colleges and universities, 70 were colleges for women and 169 colleges were coeducational (Carnegie Commission on Higher Education 1973 p. 71).

In the fall of 1987, undergraduate women outnumbered undergraduate men by nearly 1 million (5,979,218 to 5,068,684) and women graduate students outnumbered male graduate students 758,624 to 693,314 (*The Almanac of Higher Education*, 1989–90 pp. 23, 24).

In 1971, the Carnegie Commission on Higher Education reported that "For well over a century of American higher education, from the founding of Harvard in 1636 to the founding of the first public institution, the University of Georgia in 1785, public colleges and universities did not exist."

By 1800, however, North Carolina, Tennessee, and Vermont had established public institutions, and by 1900 a total of 47 states had established public colleges and universities. With federal provision of public financial support for veterans of military service following the Second World War and generous student financial assistance programs in the 1960s, financial barriers to college attendance were beginning to come down. By 1969, enrollment in private colleges and universities had dropped to 28 percent of the total (Carnegie Commission on Higher Education 1971).

Opportunities for students to obtain public higher education were increased in the early decades of the twentieth century as a system of two-year colleges was developed.

Established by counties or special two-year college districts, these institutions gave high-school graduates opportunities to begin their college studies close to home, or to pursue further educational preparation for employment. Some of them also became centers of adult education in the districts they served. By 1987, two-year colleges constituted 40 percent of all institutions of higher education in the United States and enrolled 36 percent of the country's college students (Carnegie Foundation for the Advancement of Teaching 1987 p. 7).

Higher education in the United States is less a rational system than it is an intricate assortment of diversified institutions put into order after the fact for the sake of analysis and discussion. Even the names of institutions may be misleading because "college" and "university" frequently describe aspirations more accurately than they do programs.

To facilitate appropriate comparison and analysis of institutional development, in 1973, a classification of institutions of higher education in the United States was developed by the Carnegie Commission on Higher Education under the direction of Dr. Clark Kerr. It was updated by the Carnegie Council on Policy Studies in Higher Education, also under Dr. Kerr's direction in 1975, and was most recently updated by the Carnegie Foundation for the Advancement of Teaching under the direction of Dr. Ernest Boyer in 1987.

Definitions of the categories and the number of institutions in each classification in 1987 are given below.

Research universities (104 institutions—71 public, 33 private) offer a full range of baccalaureate programs, are committed to graduate education through the PhD degree, and give high priority to research. They receive at least $12.5 million for research from the federal government and award at least 50 PhD degrees each year. In 1987 they enrolled 4,008,000 students.

Doctorate-granting universities (109 institutions—63 public, 46 private) offer a full range of baccalaureate programs. In addition, the mission of these institutions includes a commitment to offer graduate education through the doctorate degree. They award at least 10 PhD degrees annually in three or more academic disciplines, and in 1987, they enrolled 1,220,000 students.

Comprehensive universities and colleges (595 institutions—331 public, 264 private) offer baccalaureate programs and, with few exceptions, graduate education through the master's degree. More than half of their baccalaureate degrees are awarded in two or more occupational or professional disciplines, such as engineering or business administration. Institutions in this group enroll at least 2,500 students. In 1987 they enrolled 3,303,000 students.

Liberal arts colleges (572 institutions—32 public, 540 private). These are primarily undergraduate colleges and award more than half of their baccalaureate degrees in arts and science fields. About half of them have highly selective admissions policies. In 1987 they enrolled 584,000 students.

Two–year community, junior, and technical colleges (1,367 institutions—985 public, 382 private) offer certificate or degree programs through the Associate of Arts and, with few exceptions, offer no baccalaureate degrees. In 1987 they enrolled 4,518,600 students.

Professional schools and other specialized institutions (642 institutions—66 public, 576 private) offer degrees ranging from the bachelor's to the doctorate, but at least 50 percent (usually many more) of the degrees they award are in one specialized field. The category includes: theological seminaries; Bible colleges and other institutions offering degrees in religion (210 institutions—all private); medical schools and medical centers (56 institutions—32 public, 24 private); health profession schools—in chiropractice, pharmacy, or podiatry (38 institutions—2 public, 36 private); engineering and technology (31 institutions—3 public, 28 private); schools of business and management (33 institutions—1 public, 32 private); schools of art, music and design (63 institutions—4 public, 59 private); law schools: (19 institutions—1 public, 18 private); 52 other specialized institutions (8 public, 44 private); and 21 corporate colleges (all created and operated by corporate businesses to provide specialized instruction for their employees). In 1987, there were 640 specialized institutions enrolling 467,000 students.

2.1 Admissions Policies and Selection

There are no standard admissions requirements for colleges and universities in the United States. The prevailing informal policy, however, is for schools to encourage as many Americans as possible to pursue education to the highest level of their interest and ability, and the diversity of the functions and levels of instruction of American institutions make that policy feasible.

In practice, there is a dual system of institutions with "open" and "selective" entrance requirements. Institutions with "open" requirements admit persons, regardless of age, who have satisfied secondary-school graduation requirements or demonstrate educational achievement at the level expected of secondary-school graduates. They include most public two-year colleges, many state colleges, and some private institutions. Although philosophically committed to open access policies, some of these institutions may adopt more selective admission procedures when demand for entry exceeds the availability of places for new students.

Institutions with "selective" admissions policies may require that applicants demonstrate above-average academic achievements. These institutions include most major research universities and many prestigious colleges and universities in both the public and private sectors.

Graduates of secondary schools using A to F grading systems (with A as the highest grade and F as failure), usually need to have average grades of B or better in academic subjects to meet the entrance requirements of selective colleges. These subjects would include mathematics, science, English language and literature, and foreign languages. (On a numerical scale where A is valued at 3, B is valued at 2, and C is valued at 1, selective colleges admit few if any students with grade point averages under 2.5.)

In addition to academic grades and test scores, admissions officers are also interested in students' extracurricular interests and achievements and may request that samples of a student's writing be included in application materials.

A national study by the American Association of College Registrars and Admission Officers, the College Board, the American College Testing Program, Educational Testing Service, and the National Association of College Admissions Counselors in 1985 indicated that institutions of higher education may be tightening entrance requirements. Between 1979 and 1985, while the percentage of public colleges requiring high-school study of English increased from 56 to 71, the percentage requiring the study of mathematics increased from 51 to 61; the percentage requiring study of biological science in high school dropped from 41 to 39 percent; the percentage requiring social studies increased from 36 to 43, and the percentage requiring study of foreign languages was 15 in both years.

It also found that 72 percent of private colleges required study of English in both 1979 and 1985. Between those years, the percentage of private colleges requiring previous study of mathematics decreased from 70 to 68 percent, the percentage requiring biological science decreased from 57 to 53; the percentage requiring social studies increased slightly from 63 to 64; the percentage requiring physical science increased from 51 to 52; and the percentage requiring foreign language decreased from 38 to 33 (Boyer 1987 p. 30).

Colleges with selective admission policies also may expect candidates for admissions to score high on national tests that purport to ascertain students' ability to succeed academically. The most widely used examinations for this purpose are the SAT (Scholastic Aptitude Test) which yields measures of verbal and mathematical ability, and the ACT (American College Testing) examination in English, mathematics, science, and social studies. Every year, the SAT is administered to about 1 million students, and the ACT is administered to about 1.6 million.

The SAT is scored on a scale of 400 to 800 on verbal ability and mathematics with a possible total of 1,600; the ACT is scored on a scale of 1 to 36. In 1988, the average ACT score nationally was 18.5. The average SAT score was 428 on its verbal section and 475 on its mathematical section (*The Chronicle of Higher Education Almanac*, September 6, 1989 p. 15).

Academic requirements for admission to graduate school are very selective and include not only excellent academic records during undergraduate studies, but also strong recommendations from faculty members and high scores on such assessments of undergraduate achievement as the Graduate Record Examination. In 1984 to 1985, 272,000 college graduates and "soon to be graduates" took the Graduate Record Examination and 77,000 took one of 17 Graduate Record Subject Tests (Center for Education Statistics, 1987, p. 106).

The national tests are a matter of controversy among educators. Critics claim that they measure test-taking ability rather than academic potential, and that students who can afford to be coached for the tests have an unfair advantage over those who cannot. Critics also claim the tests are unfair to members of minorities because their frames of reference are those most familiar to the "White majority."

The tests are defended, however, by college officials who say that school grades do not always reflect a student's readiness for college. Tests, on the other hand, provide impartial measures of students' academic progress, and by using both test scores and grades, these officials claim, college admissions officers can make fairer judgements about applicants.

2.2 Quantitative Developments in Higher Education

In 1987, 12,768,307 students were enrolled in United States colleges and universities. That was an all-time record, exceeding the previous high in 1986 by 44,202 students.

The 1989 enrollment included 6,836,242 women and 5,932,131 men (*The Chronicle of Higher Education Almanac* September 6, 1989 p. 7).

Beginning in 1970, higher education enrollment in the United States increased year by year from 8,581,000 to 1983 when it reached 12,465,000. In 1984, it decreased by 223,000 students but has been increasing steadily since that time.

The five states with the largest enrollments in 1987 were: California, 1,788,012 students; New York, 992,544; Texas, 802,226; Illinois, 686,954; Pennsylvania, 554,370. The five states with the smallest enrollments were: Wyoming, 26,062 students; Alaska, 26,937; South Dakota, 31,755; Vermont, 33,242; and Montana, 35,882 (*The Chronicle of Higher Education Almanac* September 6, 1989, pp. 8, 9).

Because of the decreasing size of the college-age group, enrollments were expected to decline in the 1980s. Instead, they continued to increase. The 18 to 24-year old population decreased by 6.3 percent between 1980 and 1985, but enrollment actually increased by 10 percent during that period. Although there were fewer college age students at this time, a larger proportion of them were actually enrolling in institutions of higher education (Office of Educational Research and Improvement, Center for Education Statistics: The Condition of Teaching, Washington, DC 1987).

In 1971, the Carnegie Commission on Higher Education published a policy report on 105 colleges founded for Black students. It estimated their enrollment to be about 150,000 and predicted that it might reach 300,000 by the year 2000. In 1988, there were 106 colleges originally founded for Black students and they enrolled 230,760 students.

Table 2 shows that participation of all minorities in higher education has increased steadily in the

Table 2
Racial and ethnic group college enrollment in the 1980s

	1980	1982	1984	1986
American Indian				
All	84,000	88,000	84,000	90,000
Men	38,000	37,000	38,000	40,000
Women	46,000	48,000	46,000	51,000
Asian				
All	266,000	351,000	390,000	448,000
Men	151,000	189,000	210,000	239,000
Women	135,000	162,000	180,000	209,000
Black				
All	1,107,000	1,101,000	1,076,000	1,081,000
Men	464,000	458,000	437,000	436,000
Women	563,000	601,000	643,000	644,000
Hispanic				
All	472,000	519,000	535,000	624,000
Men	232,000	252,000	254,000	292,000
Women	240,000	267,000	281,000	332,000
White				
All	9,833,000	9,997,000	9,815,000	9,914,000
Men	4,773,000	4,830,000	4,690,000	4,646,000
Women	5,060,000	5,167,000	5,125,000	5,268,000

Source: US Department of Education as presented in *The Almanac of Higher Education* 1989–90, pp. 30, 31

1980s. The one significant exception is that of Black men, whose participation dropped significantly in 1984 and 1986.

2.3 Structure of Qualifications

The first degree offered by colleges and universities is the associate degree, which may be awarded after the completion of the first two years of higher education and is the standard degree offered by two-year community or junior colleges.

The bachelor's degree (usually in "arts" or "science") is awarded after four years of study and is the most common degree awarded at the conclusion of undergraduate studies.

The most familiar graduate degrees are the master's, awarded after two or more years of post-graduate study and the doctor's degree, a research degree normally earned after four or more years of postgraduate study. The exact length of time required to obtain graduate degrees is closely related to the time-requirements of the research and reporting on which they are based, however, and often exceeds minimum requirements. The most frequently awarded advanced degrees are the Master of Arts (MA) or Master of Science (MS), and Doctor of Philosophy (PhD).

There are specialized forms of degrees to accommodate specific disciplines or professions. Examples include BSEd, Bachelor of Science in Education; MEng, Master of Engineering; and ScD, Doctor of Science. The two most familiar degrees in health fields are the MD, Doctor of Medicine; and the DDS, Doctor of Dental Surgery (or Dental Science).

3. Governance, Administration, and Finance

In 1973, the Carnegie Commission on Higher Education reported:

> The governance of higher education in the United States has features that distinguish it from systems elsewhere. One of its unique features is the great diversity of forms between and among institutions—more so than in most other nations where greater internal uniformity applies. Our system, with all its internal variations, however, has been especially characterized by these general features:
> 1. Absence of centralized control by the national government—essential authority residues with state governments and with boards of trustees.
> 2. Concurrent existence of strong public and private systems.
> 3. Trustee responsibility—basic responsibility for governance of individual institutions has been in the hands of lay boards in both public and private institutions.
> 4. Presidential authority—the president has substantial executive authority delegated by the lay board.
> 5. Departmental authority—within the faculty, the department has been the key unit of academic organization over most of the past century.

The Carnegie Commission traced the reasons for these principles to these influences in the American experience more generally:

(a) The separation of church and state, which helped to separate higher education and the state, since many of the early colleges were started by religious groups.

(b) A democratic and pluralistic system with many centers of power.

(c) Private institutions governed by their own boards of trustees and financed almost entirely by income from tuition and other charges to students, and by income from gifts, endowments, and contract services.

(d) State colleges and universities operated much like private institutions except for the fact that their programs are subject to review by public commissions or officials before they can be executed.

3.1 National Administration

Authority for the development of private colleges and universities resides in their individual governing boards, which are self-perpetuating and are responsible for overall institutional policy, and for the development of the institution's administrative procedures, personnel, physical facilities, and financial management.

Privately controlled colleges and universities are independent of government control although their programs and facilities may be taken into consideration by state education planners when they evaluate proposals for the establishment of new institutions or the introduction of new programs of study. Because they are public-service institutions, they are exempt from taxation at the state and federal level.

Responsibility for the development and coordination of four-year public higher education resides primarily in the states, which exercise that responsibility through legislative committees, state coordinating boards, public administrative departments, or combinations of such authorities. In some states, higher education institutions often are relatively independent in practice. Although they are financed primarily by state governments, they are organized and operate under the immediate authority of independent governing boards. Members of such boards are usually appointed by state governors, who, themselves, may be ex officio trustees or regents. In some cases, California being one, members of college and university boards of trustees have long terms of office, which help to shelter them from political control or influence.

The most powerful instruments of public control of higher education, of course, are the state budgets, which are usually incorporated in the budget proposals of state governors and reviewed and approved by state legislatures annually.

Public two-year colleges also are governed by their own boards, but they are created by counties or districts within states, and their public members are often elected.

Coordination of public and private higher education is essentially voluntary, but may be formalized through the inclusion of public officials on the governing boards of private institutions or the creation of statewide coordinating committees. However coordination is accomplished, public higher education authorities must work closely with private institutions to avoid needless duplication of effort and monitor the adequacy of existing higher education policies and programs for meeting local and state needs.

3.2 Finance

Colleges and universities in the United States are financed from a variety of sources. Public institutions of higher education receive funding in the form of public appropriations supplemented by student fees and income from government and private support of research and special programs. Private institutions are supported by income from endowments, voluntary gifts and grants, and tuition charges. But the differences between the financing of the two sectors are not very neat. The amounts from each source vary, but both sectors receive income based on student attendance whether it is in the form of direct tuition payments, "incidental" fees, or public funding based on "average daily attendance." Institutions in both sectors receive income from private donors, and, in various forms, from governments.

Between 1980 and 1986, annual revenues for public colleges and universities increased from $43,195,617,000 to $65,004,632,000, and revenues for private colleges and universities increased from $22,389,172,000 to $35,432,985,000. In the same period, public college and university expenditures increased from $42,279,806,000 to $63,193,853,000 and private college and university expenditures increased from $21,773,132,000 to $34,341,839,000 (US Department of Education figures reported in the Chronicle of Higher Education's *Almanac of Higher Education*, 1989–90).

The differences in the financing for the two sectors are dramatically illustrated by a report on the shares and sources of revenues for the two sectors issued by the US Office of Educational Research and Improvement in 1987. They are compared in Table 3.

The cost of going to college in the United States is not modest. In 1987, Ernest L. Boyer, president of the Carnegie Foundation for the Advancement of Teaching reported that "fewer than 30 percent of prospective college students feel they can attend the college of their choice without financial aid from a college or government assistance program. Further,

Table 3

Percent of revenue shares for public and private colleges and universities, 1985

	Public institutions	Private institutions
Tuition and fees	17.5	54.8
State and local appropriations	56.9	1.3
Federal grants and contracts	13.2	17.0
Private gifts, grants and contracts	3.8	13.1
Other (including endowment income)	8.6	13.8

Source: Center for Education Statistics, Digest of Educational Statistics in *The Condition of Education—Statistical Report*, 1987 edn., p. 117

61 percent said they would need scholarships, loans, or part-time work to attend *any* institution on their preferred lists" (Boyer 1987, p. 21). The average annual cost of attending a public college or university in the United States is about $5,200, and students attending private institutions probably pay more than twice that amount.

Boyer also reported that, on average, a student's family "or someone" must invest about $20,800 to $42,000 in a four-year undergraduate degree. For students attending the most prestigious private institutions, the cost could be $60,000 or more.

To assist students from low-income families, some states have had financial aid programs for many years. In the 1960s, the federal government began to play a significant role in providing financial assis-

Table 4

Average amounts of student assistance received in current dollars, by federal postsecondary student aid program: 1973–74 to 1986–87

	1974–75 $	1978–80 $	1984–85 $	1986–87 $
Pell[a] Grant	631	868	1,073	1,330
SEOG	506	555	573	550
CW–S	518	650	877	880
NDSL	647	679	971	935
SSIG	280	592	628	550
GSL	1,215	1,976	2,326	2,375

Source: Center for Education Statistics, The Condition of Education-A Statistical Report, Office of Educational Research and Improvement, US Department of Education, Washington, DC 1987
a Pell Grant; SEOG (Supplemental Educational Opportunity Grant); CW-S (College Work Study); NDSL (National Direct Student Loan); SSIG (State Student Incentive Grant); GSL (Guaranteed Student Loan)

Table 5
Number of recipients (in thousands), by type of secondary student aid program: 1973–74 to 1986–87

	1973–74	1979–80	1984–85	1986–87
Pell				
Grant	557	2,716	2,830	2,619
SEOG	395	606	652	689
CW–S	570	926	735	753
NDSL	680	958	697	896
SSIG	136	259	241	264
GSL	938	1,510	3,403	3,610

Center for Education Statistics: The Condition of Education—A Statistical Report, Office of Educational Research and Improvement, US Department of Education, 1979 edition

tance. The extent of these programs is illustrated in Tables 4 and 5. The assistance takes various forms:

(a) Pell Grants/Basic Education Opportunity Grants—BEOG: student financial assistance provided by federal legislation in 1972 and named for the program's sponsor, United States Senator Claiborne Pell. Pell grants, based on financial need, are made directly to students.

(b) Supplemental Education Opportunity Grants—SEOG: provide student aid flexibility in relation to tuition costs.

(c) State Student Incentive Grants—SSIG: provide federal funds to match state student aid appropriations (on a 50–50 basis).

(d) College Work Study—CWS: a program in which the federal government pays a major share of earnings of students who are given jobs on a campus or in nonprofit organizations.

(e) Guaranteed Student Loans—GSL: formerly "National Direct Student Loans," a program providing federally-funded loans to needy students.

(f) National Direct Student Loan Program: loans are made by institutions although the federal government provides 90 percent of the funds. Students pay no interest as long as they engage in public service. When their service is completed, however, they are charged 3 percent interest on any unpaid loan balance.

3.3 Institutional Administration

The highest authority in United States colleges and universities resides in their governing boards, which are variously named but most frequently called Boards of Trustees or Boards of Regents. The power invested in these boards acknowledges the importance of colleges and universities to the society from which trustees are drawn. It includes authority to name presidents and other key administrators and hire, promote, and dismiss senior leaders of the institution. Not the least of their responsibilities is to approve annual budgets and secure funding for institutional development.

Members of governing boards who do not serve by virtue of institutional office or, in the case of private institutions, relatives or representatives of the founders, are selected carefully because of the weight of their authority and power and the length (in some cases as many as 16 years) of their terms. At state institutions, governing boards may include key state officials including governors, superintendents of public education, and legislative leaders as ex officio members.

At many institutions, students are also considered to have legitimate concern for the general condition of their colleges and universities and are invited to send ex officio representatives (often elected presidents of the student body) to meetings of the faculty and governing boards of their institutions.

In United States colleges and universities the basic unit of organization is the department of instruction. It is here that the academic work of teaching and research is assigned and accommodated by allocations of time, space, and budget. It is also here that staff members who teach and do research in what are sometimes narrowly defined subjects find common ground and become best known to their peers. When faculty members are reviewed for promotion, their departments are usually their sponsors and offer the best-informed testimony concerning candidates' abilities and achievements.

At large institutions, departments with similar academic interests—languages, science, or the arts—may be brought together in schools or colleges that facilitate cross-discipline interaction and represent common interests of departments to the central administration. In very large universities, these units may, by virtue of the reputations and scholarly achievements of their faculties, emerge as nationally influential centers of research and instruction attracting strong support within and from beyond the institution.

In some ways comparable to academic departments at large research universities, are research institutes. Often supported substantially by outside agencies, they bring together expert staff and sophisticated facilities for advanced specialized research that can lend enormous prestige to the institutions where they are effective and often attract very large grants of money for the support of their research, and, indirectly, their institutions.

Academic policies broadly defined are determined virtually independently of institution governing boards and administrations. These functions are performed by institution-wide faculty councils in which all faculty members may hold membership. Two of the most important functions of these councils—though they vary widely from institution to institution—are the approval of new courses and academic programs, determination of procedures for academic personnel actions, and approval of the curricula of an institution's departments, schools, and colleges.

Traditionally, the subject matter of United States higher education has been divided into horizontal divisions corresponding to fields of knowledge, and vertical divisions according to the depths (or heights) to which knowledge is to be explored and taught. Within complex institutions of higher education, the distinction between terms like "school" or "college" was once determined by whether or not their courses of study were "occupational," "professional," or "general," or led to the PhD degree. Time and practice have so blurred these distinctions, however, that, while the historic divisions continue to exist, they are no longer functionally useful in describing the academic enterprise.

Higher education in the United States is now organized to present knowledge in increasingly broader contexts. The general pattern is as follows:

(a) Department: This is the smallest academic unit, in which the depth, breadth, and findings of a relatively discrete body of knowledge can be subjected to disciplined examination in detail.

(b) College: This may be a free-standing institution or unit of a university where people, equipment, and resources of several academic departments are brought together within a professional intellectual tradition to enlarge the understanding and application of knowledge they share.

(c) University: This is the most complex institution, one in which people, equipment, and resources of several colleges and departments come together to test the limits of understood truths and the possibilities of crossing such limits to expand disciplines and merge findings across disciplines. By so doing, they increase the dimension and potential of intellectual endeavor.

4. Faculty and Students: Teaching, Learning, and Research

Colleges and universities in the United States have three basic functions: teaching; research; and public service. Individual colleges and universities often perform all three functions but emphasize one or two.

Teaching is a dominant function of faculty members at United States colleges and universities, but research effort is expected even of faculty members in institutions at which teaching is most emphasized (see Tables 6 and 7), and Clark emphasizes this point at the beginning of a chapter on "The Imperatives of Academic Work" in his 1987 study of the academic profession:

> In the allocation of faculty time . . . what we can take primarily from the national survey is the immense variation by type of institution for the two core tasks of instruction and inquiry. The variation is so extensive that any stated averages for the system at large obscure more than they reveal. Standard comments about the American professor as one who engages in both teaching and research are false: Nearly all members of the profession teach, but only a minority are significantly involved in research. (Clark 1987 pp. 80–81)

At research institutions, senior full-time faculty members often teach more graduate than undergraduate courses. Some prefer undergraduate teaching, however, and attempt to arrange their schedules to include instruction at both levels.

Even tenured faculty members do more than teach and conduct research. Clark reports that:

> Beyond the two basic lines of work—formal instruction and inquiry—there is a plethora of other activities, such as administration, preparation for teaching, informal advising, formal counseling, outside consulting, outside professional practice, and participation in professional associations in which professors up and down the institutional line are variously engaged. (Clark 1989 p. 79)

Table 6
Average number of hours per week faculty devote to classroom instruction in undergraduate courses (percent responding), by institution type

Institution types	None	1–4	5–10	11–20	20+
All institutions:	14	21	38	25	2
Research universities	26	35	30	8	1
Doctorate granting universities	14	24	41	19	2
Comprehensive universities and colleges	8	13	41	36	2
Liberal arts colleges	3	13	43	38	3

Source: The Carnegie Foundation for the Advancement of Teaching, National Survey of Faculty, 1984 as presented in E L Boyer, *College*, Harper and Row, New York, 1984

Table 7
Average number of hours per week faculty members devote to research (percent responding by type of institution)

	Hours per week devoted to research				
	None	1–4	5–10	11–20	20+
All institutions	17	25	26	17	15
Research universities	8	13	24	26	29
Doctorate granting universities	11	27	29	18	15
Comprehensive universities and colleges	23	32	27	12	6
Liberal arts colleges	33	36	19	10	2

Source: The Carnegie Foundation for the Advancement of Teaching Survey of Faculty 1984 as cited in Boyer, E L, *College*, New York, Harper and Row Publishers, 1987

Table 8
Faculty of colleges and universities in the United States
1969–89

1969–70	1970–75	1975–80	1980–85	1988–89
474,000	628,000	686,000	724,000	825,000

4.1 Faculty

Quantitative developments in numbers of faculty are shown in Table 8.

In United States higher education, the primary qualifications of the teacher are assumed to be general command of a discipline and familiarity with the planning and conduct of research. Academic achievement of those qualifications is certified by the awarding of the Doctor of Philosophy (PhD degree). In its 1984 survey of faculty members in the United States, the Carnegie Foundation for the Advancement of Teaching found that 48.8 percent of them held PhD degrees and 31.7 percent were "working" for one (Carnegie Foundation for the Advancement of Teaching 1984 pp. 47–48).

Graduate students acquire teaching experience by assisting faculty members as readers of examinations and by meeting regularly with small groups of undergraduates to discuss information and concepts presented in the text and their professor's lectures for a course. Graduate students who are strongly attracted to research may join the staffs of academic research projects where they not only have opportunities to practice research skills but also may participate in seminars on project-related research.

There are three academic ranks on the "tenure-track" of academic employment: assistant professor; associate professor; and professor. Within these ranks there may be several steps (1, 2, 3 etc.) with specified salary ranges, and duration (two years per level, for example). At institutions with such systems, faculty members may serve as many as eight years within one rank before being eligible for promotion.

In May 1989, the American Association of University Professors reported results of a national survey that indicate that the average salary across all ranks and at all types of institution was $39,640. As published in *The Chronicle of Higher Education* for May 3, 1989, the results of the survey found the highest average salary to be $64,290 paid to professors at private institutions. The lowest was $21,300 paid to instructors at church-related colleges. By rank, the average salaries for 1988 to 1989 at all institutions was reported as follows:

Professor	$50,070
Associate professor	37,890
Assistant professor	31,680
Instructor	23,890
Lecturer	25,360
All ranks	39,640

Although faculty salaries increased at an average of 5.8 percent annually at all levels, adjustments for inflation decreased the size of the increases to 1.3 percent.

Beyond the usual salary range for academic personnel are "chairs," often endowed by private donors, which are filled by individuals of special distinction and achievement. Promotions within the faculty are made after the evaluations of the candidates by faculty committees and testimony from outside authorities in a candidate's field. The decision to promote a faculty member is usually made by a department chairman subject to approval by the institution's academic dean and other key administrators. Whoever makes the final decision, a faculty member is supposed to have the right to be observed and judged by his or her peers. For that reason, the whole procedure of appointments and promotions is usually initiated at the department level.

In 1989, *The Chronicle of Higher Education* (July 12, page A16) reported that 1,207 campuses with 226,875 faculty members were represented by certified academic staff bargaining agents. These campuses accounted for about one-third of the nation's colleges and universities and 58 percent of the faculty members.

There is ambivalence about collective bargaining in higher education. In the historic model of colleges and universities, professors considered themselves to be professionals rather than employees. The expansion of the public sector of higher education over the years has clearly made a difference. Of the institutions represented by bargaining agents in 1989, 942 were public institutions and only 58 were private institutions.

4.2 Students

Undergraduate education in the United States has two components: general education; and a concentration, or "major." The general education program is designed to give students a "well-rounded" education that draws upon several disciplines, but especially, those that broaden the knowledge of the "educated" man or woman. It tends to echo, at a higher level of sophistication, the basic education of the college preparatory student in high school: language; literature; history; basic science; and mathematics.

The "major" is a concentration of studies on one subject or in one department. It usually is related to one's preparation for future employment or continuing study to earn postbaccalaureate degrees.

Table 9 presents the percentages of male and female students choosing the various majors offered by colleges and universities. The most popular majors are business and engineering, both of which, obviously, have occupational application. The large percentage of women majoring in "medicine and

Table 9

Percentage of men and women majoring in undergraduate fields of study at American colleges and universities in 1985

Major Field	Men	Women	All
Agriculture	1.6	1.5	1.5
Architecture	1.8	1.8	1.8
Arts	4.3	6.1	5.4
Biological sciences	4.5	4.7	4.6
Business	16.3	14.4	15.1
Education	5.2	11.5	8.8
Engineering	24.3	2.3	11.7
Geography	0.3	0.2	0.2
General education	1.2	1.5	1.4
Home economics	—	0.7	0.4
Humanities	6.1	9.2	10.0
Law	0.9	2.1	2.1
Library Science	1.9	2.3	2.1
Mathematics	3.7	2.0	2.7
Medicine and nursing	2.6	16.1	11.3
Physical sciences	4.7	1.5	2.8
Social sciences	8.9	7.7	9.2
Other	10.4	13.8	8.1

Source: The Carnegie Foundation for the Advancement of Teaching, 1984 Surveys of College Faculty and Undergraduates, Opinion Research Corporation, Princeton, New Jersey, 1985

nursing" includes some future doctors but mainly represents nursing students. The strong showing of the humanities and social sciences reflects the ubiquity of these subjects as a useful foundation for future teachers (including college professors), lawyers, politicians, and others whose specialized interests draw heavily on the understanding of evolving conditions and concerns of humankind.

In the American academic tradition, students are novices in scholarship who are entitled (because they are college patrons) to convenient access to able teachers and good libraries. On the campuses, that tradition is generally observed, although it may compete with another view of students as tyros in life and aspirants-in-training for nonscholarly professions and occupations.

Beyond the classroom and library, student life is often disconnected from scholarly endeavors. Much of a student's education takes place outside the classroom as part of what is vaguely referred to as "student life," and one of its key components is work.

In 1984, more than 30 percent of full-time students and 84 percent of all part-time students responding to the Carnegie Foundation for the Advancement of Teaching's survey of undergraduates worked more than 21 hours a week to earn money that would help them meet the expenses of going to college. But college is not all study and work. Thirty-one percent of the students participating in the survey reported devoting more than ten hours a week to informal conversation with other students. Fourteen percent

spent more than ten hours a week in front of the television set, and the typical student devotes between one and two hours a week to leisure reading.

Although the life of American students is determined largely by requirements for degrees and classroom assignments, there is a large domain of extracurricular activity, including clubs, publications, and recreation that is subject to student control. Usually authority in such matters is delegated to student governments by an institution's faculty and administration.

Even student government is usually a voluntary membership "activity." It may have authority over many of the campus facilities used by students (including student stores and restaurants), and have limited responsibility for the behavior and activities of individual students, but, for some students, the formal organization of their living groups, the clubs they join, and student organizations formed by academic departments may be more significant influences than campuswide student government.

The most highly publicized activity of United States colleges and universities takes place on the playing fields and in the gymnasiums and stadiums of their sports complexes.

Intercollegiate athletic competition, particularly in popular sports like football, basketball, baseball, and track and field are highly publicized—so much so, in fact, that some institutions owe at least as much of their reputations to the prowess of their athletes as to the excellence of their academic facilities and personnel, and student academic performance.

Intramural athletics involves many more students as participants than intercollegiate sports do. The number of "leagues" involved seems virtually unlimited and may include departmental leagues, living group leagues, faculty leagues, and student activity leagues. More than that, as is the case with almost all of the extracurricular attractions of colleges and universities, sports focus interest and loyalty of students that carries over into their attitudes toward the institution after they become alumni.

5. Conclusion

The most remarkable thing about United States higher education is that despite its involvement of relatively few individuals (in proportion to the total population) it has penetrated deeply into the structure and development of the nation's economic, political, and social life. Even Americans who have never attended college are affected by higher education's influence on the nation's institutions and achievements, and they are becoming accustomed to seeking, almost instinctively, the help of higher education when they become desperate for solutions to their society's problems.

The remarkable thing about the response of colleges and universities to these expectations is that, so far, they have been able to respond to the nation's demands without losing their souls—their sense of what they are. They may, however, be in danger of losing their perspective, promising more than they can deliver, subconsciously revising their mission and their character as they go along.

Evolutionary change is unavoidable and usually desirable, but, in an educational enterprise it is important to avoid being too ready to reshape vital institutions to fit the molds of shifting societal exigencies. As colleges and universities serve the larger society, it is important that they do so in the secure knowledge of their own missions.

The time has probably come for United States colleges and universities to become more thoughtful about the long-term consequences of their responsiveness to every call for help coming from external institutions and contemplate what they might be able to achieve by better understanding themselves and daring to determine and pursue more of their own education initiatives.

Bibliography

Act of Congress of the United States approved July 2, 1862 12 US Statutes at Large, article 7, section 4, 503

Boyer E L 1987 *College: The Undergraduate Experience in America*. The Carnegie Foundation for the Advancement of Teaching, Princeton University Press, Princeton, New Jersey

Brubacher J S, Willis R 1976 *Higher Education in Transition: A History of American Colleges and Universities, 1636–1976*, 3rd edn. Harper and Row, New York

The Carnegie Commission on Higher Education 1971 *The Capitol and the Campus: State Responsibility for Postsecondary Education*. McGraw-Hill, New York

The Carnegie Commission on Higher Education 1973 *Governance of Higher Education: Six Priority Problems*. McGraw-Hill, New York

The Carnegie Commission on Higher Education 1976 *The States and Higher Education: A Proud Past and a Vital Future*. McGraw-Hill, New York

The Carnegie Council on Policy Studies in Higher Education 1979 *Next Steps for the 1980s in Student Financial Aid*. Jossey-Bass, San Francisco, California

The Carnegie Council on Policy Studies in Higher Education 1980 *A Summary of Reports and Recommendations*. Jossey-Bass, San Francisco, California

The Carnegie Foundation for the Advancement of Teaching 1987 *A Classification of Institutions of Higher Education*. Princeton University Press, Princeton, New Jersey

Chronicle of Higher Education 1989 September 6, 1986, p. A32; September 6, 1989

Clark B 1987 *The Academic Life: Small Worlds, Different Worlds*. Princeton University Press, Princeton, New Jersey

Cremin L A 1970 *American Education: The Colonial Experience 1607–1783*. Harper and Row, New York

Editors of The Chronicle of Higher Education: *The Almanac of Higher Education, 1989–90*. University of Chicago Press, Chicago, Illinois

Education Commission of the States 1988 *Postsecondary Education Structures Handbook*

Greeley A M 1972 *From Backwater to Mainstream: A Profile of Catholic Higher Education*. McGraw-Hill, New York

Hines E R 1988 *Association for the Study of Higher Education*. Texas A and M University, Department of Educational Administration, College Station, Texas

Kennedy D 1988 In: Lindsay A W and Neumann R T (eds.) 1988 *Challenge for Research in Higher Education: Harmonizing Excellence and Utility*. ASHE-ERIC Higher Education Reports, 1988, p. 9

Kerr C 1982 *The Uses of the University*, 3rd edn. Harvard University, Cambridge, Massachusetts

Kerr C, Gade M 1985 *The Many Lives of Academic Presidents: Time, Place and Character*. Association of Governing Boards of Universities and Colleges, Washington

Levine A 1978 *Handbook on Undergraduate Education*. Jossey-Bass, San Francisco, California

Newman, F 1985 *Higher Education and the American Resurgence*. The Carnegie Foundation for the Advancement of Teaching, Princeton University Press, Princeton, New Jersey

Pace C R 1972 *Education and Evangelism: A Profile of Protestant Colleges*. McGraw-Hill, New York

Rudolph F 1977 *Curriculum: A History of the American Undergraduate Course of Study Since 1636*. Jossey-Bass, San Francisco, California

V. Stadtman

Uruguay

1. Higher Education and Society

With a population of slightly more than three million inhabitants, Uruguay is one of the smallest countries in Latin America. Data for the five-year period 1985 to 1990 show the annual birthrate (18.9 per thousand) to be the lowest in the region, with the mortality rate rising to 10.2 per thousand. The annual rate of population growth is 0.8 percent, which is less than half the regional average. Between 1970 and 1975 the population showed virtually no increase (0.1% annual rate) as a result of international emigration (*Annuario Estadístico de América Latina y el Caribe*, CEPAL-UN 1988).

Uruguay is atypical due to its early modernization. The nation was one of the few so-called White settler colonies (along with Argentina, Australia, Canada, and New Zealand) which were favored economically under the British Empire. Since the beginning of the twentieth century, Uruguay has enjoyed a modern social and economic structure, based on its extensive cattle production. On this basis, the nation industrialized and developed a tertiary market notably advanced for the period. Additionally, the nation's social stratification has been more similar to that of Europe than the region.

Politically, Uruguay has also been atypical. High democratic stability, the consolidation of political institutions, political parties with long historical traditions, and an extensive network of interest-mediating organizations are characteristic. These trends have been joined by a premature welfare state, advanced social legislation, and secularization of all areas of public life.

Culturally, Uruguay is a homogeneous society, formed by transatlantic immigrants (Europeans with a predominance of Spaniards) and without significant regional, linguistic, ethnic, or religious differences.

The higher education system, since the creation of the *Universidad de la República* (University of the Republic) (1849), and the reforms since 1965, have played a fundamental role in this modernization process. Higher education has contributed to the formation of the citizenry and the development of human resources, and has served as an instrument for social mobility and middle-class consolidation (Rama 1985, Paris 1958).

With the economic crisis unleashed in the mid-1950s and the stagnancy which has followed for more than 30 years, the socioeconomic and political model eroded, culminating in the 1973 coup d'état. Like most areas of life in Uruguay, the higher education system has been affected by these transformations.

2. The Institutional Fabric of the Higher Education System

The University of the Republic is unique in the breadth of its disciplinary coverage and in the diversity of its functional attributes. Almost all of the nation's university level students (61,340)—covering the entire gamut of disciplines and professions—attend this institution. The University accounts for 51 percent of all investigation units, and 56 percent of the ongoing projects and researchers involved in the nation's science and technology system; the remaining investigation is distributed in the minis-

tries, central administration, the public sector and private institutes (Argenti et al. 1988).

In addition to the University of the Republic, Uruguay is the site of the Damaso Antonio Larraña University, a private Catholic institution with 734 students in 1988, and the ORT, an institute specializing in computer science. Both of these institutions are accredited. Finally, since the dictatorial period, six private investigation centers in the social sciences have been formed, as well as other institutions.

Given the central role of the University of the Republic in the higher education system, this brief survey will refer to it alone. The University is entirely free, there are no enrollment limits, quotas, or entry tests. Consequently, admission is unlimited in principle and depends on the level of demand, the aspirations of the student population, and the nation's educational priorities. The University has experienced a notable expansion. The available data show a quadrupling of the University's enrollment in less than 30 years which now reaches 26 percent of those between 20 and 24 years of age (see Table 1).

University admission requires the completion of the *bachillerato* or six-year middle- and high-school program, with professional specialization beginning in the fifth year. One may also enter the University from a technical high school.

Degrees are offered in the liberal arts and scientific professions as well as intermediate degrees of a diverse nature (e.g., paramedic degrees). The University does not have graduate degree programs. However, there have been specializations at the graduate level. In 1989, graduate courses in social sciences were initiated in the newly created Graduate Studies and Investigation Center (CEIPO). Additionally, in 1987, a development program in natural sciences (PEDECIBA), was started, dedicated to research and graduate education in mathematics, biology, chemistry, physics, and computer science.

The University is essentially professionally

Table 1
Evolution of university students in four census periods 1960–88

Year	1960	1968	1974	1988
Students	15,320	18,650	26,220	61,340
Index 100=1960	100	122	171	400
Annual percentage growth rate	—	2.75	8.21	16.41
Percentage of students per persons aged 20–24	8.1	9.3	12.9	26.1
Number of students divided by total population	166	146	106	49

Source: Lémez and Diconca *Primeras aproximaciones a los resultados del IV Censo General de Estudiantes Universitarios* (mimeograph) University of the Republic, Montevideo, 1989

oriented and is structured in faculties and schools. Scientific research is neither autonomous nor organized in independent bodies. Instead, it is undertaken in institutes and centers dependent on the faculties. Formal approval has been granted for separate faculties in natural and social sciences and the humanities. These new faculties will soon be adding their own centers and institutions, which until now have been dispersed in the professionally oriented faculties.

3. Governance, Administration, and Finance

According to existing legislation (the Organic Law of 1958), the University is independent of the state, although it is financed through the national budget. The University is independent with regard to its general orientation, academic development policy, research, and extension. Mechanisms of control or coordination with other educational levels or with the Ministry of Education do not exist.

The institution is governed by faculty, students, and graduates. The highest ruling body is the Central Directive Council composed of 20 members: the president; the deans of the faculties or alternate faculty members; three student representatives; and three graduates. The council's functions are executive and, in practice, legislative. The president and vice-president are granted executive, administrative, and representative powers.

The faculties each have their respective directive councils composed of six faculty members, including the dean, three students, and three graduates. The schools have equivalent organisms proportionately equal in their representation of the three orders.

Above this structure is the General University Council consisting of 77 members (seven per faculty or school) and the faculty councils, all with similar proportional representation given to the three orders. The most important attributes of these bodies are "legislative" and entail the naming of presidents and deans, the approval of reforms in the curriculum or study plans, the creation of institutes and departments, and other major changes in the higher education system.

The University budget is almost totally publicly funded. Other revenue sources such as donations, loans, or research and development contracts are, in practice, quite limited. The annual budget for the 1987 school year was US$53 million or less than 0.7 percent of the Gross National Product (GNP). This figure includes the budget of the Clinical Hospital of the faculty of medicine which provides assistance services comparable to those of the public health sector, and which represents approximately one-third of the University budget and half of the non-university faculty positions. Without the Clinical Hospital, the University budget would be US$36 million.

Since the University budget has not grown with enrollment, the resources per student have deteriorated considerably. Whereas in 1974 the annual expenditure per student, excluding the Clinical Hospital's service budget, was US$822, in 1988 this expenditure fell to US$588.

Certainly these represent some of the lowest comparative figures for higher education at both the regional and international level (Corbo et al. 1989).

4. Faculty and Students: Teaching, Learning, and Research

The extraordinary university expansion has been accompanied by the following quantifiable characteristics: (a) the student body has been "feminized"—in 14 years the percentage of female students has risen from 45 to 58 percent; (b) the average age upon graduation is 27, the average length of study being 7.5 years in the faculties and 4 years in the schools; (c) the percentage of students enrolled in more than one faculty has risen in the past 4 years from 10 percent to 23 percent of enrollment and from 16 percent to 28 percent of graduating students; (d) in 1983, 29 percent of students were employed. (In 1986 this percentage rose to 38 percent. Of those students graduating in 1989, 68 percent were employed.); (e) although the traditional careers (law, medicine, and social sciences) have lost ground, they maintain their preeminence accounting for 58 percent of those enrolled; (f) the student body is increasingly composed of public school graduates (69 percent); (g) lastly, the schools (institutions granting intermediate degrees) have expanded more than the faculties: while the former have experienced a 360 percent growth rate, the latter have only grown 40.9 percent (Lémez 1989).

In general, the social base of the University has been expanded, a change which has been accompanied by a reorientation towards shorter career paths rather than the longer, more prestigious fields of study.

5. Conclusion

A final balance of Uruguay's higher education system in all its complexity cannot be undertaken here. It should be noted, however, that the "virtuous cycle" which previously characterized the University and the society has experienced a deep rupture. The University, at present, does not have the conditions necessary to respond to the nation's demands of innovation, creativity, and the generation of knowledge.

On the one hand, the University has suffered from an incapacity to transform itself. The University's organizational pattern still corresponds to the Napoleonic model which has inspired the institution since its foundation. Modernizing thrusts have existed, although these may be better characterized as timid gestures within an unchanged structure rather than as radical innovations. The University continues to be organized around the college level professional faculties, and power rests in these bodies. Neither curricular standardization nor flexible credit systems exist. The career structure is terminal, and only since the 1980s have graduate research programs been initiated.

On the other hand, the decision-making structure of the University is collegiate, honorary, parliamentary, and extraordinarily diverse with multiple foci of corporative power. Virtually all decision-making processes imply complex and successive mediating mechanisms which involve an elevated and diversified number of individual and collective actors (councils, orders, guilds). This results in a slow, difficult process which favors inertia, blockages, and mutual vetoes.

Lastly, economic constraints make it difficult to conceive of a reasonably efficient higher education system in a completely impoverished university. Without a substantial increase in the resources of the central administration, the enrollment overflow renders practically impossible any new undertakings.

Summarizing, it is unlikely that the above-mentioned characteristics—professionally oriented structure, complex decision-making system, and the lack of economic resources—can be significantly changed in the short run. However, given this background, it is important to note what has been done by the University after the impact suffered during the military intervention (1973–84), and to highlight some transformations and promising indicators. Foremost among these changes has been the impulse given to university–government relations, manifested in the following: research and development contracts and other arrangements; receptivity to alternative sources of finance; and promotion and participation in joint graduate and investigation programs (e.g., PEDECIBA and CONICYT). Also worth noting are the cooperative arrangements with private institutions, the creation of faculties in natural and social sciences, and the formation of a Graduate Social Science Center.

Bibliography

Argenti G, Filgueira C, Sutz J 1988 *Ciencia y Tecnología: un diagnóstico de oportunidades.* Ministerio de Educación y Cultura—CIESU, Montevideo

Corbo D, Menéndez W, Peri A 1989 *La Evolución de los Gastos Públicos en Educación en el Uruguay en el Período 1961 a 1987.* CELADU, Montevideo

Filgueira C, Geneletti C 1981 *Estratificación y Movilidad Ocupacional en América Latina.* CEPAL, Santiago de Chile

Lémez R 1989 *Educación y Sociedad en el Uruguay: realidades y desafíos de cara al Siglo XXI.* FESUB, Montevideo

Paris B 1958 *La Universidad de Montevideo en la Formación de Nuestra Conciencia Liberal, 1849–85.* Universidad de la República, Montevideo

Rama G W 1985 *Education et Société. Problèmes d'Amérique Latine* 77(3), Paris

C. Filgueira

V

Venezuela

1. Higher Education and Society

Venezuela is located on the northern reaches of the Caribbean shores of South America extending over an area of 916,490 square kilometers. It borders Colombia in the west and southwest, Brazil in the south, and Guyana in the east. In 1988, it had a population of approximately 18,650,000, with an estimated annual population growth rate of 2.7 percent. This rate has gradually declined over the last few decades, falling from an average of 4 percent in the period 1951 to 1961, to 3.4 percent from 1961 to 1971, and then to 3.1 percent from 1971 to 1981 (CORDIPLAN 1989).

Since 1958 Venezuela has enjoyed a significantly stable period of democracy. This has been accompanied by: (a) the availability of public funds from oil exports, allowing the needs and aspirations of all social classes to be satisfied to a greater or lesser extent; and (b) the consolidation of a mainly two-party political system, the Social-Democratic *Acción Democrática* Party and the Social Christian *Copei* Party.

In response to criticism, in 1984 the government established the Presidential Commission for State Reform (COPRE). Since 1986, reform projects have been initiated in the following areas: the democratization of the state and society; political reforms; the modernization of public administration; the rationalization of public policies; and the strengthening of community organizations.

With the establishment of the democratic regime in 1958, Venezuela began to consolidate a model of economic development based on import substitution. In 1973 the sharp increase in oil prices enabled the national government to set up an ambitious public investment program in basic industry, essentially in the areas of steel, aluminium, and electricity. Since 1979, however, the economy began to show signs of recession, and by 1982/83 the worst economic figures in recent times were being recorded. From 1984 to 1985, an economic adjustment plan was introduced, aimed at correcting the balance of payments problem and reestablishing economic growth. In 1986 to 1987 the price of crude oil and refined petroleum products fell significantly causing a drastic reduction in export revenue and a change in economic policy. According to some experts, the Venezuelan economy has still not been able to adjust itself to a situation of diminishing export earnings, to the payment of the foreign debt, or to the economic, political, and social consequences of the fall in the standard of living of most of the population. Indeed, although the distribution of wealth between 1959 and 1979 showed signs of levelling out, since 1980 Venezuelan society has gradually become more polarized (Valencillos 1989).

By 1988, the labor force represented some 35 percent of the total population. The distribution of economic activity is estimated to be as follows: agriculture 13.3 percent; mining and petroleum 1.1 percent; manufacturing 18 percent; construction 8.4 percent; public utilities 1 percent; commerce 19 percent; transportation 6.1 percent; services in general 32.3 percent (OCEI 1988).

The percentage of university educated, high-level decision-makers rose from only 9 percent in 1961 to 45 percent in 1985 (Valencillos 1989). This has been possible due to the great development in higher education in the country, which has increased from 20,000 university students in 1960 to approximately 500,000 in 1988. Approximately 25 percent of the 20 to 25 year old population is enrolled in higher education, in comparison with 5.7 percent in 1965, 8.2 percent in 1970, 17.7 percent in 1975, and 21.5 percent in 1980 (CNU–OPSU 1989).

2. The Institutional Fabric of the Higher Education System

As can be seen in Table 1, more than 80 institutions of higher education have been established in the country over the last 30 years. An outstanding feature of this expansion has been its institutional diversification, both at public and private levels. The 91 institutions of higher education that exist may be broken down as follows: (a) 28 universities, of which four are autonomous national universities, 12

Table 1
Venezuela—higher education institutions (1960–88)

Year	1960	1965	1970	1975	1980	1985	1988
Universities	7	9	10	15	18	21	28
(private)	2	3	5	5	5	8	12
Nonuniversities	2	3	3	36	55	62	63
(private)	—	—	—	12	20	26	28
Totals	9	12	13	51	73	83	91
(private)	2	3	5	17	25	34	40

Source: Departamento de Estadísticas 1989 CNU–OPSU

793

Table 2
Venezuela—enrollments in higher education (1960–88)

Year	1960	1965	1970	1975	1980	1985	1988
Universities	20,652	37,719	66,218	165,238	236,562	285,785	325,511
(private)	2,634	5,724	4,736	18,126	24,649	42,825	52,113
Nonuniversities	1,436	2,708	4,598	28,024	60,164	97,752	141,863
(private)	—	—	—	3,070	14,220	28,095	46,641
Totals	22,088	40,427	70,816	193,262	296,726	383,537	467,374
(private)	2,634	5,724	4,736	21,196	38,869	70,920	98,754

Source: Departamento de Estadísticas 1989 CNU–OPSU

national experimental, and 12 private; (b) 63 non-university institutions, made up of seven colleges of education (six public and one private), four national polytechnics, 46 technological institutes and university colleges, which are similar to junior colleges in the United States, (21 public and 25 private), four military university institutes, and two university institutes specializing in ecclesiastical studies.

The private universities have more than doubled in number in less than 10 years, increasing from 5 in 1980 to 12 in 1989. But the greatest expansion has occurred in nonuniversity institutions, both public and private, which have increased from zero in 1970 to 63 in 1988. However, although the private sector has expanded rapidly, it still comprises only 21 percent of the total number of students enrolled in institutions of higher education. This is mainly due to the great number of students enrolled in the autonomous national universities, not least among them the *Universidad Central de Venezuela*.

The number of students enrolled in higher education has grown steadily (see Table 2). As in most other Latin American countries, this was favored in the 1960s by official policies aimed at educational democratization and the formation of the human resources necessary for development. In addition, the labor market made its own demands on human resources linked to the process of development during this period. The very heavy demand for higher education continues. However, the capacity of the higher education system to expand seems to have reached its limits, insofar as available financial resources are concerned.

In view of this, in 1984 the academic aptitude test became mandatory, thereby modifying and reorganizing the criteria on admissions that had been used since 1973. These changes involve the use of what is known as the Academic Index as the basis for selection. This index is derived from taking the average grades obtained in the first four years of high school (a factor which is given a weight of 60 percent), along with the result of the academic aptitude test (20 percent verbal reasoning and 20 percent numerical ability).

The number of students at graduate level has also grown significantly over the last two decades. From 1970 onwards graduate studies, both master's and doctoral degrees, underwent a gradual process of consolidation and institutionalization. In 1984, the National Advisory Council on Graduate Studies was established. This body advises the National University Council (CNU) on matters of policy related to graduate programs. The Advisory Council is also responsible for accrediting graduate programs in universities and other institutions of higher education. By 1988, 571 graduate courses were offered, of which 59 were at the doctoral level, 262 at the master's level, and 250 specialized (see Table 3).

In 1974 as graduate programs were developing, the government began to send large numbers of students abroad to study, using a specially created foundation—the *Gran Mariscal de Ayacucho*. During its most important phase, from 1974 to 1983, 6,698 scholarships for study in foreign universities were awarded (Fundación 1984).

The institutionalization of research in Venezuela began seriously in the 1950s when a group of researchers established the Venezuelan Association for the Advancement of Science (ASOVAC) in order to promote and support the growing research community. Over the last 25 years, scientific and technological activity in institutions of higher education

Table 3
Venezuela—distribution of graduate courses (1985–88)

Year	1985		1988	
Type of Degree	Totals	University	Totals	University
Doctorate	36	33	59	50
Masters	215	184	262	216
Specialization	206	186	250	242
Totals	457	403	571	508

Sources: Boletín Estadístico 1987. CNU–OPSU; Directorio Nacional de Estudios de Postgrado 1988. CNU

has been promoted. In 1958, the Law on Universities established the basis for the development of a university research policy. This law created a Scientific and Humanistic Development Council at each university that stimulates and coordinates research in the natural, social, and human sciences. The Council is responsible for assessing the state of research in the universities and for promoting research activities. They also sponsor programs which provide financial assistance to researchers, travel funds to attend scientific meetings and to take study trips, as well as subsidies for the purchase of publications, research projects, and for the upkeep and improvement of libraries, laboratories, equipment, and so on. In 1967, the government established the National Scientific and Technological Research Council (CONICIT), which has since played an important role in supporting and promoting the efforts of institutions of higher education and the training of researchers.

The number of researchers has steadily increased, growing from 2,500 in 1970 to around 4,500 in 1983. The number of research projects and units has correspondingly risen: from 300 units in 1970 to over 6,000 in 1983 (CNU–OPSU 1986).

3. Governance, Administration, and Finance

3.1 National Administration

The system of higher education in Venezuela is comprised of (a) the university sector and (b) the university colleges and institute sector.

The university sector is coordinated by the National University Council (CNU), which is responsible for: (a) defining the general policies which guide the development of the university system, establishing detailed policies and objectives and assessing the universities that make up the system; (b) coordinating university activities throughout the country; (c) establishing the requirements for the creation, elimination, or modification of faculties, schools, institutes, and other equivalent divisions in all the universities; (d) evaluating projects, public or private, for the establishment of new universities, university institutes and university colleges; (e) providing the national executive with the annual budget requests for the universities and distributing the funds approved by the Congress; and (f) ensuring compliance with the law as it concerns the universities.

A Law on Universities exists, which governs the national autonomous universities and authorizes the experimental ones to function by way of special exception clauses. The private universities are also subject to certain provisions of the Law, and the Ministry of Education exercises a certain amount of control especially regarding the awarding of degrees.

The university colleges and institute sector is governed by a regulation promulgated by the National Executive in 1974. The Ministry of Education, through its Office on Higher Education, essentially establishes general policy guidelines regarding institutional development, as well as the supervision, control, coordination, and assessment of these institutions. This office basically fulfills for this sector what the National University Council and its backup offices do for the university sector.

3.2 Institutional Administration

The national autonomous universities constitute the oldest, most prestigious and largest institutions of higher education in the country. This group includes: the *Universidad Central de Venezuela* (1721); the *Universidad de Los Andes* (1810); the *Universidad del Zulia* (1891); and the *Universidad de Carabobo* (1892). The *Universidad Central* is located in the capital, Caracas, and the other three in important provincial state capitals.

This type of university enjoys organizational, academic, administrative, economic, and financial autonomy, and is governed along collegial lines with distinct hierarchical levels, and an academic structure built around faculties. These, in turn, are made up of schools, institutes, and research centers. The bodies responsible for running these universities are, in order of importance: the University Council; faculty assemblies; the faculty; and the school councils.

Each university has its own cultural office, which promotes and directs the institution's cultural activities, and a sports center to stimulate, develop, and coordinate sports of all kinds.

The national experimental universities are institutions created by the state in order to experiment with new academic and administrative approaches to higher education. They enjoy autonomy under the legal provisions for experimental education. Their organization and operation is set out by executive decree (Article 10 of the Law on Universities).

In most of the experimental universities, the Minister of Education or the president of the republic appoints the university authorities (rector, vice-rectors, and secretary). In some cases, the institutions themselves propose candidates to the executive through an internal voting process in which members of the teaching staff and the student body participate.

With some exceptions, authorized by the National Council of Universities, private universities must comply with the following norms concerning internal governance and organizations: (a) they must maintain the same academic structure as the national nonexperimental universities; (b) only those faculties approved by the National University Council are allowed to function; (c) legally, a minimum number of three academically distinct faculties are required before the university may receive students; (d) the university authorities, teaching staff, and researchers must fulfill those conditions established in the Law

Table 4
Venezuela—comparative chart of higher education's budget in relation to the national and education budgets in US$[a]

Year	1965	1970	1975	1980	1985	1988
National budget	1,764,465	2,392,093	9,273,953	16,946,186	7,386,135	5,177,513
Education budget	203,116	388,046	1,120,232	2,406,418	1,131,721	780,010
Education percentage	11.5	16.2	12.1	14.2	15.3	15.1
Higher Ed. budget	49,697	122,534	425,441	870,953	383,507	300,115
Higher Ed. percentage	24.4	31.6	38.0	36.2	33.9	38.5

Source: Departamento de Estadísticas 1989. CNU–OPSU
a For the years 1965–80 the value of the dollar was 4.30 bolivares; in 1985 there were 14.0 bolivares (on average) per dollar; and in 1989 36 bolivares (on average) per dollar

on Universities; (e) the degrees and certificates awarded by the university are only legal upon ratification by the National Executive.

Each university institute or college establishes its own procedures and rules of self-governance. These rules have to be approved by the Ministry of Education and, in the case of official institutes not dependent upon this ministry, they must also seek the approval of the ministry or public body to which they are attached. In every university institute and college, there is an administrative council, an academic council, a director, and one or two subdirectors.

3.3 Finance

Since public higher education is free, public sector institutions depend almost entirely upon financing from the national budget. Revenue obtained, where the case may be, through the generation of income (especially from graduate courses, enrollment fees, and extension courses) is negligible. Indeed, the state provides around 95 percent of all financial support.

Higher education spending has gone through three distinct stages: first there was a period of "slow growth" until 1973. During this period, the three sources of financial support (national budget, Ministry of Education budget, and the budget set aside for higher education) were subject to gradual increases and did not differ from one another to any large extent. In 1972, the budget for higher education rose significantly (by 80 percent in comparison to the previous year). Second came a period of "explosive growth" from 1972 to 1981. During this period the three types of budgets mentioned grew apace, fed by the more than healthy financial state of the country which was a product of the oil boom and the high levels of economic activity registered until 1977. The recession, which began in 1978 did not, however, affect the education budget, particularly that part devoted to higher education. In the third period, 1981 to 1985, the budget for higher education grew by only 1.6 percent, at a minimum biannual rate of only 0.39 percent. The national budget rose by a mere 2.3 percent, and that of the Ministry of Education by 3.6 percent (Silva Michelena 1988). In 1988, however, the higher education budget rose sharply once again, representing 38.5 percent of the total spent on education that year. This was mainly due to the payment of wage demands to university professors (see Table 4).

Table 5
Venezuela—academic teaching staff in higher education (1960–88)

Year	1960	1965	1970	1975	1980	1985	1988
Universities	1,899	3,641	6,799	11,661	20,369	20,791	22,987
(private)	289	200	689	1,002	1,399	2,297	3,303
Nonuniversities	155	294	499	2,943	6,264	8,405	13,179
(private)	—	—	—	374	1,393	2,575	3,919
Totals	2,054	3,935	7,298	14,604	26,633	29,196	36,157
(private)	289	200	689	1,376	2,792	4,872	7,222

Source: Departamento de Estadística 1989. CNU–OPSU

4. Faculty and Students: Teaching, Learning, and Research

4.1 Faculty

In the 15 years from 1965 to 1980, the number of teachers employed at the higher level almost doubled every five years. Since 1980, though, the rate of expansion has slowed to some extent. However, the number of teachers in the nonuniversity sector and in the private universities has grown steadily, a product of the institutional growth with its corresponding increase in student numbers mentioned above (see Table 5).

According to the type of contractual agreement, teaching staff can be classified as: (a) "exclusive," full-time teachers, who must not teach elsewhere or hold other employment and are generally expected to work around 40 hours per week; (b) full-time teachers, working between 30 and 36 hours per week and who are thus permitted to take up paid work outside these hours; (c) teachers who work half-time; and (d) part-time staff paid on an hourly basis. In 1985, the percentage of "exclusive," full-time teachers was 62.2 percent, whereas the percentage of part-time (half-time and hourly paid) was 37.8 percent (CNU–OPSU 1987).

University teaching and research staff are categorized and promoted, both in the national autonomous universities and in the private ones, in accordance with the regulations stipulated in the Law on Universities. The experimental universities have been permitted to establish a slightly different system in terms of placement and promotion. For university institutes and colleges, there exists a special regulation, established by the National Executive in 1974, which determines the system to be adopted in these institutions. This regulation establishes the same categories stipulated in the Law on Universities, but lays down a different system when it comes to the classification and promotion of personnel.

Teaching and research staff are placed into four categories: ordinary; special; honorary; and retired. The ordinary members in the universities and, with some exceptions, in the university institutes and colleges, enter through open competition and are placed on the scale, and rise up it, according to their credentials, scientific and professional merits, and years of service. Furthermore, to ascend one place up the scale, staff members must produce an original piece of research, which is then placed before a committee or jury as evidence of merit.

In the universities, all new teachers begin their careers as instructors, the lowest level on the scale, unless they are permitted to enter at a higher level, as laid down in Article 91 of the Law on Universities. The subsequent categories after instructor are: assistant professor; aggregate professor; associate professor; and, at the top, full professor. Teachers usually spend four years at each level and, apart from

Table 6
Venezuela—distribution of students across the main subject areas (1980, 1985, 1987)

Year	1980	1985	1987
Exact sciences	117,405	165,640	177,946
Social sciences	89,867	160,847	178,682
Humanities and education	46,528	93,140	101,154
Unknown	54,103	23,856	—
Totals	307,903	443,422	457,782

Source: Boletín Estadístico 1987 CNU–OPSU; Departamento de Estadística 1989 CNU–OPSU

submitting the research work previously mentioned, in order to rise to the level of associate professor, a doctoral degree is required.

In the university institutes and colleges, the system is different. Teachers may enter as instructors, assistants, or aggregate professors according to previous experience and their credentials.

There are two federations of teachers' unions at the national level: the Venezuelan Federation of University Professors Associations (FAPUV) and the Venezuelan Federation of University Colleges and Institutes Teachers' Association (FAPICUV). These unions have striven to obtain a greater degree of power and participation in the administration of higher education, as well as in decision-making itself. These organizations have increased their activities in order to obtain better working conditions and improved salary structures for their members, using such pressures as strike action, which has led to the occasional paralysis of academic activities.

4.2 Students

Information on student distribution by areas of study is very scarce; however, the information that is available points to a fair proportion of students in the natural sciences. This proportion has been maintained throughout the 1980s (see Table 6), due to the fact that the private sector of higher education has tended to develop areas of study in the social sciences and humanities because of their cost effectiveness and because of the employment opportunities for graduates (in fields such as economics, administration, law, education) (García-Guadilla 1988).

The significant growth in the number of graduates that has occurred since 1960 is illustrated in Table 7.

The distribution of students according to gender for the year 1984 is quite homogeneous, and even shows a higher percentage of women than men both in total (53.6 percent women) and in the university sector alone (54.5 percent) (see Table 8). However, in spite of the progress achieved by women in edu-

Table 7
Venezuela—higher education graduates (1960–87)

Period	1960–64	1965–69	1970–74	1975–79	1980–84	1985–87
Universities	10,100	18,096	29,096	50,366	68,802	57,864
Totals	11,194	20,311	33,185	65,790	106,037	89,290

Sources: Barrios 1984; Departamento de Estadísticas 1989 CNU–OPSU

Table 8
Venezuela—female university students 1984

Sector	Totals	Women
Universities	251,696	137,297
Nonuniversities	97,752	50,189
Totals	349,448	187,486

Source: Boletín Estadístico 1987 CNU–OPSU

cation and, despite the fact that women make up a significant number of professionals and technicians, their participation in management and in executive positions continues to be slight.

Regarding student social classification, Table 9 illustrates that 32 percent of the university population belongs to the upper or middle classes.

5. Conclusion

Over the last 30 years, higher education in Venezuela has undergone far-reaching changes. One significant feature has been the energetic role the state has played in providing more educational opportunities. Through this process of expansion, access has been given to sectors of society traditionally excluded (especially women and the lower-middle class). At the same time, higher education has also become more complex by providing undergraduates and graduates with numerous educational options.

In 1991 however, the system is facing serious financial difficulties as a result of the country's econ-omic instability. The better public institutions, where graduate programs and research projects are usually conducted, are financially dependent upon the state, therefore, the economic recession is making deep inroads into their day-to-day operation. But this has not altered the demands of the teachers' unions for pay increases in accordance with the rate of inflation. However, the government is considering the fact that higher education receives more than its fair share of budget resources in comparison with the other educational levels, especially since in the free public institutions of higher education a good many of the students come from comfortable middle-class backgrounds. Thus a significant amount of public money assigned to education is dedicated, in practice, to a select group of people belonging to upper-middle and higher social classes, a group that, in most cases, has received an expensive private education before entering the university.

In spite of the above, few have yet realized that the new situation facing the country demands the search for new alternatives so as not to waste the advances made by higher education over the last 30 years. It is not easy to predict the changes that might occur insofar as the organization and administration of higher education are concerned. Even though everything would seem to suggest that the situation should be tackled from a different point of view, it is only in some circles—as yet very small—that discussions have begun regarding the need to create alternative sources of revenue to augment those provided by the state. Measures to ensure the efficient use of resources have also been considered. Other alternatives include offering the services of the university to the community and to the other educational levels completely free of charge as a way of repaying the nonuniversity society that which the state has invested in this higher educational level.

Table 9
Venezuela—new university students accepted by social stratum 1985

Social stratum	Number	Percentage
High	5,092	8
Medium-high	15,092	24
Medium-low	27,693	42
Manual worker	16,490	25
Marginal	1,439	2

Source: Boletín Estadístico No. 12 1987 CNU–OPSU

Bibliography

Albornoz O 1987 *Reforma del Estado y Educaciòn*. Ediciones de la COPRE, Caracas

Barrios M 1984a *Análisis del Comportamiento de la Demanda de Oportunidades de Estudios de Educación Superior*. CNU–OPSU, Caracas

Barrios M 1984b *La Educación Superior en Venezuela*. CRESAL/OPSU, Caracas

Briceño C, Piñango R 1984 *La Estratificación Social de las Instituciones de Educación Superior.* OPSU–IESA, Caracas

Bronfenmajer G, Casanova R 1982 Democracia Burguesa, Crisis Política y Universidad Liberal. In: Rama G (ed.) 1982 *Universidad, Clases Sociales y Poder.* Edit. Ateneo, Caracas, pp. 269–309

Banco Central de Venezuela 1987 *Informe Económico.* Banco Central, Caracas

Cárdenas A 1988 Investigación y Universidad. *Revista Investigación y Postgrado,* 1988 3(4): 9–24

Casanova R 1986 *Postgrado en América Latina. Investigación sobre el Caso de Venezuela.* CRESALC/UNESCO, Caracas

Casanova R 1989 *La Crisis de la Idea de Universidad.* CENDES–UCV, Caracas

CENDES-Asociación de Profesores UCV-CDCH 1985 *Análisis del Proyecto de la Ley de Educación Superior.* Foro-Seminario, Caracas

Comisión Presidencial para la Reforma del Estado (COPRE) 1989 *Proyecto de Reforma Integral del Estado.* COPRE, Caracas

Congreso Nacional de Educación 1989 *La Educación Superior.* Congreso Nacional de Educación, Caracas

Consejo Nacional de Universidades, Oficina de Planificación del Sector Universitario (CNU–OPSU) 1986 *División de Estadísticas, Ciencia y Tecnologia en Cifras,* No. 3. CNU–OPSU, Caracas

Consejo Nacional de Universidades, Oficina de Planificación del Sector Universitario (CNU–OPSU) 1979–1987 *Boletines Estadíscos, 1989.* Datos obtenidos en el Dpto. de Estadística, Caracas

Consejo Nacional de Universidades, Oficina de Planificación del Sector Universitario (CNU–OPSU) 1988 *Directorio Nacional de Estudios de Postgrado.* CNU–OPSU, Caracas

Esté N, Liprandi R 1984 *Estrategias Sociopolíticas en la Educación Superior Venezolana.* CENDES, Caracas

Fajardo V 1988 Perspectivas de la Economía Venezolana. *Cuadernos del Cendes* 1988 8: 11–34

Fundación Gran Mariscal de Ayacucho 1984 *Memoria y Cuenta.* Fundación Gran Mariscal de Ayachucho, Caracas

Gamus E, Hung L 1989 Educación Superior y Mercado de Empleo en el Sector Industrial en Venezuela. In: Morales D, Gallart M (eds.) 1989 *Tendencias en Educación Superior y Trabajo en América Latina.* IDRS, pp. 5–30

Garcia-Guadilla C 1986 El Acceso a la Educación Superior desde la Perspectiva de los Estudiantes. In: Tedesco J C (ed.) 1986 *La Juventud en América Latina.* CRESAL/ILDIS, Caracas, pp. 69–131

Garcia-Guadilla C 1988 Expansión y Diferenciación del Sector Privado de la Educación Superior en América Latina. *Revista de Educación Superior para América Latina y el Caribe* 26: 37–64

Garcia-Guadilla C 1989 Educación Superior en América Latina: Areas Críticas y Desafíos Conceptuales. *Revista Latinoamericana de Estudios Educativos* 1989 4(14): 53–92

Godoy C R 1987 *El Financiamiento de la Educación Superior en Venezuela.* Consejo Nacional de Universidades, Caracas

Gómez C L 1988 La Democracia Venezolana entre la Renovación y el Estancamiento. *Pensamiento Iberoamericano, Revista de Economía Política* 14: 181–95

Klubitschko D 1984 El Origen Social de los Estudiantes Universitarios. El Caso Venezolano. In: Graciarena J (ed.) 1984 *Universidad y Desarrollo en América Latina y el Caribe.* CRESALC/UNESCO, Caracas, pp. 143–82

Lerner de Almea R 1988 Treinta Años del Binomio Democracia-Educación en Venezuela. *Opinión Pedagógica* 1988, July to December, Caracas, pp. 15–32

Marta Sosa J 1984 *El Estado y la Educación Superior en Venezuela.* Equinocio, Caracas

Núcleo de Vice-rectores Administrativos 1987 *Escenarios Financieros.* CNU–OPSU, Caracas

Oficina Central de Estadística (OCEI) 1988 *Indicadores de la Fuerza de Trabajo. Segundo Semestre, 1988,* OCEI, Caracas

Oficina Central de Información y Planificación (CORDIPLAN) 1986 VIII Plan de La Nación, Caracas

Oficina Central de Información y Planificación (CORDIPLAN) 1989 *Diasper,* Caracas

Pérez M A, Hernández A, Layrisse M, Guedez V, Alva Soler F 1989 Politicas y Prospectiva de la Educación Superior en Venezuela. *Universitas 2000,* 13(1), pp. 13–45

Silva M, Castillo D 1985 *La Admisión en la Educación Superior Venezolana.* CNU–OPSU, Caracas

Silva M 1987 *El Carácter Diferenciador de la Educación Media Privada.* CNU–OPSU, Caracas

Silva Michelena J A (ed.) 1987 *Venezuela hacia el 2000. Desafíos y Opciones.* Edit. Nueva Sodiedad, ILDIS-UNITAR-PROFAL, Caracas

Silva Michelena H 1988 *El Colapso de la Universidad Venezolana: ¿Proximidad o Lejanía?* Universidad Central de Venezuela, Caracas

Valencillos H 1989 Regresión en la distribución del Ingreso. Perspectivas y Opciones de Política. In: Nissen H, Mommer B (eds.) 1989, *¿Adios a la Bonanza? Crisis de la Distribución del Ingreso en Venezuela.* ILDIS/CENDES, Editorial Nueva Sociedad, Caracas, pp. 63–93

C. Garcia-Guadilla

Vietnam

1. Higher Education and Society

Vietnam is situated in Indochina and covers 330,000 square kilometers. It spreads out along the meridian, bordered by the Pacific Ocean on the east. Apart from large delta regions in the north, south and center of the country, the rest of the land is mountainous. According to the 1989 census, the total population of Vietnam is 64 million, with an average density of 200 per square kilometer. The distribution is not equal: about 800 per square kilometer in the Red River delta, and about 100 per square kilometer in the midland and mountain areas. The population is ethnically mixed, with the majority being Viet (87%), and minorities including Tay, Thai, Hoa, Khmer, Muong and Nung (about 1% each). Religious beliefs play a significant role in Vietnam. The most important is Buddhism, followed by Roman Catholicism, but no single religion is over-powerful in the spiritual life of the Vietnamese people. The biggest cities in Vietnam are Ho Chi Minh City, with about 4 million inhabitants, Hanoi, with 3 million, and Haiphong, with 1 million.

Vietnam became a French colony in 1883. By then the French were already in control and they established a feudalist puppet state. During the French colonial period, the struggle for independence was an underground movement. In August 1945 a revolution broke out eliminating the French regime, and establishing a democratic state with Ho Chi Minh as its president. Immediately the new state led a nine-year resistance war against the return of the French. In 1954, after the Dien Bien Phu victory, Vietnam was divided into two zones by the Geneva agreement: the north was controlled by the revolutionary government and the south came under the United States' influence. Vietnam then began a 21-year war against the United States, which ended in April 1975 when North and South were reunited as the Socialist Republic of Vietnam.

Vietnam was a backward agricultural country after enduring 30 years of war. This justifies its slow development. Farming occupies 72 percent of the labor force, industry 16 percent, and 12 percent are in the armed forces.

Before 1987, the Vietnamese economy was centralized, an economic model from wartime. After 1987 there was a great change in state economic and social policies, based on the government's recognition of the existence of a multisectored economy (state, collective, private, and social). This is changing a centralized subsidized system to a marketing system.

Central government is responsible for political and social leadership. The country is divided into small administrative units: 40 provinces and some big cities, each of which is controlled by its local authorities. The national educational system is directed by the Ministry of Education and Training.

As a country with an ancient culture, Vietnam has had a traditional educational system since the tenth century AD. The first university institution in Vietnam, Royal College (*Quoc Tu Giam*), was founded at the beginning of the eleventh century. Its task was to train candidates, mainly children from aristocratic families, for national exminations. This system of education and examination were regularly practiced until the early twentieth century.

Under French domination the traditional educational system was gradually removed, being replaced by a type of colonial education with a very small number of primary and secondary schools. These were organized after the low-grade school model in France. As for higher education, there were a few institutions which trained middle-level medical workers and technicians. It was not until 1940 that the French-run Indochinese authorities officially founded the University of Indochina for the three

colonial countries in this region: Vietnam, Laos, and Kampuchea. Even during the years of its greatest expansion, this university was composed of only three major faculties (medicine, law, and sciences) together with some institutions providing higher professional courses on agriculture, civil engineering, and a few other technical fields. The total number of students was not greater than 1,000. Professors and teachers were mostly French.

After 1945, the revolutionary government considered the development of education as one of the most important tasks of the newly independent Republic of Vietnam. In September 1945 the University of Vietnam was established on the basis of the former University of Indochina, but the war waged by the French colonialists hindered its activities. Its medical faculty, teacher-training and civil engineering colleges had to evacuate to rural areas or jungles to continue training cadres to serve the resistance war and people in the liberated zones. Due to the difficulties caused by the war their activities were limited.

After the 1954 Geneva agreement, higher education in the North embarked on a new stage of development. Up to 1965, there were about 16 higher educational institutions in North Vietnam with a total number of about 30,000 students. This system provided cadres for postwar reconstruction work and for the socioeconomic development of the Democratic Republic of Vietnam. In South Vietnam, during the period from 1954 to 1963, higher education was gradually restored and developed. The Higher Educational Institutes of Saigon, Hue, and Dalat were successively founded and training opportunities expanded.

Between 1965 and 1975 war spread from North to South Vietnam. In the North, despite great difficulties caused by United States bombings, higher education still continued to develop. Some new colleges such as the College of Forestry, the College of Marine Products, the College of Geology and Mining, and the College of Finance were established. Up until early 1975 there were 36 higher educational institutions in operation with over 75,000 students in the North. At the same time, in the cities of the South higher education also widened its scope. At the beginning of 1975, there were seven state-owned and private universities, two central institutes of technology, and some specialized colleges with over 93,000 students. After the liberation of the whole country in 1975 all the higher educational institutions in Vietnam were integrated into a unified national higher educational system.

2. The Institutional Fabric of the Higher Education System

Before 1987, the higher educational system of the Socialist Republic of Vietnam had the following

Table 1
Development of the Vietnamese higher education system

	1975–76	1980–81	1982–83	1984–85	1986–87	1988–89
Institutions	59	95	94	93	98	102
Teaching staff	9,642	17,297	18,375	18,717	18,702	20,212
Students	92,097	145,636	140,636	124,524	125,048	128,751

characteristics: the function of higher education was to train cadres for governmental offices and specialists for the state and collective economic sectors, according to the centralized state plans. All expenditure on higher education was granted by the state and graduates were assigned jobs according to government economic planning.

Since 1987, thanks to the new socioeconomic policies, measures have been taken to reform the higher educational system so that it would be responsible for the improvement of the people's knowledge and the supply of qualified staff for various economic sectors.

In the 1988–1989 academic year, there were 70 higher education institutions and 32 junior high schools in Vietnam. The higher education institutions comprise nine universities; nine teacher-training colleges; 14 colleges of engineering; 10 colleges of agriculture, forestry, and fishery; eight colleges of economics; 13 colleges of pharmacy, medicine, gymnastics and sports; and seven colleges of culture and arts. The total number of teachers and students are about 20,000 and 130,000 respectively.

Table 1 shows the variation in the number of higher education institutions, teachers, and students from 1975 to 1989. Growth was at its peak in 1981–1982 then began decreasing due to state financial difficulties. Since 1987 the decrease has stopped owing to new policies.

The higher educational institutions and junior colleges are distributed throughout the country as follows: Hanoi (30), Ho Chi Minh City (16), Hue (6), Haiphong (3), Danang (2), Ha Son Binh (6), Thainguyen (5), Cantho (6).

The majority of the higher educational institutions in Vietnam in the 1990s are state-founded. In early 1989, the state allowed a pilot private institution (Thang Long Center of Higher Education) to be established on a small scale, in which teaching subjects such as mathematics and computer science require less expensive equipment.

In Vietnam higher education consists of undergraduate and graduate programs. The undergraduate program is of two types: long-term (higher education) and short-term training (junior high education).

The long-term program lasts six years in medical college, five years in some colleges of engineering and foreign languages, and four years in others.

In the early 1990s, under the reform of the higher education system, the training program is divided into two phases: phase 1, lasting two years, equips the students with a basic knowledge of science and technology; phase 2, lasting two to four years, provides the students with specialized knowledge. Students who have passed phase 1 are granted a diploma of general higher education. With this diploma they can take examinations to enter phase 2 for appropriate specialist fields. At the end of phase 2, students have to write a thesis or design a project and are awarded a degree.

The short-term program (junior high education) is a lower-level higher educational system which produces cadres with a more practical knowledge than that of the long-term program. These cadres can put their knowledge at the service of the districts, cooperatives, and mountainous regions, or work as teachers of basic general schools. The short-term program is located beside the long-term one within each institution. Students enrolled into this program are all those who have finished vocational or job-training schools, and workers who have graduated from the secondary general schools. All those who have obtained the diploma of general higher education, but are unable to enter phase 2 can attend the last year of this short-term program, which normally lasts two to three years.

There are two types of training courses in the higher educational programs: full-time and inservice. The inservice courses are to meet the requirements of people at work, and may also be long-term or short-term.

There are two types of training at the graduate level: the master's program and the doctoral program. The master's program is for those who have achieved outstanding results in their higher education courses or for those who have a higher education degree and want to improve their qualifications. This program lasts up to two years, with the aim of equipping students with theoretical and practical knowledge in a certain field. Students have to write a thesis or design a major project.

Doctoral candidates have to learn and pass "minimum" examinations in one social science, one foreign language, and a specialized subject (research field). A doctoral thesis must show creativeness on theory or on practical applicability to a narrow speciality. The program lasts at least four years. Those who have

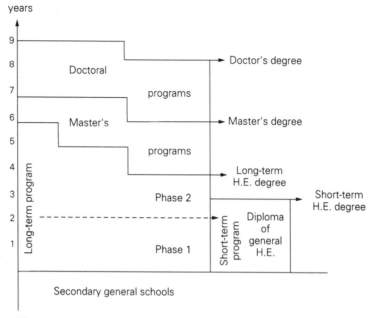

Figure 1
Vietnamese higher education system

a master's degree are exempted from the "minimum" examinations, and can concentrate their efforts on their thesis. After their thesis is successfully defended, a specialized doctoral degree is awarded.

The Vietnamese higher educational system is illustrated in Fig. 1.

Both long-term and short-term programs operate on a credit system. The short-term program requires 150–170 credits; while the long-term program requires 200–270 credits, according to the length of the program. The credit is estimated by one theoretical class hour in one semester (15 weeks) or by a number of hours spent on other equivalent study activities (practice, seminars, theses, etc.).

Table 2
Percentage of study devoted to particular areas of learning

Areas of learning	Long-term percentage	Short-term percentage
General subjects: social sciences, gymnastics, military training, and foreign languages	10–20	8–10
Basic sciences and technology	60–70	18–20
Specialized subjects	18–22	70–72

Areas of learning are approximately distributed as shown in Table 2.

3. Governance, Administration, and Finance

The Ministry of Education and Training directly manages (i.e., directly grants expenditure and assigns personnel) the 38 most important universities and colleges and the nine teacher-training colleges. Other ministries run a few other colleges which provide specialized staff for them. The provincial authorities also directly manage some junior high schools in their localities. However, whichever ministries or localities these institutions may belong to, their specialities are under the control of the Ministry of Education and Training, which approves the teaching programs and training fields; and issues regulations on enrollment, examinations, and the granting of degrees and diplomas.

The organization of Vietnamese higher educational institutions is as follows: the rector is appointed by the Minister. To assist the rector are vice-rectors and such offices and departments as administrative; coordination of study; scientific research management; labor and production; personnel and accounts offices. Also advising the rector are the Institution Council, consisting of representatives of all faculties, departments, offices, and some professors and students; and a Scientific Research and Training Council consisting of experienced scientists and educationalists inside and outside the institution. The institution is composed of various faculties covering a study field (or groups of study fields); below the faculty are various specialist sections.

The scale of a Vietnamese college is generally small, each having a teaching staff of less than a thousand. Under the reform of higher education there has been a tendency to merge smaller institutions.

Before 1987, the higher education budget was granted by the state and was estimated to occupy from 3 percent to 5 percent of the general budget. All students were granted almost the same scholarships. Since 1987, financing for all institutions has come from different sources: from the state (central and local), from scientific contracts and production, from foreign aid, and students' contributions. At present, the budget from other sources is about 50 percent of the amount subsidized by the state. This figure varies depending on the type of the institution. Students who are granted scholarships by the state make up about 50–70 percent of the total number. The granting of scholarships is based on social policies (i.e., war martyrs' children, orphans, and minority group children) and also on the results of the students' study. Scholarships are not the same for every student as before, but classed into various levels. Students who are not included in the social policies and whose study results are bad have to pay tuition fees.

4. Faculty and Students: Teaching, Learning, and Research

4.1 Faculty

The number of college and junior high school teachers estimated in the 1987–88 academic year is 20,212. Women account for 30.8 percent, doctors and masters 10.1 percent and minority groups 1.7 percent.

Teachers in higher educational institutions are ranked according to their titles: professor grade 2, professor grade 1, senior lecturer, lecturer, lecturer assistant. The titles of professor grade 2 and grade 1 are certified by the chair of the Council of Ministers on the proposal of the Central Council of Scientific Title Awards Approval. The titles of senior lecturer and lecturer are certified by the Minister of Education and Training. The title of lecturer assistant is certified by the rector.

A college teacher's tasks include (a) lecturing to undergraduate and graduate students and educating them in ideology and morality; (b) carrying out scientific research and applying it practically; (c) educating students in scientific subjects and participating in social and economic activities; (d) taking part in institution management; and (e) participating in possible international cooperations.

To increase the number of teachers with higher titles, the state has evolved a policy of sending them on master's and doctoral courses both at home and abroad.

The teachers have a right to join the Educational Trade Union and the professional leagues, either national or international. Apart from the time working for their employers, the teachers can work on contract with other universities or research institutions.

Teachers are assigned the same number of hours of teaching and research work defined by the Ministry, and are paid for extra hours. Their teaching is annually assessed in their departments.

4.2 Students

The enrollment of students is annually carried out through an entrance examination. Candidates are permitted to take the entrance examinations if they have graduated from secondary general schools or secondary vocational schools, are in good health, and are under 32 years of age (under 35 for women, for those who have taken part in production work or served in the army for over three years, and for minority groups). Before 1987, enrollment was organized by the Ministry for all institutions throughout the country. Since the 1987–88 academic year enrollment has been organized by each institution, but they must observe the regulations forwarded by the Ministry.

Of the total number of students in higher educational institutions and junior high schools for the 1987–88 academic year women occupy 39 percent and minority group students 5.4 percent.

Since 1976, the government has officially decided to organize graduate courses. Up to 1988, 64 institutions and institutes of scientific research have been allowed to train graduate students. Out of 2,105 graduate students 798 have successfully defended their dissertations.

In their institutions and schools, students can join trade unions, the Ho Chi Minh Communist Youth Union, the Students' Union, or the Women's Union. They can also join cultural and scientific groups.

Before the 1987–88 academic year the teaching program was mainly organized according to "academic year" regulations taking the academic year as the major study unit. In this way, students were arranged in fixed classes with the same curriculum and timetables. Their study was assessed at the end of each academic year. Those who were unable to pass the examinations had to resit them. Since the 1988–89 academic year some institutions have organized their teaching program according to the credit system. In this way, students can accumulate subjects and get credits. Each student can work out his or her own plan.

Before the 1987–88 academic year students were required to attend all the given classes. Those who missed one-fifth of the classes were stripped of the right to take the final exams.

According to the new regulations, besides the marks for each unit, after each academic year, the general mean marks are also taken into consideration. These general mean marks make it possible not only to classify students but also to rank them. This placement is the most important factor to take into account when granting scholarships to students.

Students who achieve outstanding results in their examinations can be directly transferred to master's or doctoral programs or may be employed by important research or production establishments. Other students may be employed by the state or may have to look for a job themselves.

5. Conclusion

Higher education in Vietnam is still at a low level and meeting with great difficulties in its development. However, the socioeconomic situation in Vietnam is under renovation which is bringing about a change in the higher educational system. The Vietnamese people will spare no efforts to catch up with the world educationally.

Bibliography

Giang Lê Văn 1985 *Lịch sử Dại hoc và Trung học chuyên nghiệp Vietnam*. Research Institute of Higher and Vocational Education, Hanoi, 1985

Ministry of Higher and Vocational Education 1989a *Dôi mói giáo dục dại học Vietnam*. Higher and Vocational Education Publishers, Hanoi

Ministry of Higher and Vocational Education 1989b *Niên giám của Vụ KH và Tài vu*. Higher and Vocational Education Publishers, Hanoi

L. Q. Thiep

Y

Yemen

1. Higher Education and Society

Yemen is a low–middle income country with an average per capita income of US$590 in 1987, and is dependent largely on agriculture and migrant earnings from petroleum-rich neighboring Arab countries. It came into being following the September 1962 Revolution which ended the feudal rule and the isolationist policy of the Hamid al-Din dynasty (1890–1962). Except for a few exclusively male and urban elementary and secondary schools providing an Islamic education with some modern refinements, education in the modern sense was practically non-existent. A protracted civil war (1962–68) and the lack of a requisite pool of secondary school graduates, frustrated attempts to establish a modern tertiary institution to train a high-level labor force needed for Yemen's development strategy.

On May 22, 1990 North Yemen and South Yemen unified to form the Republic of Yemen (ROY). The two governmental administrations have joined forces at the cabinet level and are now in the process of aligning forces at the lower ministerial levels. There will continue to be a transition period during which some separate institutions, policies, and practices will coexist at the subsectoral level. The government proposes to introduce the first budget for the newly formed Republic of Yemen in 1991 and development plans in 1992. This article is focused on the University of Sana'a, the sole higher education institution in North Yemen before unification.

Prior to 1962, the only option for aspiring Yemeni students with appropriate qualifications was to travel to neighboring Arab and other countries to study in universities and higher educational institutions. Most went to Egypt, the Soviet Union, Eastern Europe, and China. In 1960–61 around 1,030 Yemeni students were attending postsecondary institutions in about twelve countries. Most of them studied medicine, engineering, agriculture, and science. Others were in progams for higher degrees such as master's, doctorates or postgraduate diplomas in specialized fields. These students were either privately financed or supported by the host countries. Overseas study both at the undergraduate and postgraduate level plays an important role in Yemen's high-level labor force training. Until 1987, the Yemen government sponsored at undergraduate level only courses that were relevant to national development and not available at the University of Sana'a.

In November 1970 the government established the University of Sana'a by upgrading a teacher-training institute. This publicly financed university was under the authority of the Ministry of Education, with Arabic as the main medium of instruction and English as the language of instruction in science, engineering, and medicine. The main arguments advanced by the government in favor of establishing a national university were to: (a) accelerate the process of Yemenization, replace expatriates, and conserve foreign exchange; (b) provide higher education opportunities to qualified female students, since overseas study presented a cultural barrier to them; (c) redress a decline of the knowledge in the *Sharia* (Islamic Law)—a concern voiced by the articulate religious leadership; and (d) respond to the demand from the educated public for a national university system. According to the current Law No. 89 of 1977 the main goals of the University are: (a) to develop and provide a higher education system responsive to the needs of the nation and its citizens; (b) to conduct and encourage scientific research that will create scientific and cultural links with other Arab and foreign universities and scientific institutions; and (c) to preserve, transmit, and enhance the accomplishment of national goals with special attention to Arabic–Islamic values and tradition (Moltahar 1986 p. 4).

Other specialized institutions, but not necessarily high level ones, include the National Institute for Public Administration, the Telecommunications Institute, the Health Labor Force Training Institute, the Police College, the Center for Educational Research, and the Yemeni Research Center.

Since its establishment, the University of Sana'a has expanded its facilities significantly. It now has two campuses in Sana'a and four satellite faculties of education in Hodeida, Taiz, Ibb, and Hajjah. The University's two campuses house all eight faculties located in Sana'a. In the medical faculty building, donated by Kuwait at a cost of US$35 million, the present enrollment has not reached full capacity but as many as 2,000 students can be accommodated when fully functional. The University began its operation with 64 students and nine teaching staff in two faculties—the faculty of *Sharia* (Islamic Law) and law and the faculty of education, with arts (liberal arts) and science departments. In 1973, the arts and science departments were split into two independent faculties and a third faculty of commerce and economics was added. The faculties of medicine and health sciences, engineering, and the language center were established in 1983, while the faculties of agriculture, postgraduate studies, and scientific research were opened in 1984. A satellite faculty of education of the University was established in the Governorate of Taiz in 1984. Since then, three more faculties of education have been established in the governorates—in Hodeida (1987), Ibb (1988), and Hajjah (1989). Thus the University has a total of 12 faculties.

In less than two decades, the University of Sana'a has evolved as a fully fledged modern multifaculty, multicampus, and largely a nonresidential mass-university system with an undergraduate training focus and a student population of about 36,700 in 1989–90. It continues to expand rapidly in terms of student enrollments. However, the University's resources, its staff members, and facilities have far from kept pace. All its graduates have so far been employed, because of the government's guaranteed employment policy.

2. The Institutional Fabric of the Higher Education System

The initial academic year and curriculum of the University was structured along the lines of that of the Ain Shams University in Cairo, a continuous nine-month calendar from September to May, with Arabic as the main medium of instruction. In 1980, the University adopted a two-semester and credit-hour system. The curriculum is divided into four semesters of general education and four semesters of professional education structured around the American system of flexible semester credit hours. The academic year lasts from September to July, with two semesters of 18 weeks each, called a two-term system. This system was preferred as it facilitated the particular needs of each individual student and enabled development of part-time programs for working students. It also helped to reduce the repeater and dropout rates, while the earlier continuous nine-month academic year system accompanied by a rigid examination system at the end, produced a high attrition rate and consequently a low graduation rate.

At the end of each semester examinations are held. Students in some faculties, in addition to passing their end of semester examinations, must have satisfactory course grades and credit hours of attendance in order to proceed to the next academic year. A limit is placed on repetition—only one for each year of studies and a maximum of four during the four-year cycle. However, if they fail they are allowed to resit during the academic year. The credit hours required for graduation vary from faculty to faculty, from 132 credit hours for arts graduates to 171 credit hours for engineering graduates, including lengthy laboratory training. The normal duration of study for students doing a first degree is four years, while agriculture and engineering students take five years and medical students six years.

A university-wide core curriculum of 15 credit hours, consisting of Islamic culture, Arabic and English language, was adopted in 1980 for all incoming students for the first two academic years. This was further reinforced by a faculty-wide requirement of 15–30 credit hours. The objective of these two requirements in the first two academic years was to provide all students with knowledge beyond the required chosen major and minor course of specialization. Department requirements were between 45 and 70 credit hours for major and minor specializations. Finally, students were allowed to do elective coursework of 15 credit hours which could be counted towards their major and/or minor. It is expected that through an exposure to the University and college-wide core curriculum, students would be better equipped in intellectual skills such as creative thinking and problem solving, while their major and minor courses would enhance their academic knowledge and professional skills.

Course offerings are made across faculties to avoid duplication of classes and teaching facilities. The English course requirements for all students are taught by the Language Center, while the Faculty of Science teaches all the basic science courses for students from the faculties of agriculture, education, engineering, and medicine. Similarly, the Faculty of Arts teaches the basic academic courses to education students. This system of course coordination between faculties and sharing of facilities among faculties, apart from being cost-effective, provides for cross-fertilization of both students and staff from different faculties. Teaching in the science and technology-based faculties, such as medicine and engineering, is done mainly in English. However, the lack of an adequate general and technical vocabulary and communication skills in English among the majority of students have put them at a disadvantage, particularly in comprehending textbooks and references, which are largely in English. From the very outset, Arabic and Islamic cultures were made the university-wide core courses, thus protecting the cultural and religious heritage and satisfying the demands of the religious leadership as well as counterbalancing the potentially overwhelming influence of the Western-oriented curriculum.

In Yemen, all students with a secondary school-leaving certificate are entitled to enroll in the University. This includes qualifications obtained in postprimary institutions such as the religious ones which are deemed to be equivalent to secondary school-leaving certificates. The student intake is only at the beginning of the academic year. Though admission into the University is automatic, students are not guaranteed their field of choice. Placement is determined by the student's secondary school stream, the choice the student makes, and the grades at matriculation. In South Yemen, students used to be admitted on the basis of performance at the school-leaving examinations and on interview for available slots in each of the University's faculties. The number of slots were determined through labor force planning (Sanyal and Yaici 1985). Admission standards vary among faculties. Because of the high competition for admission and the limited facilities, the faculties of medicine and engineering demand higher secondary school matriculation results. Admission grades on secondary school final examinations for the faculties vary between a minimum of 55 to a maximum of 95. To further screen the candidates, the faculties of engineering, medicine, and education (for English only) hold interviews. Students with the lowest grades, who therefore do not qualify to enter the faculty of their choice, are compelled to join the faculty of arts as a last resort.

The government of Yemen has adopted a policy of guaranteed employment in the public sector for all Yemeni graduates, even those from overseas universities. They are obliged to work for at least two years in the public sector before they can move into the private sector. Employment in the private sector is more attractive, as wage levels are two or three times higher than those in the public sector. However, graduate employment opportunities in the private sector are very limited.

Until 1988, the process of Yemenization has enabled the Ministry of Civil Service and Administrative Reform (MOCSAR)—the agency responsible for graduate placement—to place all graduates in the public sector, mainly from the faculties of arts, *Sharia* and law, and commerce and economics, in spite of the rise in their numbers from 417 in 1981 to 1,588 in 1986. However, the supply of humanities and social science graduates, with many returning from Saudi Arabia, is fast outstripping demand in the public sector. In 1989, MOCSAR had 4,000 graduates for placement, the bulk of them having qualifications in the humanities. However, MOCSAR is facing increasing difficulties in placing them within the public sector in line with the government's guaranteed employment policy.

3. Governance, Administration, and Finance

From the beginning, university financing depended substantially on donor assistance, mainly from the neighboring high-income oil-exporting Arab country of Kuwait with some assistance from UNESCO and Western countries in the form of fellowships. The University grew rapidly despite the relatively small initial government contribution of less than 8 percent of the total operating cost. Kuwait made major contributions towards facilities at the new campus and the payment of competitive salaries for the non-Yemeni staff. However, declining oil revenues have reduced donor assistance and significantly increased the government's share. The government's share of the University operating cost rose from 50 percent in 1985–86 to 60 percent in 1989–90; and to 65 percent for 1990–91.

Table 1 shows the University of Sana'a's budgetary expenditure over the period 1987–90. Total real expenditures grew at an average annual rate of 31.2 percent, although this rate slowed considerably to 4.5 percent in 1990. Growth has varied according to expenditure categories. Capital expenditures, for instance, have been the most rapidly expanding item at an average annual rate of 46.9 percent. Expen-

Table 1
University of Sana'a annual budget expenditure 1987 (in thousands US dollars)

Item	1987	1988	1989	1990	Average rate of increase in %
Salaries	5,260	5,874 (11.7)[a]	8,173 (39.1)	9,865 (20.7)	23.3
Goods and services	3,578	4,930 (37.8)	7,008 (42.1)	8,046 (14.8)	31.0
Capital expenditure	2,358	3,578 (51.7)	9,104 (154.4)	7,482 (−17.8)	46.9
Subsidy expenditure	75	66 (−11.8)	57 (−13.4)	52 (−9.5)	−11.6
Total	11,271	14,449 (28.2)	24,342 (68.5)	25,445 (4.5)	31.2

Source: University of Sana'a
a Figures in brackets are the percentage increase over the previous year.
b Source of GDP deflators is World Bank Memorandum (1989)
Note: 1989 and 1990 figures are estimated using average deflator figures for the past seven years.

ditures on goods and services and salaries have grown annually by 31 percent and 23.3 percent respectively, while subsidy expenditures have consistently fallen by an average of 11.6 percent.

In 1974 the government established an autonomous governing council, presided over by the Minister of Education, to control and administer the University. Although the University enjoys considerable autonomy in its actual delivery of academic teaching and research, staff appointments and administrative management, its overall policy, planning, and finance is under the government's direction. The University is administered by a rector, nominated by the chairperson of the governing council of the University and appointed by presidential decree. In 1988, the organizational structure of the University was reconstituted to have: (a) a higher council of the University; (b) the University council; (c) the rector of the University; (d) faculty councils; and (e) department councils. This organizational structure is highly hierarchical and centralized, with clearly delineated responsibilities at each level.

The higher council establishes and implements policy for the University, ensuring its consistency within the overall framework of the government's higher education policy and overseeing its implementation. It also attempts to link graduate and research outputs with the labor force and development needs of the country and approves the annual recurrent and capital budgets. The higher council is now headed by the deputy prime minister, who represents the University in the cabinet. Other members of the council include: the Minister of Education; the Minister of Public Service; the Minister of Justice; the Minister of Finance, the Minister of Labor and Social Services; and the Assistant Minister of Planning. The council, through its dominant role in policy formulation, planning, and finance determines the development of the University allowing the government to maintain tight control.

The university council, composed of senior academics and administrators, comes under the direction of the higher council. It prepares the rules, regulations, and statutes for implementation in areas such as curricula, examinations, the University's annual recurrent and capital budget, student admission criteria, research projects, and university exchange. It acts as the main link between the University's policy and planning decisions taken by the higher council and its implementation at the faculty and departmental level.

The rector is appointed by presidential decree, based on the recommendation of the chairperson of the higher council and has the rank of a cabinet minister. As executive head of the University, he or she controls all academic, administrative, and financial matters, as well as executing the University's laws and regulations. He or she is assisted by the vice-rector, also appointed by presidential decree. The various academic faculties and centers, the administrative, financial and service directorates, the various functional units of the University, the heads of all these units—the deans and director general are all responsible to the rector via the vice-rector. Although policy-making powers are concentrated in the higher council and the University council, the rector and the vice-rector, in consultation with the relevant deans, play a central role in initiating and formulating academic policy, including admission. The content of courses is determined in consultation with the deans and heads of departments. There is a high degree of centralization of power in the hands of the rector, especially in the areas of academic and administrative appointments and provision of finance to the faculties, departments, and administrative units. The rector has the sole prerogative in the appointment of deans, deputy deans and chairpersons of departments.

Each of the 12 faculties, headed by a dean and assisted by vice-deans, are governed in academic matters by a council, chaired by the dean and composed of the vice-deans, department chairpersons, and professors selected from each department on the basis of seniority, and two annually elected members, from the ranks of assistant professors and lecturers. The faculty council sets the curricula and program of instruction, coordinates the activities across the departments, specifies the examination system, and presents to the University council the faculty's planned changes in curricula, examination system, graduation requirements, and so forth. The dean is responsible for the execution of the University's laws and regulations, and for carrying out the decisions of the University's council. In this task he or she is assisted by the vice-deans. The dean, vice-deans and the chairpersons of departments are appointed by the rector from the rank of professors.

The chairperson is the head of the department and presides over the departmental council. The council is made up of all professors and assistant professors plus two lecturers in the departments, and are elected to serve the council according to seniority The departmental council is responsible for all matters pertaining to instructional, scientific, and social activities of the department.

4. Faculty and Students: Teaching, Learning, and Research

The University appoints members of its academic and administrative staff either on tenure or contract. All Yemenis are appointed to tenure positions, while non-Yemenis are on contract. The shortage of middle- and high-level labor force forced the University to employ expatriate teaching and non-teaching, that is technical and administrative staff from neighboring Arab country universities, predominantly from Egypt, and to a lesser extent from Syria, Iraq, Sudan, Jordan, and Morocco. For foreign language teaching, and in those fields where English is the medium of instruction, such as medicine and engineering, non-Arab expatriates are recruited. The University has not faced any difficulty in recruiting them for two reasons. First, the relatively attractive salaries and fringe benefits of the expatriate staff are largely covered by funding from Kuwait and second, the working conditions are reasonable.

The national development plans, as well as the University's higher council policies, have consistently emphasized the Yemenization of the academic staff. Therefore, since the University's inception a number of qualified Yemenis, graduating both from the University of Sana'a and from overseas institutions, have been included for overseas fellowships under the University staff development program for master's and doctoral degrees to upgrade teaching and administrative capability. In 1988, there were 223 Yemeni staff training for higher degrees in various foreign countries such as Egypt (109), the United States of America (63) and the United Kingdom (30). However, few women are in this program, because Yemini tradition prevents them from studying overseas, unless accompanied by a male member of the family. As in many other Arab countries, this custom of severely limiting women's access to overseas higher education is creating a two-tier staff composition. The majority of staff are overseas trained men, while the handful of women staff have largely been trained at the University of Sana'a. Until a change in this tradition occurs, the staff will continue to be predominantly male and overseas trained. Many of the overseas training fellowships have been provided by donor agencies and by joint donor and University contributions. On completion of the program, University sponsored fellowship holders must serve the University for a minimum of twice the supported years.

Since 1976, in spite of competition from neighboring oil-rich Arab countries for professionals, the University has successfully recruited faculty members, through which it has attracted qualified Yemenis from overseas to take up academic and administrative positions. In the 1988–89 academic session, out of a total staff of 470, 273 or 58 percent were Yemenis, and over 90 percent of those were men. In June 1989, of the 111 academic staff members in the then only four faculties of education, 9, (or 8%) were women.

The government policy from the outset in 1970 was for the University to "balance the University enrollment to the capacity of the market place to absorb highly educated individuals." Thus, during the first decade, student enrollments grew and broadened from 64 in 1970 to 4,500 in 1979 with an overall student–staff ratio of 23:1. This gradual enrollment

Table 2

Number of instructional staff in selected faculties

Faculty	Yemeni		Non-Yemeni	
	1982–83	1988–83	1982–83	1988–89
Law	5	20	13	8
Arts	22	52	46	39
Science	13	40	72	62
Commerce and Economics	26	39	18	14
Education	11	50	5	21
Total	77	201	154	144

trend developed despite the provision of free higher education, a job guarantee with high remuneration, and the social prestige of a university degree. The growth kept up with the labor force needs of Yemen. However, this low growth was not because of a deliberate labor force planning policy, but rather due to the limited pool of secondary school graduates who were qualified to enter the University. In 1981 student enrollment increased to 6,634. After 1985, this trend accelerated. Student enrollment experienced an explosive growth owing to the high priority given to the expansion of secondary education in the late 1970s. In the 1985–86 session, 2,163 new students were enrolled, and this increased the total student population to 12,881. Figure 1 below shows that especially in the 1988–89 and 1989–90 academic years there was an enrollment explosion in all the 12 faculties and the Language Center. The student intake numbered 5,800 in 1988–89 and about 13,253 in 1989–90, the latter intake far outstripping the Third Five-Year Plan projected intake of 3,680 students in that year.

Within a three-year period, total student enrollments increased greatly, from 17,000 in 1987–88 to 23,447 in 1988–89 and 36,700 in 1989–90, which was about 9,000 to 10,000 of those enrolled in the four satellite faculties of education. (A small number of students included in this are part-time students, some of them not actively pursuing their studies.) There were 715 non-Yemeni students in 1988–89, largely from Palestine. As a result, a high proportion of the student enrollment, about 40 percent, were first-year students. Further growth of enrollment is expected throughout the 1990s. In the 1990–91 session, student enrollment reached 44,000 and by the year 2000, it is projected by the World Bank mission, that, at the present rate of intake, it will reach 79,000. In spite of the fact that the University of Sana'a is a "mass university," the higher education enrollment ratio is less than 1 percent of the age cohort, one of the lowest in the Arab world. Female participation in the University's student composition

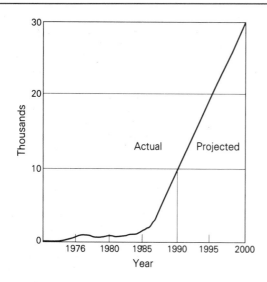

Figure 1
Education faculty enrollment 1970–2000
Source: University of Sana'a Projection based on World Bank
Mission Data

remains low, at 14.5 percent. However, due to an absence of data, it is difficult to ascertain the equity aspects of this enrollment explosion, particularly in terms of socioeconomic background and rural–urban origin.

Student health service and sports facilities are provided. There is also scope for social and cultural activities through student clubs. Because of large student numbers and meager resources, these facilities are overstretched, currently serving about five times the number of students they were intended to serve in some cases.

Though the primary emphasis of the University is on teaching, achievements in research and publications are criteria for staff promotion. Teaching loads are determined by rank. Professors are expected to teach between 8 and 10 hours a week, the norm for assistant professors, lecturers, and assistant lecturers being between 10–12, 12–14, and 14–16 hours respectively. Recruitment to academic positions depends on academic credentials, rather than teaching skills. Little research is being conducted for lack of funding. The Faculty of Graduate Studies and Scientific Research seeks to orient all research toward the needs of Yemen. Through its Center for Science and Technology, the faculty hopes to conduct applied research in the field of industry, energy, agriculture and irrigation, and health and environment.

In 1983 the University was granted the license to confer graduate degrees, and began offering graduate studies in the 1984–85 academic year at the

Faculty of Graduate Studies and Scientific Research. Yemeni graduates are encouraged to obtain higher degrees to replace non-Yemeni staff. Total graduate enrollment increased from 234 in 1988 to 341 in November 1989. Lacking human and material resources, the program offers a limited range of graduate studies: most students studying for a one-year diploma in education, commerce, and *Sharia* and law, a few students studying for the master's, lasting two to three years in the faculties of arts and science; and only one student studying for a PhD in sociology. A joint PhD program has been instituted with the Universities of Al Azhar and Cairo in Egypt. The University so far has produced one PhD candidate in chemistry in 1987. Diploma programs have also been instituted in international politics, accounting, development economics, and planning.

5. Conclusion

The unprecedented growth of student enrollment at the University of Sana'a departs from the government's initial policy to rationalize student admission by linking the University output to the absorptive capacity of the labor market. It has created problems of overcrowding, insufficient staff resources, overstretched amenities, deterioration in physical plant and equipment, inadequate provision of educational materials and equipment, and mismatch in the output. This threatens a major decline in the quality and size of output in several programs. The government would do well to develop a medium- and long-term policy and strategy for its higher education investment, and take into consideration the country's medium- and long-term needs, resource constraints, and the growing social aspirations of the people. Yemen's higher education system has reached a stage that demands some rethinking of its development over the next decade, and possibly beyond. This should help initiate medium- and long-term policies and strategies and make higher education a more efficient and effective investment, consistent with the country's needs and resources.

Bibliography

Kuwait Engineering Office *Sana'a University Phase I: The Master Plan*. Kuwait Engineering Office, Kuwait
Al-Moltahar M 1986 *Evaluating the Consequences of an Academic Innovation: The Case of the Calendar Curriculum Change at Sana'a University in the Yemen Arab Republic*. PhD dissertation, University of Michigan, Ann Arbor, Michigan
Sanyal B, Yaici L 1985 *Higher Education and Employment in the People's Democratic Republic of Yemen*. UNESCO, Paris

V. Selvaratnam; O. Regal

Yugoslavia

1. Higher Education and Society

Until 1918 Yugoslavia was a part of the Austro-Hungarian Empire. After its collapse Yugoslavia became a multicultural kingdom of Serbs, Croats and Slovenians. In 1941 Yugoslavia was occupied by the German and Italian armies. During the occupation, the partisans' liberation movement was active all over the country, and by 1943 part of Yugoslavia was free. On November 29, 1943, 208 delegates from all regions of the country decided to make Yugoslavia a federal republic. After the Second World War Yugoslavia became a federal people's republic and was recognized by the allies and other countries as independent. Today Yugoslavia is a socialist federal republic located in an area of 255,804 square kilometers, with 23,559,000 inhabitants, six republics, two autonomous provinces, over 21 nations and nationalities (or national minorities) and five official languages.

Yugoslavia is a multinational state, a community composed of equal Yugoslav peoples and other nations, nationalities and national minorities. According to the census of 1981, Yugoslavia had a total of 22.4 million inhabitants (1988 23,559,000), of whom 36.3 percent declared themselves Serbs, 19.8 percent Croatians, 8.9 percent Moslems, 7.8 percent Slovenians, 7.7 percent Albanians, 6.0 percent Macedonians, 5.4 percent Yugoslavs, 2.6 percent Montenegrins, 1.9 percent Hungarians, and less than 1 percent Gypsies, Turks, Slovaks, Bulgarians, Vlachs, Ukrainians, Italians, Czechs, Slovakians, Romanians, and so forth. Seventy-three percent of the Yugoslav population speak the Serbo–Croatian language (Serbs, Croats, Moslems, Montenegrins and Yugoslavs). Others usually speak their mother language as their first and Serbo-Croatian as their second language. Hence, Yugoslavia does not have one single official language. In the federal institutions people can use one of five languages (Serbo-Croatian, Slovenian, Macedonian, Hungarian, and Albanian). The formal equality of all nations and nationalities in Yugoslavia emerges in the highly developed system of schooling in the different languages. Given this policy, studies at university faculties in the autonomous provinces of Vojvodina and Kosovo, where the greatest mixture of the nationalities live, are frequently bilingual, in Serbo-Croatian and the local minority language. This provides possibilities for all to uphold cultural identity, and to develop their own culture.

The Yugoslav people have a long cultural tradition. During the time of the medieval independent states, they accomplished significant results in material and cultural development; and, of course, the West–East influence affected Yugoslav culture and education permanently. Because of this influence they were able to take advantage of both and to recreate their original artistic expression, which is known and recognized in Europe and elsewhere through the scientific works of Nikola Tesla, Mihailo Pupin, and Rudjer Bošković and through the Nobel prizes awarded to Ivo Andrić (literature) and Fridrich Pregl and Lavoslav Ružička (science).

The inherited backwardness of an agrarian economy, devastated by the Second World War, was only to be overcome by concentrating all the country's forces and resources on its reconstruction, electrification and industrialization. From being an agrarian and in every aspect a backward country, Yugoslavia steadily built up its productive forces and eventually achieved a medium level of development.

After the Second World War population growth was intensive. During the war, 1.7 million Yugoslavs were killed, so the government encouraged population growth by special measures such as one year's paid leave from work after childbirth for women, monthly allowances for each child, child care, and so forth. According to the 1948 census there were 15.7 million inhabitants, and in 1988 23.55 million, with 19.9 percent living in rural areas, 33.6 percent in the suburbs and 46.5 percent in cities. The number of employed persons has increased from 2 million in 1947 to 6.5 million in 1985. The public sector employs 98 percent of workers and the private sector only 2 percent. In the former 83 percent of the total labor force were engaged in economic activities and 17 percent in public services. The active private farming population was 3.2 million in 1981.

After the Second World War Yugoslavia's main task was to renew and rebuild industry, develop a material and spiritual culture, and to create a new socialist and democratic way of life. The aims of higher education were to provide people with a general background knowledge of their culture, essential professional skills, readiness for successful social life, and world citizenship.

The level of education and skills of workers has steadily improved. Plans to improve the occupational structure of the working force and to induce young people to study technical sciences are in hand.

From Table 1 it is possible to see that the relation between the primary, secondary, and tertiary sector has not changed much since 1975. The reason for this is slower economic development as well as economic crisis, which follows the social development during past years.

The school system developed slowly under the West–East influence. During the Ottoman and Austro-Hungarian occupations there was a strong tendency to impose those cultures and education on the Yugoslav people. But thanks to the education within family units and parochial schools, Yugoslavs preserved their national identity in the process of fighting for national freedom and independence during the eighteenth and nineteenth centuries. This culminated

Table 1
Percentage of employees according to sector

Year	1960	1965	1970	1975	1980	1985	1987
Primary sector[a]	8.06	8.12	10.74	5.13	4.38	4.62	4.59
Secondary sector	47.05	48.40	47.93	48.94	48.74	48.47	48.70
Tertiary sector	44.89	43.48	41.33	45.93	46.88	46.91	46.71

a Private farmers are not included here

with Tito's vision of unification in 1943. There were two kinds of education: public schools, organized by local state authorities, and people's education, planned by different kinds of organizations and churches.

In the nineteenth and early twentieth centuries higher education evolved on lines similar to Western Europe, but was less developed than in France, Austria, or Germany. Nevertheless, the University of Zagreb was founded in 1669 as the Academy of Philosophy. The Kingdom of Yugoslavia tried to establish a more flexible and acceptable school system but did not succeed. The school system had to contend with a high percentage of illiteracy (over 50%). Secondary general schools (*gymnasiums*), technical schools, and university training were accessible mostly for middle- and upper-class students. The 1938–39 data on school enrollments showed some 200,000 students in all kinds of secondary education and by 1977–78 there were over 1 million students. In 1938–39 there were 17,000 students in higher education and by 1977–78 425,000 students. During the 30 postwar years 607,000 students graduated from the Yugoslav institutions of higher learning. In addition 9,176 obtained doctorates and 10,447 obtained master's degrees. Thus, an average of some 20,000 persons a year obtained bachelor's degrees and in the most recent period this number has increased to 40,000 (that is to say, 20 times more students now obtain bachelor's degrees each year than in the total period between the wars).

The first university was founded in Zagreb in 1874. (The Academy of Philosophy was founded in 1669, but from 1776 had existed as the Royal Academy of Sciences with faculties of philosophy, law, and theology.) The University of Belgrade was founded in 1905 and Ljubljana in 1919. The University of Zagreb had faculties of theology, law, philosophy, and medicine.

After the Second World War the following universities were founded: Skopje and Sarajevo 1949, Belgrade Art University 1957, Novi Sad 1960, Niš 1965, Priština 1971, Rijeka 1973, Titograd and Split 1974, Osijek, Maribor, and Banja Luka 1975, Kragujevac and Tuzla 1976, Mostar 1977, and Bitola 1979. Their development was influenced by intensive social, economic, and cultural change which needed a highly educated labor force.

Until 1960 Yugoslav faculties granted only one type of degree, awarded after four, five, or six years according to the subject. Recent regulations adopted for higher education introduced a three-phase system: the first, lasting two years, confers a practical professional qualification, the second, lasting four or five years, offers possibilities for gaining university diplomas in certain fields (medicine, law, mechanical engineering, etc.); and the third, lasting a further one to two years, trains specialist academic researchers and gives the *magisterium* degree. Traditionally the university has the right to give the title of doctor of sciences after submission of a doctoral thesis.

The main purpose of the university was to undertake research, to create knowledge and to disseminate that knowledge through programs, different kinds of publications, and practical activities. Universities have developed into cultural and social centers, also to improve social life, the economy and culture. Throughout history, university education has had multiple purposes.

Today, the explosion of knowledge, scientific and technological development, and social needs impose new functions on university education as follows:

(a) *Professional*—to prepare experts for certain professions and for research and practical work in order to improve the economic, intellectual, cultural, and aesthetic potential of society.

(b) *Research*—to prepare students for scientific work, to solve scientific problems and to improve university teaching.

(c) *Education*—to contribute to the upholding of cultural, moral, and social values, and to the training of youth for citizenship and self-management and to prepare students for active participation in society.

Higher education is an integral part of economic and social development. It is not only a precondition of dynamic and social improvement but also an active agent contributing to this end and accelerating material and social changes.

Yugoslavian higher education is free of charge, but students buy their own textbooks and other materials. In future, students who do not study and pass their examinations regularly within the allotted period will have to repay a portion of the cost of their prolonged studies. Sociopolitical communities (from the communes to the republics and provinces), self-management communities of interests, scientific institutions, and major industrial organizations provide a large number of scholarships for students in those faculties and high schools that provide the training and skills they need. All students may apply for and get credits under favorable conditions during their studies.

Throughout history, religious communities have influenced the development of primary, secondary, and higher education. The first educational institutions were both religious and secular. After the Second World War religious communities were separated from the state and became free to conduct services and found schools. In Yugoslavia there are 30 secondary schools, one college, eight higher schools and six theological faculties, where several thousand students train for a religious vocation. Religious communities have the right to freely present their teaching through religious instruction, assemblies, and publishing activities. However, in the last 44 years religious communities did not influence the development of mainstream higher education.

2. The Institutional Fabric of the Higher Education System

In Yugoslavia there are no private higher education institutions. They are all publicly owned and supported. Public institutions are organized in 19 universities, 211 faculties, 20 art academies, and 91 higher education institutions. Under such conditions, higher education is an integral part of economic and social development.

Three or more faculties and research institutes can be organized into a university which is a free association of faculties and institutes. Each faculty, according to the law constitution, is an entirely independent body. The faculty is the highest organization for teaching and research in all subjects. Normally, faculties are organized into departments, sections, and groups. Some have research institutes as independent organizations. The formal responsibilities of the base units are to organize teaching, exams, solve students' problems and organize social life. At the higher educational level there are three types of institutions: high and higher schools, training experts for various fields of work (lasting two or three years); art academies (lasting four years); and faculties associated with universities (lasting four or six years), which train both specialists to the highest level and researchers. Graduate studies last one to two years and the preparation of the doctoral thesis from three to five years.

Yugoslavia has three types of research institutes: independent institutes, research and developmental

centers founded by industrial organizations, and research organizations and units associated with a certain faculty. The research system is organized in parallel bodies and as an integral part of the higher education system as well.

The intensive development of higher education institutions from 1960 to the present is given in Table 2. The exceptions are higher schools, which have declined since 1980, most of them becoming high schools and faculties, some of which are now closed. Independent scientific and research organizations and research organization in the field of economics merged, so their number declined from 1980 to 1985, but now that number has gradually risen.

Faculties, where courses last four or five years, train highly skilled professional personnel for various branches of the economy and social activities. They take part in scientific work and organize graduate studies. The following faculties exist in Yugoslavia: mathematics and natural sciences, architecture, civil engineering, geodesy, mechanical engineering, traffic and communications, shipbuilding and metallurgy, geology, chemistry and technology, food processing and technology, industrial safety, medicine, dentistry, pharmaceutics, agriculture, forestry, veterinary sciences, economics, tourism and foreign trade, law, political sciences, organizational sciences, philosophy (liberal arts), philology, industrial design, pedagogy, defectology, pedagogy and technology, physical culture, and so on. Interfaculty studies are organized at university level. The faculties have

Table 2
High school institutions and research organizations

Year	1960	1965	1970	1975	1980	1985	1987
Faculties	78	96	107	150	209	207[a]	211[a]
Art academies	11	14	13	16	19	20	20
High schools	10	16	9	6	4	—	—
Higher schools	106	140	117	132	124	103	91
Total	205	266	246	303	356	330	322
Research organizations	231	276	261	270	479	287	307
Research and developmental centers within enterprises	105	120	173	195	89	53	65
Research institutes linked with universities or faculties	27	36	29	36	259	302	305
Total	363	432	463	501	826	642	677

a The figure includes high schools from the Republic of Slovenia

departments or courses which provide education and training for more specialized professional profiles.

Faculties of art and art academies, where studies last four years, have the same rank and function as faculties. They train and educate highly skilled personnel in the plastic and performing arts. These include art academies, academies of music, academies of drama, the faculty of drama, and the faculty of applied arts.

Four-year schools of higher learning have an equal rank and the same functions as faculties. However, they do not organize graduate studies or scientific work, or do so to a lesser extent. There are technical schools of higher learning, schools of higher learning in commerce and economics for the organization of work, music, and physical culture. The name "school of higher learning" is gradually being changed to "faculty." In several republics, the faculties and schools of higher learning are being transformed into institutes, which are deeply engaged in research work in their respective fields, and organize education and instruction in these fields.

Two-year schools of higher learning give higher professional training to personnel with an incomplete academic training. At some faculties, after two years, that is, after the so-called first degree, diplomas

certifying two years of higher learning are issued for specific professions. The following two-year schools of higher learning exist: engineering, traffic and communications, medicine, agriculture, economics, administration, statistics, pedagogy (pedagogic academy, etc.), welfare, internal affairs, organization of work, and so forth. Depending on their profession, persons who complete faculties or four-year schools of higher learning acquire the title of engineer, doctor, diplomate philologist, and so on. Those who complete the corresponding two-year school of higher learning acquire a title without an attribute (e.g., lawyer) or some other corresponding title (formroom teacher, etc.).

Enrollment at higher education institutions is possible for all who pass the final examination in secondary schools and who succeed in the entrance examinations, the conditions of which are set independently by each institution of higher learning. Entrance examinations exist only at those institutions to which more candidates apply than are places. Requirements for enrollment in *numerus clausus* subjects are good results in secondary education in general, good marks in subjects important for future study, the results of a qualification exam, success in an aptitude test, results of testing special abilities and

Table 3
Enrollments in higher education

Year	1960–61	1965–66	1970–71	1975–76	1980–81	1985–86	1987–88
Faculties and art academies							
Full-time	77,817	86,810	139,098	193,433	212,605	203,621	210,188
Part-time	28,476	22,533	33,471	66,541	90,240	56,356	56,839
Total	106,293	109,343	172,569	259,974	302,845	259,977	267,027
High schools							
Full-time	1,710	3,460	3,902	4,290	3,285	1,034	1,660
Part-time	378	3,470	3,658	6,062	3,359	1,511	1,648
Total	2,088	6,930	7,560	10,352	6,644	2,545	3,308
First-phase education							
Full-time	—	—	—	—	—	14,516	17,083
Part-time	—	—	—	—	—	9,548	8,540
Total	—	—	—	—	—	24,064	25,623
Higher schools							
Full-time	15,179	31,563	81,074	43,322	46,644	34,280	27,909
Part-time	17,014	37,087	37,968	80,153	55,043	28,147	22,920
Total	32,193	68,650	119,042	123,475	101,687	62,427	50,829
Total in higher education							
Full-time	94,706	121,833	180,968	241,045	262,534	253,451	256,840
Part-time	45,868	63,090	80,235	152,756	148,641	95,562	89,947
Total	140,574	184,923	261,203	393,801	411,175	349,013	346,787

success in tests of general knowledge. An agreement was reached at the federal level that 50 percent of the points are awarded according to secondary school results and 50 percent on the basis of the results of the entrance examination.

Candidates who are holders of special diplomas for exceptional results in secondary education are accepted mostly without having to sit for entrance examination. Foreigners may also study at universities and other schools of higher learning. Students without complete secondary education must pass a special examination.

Research carried out in Sarajevo has shown that criteria used for enrollment satisfies neither teachers nor students. Work is now under way to improve them.

Enrollment planning for each high school institution is carried out separately in each republic and province by associated labor which needs cadres in conjunction with self-managing communities which are interested in financing education. Those plans are drawn up at assembly meetings of communities each year in May, and enrollment is in June. Teaching starts in September and lasts two semesters, the second lasting from 15 February to 30 June. The length of first degree studies is four years for social sciences and humanities and five years for technical and medical subjects. The title of the first diploma is BA, BSc or BM. The duration of studies is a cause for some dissatisfaction. In schools where studies last two years, the average time to graduate is 3.7 years. In schools where programs last four years, the average duration is 6.1 years, while students in five-year schools on average graduate after 7.1 years.

Graduate studies are organized by faculties, academies and four-year institutions of higher learning. There are two kinds of graduate studies: specialization, lasting one year leading to the academic qualification of specialist in a corresponding subject, and the *magisterium* lasting two years, which leads to the academic qualification of *magister*. In both cases, candidates must pass the exams and defend a thesis. The title of doctor of sciences is the only higher university degree, acquired after a *magisterium* or specialization, and lasting three to five years. The candidates must also defend their doctorate thesis. However, the doctorate can also, exceptionally, be acquired on the basis of a number of prominent scientific works and a successfully defended doctor's thesis without taking an oral examination.

3. Governance, Administration, and Finance

The socioeconomic system is based on freely associated labor with the means of production under public ownership and worker self-management both in production and distribution. The right of workers in associated labor is to manage the entire labor and business of an organization of associated labor, to regulate working relationships, to decide wage levels, and to earn a personal income. The entire process of decision making in basic and other organizations of associated labor is carried out electorally, either directly by the employees or through delegates elected to workers' councils. The obligations of workers in associated labor is to use their right to work with public resources for the common and general interest in a responsible and economically appropriate manner and to constantly renew, expand, and improve them.

The presidency of the republic is the collective head of state and is made up of eight members from each of six republics and two provinces. The federal executive council is the executive arm of the federal assembly. Each republic or province has its own executive council, constitution, flag, and coat of arms. The commune also has an assembly and executive council.

The assemblies are the highest organ of self-management and self-government within each sociopolitical community (i.e., commune, republic, province and federation). They are made up of delegates elected to each of the two or three chambers (two federal, three republic). The assembly decides on all matters of general interest within the competences of the community, and lays down policies on the principal questions in the economic, social, and cultural life of the community and its further development.

According to the constitution, republics and provinces are responsible for the policy, organization and development of the educational system. Uniformity of the nationwide education system is assured by the republics and provinces through mutual agreements, so-called compacts, which lay down the principles of a standard system of education, from primary school to university level studies. The assemblies of each republic, the Ministry of Education, and self-managing communities interested in higher education plan, regulate, establish educational standards, and provide money and other conditions for the normal functioning of higher education. Self-management planning of education is a component part of the system of self-management decision making in relation to a free exchange of labor among organizations in education, industry, and other sectors. Planning and implementation belong to the republic institutions. Evaluation of students' preparation belongs to the institutions of higher education.

The decrease in the percentage of gross national product devoted to higher education is the result of economical depression which started in the early 1980s and still influences the Yugoslav economy, the development of higher education and the future of young people. Since 1980 most republics and provinces have attempted to rationalize higher education and to bring it into line with real social needs, particularly in relation to employment opportunities.

Table 4
Proportion of GNP devoted to higher education

Year	1960	1965	1970	1975	1980	1985	1987
Percentage	0.59	0.63	0.68	0.76	0.82	0.61	0.71

In Yugoslavia the system of financing of education is complicated. Resources are pooled within interested self-managing communities (social institutions responsible for financing of education) and are used on the basis of annual programs of educational institutions and organizations, and the financial projects adopted by self-management organs—assemblies of interested self-managing communities. Resources are fixed and distributed in accordance with the financial plan, which is drawn up annually and is brought into line with the long-term and annual plan of the appropriate community. The self-management system of education financing should prevail over the budgetary financing of education. It was expected that the establishment of the self-management sys-

tem would reduce the involvement of the state in the organization and activities in the field of education, reduce and eliminate intermediaries, and prevent monopoly and manipulation in education generally. Education financing, based on the delegate system, within interested self-managing communities, should determine the methods of acquiring resources from the organization of associated labor, from the economic sector and other resources. This is a more democratic way, and it socializes the distribution of resources.

The practice of exchange and pooling of labor and resources cannot easily be understood, without knowing the principle beneath the income flow within the organizations of associated labor in the economy and other spheres. Organizations of associated labor in the economic sector acquire income through the free exchange of labor, the sale of products and services, various forms of compensation, and the like. When resources for production and amortization are set aside from the total income acquired, the net income of the organization of associated labor remains. Contributions (resources) for public services and other amenities are provided for by

Table 5
Staff at the higher schools

Year	1960–61	1965–66	1970–71	1975–76	1980–81	1985–86	1987–88
Teaching staff (permanent)							
Professors	513	932	1,179	1,552	2,006	2,116	1,724
Lecturers	148	432	465	818	1,612	1,018	900
Secondary-school teachers	73	24	20	23	—	—	—
Subtotal	734	1,388	1,664	2,393	3,618	3,134	2,624
Part-time	1,043	1,752	1,478	1,733	—	—	—
Total (permanent and part-time)	1,777	3,140	3,142	4,126	—	—	—
Other teaching staff							
Assistants	14	126	141	170	403	283	227
Lecturers	1	8	7	—	13	13	6
Assistant trainees	—	—	—	87	147	77	31
Assistant professionals	—	—	—	25	—	—	—
Secondary-school teachers	16	5	6	25	—	—	—
Other	30	151	153	70	287	151	75
Subtotal	61	290	307	377	850	524	339
Part-time	303	454	504	540	—	—	—
Total (permanent and part-time)	364	744	811	917	—	—	—
Total (professors and teaching staff)	2,141	3,884	3,953	5,043	4,468	3,658	2,963

law, among which are included children's and social welfare, education, science, culture, and so on.

In all self-management communities interested in education, the assembly is an organ that manages the affairs of the community. In most republics or provinces assemblies consist of two chambers: the chamber of workers' delegates attached to organizations of associated labor which perform educational activities (the chamber of educational workers) and the chamber of delegates of working people and citizens whose needs and interests in education are being satisfied and who provide resources for education.

In the university, the highest self-managing body is the assembly in which all teachers, students, and university workers, as well as the community, all have their representatives. The highest professional body is the scientific council. It consists of staff and students' representatives. The head of the university is a rector with four vice-rectors of whom three are professors and one is a student. The highest self-managing body at faculty level are councils, consisting of professors, assistants, students, and representatives of the external community, and the teaching board—the highest professional body, composed of all professors and representatives of assistants and students. The head of the faculty is a dean with three vice-deans, one of whom is a student. Membership of the bodies is elected by secret or open balloting of teaching staff and workers in the institutions. The representatives of the external community are nominated by the assembly of republic or province. Self-managing bodies determine work policy, working plans, and programs, take care of material and financial, as well as other problems of working people. All important questions are dealt with by self-managing and professional bodies. Academic work is organized in faculties and departments. The base units discuss the proposals which are submitted to the faculties and departments in the field of research and teaching.

4. Faculty and Students: Teaching, Learning, and Research

At the universities, that is, faculties, educational work is performed by university professors, holders of doctorates (docents, associate, and full

Table 6
Staff at the faculties, art academies and higher schools

Year	1960–61	1965–66	1970–71	1975–76	1980–81	1985–86	1987–88
Professors (permanent)							
Full professors	660	1,033	1,318	2,024	3,054	4,280	4,363
Associate professors	738	943	1,388	1,834	2,722	2,655	2,842
Assistant professors	877	1,336	1,523	2,092	2,757	3,401	3,534
Teachers	88	688	693	932	1,888	2,034	2,047
Other	4	79	39	170	828	2,104	340
Subtotal	2,367	4,079	4,961	7,052	11,249	14,474	13,126
Part-time	979	1,914	1,653	1,791	—	—	—
Total (permanent and part-time)	3,346	5,993	6,614	8,843	—	—	—
Other teaching staff (permanent)							
Assistants	2,964	3,868	4,031	4,529	5,755	4,842	6,181
Research and professional associates	154	250	369	380	760	644	1,097
Lectors	15	147	180	274	322	274	329
Other	75	72	183	1,197	1,683	1,737	1,977
Subtotal	3,208	4,337	4,763	6,380	8,520	7,495	9,584
Part-time	1,538	1,546	1,453	1,330	—	—	—
Total (permanent and part-time)	4,746	5,883	6,216	7,710	—	—	—
Total (professors and teaching staff)	8,092	11,876	12,830	16,553	19,769	21,969	22,710

Table 7
Graduation from higher education courses

Year	1960	1965	1970	1975	1980	1985	1986
Faculties and art academies							
Full-time	9,184	10,551	11,423	18,626	25,361	22,991	22,744
Part-time	841	1,677	2,004	2,909	5,336	5,567	5,405
Total	10,025	12,228	13,427	21,535	30,697	28,558	28,149
High schools							
Full-time	39	575	358	289	326	141	—
Part-time	4	207	427	178	207	131	—
Total	43	782	785	467	533	272	—
First-phase higher education							
Full-time		4,314	1,078	1,466	3,364	5,145	5,259
Part-time		1,350	796	1,079	2,783	4,186	3,189
Total		5,664	1,874	2,545	6,147	9,331	8,448
Higher schools							
Full-time	3,913	5,903	8,825	9,206	9,165	7,025	7,360
Part-time	767	3,375	6,960	10,161	9,828	6,291	5,747
Total	4,680	9,278	15,785	19,367	18,993	13,316	13,107
Higher Education total							
Full-time	13,316	21,343	21,684	29,584	38,216	35,302	35,363
Part-time	1,612	6,609	10,188	14,327	18,154	16,175	14,341
Overall total	14,928	27,952	31,872	43,911	56,370	51,477	49,704

professors). They are required to be active researchers. Assistants and assistant trainees help university professors as instructors. Teaching is also done by junior lecturers and language lectors. Persons in full-time research working at research institutes are scientific workers, high scientific workers, and scientific advisers. The election of university or faculty teachers are realized on the basis of the law on higher education. Assistant lecturers must have completed undergraduate study; an assistant must have a master's degree; a docent a doctor's degree; an associate professor a doctor's degree plus published works; and a full professor has to have made important contributions to teaching and to scientific advancement as well as a doctor's degree. University teachers are usually elected, every four to five years on the basis of open competition to which everyone duly qualified can apply. On the basis of assessment, given by the committee, the teaching board elects the best candidates. The election has to be confirmed by the university bodies and faculty council. Election of teachers at *viša školas* is made among well-known specialists with practical experience, holding either master's or doctor's degrees.

In research institutes promotions follow the same principle as in faculties. University teachers have freedom of scholarship and art creativity, freedom of speech, and an opportunity to formulate research policy, higher education, working conditions, and material status. University teachers and scientific workers are organized in trade unions, unions of university teachers and scientific workers, and in their professional circles (historical, philosophical, law, technical, etc.). Through them, they represent their interests and participate actively in self-management and community matters. Working conditions of academics are separately regulated by statute for each institution. Assistants usually have six to twelve classes and lecturers four to six classes per week. How much time teachers and assistants assign to research work is not regulated, but promotion to higher positions depends on their success in teaching and scholarships, and because of that they are motivated to do research.

Thirty years ago only 1.6 percent of young people between 19 and 25 years of age attended higher education and college. Today the figure is 12.4 percent. The social class of students has changed considerably. In 1949–50, 8.2 percent of students were children of industrial, building and mining workers and craftsmen. In 1977–78 this percentage was 21.4. Children from workers' families and from farmer's families accounted for over 40 percent of the total number of students. At some faculties and schools of higher education (particularly the latter) up to four-fifths of the total number of students come from workers' and farmers' families. Today, female students account for over 40 percent of the total number of students while in 1952–53, for instance, 31 percent of the students were girls.

Almost all students are members of students' organizations which work within the faculty and university. Students also have their representatives in all professional and self-managing bodies at the faculties and universities. In *viša škola* organizations students' representatives are vice-deans and vice-rectors, and this way can solve student issues and improve work at faculties and higher schools.

The high school institutions are quite independent in examinations. Some are taken during the year others at the end of the year and final exams at the end of year two at *viša škola*, and years four or five in faculties. Final examinations usually consist of written diploma work and oral examinations. Specialist's and master's degree candidates are examined during the first and second year in certain fields, and at the end they defend their specialist's and master's thesis. Doctoral candidates usually take and defend a doctoral thesis alone. Candidates who have not acquired a master's degree and have not published works, must take an oral doctoral examination and defend their thesis. Undergraduate studies are organized around subjects in general education (foreign language, physical training and social education), professional subjects, and the practice of students. Hence Yugoslavia has both single subject courses and broad general content ones. There is no credit unit system.

5. Conclusion

In addition to quantitive growth in higher education, significant qualitative improvements have also been achieved. The plans for the future development of higher education include rationalization of study programs and their updating, in keeping with the requirements of social and economical development, scientific achievements and the needs of young people. The economic crisis also influenced education. It did not, however, reduce the right to education, but caused great difficulties of a material and financial nature. This coincided with the need to improve the quality of education and to pay professors better for the additional efforts they made in implementing new programs. The future of the university in general depends on the renewal of human resources, and on the dynamic in flow of young people with new ideas, enthusiasm, and abilities. This may ensure vitality of teaching and scholarship. Yugoslavian society is undergoing a number of changes in its structure, policy, and function.

Bibliography

Belgrade University 1967 *The Collection of Codes of the Belgrade University*. Scientifics Book, Belgrade

Bureau of Yugoslav Academy 1969 *Memorial Book for 300th Anniversary of Zagreb University*. Zagreb

Federal Administration for International Scientific, Educational, Cultural and Technical Cooperation 1973 *Higher Schools of Law and Higher Schools of Administration*. Higher Schools of Economics, Belgrade

Federal Administration for International Scientific, Educational, Cultural and Technical Cooperation 1980 *Conditions, Problems and Policy of Education in Yugoslavia*. Federal Administration for International Scientific, Educational, Cultural and Technical Cooperation Belgrade

Federal Institute for Statistics 1961, 1962, 1966, 1971, 1977, 1982, 1987, 1988 *Statistical Year Book of Yugoslavia*. Federal Institute for Statistics, Belgrade

Federal Institute for Statistics 1960–1988 *Statistical Pocket Book of Yugoslavia*. Federal Institute for Statistics, Belgrade

Federal Institute for Statistics 1963. *Statistical Bulletin, Number 255, High Schools 1959/60 and 1960/61*, Federal Institute for Statistics, Belgrade

Federal Institute for Statistics 1966 *Statistical Bulletin, Number 439, High Schools 1965/66*. Federal Institute for Statistics, Belgrade

Federal Institute for Statistics 1967 *Statistical Year Book, Number 469, Graduated Students 1965*. Federal Institute for Statistics, Belgrade

Federal Institute for Statistics 1973 *Statistical Year Book, Number 525, High Schools 1970/1971*. Federal Institute for Statistics, Belgrade

Federal Institute for Statistics 1972 *Statistical Bulletin, Number 714, Graduated Students 1970*. Federal Institute for Statistics, Belgrade

Federal Institute for Statistics 1973 *Stastical Bulletin, Number 781, High Schools, 1970/71*. Federal Institute for Statistics, Belgrade

Federal Institute for Statistics 1977 *Statistical Bulletin, Number 1099, Graduated Students 1975*. Federal Institute for Statistics, Belgrade

Federal Institute for Statistics 1978 *Statistical Bulletin, Number 1103, High Schools 1975/76 and 1976/77*. Federal Institute for Statistics, Belgrade

Federal Institute for Statistics *Census for 1981*. Federal Institute for Statistics, Belgrade

Federal Institute for Statistics 1982 *Statistical Bulletin, Number 1292, Graduated Students 1980*. Federal Institute for Statistics, Belgrade

Federal Institute for Statistics 1982 *Statistical Bulletin, Number 1312, High Schools 1980/81*. Federal Institute for Statistics, Belgrade

Federal Institute for Statistics 1981 *Census for 1981, Book I, Population and Household*. Federal Institute for Statistics, Belgrade

Federal Institute for Statistics 1987 *Statistical Bulletin, Number 1611, Graduated Students 1985*. Federal Institute for Statistics, Belgrade

Federal Institute for Statistics 1988 *Statistical Bulletin, Number 1682, High Schools 1985/86—Teaching Staff.* Federal Institute for Statistics, Belgrade

Federal Institute for Statistics 1988 *Statistical Bulletin, Number 1684, High Schools—Enrolled Students.* Federal Institute for Statistics, Belgrade

Federal Institute for Statistics 1988 *Statistical Bulletin, Number 1690, Graduated Students 1986.* Federal Institute for Statistics, Belgrade

Federal Institute for Statistics 1988 *Statistical Bulletin, Number 1711, High Schools 1987/88—Teaching Staff.* Federal Institute for Statistics, Belgrade

Federal Institute for Statistics 1989 *Statistical Bulletin, Number 1734, High Schools—Enrolled Students.* Federal Institute for Statistics, Belgrade

Filipovic M 1971 *Higher Education in Yugoslavia.* The Federal Council for Education and Culture and Federal Commission for Cultural Relations with Foreign Countries, Belgrade

Jelicic B 1976 *Financing of Education.* School Book, Zagreb

Juhas M 1975 *Education and Its Reform in Yugoslavia.* Institute for Studies in Education, Belgrade

Micunovic V et al. 1987 *Handbook on Yugoslavia.* Exportpress, Belgrade

Polic V 1983 *Economy and Planning of Education.* School Book, Zagreb

Ristanovic S 1979 *Social Inequality in Education.* Republican Institute for Improving Education, Belgrade

University Today 1985 *Journal of Yugoslav University Association.* Nos. 3–4

P. D. Mandic

Z

Zaire

1. Higher Education and Society

Zaire, once a colony of Belgium, is situated in the heart of Africa and covers an area of 2,345,550 square kilometers.

Its population, 14,523,000 in 1959 (Tshibangu 1982 p. 30), doubled in 20 years (26,377,000 in 1979) and is almost three times larger today: more than 35,000,000. In spite of a strong exodus from the countryside and rapid urbanization, 80 percent of the population still reside in rural areas and work in agriculture.

Three large cities constitute the country's economic poles: Kinshasa, the capital, with more than three million inhabitants, in the west; Lubumbashi, the copper center, in the south; and agricultural Kisangani in the northeast.

Several hundred tribes inhabit this vast territory and speak more than 200 Bantu and non-Bantu languages.

The country has been politically and socially stable since the military regime of Marshal Mobutu was established in 1965. However, the economic fabric has continued to deteriorate, and in the early 1990s the potential wealth of the country is in no way comparable to the excessive poverty of the population. Political efforts, development plans, and several strategies are in place to change this situation.

2. The Institutional Fabric of the Higher Education System

The first institution of higher education recognized by the colonial power was the *Centre Universitaire Congolais Lovanium*, founded in 1949. This gave birth to the first Catholic university, the *Université Lovanium*, in Kinshasa. From that time on, the development of higher education in Zaire was continuous, characterized by three stages: expansion, centralization, and regrouping.

The period 1954–70 is characterized by the creation of universities and institutes of higher education of different types. However, it was after Independence that higher education in Zaire really developed, responding to the country's concern to have competent local cadres. In 1970, Zaire had three universities with 8,059 students and 27 institutes of higher education with 5,077 students.

All these institutions are truly autonomous. Verhaegen (1978) has characterized them as having diverse status, diplomas, recruitment criteria, and a pluralism of ideological influences, as well as material and intellectual gaps between the different institutions.

1971 marks an important stage in the history of higher education in Zaire: the National University of Zaire was founded. All the universities and institutes of higher education were fused together into this single official institution. It was a policy of "centralizing power and programs, standardizing rules and programs, and placing the University at the service of the state" (Verhaegen 1978).

The need for this centralization was based on a series of academic and political problems. Indeed, in spite of the great progress made on both the quantitative and structural level, "higher education had accumulated academic, administrative, and financial problems, which had the student protests as a background" (Ekwa 1973). The reform had three objectives: politicization, specialization, and professionalization (Isango 1980 pp. 122–26).

The incorporation of all the institutes into one university led to the inauguration of one scale of degrees and levels, and consequently, in the rejection of the dualism between faculties and institutes. However, the excessive centralization in a country of gigantic size with poor means of communication, the multiplication of consulting agencies, and the bureaucracy, hindered day-to-day administration (Comeliau 1974, Gakodi 1979). The difficulties led to the counter-reform of 1981.

A 10-year experience of centralized administration gave way, for the reasons mentioned, to the return to the old universities and several autonomous institutes of higher education. However, both kinds of institutions have been changed in several ways by being part of the National University of Zaire for 10 years.

In order to protect the gains of the 1971 reform, the universities, the teacher-training institutes, and the technological institutes are headed by three different administrative councils and each institution has some autonomy.

Higher education in Zaire includes universities and institutes of higher education. Three universities function respectively in Kinshasa, Lubumbashi, Kisangani, and a faculty institute in Yangambi. These four institutions have 19 faculties among them.

There are 14 teacher-training institutes and 18 technological institutes. The teacher-training institutes were founded to meet the country's need for competent and qualified teachers. Each region of the country has at least one of these institutes. The

Table 1
Growth of student population

Institution	1960–61		1964–65		1970–71		1974–75		1980–81		1985–86	
	Numbers	%	Numbers	%	Numbers	%	Numbers	%	Numbers	%	Numbers	%
Universities	567	74.3	1,838	63.9	8,059	63.7	14,748	66.28	9,927	34.84	16,239	39.76
Technological institutes	176[a]	23.1	580	20.2	2,216	17.5	3,139	14.11	10,045	35.25	13,678	33.49
Teacher-training institutes	20	2.6	457	15.9	2,381	18.8	4,363	19.61	8,521	29.90	10,928	26.75
Total	763	100	2,875	100	12,656	100	22,250	100	28,493	100	40,845	100

a Former high schools

technological institutes seek to train middle-level technicians in several fields of the country's economic life.

All these institutions are public and are under the Department of Higher Education, University and Scientific Research. There are, however, some private institutions, including the faculties of Catholic Philosophy and Theology and of Protestant Theology, both of which are in Kinshasa.

Besides these institutions, more and more private institutes are being founded in Zaire. These are emerging as society's response to the incapacity of the state universities and institutes to respond to the demographic pressure. Unfortunately, these institutes are not governed by any regulations and the diplomas they give, under very variable conditions, are still not recognized by the state.

The 1971 reform made it possible to have the same admissions requirements for the university and the institutes. However, after the entrance examination was terminated, the criterion became the grade obtained on the state diploma, which closed the door to higher education to a good many high-school graduates. In practice, the main condition for admission is to have a state diploma.

Higher education grew quickly. The number of students went from 763 in 1960 to 40,845 in 1985, an annual growth rate of 10.4 percent (Tshibangu 1982 p. 29).

The universities have progressively lost students to the institutes, especially since 1980. The desired percentages were obtained in 1985: 40 percent in the universities and 60 percent in the institutes. Several factors were at play here: the universities were saturated; new institutes were constantly being founded; cutbacks on scholarships (travel, room and board, tuition) induced students to study close to home, usually at an institute.

Scientific research is an integral part of the university in Zaire. But since the 1971 reform, several institutes have set up research centers, most of which are recognized by the ministry that supervises them.

The majority lack funds and full-time researchers. The researchers are usually faculty members of the parent institution. Departments and faculties without specific centers also do some research. Indeed, almost all the faculties and institutes have a journal to publish their research results.

There are also autonomous centers, dedicated completely to theoretical or applied research, for example, the Research Center for the Natural Sciences in Lwiro (Katana) and the Research Center for the Human Sciences in Kinshasa.

All the centers face problems of finance, dissemination, and coordination.

Studies are structured in the same way for both the universities and the institutes.

The first stage (pregraduate) entails three years of study and leads to graduation. The second stage lasts two years and grants the licentiate, except for the medical faculties (human and veterinary) where the same stage is three years long and grants the doctor of medicine degree. The third stage is mainly comprised of a program of higher studies (DES). This program lasts two years and includes a certain number of courses and seminars along with the presentation of a dissertation. After obtaining the DES, the candidate can register in a doctoral program and prepare the thesis. The fourth stage leads to the doctorate. The time spent varies; it averages from four to seven years.

The programs which are set by the political authority are conceived in such a way that at the end of each stage they enable students to adopt a profession. This professionalization is stronger in the institutes than in most of the faculties.

3. Governance, Administration, and Finance

3.1 National Administration

Administration in higher education in Zaire is centralized. The State Commission (the ministry) of Higher Education and Scientific Research is the most authoritative body. It controls several specialized services. All the important decisions are made on this level: appointments of academic and administrative authorities, setting the number of students to be admitted, and so on.

Three administrative councils coordinate the activities of the universities with the teacher-training institutes (CA-ISP) and with the technological institutes (CA-IST). They define overall policy and objectives, decide on new courses, and calculate the number of hours per subject, and so on. The real power, however, lies with the State Commission; the councils simply communicate its decisions. They function more as consultative bodies. A permanent office deals with day-to-day problems.

3.2 Institutional Administration

Each institution has a university or institute council, an administrative committee, faculties (or sections), and departments. The university or institute council is the highest authority. It is comprised of the administration committee, the deans (section heads), a faculty representative, a student representative, a representative of the administrative personnel, and the head librarian. Within the limits placed on it by law, this body coordinates the academic and scientific policy of the institution.

The administration committee runs daily operations. Paradoxically, its members are not elected by their colleagues but appointed by the central power. This often leads to the control of other bodies by the administration committee or to conflicts involving competency.

Table 2
Distribution of students by field of study

Field of study	1970–71 Numbers	%	1985–86 Numbers	%
Sciences				
Medicine and pharmacy	1,149		3,504	
Veterinary medicine	86		326	
Science	948		1,524	
Agronomy	451		489	
Polytechnic studies	280		1,169	
Total sciences	2,914	34.7	7,012	43.7
Arts and Humanities				
Arts	782		643	
Law	941		2,212	
Education	899		1,002	
Total arts and humanities	2,622	31.2	3,857	24.0
Social sciences				
Economics	1,340		2,374	
Social science, politics, and administration	1,520		2,817	
Total social sciences	2,860	34.1	5,191	32.3
General total	8,396	100	16,060	100

Sources: Verheust 1974 pp. 29–30; Commission Permanente des Etudes 1986

The section or faculty council is exclusively concerned with the academic and scientific problems of that faculty or institute. It comprises full professors and department heads. The department council is the source of academic life in the universities. It comprises full professors who elect the department head.

4. Faculty and Students: Teaching, Learning, and Research

4.1 Faculty

The teaching staff is divided into scientific and academic personnel, with both under the same regulations. Criteria for recruitment and advancement as well as salaries are the same in all institutions.

There are five levels: assistant, project head, associate professor, professor, and full professor. An assistant must have a licentiate or its equivalent, and is named for a two-year period, twice renewable. A project head needs four years as assistant and two publications in a scientific journal. An associate professor must have a first-level doctorate. Promotions require four years on the previous level together with several publications. Salaries are determined by the number of hours taught or worked, which increases with rank.

4.2 Students

The number of students in higher education has grown rapidly (Table 1). The distribution according to field of study is shown in Table 2. Most of the students are from the lower social strata (Payanzo et al. 1980 pp. 37–41) who form the majority of the population of Zaire. They receive government scholarships. The high cost of higher education due to the increase in the number of students has led to a review of this policy. In the early 1990s the amount granted covers very little of a student's expenditure. Their material situation has deteriorated and parental income is more than ever a determining factor for higher studies.

5. Conclusion

Since the first university was founded, considerable efforts have gone into a whole system of higher education. Thanks to those efforts, Zaire has competent professionals in all domains.

The future of the system depends on how it solves the serious problems it faces. Failure to deal with these problems successfully could cause the whole system to deteriorate. These problems can be summarized in a few words: "the exponential development of the student population, exhausted resources, and the depreciation of existing infra-structure" (Tshibangu 1982).

In the social and scientific domains, the system will have to allocate more resources to scientific research. Such research could help the university play a larger role in the social and economic fabric of the country by finding solutions to general problems. The wall separating education from everyday life must be removed. Given available resources and the unre-strained social demand, the private sector will have to play an increasingly important role in this expansion.

Bibliography

Benekabala L, Bongeli Y 1980 Aspirations, attitudes et conditions de vie des étudiants de l'UNAZA. *Les Cahiers CRIDE* 39–40:
Comeliau C H 1974 L'université dans la Nation: Options et propositions pour l'avenir. *Zaïre-Afrique* 84: 207–20
Ekwa bis Isal 1973 Le point de la réforme universitaire. Propos en marge d'un colloque. *Zaïre-Afrique* 77: 397–406
Eyamba G B 1986 Education and Development in Zaïre. In: Nzongola-Ntalaja(ed.) 1986 *The Crisis in Zaïre: Myths and Realities*. Africa World Press, Trenton, New Jersey, pp. 191–218
Gakodi G 1979 Problématique actuelle de l'UNAZA. *Zaïre-Afrique*, 136: 349–60
Isango I W 1980 La politique d'éducation au Zaïre: Essai d'analyse des conditions d'adaptation de l'enseignement. Doctoral dissertation, Lubumbashi
Lacroix B 1972 Pouvoirs et structures de l'Université Lov-anium. *Les Cahiers du CEDAF* 2/3:
Tshibangu T 1982 *La crise contemporaine, l'enjeu africain et l'université de l'an 2000*. P.U.Z., Kinshasa
Tshimanga M, Kabanga M 1986 Organisation académique des ISP. Réflexions et étude critique. *Coll. Etudes*, 14, Bukavu, CERUKI
Verhaegen B 1978 *L'enseignement universitaire au Zaïre. De Lovanium à l'UNAZA 1958–1978*. L'Harmattan-CED-AF-CRIDE Paris-Bruxelles-Kisangani
Verhaegen B 1986 Propositions pour l'Université de demain. *Revue de l'IRSA* 1: 54–64
Verheust Th 1974 L'enseignement en République du Zaïre. *Les Cahiers du CEDAF* 1: 1–47

M. Magabe

Zambia

1. Higher Education and Society

The Zambian higher education system has developed against a colonial, and then a post-Independence backdrop. The colonial higher education system was characterized by limited provision of facilities and restrictive access to apprenticeship training. Zambia (then Northern Rhodesia) shared the services of a common institution, the University of Rhodesia and Nyasaland, with Southern Rhodesia and Nyasaland.

Upon Independence in 1964 the Zambian govern-ment set out to reform the previous restrictions and deprivations in the system. It was decided to establish a university in Zambia and to reorganize technical education and vocational training. In 1966 the Uni-versity of Zambia was opened.

The development and expansion of higher edu-cation was an attempt to address the acute problem of shortage of educated and skilled labor force among the local people. Politically, too, there was the long-term need for Zambia to develop a cadre of highly educated Zambians who could participate effectively in the management and control of the country's econ-omic and social sectors.

The population of Zambia, which stood at 3.5 million in 1963, increased to 4.4 million in 1969 and 5.7 million in 1980. The population further increased to 6.4 million in 1984 and to 7.5 million in 1988. At Independence in 1964 the majority of Zambians lived in rural areas. The 1963 census showed that only 20.5 percent of the population lived in urban areas. By 1969 the proportion had increased to nearly 30 percent. In 1980 about 40 percent of the total popu-lation were urban dwellers. The high level of urban-ization is a result of both past colonialist policies and post-Independence factors, such as industrial growth.

The internal structure of the Zambian economy is dependent on one major export commodity, copper. The agricultural sector has gained importance as a growing source of Gross Domestic Product (GDP), employment, and exports. In 1988 the agricultural sector exceeded the previous year's level by 6.4 per-cent. Improved marketing facilities, access to credit facilities, and good weather conditions have enhanced the performance of this sector. However, it has continued to face operational and structural contraints which have yet to be overcome completely.

The manufacturing sector has made important stri-des in its performance. Because the sector was recently able to secure sufficient allocation of foreign exchange for the importation of raw materials inputs, the sector was able to increase its production capacity. Lack of foreign exchange and its effects on importation of production inputs have remained the major constraints on the sector's performance.

1.1 Structure of Government and Main Political Goals

Zambia entered its independent political life as a pluralist system dominated by the ruling United National Independence Party (UNIP). However, pluralism was short-lived. In 1973 a one-party po-litical system was introduced by UNIP after a national referendum. UNIP's central committee is divided into standing subcommittees. These are responsible for broad national policy matters concerning political, social, and economic affairs. Two subcommittees are responsible for general and higher scientific and technological education. UNIP's main political goals since 1964 have been: to consolidate its power base at home, to introduce measured decentralization in local government, to maintain political neutrality internationally, to support the liberation of Southern African countries that had been under colonial rule, and to work toward the creation of a democratic South Africa.

Since the late 1980s, especially after the collapse of communism in many Eastern European countries, UNIP has come under increasingly severe criticism within Zambia. The pressure on UNIP has been such that in 1990 it agreed to repeal Article 4 in the Zambian constitution to allow the reintroduction of a pluralist political system. By the end of 1990 four new political parties had been formed.

1.2 Religious Bodies

During Zambia's colonial period, a partnership existed between Christian missionaries and the government with the aim of providing education and training. In 1991 the education sector is dominated by institutions run by Christian bodies with, in addition, one Islamic Education Trust institution. There are over 12 institutions in this category. They provide courses in teacher training, theological education and training, business management, and applied arts.

2. The Institutional Fabric of the Higher Education System

Higher education in Zambia consists of the public sector, the private sector, and a small grant-aided establishment. The public sector comprises two universities and several technical, business, agricultural, applied arts, and teacher-training colleges. This subsection is distinguished by its centralized administrative framework and total dependence on public funding. Four ministries and the Cabinet Office share the responsibility of organizing and administering public sector institutions. The Ministry of Higher Education, Science, and Technology (MHEST) is in charge of the universities, the four secondary school teacher-training colleges, and all the institutes and colleges run by the Department of Technical Education and Vocational Training (DTEVT). The Ministry of Power, Transport and Communication runs the Zambia Air Services Training Institute (ZASTI), the Ministry of Agriculture and Water Development administers agricultural and veterinary colleges, the Cabinet Office runs the National Institute for Public Administration (NIPA), and the Ministry of Health is responsible for running three nursing schools for state-registered nurses.

Of all the higher education institutions, it was the technical education and teacher-training colleges which experienced the most rapid growth between 1965 and 1990 (see Table 1). These were the institutions that were designated the task of rapidly producing an adequate middle-level labor force. After 1975 a general decline was experienced in economic development in all social sectors including higher education. Severe financial constraints due to falling copper prices and rising international oil prices forced the government not to undertake new capital projects. Ongoing capital projects suffered long delays in their completion schedules.

The private sector includes a mixture of religious and secular training institutions. These range from in-house and public training institutions to small colleges run by individuals. In 1990 there were 196 institutions registered with the Department of Technical Education and Vocational Training (DTEVT 1990). Of these 18 are owned and administered by state-owned corporations and 10 are run by private corporations. The rest have different forms of ownership. Institutions in this category are characterized by autonomy and independence in areas of policymaking, operations, financing, and administration.

Table 1
Public sector higher education institutions 1965–90

	1965	1970	1975	1980	1985	1990
Universities	—	1	1	1	2	2
Teachers colleges	—	—	2	2	16	16
Agricultural colleges	6	6	6	6	6	6
Veterinary colleges	1	1	1	1	1	1
Forestry colleges	1	1	1	1	1	—
Technical colleges	2	13	13	13	13	12
Nursing colleges	1	3	4	4	4	4
Business/Applied arts colleges	2	2	2	2	2	1
Business colleges	1	2	2	2	2	1

Sources: Southern African Countries Development Conference 1987 *Inventory of Regional Training Facilities* A handbook of post-secondary programs, Mbabane, Ministry of Education Annual Reports, Government of the Republic of Zambia Institutional Reports

Table 2
Enrollment in selected higher education and training institutions 1966–89

	1966	1970	1975	1980	1985	1989
Universities	312	1,232	2,354	3,986	4,680	5,367
Technical/vocational training colleges	148[a]	3,656	5,421	5,338	4,692	—[b]
Teacher training colleges	1,571	2,211	3,334	4,680	4,549	—[b]
Nursing (SRN) colleges	50	94	174	215	—[b]	—[b]

Sources: Institutional Annual Reports MHEST 1990 Report of the Working Party on Student Loans, p. 12
a Enrollment for Everlyn Hone College and Northern Technical College alone b Information not available

However, the establishment of private business and technical colleges has to be approved by the Ministry of Higher Education, Science, and Technology's Department of Technical Education and Vocational Training.

2.1 Admissions Policies and Selection

Admission to all public sector higher education institutions is regulated by ministerial, departmental, and institutional policies. The legislation which created the institutions did not specify admissions and selection criteria (Nurses and Midwives Act 1970; University of Zambia Act 1987; Copperbelt University Act 1987). The power to formulate policies was entrusted to institutional bodies specified in the Acts. However, admissions of students have always reflected national priorities in labor force development. For example, the national emphasis on science and technology has been reflected in the higher proportion of students being admitted into natural sciences, engineering, and related education and training courses. Academic performance and achievement in selection examinations have remained the only criteria for admission and selection.

Admission into universities is guided by the university senate regulations. Senate determines the number of students to be admitted and the distribution across the schools and centers. However, the universities have a policy which limits the intake of non-Zambian students to 5 percent of the total intake. Entry qualifications into the universities have been maintained at O- and A-level passes or possession of a diploma recognized by the university. However credit level passes in specified subjects are a prerequisite for selection by schools and centers. A credit level pass in English language is demanded by most study programs.

2.2 Quantitative Development

The University of Zambia initially had schools of education, humanities and social sciences, and natural sciences. By 1970 new schools had opened, thereby increasing student enrollment. The opening of a new university in the Copperbelt (1987) also had an impact on the quantitative development of the

sector. Other institutions experienced enrollment growth too, especially in the early 1970s.

2.3 Structure of Qualifications

There are five higher education and training qualifications. The universities offer three types of qualification: degrees, diplomas, and certificates. Nonuniversity colleges in the public sector offer diplomas and certificates only. Three theological colleges offer degrees which are underwritten by other colleges and universities. The length of study for first-degree programs is generally four to five years, though the BVetMed program lasts for six years, and the MBCHB program for seven.

Graduate studies are offered at the two universities. An acceptable first degree or diploma forms the minimum entry qualifications for postgraduate programs. Previous experience as well as appropriateness of research topic are also important considerations. University postgraduate studies are the only base for formal research training in the country. Additional formal training is provided by overseas training programs.

3. Governance, Administration, and Finance

The University of Zambia Act, 1987 and the Copperbelt University Act, 1987 provide for the establishment of university councils and senates to administer the affairs of the two universities. Council members are appointed by the chancellor (the head of state) on the recommendation and advice of the relevant authorities. Members are drawn from the university community, local authority area, parliament, selected ministries (Agriculture, Finance, Health, and MHEST), the international academic community, and the Zambian public. The council is responsible for the general control of the universities.

The senate is the academic authority in each university. It organizes, controls, and directs the entire academic life of the university in teaching, research, assessment, and general standards of education. Senate members are appointed mainly from the university communities. Deans and directors are members. Other members include the librarian, dean of students, and professorial and nonprofessorial aca-

Table 3
Proportion of Gross Domestic Product (GDP) devoted to higher education 1970–88[a]

	1970	1975	1980	1985	1988
GDP (US$ million)	1,659.4	2,454.2	3,860.1	2,545.8	3,655.4
Percentage	0.3[b]	2.5[c]	1.1	1.2	1.2

Source: Government of the Republic of Zambia *Estimates of Expenditure*
a Proportion of government grant to the University of Zambia only; department of technical education in the process of reorganization b Department of Technical Education and Vocational Training had capital grant of k23.8 million

demic staff. Non-university members are very few and are appointed by the vice-chancellor.

A collegial system of authority and participation forms the administration of the universities. Formal committees at different levels allow wide participation by both academic and nonacademic staff in decision- and policy-making processes. The University Act allows membership of most of the key bodies and their standing committees by academic and nonacademic staff. Academic staff are represented on the university council and its standing committees, the senate, boards of studies, and other university and departmental base unit committees. Nonacademic staff are represented on the university councils and all their subcommittees except the appointments, finance, and disciplinary committees.

Governance and administration of higher education and training in the nonuniversity public sector is centered on each ministry and its institutions. Each ministry runs its own institutions without close coordination with the others. Ministries oversee the development of the sector through planning the physical development of the institutions, budgetary provision, and exercising policy controls in such areas as student admissions, staff recruitment, examinations, certification, and curriculum development.

Zambia's five-year national development plans incorporate details of government objectives and goals for higher education and training. Development goals are transmitted to institutions by ministerial policy directives. It is the responsibility of the departments and institutions concerned to implement these policies.

Assessment and evaluation of goal achievement has tended to concentrate on examining completion of development projects and measuring output of graduates from the system. Both broad and in-depth assessments and evaluations of the higher education process have been constrained by the sector's reliance on the severely underresourced inspectorate. The universities, too, rely on inadequate mechanisms of assessment and evaluation. Aid donors do provide assessments and evaluations of the working of some aspects of the system, but these often have a specific, and usually narrow, focus.

The primary source of funding for higher education in the public sector is the central government. Funds

are allocated nationally by the Ministry of Finance. From the mid-1970s the government has faced severe financial constraints arising from the country's unfavorable economic conditions. Consequently, not only has higher education been facing keen competition from other sectors regarding resource allocation, but parallel cuts in capital and recurrent expenditure allocations have created numerous operational problems in the sector. This forced the government to introduce a cost-sharing financial policy in the higher education sector, in 1989 (MHEST 1989). University students are required to pay small fees towards the total cost of their education. Primary school teacher-training college students pay 409 Kwachas per term for board and lodging (1991 academic year). The government is working towards introducing a comprehensive student loan scheme (MHEST 1990).

The government gives financial support to four teacher-training colleges run by Christian churches. MHEST provides 75 percent of the total budget and also provides trained teachers. Private colleges do not receive any financial grants from the government. Table 3 shows the proportion of the country's Gross Domestic Product (GDP) devoted to higher education since 1970. The fact that the figures more than double between 1980 and 1985, and subsequently show a large increase, is due to the redesignation of the status of many institutions following the establishment of MHEST in 1982. Primary school teacher-training colleges, for example, were transferred to the higher education sector.

The organization of academic work is centered around schools, bureaus, centers, institutes, and departmental base units. The formal responsibilities of base units are to plan and execute courses, teaching, and research, and to provide administrative support.

4. Faculty and Students: Teaching, Learning, and Research

4.1 Faculty

The University of Zambia faced a severe shortage of highly educated and skilled local labor force, when it was created. This position gradually improved after the launching of the staff development program in

Table 4
Full-time university teaching staff[a] 1966–90

	1966	1970	1975	1980	1985	1990[b]
Zambian	5	12	50	115	194	287
Non-Zambiam	44	185	250	236	216	118
Total	49	197	300	351	410	405

Source: University of Zambia Computer Center *Annual Reports*
a Staff on study leave not included   b Figures as at 11.26.90

1969. Table 4 shows the growth of university teaching staff since 1966.

The recruitment of teaching staff is the responsibility of each university. Staff members are appointed by the university council. The minimum qualification for a teaching appointment is a master's degree.

Zambian citizens are appointed on local permanent and pensionable conditions of service, whereas expatriates are generally appointed by contract. People appointed to university posts are required to serve a probational period of twelve months (UNZA 1990), with the exception of those appointed to the rank of senior lecturer and above.

The universities contain senior staff associations, which are social organizations of teaching, administrative, and technical staff. The representation of corporate interests, settlement of disputes, and any related matters concerning academic teaching staff are dealt with on an ad hoc basis.

4.2 Students

Until 1988 when Statutory Instruments Nos. 99 and 100 sought to replace the old student unions with new student representative councils, the University of Zambia and Copperbelt University had strong and quite effective student unions. The move to create new representative structures has met with opposition from the student bodies. Consequently, in 1991 the government was forced to revoke its earlier decision (Statutory Instrument nos. 38 and 39; Times of Zambia, March 19, 1991). The restoration of the old student union structure will once again enable students to be represented on key university committees. Nonuniversity institutions have generally flexible student organizations. Most colleges have student representative councils which are run on general college guidelines rather than adhering to any firm constitutions. The Zambia National Union of Students (NUZS) was very active in the mid-1960s until the mid-1970s but in 1991 this is no longer the case.

The structure of first degrees is defined by the senate in consultation with the schools and centers. Any new study programs have to be approved within the university establishment by the appropriate committees. For a long time the universities have subjected the final year undergraduate and all graduate examinations and results to external scrutiny.

The methods by which students are assessed are essays, tests, project work, research papers, internships (in education, medicine, social work, etc.), and examinations. The weight given to continuous assessment and examinations varies according to course program.

5. Conclusion

Higher education has undergone tremendous growth and diversification since 1965. Significant achievements have been made regarding the objectives and goals set up for higher education and training. However, since the start of the 1980s the sector has been operating under severe constraints, as a result of the country's ailing economy. This has seriously affected the quality of service output. The government also faces the problem of coordinating institutions in the higher education sector.

Set against a background of political change and continuing economic problems, the sector's prospects for the future are unclear. What is certain is that both economic recovery measures being implemented by the government, and the general liberalization of institutional ownership and operations are going to have a profound impact on higher education's future profile and objectives. They will also affect the private and social demand for higher education and training from the Zambian public.

Bibliography

Kelly M J 1988 *The Financing of Education in Zambia.* IIEP, Paris
Ministry of Education *Annual Reports*
Ministry of Health 1990 *List of training hospitals.* Ministry of Health, Lusaka
Ministry of Higher Education, Science, and Technology 1989 *New Policies for Financing Higher Education.* MHEST, Lusaka
Ministry of Higher Education, Science, and Technology 1990 *Report of a working party on student loans.* MHEST, Lusaka
Ministry of Higher Education, Science, and Technology *Annual Reports*
Segestrom J, Deguefu-Dawit D, Dougherty C, Fuller C, Johnson A, Leonor M 1986 *Zambia Specialised Training Study.* World Bank, Washington, DC
Southern African Countries Conference on Development 1987 *Inventory of Regional Training Facilities: A Handbook of Postsecondary Programs.* SACCD, Mbabane
The University of Zambia 1986 *Management Statistics.* UNZA, Lusaka
The University of Zambia 1990 *General Entrance Requirements for Admission.* UNZA, Lusaka
The University of Zambia 1990 *Terms and Conditions of Service for Permanent and Pensionable Academic and Senior Administrative Staff.* UNZA, Lusaka

The University of Zambia *Annual Reports*

United National Independence Party 1985 *Policies for the Decade 1985–1995*. Freedom House, Lusaka

United National Independence Party 1988 *Science and Technology Five Year Work Programme*. Freedom House, Lusaka

L. H. Kaluba

Zimbabwe

1. Higher Education and Society

In Zimbabwe, higher education generally covers postsecondary institutions such as the university, the polytechnic, teachers' colleges, technical colleges, and a number of institutions in government ministries, parastatals, the private sector, and other nongovernmental organizations that provide in-house training for their specific needs. The term "postsecondary" can however be misleading within the Zimbabwean context. A full secondary education comprises six years of postprimary study with external public examinations every two years at junior certificate, Ordinary, and Advanced levels. Before Independence in 1980, the majority of African pupils who had succeeded in getting a secondary-school place dropped out at junior certificate level to train generally as teachers, agricultural extension demonstrators, and medical assistants. Only a few proceeded to do Ordinary level with yet a small minority of these proceeding to Advanced level. A more than 600 percent expansion in secondary education since Independence has ensured that few pupils drop out at junior-secondary level. The World Bank Report on education in Sub-Saharan Africa (World Bank 1988) notes that Zimbabwe is close to achieving universal primary education. About 80 percent of the students completing primary school proceed to secondary education in Zimbabwe. Postsecondary education thus now refers to post-Ordinary level and Advanced level education. For the purpose of this article experiences from the university, the polytechnics, technical colleges, agricultural colleges, and teachers' colleges will be highlighted as representing higher education.

The epistemological dualism between the pure and academic and the applied and practical was most evident before Independence where higher education generally referred to university education and further education was used to refer to all technical training in the polytechnic and the technical colleges. Since Independence, however, the new Black government, inspired by its Marxist views of knowledge that regards true knowledge as both theoretical and practical, has attempted to bridge this epistemological divide culminating in the formation of the Ministry of Higher Education in 1988.

Zimbabwe is the southernmost country of intertropical Africa extending from 15°30s to 22°30s and lying between 25°E and 23°E. It shares borders with Zambia in the north, Mozambique in the east, South Africa in the south, and Botswana and Namibia in the west. It covers an area of about 576,000 square kilometers (Kay 1970). It is a relatively high region composed of a series of plateaux, the highest of which, known as the high veld, lies mostly between 4,000 and 5,000 feet above sea level and constitutes about 25 percent of the total area. The high veld is flanked on each side by the middle veld which lies between 4,000 and 3,000 feet above sea level and constitutes about 40 percent of the total area. According to Atkinson (1972) this altitude has an important moderating influence on the climate of an area which is entirely contained in the tropics making it suitable for permanent habitation by Europeans—a factor which has significantly influenced the history and economic and political development of a country that is otherwise African. The rest of the country—the low veld—lies below 3,000 feet and comprises mostly the river valleys. Only very restricted parts of the highlands receive more than 50 inches of rain in a year and more than two-thirds of the country receive less than 30 inches.

Vincent and Thomas (1961) surveyed the natural controls governing agricultural land use and divided Zimbabwe into five natural farming regions with a sixth unsuitable for farming. These range from the rich well-watered regions of the highlands that cover about 1.6 percent of the country and are suitable for specialized and diversified farming to the low-rainfall areas in the low veld generally suitable for raising livestock.

Of Zimbabwe's population estimated at about 9.4 million, the Shona constitute the biggest single ethnic group and have been in Zimbabwe the longest. The exact date of their arrival is not known, but Portuguese records indicate contact between the Shona and the Portuguese missionaries and traders as early as the sixteenth century. Apparently they had settled all over the country in small groups under a chief or headman practicing shifting cultivation.

The Ndebele, the next biggest ethnic group, fleeing from Tshaka the Zulu king under their leader Mzilikazi, cross the Limpopo River that borders Zimbabwe and South Africa in 1832. Mzilikazi, an *induna* (lieutenant) of Tshaka had incurred the wrath of his king by refusing to hand over all the loot from a raid. The Ndebele, a warlike tribe, lived on plunder and raiding the Shona for cattle, grain, women, and young men to boost their *impis* (fighting groups, regiments, armies). Their sporadic raids altered the Shona way of life considerably. The Shona left their fertile low-lying plains to live near mountains where they could easily detect the invaders.

The first big group of Europeans to settle in Zimbabwe were members of Cecil John Rhodes's Pioneer

Column that left Kimberley in South Africa and flew the Union Jack at Fort Salisbury on September 12, 1890, having established forts at Tuli, Fort Victoria, and Charter. The Pioneer Column was sponsored by Rhodes's British South Africa Company and had been promised land for farming and mining as part of Rhodes's grand strategy of extending the British Empire from the Cape to Cairo. The country was known as Rhodesia after Rhodes up until Independence in 1980 when it changed to Zimbabwe, the name of a sixteenth-century fort in the south of the country.

The Shona and the Ndebele rebelled against White occupation but both rebellions were quashed due to the superior weapons of the Europeans. The new White administration stopped the Matabele raids into Mashonaland and the land was divided into European and African land. Through a series of land legislations, notably those of 1930, 1951, 1963, and 1969, Rhodesia was divided more or less equally between Europeans and Africans although the Africans outnumbered Europeans by almost 20:1. European land fell in the best first three regions whereas Africans were largely in regions four and five where the soil was poor and rainfall unreliable. A policy of racial segregation was introduced where the economic, social, political, cultural, and educational interests of the two races would be different. The ultimate goal was to entrench European supremacy in all aspects of Rhodesian life:

> We do not intend to hand over this country to the native or admit him to the same social or political positions as we occupy ourselves, he will always be a hewer of wood and drawer of water for his master the European. (Bull 1967 p. 69)

Thus, European immigrants were encouraged and assisted to buy land (a land bank was set up as early as 1912) and mining concessions, whereas Blacks were expected to provide cheap labor. To each and every White man, woman, or child there were four Black laborers. On average, farmers employed one native laborer for every four acres of cultivated land. Wages ranged from £0.37p for boys of between 10 and 15 years of age to £1.12 for adults per month. In the early 1990s, about 5,000 White commercial farmers still own about 40 percent of the land.

Socially, residential areas were separated along racial lines in towns, mission stations, and on farms. This in turn meant the provision of separate health and educational facilities. European education was intended to provide labor force in the higher echelons of government and the private sector, whereas, African education was intended to produce low-level labor force such as clerks, messengers, teachers, and medical assistants for general African upliftment through rural development. White education was the responsibility of the government and was universal and compulsory up to the age of 15. African educa-tion, on the other hand, was the responsibility of various groups including missionaries, councils, commercial farmers, and very peripherally the government itself. African education was not compulsory as there were not enough schools for school-going children of all ages. In 1976, for example, an estimated 4,500 children of school-going age at primary level failed to find places in existing schools. At the secondary-school level, the policy after 1965—when the Rhodesian government unilaterally declared Independence from Britain for fear that the British would hand over power to the Blacks—was that only 12.5 percent of African students completing primary school would find places in academic secondary schools (a figure close to the number of European children in secondary schools). An additional 37.5 percent had access to vocational secondary schools, and the remainder were not catered for in the formal system. However, even this was not achieved, for by 1980 when Zimbabwe gained Independence (after a protracted war between the Blacks and the Whites), only 18 percent of all African students completing primary school were in secondary schools of both types.

2. The Institutional Fabric of the Higher Education System

2.1 Historical Background

Before Independence, what is now higher education was divided into four subcategories: (a) higher education, which referred to university education; (b) further education, which included technical colleges and the polytechnics; (c) teachers' training, which until the early 1960s was restricted to the training of primary-school teachers; and (d) agricultural training, which was part of the Ministry of Agriculture.

The origin of the University of Zimbabwe can be traced back to the last years of the Second World War, when a group of White business and professional people, primarily interested in an institution providing a university education for White Rhodesian youths, formed the Rhodesia University Association. In addition to this group, there was also a much smaller group of White liberals, mainly missionaries and clergymen, who were interested in the provision of university education for Rhodesian Blacks. The latter had the support of the British government, which was concerned with the provision of higher education for Blacks in the three territories of Central Africa, namely, the then Northern Rhodesia (Zambia), Southern Rhodesia (Zimbabwe), and Nyasaland (Malawi). The Rhodesia University Association later promoted a bill in the Southern Rhodesia parliament establishing an inaugural Board, which was to lead to the formation of the university.

Little attention was given to university training for Blacks, since there was only one secondary school providing education through to Ordinary level. However, thought was given to the possibility of a college for Africans close to the university so that there might be a sharing of staff. The teaching at the Whites-only university would be in such pragmatic courses as accountancy, business studies, social administration, agriculture, and engineering—courses which provided for jobs dominated or rather exclusively reserved for Whites in the White-dominated economy.

A commission, which had been interested in higher education for Blacks, in the three territories had been promised finance by the British government plus the model of a linkage with a British university, which would facilitate development and ensure academic standards. Eventually, the concept of multiracialism gradually became accepted due to the need for a university-trained Black labor force especially in the field of education. There was also an awareness that significant numbers of Blacks were making their way overseas for such education with the possibility that they would be exposed to "harmful ideas and influences." In 1950, the South African government announced that it would no longer give Rhodesian Blacks access to the same facilities as Whites at the universities of Cape Town, Witwatersrand, and Natal. Blacks would only be accepted at Natal for medicine and Fort Hare for other courses. There was therefore a need for alternatives for Blacks. The formation of the Central African Federation in 1953, based on the principle of partnership, required for purposes of legitimacy, that compliance with the principle of multiracialism be observed.

Thus the combined weight of the above factors led to an agreement to establish a multiracial university college affiliated with the University of London and based on the English civic university model. The university was seen as a self-governing cooperation, with its policies determined by senior member academics but moderated by the presence of a predominantly lay council, which represented the public interest. A royal charter dated February 10, 1955 brought the infant university into legal existence as an autonomous body with all the powers of the university college vested in a council charged with the duty of governing the institution. The charter stipulated the creation of an Academic Board to control, regulate, and supervise instruction, education, and research, subject to review by the council. The power to appoint staff members was vested in the council on the advice of a selection board drawn from the academic staff. The council itself consisted of 10 academics, 7 nominees from government bodies, and 7 nominees from the business and professional sectors.

The university was started at a time in Rhodesian history when the liberal, assimilationist, meritocratic perspective in White Rhodesian politics, always

Table 1
Student statistics 1957–88

Year	1957[a]	1960	1965	1970	1975	1980	1985	1988
Black	8	49	174	363	707	1,427	4,318	7,264
White	68	153	454	489	561	693	231	300
Other	—	5	43	85	93	121	193	135
Total	77	207	671	937	1,361	2,240	4,742	7,699

Source: University of Zimbabwe Registry
a The year the university started

present but never ascendant, was perhaps in its most favorable position to make its weight felt. Still Whites by and large saw the university as an instrument to perpetuate White racial sovereignty through the inculcation of skills and values consistent with this goal. There were concessions made to racism, for example, segregated accommodation between 1957 and 1962. The White government directed Africans to courses such as teaching, medicine, and agriculture by restricting awards of grants and loans to Africans doing these courses. Murphree (1982) postulates three distinct stages in the life of the university. The first stage, 1957 to 1971, he called the integrationist stage when Blacks were outnumbered but were prepared to experiment with the integrationist philosophy. The second stage, 1962 to 1973, was characterized by growing militancy against racism with a growing awareness of the structural basis of racism in society. In 1973, 100 Black students were arrested for political activities and were effectively barred from end-of-year examinations. During the third phase, 1974 to 1980, Blacks came to outnumber Whites for the first time in 1975 (see Table 1). This was mainly because White youths were on military service to fight Black nationalist guerrillas, who were fighting for Black majority rule.

At no stage in the life of the university during the colonial era was there ever genuine integration across racial lines.

Due to pressure from White trade unions that feared competition from Blacks for artisan jobs, there were hardly any Black apprentices until the late 1970s. Since access to the polytechnic and technical colleges was largely through sponsorship by an employer, these institutions remained until the 1970s reserved for training and developing the skills of Whites. The effect of this on the economy was that Blacks largely provided semiskilled and unskilled labor while Whites provided most of the skilled labor.

In the area of teacher education, the university provided secondary-school teachers for both the African and European divisions of education, although most teachers for the European division were recruited from abroad. Not until the 1960s did Bulawayo Teachers' College for Whites, Asians, and

Coloreds, and Gweru Teachers' College for Blacks produce standard qualified teachers through the associateship scheme with the University of Zimbabwe. Previously, most teachers in African schools were trained by missionaries in their small teacher-training schools that lacked both human and material resources. Teachers for the lower-primary, upper-primary, and infant classes in European schools had been trained in Bulawayo since 1918. The training school closed in 1938 and was reopened in 1958. Between these dates, teachers for the White schools were recruited from abroad and teachers were trained in England and in South Africa.

In agriculture, Gwebi College of Agriculture started in the early 1950s with a view to training young Whites who would become farmers themselves. They were assisted through various schemes to lease or buy land in order to keep White commercial agriculture viable. Chibero College of Agriculture for Africans was intended to produce Black agricultural officers who would serve among the Black peasant farmers. The graduates were not encouraged to buy land themselves or to work with White commercial farmers as managers.

The above policies and conditions almost inevitably led to the rise of African nationalism especially amongst those Africans who had received missionary education. African nationalism initially found more organized expression through the trade-union movement and progressively through political parties. The main grievances centered around the abolition of racial segregation in all aspects of Rhodesian life. When successive colonial governments responded by further repression such as banning African political parties and detaining their leaders, the Africans resorted to armed resistance. Between 1966 and 1979 the country was locked in a racial civil war, which ended through the intervention of the international community. The British convened a constitutional conference at Lancaster House in London where the contending parties agreed on a nonracial constitution with guarantees to protect the interests of the White minorities for at least the first ten years of Independence. A Black majority rule government was established in 1980.

The new Black government adopted a Marxist–Leninist ideology as a means of redressing the inequalities of the past and establishing a new egalitarian society through policies that were intended to stimulate economic growth with equity. Among its priorities were the resettling and rehabilitation of the war-displaced through land redistribution. It aimed at correcting disparities in incomes and quality of life through creating full employment, especially for ex-combatants and youth who had failed to complete their schooling. The instruments used by colonial regimes to uphold the inequitable social order, such as educational and labor force training practices, were reviewed and changed to serve the objectives of the new government through desegregation and improving access to secondary schools, apprenticeships, and institutions of higher and further education.

However, there were problems. To start with the more strategic sectors of the economy such as finance, mining, and manufacturing were dominated by foreign and private investment with up to two-thirds of the invested capital in the economy being foreign. The state only controlled such infrastructural sectors as transport, energy, health, and education. It did not have sufficient financial muscle to implement its programs. Indeed between 1980 and 1983 profits remitted abroad in scarce foreign exchange amounted to z$330 million. The economy also depended largely on export of agricultural and other raw materials and had few secondary industries. Population growth of about 3 percent per annum was one of the highest in Africa with a high-dependence younger-age (up to 14 years) ratio making up 47.3 percent. The flight of White labor force skills through emigration and the Africanization of the public sector meant that for some time both the private and public sectors lacked experienced technical, managerial, and professional leadership desperately needed at a time of envisaged rapid change. For some time there was a gap between stated policy and actual practice in both the private and public sector institutions.

2.2 Quantitative Developments in Higher Education

At Independence, fundamental changes had to take place if the new government was to be viewed as addressing African grievances.

At the University of Zimbabwe, the new Black vice-chancellor addressed the need for change in the following words: "The informing ideals which created the university had their genesis in a milieu of an old-fashioned liberalism" (Kamba 1981). There was therefore a need for a new orientation guided by a commitment to excellence and relevance. He continued "I regard the University of Zimbabwe as first and foremost a developmental university which is singularly animated and concerned rhetorically and practically with the search for solutions to the concrete problems of national development." He was supported by the then prime minister of the country Robert Mugabe who said: "Higher education is too important a business to be left entirely to deans, professors, lecturers and university administrators" (Mugabe 1981 p. 6). Thus, higher education was seen essentially as serving the developmental needs of the new nation, especially in the context of the exodus of White skills which had formed the backbone of the country's economy. Enrollment figures increased at all the institutions of higher education.

Entrance into the polytechnic and the technical colleges no longer depended on sponsorship by employers. It was centralized and college tutors worked closely with employers to place their students for industrial experience. The aim of government was to produce a more skilled labor force without depending on the apprenticeship needs of the private sector, which it did not control. This however created other problems. On the one hand, central recruitment into technical colleges did not guarantee availability of places for industrial experience by the recruits. On the other hand, those already in industry as apprentices or those trade-tested but needing the theoretical inputs of their trade did not always get places in technical colleges when necessary. Thus, there was a genuine fear that the product of this type of labor development strategy would receive inadequate training. Furthermore, there was the fear that since centralized recruitment and training did not necessarily reflect on the expansion, ability, and performance of the economy to create more jobs, this would eventually create skilled unemployment.

In teachers' colleges, enrollments had to be increased in both secondary- and primary-teachers' colleges in order to meet the high demand for trained teachers in the expanded system of education. This was achieved through restructuring the conventional programs from three years' full-time study to four years with students spending the first and third years of training in college and the second and fourth in schools teaching on a full-time basis. Additionally, through the introduction of a four-year training program, the Zimbabwe Integrated Teacher Education Course (Zintec) was introduced. This program was directed at the untrained primary-school teachers who spent the first and last 16 weeks of the four-year program in college. The rest of the time they were in schools teaching but receiving instruction through visits from tutors and through distance-education strategies. This increased the number of student teachers significantly.

The government's policy of land distribution to individuals and cooperatives through its resettlement schemes required both technical and professional skills, especially if the land that had been appropriated from former commercial farmers was to retain or even increase its productivity. The two agricultural colleges increased their enrollments and Gwebi, which was previously reserved for Whites only, became multiracial. The emphasis changed from producing potential commercial farmers to generating a labor force for the agricultural and other agro-chemical industries in general.

2.3 Admissions Policies and Selection

Entry requirements for students include a minimum of two principal passes at Advanced level but due to pressure for places only those with higher grades secure university places. Prospective students apply through central administration indicating their faculty preferences. Once they have met the arbitrary cut-off point for that year, which depends largely on the quality of Advanced level results for that year, their names are forwarded to their preferred faculty for final selection to departments and subjects. There is also a mature entry route for mature students and a special entry route for those with experiences and qualifications deemed equivalent to the normal entry qualifications.

In the arts and science faculties, students generally take three years to complete a degree which can be passed at first class, upper second class, lower second class or third class grades. Generally in the first year, they take three subjects, and two for the second and third years. Honors students can however take one subject from the second year onwards. Those in professional faculties like veterinary science, medicine, engineering, and to some extent education, have different arrangements intended to meet the needs of their clients.

3. Governance, Administration, and Finance

At Independence, the University Charter was replaced by the University of Zimbabwe Act (1982), which democratized the governance of the university by, for example, increasing the membership of council to 36. According to the vice-chancellor, the Act "provided a framework within which to evolve a new orientation and a new identity which places the university at the centre and not at the periphery of national development." A second rotational pro-vice-chancellorship was created to increase the range of administrative skills at higher levels in the university. In the departments, where power and influence had been concentrated in the professor and head of the department for life, an ordinance (Ordinance 25) was promulgated separating the professorship from the headship. Instead the vice-chancellor, in consultation with one of the pro-vice-chancellors, dean of faculty, and members of the department concerned, appoints a rotational chairman for three years. The ordinance ensures that appointment to professorship depends on published research and not necessarily on administrative responsibilities. As a result of this ordinance, some 25 Black lecturers were immediately appointed chairs of departments, ranging in rank from lecturer to professor, as opposed to only two heads of department before the ordinance. Whereas there were two Black deans of faculty out of seven faculties in 1982, by 1988 seven of the ten deans were Black. Ordinance 25 also gives a lot of power to the department through its Departmental Board, which comprised the dean of faculty, his or her deputy, the chairperson of the departments, all academic members of the department, and representatives of the technical and secretarial staff. The main aims in establishing the Departmental Board were: to encourage collegiate decision making in such issues as initial vetting of applicants for all departmental posts—academic, administrative, technical, and secretarial; to recommend colleagues for promotion; to decide on syllabi; to assign tutorial and other responsibilities to members; and to act as a panel of examiners prior to candidates being presented to the Faculty Examining Board and Academic Committee. The Chairperson takes most of the recommendations of the Departmental Board to the relevant committees of the university depending on the nature of the issue.

Unlike the university—which operates under an Act of Parliament, the nonuniversity institutions are administered directly from the parent government ministries except that for purposes of examination and certification, the Bachelor of Technology degree of the polytechnic is offered by the university and so is the Certificate in Education taught by teachers' colleges. However, the national Diploma in Agriculture is issued by the Ministry of Agriculture. The principals of the above institutions report directly to the relevant directors in their ministries on administrative issues. On academic matters they work through the local academic boards, which comprise department heads and other senior academics. These make recommendations to the relevant examining authority.

The increase in university student numbers from 2,240 in 1980 to 9,288 in 1989 has necessitated huge financial inputs in capital and recurrent expenditure. Capital expenditure included construction of lecture rooms, lecture theatres, halls of residence for students, recreational facilities, and extensions to the library. Recurrent expenditure included increases in salaries and wages for both academic and nonacademic staff, loans and grants for students, vehicle and machinery maintenance, research and general consumables, stationery, and postage. The government has largely been the main provider of funds except for projects funded by donors such as the European Community, United States Agency for International Development, the Swedish International Development Authority, and the International Development Research Center of Canada, among others. In 1980 the government recurrent expenditure on the university was Z$10,985,000 (US$100=Z$2.00), rising to Z$26,289,000 in 1985 and Z$49,050,000 in 1989. Capital expenditure was Z$1,069,000 in 1980, rising to Z$13,044,000 in 1985, reaching a peak of Z$13,130,000 in 1987 and then falling to Z$7,897,000 in the 1988/89 financial year. Using 1980 as a base, cost per student in real terms was Z$4,904,000 decreasing to Z$2,800,000 in 1985 and Z$2,565,000 in 1987. Since Independence, education and defense have vied for top place in claiming the lion's share of the national budget.

Except for a few donor-funded projects, the government has been the main source of both capital and recurrent expenditure in the nonuniversity institutions.

4. Faculty and Students: Teaching, Learning, and Research

4.1 Faculty

The minimum qualification to teach in the university has always been an honors degree, but in practice most lecturers have at least a master's degree. Those with lower qualifications would most likely work as teaching assistants or staff-development fellows while studying for higher degrees.

In the event of a post being vacant or arising due to expansion, the chairperson of the department prepares a suitable advertisement which he or she sends to staff registry for placement in both local and international newspapers or educational supplements. Applications are circulated among members of the department and at a subsequent meeting called by the chairperson, a few are shortlisted for consideration by the Academic Appointments Board (AAB). This comprises the vice-chancellor or his representative, a pro-vice-chancellor, dean of the faculty, chairperson from the faculty, and the administrator of the faculty. The chairman of the department presents all the applicants and also the short-listed candidates and the AAB makes the final decision on who should be called for an interview. Generally shortlisted candidates from Africa are invited for an interview to Harare, while applicants from America and Europe are interviewed locally through approved institutions. The number of Black staff has steadily been increasing since Independence (see Table 2).

Lecturers fall into four main grades of lecturer, senior lecturer, associate professor, and professor. On appointment, a member below the rank of associate professor serves a probationary period of two years before he or she is confirmed and given tenure. Once tenured, they are free to apply for promotion to the next grade. Criteria for promotion are set out in Ordinance 28 promulgated after Independence. For promotion to senior lecturer applicants must satisfy their Departmental Board on required criteria which in turn will recommend them to the pro-

Table 2
Academic staff statistics 1983–86

	1983	1984	1985	1986
No. of posts vacant	60	115	132	170
No. of posts filled	349	346	371	402
Expatriate	54	62	80	87
Non-Zimb.	27	24	21	17
Zimb. Blacks	99	105	126	148
Zimb. others	169	155	144	150
Total no. of posts	409	461	503	572

Source: University of Zimbabwe Registry

motions committee of the university. Applicants must satisfy the Departmental Board that they have performed well in the three areas of teaching, research, and university service (which includes public service). In addition they must be deemed outstanding in one of the three. In reality, however, only those who have proved to be outstanding in research have been promoted, as university service and teaching are deemed to be difficult to assess. For promotion to associate professor, research is the dominant criterion and ability to sustain that level of research output qualifies one for a full professorship. The university has retained departmental chairs as well. The Association of University Teachers has attempted to provide a forum for organized staff activities, but it tends to be active only when there are controversial issues.

4.2 Students

The University of Zimbabwe started as a residential university. It attempts to provide accommodation for up to 60 percent of its full-time students. At the beginning of the 1990 academic year the university had accommodation for 4,100 students with an anticipated student population of 10,000. Thus, the rest of the students have to look for accommodation elsewhere. However, due to transport problems in metropolitan Harare, students sometimes spend between three and four hours daily getting to and from the university.

Due to a shortage of foreign currency, the university library has not been able to retain all its pre-Independence journal titles nor purchase all the books required by departments. This has been a problem for both staff and students. Where donor assistance has been solicited for books, equipment, or computers, it has not always been easy to get these through the local customs officials. In spite of these problems, a lot of research, both basic and applied, is taking place in the university with research by Dr J. Gopo and Professor Chetsanga in biotechnology having received international acclaim.

5. Conclusion

The development of higher education in Zimbabwe has been both retroactive, in relation to redressing past imbalances, and proactive in terms of its attempts to produce a large-enough labor force to implement new government policies that are inspired by its socialist ideals. The major constraints in implementing the new programs include a shortage of labor force to operate the expanded training institutions; for example, none of the technical colleges have been able to enroll above 70 percent of student capacity due to shortages of both human and material resources. Training institutions cannot offer the same level of remuneration as the private sector and par-

astatals so they lose out to these. The acute shortage of foreign exchange has also resulted in shortages of resources; for example, some of the technology available in industry and in technical colleges is said to be at least 20 years old. Zimbabwe is therefore training its apprentices through an obsolete technology. The rapid expansion at the university has also meant a readjustment downwards in terms of resources and facilities available to both staff and students. Unless this is checked soon, this might progressively lead to a dilution of the quality of teaching and learning that goes on in the university.

Higher education in Zimbabwe is caught up in the on-going process of transforming a White-dominated capitalist economy to an envisaged socialist multiracial one. Success as well as major challenges have been encountered. Still bold decisions have to be made in the area of job creation, as an estimated 300,000 graduates a year are expected from 1990 onwards. The economy so far has not been able to produce more than 11,000 jobs a year. Therefore, there is a need to involve all the productive sectors of the economy in a debate on labor force training and job creation through higher education.

Bibliography

Atkinson N D 1972 *Teaching Rhodesians*. Longman, London

Bull T 1967 *Rhodesia Perspectives*. Michael Joseph, London

Hayden H 1967 *Higher Education and Development in South East Asia. Vol I: Directors' Report*. UNESCO and the International Association of Universities, Paris

Kamba W J 1981 The University: From this time on. In: Chideya N T, Chikomba C E M, Poongweni A C J, Tsikirayi L C (eds.) 1981 *The Role of the University and its Future in Zimbabwe*. Harare Publishing House, Harare

Kay G 1970 *Rhodesia: A Human Geography*. University of London Press, London

Mugabe R G 1981 Opening speech. In: Chideya N T, Chikomba C E M, Pongweni A J C, Tsikirayi L C (eds.) 1981 *The Role of the University and its Future in Zimbabwe*. Harare Publishing House, Harare

Murphree M W 1982 The Birth of the Non-Racial Island. Unpublished manuscript

OHMS 1955 *Charter: The University College of Rhodesia and Nyasaland . . . at the Court of Buckingham Palace, the 10th day of February 1955*. HMSO, London

University of Zimbabwe. *Five-year Report 1981–85*. University of Zimbabwe, Harare

University of Zimbabwe *Vice-Chancellor's Annual Reports for 1982 and 1983*. University of Zimbabwe, Harare

Vincent V, Thomas R G 1961 *An Agricultural Survey of Southern Rhodesia. Part I: Agro-Ecological Survey*. Federation of Rhodesia and Nyasaland, Salisbury

World Bank 1988 *Education in Sub-Saharan Africa: Policies for Adjustment, Revitalization and Expansion*. The World Bank, Washington, DC

O. E. Maravanyika